POWER STATION AND SUB-STATION PRACTICE

[A Practical Hand Book on Alternators, Transformers, HV/EHV/HVDC Substations and Protective Relays, etc.]

POWER STATION AND SUB-STATION PRACTICE

[A Practical Hand Book on Alternators, Transformers, HV/EHV/HVDC Substations and Protective Relays, etc.]

M.P. KRISHNA PILLAI

STANDARD PUBLISHERS DISTRIBUTORS

1705-B, NAI SARAK, POST BOX No.: 1066, DELHI-110006

Phones: 23262700, 23285798, Fax: 011-23243180

www.standardpublishers.com www.engineeringbooks.co.in email: stpub@vsnl.com

Published by:
A.K. Jain
For Standard Publishers Distributors
1705-B, Nai Sarak, Delhi-110006.

First Edition: 2008
Reprint 2015

Price: Rs. **850.00**

ISBN: 81-8014-116-0

Laser Typesetting by: Bhargave Laser Printers, Delhi.
Printed by: Meenakshi Art Printers, Delhi.

PREFACE

Power generation, transmission and distribution, is one of the most essential aspect in the electrical industry. The aim of this book is to share with the reader's the practically gained experience of the author, especially in modern power stations, high voltage and extra high voltage substations and medium voltage power distribution system. To make the subject more realistic, understandable and approachable, there are 734 illustrations/ circuit diagrams/test diagrams collected from various worlds vide manufacturers, which are presented in an easy-to-follow, step-by-step procedure duly supported with practical questions and answers.

The area covered includes installation, testing, commissioning, operation, maintenance and trouble shooting of electrical equipments such as brush type and brushless alternators, power and distribution transformers, high voltage motors and controllers, low and medium voltage switchgears and circuit breakers, high voltage and extra high voltage substations, substation equipments and circuit breakers, high voltage direct current system etc. In addition to that, selection, application, testing and setting of protective relays for generators, power transformers, transmission feeders and bus protection etc are included.

The standard, which follows throughout the book is, IEC (International Electro-technical Commission) standard. Occasionally BS (British Standard) and ANSI (American National Standards Institution) standards are referred. No doubt it should prove invaluable as a source of practical information for almost all generation, transmission and distribution equipments and modern control circuitry. However low, medium, high and extra high voltage cables are not included, except technical data and current ratings given in Appendix 1 to 4. Reader's who wish to gather more practical information on low, medium, high and extra high voltage cables and fiber optic cables, OPWG cables etc. are requested to read *"Practical hand book on electrical communication and networking cables"* written by the author and published by Standard Publishers, New Delhi 110006 (ISBN 81-8014-071-1).

New Year Day,
1-1-2008

—M.P. KRISHNA PILLAI

CONTENTS

SYMBOLS

(1) SYMBOLS FOR ELECTRICAL/MECHANICAL INSTRUMENTS

MW	ACTIVE POWER MEASUREMENT
MVAR	REACTIVE POWER MEASUREMENT
A	CURRENT MEASUREMENT
V	VOLTAGE MEASUREMENT
Hz	FREQUENCY MEASUREMENT
kWh	ACTIVE ENERGY METERING
kWARh	REACTIVE ENERGY METERING
PF	POWER FACTOR
h	RUNNING TIME MEASUREMENT
26W	WINDING TEMPERATURE INDICATOR
26O	OIL TEMPERATURE INDICATOR
63B	BUCHHOLZ RELAY
PRD	PRESSURE RELIEF DEVICE
SCS	SUBSTATION CONTROL SYSTEM
DCS	DISTRIBUTED CONTROL SYSTEM

n	LOCAL TEMPERATATURE INDICATOR FOR TEST ONLY
PI	LOCAL PRESURE INDICATOR CONTINUOUS MEASURING
PICA H/L	PRESSURE TRANSMITTER FOR - CONTROL BY UNIT CONTROL SYSTEM - REMOTE INDICATION AT UNIT CONTROL ROOM - HIGH / LOW ALARM CONTACTS
UCZ HH/LL	LEVEL TRANSMITTER FOR - CONTROL BY AUTONOMOUS CONTROL SYSTEM - REMOTE INDICATION AT LOCAL PANEL - HIGH HIGH/ LOW LOW TRIP CONTACTS
FICA L FI	FLOW TRANSMITTER FOR - CONTROL BY AUTONOMOUS CONTROL SYSTEM - REMOTE INDICATION AT LOCAL PANEL - LOW ALARM CONTACT AT LOCAL PANEL - REMOTE INDICATION AT UNIT CONTROL ROOM
α pH	MEASURING FOR pH VALUE FOR TEST ONLY
LSAZ HH/LL H/L	LEVEL SWITCH - CONTROL INTERLOCK BY UNIT CONTROL SYSTEM - HIGH/LOW ALARM CONTACTS - HIGH HIGH/ LOW LOW TRIP CONTACTS
PS H	PRESSURE SWITCH - CONTROL INTERLOCK BY UNIT CONTROL SYSTEM

(2) SYMBOLS FOR POWER STATION/SUBSTATION EQUIPMENTS:

SURGE ARRESTOR

EARTHING

UG CABLE

TAPPED LINE

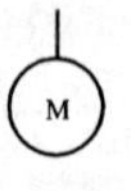

ELECTRIC MOTOR

GENERATOR

SYNCHRONIZATION

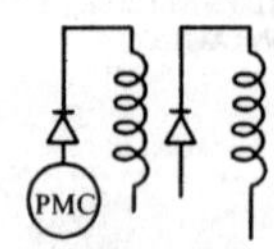

BRUSHLESS EXCITATION
WITH PERMANENT MAGNET GENERATOR

VOLTAGE TRANSFORMER
TWO WINDING

VOLTAGE TRANSFORMER
THREE WINDING

MOTORISED DISCONNECTOR

DISCONNECTOR

MOTORISED EARTH SWITCH

CIRCUIT BREAKER

CURRENT TRANSFORMER

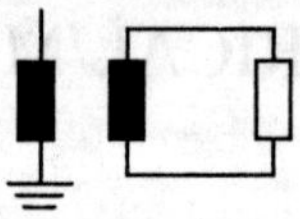
GENERATOR NEUTURAL CONNECTION

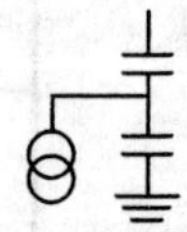
CAPACITOR VOLTAGE
TRANSFORMER

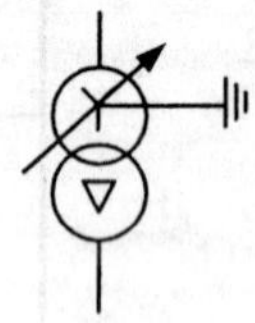
GENERATOR TRANSFORMER WYE-DELTA
-WYE CONNECTION, NEUTRAL POINT
SOLID EARTH, ONLOAD TAP CHANGER

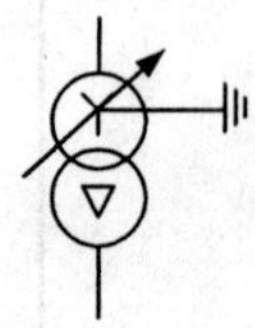
STATION TRANSFORMER WYE-DELTA
CONNECTION, NEUTRAL POINT
SOLID EARTH, ONLOAD TAP CHANGER

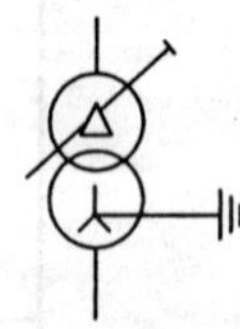
UNIT/AUXILIARY TRANSFORMER DELTA
-WYE CONNECTION WITH OFF-LOAD
TAP CHANGER AT DELTA SIDE
SOLID EARTH

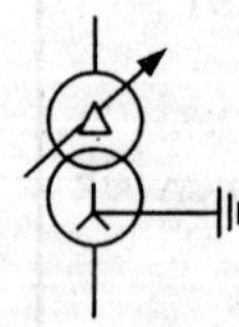
AUXILIARY TRANSFORMER DELTA
-WYE CONNECTION WITH OFF-LOAD
TAP CHANGER AT DELTA SIDE
SOLID EARTH

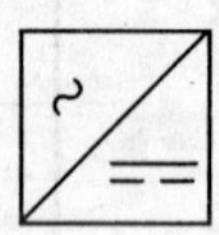
BATTERY CHARGER

AUTOMATIC VOLTAGE REGULATOR

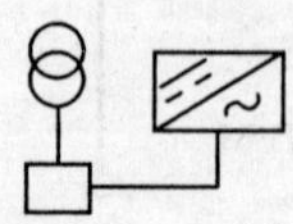
UN INTERRUPTED POWER SUPPLY

(3) GRAPHICAL SYMBOLS FOR SWITCHGEARS AND APPARATUS.

 SQUIRREL-CAGE INDUCTION MOTORS & GENERATORS

 WOUND-ROTOR INDUCTION MOTORS & GENERATORS

 SYNCHRONOUS GENERATORS, MOTORS & GENERATORS

 SYNCHRONOUS CONVERTORS

 D – C GENERATORS, MOTORS & EXCITERS

 POWER RECTIFIERS

FIXED RATIO POWER TRANSFORMER:

 2 WINDING

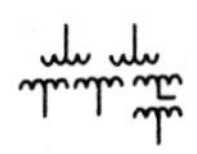 3 WINDING

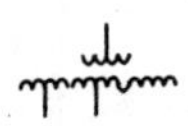 4 WINDING

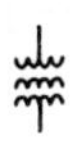 WITH TERTIARY NOT BROUGHT OUT

 AUTOTRANSFORMER

 CONSTANT-CURRENT TRANSFORMER

 INDUCTION REGULATOR

 NONMAGNETIC CORE REACTORS

 MAGNETIC CORE REACTORS

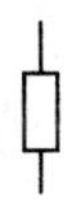 RESISTORS

 STATIC CAPACITORS

 AIR BREAK SWITCH, DIRECT MANUALLY OPERATED, SINGLE THROW

 AIR BREAK SWITCH, DIRECT MANUALLY OPERATED, DOUBLE THROW

 AIR BREAK SWITCH, REMOTE OPERATED, SINGLE THROW

 AIR BREAK SWITCH, REMOTE OPERATED, DOUBLE THROW

 AIR BREAK SWITCH, REMOTE OPERATED, DOUBLE BLADE SELECTOR TYPE

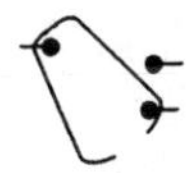 AIR BREAK SWITCH, REMOTE OPERATED, SINGLE BLADE SELECTOR TYPE

 CONTACTOR WITH NORMALLY OPEN CONTACT

 CONTACTOR WITH NORMALLY CLOSED CONTACT

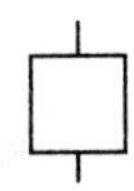 CIRCUIT BREAKER

 FUSES

 LIGHTNING OR SURGE ARRESTER

 PROTECTIVE GAP

 SURGE CAPACITOR

CURRENT TRANSFORMERS:

 SINGLE RATIO SINGLE SECONDARY

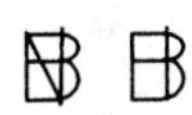 DOUBLE RATIO SINGLE SECONDARY

 SINGLE RATIO DOUBLE SECONDARY

 BUSHING TYPE

POTENTIAL TRANSFORMERS:

 2 WINDING SINGLE RATIO

 2 WINDING WITH TAPPED SECONDARY

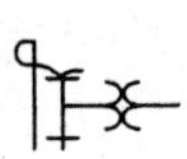 CAPACITANCE BUSHING POTENTIAL

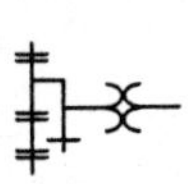 COUPLING CAPACITOR POTRNTIAL

(4) SYMBOLS FOR PUMPS AND PIPELINE COMPONENTS:

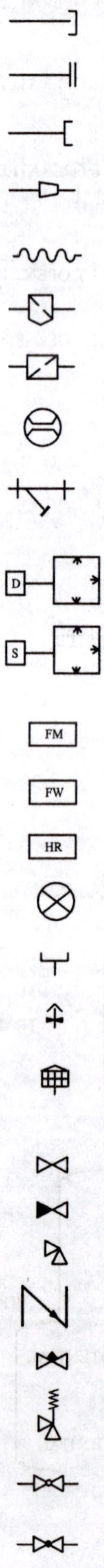

PIPELINE COMPONENTS / ACCESSORIES

- SCREWED CAP
- BLIND FLANGE
- HOSE CONNECTION
- REDUCER
- FLEXIBLE HOSE
- SCREEN / STRAINER
- FILTER / STRAINER
- FLOW METER ORIFICE / VENTURI TYPE
- STRAINER (Y - TYPE
- SPRAY NOZZLE (DELUGE)
- SPRAY NOZZLE (SPRINKLER)
- FROM MONITOR
- FROM WATER MIXER STATION
- HOSE REEL SYSTEM
- HYDRANT
- OPEN PIT DRAIN
- VENT TO ATMOSPHERE
- FLASHBACK ARRESTER

VALVES

- VALVE GENERAL (NORMALLY OPEN)
- VALVE GENERAL (NORMALLY CLOSED)
- ANGLE VALVE (GENERAL)
- ANGLE VALVE (GENERAL)
- CONTROL VALVE (GENERAL)
- PRESSURE RELIEF VALVE
- GLOBE VALVE (NORMALLY OPEN)
- GLOBE VALVE (NORMALLY CLOSE)

PUMPS

- FLUID PUMP GENERAL
- CENTRIFUGAL PUMP
- PISTON PUMP
- DIAPHRAGM PUMP
- SCREW PUMP

DRIVES/GENERATOR/COUPLINGS

- ELECTRIC MOTOR
- DIESEL ENGINE
- ELECTRIC GENERATOR
- STEAM TURBINE
- GAS TURBINE
- SILENCER
- BELLOW

ACTUATORS

- ELECTRIC MOTOR
- PISTON (HYDRAULIC)
- TYPE OF VALVE SUITABLE TO MEET SPECIFICATION
- SPRING (LOADED)
- HANDWHEEL (MANUAL)
- PHEUMATIC

CHAPTER # 1

ALTERNATORS FOR POWER GENERATION

CONTENTS:

1.1 PRIME MOVERS FOR POWER GENERATION.

Alternator is a rotating machine used to generate alternating current by rotating conductors through a magnetic field. Prime mover is a device supplying turning force necessary for rotating (driving) the shaft of a generator (alternator). Alternator generates alternating current (AC). Alternating current is the current that reverses its direction of flow periodically. Reversals generally occur at regular intervals.

Turbine is a rotary type, prime mover, which converts heat or kinetic energy in to rotary mechanical energy to drive generator shaft. Turbine and generator rotor are mounted on the same shaft or coupled together. Governor controls the input to turbine to govern synchronous speed and thus control the output (load) in the generating unit. Synchronous speed means the rotor rotates at the same speed of the rotating magnetic field.

Turbines are classified as:

(a) Combustion turbine: An electrical generator powered by exhaust gases from an oil or gas fired turbine rather than by heat-created steam.

(b) Gas turbine: A combustion turbine that converts energy of hot compressed gases (produced by burning fuel in compressed air) in to mechanical energy that can be used to generate electricity and compress more air.

(c) Hydraulic turbine: A turbine in which the force of water directed against blades fastened to a vertical or horizontal shaft produces mechanical energy.

(d) Steam turbine: A turbine in which heat energy in steam is converted in to mechanical energy for the force of a high velocity flow of steam directed against successive rows of radial blades fastened to a central shaft.

(1) Hydroelectric power stations:

Hydroelectric power stations are situated where there is greatest fall of large quantity of water, i.e. at the bottom of a deep and steep-sided valley or gorge, or near the base of dam having large catchments areas. Dams can be of two types (1) impounding (non-overflow), and (2) spillway (overflow). If impounding dams are built, means must be provided to release excess flow, by providing spillway gates. Spillway dams are always concrete, and for low head power stations. A hydroelectric generating unit consists of steel penstocks with motor operated steel head gates (water-inflow), water turbine (hydraulic turbine) to convert the water energy into mechanical energy, an electric generator to convert mechanical energy into electrical energy, and governor for regulating water pressure. After the water has given up its energy to the turbine, it is discharged through tailrace. The amount of energy available from water depends on both the quantity of water and its pressure at the turbine. The pressure depends on the water head, and is measured as the height that the surface of the water above the turbine. The electrical apparatus is usually housed in the superstructure. Transformers are located within the superstructure or over the draft-tube extension. High voltage switchgears are located outdoors adjacent to the powerhouse and are not an integral part of it. Electrical overhead traveling crane consists of bridge (for longitudinal movement), trolley (for transverse movement), and main and auxiliary hoists (for lifting and lowering of load) is installed above the service bay with traveling facility over the machine hall to handle the heaviest parts such as turbine runner, generator stator and rotor etc. Figure 1.1 (a) illustrates the typical diagram of a hydroelectric scheme.

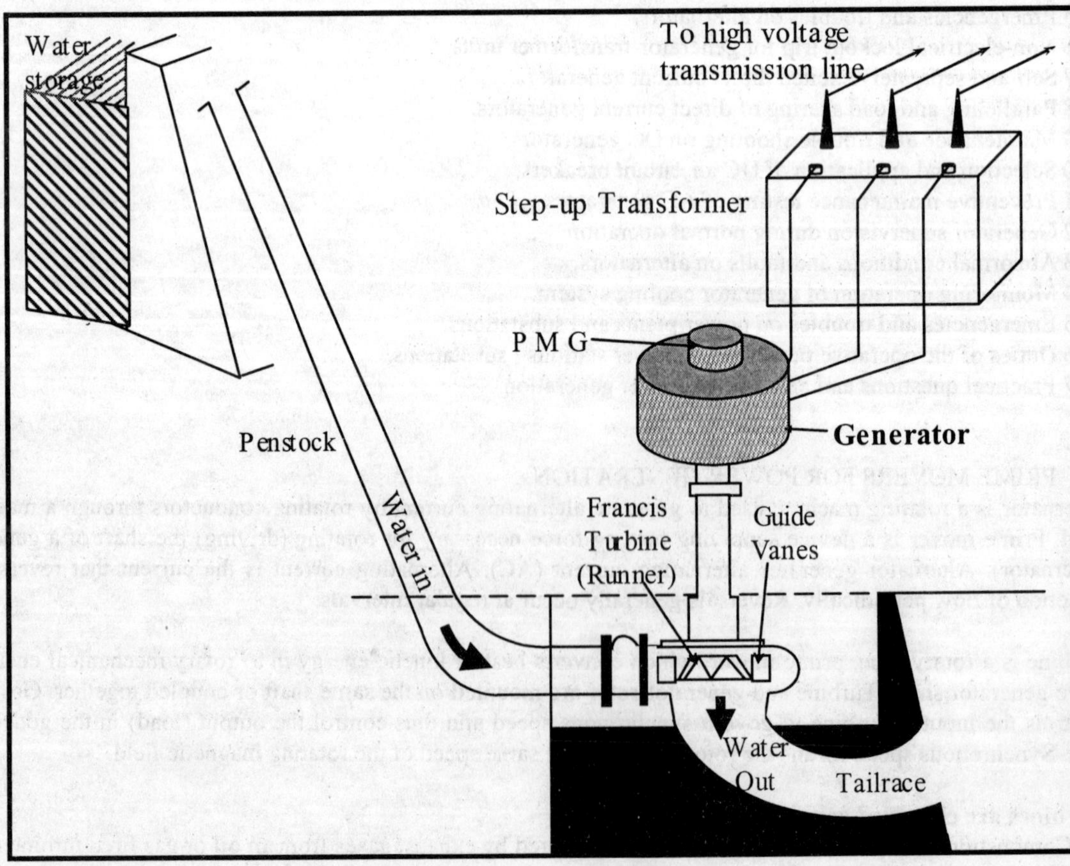

Fig. 1.1 (a): The diagram of hydroelectric scheme.

The three main types of water turbines (named after their inventers) are: (1) Pelton wheels turbine; (2) Francis turbines; (3) Kaplan turbine (Propeller type); all that can be mounted vertically or horizontally. Francis turbine is used where a large flow and medium head of water is involved. Francis turbine has spinning wheels with fixed blades in between two rims. This wheel is called a 'runner'. A circle of guide vanes (wicked gates), surround the runner and controls the amount of water driving it through hydraulic servomotors. The Francis turbine shown in Figure 1.1 (b) consists of:

- A spiral casing, which serves to guide the water up to the guide vanes ring;
- A ring with movable guide vanes, which actually controls the admission of water to the turbine runner;
- A Francis runner, mounted on a shaft provided with guide bearings, a thrust bearing and a seal. The flow through the runner is purely radial for large heads, becoming almost axial for lower heads;
- A control system, which controls the opening of the guide vanes by speed and loading set values given to controllers, which are either mechanical or electronic;
- A draft tube, the purpose of which is to recover the residual energy at the runner outlet.

Pelton wheel is used where a small flow of water with a large head is available. The Pelton wheel has small 'buckets' all around its rim. Water fed through nozzles at very high speed hitting the buckets, pushing the wheel around.

Kaplan turbines are designed for large flows or a small head of water is involved. These turbines resemble ship's propellers. The angle of the blades, are altered to suit the water flow. Kaplan turbines are normally used for flows over 30 m^3/sec, with heads up to 60metre and when there is a large head variation. The number of blades increases in accordance with the water head.

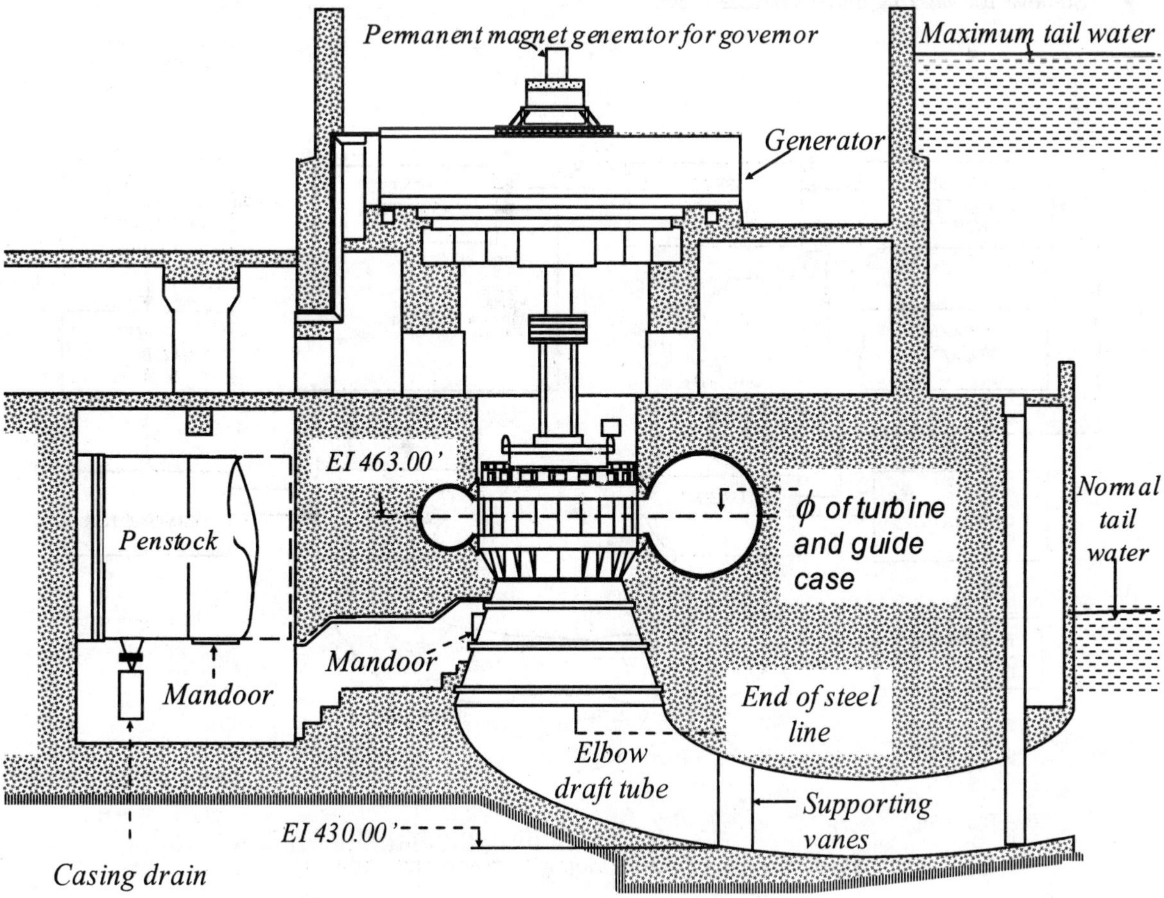

Fig. 1.1 (b): Plate-steel spiral-case setting of a vertical Francis turbine.

Kaplan turbine fundamentally comprises:

- A spiral casing to guide the water to the guide vane ring;
- A guide vane ring with moving guide vanes;
- A Kaplan driving runner fitted on a shaft equipped with guide bearings, thrust bearings and seals;
- A mechanical or electronic speed regulation device;
- A draft tube for the purpose of recovering the residual energy obtaining at the runner exit

A large number of hydroelectric stations are of the pumped storage type. Such stations re-uses the discharged water, by storing it in catchments areas (below the station) and then pumping it back up to the higher catchments of the dam (above the station) in a closed circuit arrangement in "off-peak" times. The principle of its operation is to store electrical energy by pumping water from a lower reservoir in to an upper reservoir by means of the generating set, which runs as a motorized pump during the late night hours, and then return this energy to the power grid when the set runs as a turbo-generator usually during peak hours. This generating set runs in one direction as a turbo-generator, and in the other direction as pump motor. Pumped storage power plant may also be used as synchronous compensator to generate reactive energy demanded by the power grid.

The bulb units are axial flow hydroelectric generating sets in which the water flows through the set in a straight line. The bulb unit essentially consists of a horizontal shaft Kaplan turbine, with fixed or movable guide vane ring, driving an AC generator mounted inside a waterproof housing (the bulb) placed in the middle of the flow of water. For the bulb turbine, the feature is:

- A higher speed of rotation;
- An improvement in the turbine efficiency and smaller loss of efficiency under partial loading;
- Suitable for working under variable heads.

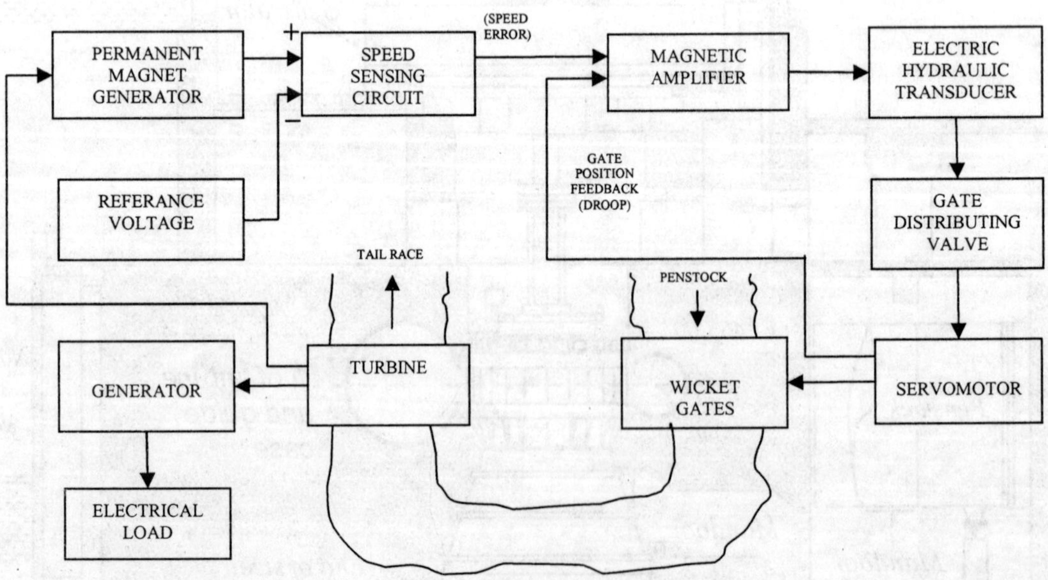

Fig. 1.1 (c): Block diagram of closed loop governor control system.

Figure 1.1 (c) shows the block diagram of a closed loop turbine governor control system. Essential elements of the basic control are briefly described below.

1) A permanent magnet generator mounted on the generator shaft, which rotates at turbine speed and transmits to the governor sensing circuit a voltage signal proportional to the turbine speed.
2) An electric speed sensing circuit, which compares the speed signal from the permanent magnet generator to a stable voltage known as the reference voltage.
3) A magnetic amplifier to convert the error signal and other auxiliary control signals in to a useful electrical output.
4) An electric-hydraulic transducer to transform the electrical signals in to a hydraulic fluid flow that is proportional to the electrical signal.
5) A gate distributing valve or relay valve to amplify the fluid flow to a valve sufficient to operate the servomotor.
6) A servomotor that is moved according to the rate of flow of the hydraulic fluid. This is an "integrator" in that its final position is determined when the hydraulic flow ceases.
7) A sets of wicked gates operated by the servomotor to control the flow of water to the turbine blades.
8) A turbine-generator that revolves at a speed dependent upon the water velocity and the load on the generator.

The above sections, comprises the primary closed loop governing system. All of the dynamic characteristics of each section are related to the overall performance of the entire loop.

Percentage speed droop = $\frac{\textbf{Zero gate speed} - \textbf{Full gate speed}}{\textbf{Normal speed}}$

(2) Steam turbine power plants:

A turbine in which heat energy in steam is converted in to mechanical energy by the force of a high velocity flow of steam directed against successive rows of radial blades fasten to a central shaft. Steam power station is equipped with boiler, turbine, generator, feed water system, air for combustion, exhaust gas system, condenser, cooling tower, fuel handling and feeding system etc.

In a conventional coal-fired thermal power station each generating unit consists of a boiler, a steam turbine, and the generator itself. The modern steam turbine has three stages. The high-pressure section has small blades because the incoming steam has very high energy (about 2,500 pounds per square inch at 1000 degrees Fahrenheit). After the steam passes through the high-pressure section, it is sent back to the boiler to be reheated to 1000 degrees Fahrenheit. The steam is then sent to the next section of the turbine, called the intermediate pressure section. The blades here are larger than those in the high-pressure section. After passing through this section, the steam is sent to the low-pressure section of the turbine. Because much of the energy has already been removed from the steam, the blades here are the largest in the turbine. The steam exits the turbine through the bottom, where it is condensed back in to water. From there it is sent back to the boiler to be made in to steam again.

Single stage steam turbine:

Figure 1.1 (d) shows a typical single stage steam turbine driving an alternator. Such a machine is suitable for industrial applications requiring powers up to 500 KW steam conditions 120 bar, 530°C and rotational speeds below 5000 rpm.

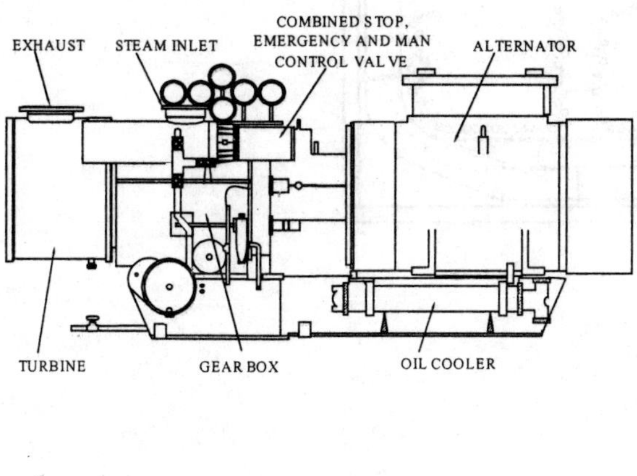

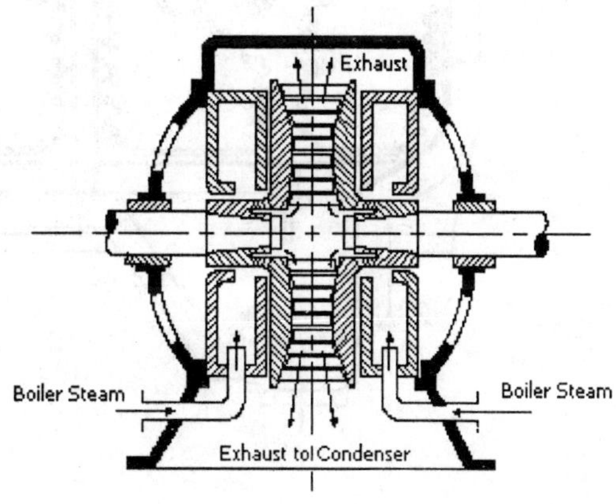

Fig. 1.1 (d): A single stage steam turbine. Fig. 1.1 (e): Radial flow double motion reaction turbine.

Reaction turbine: A turbine in which the flow of water is under pressure.
Figure 1.1 (e) shows the radial flow double motion reaction turbine, in which the steam flow is radially outward or inward, passing through groups of blades set in concentric rings. In such an arrangement the steam leakage and machine efficiency deterioration have tended to discourage the selection of these types.

A typical axial flow condensing-turbine is shown in Figure 1.1 (f). In the multi-stage axial flow designs the blade is of the impulse type or of the reaction type having following features.

1. Velocity-compounded impulse wheels followed by several single-row impulse wheels. This is a combination of the Curtis and Rateau types.
2. Velocity-compounded impulse wheels followed by impulse reaction stages (Curtis-Parsons type).
3. One or more impulse stages followed by several stages of impulse reaction blading (Rateau-Parsons type).

The turbo-generator speed must be maintained within limits if it is to generate power and the control system must also be capable of preventing over-speed upon sudden rejection of load. For this requirement fast acting valves are equipped with full modulation within 0.5 sec. The security of the turbine is also dependent upon the lubrication of the bearings, and the control systems are closely linked with the various lubricating systems of turbine, gearbox and alternator.

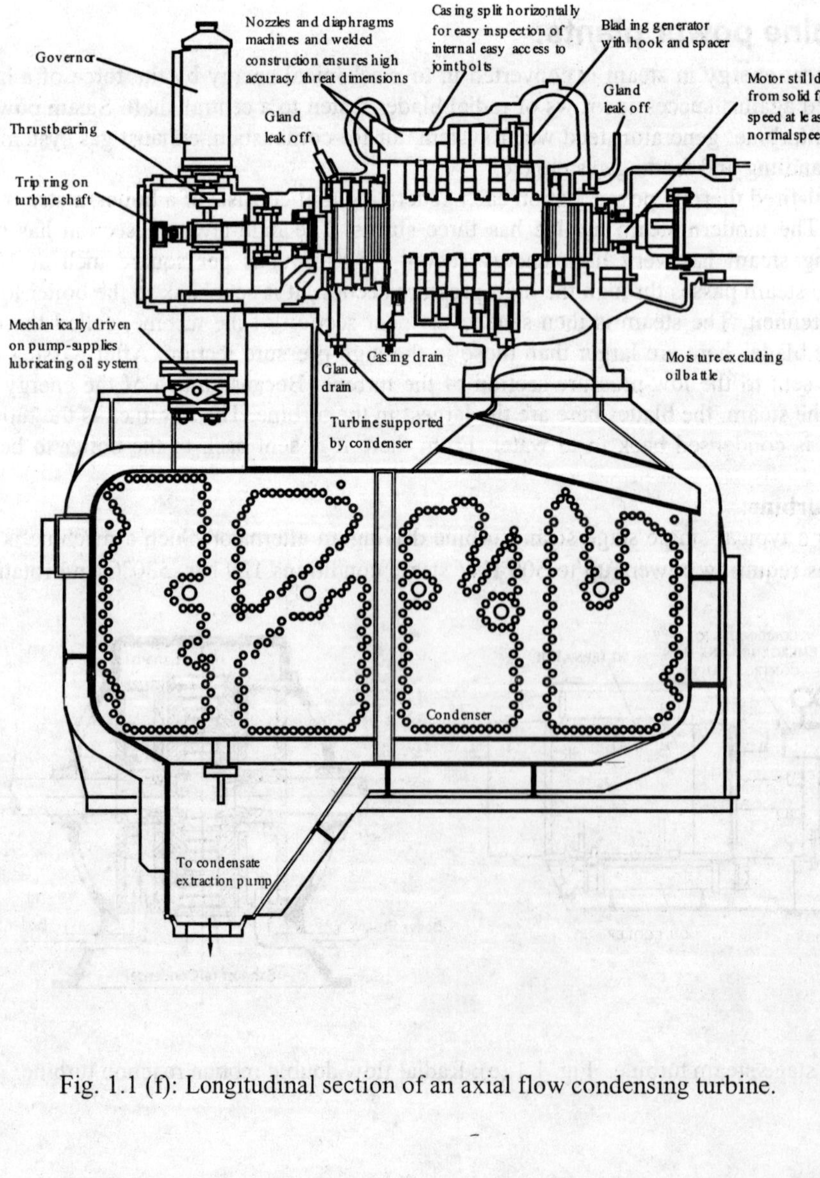

Fig. 1.1 (f): Longitudinal section of an axial flow condensing turbine.

Condenser: A device that condenses steam in to water after the steam has gone through the turbine and before it is fed back into the boiler for reuse. Following are the functions of a condenser unit in a thermal power plant:

(1) To provide vacuum at outlet of steam turbine;
(2) To condense the steam and pass on the condensate to boiler feed;
(3) To remove moisture, gases, air from the condenser chamber.

Cooling towers: A structure that helps remove heat from water in a power generating plant especially in thermal and nuclear power station. Three types of cooling towers are available:

(1) Forced drift tower: In forced drift tower, air is forced in to the tower;
(2) Cross-flow induced drift tower: In induced drift tower, air is thrown out of the tower to induce a draft of cool air.
(3) Byperbolic natural drift tower: In this construction cooling air is forced in to hot water for cooling purpose.

Speed governed turbine control:

A typical high-pressure, quick-response governor and lubricating system for a speed-governed turbine is shown in Figure 1.1 (g). Basically, a speed governor controls the oil pressure supplied to the servo-operated control valves, which are arranged so that they open in sequence to ensure maximum steam economy. Other types of control systems can be incorporated with the basic speed-governed system to provide backpressure, inlet-pressure and pass-out pressure governing.

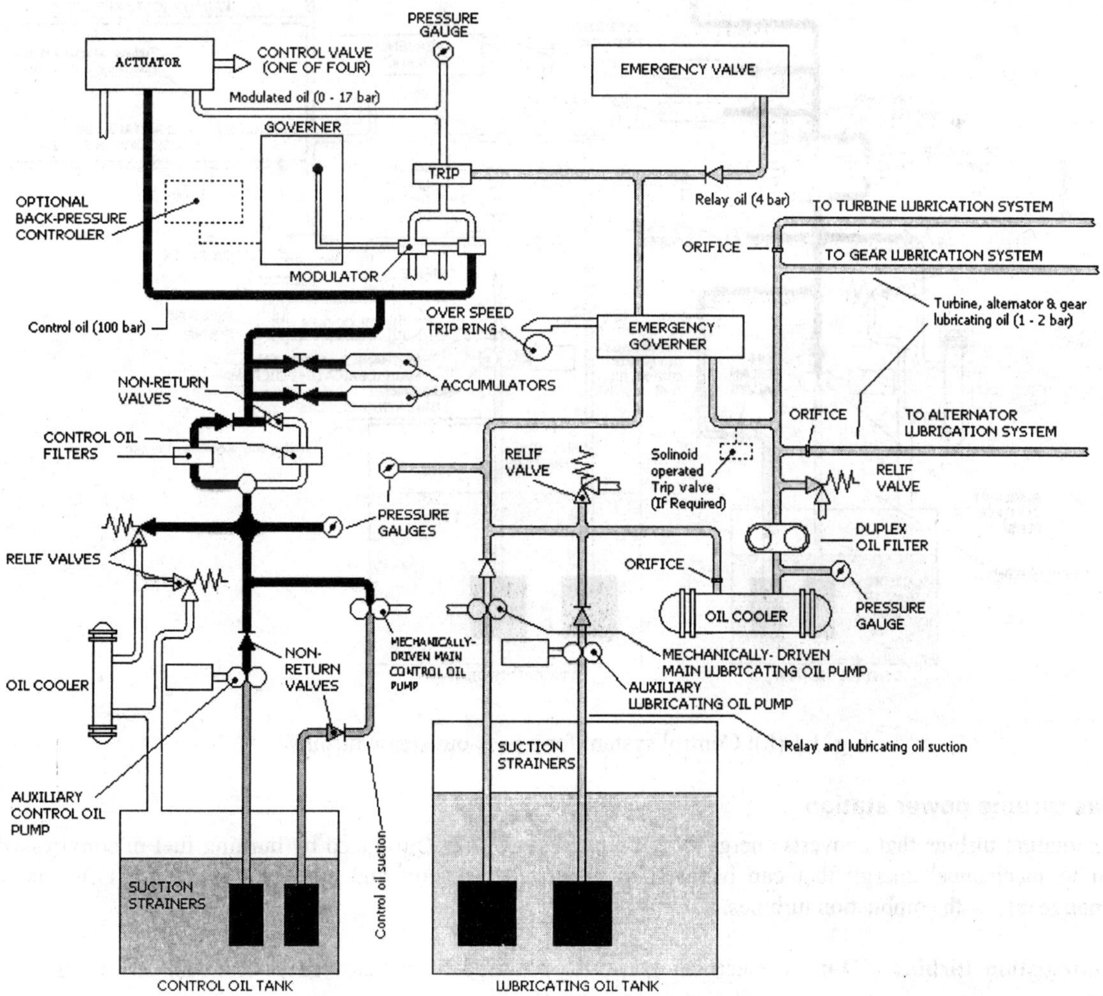

Fig. 1.1 (g): Control system for a speed governed steam turbine.

Pass-out steam turbine control:
A typical fully interlinked control system for a pass-out system is shown in Figure 1.1 (h). Oil is supplied to these systems by a pump normally driven from the turbine rotor, with an auxiliary pump for use when starting the turbine. The main lubricating oil pump draws oil through a suction strainer and discharges to the emergency valve and hence through a cooler and filter to the lubrication system. A separate auxiliary lube-oil pump is fitted for supplying oil to the bearings when stopping and starting and to lift the emergency valve at start-up.

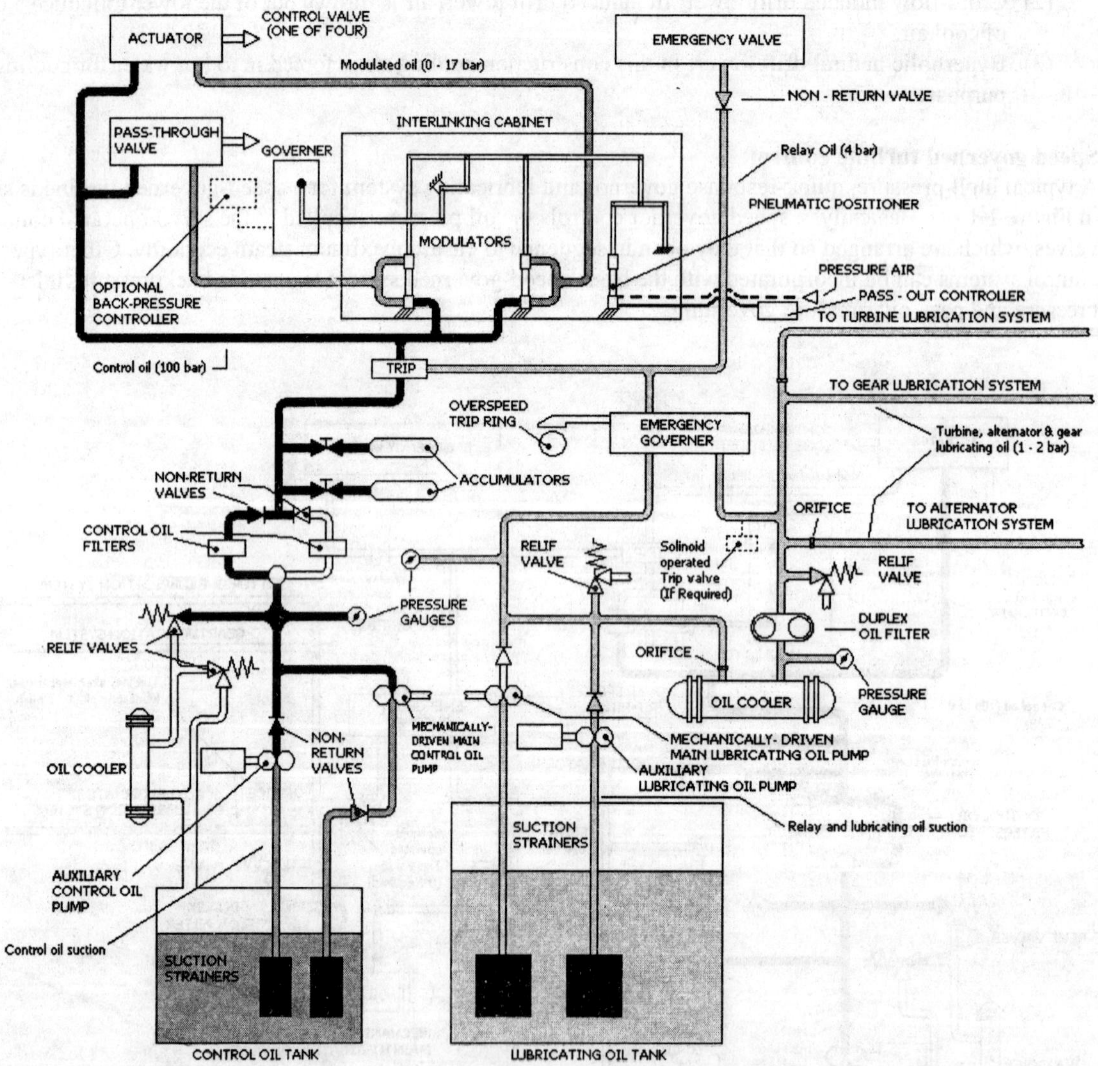

Fig. 1.1 (h): Control system for a pass-out steam turbine

(3) Gas turbine power station

A combination turbine that converts energy of hot compressed gases (produced by burning fuel in compressed air) in to mechanical energy that can be used to generate electricity and compress more air. Often used interchangeably with combustion turbines.

(a) Combustion turbine (CT): An electrical generator powered by exhaust gases from an oil-or gas-fired turbine.

(b) Simple cycle gas turbine:
Schematic diagram for a simple-cycle (single shaft) gas turbine generator set is shown in Figure 1.1 (i). Air enters the axial flow compressor at ambient conditions. Air entering the compressor is compressed to higher pressure. Compression raises the air temperature so that the air at the discharge of the compressor is at a higher temperature and pressure. Upon leaving the compressor, air enters the combustion system, where fuel is injected and combustion occurs at essentially constant pressure. Although high- temperatures are reached within the primary combustion zone, combustion system is designed to provide mixing, burning, dilution and cooling. Thus, by the time the combustion mixture leaves the combustion system and enters the turbine at a mixed average temperature.

In the turbine section of the gas turbine, the energy of the hot gases is converted in to work. This conversion actually takes place in two steps. In the nozzle section of the turbine, the hot gases are expanded and a portion of the thermal energy is converted in to kinetic energy. In the subsequent bucket section of the turbine, a portion of the kinetic energy is transferred to the rotating buckets and converted to work. The compressor rotor and turbine module form a single shaft, which rest in two standard hydrodynamic bearings. Frequency controlled electric starter motor connected to the speed reduction gear is used for starting the turbine during the start-up sequence.

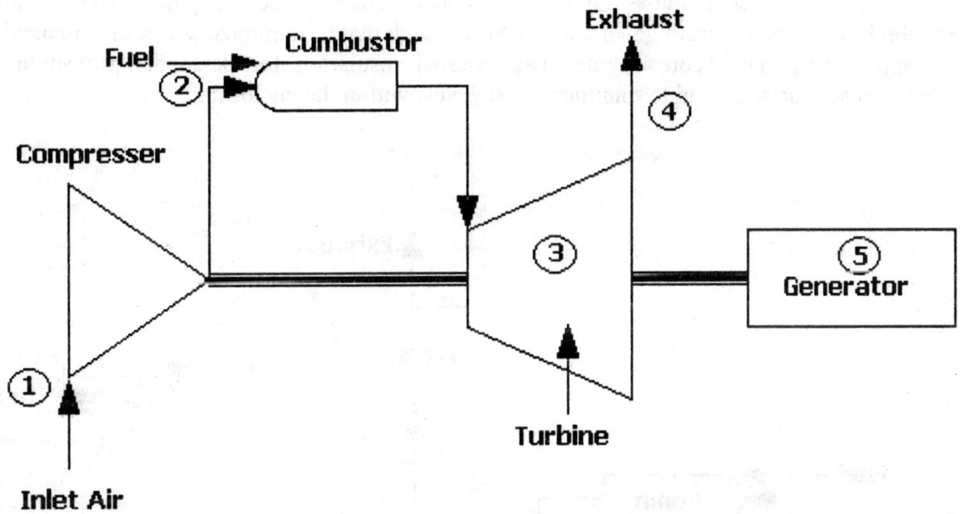

Fig. 1.1 (i): Simple-cycle, single shaft gas turbine.

Some of the work developed by the turbine is used to drive the compressor, and the remainder is available for useful work at the output flange of the gas turbine. Typically more than 50% of the work developed by the turbine section is used to power the axial flow compressor. Single shaft gas turbines are configured in one continuous shaft and therefore, all stages operate at the same speed. These units are typically used for generator drive applications where significant speed variation is not required. Double shaft units are for variable speed applications.

(4) Combined cycle gas turbine power stations:
The combined cycle is generally defined as one or more gas turbines with heat-recovery steam generators (HRSG) in the exhaust, producing steam for a steam turbine generator, heat-to-process, or a combination thereof. Figure 1.1 (J) shows a combined cycle gas turbine in its simplest form. High utilization of the fuel input to the gas turbine can be achieved with some of the more complex heat-recovery cycles, involving multiple pressure boilers, extraction or topping steam turbines, and avoidance of steam flow to a condenser to preserve the latent heat content.

Compressor:
The compressor is of aerodynamic design, uses controlled diffusion airfoils for high efficiency. The first 3 stages have variable geometry. To minimize leakage over the blade tips, seals are applied to remaining stages.

The vane carrier of the high-pressure section, where the blades are shortest, is made from a low-expansion material that helps keep clearances to a minimum. The compressor rotor is built up from discs, which are welded together in to a robust unit using electronic beam welding, a design giving minimum vibrations and very reliable operation. Cooling air for the hot sections of the turbine is extracted from the compressor externally/internally at different stages.

Combustor:
The combustor is of the annular type and is made from welded sheet metal, which is externally convection cooled. The internal surfaces of the combustor, has a thermal barrier coating, which reduces the level of heat transfer and extends the life of the combustor. The combustor has several numbers of burners with built-in dual-fuel (liquid as well as gaseous) dry low emission capability. Combustion system is designed to provide mixing, burning, dilution and cooling.

Turbine:
The multi-stage turbine is built as one module for ease of maintenance and bolted to the stub shaft of the compressor. It has an advanced aerodynamic design with a fully 3D-analyzed flow path with cylindrical sections. The turbine stator flanges are cooled by compressor air to reduce clearances and improve efficiency. The cold-end drive arrangement allows an optimized axial diffuser section. The design of the diffuser connection to the Heat recovery steam generator (HRSG) is such that to minimize losses in combined cycle and cogeneration applications. The "core engine" has external insulation for personnel protection to reduce temperature on exposed surfaces, and to minimize noise levels within the enclosure.

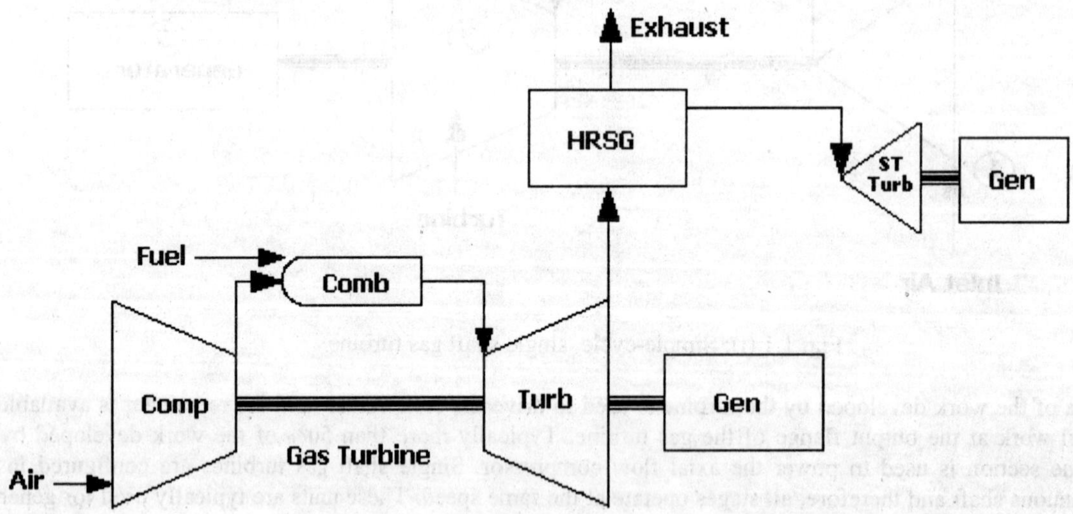

Fig. 1.1 (J): Combined cycle gas turbine arrangement

Start-up drive:
Gas turbines require a start-up drive capable of achieving a high rotational speed so that they can become self-sustaining. The power consumption of the start-up device will be between 5 to 10 % of the machine rating. Electric motor or diesel engine is used for initial priming of the turbine. At idle speed the start motor disengages.

Protection system concept for combined cycle gas turbine unit: Figure 1.1 (k) shows plant interlock and protection system concept scheme of a combined cycle gas turbine generating station consisting two gas turbine generators and one steam turbine generator. Logic diagram is divided in to three groups representing three generators of the combined cycle system. The function of “AND GATE”, “OR GATE”, and “NOT GATE” indicated in the logic diagram is described in the respective symbols.

LEGEND:

1A: Combined cycle gas turbine 1 unit A.
1B: Combined cycle gas turbine 1 unit B.
CB: Circuit breaker
GT: Gas turbine
GTG: Gas turbine generator
HRSG: Heat recovery steam generator
ST: Steam turbine
STG: Steam turbine generator

LOGIC SYMBOL

A, B — C	OR GATE LOGIC OUTPUT 'C' EXISTS IF ONE OR MORE OF LOGIC INPUTS A, B EXISTS
A — C	AND GATE LOGIC OUTPUT 'C' EXISTS IF ALL OF LOGIC INPUT A, B EXIST
A, B — & —	NOT GATE LOGIC OUTPUT 'C' EXISTS IF LOGIC INPUT 'A' DOES NOT EXIST

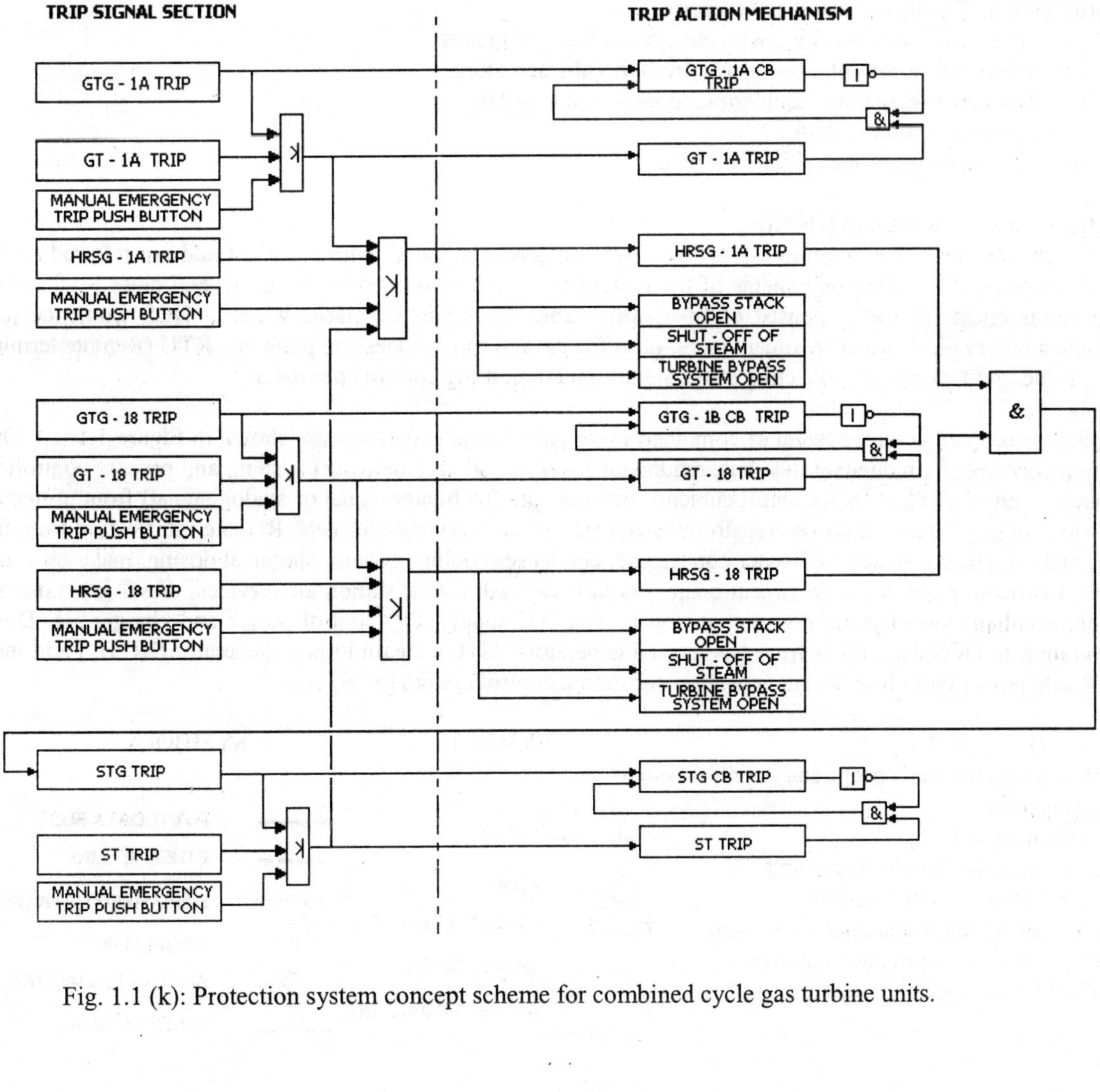

Fig. 1.1 (k): Protection system concept scheme for combined cycle gas turbine units.

Following are the conditions for forced shutdown of gas turbine generator unit A:
(1) Initiation of trip signal for gas turbine generator A and trip coil No 1 of generator circuit breaker energizes to clear the fault by opening the circuit breaker. If not tripped:
(2) Initiation of shutdown signal for gas turbine unit A.
(3) Emergency pushbutton of gas turbine unit A operated.
If any of the above conditions may fulfill, the gas turbine unit A will shutdown and simultaneously trip coil No 2 of generator circuit breaker will energize to open the breaker. Upon gas turbine unit A shutdown, HRSG A will close by shut-off of steam, turbine bypass system open and bypass stack open.

Conditions for forced shutdown, of gas turbine unit B is similar to unit A described above.

Following are the conditions for forced shutdown of steam Generator unit.
(1) Both HRSG A and B shutdown causes steam generator circuit breaker opens and steam generator shuts down.
(2) Initiation of shutdown signal to steam turbine unit.
(3) Manual emergency pushbutton of steam generator operated
If any of the above conditions may fulfill, the steam turbine unit will shutdown and generator circuit breaker will trip open.

Control and instrumentation:
Typical microprocessor controlled gas turbine control system is demonstrated in section 1.8 of this Chapter. In combined-cycle installations the control and monitoring system would be linked in to the higher-level station control system. The instrumentation comprises:

a) Speed and load governing with electro-hydraulic actuators;
b) Temperature control, also via electro-hydraulic actuators;
c) Temperature, pressure and vibration monitoring systems
d) Flame-detection system;
e) Automatic sequential control system.

Distributed control system (DCS):
DCS provides "real-time" monitoring and control of a given "process" within a plant and are referred as "in-plant" systems. All major components of the system are usually confined to one or several close by facilities. The communications media consist of fiber optic cable. Examples of places where a DCS would be used include a power plant, water treatment plant, oil refinery, and food processing plant etc. RTU (Remote terminal unit) is the unit tasked with collecting status signals and outputting control commands.

Typical distributed control system of combined cycle gas turbine generators are shown in Figure 1.1 (L). DCS system consists of a redundant data bus, redundant LAN (Local area network) system, and process controllers. Process controller (Plant DCS control cubicle) receives data (by binary signal or analog signal) from protection relays of all generators, all power transformers and station auxiliary transformers. Remote information from fuel gas, fuel oil, HRSG, steam feed water condensate, condenser cooling system, chemical dosing, make-up water, waste treatment plant, water treatment plant, gas turbine wash water, station air services, diesel generator set, medium voltage switchgears, essential station service AC supply, DC control power and charger etc. Direct integration to DCS data bus is from gas turbine generators (GTG), steam turbine generator (STG), Field input (Fail-safe power type) from steam generator, substation control system (SCS) etc.

LEGEND [Figure 1.1 (L)]: SYMBOL: SYMBOL
MPCS: Manufacturer's proprietary control system.
DT: Gas turbine
ST: steam turbine
CIU: Communication interface unit
SCS: Substation control system
SWAS: Steam and water analysis system
AAMS: Ambient air monitoring system
MMS: Meteorological monitoring system

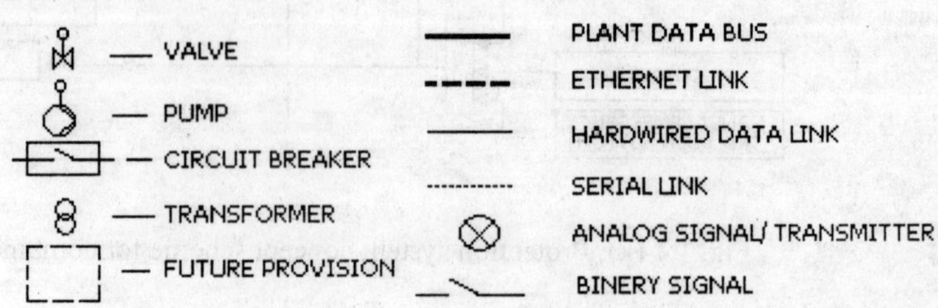

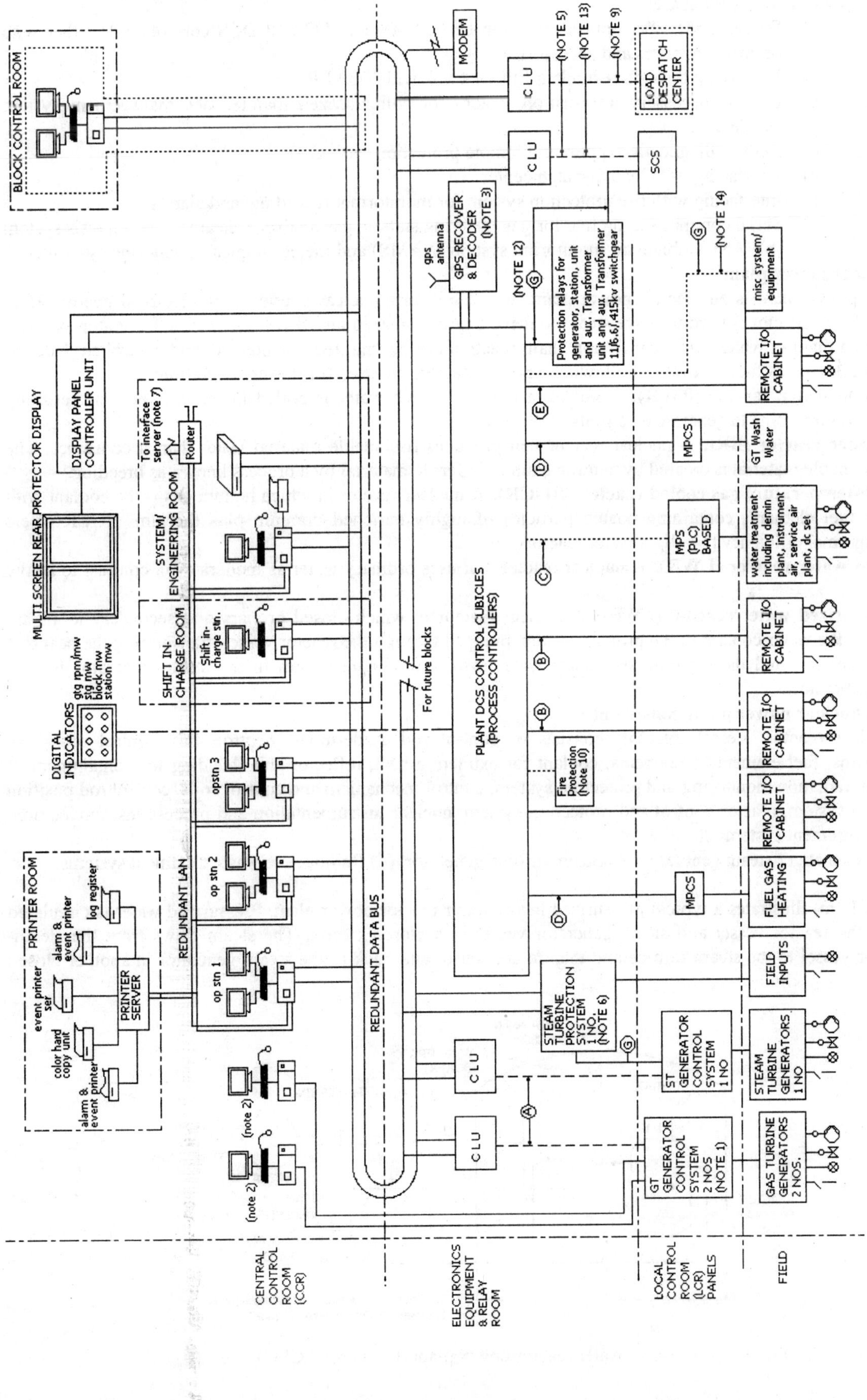

Fig. 1.1 (L): Typical distributed control system of combined cycle gas turbine generators.

Other features of DCS system are:

a) Single mode fiber optic connection between remote I/O and DCS controllers together with optical converters and accessories.
b) Interfacing through redundant Ethernet link with TCP I/P.
c) Provide necessary information system for computerized maintenance management system (MMS).
d) Remote diagnostic support and remote protection setting.
e) Interfacing with load dispatch center
f) Interfacing with fire protection system for monitoring, recording, and alarms.
g) Serial communication line for gas metering station, gas analyzer, steam water analysis system (SWAS), ambient air monitoring system (AAMS) and meteorological monitoring system etc.

(5) Nuclear power plant

Nuclear power plant is an electric power plant, which converts nuclear energy in to electrical energy. Heat produced by a reactor is used to make steam to drive a turbine that in turn drives an electric generator. Nuclear reactor is a plant in which a nuclear fission chain reaction can be initiated, maintained, and controlled. Nuclear Isotopes are used as fuel in reactor. Following types of reactors are used for power generation:

(a) Boiling water reactor (BWR): A nuclear reactor in which water is boiled in the core and the resulting steam drives a turbine to generate electricity.

(b) Breeder reactor (BR): A nuclear reactor that produces fissionable material faster than it consumes. The new fissionable material is created by neutron capture in fertile material by a process known as breeding.

(c) High-temperature gas cooled reactor (HGCR): A nuclear reactor in which helium gas is the coolant with graphite fuel elements containing coated particles of highly enriched uranium plus thorium. HGCR offers greater thermal efficiency than light water reactors.

(d) Light water reactor (LWR): A nuclear reactor that uses ordinary water as moderator in contrast to heavy water.

(5) Pressurized water reactor (PWR): A nuclear reactor in which closed primary and secondary loops are used, with the water coolant in the primary system pumped through the reactor vessel, transporting the heat to a steam generator, and the separate secondary water system producing steam in the steam generator for the turbine generator.

Typical nuclear power plant consists of:

(a) Nuclear reactor: Vessel internals consists of control rod guide-tubes; neutron flux control rod drive mechanisms; fuel element components; coolant for extracting heat, reflector and shielding for containment of radiation, radiation monitoring and protection system, control mechanism and control coils, control rod position indication system, reactor control and protection system, nuclear instrumentation and process instrumentation, flux measurement systems etc.

(b) Heat exchanger steam generator: (c) Steam turbine generator; (d) Radioactive waste treatment systems.

Figure 1.1 (m) illustrates a typical pressurized heavy water reactor power plant. Pressurized water is circulated through the reactor vessel and steam generator vessel in a closed circuit. The steam flows from the steam-generator vessel to the steam turbine and then to condenser and back to the steam generator in another closed circuit.

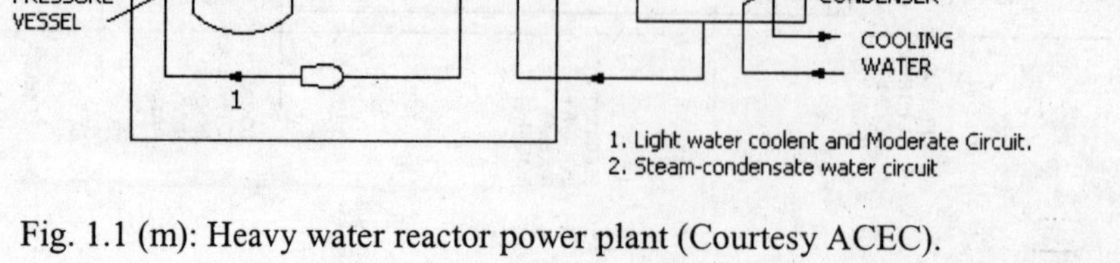

Fig. 1.1 (m): Heavy water reactor power plant (Courtesy ACEC).

(6) Wind turbine power plant:

Wind power is the energy extracted from wind to generate electricity; generally requires wind speed in excess of 16 kilometres per hour (10 miles per hour). The governing equation is as follows:

Wind power = Area of blades in square metre x Power density in watt/square metre

Power density in watt/square metre = KVw^3

K = Constant = 0.6386

Vw = Wind speed in turbine axis, m/s.

There are two types of wind turbines:

(1) Horizontal shaft wind turbine with 3 blades. Generator and turbine are installed on a tall tower. The unit consists of tower, wind turbine (blades, shaft and bearings), generator, Gearbox and mechanical transmission, Power and control cable, Wind direction sensor, Switchgear, microprocessor controlled control and protection panel etc.

(2) Derrius rotor with an oval blade in vertical plane rotating around vertical axis. The generator is located on ground at the base of the vertical axis.

A wind farm has several wind turbine generator units operating in Parallel. There are three different types of generators which are diagrammatically illustrated in Figure 1.1 (n)]: (1) Variable speed asynchronous AC generator with rectifier and inverter; (2) Synchronous generator; (3) DC generator with inverter. In all the three cases the output obtained is of constant frequency AC supply.

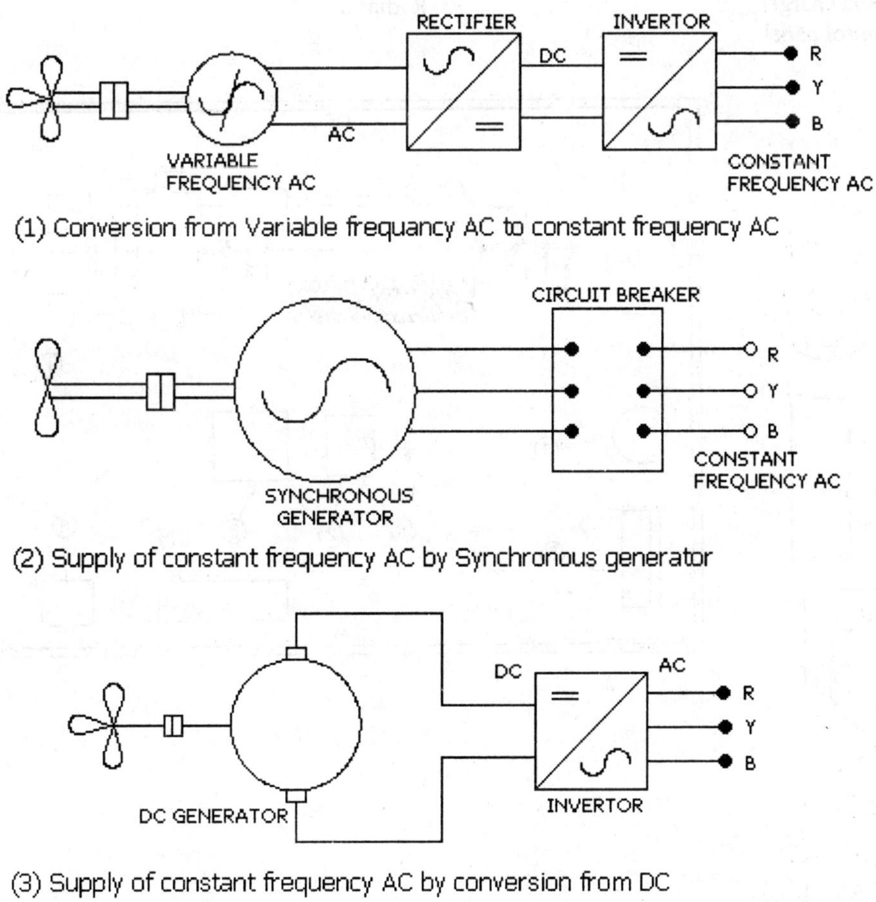

Fig. 1.1 (n): Typical generation systems for wind powered generators.

(7) Diesel power plant

When driving a generator the diesel engine is usually a multi-cylinder machine required to operate at synchronous speed which is, in turn, dependent upon the required frequency (f) and the number of generator poles (p).

Hence engine speed, $N = \frac{120\ f}{P}$ revolution / minute

Typical block layout of a diesel engine room is shown in Figure 1.1 (o). The engine foundation requirements (including anti-vibration mounting pads), data will be provided by the generator set manufacturers. While ventilation considerations (excluding combustion air requirements) heat recovery equipments are required to overcome 8% of the engine rating which will be radiated as heat. The compression ignition engine can operate on a variety of liquid fuels and gases. The engine may also operate in a dual-fuel mode, using a mixture of gas and air with the option to revert to a liquid fuel in the event of any interruptions to the gas supply. Thus a more complex control and protection system is required in order to give modulation for both the oil and gas flows.

LEGEND

1. Diesel generator set
2. Jacket water header tank
3. Lubricating oil service tank
4. Air receiver
5. Diesel driven compressor
6. Batteries and charger
7. Engine control panel
8. Pneumatic control panel
9. Fuel oil control panel
10. Engine exhaust silencer
11. Charge air filter
12. Daily service fuel oil tank
13. Radiator

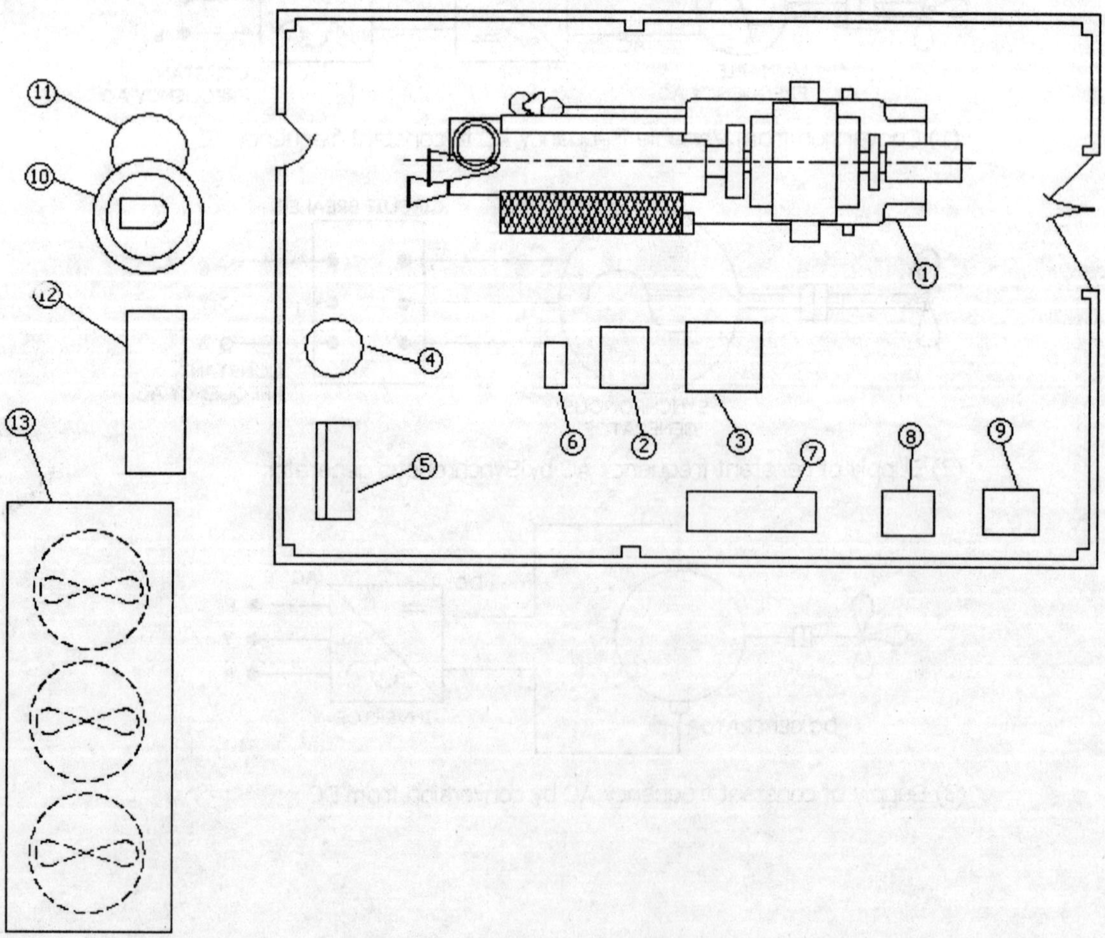

Fig. 1.1 (o): The layout of a typical Diesel generator plant.

For small engines below 500 KW output, air-cooling is considered. However, fan cooling and/or water-cooling by circulation of water through cylinder jackets is the method normally used for larger diesel generator plants. As an alternative to the cooling tower, when a good source of raw water is available, this can be used on one side of the heat exchanger. A typical closed circuit secondary cooling system is diagrammatically shown in Figure 1.1 (p).

Starting diesel engines:

There are two methods of starting diesel engines:

(1) Electric starter motor: When the start push button is pressed or remote auto-start signal is initiated, battery current will flow through starter motor magnetic switches and energizes pinion solenoids. This causes the start motor to crank the engine. When engine starts to run and the r.p.m increases to the speed of the crank terminate speed setting, the speed switch will open to disconnect the start motor.

(2) Air starter: If engine has an air starter motor, current will flow through DC operated air-start solenoid valve, when start pushbutton is pressed or remote start signal is initiated. Air solenoid will open the air supply to the air-start motor, which will crank the engine. The engine will now start to run and the r.p.m increases to the speed of the crank terminate speed setting. Speed switch will now operate to stop current flow to the air-start solenoid. This will cause to shut-off air supply to the starter motor.

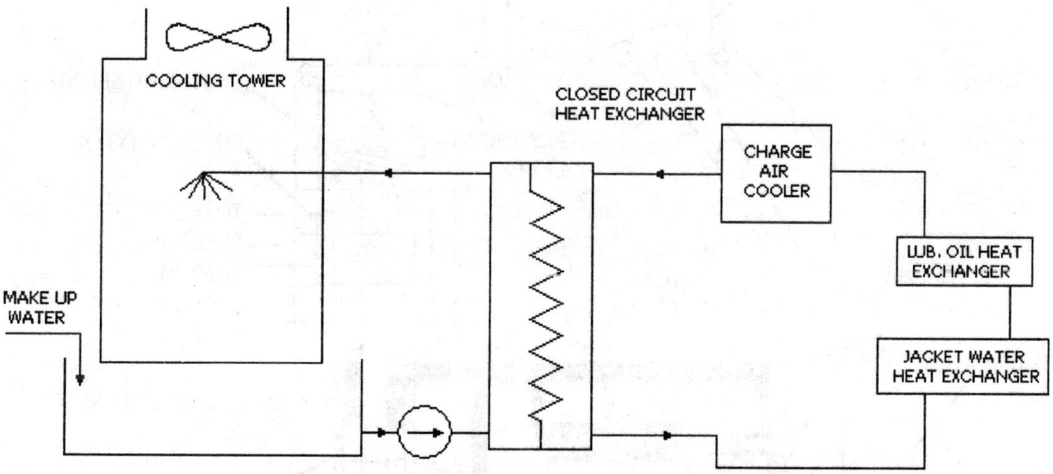

Fig. 1.1 (p): Typical closed circuit secondary cooling system.

Governor: Governor is a device, which controls engine speed and thus the generator output frequency. Engine speed is controlled by the use of variable speed governors, which can be mechanical, mechanical-hydraulic or electronic. Electric fuel control governor shown in Figure 1.1 (q) is an isochronous (same speed at no load and full load) or speed droop governor that consists of a magnetic pickup unit (MPU), a governor control (load sharing and speed control device), and an electric governor actuator (EGA). The actuator is mounted within the fuel pump housing. Parallel load sharing control system has two functions: (1) Precision engine speed control; (2) Kilowatt load sharing unit; which measures engine speed constantly and makes necessary corrections to the engine fuel setting through an actuator connected to the fuel system. The engine speed is felt by a magnetic pickup. As the teeth of the flywheel ring gear go through the magnetic lines of force around the magnetic pickup, an AC voltage is produced. The ratio between the frequency of this voltage and the speed of the engine is directly proportional. An electric circuit inside the parallel load sharing control box senses this AC voltage. In response, it sends a DC voltage from the control, which is inversely proportional to the engine speed, to the actuator.

The actuator is connected to the fuel system by linkage. It changes the electrical input from the control box to mechanical output that changes the engine fuel setting. For example, if the engine speed is more than the speed setting, the control box will decrease fuel to the engine. Actuator will now adjust a new fuel setting to make the engine speed same as the speed setting in the electric governor. Actuator pilot valve plunger is connected to permanent magnet that is spring suspended in the field of a twin coil solenoid. The output signal from the electric speed control unit is applied to the solenoid coils to make a magnetic force, which is proportional to the current in the coils. This force always tries to move the magnet and pilot valves plunger in the down direction to increase fuel. The centering spring at the top of plunger force always tries to move the magnet and pilot valve plunger in the up direction to decrease fuel. When the unit runs on normal speed, at steady state conditions, these two forces are equal but in opposite directions. The pilot valve plunger at this time will be centered. If there is an increase in engine speed, the input voltage to the actuator solenoid coils will be decreased. The magnetic force of the solenoid coils also will now be decreased. This allows oil under the power pistons to drain to sump, and the down movement of the power piston will cause rotation of terminal shaft in the decrease fuel direction. Similarly, if there is a decrease in engine speed voltage and magnetic field in the actuator solenoid coil will be increased. Now the pilot valve plunger will move down to allow to pressure oil under the power piston. Kilowatt load sharing between groups of engine driven generating sets is made possible by electric circuits in the control box. The load on each generator in the system is measured constantly by, its control box. The load sharing circuits in the control box make constant corrections to the voltage sent to the actuators. This gives Kilowatt load sharing.

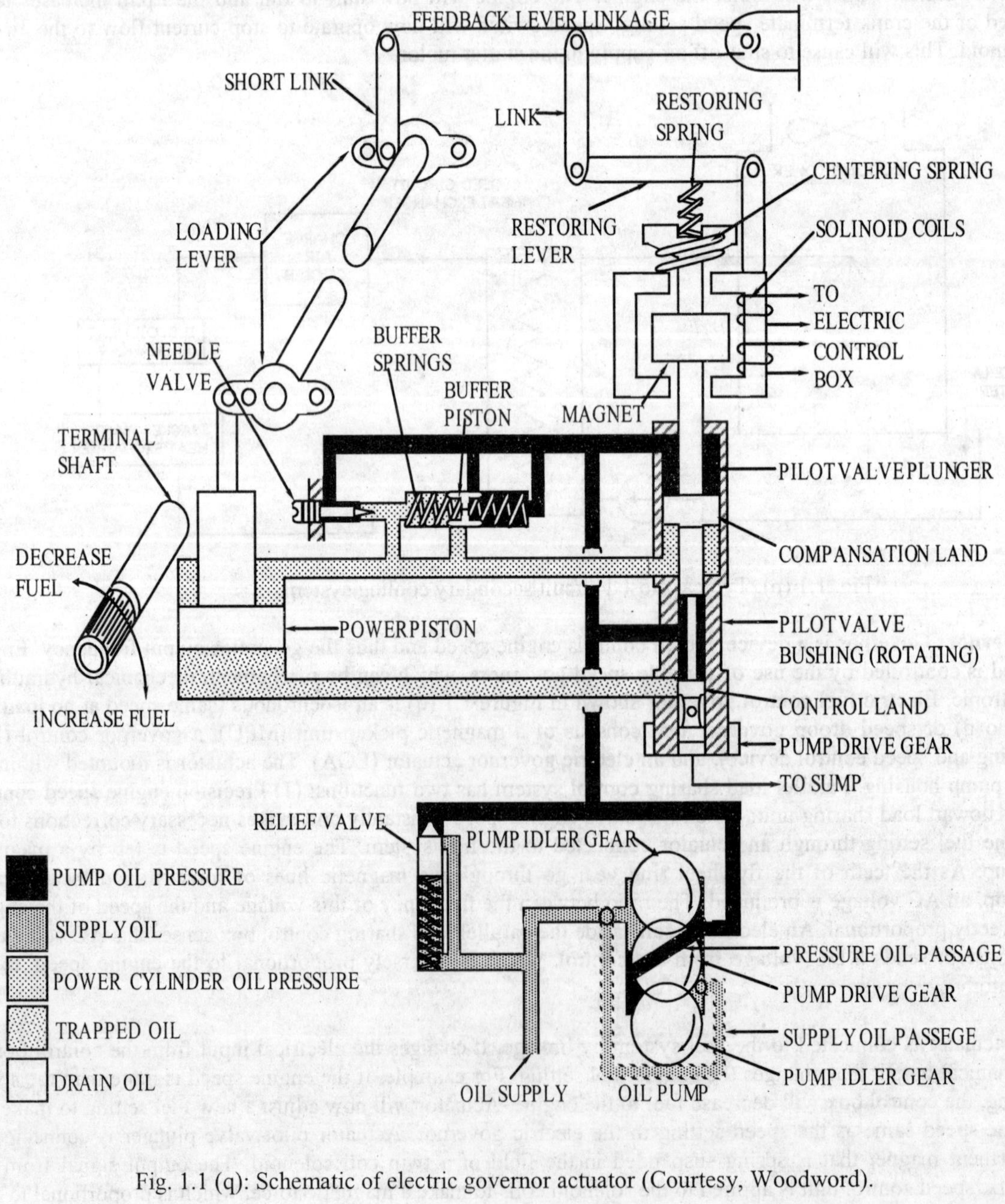

Fig. 1.1 (q): Schematic of electric governor actuator (Courtesy, Woodword).

Typical signal monitored and recorded are:

1. Engine and turbocharger speeds;
2. Lubricating oil pressure and temperature;
3. Cooling water temperature;
4. Exhaust temperature

Typical alarms and annunciations are:

a) Engine cooling water high outlet temperature
b) Engine lube oil system low inlet pressure;
c) Fuel system: (1) Service tank low level, and (2) Engine inlet low pressure
d) Over-speed

Figure 1.1 (r) shows the wiring diagram of an electric governor actuator connecting the stop solenoid and fuel shutoff valve. Governor control unit has several built-in protections and settings.

(a) GAIN and STABILITY setting: Set the potential meters "GAIN" and "STABILITY" to the center position. During operation, turning the "GAIN" potentiometer clockwise will increase the governor reaction with changes in load. Turning counter-clockwise will give a slower reaction. Turning the stability control clockwise will shorten the time for the system's recovery after a change in load. Turning counter-clockwise will give a longer recovery time for the system.

(b) Speed potentiometer setting: The speed potentiometer is to be adjusted to obtain normal running speed and frequency. Run the engine without load and turn the gain control clockwise until instability occurs. Then turn back the control until stability is obtained and then an additional 1/8 turn. Adjust the stability control in the same way as for the gain above. Repeat the gain and stability adjustment after loading the generator.

LEGEND:

1. Control unit	5. Fuse	9. Engine speed monitoring
2. Actuator	6. Switch / MCB	10. Over-speed switch.
3. Magnetic Pickup	7. Stop-solenoid	11. Relay
4. External speed trim	8. Fuel shut off valve	12. Battery

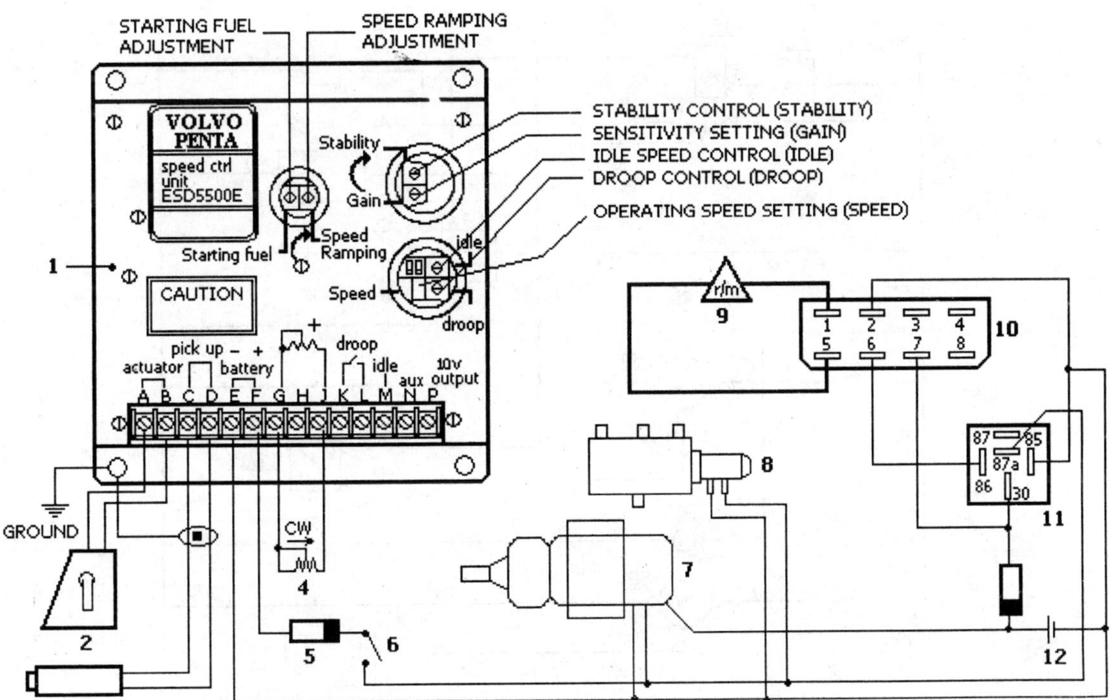

Fig. 1.1 (r): Wiring diagram of an electric governor actuator (Courtesy, Volvo Penta).

Figure 1.1 (s) shows the wiring diagram of typical battery start engine of a diesel generator set. Engine will automatically shutdown due to the operation of over speed switch, low oil pressure switch, High engine temperature and fail to start. Starter motor cutout is preset at 40% normal running speed. The over-speed trip is preset at 110% of the normal speed. Auto start-stop circuit is shown in figure 1.3 (i).

LEGEND:

1. Battery
2. Switch
3. Starter motor (M)
4. Alternator (G)
8. Fuse
10 Oil pressure sender
11 Temperature switch
14 Oil pressure switch,
15 Temperature switch
16 Relay
17 Stop solenoid
18 Signal horn
46 Water level switch.
52 Start button
52a Start relay
53 Interlocking button.
54 Stop button
57 Charging control lamp
58 Oil pressure gauge
59 Water temperature gauge
61 Hour meter
65 Switch for instrument light
66 Instrument light
84 Holding current relay.

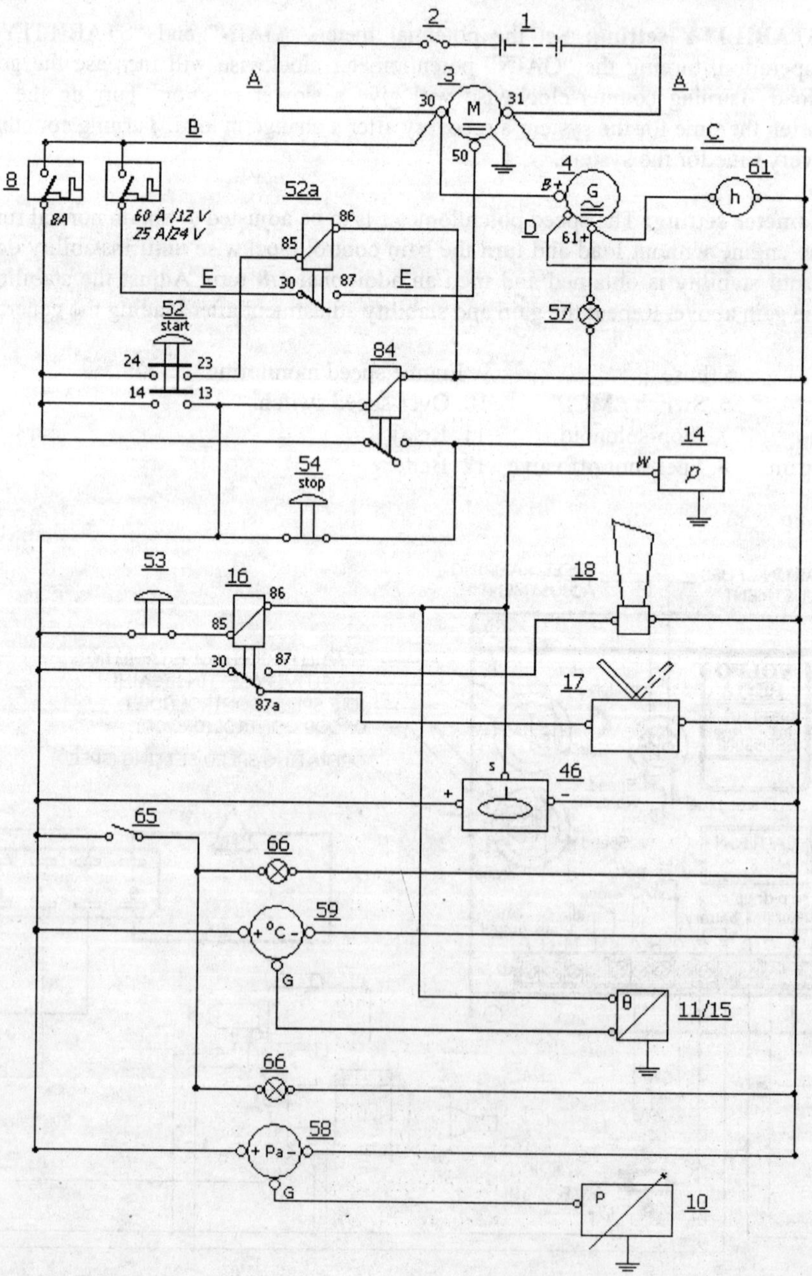

Fig. 1.1 (s): Wiring diagram for battery start engine of a D.G. Set (Courtesy, Valvo Penta).

Various types of power plants (generating stations), type of prime mover and primary energy source etc. are listed in Table 1.1 (1).

Table 1.1 (1): Prime movers for power generation.

S/No	Plant type	Primary-energy source	Turbine type	Technical requirements
1	Hydro-electric plants	Water stored in dams	Hydro-turbine (Petton wheel /Francis turbine / Kaplan turbine)	Convert water energy stored in high head dam reservoir in to electric energy. Water flows through penstocks to drive the turbine. Water pressure is controlled by wicked-gates
2	Coal fired steam thermal plants	Coal obtained from Coal mines	Steam turbine	Steam expands through turbine blades to drive turbine shaft. The exhaust steam is condensed in the condenser and re-use.
3	Gas turbine plants	Air/gaseous/liquid fuel	Gas turbine	Hot compressed air and gaseous/liquid fuel are burnt in the combustion chamber and expanded through blades of gas turbine.
4	Combined-cycle gas/steam plants	Natural-gas /methanol Ethanol /petroleum	Gas-turbine and steam turbine	Unit consists of minimum two gas turbines and one steam turbine. Heat-recovery steam generator, which recovers heat from exhaust and feeds it to the boiler.
5	Nuclear-power plants	Nuclear-fuel, uranium	Steam turbine	Pressurized water is circulated through the reactor-vessel and steam-generator vessel in a closed circuit. The steam flows from the steam-generator vessel to steam turbine and then to condenser & back to steam generator
6	Oil fired thermal plants	Petroleum /crude oil	Steam turbine	Steam is produced by burning of oil
7	Wind power plants	Wind energy	Wind turbine	Operates only windy periods. Blades mounted on the rotor shaft are driven by the wind energy.
8	Diesel-electric plants	Diesel	Diesel Engine	High speed diesel engine with electronic governor and engine monitoring system
9	Geo-thermal plants	Geo-thermal brine (hot fluid) Hydro-carbon hot gas	Gas turbine	Gas turbine driven by expanding high temperature high-pressure gas. Exhaust of gas is condensed in condenser.
10	Ocean-thermal plants	Warm-water from Ocean	Gas turbine	Heat exchanger transfers heat to vapourise. Liquid vapours drives gas turbine.
11	Ocean-waves plants	High waves from Ocean	Air turbine	Shoreward waves in the sea create pressure on piston of air cylinder. The air, get compressed and drives air turbine.
12	Waste incineration plants	Municipal waste	Steam turbine	Steam is produced by burning of municipal waste

1.2 BRUSH-TYPE AND BRUSHLESS ALTERNATORS.

AC generators (Alternators) used for generation of electricity are classified in to (a) Asynchronous generators (b) Synchronous generators. Asynchronous generators are induction machines (less than 5 MW) operated at super synchronous speed. Synchronous generators are operated at synchronous speed and the terminal voltage and power factor of operation are controlled by the excitation.

Single-phase alternators:

In a single-phase alternator [Figure 1.2 (a)], the stator coils are connected in series, voltages therefore, add to produce a single-phase AC voltage. "Phase" relates to the timing of the magnets passing over the coils at different times. "Out of phase" means out of time. With single phase the magnets and coils all lineup with each other and are said to be in phase. Figure 1.2 (b) shows the step-by-step development of the induced voltage during one revolution of armature in magnetic field.

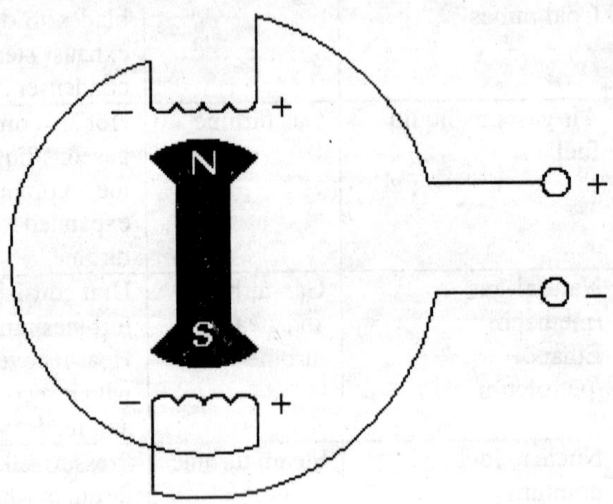

Fig. 1.2 (a): Stator connection of a two pole single-phase generator.

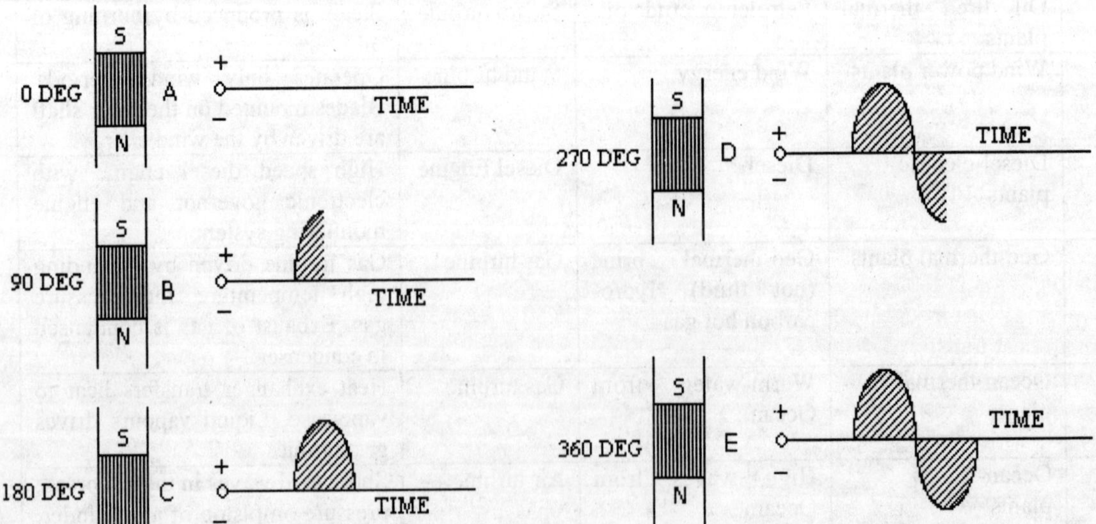

Fig. 1.2 (b): The step-by-step development of the induced voltage during one revolution.

The diagram in Figure 1.2 (c) shows single-phase connection of a 4-pole (2 pair) alternator. Stator coils are wound opposite to the first i.e. one is wound clockwise (North pole) and next is counter clockwise (South pole). If the unit, have 8 magnets (8 poles) then it would also have 8 coils connected in series in order for the voltage induced in the windings to add together for a single output. Figure 1.2 (d) illustrates the typical connection diagram of a self-excited, self-regulated single-phase four-pole alternator. The rotor has two coils designated as main winding and auxiliary winding and its rectified output is connected to the quadrature axis winding.

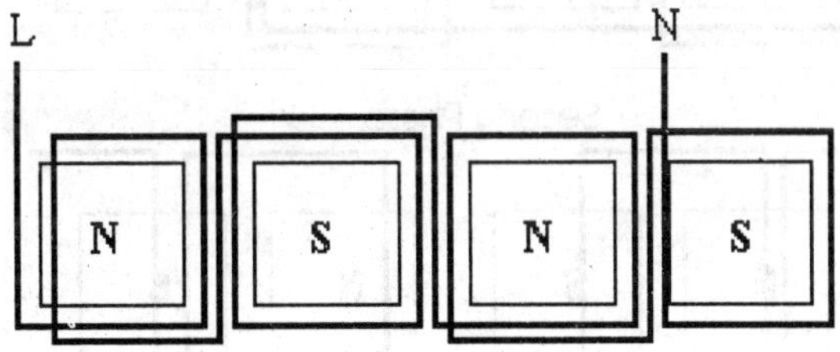

Fig. 1.2 (c): Stator connection of a 4-pole single-phase alternator.

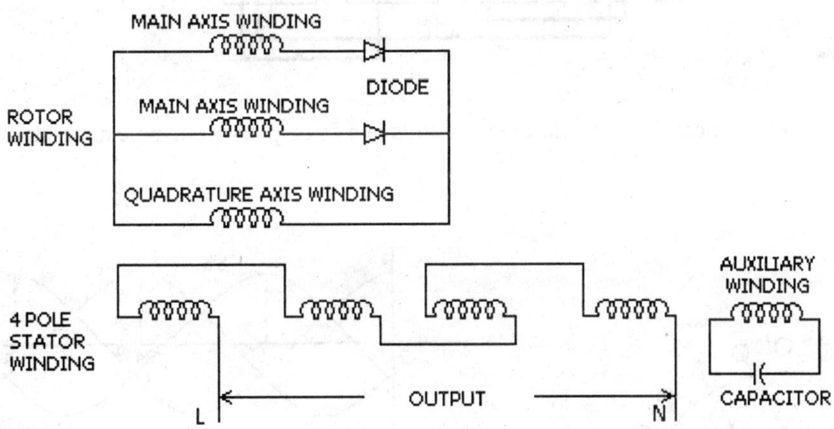

Fig. 1.2 (d): Connection diagram of self-excited, self-regulated, single-phase 4-pole alternator.

The stator frame is fabricated with standard steel, designed to ensure proper distribution of airflow over core and winding. Stator core is made up of low loss silicon steel lamination. High-efficiency-fan provides maximum heat transfer. To ensure minimum vibration during operation rotors are dynamically balanced. Non-drive end has grease lubricated sealed bearing. Drive end has roller/ball bearing. Generator stator windings are impregnated with resin/varnish. Epoxy coating is provided on the winding overhangs for protection against saline and dust contamination.

Three-phase alternator:

Three-phase system would have minimum three coils for each pair of magnets. A pair means one north- pole, and one south-pole magnet. There are many combinations for any one setup. For example, three sets of four coils in series. Figure 1.2 (e) shows the diagram of four magnets with the placement of each of the coil sets. First phase covers only the north-pole magnets and are wound all the same direction. The second phase and third phase are identical to the first with the exception they are offset equally. Starting end wires are labeled R1, Y1, B1 and the finishing end wires labeled R2,Y2, B2 respectively.

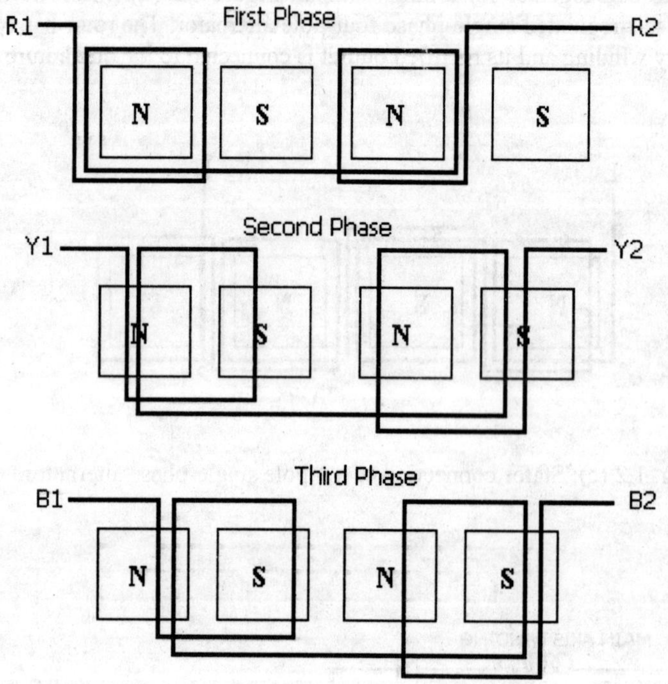

Fig. 1.2 (e): Typical arrangement of stator coils in a three-phase four-pole alternator.

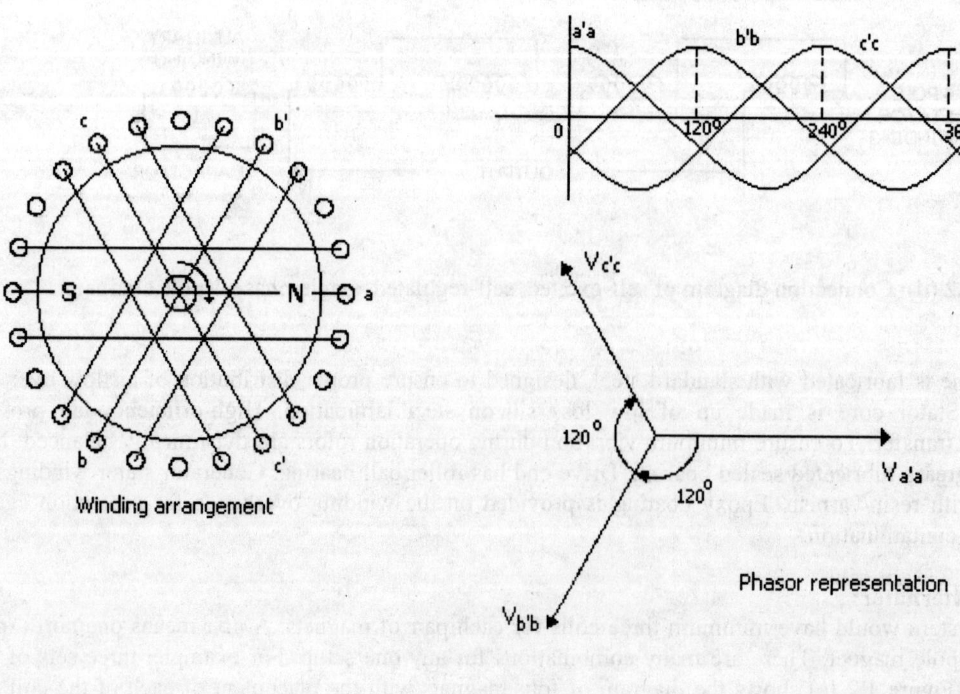

Fig. 1.2 (f): Development of three-phase sine wave.

Figure 1.2 (f) shows typical winding arrangement, phasor representation and development of three-phase sine waves in an alternator. The stator winding of a rotating-field AC generator consists essentially of a number of coils contained in slots on the inner periphery of an annular stator core built up of sheet steel laminations (see winding arrangement). The coils are so proportioned and interconnected as to produce the required number of phases, the required number of poles, and the required voltage. In the three-phase system (see phasor representation), three electrically discrete phases, mutually displaced in time/phase by one-third of a complete cycle (i.e. by 120 electrical degrees or $2\pi / 3$ radians) have been combined in to a star neutral connection. Figure 3 of 1.2 (f) represents one complete 360°cycle of the sinusoidal voltage waveforms of a three- phase system. Figure 1.2 (g) shows the production of a rotating field in a synchronous motor or induction motor, which is fed by a three-phase alternator. The m.m.f contributed by the three balanced currents, are represented in (A). The instantaneous value of the currents, are shown in (B). Positive currents in the concentrated windings produce m.m.f's in the directions indicated in (C). At the instant wt = 0°, say, Ia is a positive maximum and Ib and Ic are negative and one-half maximum. Assuming a linear magnetic circuit, the principle of superposition applies, and the flux contributions of the three currents are as shown in (D). The stator flux is the vector sum of the three contributions. At wt = 30°, the relative magnitudes of the three currents have changed and the rotor position of the resulting stator flux has shifted 30°, i.e a rotating magnetic field exists because the position of maximum flux rotates at synchronous speed.

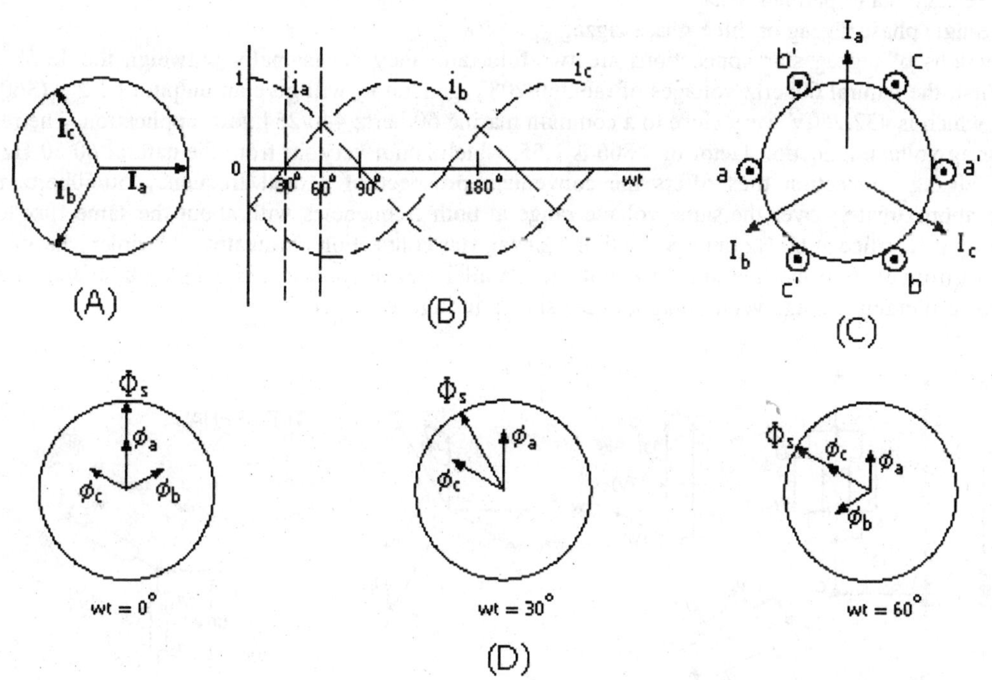

Fig. 1.2 (g): Production of a rotating stator field in a synchronous motor.

There are basically two ways to connect a three-phase alternator for obtaining a three-phase output. Figure 1.2 (h) shows star connection (called wye in USA) and delta connections of a three-phase alternator. With delta configuration, lower output voltage and higher output amps, but with star configuration, higher output voltage and lesser output amps will obtain.

In star connection, line current = phase current, and line voltage = Phase voltage x √3.

In delta connection, line current = phase current x √3, and line voltage = phase voltage.

In both case, power output will be same

A delta is a closed circuit, and although the fundamental voltages naturally balance each other out round it, any third harmonic voltages do not. On the contrary they are in time-phase with each other. They thus add up directly round the closed delta, with only the leakage inductances and the resistances to limit the circulating current produced. Star connections have the advantage of an earthed neutral and for low voltage system, a 3-phase 4-wire service.

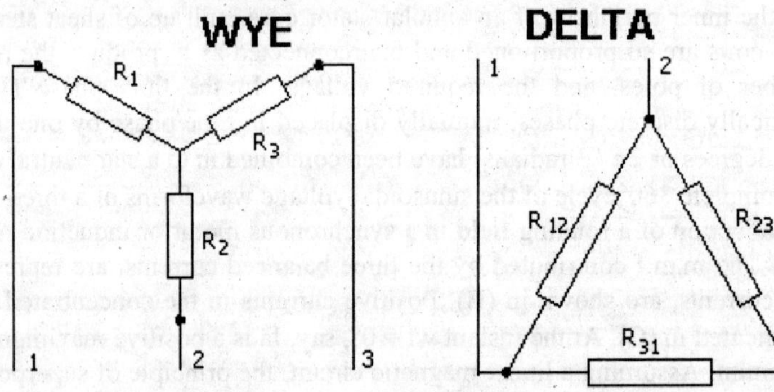

Fig. 1.2 (h): Three-phase alternator stator winding, Star & Delta connections.

12 coil stator windings are usually adopted for connecting the system in the following manners:

1. Series star or Parallel star
2. Series delta or parallel delta
3. Single phase zigzag or three-phase zigzag

The attractions of zigzag star connections are two-fold, and they occasionally outweigh the 13.5% loss of output. First, the natural 60hertz voltages of the 360/208V generator, will give an output of 1.2 x (360/208) at 50 hertz, which is 432/250V, very close to a common marine 60 hertz 440/254 volts application. The reciprocal of the zigzag voltage reduction factor of 0.866 is 1.55, which is not very far from the natural 60/50 Hz ratio of 1.2. The zigzag connection thus offers the convenient prospect of a dual frequency 50/60hertz machine operating approximately over the same voltage range at both frequencies with about the same flux level and with an output sacrifice at 60 Hz only. Second, the zigzag star connection eliminates all "triplen" harmonics (3rd 9th 15th etc) from even to the line to neutral voltage. Parallel zigzag connections, single-phase and three-phase and the corresponding voltage vector diagrams are shown in Figure 1.2 (i).

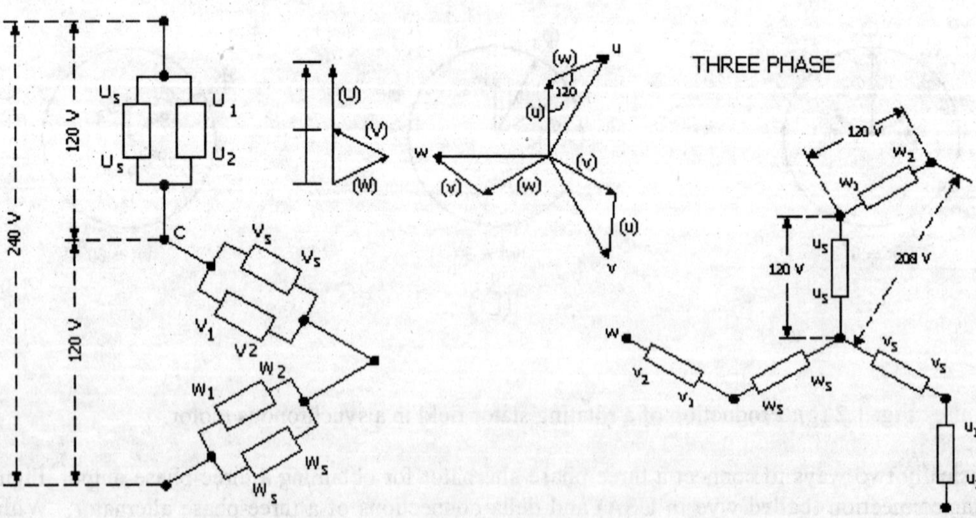

Fig. 1.2 (I): Parallel zigzag connections, single phase and three-phase.

In series delta connection, by tapping in to the mid-point of one phase, giving a center-tapped delta, limited amounts of "half voltage" power can be obtained. Too much unbalance between the two halves of one phase could produce secondary ill effects, and it is customary to limit the difference between the currents in the two sections of the tapped phase to 10 – 15 percent of the rated phase current. Parallel delta, in which, the "paralleled" phases of Figure 1.2 (J) are simply connected in to delta. This connection provides a three-wire low voltage system without neutral conductor..

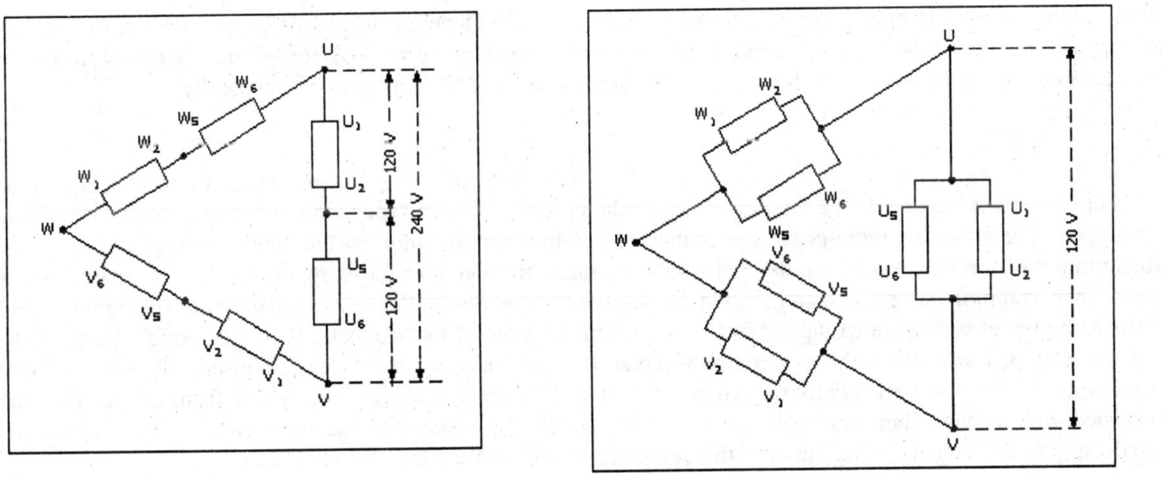

Fig. 1.2 (J): Series delta and parallel delta connections.

In series star connection, two in-phase sections in series per phase and have then connected the three phases into a star. Because the voltages of the two sections of each phase are exactly equal and exactly in-phase, the two sections can safely be paralleled giving the parallel star of Figure 1.2 (k).

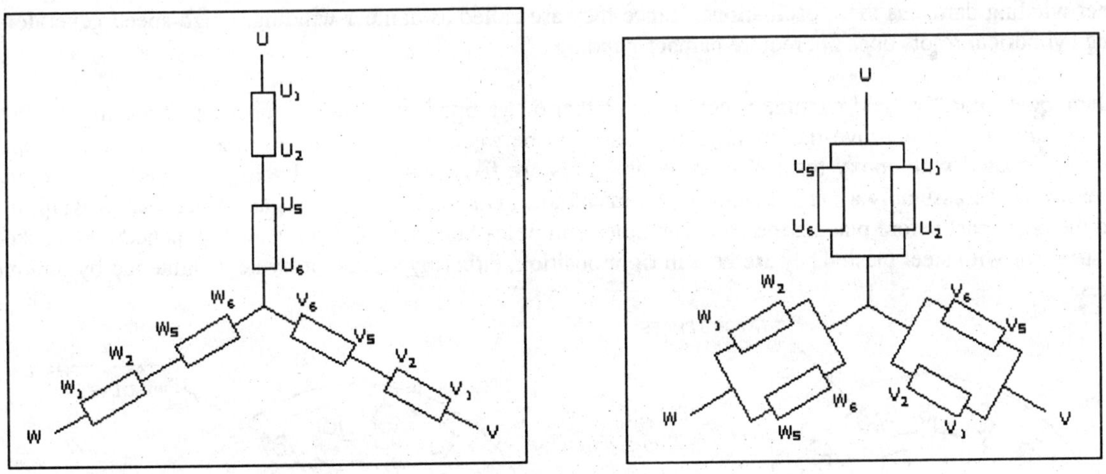

Fig. 1.2 (k): Series star and parallel star connection.

Principal features of synchronous generators relate to: (1) The method of excitation; (2) The method of cooling; (3) Temperature rise classification; and (4) Insulation system. The excitation system provides the magnetizing current necessary for the generator to operate at the desired voltage and, when in parallel with other generators, supplies the required amount of reactive current. Excitation systems are demonstrated in section 1.4.

Cooling generators is classified according to the nature of the coolant, and designated on the arrangement of the cooling system (first numeral) and the method of supplying power to circulate the coolant (second numeral). For machines with more than one cooling system a complete coding system is used including the nature of the coolant and the means of circulating. For example:

TAH or TCH: Hydrogen-cooled turbo-generators;

TCC: Inner-cooled turbo-generators;

TCO: Inner-cooled generator with water-cooled stator winding. (Refer section 1.24)

The winding insulation must remain intact with respect to both electrical insulating properties and mechanical strength for the life of the machine. Temperature rise above an assumed ambient temperature are used to specify the requirements of the insulation. Insulation classification utilized for generators are typically:
Class A 105°C; Class B 130°C; Class F 155°C, Class H 180°C

Typically, insulation limited to class B and class F temperature rises will employ inorganic materials such as mica or glass fiber bonded with a thermosetting synthetic resin. Class H type insulation may also include silicon elastomers. The stator has three-phase star connected winding and the rotor has DC field winding.
Regarding medium type machines, the coil which are made from copper flat-wires insulated with enamel and a glass-fiber wrapping, are packed and shaped, before being lapped with the base-insulation consisting in several coats of highly absorbent mica tape. After being put in the slots of the magnetic core, the straight parts of the coil are clamped with the help of wedges, whereas the end turns by means of felt inserts. Regarding large machines, coil parts are essentially composed of bars or half coils which are also made from copper flat-bars insulated with a glass-fiber wrapping, used together, according to the size and the cooling type, with hollow conductors for hydrogen circulation or with hollow copper alloys for water circulation.

The rotor is either salient pole construction or cylindrical construction. Salient pole rotor [Figure 1.2 (l)] is used for low speed generators, for example, hydro-generators. The cylindrical rotor [Figure 1.2 (m)] is used for high-speed generators, for example, gas or steam turbine generators. **Damper winding of a generator is an additional short-circuited (copper bar) winding on the surface of a salient pole rotor.** The damper winding improves the waveform of current under fluctuating conditions of load angle. Load angle is the angle between stator-magnetic-field and rotor-magnetic-field both rotating in synchronous speed. When the load of a synchronous generator changes the rotor angle oscillates about the new position. This is known as hunting. The damper winding dampens these oscillations. Hence they are called as damper winding. High-speed generators, having cylindrical rotors does not require damper winding.

In salient pole rotor, the field winding is composed, either of wrapped and wound copper, or of rectangular flat-coils, so staggered to improve the cooling, and insulated between them by interposition of polyamide paper strips impregnated with epoxy resin. The excitation coils are fixed with recessed wedges by hollow wedging keys ensuring the assembly a perfect rigidity. An insulation made up of an epoxy glass-fiber web is wrapping round the polar part before placing the coil. The poles and pole-shoes are carried out with punched and stacked steel sheets or with steel mast. They are kept in right position, either by screws or by keys tightened by oblique wedges.

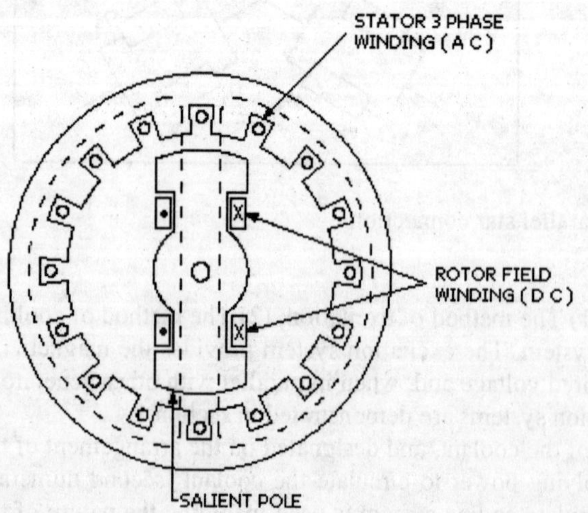

Fig. 1.2 (L): Salient pole rotor and stator

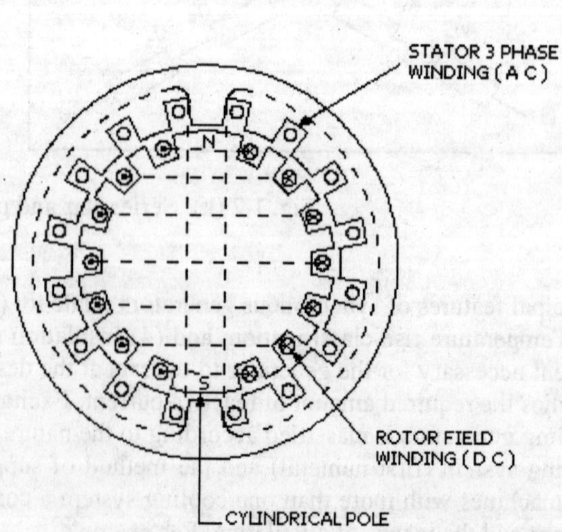

Fig. 1.2 (m): Cylindrical rotor and stator

In cylindrical rotor (Turbo-generators with surface rotor), the rotor winding is carried out with silver copper profiles directly ventilated by the cooling gas. To ensure an-insulation between coil-turns, insulated material is closely adhering to the copper, whereas an-insulation to earth is ensured by profiles filling the groove.

Separately excited Alternator (Slip-ring type/Brush type Alternator):
The rotor of a synchronous machine needs DC field current. The field current is supplied and controlled by the excitation system. Exciter is a DC generator (driven by an AC motor), which is connected to the rotating rotor field through slip rings and carbon brushes. Slip rings are circular bands of metal (brass or stainless steel) placed in the rotating part of the machine. Carbon brush, riding in contact with the slip ring provides connection to the external circuit. Brush is a sliding contact, generally made of carbon, used to provide connection to rotating parts of machines.

Excitation voltage and excitation current is controlled through an automatic voltage regulator (AVR). Excitation current is the direct current used to produce electromagnetism in the fields of the rotor of an alternator or synchronous motor. Figure 1.2 (n) illustrates the stator and rotor connection diagram of a separately excited brush type synchronous generator. In this excitation method, the DC field current for the synchronous generator is obtained from a separate DC generator known as an exciter. The exciter is a shunt-wound or compound-wound DC generator that is either driven by the alternator itself or by a separate AC induction motor.

The shunt field of the exciter is separately excited by the solid-state control. Excitation controls automatically regulate the synchronous generator field in a closed loop configuration designed to maintain adequate field strength for varying loads or to maintain a constant power factor. The exciter shunt field strength controls the DC output of the exciter, which is picked off by the commutator brushes, bused to the slip-ring brushes, and applied via the slip rings to the main rotating field of the synchronous generator. The field current is applied to the rotor by closure of the field circuit breaker (Device No: 41).

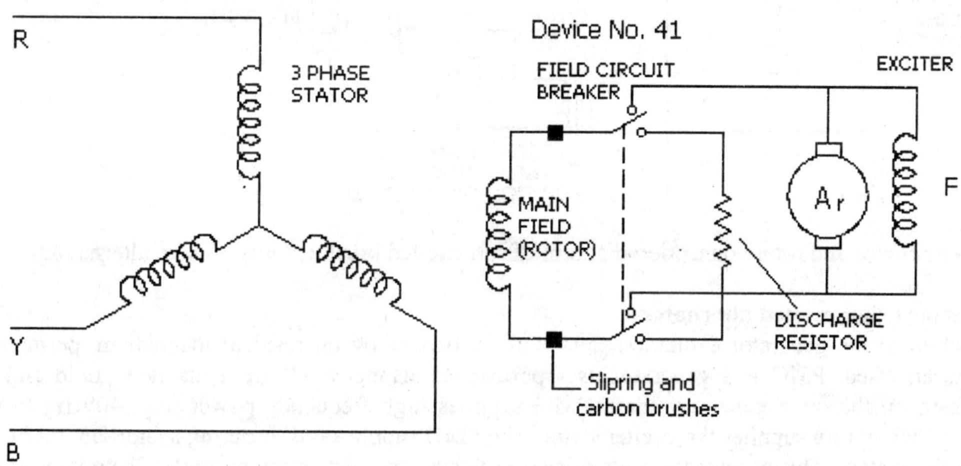

Fig. 1.2 (n): Stator and rotor connection diagram of a brush type alternator.

Brushless Alternators (Self excited Alternators):
Self-excited brushless system consists of a rotating rectifier assembly, exciter assembly and main generator assembly. The e.m.f induced in the three-phase exciter rotor winding is rectified through the full wave rotating diode assembly and fed to the DC field winding on the alternator rotor. Thereby the need for slip rings and brushes are eliminated. Initially the generator generates no load voltage due to residual magnetism in the exciter. This induced voltage is used to feed the AVR power circuit and control circuit. Rectified output of the power circuit is given to the exciter stator. Connection diagram of brushless self-excited alternator is illustrated in Figure 1.2 (o). Self excited generators are usually low voltage generators.

The induced voltage in the main armature is sensed by AVR control circuit and input to the exciter field is varied accordingly to get the rated voltage. This process is repeated whenever there is a load variation. Diode is a two terminal solid-state device, which permits current to flow in one direction, but not in the other. In AC circuits, a diode will permit half cycle to flow but will resist the flow of the opposite half cycle of current. Thus, AC is converted to direct current by a diode. Heat sink is a device, which absorbs heat from electrical devices such as diodes and SCR's and dissipates the heat to the surrounding air. Varistor mounted on the heat sink assembly protects diodes by suppressing any abnormal transient peak voltages. For large generators positive side of the rotating rectifier assembly is connected to the generator shaft through a resistor to prevent voltage build up due to electrostatic charges created due to air friction on the windings and heat sinks. Surge suppressor is a device capable of conducting current in either direction in the presence of high transient voltages thus protecting devices that could otherwise be damaged.

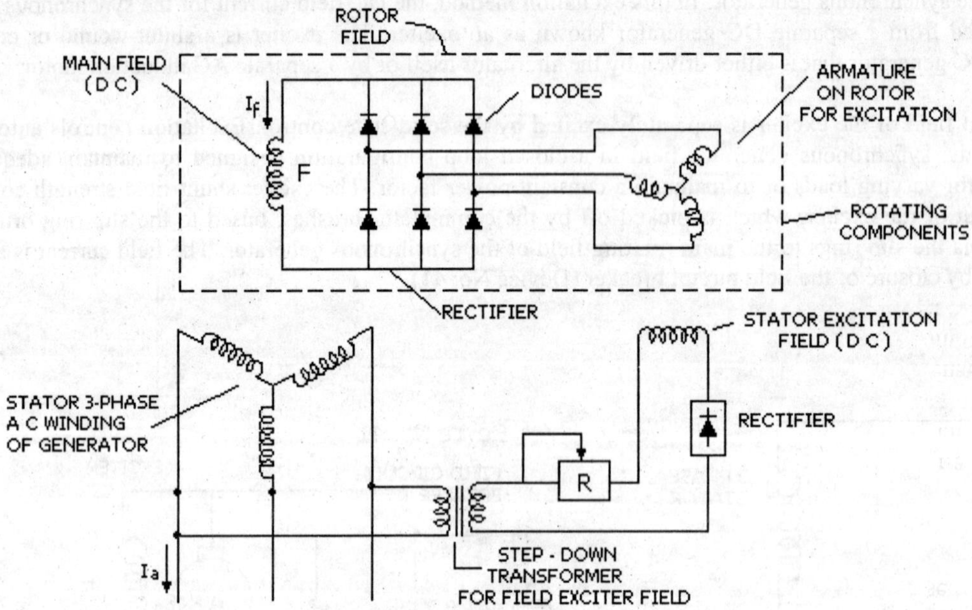

Fig. 1.2 (o): Stator and rotor connection diagram of self excited brushless low voltage alternator.

Brushless Alternator (Pilot excited alternator):

To provide excitation to the generator excitation field without depending on residual magnetism, permanent magnet generators are used. PMG is a generator uses permanent magnet to create a magnetic field and its armature is mounted on the main generator shaft. PMG supplies high frequency power (e,g. 400Hz) to the voltage regulator, which in turn supplies the exciter stator. The PMG supplies power during a short circuit of the main generator or the system. This permits the main generator to sustain short circuit currents. The output of the permanent magnet generator is electrically isolated from the main generator output and is not adversely affected by main generator output waveform distortion such as from semi-conducting rectifier (SCR).

Following are the advantages of PMG:

1. PMG voltage is independent of the generator voltage. Fluctuations in power system during abnormal conditions (e.g. short circuit/earth fault) will not fed back in to the exciter.
2. No need transformer to step down the voltage
3. 300% Short circuit sustaining capability
4. High frequency interference resulting from switching transients can be avoided.
5. Improved voltage recovery and waveform, reduced telephone interference and radio frequency interference.

Pilot excited alternator consists of a three-phase star connected rotating exciter armature and silicone diode rectifier assembly mounted on the main generator rotor shaft, which feeds power direct to the rotor winding of the AC alternator. Figure 1.2 (p) illustrates the stator and rotor connection diagram of a brushless PMG excited, medium voltage alternator. The exciter provides a controlled DC output using feedback signals and a reference point established by the setting of the voltage regulator. A transfer switch provides for selection of automatic or backup automatic regulator control. Voltage regulator DC output is fed to the stationary field of the rotating exciter. Three-phase, high frequency AC output from the rotating armature is rectified and applied to the generator field. Field ground indication is provided without slip rings by means of a transmitter mounted on the diode wheel assembly. A light signal is sent across the air gap to a stationary receiver and relay to indicated presence of a ground. [Refer figure (g) in section 1.6 for stator rotor connection of permanent magnet generator]

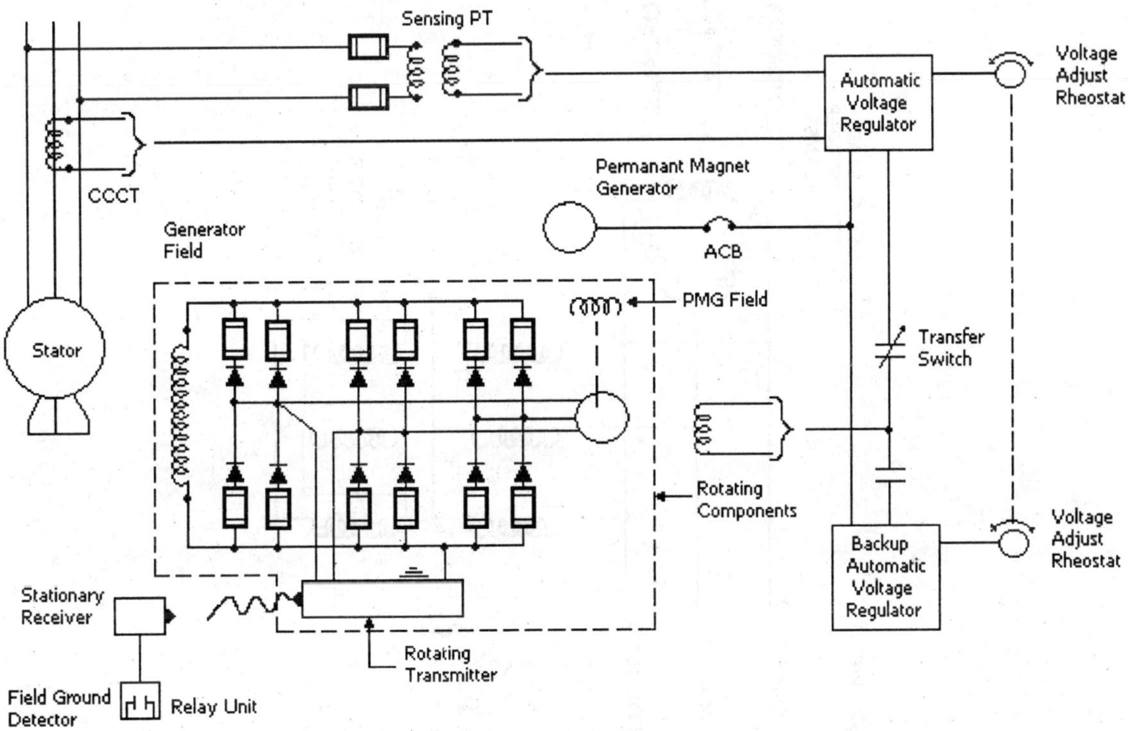

Fig. 1.2 (p): Functional diagram of exciter with permanent magnet generator.

One or more open rectifiers in the rotating rectifier assembly can cause a decrease in the available field power for the main generator field. This can lead to the failure of more rotating rectifiers or the excitation system as it is forced to increase its output to compensate for the defective brushless exciter diodes. In large units exciter diode monitor is employed, that detects open circuited or shorted rotating rectifiers and sends an alarm to annunciate the condition so an orderly shutdown can be made.

Combined generator-transformer unit: The GT unit consists of a star connected generator and a delta/star step-up power transformer connected through a bus-duct as shown in Figure 1.2 (q). Generator star point (neutral) is grounded through a grounding transformer. Power transformer secondary is earthed directly or through a earth resistor. Broken delta secondary of the potential transformer is connected to an over-voltage relay for ground fault protection.

In a combined generator-transformer unit, transformer may fail due to over fluxing if voltage is maintained during starting the unit or low frequency running or when a loaded generator breaker trips without unloading the load. The flux density (β) of a transformer depends on the V/f ratio. At higher flux density core gets saturated. The flux then passes through core bolts and the insulation gets damaged and core bolts get heated and core fault develops in the transformer. In case of generator transformers, unit auxiliary transformers, the conditions of over-fluxing occurs if excitation is applied to the generators before attaining full synchronous speed or during under-speed operation or when the load is rejected. To overcome over-flux problem, during starting brush type generators, the field breakers provided in the generator rotor is switched on through a speed switch, which operates at synchronous speed. Similarly, while stopping the generator field generator will trip simultaneously with main breaker. In addition to the above, voltage per hertz relay is provided to protect the equipment during over-fluxing conditions. [Refer Chapter # 6, section 6.14]

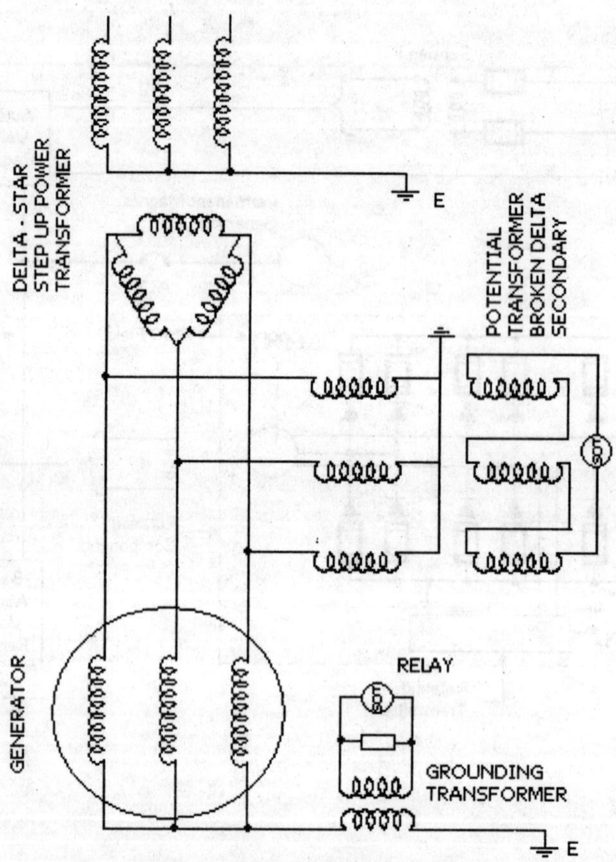

Fig. 1.2 (q): Connection diagram of a combined generator-transformer unit.

1.3 BASE LOAD GENERATORS AND STANDBY GENERATORS.

The term "standby" is used where some generators are brought in to operation only on mains power (utility power) failure. Many "prime power sets" operate continuously in situations where mains power supply is not available or during peak load hours. It is of course essential not to confuse continuous and stand by ratings of an alternator. Base load generators are either synchronized with utility network [as shown in figure 4.1 (e) of chapter # 4] or for direct distribution as shown in Figure 1.3 (a). Direct distribution means several units running in parallel to share the load of an independent distribution network.

Direct distribution system:

Figure 1.3 (a) shows the single line diagram of a diesel generator plant designed for direct distribution. Four numbers 13.8 KV 60 Hz. Generators (6 MVA and 10 MVA) are installed with provision for paralleling. In the base load system, both the generation and distribution voltages are at the same potential level. Bus bars are rated for 3000 A nominal continuous current and designed for a system fault level of 750 MVA. Bus is divided in to two sections (Bus A and Bus B) and tied with 2500 A bus-tie breaker. Outgoing feeders are designed for radial or ring system (overhead line or underground cable) distribution. Station auxiliary load is connected to the low voltage side of the station transformers of respective bus section. All feeder circuit breakers and generator circuit breakers are rated for 1250 A nominal current and 31.5 KA short-circuit current.

Current transformers (with multi core secondary) and potential transformers are employed for protection relay and measuring instrument connections. (13.8 KV, 60 Hz. systems, is the standard voltage in USA, Soudi Arabia and various other countries).

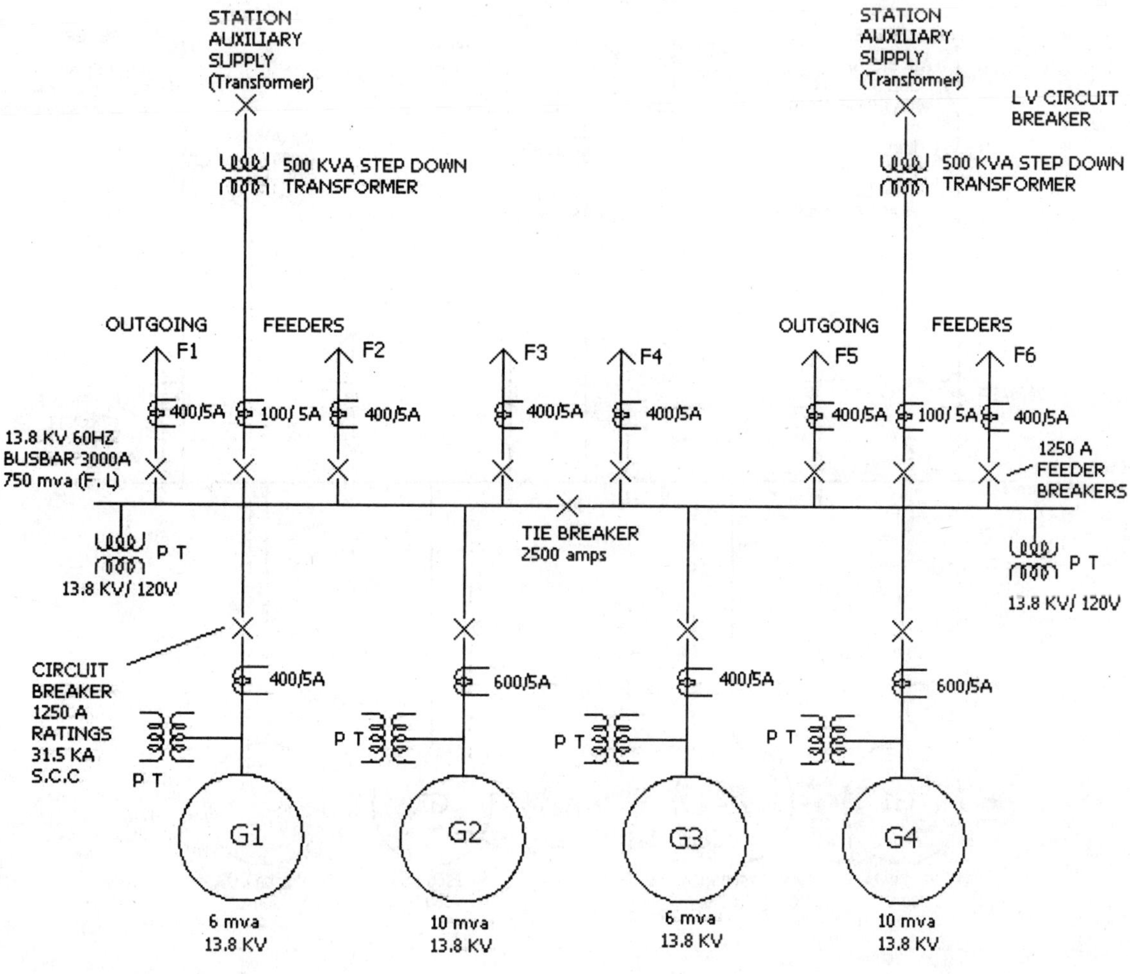

Fig. 1.3 (a): Single line diagram of a typical 13.8 KV generating station, direct distribution.

Figure 1.3 (b) shows the single line diagram of a low voltage diesel generating plant. Four numbers 2500 MVA 380 volts 50 Hz. Generators (5000 A 46 KA circuit breaker) are installed with provision for paralleling, and facility for auto start and auto stop. Station auxiliaries are fed from an independent feeder. Six numbers outgoing feeders (3000 A 46 KA circuit breaker) are for direct distribution of generation voltage. Two feeders are provided with step up facility, so that 380 volts supply can be stepped up through 1600 KVA step up transformers to match utility system voltage 10 KV 50 Hz, which is the standard secondary distribution voltages in most of the European countries.

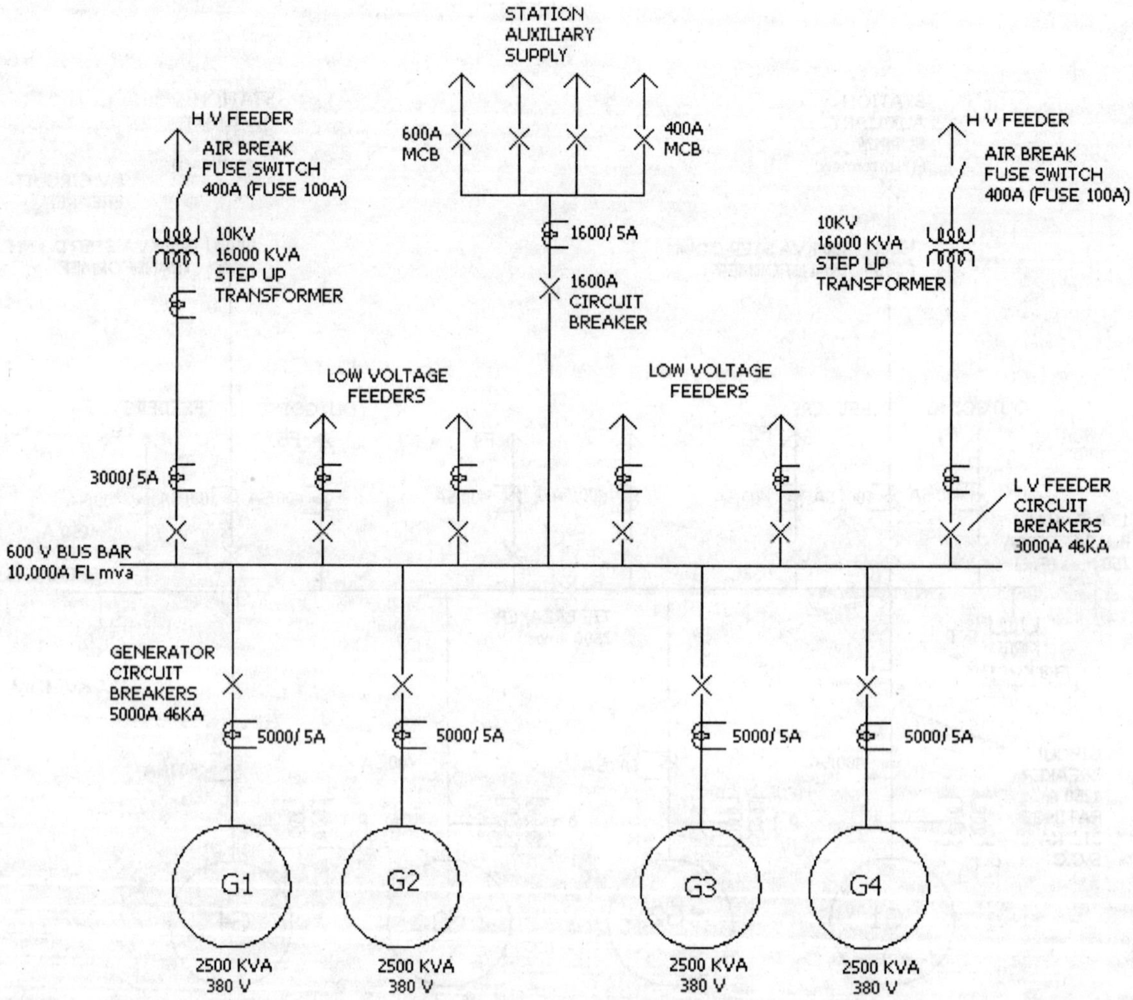

Fig. 1.3 (b): Single line diagram of low voltage diesel generating plant with step up facility.

Micro power plant

Micro or mini power plants described here are of water turbines consisting axial runner with adjustable runner blades at standstill, and fixed guide ring, driving a generator at high speed by belt. Flat-sliding type gates are installed down-stream and used for starting and stopping the generator, and emergency closing of the unit. Generators are either synchronous generators with static excitation or asynchronous type with permanent magnet generator. The complete unit (Low voltage or medium voltage) is assembled and grouped in pre-cabled container with integrated microprocessor for automatic starting/stopping and synchronizing by remote control or by water level control. While using asynchronous generator, the compensation of power factor is carried out by capacitor bank installed in the plant. Synchronous generator contributes reactive power to the utility. In case of several units, starting bus bars are employed for automatic synchronization and transfer to the main bus bar. For isolated networks (not synchronized with utility) dissipation resistance and regulation thyristor is used for dissipation of excess energy generated. Figure 1.3 (c) shows an electrical single line diagram of an interconnected hydroelectric micro-power plant.

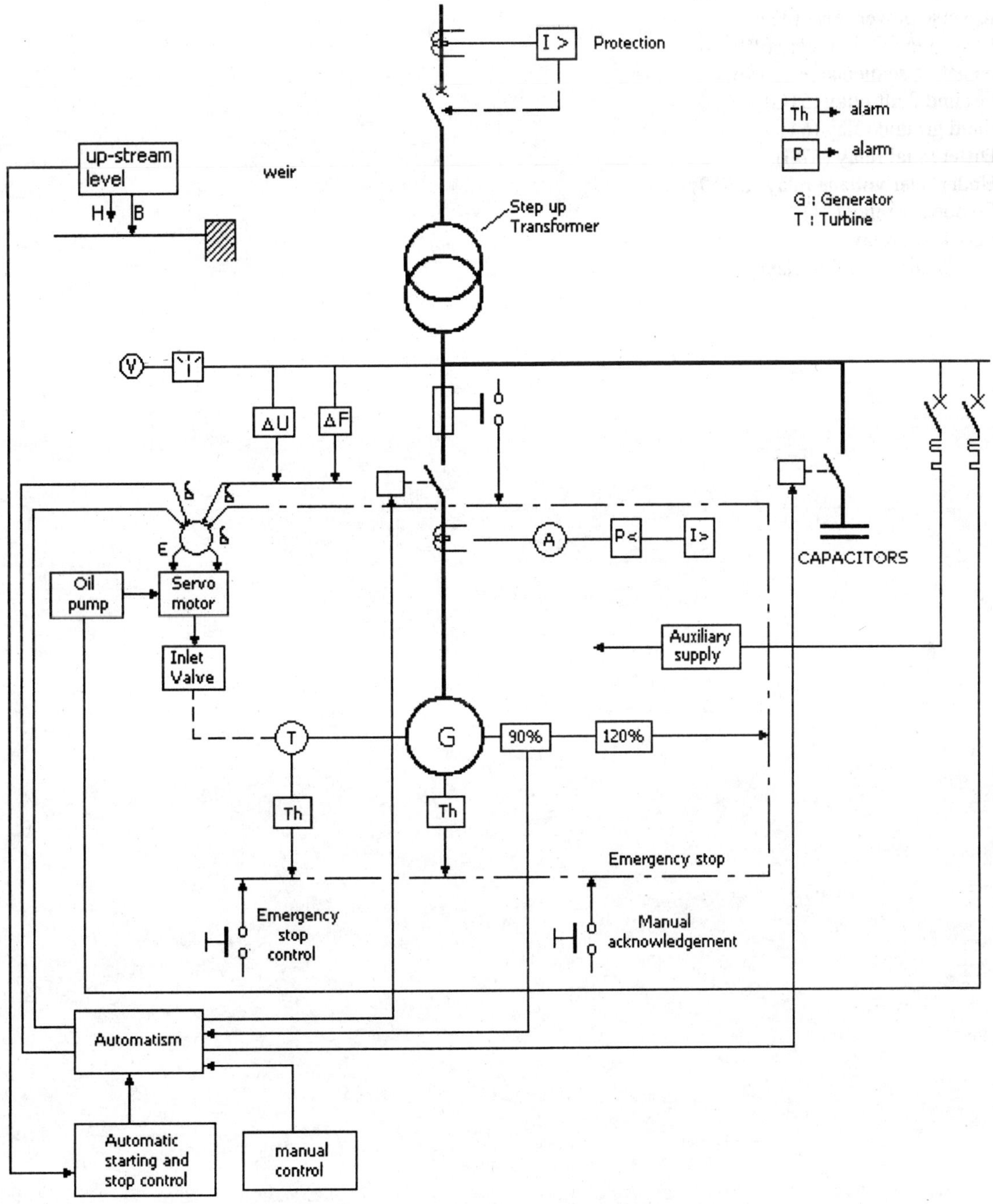

Fig. 1.3 (c): Single line diagram of an interconnected micro-power plant.

Figure 1.3 (d) shows the schematic diagram of a typical medium voltage alternator consisting (a) generator cubicle; (b) NGR cubicle; (c) HV switchgear cubicle (d) Control and relay cubicle. Generator cubicle is equipped with cable termination chamber and current transformers for voltage-restrained over-current protection / differential protection / automatic voltage regulator (AVR) etc. NGR cubicle is provided with neutral circuit breaker, neutral grounding resistor and current transformer for earth fault relay connection. HV switchgear cubicle is designed for generator circuit breaker, medium voltage cable termination chamber with earth fault sensor, potential transformer (star /star connected) for synchronizing / measuring circuit, and current transformers for bus bar protection /differential protection / measuring instruments etc.

Relay and control cubicle is provided with:

1) Voltage restrained over-current relay (51V)
2) Reverse power relay (32)
3) Loss of excitation relay (40)
4) Negative sequence relay (46)
5) Ground fault relay (51G)
6) Field ground relay (64)
7) Differential relay (87G)
8) Under/over voltage relay (27/59)
9) Frequency relay (81)
10) Lock out relay

(Refer Chapter # 6 for relays)

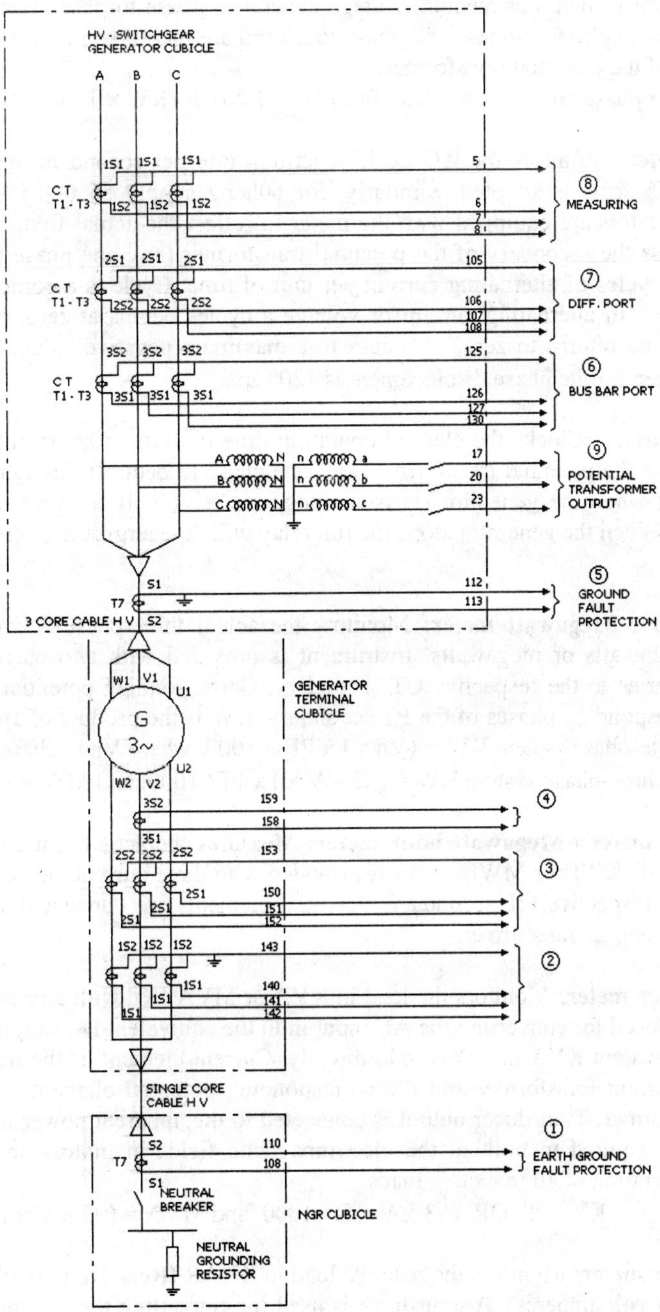

Fig. 1.3 (d): Schematic diagram of a typical medium voltage alternator.

Measuring instruments: [Refer figure 1.3 (e)]

Following instruments are required to be installed in the generator control desk.

1) **Ammeter:** Monitors the load current of the generator in amperes or kilo-amperes. This value changes depends on the actual load on the generator. Either independent ammeters for each phase or single ammeter with phase selector switch is the alternative arrangement. Indication will appear in amps when an external load is applied to the generator, by closing the circuit breaker. Ammeters are wired in series to the current transformer (CT) secondary. If phase selector switch is used, ensure that C.T connections to the selector switch terminals remain shorted while the switch is in the off position. Current I in a 3 phase circuit = (KVA x 1000) / (V x 1.73) or (KW x 1000) / (V x 1.73 x PF)

2) **Voltmeter:** Monitors the output potential in volts or kilo-volts for the position selected on the voltmeter selector switch. For medium voltage generators phase-to-phase voltage is indicating, but for low voltage system phase-to-phase and phase to neutral are measured. Voltmeters are connected across the secondary of the potential transformer.
Voltage V in a 3 phase circuit = (KVA x 1000) / (I x 1.73) or (KW x 1000) / (I x 1.73 x PF)

3) **Frequency meter:** Monitors the AC cycle repetition rate per second in units of hertz. For 50hertz supply 45 to 55 scale is adopted. Similarly, for 60hertz supply 55 to 65 scale is marked. In-built frequency converters are equipped with the meter to reflect the actual frequency. Frequency meter is connected across the secondary of the potential transformer (any one phase to neutral). Frequency is the number of cycles of alternating current per unit of time. Cycle is a complete set of events before repetition occurs. In alternating current or voltage a cycles begins at zero, continues to a maximum positive value and returns to zero, continues to a maximum negative value, and returns to zero. In a three-phase generator the phase displacement is 120° apart.

4) **Elapsed time meter:** Clocks the elapsed operating time in units of hours and tenths of an hour. It is connected across the potential transformer (any one phase to neutral) through generator run relay NO contact, so that when the generator starts running, run relay will energize to keep the elapsed time meter running. When the generator stops the run relay will de-energize to stop the clock.

5) **Kilowatt meter / Megawatt meter:** Monitors the actual three-phase active load delivered by the generator in kilowatts or megawatts. Instrument is provided with two current elements, which are connected in series to the respective CT secondary. Corresponding potential elements are connected across the corresponding phases of the PT secondary. KW is the product of apparent power and power factor. In a single-phase system KW = (Vn x I x PF) / 1000, where Vn is phase to neutral voltage.
Similarly, in a three-phase system KW = ($\sqrt{3}$ x V x I x PF)/1000; and MW = KW/1000.

6) **Kilowatt-hour meter / Megawatt hour meter:** Measures the actual unit consumed in KWH/MWH during generation. KWH or MWH meter is provided with three current elements, which are connected in series to the respective CT secondary. Potential elements are connected across the corresponding phases of the potential transformer.

7) **Apparent-power meter:** Monitors the load in KVA or MVA (Kilovolt ampere or Mega-volt ampere). A transducer is used for converting the AC input in to the equivalent DC output. The scale is calibrated to read the equivalent KVA or MVA load directly. Current element of the transducer is connected in series to the current transformer and the corresponding potential elements are connected across the potential transformer. Transducer output is connected to the apparent power meter. Apparent power is the AC power required to buildup the electromagnetic fields in motors and transformers etc. It is essential for operation of all inductive loads.
Three phase KVA = KW /PF; OR ($\sqrt{3}$ x V x I) / 1000, and MVA = ($\sqrt{3}$ x V x I)/100,0000

8) **Reactive power meter:** Monitors the reactive load in KVAR (Reactive kilovolt amperes) or in MVAR (Reactive Mega-volt amperes). A transducer is used for converting the AC input to the equivalent DC output. The scale is calibrated to read the equivalent KVAR or MVAR load directly. Current element of the transducer is connected in series to the respective CT secondary. Potential element is connected across the PT secondary. Phase shifting is obtained by interchanging the leads of the potential element connection. The current element of the transducer R phase is connected from R phase CT, whereas the corresponding potential element is fed from Y phase PT. Other phase elements are also connected similarly. Transducer output is connected to the reactive power meter. Reactance power constitutes a nuisance load on cables and other equipments.

Three phase KVAR = $\sqrt{3}$ x V x I x ($\sqrt{1 - PF^2}$) / 1000, where V represents the voltage between any two Phases and PF = Power factor..

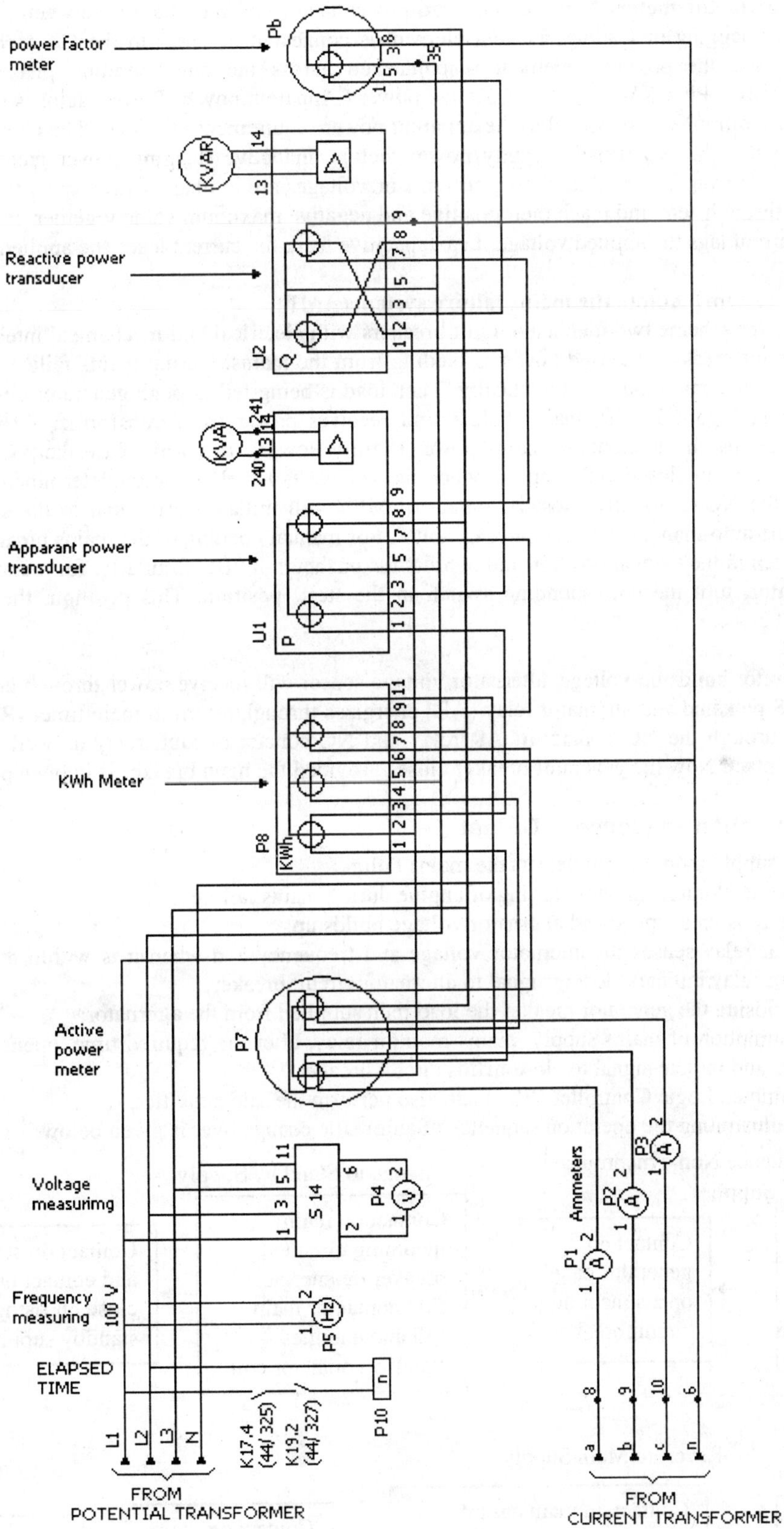

Fig. 1.3 (e): Instrumentation circuit for a typical medium voltage generator.

9) **Power factor meter:** Monitors the load power factor and the relation between voltage and current whether lagging or leading. Current element is connected in series to the CT secondary of any one phase and the potential element is connected across the corresponding phase of the potential transformer. PF = KW / KVA i. e, Active power / Apparent power. Power factor is the ratio of the true power requirements of a load to the apparent power requirement of a load. The combined loads power source may have a resistive (unity power factor), inductive (lagging power factor), and capacitive (leading power factor). Alternating currents or voltages are in phase with respect to each other if they cross through zero and reach their positive and negative maximum value together. In an inductive load, the current lags the applied voltage. In a capacitive load, the current leads the applied voltage.

Auto-transfer system / Automatic mains failure system (AMF):

In the auto transfer scheme two identical circuit breakers with electrical and mechanical interlock is employed. When main circuit breaker is closed power is feeding from the mains. During mains failure the mains breaker will open and the generator starts automatically. Then load is being fed through generator circuit breaker. Auto transfer circuit in Figure 1.3 (f), mains failure unit receives power from transformer T2. Automatic mains failure (MFU) senses the three-phase mains power (Utility Power). In normal case the NO (Normally open) contact of MFU remain closed and open out when the voltage falls below the predetermined set value. During power failure, the NC (Normally Closed) contact of MFU will initiate start signal to the stand by generator provided the "off-auto-manual-test" switch is in 'auto'. For manual opening of the mains breaker, keep the auto-manual-off switch in the manual position and depress the pushbutton PB5. Similarly, for maintenance test of the standby generator, turn the corresponding switch in the 'test' position. This position, the generator circuit breaker will not close.

When the generator builds up voltage, alternator voltage sensor will receive power through control transformer T5. Hence AVS picks up and alternator relay (AR) energizes through return to main timer (RMT). Timer GCT now picks up through the NO contact of AR relay and NC contact of fault relay as well as circuit breaker auxiliary NC contact. Now the generator breaker closes provided the main breaker is in open position.

Automatic operation sequence of DG set

1. Mains supply monitor unit detects the mains failure;
2. The mains monitor initiates starting of engine during mains failure;
3. Engine runs up to speed and alternator voltage builds up;
4. Detector relay senses the alternator voltage and frequency and when it is within the required limits, detector relay initiates closing signal to alternator circuit breaker;
5. Upon closing the generator breaker the load then supplied from the alternator;
6. On resumption of mains supply, mains monitor relay, after the required time, opens alternator circuit breaker and initiate signal to close mains circuit breaker;
7. Programmed Logic Controller (PLC) can also perform the said activities.

Block diagram illustrating the operation sequence of automatic change over is given below.

Operation Sequence Non-synchronised Supplies

Change to Stand by Supply

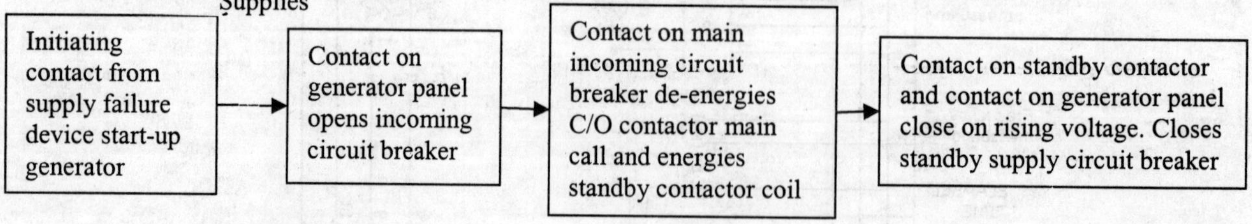

Revert to Main Supply

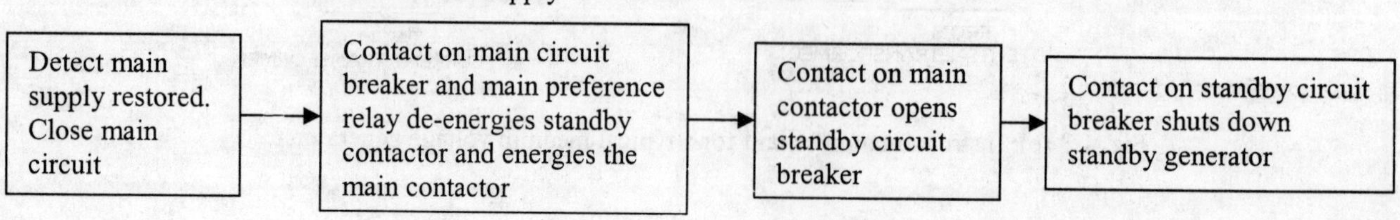

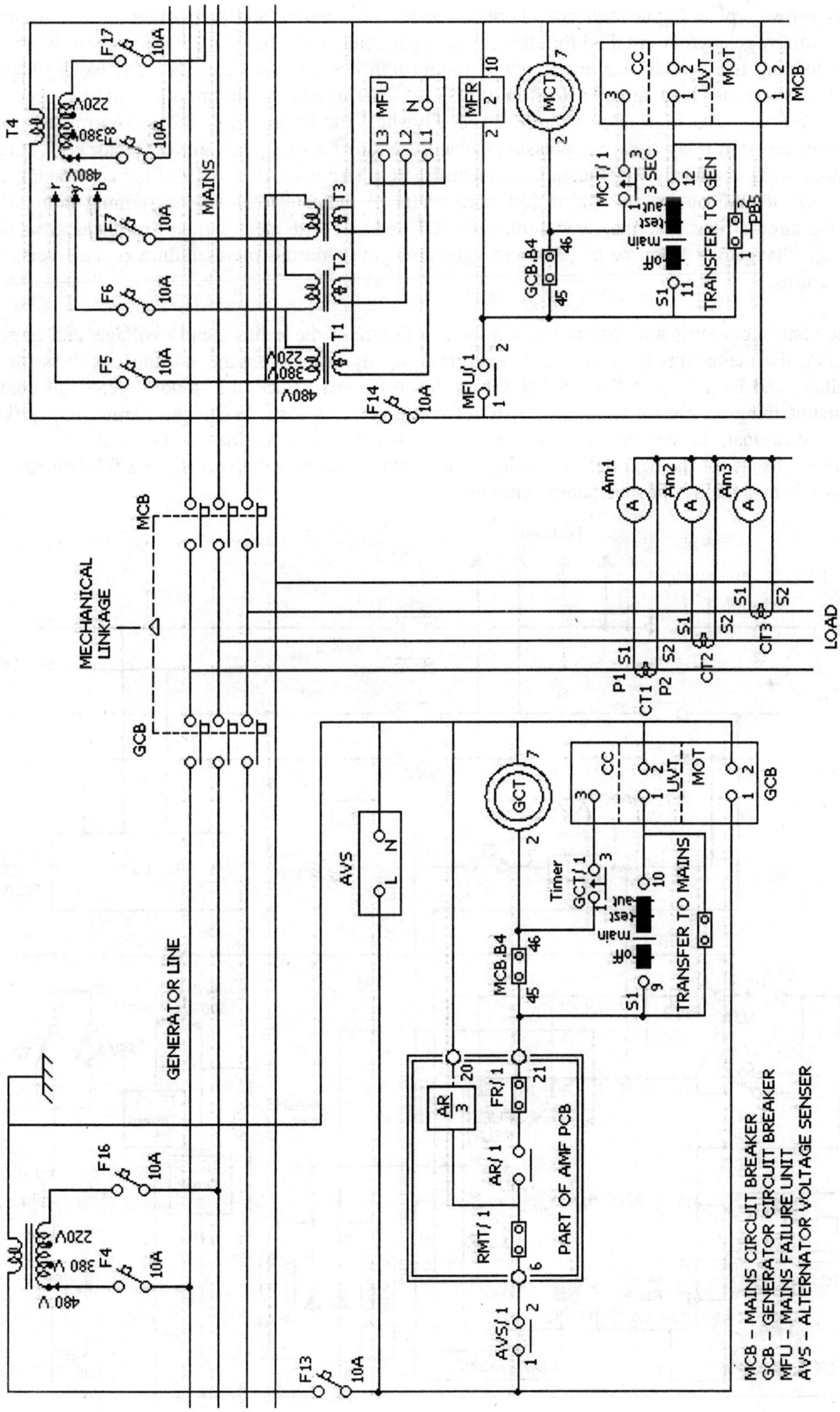

T4
T5
220V
380V
480V
F4
F5
F6
F7
F8
F13
F14
F16
F17
10A
T1
T2
T3
MAINS
MFU
L1
L2
L3
N
MFR
MCT
MFU/ 1
GCB.B4
MCT/ 1
3 SEC
test
aut
main
off
S1
PB2
TRANSFER TO GEN
CC
UVT
MOT
MCB
MECHANICAL LINKAGE
GCB
Am1
Am2
Am3
CT1
CT2
CT3
P1
P2
S2
LOAD
GENERATOR LINE
AVS
L
GCT
Timer
GCT/ 1
MCB.B4
TRANSFER TO MAINS
AR
FR/ 1
AR/ 1
RMT/ 1
AVS/ 1
PART OF AMF PCB
MCB – MAINS CIRCUIT BREAKER
GCB – GENERATOR CIRCUIT BREAKER
MFU – MAINS FAILURE UNIT
AVS – ALTERNATOR VOLTAGE SENSER

Figure 1.3 (g) shows typical application circuit for automatic changeover and engine loading circuit usually employed for standby generators installed for airport runway lighting and other similar applications where auto-start and auto-loading is essential. Automatic mains failure unit operates on 12 or 24 volts battery supply is provided for auto-start, auto-loading and auto stop of D.G set. Alarm contacts are provided for over-speed, start failure, low oil pressure and high engine temperature. Flywheel diodes are provided across run relay (load relay), Fuel relay and start relay coils. Suppression capacitor is fitted across generator contactor coil. Magnetic pick-up for monitoring engine flywheel teeth is connected across terminals 18 and 19 of the auto mains failure relay. Tachometer to indicate engine speed and hour meter to indicate total engine running hours is also employed in the circuit. Four pole magnetic contactors (C1 and C2) with electrical and mechanical interlocks are provided for changeover from mains power to generator power during mains failure or vice versa when mains power returns.

The automatic control circuit is arranged to sense a fault or failure of the mains supply voltage, and on receipt of such a signal, the mains supply contactor de-energizes, opens and the engine starting circuit is initiated. When the voltage and frequency of the standby set are up to normal values, the standby generator contactor closes, thus maintaining an electrical supply to the essential services load. When the mains supply (Utility supply) returns to normal, the standby sets automatically shuts down after the load is transferred to the mains, and the equipment resets for the next duty operation. The starting battery is maintained in a fully charged state when the set is idle by a mains operated battery charger.

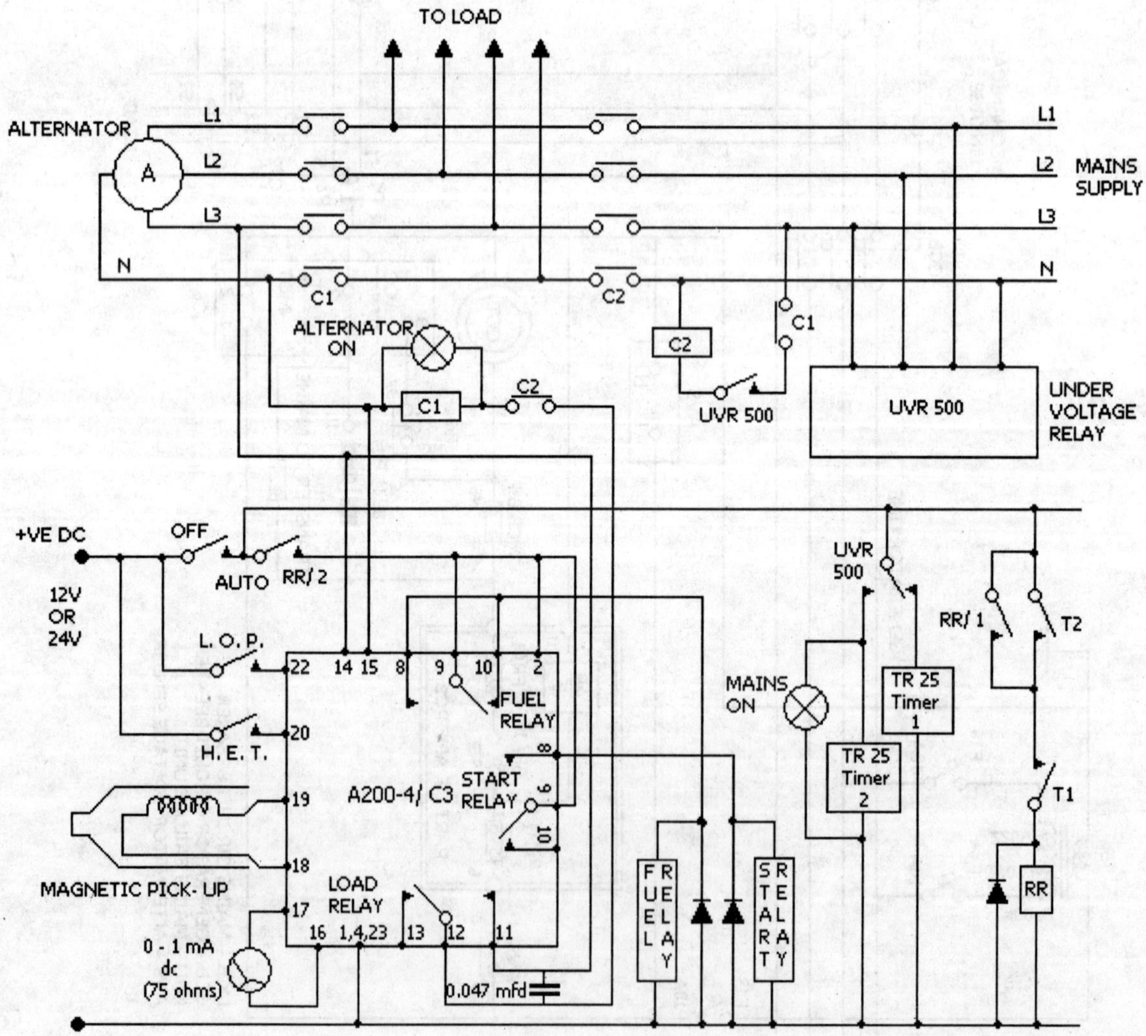

Fig. 1.3 (g): Typical application circuit for automatic changeover and engine loading.

Figure 1.3 (h) shows a 3.3 KV continuous duty generator set installed for industrial applications. During mains power failure the generator will work as a standby generator and feed the 11 KV industrial-networks through the step up transformer. During peak load hours the generator can be synchronized with the mains power 12 KV substation bus to share the load and improve voltages in the distribution network. Synchronism check relay is employed for synchronizing the generator to the mains power by closing recloser circuit breaker B.

DEVICE NUMBER: [Refer Chapter # 6 for Generator protection relays]

27-I: Instantaneous under-voltage relay.
27T: Time delayed under voltage relay
32: Over power relay (Reverse power relay)
51-V: Voltage restrained over current relay
59-I: Instantaneous over-voltage relay
59-T: Time over voltage relay
74: DC under-voltage relay
81-Under / Over frequency relay

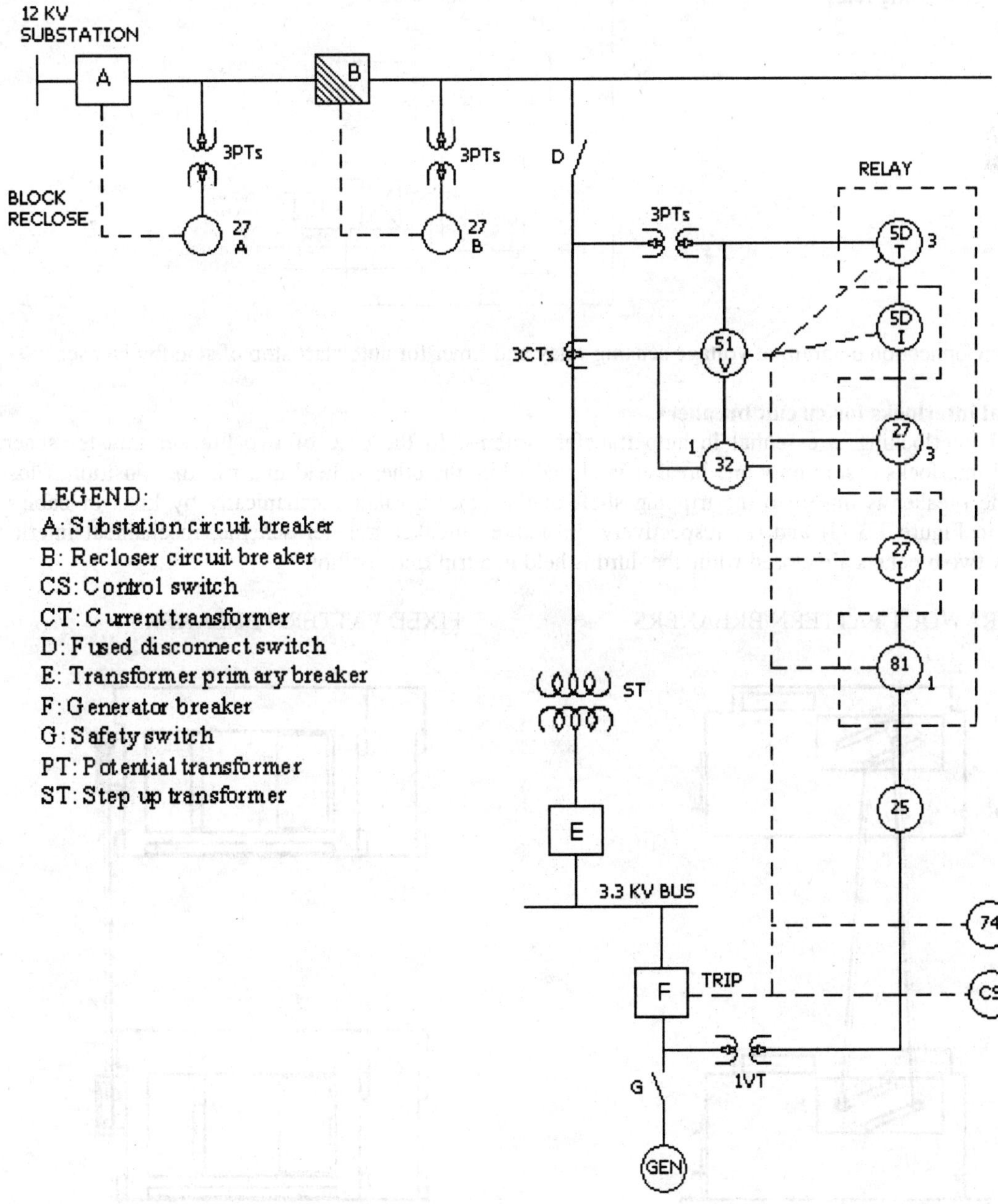

Fig. 1.3 (h) Interconnection generator for Industrial installation (Courtesy, Pride Relay).

Voltage sensing relay:

Figure 1.3 (i) shows the connection diagram of mains failure voltage sensing relay used for auto starting of standby diesel generator set. During mains power failure or the mains voltage drops below the set value, the MSR relay de-energizes and its NC contact initiate auto start signal to the engine, provided the auto-off-manual switch is in auto position. When the mains power returns and the voltage is slightly above the pickup setting, through the NO contact of MSR relay, the timer MT starts timing. After elapsing the set time value (3 or 5 minutes) the timer NO contact initiate auto stop signal to the engine and engine stop after 3 to 5 minutes idle running. This allows the lubricating oil and the engine coolant to carry heat away from the combustion chamber and bearing.

LEGEND:
NF: HRC fuse
MSR: Voltage sensing relay
MT: Timer

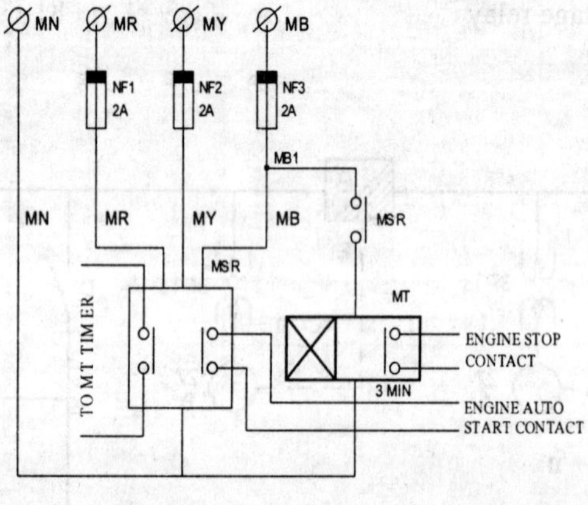

Fig. 1.3 (I): Connection diagram of voltage sensing relay and timer for auto start/stop of standby DG set.

Mechanical interlocks for circuit breakers.

Mechanical interlocking is essential in auto transfer systems. In the case of two breaker transfer scheme, mechanical interlocks ensure only one breaker is closed while the other is held in a trip free position. Closing shaft of one breaker is linked to the tripping shaft of the other breaker mechanically by links or cables as illustrated in Figure 1.3 (J) and (k) respectively. In a three breaker transfer scheme, mechanical interlocks ensure only two breakers are closed while the third is held in a trip free position.

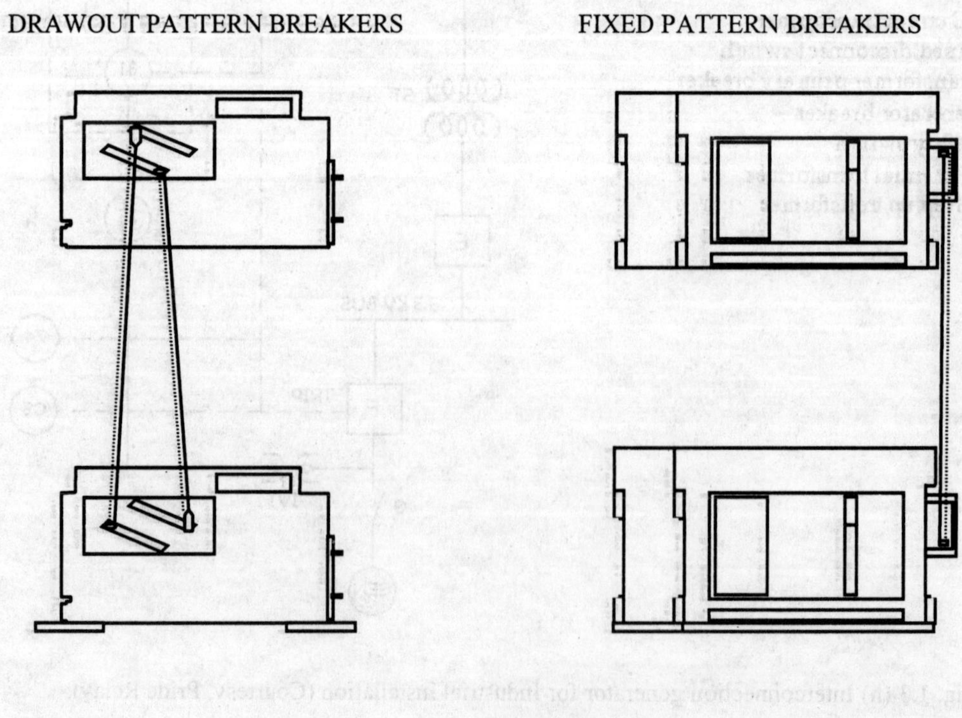

Fig. 1.3 (J): Mechanical interlocking by links for 2 draw-out & fixed pattern stack-mounted breakers.

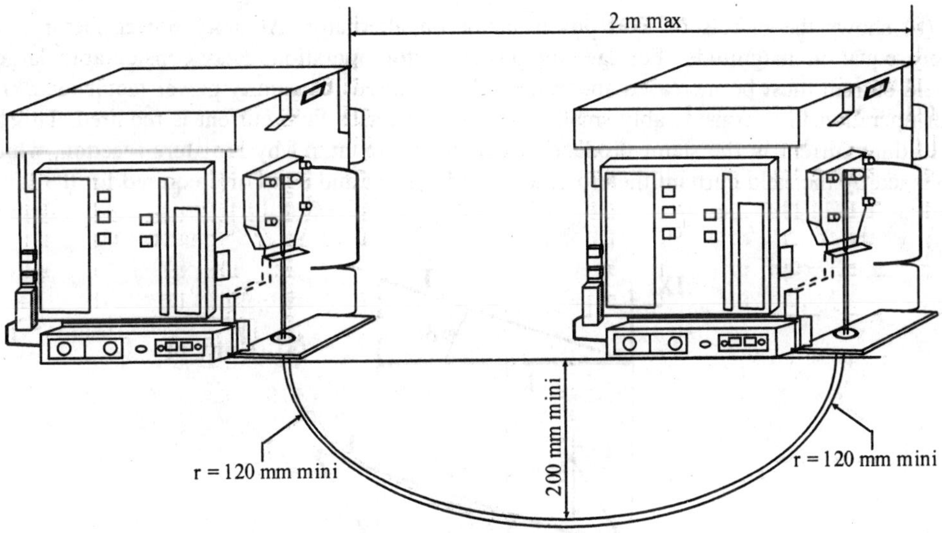

Fig. 1.3 (k): Interlocking by cables for 2 side-by-side mounted, fixed or draw-out pattern breakers.

1.4 ALTERNATOR CHARACTERISTICS, POWER FLOW AND EXCITATION SYSTEMS

Equivalent diagram of an alternator

Figure 1.4 (a) illustrates the equivalent circuit and phasor diagram of a balanced three-phase synchronous or constant speed generator.

E = Induced e.m.f (No load voltage)
V = Terminal voltage per phase
Xs = Internal reactance per phase
Ra = Internal resistance of the stator winding (main generator)
Ia = Stator current
Vt, terminal voltage for cylindrical rotor = E - Ia (Ra + ȷXs)

Zs, synchronous impedance = $\sqrt{Ra^2 + Xs^2}$
In case of salient pole rotor the total synchronous reactance is split up in to two parts Xs = Xd + ȷXq
Xd = Direct axis reactance (similar to the synchronous reactance of cylindrical rotor machine)
Xq = Quadrature axis reactance which is considered to be perpendicular to Xd.

Assume that Ra is neglected and E = k' I_f for a linear magnetic circuit. The external characteristic is defined by
$V = E - I\,(Ra + ȷX_S) \cong E - ȷIX_S$
$E = V + ȷIX_S$
The corresponding phasor diagram of an inductive load shown in the figure, Generator terminal voltage (V) is taken as horizontal reference and current (I) is drawn at a lagging angle θ. Reactive drop (ȷIXs) is 90° ahead of I, and e.m.f induced in the winding (E) is the vector sum of V and ȷIXs. Since E is directly determined by the rotor flux, and V bears a similar relation to air gap flux linking the stator, the angle between E and V is δ, i.e. the angle between rotor flux and air gap flux.

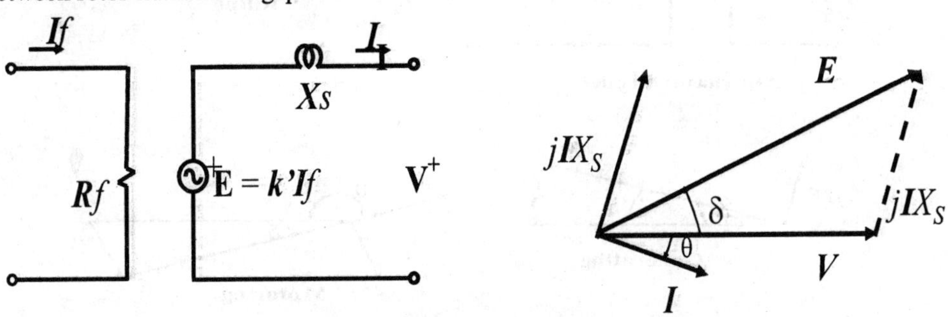

Fig. 1.4 (a): Equivalent circuit and phasor diagram of an alternator.

Figure 1.4 (b) shows the effects of load power factor on alternator. At unity power factor E and V are approximately equal in magnitude. For lagging power factor operation, E is considerably larger than V; therefore, field current must be increased above the value required for a unity power factor load. For leading power factor operation, E is considerably smaller than V and lesser field current is required. This behavior is because of leading current in the stator produces a component of m.m.f by armature reaction, which aids the m.m.f established by the field current; therefore, less field current and e.m.f are required for the same terminal voltage (V).

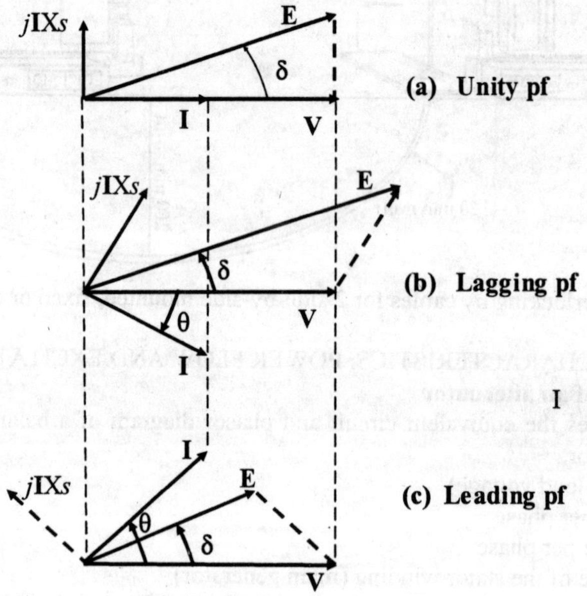

Fig. 1.4 (b): Effect of load power factor on alternator.

An alternator supplying constant electrical power at a constant speed would develop a constant torque. For constant torque, δ must remain constant or the stator flux must move in synchronism with the rotor flux. By changing the direction of power flow the alternator becomes a motor. In a DC machine, the direction of current flow is reversed by, changing the field current and thereby changing the generated e.m.f. But Figure 1.4 (c) indicates that in a synchronous machine there may be large changes in E with no change at all in the power delivered by the alternator. Consider an alternator driven at synchronous speed is synchronized with utility power supply, let V be one phase voltage and field current be adjusted so that E = V. Under this condition, I = 0 and there is no power transfer to the utility; the alternator is idling.

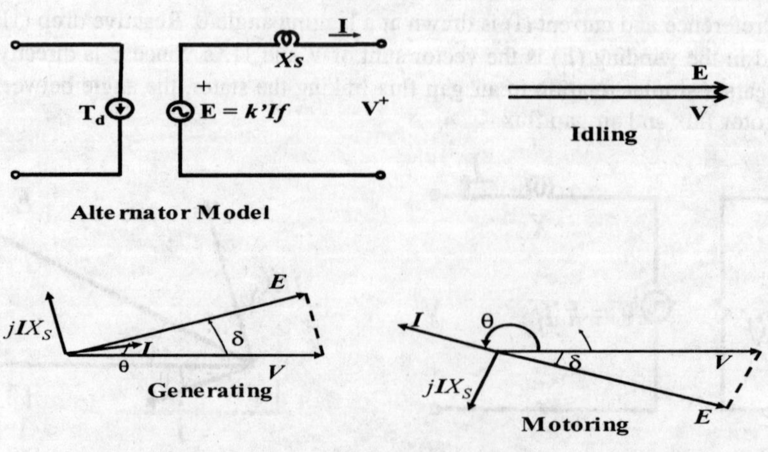

Fig. 1.4 (c): Idling and motoring power flow in a synchronous machine.

Assume an engine driven generator and attempt to accelerate the rotor. As the rotor is driven ahead of the stator field, there is a voltage difference between E and V, and current I flows (magnitude of E does not change). The electrical power output must be matched by a corresponding mechanical input. If the engine speed is returned to the idle position, the torque angle returns to zero and the rotor continuous to turn at synchronous speed. If the engine fuel flow is closed, the rotor tends to slow down; the engine is now, in effect, an air compressor acting as a load on the synchronous machine. As the rotor shift back through an angle delta, the e.m.f E is retarded in phase with respect to V and a voltage difference exists across Xs. The resulting current I is nearly 180° out of phase with V. The electrical output becomes ***negative,*** or the machine is absorbing electrical power from the utility and delivering mechanical power to the shaft. It is operating as a synchronous motor.

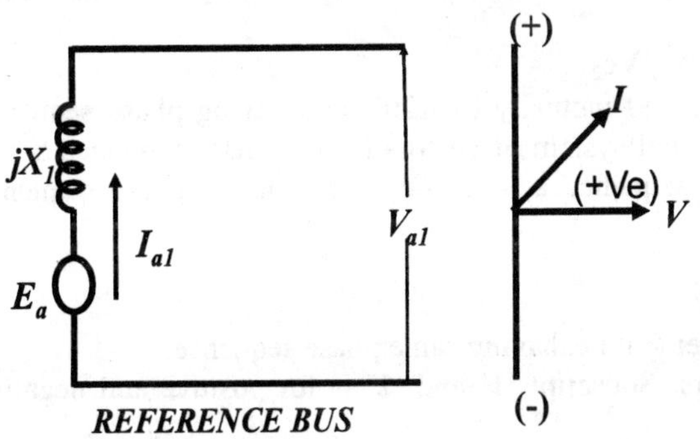

Fig. 1.4 (d): Positive sequence network.

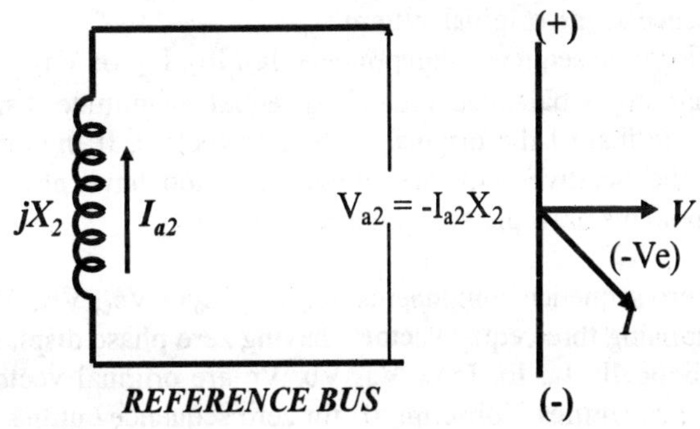

Fig. 1.4 (e): Negative sequence network.

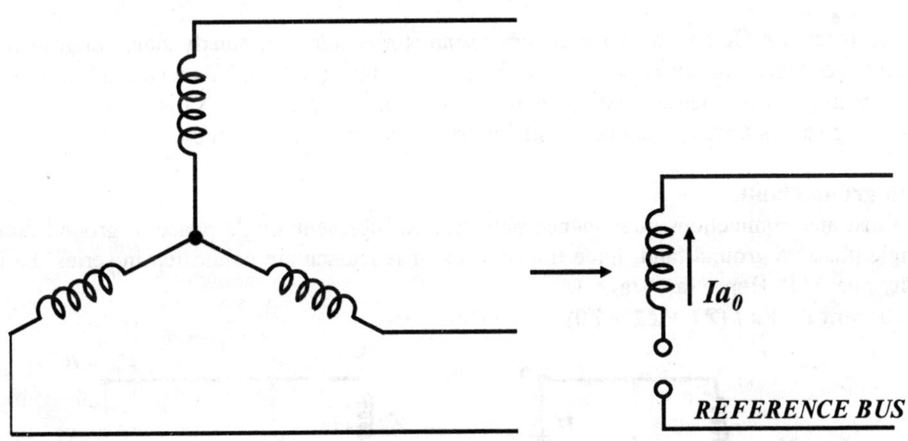

Fig. 1.4 (f): Zero sequence network of neutral ungrounded alternator.

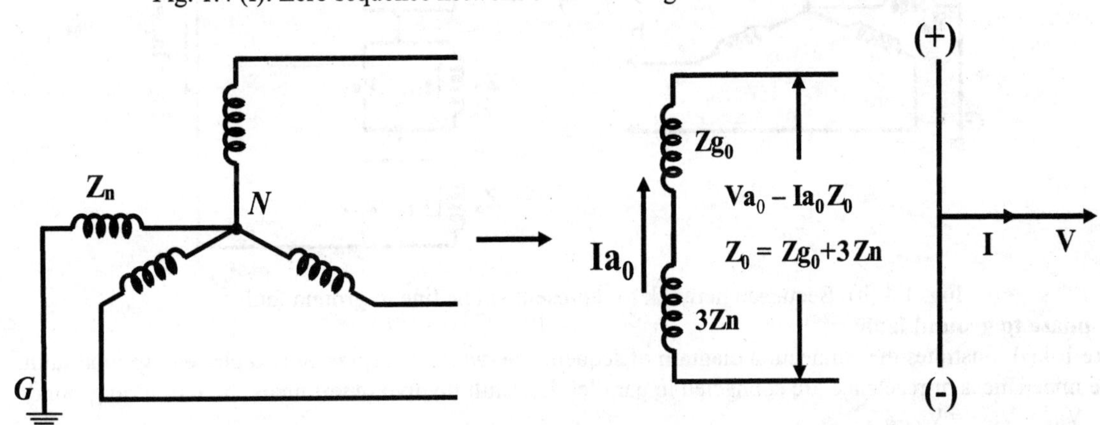

Fig. 1.4 (g): Zero sequence network of neutral grounded alternator.

The effect of flux due to armature current on the main field is called armature reaction. In a salient pole machine (low speed) the armature reaction should be considered with respect to pole axis (direct axis) and quadrature to pole axis. The cylindrical rotor (wound rotor) synchronous machines have uniform air-gap between the stator and rotor. Hence synchronous reactance Xs is considered as direct axis reactance Xd. Armature leakage reactance (XL) is the reactance, which results from stator leakage flux.

Positive, negative and zero sequence reactance:

In unbalanced system of 3 vectors Ia, Ib, Ic or Va, Vb, Vc can be resolved in to 3 balanced systems of vectors.

(1) Positive sequence components: Ia_1, Ib_1, Ic_1 or Va_1, Vb_1, Vc_1;

Comparing 3 balanced vector's of equal magnitude, displaced mutually by 120° and having the same phase sequence as the original system.

(2) Negative sequence components: Ia_2, Ib_2, Ic_2 or Va_2, Vb_2, Vc_2

Comparing 3 balanced vector's of equal magnitude displaced mutually by 120°, and having phase sequence opposite that of the original system of vectors. If the original system of vectors have a phase sequence a-b-c; then the positive sequence components too have phase sequence $a_1 - b_1 - c_1$ but negative phase sequence components have phase sequence $a_2 - b_2 - c_2$

(3) Zero sequence components: Ia_0, Ib_0, Ic_0 or Va_0, Vb_0, Vc_0

Comprising three equal vector's having zero phase displacement i.e. having same phase sequence.

Symbolically Ia, Ib, Ic or Va, Vb, Vc are original vectors. Subscript '1' and '2' is for positive and negative sequence entities. Subscript '0' for zero sequence entities.

$Va = Va_1 + Va_2 + Va_0$ and $Ia = Ia_1 + Ia_2 + Ia_0$

$Vb = Vb_1 + Vb_2 + Vb_0$ and $Ib = Ib_1 + Ib_2 + Ib_0$

$Vc = Vc_1 + Vc_2 + Vc_0$ and $Ic = Ic_1 + Ic_2 + Ic_0$

Positive sequence reactance (X_1) is the same as synchronous reactance for steady state conditions. Reactance offered to negative sequence current is negative sequence reactance (X_2). Unbalanced load current or fault on generator produces negative sequence rotating field. Zero sequence reactance (X) is caused by zero sequence components, which gives a stationary magnetic field alternating at supply frequency.

Single-phase-to-ground fault.

Figure 1.4 (h) illustrates connections of sequence networks to represent single phase to ground fault on phase 'a'. During single phase to ground fault, three impedances or reactance are connected in series. Ea is the e.m.f induced in faulty phase 'a'. Hence $Ia_1 = Ia_2 = Ia_0$

Va = 0, Fault current I = Ea / (Z1 + Z2 + Z0)

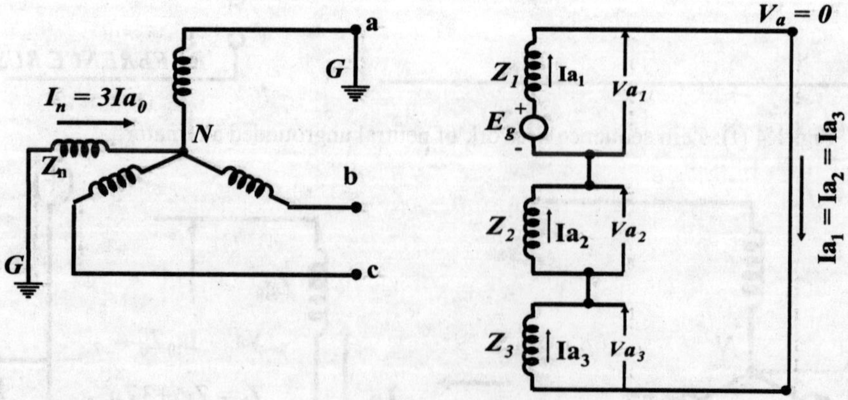

Fig. 1.4 (h): Sequence network to represent single line to ground fault.

Two-phase to ground fault

Figure 1.4 (i) illustrates the connection diagram of sequence networks to represent two phase to ground fault. Three impedances or reactance are connected in parallel. Let fault involve in terminals 'b' and 'c' to ground.

$Va_1 = Va_2 = Va_0 = Va / 3$

$Ia = Ia_1 + Ia_2 + Ia_0 = 0$, Hence fault current I_f = **Ea / Z1 + (Z2 Z0 / Z2 + Z0)**

Phase to phase fault and three-phase fault

Figure 1.4 (J) illustrates the connection diagram of sequence networks to represent line-to-line fault. Let a-b-c be the three-phases of a generator whose neutral is grounded through impedance Zn. Fault does not involve ground. Hence Z1 and Z2 only persisting and they are connected as shown in Figure.

$Ia_1 = (-)\ Ia_2$; Two phase fault current $I_f = Ea / (Z1 + Z2)$

$Va_1 = Va_2$; Three-phase fault current $I_f = Ea / Z1$ Ground fault in phase 'a' represents 3 phase ground fault

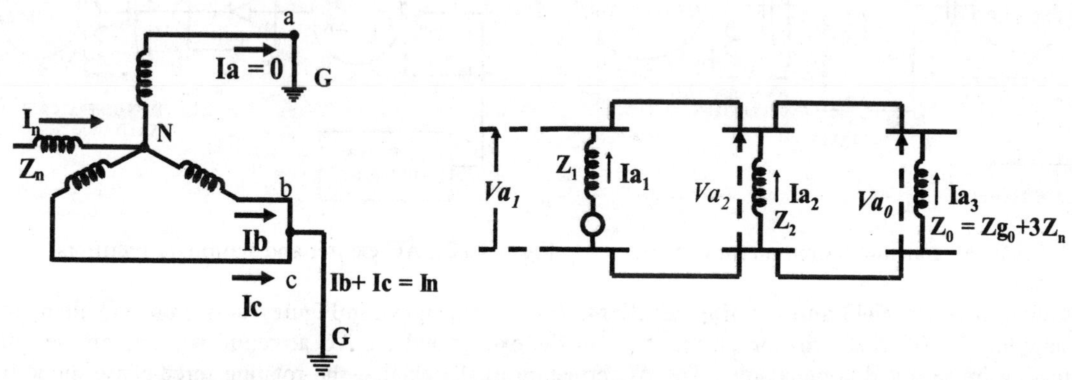

Fig. 1.4 (I): Sequence network to represent double line-to-ground fault.

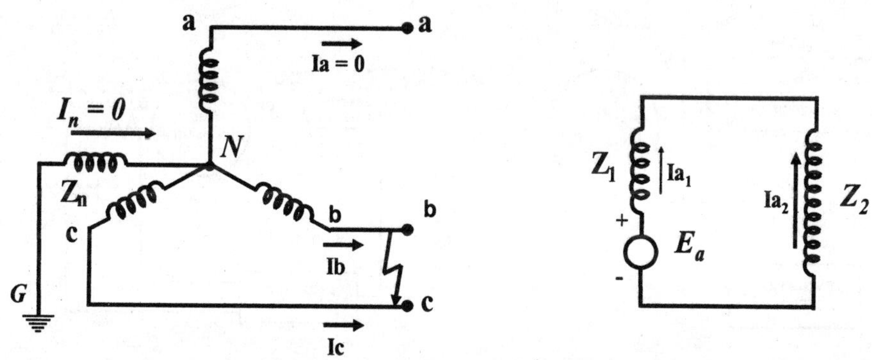

Fig. 1.4 (J): Sequence network to represent line-to-line fault.

Short circuit ratio of an alternator = Ifo/Ifs

Ifo = Field current required to-produce the rated open circuit voltage

Ifs = Field current required to-produce rated stator current during short-circuit test.

EXCITATION SYSTEMS:

There are four basic types of excitation systems used to control the output of AC machines

(1) System with DC generator commutator exciter: In this system a DC control signal is fed from the excitation control to the stationary field of the DC exciter. The rotating element of the exciter then supplies a direct current through a field circuit breaker to the field winding of the AC generator as shown in Figure 1.4 (k). The rotating armature of the DC exciter is either driven from the shaft as the rotating main field of the generator or can be on a separate motor-driven shaft. In either case a DC commutator is required on the exciter and brushes as well as collector rings are required on the rotor to transmit the main generator field current. This system is used only in very old machines.

(2) System with AC exciter and stationary rectifiers: To eliminate the problems of high current commutation for medium and large machines, the DC exciter, is replaced by, an AC exciter with rectifier. The system shown in Figure 1.4 (L) uses an alternator (AC exciter) with a rotating DC field winding driven from the shaft of the main AC generator. Current for this field winding is obtained from the excitation controls through brushes and collector rings. The three-phase AC output of the alternator is rectified through a stationary three-phase diode bridge and the direct current output is fed to the field winding of the generator through brushes and collector rings.

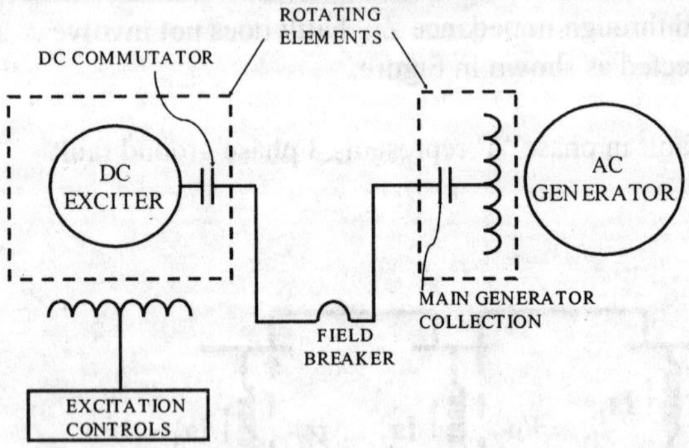

Fig. 1.4 (k): DC generator commutator exciter.

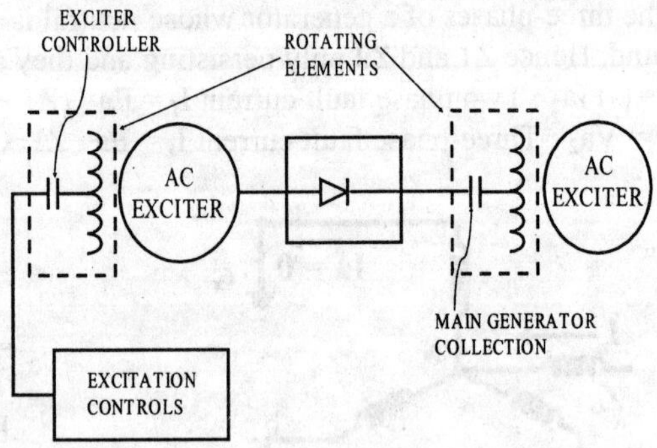

Fig. 1.4 (L): AC exciter and stationary rectifiers.

(3) Exciter with DC field and rotating rectifiers: The system shown in Figure 1.4 (m) uses an alternator but by mounting the DC field winding on the stator of the exciter and the AC armature winding on the rotor by eliminating brushes and commutators. The AC armature of the exciter, the rotating three-phase diode bridge rectifier and the main field of the AC generator are all mounted on the rotating rotor shaft. All electrical connections are made along or through the center of the shaft.

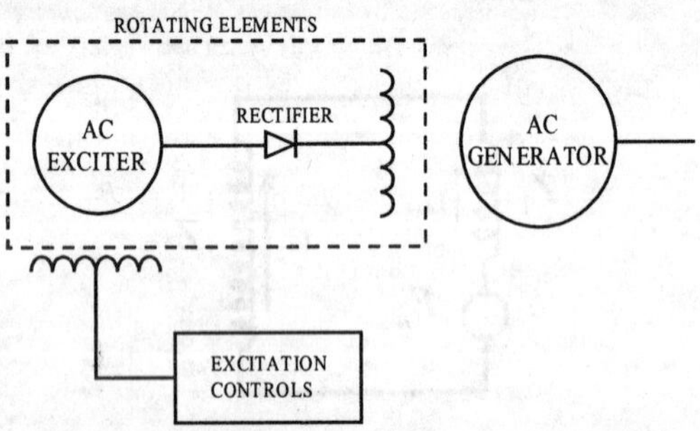

Fig. 1.4 (m): Exciter with DC field and rotating rectifiers.

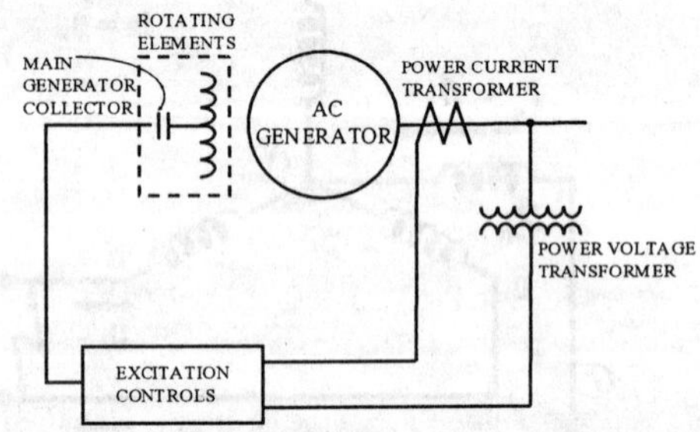

Fig. 1.4 (n): Static exciter feeding from CT and PT.

(4) System with static exciter: The preceding schemes utilize the energy directly from the prime mover shaft to obtain the required excitation power. Static excitation systems obtain this power from the electrical output of the generator or the connected system. In Figure 1.4 (n) the external current transformer and/or voltage transformers feed rectifiers in the regulating system, which in turn, supply direct current to the main field winding of the generator through brushes and collector rings. Some systems use only potential transformers as input power, while some use additional current transformers to boost the input during fault conditions when the terminal voltage is reduced.

1.5 NEUTRAL GROUNDING METHODS FOR ALTERNATORS.

Earth grid for large generating stations and substations are demonstrated in section 4.29 of Chapter # 4. The purpose of grounding the generator neutral is to facilitate protection of the stator winding and associated system. Direct connection of Generator neutral to the earth grid is limited to low voltage generators:
(1) To limit the mechanical stresses and fault damage; (2) To limit transient voltage during fault;
(3) To provide means for detecting ground faults within the machine.
Impedance (resistance or reactance) is inserted in the earthing of medium voltage generators: (1) To limit the magnitude of the earth fault current; (2) To limit system over-voltage during ground fault; and (3) to avoid tripping of the generator on momentary or high resistance ground fault, in order to keep the continuity of power.

Following are the different methods of neutral earthing.
(1) Solid earthing: Generator winding star point (neutral) is directly connected to the earthing system.
Applicable only for low voltage generators because the earth fault current is limited to phase-to neutral voltage

divided by earth resistance measured at site i.e. 230 / 1.0 = 230 amps (maximum) at one ohm earth resistance. For solidly earthed medium voltage generators, the earth fault current value will be very high. Figure 1.5 (a) shows solid earthing connection of an alternator. The line-to-ground bolted fault current (I_G) at the terminals of a solidly-grounded generator is given by the equation

I_G = (3 x Line to Neutral voltage) / (X1 + X2 + X0)

X1 = Direct axis sub-transient reactance;

X2 = Negative sequence reactance; X0 = Zero sequence reactance

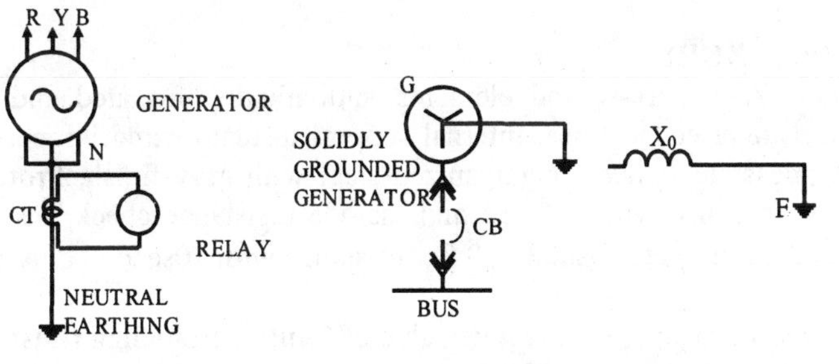

X_0 = Zero sequence reactance of the generator.

Fig. 1.5 (a): Solid earthing for low voltage generator neutral.

(2) Resistance earthing: Generator neutral is connected to the earthing system through a neutral grounding resistor (NGR) as shown in Figure 1.5 (b). Applicable for medium voltage generator(s) directly connected to a common bus for power distribution. Severe arcing to the machine core burns the iron at the point of fault and welds laminations together. Replacement of the faulty conductor may not be a very serious matter but the damage to core cannot be ignored. It may be necessary to rebuild the core down to the fault, which would involve extensive dismantling of the winding. If the earth fault current is limited to a safe value, burning of the core will not readily occur. Hence generator neutral is grounded through a resistor to limit the earth fault current. For example, in an 11 KV generator the phase to neutral voltage is 11000 / √3 = 6351 volts. If a 10 Ω resistance is introduced in the circuit the maximum earth fault current is limited to 6351 / 10 = 635.1 amps, assuming that the actual earth resistance is less than one ohm. In addition to the above, resistance grounding eliminate harmonic current.

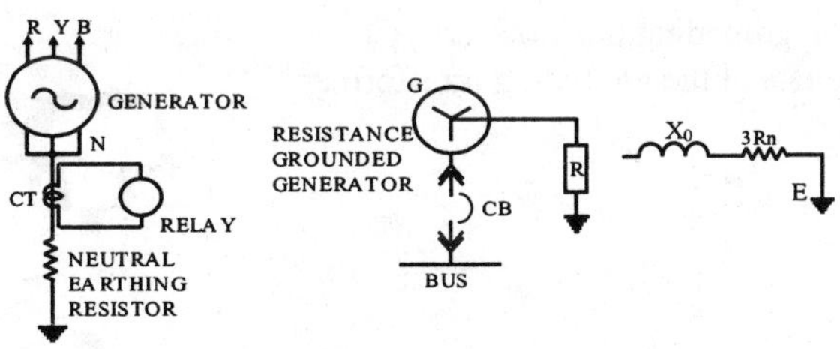

X_0 = Zero sequence reactance of the generator.

Rn = Resistance of grounding resistor.

Fig. 1.5 (b): Resistance earthing for medium voltage generator neutral

(3) Reactance earthing: Generator neutral is connected through the high voltage winding (primary) of a single-phase reactance transformer as shown in Figure 1.5 (c). The secondary of the reactance transformer is connected to a resistor. Resistor has been introduced in the secondary to prevent the generation of high transient over voltage in the event of an arcing earth fault. Applicable for generator transformer combined units. Assume that an 11 KV generator is supplying to a 132 KV bus through a step up transformer. The unit is called combined generator-transformer unit. In this system the generator winding and the transformer primary winding can be treated as an isolated system, which is not influenced by the transmission line earthing system. The reactance connected between neutral and ground provides a lagging current which neutralizes the capacitive current from the line, i.e. reactance provides the necessary phase opposition between capacitive line current and fault current.

Ground fault neutralizer:

When the power plant is being operated as a 3-phase 4 wire system with a loaded and earthed neutral, the alternator star point (N) is often connected to the star point of one or several transformers or with the star point of one or more alternators of different power ratings (KVA ratings). Large circulating currents of three times the mains frequency can flow in the neutral lead of such systems. These circulating currents should not exceed 20% of the rated current of the smallest alternator running in parallel. Connection of a star point choke (Petersen coil or arc suppression coil) in the neutral conductor for the suppressions of these circulating currents is the best solution. With the choke connected between neutral and earth, power frequency current between line and earth due to capacitance of healthy lines and earth is equal and opposite to the current in the earth connection. When the neutrals of alternator of like power and like type are connected without connection to a transformer neutral conductor no circulating current will flow, and a star point chock is superfluous.

Neutral grounding resistor (NGR):

NGR is made of stainless steel wire-wound elements, individually insulated and supported on aluminium frames with stainless steel inner connections, internal support insulators and jumpers. Enclosure is made of 2 mm thick grade 304 stainless steel sheet or galvanized steel with gray finish, Protection classification IP23. NGR is to be tested in accordance with IEEE32 and include resistance check, insulation test and flash test, temperature rise (760°C maximum) etc. Usually 10 Ω, resistance with 10second duty is sufficient for grounding an 1.1 KV generator.

I = (System line to line rated voltage) / (√3 x Ohmic value of Neutral grounding resistor unit).

Cast resin neutral grounding transformer:

Single phase cast resin type, Class B / F, 10 amps 10 second rated transformer is sufficient for reactance grounding. Primary (rated to 1.5 times the generator phase-to-neutral voltage) is connected to the generator neutral and station earthing. Secondary low voltage winding is connected across a resistor and an over-voltage relay as shown in Figure 1.5 (c). Protection classification for the indoor type air insulated transformer is IP00. To avoid the possibility of harmfully high transient over-voltage because of ferroresonance, the ohmic value of secondary external resistance should not exceed $X_c / 3N^2$

Xc = Total phase to ground capacitive reactance per phase of the generator stator windings + the surge protection capacitors/lightning arrestors + the leads (cable or bus duct) to the main and station service transformers and the primary windings (generator side) of the transformer(s).

N = Open-circuit voltage ratio or turn-to-turn ratio of the high voltage to low voltage winding of the neutral grounding transformer.

The KVA rating of the neutral grounding transformer is derived by using the formulae: $1000\ V_G\ V_T / \sqrt{3}\ N^2\ R$

V_G = Phase to phase voltage of the generator in KV

V_T = High voltage rating of the grounding transformer.

R = Secondary external resistance of the grounding transformer

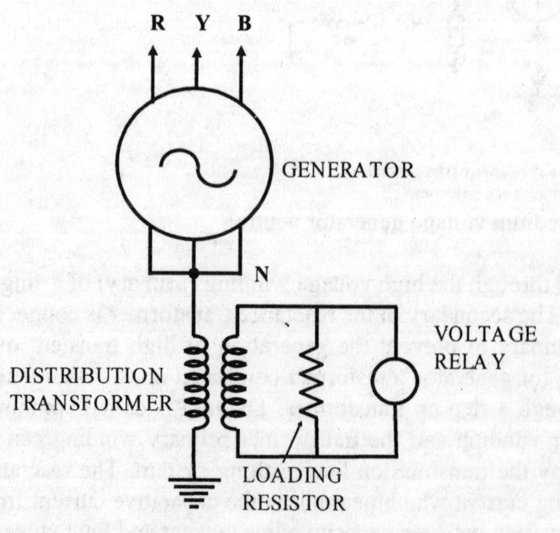

Fig. 1.5 (c): Reactance grounding for combined GT unit.

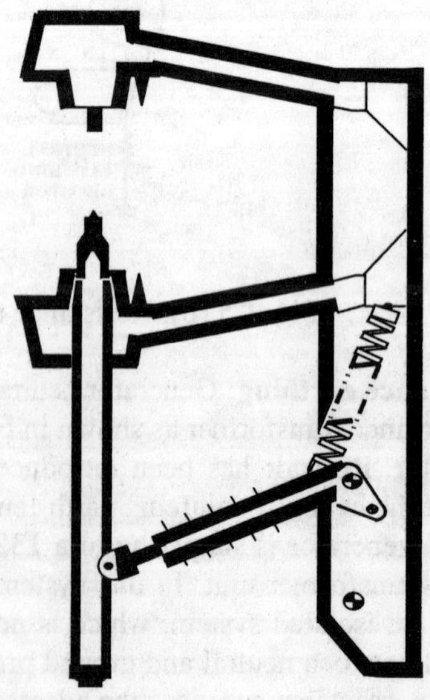

Fig. 1.5 (d): Single pole air break circuit breaker.

Neutral grounding circuit breaker

Figure 1.5 (d) shows a typical single pole air break circuit breaker designed for switching neutral grounding resistor. If several resistance-grounded identical generators installed in a power station are working in parallel, only one NGR of running unit (base unit) is sufficient. Neutral grounding resistance of remaining generators will remain open. If the base unit is tripped due to any reason, provision shall be made to close the neutral circuit breaker of the generator under priority number II

1.6 AUTOMATIC VOLTAGE REGULATORS FOR BRUSH TYPE/BRUSHLESS ALTERNATORS.

Voltage regulator is a device that or circuit that maintains a constant value of voltage at varying load conditions. AVR maintains the set terminal voltage within ± 1%. Other advantages are under speed protection (V/F), inbuilt volt trimming port and quadrature droop compensation facility. Automatic voltage regulators are shunt-regulators, because they tap off field current from the alternator, which control the voltage or the power factor of the alternator by adjusting the field current in the exciter stator coil.

Following are the protective features of AVR.

1. Loss of sensing
2. Under frequency
3. Over excitation
4. Over temperature
5. Field current limit
6. Generator current limit

Figure 1.6 (a) and (b) shows the block diagram and wiring diagram of an automatic voltage regulator. The voltage regulator senses the generator voltage, compares a rectified sample of that voltage with a reference (zener) diode voltage and supplies the field current required to maintain the predetermined ratio between the generator voltage and the reference voltage. This unit consists of five basic circuits. These are sensing circuit, an error detector, an error amplifier, a power controller and a stabilization network. Sensor circuit will sense the generator voltage, rectify and filter this voltage and apply the resultant DC signal to the error detector and error amplifier. Error detector provides a DC signal that is proportional to the generator voltage, and compared with reference voltage to develop the error signal, which is applied to the error amplifier.

Error amplifier providing phase angle control of the firing signal applied to the SCR's (thyristors) in the power controller. Power controller consists of thyristors and diodes in a bridge rectifier circuit. This circuit, compare the power source and the exciter field. Stabilization circuit provides stable operation under all operating conditions.

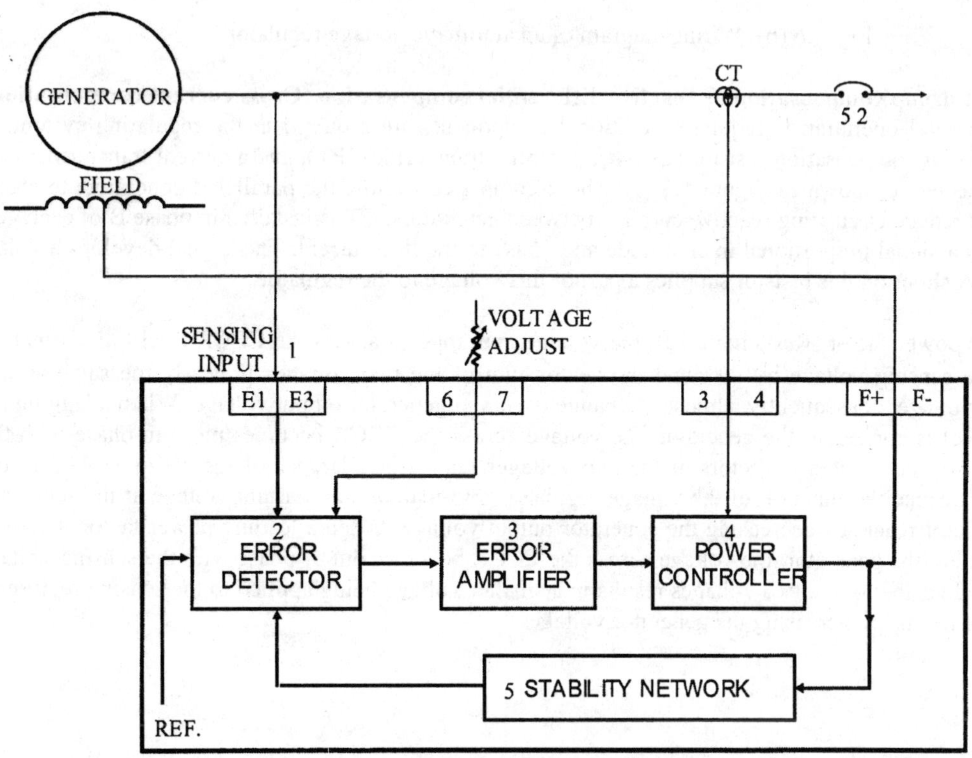

Fig. 1.6 (a): Block diagram of an automatic voltage regulator (Courtesy, Basler Electric).

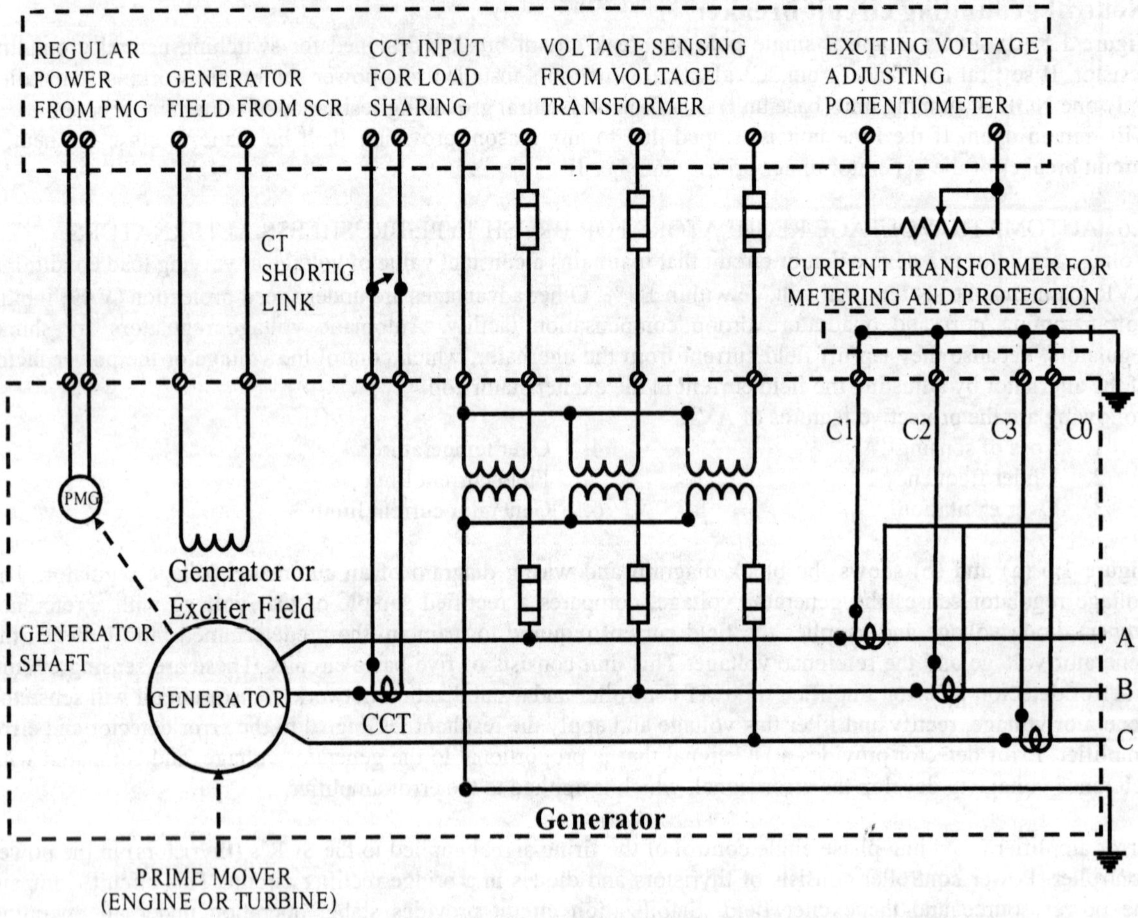

Fig. 1.6 (b): Wiring diagram of an automatic voltage regulator.

Reactive droop compensation or reactive differential compensation (Cross current compensation)
When parallel operation is required, additional components are required in the regulating system. These are cross current compensation resistor (CCCR), potential transformer (PT), and a current transformer (CT). These are connected as shown in Figure 1.6 (c). These components allow the paralleled generators to share reactive load and reduce circulating reactive currents between generators. CT is installed in phase B of each generator. It develops a signal proportional in amplitude and phase to the line current. This signal develops a voltage across CCCR. A slider on this resistor supplies a part of this voltage to the regulator.

At unity power factor (Resistive load), the voltage that appears across the CCCR (and transformer windings), leads the sensing voltage by 90°, and the vector sum of the two voltages is nearly the same as the original sensing voltage; consequently, almost no change occurs in generator output voltage. When a lagging power load (Inductive) is applied to the generator, the voltage across the CCCR becomes more in-phase with the sensing voltage and the combined vectors of the two voltages results in a larger voltage being applied to the sensing rectifiers. Since the function of the voltage regulator is to maintain a constant voltage at the sensing rectifiers, the regulator reacts by decreasing the generator output voltage. When a leading power factor (Capacitive load) is applied to the generator, the voltage across the CCCR becomes out of phase with the sensing voltage and the combined vectors of the two voltages results in a smaller voltage being applied to the sensing rectifiers, then the regulator reacts by increasing the generator voltage.

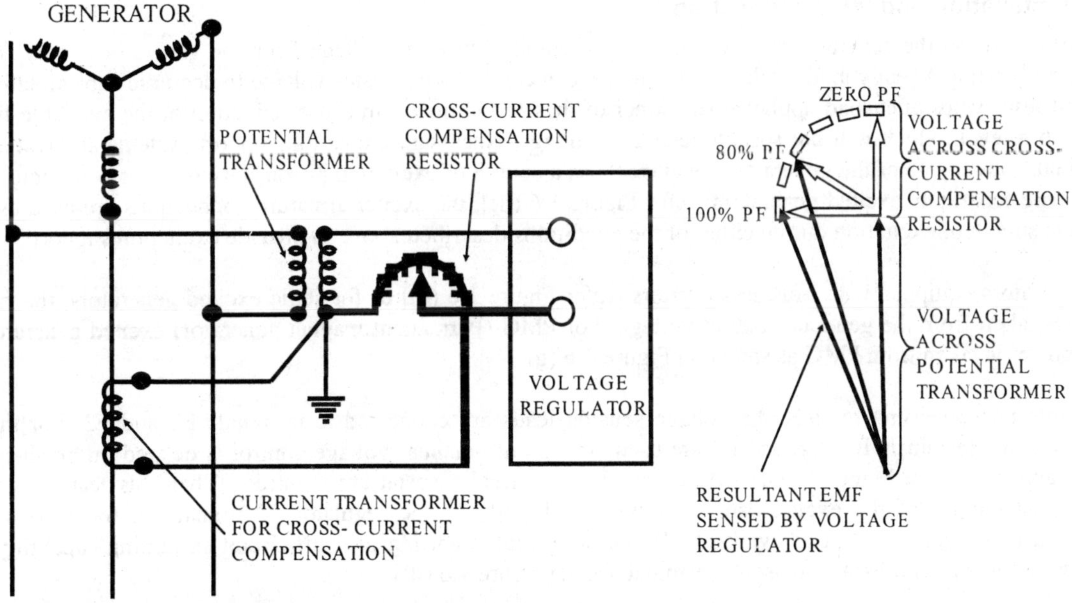

Fig. 1.6 (c): Cross current compensation circuit (Courtesy, Basler Electric).

When two generators are operating in parallel, if the field excitation on one generator become excessive and causes a circulating current to flow between generators, this current will appear as a lagging power factor (inductive) load to the generator with excessive field current and a leading power factor (capacitive) load to the other generator. The parallel compensation circuit will cause the voltage regulator to decrease the field excitation on the generator with the lagging power factor load, and increase the field excitation on the generator with leading power factor load, so as to minimize the circulating currents between the generators.

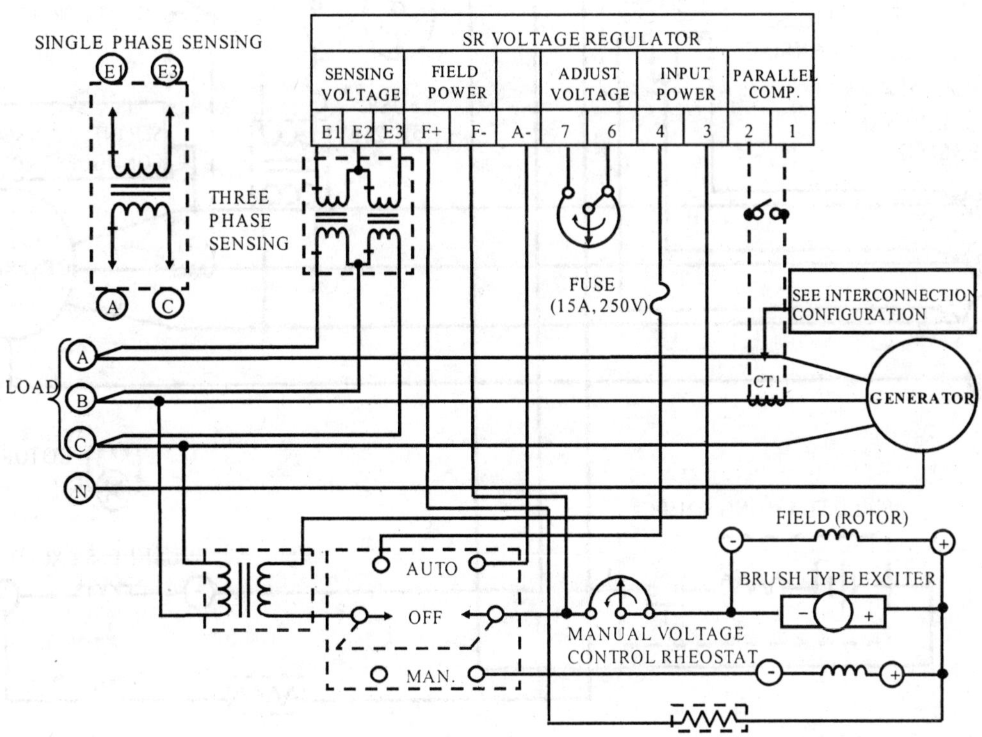

Fig. 1.6 (d): Connection diagram of voltage regulator used in brush type alternator (Courtesy, Basler Electric).

AVR installation and inter connection

A short circuit on the generator terminals or out put could reduce the voltage from the generator nearby zero. Similarly, starting a heavy load, such as large motor, can cause the generator voltage to decrease substantially at the first few cycles after load applications. Either of these conditions can cause reduction of the available field power to a level, which will not sustain generator voltage. Necessary excitation support systems are available which take advantage of the generator line currents as a source of excitation power during either condition. For brush-type separately excited generators [refer Figure 1.6 (d)], the exciter armature connections are used as an alternate source of excitation during either of the conditions described above to provide excitation support.

For generators equipped with brushless exciters [refer Figure 1.6 (e)] or for static excited generators, the field power is taken from the generator output voltage. For PMG (Permanent magnet generator) excited generators, input power is taken from PMG as shown in Figure 1.6 (g).

For single phase sensing models, the voltage sensing leads are connected to terminals E1 and E3. For three phase sensing, terminals E1, E2, and E3 are used. When auto-manual voltage control is desired on brush-type exciter applications, a Manual – Off - Auto switch and a field rheostat are required. When this feature is not desired, the output of the exciter can be connected directly to the regulator (Terminal A), to allow self-excitation during short-circuit or overloads. When large motor starting or short-circuit sustaining capability is not required it is not necessary to use A- terminal. [Refer figure 1.6 (d)].

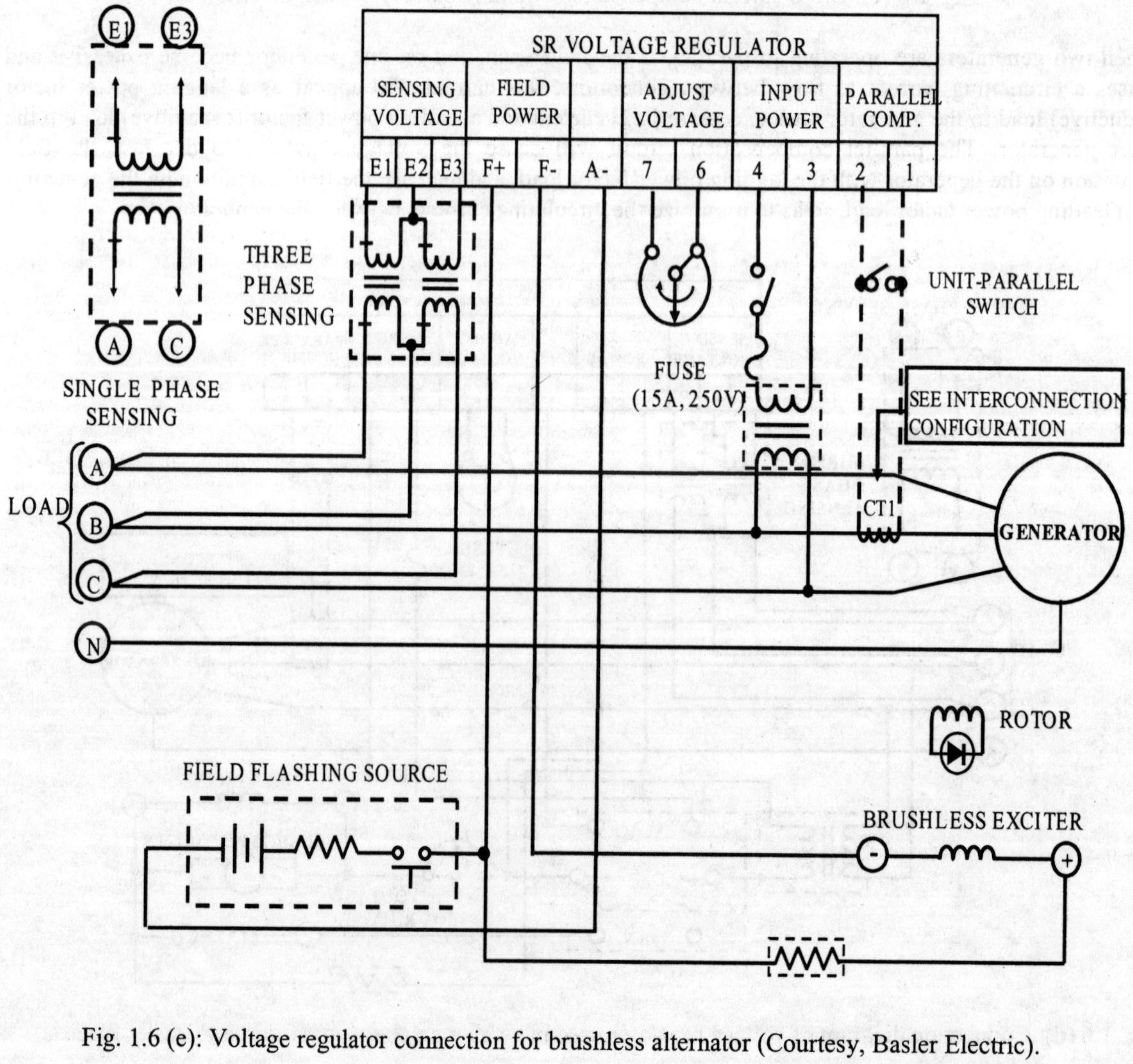

Fig. 1.6 (e): Voltage regulator connection for brushless alternator (Courtesy, Basler Electric).

The phase relationship of CT signal to the voltage regulator sensing circuit must be correct or otherwise, the system will not perform parallel operation properly. On three phase sensing model the CT must be installed in the line (phase) that supplies sensing voltage to regulator terminal E2. For single phase sensing, the CT must be installed in the line of the three-phase regulator that does not supply sensing voltage to the regulator. [Refer figure 1.6 (d) or (g)]. Figure 1.6 (f) shows the correct CT polarity for A-B-C rotation. If the phase rotation sequence is A-C-B, the CT's secondary leads must be interchanged. A unit parallel-switch (Circuit breaker auxiliary NC contact) shorts the parallel CT secondary to prevent any droop signal from being injected in to the regulating system during non-paralleled operation. The switch may not be required on parallel droop compensation applications where a voltage drop is not objectionable especially in smaller units.

PARALLELING CT POLARITIES:

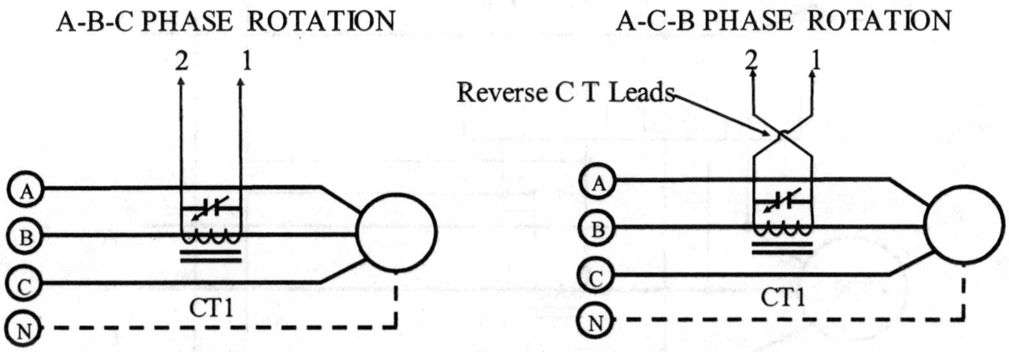

Fig. 1.6 (f): Interconnection configuration for brushless rotary exciter or static exciter.

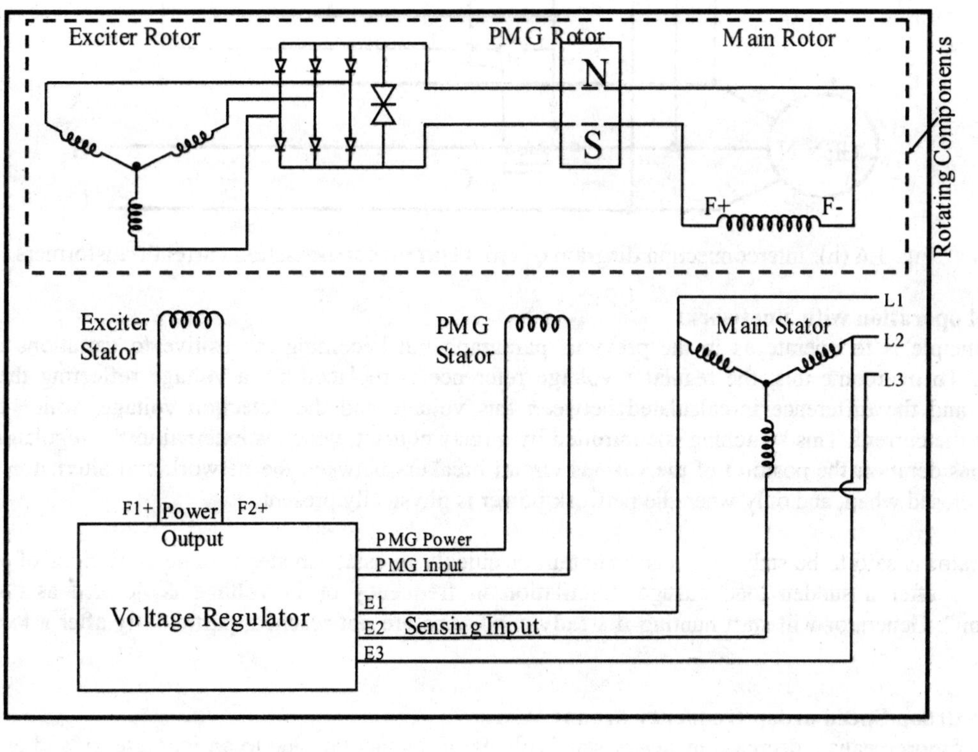

Fig. 1.6 (g): Voltage regulator connection for PMG excited generator.

For reactive differential compensation of parallel running generators, connect each CT to its, respective regulator. Then connect the finish of the first CT to the start of the second CT, the finish of the second CT to the start of the third CT, etc. Continue until all CT's are connected in series. The final step will be to connect the finish of the last CT to the start of the first CT as shown in Figure 1.6 (h).

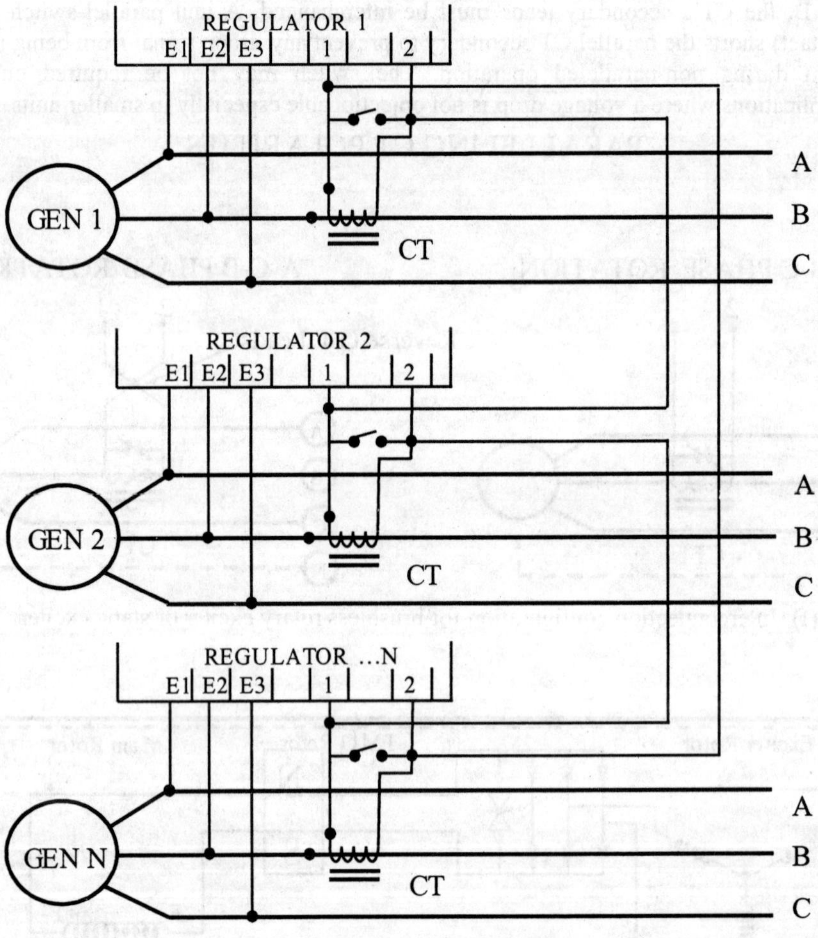

Fig. 1.6 (h): Interconnection diagram of cross current compensation current transformers.

Parallel operation with a network:
The principle is to operate as in the previous paragraph but becoming insensitive to variations in network voltage. To overcome this, the regulator voltage reference is replaced by, a voltage reflecting the generator voltage and the difference is calculated between this voltage and the detection voltage, which takes in to account the current. This switching is controlled by a relay contact, which is external to the regulator and takes in to consideration the position of the various circuit breakers between the network and alternator. This relay contact closed when, and only when the network power is physically present.

A generator is said to be stable if it can maintain or quickly re-establish steady-state conditions of voltage and frequency after a sudden load change. Oscillation in frequency or in voltage is defined as "out of step condition". Generator will start hunting if steady conditions are not reached, particularly after a load transient change.

Voltage droop/Speed droop/frequency droop:
Voltage droop means a decrease in steady-state voltage of a generator due to an increase in load applied. This decrease in voltage from the no load voltage is expressed as a percentage of the full load voltage or:

$$\text{Percentage voltage droop} = \frac{(\text{No load voltage} - \text{Full load voltage}) \times 100}{\text{Full load voltage}}$$

Operation of generators in parallel requires voltage droop as reactive load is increased. For providing voltage droop function, droop transformer and droop rheostat is incorporated in the voltage regulator circuit. Transformer senses load current and droop-rheostat provides adjustment of droop voltage. Voltage adjusting rheostat provides a no load voltage adjustment approximately ± 10%. Voltage gain rheostat provides an adjustment to compensate prime mover r.p.m. This rheostat can be adjusted to keep the same terminal voltage at no load and full load.

On parallel operation, for reactive differential compensation applications a normally closed (NC) breaker auxiliary contact should be used to shortening the paralleling current transformer secondary when the generator is not paralleled to the bus. If this NC contact is not used a voltage droop will be introduced in the system. This is due to the unloaded generator parallel CT not supplying its compensating signal, but allowing a voltage drop to occur across it. Lack of this shortening contact will also cause the voltage of the incoming generator to fluctuate prior to paralleling. This contact opens when the circuit breaker is closed.
Speed droop means a decrease, in steady-state speed of a prime mover due to an increase in applied load. This decrease in speed from the no load speed is expressed as a percentage of full load speed, hence:

$$\text{Percent speed droop} = \frac{(\text{No load speed} - \text{Full load speed}) \times 100}{\text{Full load speed}}$$

Frequency droop means a decrease in steady-state frequency output of a generator due to an increase in load. This decrease in frequency from the no load frequency is expressed as a percentage of the full load frequency, hence:

$$\text{Percent frequency droop} = \frac{(\text{No load frequency} - \text{Full load frequency}) \times 100}{\text{Full load frequency}}$$

Gain setting for governor or regulator:
The increase in signal power that is produced by an amplifier is usually given as the ratio of output to input voltage, current or power. In generators, a low gain setting on the electric governor or electronic voltage regulator provides a relatively small signal to correct variations of frequency or voltage. The frequency and/or voltage may wander or may be slow in recovering to stable conditions after a load change. A high gain setting provides a relatively large signal to correct variations of frequency and/or voltage. If the gain is set too high, the electric governor or voltage regulator may overcorrect. This may probably produce hunting of the frequency and/or voltage.

Circulating current (cross current):
Current, which flows between paralleled generators, most apparent with no load on the paralleled generators. Circulating current is caused (1) by unequal excitation of the generators (reactive current, which may be reduced by changing the voltage regulator adjustment); and (2) by unequal power from the prime movers that are driving the generators real current/power, which can be eliminated by governor adjustments..

Cross current compensation / Reactive differential compensation / Reactive droop compensation:
Cross current compensation: A circuit arrangement that made paralleled generators share the reactive component of load current in proportion to the generator ratings. The circuit arrangement could also essentially eliminate the reactive component of circulating current flowing between paralleled generators.

Reactive differential (cross current) compensation: It is a circuit arrangement for operating generators in parallel with out generator voltage droop. Reactive differential compensation is accomplished by a differential interconnection of the secondary of the generator current transformers used for reactive droop compensation. This arrangement is very difficult to set up when paralleling generators of different capacities.

Reactive droop compensation: A circuit arrangement that creates a droop in generator output voltage that is proportional to the reactive load current. This circuit arrangement makes paralleled generators share the reactive component of the load current in proportion to the generator ratings. It also can essentially eliminate the reactive component of circulating current, which may flow between paralleled generators. The reactive droop compensation arrangement is commonly called the generator-paralleling module.

Voltage droop compensation: A system which permits paralleled generators to share load currents in proportion to the generator ratings.

1.7 PARALLELING AND LOAD SHARING OF ALTERNATORS.

Synchronism means the condition where two or more generators are operating at the same frequency and output voltage and are in phase with one another. Synchronizing is the procedure of matching the frequency, phase rotation, voltage and phase relationship of one generator to another for purposes of paralleling the units on to a common bus. Parallel operation is the method by which two or more generators having the same voltage and frequency characteristics are connected to a common load. Following are the conditions for paralleling alternators:

1. The voltage and frequency must be same.
2. Same phase displacement and voltage regulation characteristics
3. Same phase rotation and phase sequence
4. Prime movers should have the same speed regulation characteristics
5. Provision shall be made available for (1) voltage regulator paralleling; (2) current transformer paralleling; (3) governor controls paralleling (4) auto-synchronizer or synchronism check relay and synchroscope for manual synchronizing.

Out of phase paralleling

Figure 1.7 (a) illustrates that an armature rotating within a magnetic field induces a sinusoidal waveform. The relationship of rotor position to the output waveform at several points in the cycle is also shown. The output voltage of a generator at any instant in time is directly related to the position of the rotor with respect to the stator. When generators are paralleled out of phase, the voltage waveforms are forced in to synchronism and the rotors are forced to new positions almost instantaneously.

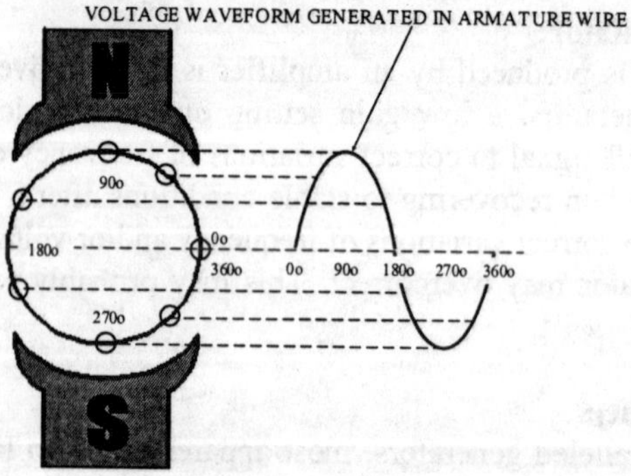

Fig. 1.7 (a): Typical armature and sinusoidal waveform.

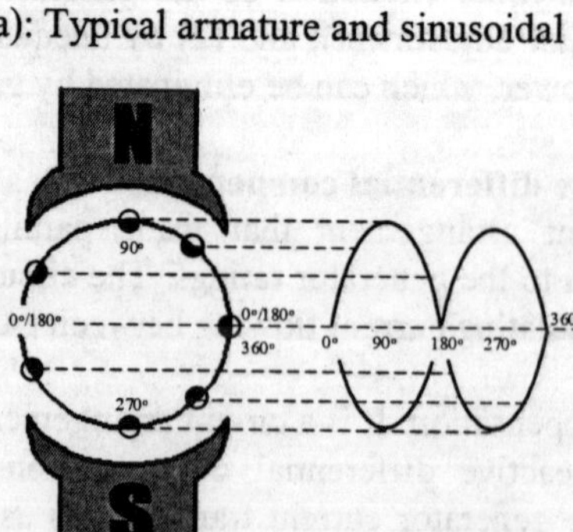

Fig. 1.7 (b): Armature out-of phase waveform.

In Figure 1.7 (b), two armatures are superimposed on the same axis, with the same magnetic field. The two armatures are rotating in the same direction and at the same speed, but they are 180° out-of phase. This is illustrated in the associated output waveforms. If the two generator outputs were paralleled at this time, the resulting high currents and mechanical forces exerted on the generator sets would have catastrophic results. **Damage to the generator sets could involve prime mover failure, rotor lamination slippage, excitation system damage and power cable damage**. The magnitude of damage is a function of the phase differential and the relative size of the generator sets being paralleled. Out-of phase paralleling with a utility source will cause severe damage.

Figure 1.7 (c) shows the effect of the addition of the harmonics to a voltage waveform (50 or 60 Hz). Note that the two dissimilar waveforms in the figure have the same cycle length and RMS voltage value, but that their shapes (Peaked shape and flattened shape) are completely different due to the addition of the harmonics to the system. Because the harmonic content of a generator waveform varies with the load, the negative effect of operating with dissimilar generators may be more apparent at some load levels than others.

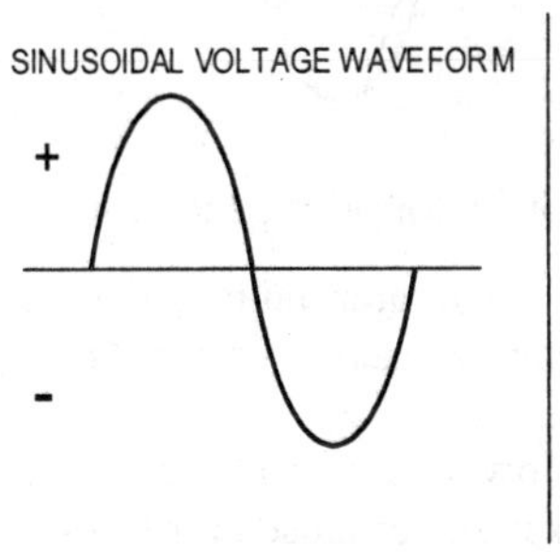

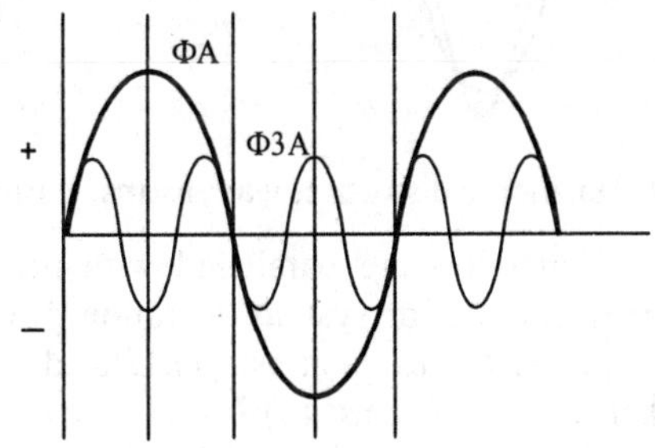

Fig. 1.7 (c): Effects of harmonics on waveform shape. Fig 1.7 (d): Third harmonic current waveform.

Sinusoidal wave having a frequency that is, an integral multiple of a fundamental frequency. Fundamental complex wave whose frequency is twice that of the fundamental frequency is called the second harmonic. Figure 1.7 (d) represents the waveforms of fundamental current (φA) and (180Hz) third harmonic current (φ3A). Similarly Figure 1.7 (e) represents the waveforms of fundamental current (φA) and (300Hz) fifth harmonic current (φ5A).

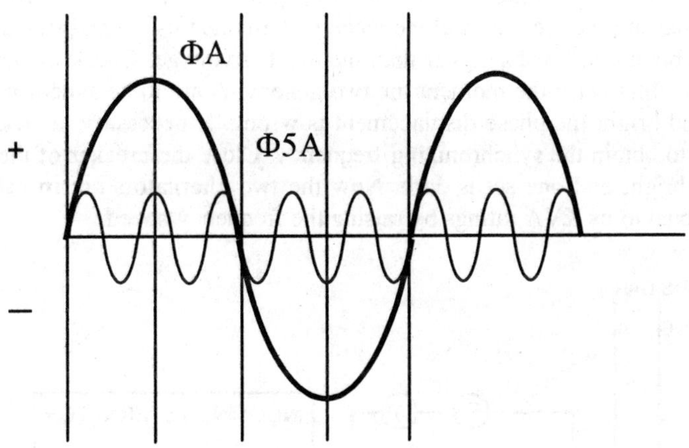

Fig. 1.7 (e): Fifth harmonic current waveform.

Figure 1.7 (f) shows harmonic distortion waveforms representing harmonic additive to peak and harmonic subtractive from peak. Harmonics in a power system cause distortion of the normal sinusoidal waveform.

When generators are paralleled, their voltage waveforms are superimposed upon one another as shown in Figure 1.7 (g). At any point in the cycle where there is a voltage difference between the generators, current will flow between the machines. This is known as circulating current. This circulating current is not adjustable by manipulation of cross current compensation (Refer section 1.6) or other devices. Due to the design of the individual components, circulating current is inherent in the system. The circulating current may or may not be damaging; depending on the magnitude of the current, the ratings of the generators in the system, and the susceptibility of load devices in the system to harmonic currents.

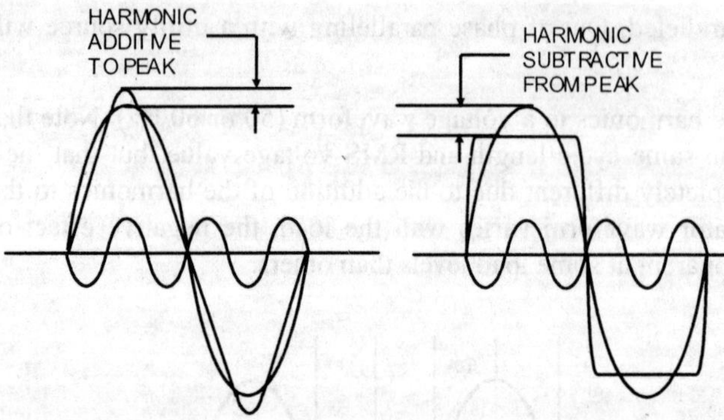

Fig. 1.7 (f): Harmonic distortion waveforms.

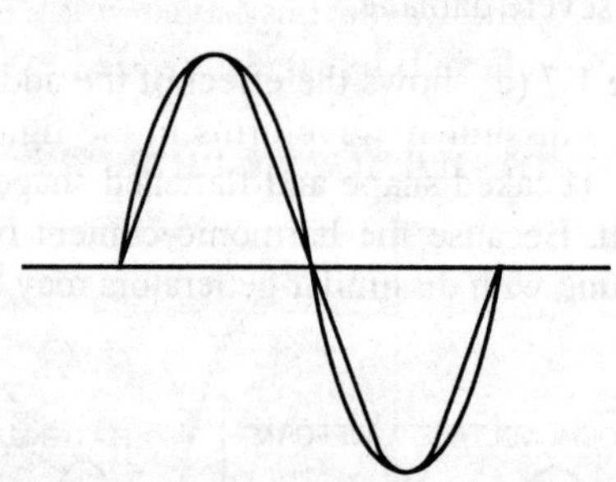

Fig. 1.7 (g): Superimposed voltage waveforms of generators.

If dissimilar generators are paralleled with their neutrals connected; premature generator failure, degraded generator performance, or system operation problem can occur. The system designer has several options to avoid harmonic problems such as: (1) Use identical generators; (2) Use of resistance grounded neutral will eliminate harmonic problems; (3) Install reactors in the neutral to limit current flow at third and higher order frequencies. (4) Install neutral circuit breakers to connect the neutral only on the first unit to close to the bus.

While paralleling alternators the running machine is the machine connected to the load bus and the incoming machine is the machine to be synchronized to share the load on the bus. When the bus bar is not energized it is said to be dead bus. On dead bus closing the dead bus-closing relay will energize and give a closing command to the breaker provided proper frequency and voltage is build up in the incoming generator.

Manual synchronizing by dark lamp method:

Figure 1.7 (h) illustrates the synchronizing check by using two sets of bright lamps and one set dark lamp for manual synchronizing of two or more low voltage alternators. Start any one machine and check that the voltage and frequency is correct. Connect to the load bus by closing the circuit breaker, provided the load bus is dead (not energized). After starting the second machine when it is attained its normal speed (idle speed) its excitation should be adjusted to obtain a few volts higher than the bus bar voltage. Check the lamps connected across the two circuits. They are extinguished the moment the two generators are to be synchronized. If the two lamps are simultaneously dark and bright the phase displacement is wrong. If necessary, increase or reduce the speed of the incoming machine to obtain the synchronizing frequency. Close the breaker of the incoming machine when two sets of lamps are bright and one set is dark. Now the two alternators are in parallel. Load the machines equally but in proportional to its KVA ratings by raising the frequency/speed.

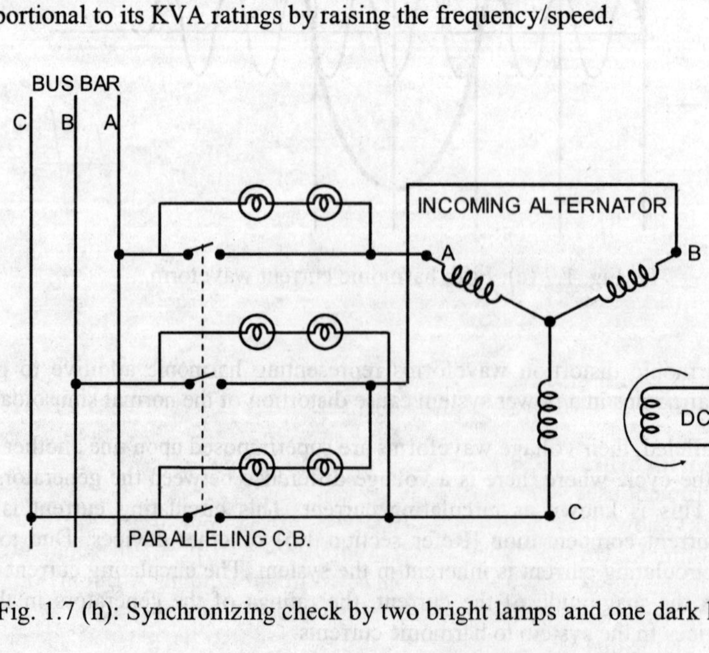

Fig. 1.7 (h): Synchronizing check by two bright lamps and one dark lamp.

Figure 1.7 (i) shows two in-phase waveforms on the left and two out-of-phase waveforms on the right. In both examples, the waveforms have the same amplitude and frequency. In the out-of-phase example, waveform A leads waveform B by 90 electrical degrees.

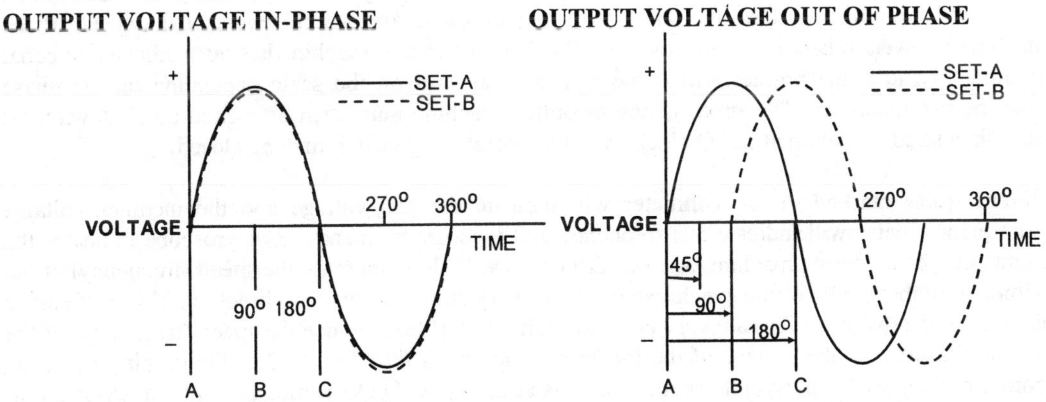

Fig. 1.7 (i): Synchronization lights: In-phase and out-of-phase waveform.

Figure 1.7 (J) shows the output waveforms of two out-of-phase generators. The lower graph shows the voltage differential across the synchronizing lamps as the two sources drift in and out of phase. At point X, the two sources are in-phase and the voltage differential is zero. The lamps are dark and it is safe to parallel. At point Y, the two sources are 180 degrees out-of-phase, providing the maximum voltage differential between the sources. At this point, the synchronizing lamps burn brightly. At point Z, the two sources are shown in phase again.

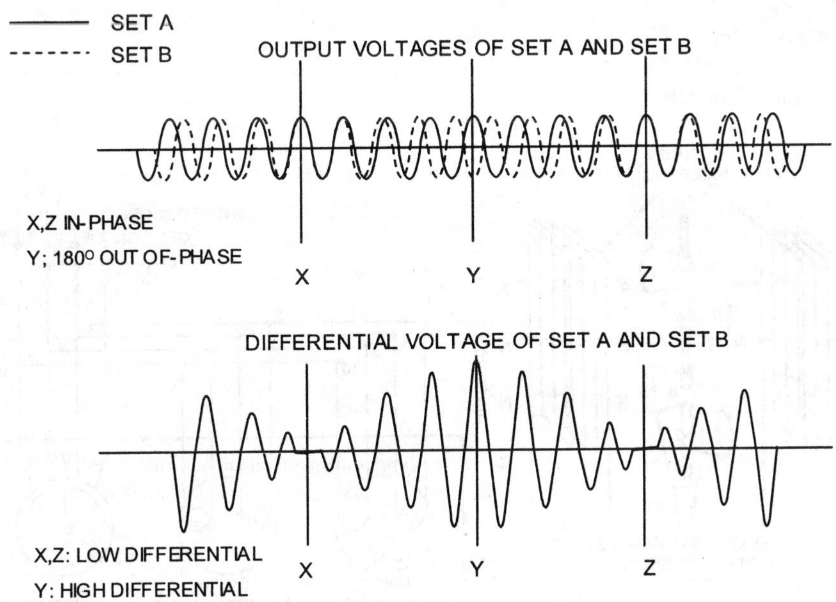

FIG. 1.7 (J): Synchronization lights: Out-of-phase waveforms and voltage differential.

Manual synchronizing with synchroscope:

Synchroscope is an instrument used for measuring the phase displacement of two paralleling power sources or alternators. Figure 1.7 (k) shows the internal and external connection diagram of a rotating synchroscope with frequency meter and voltmeter. In the rotary synchroscope the axial polarizing coils are energized from the 'incoming' source, while the radial field coils are connected to the 'running' machine or bus circuit. If there is no difference between the two circuits either in phase angle or frequency, the pointer will remain motionless at the 12, O clock position on the dial of the rotating synchroscope. With no frequency difference, any phase angle difference will cause the pointer to take up a position away from this point, in the similar fashion to the action of the power factor indicator. If, however, there is a difference in frequency between the two machines, this phase relationship will be constantly changing and the pointer will consequently rotate continuously in one direction or the other at a speed corresponding to the difference in frequency. If the 'incoming' machine is at a higher speed than the 'running' machine the pointer rotates clockwise and anticlockwise if the speed of the 'incoming' machine is lower. When the frequency (speed) of the 'incoming' machine has been adjusted to equal that of the running machine, the pointer will come to rest at a point on the scale depending on the phase displacement of the two machines. The speed of the incoming machine must then be inched up or down until the pointer takes up a steady position at 12' O clock, when the paralleling switch may be closed.

The two different scales marked in the voltmeter will indicate the bus voltage and the incomer voltage. Similarly the frequency meter will indicate bus frequency and incomer frequency. Synchroscope indicates the phase displacement of the incoming machine whether fast or slow. If slow, increase the speed (frequency) of the incoming machine until the needle of the synchroscope move very slowly in the fast direction. This will ensure that the frequencies of the two machines are very close to each other. If fast, reduce the speed (frequency) of the incoming machine. Ensure that the voltage of the incoming machine is little higher than the running machine. Close the incomer breaker when the synchroscope needle is at zero (12' O clock) position. It is always safe to close at an angle less than 5° "fast" to match the closing time of the circuit breaker. Switch off the synchroscope after synchronizing. If the synchronizing is not done at the proper time the generator and bus bar voltage will get heavy jerk. If synchronism check relay is employed the breaker will close only if the check relay contact is closed. Similarly, when the breaker closes the synchroscope connection de-energizes through breaker auxiliary NC contact.

LEGEND:

U1-V1: Incoming generator voltage;
U2-V2: Bus voltage
Sy: Synchroscope
Hz: Double frequency meter
V: Double voltmeter
SW: Synchroscope on-off switch

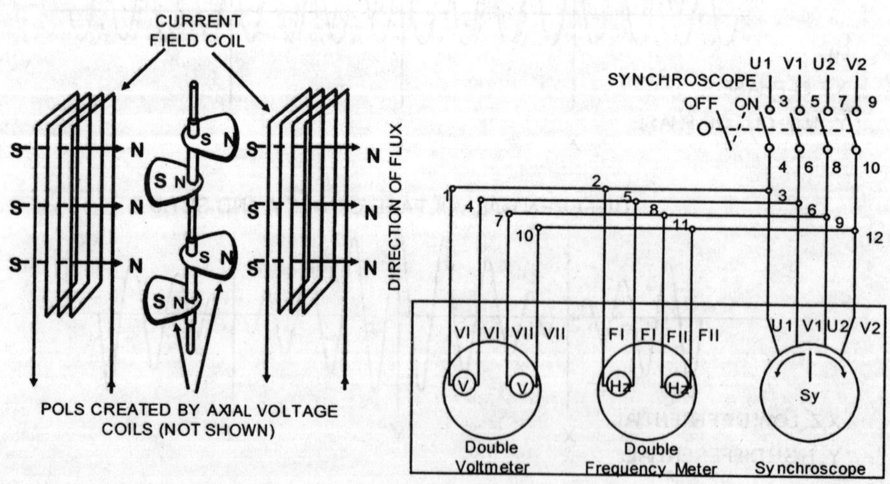

Fig. 1.7 (k): Internal and external connection diagram of a rotary synchroscope.

Auto-synchronizer with speed and voltage matching relays:

Figure 1.7 (L) illustrates the typical wiring diagram of an auto-synchronizing circuit. An auto- synchronizer (Device No: 25) contains various outputs such as; (1) Generator voltage increase: (2) Generator voltage decrease; (3) Prime mover speed (frequency) increase; (4) Prime mover speed (frequency) decrease; and (5) Circuit breaker closing while synchronizing.

Synchronizing relay measures the speed of the AC generator relative to the system frequency, the phase angle between the generators or incoming generator and running bus power system (in grids) and then gives a closing impulse to the breaker at the correct angle in advance of synchronism to ensure that the breaker poles will close when the machines or machine and the power system are in phase provided the auto-synchronizer is correctly set. Typical limits of closing angles are ± 10% electrical degrees. Typical frequency difference is less than 0.067 Hertz. Voltage matching limit is + 5%.

Speed matching relay: SPM, which is an integral part of an auto-synchronizer automatically match the incoming generator frequency to the system frequency (Bus frequency in a live bus). Relay produces impulses, which can be used to raise or lower generator speed by driving governor speed-adjusting rheostat. Frequency control by using servomotor is shown in Figure 1.7 (m). In general the incoming generator speed is to be adjusted slightly higher than bus frequency to prevent motoring or tripping during synchronism.

Voltage matching relay: VMR, which is an integral part of an auto-synchronizer automatically match the generator voltage to the system voltage (bus voltage). Relay produces impulses, which can be used to raise or lower the incoming generator voltage by driving the voltage-adjusting rheostat. Voltage control by using servomotor is shown in Figure 1.7 (n).

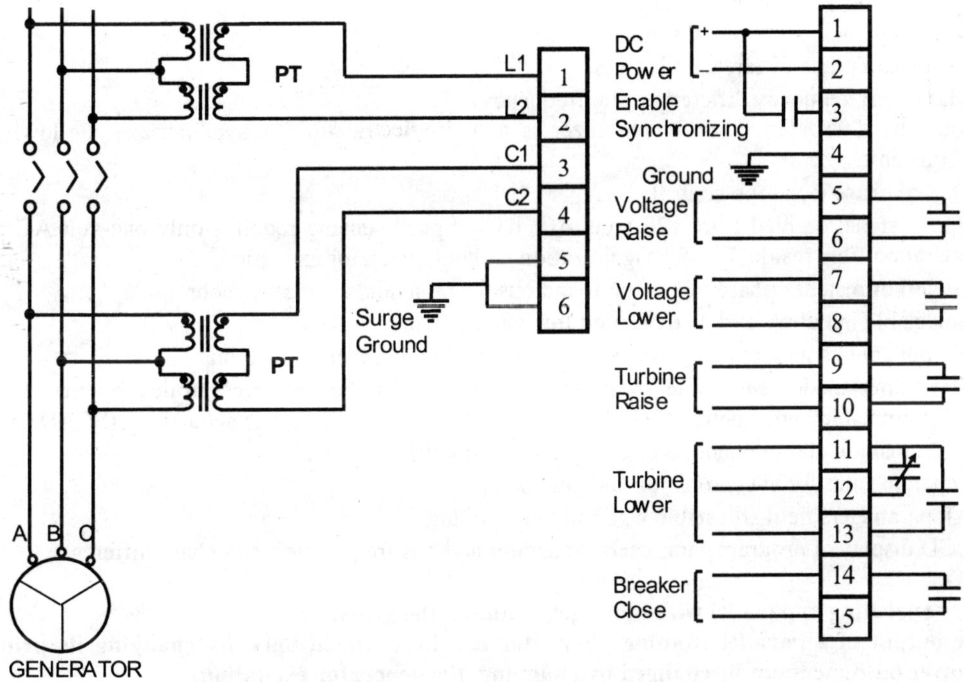

Fig 1.7 (L): External connection diagram of auto synchronizer (Courtesy, Clifton Lab)

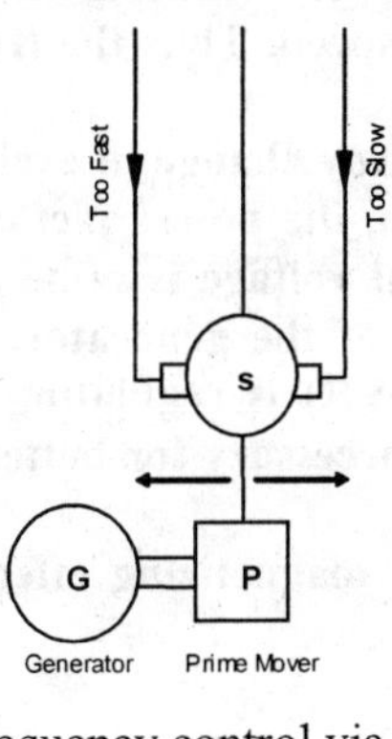

Fig. 1.7 (m): Frequency control via servomotor.

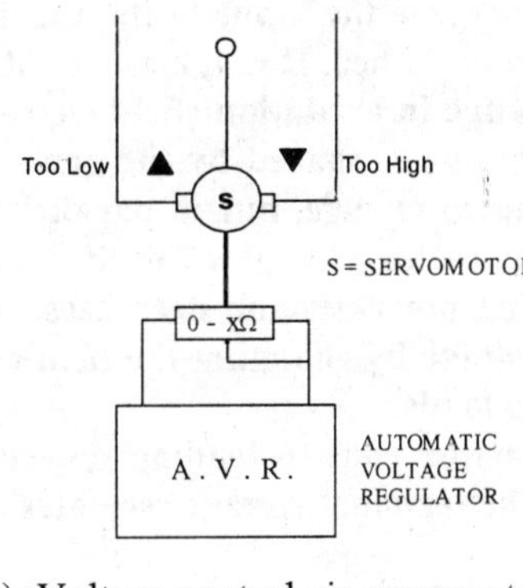

Fig. 1.7 (n): Voltage control via servomotor.

Clifton Labs Hyd-Syn 100 is designed to directly control gas or steam turbines when paralleling to utility systems where speed regulation is required only for synchronizing. Advanced digital technology locks the phase of the generator to the bus before initiating breaker closing. The very low slip frequency (less than 0.01Hz) eliminates the uncertainties inherent in breaker closing time compensation schemes.
Following are the features of this unit.

- Contacts outputs are capable of drive hydraulic solenoid valves or motor contactors of electric actuators.
- Matches frequency and controls phase angle difference between generator and bus.
- Contacts outputs to raise/lower voltage compatible with analog voltage regulators.
- Contact output to initiate breaker closing when voltage, frequency, and phase difference are all within specified windows.
- Keypad and LCD display for setting control parameters and monitoring operation.

Adjustable Parameters

- Maximum rate of actuator movement
- Frequency ramping rate up to 95% nominal frequency
- Proportional gain / Integral gain / Phase gain
- Minimum and maximum bus voltage
- Maximum phase difference (degrees)
- Maximum frequency difference (slip frequency)

The Clifton labs Z-180 Governor/Synchronizer is a hydroelectric turbine synchronizer. Following are the features of this unit.

- Digital phase lock loop control
- Speed signal derived from 120 volts AC, PT's. Speed sensing requires only one-volt AC permitting operation from residual rotor magnetization without generator excitation.
- Governor matches phase of generator and bus for rapid and accurate synchronizing.
- Selectable initial wicked gate position for synchronizing
- Output contact indicating phase and frequency match of generator and bus.
- Governing modes selectable by external contacts. Can be easily controlled by manual switches, Programmable logic controller (PLC), or Supervisory control and data acquisition (SCADA) system.
- Gate position output connects directly to servo amplifier
- Separate gains for synchronizing and generating
- All parameters field adjustable while field is running
- LCD display of program parameters, generator and bus frequencies, and phase difference

Generators operating in parallel with other generator or the grids:

(1) Power output of a parallel running alternator can be changed only, by changing its prime mover output. Power output cannot be changed by changing, the generator excitation.

(2) Frequency of the generator stator current will be the same as the bus bar frequency. The turbine input is controlled by, the governor. As the load increases the frequency tends to dropout, but the governor increase the input to the turbines so as to maintain constant speed. Thus the frequency of the bus bar is maintained. If not, load shedding is required.

(3) The change in excitation (field current) changes the induced e.m.f. Any change in excitation changes the reactive power shared by the generator. By changing the excitation, the power factor and terminal voltage tend to change, but in parallel running generators the terminal voltage is same as the bus bar voltage. Hence the change in excitation will change the power factor of the generator. When voltage increases the power factor decreases. Automatic voltage regulator (AVR) is regulating the generator terminal voltage by changing the field current. Higher field current is necessary for better power factor during high loads.

(4) If alternator runs in leading power factor, the load current has a magnetizing effect of armature reaction. The terminal voltage escalates on its own.

Load sharing of alternators:

When two alternators are running in parallel on a common bus bar, they behave as if the sets are coupled together. If the speed of one of the machine is raised the load on this machine will increase. Simultaneously the load on the other machine will decrease. It is necessary that the parallel running machines have identical speed regulation for satisfactory parallel operation. If the speed is considerably attempt to increase it will take the whole load, but in addition drive the other machine as a synchronous motor. To geared against the generators working in parallel are invariably provided with reverse current protection. While the generator is connected to the utility having KW or KVAR import and export requirements, KW and KVAR load sharing units shown in Figure 1.7 (o) and (p) are used for load sharing applications. Maximum and minimum limit of the KW or KVAR is set in the respective units, to prevent overloading or motoring the generator or to keep the generator running at the desired power factor.

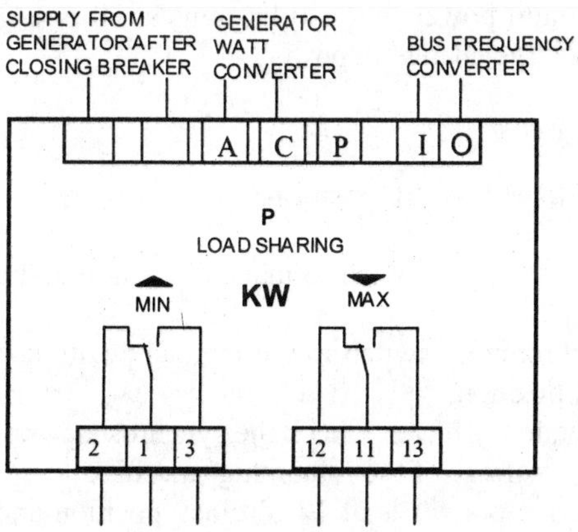

Fig. 1.7 (o): KW load sharing unit.

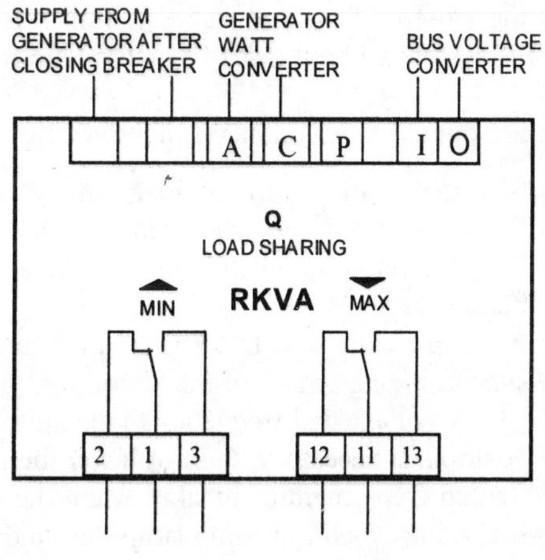

Fig. 1.7 (p): KVAR load sharing unit.

The power of each generator is measured by using a watt transducer and its DC output then controls input 'P' of the load-sharing unit. The bus bar frequency is measured by using a frequency converter. The output of the converter then controls input 'O' of the load-sharing unit. The load is subsequently automatically shared between the generators and the frequency is being controlled to the rated frequency. The load-sharing unit is placed in operation only after synchronizing the unit. Signal from the KW load-sharing unit drives the servomotor of the governor to increase or decrease the speed or frequency or kilowatt. Similarly, signal from the KVA load-sharing unit drives the servomotor of the voltage-adjusting rheostat.

Consider two alternators are running in parallel and sharing equal loads (loads proportional to its KW ratings). If excitation of one machine is increased, it will draw more lagging reactive current. Any inequality of excitation is equalized by, a circulating reactive current passing from the overexcited machine to the other.
Following are the effects of voltage and speed adjustment in parallel running alternators:

- **Generator voltage increase: Reactive KVA increases and power factor decreases.**
- **Generator voltage decrease: Reactive KVA decreases and power factor improves.**
- **Generator speed increase: KW load increase**
- **Generator speed decrease: KW load decrease**

Parallel running turbo-generators and Hydro-generators:
The frequency of parallel running generators will be the same as the bus bar frequency. As the load increases the frequency tends to dropout. Meanwhile the governor automatically increases the input to the turbine in a turbo-generator so as to maintain synchronous speed which is equal to 120 F/P. Where as in a hydro-generator governor automatically give signals to reposition the wicked gates to flow the required water pressure to increase the speed of the runner. Thus the frequency of the bus bar is maintained within targeted limits. As the load is reduced, the frequency trends to increases. Then the governor will automatically actuate to maintain the synchronous speed or bus frequency.

Behavior of AC synchronous machine:
An AC synchronous machine will behave depending on the operation of the machine such as:

- As a generator driven by a prime mover contributing active power
- As a motor (driving load) drawing active power
- If overexcited contributing reactive KVA
- If under excited drawing reactive KVA

(2) Ability of a synchronous machine to remain in synchronism is called stability.
(3) Steady state stability means the ability of a system to respond to small, gradual change in power at a given point of the system. Steady state stability limit is the maximum possible power that can be transferred without loss of synchronism, which vary with gradual increase in power.
(4) The term transient stability means the ability of a system to respond sudden large change in power at a given point of the system. Transient stability limit refers to the maximum power that can be transferred to a given point of the system without loss of synchronism for given sudden large change in power.

Sequence of operation for manual synchronizing/manual switching off:

1. Start generator by turning the generator unit start switch to MANUAL position.
2. Make sure the voltage and frequency is correct.
3. For connecting to a dead bus turn the auto-manual synchronizing switch to manual position and close the breaker.
4. For connecting to a live bus turn the auto-manual synchronizing switch to the manual position. Turn synchronizing switch of the 'incoming' generator to ON position.
5. Check voltage and frequency in the double voltmeter/frequency meter. Check the synchroscope pointer position. If necessary, raise or lower the frequency and or voltage of the 'incoming' machine
6. Switch ON generator breaker when the rotary syncroscope pointer is at 12 o' clock position and the flickering synchronization lamps are in dark (off) position.
7. After closing the generator breaker turn OFF synchronizing switch. (Breaker NC auxiliary contact will open and disconnect the power to the synchroscope). Breaker ON indication will appear.
8. For loading the synchronized generator increase the prime-mover speed by using frequency control switch. If necessary, reduce load from the other parallel running generators simultaneously.
9. For adjusting the power factor (KVAR load) raise or lower voltage control switch. If necessary, increase or decrease KVAR from the other parallel running machines simultaneously.
10. Share load proportionally in all parallel running generators based on its KVA or MVA ratings.
11. Before stopping any generator unload the load by using frequency control switch. After unloading 90% load, switch off the generator breaker. Breaker OFF green light will appear.
12. Stop the prime-mover if the breaker is off and the cool down time is elapsed.

Sequence of operation for automatic synchronizing/automatic switching off:

1. Turn the generator unit start switch to AUTO position.
2. Turn the synchronizing switch to AUTO position.
3. Turn the generator breaker control switch to AUTO position.
4. If the bus is dead (not live) the breaker will close automatically after building up the correct frequency and voltage.
5. If the bus is energized the auto-synchronizing relay will sense the conditions for paralleling the system.
6. If the 'incoming' frequency is not matching with the bus frequency the auto-synchronizing relay will send impulse to the speed-adjusting servomotor to raise or lower the speed.
7. If the voltage of the 'incoming' generator is not matching to the bus voltage the auto-synchronizing relay will send impulse to the voltage adjusting rheostat servomotor to raise or lower the voltage.
8. When all the paralleling conditions (Voltage, frequency, and phase relationship) are met, the auto-synchronizing relay will send impulse to close the generator breaker.
9. Breaker ON indication appears in the mimic panel. When the breaker closes the normally closed auxiliary contact of the breaker will disconnect the power to the auto-synchronizing relay.
10. KW load sharing unit will automatically activate to load the generator.
11. KVAR load sharing unit will automatically activate to control the KVAR load and power factor.
12. If stop signal is initiated, the KW and KVAR load sharing units will actuate to unload the generator before switching off the breaker. Prime mover will automatically stop if the breaker is OFF and the set cooling time is elapsed.

1.8 P.L.C BASED INTEGRATED GAS TURBINE CONTROL SYSTEM.

PLC based integrated Gas turbine generator set control system described in this section is **PETROTECH product Bulletin 96053**. Figure 1.8 shows the schematic diagram of the unit. The system provides turbine fuel control, temperature control, turbine and generator sequencing/complete turbine control, load control, DCS interfaces, communication interfaces (SCADA, MODBUS, Ethernet, etc.), and a graphic operator interface for system status, trending and data logging. Turbine fuel control and sequencing / protection are integrated in to a single platform. This eliminates the need for additional hardware and communication links, thereby providing an excellent solution. All control functions are performed by, the PLC equipment. Communication tasks are handled with a separate, dedicated module in the PLC, increasing data rate and simplifying network installation.

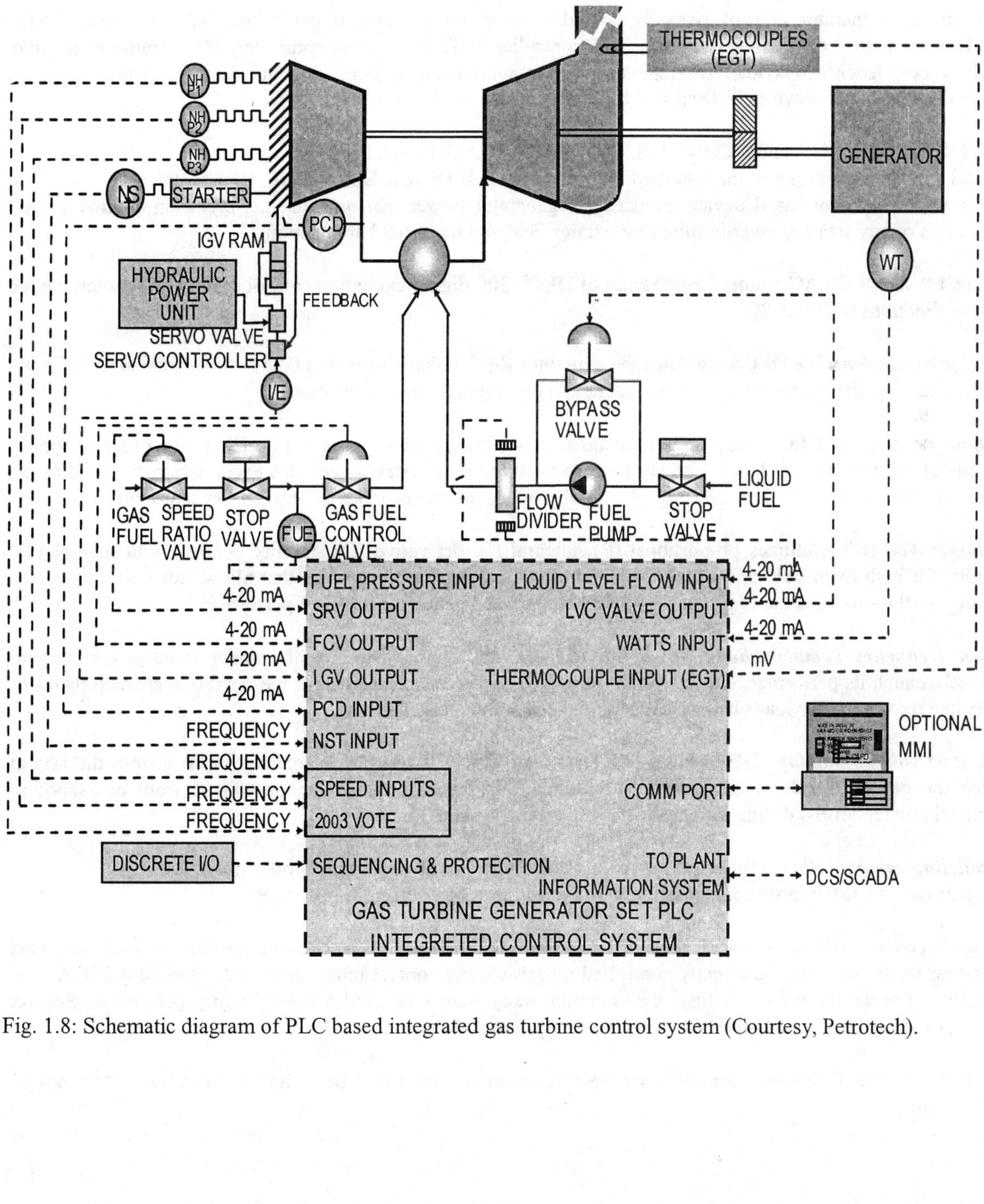

Fig. 1.8: Schematic diagram of PLC based integrated gas turbine control system (Courtesy, Petrotech).

Fuel regulation: Fast loop sampling rate, combined with modern digital control techniques improve steady-state set-point control, and reduce overshoot during transients.

Start-up reliability: Special "lean light-off" procedure ignites all burners with essentially 100% reliability, and with greatly reduced thermal stress.

Exhaust temperature monitoring and control: Advanced statistical algorithms detect turbine hot/cold spots and automatically reject failed thermocouples.

Fail-safe features: Redundant over speeds; open/short monitoring of mA and thermocouples; read back monitoring of outputs, and special self-check features improve safety.

Gas turbine Generator control typically includes firing ramp, start-up controller, NHP controller, NHP acceleration and deceleration scheduling, EGT controller, EGT rate of rise controller, EGT controller for inlet guide vanes, Isochronous load sharing, combustion monitoring system with automatic rejection of failed thermocouples, Cool down stop, Dual fuel capability with bumpless on-line transfer etc.

1.9 DIGITEL EXCITATION CONTROL SYSTEM FOR ALTERNATORS.

Digital excitation control system described in this section is **BASLER ELECTRIC DECS 300**.
It is a microprocessor-based device intended for generator power management, i.e. precision control for AC generators of any size and equally suited for exciter field and main field application.

Figure 1.9 shows the AC connection diagram of DECS 300 digital excitation control system. Following are the control functions of DECS 300.

Voltage regulation: The DECS regulates the generator RMS voltage to within 0.25% from no load to full load. It does this by utilizing digital signal processing and precise regulation algorithms.

Output signals: The DECS sends an output signal of 4-20mA, 0-10V DC or ± 10V DC to the firing or control circuits of external power stages. The DC current from the power stages provides excitation to the field of the main generator or exciter. Hence the unit is suitable for use on synchronous generators / synchronous motors.

Stability: The DECS utilizes proportional (P), integral (I), derivative (D) stability control, with several PID settings for both main field and exciter field. The DECS has a stability range that allows for customizing the stability settings to fine tune to provide optimum customized generator transient performance.

Under frequency compensation: DECS provides the ability to customize the under frequency setting to precisely match its performance to the prime movers, i. e. precisely matched to the operating characteristics of the prime mover and the loads being applied to the prime mover /generator.

Soft start voltage buildup: DECS has a soft-start feature with a user-adjustable setting to govern the rate at which the generator voltage is allowed to buildup. This prevents the generator voltage from overshooting (nominal voltage levels) during start-up of the generating system.

Paralleling compensation: DECS has provisions to parallel two or more generators using reactive droop or reactive differential compensation with the addition of a current transformer.

Set-point control: DECS has means for external set-point adjustment of the controlling mode of operation. This operating modes set-point be directly controlled by raise/lower contact input (auxiliary inputs of 4-20mA or ± 10V DC). The auxiliary input adjusts the operating mode across its predetermined adjustment range. Second method of set-point control can be through a power system stabilizer.

The third method of set-point control is via RS-232 communication port by using PC software, or Modbus or Rs-485 port.

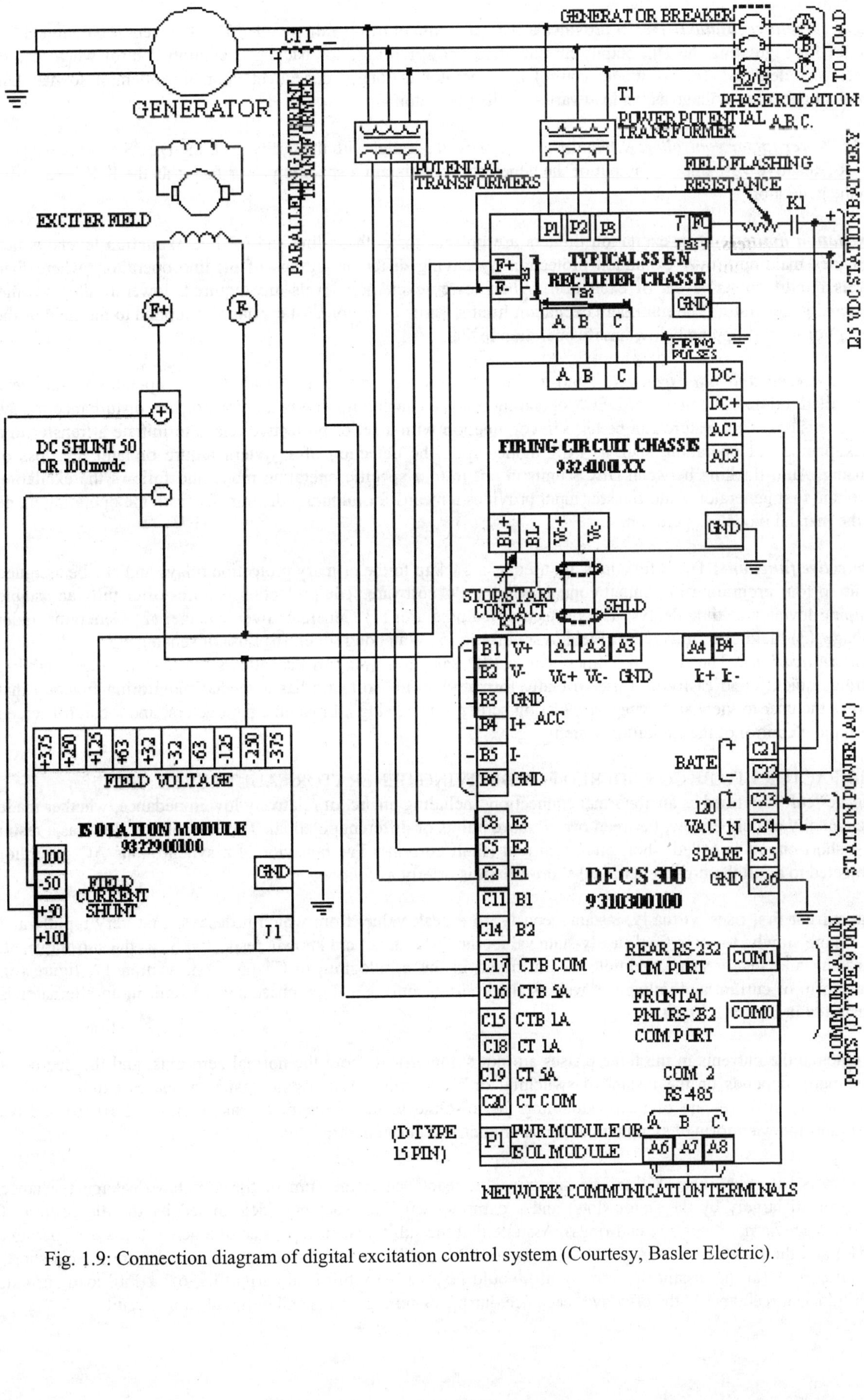

Fig. 1.9: Connection diagram of digital excitation control system (Courtesy, Basler Electric).

Field current regulation: DECS provides a manual channel of operation called Field current regulation (FCR mode) for regulating the DC output current of the power bridge for backup excitation control when loss of sensing is detected. In this mode, control of generator is totally dependent upon the operator to maintain nominal generator voltage as the load varies on the generator.

VAR/Power factor controller: When the generator is in parallel with the utility grid, the DECS can regulate the VAR (Reactive volt ampere) output of the generator to maintain a specific power factor as the KW load varies on the generator.

Excitation limiters: Over-excitation limiters are present for both on-line and off-line excitation levels, which provides maximum over excitation protection by having different settings of off-line operation, where load levels require lower levels of excitation. When lower excitation levels are required, lower limiter settings protect the generator. The minimum excitation limiter limits the amount of excitation supplied to the field of the generator from dropping below unsafe operation levels.

Auto-tracking and auto transfer: Auto-tracking between operating modes allows the operator to initiate a controlled, bumpless transfer of DECS operating modes, causing minimum amounts of line disturbance for the power system. This feature can be used in conjunction with a set of protective relays to initiate a transfer to a backup mode of operation, such as FCR mode, upon the detection of a system failure or fault, i.e. loss of sensing. Auto-tracking between DECS units is put in to a specific operating mode and follows the excitation level the first generator. Auto transfer input provides a means for initiating the transfer from the operating mode to the manual mode of operation.

Protective functions: These functions are used as a backup to the primary protection relays and can be assigned to up to four programmable output contacts via the PC software. The protection features offer fully adjustable tripping levels and time delays. The protective features are: (1) Generator over voltage; (2) Generator under voltage; (3) Field over voltage; (4) Field over current; (5) Watchdog timer; (6) Loss of sensing etc.
Communications: The software comes with a PID selection program that allows the user to select stability settings quickly and easily in a user-friendly format. The PC software has a special monitoring function that allows the user to view all settings, a metering screen for viewing all machine parameters, and a control screen for remote control of the excitation system.

1.10 FACTORS TO BE CONSIDERED FOR DERIVING GENERATOR FAULT LEVEL.

Short circuit is defined as an abnormal connection, including an arc, of relatively low impedance, whether made accidentally or deliberately, between two or more points of different potential. The current that flows as a result of a short circuit is called, short circuit current (fault current). The behavior of a synchronous AC generator subjected to a full three-phase terminal short-circuit is briefly as follows.

The current first rises, virtually, instantaneously, to a peak value, from which it decays, first very rapidly and then more slowly, to some final steady-state value, the three stages are known, respectively, as the sub-transient, transient, and steady-state conditions as illustrated in the oscillogram in Chapter # 3, section 11, figure (e). Waveform of current and voltage as well as field current during a three-phase short circuit in an alternator is illustrated in Figure 1.10 (a).

In practice the currents in the three phases are not symmetrical about the normal zero axis, and the degree of asymmetry depends on the instant of switching or short-circuit. Usually at least two phases exhibit marked asymmetry, to the extent of nearly doubling the absolute value of the first peak. Figure's 1.10 (b) and (c) illustrates the waveform of symmetrical and asymmetrical currents respectively.

Sub-transient reactance (Xd"): The sub-transient reactance is the sum of the armature leakage reactance (determined largely by the stator slots) and a damping winding reactance (determined by the disposition of squirrel cage damper bars and end-rings). Assume that the sub-transient reactance of a generator is 0.15 per unit (15%) and the time constant might be 0.05 second (2.½ cycles at 50Hz system); the initial symmetrical short-circuit current (at the instant of short circuit) would be (1/0.15) x full load current i.e, 6.7 x Full load current. Sub-transient reactance is the effective reactance during switching events and terminal short circuit.

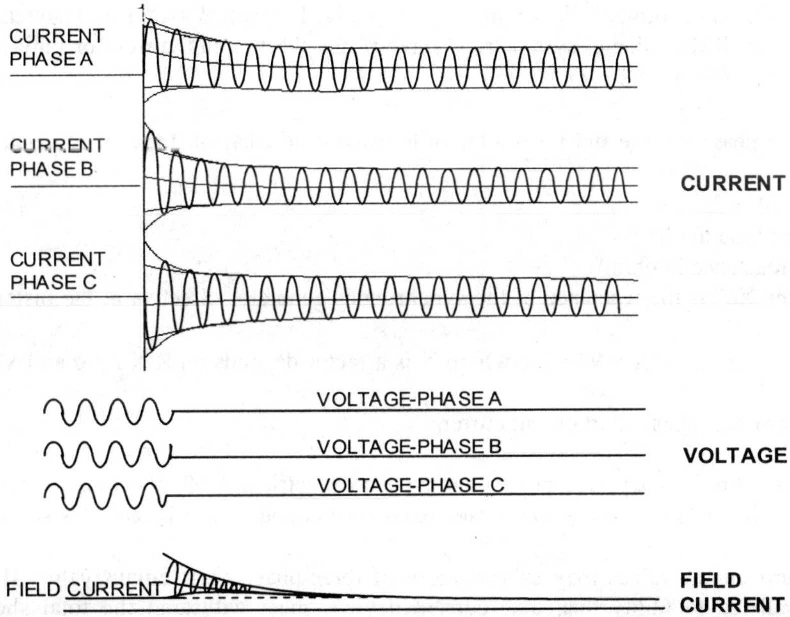

Fig. 1.10 (a): Waveform of current and voltage during a three-phase short-circuit in an alternator.

Transient reactance (Xd'): During electromechanical transients **or power swings,** the effective reactance is reduced by the tendency of the short-circuited field winding to hold flux constant for a short period. Transient reactance is applicable when armature mmf is changing to meet the above situation. The transient reactance is the sum of the armature leakage reactance and a field leakage reactance, the value of which is determined largely by the relative geometry of the adjacent pole-tip and pole leakage surfaces. It is a field-influenced quantity; its rate of decay is determined by a corresponding transient time constant. Assume that typical value of a generator is 0.23 per unit (23%) and transient time constant (the ratio of transient inductance to the armature-plus-equivalent-field resistance) is 0.5 seconds (25 cycles at 50Hz system).

Synchronous reactance (Xd): During normal operation of alternators, the rotor is rotating in synchronism with the magneto motive force. The reactance obtained thus is known as synchronous reactance or steady state reactance. Normally this value will be 5 to 10%.

Initial surge of current would be limited by the sub- transient reactance of the machine, which is normally 8 to 12%. This would produce a current of approximately 10 times the generator full load current during a short circuit and if the short were initiated as the voltage waveform is passing through zero, the DC offset component would multiply this figure by 1.6. Hence 1.6 x 10 = 16 times normal full load current will produce a tremendous mechanical thermal stress on the generator, but modern machines are designed to withstand these stresses for a short time during which they exist. Method of measuring synchronous reactance is given in section 1.13. Since the ratio of reactance to resistance is very large, the power factor of a short-circuit load is practically zero. Hence the prime mover load is actually reduced, if the governor does not act. Under short-circuit condition the voltage output at the terminals of the generator will be zero.

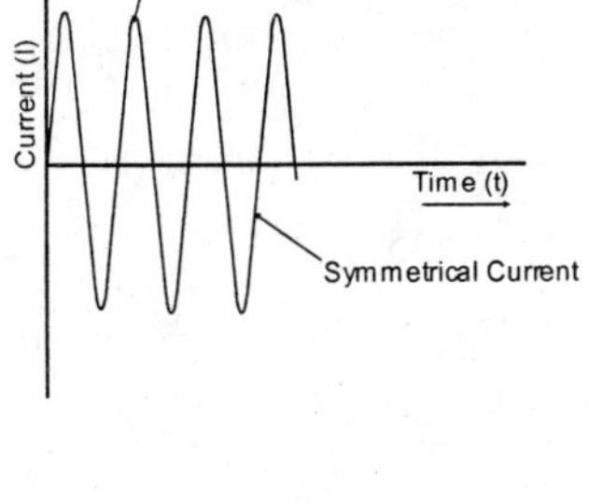

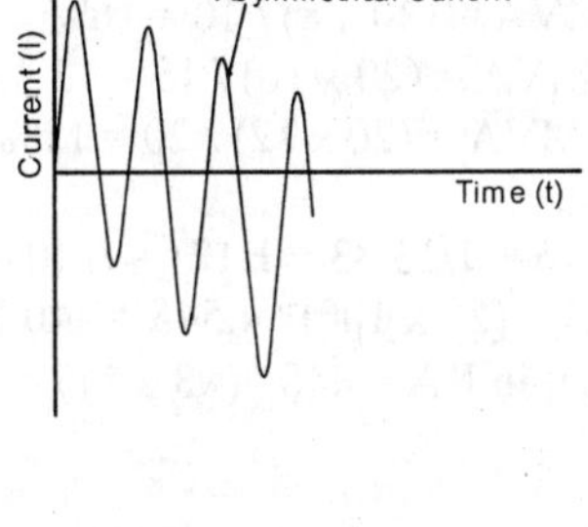

Fig. 1.10 (b): Waveform of symmetrical current Fig. 1.10 (c): Waveform of asymmetrical current.

Short circuit current: RMS value of symmetrical three-phase short circuit current or initial symmetrical short circuit current, Isc = (1.1x V) / (√3 x Z).

Where V = Phase-to-phase voltage and 1.1 is a factor to be considered against the raise in generator voltage

Z = Impedance = $\sqrt{R^2 + X^2}$
R = Resistance per phase in ohm;
X = Sub-transient reactance in ohm.
The initial reactance Xd" is the reactance of the synchronous generator effective at the instant the short circuit occurs.
Peak short circuit current: Is = X x √2 x Isc where X is a factor depends on R/X ratio and √2 is for converting RMS to peak.
Isc = Initial symmetrical 3 phase short circuit current

Another formula used for deriving three-phase first cycle, symmetrical, RMS short circuit current developed by a generator is: Isc = Ir / X"d where Ir = Generator rated current and X"d = Direct axis sub-transient reactance per unit value.
Line-to neutral short circuit values may exceed those of three-phase short circuit value. If generators are in parallel, or if paralleled to utility bus, over-current devices must withstand the total short circuit current developed by all generating devices including utility. Synchronous and induction motors feed additional short circuit current to the fault at a value which is approximately equal to their locked rotor current. If a circuit breaker is used, additional protective devices upstream of the breaker may be required when connected to utility.

Fault level of a single generator:

Fault level in MVA = Generator capacity in MVA x 100 / Percentage reactance

Fault current in KA = Fault level in MVA / (√3 x Phase-to-phase voltage in KV)
For example, consider a 3 phase 440 volts, 50 Hertz 1000 KVA generator with 8% sub-transient reactance. (1 MVA = 1000KVA)
Fault level in MVA = (1 x 100) / 8 = 12.5
Fault current in KA = 12.5 / √3 x 0.44 = 16.4 KA = 16400 Amps

Fault level and fault current in paralleled synchronous generators:

% Reactance of a machine = (I x X) / E
I = Full load current in ampere;
X = Reactance in ohm;
E = Rated voltage (phase-to-phase)
Short circuit current Isc = E / X = (I x 100) / %X
Per unit reactance = % reactance / 100 or Actual reactance / Base reactance

Short circuit ratio of a synchronous generator = No load excitation current / Full load excitation current observed during S/C test

For example, consider 3 Nos 11 KV generators 10MVA, 15 MVA and 20 MVA running in parallel have 8%, 10% & 12% sub-transient reactance respectively.
Assuming a common base level of 20 MVA, convert all impedances in to this common base level:
8% at 10 MVA = (20 x 8) / 10 = 16%
!0% at 15 MVA = (20 x 10) / 15 = 13.33%
12% at 20 MVA = (20 x 12) / 20 = 12%

Z = 1 / (1/16 + 1/13.33 + 1/12) = 1/ (0.0625 + 0.075 + 0.0833) = 1/ 0.220 = 4.545%
1Fault level = (20 x 100) / 4.545 = 440 MVA
Fault current in KA = 440 / (√3 x 11) = 23.095 KA

1.11 PHASE SEGREGATED TUBULAR BUS DUCTS FOR GENERATOR CONNECTION.

Isolated phase bus is a bus in which each phase conductor is enclosed by an individual metal housing separated from adjacent conductor housings by an air space. The bus may be self cooled or may be forced dry air-cooled, or SF6 gas insulated. Tubular construction is commonly used. For connection between large generators and generator circuit breakers and / or step up power transformers, three single-phase isolated tube bus ducts made of aluminium alloy are being employed.

Up to 4000 A, generator bus ducts are generally shaped as shown in figure 3.4 (e) of Chapter # 3, i.e. copper or aluminium three-phase bus bars. When laid in a aluminium enclosure, the bars are protected against safety and contamination. Added protection is provided by partitions between the phases, thus preventing phase to phase short-circuits and reducing dynamic forces. With these non-segrigated constructions, the disadvantages are:

a) Progressive rise of conductor temperature due to skin effect.
b) Heating of concrete reinforcement and other nearby conducting material by the magnetic field of the conductors.
c) High forces on main and component conductors in the event of a short circuit.

Beyond 4000 A, therefore, isolated-phase bus ducts are used. As a rule, these take the form of tubular aluminium or copper conductors, contained in a tubular aluminium enclosure. Moulded resin insulators hold and insulate the conductor in the duct. Natural air-cooling is acceptable up to 25 KA; providing means of forced cooling allows current ratings up to 40 KA. Current ratings of indoor aluminium tubular bus bars are given in Table 4.12 (1) of Chapter # 4.

Isolated-phase bus duct (IPB) consists of:

(1) Aluminium alloy tubes as bus with enclosure made of 3mm thick aluminium sheet and bus supports consisting three cast resin insulators (Protection class IP65) as shown in Figure 1.11(a). Dull black coating is applied to the Aluminium tube outer surface and aluminium duct inner surface to improve the heat dissipation. Rust protection for aluminium duct surfaces is not necessary.
(2) Flexible phase connection to the generator side and circuit breaker or transformer side consisting press welded, laminated copper strap with silver plated contact surface, bolts and nuts etc. Expansion joints are also provided at every 6M intervals.
(3) Hot dip galvanized steel support structures (suitable for maximum wind speed 100 km/h) are provided at every 1metre intervals.
(4) Pressurizing system (Oil and dust free dry air 8 to 10 bar pressure) with connection to the compressed air system, air volume approximately 1 M^3 / h for 5m bar.

Technical data for a typical 11 KV bus duct used for a 63 MVA generator:

Power frequency withstand voltage 28 KV, 1minute.
Impulse withstand voltage (BIL) 75 KV (1.2 / 50μs).
Thermal short-circuit current (1 second) 51 KA.
Dynamic short-circuit current (Peak) 130 KA.

Ambient temperature 40°C
Enclosure temperature 65°C
Conductor temperature 85°C
Section length maximum 9 Metre

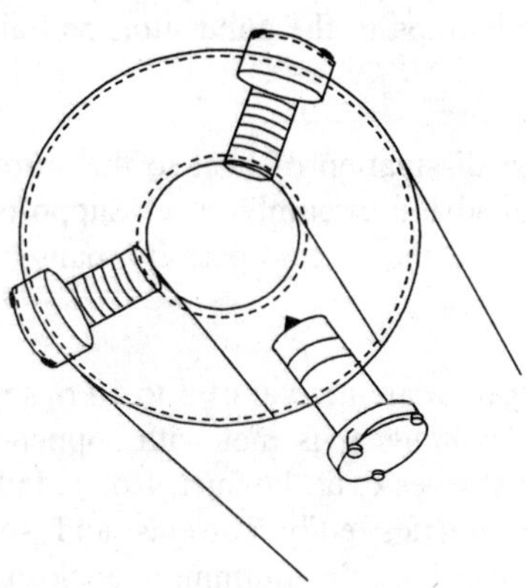

Fig. 1.11 (a): Cross section of an isolated phase bus duct.

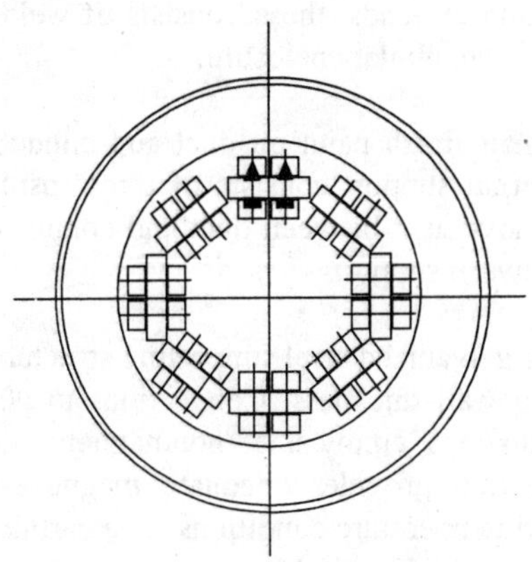

Fig. 1.11 (b): Flexible connection unit.

IPB conductors are connected to generator circuit breaker at one end and generator terminal at the other end. For combined generator-transformer unit, the IPB conductors are connected to the generator terminals and power transformer terminals. Cross section of a typical flexible connection of IPB is shown in Figure 1.11 (b).

Cooling air flow diagram of a typical 30,000 Amps bus duct is illustrated in Figure 1.11 (c). Air velocities up to 25 m/s need no aerodynamic measures or silencing, but raise the current carrying capacity by 50 to 100%. Should the cooling system fail, the bus duct can carry 60 to 70% of the rated current.

LEGEND

1, Generator bus duct

2. Cooling unit with fans (a) Standby fans; (b) Flap valves; (c) Cooler; (d) Standby cooler

3. Damper valves for flow distribution

4. Cooling-water circuit with motor operated valves for flow to cooler and standby cooler.

5. Air make-up with filter and drier.

6. Alternative to item 5 above: Air make-up from station air system via reducing valve and air filter.

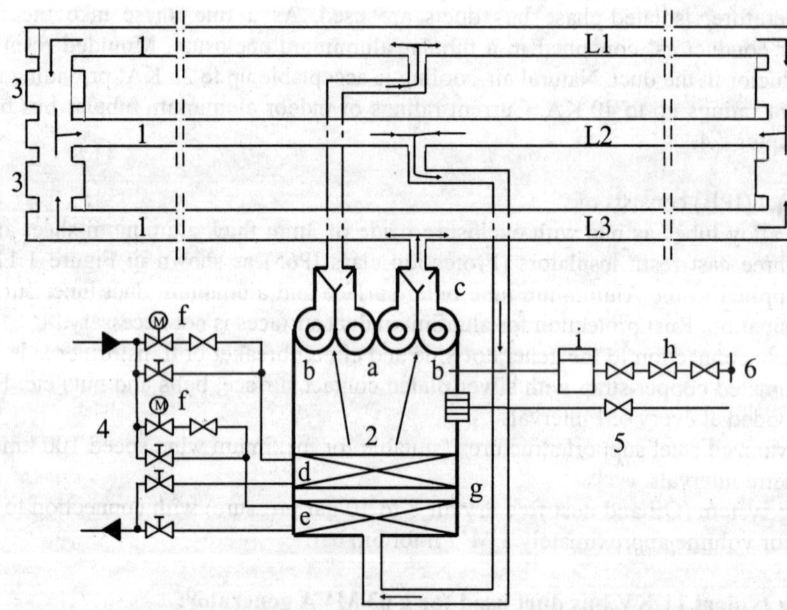

Fig. 1.11 (c): Cooling air flow diagram for a typical generator bus duct.

The material of the aluminium tube (conductor) is extruded aluminium alloy E-A1 99.5 F7 to DIN standard 40501 or equivalent. The number and shape of sub-assemblies of a generator bus duct depends on its layout (straight sections, bends, branches, etc.). Expansion due to-heat are taken up by expansion joints in long straight sections and at bends; these consists of welded aluminium laminated straps in the conductor, and aluminium bellows in the tubular enclosure.

Special matt finish paint on duct and conductor greatly improve the dissipation of heat to the surroundings. Each internal support consists of three insulators evenly spaced round the circumference. Supports prevent relative movement between duct and conductor. The high strength of tubular section permits spans of about 7 Metre between supports.

The outer galvanized steel supporting structure for the bus duct is placed at an interval of 5 to 10 m span length depending wall thickness. Connections to generator / transformer / switchgear is met with copper braids or laminated straps, amply sized nonmagnetic bolted joints and resilient sleeves over the duct. Isolated phase type of connection provides adequate magnetic-field compensation, eliminates eddy currents and so ensures controlled temperature conditions. The earthing system of the bus duct utilizes the aluminium enclosures of the three phases as an earth. Motor operated earth switches are provided for maintenance earthing of bus ducts. Fig. 1.11 (d) illustrates the installation arrangement of a generator bus duct.

LEGEND
(1) Generator; (2). Neutral; (3). Short-circuit and earthing gear; (4). Instrument-transformer cubicle; (5). Exciter-transformer; (6). Generator-circuit breaker; (7). Capacitor and instrument transformer cubicle; (8). Station-service transformer; (9). Expansion joint in bus duct; (10) Lightning arrester; (11).Generator transformer.

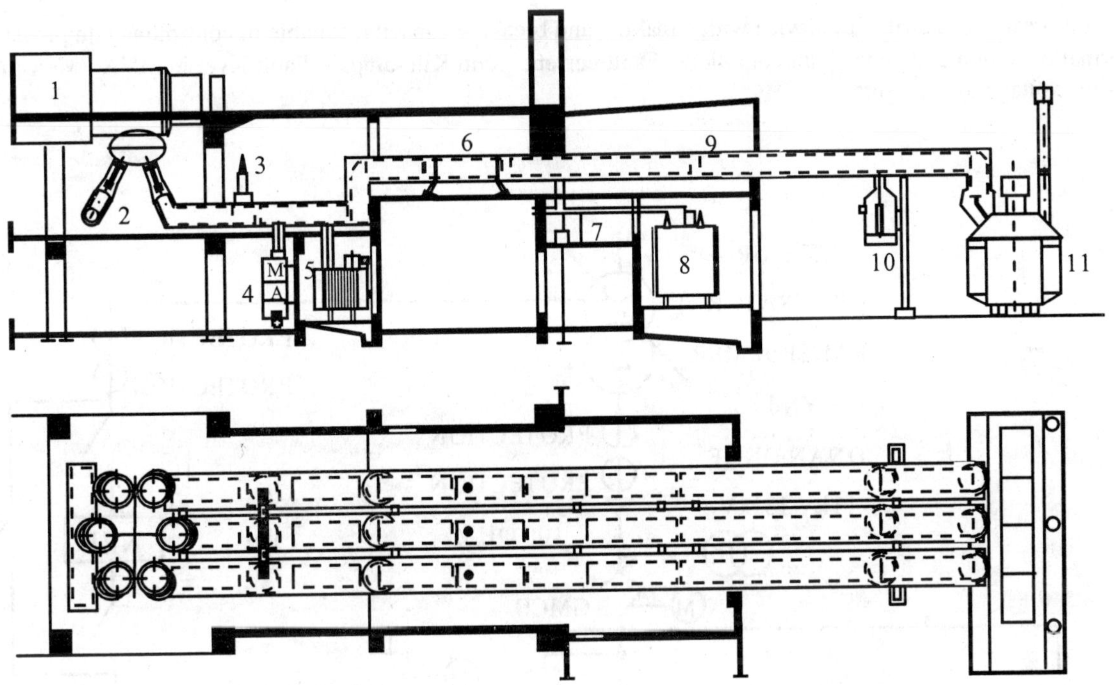

Fig. 1.11 (d): Typical generator bus duct installation.

1.12 SF6 GAS INSULATED GENERATOR MAINS CIRCUIT BREAKER.

Generator circuit breakers (GMCB) for large alternators (63 MVA and above) are incorporated between Generator and step up power transformer. Employing a generator breaker (GMCB) has following advantages.

(a) Disconnect generator from station services supply during start up.
(b) Synchronizing on low voltage side of generator transformer.
(c) Isolate fault in generator transformer or in station service transformer.
(d) Isolate fault in generator
(e) Isolate fault on line from power plant to next transformer or switching station.
(f) Use in Nuclear power stations (improves security of no-break station service power supply).

Figure 1.12 (a) shows the single line diagram of a steam turbine generator with provision for segregated tubular phase bus duct for connecting generator-to-mains circuit breaker (GMCB). Following are the equipments/devices provided with the alternator.

a) Neutral grounding transformer and ground fault protection relay
b) Current transformer for power measurements
c) Differential protection current transformer
d) Steam turbine as prime mover with high voltage brushless alternator as main equipment
e) Protection, measuring and metering CT's (including generator differential protection CT).
f) Isolated phase bus duct for connecting generator-to-generator circuit breaker.
g) Lightning arrester and earth switch
h) Three winding potential transformer for protection, excitation, measurement, metering and synchronizing.
i) Generator mains circuit breaker (GMCB)
j) Potential transformer (Transformer side)
k) Isolated phase bus duct between generator circuit breaker and step up power transformer.

l) Protection CT's (Transformer Primary side).
m) Step up transformer delta/star connection and on load tap changer (Vector group YNd1). Cooling air natural/forced air
n) Transformer Neutral earth resistor with disconnector and bypass switch
o) Earth fault protection CT's.

Circuit breaker is a switching device with a making and breaking capacity, capable of controlling equipments in normal operation and under fault conditions. Fault current Isc in Kilo-amps = Fault level in MVA / √3 x Line-to-line voltage in kilo-volts.

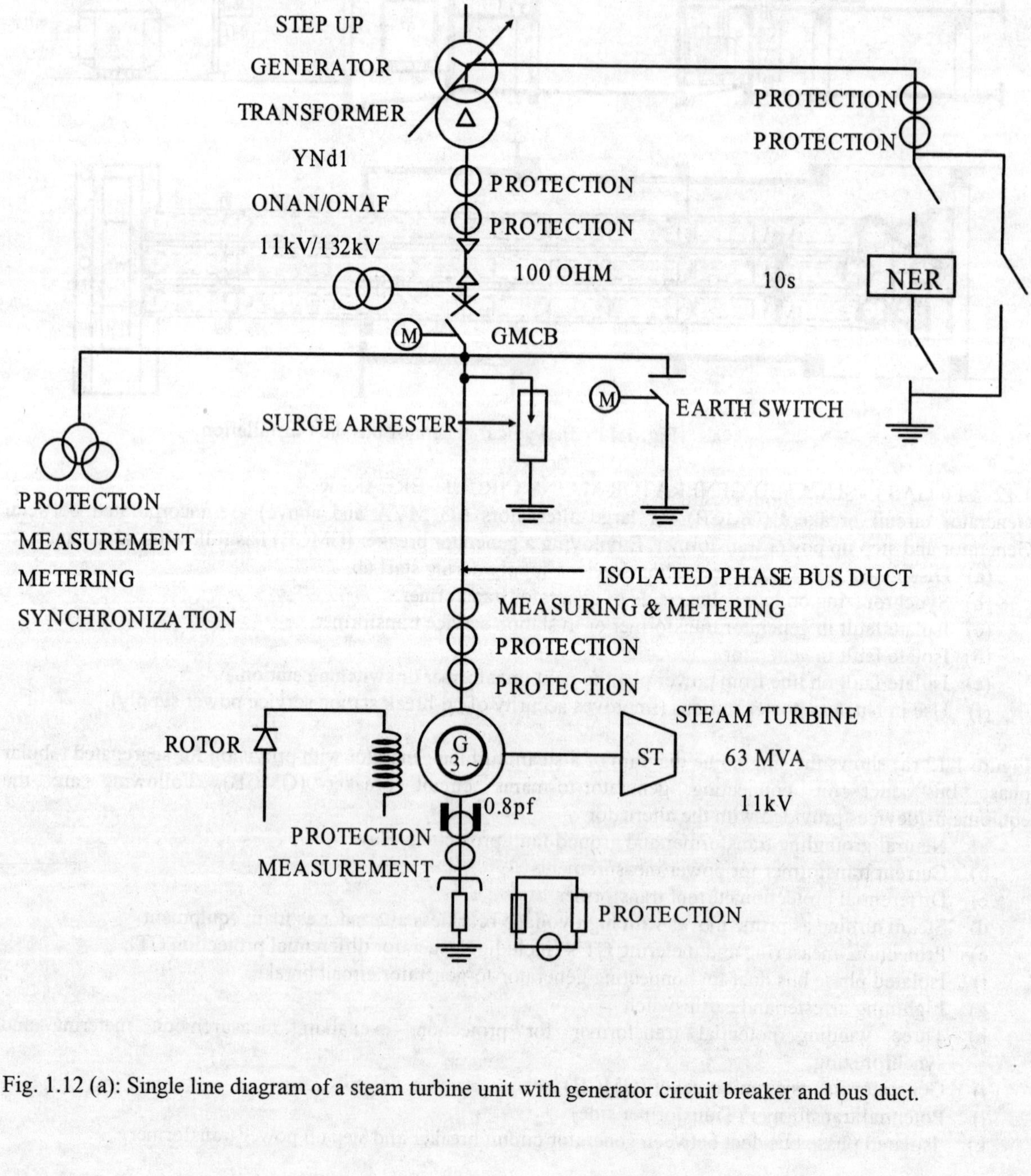

Fig. 1.12 (a): Single line diagram of a steam turbine unit with generator circuit breaker and bus duct.

Figure 1.12 (b) illustrates typical arrangement of combined generator transformer unit for power stations. In this scheme GMCB is not applicable and the provision for circuit breaker is in the secondary side of power transformer and secondary side of station service transformer. Figure 1.12 (c) illustrates typical application of GMCB for large units. Power transformer is provided with circuit breaker both in the primary and secondary. Station service transformer has circuit breaker in the secondary only.

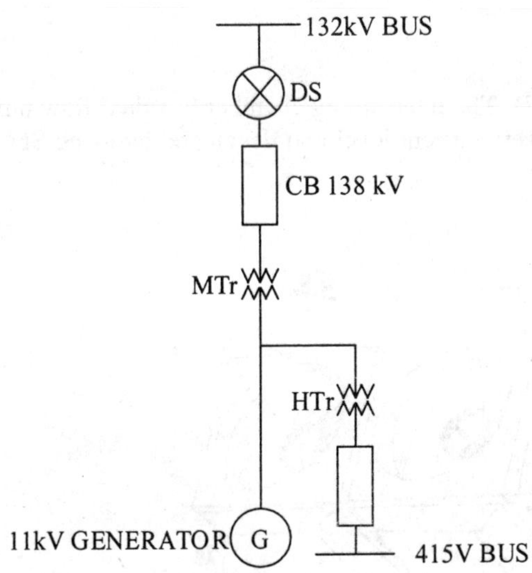

Fig. 1.12 (b): Combined generator-transformer unit.

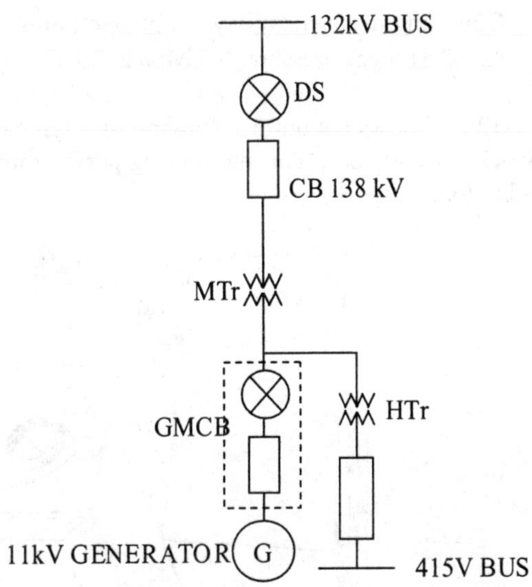

Fig. 1.2 (c): Generator with GMCB.

Generator mains circuit breaker chamber shown in Figure 1.12 (d) consists of:

1. Series disconnector switch
2. Circuit breaker (Device 52)
3. Surge capacitors (both generator side and transformer side)
4. Potential transformer (both generator side and transformer side)
5. Surge arrester (Transformer side)
6. Earth switch (Generator side)
7. Current transformers (Generator side)

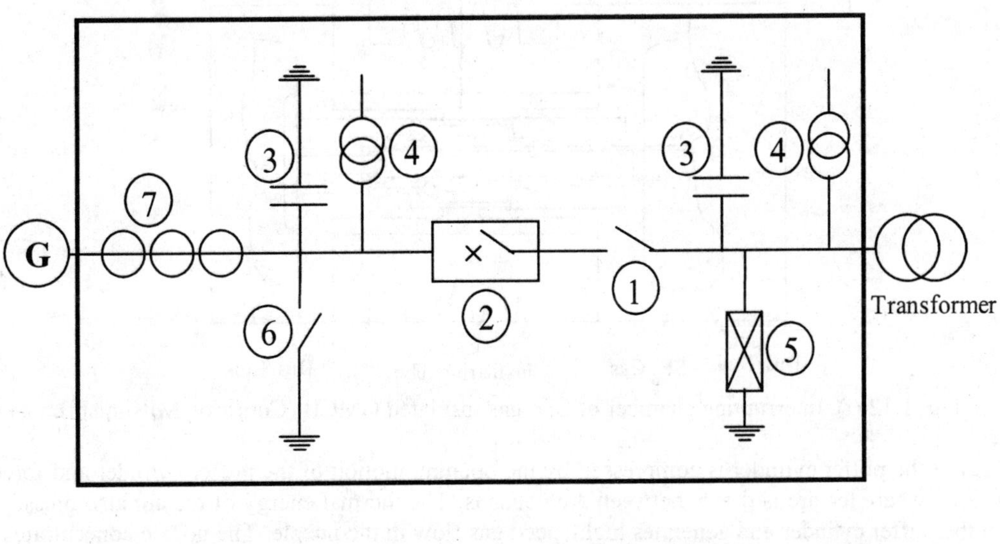

Fig. 1.12 (d): Single line diagram of a typical GMCB cubicle (Courtesy, Mitsubishi).

Generator circuit breakers are manufactured in conformity with IEEE standard: C37 013-1997. "Standard for AC high voltage generator circuit breakers rated on symmetrical current".

Specification (Typical example)

- Rated current: 8KA
- Rated breaking current: 100KA
- Rated opening time: 25ms
- Operating mechanism: Hydraulic operation
- Rated SF6 gas pressure: 0.5 Mpa at 20°C

Figure 1.12 (e) shows the outline drawing of a typical GMCB. The interrupting chamber is a dual flow puffer-type, which have an excellent interrupting performance at every current level and developed by using SF6 gas flow technologies.

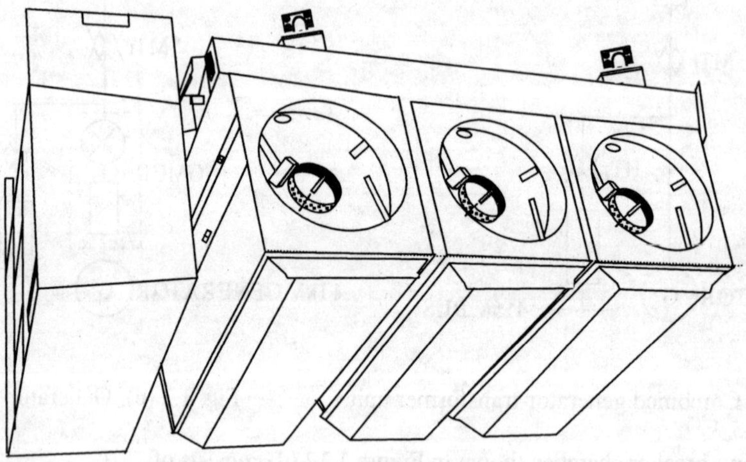

Fig. 1.12 (e): Out line drawing of generator mains circuit breaker (Courtesy, Asia Brown Boveri).

Figure 1.12 (f) shows the construction of the SF6 interrupting chamber of a GMCB. When closing signal ia applied, current runs through the main fixed contact, the puffer cylinder, and the finger contact. When trip signal is applied, movable parts including the puffer cylinder start opening processes. At first main contacts separate, and then arc contacts separate, accordingly arc-arise between arc contacts.

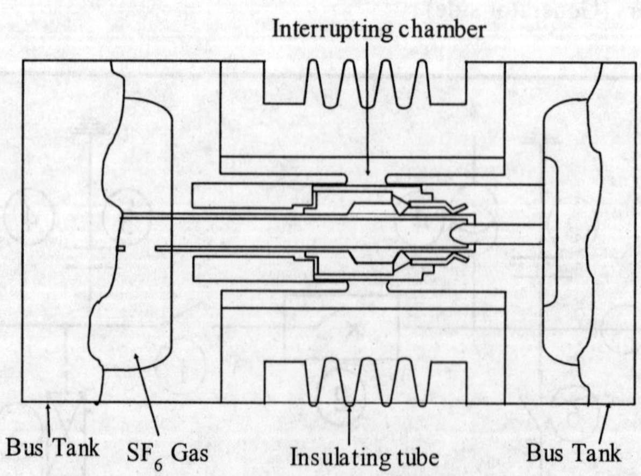

Fig. 1.12 (f): Interrupting chamber of SF6 gas insulated GMCB (Courtesy, Mitsubishi).

The SF6 gas in the puffer cylinder is compressed by the opening motion of the puffer cylinder and forced in to the nozzle area where the arc is drawn between arc contacts. The thermal energy of the arc also pressurizes the SF6 gas in the puffer cylinder and generates high-speed gas flow in the nozzle. The nozzle concentrates the gas flow to the arc and that gas flow cools it efficiently.

Trip circuit for a medium voltage turbo-generator is similar to the one shown in figure 2.16 (a) of Chapter # 2 except that the device numbers will change as listed in Table 1.12 (1). Function and application of protective relays are demonstrated in Chapter # 6. Table 1.12 (1) shows the list of Protective devices required for a Turbogenerator. On the event of a fault in the generator (internal or external) the corresponding protective relay operates to initiate a trip signal. This causes to energize electrical lockout relay (Device No: 86E) and/or non-electrical lockout relay 86NE.

If the circuit breaker is closed, normally open auxiliary contact of the circuit breaker closes; which is wired in series to the trip coil. Through NO contact of lockout relay 86E/86NE, the trip coil energizes and the circuit breaker trips open. Lockout relay is either hand reset or electrical reset. Before attempting to restart the generator, the concerned protection relay as well as lockout relay(s) has to rest. Non-electrical fault trip circuits are connected to non-electrical lockout relay, which causes mostly to shut down the unit. Relays employed for protection against internal fault on generator and transformer (incase of combined generator-transformer unit) are connected to shutdown the prime mover in the event of operation of those relays..

Table 1.12 (1): Generator Protection relays.

Device #	Protection	Device #	Protection
12	Over-speed switch (Non-electrical)	87SP	Split phase relay (Gen: inter-turn fault)
27	Under voltage relay	64F	Field ground relay (Rotor earth fault}
59	Over-voltage relay	71	Oil level switch (Non-electrical)
32	Reverse power relay	78	Loss of synchronism relay (Pole slip)
40	Loss of excitation relay	81	Under/Over frequency relay
46	Negative sequence relay	86	Lockout relay (Unit shut down/CB trip)
49	Thermal relay	87G	Generator differential protection relay
51	Time over-current relay	39B	Boiler overheats
51V	Voltage restrained over-current relay	39V	Loss of vacuum
59GN	Voltage relay (Grounding transformer earthed generator neutral only)	39OF	Lubricating oil system failure
51GN	Earth fault relay (Resistance earthed generator neutral only)	39CF	Generator cooling system failure
60	Voltage balance relay (PT fuse fail)	26T	Bearing temperature highest

1.13 PRE-COMMISSIONING TESTS ON SYNCHRONOUS MACHINES.

(1) Dielectric absorption and polarization index test: The standard voltage of a generator range from 220 V to 600 V in low voltage system and 3.3 KV to 26 KV in medium voltage or high voltage system. The system frequency is either 50 Hz or 60 Hz. The insulation resistance test is often used as a measure of the condition of the winding. Insulation resistance measured in mega-ohm indicates the dielectric strength of the generator winding. It is the ratio of the applied voltage to the current at some specified time after the voltage applied. Megger used for measuring insulation resistance generates DC voltage. For rated AC voltage up to 600 volts, 1000 volts megger is sufficient. For rated AC voltage 3.3 KV to 7.2 KV, 2.5 KV megger is being used. Above 7.2 KV, 5 KV megger is required. Insulation resistance of the field windings can be measured by using a 1000 V megger. Although the operating voltage of the field winding is below 600 volts, during interruption of full load field current (Transient conditions) the voltage will rise several times rated volt for a short duration. Hence the same insulation classes, as stator winding is applied to field winding also.

The insulation resistance value obtained after an interval of one minute is the leakage current over the winding surface and conduction through the insulation material. Similarly, the value obtained after ten minutes is the absorption currents in the insulation.
Dielectric absorption value = one minute reading / 30 seconds readings
The ratio of 10 minutes reading to one minute reading is called the polarization index value.
Polarization Index (PI) = 10 minutes reading in mega-ohm / One minute reading in mega-ohm.
The minimum value of polarization index for class A insulation should be 1.5, and for class B 2.0. Figure 1.13 (a) illustrates the method of testing insulation resistance of an alternator by using motorized megger tester.

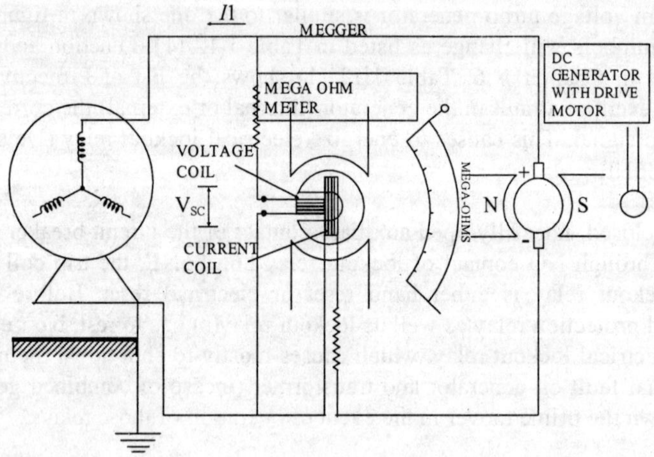

Fig. 1.13 (a): Dielectric absorption and polarization index test on AC generator by using Megger tester.

As per IEEE recommendations the minimum acceptable value of insulation resistance of a rotating machine winding (Generator or motor) at 40°C is 1 MΩ for every 1 KV rated voltage + 1 MΩ. For example, the minimum value of insulation resistance of an 11 KV generator at 40 °C should not be less than 11 + 1 = 12 MΩ. However, manufacturers factory test report is the reference value for site tests.

(2) High potential dielectric test: For evaluating insulation capability and condition of alternators AC or DC high potential is applied across the winding to earthed body for a duration of one minute by using a high voltage test set. Test connections are shown in Figure's 1.13 (b) and (c). ANSI standard recommends as follows:
The AC voltage to be injected across the stator winding and earthed body = (2 x generator rated voltage) + 1000 volts. For example in a 13.8 KV generator, the AC voltage to be applied for 1 minute duration is (2 x 13800) + 1000 = 28,600 V.
If it is desired to use DC test voltage instead of AC apply 1.7 times AC test voltage only for a test duration of one minute.

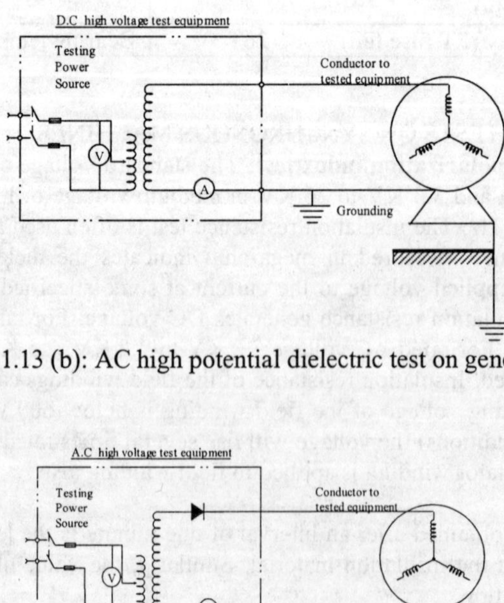

Fig. 1.13 (b): AC high potential dielectric test on generator.

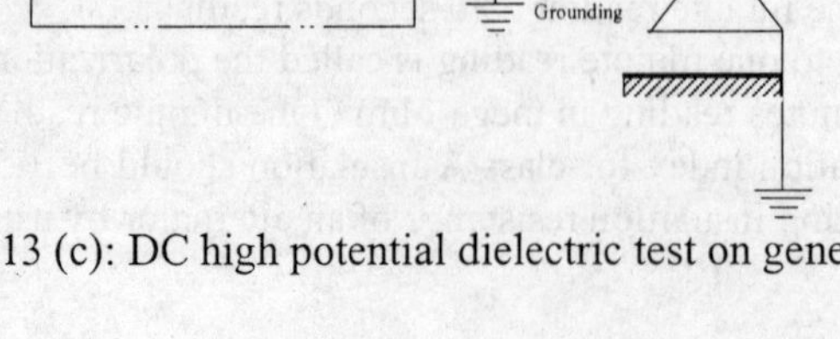

Fig. 1.13 (c): DC high potential dielectric test on generator.

In both case during the test, the leakage current is to be measured in micro-amps or milliamps and recorded. It is a severe test and is conducted only after ascertaining that the winding is dry and clean.

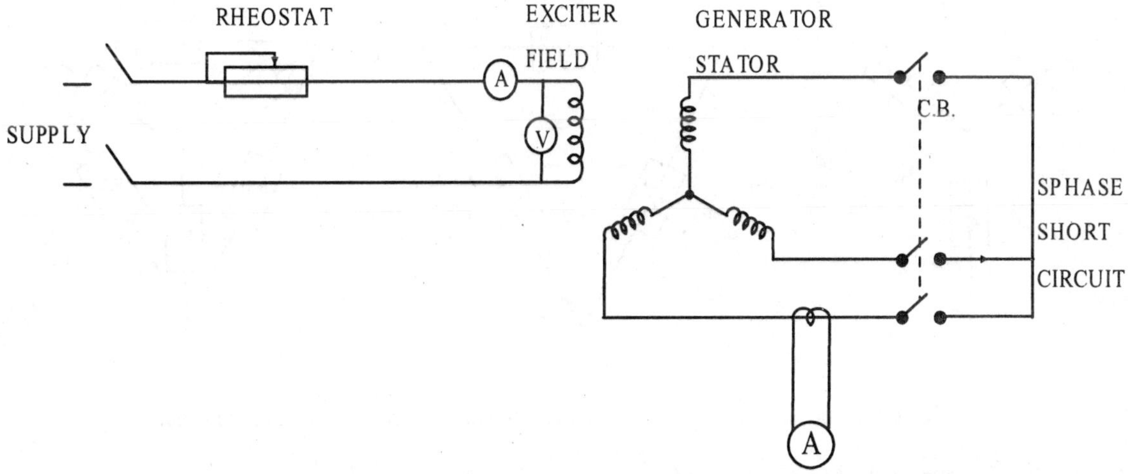

Fig. 1.13 (d); Open circuit and short-circuit test connection for AC generator:

(3) **Open circuit, short-circuit, and full load test:** To observe the no-load losses, the alternator being tested is mechanically coupled to a driving motor and driven at rated speed. Stator terminals are open-circuited and rotor is connected to the exciter. Excitation is varied from 30% to 130% of the rated voltage by using a rheostat. Simultaneous readings of excitation current and terminal voltages, is taken for plotting the open circuit saturation curve. If the power input to the driving motor is measured and its losses are known, the input to the alternator can be determined. This value represents windage, friction and core loss.

To obtain short-circuit saturation curve, same test may be repeated by short-circuiting the stator terminals. Excitation is so adjusted that the stator current can vary from 30% to 130% by using a rheostat. The input to the driving motor measured during the test is the sum of losses of the driving motor, the no-load losses described above, plus armature copper loss. Hence, armature copper loss can be obtained by short-circuit test by subtracting no load losses and losses of the driving motor. The test connection is shown in Figure 1.13 (d). During open circuit test, the circuit breaker is kept in open position. During short-circuit test the breaker remain closed.

For load test, water resistance or metal resistance load banks are being used. Winding temperature is recorded during load test. Resistance temperature detectors embedded in the stator winding is measuring the winding temperature.

(4) **Measuring winding resistance:** Winding resistance of stator or rotor is usually measured by using a Kelvin bridge. During measurement the temperature of the winding is to be recorded. Then the measured value is to be corrected to the temperature to compare with the records available in the test data.

R1 = R2 X (K + T1) / (K + T2)

R1 is the winding resistance recorded earlier at temperature T1

R2 is the measured temperature at temperature T2.

K is a constant indicating the electrical conductivity depending upon the material used for winding (Copper 234.5 and aluminium 225).

As shown in Figure 1.13 (e), if the star connection is made integral to the machine and only three leads are available, then the resistance of each phase winding R1, R2, R3 can be obtained by using the formula:

R1 = (R12 + R31 – R23) / 2 ohms.

R2 = (R23 + R12 – R31) / 2 ohms

R3 = (R31 + R23 – R12) / 2 ohms

R12 is the resistance measured between terminals 1 & 2 of star connected winding. Similarly, R31 is the resistance between terminal 3 & 1, and R23 represents the resistance across terminals 2 & 3.

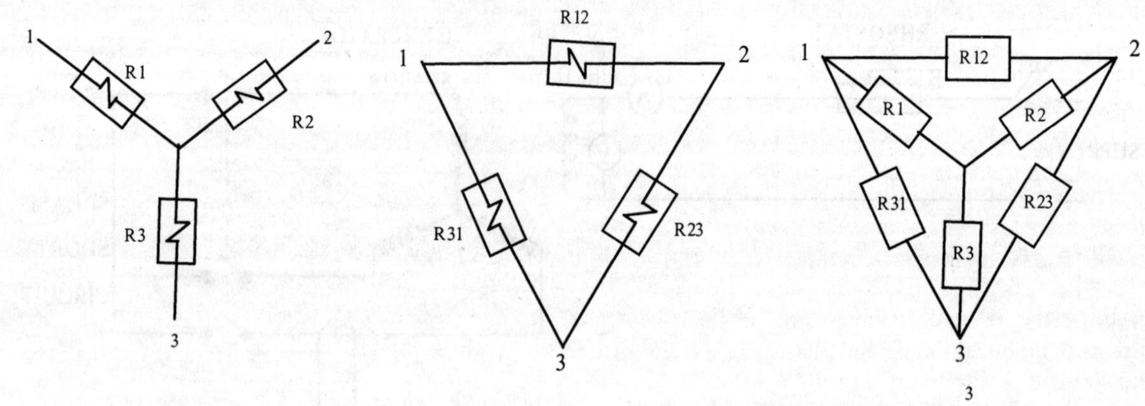

Fig. 1.13 (e): Method of measuring winding resistance on star and delta connected alternator.

If the winding is delta connected R1, R2 and R3 can be obtained by using the formula:

$$R1 = \frac{R12 \times R31}{R12 + R23 - R31} - \frac{R12 + R23 - R31}{2} \text{ ohms}$$

$$R2 = \frac{R23 \times R12}{R23 + R31 - R12} - \frac{R23 + R31 - R12}{2}$$

$$R3 = \frac{R31 \times R23}{R31 + R12 - R23} - \frac{R31 + R12 - R23}{2}$$

R12 is the resistance between terminals 1 and 2 of delta-connected winding in Figure 1.13 (e). R23 is the resistance between terminals 2 and 3 of the delta-connected winding. Similarly, R31 is the resistance measured between terminals 3 and 1.

An alternative method of measuring winding resistance is drop of voltage method, which is illustrated in Figure 1.13 (f). A 12 V battery supplies the circuit, while a variable resistance permits varying the value of the current. Voltmeter and ammeter are incorporated in the circuit. DC resistance = Voltmeter reading / ammeter reading By using the formula given above the resistance of each phase at 75°C can be calculated.

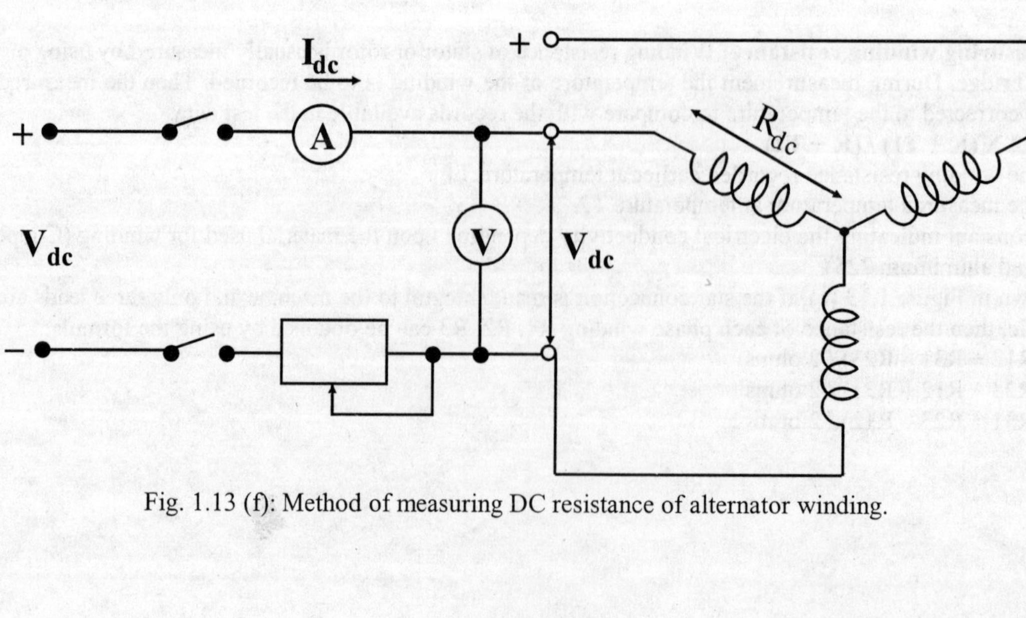

Fig. 1.13 (f): Method of measuring DC resistance of alternator winding.

(5) Measuring reactance: Synchronous reactance can be determined by applying a positive sequence voltage to the armature (stator) windings with no field current while the machine is rotated slightly below or slightly above rated speed, and measuring the maximum and minimum value of the varying current,
Direct axis synchronous reactance = Voltage applied / Minimum value of the current.
Quadrature axis synchronous reactance = Voltage applied / Maximum value of current.

The negative sequence reactance is applicable with an armature m.m.f rotating backward at synchronous speed while the rotor m.m.f is rotating forward at synchronous speed. Such situation results from unbalanced loading or certain type of faults. Negative sequence reactance can be determined by applying a negative sequence voltage at the armature (stator) windings while the machine is rotated at rated speed in the positive direction, with its field winding short-circuited.

Zero sequence reactance is applicable to situations in which all the three phases of the armature have identical currents in both magnitude and phase, such as would arises from a ground fault. Zero sequence reactance can be determined by applying a single phase AC supply across the stator (armature) neutral and phases, with three phase winding terminals connected together (in parallel). With the machine rotated at rated speed, and with its field winding short-circuited.
Zero sequence reactance = Applied voltage / current.

Pre-commissioning check

1. General cleaning and tightness of nuts, bolts, safety guards and earthing connections
2. Air gap check, bearing tolerance, noise level, vibration etc
3. Paint finish, ventilation paths, cable box, cable glands, heater supply, coupling
4. Cooling system, bearing oil level, fire protection system, fire fighting system etc
5. Winding resistance (a) stator (b) rotor (c) exciter stator (e) exciter rotor (f) permanent magnet generator
6. Insulation resistance check (continue on item 5 listed above)
7. Control circuit, function check on protection system (Including primary and secondary injection test)
8. Function check on trip circuit, alarm/annunciation, battery bank and battery charger etc
9. Closing and tripping time of generator circuit breaker
10. Rotor alignment/bearing oil level etc.
11. Earth connection of neutral and body including earth resistance measurements.

Additional tests on slip ring type machines:

1. Brush grade, brush gear, brush bedding, brush staggering etc
2. Neutral axis of brushes, brush box clearance
3. Cleanliness of commutator surface and slip-ring surface
4. Exciter check (repeat item 1 to 3 above)
5. Closing and tripping time of field circuit breaker

Commissioning check

(a) Polarization index (Insulation resistance at 10 minutes / Insulation resistance value at 1 minute) minimum value must be above 1.2
(b) Check danger notice, nameplate data's, relay settings and voltage regulator settings, synchronizing relay setting etc.
(c) Check phase sequence, Phase to phase and phase to neutral voltage at PT terminals
(d) Check speed, frequency and conduct over speed test.
(e) Full load current at CT secondary.
(f) Bearing temperature, oil temperature and winding temperature.
(g) Cooling water flow, cooling water pressure, cooling water inlet and outlet temperature.
(f) Measure noise level and vibration.

1.14 MAINTENANCE AND REPAIR OF ALTERNATORS

The following maintenance procedures should be followed to insure long equipment life and satisfactory performance. Maintenance intervals may depend upon total running hours, operating conditions, and manufacturer's recommendations.

1. Periodically check the bearing for smooth, quit operation. Vibration of bearing can be measured by a set of 3 Orthogonal accelerometers fixed on each bearing. The measured value should be within the tolerance limit recommended by the manufacturer. Check the bearings for damage or wear.
2. Inspect all electrical connections to be sure they are clean, tight, and properly insulated.
3. Check and clean intake and exhaust air screens. Clogged screens will increase operating temperatures, and reduce the generator's life. For large generators check the cooling system against clogging.
4. Inspect the unit for buildup of contamination on the windings, which may inhibits heat transfer, and can lead to shortened insulation.
5. Over speed check: Increase prime mover speed 110% of normal speed and check the operation of speed switch alarm and trip signal.
6. Audible noise check: Noise is caused by magnetostriction, aerodynamics, Bearings of rotating shaft, speed and power effect, ventilation etc. Measurements are taken at a distance of one metre from the machine surface in direction perpendicular to the shaft.
7. Insulation resistance should be measured in the following windings by using a calibrated megger: (a) Main generator stator (after opening the circuit breaker as well as ground connections to neutral leads) (b) Main generator rotor (c) Exciter stator (after disconnecting the wires connected to voltage regulator) (c) Exciter rotor and (d) permanent magnet generator stator. Compare the readings with the original test certificate data's. Deterioration of winding insulation reduces the insulation resistance value. Clean the winding with dry and hot air, remove dust and dirt accumulated.
8. Functional check of protective devices and closing and opening time of generator circuit breaker and field circuit breaker of separately excited generator.
9. Rectifier block testing of self excited generators by using calibrated digital precision multi-meter. Set the multi-meter in the diode range (positive lead on cathode) and observe the resistance reading. Reverse the lead and measure the resistance again. A good diode will indicate very low resistance value when the leads are reversed. The continuity tester will have the light "on" in one direction, and "off" in the other. In a shorted diode Ohmmeter reading will be zero, or very low in both directions and continuity tester light will be "on" in both directions. In open conditions Ohmmeter will have an infinity reading in both directions and continuity tester light will be dark or off in both directions.
10. Varistor check by measuring the resistance between the positive rectifier terminal and the negative rectifier terminal and compare with manufacturers test report.
11. Check the exciter stator, rotor and PMG for loose, frayed or burnt winding. Measure winding resistance and compare with manufacturers test report.
12. Check the exciter, rotor and PMG for burns on the mating surfaces. Look for score marks on the outside diameter of the armature core caused by rubbing.
13. Apply antifriction, high quality, multipurpose lithium base grease for bearing lubrication if applicable.

REPAIR PROCEDURES:

1. Drying generator winding: The method of drying generator windings are: (a) By using space heaters (b) By using electric oven (c) By applying forced hot air and (d) Short circuiting the stator winding.

Short-circuit the stator winding at its outgoing terminals. Apply DC (10% of the rated voltage), through a rheostat to the rotor winding while the machine is running at 50% speed. Increase the DC voltage gradually until the rated full load currents circulate through the stator winding. Temperature of the stator is to be checked and controlled. When the polarization index value is 1.2, stop the drying out procedure.

2. Impregnation of generator winding: The process of coating electrical winding with insulation varnish is called impregnation. By covering the coils with a good insulation varnish the air spaces are filled up and sealed. Thus the winding get protected against ingress of moisture. Hot dip impregnation method is demonstrated in Chapter # 9, section 9.22 Part 'C'..

The Vacuum impregnating plant consists of a large airtight double-jacked, vacuum impregnating chamber with a removable lid. The interior of the tank can be heated by circulating steam or hot oil through the jacket. The insulation varnish (baking type) is kept stored in another storage tank. A motor-driven compressor- cum-vacuum exhauster is provided with suitable valves to create either vacuum or pressure as required. The process is as follows:

Place the rotor inside the vacuum tank with the help of an overhead crane. Close the top cover (lid) and heat-up the chamber at 100°C at least four hours by circulating steam or hot oil through the jacket. During this period air inside the tank is pumped out and vacuum is maintained. By this process, all the air and moisture inside the coil is completely driven out since all liquids vapourise very rapidly in vacuum.

Now allow insulating varnish (by opening the valve) to flow in the chamber, until the rotor is fully immersed. Apply sufficient pressure in to the space above the varnish level inside the tank after closing the varnish outlet valve. The varnish will now be forced by pressure in to all the porous spaces in the interior of the coil. After half an hour, allow all the varnish to flow back in to the storage tank under air pressure and the excess varnish in the coil to drain out. Bake the winding for 4 to 8 hours at a temperature of 100 to 110°C. This will cause the varnish in all portions of the coil to set and become bone dry.

3. Static and dynamic balancing of rotor: The applicable method is demonstrated in Chapter # 9, section 9.22 Part 'C'..

4. Restoring residual magnetism: To restore the residual magnetism necessary to begin voltage buildup in a self excited alternator, connect a 12volt battery to the exciter field for 5 to 10 seconds time (after disconnecting the exciter field leads F+ and F- from the voltage regulator) while the generator is at rest. Repeat the procedure if the generator fails to build voltage while starting.

1.15 EMERGENCIES AND TROUBLES ON ALTERNATORS.

The main causes of trouble in the stator are:

(1) Defect in the slot insulation or turn-to-turn insulation of the stator winding.
(2) Mechanical damage to the winding insulation due to vibration of the core steel laminations resulting from weakening of the clamping pressure on the core stacks.
(3) Poor joints in the end winding due to the damage of silver solder connection.
(4) Mechanical wear due to shifting of bars of the stator winding due to improper seating and lacking.
(5) Due to corrosion in the core steel laminations. It should be cleaned and re-insulated with insulating varnish of suitable grade.
(6) Overloading the generator or failure to trip during, a short- circuit or any major faults.
(7) Out of step paralleling.

Rotor troubles:

(a) Very high mechanical and non-magnetic requirements have to be met by the end winding retaining rings on turbo-generator rotors. These rings are generally made of a non-magnetic material to avoid them becoming heated due to a loss in balance of the magnetic fields or some other cause. During overhaul make sure that there are no signs of temper colours, indication of overheating or any signs of hairline or cracks etc. This is a matter of great importance because a defect in the retaining ring or a weak fit of the ring may become the cause of breakdown.

(b) When vibration of machine begins to exceed permissible limits, measures are to be taken to eliminate the causes. This may probably due to turn-to-turn short circuit in the rotor winding. By measuring the value of rotor winding resistance and comparing with original test report, this can be detected.

(c) Brushless generators are not equipped with field circuit breakers. Hence flow of reverse power in an idle generator will damage the rectifier or rotor.

(d) Generator breakdowns have also been caused by rotor balancing weights, which flow off during service.

(e) Double earth fault of the rotor winding may cause complete destruction of the generator and damage the rotor.

Exciter troubles:

(1) Prolonged sparking in the brushes, which suddenly develops in to a flashover round the commutator, the causes of which are accumulation of deposits on the surface of the commutator and a drop in the armature insulation resistance due to excessive gathering of the graphite dust from the brushes on the surrounding surfaces. A flash over will result in the fusing of the brush holder boxes, burning of the brushes, and scorching of the commutator surfaces.

(2) In brushless generator, failure of the automatic voltage regulator or failure of the rotating rectifier may cause failure of excitation. Hence, the paralleled generator begins to operate in the asynchronous running condition.

Failure of cooling system:
Failure of the stator cooling system (air, hydrogen, water) may cause to overheat the stator winding and the winding impregnating compound may bleed in to stator cores. Hence, insulation resistance and polarization index value will come down.
Trouble shooting on alternator:
(1) Generator produces no voltage or residual voltage: No regulator input or regulator fuse blown; Defective diodes or surge suppressor; Voltage regulator protective shutdown circuits are operating, PT fuse blown.
(2) Generator voltage increases when loaded: Leading power factor or switching on long distance high voltage cables with light load.
(3) Generator voltage is fluctuating: Incorrect or unstable speed, Defective or loose connections, defective voltage regulator or defective voltage adjusting rheostat, won bearing or uneven air-gap.
(4) Generator builds voltage but then reduces: Voltage regulator protective shutdown circuit is operating.
(5) Motor or other equipment runs on utility power but will not run on generator set: Wave form distortion due to excessive thyristor (SCR) load, improper generator voltage and or frequency, incorrect regulator adjustment.
(6) Generator voltage reduces when load is applied: Excessive load, very low power factor, incorrect voltage droop setting for paralleled generators.
(7) Generator produces high voltage at no load: Diode polarity wrong or defective voltage regulator or breaker tripping at full load.
(8) Generator overheats: Overload, failure of cooling system, clogged ventilation, core faults, unbalanced stator current, un-cleared external short circuit or earth fault, circulating current in a paralleled generator.
(9) Excessive vibration: Short circuited turns on the rotor or double earth fault on the rotor, defective bearing, improper alignment, inadequate foundation or poor balance of the rotor.

1.16 NON-ELECTRICAL LOCKOUT TRIP FOR GENERATOR-TRANSFORMER UNITS.

Trip circuit for a generator is classified in to electrical lockout trips and non-electrical lock out trips. Protective relays employed for electrical lockout trips are listed in Chapter # 6. Non- electrical lockout trips of turbo-generators are over-speed protection, boiler protection, loss of vacuum, high bearing temperature, lubricating oil failure and rotor distortion etc.
The speed of a turbo-generator rises when the steam input is in excess of that required for the load. The speed governor can normally control the speed and in any case a parallel running set cannot accelerate much independently even if synchronism is lost. If the circuit breaker is tripped suddenly, (without unloading load on the generator) the speed will increase. The speed governor is designed to prevent a dangerous speed rise even with a 100% load rejection, but an additional centrifugal over-speed trip device is provided to shut off the emergency steam valves if the over-speed exceeds the desired value. Despite the safety measures, a risk still remains if the steam valve fails to close completely.
Boiler may overheat if: (1) The water level falls because of an interruption of the feed water supply; (2) The steam demand ceases when the turbine steam valves are unexpectedly shut off. In this case the super-heater or the pre-heater tubes will overheat. Loss of boiler water is detected by a device, which trips the boiler firing immediately and initiates shutdown of the unit. A similar action is initiated by, the valve relay fluid switch when the turbine valves are shut off. Loss of boiler firing is detected by a fall in steam pressure. A pressure sensitive device operates on the governing system, in the event of fall in pressure below 90% of normal, to unload the unit and finally to shutdown the turbine.
A failure of the condenser vacuum in heating which, produces strain in the condenser tubes and so on, and also a rise in temperature of the low pressure end of the turbine. Vacuum pressure devices initiate progressive unloading of the paralleled unit and eventually cause a non-electrical shutdown.
In some turbo-generator units the bearing oil is derived from the same pump that supplies serving system controlling the governing valves. These valves are arranged to close if the oil supply fails. So that separate action need not to be taken. Many units, the valve control fluid is separate from the lubricating oil. An oil flow device is therefore needed to detect bearing oil failure and trip the unit..

The cooling rates after a shutdown are different at the top and bottom of the turbine casing. This may distort the rotor slowly during the cooling period. Turbines are equipped with barring gear for this purpose, the tendency is to use higher barring speeds, which assists the circulation of air within the casing and equalize the temperature in transverse plates for the turbine as a whole. The rotors of large turbines weigh several tons and a 0.1mm displacement of the center of gravity of a rotor from the axis of rotation will produce a centrifugal force equal to its weight. The rotor will tend to revolve about an axis through its center of gravity; if the latter does not coincide with the geometric center of the shaft at the bearings, relative transverse motion will take place and the shaft will appear to be eccentric. Eccentric running of the shaft will be detected by a pair of electromagnets mounted rigidly on the bearing housing and opposed diametrically across the shaft. The magnets are connected in to a bridge circuit energized by a high frequency signal. The signal is amplified to energize display and recording instruments.

Figure 1.16 illustrates typical tripping diagram of a turbo-generator-transformer combined unit. All non-electrical protections and certain electrical protections such as differential protection, reverse power protection will simultaneously trip the generator circuit breaker, and field circuit breaker of brush type generator and shut down the prime mover. Other protective relays will initiate trip signal to the circuit breaker.

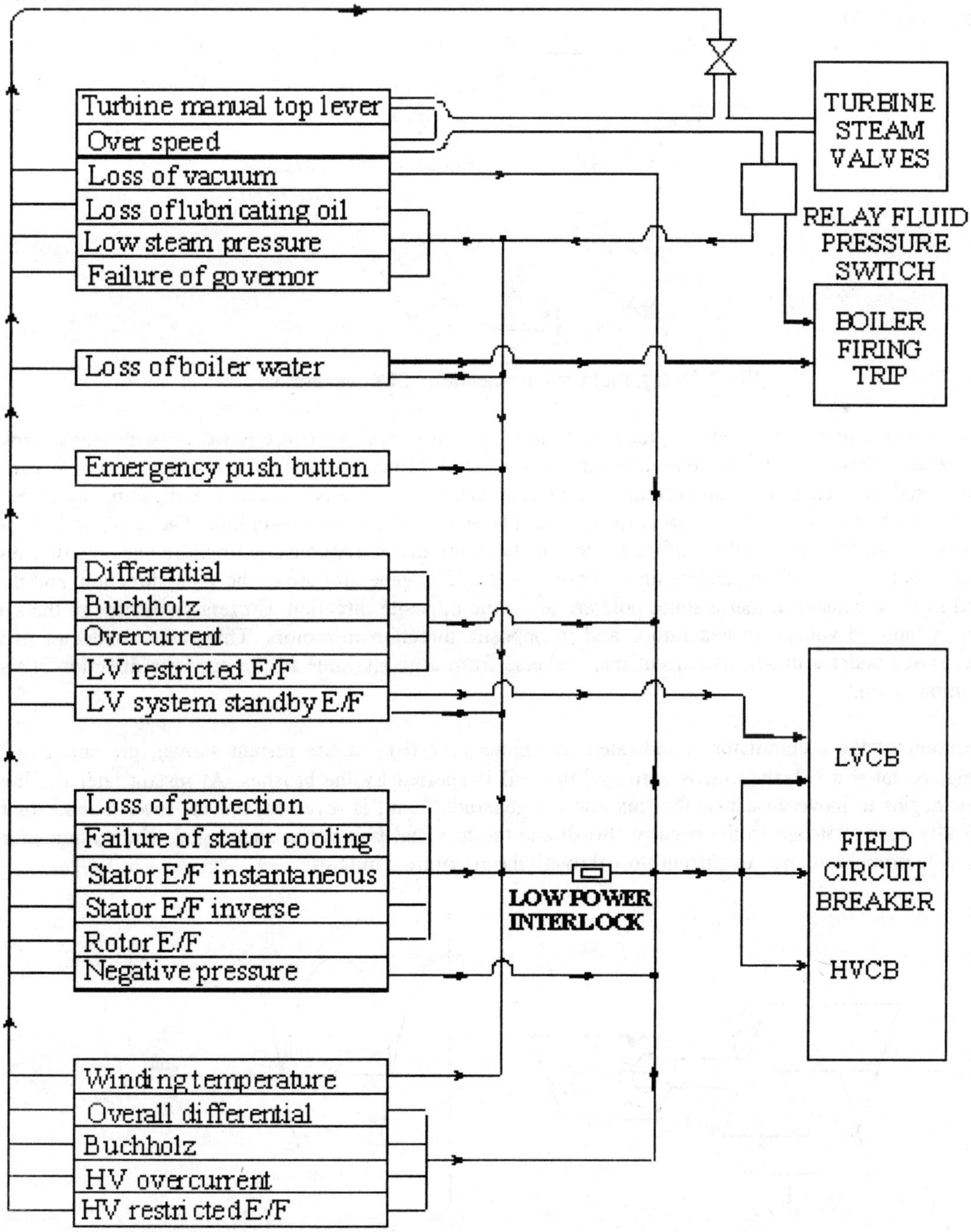

Fig. 1.16: Typical tripping diagram of a high voltage turbo-generator-transformer combined unit.

1.17 SELF AND SEPARATELY EXCITED DIRECT CURRENT GENERATORS.

Direct current means current that flows only in one direction or current that does not reverse its direction of flow. DC generator is a device that used to convert mechanical energy in to (direct current) electrical energy. Based on field winding connections, the self-excited direct current generators are classified in to (1) Series field generator (2) Shunt field generator (3) Compound wound generator. The standard DC voltages are 250 V, 750 V, 1000 V, 1500 V, and 3000 V.

In an AC generator, the induced current in the coil flows first to maximum value in one direction, then reverses and flows to maximum in the opposite direction. If it is desired to have a direct current in the output terminals of the generator, the alternating current in the rotating armature is converted in to direct current by means of a commutator. Field coils placed over pole pieces or pole shoes are fastened to the steel frame of the generator. Figure 1.17 (a) illustrates the field coil connection of a DC generator. These electromagnets, produces a strong electromagnetic field.

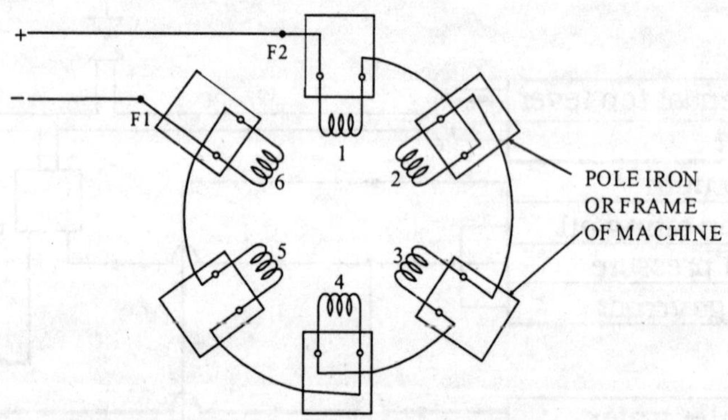

Fig. 1.17 (a): Field coil connection of DC generator.

The revolving armature is suspended in the case with proper bearings. Armature is wound with many turns of wires. External connections to the rotating armature are made through commutator sections. Strips or bars of metal, insulated from each other and arranged around an armature is the commutator. Carbon brushes ride on the commutator bars carry the load current from the armature coil to the external circuit. The brush holders hold the brushes against the commutator surface by springs to maintain a fairly constant pressure and smooth riding. The voltage generated in all conductors under a north pole of DC generator are in the same direction, and those generated in the conductor under a south pole are all in the opposite direction. Currents will flow in the same direction as induced voltage in generators, and in opposite direction in motors. Thus, as a conductor of the armature passes under a brush, its current must reverse from a given value in the opposite direction. This is called commutation.

The operation of the commutator is indicated in Figure 1.17 (b). At the instant shown, the coil e.m.f is decreasing, At $\omega t = \pi / 2$, the emf is zero and the coil is shorted by the brushes. At instant later the lower conductor begins to move up across the flux and the generated e.m.f is reversed; but the lower conductor has automatically been switched to the negative brush and the terminal polarity is unchanged. The commutator is used to insure proper direction of current flow through the armature windings.

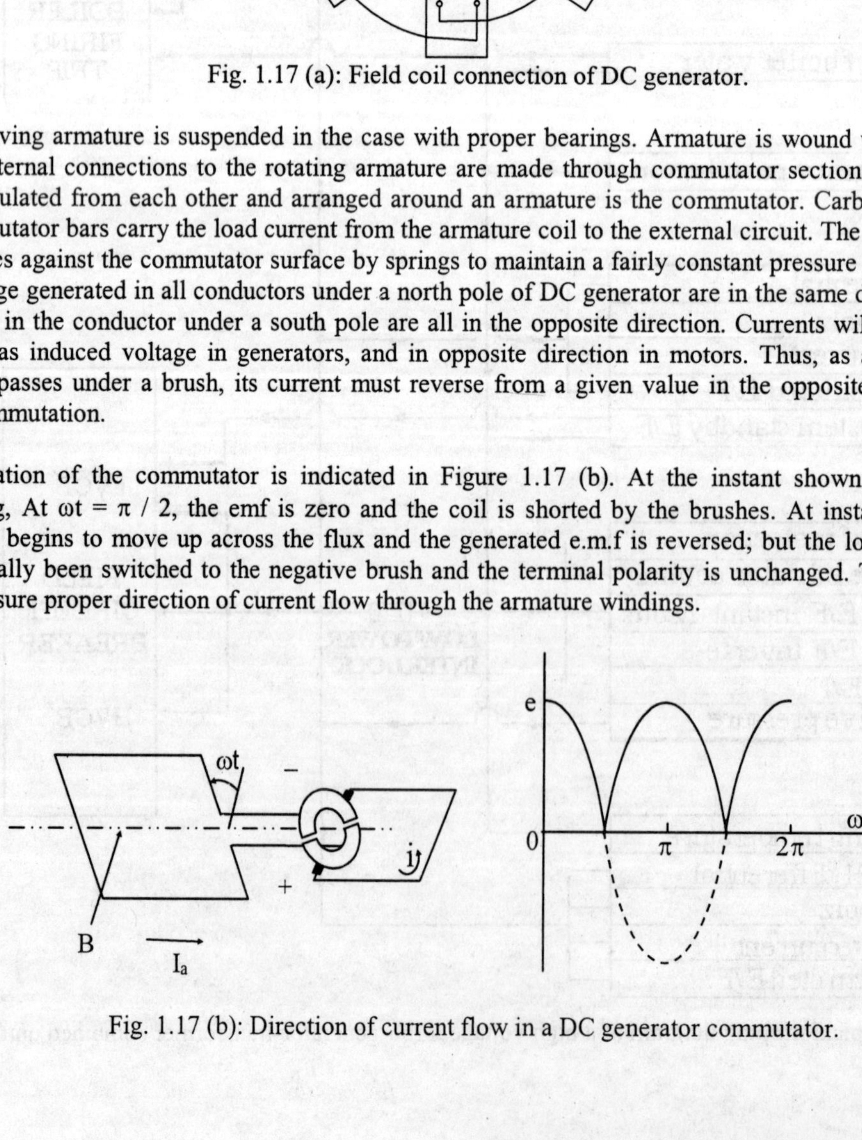

Fig. 1.17 (b): Direction of current flow in a DC generator commutator.

The armature windings in the generator are wound on an iron core (cylindrical iron rotor), which is slotted to hold the coils as shown in Figure 1.17 (c). If the core is a solid block of iron, voltages would be inducing in the core causing an alternating current to flow in the core. These, alternating current in the core are known as eddy currents. They produce heat, which is a loss of energy. To reduce this loss to a negligible value, the core is built up of thin sections of laminations. Each lamination is insulated from the others by lacquer. Laminating the core reduces voltage in the core, and increases the resistance to eddy currents. Eddy current will increase in the core, as the speed of rotation increases or the field density increases.
The effect of magnetic field of the armature current on the main field is called armature reaction. Due to armature reaction in DC machines, the main field gets distorted. To overcome the effect of armature reaction, the brush is slightly shifted from neutral axis when the load on the machine is increased. The direction of shifting of brush-gear in a generator is in forward direction. Where as in a motor, the direction of shifting is in reverse direction.

The stationary field windings establish a high and nearly uniform flux density in the small air-gap. The e.m.f generated in a single conductor is also indicated in e_1. In a practical machine there are many conductors and many commutator segments. At any instant many coils are connected in series between brushes and a few coils are short-circuited by the brushes as they are being switched from one circuit to another as in indicated in e_1 to e_4. The net results of e.m.f generated, is shown as rectified output. As the armature rotates, the flux density remains fixed in space at the optimum torque angle 90°. The resulting developed torque is clockwise and in a generator, must be overcome by the mechanical power source. If direct current from an electrical source is introduced at the brushes, a constant unidirectional torque is developed and the machine functions as a motor.

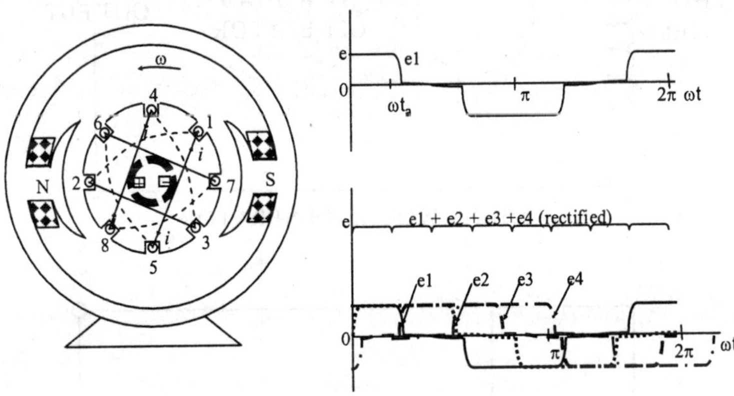

Fig. 1.17 (c): Two pole direct current generator

Commutating field used in direct current machines to help overcome the problems of armature reaction. The commutating field connects in series with the armature and is also known as inter-pole winding.

Self-excited DC generators:
Self-excited generator excites its own field. The initial generator voltage is produced when the armature windings cut across a small magnetic field caused by the residual magnetism in the pole shoes or field coil cores. Proper voltage is build up when the armature speeds up.
(1) Series field generator: The field coils (wound with large size wire and few turns) are connected in series with the armature as shown in Figure 1.17 (d) i.e. current that flows through the armature flows through the series field winding, with the result that the voltage developed rises with load. In a series wound generator, output voltage varies directly with the load current. Hence series field generators are not in common use.
(2) Shunt field generator: The shunt field (wound with small wire having many turns) is connected in parallel to the armature terminals as shown in Figure 1.17 (d). The voltage generated by a shunt generator is more or less constant if the speed is steady. It has a drooping characteristic, i.e. the voltage drops down slightly as the load increases from no load to full load. This is mainly because of the voltage drop (IR) in the armature and carbon brushes, due to load current. In a shunt wound generator, output voltage varies inversely with the load current. Output current always varies according to the actual load. The field flux does not vary to a great extent, so the terminal voltage remains constant under varying load conditions..

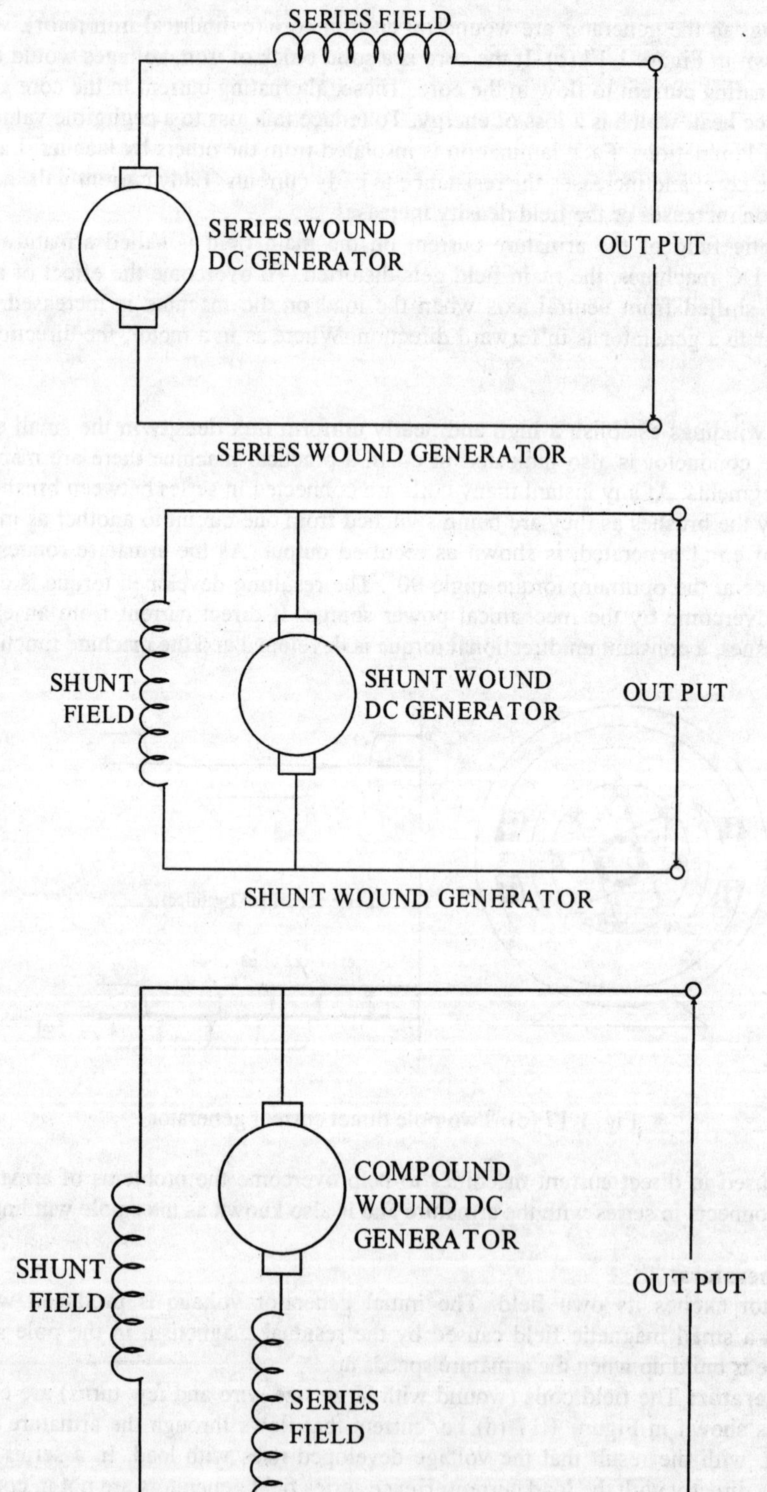

Fig. 1.17 (d): Conventional diagrams of DC series, shunt, and compound wound generators.

(3) Compound wound generator: The compound wound generator employs both series and shunt windings in the field as shown in Figure 1.17 (d). The series windings are usually a few turns of relatively large wire and are mounted on the same poles with the shunt windings. Both winding contribute to the field strength of the generator. The series winding is connected to strengthen the main shunt field when load current passes through it. The series winding compensates for the voltage drop occurring in the shunt wound generator. The currents passing through the series field and the degree of the compensation can be adjusted by a variable resistance called "diverter' which is connected across the series field winding. The diverter permits the modification of the characteristic curve of a DC generator as required.

If both series and shunt winding act in the same polarity, an increase in load would cause an increase of current in the series coils, thus increasing the magnetic field and increasing the terminal voltage of the output. The fields of both the coils are then additive, and the resultant field would be the sum of both coils. However as the load exceeds the limit, the current through the series winding may produce magnetic saturation of the core and result in a decrease of voltage as the load increase. The manner-in, which the terminal voltage behaves, is depending up on the degree of compound.

In a level compounded generator, the voltage at the full load is the same as the no load voltage. In the over-compounded generator, the voltage at full load is higher than the no load (Over compounded generator). This rise in voltage could compensate for the voltage drop in the load lines so that the voltage may be maintained at the correct level, irrespective of load fluctuations. Compound DC machines may be connected long-shunt, short shunt, cumulative compound, or differential compound. Compound wound generator has a constant output voltage in varying load conditions (Flat compounded generator).

Separately excited DC generator:

DC generator output is determined by the strength of the magnetic field and the speed of rotation. The strength of the field is measured in ampere-turns. Hence, an increase in current in the field winding will increase the field strength. Since output voltage is in direct proportion to field strength times the speed of rotation, most output regulating devices depends up on varying the current in the field. The field winding is connected to an external source of DC voltage as illustrated in Figure 1.17 (e). Since the speed of the prime mover is constant, the output may be varied, by controlling the exciting voltage of the external DC source by inserting a variable resistance in series. This type of generator is called separately excited DC generator.

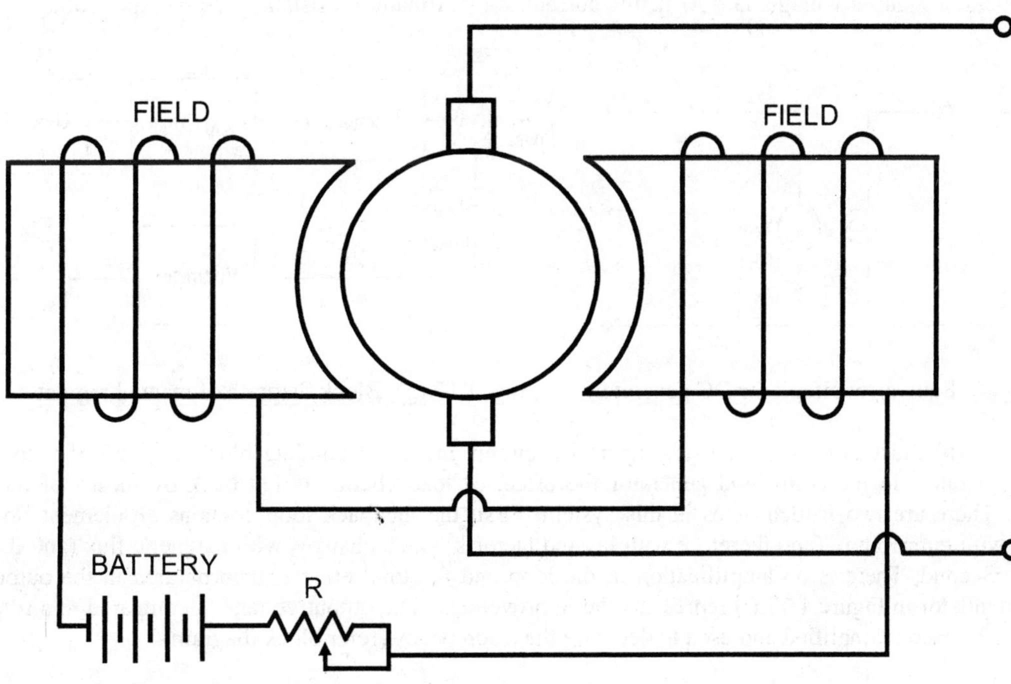

Fig. 1.17 (e): The diagram of a separately excited field, DC generator.

Efficiency and losses in a DC generator:

All of the mechanical power used to drive the generator is not converted in to useful electrical power. Losses resulting from the resistance in the winding are classified as copper losses. Copper loss = $I^2 R$.

AS the armature rotates in the fixed magnetic field, many of the magnetic particles in the armature core remain in a lineup position with the fixed field. This causes a rotation of these particles in respect to those, not in alignment with the field. This rotation causes internal friction between the magnetic particles and creates a heat loss (hysteresis loss). Silicon steel has a low hysteresis loss. Losses are segregated as follows:

1. Armature copper loss ($I^2 R$).
2. Compensating, commutating, and series field losses.
3. Brush loss and brush friction loss.
4. Load loss
5. Iron loss and eddy current loss (Shunt field loss).
6. Friction and windage loss.

Efficiency = Output / (Output + Losses).

Voltage and current regulation in a DC generator:

Voltage regulation is defined as the percentage of voltage drop between no load and full load.

$$\% \text{ Regulation} = \frac{(\text{No load voltage} - \text{Full load voltage}) \times 100}{\text{Full load voltage}}$$

It is desirable to maintain the output generator voltage at a fixed value at varying load conditions. Output of a DC generator is depending upon the field current. Current varies inversely with resistance. Therefore, by introducing a resistance in the field circuit, the voltage output of the generator can be varied. The purpose of a voltage regulating system is to hold the controlled voltage within specified limits in spite of changes in load or other operating conditions. Electronic voltage regulators are employed to control the output voltage of a generator at varying loads.

The output voltage of the separately excited, constant speed, DC generator in Figure 1.17 (f) varies with changes in load current because of the armature-resistance voltage drop. The variation can be reduced by "closing the loop" through an operator with his eye on the voltmeter and hand on the field rheostat as illustrated in Figure 1.17 (g), the block diagram of manual voltage regulator. The "controller" notes the "error" between the voltmeter pointer position and the "reference" and takes the necessary "action" to reduce the error to zero.

Key: Vf = External field voltage; Rf = Field resistance; Lf = Field inductance; If = Field current; Eg = Generator induced voltage; Ia = Armature current; Ra = Armature resistance; Vc = output voltage

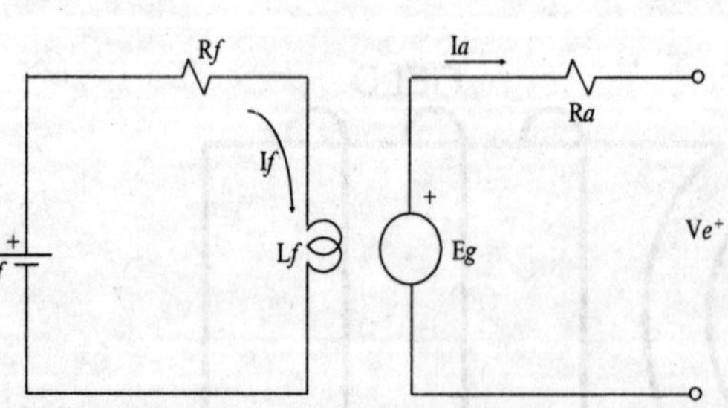

Fig. 1.17 (f): Equivalent circuit for DC generator.

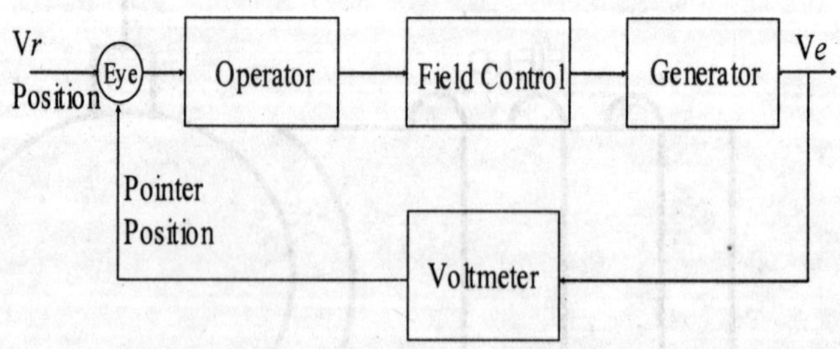

Fig. 1.17 (g): Block diagram of manual regulator.

Figure 1.17 (h) illustrates the steady-state operation circuit and corresponding block diagram of a compound wound generator. In the compound generator the effect of load change is fed back by means of the series winding. There are two inadequacies in this system; First, the feedback loop contains an element Ra which changes with temperature (and therefore with Ia) and factor k which changes with magnetic flux (and therefore with Ia). Second, There is no amplification in the loop and the total error is incorporated in the output. The voltage regulator in Figure 1.17 (i) represents the improvement. The output voltage is compared to a reference, and the difference is amplified and used to decrease the discrepancy (refer block diagram).

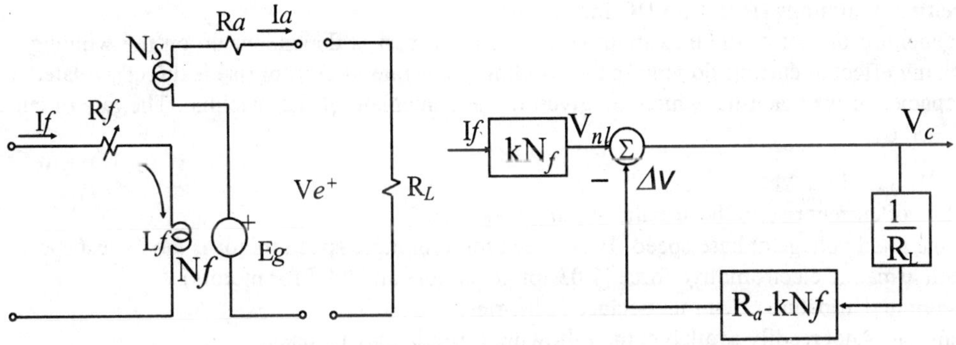

Fig. 1.17 (h): Steady state operation of a compound wound generator

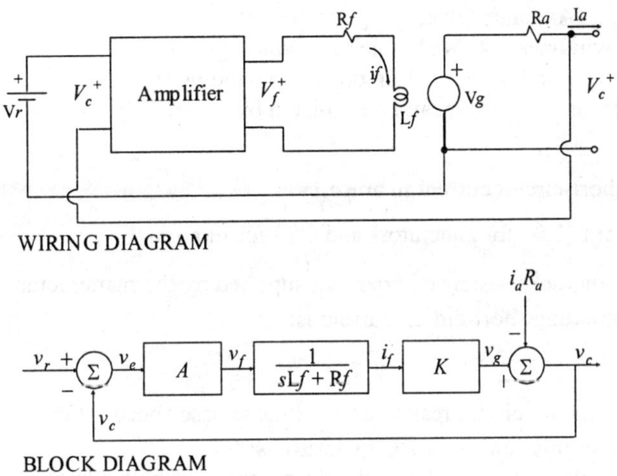

Fig. 1.17 (I): Wiring and block diagrams of DC generator voltage regulator.

An alternative method is the use of permanent magnet generator as shown in Figure 1.17 (J). PMG is mounted on the DC generator to provide AC power for the generator voltage regulator circuitry. In this method the voltage regulator, powered by the PMG, senses the DC output of the generator and regulates the generator field current to maintain the generator output at rated voltage.

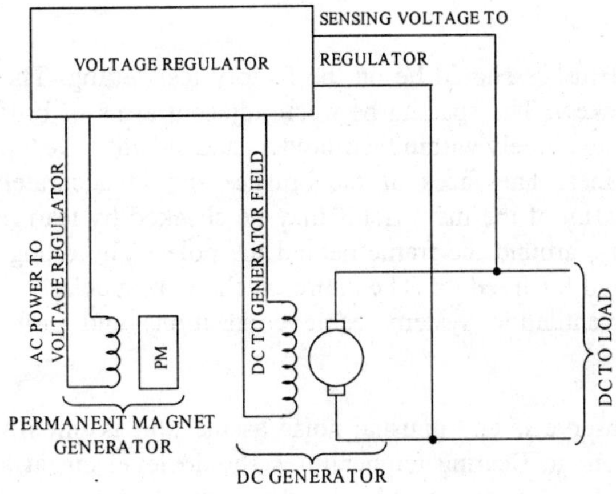

Fig. 1.17 (J): PMG used as power source for voltage regulation on a DC generator.

Short circuit calculations (Rotating DC machines)

In a DC generator or motor, the maximum short circuit current is dependent up on the winding and upon the demagnetizing effect of current flowing in the windings. The rate of current rise is directly related to the voltage and the capacity of the machine, which are given in the nameplate of the machine. The rate of current-rise can be determined by:

$(di_a /dt) = (V_1\, e_a \,/ La')$ where:
di_a /dt = Rate of current rise in the armature in amperes / sec.
V = Machine rated voltage at base speed (Base speed for a multiple speed motor is the lowest speed.
e_a = Per unit armature electromotive force (1.03 for generators and 0.97 for motors)
La' = Unsaturated armature circuit inductance in henries.
In the event La' is not readily available, the following formula may be used:

$(di /dt) = (PN_1\, Ia\, e_a) / 19.1C_a)$ where:
P = Number of poles; N_1 = Base speed in RPM; Ia = Rated current in ampere;
Ca = Inductance coefficient. (Average values are given below).
Motor: Without pole-face windings 0.4; With pole-face windings 0.1.
Generator: Without pole-face windings 0.6; With pole-face winding 0.2.
The magnitude of the short-circuit current can be estimated by:

Ia' = (Ia ea) / rd' where:
Ia = Maximum armature short-circuit current in amperes.

ea = Per unit armature e.m.f (1.03 for generators and 0.97 for motors)

rd' = Effective transient armature resistance in per unit supplied by the manufacturer.
Alternative method for estimating short-circuit current is:

Ia' = $(V_1$ ea) / Rd' where:

Rd' = Effective transient armature circuit resistance in ohms at base speed = (V_1 / I_a) x ra'

Installation, testing and commissioning of DC generators:

If the generator is dry and clean, the windings should be checked with a megger for insulation resistance to ground measurements. Reading less than one MΩ is not acceptable. After the machine is installed and grouted to the foundations, alignments of shafts finally checked as per manufacturers guidelines. Shafts should be rotated 180 degrees and rechecked by using magnetic dial indicators. The frame should be set on the magnetic center of the core. This position can be located by setting the armature in rotation and forcing it to oscillate longitudinally the full end play of the bearing by pushing on the end of the shaft. While the rotor is coasting and oscillating freely, excite the main field. The stator can then be shifted so that the rotor position with excitation coincides with the center of bearing endplay. Air-gaps between the rotor and poles should be uniform. A typical limit of variation is 2.5mm. The brushes should ride properly on the commutator surface at both extremes of bearing endplay.

Pre-commissioning check: Brushes should be on the factory test setting. The toes of the brushes should be aligned and should have no skew. The spacing between adjacent arms of brushes should be identical within 0.8mm. The brushes should move freely within their holders and should have a pressure against the commutator as per manufacturers guidelines. The faces of the brushes should accurately match the curvature of the commutator surface. The polarity of the main fields may be checked by lead markings or by slightly exciting the fields and using a compass around the frame behind the poles. The oiling system for bearings should be checked and the oil rings tested for freedom. The entire machine, particularly its air-gaps, should be inspected for foreign materials. The ventilation system, cable connections and protection settings should also be examined.

No load running check: Observe if any unusual noise as the unit is initially brought up to normal speed. Measure noise level and record it. Bearing temperatures should level out at acceptable values within a few hours. The voltage should be slowly raised at no load and commutation observed. If satisfactory, voltage should be raised up to 110% of rated voltage and then reduced. The generator may then be loaded gradually, while commutation is observed. If commutation at full load is satisfactory until stable temperatures are achieved, the generator can place under continuous operation. Protection employed for DC generators are over-current relay and earth fault relay. Reverse power relay is seldom used for generators operating in parallel

No load and load test:

Separate excitation is used for determination of open circuit characteristic or magnetization curve of DC machine. Test connections are made as shown in Figure 1.17 (k). The field current is gradually increased and the readings of field current and open circuit armature voltage are taken while increasing and decreasing the current to plot the characteristic curve as illustrated.

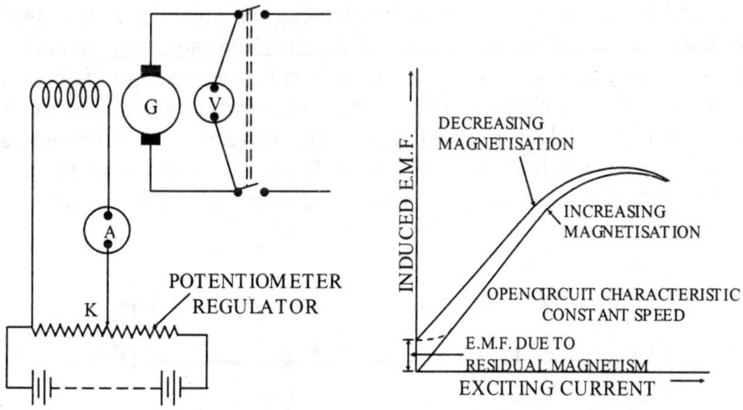

Fig. 1.17 (k): Open circuit characteristic and magnetization curve of a DC machine.

Load characteristic gives relation between load current and terminal voltage of DC generators. Test connection for load test on a separately excited generator is shown in Figure 1.17 (L). The load current is gradually increased, by changing the resistance in the load circuit. The magnitudes of load current and terminal voltages are taken to plot the external characteristic (Refer Figure 1.17 (m).

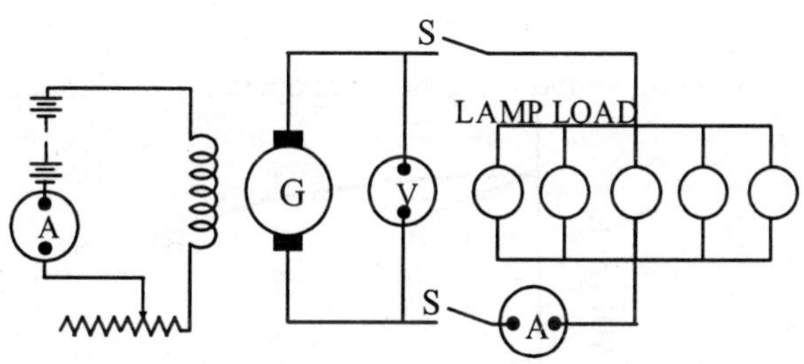

Fig. 1.17 (l): Connection for load test on DC generator.

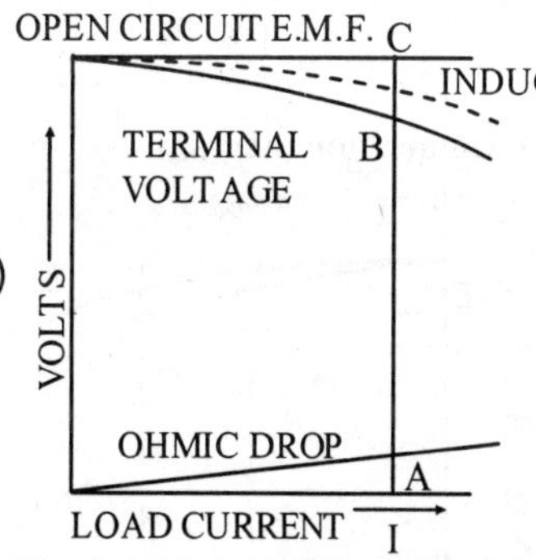

Fig. 1.17 (m): External characteristic curve.

1.18 .PARALLELING AND LOAD SHARING OF DIRECT CURRENT GENERATORS.

Following are the conditions for paralleling DC generators:

1. Generator voltage regulation characteristics must be similar.
2. Polarities of the generator connection must be the same (Positive to positive and negative to negative connection)
3. The terminal voltages of the generators must be equal.

When one generator is fully loaded, the second one will have to be started-up and paralleled with the running generator to meet the increased demand. After the second machine has attained its normal speed, by adjusting the field regulator the voltage of the incoming generator may be kept little higher than the first machine. The new machine can then be switched on to the bus bars. It will absorb some load immediately as its voltage was a few volts above the bus bar voltage. If the field excitation of the machine is increased, a higher voltage will be developed and it will, therefore, take a greater portion of the load. By adjusting the two regulators the load sharing can be controlled. **Speed regulation of the prime mover has no effect in DC machines if it is running in parallel.** DC generators intended for parallel operation must have similar voltage regulation characteristics. Unless this can be secured, proper sharing of the load between generators cannot be ensured automatically. As the field current of any one machine is raised, it takes more and more of the load, until the whole load is taken by it and the other machine running in parallel is unloaded. If the voltage of the loaded machine is increased further the unloaded machine will start to run as a motor, and drive the prime mover to which this generator is coupled, drawing power from the loaded generator. To prevent this, the generators intended for parallel operation should be protected by reverse current relays.

Shunt generators in parallel: Figure 1.18 (a) illustrates the connection diagram of two shunt wound generators operating in parallel. A and B are two similar generators feeding the same bus bars C and D. If A tends to take more than its share of the total load (overloaded), its voltage falls and more load is automatically thrown on B. Also if the driver of one of the generators slows down, the e.m.f of the machine falls until the other generator begins to drive it as a motor. This continuous until it's driver takes over again. The external characteristics of two machines are shown in Figure 1.18 (b). At voltage E, the currents in the generators are Ia and I_b, and the line current is Ia + I_b. To make machine A more of the load, its excitation must be increased to raise its characteristic curve. If a 1000 KW generator and a 500 KW generator have the same regulation curves, the machine will share the load according to their respective capacities.

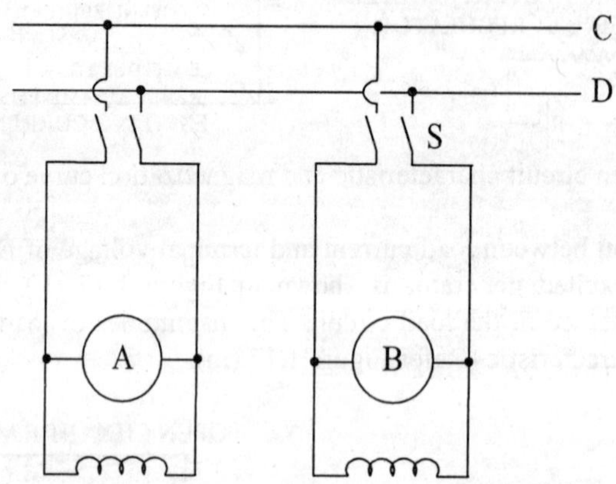

Fig. 1.18 (a): Connection diagram showing two, shunt wound DC generators operating in parallel.

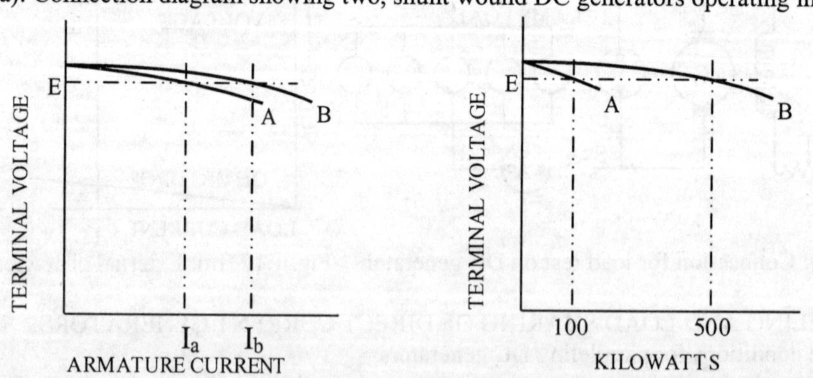

Fig. 1.18 (b): External characteristic of two shunt wound generators operating in parallel.

Figure 1.18 (c) illustrates the connection diagram of two compound wound generators in parallel. The system is connected to the positive bus bar, negative bus bar and equalizing bus bar. The bus connecting series fields in parallel is called equalizer bus. There are two basic functions of equalizer connection; (1) The division of load between generators remains in accordance with their respective ratings; (2) The current in series field does not get reversed in case a generator starts motoring. Suppose that the equalizing bar switch is open, and if the speed of one generator rises slightly, it will take more load, and therefore the current flow in the series field will increase. This will further increase the terminal voltage of the generator and subsequently, the load will increase. This process continues until the second generator runs as a motor instead of as a generator. To avoid this condition an important precaution to be observed is to close the equalizer switch before connecting the generators in parallel provided both generators are running at rated speed. When the equalizing switch is ON, the load current passes through both the series fields as they are in parallel, therefore the voltages of both the sets are same while working in parallel.

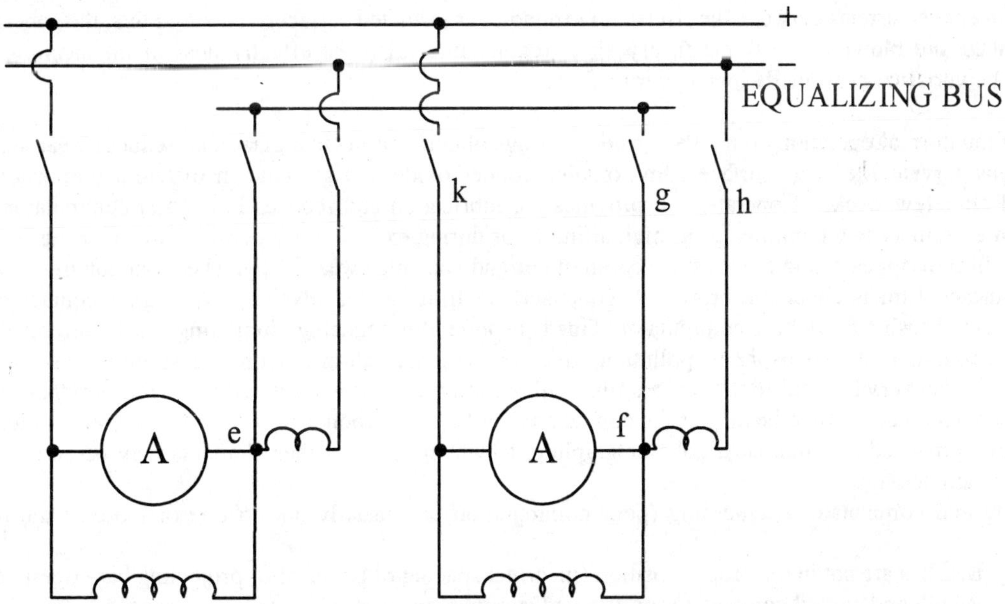

Fig. 1.18 (c): Connection diagram showing two, compound wound DC generators operating in parallel.

Generator having higher field current has more e.m.f and shares more DC load. Hence to increase the load shared by the DC generator, it's field current should be increased by reducing the resistance in the shunt-field circuit. Reversal of polarity of a DC generator is caused by either reversal of direction of rotation or due to reversal of field current.

Operation sequence for paralleling DC generators:

Generator No: 1

1) Ensure that the DC circuit breaker or contactor is opened and the disconnecting link is in connected position.
2) Voltage regulator is in auto.
3) Start the prime mover (Electric motor or Engine).
4) Observe rated speed and rated voltage is attained. Close the DC circuit breaker.
5) Ensure that the generator is loaded.

Generator No: 2

1) Follow procedure 1 to 3 above and ensure that speed and voltage of the second unit is equal to the first unit. If not adjust it.
2) Check the polarity of the incoming generator voltage and the bus bar voltage (across the circuit breaker) through a filament lamp or DC voltmeter. The voltage between positive to positive must be zero. Close the circuit breaker of the incoming generator.
3) If necessary adjust the voltage regulator of the incoming generator to raise direction and loaded generator on lower direction until both generators share total load in proportion to their KW capacity. (Adjust field rheostat for manual control).
4) Before stopping the generator, unload the generator to be stopped by transferring the load to the other generator. Then initiate trip signal to the circuit breaker and shutdown the prime mover.

1.19 MAINTENANCE AND TROUBLE SHOOTING ON DC GENERATORS.

Maintenance of DC machines differs little from that of other rotating electrical machines except for the commutator and its brushes. Proper lubrication must be provided for the bearings, and the machine must be kept clean and dry. In addition, the brushes should be checked periodically for commutation, riding ability, freedom of motion in the brush holders, pressure, and length of the carbon brush. Because of the commutator necks are not insulated and receive full voltage, conducting dust from brush wear or from ventilating air can cause creepage currents between the risers and ground over insulated surfaces. To avoid this, the generator must be cleaned and blown out with clean, dry air at regular intervals. The effectiveness of the cleaning program should be verified occasionally by megger readings.

During the normal operation commutator and slip rings obtain a protective glaze that reduces wear and thereby lengthens service life. This surface film contains copper oxide and graphite in different proportions and is formed after few weeks of operation. It provides the lubrication and reduces brush and commutator wear. In areas of extremely low humidity, as at high altitudes or during extended dry periods of cold winter months the surface film disappears, and the brushes, commutator and slip rings wear badly. The most common colour of a good surface film is chocolate brown. A good surface film has an advantage of higher contact resistance between the brush face and the commutator. This is beneficial in reducing circulating brush currents that occur during commutation. Atmospheric pollution, like oil vapours, salt-air, hydrogen sulphide gas, or silicone vapours is also very harmful to the surface film. Oil pollution is indicated by, a thick black film that cause poor brush contact and excessive heating at the conducting spots. The carbon brushes used with commutator and slip rings are composed of lampblack, coke or graphite, to which various other elements may be added to obtain special characteristic.

Sparking and commutator bar burning (poor commutation) are usually due to one or more of the following causes

1. Brushes are not in the proper position (incorrect spacing of brushes) or projecting bar-edge-mica
2. Rough and burned commutator or grooved commutator
3. Poor brush contact or worn brushes or wrong size or grade, incorrect spacing of brushes.
4. Stikking or chattering brushes, worn brushes replaced by wrong size.
5. Vibration due to poor alignment or inadequate foundation or unbalanced rotor.
6. Short-circuited turns on the commutating or compensating fields.
7. Open or very high resistance joints between the commutator neck and the coil leads
8. An open or broken armature coil
9. Short-circuited or reversed main field coils.

Trouble shooting on DC generators:

(a) Shorted shunt field turns: Shorted turns in the field coil of a DC machine can be located by applying 120 or 230 volts AC supply to the field circuit after removing the armature. Figure 1.19 (a) shows the test circuit. Measure the voltage drop across each field coil by using an AC voltmeter. If voltage across every coil is equal, it can be considered that there is no short-circuit in the field coils. If voltage drop in any one of the coils is considerably less than the average, then the coil is defective. Faulty coil should be removed and replaced. Assume that the stator has 4 poles and 240 volts AC is applied, 60 volts will indicate across each coil.

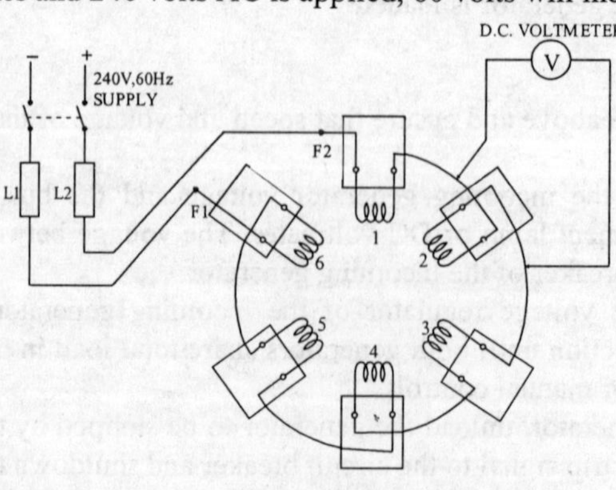

Fig. 1.19 (a): Tracing shorted field coils in a DC generator winding.

(b) Tracing open circuit: Open circuit in the field coil of a DC machine can be located by using a continuity tester or multi meter. To segregate the exact coil, connect the field coil to rated DC supply voltage (after removing the armature) as shown in Figure 1.19 (b). Measure voltage between positive terminal and terminals of each coil by using a DC voltmeter. The coil with open circuit will indicate full supply voltage across it. The other coils will show lesser voltage corresponding to the IR drop.

(c) Tracing earth fault: Earth fault in the field coil of a DC machine can be located by using 500 V megger. To identify the exact location of fault, connect the field coil at rated DC voltage or less than rated voltage. Measure the voltage drop between each coil and the pole shoe as shown in Figure 1.19 (c). The coil, which indicates very low voltage or zero voltage between its terminals and earth is likely to have an earth fault. Earth fault by puncture of insulation calls for replacement of the coil.

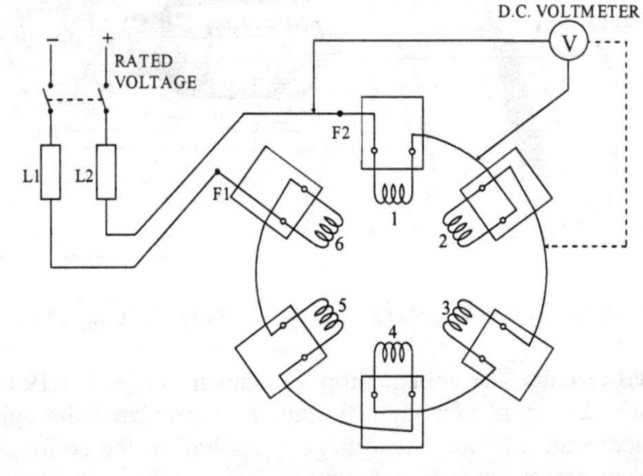

Fig. 1.19 (b): Locating open field coils in a DC generator winding.

(d) Polarity check: Apply rated DC voltage to the field coils. The alternative poles should have opposite polarity. This can be checked by, using a compass. Alternatively, take two soft iron pieces. Keep one end of each piece on neighboring poles and the other end bring close to each other. If neighboring poles are of opposite polarity, the soft iron pieces will attract each other.

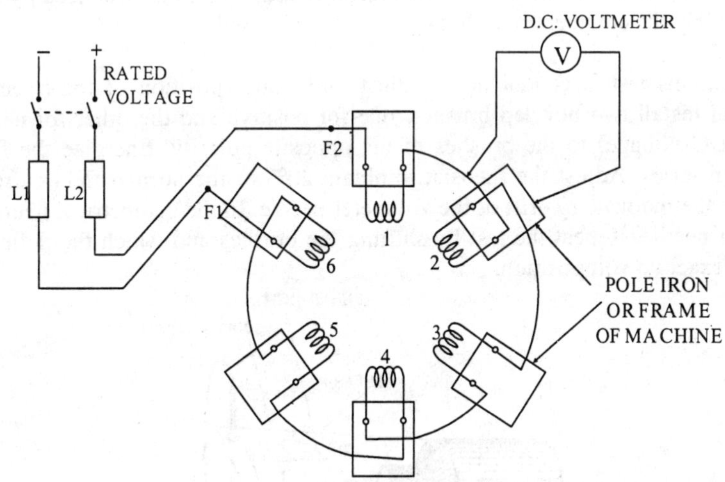

Fig. 1.19 (c): Locating earth fault in shunt-field coils of DC generator.

(e) Testing armature for grounded circuit: Armature growler is used to test the armature loops or grounded, open or short circuits. To test the armature for ground, place the armature on to the growler as shown in Figure 1.19 (d) and switch on the test probe circuit. Hold one test probe on the armature shaft or iron core and slide the other probe over and around the commutator. The test light will go ON when one or more loops or the commutator are grounded to the armature shaft, in which case the armature should be repaired or replaced.

(f) Testing armature for short circuit: Place the armature above the growler as shown in Figure 1.19 (e) and switch on to energize the growler coil winding (230 V, AC). The current flow through the coil windings creates a magnetic field, which induces a voltage in the armature under test. Rotate the armature by hand. Hacksaw blade placed above the armature will vibrate if there is any shorted turn in the armature.

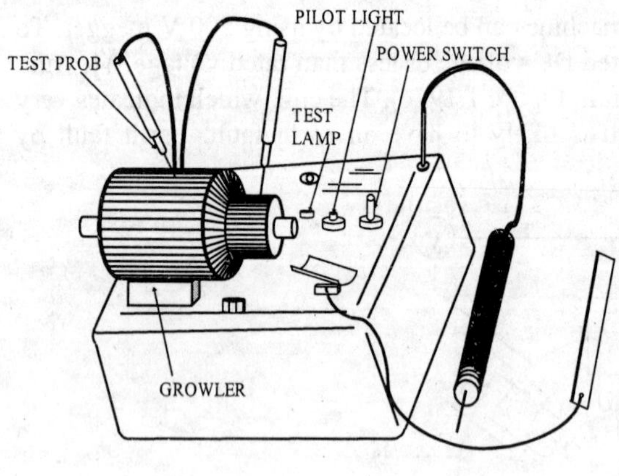

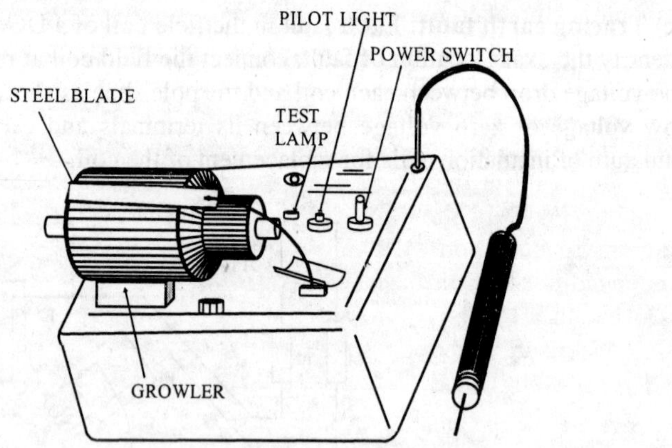

Fig. 1.19 (d): Ground test on armature of a DC generator. Fig. 1.19 (e): Tracing shorted turns on armature.

(g) Testing armature for open circuit: The voltage drop test shown in Figure 1.19 (f) reveals open circuits or high resistance in the armature. A current of about 10 ampere is circulated through the armature circuit by adjusting the variable resistance control knob. The voltage is applied to the commutator across diametrically opposite poles. The voltage drops across adjacent commutator bars are measured by sensitive wide scale milli-voltmeter or digital multi-meter. The readings are taken between each consecutive pairs of commutator bars. The readings should be within ± 5% of average reading. If any particular reading is high, it indicates loose end soldering or open circuited coil.

(h) Polarity check on armature: Heavy sparking on load in a DC machine is generally due to the reversal of polarity of inter-pole winding or commutating pole windings. If such sparking is reduced by shunting any of the inter-pole winding definitely the connection of that inter-pole is reversed.

(i) Inductive kick test: This test is conducted to adjust the neutral position of the brushes if it is shifted. Remove the brushes and install two beveled brushes, one for positive and the other for negative. Connect an analogue multi-meter (DC voltage) to the brushes of the opposite polarity. Energize the field through a DC source with a rheostat in series. Adjust the rheostat to obtain 20% of the normal field current. Switch off the field supply and observe the momentary drift of the voltmeter needle. In the geometrical neutral position there is no kick in the voltmeter needle. Repeat the test by shifting the brushes and watch the deflection. Finally shift the brush holders to the exact no volt position.

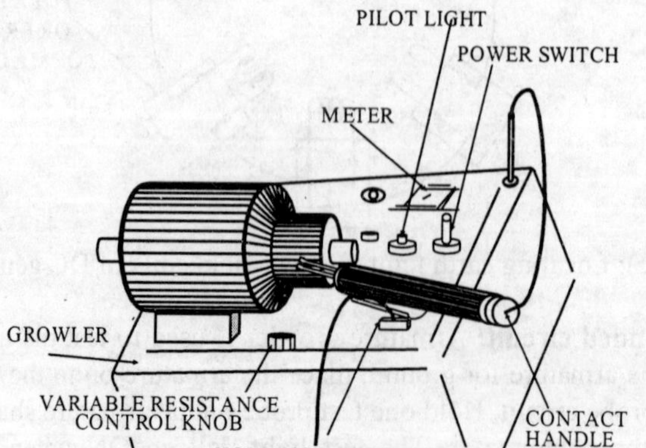

Fig. 1.19 (f): Tracing open circuit on armature of a DC generator.

1.20 SELECTION AND APPLICATION OF DC AIR CIRCUIT BREAKERS.

The more important source of DC power is motor-generators, rectifiers, rotary converters and battery banks etc. General voltage classes for dc systems in common use are; 250, 750, 1000, 1500 and 3000 Volts. The selected air circuit breaker must have an assigned continuous current rating equal to or greater than the maximum continuous load current expected-to-be encountered on the circuit. Transitory over-currents of short duration, i. e, motor starting current, are permitted to exceed the continuous current rating of the breaker.

The proposed air circuit breaker should have an assigned interrupting rating in amperes equal to or greater than the fault current in amperes capable of being developed on the circuit on which it is to be applied. Current limiting breakers should be applied with the specified limits of rate-of-current rise. For reasons of remote / automatic operation a DC air circuit breaker is normally electrically operated, but it may also be manually operated provided the short-circuit current does not exceed 50 KA. Following are the rules governing the use of DC circuit breakers:

1. Each DC source and contributing source must be protected by a circuit breaker having an interrupting rating equal to or greater than the maximum short-circuit current capable of being developed by the source.
2. Each circuit breaker must be equipped with an instantaneous trip device set as low as possible, in any event not over five times the rated continuous current of the source.
3. For protection of personnel, the circuit breaker must be enclosed and arranged for remote operation.
4. After each fault trip, the circuit breaker must be inspected and repaired, if necessary, before again placing in service.
5. *AC breakers should not be used for DC applications.*
6. Semi-high speed breakers may not be applied on a circuit capable of developing 250 KA or more at 0.025 seconds.
7. High-speed breakers may not be applied on a circuit capable of developing 250 KA or more at 0.008 seconds.

There are four distinct types of DC air circuit breakers:

(1) General purpose breaker: These types of breakers are used extensively at voltages up to 250 V on a wide variety of circuits with short circuit currents of 100 KA. This breaker has an interrupting time of 0.03 to 0.04 seconds and generally will not limit the fault current. For example, Field discharge breaker.

(2) Semi-high speed breaker: These types are employed on 250 to 1000 V circuits requiring either a high continuous current rated breaker or a device to limit the fault current to permissible values or both. Maximum available fault current may not exceed 125 KA. Development of high-speed breaker has made the use of semi-high speed breakers obsolete.

(3) High speed breaker: Suitable for 250 to 1000 volts DC circuits capable of developing very large values of short circuit currents. The breaker is designed for application on systems with initial rate-of-current-rise of 15 million amperes per second and below; if applied above this rating the maximum available fault current must not exceed.

(4) High speed anode breaker: Connected to the anode of a power rectifier unit. It trips automatically only on reverse current and starts reduction of current in 0.008.

Field discharge circuit breaker is a two pole general purpose DC breaker without overload device but with an auxiliary discharge contact, which short-circuits the field of a brush-type generator or motor through a resistor immediately preceding the opening of the main contacts. This same contact disconnects the field from the short-circuiting resistor at the instant immediately following the closing of the main contacts. A field breaker will protect the field winding from the high recovery voltage normally experienced on open or closing a highly inductive field circuit. Field breakers are generally rated for 1000 volts DC and are available in continuous ratings of 1200 A to 12,000 A. The interrupting capacity is adequate to safely interrupt any fault current on DC circuits where the rate of rise of fault current is 15 million (15×10^6) amperes.

DC breakers are built in single pole construction for use on grounded systems and in two-pole construction for two-wire ungrounded DC systems. Breakers are manufactured either in fixed version or draw out version similar to the one illustrated in figure (a) of section 3.23. The draw-out cradle serves as a disconnecting device and eliminates the dangers attendant to opening a disconnect switch under load, since the breaker cannot be racked to the test or disconnected position until the breaker is switched off. Draw-out design permits quick removal of the breaker for easier, safer, more efficient maintenance. In a manual closing breaker, a pair of powerful springs actually closes the contacts. The operator provides energy to the spring, by pulling the semi-flush closing handle downward through approximately 90 degrees. The initial 80 degrees of handle motion fully charges the closing springs and the remaining motion releases the spring energy to drive the contacts smoothly to the closed position. Electrically operated breakers are closed by an AC / DC electric motor driving a simple toggle linkage. This mechanism produces very fast closing, which minimizes arcing when closing against load. The total closing time is 0.1 to 0.2 seconds.

The breaker is held in the closed position magnetically. The magnetic holding device, known as flux shifting magnet, also embodies the high speed tripping function. In tripping, the fault current flowing through the breaker sets up a magnetic flux, which reduces the magnetic hold-closed force and allows the breaker contacts to open under the action of a powerful opening spring. DC breakers are mechanically and electrically trip-free at all stages of closing travel. Shunt tripping of the breaker is accomplished by closure of a contact to energize a trip coil, which bucks down the holding magnet coil flux. Electrically operated breakers are equipped with a non-repeat closing relay and a manual maintenance-closing handle. The closing mechanism and the holding coil on the flux-shifting magnet are wired to a terminal block or to draw-out type secondary disconnect contacts. When an AC control source is used, a rectifier is mounted on the breaker to supply DC to the holding coil.

Each breaker is equipped with a set of main contacts and a set of arcing contacts. During each closing operation of the breaker a high pressure wiping action is imparted to the moving contacts as the contact pressure is applied. The contact pressure is supplied by self-aligning stainless steel springs. Each main moving contact has an individual springs as does each arcing contact. Arc chutes consisting of a number of steel cross plates or ceramic cross plates mounted in a moulded housing, are provided for quenching the arc produced during operation of the breaker. DC breakers employ the magnetic blow out principle whereby the flux is forced upward in the arc chute by a transverse magnetic flux. This blow out flux is produced by, a single turn coil on each side of the arc chute. These, blowout coils are in the circuit at all times maintaining blow out flux to act on the arc from the instant it forms. This arc quencher is very effective at low values of load current as well as on fault currents. A dual over-current device incorporating delayed over current, instantaneous over-current, and reverse current -protection is provided in one pole of the breaker.

1.21 PREVENTIVE MAINTENANCE TESTING OF AC GENERATORS.

Following commissioning, each machine should regularly undergone certain preventive maintenance inspections and tests. The most essential tests are discussed below.

Insulation resistance measurements of the stator, rotor, exciter armature and exciter field circuit.

These measurements are taken with a 1-2.5-5 KV megger. To avoid any error in the measurement that may be introduced by charges still remaining on the insulation. Each winding under test should first be earthed at-least two minutes. The insulation resistance measurements should be taken after 15 seconds and 60 seconds interval of time, counted off from the moment the full megger potential is applied to the winding. This is for plotting absorption factor curves. The value R60/R15 is the absorption factor, which will indicate whether the winding is in a fit condition or not. At a temperature between 15 and 30°C, a dry winding will have an absorption factor 1.2 to 2. Moist winding or dirty winding will have an absorption factor 1 or less. In the course of a general overhaul, the insulation resistance of each phase or parallel phase branch in the stator winding is measured with all the other phases shorted to ground. The measured value is compared with previous test values. However the insulation resistance of the rotor winding should not be less than 0.5 Meg-ohm, that of the excitation circuit at least 1 Meg-ohm, and that of the exciter armature winding at least 0.5 Meg-ohm. Figure (a) of section 1.13 illustrates the circuit connections used in measuring the insulation resistance of generator stator winding.

Measurement of the insulation resistance of the insulated liners placed under the bearing pedestals.

In vertical shaft waterwheel generators insulated liners are used to electrically isolate the stator frame from the brackets and thrust bearing. It should be checked frequently. Weak insulation may lead to the appearance of bearing currents. These currents may damage the bearings because they will pass through the shaft journal or thrust plate, the oil film, and the bearing liners or pads if allowed to find a closed path back to the shaft.

In turbo generators, horizontal shaft water wheel generators and synchronous condensers, the bearing pedestal at the exciter end, as well as the exciter bearing pedestals, are isolated from the bedplate by a sheet of insulation.

To avoid bearing troubles due to bearing current produced in the shaft, the condition of the insulating liners should be checked regularly. Two methods are used: (1) The insulation resistance of the insulated liner or sheet should not be less than 1 Meg-ohm; (2) First the voltage across the ends of the turbo generator shaft is measured. Then the oil films on both the bearings, are shunted by, jumpers and the voltage across the insulating pad is measured (between the bearing pedestal and the bed plate). If the voltmeter readings are identical then the insulating liners are satisfactory.

In the case of a vertical shaft water wheel generator, when determining the condition of the insulation at the thrust bearing and upper guide bearings, the voltage across the generator shaft is measured. Measurements of the leakage current to earth may be taken to determine whether or not a potential has been set up along the generator shaft.

Winding resistance of stator, rotor, exciter field winding, Permanent magnet generator:
By using a micro-ohm meter or ammeter-voltmeter method (as described in section 1.13) the resistance of stator winding, rotor winding, exciter field winding, permanent magnet generator winding etc shall be measured and compared with the test report value. The value may differ due to winding temperature, turn-to-turn short circuit as well as unsatisfactory solder joints (hotspot).

AC high voltage test / DC high voltage test:
After every general overhaul before placing the machine in to service, the windings are subjected to a stepped up voltage test (as described in section 1.13) to reveal any weakness in to insulation that cannot be detected by external inspection or an insulation resistance test. The stator winding is tested with AC voltage 1.5 times (phase to earth) the rated voltage for one-minute duration. Besides this, DC voltage equal to 2 to 2.5 times the rated voltage of the machine under test is applied for one-minute between the stator winding and earth. A high-rectified voltage test serves as a more effective means for checking the end windings since it leads to a more uniform distribution of the potential in them. During this test each phase is measured for its leakage current in microampere in order to judge the presence of defects in the insulation of the end windings. High voltage testing of water-cooled generator windings differ somewhat from the test discussed above. In water cooled generator the water must be kept in continuous circulation during the test, otherwise the water in the hoses will rise to a temperature of 95°C and damage the header packing of the winding. **It is practically impossible to conduct a DC high voltage test on a water-cooled generator.** When carrying out the preventive maintenance test the exciter winding can be subjected to an AC test voltage of 1000 V for one minute between winding to earth.

Air-gap measurement:
Correct centering of the rotor within the bore of the stator is a matter of significant importance. The difference between the air-gaps of any two points diametrically opposite to each other should not exceed 10% of the average air-gap in a turbo-generator or 20% in a water wheel generator. Air-gap feeler gauges of various designs are used for this purpose. Air-gap difference in excess of the values given above can considerably unbalance the magnetic field and may become the cause of increased vibration and damage of the unit.

1.22 GENERATOR SUPERVISION DURING NORMAL OPERATION.

The method of supervision used in the operation of generators depends on the kind of power station hydel, thermal, diesel etc. A general external inspection is made in each shift. Routine maintenance of the exciter commutator and collector ring of separately excited alternator is carried out once in a day. Work involved blow-off of the commutator and slip rings with clean dry compressed air, replacement of the brushes or adjustment of the brush pressure when the need arises. The temperature of the stator winding in air-cooled or indirectly gas cooled generators should be checked once every shift, particularly peak load hours. The temperature should be measured at intervals of one hour for directly and indirectly gas cooled turbo-generators. Following hourly reading should record on the shift log sheet: (a) Active and reactive load of the station; (b) The MW load shared by each generator; (c) Stator and rotor current of each generator; (d) Generator terminal voltage and power factor.

Machine hall operator of the turbo-generator has to attend the following works:
(1) Maintain and watch-over the bearings of the load sharing generators including bearing oil level and temperature etc.
(2) Check and adjust the air temperature and the gas cooler, water temperature, water pressure etc.
(3) Maintain and watch-over the gas oil system of a hydrogen-cooled generator. See that coolant flow is continuously maintained in the circuit of a liquid cooled generator. Check hydrogen pressure and purity.
(4) Keep watch-over the operation of the annunciation and indications.

Generator operator in the machine hall should inform the control engineer of any abnormality that arises in the machine, for example, an increase in vibration, excessive sparking at the brushes, a failure in the flow of cooling liquid, appearance of smoke or flame etc.
Because of some emergency, failure to maintain the necessary operating conditions such as atmospheric disturbances, sudden overloading or short time overload, momentary voltage dip or power swing, overloading excitation system, failure of cooling system etc, it become necessary to continue operation under strict watching of the defective unit. For emergency shutdown of the generating unit Emergency pushbutton is provided in the machine hall control panel. In order to prevent it being depressed accidentally, "ATTENTION! MACHINE DANGER" pushbutton is fitted with a guard that easily collapse when intentionally pressed.

To provide operative communication between the machine hall and main control room visual display units (VDU) connected to the local area networks (LAN) are being used. Computers connected with (DCS) Distributed control system [refer figure (L) in section 1.1] can also be used for communication as well as status display with mimics of each generating unit.
To fight a fire in a generator (either indirect hydrogen cooling or direct water or air-cooling) use is made of carbon dioxide. The CO2 is taken from the cylinders connected together to form a bank. In the event of a fire in the generator, the heat detectors initiate automatic signal to energize the solenoid valve to discharge the carbon dioxide bank. In order to prevent the generator shaft from developing a bend during one-sided heating due to fire, keep the machine rotating at a slow speed (about one-tenth rated speed.). This may also be done in a turbo generator with the electrical turning gear by means of which the set is slowly rotated for inspection after overhaul.

1.23 ABNORMAL CONDITIONS AND FAULTS ON ALTERNATORS.

Abnormal conditions and faults, which requires automatic shutdown of the generator are as follows:
(1) Stator earth fault: Medium voltage generators are either resistance or reactance earthed neutral system. When one of the stator phase faults to earth, the voltage of the other two phases may rise as high as 1.73 times the rated phase-to neutral voltage or equal to phase-to-phase voltage. At the same time neutral of the stator winding acquires a potential equal to the phase voltage. If the earth fault current exceeds the set value, the earth fault relay will operate to shutdown the generator.

(2): Earth fault in the excitation circuit. Earth fault may probably develop in the exciter, field breaker and field rheostat of separately excited generators, or some other piece of equipment in the excitation circuit due to ageing, deposit of dirt, due to mechanical faults developed in the exciter etc. This is considered as an abnormal condition. Field ground relay demonstrated in section 6.17 of Chapter # 6 can be used for protection against field ground.

(3) Earth fault in the rotor winding: Such a fault may arise in the collector rings, in the leads running up to the rotor winding, in the end windings or in the slots portion of the rotor winding. A fault in the rotor winding can be located by measuring the voltage drop between one of the collector rings and the rotor core with the rotor winding energized. If the voltmeter reads absolutely zero it indicates that the fault is in the ring of the lead connecting it to the winding. If the fault exists at some point along the winding it may be located approximately from the ratio of the voltage obtained in the voltmeter during the test. In locating the fault after the rotor has been withdrawn from the stator, it is possible to apply a 24 Volts DC supply across the ends of the rotor shaft through a variable rheostat. A milli-voltmeter is connected, one lead to the collector ring and the other lead to a probe which is held against the core and is moved along the rotor, very near to fault the milli-voltmeter read its lowest value.

However, single fault to earth is not a direct dangerous. Occurrence of another fault to earth in the rotor circuit may lead in to considerable flow of current, vibration, unbalancing of the generator field, and to serious damage. In water wheel generators (Hydroelectric generators) owing to their silent pole construction, the rotor can become so unbalanced magnetically that the air-gap cannot be maintained. Hence the first fault itself considered as an abnormal condition. Field ground relay demonstrated in section 6.17 or method illustrated in figure 1.24 is used for detecting rotor earth fault.

(4) Loss of excitation of paralleled generators: If a parallel running generator losses its excitation, the rotor field will drop below that of the revolving stator field, determined by the frequency of the other generator running in parallel with the given unit. Generator stator will now draw its exciting current (no load current) from the bus. By the magnetic field produced by the stator winding circulating current of slip frequency are induced in the rotor core, and damper winding (for silent pole rotor). This is called asynchronous running, during which the machine develops a resisting torque and run as an induction generator capable of carrying certain active power loads. **When the generator losses its excitation, the rotor ammeter and voltmeter will indicate zero reading. The pointer of the KVAr / MVAr meter will swing over to the negative side of the scale because the generator is drawing reactive power.** Similarly, power factor meter will show leading. Stator ammeter will show that the machine carries a current greater than normal. Hence the circuit breaker must be tripped the instant the excitation fails. Loss of excitation relay / Field failure relay employed for protection is demonstrated in section 6.10 of Chapter # 6.

(5) Power swings: On the occurrence of a heavy disturbance in the system a decrease in static and dynamic stability may results in power swings and tripping of the generator circuit breaker by the respective protections. During such moments the generators will begin to rumble in a characteristic similar to pulsating manner at the same time the voltmeter will oscillate at a low value of voltage, while the stator ammeter show that the current surging (hunting) to high values. Only the immediate remedy is to reduce the active load (KW / MW) on this unit, of the machine showing instability. Generator backup protection relay demonstrated in section 6.19 protect the generator during out of step conditions.

(6) Unbalanced load: An unbalanced load may appear when the conductor breaks on one of the power transmission lines. A generator operating under such unbalanced conditions will experience increased heating and abnormal vibration. Negative phase sequence relay demonstrated in section 6.12 of Chapter # 6, is for protecting the generator under unbalanced condition. Effect of unbalanced load is given in Q2 of section 1.27.

1.24 MONITORING OPERATION OF GENERATOR COOLING SYSTEM.

Air, hydrogen, and water are used as cooling media for generators. Air-cooling may be provided with an open circuit or closed circuit system. Hydrogen cooling is employed for cooling generators with a rating above 25 MVA. Hydroelectric generators are water-cooled generators. If the heat is removed by a gas or liquid (water or oil), this is called direct cooling. In the indirect cooling system, the heat of the generator is removed by external cooling system such as air or hydrogen.

Cooling systems of machines are identified as follows:

1. Generators, whose stator and rotor windings are, respectively, directly and indirectly cooled with hydrogen.
2. Generators, whose rotor winding is directly cooled with hydrogen and stator winding is directly cooled with water.
3. Generators, whose rotor and stator windings are directly cooled with hydrogen.

If a leak allowed to-develop at the joints of hydrogen-cooled turbo-generators, in their sheathing will lead to-excessive hydrogen losses. To detect the points of leakage, all the welded seams and joints in the sheath should be wetted with a soap solution with the pressure of the hydrogen within the machine raised to its highest possible value. Soap bubbles will usually form wherever the leakage is excessive. Sweating of gas coolers may occur incase when driers, filled with calcium chloride or coarse grain silica, become exhausted. This condition is indicated by water seen dripping in the glass and appearance of respective warning signal. Handheld portable gas leak detector with sensing probe can also be used.

The purity of the hydrogen is of great importance. During generator operation, the hydrogen in the machine should have a purity not less than 96 – 98%; an oxygen content not greater than 1.2%, and a moisture content not exceed 10 – 15 gram / m^3. The relative humidity of the cold gas should not exceed 85%. If the purity is reduced it leads to less efficient cooling and greater heating of the active parts and a drop in efficiency. A drop in hydrogen purity to 92 – 93% necessitates blowing out of the generator with pure electrolytic hydrogen having a purity of 99.5%. In thermal power stations with hydrogen-cooled turbo-generators, electrolytic hydrogen generating equipment is installed especially for this purpose.

Constant monitoring of the purity of the hydrogen is accomplished by using an electric gas analyzer, while the pressure is watched with the aid of a pressure differential gauge. Daily analysis of the composition of the gas samples taken from given points in each machine is essential. Hydrogen containing 5 to 75 percent oxygen forms an explosive mixture that can be ignited by a spark. To guard against a hydrogen explosion within a generator, the hydrogen must be maintained at a pressure greater than the atmosphere and its purity should not be allowed to drop below 92%.

In operating and repairing hydrogen-cooled machine, it is necessary to make certain measures to ensure safety. No work should be done with naked flames. Smoking is strictly prohibited. Carbon dioxide cylinders with rubber hoses may be used for fire fighting. No inflammable or explosive materials are allowed to be stored in the machine hall. It is also forbidden to carry out chemical analysis of the air or do any arc or gas welding in the machine hall if the air contains 3% hydrogen.

For filling hydrogen or displacing hydrogen from the generator is carried out with the aid of carbon dioxide. The operation takes from 8 to 15 hours to complete. If it is necessary to changeover from hydrogen to air-cooling or vice versa in a generator carbon dioxide is used to displace the hydrogen.

1.25 EMERGENCIES AND TROUBLES IN POWER STATIONS AND SUBSTATIONS.

Particular importance in handling power system emergencies is strict operating discipline and the efficiency and knowledge of the operational team. When an emergency occurs in a power system, it is the duty of the shift in-charge to supervise its elimination. Following immediate measures are recommended during an emergency.

1. Switch off any equipment whose further operation directly endangers the life of human beings.
2. Switch off any piece of equipment that fails in service and then take immediate measures to maintain the rest of the equipment in normal operation.
3. Disconnect from supply any piece of equipment that is in danger of a breakdown or damage.
4. Immediately put in service an operating generator, which has obviously been falsely disconnected.
5. Restore supply to the station and substation auxiliaries.
6. In case of load demand or instructions from load dispatch center start-up or switch-in the requisite standby or reserve equipment.

A considerable percentage of emergencies, and accident that occur in power system is of due to following reasons:

(a) Wrong operation due to the result of a mistake of an operator.
(b) Insufficient knowledge or improper training.
(c) Lack of attentiveness / mistakes in performing the given operation.
(d) Lack of firm knowledge of the operating procedures.
(e) Failure to follow the safety rules for handling apparatus.
(f) Lack of training in handling portable fire fighting equipments.

In the event of an emergency or failure, the first task of the shift personnel is to gain an accurate picture of what has actually happened, this being done by reading the indications of the instruments on the respective control boards (or DCS / SMS in modern power stations and substations), taking notice of the warning and alarms (annunciation windows), and looking at the relay targets (or status mimic display in digital relays), which have been brought in to action.

Certain cause of emergencies, which arise in power stations may lead to full or partial loss of auxiliary supply, causing the disconnection of one or several generators and even the entire station. Most of the power stations have standby auto-start diesel generator sets to meet the emergency requirements of AC auxiliary power supply.

Emergencies, which develop because of low station battery voltage, can be very severe. Usually two chargers with 2 battery banks for power plant generating system and another dual charger for HV/EHV substation attached with the power station. Station battery system has means for automatically maintaining DC voltage, charging the batteries and sharing station DC load.

Handling of emergencies:

Minor defects may lead to breakdowns, destruction of the equipment, or fatal accident if not rectified on the spot. Besides taking every possible precaution to prevent an emergency the operator must act independently and immediately as required by the operating instructions and restore normal operation of the electrical equipment and circuit should an emergency occur within this equipment. Actions should be based on the following:

(1) Immediate action should be taken to protect human lives and the equipment from impending danger, should this be impossible, the installation or equipment should be switched off on an emergency basis. A generator can be stopped by, pressing emergency pushbutton if there is no other alternative.

(2) It is forbidden to interfere with the operation of automatic devices and controls. Never bypass any interlocks in the control circuitry and if it does to meet the emergency, it should be displayed in the panel.

(3) Measure should be taken to continue operation of the units not effective and all power station and substation auxiliaries still remaining in service and also switch on or start-up the standby equipment.

(4) To judge quickly as what has happened and where, and estimate the nature and extend of the emergency. The operator should immediately check the indicating instruments, note the alarms displayed, protective relays operated (flag or LED), and look for external visible signs of the trouble if any. While handling the emergency the operator should act fast and precisely, but without panic or excitement as this may impede or aggravate the situation.

(5) When no means of communication with the shift control engineer is possible, the operator must inform and coordinate his step-by-step actions with those of the associated or controlling stations. Disturbance or emergency may be brought in to the notice of the superiors.

A list of the mistakes that lead to emergencies and damages/accidents within the power stations and substations are given below.

(a) Opening of an isolator while it is carrying the load current.
(b) Energizing a circuit in which the safety earthing conductors, have not yet been removed.
(c) Earthing of a live circuit.
(d) Wrong switch-off of operating and essential auxiliaries.
(e) Lack of knowledge of the operating guidelines.
(f) Accidental failure of DC control power.
(g) Disturbing off-load tap changer when the transformer is in service

A list of emergencies caused by shortcomings in the circuit configurations and by defects in the electrical apparatus are given below:

1. Unsatisfactory sectionalization of the auxiliary supply system.
2. Incorrect selection of key position in key interlocked circuit breakers.
3. Unsatisfactory condition of the protections provided for the auxiliary supply system.
4. Developing earth fault in the DC control power.
5. Defects in Uninterrupted power supply units used for precision drives and circuit breaker spring charging motors.

1.26 DUTIES OF THE OPERATIVE PERSONNEL IN POWERSTATIONS / SUBSTATIONS.

Primary duties and responsibilities of a power plant and associated substation operator is for carrying out the following functions:

1. Switching operation of the equipment in normal and emergency cases.
2. Providing shutdown, and apply the safety earthing and issue permit to work.
3. Starting and synchronizing generators to the bus.
4. Divide the load amongst all paralleled generators in proportion to their MVA ratings. If all generators are same capacity the load will be shared equally to attain the most economical conditions of operation.

5. Watch the indications of the instruments provided on the main control and local control boards and on the unit and station service boards and control panels. Modern power stations with Distributed control system and Substation management system the required information is displayed in the computer.
6. Replace fuses, indication lamps etc. effect minor repairs and remedy defects requiring immediate attention.
7. Render first aid to any person who has suffered an injury or burns. Apply artificial respiration to a victim of electric shock who has lost consciousness.
8. Take immediate measure to fight a fire, which breaks out and inform fire station if necessary.
9. Ensure that all lighting including emergency lights, ventilation system and air conditioning system are maintained in a good condition.
10. See that the equipments are operating with adequate lubrication and the cooling system is functioning properly.

According to standard practice, personnel responsible for operation of electrical equipments in power stations and substations are obliged to know:

a) Operating procedures of electrical equipments.
b) The rules for safety and prevention of fire.
c) Maintain shift log sheet.
d) Emergency procedures.
e) Layout of the main structures, premises, function etc.
f) Single line diagram of the complete system
g) Mimic diagram of the switchgear.
h) Layout diagram of transformer oil – water-cooling system, airline system, generator cooling system, fire fighting water mains and sprinkling system, carbon dioxide bank etc.
i) Familiar with control and protection circuit, synchronizing circuit etc.
j) Electrical performance characteristics and permissible limits of loading and temperature rise of the equipment such as generators, transformers, batteries etc.

The person in-charge of the keys must strictly comply with the standing instructions for handling the keys. The keys are classified as follows.

1. Premises keys; Example: keys of main gate, buildings, stores, tool room, laboratory etc.
2. Switchgear keys; Example: keys of switchgear cubicles, cells and control cubicles etc.
3. Electromechanical interlock keys; Example: Disconnectors, Earth switches, changeover switches etc.
4. Padlock keys: Example: Keys for locking isolator and earth switch operating mechanism, CO_2 bank etc.

1.27 PRACTICAL QUESTIONS AND ANSWERS ON POWER GENERATION.

Q1: What do you mean by brushless alternator?

Ans: Brush is a sliding contact, generally made of carbon, used to provide connection between to rotating parts of machines. Three-phase AC generator without slip rings and carbon brushes are said to be brushless alternator. It consists of exciter, rotating rectifier assembly and main generator assembly. Low voltage generators are self excited generators and high voltage generators are permanent magnet/pilot excited generators.

Q2: What will be the effect of unbalanced load current in a three-phase alternating current generator?

Ans: A three-phase balanced load produces a reaction field, which is constant and rotates synchronously with the rotor field system. Any unbalanced condition can be resolved in to positive, negative and zero sequence components. Positive sequence component is similar to normal balanced load. The negative sequence component produces a flux, which cuts the rotor at twice the rotational velocity thereby inducing double frequency currents in the field system and in the rotor body. The resulting eddy-currents are very large and cause severe heating of the rotor. Negative sequence relays (measuring unbalanced phase currents) are employed to trip the generator circuit breaker to prevent overheating of the winding. Zero sequence components will not produce the armature reaction. Twisting or bending of the main magnetic field of a motor or generator is called armature reaction. Armature reaction is proportional to armature current. Negative sequence relay is demonstrated in section 6.12 of Chapter # 6.

Q3: What will be the effect of double earth fault in a AC generator rotor?
Ans: Since the DC system of a generator is not earthed, if an earth fault occurs no fault current will flow and the need for quick action will not be evident. Danger arises if a second earth fault occurs at a separate point in the DC system because a parallel path will form to divert current. This will cause the rotor winding to burn, moreover the flux and the attracting force is large on one pole and weak on the opposite pole. The result is an unbalanced force, which in large machine may be the order of hundreds of tons. This force is rotating with the rotor and hence produces a violent vibration, which may damage bearing surfaces or even displace the rotor to cause it to foul the stator. Rotor ground fault relay is employed to annunciate when an earth fault is developed in large generators. Rotor earth fault protection / Field ground protection is demonstrated in section 6.17 of Chapter # 6.

Q4: What is the effect of turn-to-turn short circuit in an alternating current generator rotor winding?
Ans: Short-circuiting of turns in the main field winding would tend to cause the automatic voltage regulator to raise the level of the field current. If not detected this would result in increased heating of the healthy positions of the field circuit. A single turn of the rotor winding being short-circuited or a single diode of brushless alternator becoming open circuited would produce no significant change in the level of excitation. Short-circuited turns on the rotor tend to cause vibration of the generator

Q5: What is the effect of failure of excitation in an AC generator?
Ans: Failure of the field system in a single generator will not produce rated voltage and current. Hence the breaker under voltage release or under voltage relay will initiate to trip the breaker. In a parallel running generator (with another generator or utility) failure of the field system will result in lossing synchronism and running above synchronous speed. The main flux being produced by wattles stator current drawn from the system. It will thus operate as an induction generator. The machine will continue to generate power, the value being determined by the load setting of the prime mover governor. Operation as an induction generator necessitates the flow of slip-frequency current in the rotor (damper winding, slot wedges and solid rotor body). However the generator is not designed as an induction machine, the damper windings are not adequate to carry the rotor slip current. Hence overloading of the stator winding and abnormal heating of rotor will take place. This can be overcome by providing loss of excitation relay. The relay will actuate to trip the generator circuit breaker during failure of excitation. Field failure relay is demonstrated in section 6.10 of Chapter # 6.

Q6: What happens if the generator may fails synchronism without failure of the excitation system?
Ans: Because of a severe system fault disturbance or operation at a high load with a leading power factor (relatively weak field) generator may go out of synchronism. In this condition, the machine is subject to violent oscillations of torque, with vide variations in current power and power factor, hence the machine must be isolated from the system. Similarly a system power shock may make a generator rotor oscillate, with consequent variations of current voltage and power factor (hunting). If the generator displacement of the rotor exceeds the stable limit, the rotor will slip a pole pitch. Hence the machine must be isolated from the system. Out of step (Backup impedance) relay is employed to trip the circuit breaker during abnormal conditions.

Q7: What happens when the prime mover of a parallel running alternating current generator fails?
Ans: When a generator operating in parallel with others or utility losses its driving force, it remains in synchronism with the system and continues to run as a synchronous motor drawing sufficient power to drive the prime mover. Loss of motive power is likely to be caused by some mechanical failure or governor failure, and continued running is likely to cause severe damage. Reverse power relays are employed to trip the generator circuit breaker. Relay will sense the direction of current flow and actuate during reverse flow of current.

Q8: Why it is necessary to use permanent magnet generator in medium voltage generators?
Ans: In a separately excited generator PMG output is connected to the governor circuit to sense the actual speed of the rotor shaft. In a self-excited generator the irregularities that occur in generator output voltage caused by load and fault conditions are likely to fed back in the exciter. Hence PMG act as a pilot exciter and supply rectified output to the exciter stator, which has no interference with generator output voltage. Connection diagram of PMG is shown in figure (g) of section 1.6.

Q9: What is the function of an Automatic Voltage Regulator when it senses generator terminal voltage?

Ans: Automatic voltage regulator senses generator voltage and regulate the flow of rectified current to the exciter stator in a self-excited generator. In a separately excited generator, AVR connected in series to the exciter shunt field winding will regulate the exciter output voltage.

Q10: Assume that 2 or more generator's of different KVA ratings are working in parallel. What happens in each occasion given below?

(a) Increase the voltage setting of one generator
(b) Decrease the voltage droop setting of one generator
(c) Voltage adjusting rheostat is turned to raise or lower direction
(d) Speed adjusting rheostat is turned in raise or lower direction

Answer:
a) Increase in setting of the generator voltage may cause an increase of ampere (ammeter reading) in that generator and ammeter reading of the other two generators will proportionally reduce
b) Uniform distribution of reactive power in all load conditions are possible for paralleled generators only if each generator has equal voltage droop settings. Decreasing the voltage droop setting will reduce the load sharing capacity of that generator.
c) Voltage adjusting rheostat connected to the voltage regulator circuit reduces or increases the power factor if the generator running in parallel. Voltage regulator controls the reactive power of the paralleled machine.
d) In a paralleled generator the speed adjusting switch is for loading (raise direction) or unloading (lower direction) the machine. Load is accepting by this machine while raising the frequency, and load is transferring to other machines while lowering the frequency.

Q11: Assume that two generators are running in parallel and DC trip circuit fuse of one generator circuit breaker has blown and the generator CB will not trip in the event of a fault. What happens?
Ans: DC under voltage release will operate to trip the circuit breaker if it is provided. Alternatively trip circuit supervision relay will operate and annunciate.

Q12: Two AC generators are running in parallel and sharing a load in the bus bar. One generator shows lagging power factor and the other shows leading power factor. What are the reasons for it?
Ans: (a) Reactive current flows between the generators. (b) Circulating current flows between the generators (c) Cross current flows between the generators.

Q13: A voltmeter designed for use with 11KV/120V PT is connected to 6.6 KV/120V PT. What will be the reading in the voltmeter?
Ans: PT ratio = 11000/120 = 91.666 i.e the voltmeter scale is marked to read 91.666 times the actual voltage applied to the voltmeter. Since the voltmeter is using for 6600/120 volt PT, the ratio is 55. The voltmeter will indicate 91.666/55 = 1.666 time's higher voltage (11 KV instead of 6.6 KV).

Q14: An ammeter designed for 1000/5A, current transformer is connected to a 500/5A, CT. What will be the reading of the ammeter if the actual current in the primary circuit is 250amps?
Ans: The ammeter scale is marked to indicate 1000 amps when 5 amps is passing through the ammeter. The ratio is 1000/5 = 200. When it is connected to 500/5 amps CT, the ratio is 100. Since the actual current is 250 amps, the current passing through the ammeter = 250/200 =1.25 amps. Ammeter will indicate 1.25 x 100 = 125 amps i.e. 50% of the actual primary current.

Q15: Explain the method of switching-off DC control power to auto-synchronizing relay after synchronizing an alternator?
Ans: Normally closed (NC) auxiliary contact of the generator circuit breaker is used for connecting the auxiliary DC power to the auto-synchronizing relay. When the generator circuit breaker is ON, this auxiliary contact opens to disconnect the supply. Auto-synchronizer is for automatic synchronizing of alternators or with utility power.

Q16: In a star connected three-phase medium voltage generator, the neutral is earthed through a grounding resistor. If a single phase to ground fault is occurred what will be the voltage in other two healthy phases measured with respect to ground provided the protection not operated and earth fault is persisting?.

Ans: Approximately 73% of phase-to-phase voltage. For example in an 11KV generator the nominal phase to ground voltage is 11000 / √3 = 6350 volts. During ground fault the phase to earth volts in other two healthy phases will be 11000 x 0.73 = 8030 volts.

Q17: What are the advantages of connecting three-phase alternating current generator winding in star?
Ans: (a) To obtain a ground neutral system (b) Winding Phase voltage is equal to line voltage / √3. Hence the insulation of winding is easier (c) To obtain a three-phase four-wire output system for low voltage generators.

Q18) Why differential protection relay is employed for alternator winding protection?
Ans: Differential relay protect the stator winding against internal short circuit or earth fault in an alternator (except turn-to-turn short circuit). Differential protection is demonstrated in section 6.5 of Chapter # 6.

Q19: What are the different types of circuit breakers employed for low and medium voltage generator switching?
Ans: **(a) For low voltage generators:** (1) ACB (Air circuit breaker); (2) MCB (Moulded case circuit breaker);

(b) For medium voltage generators: (1) MOCB (Minimum oil circuit breaker); (2) VCB (Vacuum circuit breaker); (3) SF6 insulated circuit breaker (Sulphur Hexa-flouride gas). Circuit breakers are demonstrated in Chapter # 3.

Q20: Why it is essential to provide under voltage release/under voltage protection for generator circuit breakers?
Ans: Assume that the generator is stand-still, and due to mis-operation (accidental closing) close signal is initiated to the generator circuit breaker, the breaker will not close as the under voltage release does not allow the mechanism to move. Similarly if the generator supply fails due to any reason, while the generator is running, AC under voltage release will de-energize and the breaker will trip open.

Q21: What is the symptom for a faulty voltage regulating system in an AC generator?
Ans: A high ammeter reading accompanied by a KVAR or power factor unbalance but a constant KW exists when the voltage regulator is faulty.

Q22: What do you mean by voltage dip in an alternator? How voltage dip can be estimated in a system?
Ans: A temporary reduction in voltage generally resulting from a sudden increase of load or starting currents of large motors. Voltage dip Vd = 1.05 Im x (X/100R)
Im = Starting MVA of the electric motor assuming 1 HP = 1 KVA
For direct on line motors starting KVA = 6 times HP rating of motor
Assisted starting, starting KVA = 4 times HP rating of motor
X = Sub-transient reactance of the generator
R = MVA rating of the generator
Generator capacity = 2.5 times the largest motor horse power for assisted starting

Q23: What is the direction of rotation of the alternator?
Ans: Clockwise, when looking from drive end.

Q24: What is brushless excitation, and what are the differences between self-excited generator and pilot excited generator?
Ans: Refer section 1.2, along with illustrations in Figure 1.2 (o) and (p).

Q25: What are the points to be considered while selecting a standby generator?
Ans: (a) Type of generator and excitation; (b): Fault level, system voltage, and supply frequency
(c): Method of starting, cooling and neutral earthing; (d): Impedance of the generator; (e): Generator protection; (f): Transient performance (The capability of the generator to maintain the output voltage when a sudden load is applied).

Q26: What is the formula used for determining generator-running speed, if KW and KVA are given?

Ans: Speed = Speed at no load x (Available KW / Rated KW) x (Speed at no load – Rated speed at full load.).

Q27: What is the formula used for determining standby generator capacity for starting a large motor?

Ans: **(a) Direct on line starting of largest motor:**
Generator capacity in KVA = (Largest motor H.P x 100 x Starting KVA per H.P) / (Start factor x % available KVA)
Starting KVA / H.P is 5.5 for D.O.L start; Start factor is 1.0 for D.O.L start; % avail KVA = 100
However the voltage drop should not exceed 15% while starting the largest motor.

Ans: **(b) Assisted starting of largest motor:** Use the formula given for DOL starting considering the following factors:
Starting KVA / H.P is 5.5; Start factor is 4 for assisted starting; % avail KVA = 100
Generator voltage drop should not exceed 20% while starting the largest motor

Q28: What are the four basic functions of engine modular or electronic speed switch in a D.G. set?
Ans: (1) Engine over-speed: This switch operates when the engine speed exceeds the set value. This will cause to close the inlet air and the fuel to the engine.
(2) Crank-terminate: This switch opens when the engine speed reaches cranking speed. This condition will cause to stop current flow to starter motor circuit and the starter motor pinion gear will then disengage from engine flywheel ring gear.
(3) Engine reversal: This will switch off the fuel to the engine if a condition persists that the engine may run in reverse direction.
(4) Oil pressure failure: This stop the engine from a failure caused by not enough oil pressure to maintain desired engine speed.
These are the four main reasons for obtaining non-electrical shut down in a Diesel Generator set.

Q29: What are the features of employing an electronic engine monitoring system in a D.G set?
Ans: Electronic engine monitoring system is microprocessor-based device built for monitoring and control of equipment. Basic programs provide selectable auto or manual start/stop and first-out shutdown/alarm for engine functions such as pressure, and temperature level and over-speed. Time delays for lockout during start up can be adjusted. Other features are: (1) Field adjustable parameters; (2) Shut down history file; (3) Engine servicing reminders; (4) Four or more communication ports and external P.C card reader; (5) Back lit Alphanumeric display; (6) RTU (Remote transfer unit) to interface with SCADA (Supervisory control and data acquisition system) applications and other control platforms.

Q30: What is the symptom for a faulty speed regulating system in an AC generator?
Ans: A high ammeter reading accompanied by a large KW unbalance condition exists, when the speed regulating system (Governor) is faulty.

Q31: What are the equipments and instruments mounted in the DC/AC control panel of a D.G set?
Ans: (a) DC panel for monitoring the engine is provided with:
* Oil pressure gauge: Indicates pressure of lubricating oil in engine.
* Oil temperature gauge: Indicates lubricating oil temperature
* Water temperature gauge: Indicates temperature of circulating coolant in engine.
* Instruments: Tachometer, hour run meter, DC voltmeter etc.
* Indication lamps: Monitoring system for over-speed, over-crank, low oil pressure, high water temperature, and engine started indication.

(b) AC panel for monitoring the generator is provided with:

- Ammeter with selector switch indicates load currents in amps.
- Voltmeter with selector switch indicates generator terminal voltage.
- Frequency meter indicates generator output frequency in hertz.
- Duty selector switch (Auto-Off-Manual)
- Battery charger with DC voltmeter and DC ammeter

- Buzzer for alarm during abnormal conditions persists.

Q32: Which formula is used for finding the three-phase symmetrical RMS short circuit current developed by a generator?
Ans: Three-phase first cycle, symmetrical, RMS short-circuit current Isc – Ir / Xd".
Ir = Rated generator ampere.
Xd" = Direct axis sub-transient reactance per unit value.

Q33: Explain the guidelines (procedures) for starting and stopping a stand by D.G set?
Ans: Automatic starting: Place the Auto-Off-Manual switch in the Auto position if an auto mains failure system is used. The function enables the auto transfer switch to load the generator set if a power outage occurs and stop the generator set 10 to 15 minutes after idle running when the power returns.

(c) Exercise period: Generator sets on continuous stand by must be able to perform a cold start. This can impose a severe burden on engine parts. Regular exercising (once in a week minimum 30 minutes running on load) keeps engine parts lubricated, prevents oxidation of electrical contacts and in general helps to provide reliable engine starting.

Q34: What are the minimum clearances required for a D.G set installation?
Ans: (a) Minimum height of the generator room shall be 5 metre with provision for ventilation and exhaust fan; (b) Minimum clearance shall be 1 metre in all the four sides. Between generators minimum 2 metre; (c) Exhaust pipe shall maintain minimum 2.5 metre above ground level. (d) For manual changeover system, castel key interlocks are required. For auto changeover both mechanical and electrical interlocks are required.

Q35: what are the two types of battery banks used in power stations?. Compare the advantages and disadvantages?. What is the purpose of installing battery banks in power stations?
Ans: (1) Lead acid batteries (2 volt per cell) with electrodes of lead, and lead compounds, and dilute sulphuric acid (specific gravity 1240 at 20°C) as electrolyte. (2) Nickel cadmium batteries with positive electrodes of nickel compounds, negative electrodes of cadmium and dilute potassium hydroxide (specific gravity 1240 at 20°C) with lithium hydroxide as additive as electrolyte. Hydrometer is used for measuring specific gravity of electrolyte. To obtain specific gravity at other temperature, above 20°C, add 0.0007/degree and below 20°C, deduct 0.0007/degree.

Nickel cadmium batteries have the advantages of: (a) Great mechanical strength; (b) Easy to maintain; (c) Longer life; (d) Space requirement and weight significantly smaller (e) Fully discharged sealed nickel cadmium batteries can be recharged even after few days.

Nickel cadmium batteries have the disadvantages of: (a) Lower cell voltage (1,2V/cell); (b) Voltage rise on charging up to 50%; (c) Voltage drop on discharging up to 20%; (d) Efficiency only 75% in terms of ampere hour; (e) Sensitive to temperature, usable only up to 45°C. (f) Higher consumption of distilled water.
The purpose of installing battery bank is: (a) Share the load when the charger fails; (b) Share the temporary load, which is in excess of the charger capacity; (c) Serve as a standby source control power for switchgears.

Q36: What is control power? Why DC is preferred as control source?
Ans: Control power or operative current in switchgear is a current feeding the remote control circuits of circuit breakers, operative circuit of protective relay schemes, and various types of indication and alarm schemes. The standard voltage is 110 volts direct current obtained from a dual battery charger, duly equipped with dual battery bank

The basic requirement for a DC control power source is that in the event of a short circuit or abnormal operating conditions in the AC system, the voltages of the control power should be high enough to actuate the protection and control of every automatic devices associated with the switchgears and circuit breakers. To enhance reliability DC source from storage battery is preferred.

Q37: What is UPS? Why it is required in modern power stations?

Ans: UPS is an abbreviation used for Uninterrupted Power Supply. A power supply that will continue to operate after the loss of AC input power. A UPS normally uses some type of battery backup system.

Uninterrupted power supply system is an electronic-equipment for inverting DC power in to AC to avoid interruption of power supply. UPS provides reliable precisely regulated AC power for supporting critical loads in power stations such as computerized Substation management system (SMS), Distributed control system (DCS), Process control instruments, Communication links, Spring-charging motors of MV, HV and EHV circuit breakers etc. Battery bank made of sealed lead acid batteries are being used as backup DC source.

The UPS consists of a rectifier unit to supply load current and battery charging current, an inverter to obtain AC power from the battery system, and an electronic by pass system. The UPS modules are capable of being paralleled with additional units of like rating for increased system capacity or redundancy. Its output is defined in KVA.

During the normal operation, the AC input feeds the rectifier. The rectifier converts AC in to DC and charges the battery bank equipped with the UPS. Simultaneously, the rectified supply is inverted to AC by inverter. Whenever AC power fails, the battery bank will takeover the AC load through the inverter. Hence the uninterrupted (continuous) AC supply is made available during a power interruption. Usual practice is that the battery capacity is limited for full load rating of 1 or 2 hours. For longer duration of power failure, standby generator, will takeover the load and battery charging process.

A static switch and bypass circuit is provided as an integral part of the system. It contains an automatic transfer control circuit that senses the status of the inverter logic signals and operating conditions to provide an uninterrupted transfer of the load to the alternate source. The static transfer logic will automatically turn on the static switch, transferring the critical load to the by pass source, within 150 micro-seconds after the transfer logic senses the following:

- Inverter overload;
- Critical AC bus over / under voltage;
- Battery under voltage;
- UPS inverter failure.

Q38: What do you mean by, phase-sequence in a three-phase system? How it can be checked?
Ans: The phase sequence is the order in which the currents or voltages of a three phase AC system attain their peak position with reference to time. Three-phase voltage sin-wave given in section 1.2, Figure 1.2 (f) shows that at-first phase 'a' reaches peak value, followed by phase 'b' and 'c' and the direction of rotation is clockwise. If a phase sequence meter is connected to the circuit in a-b-c sequence, the dial will rotate on clockwise direction. If any two leads are reversed, it will rotate on anticlockwise direction.

Q39: Explain the term short circuit current, symmetrical and asymmetrical short circuit current?
Ans: The practically non-resistive connection established between live conductors, resulting in the current becoming a multiple of the load current. This may lead to thermal or mechanical overloading of the equipment connected. Damage and destruction can only be prevented by, employing the appropriate short circuit protection. A distinction is made between a three-phase short circuit, two-phase short circuit, and an earth fault. The prospective current, which will flow under the conditions of a terminal short-circuit is defined as short-circuit current. [Refer figure 1.10 (a), (b) and (c) of Chapter # 1]

DC component indicates the amount by which the normal sinusoidal current wave deviates from the zero axis. The DC component occurs briefly on short circuit, for example, its magnitude is a function of the cos φ and of the instant at which the short circuit current starts to flow. The DC component and the symmetrical short circuit current add up to the asymmetric short circuit current. The short circuit current increases by the amount of the DC component, and the interrupting conditions for the switching device are thus aggravated. The DC component can equal the peak symmetrical short circuit current, but in conventional low voltage networks it is usually not more than 50% of this current.

The AC component of the short circuit current, whose maxima and minima are equidistant from the zero axis about which the sinusoidal current alternates. The DC component makes the short circuit current asymmetric since it causes the zero axis to be raised or lowered to a positive or negative maximum. The zero-axis, offset in this manner, gradually returns to its normal position, the delay depending on the network inductances.

In the case of a fault close to a generator, the symmetrical short circuit current decreases from the initial value to the level of the sustained short circuit current. If a fault occurs away from a generator, the symmetrical short

circuit current is almost constant during the entire fault duration, i.e. the initial symmetrical short circuit current is thus equal to the sustained short circuit current.

(40) Explain the requirement of installing programmable logic controller in a standby diesel generating plant?
Ans: Programmable logic controller (PLC) is using for automatic operation of standby DG plant. It receives its analogue input from transducers connected through current and potential transformers. Output command will actuate the operation of equipments or devices as programmed. Following automatic operations are usually programmed:

1) Starting and synchronizing of alternators up on mains power failure.
2) Loading and unloading of alternators as and when required.
3) Walk-in and walk-off of alternators based on priority setting and load requirement.
4) Load shedding if overloaded.
5) Auto-transfer scheme

For single unit standby generator microprocessor is employed to perform such functions which is applicable.

Q41: What are the precautions to be taken while erecting/connecting/earthing of alternators?
Ans: (a) A dry, clean room, free from vibrations with correct ventilation conditions is a favorable site for electrical machines. The ventilation system for the room containing the alternator must be such that the cooling air does not exceed the permissible temperature.
(b) The inlet and outlet cooling air is not obstructed. The warm outlet air should not find entry to the inlet ports of the machine. During erection the transport securing devices and blocking plates should be removed. The corrosion protection on the shaft or on the flanges should be removed with a suitable solvent.
(c) The substructures such as foundation plates, base frames, bedplates should be very solidly constructed in order to free from vibration. The concrete foundation should be carefully built with the certified dimension sheet of the machine and the foundation plan drawing.
(d) The alternator is dynamically balanced with either full feather key or full key. The coupling, pulley or pinion must be balance with open key way, i.e. without key. After assembly, both halves of the couplings should be checked with a clock gauge for trueness of rotation. The measured value should not exceed =/- 0.01 mm.
(e) The alternator is placed on the foundation after the driving machine has been completely aligned, then carryout the axial and radial alignment. Taper pins are used to finally locate the precise alignment is completed.
(f) Connections from generator to generator breaker or power transformer is made either by using cables or bus ducts. The phase sequence R-Y-B or U-V-W is used for right-handed sense of rotation as seen from the drive side.
(g) When single core cables are used as power cables, non magnetic materials like aluminium plate, bakelite sheet, stainless steel plate etc are used as gland plate to prevent overheating the cable and gland plate due to stray current formed in the glanding area. For low voltage cables, this difficulty can overcome by using aluminium glands. All single core power cables shall be laid in tri-foil formation and tied together with stainless steel cable ties. (For medium voltage single core cables, tri-foil cable clamps designed to suit for the rated system fault level must be used). If several single core cables are connected in parallel, each group of tri-foil formation is formed with one cable of all the three phases, failing which, paralleled cables will not share equal loads.
(h) When control cables are connected to the electronic equipment, shielded cables must be used. The shielding should be earthed at one end only and the other end being unearthed. Shielding of the cable guarantees that no external disturbances, e.g, magnetic stray fixed around the cable can induce disturbance in the system i.e. voltage regulator.
(i) For safety reasons the earthing of the machine body is of great importance, and should therefore be earthed on the foot of the machine at two locations and the terminal box.
(j) Neutral (star point) of low voltage generators are solidly grounded and medium voltage generators are connected through neutral grounding resistor. For combined transformer-generator unit, neutral is grounded through the grounding transformer. If several solidly grounded low voltage generators (or transformers) of

different types and KVA ratings are connected in parallel, large circulating currents of three times the mains frequency can flow in the neutral lead of such systems. These circulating currents should not exceed 20% of the rated current of the smallest alternator running in parallel. When the neutrals of alternators

(or transformers) of similar type and ratings are connected, no circulating current will flow, and a star point choke is superfluous.

Q42: What are the fire protection and fire detection requirements required in generating stations based on NFPA recommendations?

Ans: Table 1.21 (1): NFPA (National Fire Protection Association) recommendations for fire protection system in power generating stations.

Area or equipment to be protected	Protection system	Detection system
Turbine generators (Hydro electric / steam / gas turbines)	High pressure carbon dioxide (CO_2) Fire extinguishing system (NFPA 12)	Smoke / heat detectors (NFPA 72) & (For steam generators UV/IR detectors additional)
Turbine building/Machine hall	Foam water mixer station NFPA11 Hose-reel-(NFPA14) Portable extinguisher (NFPA 10)	Smoke detectors and alarm system (NFPA 72)
Control building / work shop / store building /water pump house / fire pump house	Automatic sprinkler system NFPA-13 Hose-reels-(NFPA-14) Hand held portable fire extinguisher (NFPA 10)	Smoke / heat detectors and alarm system (NFPA 72)
Water treatment plant / Effluent treatment plant/ Chemical dosing station / Laboratory	Hose-reels (NFPA 14) and hand held portable fire extinguisher	Smoke / heat detectors and alarm system (NFPA 72)
Distillate storage tank	Fixed foam system for surface of fuel in tank (NFPA 11 and 16) Automatic fixed spray water deluge system (NFPA 16)	Break glass manual call point
Fuel gas station	Water hydrant (NFPA 24) and hand held portable fire extinguisher	Heat / smoke detectors and alarm system

CHAPTER # 2

POWER AND DISTRIBUTION TRANSFORMERS

CONTENTS:

2.1 TRANSFORMER CAPACITY, CONNECTIONS AND VECTOR GROUPS.

Transformer is a static-machinery used for transferring electrical energy from one circuit to another by magnetic induction, usually between circuits of different voltages and having following features: (a) Stepping up the voltage (b) stepping down the voltage (c) Varying the voltage and (d) Isolating the circuit. Transformer capacity is always given in KVA (Kilovolt ampere) or MVA (Mega-volt ampere). Rating of a transformer is the numerical value assigned under specified operating conditions, which denote the capabilities of the transformer.

In a transformer, the available output is limited by, transformer heating by losses. The losses are determined by, voltage and current and are unaffected by power factor. Hence the size of the single-phase transformer is the product of its voltage and current. For three-phase transformer the capacity is $\sqrt{3}$ E x I, volt-amps. 1 KVA = 1000 volt-amps.

1MVA = 1000 KVA = 1000,000 Volt-amps

Star connection:

Connections of three electrical coils made in such a manner that one end (for example, finishing ends) are connected together to form star point. Three phase supplies are connected to the other ends of the respective phases as shown in Figure 2.1 (a). In a star connection, line current and phase current are same. $I_L = Ip$, and the line voltage is higher than the phase voltage by a factor of the square root of 3. i.e. $E_L = \sqrt{3}\ Ep$

Delta connection:

Circuit formed by connecting three electrical coils in series to form a closed loop. Starting end of one coil is connected to the finishing end of the other coil and so on as shown in Figure 2.1 (b). In a delta connected system, the line voltage and phase voltage are the same. $E_L = Ep$, and the line current is higher than the phase current by a factor of the square root of 3. i.e. $I_L = \sqrt{3}$ Ip

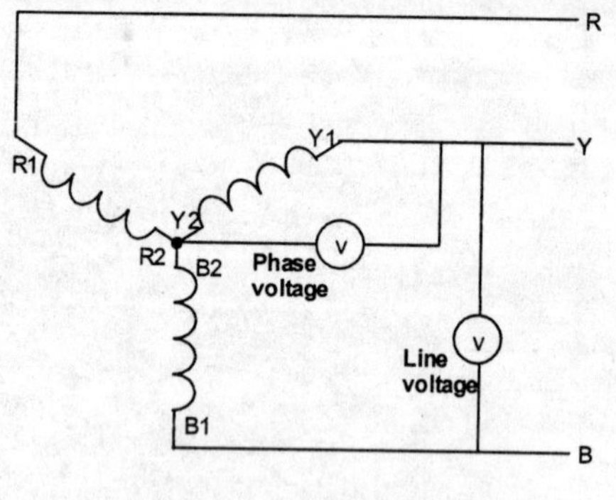

Fig. 2.1 (a): Star connection

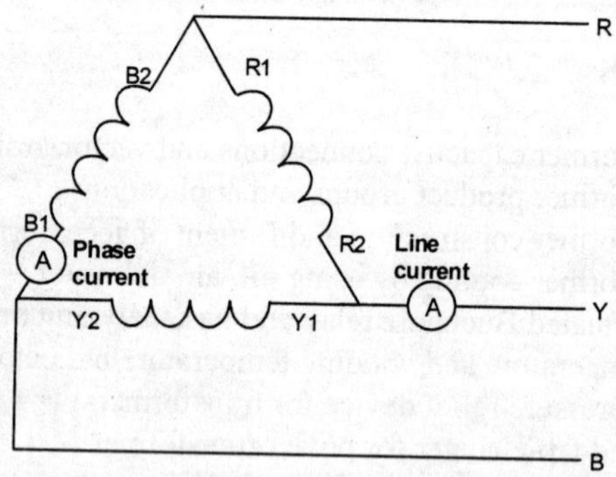

Fig 2.1 (b): Delta connection

Different types of connections employed in three phase transformers are (a) Star/Delta connection (b) Delta/Star connection (c) Star/Star connection; (d) Delta/Delta connection; (e) Zigzag connection (refer figure 5.2 (c) of Chapter # 5); (f) Open delta connection. In the open delta connection shown in figure 5.2 (d) of Chapter # 5, two single-phase transformers provides a three-phase output, but the capacity is being reduced to 87% of the total ratings.

Vector group: Vector group is the phase displacement between the primary and secondary windings. In a three-phase transformer, the primary and secondary windings can be connected in the same polarity (0 degree phase displacement YY0) or in the opposite polarity (180 degree phase displacement YY6). Figure 2.1 (c) shows the internal arrangement of connections and vector diagram for YY0 vector group. Similarly Figure 2.1 (d) shows the connection arrangement and vector diagram for YY6 vector group. Vector group indicates the connection of the transformer windings. The first alphabet, represents the primary side connection and the second alphabet, represent secondary side. Y = star, D = delta, Z = zigzag, n = Neutral brought out, and the numerical number indicates the phase displacement between primary voltage and secondary voltage. This value is to be multiplied by 30 for obtaining the actual degree. For example, assume that the vector diagram given in the nameplate of a 1000 KVA, 11KV / 415 Volts distribution transformer is DYn11.

Dyn11 means:

D = Primary delta connected (11000V)

Y = Secondary star connected (415V)

n = Secondary neutral brought out (Bushing)

11 = Phase displacement 11 x 30 = 330°

LEGEND:

A1, B1, C1 Starting ends of primary windings

A2, B2, C2 Finishing ends of primary windings

a1, b1. c1 Starting ends of secondary windings

a2, b2, c2 Finishing ends of secondary windings

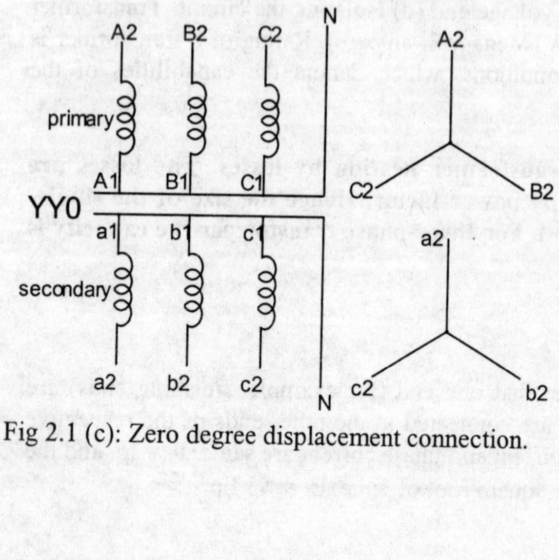

Fig 2.1 (c): Zero degree displacement connection.

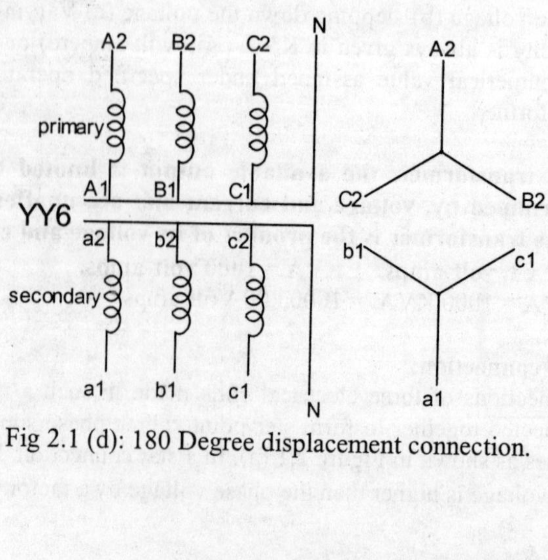

Fig 2.1 (d): 180 Degree displacement connection.

Typical vector groups, connection diagrams with turns-ratio of three-phase transformers are given in Figure 2.1 (e). Turns ratio express the number of turns in the secondary winding of the transformer for every turn in the primary winding.

Vector Group	Vector Diagram / Circuit configuration	Ratio $V_1:V_2$
Dd0	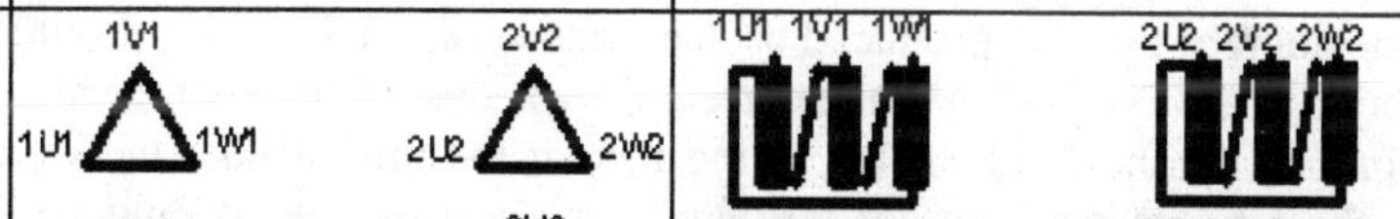	$\frac{N_1}{N_2}$
Yy0	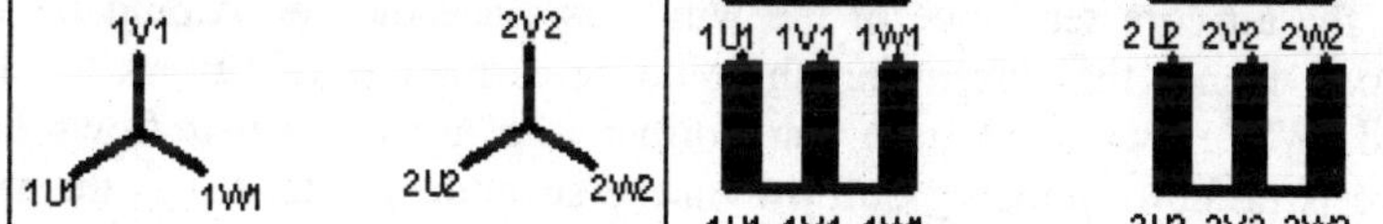	$\frac{N_1}{N_2}$
Dz0	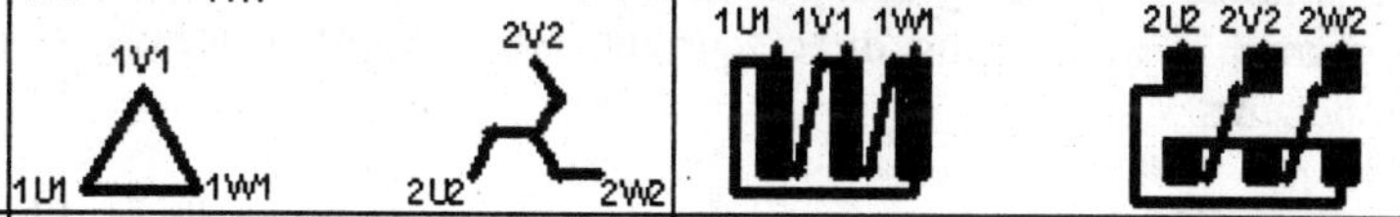	$\frac{2N_1}{3N_2}$
Dy5	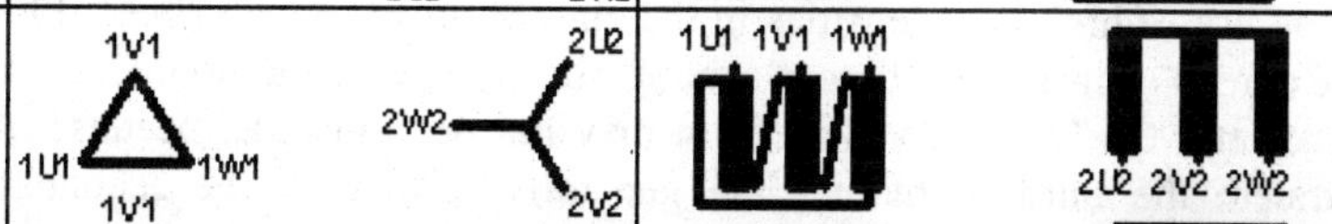	$\frac{N_1}{\sqrt{3}N_2}$
Yd5	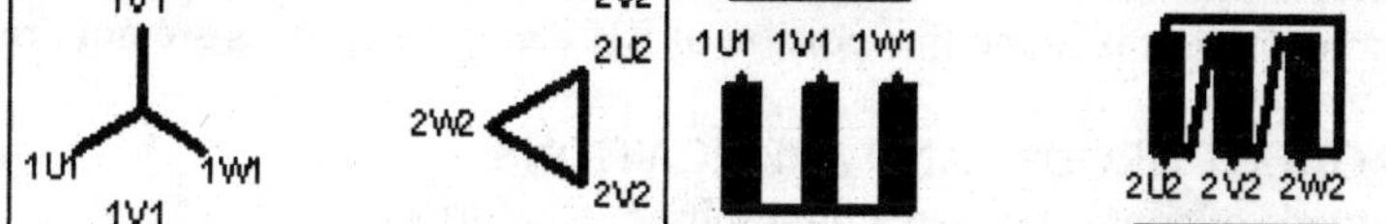	$\frac{\sqrt{3}N_1}{N_2}$
Yz5	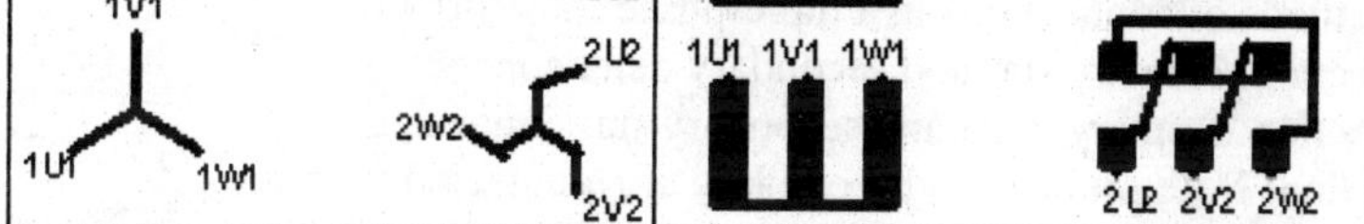	$\frac{2N_1}{\sqrt{3}N_2}$
Dd6		$\frac{N_1}{N_2}$
Yy6		$\frac{N_1}{N_2}$
Dz6	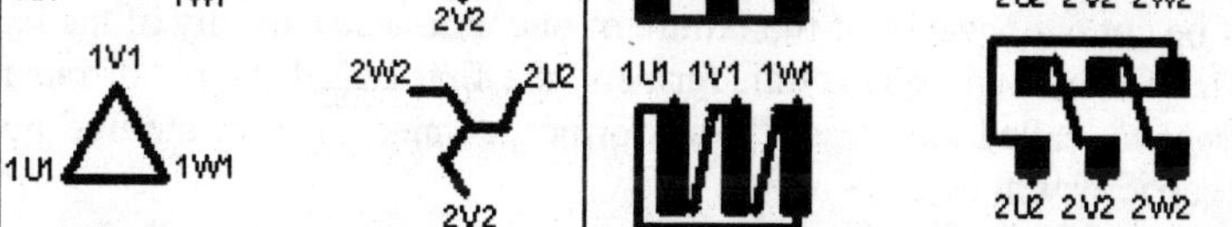	$\frac{2N_1}{3N_2}$
Dy11	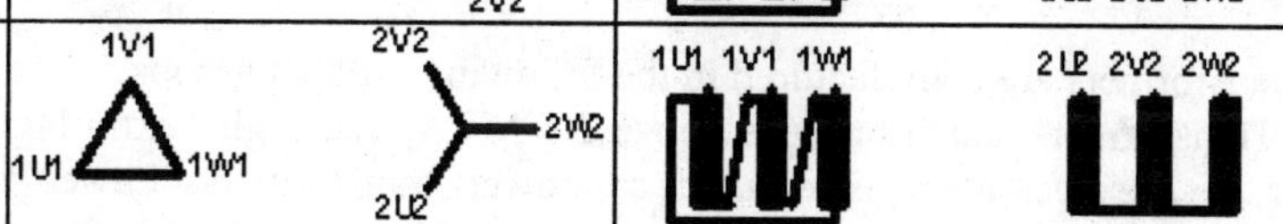	$\frac{N_1}{\sqrt{3}N_2}$
Yd11	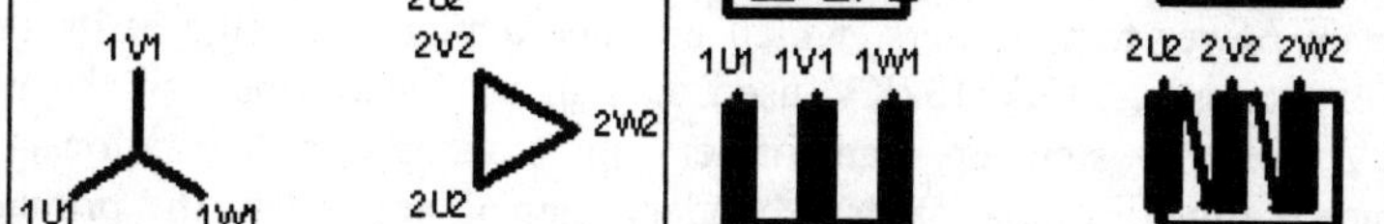	$\frac{\sqrt{3}N_1}{N_2}$
Yz11	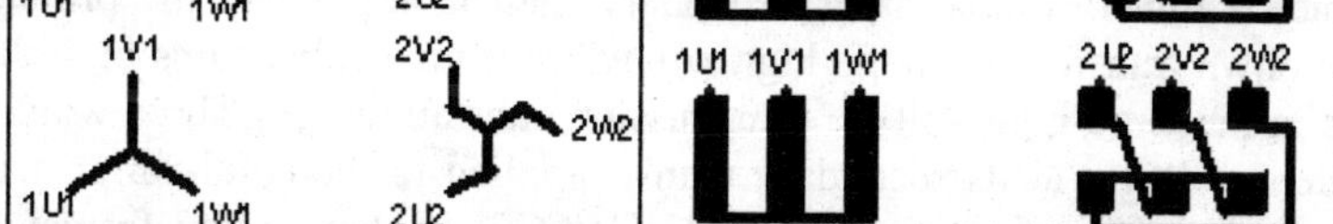	$\frac{2N_1}{\sqrt{3}N_2}$
Ya0	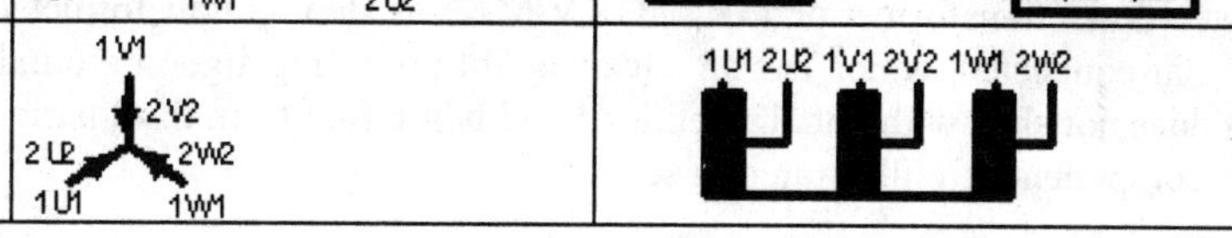	

Figure 2.1 (e) Vector group connections for transformers.

Current Inrush and harmonics:
The fundamental principle of the transformer is that the voltage applied to the primary is nearly counterbalanced by the back e.m.f produced by the alternating magnetic flux in the core. When a transformer is switched off, the primary circuit opens at zero current-wave but the secondary current takes a short time to decay to zero. This leaves a residual flux in the core of the transformer. At the instant of switching on (energizing) a transformer, the back e.m.f, which develops is dependent up on the value of the residual flux, which may either be in opposition to the flux produced by the impressed voltage, as it should be, or it may be assisting it. Therefore, at the instant of switching in the current flow is determined by the value and direction of the back e.m.f and, therefore, up on the residual flux in the core at the time. Under the worst condition this current is limited only by the air-core reactance of the windings since the core would be saturated and its impedance is greatly reduced. Hence the current inrush could be as high as five times full load current and persists nearly one second. While switching on a transformer, the inrush current flows only through the primary winding, and there is no corresponding outflow on the secondary side. It has the same effect as an internal fault. The inrush current is a pulsating direct current, which rapidly decays. It contains a large percentage of harmonic components.

Harmonics are caused by the use of high flux densities in the core of power transformers. Flux density should not exceed 1.4 Tesla. If the core is of insufficient cross-section, the core gets saturated. Even if primary voltage might have sinusoidal waveform, the secondary waveform may not be sinusoidal because of magnetic core. When the core gets saturated, the third harmonics are generally present in the secondary waveform. If operating point of magnetizing current is in the line portion of BH curve, harmonics are not present.

2.2 TRANSFORMER PRODUCT GROUPS AND APPLICATIONS.

There are four standard methods of connections in a three-phase transformer.

1) Star / Delta connection: Primary star and secondary delta connected.
2) Delta / Star connection: Primary delta and secondary star connected.
3) Star / Star connection: Both primary and secondary are connected in star.
4) Delta / Delta connection: Both primary and secondary are connected in delta.

In a delta / star transformer, the load (except balanced 3-phase load with out neutral i.e, motor) shall be connected to line to neutral only. In a star / star transformer, the source (primary) neutral shall be connected back to the source. If one of these two conditions is not maintained, the neutral will shift, reducing the voltage of the loaded phase and increasing the voltage of other two phases.

'V' Connection is an unsymmetrical connection, which is used if one transformer of a bank of 3 single-phase delta connected units must be cut out because of the failure of one unit. The capacity of the bank will be 57.7% only. The 'T' connection uses two single-phase transformers, the first called the main transformer connected from line to line and the second, called the "teaser" transformer, connected from the mid point of the first to the third phase (line). The capacity will be 73% only.

Based on its application, transrormers are manufactured in the following product groups.

1) Power transformers: Transformers usually ratings above 2.5 MVA, and high / extra high voltage supply either in the primary or in the secondary is defined as power transformers. Power transformers are discriminated as: (a) Step up power transformers, which produce a higher voltage at its secondary than is applied to the primary. For example, 11KV/132KV used as step up transformers in the power generating stations or 380KV/765KV used as step up transformers in transmission substations. (b) Step down transformers, which produce a lower voltage at its secondary than is applied to the primary. For example 110KV/33KV used as step down transformer in the high voltage receiving substations or 440KV/220KV used as step down transformers in the extra high voltage transmission substations. (c) Three winding transformers, which produces two different voltages at its secondary than is applied to the common primary. For example 220KV/110KV/66KV as step down transformer or 11KV/33KV/66KVas step up transformer. Most of the step up transformers are delta / star connected, which has an advantage of providing a good grounding point on the star connected side, which does not shift with unbalanced load and being free from third harmonic voltage and current. Power transformer components are illustrated in section 2.3.

2) Distribution transformers: Delta / star connected step down transformers used for distribution of power for domestic, commercial and industrial purposes are called distribution transformers. Medium voltage (3.3KV to 33KV) as Primary voltage and secondary is three-phase four-wire, (grounded neutral) low voltage supply. Distribution transformers 25 KVA to 315 KVA are suitable for pole mounting/ground mounting. 350 KVA to 2500 KVA are ground mounting type. Distribution transformers are classified in to (1) Resin moulded dry type air-cooled indoor transformer [refer figure 2.14 (c)]; (2) Oil immersed conventional transformer with conservator and (3) Oil immersed hermetically sealed transformer Nitrogen gas cushioned as illustrated in figure 2.2 (a)].

Dry type transformers are widely used as unit auxiliary transformers in generating stations, high rise buildings, petrochemical refineries, offshore drilling rigs, mining and marine applications and indoor use in nuclear power stations. Its advantages are reduced maintenance, elimination of fire hazard, reduced space requirements etc.

Hermetically sealed transformers have neither conservator nor breather and the oil variations are taken up by, the elastic cooling fins. The system prevents oxygen, moisture and any harmful gases from entering the oil. These transformers, does not require any oil maintenance. Sealed transformers are completely filled with transformer oil by the manufacturers. The heating of the oil core assembly is absorbed by the transformer oil, which may then increase or reduce the volume of oil depends on the temperature. This is taken up by the elasticity of the cooling fins (radiators), the inert gas cushion or a combination of both the above. Nitrogen is the inert gas used to pressurize the empty space above the oil. The changes in volume of the oil, causes changes in pressure in the tank because the oil is not compressible. The eventual gas cushion is used to keep this pressure between acceptable values. Due to the fact that there is no contact between the oil and ambient air, the oil cannot absorb any moisture so that the dielectric strength of oil cannot deteriorate. The aging process of the insulation material by oxidation is avoided as no oxygen is taken up. Even the gaskets of the bushings are under oil so that this gasket will not dry out. Sampling and testing of oil is not allowed as the air may enter inside the tank.

CONSERVATOR TYPE **HERMATICALLY SEALED TYPE**

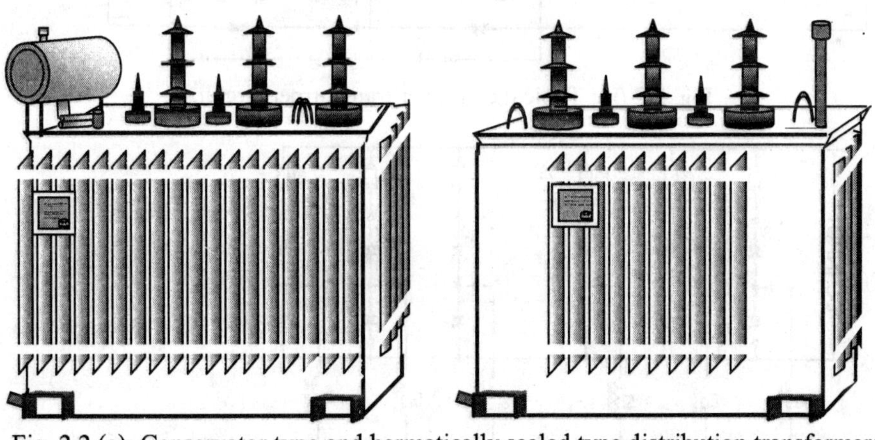

Fig. 2.2 (a): Conservator type and hermetically sealed type distribution transformers.

3) Converter transformer: Converter transformers with single secondary or multiple secondary windings are used with AC/DC converters or for slip energy recovery schemes. Its application is mainly for steel plants, cement factory, traction substations, electrolysis plant etc: The advantages of employing converter transformers are: (a) Multiple secondary windings; (b) Reduces stray losses due to harmonics; (c) Prevention of electrostatic transfer of higher surge voltages to the converters. Three-phase converter unit consists of an isolation transformer with delta-connected primary and two secondary windings one in star and the other in delta as shown in Figure 2.2 (b). With such a combination, phase shift of 30 electrical degrees between two six pulse units connected in series can be obtained to get a 12 pulse converter. The two sets of secondaries generate six different phases to be rectified by the 12 semiconductor rectifiers (SCR's). Each secondary feeds a full wave bridge rectifier.

(4) Inverter Transformer: DC power is used as input power for the inverter. The DC power is converted to AC power utilizing silicon devices (SCR;s). The inverter legs constitute bridge circuits, which supply quasi-square waveforms to each of the primary windings of the inverter output transformer. Waveform created by summing several quasi square waves together which leads to an approximate sin wave. 12 Pulse inverter transformers is a double delta primary unit. The secondary is connected in zigzag as shown in figure 2.2 (c). Filter circuit and reactive impedance is employed in the AC side for obtaining a sinusoidal wave and reducing short-circuit current.

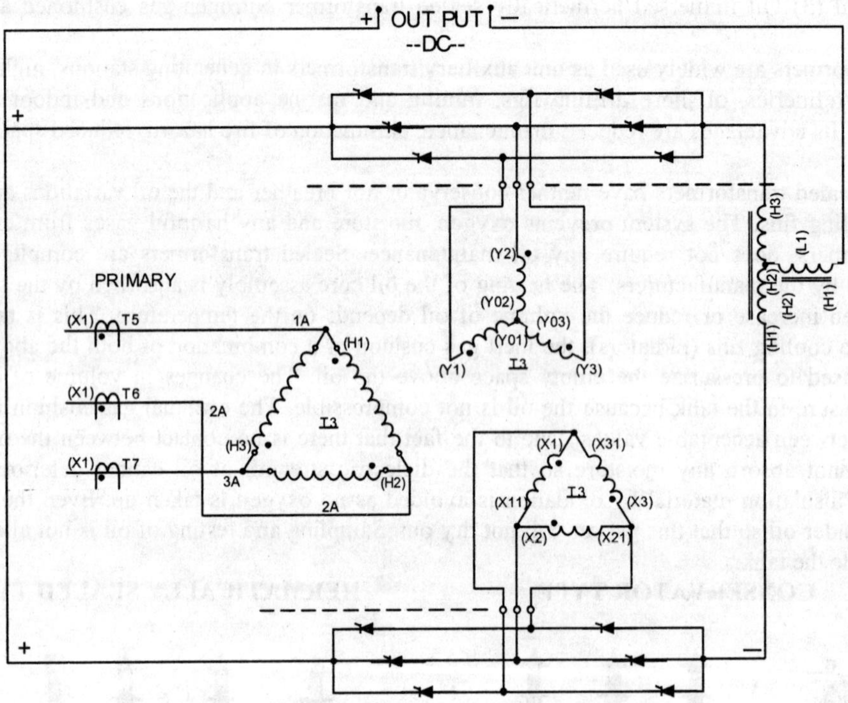

Fig. 2.2 (b): Typical converter transformer circuit.

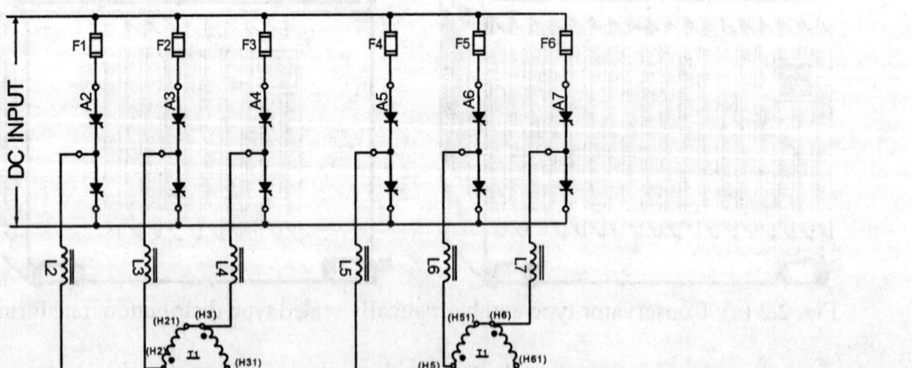

Fig. 2.2 (c): Typical inverter transformer circuit.

5) Rectifier transformers: Rectifiers are used for electric traction, electrolytic applications, DC motor drives, cyclo-converter etc. Three-phase rectifier transformer has a star connected primary and the secondary as shown in Figure 2.2 (d) or double star, zigzag or double zigzag and bridge connection. For example, 6, 12, 24 pulse bridge rectifier. Figure 2.2 (e) shows a typical 6-pulse full wave rectifier circuit.

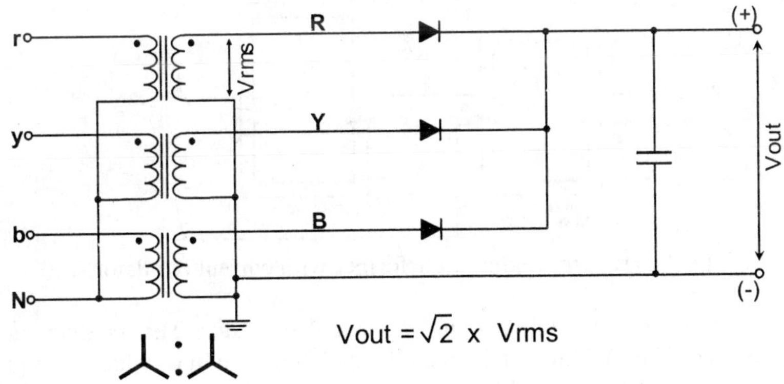

Fig. 2.2 (d): Rectifier circuit with star / star transformer

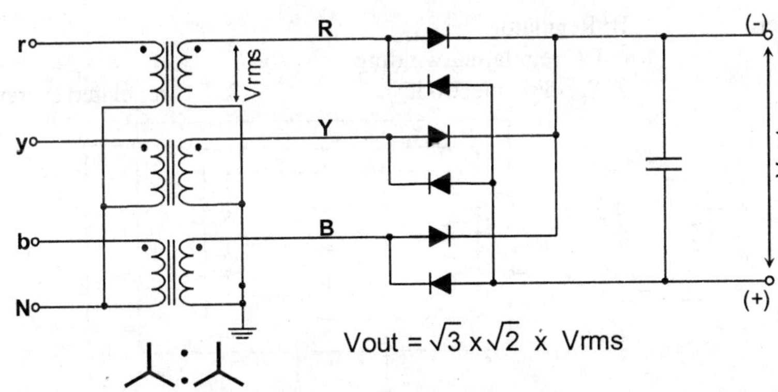

Fig. 2.2 (e): Six pulse full wave rectifier circuit

5) **HVDC transformers:** The converter or inverter transformers are the heaviest equipment in a High voltage direct current (HVDC) station. Single units have 200 to 400 tons weight. Converter transformers connected the AC network to the thyristor, and adjust the voltage to a suitable level based on the DC voltage used for the transmission system. The transformers can be of different design depending on the power to be transmitted and possible transport limitations. The most common type is single-phase-three-winding design. Three identical transformers are then needed per converter. The converter transformer serves several functions:

6) (1) Supply of AC voltages in two separate circuits with a relative phase shift of 30 electrical degrees for reduction of low order harmonics, especially the 5th and 7th harmonics.
(2) Act as a galvanic barrier between the AC and DC systems to prevent the SC potential to enter the AC system.
(3) Reactive impedance in the AC supply to reduce short circuit currents.
(4) Voltage transformation between the AC supply and the HVDC system.
(5) A fairly large tap range with small steps to give necessary adjustments in supply voltage.

7) Welding transformers: Welding is a process of joining together two metal parts (or surfacing) by, heating them to melting point. In electric arc welding the metal to be welded is heated by electric arc by using welding rods of different gauges. Arc welding transformer consists of single phase or two-phase low voltage primary and 20 to 100 volts, 100 to 1500 amps secondary. Transformer is either air-cooled or oil filled depends on the amperage capacity. A variable reactor (choke) is used for regulating the secondary current of the transformer as shown in Figure 2.2 (f).

Key: 1. Terminal to welding elements 2. Terminal to work-piece (earthed) 3. Power supply

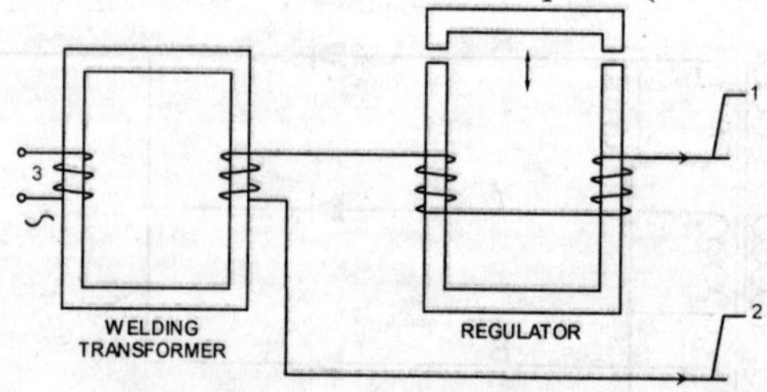

Fig. 2.2 (f): Arc welding transformer with current regulator.

Figure 2.2 (g) shows another type of welding transformer and regulator. The welding transformer supplies current via saturable reactor. The DC current is central regulating winding, which is regulated by external means. Any increase in current in the external DC regulated current circuit gives increased DC components in the core and it leads to saturation of the core. The reactance reduces and welding current increases. By varying DC current in the regulating winding, the welding current supplied to the welding electrode can be easily controlled..

KEY:

A: Welding transformer B: Regulator
b: Series winding c: DC regulating winding
1: Power supply 2: Welding electrode 3: DC regulated current circuit

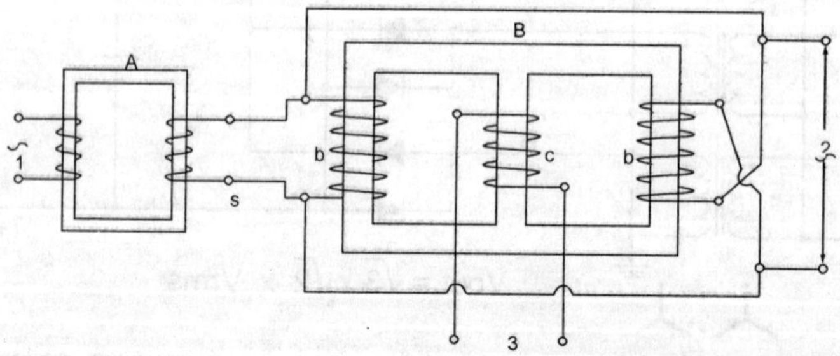

Fig. 2.2 (g): Welding transformer with DC regulated current circuit

8) Traction transformers: Traction transformers are used for traction power supplies tò Railway, electric locomotive (train), trolley bus, and electric rail tramway (Passenger train) system etc. Converter transformers demonstrated above are also used in traction substations.

9) Mining transformers: Transformers specially designed for mining applications are called mining transformers. Following types of transformers are used in mines depending on the area classification: * Impregnated dry type air-cooled transformers; * Cast resin type air-cooled transformers for underground mines; *Oil filled transformers (mineral oil) for open cast coalmines; * Flameproof transformers for underground coalmines. Flameproof transformers have flameproof enclosure and high quality insulation materials to achieve total safety and reliability.

10) Isolation transformers: A transformer whose secondary winding is electrically isolated from its primary winding, but symmetrical windings with 1:1 turns-ratio, used to decouple two circuits. It is used for electronic and lighting applications.

Audio line isolation transformer prevents humming caused by ground loop. Isolation transformer enhances the quality of the power system by reducing common mode noise, while the internal surge suppression system minimize high-energy transients and normal mode noise that can disrupt the operation of sensitive electronic equipments. Isolation transformers are essential for computer and peripherals, telecommunication system, medical and laboratory instrumentation, process control applications, office automation, security system, audiovisual equipments, aircrafts and as a bypass transformer for uninterrupted power supply (UPS). Lighting transformers prevents flickering of discharge lamps during momentary line faults in the primary circuit. Audio and telecommunication transformers are manufactured by using nickel alloy laminations.

Personal computer, fax machines, photocopiers, electronic ballasts, variable speed drives, and various types of medical equipment, they only demand current during part of the cycle. This type of load creates harmonic currents, which in turn generate heat in the transformer. The temperature rise limit of the winding insulation is usually 150 or 200°C. When this limit is exceeded the insulation breaks down destroying the transformer. The term for the total amount of harmonic current present is called "Total Harmonic Distortion" (THD). This is where K-factor comes in. K-rated transformers are classified as follows:
K1: Incidental electronic equipment representing <5% non-linear current.
K4: Harmonic producing equipment representing <35% non-linear current (Harmonic current up to 4th harmonics + 100% linear load).
K7: Harmonic producing equipment representing <50% non-linear current (Harmonic current up to 7th harmonic + 100% linear load)
K13: Harmonic producing equipment representing <75% non-linear current (Harmonic current up to 13th harmonic + 100% linear load)
K20: Harmonic producing equipment representing <100% non-linear current (Harmonic current up to 20th harmonic + 100% linear load)
K rated transformers are manufactured with heavier gauge copper wire and a double sized neutral conductor and have higher magnetic to resistive properties than a standard transformer of the same capacity, which enables them to handle the heat generated by harmonic currents.

11) High frequency transformers: Switch-mode transformers for high frequency electronic applications. Its range is 25 Kilohertz to 1 Megahertz. Ferrite is a ceramic magnetic core material composed of ferric oxide and a combination of manganese, zinc or nickel. Lamination made in the stamped letter shape EE, PQ, UU, ETD and dual-slab are used for manufacturing high frequency transformers. Switching power transformers are of high efficiency, very small size and called buck-boost transformers, converters and inverters. Operated from DC power that is typically switched at a rate of 50 to 100 KHz. Switching speeds of almost one MHz can be achieved. Switching power transformers are designed for a specific application such as fly-back, forward, push-pull or bridge. Fly-back transformers (limit 100VA) are storing energy when the switch is 'ON', and delivering energy when the switch is 'OFF'. Forward transformers (limit 500VA) transfer power to the load during the 'ON' time and re-setting in the 'OFF' time. Push-pull transformer (limit 1 KVA) delivers power to the load during the whole input cycle. Half bridge is a dual forward converter using two power switches. Four power switches are used in the full bridge system. Full supply voltage is obtained in both the directions.

12) Toroidal transformers: These are made with tape wound cores. The tape wound cores provides a perfect magnetic circuits to minimize losses, fringing, leakage, distortion, and provide good magnetic shielding. Toroids are circular, non-radiating magnetic cores made of nickel and cobalt alloys, metallic glass, ferrite and powdered iron. Available in 10VA to 750VA range, suitable for use power magnetic, EMI, RFI filters etc. Other features are: * Low magnetic noise; * Very low magnetizing current; * High efficiency and excellent load regulation.

13) Autotransformer: Transformer that uses only one winding per phase for both primary and secondary. In an autotransformer, KVA for primary winding is equal to KVA for secondary winding. Autotransformers are used as power transformers where the primary and secondary voltages are not far apart. (For example, 110 KV, primary voltages and 66 KV, secondary voltages). Such autotransformers are usually connected in star with the neutral grounded and are provided with a delta connected tertiary winding to provide a path for the flow of the third harmonic of exciting current. The disadvantages of autotransformers are (1) low impedance and high short circuit currents for short circuits in secondary side. (2) If winding common to both primary and secondary is opened, full primary voltage will appear across secondary resulting in higher voltages across secondary side.

Figure 2.2 (h) shows the circuit diagram of a three-phase star connected autotransformer with neutral solidly grounded. An additional delta winding called tertiary winding wound on the same core is provided. The purpose of delta tertiary is to provide an internal path to the third harmonic currents required for excitation and thus eliminating them from the AC network. The delta tertiary also helps to stabilize the neutral with reference to line voltage.

LEGEND:

1. Auto transformer Star / Star 2. Delta connected tertiary

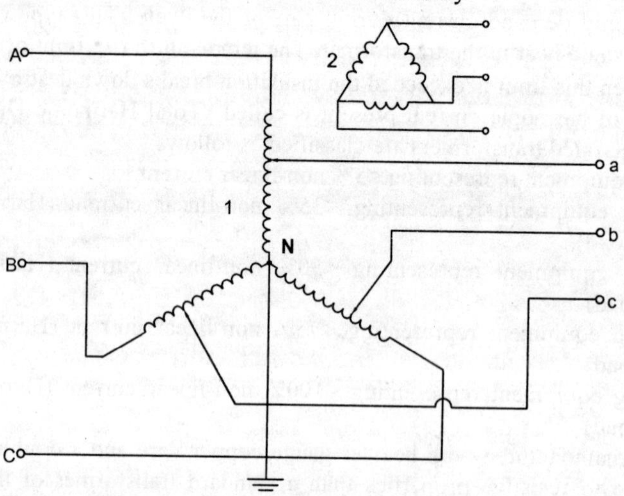

Fig. 2.2 (h): Three-phase autotransformer with delta tertiary winding.

As a rule, star/star connected autotransformer is provided with delta tertiary for stabilizing the phase-to-phase voltages during unbalanced load on secondary side. During single-phase loads the current in unloaded phases is purely exciting current. There is no induced current. By saturation effect phase voltage get deformed. Stray fluxes increase and the tank gets heated. By incorporating a delta tertiary the balanced ampere-turns are obtained in all the three phases of tertiary. These windings are on the same core. Hence the magnetizing currents are balanced in all the three phases. Thus the problem of shifting the neutral and unbalanced voltage is eliminated.

Figure 2.2 (i) shows autotransformer connections with tap changer. The arrangements are: (1) Tap position between series and common winding; (2) Tap position at the end of series winding; (3) Tap position at star point; (4) Tap position at lower voltage terminal (Fork-connection)

Autotransformers can be used for reduced voltage starting of three-phase low voltage and medium voltage motors. Variable voltage autotransformer is used for variable voltage applications as demonstrated in Chapter # 5, section 5.14. Where accuracy of voltage is essential, regulating transformer with on-load tap changer is used to get the desired voltage.

LEGEND:
SW: Series winding
CW: Common winding
TW: Tapped winding

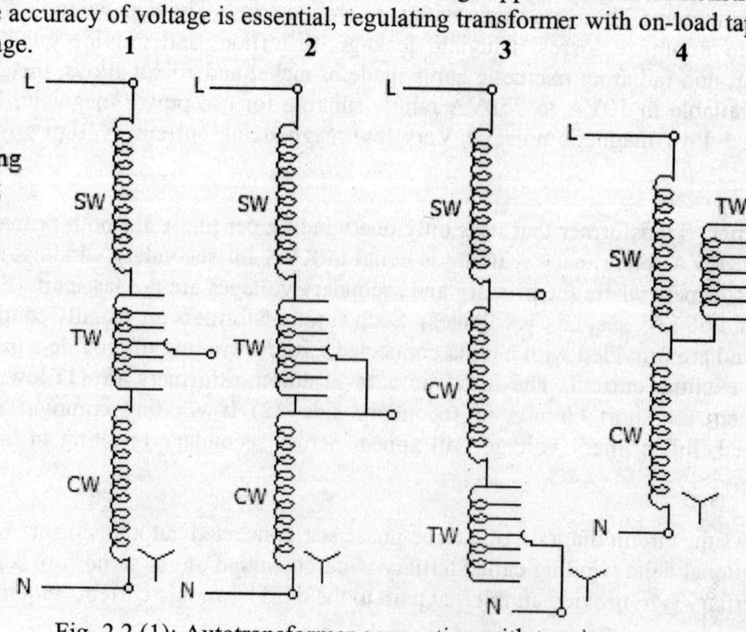

Fig. 2.2 (1): Autotransformer connection with tapping.

14) Control transformer: An isolation transformer used to supply control power to the switchgear by stepping down the mains voltage in a very low potential suitable for the control circuitry. It is connected to the main switchgear bus as its power source, usually single phase only and having 120 to 415 volts output. For example, in a 6.6 KV Medium voltage motor control center (MCC), assume that the control power for the medium voltage vacuum or SF6 contactor is 415 volts AC. A step down transformer (6600/415 V) having 200 to 500 volt-amps rating is required to feed the control circuitry of the medium voltage motor. Following are the advantages of providing a control transformer…

1. To obtain a safety output (extra low voltage)
2. To obtain an earthed secondary output.
3. Reduce the voltage ratings of the auxiliary (NO/NC) contacts.
4. Conversion from AC to DC is easy.

One of the major disadvantages is that due to voltage drop the length of the secondary circuit is limited. Figure 2.2 (j) shows the connection diagram of a typical control transformer in which primary is 2 phase 380 volts and the secondary is 110 volts single phase (one side earthed).

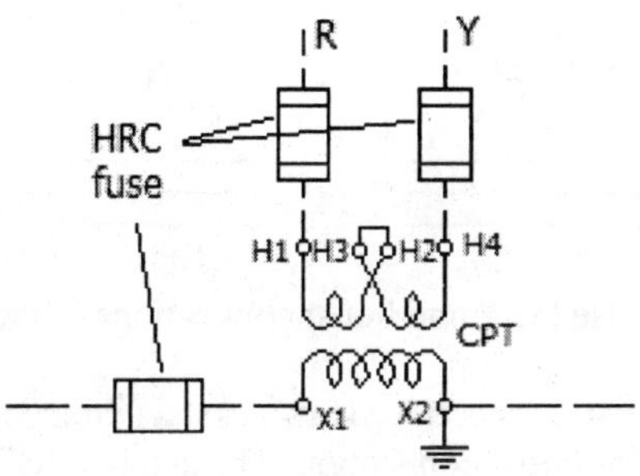

Fig. 2.2 (j): Typical control transformer circuit

15) Booster transformer: Figure 2.2 (k) illustrates the connection diagrams of various types of single-phase booster transformers.

LEGEND: SW: Series winding; CW: Common winding; PW: Parallel winding;

1. Primary; 2. Secondary

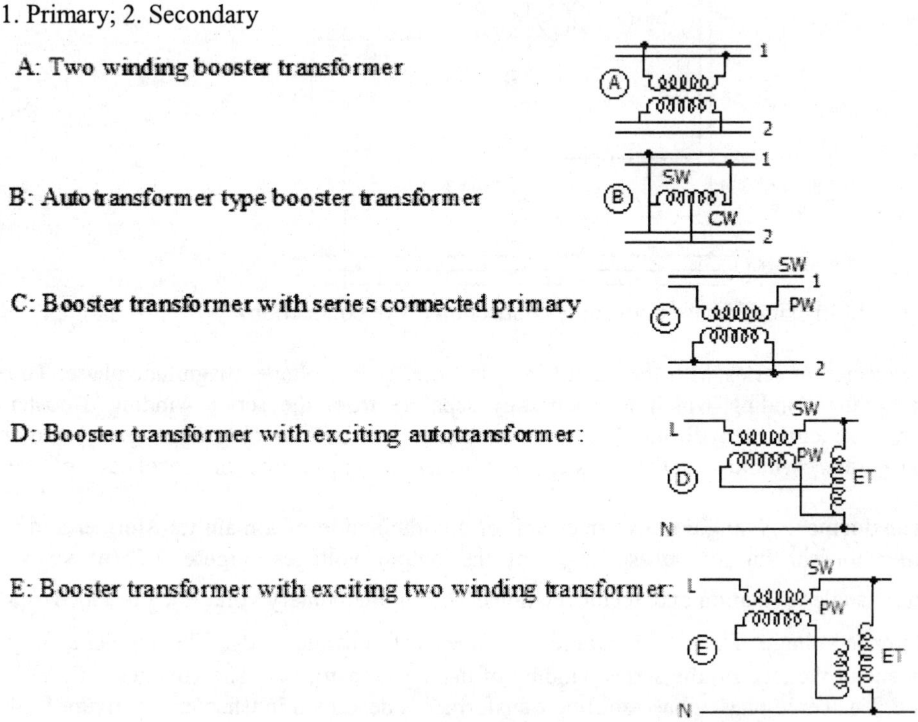

Fig. 2.2 (k): Single-phase booster transformers.

Figure 2.2 (L) shows three-phase buck and boost connections. Open delta diagrams are for boost connection. For buck connection reverse input and output. The symbol "O" used in these connection diagrams indicates where to install over-current protective device.

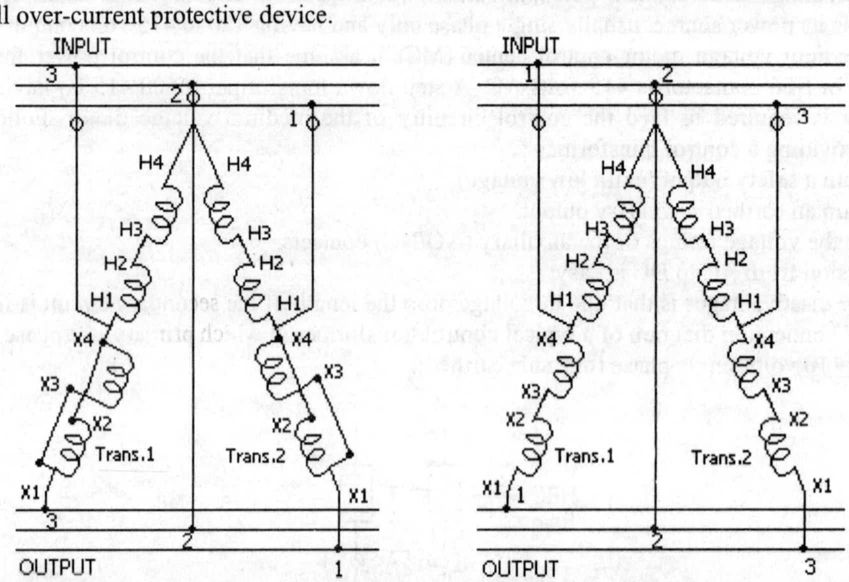

Fig. 2.2 (L): Three-phase buck and boost connections (Open delta connection).

Figure 2.2 (m) shows three-phase boost connection. In wye (star) connection the input and output cannot be reversed. Hence this diagram is only for boost connection. The symbol "O" shows the location for over-current protection.

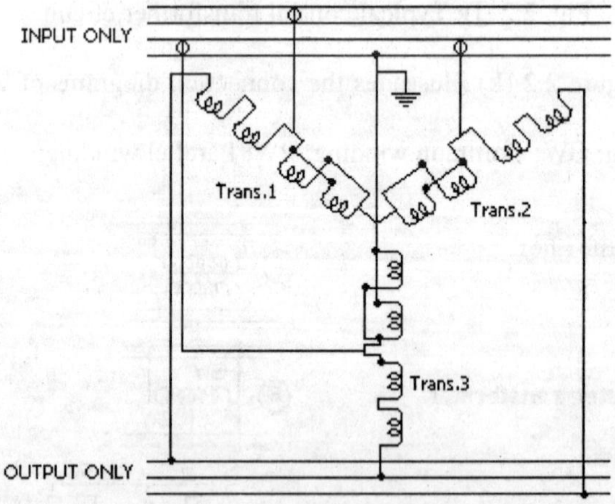

Fig. 2.2 (m): Three-phase boost only connection (Wye connection)

One of the winding is connected in series with the circuit in order to alter its voltage, magnitude/phase. The other winding is an energizing winding which is electrically separate from the series winding. Booster transformer set consists of an exciting transformer (an autotransformer or a two winding transformer) and a booster transformer. The parallel winding of the booster transformer is supplied by the secondary of the exciting transformer.

16) Phase regulating transformer: A single transformer unit or a combination of a main transformer and a supplementary transformer for shifting the phase angle of the output voltages. Figure 2.2 (n) shows connections for direct phase angle regulation and vector relations. The supplementary voltage e_2 is added at a phase angle ϕ to the reference voltage. Thereby the angle δ changes with change in e_2**.** The supplementary voltage is changed by means of the taps on the series winding of the autotransformer. The voltages Va', Vb', Vc' are lesser than Va, Vb, Vc. Three-phase phase-shifting transformer is described in Chapter # 5, figure 5.14 (e).

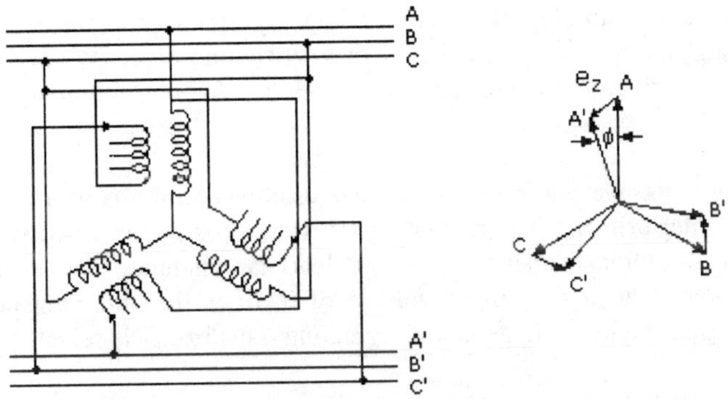

Fig. 2.2 (n): Direct quadrature phase regulation transformer.

Figure 2.2 (o) shows the connection diagram of two transformers for phase angle control. Two transformers are often necessary for reasons of dielectric or short circuit strength. The first transformer serves to supply the second supplementary or series transformer. It is quite possible to use an existing power transformer to provide excitation for the unit.

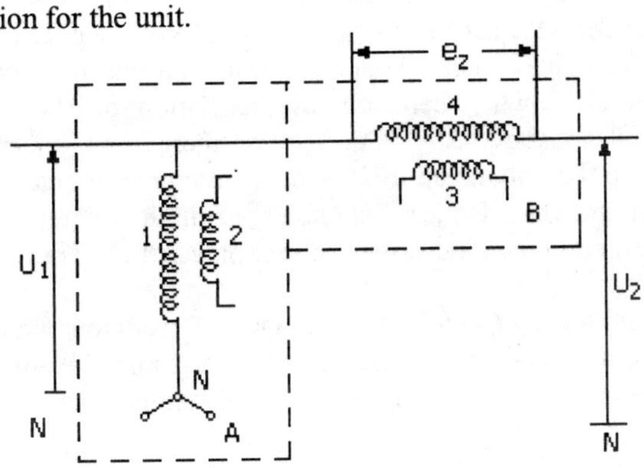

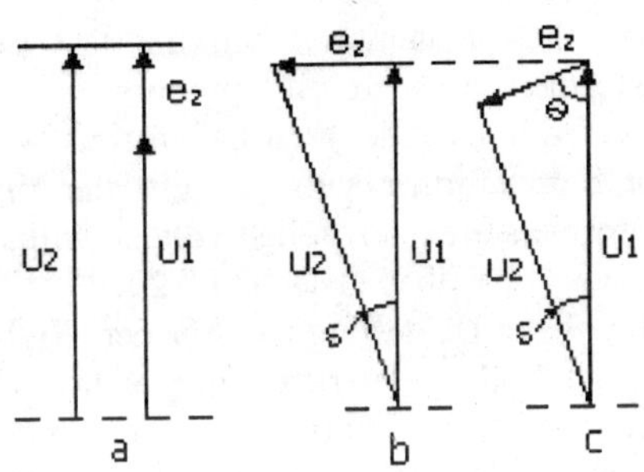

Fig. 2.2 (o): Phase angle control by, two transformers. Fig. 2.2 (p): In-phase quadrature, phase angle regulation

Figure 2.2 (p) illustrates the vector diagram of in-phase, quadrature, phase angle regulation of transformer lines.

In-phase voltage regulation method: Only magnitude of output voltage is regulated without change in phase angle.

Quadrature voltage regulation method: The supplementary voltage is added in quadrature to get phase angle shift. Phase angle regulation method: Supplementary voltage is added at an angle to achieve regulation of load angle δ.

17) Inter-phase transformer: These transformers are necessary between two parallel running rectifier transformers, on rectifier side to absorb the differences in DC voltages and reduce circulating currents through windings. They have a core with windings. The reactance in the path absorbs the difference in voltages of two rectifier transformers and limits the circulating currents. Typical inter-phase transformer circuit is shown in Figure 2.2 (q).

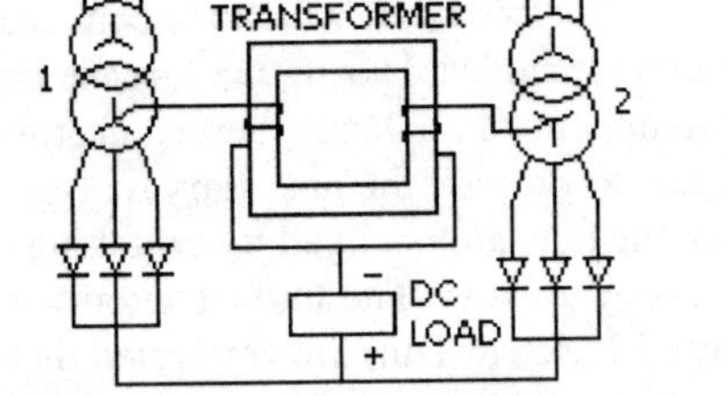

Fig. 2.2 (q): Inter-phase transformer circuit.

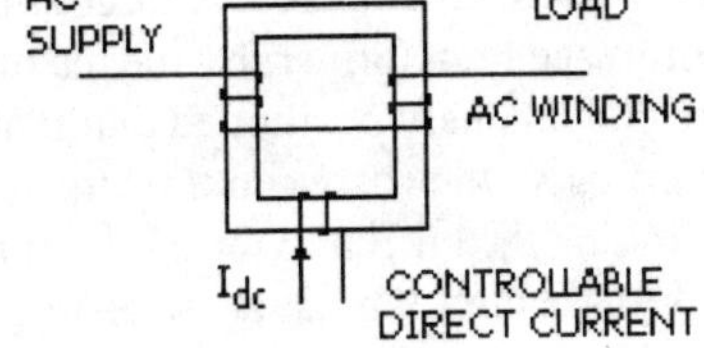

Fig. 2.2 (r): Transductor connection

18) Transductors: It has a core with controlled DC winding. By varying the current in DC winding, the flux in the core is varied by using the non-linear portion of magnetization curve. By varying exciting DC current, the reluctance of the core is varied and impedance changes. Hence AC current changes. Figure 2.2 (r) shows transductor circuit.

19) Regulating transformer: Regulating transformer receives power from mains at mains supply voltage and supplies to rectifier transformer primary. The regulating transformer is either a two winding transformer with on-load tap changer or an autotransformer with an on load tap-changer. Tap changing is automatically controlled to achieve the variation in the output voltage of rectifier for obtaining power control. Thus for higher power output of rectifier, higher voltage tap of regulating transformer is selected.

20) Testing transformers: Based on its application, testing transformers are classified in to:

(a) Short-circuit testing transformer: These transformers are for factory testing of LV and HV switchgears. It is capable of withstanding repeated short circuits, elimination of distortion in recovery over voltages, meet X/R ratio.

(b) High voltage testing transformer: For routine high voltage tests on other electrical apparatus and also special tests like measurements of potential difference etc. High voltage testing transformers are either autotransformers or single-phase isolation transformers. Primary is connected to 220 volts supply and the secondary is 60 to 100 KV or above. The testing transformers are subjected to transient over-voltage during their operation when the test piece, break down. Therefore, the insulation of HV testing transformers are carefully proportioned. For voltage above 100 KV, two or more transformers are connected in cascade. First transformer will step up the voltage up to 50% of the required output and the second transformer will provide the final test voltage. Typical examples of high voltage testing transformers are (1) Applied voltage withstand test equipment described in section 2.20; (2) Transformer oil test set described in section 2.23.

(c) High voltage DC testing transformer. High pressure testing (up to 1200 KV, DC) of insulating materials, cable and other electrical equipments, HV electron tubes etc. This is a power source for impulse generators, X-ray equipment, radar controls etc. It is used for electrostatic applications such as spray painting, dust precipitation, pollution control etc.

21) Grounding transformers: Following types of earthing transformers are used for neutral grounding of power transformers and AC generators: (1) Single-phase distribution transformers for grounding the neutral of Generator-transformer combined unit. (Refer figure 1.5 (c) of Chapter # 1); (2) Zigzag transformer described in figure 2.13 (g). (3) Three-phase star / delta neutral grounding transformer described in figure 2.13 (h): Three phase grounding transformers are used in continuous process industries, like steel plants where power interruptions due to arcing faults cannot be tolerated. Star/delta connected / Inter Star connected (10 to 60 second ratings with auxiliary winding) dry type or mineral oil filled earthing transformers are used for system earthing, where no neutral is available. Neutral grounding transformer has special winding arrangements to achieve required zero sequence impedance.

Arc suppression coils are also used for neutral grounding to limit the fault current of generators and transformers. They are specially constructed to achieve the required saturation characteristics.

22) Instrument transformers: Instrument transformers are classified in to (1) Current transformer (2) Potential transformer. Both CT and PT are demonstrated in Chapter # 5, section 5.1 & 5.2 respectively.

23) Arc furnace transformer: Furnace transformer is a two winding transformer with OFF load tap changing in the 11 KV or 33 KV primary side. The secondary voltages are between 80 to 500 volts and secondary currents are several thousand amperes. A three-phase furnace has three electrodes, which are connected to the secondary of the furnace transformer, by means of flexible high current cables. During the furnace operation, the electrodes are continuously positioned automatically for obtaining current balance. Series reactors are connected in the primary side (between transformer and switchgear) to provide the necessary reactance to stabilize arc by limiting the current. During the furnace operation, the taps are changed by switching off the medium voltage furnace circuit breaker, so as to get desired secondary voltage. The furnace circuit breaker is suitable for intermittent operation. Very large furnace units (above 50 Metric Ton) are connected through 66

KV to 220 KV supply with automatic ON load tap changers. While selecting the power supply for an arc furnace, the power line should be taken direct from substations to maintain the system fault level.

24) Coreless induction furnace transformer: Coreless induction furnaces are very popular with cast iron and aluminium melting foundries. It is a two winding star / star transformer with primary fixed taps and secondary ON load automatic tap changer. The three-phase power to the furnace is through a starting contactor via series connected starting resistors. The power requirement in the initial heating stage is more and reduces for the subsequent heat and automatically changeover from starting contactor to main contactor. The furnace heating-coil is connected to two phases. Fixed and switching capacitors are provided across the two loaded phases for maintaining power factor between 0.8 to unity. Generally no electrical protection is required in the low voltage side. Transformer is fitted with Buchholz relay, temperature indicators, cooling water failure alarm etc.

2.3. TRANSFORMER CONSTRUCTION AND FITMENT OF ACCESSORIES.

Oil filled power transformer consists of the assembly of following components:

(1) Core assembly: The cores are made of low loss grain oriented silicon steel lamination sheet, which form a closed magnetic circuit, and are so designed as to yield low iron losses, to meet IEC publication 76. The laminated core are then clamped strongly to ensure a good mechanical strength and to reduce vibration and the noise level.

(2) HV/LV windings: Windings are designed and constructed to withstand an over voltage and impulse voltage as specified in IEC 76. The windings are made of PVF grade enameled copper wire or paper wrapped flat copper wire. Insulation between layers of winding normally comprises of Class A insulation paper. The windings are so constructed, so as to meet besides the required dielectric strength, but also a sound mechanical strength. Low copper losses and standard percentage impedance and smooth circulation of oil through the windings (good heat transfer) provide good performance. Winding must be capable of withstanding internal and external short circuit stress for a specified period.

(3) Core and winding assembly: The core and coil of the transformers are then assembled together and heated and dried in a vacuum drying oven until the insulation resistance goes up to several mega-ohms. After drying out process tanking and bolting of lid is to be carried out. Gasket used is of nitrite-rubber, which besides, its high temperature withstand capability also have an excellent oil resistant characters.

(4) Main tank and lid: The tank and cover is fabricated from mild steel plate, bended and welded to construct them as required size and shape. The fabricated tank (before going to coating/painting process) is subjected to pressure test to ensure no oil leakage occurred during test. The coating of tanks strictly follows a standard procedure: (1) pre-treatment process (Shot blast process), which help to eliminate the grease and rusts on tank surface, followed by phosphating process by dipping the tank into a phosphating tank. (2) Base coat (primer) is to be applied after the pretreatment. Then after being baked properly, followed by (3) Final coat / surface coat up to the required thickness by using oil and heat resistant grade dark gray paint (Colour code No: RAL7003), which reflects the Sun radiation. Tank assembly consists of: (a) Sliding channels; (b) Trolley truck (Steel carriage with flanged caster wheels placed on rails); (c) Anchor foundation-bolts (stopper clamps for rail mounted transformers); (d) Lifting hooks; (e) Hydraulic jack pad; (f) Grounding connection between tank parts and grounding terminals; (g) Vacuuming, oil draining, oil filling, and oil sampling valves; (h) Ladder (i) Rating plate as required under IEC standard 76.

(5) Transformer insulating oil: Shell Diala B grade mineral oil (or equivalent) manufactured from quality petroleum base stocks, blended with selected additives and conforming to IEC 296 class 1-1A, 2-2A is used as transformer oil, which has critical electrical properties like breakdown voltage, Tan delta and ageing profile. Selection of the low viscosity index Naphthenic base oils ensures excellent cooling characteristics. The colour of new transformer oil is Pale-amber. Sampling and testing instructions are given in section 2.14

Following are the disadvantages of transformer oil:

(1) Arc produced in the oil is inflammable and explosive. If arc is not extinguished the pressure in the tank may rise above the safe limit and explosion may occur.
(2) Oil absorbs moisture and dielectric strength reduces by carbonization, which occurs during arcing.
(3) Oil needs periodic testing and filtration and replacement.
(4) The dust particles and sludge can create flashover due to tracking.

6) Conservator tank: Fabricated steel tank fitted with air cushion, (in the top of the transformer main tank) for accommodating the transformer oil created due to expansion or contraction in the main tank. Conservator is provided with oil level indicator, oil draining valve, air valve, and diaphragm. For OLTC, either separate conservator or partition in the main conservator is required. Oil conservator shall have a volume of at least 11% of the transformer oil volume. Control cubicle and OLTC cubicle should not be mounted below the conservator

7) Radiators: Radiators are manufactured from cold rolled steel sheets, cold drawn and seam welded to form its desired dimension and then galvanized after fabrication. The purpose of radiators is to limit the temperature of oil and winding in a transformer by dissipating heat that is generated due to losses within the transformer while in service. Radiator is provided with air release plug, oil drain plug, shut-off valve to stop the oil flow if the radiator is leaking. Where built-on type radiators are used each radiator shall be connected to the main tank through flanged valves.

8) Cable box / bus duct termination box: For transformers with medium voltage secondary usually cable boxes with stainless steel bottom plates are provided for glanding and termination of multiple single core XLPE insulated cables. Usually brass-wiping glands are bolted to the base plate for glanding cables. Bus bars are provided to connect the multiple cables single-core cables by using crimp type lugs. For large transformers bus ducts are used. Expansion type flexible connectors are used for connecting the bus duct to the transformer bushing terminals.

9) Cooler banks:
Each cooler bank is provided with:
(a) A valve at each point of connection to the transformer tank.
(b) Loose blanking plates for blanking off the main oil connections.
(c) A 50 mm filter valve at the top of each cooler bank. For oil filter connection.
(d) A 50 mm drain valve at the lowest point of each inter connecting oil pipe.
(e) A thermometer pocket fitted with captive screw cap in the inlet and outlet oil pipes.

10) Valves on main tank, conservator and Tap-changer:
(a) A 50 mm bore filter valve located near to the top of the tank for filter machine hose connection.
(b) A 50 mm bore filter valve located near to the bottom of the tank for filter machine hose connection.
(c) A 50 mm drain valve located such that the main tank can be completely drained or for oil sampling.
(d) A drain valve for oil conservator.
(e) One valve between the conservator and Buchholz relay of the main tank.
(f) One 50 mm drain valve for tap-changer tank.
(g) One 50 mm filter valve for filter machine hose connection to tap changer.

11) Oil pipes and flanges:
Oil piping necessary for connecting the transformer to its conservator and cooler banks etc should be of approved material with machined flange joints. Dimensions of steel pipes may be in accordance with BS 3600. Expansion piece is provided in each oil pipe connection between the transformer and each oil cooler bank. Proper supports and foundation bolts are to be provided for the oil piping and all other attachments. It should be possible to drain any section of pipe-work independently of the rest and drain valves or plugs must be provided as necessary.

12) Rating diagram and valve plates:
The following rating diagrams made of stainless steel plate are to be fixed to each transformer:
(a) A rating plate bearing the data specified in IEC 76-1, including primary / secondary voltage, full load current, short-circuit current rating, percentage impedance etc.
(b) A diagram plate showing the internal winding connections and the voltage vector relationship of the several windings in accordance with IEC 76-1, including the transformer voltage ratio of each tap and physical relationship of the terminals etc.
(c) A plate showing the location and function and position of all valves and air release cocks or plugs

Figure 2.3 (a) to (c) respectively illustrates the outline drawings of a typical ONAN/ONAFPower transformer front view, top view, and side view respectively.

LEGEND: [Figure 2.3 (a)]

1. Shut-off valve (Buchholz relay)
2. Buchholz relay main tank.
3. H.V. Neutral bushing.
4. Lifting lugs for transformer.
5. H.V. Phase bushings
6. Lifting lug for core and coil.
7. Over pressure relief device main tank.
8. Drainage oil filter valve bottom.
9. Bottom oil sampling valve.
10. Grounding pad
11. Throttle valve for radiators.
12. Jacking bosses
13. Skid base
14. Anti-vibration pad
15. Motor drive unit for OLTC.
16. Gas sampling device.
17. Dehydrating breather for OLTC.
18. Drain valve conservator main tank.
19. Drain valve conservator OLTC.
20. Dehydrating breather for main tank.

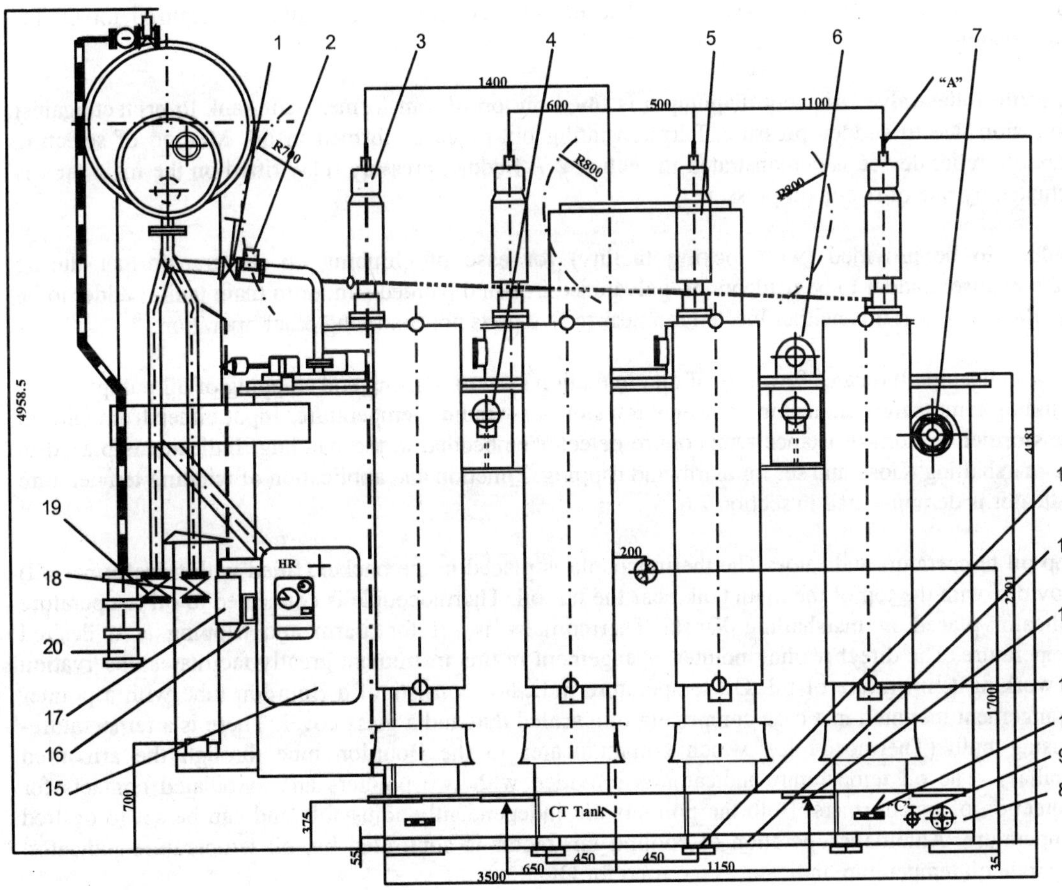

Fig. 2.3 (a): Outline drawing indicating accessories of a typical ONAN/ONAF power transformer (Front view) (Courtesy, Pauwels Trafo)

13) Accessories mounted on power transformers:

1. Buchholz relay: The relay is fitted in the oil connection between conservator and tank. The relay comprises a housing containing two pivoted buckets / floats counter balanced by dead weights. Due to gas collection, the oil level inside the relay drops and the upper bucket moves down. This tilts the mercury switch bringing fluid mercury in such a position that it bridge, the normally open contacts. For large transformers Buchholz relay shall be fitted with a gas-sampling valve at ground level (1500 mm above ground) gas receiver and indicator. The function and application of Buchholz relay is demonstrated in section 2.5. OLTC is provided with surge relay, which is illustrated in figure 2.8 (c).

2. Silica gel dehydrating breather: Whenever there is a change in the ambient temperature or in the load of an oil immersed transformer, there is a change in oil temperature and, hence in the volume of oil. Increase in oil volume, causes the air above the oil level in the conservator to be pushed out and decrease in oil volume causes air to be drawn in. Thus the transformer "breathes". When air is breathed-in, there is a possibility of moisture and dust from atmosphere to be sucked in. These contaminants deteriorate the insulation properties of oil. Hence silica gel breather is provided which arrests moisture and dust from the air drawn in. Installed in a pipe from conservator, filled with dry silica gel (pink colour). Silica gel absorbs the moisture and admits only dry air and becomes blue colour, can be dried by heating during periodic maintenance, to obtain pink colour. Silica gel breather shall be mounted 1500 mm above ground level. Separate silica gel breather is required for OLTC conservator.

3. Pressure relief valve: Air vent diaphragm is fitted on top of transformer main tank to protect against explosion due to sudden pressure. Permit venting out of gases formed in oil. Method of selecting pressure relief device is demonstrated in section 2.7. Sudden pressure relay fitted on the main tank is actuated by rate of rise in oil pressure.

4. Ladder to be provided (with locking facility) for ease of climbing up the transformer during maintenance. Ladder to be made up of, galvanized iron and painted similar to main tank. Ladder to be installed such that it is neither located too near to live parts nor hindering other operation.

5. Flow indicators: Indicates flow rate of oil circulation system, starting and stopping of oil pumps.
6. Winding temperature indicator: Indicates transformer-winding temperature. Input either from current transformer or from resistance temperature detector embedded in the winding. Indicator is placed in the marshalling Kiosk and set for alarm and tripping. Function and application of winding temperature indicator is demonstrated in section 2.6.

7. Top oil temperature indicator: The thermocouple is placed in the pocket (filled with transformer oil) provided with the top of the main tank near the hot oil. Thermocouple is connected to oil temperature indicator placed in marshalling Kiosk. Thermometer is set for alarm and tripping at a desired temperature. The direct reading pointer arrangement in this instrument greatly facilitates observation of working temperature of oil. Oil temperature indicator consists of a Bourdon tube with a pointer arrangement mounted in a case comprising of a scaled dial and a glass cover. There is a temperature-sensing bulb (Thermocouple), which communicates to the Bourdon tube through the armoured capillary. The oil temperature indicator is provided with two pointers and associated contacts for protection of transformers. Both the pointers are independently adjustable and can be set to desired temperature. Automatic operation of cooling fan motor is controlled by, oil temperature indicator. Separate oil temperature indicator is required for OLTC.

8. On load Tap changer (OLTC) with conservator: On load tap changer is connected to either primary or secondary winding of a power transformer. For star connected winding with solidly grounded neutral the tap is generally placed on the grounded neutral end of the winding. By placing the tap nearer to the neutral end, the voltage rating of the tap changer can be minimized. For automatic voltage control of transformers, voltage control relays are employed. Relay sense the voltage from the voltage transformer and gives command to on load tap changer drive motor to raise or lower the voltage. On load tap changers and voltage regulating relay are demonstrated in section 2.8 and 2.9 respectively.

9. Impact recorder: Impact recorder is temporarily installed for observing shake during transit (shipping). After unloading the transformer on its bay (foundation) the impact recorder shall be removed and the graph plotted is to be examined against any shake. This is required only during shipping or transporting.

LEGEND: [Figure 2.3 (b)]

21. Drain and filling valve of OLTC.
22. Oil filter valve (top)
23. Over pressure relief device OLTC.
24. LV Neutral bushing
25. C.T terminal box (Winding temperature)
26. C.T terminal box (L.V.Neutral).
27. L.V. phase bushings
28. Tertiary bushings
29. Towing lug.
30. Core and frame earthing bushings.
31. End frame earthing plate.
32. Lockable ladder
33. Core earthing plate
34. C.T. Terminal box (HV).
35. Winding temperature indicator
36. Spare thermometer pocket
37. ON-Load tap changer.
38. Shut off valve OLTC connectiom.
49. OLTC protective relay.
40: Equalizing valve main tank.
41. Equilizing valve OLTC.
42. Equalizing valve vacuum process
43. Vacuum pulling range

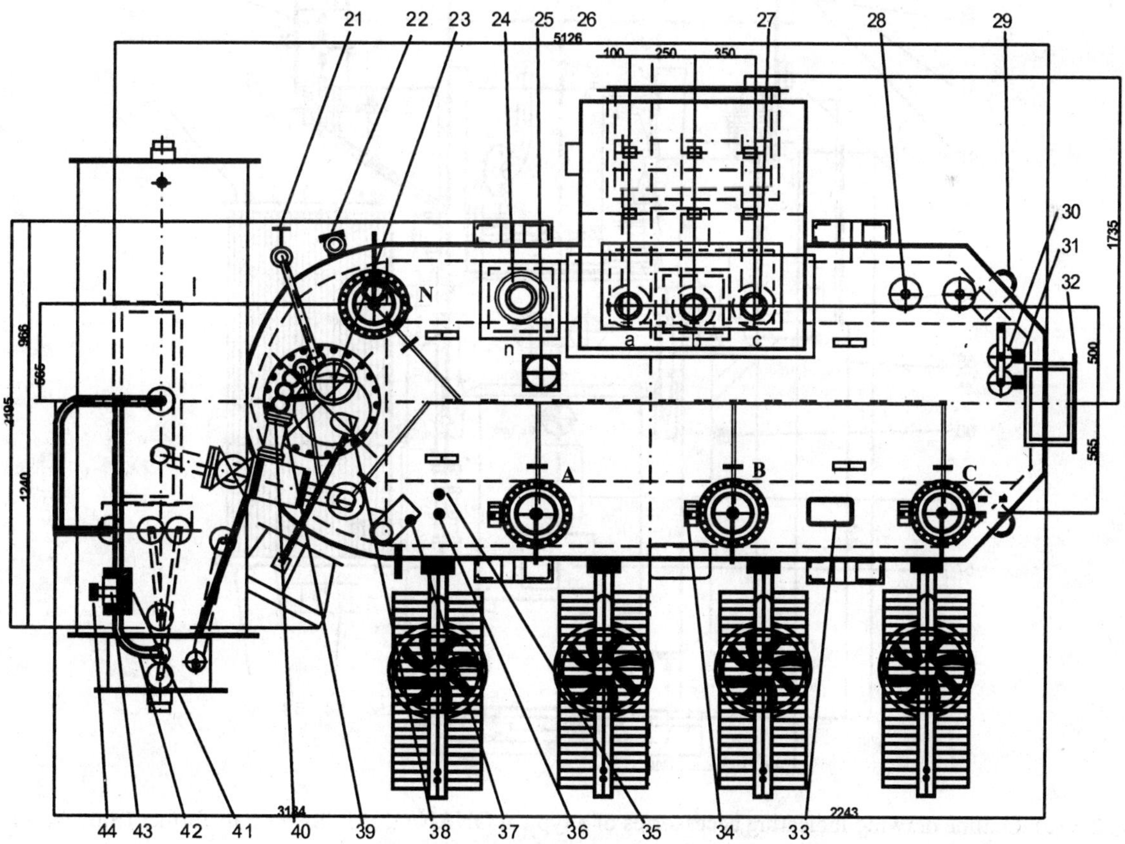

Fig. 2.3 (b): Outline drawing indicating accessories of a typical ONAN / ONAF Power transformer (Top view). (Courtesy, Pauwels Trafo)

10) Marshalling Kiosk:

Power transformer is provided with marshalling kiosk or tank-mounted cubicle. It is used for housing oil temperature indicator, winding temperature indicator, fan and pump controls, current transformer terminals, anti condensing heaters etc. These equipments are having electrical contacts or terminals to be connected to the protection schemes to give alarm / annunciation or shutdown under abnormal conditions. Incoming AC power supply cables to OLTC, pumps and fans etc, as well as DC control power cable is also terminated in the marshalling box by using double compression cable glands. Control cubicle (Kiosk) should not be installed below the conservator. .

LEGEND: [Figure 2.3 (c)]

45. Magnetic oil level indicator main tank.
46. Conservator end plate bolted type
47. Air vent
48. Drain plug for radiator.
49. Conservator for OLTC.
50. Magnetic oil level indicator OLTC
51. Air vent for radiator
52. Drain plug for radiator.
53. Detachable radiators
54. Cooling fans
55. Winding temperature indicator.
56. Warning notice/Operating instructions
57. Rating and diagram plate.
58. Oil piping and valve locating plate
59. Top oil temperature indicator
60. Anchor lug for transport

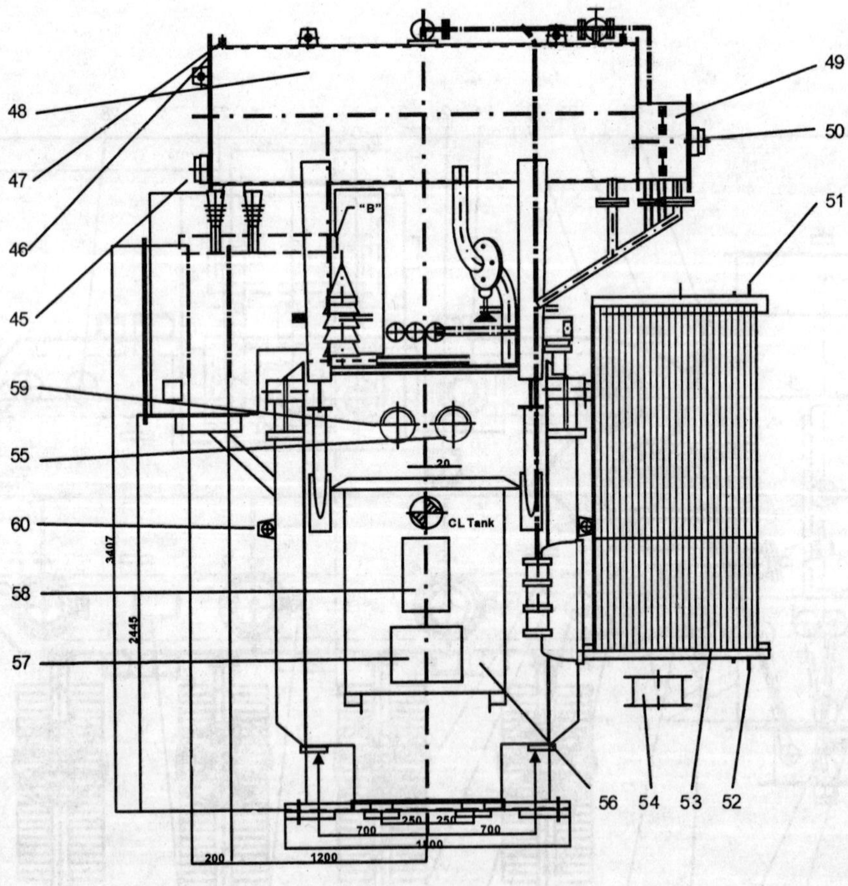

Fig. 2.3 (c): Outline drawing indicating accessories of a typical ONAN/ONAF Power transformer (Side view).
(Courtesy, Pauwels Trafo)

11) Power transformer bushings: Transformer primary/secondary/tertiary/zigzag windings are connected to the external circuit through terminal bushings manufactured in conformity with IEC standard 137. The bushings are installed on the lid of transformer main tank or, on sidewalls of the transformer tank. The lower ends of the bushing protrudes in to the tank and at both their ends are provided with suitable fasteners to connect the line leads inside the transformer and external conductors outside it. Generally, condenser bushings are used for 66 KV and above. These bushings contain their own oil and are sealed to retain the same. Whenever these bushings are mounted on bushing pockets or raised truncated portions, air vent pipes are provided for carrying away air or gas from these pockets to Buchholz relay during service. Figure 2.3 (d) illustrates a typical condenser bushing. The main electrical insulation is a condenser body, made of a continuous sheet of pure craft paper, wound around a tube or copper conductor rod. The paper is "dried" by placing in heated cylinders and infrared rays during winding, to reduce the water content to the Paper. During a sequence of aluminium foils, cylindrical shape and coaxial disposition is inserted between the layers of paper. These foils grade the best possible distribution of the radial and longitudinal electrical gradient between the conductor and the fixing flange, which is grounded. After the winding the bushing is assembled and placed in to an oven at 106°C, treated under vacuum. The impregnation is made under pressure in order to obtain the best impregnation and to test the perfect tightness. After impregnation the head of bushing is filled with nitrogen cushion. All this process is automatic. The airside envelope is made of porcelain brown colour or fiberglass envelope covered by silicone sheds with creepage for very high-polluted area 31mm/KV. Creepage (leakage) distance is the shortest distance along the surface of an insulator from one conducting part (terminal) to another conducting part, which may be energized or at ground potential. Bushing type current transformer termination box shall be designed such that ingress of water should not occur.

KEY AND CONSTRUCTION DETAILS: Refer Figure 2.3 (d).

1: Terminal for connection of tubular (Aluminium or copper) bus bar or AAAC (all aluminium alloy conductor).
2: Assembly of central tube and conductor in the bushing.
3: Aluminium casted head with oil expansion chamber and oil level indicator. The chamber is hermatically sealed.
4: COT bushings are filled with dried degassed insulating oil
5: Porcelain insulator made of high-grade electro-technical porcelain conforming to IEC 815. The insulator is connected to the mounting flange using Portland cement and sealed with O-ring gasket.
6: Central tube and conductor made of oil impregnated wide band paper with layers of aluminium foil to control the field strength radially and axially. Depending on the current rating, the paper and foil are wound on either a central tube or a solid conductor.
7: Mounting flange with integrated test tap made of corrosion free aluminium alloy machined to ensure that an excellent seal between the bushing and the transformer.
8: Current transformer pocket suitable for mounting multi core current transformer for protection and metering.
9: Epoxy resin insulator on the oil side of the transformer tank is made of an epoxy resin tube. It is designed to withstand 130° Celsius temperature, as the temperature may arise during the dry-out processes of the transformer.
10: End-shielding: Special aluminium electrode is cast in to the end of the epoxy resin tube. The end-shield controls the electrical field strength in this area.

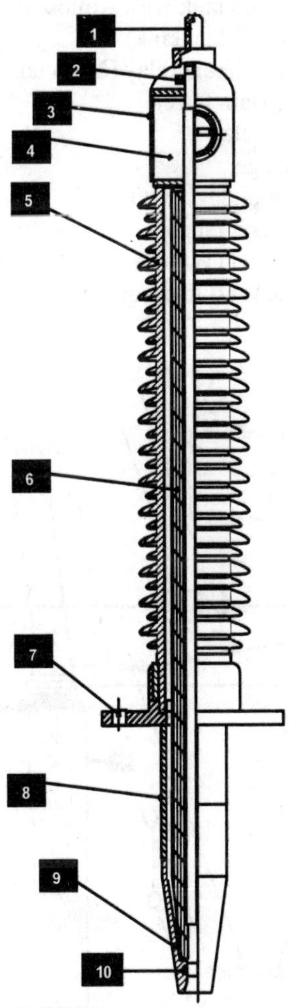

Fig. 2.3(d): Cut view of typical high voltage bushing

11) Arcing Horn: Bushings used in outdoor transformers are equipped with arcing horns [refer figure 4.11 (c) of Chapter # 4] to discharge the arc produced due to lightning surges. On the bushing flange there are threaded holes for fixing the lower arcing horn. The upper arcing horn is fixed with one of the screws used for the fixing of the terminal. The suggested discharge distance for High voltage range is given below.

Rated voltage (KV)	52	72.5	100	125	145	170	245
Discharge distance of Arcing horn: (mm)	320	500	600	750	900	1000	1450

12) Oil piping and valve locations.

Figure 2.3 (e) illustrates the oil piping and valve locations for a typical ONAN/ONAF power transformer. **All Pipes must be properly secured to the tank in order to avoid excessive vibration.**

LEGEND:

1. Magnetic oil level indicator (OLTC).
2. Conservator for OLTC.
3. Equalizing valve for vacuum filling (OLTC).
4. Equalizing valve for vacuum filling (Main tank)
5.Equilizing valve for filter pricess (Main tank).
6.Equalizing valve for vacuum filling (Atmoseal)
7. Conservator oil filling pocket
8. Conservator air vent
9. Conservator for main tank with Atmoseal
10 Magnetic oil level (Main tank)
11 Shut-off valve, Buchholz relay (Main tank)
12 Buchholz relay (Main tank)
13 OLTC protective relay
14 On-load, tap-changer
15 Over pressure relief device (OLTC)
16 Thermometer pocket (spare)
17 Thermometer pocket (Winding temperature)
18 Thermometer pocket (Oil temperature)
19 Over pressure relief device Main tank
20 Throttle valve for radiator
21 Air vent for radiator
22 Drain plug for radiator
23 Radiator disconnectable
24 Drain oil filter valve bottom
25 Bottom oil sampling valve
26 Winding temperature indicator (LV)
27 Control cabinet for cooling fans
28 Top oil temperature indicator
29 Gas sampling device
30 Oil filter valve top
31 Shut-off valve OLTC conservator
32 Drain and filling valve of OLTC
33 Drain valve conservator main tank
34 Dehydrating breather main tank
35 Dehydrating breather OLTC
36 Drain valve conservator OLTC

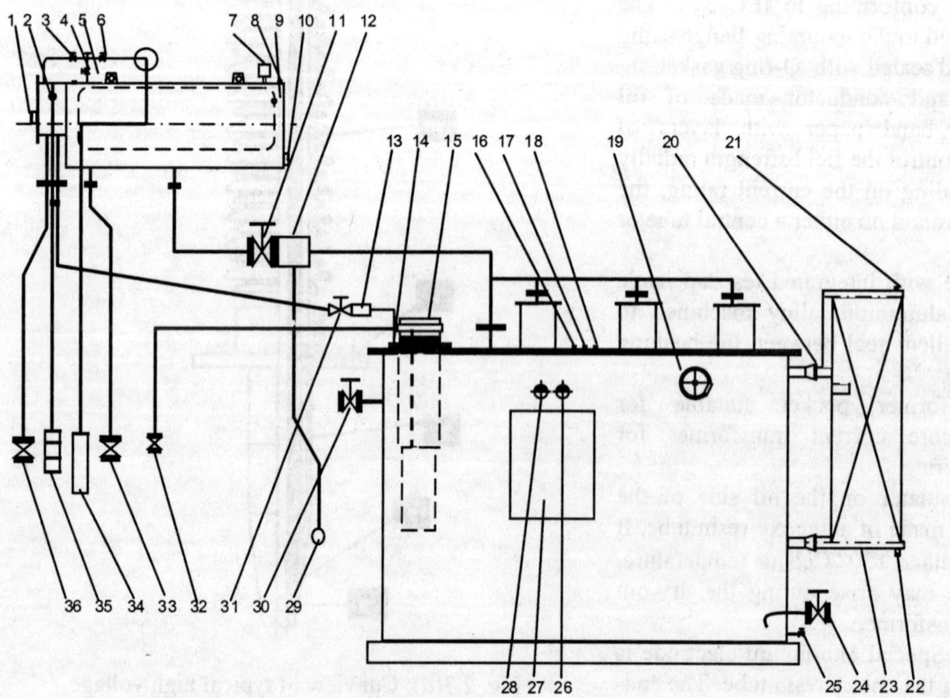

Fig. 2.3 (e): Oil piping and valve location drawing of a typical ONAN/ONAF Power transformer.
(Courtesy, Pauwels Trafo)

10. Magnetic oil level indicator with maximum and minimum oil level contacts for alarm/annunciation: For large power transformers dial type oil level indicators as shown in Figure 2.3 (f) are used. For distribution transformers conventional glass oil level indicators are used. These compartments are sealed against leakage of oil by a metallic diaphragm. On the oil side compartment, there is a bevel gear wheel and it is positioned near the diaphragm. Movement of the float duc to rise and fall of oil level in the conservator results in to circular motion of the driving magnet. A follower magnet is positioned in the pointer side compartment near the diaphragm. This magnet has its poles face to face to the poles of driving magnet from the oil side compartment coupling them magnetically. The movement of float is, therefore, transferred through the diaphragm, eliminating direct oil light mechanical coupling. The other end of the axis of the driven magnet an indicating pointer is fitted. The dial is calibrated to show the oil level in the conservator. The dial and the pointer are housed behind the front glass. The dial has three positions marked. The follower magnet has also a cam fitted on it, which operates a mercury switch. When this magnet is at a position corresponding to low oil level the mercury switch closes the normally open contacts. These contacts are normally wired to give audible alarm. **Magnetic oil level indicator mounted on the conservator shall be slanted towards ground so that it can be read from ground level without causing parallax errors.**

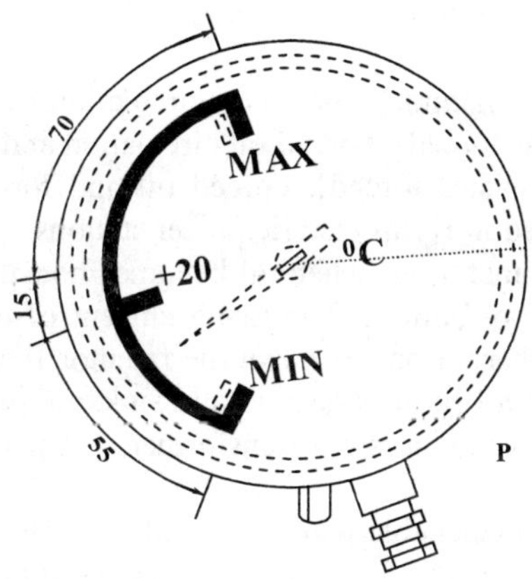

Fig. 2.3 (f): Magnetic oil level indicator.

2.4 TRANSFORMER COOLING BY USING OIL, AIR, AND WATER.

Transformer oil is a refined fraction of mineral oil boiling in the temperature range from 250 to 300°C. After refining, the oil is chemically very pure and contains exclusively liquid hydrocarbons. **In service the function of the oil is: firstly it acts as electrical insulation and secondly it carries off heat from the active parts to the coolers.** As such the requirements of the transformer oil as an electrical insulating and cooling medium has risen.

The electrical characteristics are very good if the oil is pure. The cooling ability is high and also the pour point (solidification point) low if the viscosity is low. However, the viscosity cannot be lowered beyond the limit, because lowering the viscosity also lowers the flash point and this is harmful with regard to the fire safety. A flash point of 130°C is taken as the lower limit. At the same time the viscosity may be sufficiently low to give a pour point better than (-) 40°C. There are two fundamental requirements of the oil to be used in a transformer.

1) The oil must be clean, i.e. free from impurities such as suspended solid matter, detrimental chemical compounds and water contents.

2) The oil must be chemically, stable, i.e. its deterioration by the attack of heat and oxygen at the service temperatures must be as slow as possible.

The impurities effect, primarily the electrical characteristics of the oil. The effect, however, depends up on the type of impurities present:

a) Solid particles larger than about 15 μm in cross section and water droplets reduce the dielectric strength of the oil.
b) In the presence of solid particles the dielectric strength is further reduced by water dissolved in the oil.
c) Very small solid particles (< 15 μm) as well as dissolved polar compounds give in an electric field rise to dielectric losses in the oil.

Requirements on the dielectric strength in a transformer or circuit breaker according to IEC publication 422 is as follows:
Transformers: (a) Medium voltage < 60 KV; breakdown voltage > 30 KV.
(b) High voltage > 60 KV up to 245 KV; breakdown voltage > 40 KV
(c) High and Extra high voltage > 245 KV; breakdown voltage > 50 KV
Circuit breakers: (a) < 170 KV breakdown voltage > 20 KV
(b) ≥ 170 KV breakdown voltage > 30 KV
The above value is applicable for Shell diala dx or Esso univolt N 36 mineral oil.
If the breakdown voltage of the oil does not comply with the above requirements, the oil obviously contains too large a quantity of solid impurities and / or water. The maximum permissible water contents according to IEC, is 20 mg/dm^3 for voltage ratings above 170 KV and 30 mg/dm^3 for ratings below 170 KV. For the dielectric dissipation factor (tan δ), which is affected by the smaller particles and dissolved polar compounds. Generally, 400°/oo as an upper limit for tan δ as measured at 90°C.

Different types of cooling systems employed for oil immersed power and distribution transformers are:
(1) ONAN: [Oil natural, air natural]. Only radiators are provided for transformer cooling
(2) ONAF: [Oil natural, air forced]. Radiators and cooling fans (Air blower) are provided for cooling
(3) OFAN: [Oil forced air natural]. Forced oil circulation by using oil pump and cooler
(4) OFAF: [Oil forced air forced]. Forced oil circulation and forced air cooling.
(5) OFWF: [Oil forced water forced]. Forced oil and forced water circulation; For example, Transformers installed in Hydroelectric power stations.

(1) ONAN (Radiator Cooling): In a transformer when oil becomes hot, it becomes lighter and therefore rises up, drawing in its wake, colder oil from bottom. The rising current of oil takes the heat away from the oil surfaces to the top of the tank. From there it passes down the radiator fins where the heat is reduced out in to the atmosphere. As the oil gets cooled it becomes heavier and sinks to the bottom of the tank. The number of sections per radiator and the number of radiators per transformer is depends up on the losses and permissible temperature rise.
Power transformers are provided with detachable panel type radiators [Figure 2.4 (a)] with individual radiator valves for ease of maintenance or replacement. Each radiator consists of number of sections made from pressed CRCA sheets forming channels for oil flow. These sections are welded to header pipes at top and bottom. Detachable radiators are provided with M.S flanges at top and bottom. Flanged radiators are fitted with air release plug, oil drain plug, lifting lugs etc. Bracing straps, made from M.S flat are fitted on radiators to prevent vibration of sections. Recommended oil and winding thermometer settings for ONAN transformers are given in Table 2.6 (1) of section 2.6.
Radiator protection against corrosion:.
(1) Hot dip galvanized or
(2) Cold phosphate treated before painting
(3) Intermediate quote: Epoxy primer
(4) Top coat: Polyurethane RAL 7033
(5) Internal coat: Celerol reaction primer

2) ONAF: In this system in addition to panel type radiators, air blowers are provided for forced air-cooling. Automatic control of air blowers, are through winding thermometer or oil thermometer. Combined ONAN / ONAF transformers have dual ratings. For example: 12/16 MVA, 33/11KV, ONAN /ONAF Transformer. This transformer will deliver 12 MVA as ONAN (Oil natural and air natural) and 16 MVA as ONAF (Oil natural Air forced) conditions. Recommended oil and winding thermometer settings for ONAF transformers are given in Table 2.6 (1) of section 2.6.

3) OFAN: Oil forced air natural system consists of conservator, cooler, and oil pumps. As shown in Figure 2.4 (b), oil is circulated through external cooler unit. Automatic control of the oil pump / stand by oil pump is maintained by the pressure switch.

4) OFAF: This system (Oil forced air forced) is similar to OFAN, but cooler is exposed to forced air to exchange heat from oil to air (Forced oil to air heat exchangers). Recommended oil and winding thermometer settings for OFAF transformers are given in Table 2.6 (2) of section 2.6.

5) OFWF: Oil forced water forced systems are widely used in Hydroelectric power stations where high-head water is available. Oil is forced through external cooler. Cooling water is circulating through closed loop of the transformer tank due to its gravity. (Forced oil to water heat exchangers)

LEGEND:

1. Element fins
2. Header pipe
3a. Round bar
3b Round bar
4. Air vent
5. Drain plug
6. Lifting lug
7. Flange
8. End plate
9. Bracket
10 Logo holder

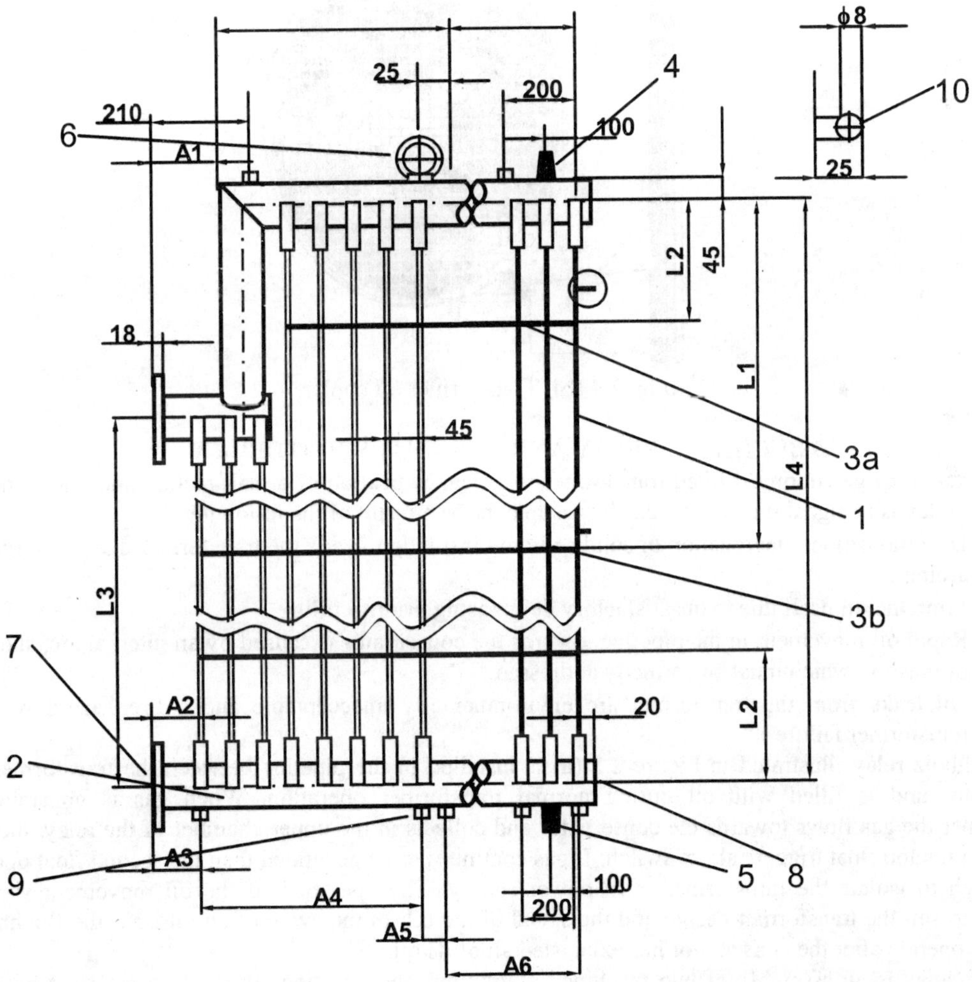

Fig. 2.4 (a): Typical radiator for ONAN/ONAF Power transformer (Courtesy, Pauwels Trafo).

Transformer oil cooler:

The forced oil/forced air cooler consists of a vacuum-proof cooler element and a three phase outdoor type fan, the casing of which is bolted to the cooler element and the oil connections are placed diagonally. The cooler element is built up of corrugated oil ducts, which are made from sheet steel welded together in pairs. The inlet and outlet sides of the oil ducts are welded to their respective header. The air-ducts are created by, a pair of steel sheets located between the oil-ducts and separated by a corrugated plate. The air-duct surfaces constitute a large heat-emitting area and the hot dip galvanizing ensures good thermal conductivity. The cooling air flows in a direction 90 degree to that of the oil flow. The entire unit is supported in a frame and tie rods ensure the cooler's mechanical stability and enable it to withstand stresses, which may arise due to vibrations in temperature. Flow monitors with pressure differential diaphragm and low oil flow switch is fitted on the headers. The impeller made of aluminium alloy mounted direct to the motor shaft is of the axial-flow type and has a diameter of 1240mm. The fan outlet is mounted to the cooler element and the inlet is protected by a wire-guard. The cooler unit can be mounted either on the transformer tank or on a freestanding framework. If several coolers are to be used, (maximum up to 4) cooling system can be connected in series with one, oil pump for the whole cooler group. The advantages are low noise level and high cooling capacity, not deteriorated by dust or insects, little maintenance. Figure 2.4 (b) shows transformer oil cooler.

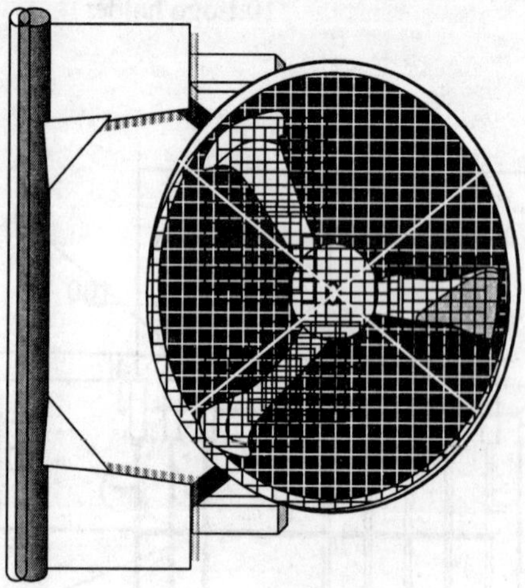

Fig. 2.4 (b): Transformer oil cooler.

2.5 GAS ACTUATED BUCHHOLZ RELAY AND GAS ANALYZING DEVICE.

The generation of gas in on oil filled transformer is a clear indication of a malfunction and one of the task of Buchholz relay is to signal this presence. The gas may be as a result of the following:

- Decomposition / degradation of solid or liquid insulation inside the transformer due to overheating, or arcing.
- From the oil itself due to unsatisfactory de-greasing prior to filling.
- Rapid oil movement in the pipeline towards the conservator is caused by an internal arc, short circuit, or hotspot, which must be correctly addressed.
- Oil leaks from the transformer are environmentally unacceptable and a fire hazard will lead in transformer failure

The Buchholz relay illustrated in Figure 2.5 (a) is installed in the pipeline between the transformer and the conservator and is filled with oil during normal transformer operation. When gas is generated in the transformer the gas flows towards the conservator and collects in the upper chamber of the relay, the oil level drops and the top float triggers alarm switch. If gas continues to be generated then the second float operates the trip switch to isolate the transformer from power supply. The operation of the oil movement vain can be adjusted to suit the transformer design and the speed of the oil. In the event of an oil leak, the Buchholz relay will only operate after the conservator has exhausted all of its oil.

Buchholz relay is an assembly of two machined aluminium alloy castings that affect a perfect oil seal. The main body of the relay is fitted with glass inspection windows with graduated scale marked in cubic centimeters to indicate the internal volume. The oil drain plug is located at the bottom of the main body. The top cover carries the frame, which contains:

- The moving parts of the relay such as the two floats and their associated switches encapsulated in glass bulbs.
- One calibrated flow valve and two permanent magnets.
- A gas discharge valve with protective cap
- Valve for pneumatically testing the alarm and isolation (trip) circuits
- A push rod for mechanically tripping the alarm and isolation circuits, with protective cup.
- Terminal box with 4 numbered terminals and one earth terminal

The relay pipe work is typically mounted at 2.5 degree to the horizontal, installation is possible with a maximum inclination of 9 degrees but special calibration is required. Operating pressure 1 bar, to be tested to 2.5 bar for 2 minutes @ of 115°C. Gas volume to trip/alarm 125cm^3 or 235cm^3.DIN standard recommendation for pipe dimension is as follows.

Transformer capacity (MVA):	5	>5 to <20	>20 to <50	>50
Internal dia of the pipe work (mm):	25	50	80	100

The following installation procedures must be observed for proper relay operation.

- The red arrow of the relay must point towards the conservator.
- Minimum oil level in the conservator must be higher than the relays breathing valve.
- The recommended inclination of relay pipe work must be 2.5 degree from the horizontal.
- The pipe from the transformer tank to the Buchholz relay must be from the top of the main tank
- The pipeline upstream from the relay has to be straight and with a length equal to 5 to 10 times the pipeline diameter, at least.
- Downstream from the relay, pipeline length has to be 3 times the pipeline diameter, only. It must rise up towards the conservator.

Routine test on Buchholz relay:

1. Hydraulic seal test in mineral oil at 90°C and 100 Kpa pressure for 30 minutes.
2. Contact operation via mechanical push rod.
3. Contact operation by lowering the oil.
4. Rate of oil flow to trip alarm/isolation contacts.
5. Electrical resistance measurement on contacts.

Field test: Following tests are performed prior to commissioning or routine (half yearly) maintenance
(a) Alarm and trip contact operation either manually by the pushrod or by introduction of air in to the relay through the valve by using a bicycle hand pump.
(b) Physical verification of trip operation of circuit breaker by repeating test in item 1 above.

LEGEND
2. Housing cover
2.41 Screw plug Pg 16
2.42 Screw gland
2.5 Double bushing
2.6 Tread guard and lid
2.66 Clamping knob
3.2 Bottom float (Tripping)
3.4 Guide rail
3.64 Permanent magnet
3.7 Clamp
3.72 Fixing screws
3.8 Dry-read magnetic switch

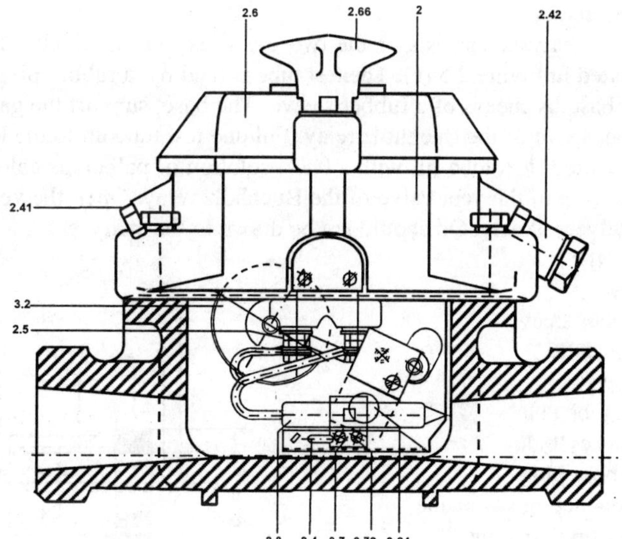

Fig. 2.5 (a): Buchholz relay

Gas sampling apparatus:

Analysis of the evolved gas can often give good indication of the type of malfunction but accessing the Buchholz relay during live operation of the transformer can be hazardous. The gas-sampling device shown in figure 2.5 (b) is the apparatus for collecting gas sample from Buchholz relay. It is manufactured from an aluminium alloy casting with following fittings:

1. A tempered glass inspection window with graded markings for volume indication.
2. A gas sampling valve 3. Bleed valve (top) 4 Bleed valve (bottom)
5 Gas inlet valve for pneumatic testing 6 Drain valve (right hand side)
7 Drain valve (left hand side)

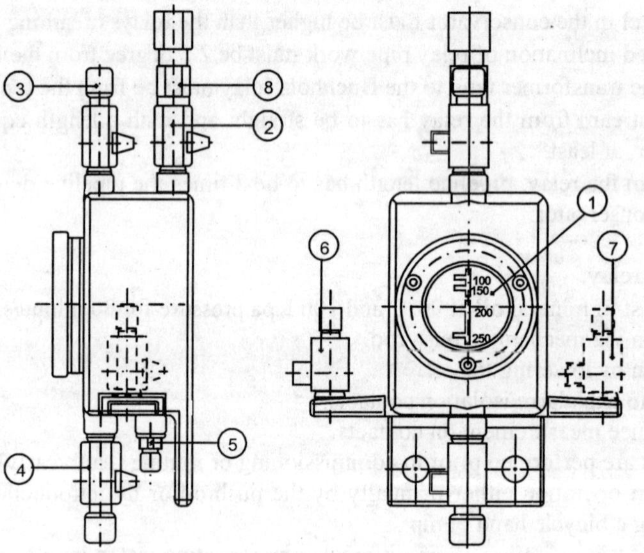

Fig. 2.5 (b): Buchholz relay gas sampling apparatus

Gas Analyzer

The gas analyzer consists of the two glass test tubes, which are connected to each other by a glass tube as illustrated in Figure 2.5 (c). The test tube is held by, a rubber plug in the glass cylinder, which itself is attached to the base by means of a rubber sleeve. The base, support the gas analyzer and has threads for screwing on to the vent valve of the Buchholz relay. Fill one test tube up to the level mark with a 5% solution of silver nitrate and the other test tube fill with a 0.2% solution of palladous chloride also up to the level mark. Screw the gas analyzer on to the vent valve of the Buchholz relay. Open the vent valve carefully and permit the gas to enter the analyzer slowly. Oil should not be drawn to the analyzer.

LEGEND:
1.Base
2. Rubber sleeve
3. Riser tube
5. Tube
7 Test tube (1)
9. Glass cylinder
11 Rubber plug
13. Connecting glass tube
15. Venting opening
17. Test tube (2)
19. Level mark

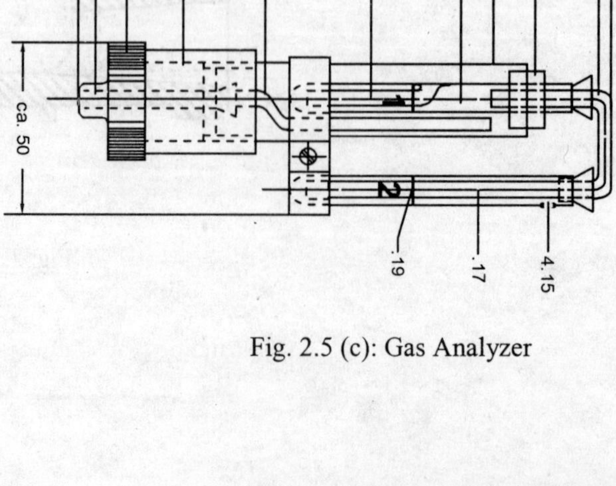

Fig. 2.5 (c): Gas Analyzer

The gas or air drawn from the relay will rise through the tube and enter the glass cylinder. It flows from there via tube in to the silver nitrate solution. After passing through the solution the gas enters the test tube via the connecting tube. It passes through the palladous chloride solution and escapes through the venting opening in the side of the test tube. Clean the test tubes and the connecting glass tube immediately after use, rinsing them thoroughly, firstly with water from the tap and then with distilled water. Remove sediment adhering to test tube, which is filling pelladous chloride with a solution of ammonia and the other test tube by using a weak solution of hydrochloric acid using a brush or cloth paper. Classification of gas analyzer reading is as follows:

(a) 0% to 0.5%, no indication of incipient fault.
(b) 0.5% to 1%, take periodic gas samples once in a month and observe test results.
(c) 1% to 5%, take additional gas samples and prepare to investigate the cause, preferably by internal inspection of transformer.
(d) Higher than 5%, at once remove the transformer from service until the cause is located and remedied.

2.6 OIL TEMPERATURE AND WINDING TEMPERATURE INDICATORS.

Winding temperature indicator shown in Figure 2.6 (a) is a conventional oil temperature indicator, supplemented with an electrical heating element. The winding temperature indicator measures the temperature (in Celsius) of the hottest part of the transformer winding. Since it is difficult to measure the temperature of the winding directly, therefore an instrument has been used by means of which a "thermal image" of the temperature can be obtained indirectly.

The winding temperature indicator is provided with a sensing bulb placed in the oil filled pocket in the transformer tank cover. The bulb is connected to the instrument housing by means of a, flexible capillary tubing. The capillary is connected to the measuring bellows of the instrument. The measuring system is filled with a liquid, which changes volume with varying temperature. A compensating bellows acts upon the measuring bellows through a linkage, compensating for variations in ambient temperature. Inside the instrument is fitted with a heating resistance, which is fed by a current proportional to the transformer load current. Both the temperature of the heating resistance and the temperature in the oil filled pocket affect the measuring bellows, whose motion is transmitted by a linkage to the pointer and the shaft with the switches. Either 2 or 4 switches are provided and each may be set independently of the others.

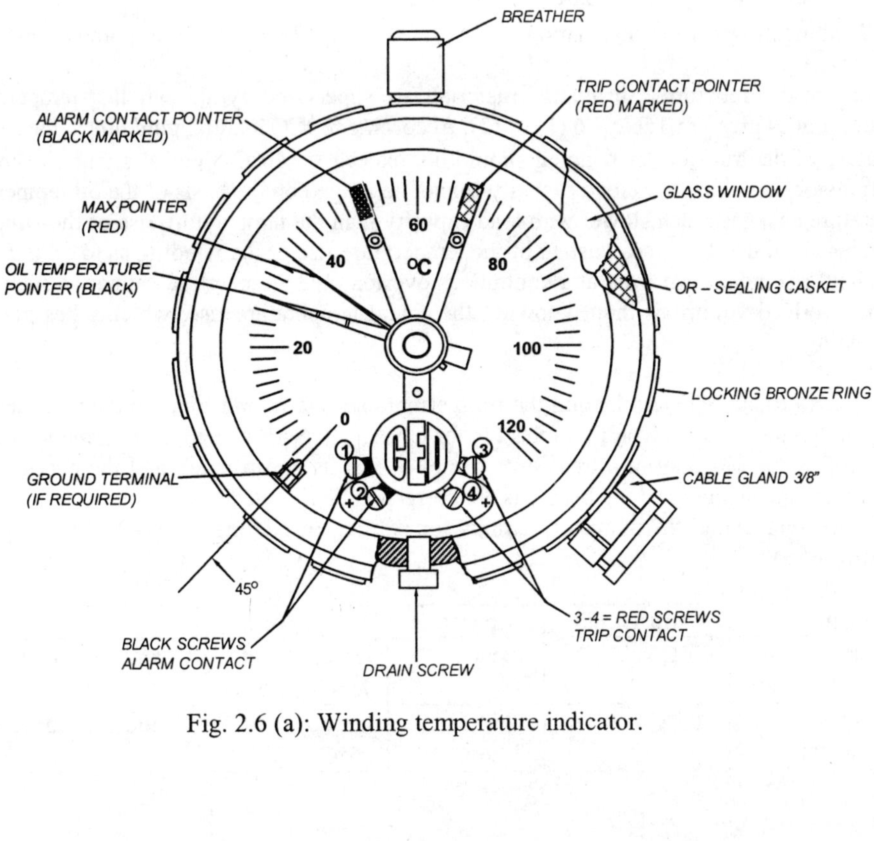

Fig. 2.6 (a): Winding temperature indicator.

The instrument has a maximum indicating pointer, which moves with the pointer when the temperature rises. The maximum pointer thus indicates the maximum temperature reached until it is reset. The temperature increase of the heating resistance is proportional to the temperature increase of the winding over the top oil temperature. The bulb of the instrument on the other hand, is located in the hottest oil of the transformer and thus senses the top oil temperature. Therefore, the measuring bellows reacts to both the temperature increase of the heating resistance, corresponding to the temperature increase of the winding above the top oil temperature, and the transformer oil temperature. In this way the instrument indicates the temperature in the hottest part of the winding, i.e "hot spot temperature". The thermal time constant for the instrument is of the same magnitude as that of the winding. Thereby the indicator gives a true "thermal image" of the winding temperature in relation to time. Installation arrangement of winding temperature indicator and oil temperature indicator are shown in Figure 2.6 (b) and (c) respectively.

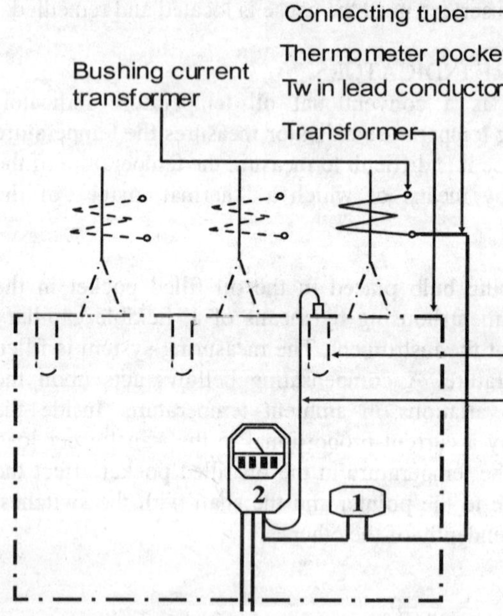

Fig. 2.6 (b): Winding thermometer installation.

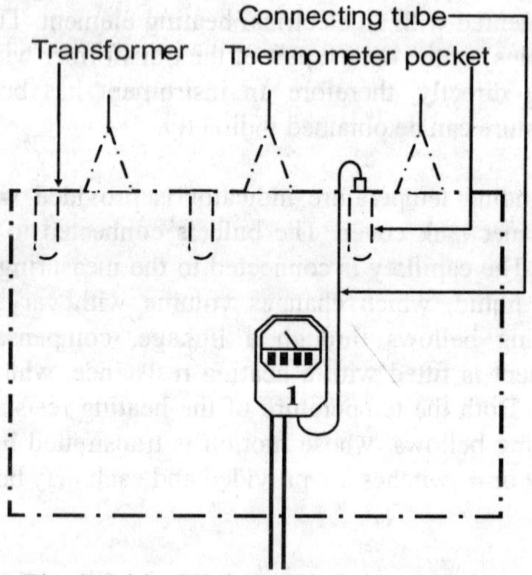

Fig. 2.6 (c): Oil thermometer installation.

The temperature of the transformer insulating materials are supervised by, the winding temperature indicator, which is set to point as given in Table 2.6 (1) or (2). According to IEC loading guidelines, the maximum short-term temperature of the transformer winding should not exceed + 140°C. Special attention should be paid to the fact that transformers short-term load capacity cannot be judged on the basis of the oil temperature, because the oil temperature changes much slower with load capacity than the temperature rise of the winding. Based on volume it can be stated that the time constant of the temperature rise of the winding as to oil is 5 to 20 minutes. However, it should be noted that even at a continuous overload the temperature cannot as such to be used for estimating the overload volume without knowing the actual temperature rise, which takes place at the rated load of the winding.

For continuous load capacity determination the oil thermometer alarm and tripping contacts are set according to the top oil temperature value given in Tables (1) for ONAN / ONAF cooled transformers and (2) for OFAF cooled transformers. Overloading of a transformer implies that its construction and the accessories used in it, such as the on-load tap changer and the bushings are correspondingly rated.

Table 2.6 (1): Recommended thermometer settings for natural air-cooling (ONAN) and forced air-cooling (ONAF) transformers.

Item	Instrument	Alarm setting	Trip setting	Starting of fans
1	Oil thermometer	90°C	105°C	Group 1, at 60°C and Group 2, at 75°C
2	Winding thermometer	105°C	135°C	Group 1, at 80°C and Group 2, at 95°C

Table 2.6 (2): Recommended thermometer settings for forced air and forced oil-cooled (OFAF) transformers.

Item	Instrument	Alarm	Tripping	Starting fans	Starting pump
1	Oil thermometer	85°C	100°C	Group 1, at 60°C and Group 2, at 75°C	≤ 40°C
2	Winding thermometer	105°C	135°C	Group 1, at 80°C and Group 2, at 95°C	≤ 60°C

2.7 FLOW PRESSURE RELIEF DEVICE FOR TRANSFORMERS.

Power transformers are the single largest capital expenses in any substation and the most vulnerable to catastrophic failure. Given the importance of protecting transformers and the impact on system reliability when it fails, it is important to provide best possible protection.

Pressure relief valves: Pressure relief valves are employed to prevent bursting of transformer tank in the case of sudden rise of the internal pressure. The design allows to-release the excess pressure in a very short time. Pressure relief valve consists of flanged body and cap in aluminium alloy (protected by paint), two sealing gasket, hardened steel spring, vent screw, presetting valve from 20 KPa (Kilopascal) up to 70 KPa (0.2 bar to 0.7 bar) and electric contact actuated by a limit switch. 100 KPa = 14 lb/in^2 = 1 Kg/cm^2 = 1 Bar

In normal operation the oil pressure works on the surface of the cap, within the area limited by the internal seal. As and when the pressure increases above the set value the cap rises up and the sealing is made by the external gasket: in this moment the pressure apply on the total area of the cap so the total force caused by the oil pressure becomes much bigger than the opposite force of the spring and the valve open suddenly to relieve the excess pressure. The valves are manufactured in 4 sizes, which have different release section.

Valve size (release section) mm	50	80	125	200
Corresponding oil volume cm^3	3000	9000	25000	45000

For tanks containing higher oil volumes it is advisable to use more valves. In order to have an immediate intervention, it is necessary, that the inside of the valve is breathed, so that the closing disc is directly in contact with oil. Valves are supplied with a protection plate, which will not offer any resistance to release the excess pressure, allows to orientate and eventually to pipe the outgoing flow towards the desired point in order to avoid damages due to hot oil flowing out. The valve is also provided with an optic signal of happened opening. It is a pin, which remains projecting in the central point of the protection cap. While operating the valve by realizing pressure, and in order to make it to return in normal position, push the pin to detain inside. OLTC tank need separate pressure relief device.

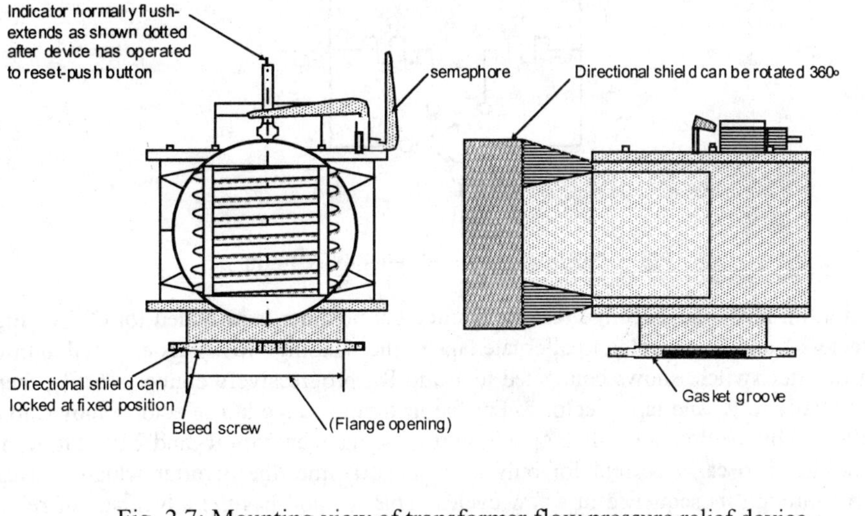

Fig. 2.7: Mounting view of transformer flow pressure relief device.

Flow pressure relief device: Flow pressure relief device is for providing protection for over pressure conditions in power transformers and other oil filled electrical equipments. Over pressure occurs when transformers are subject to fault conditions. The transformer tank can bulge or rupture releasing thousands of gallons of oil that can result in environmental and safety risks. By installing a pressure relief device reduce the risk of catastrophic failure by safer expansion of oil or gas spray. Figure 2.7 illustrates the mounting view of a typical flow pressure relief device. The standard features are:

(a) A built in directional shield (360° positionable), which ensures workers safety, discharge in any direction, environmental protection and provides hassle-free cleanup.
(b) Integrated gas-based system to allow easy release of minor gas buildup.
(c) Highly visible semaphore providing a visual alert of operation.
(d) Manually reset alarm and trip switches to provide remote indication and shutdown when the device operated.
(e) Stainless steel spring loaded valve.

2.8 ON-LOAD TAP-CHANGER FOR POWER TRANSFORMER.

Tap changer changing the voltage ratio under load by means of tapings on the higher voltage winding. On-load tap changer complying to IEC 214 or BS 4571 is suitable for power flow in both directions. OLTC is usually mounted on the tank in a separate housing and connected to winding leads through copper studs fixed on the insulated oil tight terminal board. Hence oil in the main tank need not be lowered for attending OLTC. Otherwise OLTC is housed in the main tank, by suitably mounting on the top cover. OLTC oil in which, arcing takes place is not allowed to mix with the main tank oil. The advantage of providing the tapping arrangement of the transformer (each phase) on the center part of the Higher Voltage windings is:

1. The tapings are at a lower voltage to earth.
2. The magnetic forces are better balanced, especially under a short circuit condition.

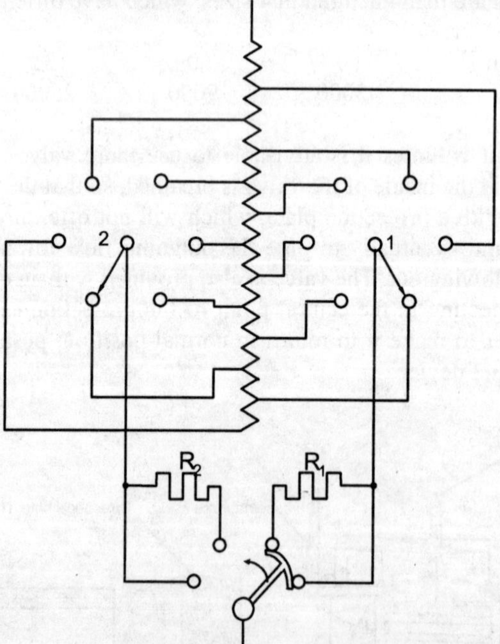

Fig. 2.8 (a): On-load Tap-changer circuit

Separate conservator, oil level gauge, Surge relay and silica gel breather is provided for OLTC. Figure 2.8 (a) shows the tap selectors 1 and 2 connected to alternate taps in the winding. Resisters are used to bridge the tap. The contactor, or diverter switch, shows connected to 1 and R_1, progressively connects or R_1, then to R_1 and R_2, then to R_2 and finally to R_2 and tap selector 2. For the next tap change tap selector 1 moves to an adjacent tap and is then followed by the diverter switch operation reverse manner from R_2 and 2 back to R_1 and 1. Since the resisters are designed to carry current for only a very short time, the diverter which is usually spring-actuated and moves through its sequence in a few cycles. This method has the advantage of relatively small size resistors but requires a transformer tap for each operating voltage, while the autotransformer circuit uses the tap bridging position for an opening voltage and thus requires half the number of transformer taps. Figure 2.8 (b) illustrates the outlook of an on-load tap-changer unit, which identify its main components.

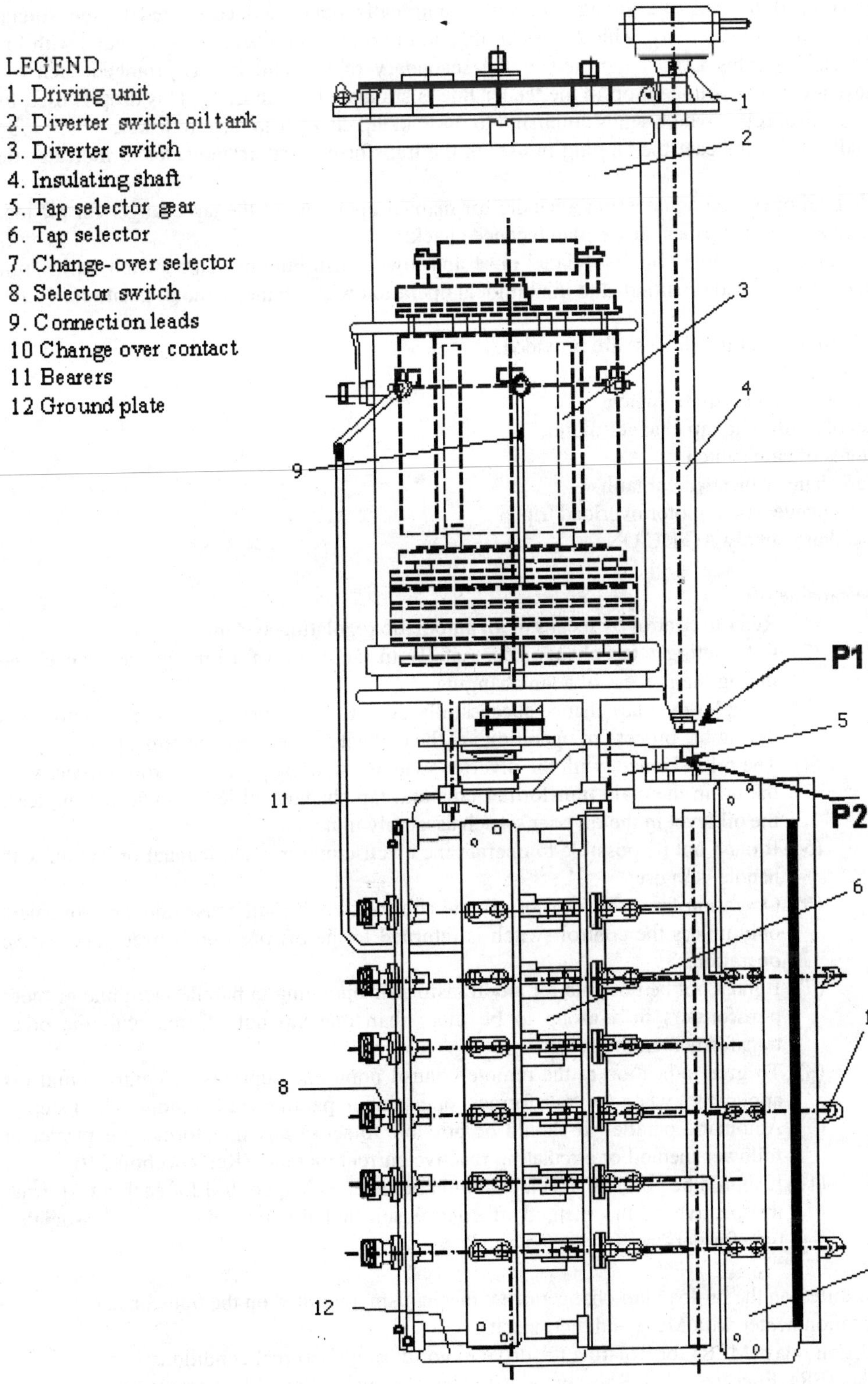

Fig. 2.8 (b): Outlook and components of a high voltage on-load tap-changer (Courtesy, Elin)

On-load tap changer consists of:-

1). Motor operated tap-changing mechanism with over-travel limit switches housed in a moisture and dust proof steel cabinet mounted on the transformer. The motor driven on load tap changer is initiated by a push button (for manual control) or sensitive voltage relay (for automatic operation) connected to the voltage transformer secondary. The Voltage relay, which gives command to on load tap-changer, is provided with line droop compensation (LDC). This LDC connected to the secondary of CT and PT, is arranged such that variation of load current causing voltage drop in the feeder line is simulated in the LDC. This drop is used for actuating the voltage control relay, which sends command to on-load tap changer to raise or lower.

2). A tap position indicator to indicate the tapping in use on the transformer and an indicator to indicates the range of tapings.

3). A non-re-settable total operation counter and a handle for manual operation of the tap changer for off load operation (after isolating the transformer) or for maintenance check.

4). A local/remote changeover switch with associated raise and lower push buttons. This switch will inhibit remote operation when in the 'local' position, and inhibit local operation when in the 'remote' position.

Following indications (light emitting diodes) are provided:

a) Tap position
b) Status of local/remote switch
c) Supply failure to tap changer motor.
d) Status of cam switch
e) Tap-changer mechanical fault
f) Tap changer drive motor overload trip
g) Auxiliary supply AC/DC ON

Tap changer must be capable of:

(1) Remote control by means of an automatic regulating system.
(2) Completing a tap change successfully in the event of a through fault occurring during the process of a tap changing.
(3) Completing a tap change successfully even if the power supply to the motor fails during the process of operation i.e. the contacts commence movement.
(4) The oil in contact with the diverter switches shall be prevented from mixing with the oil in the main transformer tank and tap changer oil level gauge will indicate the oil level in the diverter switch assembly unit.
(5) It must not be possible to operate the electric motor when manual operation with handle is in use
(6) Operation from the local or remote control switch shall cause one tap movement only unless the control switch is returned to the off position between successive operations.
(7) It must not be possible for any transformer operating in parallel with one or more transformers in a group to be more than one tap out of step with the other transformers in the group
(8) To give indication at the remote control point and supervisory control point (as applicable) when the transformers operating in parallel are operating out of step.
(9) Automatic parallel: It should be possible to select any transformer for master or follower method or circulating reactive current method. (Refer section 2.9).
(10) It should be possible to select automatic independent control for each transformer irrespective of the method of control selected for any other of the associated transformers.

List of equipments installed on the on-load tap-changer drive mechanism, mounted on the transformer:

1. Anti condensation heater with MCB and thermostat
2. Motor protection relay (MPR) for isolating the drive motor during abnormal conditions.
3. Stepping relay (SR). Energize when Raise or Lower sequence pushbutton (14) is pressed.
4. Fuse for control power
5. Raise contactor (RC). To energize the drive motor in the raise direction.

6. Position indicator-switch (PIS). Indicates actual tap position of tap-changer.
7. Drive motor with drive mechanism (DM)
8. Raise/Lower local control-switch (LCS). Actuate only when the Local/Remote selector switch is in local position.
9. Lower contactor (To energize the drive motor in the lowering direction)
10. MCB for tap changer power supply
11. Hand interlock switch (To check the control circuit with out energizing the drive motor during trouble-shooting).
12. Raise limit switch (RLS). Motor runs in the raise direction until the raise limit switch is open out.
13. Lower limit switch (LLS). Motor runs in the lower direction until the lower limit switch is opened out.
14. Raise/Lower sequence pushbutton
15. Local/Remote selector switch.
16. Control circuit transformer
17. Terminal blocks for cable termination.

Oil filling of diverter switch oil tank:

New transformer oil with a dielectric strength of >50KV/2.5mm gap, is used. When filling the diverter switch oil tank, the transformer tank and diverter switch oil tank should be jointly evacuated. The diverter switch oil tank should be vented using the vent screw and the tap selector compartment is also to be vented. For drying process during oil filtering or replacement of oil, the drain plug on the bottom of the diverter switch oil tank is to be opened before the beginning of the drying process in order to drain the condensate from the diverter switch oil tank. During the drying process in the transformer tank, the cover of the driving unit must be closed because the cover is vacuum proof. The transformer tank and diverter switch oil tank must be evacuated together using a suitable connection pipe.

Buchholz type Protective relay:

Figure 2.8 (c) shows thc mounting arrangement of protective relay (Surge relay) used for tap-changer protection. The housing consists of corrosion-proof light metal and is provided with flanges for the connection of pipes leading to the tap-changer head and to the tap-changer oil conservator. The actuating element of the relay consists of a flap valve with permanent magnet. This magnet serves for actuating the reed switch and for fixing the flap valve in service position. An inspection window is located on the front side of the housing to check the flap valve position. The terminals of the reed switch are housed in a terminal box, sealed from the oil chamber of the relay by oil-tight seals. Two test buttons in the terminal box serve for periodic checking of the tripping function of the protective relay as well as for resetting the flap valve.

LEGEND:
A: On-load tap-changer
B: Tap-changer head
C: Protective relay
D: Stop valve
E: Oil conservator.

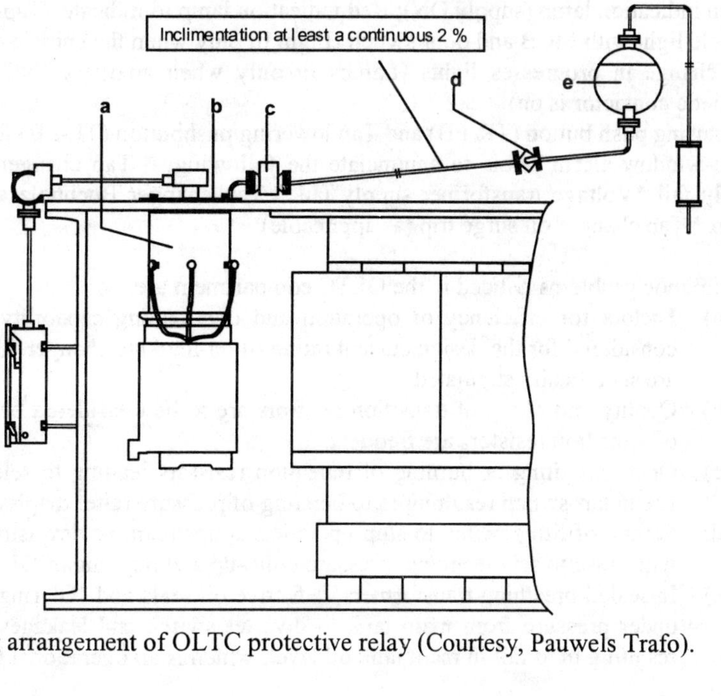

Fig. 2.8 (c): Mounting arrangement of OLTC protective relay (Courtesy, Pauwels Trafo).

OLTC Protective relay (MR brand RS 2001 model) is illustrated in Figure 2.8 (d). The protective relay responds only if oil flows occur from the tap-changer head to the tap-changer oil conservator. The flowing oil actuates the flap valve which tilts-over in to position "OFF," the reed switch is then actuated, the circuit breakers in the primary and secondary of the power transformer are tripped and the transformer is de-energized. **[LEGEND: 1. Flap valve; 2. Permanent magnet; 3. Reed switch]**

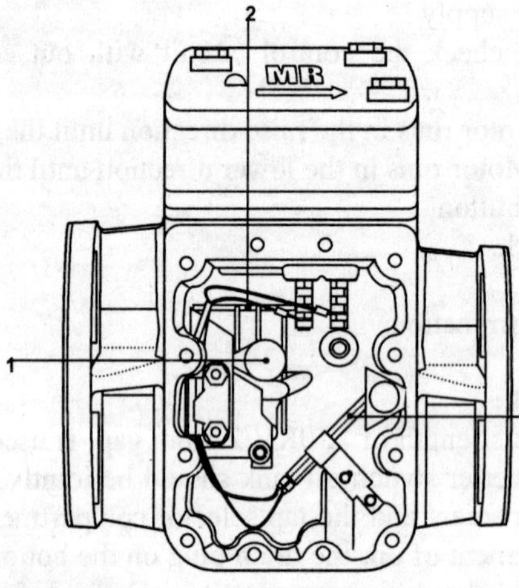

Fig. 2.8 (d): Buchholz type OLTC protective relay (Courtesy, MR)

Install the protective relay in a horizontal position and with the test buttons upwards. The reference arrow on the terminal box cover must point towards the OLTC oil conservator. Use pipe of at least 25 mm nominal diameter between protective relay and tap-changer head / oil conservator.

Remote tap changer unit:

A control cubicle with voltage sensing relay to control and supervise the on load tap changer operation. Following are the list of equipments required in the tap-changer remote control panel.

1. Anti condensation heater with MCB and thermostat
2. Auto/Manual switch to place automatic voltage regulating relay "in" or "out" of service.
3. Automatic voltage regulating-relay (Sensing voltage input from voltage transformer, and giving raise/lower signal for energizing appropriate magnetic contactors. When the voltage reaches in the set value, AVR open its contacts to stop the motor)
4. Green indication lamp (supply ON); Red indication lamp to indicate "Tap-changer in progress".
5. Cubicle light with MCB and door switch (Light lit only when the cubicle door is open for access.
6. Tap change in progresses lights (Lamps lit only when auxiliary 'NO' contact of raise or lower magnetic contactor is on)
7. Tap raising push button (TR-PB) and Tap lowering pushbutton (TL-PB) for manual raising/Lowering.
8. Multi-window alarm fascia to annunciate the following: * Tap changer out of step * Tap changer supply fail *Voltage transformer supply fail * Tap changer Buchholz alarm/trip * Oil temperature alarm * Tap changer oil surge trip (as applicable)

Some of the common problems noticed in the OLTC compartment are:

a) Factors for efficiency of operation and overloading capability of transformer have to be considered for the design current rating of on-load tap changer. Hence current/voltage ratings are specifically stipulated.
b) Quality and rating of transition resistors are to be considered because incidences of burning of transition resistors are frequent.
c) Open circuiting or burning of transition resistors leading to selector switch spark over and fire in tap-switch resulting in to bursting of pressure relief diaphragm.
d) Failure of limit switch to stop operation at upstream or downstream position of tap changer will cause to severe arcing, pressure build-up and bursting of OLTC compartment.
e) In sealed breathing transformers, defective oil seals and "O" rings might cause transfer of oil under pressure from main tank to diverter switch and leakages through silica gel breather resulting in to fall in main tank oil level, which is an operational hazard.

Figure 2.8 (e) and (f) shows the power circuit and control circuit for OLTC drive motor.

LEGEND:

F13: Automatic cutout

K1 & K2: Forward/Reverse contactor

K20: Auxiliary contactor

K30: Timer

K37: Coupling relay for automatic Passage of tap-changer position.

M1: Motor three-phase 415 V

Q1: Master contactor

S1 & S2: Cam operated switch

S3: Raise/lower control switch

S4: End position switch

S5 & S6: End position switch

S8: Safety switch

S10: Door contact

S12 to S14: Cam-operated directional switch

S15: Cam-operated non-directional switch

S22 &S23: Cam-operated directional switch

S24: Cam-operated non-directional switch

S26 & S27: End position signaling switch

S28: Hand crank signaling switch

S35: Main switch

S37: Switch for automatic transfer of positions

S38M: Position transmitter module (resistor type)

S38P: Position transmitter board

S40M: Position transmitter module (NO contact)

S40P: Position transmitter board.

X: Terminal block

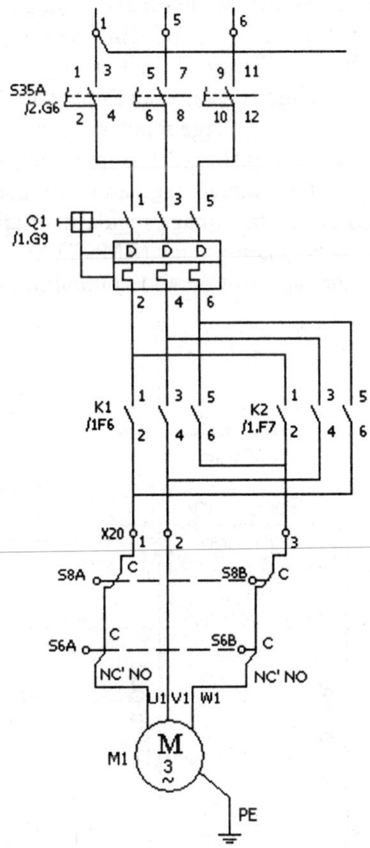

Fig. 2.8 (e): Power circuit diagram of OLTC drive motor (Courtesy, MR)

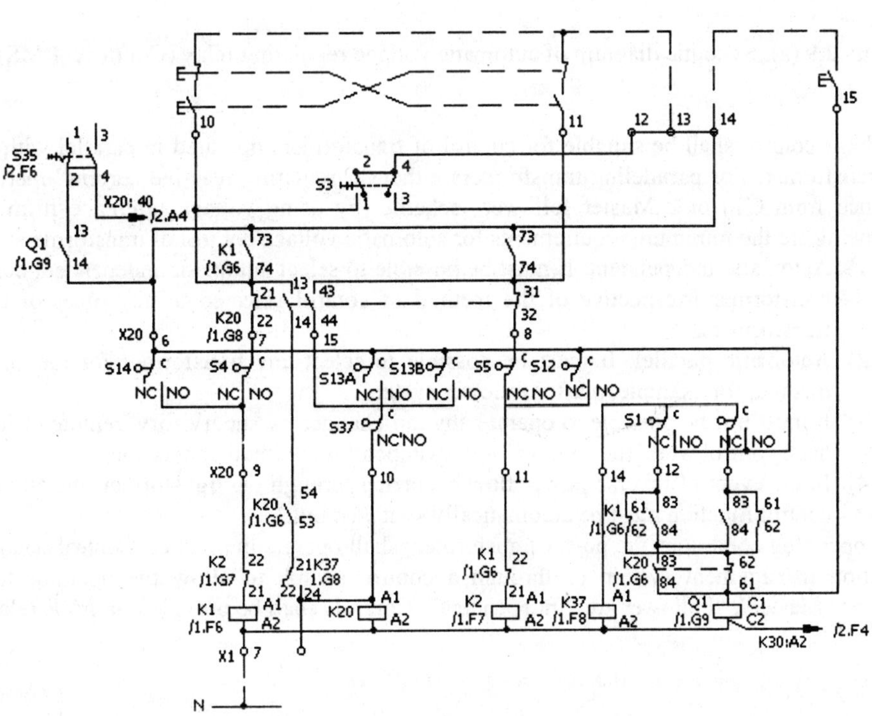

Fig. 2.8 (f): AC control circuit diagram of OLTC drive motor (Courtesy, MR)

2.9 VOLTAGE REGULATING RELAY FOR ON-LOAD TAP-CHANGER UNIT.

Voltage regulator serves for the automatic voltage control of power transformers equipped with on-load tap changer. The control of the corresponding motor drive unit follows the step-by-step principle, i.e, a single control signal results in a change of the transformer voltage by one step. A "Raise" or "Lower" control signal is generated by the voltage regulator and relayed to the motor drive whenever the measured voltage deviates from preset conditions. The voltage regulator is provided with parallel control module so that single or parallel control of two or more transformers is possible. Circulating reactive current method or Master-Follower method is employed for voltage regulation of paralleled transformers. The open-structure of the control algorithm allows to-effect the voltage regulation individually and more efficiently. As shown in Figure 2.9 (a) the automatic voltage regulating relay (RMS 2V164) receives its input from a current and voltage transformer. Transducer senses the tap position and communicates to the AVR. OLTC receives tap raise/lower command from AVR.

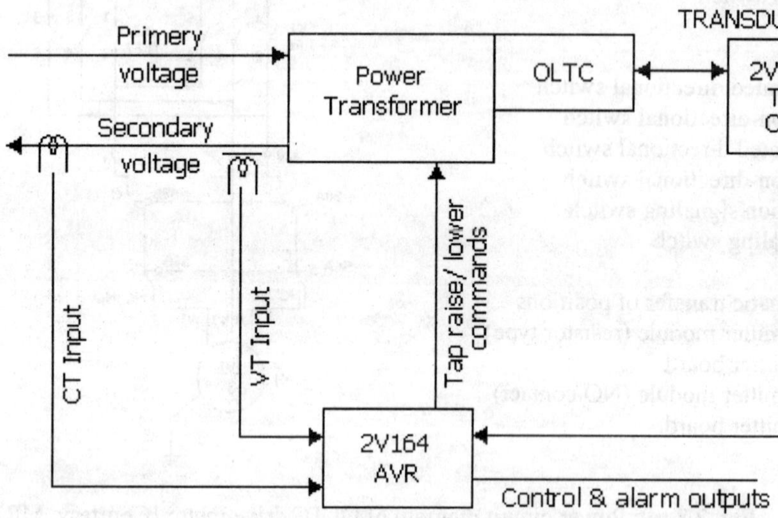

Fig. 2.9 (a): Synoptic diagram of automatic voltage regulating relay (Courtesy, RMS).

Automatic voltage control shall be suitable for control of transformers operated in parallel with provision for more future transformer. For paralleling transformers either "Circulating reactive current" method (by using current reference from CT) or " Master follower" scheme (by using voltage reference from PT) is being selected. Following are the minimum requirements for automatic voltage control of transformers:

(1) Automatic independent: It must be possible to select automatic independent control for each transformer irrespective of the method of control selected to any other of the associated transformers.
(2) Automatic parallel: It must be possible to select any transformer for the adopted control method, for example, master follower system.
(3) It must **not** be possible to operate any tap-changer by supervisory, remote or local electrical hand control while the equipment is switched for automatic operation.
(4) In the event of reverse power flow occurring through the transformer, the automatic voltage control function must be automatically switched out.

Under normal operating conditions the power transformers shall operate in parallel. Controls shall be provided on the substation management system or through a control switch to allow the operator to select each transformer to be "Master", "Follower" or "independent". Controls shall be provided on AVR relay to select voltage regulation 'Auto/Non-auto'. When Online and available and voltage regulation is set to "Auto" the master transformer shall regulate the secondary bus bar voltage using its voltage regulation parameters. When Online and available and voltage regulation is set to "Auto" the follower transformer shall attempt to follow the "Master transformer" at all times. Transformers selected as "Individual" (when Online and available) shall regulate the secondary bus to which, they are connected using their own individual voltage regulation parameters. A transformer is considered as "Online" when its primary and secondary circuit breaker is closed (energized condition).

Figure 2.9 (b) shows a typical Tap position indicator transducer (RMS model 2V200). The relay bandwidth can preferably be adjusted to any value between 1.5 and 2.5 times the transformer tap set percentage. Relay is insensitive to frequency variation ± 5% of the normal frequency.

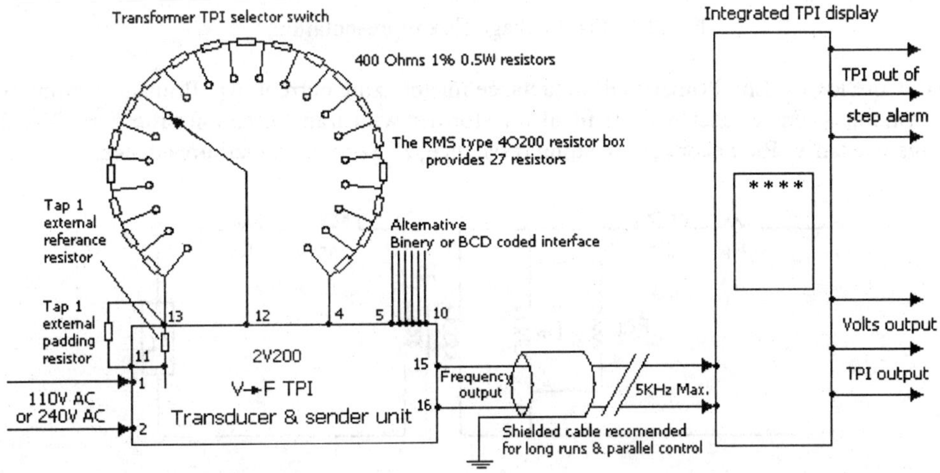

Fig. 2.9 (b): Tap position indicator transducer (courtesy, RMS).

Extended functions of tap position indicator transducer:

Under-voltage blocking facility, which renders the control inoperative (Tap changer command will be inhibited) if the reference voltage falls below 80% and automatic restoration of control when the reference voltage rises to 85%.

(5) Initial time delay setting facility with definite time and inverse time delay characteristics.
(6) Built-in line droop compensator with 1Amp or 5Amps current transformer input.
(7) System status LED indicators and simple menu setting procedure.
(8) Self-diagnosis and fail alarm/Tap change fail alarm.
(9) Independent fine and coarse voltage bandwidth windows.
(10) Over voltage and under voltage alarms.
(11) Two digital input load step stages.
(12) Line voltage/line current display.
(13) Line voltage milli-ampere output.
(14) Tap position milli-ampere output.
(15) Tap change event counter.
(16) Optical isolated RS 232 Personnel Computer link.
(17) PC programming software.
(18) MODBUS RTU compatible network protocol.

2.10 TRANSFORMER LOSSES, EFFICIENCY AND PERCENTAGE IMPEDANCE

Usually all the flux created by the magnetizing current in the primary linked the secondary windings. But some of the magnetic lines of force produced by the magnetizing current do not link the secondary. These lines of forces are called the primary leakage flux, as illustrated in Figure 2.10 (a). The reminder of the total primary flux does link the secondary and is called the mutual flux. Similarly, when load current flows in the secondary, some of the secondary magnetic lines of force do not link the primary. These lines forces are called the secondary leakage flux. The reactance of these ineffective primary turns is called the primary leakage reactance. As far as the primary leakage reactance is considered, the transformer takes on the appearance shown in Figure 2.10 (b).

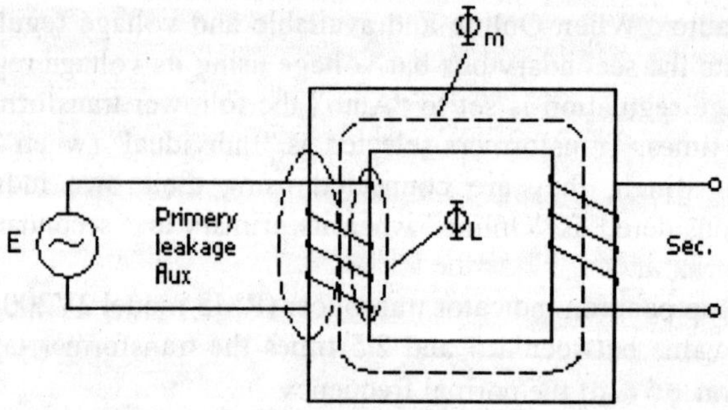

Fig. 2.10 (a): Leakage flux representation.

LEGEND: Rc_L Core losses; Lm: Primary self inductance magnetizing current; Rp: Primary winding resistance; Xp: Primary winding leakage reactance; T: Ideal transformer with transformation ratio zero. Xs: Secondary winding leakage reactance; Rs: Secondary winding resistance; Z: Secondary load impedance.

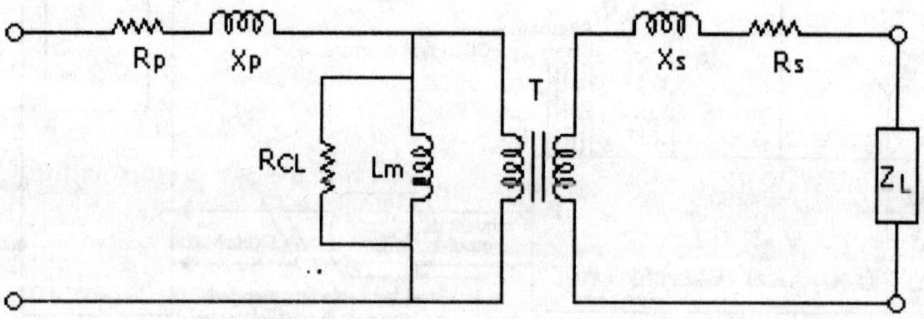

Fig. 2.10 (b): Effect of leakage reactance.

In most iron-core transformers, the primary and secondary leakage reactance's represent approximately the same percentage of their respective windings: thus, the transformation ratio of the perfect transformer portion of the equivalent circuit of Figure 2.10 (b) is still essentially Np/Ns. Since this represents a perfect transformer, up on looking in to its primary, the source "sees" a reflected load of $Zref = a^2 (Rs + jXs + Z_L)$, therefore, reduce the transformer still further to the equivalent circuit of Figure 2.10 (c). If the transformer is fully loaded, the magnetizing current in the branch of the equivalent circuit containing Rc_L and Lm is so small compared with the load current that it creates negligible voltage drop across Rp and Xp. Consequently, when it is desired to determine the effects of loading a transformer, omit Rc_L and Lm branch and simplify the equivalent circuit still further to the simple series circuit of Figure 2.10 (d).

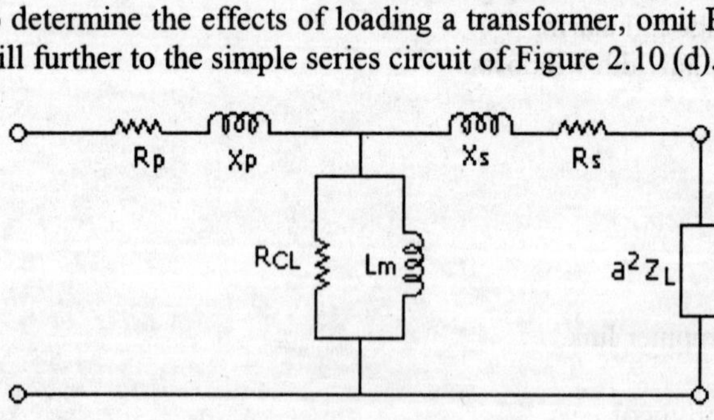

Fig. 2.10 (c): Equivalent network of a transformer.

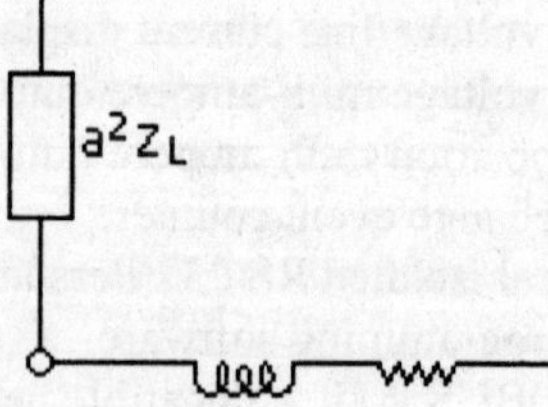

Fig 2.10 (d): Simplified equivalent network

(1) Losses in a transformer:

1) Copper loss: Power loss due to current flowing through a wire. Copper loss is proportional to the resistance of the wire and the square of the current ($I^2 R$). Copper loss in a transformer can be determined by short circuit test described in section 2 12.

2) Eddy-current loss: Eddy-current is the circular induced current in a conductor contrary to the main currents. Eddy-currents are a source of heat and power loss in magnetically operated devices. To minimize the eddy-current losses the core laminations are insulated.
3) Core loss: Core is a magnetic material used to form the center of a coil or transformer. The core is usually made of magnetic materials (Silicon iron). Core loss is the power loss in the core material due to eddy-current and hysteresis losses. Exciting current in a transformer is the current measured in the primary when the secondary is open circuited. Exciting current is the vector sum of magnetizing current and core loss current.
4) Hysteresis loss: Whenever an alternating magnetic field is passed through a core, the current varies from zero to maximum and back again to zero during every cycle of the sine-wave and the current is all the time trying to neutralize the residual magnetism. This is called Hysteresis. Silicon iron laminations are used as core material as they offer much less resistance to magnetism. Thus the hysteresis loss is get reduced. Silicon iron lamination gives higher permeability (Ability to produce stronger magnetic field) for the same magnetic current. Laminations are cold-rolled and specially annealed to orient the grains in a uniform direction. This produces very high permeability and low hysteresis loss. The maximum flux density for saturation for the best quality of lamination is about 20,000 lines per square centimeter. If a transformer is connected to a power supply having higher frequency than the design frequency, then the flux density will be lower and magnetizing current become less. It is however not possible to operate a transformer at a much lower frequency as it will over-saturate the core and exciting current will be abnormal, the iron loss will be excessive and the transformer will overheat.

5) Iron loss: Laminated sheets are used for building up the core, but in such a way as to prevent the eddy-current passing from one layer to another. The lamination should be smooth and without any burrs, coated with insulation varnish to prevent flow of eddy-current when they are stacked together. It is also necessary to provide insulating bushes over the through bolts holding the core together to prevent any metallic continuity being established between the end plates on the two sides of the core. Iron loss is approximately proportional to the square of the thickness of lamination, and therefore, the laminations should be as thin as possible. Iron loss in a transformer can be determined by open circuit test described in section 2.12..

(2) Efficiency (η):
Efficiency = Output / Input = Output / (Output + Losses) = Output / (Output + Copper loss + Iron loss). Transformer efficiency is very high (95 to 98%) because no moving parts are existing. Like alternator there is no mechanical friction, windage and other mechanical losses. **The maximum efficiency of a transformer occurs at a load factor at which the iron losses are equal to the copper loss i.e. no load loss = short circuit loss**. Efficiency of a transformer can be calculated with sufficient accuracy for given load conditions from the quoted losses as follows:

Percentage efficiency, $$\eta = 100 - \frac{\{[Po + (n^2 \times Pk)] \times 100\}}{[n \times Pn \times \cos\varphi]}$$

Po = No load losses in KW
Pk = Short-circuit losses in KW
Pn = Power rating in KVA
n = Load factor
Cos φ = Secondary power factor

Example: Find the efficiency of a distribution transformer rated 800 KVA with no load loss 1.45 KW, short circuit losses 11 KW, at half load (n = 0.5) and power factor 0.8

$$\% \text{ Efficiency} = 100 - \frac{\{[1.45 + (0.5 \times 0.5 \times 11)] \times 100\}}{[0.5 \times 800 \times 0.8]} = 100 - (420 / 320) = 98.69$$

(3) Impedance voltage: Impedance in an electrical circuit is the total opposition of current flow in the circuit. Impedance in a transformer is the vector sum of resistive current (I_R) and reactive current (I_X). **Impedance voltage of a transformer is the voltage required to-be applied to the higher voltage winding (Vsc) to circulate full load current in the lower voltage winding, when the lower voltage winding outgoing terminals are short-circuited**. Impedance = Vsc / Isc measured in ohms. Impedance of a transformer is always expressed in terms of *Impedance Voltage and is measured by conducting sustained short circuit test.* Impedance voltage is also called short circuit voltage of the transformer and expressed in percentage of rated voltage. *It is the vector sum of resistive voltage and reactive voltage.*
Impedance voltage Zv = (Vp x %Z) / 100 where Vp is the rated voltage at the higher voltage side and Z is the impedance. The rated impedance voltage is usually stated as a percentage of the voltage rating of the winding

to which the voltage is applied. Transformer with a, rated impedance 4% to 5% are used mainly in distribution network in order to keep the voltage drop small. Transformers with rated impedance 6% to 7.5% are preferably to be used in industrial networks and in high-power (33 KV) distribution networks in order to limit the short circuit stress. The rated impedance of medium size and large power transformers are even higher (13% to 15%) so as to achieve sufficient short-circuit strength.

Assume that 11000 / 440 Volts step down distribution transformer the percentage impedance is 5, Zv = (11000 x 5) /100 = 550 V, i.e, during short circuit test, for circulating full load current in the secondary winding the voltage to be applied in the primary of the said transformer is 550V. If 440voltage is applied in the primary, the circulating current will be (440/550 = 0.8) 80% of the full load current (both primary and secondary). High impedance voltage means higher voltage regulation, higher losses, low-efficiency and reduced through short circuit current.

2.11 VOLTAGE REGULATION AND DETERMINATION OF FAULT CURRENTS.

When an AC voltage is applied to the primary of a transformer, the primary winding produces a magnetic field, most of which is concentrated in the core. Some of the magnetic flux finds other alternative leakage path through the air. As the load increases, a greater portion of the flux takes the leakage path. The voltage induced in the secondary is due to the linkage of magnetic flux in the core over which the secondary is wound. Therefore, the leakage flux of the primary is not effective in inducing voltage in the secondary. It is this leakage flux, which causes voltage drop in a transformer. As such the voltage regulation of a transformer becomes worse if the leakage reactance is very high. Voltage regulation of a transformer can be improved by reducing leakage reactance. For reducing the leakage reactance the primary and secondary windings are wound in sections so that they may be interposed together as a sandwich. Air gap will reduce the magnetic flux since air offers much more resistance to flux flow than iron. While building up the core by assembling the silicon laminations, the joints are staggered at every layer for reducing the air gap as well as leakage reactance.

As the transformer is loaded, the current causes voltage drop in the impedance. Therefore, the primary applied voltage changes in the load and power factor of the connected load changes the secondary voltage. For lagging power factor load currents, the secondary voltage drops with increase in load current. For leading power factor load currents the secondary voltage improves with increase in load current. This change in the secondary voltage is generally expressed as a percentage of rated secondary voltage and is called the percentage voltage regulation of the transformers..

$$\%\ \text{Regulation of a transformer} = \frac{(\text{No load voltage} - \text{Full load voltage}) \times 100}{\text{Full load voltage}}$$

$$= \frac{\text{KVA load}}{\text{Rated KVA}} \times (\%\ IR \cos\varphi + \%\ IX \sin\varphi) + \frac{(\%IX \cos\varphi - \%IR \sin\varphi)^2}{200}$$

Sequence networks:

(1) Positive sequence impedance (Z1) of three-phase networks is the impedance per conductor as viewed from the side of the fault in the positive-phase-sequence system. In positive sequence networks only positive sequence voltage, impedance and current are effective. Positive sequence network is the same as the impedance or reactance diagram.

(2) Negative sequence impedance (Z2) of three-phase networks is the impedance per conductor as viewed from the side of the fault in the negative-phase-sequence system. Negative sequence networks are similar to positive sequence networks but differ in the following aspects.

(a) No negative sequence e.m.f source;

(b) Negative sequence impedances of rotating machines is different from their positive sequence impedance;

(c) The phase displacement of transformer banks for negative sequence is of opposite sign to that of positive sequence.

(3) Zero sequence impedance (Z0) of three-phase networks is the impedance per conductor as viewed from the side of the fault in the zero-phase-sequence system. Zero sequence networks differs greatly from the positive sequence and negative sequence networks in the following aspects.

(a) The zero sequence impedance of transmission lines is higher than that for positive sequence.

(b) Equivalent circuits for transformers are different.

(c) The neutral grounding should be considered in zero sequence-network.

As the zero sequence currents in the three phases are equal and of the same phase, consider it as single phase as regards zero sequence currents. Zero sequence currents flow only if return path is available through which circuit is completed. Figure 2.11 (a) illustrates zero sequence equivalent circuits for star connection:

(1) Ungrounded star connection: Sequence currents have no return path, and therefore, the zero sequence equivalent circuit is open. Hence no zero sequence current flows.

(2) Solidly grounded neutral: The zero sequence current flows through the ground connection. Hence in the zero sequence equivalent circuit, the point N is connected directly to reference bus.

(3) Impedance grounded system: The neutral current $I_n = 3I_{ao}$ flows through the impedance Zn connected between the neutral and ground. The zero sequence network impedance 3Zn is connected between N and reference bus, current flowing being I_{ao}

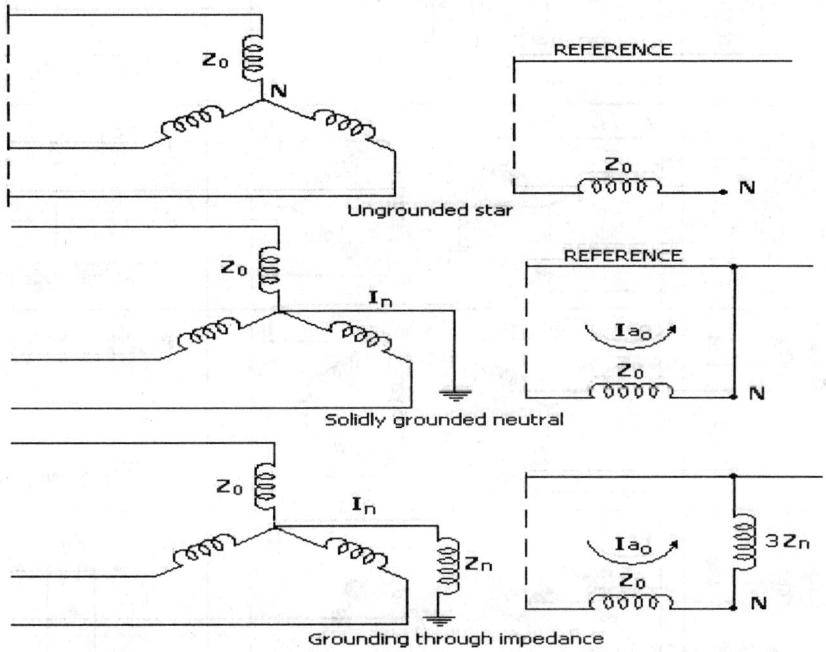

Fig. 2.11 (a): Zero sequence equivalent circuit for star connection

Figure 2.11 (b) illustrates zero sequence circuit for delta connection. The return neutral path is absent. Hence the zero sequence currents may circulate in closed delta, if any zero sequence voltages are induced in the delta.

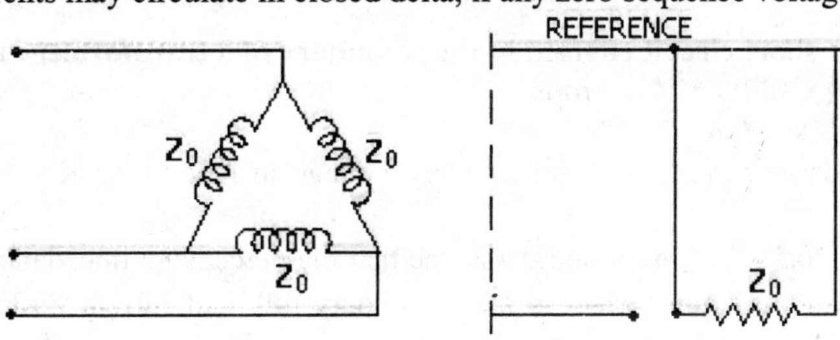

FIG. 2.11 (b): zero sequence equivalent circuit for delta connection

The zero sequence networks and equivalent circuit for following transformer connections are illustrated in Figure 2.11 (c).

(a) Star-star primary neutral solidly grounded
(b) Star-star both primary and secondary neutral grounded.
(c) Star-delta, primary neutral solidly grounded
(d) Star-delta ungrounded
(e) Delta-delta

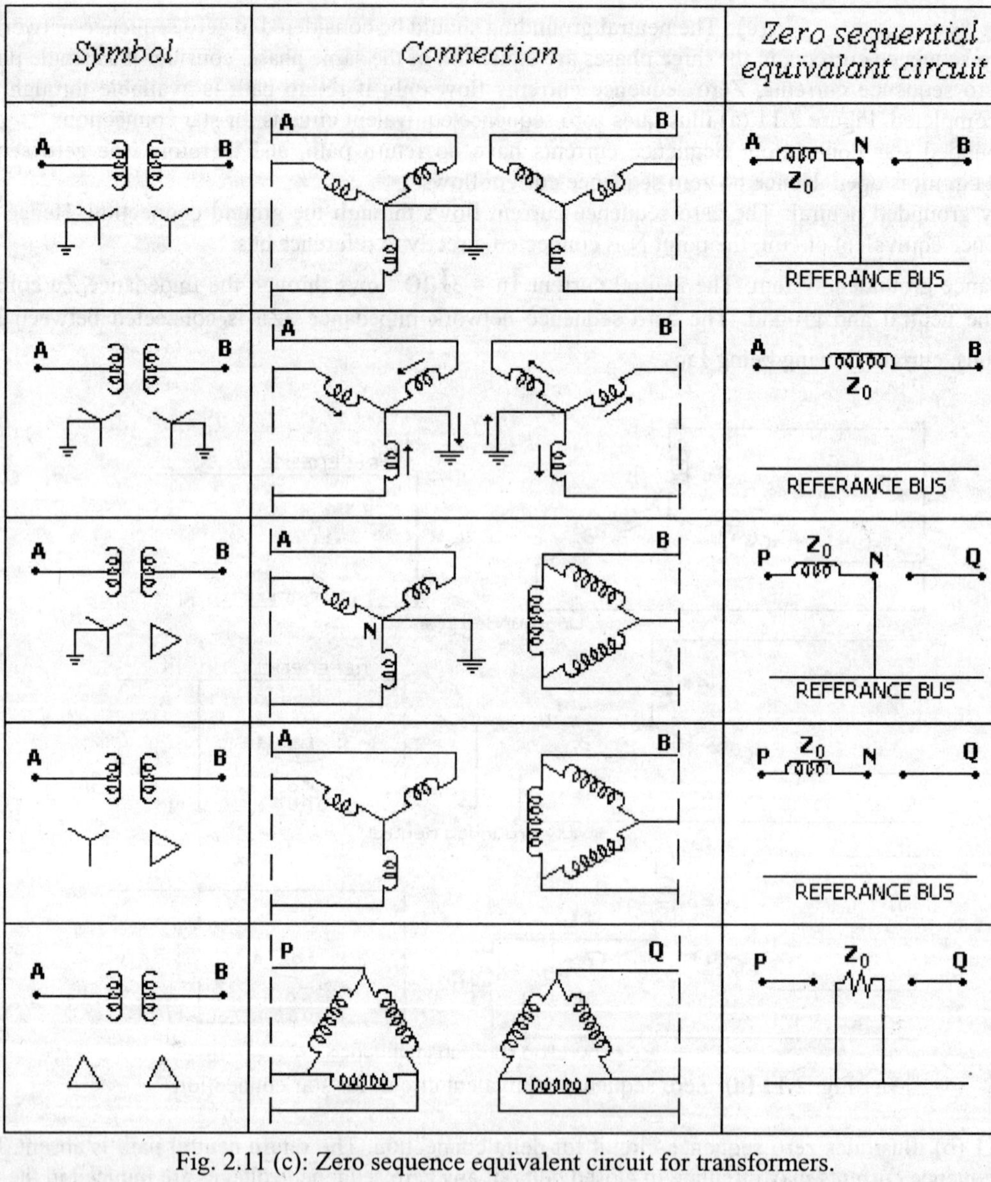

Fig. 2.11 (c): Zero sequence equivalent circuit for transformers.

Fault current: Three-phase short circuit current in the secondary of a transformer can be determined by using the formula, Isc = (In x 100) / %Z . Amps

Fault level in MVA = √3 x KV x KA

In = Full load (rated secondary) current; KV = Secondary voltage in Kilo-volts; KA = Secondary full load current in Kilo-amps.

Permissible duration, tmax = 0.5 x %Z in seconds. Assume that the percentage impedance of a three-phase 25 MVA, 66/11 KV, step down Power transformer is 9%. Secondary full load current = (25 x 1000,000) / (√3 x 11000) = 1312.20 Amps

Three-phase short circuit current in the secondary = (1312.20 x 100) / 9 = 14580 Amps = 14.58KA

Fault level in MVA = √3 x 11 x 14.58 = 277.78

Permissible maximum time for short circuit current to flow = 0.5 x 9 = 4.5 seconds. If the power is not disconnected within the permissible time, severe damages may occur in the transformer.

To determine the earth fault current in the secondary of a transformer:

Solidly earthed system, earth fault current I_{EF} = (In x 100) / (√3 x %Z).

Fault current in a Delta/Star transformer:

(1) Assume that 3-phase short circuit occurred in the star side, the corresponding fault current in the delta side (Transformation ratio is Vs/Vp, where Vs = Secondary line to line voltage and Vp = Primary line to line voltage), Isc (Delta) = Isc (Star) x (Vs/Vp), where Isc = Three phase short circuit current.

(2) Assume that phase to phase (Two phase) short circuit occurred in the star side, the star side fault current Isc in percentage = ($\sqrt{3}$ / 2) or 0.866% of 3-phase fault current (Isc), and the delta side fault current = (1/ $\sqrt{3}$) x 2 or 0.58 x 2 = 1.16 of Isc x (Vs/Vp).

(3) Assume that phase to earth fault occurred in the star side, and star side earth fault current is I_{EF}. Corresponding earth fault current in the delta side is 1/$\sqrt{3}$ or 0.58% of I_{EF}

Figure 2.11 (d) illustrates the line currents and phase currents for delta-delta and delta-star transformers during fault condition..

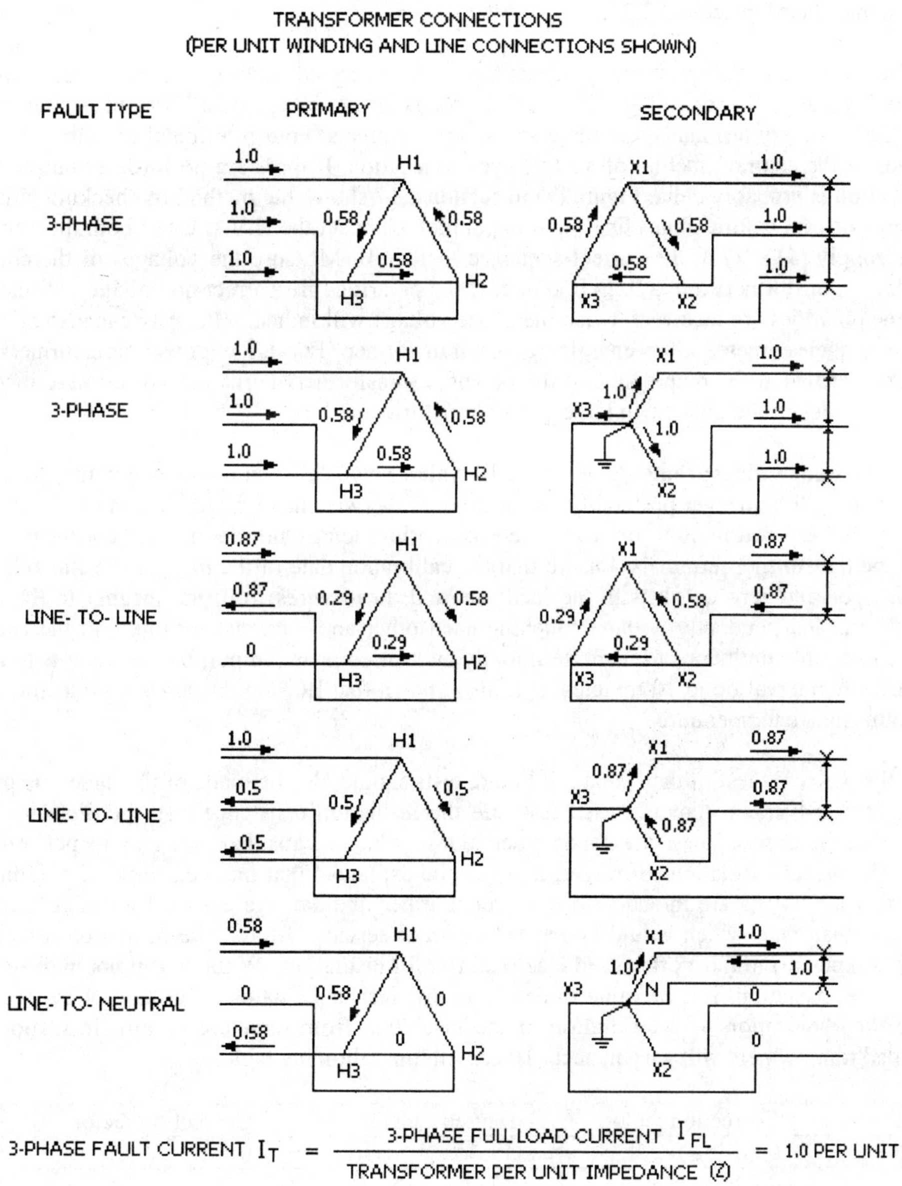

Fig. 2.11 (d): Line currents and phase currents for delta/delta and delta/star transformers during a fault.

2.12 TESTS ON POWER TRANSFORMERS AND DISTRIBUTION TRANSFORMERS.

The proper operation of a transformer relies almost entirely on the electrical properties of its windings. To ensure continued proper operation, transformers are tested to verify that their electrical properties are fully comply with, the design specification.

Following tests are recommended as routine test in a transformer in accordance to IEC 76:

- Insulation resistance test
- Winding resistance measurement
- Magnetizing current test
- Measurement of impedance voltage
- Operation of on-load tap changer

* Short circuit test
* Ratio test
* Low frequency test
* Vector group check
* Capacitance and loss angle of bushings

Lightning impulse test (Full wave and chopped wave) and temperature rise test are held under type test. Power frequency high voltage test and Impulse voltage withstand tests are demonstrated in section 2.20. Portable test equipments are introduced in section 2.23.

1) Polarity check: In a transformer primary means power incoming side and secondary means power outgoing side. Similarly, HV means higher voltage side and LV means lower voltage side. Three phase transformers will have at least three primary terminals and three secondary terminals. Fourth terminal on either the primary or secondary side are the neutral junction of a star (wye) connection. If there are no forth terminals, the internal winding connection is probably delta. Figure (a) in section 2.17 shows the method of checking polarity of two three-phase transformers before connecting them in parallel. Connect the H.V sides of both the transformers to a low voltage supply (415 V) in the correct sequence to R-Y-B. Measure the voltages of the corresponding phases in both the transformers a to a, b to b, c to c. If the polarities are correct no voltage will indicate in the voltmeter. If the polarities are incorrect, twice the phase voltage will indicate. Polarity can also be checked by, using a phase sequence meter after energizing the transformer. For large power transformers the phase sequence can be verified at the output side of the potential transformer. Turns ratio tester described in section 2.22 can be used to determine polarity in large power transformers.

2) Insulation resistance measurement: Measure IR value between windings and winding to earth with a 1000/2500/5000/10,000 V megger preferably motor driven otherwise hand driven. Before measuring clean all bushings with clean dry cotton cloth or if required use carbon tetra chloride and disconnect if any external connection in the transformer terminals. Ensure that the calibration date of the megger is valid and the infinity test with leads open and zero check with the leads shorted. Lead wires from the megger to the transformer terminal should run independently without touching each other and without any joints in the leads. The IR reading (Phase to earth) continuous to increase initially and for comparison purpose, reading is to be recorded at every one-minute interval up to 10 minutes. It is also known that IR value depends on transformer winding temperature/ atmosphere temperature.

In addition to the dielectric test of the insulating liquid, tests should also be made of the dielectric properties of the solid insulation. Several commonly used tests are the insulation resistance test, the dielectric absorption test, and the power factor test. These are nondestructive test, which means that they may be performed without the risk of damage to the insulation. However, it should be explained that incipient insulation failures are one of the results that these tests are intended to discover. Further, the damage caused by test voltage should be considerably less than that, which would be caused by an in-service failure. The insulation resistance test is probably the best known and most often used electrical test for insulation. While it will not indicate the quality or condition of the insulation, it is of value in detecting low resistance paths, to ground or between windings that result from carbonization or deterioration of the insulation from moisture or dirt. Insulation resistance value of oil filled transformers will vary in accordance with the following table:

Degree Celsius	Correction factor	Degree Celsius	Correction factor
0	0.06	30	0.5
5	0.09	40	1.0
10	0.13	50	2.0
15	0.18	60	4.0
20	0.25	70	8.0

To obtain the equivalent insulation resistance at 40°C, multiply the insulation resistance reading in mega-ohms by the correction factor. The readings will also depends on other variables such as the humidity, the size and type of transformers, and the value of test voltage and how long it is applied. Thus, it is important to record the temperature, humidity, and other variables at the time of test so that a comparison may be made with past and/or future test results and to reveal any trends. Following readings are to be recorded. (IV = Intermediate Voltage of autotransformer)

Two-winding transformer	Three winding transformer	Autotransformer
HV to Earth	HV to Earth, LV to Earth, IW to Earth	HV to LV + Earth
LV to Earth	HV to LV + IW + Earth	LV to HV + Earth
HV to LV	LV to HV + IW + Earth	LV to HV + IV + Earth
HV to LV + Earth	IW to HV + LV + Earth	HV to IV
LV to HV + Earth	IW to HV, IW to LV, HV to LV	LV to IV
LV + HV to Earth	IW: Intermediate winding	HV to LV

The dielectric absorption test is a continuation of the standard insulation resistance test for a longer fixed period of time usually ten minutes. Readings are taken at every one-minute interval during the test. The reading should be plotted on the log-log graph paper with time as the abscissa and the insulation resistance as the ordinate. Good insulation will have a straight-line characteristic with the insulation resistance increasing with time. Insulation that is contaminated, or deteriorated, or moisture soaked will exhibit a line that flattens over with time. For large power transformers core earthing and frame earthing are made through bushings. Disconnect earth connection to core and frame, check with 1000 volts insulation tester that core and frame shows infinity with earth/tank, and between core and frame.

Dielectric absorption ratio = 60 seconds reading / 30 seconds reading.
Polarization Index is the ratio of the ten minutes to one-minute insulation resistance readings. For transformers an index of 2.0 or above indicates that the insulation is in good condition, while a reading between, 1.2 to 2.0 indicates that the insulation is in questionable condition, and below 1.0 that is in very poor condition.
PI = Ten minutes reading / one minute reading

3) Magnetizing current test (No load test): This test reveals the no load loss of a transformer. Apply rated voltage in the primary with the secondary terminals disconnected. The wattmeter will indicate the no load loss and ammeter will read the no load current. No load test connection (open circuit test) for a low voltage single-phase transformer and a three-phase transformer is shown in Figure 2.12 (a). Typical no load test connection for medium voltage, high and extra high voltage transformers are illustrated in Figure 2.12 (b). Current transformers and potential transformers are being used for measurement.

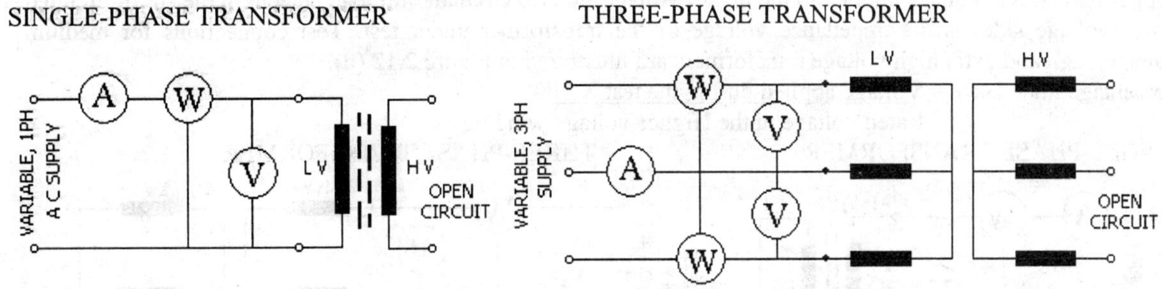

Fig. 2.12 (a): No load test circuit for a single-phase transformer and 3-phase transformer

The no load losses shall be as low as is reasonably practical using contemporary design techniques and materials. For large power transformers the manufacturer will provide guaranteed values of iron and copper losses. These losses are applied while procurement of transformers and witness test at factory will reveal that whether the transformer achieve the guaranteed losses.

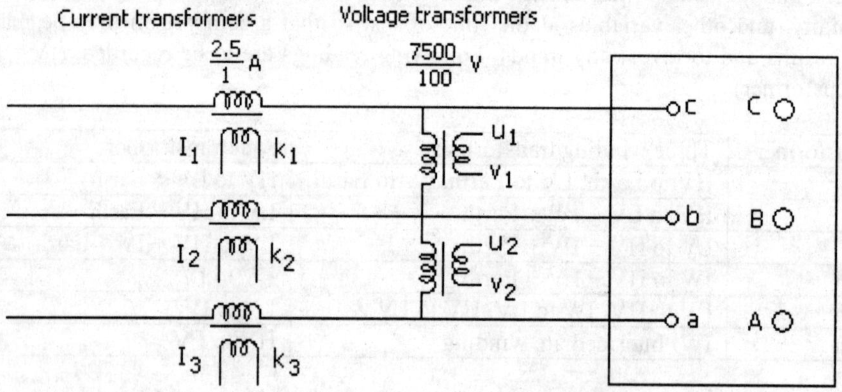

Fig. 2.12 (b): Open circuit test (no load test) connection for high voltage transformer.

4) Measurement of impedance voltage: Impedance voltage of a two winding transformer can be derived by using the formula Zv_2 = (Rated voltage in the higher voltage side x % Impedance) / 100.

For auto transformer impedance voltage $Zva = \frac{(Vp-Vs)}{Vs} \times \frac{\%Z}{100}$

Vp = Primary voltage and Vs = secondary voltage

Impedance voltage for three winding transformer can be derived by using the formula (Vh x %Z) / 100

Vh = Highest voltage i.e in an 11/110/230 KV three-winding transformer the highest voltage is 230 KV

In a generator-transformer unit (step up transformer), the nominal value of transformer percentage impedance has been coordinated with the specified reactance and transformer tap range. Transformers for transmission substations, a different combination resulting the system fault current contribution achieving the required voltage regulating range at maximum and minimum tap position is considered.

5) Short circuit test: For the higher voltage side rated voltage and percentage impedance of the transformer, it would be possible to calculate the current, which would flow in the HV side and the voltage to be applied to the higher voltage side with the lower voltage terminals short circuited to circulate full load current through the windings and also observe temperature rise during the test. This test known as short circuit test will reveal the copper loss of the transformer.

Short-circuit test connection for a low voltage transformer is shown in Figure 2.12 (c). During the test power input in watts, voltage applied to higher voltage winding, current in the lower voltage windings and higher voltage windings are observed. When the oil temperature attains 75°C, wattmeter reading indicates full load copper loss ($I^2 R$). Voltage applied to the higher voltage side (to circulate full load current in the short-circuited lower voltage side) is the impedance voltage of the transformer under test. Test connections for medium voltage, high and extra high voltage transformers are illustrated in Figure 2.12 (d).

$$\text{Percentage impedance} = \frac{\text{Voltage applied during the test X 100}}{\text{Rated voltage in the Higher-voltage winding}}$$

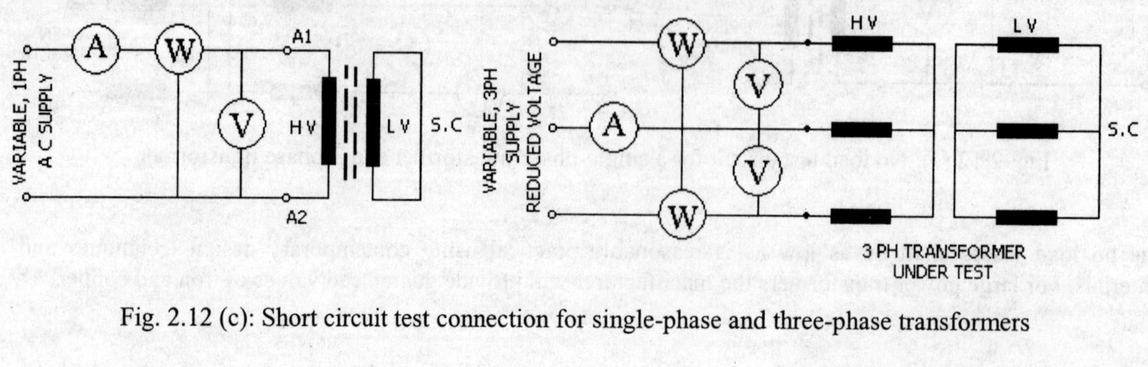

Fig. 2.12 (c): Short circuit test connection for single-phase and three-phase transformers

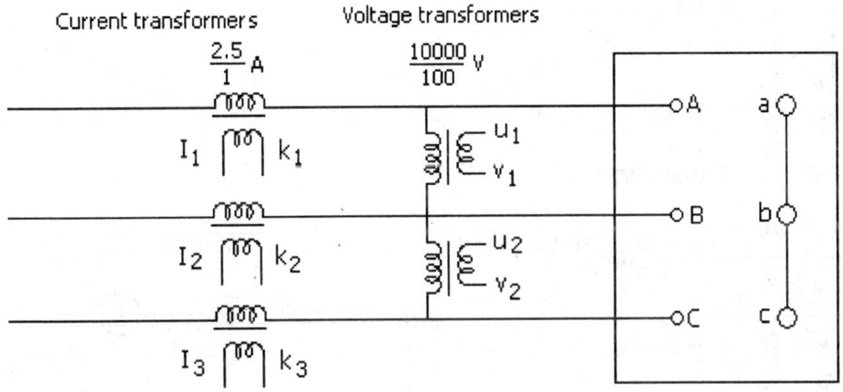

Fig. 2.12 (d): Short-circuit test connection for high and extra high voltage transformers

Example: The % impedance of a 1000 KVA, 13.8 KV / 220 Volts (3-phase 4 wire) 60 Hz, delta-star distribution transformer is 6%. For circulating full load current in the secondary how much voltage has to be applied in the primary.

Test voltage to be applied in the primary = (Primary rated voltage x % impedance) / 100

= (13800 x 6) / 100 = 828 Volts

Secondary full load current = (KVA x 1000) / ($\sqrt{3}$ x Secondary phase-to-phase Voltage)

= (1000 x 1000) ÷ (1.732 x 220) = 2624.4 Amps

Primary current during the test = (1000 x 1000) ÷ (1.732 x 13800) = 41.8 Amps

Figure 2.12 (e) shows short-circuit test by using variable autotransformer, which will supply exact voltage to the higher voltage side of the transformer during short-circuit test. **(Load means Transformer primary)**

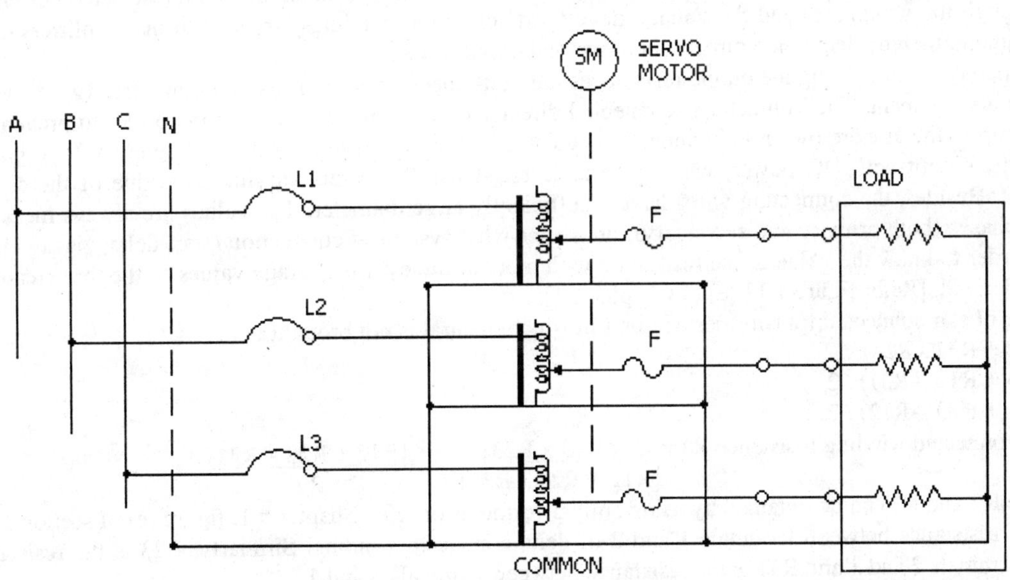

Fig. 2.12 (e): Short circuit test connection using variable autotransformer.

6) Back-to-back test on three-phase transformer for evaluating the total losses:

In the back-to-back test two identical units are connected as shown in Figure 2.12 (f). If the ratios of both units are identical no current will flow in the windings. If the ratio is changed by, changing the tap of any one unit a circulating current would flow through the two transformers. This current is predominantly reactive, and the net power taken from a supply is equal to the total power losses in the two transformers under test. If tapings are unsuitable to circulate rated full load current use a booster transformer connected in the leads between the two transformers.

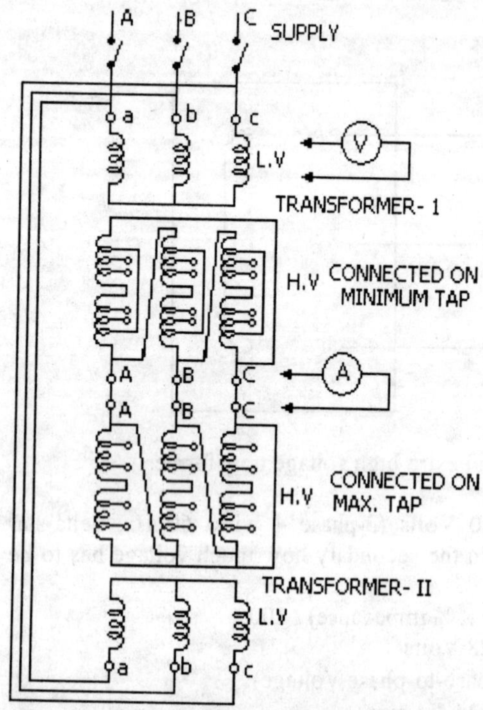

Fig. 2.12 (f): Circuit for back-to-back test.

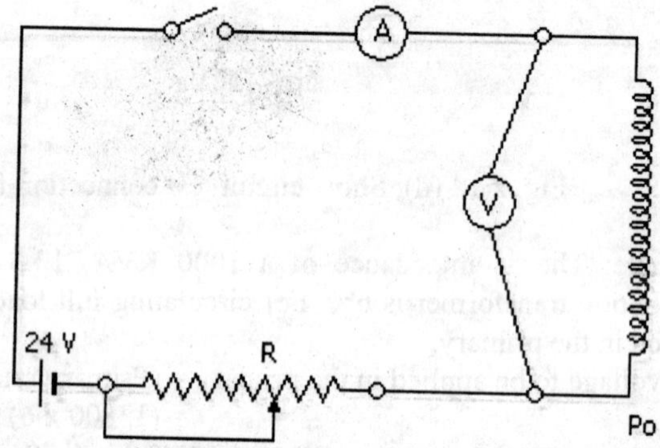

Fig. 2.12 (g): Circuit for measuring winding resistance.

7) Winding resistance measurement: winding resistance of star or delta connected transformer is measured by using a winding resistance meter. DC power source from the test instrument allows the selected currents to flows through the winding(s) and the voltage developed across the windings, are sent to the amplifiers of the test instrument, thereby displaying directly in numerical ohmic values.

Another method of measuring the ohmic resistances the volt-ampere method is used. Figure 2.12 (g) shows the schematic arrangement. The voltmeter is connected directly to the terminals of the transformer to prevent the voltage drop in the ampere meter and connection cables, affecting the results of the voltmeter. A 24 V battery supplies the circuit with DC power, while a variable resistance R permits varying the value of the current during test. Besides, the connecting wires have a sufficiently large diameter. The values are always measured between phases (both primary and secondary), no matter what system of connection (star, delta, zigzag etc) is used. In order to know the value of the resistance with more accuracy, the average values of the three readings are to be derived. [Refer figure 1.13 (e) of Chapter # 1].

Resistance of star connected transformer winding in which, neutral is not brought out:

R1 = (R12 + R31 - R23) / 2

R2 = (R23 + R12 – R31) / 2

R3 = (R31 + R23 – R12) / 2

For delta connected winding resistance $R1 = \frac{[2 \times R12 \times R23]}{[R12 + R23 - R31]} - \frac{[R12 + R23 - R31]}{2}$

Resistance R2 and R3 can be obtained by using similar formulas or refer Chapter # 1, figure (e) of section 1.13. R12 is the resistance between terminals 1 and 2 of delta-connected winding. Similarly, R23 is the resistance between terminals 2 and 3 and R31 is the resistance between terminals 3 and 1.

In general, the characteristics of a transformer are guaranteed at a winding temperature of 75°°C. Therefore, it is necessary that the losses, the impedance voltage, etc. measured at atmospheric temperature and converted to 75°C. Assume that the no load losses (iron losses) remain constant at temperature of between - 20° and + 120°C, the small changes in the structure of the magnetic sheets are negligible. Load losses vary according to the winding temperature. Certain load losses (Joule losses) are proportional to the ohmic resistance of the windings.

For pure metals the relation between resistance and temperature is = $(Rt_2 / Rt_1) = [(T + t_2) / (T + t_1)]$

The value T depends on the metal used, i.e. for copper T = 235 and for aluminium T = 225.

Suppose the resistance is measured at 20°C, using the formula below, the resistance at 75°C can be derived.

Assume copper conductor winding:

$$R75 = R20 \times \frac{[235 + 75]}{[235 + 20]} = R20 \times 1.26$$

For aluminium winding replace figure 235 by 225.
Figure 2.12 (h) represents an impedance triangle.
The symbols Ur, Ux, and Uk indicate the three sides of the impedance triangle.
Uk = %Impedance voltage during short circuit test;
Ur = %Resistive voltage at 75°C;
Ux = %Reactive voltage.

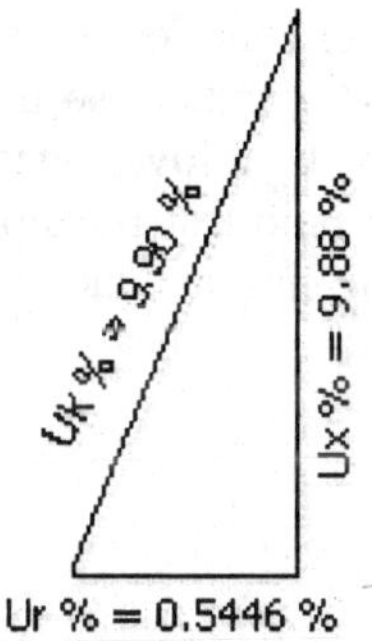

Fig 2.12 (h): Typical impedance triangle

8). Temperature rise test (Heat run test): Temperature rise test is one of the type tests conducted on transformers. It is not a routine test. This test reveals the conditions of the transformer at a continuous rated load and the temperature rise occurring during full load conditions. Short circuit test or back-to-back test prescribed in this section is the heat run test. Test is continued until the temperature of the oil is stabilized. Assume that the temperature of the oil reaches 75°C at full load current, and the atmosphere temperature is 25°C, immediately after switching off the power, the resistance of HV and LV windings are measured, while recording the time passing between each measurement. The resistances are inversely proportional to the length of time that collapses between the measurement and isolating power. The values thus obtained are transferred to a graph paper. Separate curves are formed for both HV and LV windings. Figure 2,12 (i) illustrates the circuit for temperature rise test on a single-phase transformer.

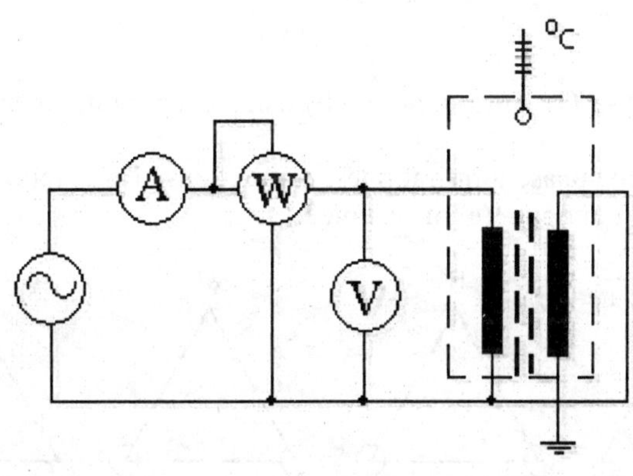

Fig. 2.12 (I): Temperature rise test on single-phase transformer.

9). Turns ratio and vector group test: Transformer turns ratio is the ratio of the number of turns in the higher voltage winding to that in the lower voltage winding. Transformer turn ratio tester is the apparatus used for measuring the turn ratio of power transformers. For small transformers 3-phase low voltage supply is being applied to the higher voltage side and measure the voltage at the lower voltage terminals at all tap positions. If off load tap changer is used power must be isolated before changing the tap, failing which heavy flash over will occur in the HV side. A digital voltmeter is being used for measuring the input and output voltages during the test.

Due to the inaccuracy of the general purpose meter a difference of few percentages may be possible. It is advisable to use a transformation ratio bridge (Keller Bridge). The bridge enables to measure the ratio between two voltages, which are in-phase and have the same sense (vectorially). Turns ratio can be read direct on the instrument. The readings are taken in every tap position for each phase. Instrument will indicate the polarity, and vector group also. Typical turns ratio tester is demonstrated in section 2.22.

Ratio tester transformer consists of a fixed primary and the secondary having a large number of taps with one coarse adjusting selector switch, so that voltage can be adjusted as required. HV winding of the transformer under test is energized by a low voltage supply, say 230 volts and its secondary output is compared with the voltage output of the ratio test transformer [refer Figure 2.12 (J)] after ensuring that the two voltages are in opposition. Circulating currents due to the difference in potential if any can be detected from the ammeter.

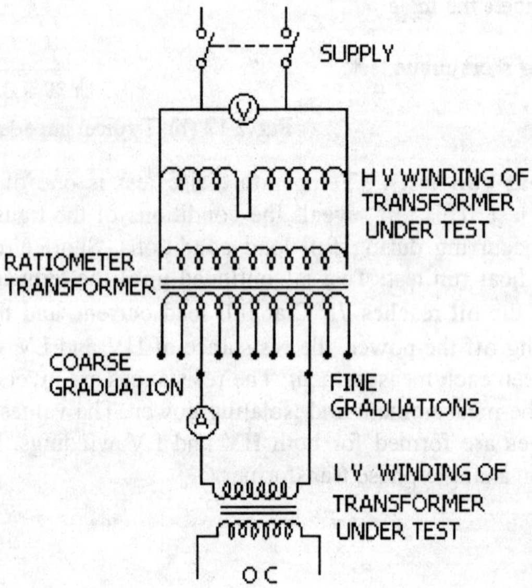

Fig. 2.12 (J): Turns ratio test by using a turns-ratio meter.

Figure 2.12 (k) illustrates the three-phase turns ratio test connections. Turns ratio of transformers connected in different vector groups are shown in figure (e) of section 2.1.

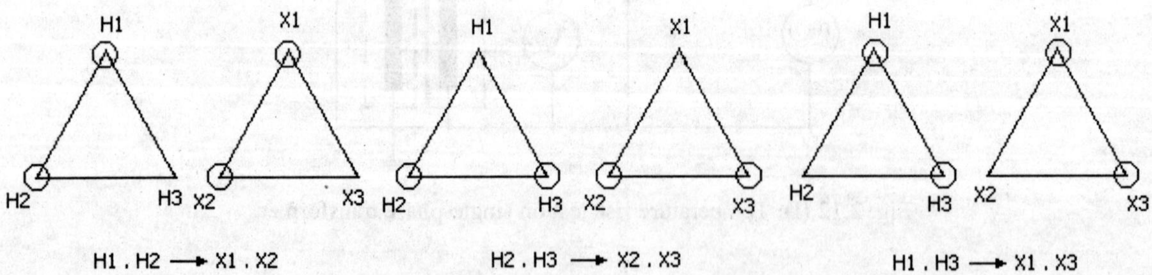

Fig. 2.12 (k): Three-phase turns ratio test connections

The phase angle deviation is the relationship between the voltage signal applied to the higher voltage winding and the voltage signal extracted from the lower voltage winding. Transformer turns ratio tester, can detect the vector group and transformer polarity also. The turns-ratio test instrument is illustrated in figure 2.22.

10) Capacitance and Tan-delta test on bushings: This test set is ideal to conduct routine diagnostic tests on solid insulating components, equipments for high and extra high voltage applications. This test equipment consists of; (1) Capacitance and Tan-Delta measurement bridge; (2) High voltage AC power supply control unit; and (3) Capacitor. Capacitance and tan delta test set if described in section 4.19 of Chapter # 4.

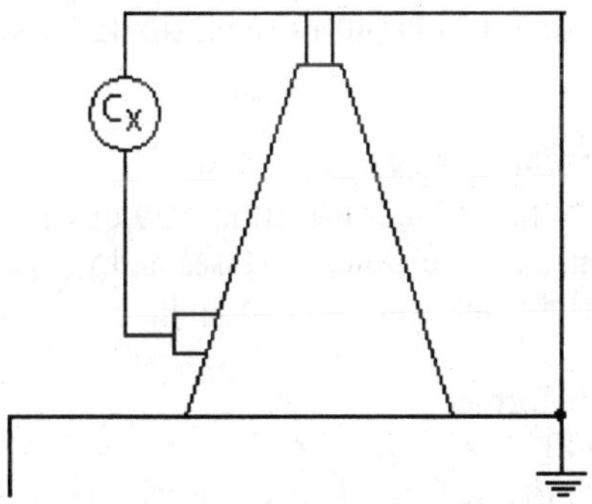

Fig. 2.12 (L): Capacitance measurement of a bushing.

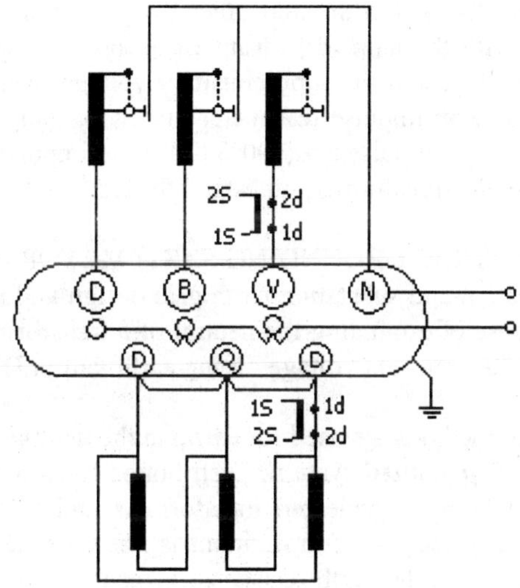

Fig. 2.12 (m): Tap-changer function test

11) On load tap-changer function test: Manual operation of the on load tap-changer can be checked at full load during short circuit test. For conducting site test to verify the function of a tap-changer, connect low voltage 230 volts supply to the bushings through incandescent lamps in series as shown in Figure 2.12 (m). Change the tap one by one and ensure that at every tap position all the lamps are illuminating. If a defective tap position the corresponding lamp will not lit.

12) Power frequency withstand voltage test:
The purpose of this test is to determine the insulating properties of the oil and windings. Assume that a 66 KV/ 11 KV, 50Hz transformer is under test. Between the primary winding and the secondary winding an alternating voltage of design power frequency is applied, the value of which depends on the insulation level of the transformer. Thus a voltage of 140 KV is applied for one minute between the primary and secondary windings. During the test the secondary winding and the tank are earthed. Between the secondary winding and earthed tank a voltage of 24 KV is applied for one minute. Power frequency Voltage test set is described in section 2.20 and the voltage to be applied on HV and EHV transformers are listed in Table 2.20 (1).

13). Induced over-voltage test: The transformer is fed by twice the nominal voltage and frequency. This is necessary to limit the no load current and to obtain the same nominal induction at 100 cycles and at 50 cycles. During this test the voltage between two adjacent windings has a value twice as high as under normal working conditions.

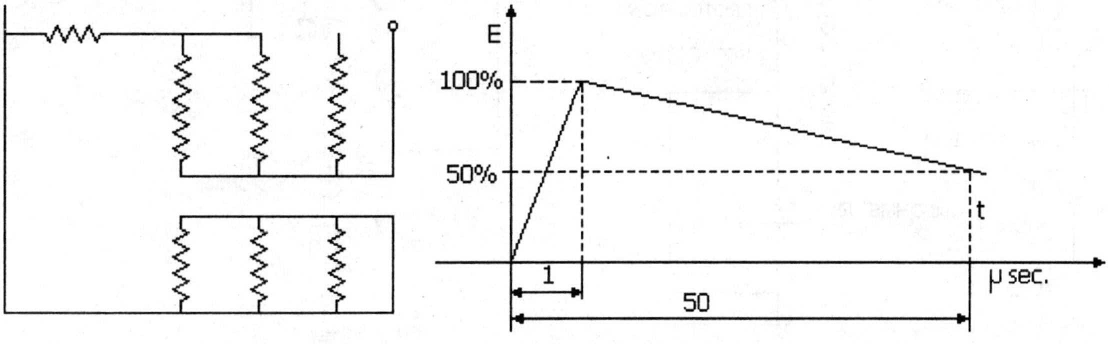

Fig. 2.12 (n): Impulse withstand voltage test on transformers.

14) Impulse voltage withstand test: The transformer is applied with a voltage in the form of 1.2/50. Impulse voltage test set is described in section 2.20 and the voltages to be applied on HV and EHV transformers are listed in Table 2.20 (1). The voltage applied is a function of the insulation level in accordance with the standards used. During the test the transformer is connected as shown in Figure 2.12 (n). One phase terminal is connected, to the test set and other two are earthed via a small shunt. The remaining terminals are earthed together with the tank. By means of an oscillograph equipped with a camera, photographs are taken of the applied voltage and the supplementary voltage over the shunt in the no load phases. The voltage is measured by means of an impulse test meter or can be gauged by a spinter meter. The transformer is subjected to the 50% full wave impulse and 100% full wave impulse. If the 50% and 100% impulses seem similar as shown in the figure, the transformer, withstand the test.

2.13 NEUTRAL GROUNDING SYSTEMS FOR POWER TRANSFORMERS.

Power station and substation earth grid design and installation is demonstrated in section 4.29 of Chapter # 4. The purpose of grounding the neutral of a transformer is: (1) Limit the mechanical stresses and fault damage; (2) Limit the transient voltage during earth fault; (3) Provide means for detecting ground fault.

Following methods are used for earthing the neutral of a power transformer:

(a) Solidly grounded system: Distribution transformers (11KV/440 V or 10 KV/380 V or 6.6 KV/ 415 V are always Delta/Star connected transformers and L.V neutral is solidly grounded to the earth electrode. The external resistance in neutral circuit is not necessary because the voltage available between line and earth is only 230 volts. The earth resistance of neutral earth is of the order of 1 ohm. The earth current is limited to 230/1 = 230 Amps.

(b) Resistance earthed system: Method of connecting the transformer star point to the ground earthing terminal, especially through a grounding resister to limit the maximum fault current to a value which will not damage the transformer and associated equipments, yet high enough to operate protective relays to clear the fault during an earth fault. By connecting the neutral through an NGR, during phase-to-phase short circuit, Phase-to earth voltage of the shorted phases falls 50% of the rated voltage. Earth fault current level is much lower than phase fault level. During phase to earth faults the voltage drops on the faulty phase no matter where the fault is occurred. Figure 2.13 (a) shows the single line diagram of a step up transformer neutral connection through NGR and single pole disconnector switches. By pass switch is employed for solid earthing if required. Figure 2.1 (b) shows the schematic diagram of transformer neutral earthing through a resistor.

Neutral grounding resisters: NGR is designed to dissipate a large amount of energy without exceeding temperature limitations. The design criteria, is based on the ohmic value of the resistance and allowable time in seconds the line-to-neutral voltage can be applied without exceeding the allowable temperature rise.
NGR ohmic value = Phase to neutral voltage / Transformer full load current at the earthed winding
Maximum earth fault current = Phase to neutral voltage / (NGR ohmic value + Earth resistance)
Assume that the 66KV side of a power transformer is connected to the ground bus through a 100 ohm 10 second rated NGR, the maximum fault current at 66 KV side will be (66000/1.732) / 100 = 381 Amps.

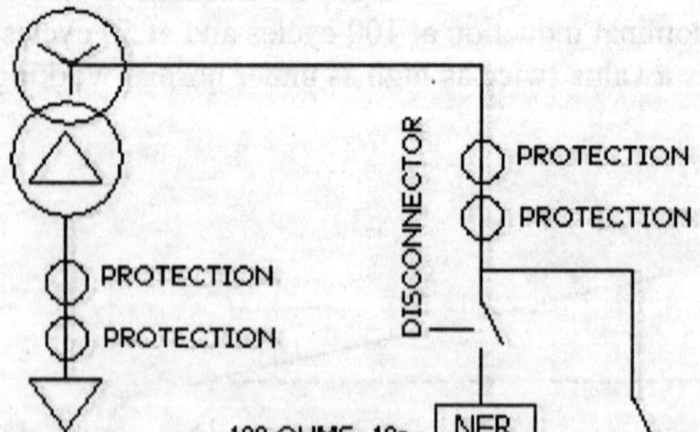

Fig. 2.13 (a): Single line diagram of NGR

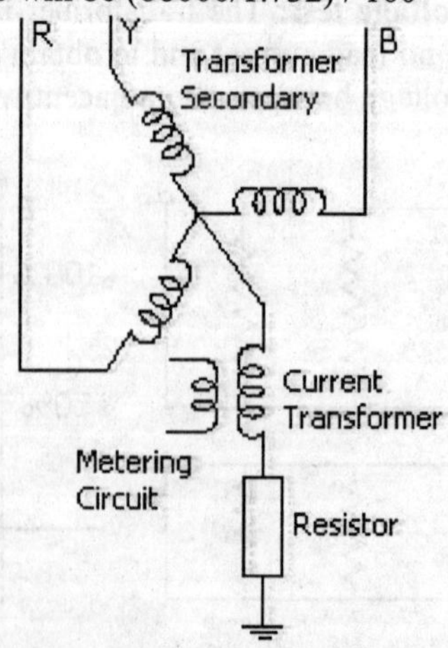

Fig. 2.13 (b): Schematic diagram of NER

Figure 2.13 (c) illustrates a typical outdoor type oil immersed NGR used for earthing the neutral of a large extra-high voltage power transformer. Similarly, Figure 2.13 (d) illustrates a typical outdoor type air-insulated NGR used for earthing the neutral of a typical extra high voltage power transformer. Usually Resisters are designed to suit the following specifications:

a) Duty: 10 seconds
b) Temperature rise: 760°C
c) Resistor: Stainless steel edge wound elements, individually insulated and supported on aluminium frames with stainless steel welded inner-connections.
d) Enclosure: Galvanized steel construction with an ANSI 61 gray finish. Outdoor, rated with a solid top, removable solid front, rear, and side covers, and a screened bottom.

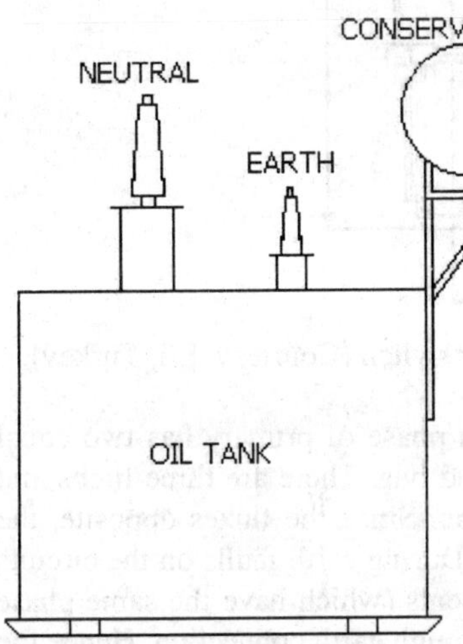

Fig. 2.13 (c): Oil immersed neutral. grounding resistor

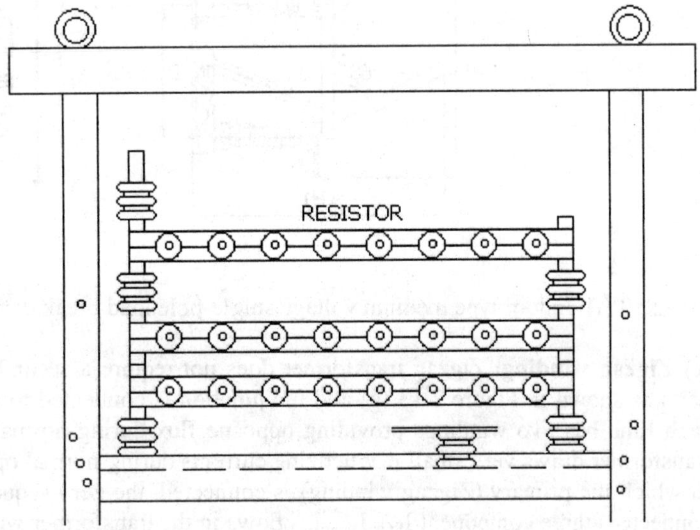

Fig. 2.13 (d): Air insulated neutral grounding resistor.

Figure 2.13 (e) shows earth bus arrangement for 2 numbers 25 MVA 132/11 KV step down power transformers. Three numbers indoor type 1000 A medium voltage single-pole load break disconnector switches mounted in a cubicle, which is suitable for out door installation is provided with each NER. Neutral earth bus facilitates any one NGR during parallel operation of transformers or interchanging the neutral grounding resistor. 1 Core 630 sq:mm medium voltage cable is used for connecting transformer neutral bushing to disconnector switch and from disconnector switch to neutral grounding resistor. NER is connected to the substation earth grid by using two numbers 300 sq:mm bare stranded copper conductors.

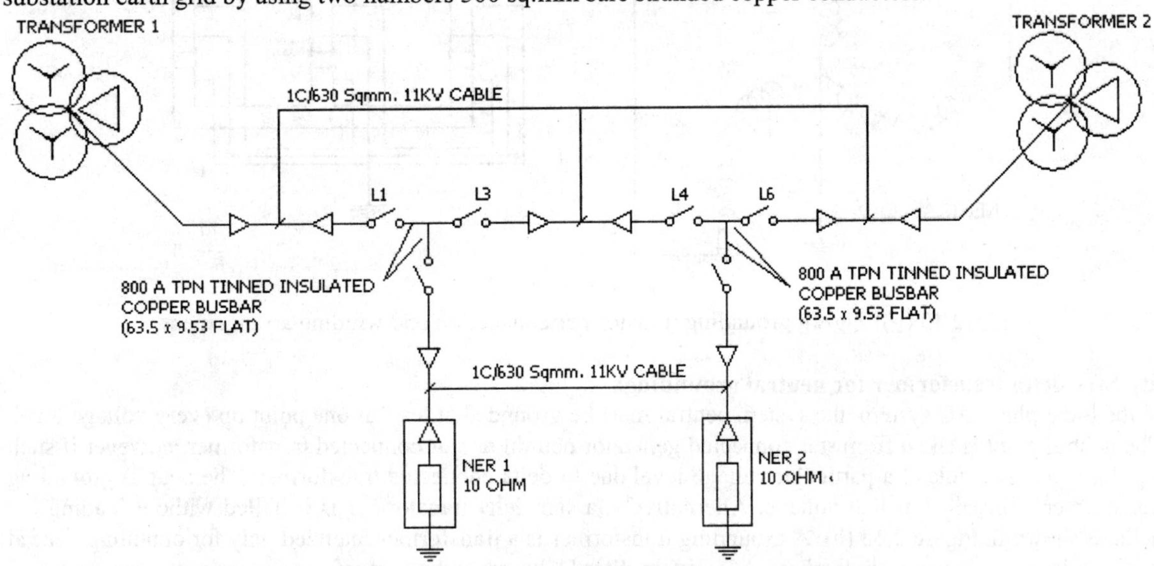

Fig. 2.13 (e): Neutral earth bus and neutral grounding resistor connection.

Figure 2.13 (f) illustrates typical indoor type load break disconnector switch suitable for mounting indoor or outdoor type cubicles.

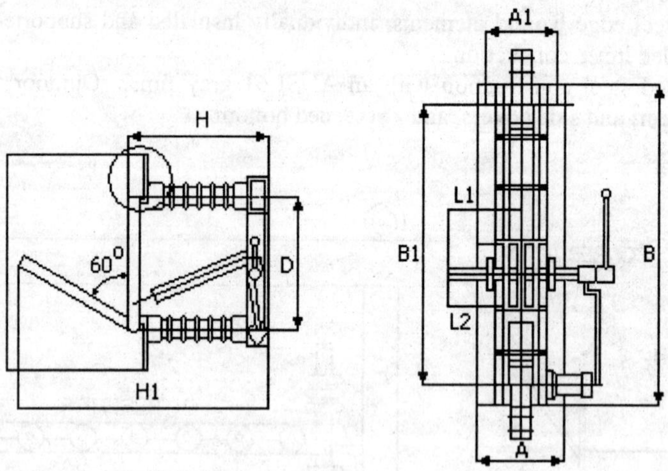

Fig. 2.13 (f): Indoor type medium voltage single-pole load break disconnector switch (Courtesy, Eli, Turkey).

(c) Zigzag winding: Zigzag transformer does not require a secondary, each phase of primary has two equal parts as shown in Figure 2.13 (g) and the junction is connected to the ground bus. There are three limbs and each limb has two windings providing opposite flux during normal condition. Since the fluxes opposite, the transformer draws very small magnetizing currents during normal operation. During earth faults on the circuits to which the primary (Zigzag winding) is connected, the zero sequence currents (which have the same phase connected) three component I_{RO}, I_{YO}, I_{SO} flows in the transformer winding through earth connection. Hence the earth fault current finds little impedance. Zigzag winding is required only if the transformer winding is delta connected. Typical application diagram of Zigzag transformer is shown in figure 7.3 of Chapter # 7. Figure 2.13 (g) also illustrates the winding arrangements of Zigzag grounding transformer. If a star connected secondary winding is provided, the out put can be used for station service applications.

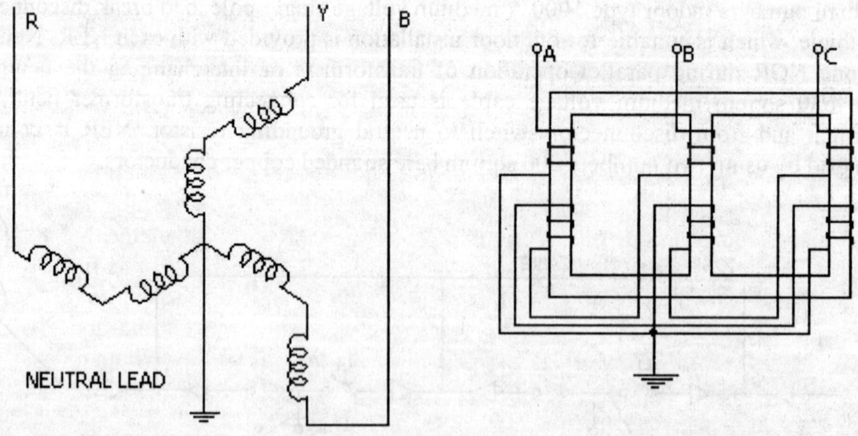

Fig. 2.13 (g): Zigzag grounding transformer connection and winding arrangement

(d). Star delta transformer for neutral grounding:

In the three-phase AC system, the system neutral must be grounded at least at one point on every voltage level. The neutral point is taken from star connected generator neutral or star connected transformer, however if such a point is not available at a particular voltage level due to delta connected transformers, the neutral grounding transformer is installed at that voltage. Alternatively, a star delta transformer is installed without loading the delta as shown in Figure 2.13 (h). A grounding transformer is a transformer intended only for obtaining neutral to ground connection in a three-phase AC system. Star/Delta grounding transformer does not serve the usual transformer functions of stepping up or stepping down the voltages because grounding transformer is short time rated (10 sec to 30 sec), therefore their size is small and they do not need cooling tubes or radiators. They are oil filled and provided with Buchholz protection.

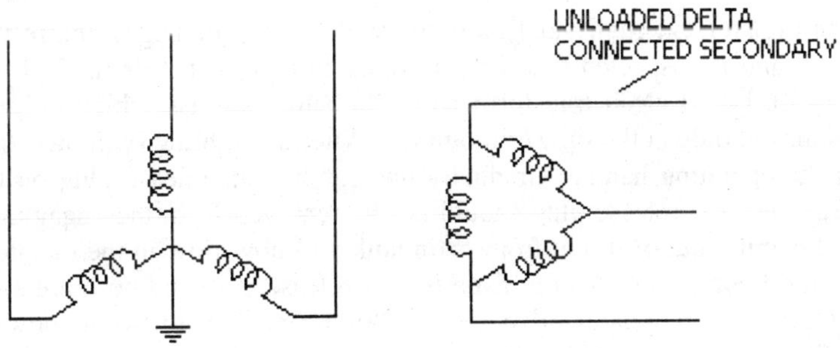

FIG. 2.13 (h): Star-delta transformer for neutral grounding.

(e) Transformer earthing for combined generator-transformer units: Assume that an 11KV generator is supplying to a 132KV bus bar through a step up transformer. In this system the generator winding and the transformer primary winding can be treated as an isolated system. Common practice is to earth the generator neutral through the primary winding of a single-phase distribution transformer. Resistor has been introduced to the secondary of this transformer to prevent the production of high transient over voltage in the event of an arcing earth fault. Typical application diagram of transformer earthing for a combined generator-transformer unit is shown in figure 1.2 (q) of Chapter # 1. Technical application of neutral grounding transformer is demonstrated in section 1.5 of Chapter # 1.

2.14 TRANSFORMER INSTALLATION, OIL TREATMENT AND OIL TESTING

Usually Power transformers are installed outdoor in the transformer bay, but occasionally installed indoor also. Transformer should be installed in a well-ventilated place, free from excessive dust, corrosive fumes and other atmospheric pollution. Adequate ventilation is necessary for radiators so that they can dissipate heat. Foundation should be firm, horizontal and dry. Where rollers are fitted, suitable rails should be provided. Necessary provision for oil draining, oil soak pits for collecting exhausted oil, water fog and deluge system and sprinkler system, fire separation walls (6M high) etc must be provided..

Main tank: Shift the transformer main tank to the foundation by using a crane and trailer if proper approach to the foundation is available. Use anti-vibration mounting pads and fasten foundation bolt to the skid base. Lock the rollers to prevent any accidental movement on rails if the transformer is shifting and installing on the rails. Draw an oil sample from the bottom of the tank and test it for breakdown voltage. Now various components dismantled for shipping are to be assembled. Transformer transported without oil is filled at the factory by dry air approximately, 0.5 bar (50 KPa) over pressure and provided with a manometer to read the pressure. While the transformer is stored at site, the pressure must be checked continuously and dry air or oxygen must be added when the pressure falls below 0.1 bar or 10 KPa. Transformer shipped without oil shall be filled with oil after transporting to the foundation rail, but before assembling the accessories. Oil filling is being carried out according to the guidelines given below.

- Connect the suction pipe of the vacuum pump to the connecting flange of the oil conservator and start the treatment under vacuum.
- Continue the suction under vacuum for 8 hours at least, and try to keep the pressure under 133 Pa = 1 torr = 1.33 mbar = 1 mmHg. Thereafter start to fill the transformer with fresh oil. The vacuum pump must be in operation.
- Pump the oil from the oil tank or oil drum slowly through the filter via the oil-filling hole to the transformer tank. The filling speed is correct if the vacuum does not considerably decrease during the filling.
- When the windings and insulation parts are below the oil level, interrupt the oil filling

Conservator: Mount the main tank conservator and OLTC conservator (if it is an independent one). Install Buchholz relay shut off valve, and piping. Install oil surge relay of OLTC along with silica jell breather for both conservators. Fill the conservator with transformer oil to prevent entry of moisture in the main tank.

Radiators: Clean the radiator externally and thoroughly check any damages before installation. If blanking plate is not in position, and is suspected that dirt and other foreign materials might have entered, clean them internally by flushing fresh and clean transformer oil. Radiators are assembled only one at a time and the blanking plates are removed only at the time of mounting. After assembling (with new gasket) open the bottom radiator valve using the operating handle. Gradually unscrew the air release plug on the top of the radiator, until the air starts escaping. Air release plug should not be removed from the engaging thread as it would be difficult to control oil coming out of it. Oil from main tank will now flow in the radiator, driving out air from air release plug. When oil comes out steadily from the air release plug and no more air comes through, close the air release plug. Open the top radiator valve. Oil level in the conservator would now have fallen which is to be filled if required. Ensure that oil is not leaking from the newly installed radiator and its gasketed joints.

Bushings: Clean the bushings by using dry clean cotton cloth and check thoroughly against hair-cracks or other damages. Test insulation resistance of each bushing with a megger. Install both higher and lower voltage side bushings as well as tertiary winding bushings (if applicable) as per manufacturers guidelines. Ensure that the electrical connection to the windings is perfect, the test tap cap is fully tightened and the arcing horn gaps are adjusted.

General guidelines: Tighten all gaskets, because they might have unfastened due to vibration during the transportation. When installation work has been completed the coating damages caused by transportation and installation have to be repainted with the paint supplied with the transformer. Clean also the transformer tank and bushings from possible oil and dirt stains. Remove the connection pipe (U-pipe) between the oil tank of the on-load tap changer and that of the transformer (if applicable), and cover the holes with blind flanges supplied with the transformer. Obtain IR value.

Oil filling: Fill the transformer with oil.

- Open the upper shut-off valves of all radiators
- Pump carefully dried and cleaned oil in to the oil conservator: the oil flow in the transformer can be followed through the gas relay window.
- Raise the oil level by following the oil indicator up to the level, which corresponds to the prevailing transformer temperature.
- Open the lower shut-off valves of radiators.
- Tightens the nuts of the shut-off valves.

Release air from the transformer in the following order:
1) From top cover by unfastening the airing screw.
2) From on-load tap changer by unfastening the airing screw.
3) From bushings by unfastening the upper gasket.
4) Gas relay by unfastening the airing screw
After airing tighten the airing screws and gaskets.

Foundation construction: The transformer is being installed on a reinforced concrete foundation to which the vertical fishes have been fastened. The transformer on rollers has to be fastened to its foundation by wedges or other fasteners so that it cannot move no the event of an earthquake. An oil pit is built under the transformer to prevent the spreading of oil and fire in case of an oil outage from transformer due to fault. Oil pit is made of reinforced concrete and big enough for the total oil quantity of the transformer can be collected. The pit is so designed that oil is extinguished when it runs to the pit. A small-eye steel net is used for extinguishing the fire. The net is installed at the mouth of the cavity built at the bottom of the pit, which leads to the oil pipe. Rough graded gravel also used for this purpose. In this case the pit will be covered by, a dense steel grating on top of which 25 to 50 cm layer of stones, then gravel spread over it. If several transformers are installed, a common oil well can be built outside the building and connected through pipes only. In the case of very large transformers it is better to provide rails to the foundation reach the transport path in the same level. The transformer can be unloaded on the rails and down to its place along the rails. The foundation must also be provided with hauling hooks for the fixing of wire ropes. Steel piling is recommended below the foundation. Transformer should not be installed near by (less than 20M) unless a protective-wall exist between them Firewalls are built between transformers to prevent spreading of fire between transformers. Steel reinforced concrete wall, which reaches to one metre above the height of the bushings and in the deep direction at least one metre on both sides of the transformer are constructed for this purpose. Protective walls can be used also when protecting the transformer against external vandalism and for suppression of noise. GRP water tank and detachable sprinkler system is provided for fire fighting. Typical foundation arrangement with firewall, oil sump, and sprinkler system for 40 MVA step down transformers are shown in Figure 2.14 (a).

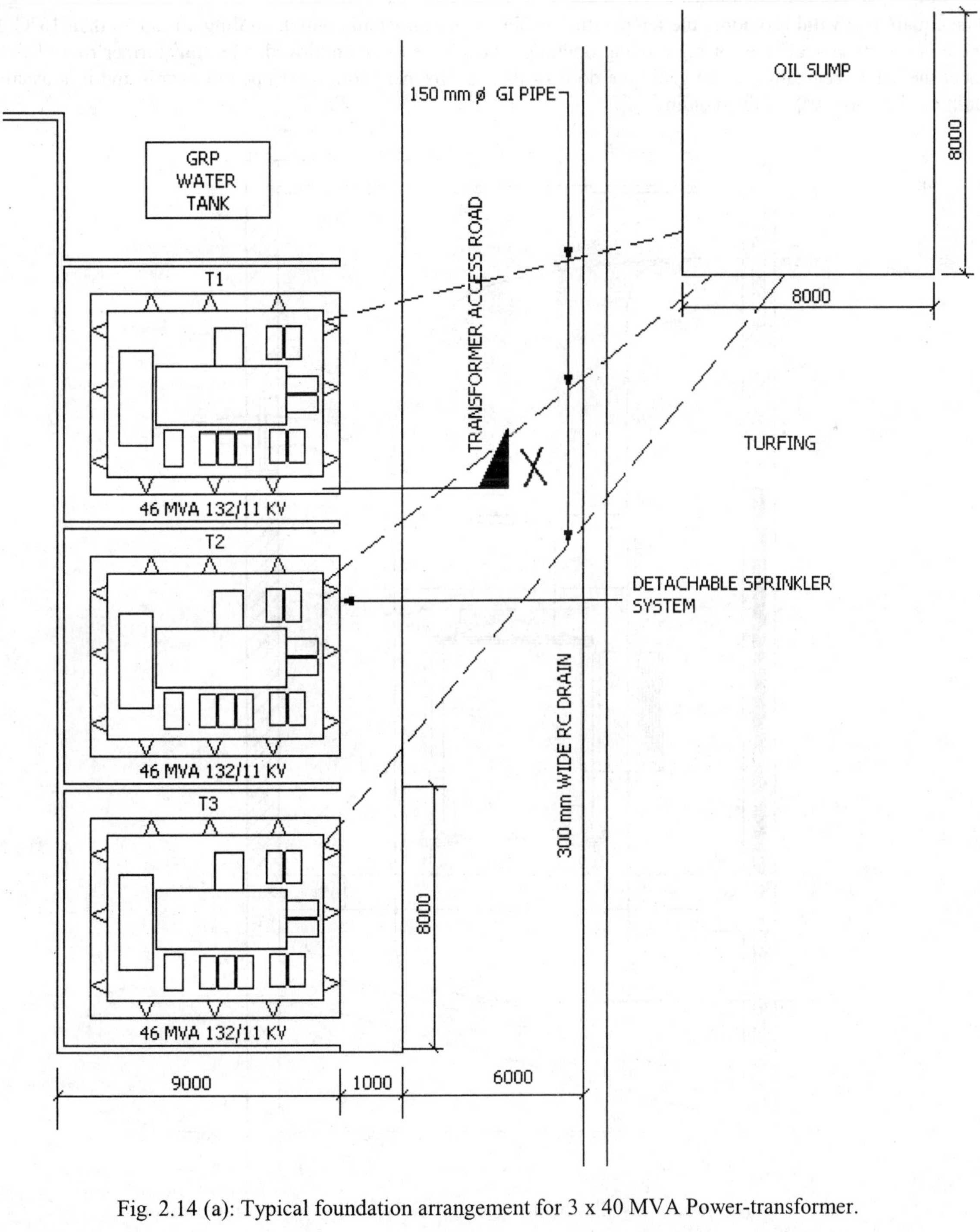

Fig. 2.14 (a): Typical foundation arrangement for 3 x 40 MVA Power-transformer.

Indoor oil immersed transformer:

For naturally cooled indoor transformers (ONAN), satisfactory ventilation must be arranged to dissipate the heat losses. The principle of the cooling system is shown in Figure 2.14 (b). A fresh air channel must be built under the transformer so that the cooling air is divided as evenly as possible between the transformer cooling elements. A ventilation duct leading to outer air must be built on the ceiling or upper part of the wall. The duct diameter has to be at least the same size as the inlet opening. The free cross section of inlet and outlet openings can be calculated from the equation: Area in square metre $= 0.12 \times P \times (KW) / \sqrt{h} \times (m)$

h = Effective height difference of draught;

P = Total losses of the transformer at full load;

The equation is valid providing the temperature differences of inlet and outlet, cooling air is less than 15°C. If there is no space available for big cooling openings, fans have to be employed. The transformer room has to meet the safety regulations. The grill type door of the transformer room must open outwards and it is usually built on the outer wall of the building.

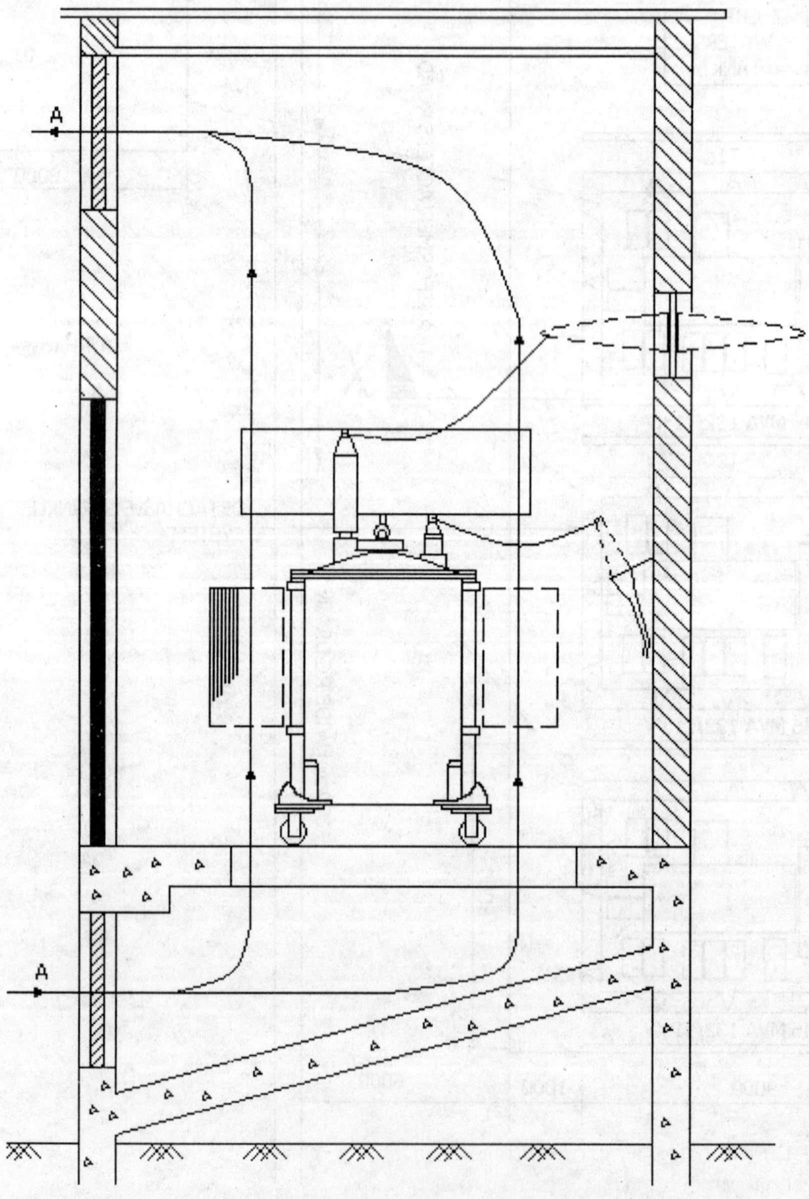

FIG. 2.14 (b): Indoor installation arrangement for oil filled power-transformer.

Dry type resin moulded distribution transformers:

Free-breathing transformers, does not require tank or oil for cooling. All windings have dry type class F insulation with air natural cooling facility. Grain oriented silicone sheet steel (insulated with carlite) is used as core laminations. This will suppress sheet steel corrosion and reduce noise level. The core is enveloped in resin. The LV and HV windings are inserted to the core and the complete assembly is impregnated under vacuum in to a class F resin. No particular precaution against fire is necessary. The dry type transformer should not be installed outdoor or indoor area liable to be wet or flooded.

The ambient temperature inside the room where the transformer is installed should in no case exceed 40°C and be lower than -25°C under normal operating conditions. Dry type distribution transformers, does not require bushings. Delta connection bars, tap-changing links, LV connection bars, HV and LV winding earthing terminals etc are provided as illustrated in Figure 2.14 (c).

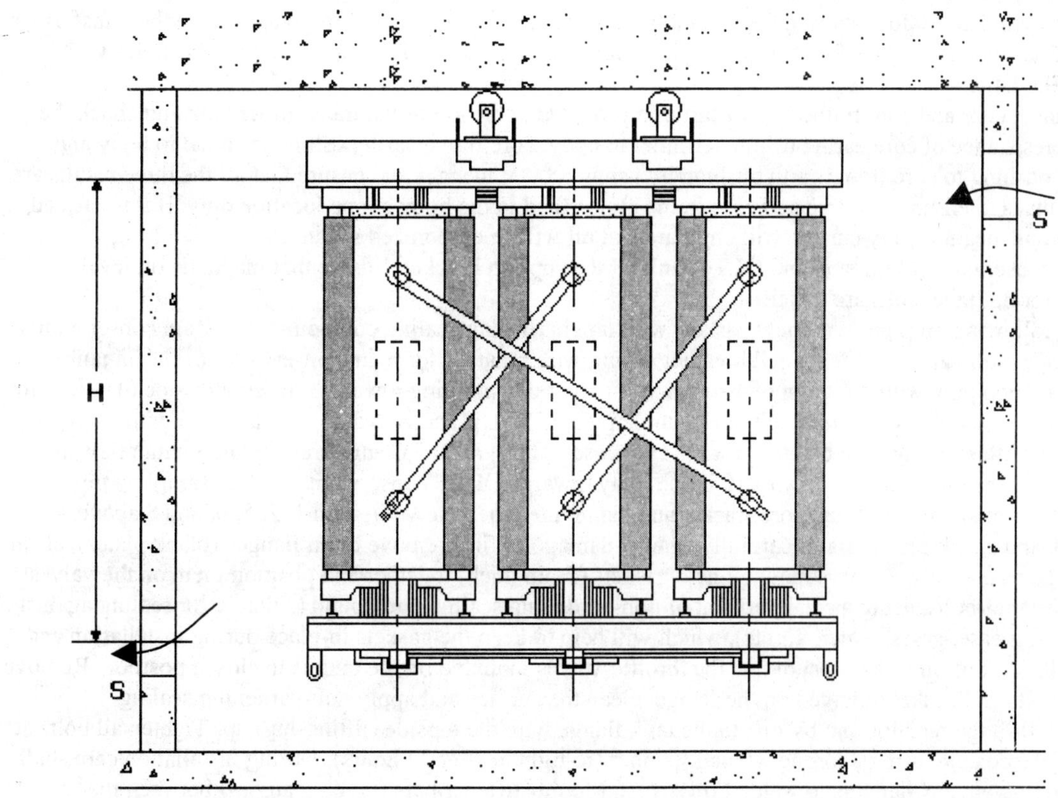

Fig. 2.14 (c): Installation arrangement of dry type transformer.

In the general case of natural cooling (AN), the purpose of the ventilation of the room or of the housing is to dissipate by free convection the heat produced by the total losses of the operating transformer. A good ventilation should consist of an inlet hole for cool air entry of section S at low level and an outlet hole of section S' diagonally opposite within the room at a height H with respect to the inlet. It should be noted that a limited airflow involves a decrease in the rated power of the transformer.

Surface of the inlet hole of cool air expressed in square meter $= \frac{0.18P}{\sqrt{H}}$ and $S' = 1.10 \times S$

P = Total losses of the transformer expressed in KW;
H = Height between the two holes expressed in meter;
S' = Surface of the air outlet hole expressed in square meter.

The equation is valid for an average ambient temperature of 20°C and a maximum altitude of 1000 Meter.

Transformer erection:

Step by step erection procedure for a 63 MVA, ONAN/ONAF transformer is described below.

(a) Inspect the availability of all parts and equipments as per packing list. If any item is missing it is not advisable to start the erection work.

(b) Inspect the impact recorder provided prior to shipping and ensure that no impact is recorded in the graph paper. If major impact is noticed, refer to manufacturer and obtain their advice.

(c) For plinth mounted transformers, provide anti-vibration mounting pad at the skid base prior to placing on the foundation.

(d) After placing the transformer to the plinth, check the alignment of the transformer by using both spirit level and water level and if necessary proceed with realignment.

(e) Inspect the inert gas pressure system (Nitrogen gas) and ensure that the pressure in the partially oil filled transformer is not less than 0.3 bar (- 4.35 Psig). If low gas pressure or no gas pressure is noticed, test the dielectric strength and moisture content of the oil. Before starting the assembling work close and detain the Nitrogen gas pipe and valve in the transformer side. Close both Nitrogen gas cylinder valves and remove the piping and cylinders. Before starting the assembly of accessories release the Nitrogen gas from the transformer tank. Remove equalizing pipe for nitrogen gas between main tank and OLTC tank and plug the holes with gasketed blank plates.

(f) Disconnect core and core frame (yoke) earthing provided at the top of the transformer tank and check the insulation resistance of core earth bushing terminal to body, core frame earth bushing terminal to body and core earth bushing to core frame earth bushing by using 1000 V megger and ensure that all the three results are infinity. This is to ensure that core and core frame are earthed to the body at one location only. If it is earthed more than one location eddy current will circulate and oil will be carbonized in due course.

(g) Install conservator (Main tank and OLTC tank) at the support bracket. Ensure that magnetic oil level indicators for both the tanks are intact.

(h) Install following oil pipes with new gaskets with non hardening sealing compound: (1) Main conservator oil drain pipe with valve; (2) Celica jell breather piping with breather for main conservator; (3) Main tank Buchholz relay piping with direction of arrow mark in the relay pointing towards conservator side (4) Pipes for connecting the bushing oil chamber to the Buchholz pipe; (5) OLTC conservator oil drain pipe with valve; (6) Celica jell breather piping with breather for OLTC conservator; (7) OLTC surge relay piping with relay and valve pointing the direction of arrow mark in the relay towards OLTC conservator: (8) Gas sampling pipe for Main tank Buchholz relay; (9) support bracket and clamp the pipes shown in item 1, 2, 5, 6, and 8 above.

(i) Unpack and check each radiator carefully against damage of fins, remove blind flanges (blank plates), clean gasket surfaces properly. Always mount 2 new gaskets (2mm thick) together and position them on the valves between the stud-bolts, using a small amount of non-hardening sealing compound (suitable for sealing against mineral oils, grease, gases, water, air etc), which will help to keep the gaskets in-place during installation and will limit the risk of oil leaks. Ensure that the throttle-valves mounted on the tank is in closed position. Remove the blank plate and gasket mounted on the flange, clean the surface and apply non-hardening sealing compound. Bolt the radiator one-by-one to the tank flange with the topside (lifting-lug) up. Tighten all bolts at the required torque by using a torque wrench spanner (re-tighten after 24 hours). During installation care shall be taken to prevent any damage to welded fin seams. Mount stiffener bars (bracing angles) between the radiators, fastened to the main tank (both top and bottom) to secure properly. Install weather-proof fan units in the appropriate locations and connect to the marshalling box mounted on the transformer.

(J) Install pressure relief discharge pipes for both main tank and OLTC tank.

(k) Bottom connected condenser bushings are designed for a current of 800 amps or more. It has a solid core to which the internal winding lead has to be connected through a separate hand hole. Draw lead condenser bushings are hollow bushings through which the insulated draw lead has to be pulled during installation. The winding lead is brazed to the terminal stud, which is fastened with pad type terminal at the top of the condenser bushing for facilitating external connection to the transformer.

(1) Installation of draw out type condenser bushing: Unpack the bushing and remove the plastic wrapped on the bushing. Inspect carefully the bushings against any crack, break, oil level etc. Clean the porcelain with clean rags (cotton cloth) moistured with Methyl hydrate. Remove the blind flange on the transformer tank where the bushing is to be mounted. Clean the gasket surface properly and place a new gasket on the cover after applying non-hardening sealant on either side of the gasket. Precaution shall be taken against accidental falling of any tools or metal pieces inside the tank. Always tie the tools to the transformer body with nylon rope to prevent accidental slipping while working. Sling the bushing at the correct angle by using nylon belt. Screw a suitable bolt on the inner threading of draw lead terminal stud and tie with a strong cord and pull it through the central

tube of the bushing. Slowly draw the draw lead cable in the bushing while the bushing is placed in to the position and fix the clamping nut and locking pin. Tight the flange bolts at the required torque to fasten the bushing with the tank. Fix the bushing head cap, provide gasket with non-hardening sealant, fix contact nut. Mount the terminal cap on the terminal stud and assemble the connecting clamp. Complete the assembly of all condenser type bushings. Record the insulation resistance of the winding by using a 5 KV megger.

(2) Installation of medium voltage porcelain bushing: Unpack the bushing and clean it. Remove the blind flange on the transformer tank and clean the gasket surface properly. Provide new gasket after applying non-hardening sealant on either side of the gasket. Screw the copper stem in the threaded hole in the internal winding connection and tighten at the required torque by providing nut and counter nut at the top end of the stem. Mount the porcelain housing together with fixation ring over the stem. Mount the upper gasket, the press ring and the locknut without tightening them. Tighten the fixation ring at first by hand and then progressively tighten the bolt with correct torque. Tighten the bushing locknut with required torque. Fix the flange bolt to fasten the bushing to the transformer tank. Assemble all porcelain bushings including neutral bushing and tertiary bushing. Record the insulation resistance to earth.

(L) Connect the transformer body to the substation earth grid at 2 earth points marked in the transformer tank.

(m) Connect back all the cables disconnected prior to shipping.

(n) Recommended tightening torque for transformer assembling bolts are given in Table 2.14 (1).

Table 2.14 (1): Recommended tightening torque for transformer assembling bolts.

Metric size bolts	Inch size bolts	Torque in Newton Metre	Torque in Foot Pounds	Torque in Kilogram force
M5	3/16	3.5	2.5	0.40
M6	¼	6.0	4.5	0.60
M8	5/16	14.5	10.75	1.5
M10	3/8	29	21.5	3.0
M12	½	50	37	5.1
M16	5/8	120	88.5	12.25
M20	¾	250	185	25.5
M22	7/8	375	276	38
M25	1.0	440	325	45

Note: 1 Kilogram metre force = 9.8066 Newton metre force;
1 foot pound force = 1.355818 Newton metre force

Oil test for high and extra high voltage transformers (66 KV to 800 KV):

1. The dielectric strength of the new transformer oil sample for medium voltage shall be minimum 65KV. Test values of new oil for high and extra high voltage transformer oil shall be in between 90 KV to 120 KV. Microprocessor controlled automatic oil test sets with digital display, zero start interlocking and door interlocks are available in the range of 50 to 120 KV. (Refer figure 2.23 (a).
2. Oil moisture content should not be above 10 ppm (Part per million).
3. The interfacial tension (sediment of sludge's) of the transformer oil should not be below 40mN/m
4. The acidity of the oil should not be greater than 0.03 KOH/g (KOH = Potassium hydroxide)
5. The dielectric dissipation factor at 90°C should not be greater than 5m rads.
6. The oil shall be entirely free of Polychlorinated Biphenyls (PCB's) and PCB content must be less than 0.1 ppm.
7. The Poly-cyclic aromatic of the oil must be more than 3 ppm
8. Shell type DIALA B is the oil used in the transformer

Oil test for medium voltage transformers up to 36 KV:

		Shell-Dial B	**Askaral**
1.	Dielectric strength (minimum)	30 KV	25 KV.
2.	Acidity test (Maximum permissible neutralization number)	0.4mg	0.1mg
3.	Maximum acceptable value of water content Parts per million	36 ppm	36ppm

4.	Colour test (Maximum acceptable colour number)	4	------
5	Tan delta or power factor dissipation factor	1%	-------

Tan delta and resistivity tester measures the dielectric constant and dissipation factor (Tan δ) up to 100% and resistivity of oil under test. Oil cell of the test equipment is fabricated out of stainless steel and Teflon is the insulation material used for isolation of the three electrodes i.e. H.T. Electrode, Guard electrode and central electrode. Heating chamber uniformly heats the test cell and oil under test up to desired temperature. Digital meter will display the test results. Typical test equipment is demonstrated in figure 2.23 (a) and (b).

Transformer oil treatment:

Where the sampled and tested oil does not meet the above requirements the oil filtering might be carried out, by using a transformer oil filter machine. Oil can be circulated through this machine for removing humidity and sludge's. If not successful, the oil shall be replaced by new oil after cleaning and vacuum processing of the main tank. Oil treatment plant must be capable of treatment of oil in accordance to IEC 296 and IEC 422. Replaceable paper filter type filter machine with following facilities are recommended:

1. Oil treatment rate not less than 4000 litter per hour.
2. Water extraction capability < 5 ppm (parts per million)
3. Reduction of dissolved gas content to 1% by volume or less.
4. Equipped with oil transfer pump, vacuum pump and heaters
5. Vacuum capable approximately 1 Torr
6. Facility to apply vacuum to transformer tank during oil replacing.
7. Wire reinforced heat and oil resistant hose coloured differently for clean and dirty oil.

Following precautions need to be taken during filtration and degassing:

(a) Don't use rubber hose since sulphur in rubber hose may react with oil.

(b) In the event of transformer provided with air cell in the conservator, the conservator should be isolated.

(c) Do not allow the oil temperature to go above 60°C. If exceeding 70°C, this may cause oxidation of oil.

(d) Do not mix OLTC oil with main tank oil during filtering.

(e) For filtration and degassing of the transformer, the inlet to the filter machine is taken from the bottom of the transformer tank and the outage is connected to the top of the tank.

(f) Connect the cooling water supply and ensure that the cooling water is circulating through the condenser of the filter machine for better condensation.

(g) Check the correct direction of rotation of all pumps

Oil first enters the preliminary filter, which is provided with a magnetic strainer and a perforated coarse filter. The magnetic particles and coarse particles are filtered here. Then the inlet gear pump allows the oil to flow through the heaters, which are controlled through a thermostat via magnetic contactors. The hot oil passes through the filter press and cartridge filter. After the moisture content in oil is reduced it is better to switchover the cartridge filter as the filter press is not meant for heavy-duty operations. Filtered oil passes through the degassing chamber where oil is subjected to very high vacuum and water as well as gas are separated. Now the oil flows to the transformer tank and circulates through filter by pumping action. The oil is tested for breakdown voltage once in 12 hours and the filtration is continued until the desired value obtained. For closing down, switch off oil pumps and close inlet/outlet valves from the transformer. Break vacuum in the degassing chamber. Drain oil from heater tank, cartridge filter press, degassing chamber and condensate tank. Close all valves and disconnect oil hoses, water supply and electric supply. Figure 2.14 (d) shows the block scheme of a degassing plant (filter machine), which is equipped with a heater and filter.

LEGEND

1. Oil pump
2. Heater
3. vacuum chamber
4. Oil pump
5. Filter
6. Vacuum chamber
7. Oil pump
8. Vacuum pump
9. Vacuum pump
10. Vacuum pump

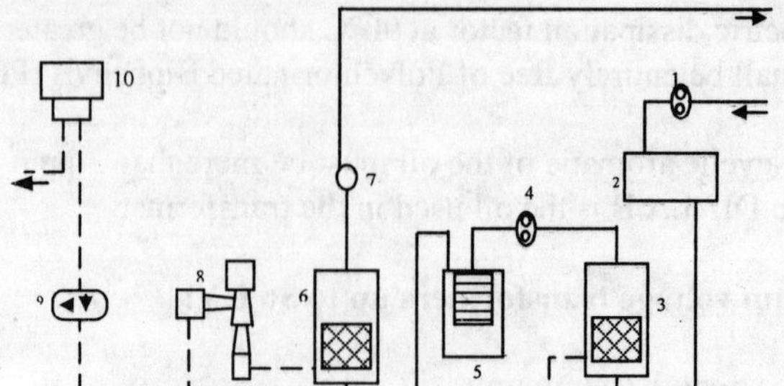

Fig. 2.14 (d): Block scheme of a transformer oil filter machine

Usually the water content of the oil depends on the moisture of the windings. Actually the distribution of total amount of water inside the transformer between the paper and oil is temperature dependent. The equilibrium state is depicted in Figure 2.14 (e). From this it is seen that water is diffused from paper to oil as the temperature increases and back again when the temperature decreases. Consequently, when the transformer is warmed up, it can gradually be dried by, drying the oil. There is, however, about 50 times more water in the paper insulation than in the oil and the diffusion of water from craft paper insulation to the oil is rather slow. Correspondingly the drying is very slow and is economical only if the transformer can be kept in service during the drying. To this end a molecular sieve dehydrator shown in Figure 2.14 (f) can be used to reclaim the oil.

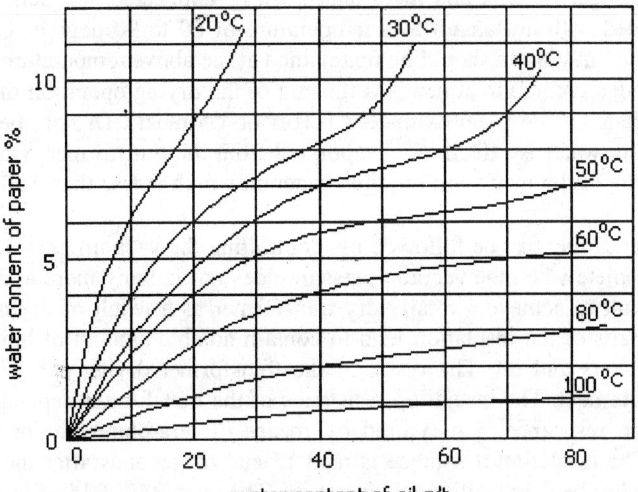

Fig. 2.14 (e): Equilibrium between water content of paper and oil.

The apparatus in figure (f) can be used for reclaiming the oil because it absorbs aging products and other polar compounds from the oil. In most cases it is more economical to replace new oil than to reclaim it. However, great care must be taken to avoid entry of ingress of air or solids in to the transformer through the connecting pipes. These could cause breakdown of the insulation when the transformer is energized.

LEGEND:
1. Transformer
2. Oil pump
3. Column filled with molecular sieve
4. Oil filter
5. Conservator

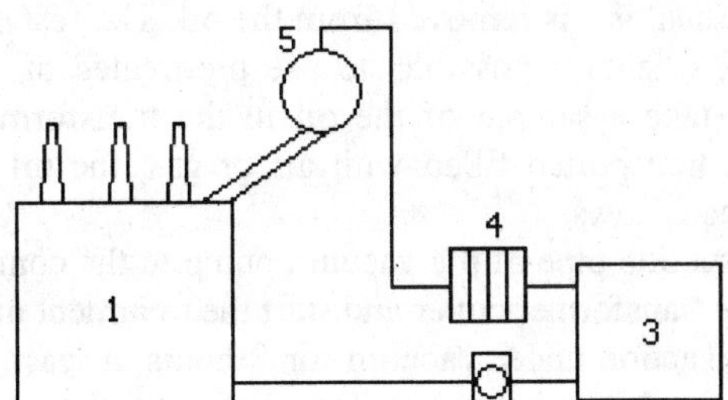

Fig. 2.14 (f): Block scheme of Molecular sieve dehydrator

Transformer oil sampling:

Following points are to be considered while taking samples for oil testing:

a) Oil samples should be taken from the bottom of the transformer (sampling valve) after draining some oil (Askaral samples should be from top)

b) Samples should be taken in clean, dry bottles (after rinsed with sample oil), tightly sealed and either of amber glass or kept shielded from the light. The stoppers of bottle may be glass, cork or oil resistant plastic. Rubber stoppers should not be used.

c) Sample should be taken in a dry day and at a time when liquid temperature is high

d) Samples should be allowed to stand in tightly sealed bottles for 24 hours prior to test.

e) It is not permitted to take any sample for test from hermetically sealed transformers because the oil will not deteriorate.

Vacuum drying and drying control:
The transformer can also be dried by vacuum treatment. Shorter drying time will be achieved, if vacuum, necessary for steaming of oil. Vacuum drying can be carried out on transformers own tank, provided the tank can withstand vacuum. The main tanks of large transformers are vacuum-proof. The suction pump of the vacuum drying equipment will be generally fastened to the connection flange of the oil conservator located on the transformer cover. In transformers provided with on-load tap changers the connection pipe (U-pipe) between the on-load tap changer oil tank and main tank must be connected. Vacuum drying ensures that the transformer interior is heated with hot air up to a temperature of 60 to 90 degrees Celsius. During vacuum drying, the temperature of the insulation should be maintained at the above temperature by applying DC power directly to the windings under vacuum treatment. At the end of the drying operation the vacuum pressure of a transformer must be less than 150 Pa (Approximately 1 Torr or 1.5 mbar). During the vacuum process while simultaneously being heated, water is effectively evaporated from the transformer windings. The evaporation of oil from the surface layers of the insulation requires vacuum, which is less than 15 Pa and a temperature of 80°C.
The progress of transformer drying can be followed by, controlling the vacuum pressure, ingress of water and temperature. Drying is complete when the vacuum pressure does not fall any more and the ingress of water is very slow. It is very difficult to achieve a totally dry transformer as a result of drying a moist oil-insulated transformer. The deepest parts of the insulation tend to contain notable amount of humidity, which will later diffuse in to the surface layers and oil. The result of the transformer drying can be checked by means of insulation resistance measurement. The insulation resistance of the transformer depends both on moisture and temperature. The insulation resistance is measured by means of tera-ohmmeter or DC-megger or Digital insulation tester (5 KV). The insulation resistance is read 15 and 60 seconds after the measuring voltage has been applied and the meter has been in continuous operation. The ratio R60: R15 of the values obtained in this measurement usually ranges from 1.3 to 3 in dry transformers. In case a final moisture value is required to be measured, it can be done with chemical methods from special paper samples inserted in to the transformer.

Filling the transformer with oil after vacuum treatment
When the transformer is proved to be dry after vacuum treatment, oil filling can begin. Oil is slowly directed to the upper part of the tank and highest possible vacuum is maintained all the time. The correct filling speed can obtain if the vacuum does not considerably decrease during filling. When the windings and insulation parts are below the oil level, the oil filling is interrupted. When deaerated oil is used, the vacuum must be maintained for several hours so that all the residual gas is removed from the oil. The rest of the oil can be filled normally. For vacuum filling, it is advisable, whenever possible, to use pre-treated oil from which air has been removed. Finally, it is recommended to take a sample of the oil in the transformer to check the dielectric strength. Transformers which, has been transported filled with air or gas, the oil filling is carried out as mentioned above. Method of filling oil is as follows:

1. Connect the suction pipe of the vacuum pump to the connecting flange of the oil conservator located on the transformer cover and start the treatment under vacuum.
2. Continue the suction under vacuum for 8 hours at least, and try to keep the pressure under 133 Pa = 1 torr = 1.33 mbar = 1mmHg.
3. Thereafter start to fill the transformer with oil, keeping the vacuum pump in operation.
4. Pump the cleaned and dried transformer oil from the transportation tanks slowly through the filter via the oil-filling hole to the transformer tank.

Transformer connection: Cable should not be laid above or near by oil sump. Cables or bus duct are to be installed such that bushings are not liable to mechanical strain. Flexible joints are to be used for connecting bus ducts to the bushings. Temperature fluctuation due to changing of load on transformers causes strains in joints. To withstand these strains the joints must be provided with flexible cup springs under the fastening screw or nut. These will help to keep the compressive force constant. In joints made of aluminium, pressure-balancing sheets must be used directly against the aluminium surface both on the fixing screw and nut side. While doing aluminium joint or aluminium copper joint following precautions must be taken:

(a) In aluminium copper joint the copper is coated with tin, or bimetal (one side copper and the other side aluminium) is being used between the joint.

(b) The aluminium surface must be massive compared to that of copper.
(c) Aluminium parts should always to be placed above copper parts so that rainwater cannot drain from the copper parts in to aluminium.
(d) The layer of oxide in aluminium shall be removed by, a steel brush. Jointing grease, which prevents the access of air and humidity in to joints, must be used in the joint. The zinch crystals of grease break moreover the layer of oxide in aluminium.
(e) Satisfactorily strong steel bolts and nuts with flat and spring washers have to be used for the tightening of the joint

Transformer earthing: Figure 2.14 (g) and (h) shows the typical ground bus arrangement for earth connection to a 66/11 KV transformer tank and neutral through neutral grounding resistor. Fabricated tinned copper bus bars duly supported with insulators are used as earth bus. All earth conductors connected to the bus are single core PVC insulated copper conductor cable green colour with yellow lining. Cable sizes are usually selected on the basis of the actual soil resistivity measured at site and design calculations made as per IEEE standard 80.

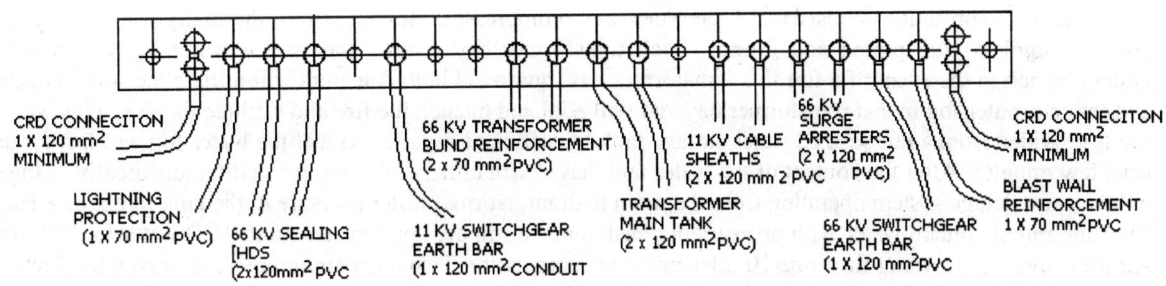

Fig. 2.14 (g): Earth bus for 110/11 KV indoor transformer

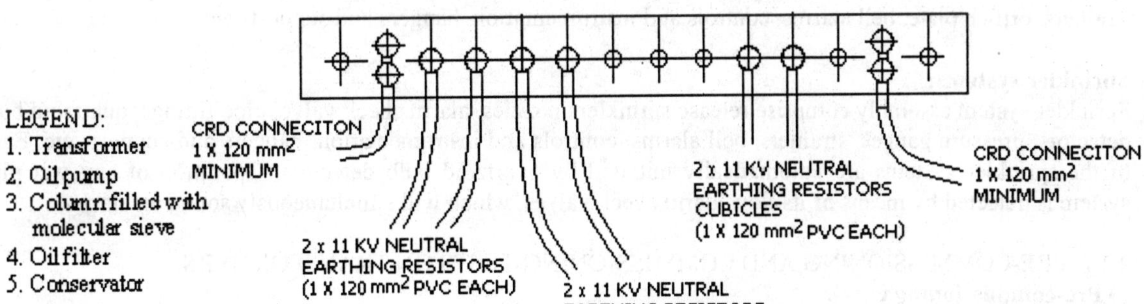

Fig. 2.14 (h): 110/11 KV Transformer neutral earth bus.

2.15 TRANSFORMER BAY, WATER FOG AND DELUGE SYSTEM.

Fire hydrant and fire fighting equipments: A cast iron cement lined hydrant main of at least 100mm diameter pipe line connected to the local water supply line is required near by the transformer bay (inside substation fencing). Hydrant system is provided with isolation valve, strainer and facilities to connect a fire-brigade booster pump located at a convenient place in consultation with local fire fighting authorities. Fire system equipment cubicle is provided to store the equipment associated with the fire hydrant and hose system. The access door to the cubicle shall face towards the transformer bay. Following equipments are to be stored in the cubicle based on the recommendation of NFPA (National fire protection association).

(a) 6 numbers 20 litter drum of foam concentric liquid including water nozzle and foam making nozzle (one each)
(b) 6 numbers 30 metre length 25mm diameter. fire hose with hose reel
(c) 1 number foam trolley extinguisher 30 liter size
(d) 3 number 5Kg portable CO2 fire extinguisher
(e) 1 number CO2 trolley extinguisher with 2 x 9Kg cylinder mounted.

Automatic water fog and deluge system:
This system in substations consists of a pressure tank, compressor, jacking pump, thermally triggered spray nozzle, complete with piping and fittings. Each transformer bay is provided with a water fog and deluge system, which in the event of a fire in a transformer bay, quartzoid bulb detectors will initiate the spray nozzle and set up a water fog in that transformer bay and will cool and quench the fire and exclude oxygen. This water fog is provided from a pressurized water storage tank of sufficient capacity so that the water fog will last for at least few minutes. After the content of the water tank have been utilized, the system shall automatically change in to a water deluge system operating from the main hydrant. Normal water pressure in the tank might be 8 bar. The tank might contain water with pressurizing cushion of air in an, approximate ratio 1/3rd water to 2/3rd air. Air pressure 8 bar or water flow rate 10 litter/minute/square metre. Two units air compressor, driven by electric motor and controlled by a pressure switch. Low pressure and high-pressure alarm with automatic change over also required. A jacking pump driven by an electric motor and a standby diesel pump is provided to maintain the water level within the pressure tank. Transformer bay might be provided with a spray nozzle, which will set up a water fog within the area between the bay's fire and blast walls.

In power stations, the system is used with a deluge valve of hydraulic actuation type directly connected with fire detection line. The detection line is always filled with water and equipped with closed type of fire detectors such as sprinklers heads. The system assembly shall comprise a release sprinklers nozzles, open spray nozzles, hydraulic actuated spray deluge system, pipe fittings, valves, quartzoid bulb detectors, pressure gauges, strainers, orifice plate, bell alarms, controls and instrumentation, hangers and supports etc.

Sprinkler systems:
Sprinkler system assembly comprise release sprinklers nozzles, alarm check valve, pipe fittings, quartzoid bulb detectors, pressure gauges, strainers, bell alarms, controls and instrumentation, hangers and supports etc. Each of the sprinkler systems are automatically initiated by quartzoid bulb detectors. Operation of any wet pipe system is detected by means of its flow alarm check valves, which will simultaneously sound an alarm.

2.16 PRE-COMMISSIONING AND COMMISSIONING TESTS ON TRANSFORMERS.

a) Pre-commissioning check:

1. Oil samples from main tank and On-load Tap-changer have passed BDV (Break down value) minimum 60 KV with 2.5mm electrode gap on oil test set [refer figure 2.23 (b)]
2. Bushing surfaces were cleaned, air released, Test-tap caps are tightened, and arcing horn-gaps are duly adjusted. Measured insulation resistance value (before connection) with 5 KV megger is not less than 5000 Mega-ohm for both HV and LV bushings. (Wash the bushings with hot oil to improve the insulation value)
3. Oil level in main conservator as well as OLTC conservator is up to mark.
4. Magnetic oil level gauge lock is released and the oil level is intact.
5. Buchholz relay: (a) Release lock; (b) Check test lever position; (c) Shutoff valves on both sides are open; (d) Close air release valve; (e) Check arrowhead pointing towards conservator; (f) release air
6. OLTC oil surge relay: (a) Release OSR lock; (b) OSR shutoff valve is open; (c) Check OSR arrowhead pointing towards OLTC conservator (d) Release air.

7. Main and OLTC silica jell breathers: (a) Colour of silica jell is blue; (b) Oil is filled in breather bottom cup up to marked level; (c) Sealing tape is removed (d) Check OLTC drive motor and mechanism operation sequence.
8. Check all butterfly valves (top and bottom) of radiators are fully open and ensure that no oil is leaking from radiators.
9. Cable box is filled with oil (if applicable) and the valve connecting oil pipe to cable box is open.
10. Oil sampling, oil draining and filtration valves and oil filling cap on conservators are fully closed and no oil is leaking from any gasketed joints.
11. No oil in explosion vent. Remove blanking plate and fix diaphragm on explosion vent. Fill transformer oil in oil thermometer and winding temperature indicator thermocouple mounting pockets.
12. For off-load tap changers set the tap in the required position and lock the operating wheel.
13. Check double ground connection from transformer tank to Earth bus, neutral earth connection to neutral bus for solidly earthed system and connection through NGR for resistance-earthed system. Check earth connection to earth bus / by pass switch /disconnectors.
14. Ensure that unused CT secondary terminals are shorted.
15. Setting of oil and winding temperature indicator alarm and trip contacts.
16. Check the direction of rotation and automatic functioning of air blowers/water pumps/oil pumps, fire pumps etc (if applicable)
17. Tightening incoming and outgoing cable or bus duct connections and check correctness of phase sequence. Check tightness of clamps and connecters in the transformer bushings and apply petroleum jelly.
18. Check foundation (Rollers are properly locked) oil drain system and fire fighting system etc.
19. Function check of all annunciation systems and trip circuits. [Refer figure 2.16 (a) & (b)].
20. Measuring earth resistance/Insulation resistance of windings and connecting cables

Figure 2.16 (a) shows the typical trip circuit of a power transformer. Following devices are usually provided for tripping the circuit breaker of a power transformer.

(1) 50/50N, Instantaneous over-current and earth fault relay;
(2) 51G, Ground fault relay transformer neutral earthing .
(3) 51/51N, Time over-current and earth fault relay
(4) 64, Restricted earth fault relay
(5) 67/67N, Directional over-current and earth fault relay
(6) 87T, Transformer differential relay
(7) 26WT, Winding over temperature
(8) 26OT, Oil temperature high.
(9) 63MT, Main tank Buchholz relay
(10) 63TC, Tap changer protective relay
(11) 63OPM, Transformer main tank over pressure
(12) 63 OPO: OLTC tank over pressure

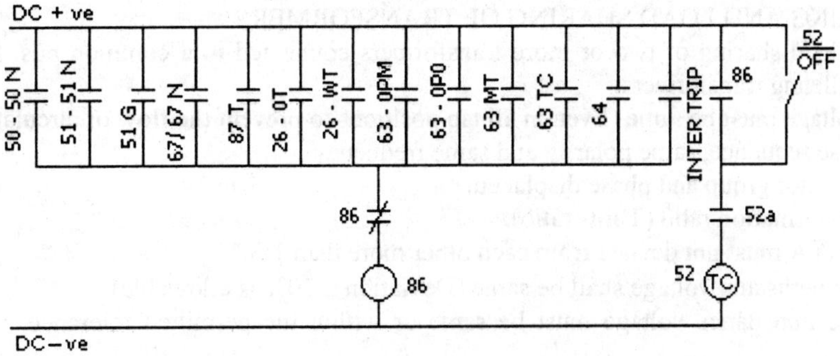

Fig. 2 16 (a): Typical trip circuit of a power transformer

Figure 2.16 (b) shows interlocking circuit for inter tripping of primary and secondary breakers. In the event of an internal fault or any external faults, which are not cleared by the secondary side relays in a transformer, primary side relays or non electrical devices will initiate to trip the primary side circuit breaker. Inter-tripping circuit is for simultaneous tripping of secondary side breaker. This circuit is very essential for parallel connected transformers and wherever stand by generator is employed.

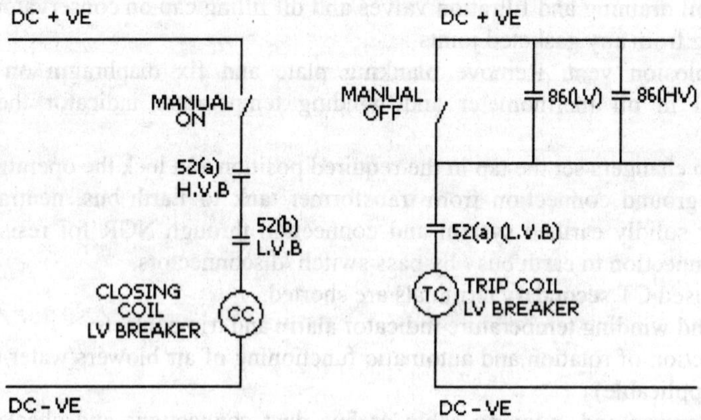

Fig. 2.16 (b): Interlocking circuit for inter-tripping of transformer circuit breakers

b) Commissioning tests:

1. Insulation resistance test: HV to LV, HV to Earth, LV to Earth. (Similar tests on Tertiary winding or Zigzag winding)
2. Primary and secondary injection tests on protective relays and final setting of relays.
3. Function check on On-load Tap-changer by mechanical operation and setting of voltage regulator.
4. Ratio test, phasing test, polarity test and vector group test by using appropriate testers. Test instruments are described in section 2.22
5. Primary and secondary circuit breaker function check.

c) Tests after commissioning:

1. Noise level (For ONAN cooling system, the noise level measured at one metre distance from the transformer should not exceed 72 dB. Similarly, for ONAF cooling system the noise level should not exceed 75 dB).
2. Measurement of voltage at various tap position and compare with original test report
3. Function check of OLTC and voltage relay. Setting of voltage relays for master/follower operation
4. Transformer oil test after commissioning
5. Observe winding and oil temperature during and after initial loading
6. Synchronism check for parallel operating transformers.

2.17 PARALLELING AND LOAD SHARING OF TRANSFORMERS

Paralleling means load sharing of two or more transformers connected to a common bus. Following are the conditions for paralleling transformers:

1. Output voltage must be same (Even in all tap positions to prevent the flow of circulating current)
2. Same phase sequence, same polarity and same frequency.
3. Identical vector group and phase displacement
4. Same transformation ratio (Turns ratio).
5. KVA or MVA must not deviate from each other more than 1:3
6. Short time withstand voltage shall be same (Deviation ± 10% is allowable)
7. Percentage impedance voltage must be same or within the permitted tolerance, i.e. maximum 1% difference
8. Same percentage regulation.
9. All paralleled transformers have identical tap changers (either off load or on-load)

Figure 2.17 (a) shows the connection diagram of two transformers of similar vector group to be connected in parallel. If two or more three-phase transformers have to be connected in parallel, it is essential that only transformers bearing identical indices (phase displacement) can be run in parallel Transformers with indices 5 and 11 can also be synchronized if the conductors of both the LV and HV sides are suitably crossed as shown in Figure 2.17 (b)

Dangerous transient currents can occur if transformers with different voltages (even different tap settings) operated in parallel. Disregarding any dissimilarity in impedance phase angle φ, the voltage difference ∇u in ratio drives through both sides a circulating current of $Ia = \frac{\text{Voltage difference in \%}}{(\%Z1 / I_{N1}) + (\%Z2 / I_{N2})}$

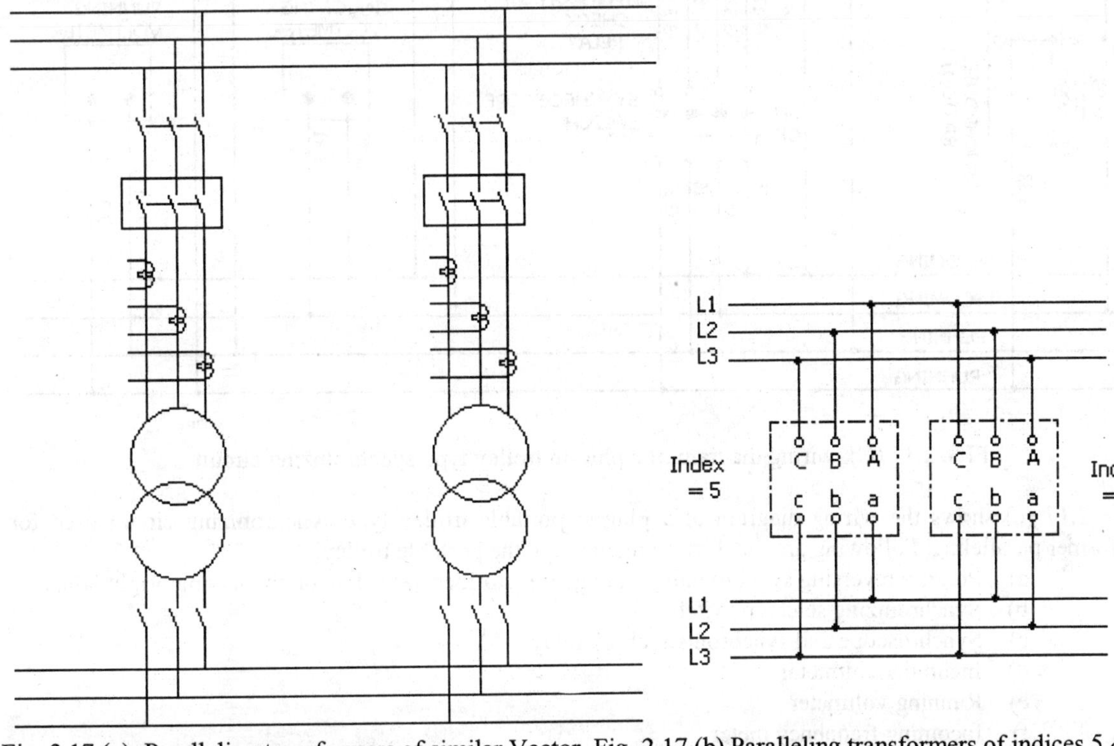

Fig. 2.17 (a): Paralleling transformers of similar Vector. Fig. 2.17 (b) Paralleling transformers of indices 5 &11

For example if percentage impedance of two transformers T1 and T2 running in parallel, Z1 = Z2 = 6%, and transformer secondary rated current I_{N1} = 910 A, and I_{N2} = 1445 A, Voltage difference ∇U = 4%.

Ia = 0.04 / [(0.06/910) + (0.06/1445)] = 0.04 / (0.000065934 + 0.000041522) = 372.25 A

The transient current is superimposed on the transformer rated secondary currents, which are fed in to the network. It is added to the current of that transformer which has the greater secondary no load voltage. Similarly, even if the off load tap settings of 2 or more paralleled transformers are set at different taps, circulating current will pass between the transformers.

Procedures for paralleling step down transformers:

(a) Connect the corresponding HV and LV terminals as shown in Figure 2.17a.

(b) Execute the common earthing of both the transformer tanks from one earth bus provided the transformers are installed next to each other or in the same yard.

(c) Close HV circuit breakers of both the transformer. The LV circuit breakers must be open and the synchronizing switch in the off position.

(d) Check for any difference in voltage between the corresponding LV phases. The source should be traded because the difference in voltage may be caused by a non-symmetrical connection or by faulty tap changer position. To raise or lower the transformer voltage on load tap changer can be used.

(e) Only when it is certain that no difference in voltage exists between corresponding LV terminals, the LV breakers are closed.

(f) Use of synchronism check relay or auto synchronizer is essential.

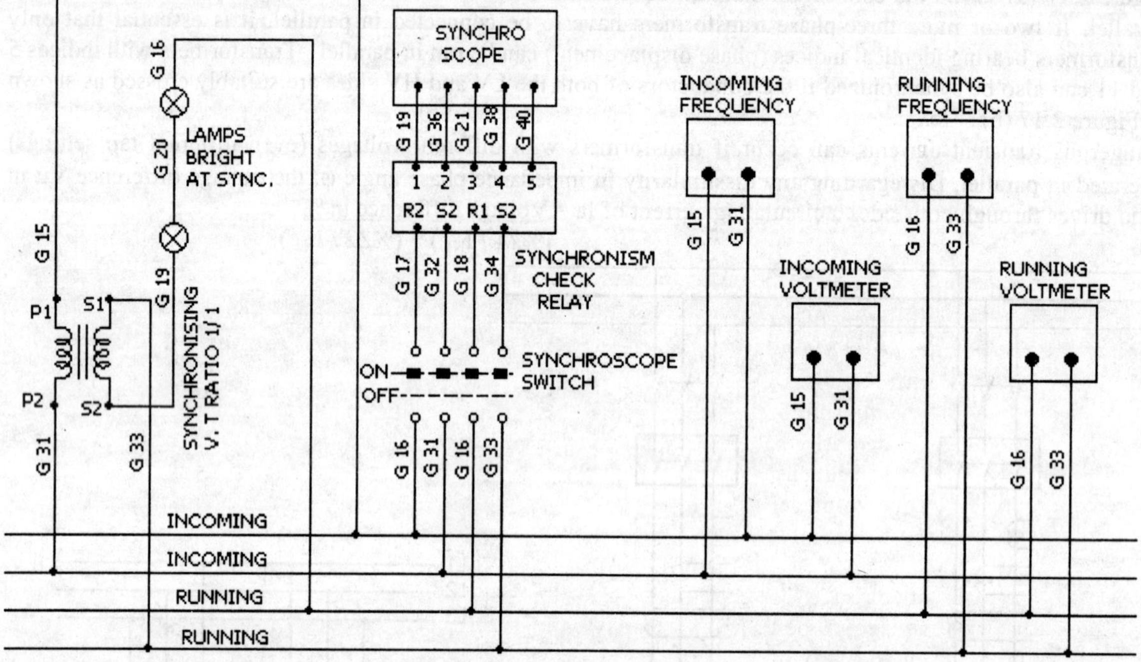

FIG. 2.17 (C): wiring diagram of a plug-in trolley type synchronizing circuit.

Figure 2.17 (c) shows the wiring diagram of a plug-in portable trolley type synchronizing circuit used for transformer paralleling. Following are the devices mounted in the portable trolley:

a) Polarity reversing synchronizing voltage transformer, ratio 1:1 for connecting bright lamps.
b) Synchronizing selector switch
c) Synchroscope and synchronism check relay
d) Incoming voltmeter
e) Running voltmeter
f) Incoming frequency meter
g) Running frequency meter

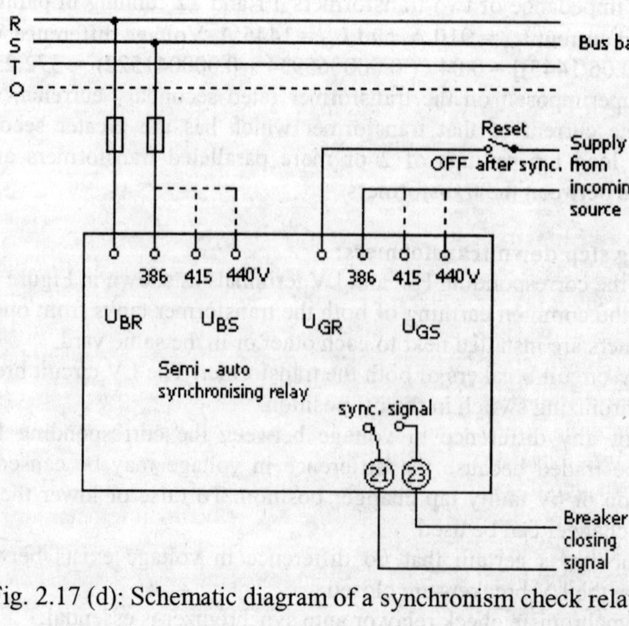

Fig. 2.17 (d): Schematic diagram of a synchronism check relay.

For initial paralleling ensure that the measured voltages between corresponding phases (incoming as well as running) are zero. If these voltages are twice the phase value connections are not in the same phase sequence.

If synchronizing is permitted manually, it may be desirable to supervise the operator with an automatic synchronizing device called synchronism check relay. Thus if both the operator and the synchronizing device are in agreement, the synchronizing breaker is permitted to close. On the other hand, if there is a disagreement between the operator and the device, closing of the breaker is blocked. Figure 2.17 (d) illustrates the schematic diagram of a synchronism check relay.

Load sharing of paralleled transformers:

1) If percentage impedance of paralleling transformers are equal, the loading of these transformers are proportional to their KVA or MVA ratings.

2) Polarity or phase relation ship of paralleled transformers must be same. To determine the polarity, energize the two transformers temporarily by connecting 415volts supply to the higher voltage side of the transformer with correct R-Y-B phase sequence. Measure the voltage between the corresponding phases (R to R) in the lower voltage side. If the voltmeter reads zero voltage the polarity is correct. If the voltage recorded is twice the polarity is not correct. Test all the three phases and ensure that the terminal markings are correct.

3) During parallel running it is common practice for the transformer with the lowest short time withstand voltage (impedance voltage) to be the most heavily loaded. When the transformer is loaded at its rated output, the maximum total output Smax of all the transformers operating in parallel can be obtained by applying the equation

$$S_{max} = \frac{[Z_{min} \times S_{N1}]}{Zi} + \frac{[Z_{min} \times S_{N2}]}{Z2} + ----$$

An example of the parallel operation of the three transformers:
Transformer No: 1, KVA capacity S_{N1} =5000 KVA; Z1 = 9%
Transformer No: 2, KVA capacity S_{N2} = 8000 KVA; Z2 = 10%
Transformer No: 3, KVA capacity S_{N3} = 10,000 KVA; Z3 = 11%

Total rated output = 5000 + 8000 + 10,000 = 23000 KVA (23 MVA).

Zmin: = 9%. Hence S1 = (Zmin x S_{N1}) / Z1 = (9 x 5000) / 9 = 5000 KVA

S2 = (9 x 8000) / 10 = 7200 KVA; S3 = (9 x 10,000) / 11 = 8181 KVA

Maximum output = S1 + S2 + S3 = 5000 + 7200 + 8181 = 20.381 KVA;

Approximately 88.6% of the total rated output.

Temperature-rise and load capacity:

When the transformer load increases its temperature will rise and the ageing of insulting materials accelerates. The aging speed will double and the corresponding lifetime will be halved, when the temperature of the hottest point in the windings rises 6 to 8°C, within the temperature range of 80 to 140°C. In addition to the temperature, some other factors such as oxygen, acids and humidity also speed up the aging. Aging sets certain limits as to the load capacity of the transformer.

According to IEC publication 354 (Loading guide for oil immersed transformers), the normal operation of air-cooled transformer is considered as the continuous operation at the rated power when the ambient air temperature is + 20°C. Continuous load capacity at different ambient air temperature at the hottest point in the winding is 98°C i.e. the same as normal operation. Table 2.17 (1) shows the continuous load capacity for air-cooled transformers (ONAN/ONAF) at different ambient temperatures in accordance with IEC loading guide.

Table 2.17 (1): Continuous loading capacity and corresponding oil temperature of ONAN/ONAF transformers.

Ambient air-temperature /°C	- 20	- 10	- 0	+ 10	+ 20	+ 30	+ 40
Continuous loading capacity	130 %	123%	116%	108%	100%	91%	82%
Oil temperature /°C	67	69	71	73	75	78	80

IEC loading guide also gives short-term overloading capacity as a function of the ambient air temperature and the loading duration provided the loading capacity at other times of the day does not exceed 90 % of the rated power.

Table 2.17 (2): Short-term load capacity as a function of the ambient air-temperature and duration of loading for air-cooled (ONAN/ONAF) transformers.

Load time hrs/day	- 20°C	- 10°C	0°C	+ 10°C	+ 20°C	+ 30°C	+ 40°C
0.5	150%	150%	150%	150%	150%	126%	118%
1.0	150%	150%	150%	150%	150%	110%	104%
2.0	150%	150%	150%	147%	132%	99%	95%
4.0	150%	148%	140%	130%	118%	95%	88%
6.0	144%	139%	132%	123%	112%	93%	86%
8.0	140%	134%	128%	119%	109%	93%	84%
12.0	137%	131%	123%	115%	105%	92%	83%

2.18 PREVENTIVE MAINTENANCE ON TRANSFORMER IN SERVICE.

Weekly maintenance (Transformer in service)

1. Oil level in conservators and on load tap changers (Refilling only after shutdown).
2. Oil temperature indicator and winding temperature indicator readings.
3. Noise/humming sound measurement (If abnormal, obtain advice from manufacturer).
4. Operation of fans/pumps/fire pumps and all other motors. Oil pump should be checked by, observing the readings of pressure gauges.
5. Condition of silica gel of both breathers (Bright blue colour) and preheating if more than 50% become pink colour. Heated in a well-ventilated oven at 135 degree Celsius till the entire quantity changes to original bright blue colour.
6. General cleaning of the transformer surroundings/external cleaning of tank and radiators.
7. Oil leaking and radiator valve positions (attend oil leaking only after shutdown).
8. Physical check against worn out earthing terminals (Neutral, body and NGR).
9. Physical check on all accessories provided on the transformer.

Quarterly maintenance (Short-term shutdown works)

1. Attend oil leakage and sampling of oil (main tank and OLTC) for dielectric strength test and moisture content test. For BDV test adjust the (12.5mm dia) electrodes to obtain a gap of 2.5mm between them. Carryout six tests on the oil, stirring the oil between each breakdown and allowing it to settle. The average value 60 KV (BDV) is acceptable. The moisture content should not exceed 15 PPM (Parts per million).
2. Cleaning bushings and examine for cracks and flashover.
3. Tightening all bolted connections.
4. Tap changer servicing, function check, refilling oil if necessary.
5. Servicing cooling fans/oil pumps/fire pumps
6. Repair of radiators (Check ventilation system for indoor transformers)
7. Makeup oil level in dehydrating breathers.
8. Replace filter in forced oil cooled transformer filtering unit. Observe oil pressure on forced oil cooled transformers and water pressure on OFWF transformers.
9. Test moisture contents of oil filled cable boxes.
10. Marshalling cubicle: Check doors and hinges, light, space heater, tightness of cable connections etc.

11. Cooling system: Clean cooling system by water flushing at high pressure to remove the dirt, insects or any air borne particles. Cooling of internal cooling surfaces of oil coolers and radiators. In the event of setting of sludge formation the same may be flushed internally with clean transformer oil. If the sludge does not get cleaned use petrol at first and then flushing with clean transformer oil. The cooler can be cleaned by taking out the tube-assembly and thereby, making them assessable for cleaning.
12. Use of thermovision camera may be made to detect any hotspot in the joints.

Annual maintenance (Long-term shutdown works)

1. Measurements of insulation resistance and compare with values observed during commissioning tests. Minimum insulation resistance for one minute value (in mega-ohm) for transformer may be determined by using the formula IR = CE / √KVA where C = 1.5 for oil filled transformers; and E = Voltage rating for one of the single phase winding. KVA = Capacity of the transformer under test. The minimum IR value at 30°C: for 11KV winding 300MΩ, for 33 KV winding 400MΩ and for HV & EHV windings 500MΩ. For other temperatures apply correction factor given in Table 2.23 (1).
2. Polarization index value should not be less than 1.5 for power transformers. If the value is above 1.5 which indicates very good condition. (PI = Ten minutes IR value / 1 minute IR value)
3. Tighten the bolts of gasketed joints evenly to avoid uneven pressure
4. Oil to be replenished in the pockets holding thermocouples of oil and winding temperature indicators. Check calibration of thermometers by using calibrated temperature controlled bath.
5. Check contamination of motor and cooling fan blades. Check starting of first stage cooling fans at 65°C and second stage cooling fans at 80°C, alarm at 110°C and breaker tripping at 125°C.
6. Check pointer of dial type oil gauge and repair/replace if necessary.
7. Painting repair or retouching if necessary.
8. Primary and secondary injection test on protective relays and function check of trip circuits.
9. Examine surge diverter and clean, adjust horn gaps if necessary.
10. If the dielectric strength of oil is below the specified value, the oil shall be reconditioned by using a filter machine.
11. Ensure that cooling tubes are not clogging and external coolers are working properly.
12. Dust, snow and salt spray deposit on the surface of the bushing must be removed.
13. Measure earth resistance value and ensure that the value measured is not higher than the design value. If the earth resistance is very high, high voltages to be impressed at neutral end of the winding during ground fault on bus or feeder. This will cause inter-turn fault on neutral end of the transformer.
14. Function check of upstream and down stream circuit breakers and associated tripping devices such as Buchholz relay, OLTC surge relay, winding temperature high, oil temperature high, Lockout relay, breaker failure protection, over current and instantaneous over current protection, earth fault protection, restricted earth fault protection, differential protection etc.
15. Check each valve for free operation and returns to "in-service" operating position.

Before carrying out maintenance work following precautions might be taken:

(1) The transformer and associated equipment should be taken out of service, isolated and earthed.
(2) Obtain a permit to work and detain all relevant keys.

Return work permit with keys and clearance for energizing the transformer after completing the work and clearing all tools and materials.

Operation checks and inspection/maintenance of on-load tap-changer (OLTC):

- Check the up and down movement of the tap-changer for the full range by inserting the handle. Drive by handle halfway and remove the handle. Now switch on power to the drive motor and ensure that motor continues to drive the tap-changer in the same direction in auto operation.
- Connect an analogue multi-meter across phase and neutral of the corresponding bushing (for delta connection phase to phase) and change the tap position from maximum to minimum and ensure that no discontinuity during the processes of test. Continue the test on other phases also.
- Check the operation of the limit switches at the minimum and maximum position.
- Check the direction of operation and measure the starting and running currents of the drive motor in both rise and lower mode with the tap changer in mid position. Set the overload relay 10% above running current.

- Move any one phase tap little bit ahead to get an out of phase situation. Energize the tap-changer circuit to ensure that out of step relay operates and alarm is activated. Repeat the other two phases also.
- Check the accuracy of mechanical and digital position indicator in all positions.
- Check the operation of tap changer incomplete alarm by driving the tap changer half way by handle, then remove handle and switch on AC/DC power to the unit.
- Check the correct operation of tap-changer operation counter.
- Check the tripping function of tap-changer surge protection relay.
- Test oil breakdown voltage and moisture content (PPM).
- Extent of arc erosion on stationary and movable arching contact.

Generally the oil temperature of OLTC compartment is a few degrees Celsius less than the main tank oil temperature. In case the OLTC oil temperature is higher, this indicates some problem in the OLTC compartment and subjected to inspection and trouble-shooting.

Transformer oil maintenance:

Since the oil is an organic compound deterioration of oil due to heat and oxygen cannot be completely avoided. Thus the oil oxidizes and polar and acid components are produced. Through the polar products the dielectric losses of the oil are increased and the interfacial tension against water is decreased. The acid compounds on the other hand have an adverse effect on the paper and pressboard insulation of the coils. A further drawback with the oil deterioration is the formation of sludge. The deterioration has then proceeded relatively far, for instance the interfacial tension has at this stage fallen from its initial value of 0.045 N/m to about 0.015 N/m. The sludge, when formed precipitates on the coils and then the coils are not effectively cooled. Recommended actions to be taken when the acidity (neutralization value) of the oil is found to be too high or sludge is found.

Neutralization value mgKOH/g	Sludge	Actions
< 0.2	Non	Non
0.2 to 0.3	Non detectable	Check at more frequent intervals reclaiming or replacement
0.3 to 0.05	Non detectable	Check at more frequent intervals or replacement
.0.5	Detectable	Replacement

In order to check the condition of the oil, various types of tests are carried out when necessary. The following scheme can be used as guidance for the choice of characteristics to be checked.

1) Breakdown voltage--------Water content---------Number of particles ≥ 15 μm
2) Interfacial tension---------Sediment or sludges---------Dielectric dissipation factor
3) Neutralization value---------------Oxidation inhibitor content

The oil must be reconditioned, reclaimed or replaced if it contains:

a) Too high a number of particles higher than about 15 μm.
b) Too much moisture (water content above 20 to 30 mg/dm^3
c) Too large an amount of deterioration products or other dissolved polar compounds (e.g. tan δ / 90°C, > 400°/oo).

Maintenance tests on transformer oil as per ASTM standard:

(1) Dielectric breakdown test: The two types of insulating liquid in general use are mineral oil and a nonflammable silicon fluid. The dielectric breakdown test measures the ability of an insulating liquid to withstand electrical stress up to the point of failure. It reveals the voltage at which the breakdown occurs. The dielectric breakdown voltage test, as covered in ASTM D-877 requires a sample of the liquid be placed in a clean "standard" cup so that it covers the two vertical disc-shaped electrodes that are one inch (2.54 cm) in diameter and have their faces one tenth of an inch apart. An AC voltage is applied across the electrodes (after filling the cup by sample oil) and increased gradually until a flashover through the liquid occurs. This test is to be repeated on at least three times from the same sample, and the average breakdown value is the dielectric strength of the liquid under test. Microprocessor controlled fully automatic dielectric test sets (Refer section 2.23) are used for determination of the high voltage breakdown strength of oil.

(2) Acid test (Neutralization number): The oxygen in air, combined with the heat will result the formation of the acid and sludge in oil during normal operation. The sludge settles on the horizontal parts of the windings and at the bottom of the tank and interferes with the normal circulation of the liquid-and thus its ability to dissipate heat. The acidity of oil is a measure of how much it has oxidized and thus deteriorated and how great is the propensity to form sludge. Acidity is measured by, a neutralization number as covered in ASTM D-1534. This measured number represents the milligram of potassium hydroxide (KOH) required to neutralize the acid in one gram of oil. A maximum permissible neutralization number for mineral oil is 0.35. Maximum permissible neutralization number for askerel is 0.10.

(3) Water content (Moisture content): Moisture is a most dangerous containment of insulating liquids. As small and amount as ten parts per million (PPM) by volume can reduce the dielectric strength of insulating oil below its minimum acceptable value. Aquameter is a Karl Fischer titrating apparatus for water determination. The regent (iodine) is generated electrochemically directly in the titration cell. This coulometric method enables traces of moisture down to the lower microgram range. Operation of aquameter is automatic and microprocessor controlled. According to ASTM D-1533, maximum acceptable value of water contents in transformer oil is 35 PPM (Particles per million).

(4) Dissipation Factor (Power factor): A dissipation factor (tan δ) is the ratio of active power to reactive power at a certain frequency. Since this factor greatly depends on temperature, very accurate temperature control is necessary during measurement.

The dissipation factor of an insulation liquid gives information about its degree of purity as well as its aging condition. Formation of oxidation products and dissolving of transformer materials such as varnishes can cause the dissipation factor to increase. **Tan δ gives an indication of the leakage currents through the oil and dielectric loss.** In contrast to the dissipation factor, measurement of the volume resistivity is made with direct voltage. Loss factor meter is used for measuring tan δ (power factor) and resistivity test. Acceptable value of power factor at 25°C (according to ASTM D-924) is 0.05% maximum.

(5) Colour test: The colour test is performed by visually comparing the light transmitted through a sample of insulating liquid with a standard colour scale. The scale ranges from 0.5 to 8.0 with new oil having a "colour number" of 1.0 or less. New oil colour is clear yellow. While a dark colour or cloud oil indicates sludge or other contamination. The maximum acceptable colour number for oil is 4, and the maximum for askarel is 2. The colour test is covered in ASTM 1524.

If any of the 5 tests indicate that an insulating liquid is not in satisfactory condition it may be restored by, reconditioning, reclaiming or replacement. Reconditioning is the removal of moisture and solid materials by, mechanical means such as filter press, centrifuges or vacuum dehydrators. Reclaiming is the removal of acidic and colloidal contaminants and products of oxidation by chemical and absorbent means.

2.19 NATURE OF FAULTS AND CAUSES OF FAILURE OF TRANSFORMERS.

Reasons for failure of transformers:

1. Improper tightening of core bolts and clamps results excessive vibration and noise. **Failure of yoke bolt insulation causes short circuit in the lamination resulting intense eddy currents.**
2. Improper supports and clamps for windings result in collapse of winding during external short circuit. High flux density causes large amount of force at the time of switching and damage winding insulation.
3. Improper soldered joints and bracings result in internal flashover during external short.
4. Oil leakage, loss of oil, absorption of moisture will overheat the windings. **Metallic part left over inside the tank during assembling may cause partial discharge.**
5. Continuous overloading, loose connection, Tap-changer failure, insulation surface contamination, and poor dielectric strength of oil will damage the transformer.
6. Dust, snow, salt spray deposit on the surface of bushings and bushing failure due to crack or flash over causes failure of transformer
7. Radiator failure or clogging of cooling medium (water or oil) causes to reduce effective cooling and overheating the winding.
8. Poor polarization index value or aging. Improper conductor insulation deteriorates under influence of high voltage stress and damage insulation.

9. Due to adverse operating conditions such as sustained overload, switching surges, lightning surges and transient surges, life expectancy of transformer will get diminished.
10. Maintenance deficiency. Preventive maintenance is strongly recommended to improve the reliability of transformer.
11. Manufacturing deficiency; for example, improper short circuit withstand capability (mechanical force).
12. All metal components not earthed: Partial discharge may start and oil quality may get affected. Bare copper for connection causes formation of oxidation and sludge's.

Nature of faults occurring in a transformer:

1). Inter-turn faults: A short circuit of few turns (turn-to-turn short circuit) of the winding will produce a heavy fault current in the shorted loop, but the terminal currents will be very small because of the high ratio of transformation. Protection from turn to turn fault in a transformer can be obtained by employing differential protection, which is sensing the difference in current between input and output.

2) Core faults: If any portion of the core insulation becomes defective, the resultant heating may reach a magnitude, sufficient to damage the winding, and breakdown of oil with an accompanying gas evolution. Either winding hot spot thermometer or Buchholz relay will protect the transformer. Core faults are usually developed due to failure of core insulation, ground strap burned away, shorted laminations, loose clamps, bolts, wedges etc.

3) Tank faults: Loss of oil through tank or radiator or clogging of cooling water or oil pipe may reduce effective cooling and produce heat. Oil sledging can also block cooling ducts and pipes, leading to overheating on load.

4) Abnormal stresses: Sources of abnormal stresses in a transformer are: over loading, system faults, over voltage, reduced system frequency etc. Overload causes increased copper loss and a consequent temperature rise. Short circuit will produce severe mechanical stresses. Transient over voltage arise from switching and lightning disturbances are liable to cause inter-turn faults. Power frequency over voltage causes both an increase in stress on the insulation and a proportional increase in the working magnetic flux, which may cause to increase iron loss and magnetizing current and destroy the winding insulation. Reduction of frequency has an effect with regard to flux density similar to that of over voltage. Protective relays are employed for protection against such faults.

5) Switching surge and re-striking voltage: When the circuit breaker provided at the primary of a transformer trips, the current gets usually broken, when the current wave is passing through zero. In the next negative half cycle, if the breaker interrupter contacts are not fully separated, the voltage crest may "re-strike" between the contacts, thereby producing a back e.m.f twice that of the normal crest voltage, on account of the electrostatic charges remaining on the system. If this re-striking takes place during subsequent voltage crest also, re-striking voltages could be as high as 4 or 6 times normal voltage. This voltage is unidirectional (DC) in nature and causes voltage transients resembling lightning surges.

6) Magneto-striction: Every transformer does make some humming noise. The noise is due to the fact that the core, which is made up of thin laminations, vibrates because of the alternating magnetic flux, and therefore expands or contracts ever so slightly with each cycle of magnetization. This causes the audible hum. The contraction caused due to magnetization is called "magneto-striction". To reduce the noise level the core is tightly clamped together and the flux density should also be reduced as much as possible. Sometimes under unfavorable conditions of poor design or construction, the hum gets multiplied hundreds of times due to resonance.

7) Failure of tertiary winding: Tertiary winding inter-turn insulation failures have been, found to be due to transferred surges. Protection of tertiary winding is necessary particularly in case of capacitive/reactive loading. Failure of tertiary windings generally have been observed because of * Over stressing and inadequate cooling; * Improper implementation of protective schemes; * Frequent switching ON/OFF of capacitive/reactive load; * Improper short circuit withstand capability.

8) Failure of on-load tap changers: The defects of OLTC are of (1) Burning of transition resistance; (2) Burning and damage of rollers and fixed contacts; (3) Misalignment of the tap-changer assembly; (4) Error in time sequence operation; (5) Defect in tap changing driving gear i.e. mis-operation of limit switches and step-by-step contactors. Failure of tap changer can also occur due to tracking, overheating, short circuits, oil leak or deterioration of oil in the tap changer housing, prolonged external faults etc.

9) Failure of bushing: Condenser type bushings are supplied with tip portion sealed and covered by porcelain rain shade and the bottom portion is covered with wax coated cotton tape. If these transient tapes are not removed at site during installation, over a period of service, the wax melted on contact with hot oil inside the tank and the cotton tape opened out and causes discharge inside the tank. Other reasons of failure of bushings are aging, contamination, cracking, flashover due to surges, moisture, low oil level etc.

10) Winding failure: In addition to inter turn fault, following are the causes of failure of winding: Lightning surges; Switching surges; External faults; Moisture; Over heating; Open joints; Deterioration; Improper blocking of turns; Ground fault and mechanical failure etc.

11) Over-fluxing: In a combined generator transformer unit, transformer may fail due to over-fluxing if: (a) Voltage is maintained during starting the unit; (b) Low frequency running of generator; (c) When a circuit breaker trips with out unloading the load. The flux density of a transformer depends on the voltage / frequency (V/f) ratio. At higher flux density core gets saturated. The flux then passes through core bolts, insulation gets damaged and core bolts get heated as such core fault develops in the transformer. To overcome over-flux problem in the main and auxiliary unit transformers, the excitation is applied to the generator rotor only when the generator speed attains near its synchronous speed. This can be controlled by, a speed switch. While stopping the generator transformer unit or tripping the main breaker the auxiliary-transformer primary and secondary breakers and field breaker must trip simultaneously. In addition to the above, voltage per hertz relay is employed to shutdown the unit during over-fluxing.

12) Miscellaneous failures such as bushing current transformer failure, bushing flange grounding, metal particles in oil, tools left out in oil, poor tank weld and treatment, auxiliary system (fan or pump) failures, over-voltage, overloads, loose connections, tracking, short circuit, ground fault, failure of neutral grounding resistor etc. Transformer may overheat due to high ambient temperature, failure of cooling system, external faults not cleared promptly, overload, and abnormal system conditions such as low frequency, high voltage, non-sinusoidal load current or phase voltage unbalance.

Mechanical detection of faults:
There are few mechanical methods of detecting transformer fault other than the electrical protection relays demonstrated in Chapter # 7. They are:

(1) Gas accumulator relay (Buchholz relay): Buchholz relay described in section 2.5 is applicable only to conventional transformers equipped with conservator tank and with no gas space inside the tank. Relay will annunciate against accumulating the gas over a period of time or for large faults, which force the oil through the relay at a high velocity and trip the circuit breakers of both the primary and secondary. Gassing of the oil is obtained due to sudden reduction of pressure.

(2) Gas detector relay: This device can be used in both conventional and hermetically sealed transformers. The relay is mounted on the transformer tank with a pipe connection from the highest point of the cover to the float chamber. A second pipe connection from the float chamber is carried to an eye level location on the tank wall. This connection is used for removing gas samples for analysis. The relay is equipped with a dial graduated in cubic centimeters and a snap action switch set to function to give an alarm when a specific amount of gas has been collected. The relay will often detect gas evolution from minor arcing before extensive damage occurs to the windings or core.

(3) Sudden gas pressure relay: Sudden gas pressure relay is applicable to all gas cushioned oil immersed transformers and is mounted in the region of the gas space. It consists of a pressure-actuated switch, housed in a hermetically sealed case and isolated from the transformer gas space except for a pressure equalizing orifice. The relay operates on the difference between the pressure in the gas space of the transformer and the pressure inside the relay. A rapid rise in pressure in the gas space of the transformer due to a fault results in operation of the relay

(4) Sudden oil pressure relay: This relay is applicable to all types of oil-immersed transformers and is mounted on the transformer tank wall below the minimum liquid level. Transformer oil fills the lower chamber of the relay housing within which a spring-backed bellows is located. The bellows is completely filled with silicone oil and additional silicone oil in the upper chamber is connected to that in the bellows by way of two small equalizer holes. A piston rests on the silicone oil in the bellows, but extends up in to the upper chamber, separated from a switch by an air gap. Should an internal fault develop, the rapid rise in oil pressure or pressure pulse is transmitted to the silicone oil by way of the transformer oil and the bellows. This then acts against the piston, which close the air gap and operates the switch.

Thermal detection of abnormalities:
Over heating shortens the life of the transformer insulation in proportion to the duration of the high temperature and in proportion to the degree of high temperature. Thermal relays for winding temperature and top oil temperature, described in section 2.6 is used for thermal protection of the transformer. A common method of simulating the hot-spot temperature is with a thermal relay responsive to both top oil temperature and to the direct heating effect of load current. In these relays, the thermostatic element is immersed in the transformer top oil. An electric heating element is supplied with a current proportional to the winding current, so that the responsive element tracks the temperature, which the hotspot of the winding attains during operation. If this tracking is exact, the relay would operate at the same time as the winding reaches the set temperature.

For calibrating thermal relays, remove the relay from the transformer and immerse the temperature sensitive element in a controlled temperature oil bath. The heating element, which provides the load current effect is an integral part of the well in which the relay sensing element is mounted, and provision is made to circulate current from a test source though this heater to check the operation of this element. Calibration procedures should ensure that the relay contacts and the temperature-dial indication are within specified limits.

2.20 POWER FREQUENCY AND IMPULSE WITHSTAND VOLTAGE TEST SETS.

Insulation coordination: The expression "insulation coordination" refers to the steps taken to correlate the insulating strength of electrical apparatus to prevent them being damaged by over voltages and to localize flashovers and thereby achieve reliability of supply. In a grid network, the surge diverters (lightning arresters) should have the lowest insulation level, followed by suspension insulators, isolating switches (disconnectors), circuit breakers and finally the transformers, which should have the highest level since they are the costliest.

Basic Impulse insulation Level (BIL): The basic impulse insulation level is defined as the combination of voltage values (both power frequency voltage and impulse voltage), which characterizes the insulation of the apparatus with regards to the capability of withstanding dielectric stresses. There are two test methods, which determine the insulation level.

(3) DC impulse withstand voltage
(4) AC Power frequency withstand voltage

Withstand voltage: The specified voltage that can be applied to insulation under specified conditions without causing flashover or puncture to occur.

AC Power frequency withstand test: AC high voltage test sets are designed for Power frequency high voltage test on transformers. The sets are capable of giving continuously variable AC high voltage from zero to maximum rated output voltage. For protecting the HV transformer (oil filled or resin cast) of the test set against overloading and short circuit, tripping mechanism is provided.

Apart from tripping mechanism and digital display meters, zero start interlocking along with over voltage alarm and indication are provided. One end of the high voltage winding of the transformer is grounded through milli-ammeter while the other end remains in floating condition as HV terminal. One minute Power frequency test voltage to be applied to the HV and EHV apparatus under test is listed in Table 2.20 (1). Figure 2.20 (a) illustrates the schematic diagram of a typical power frequency AC voltage test set.

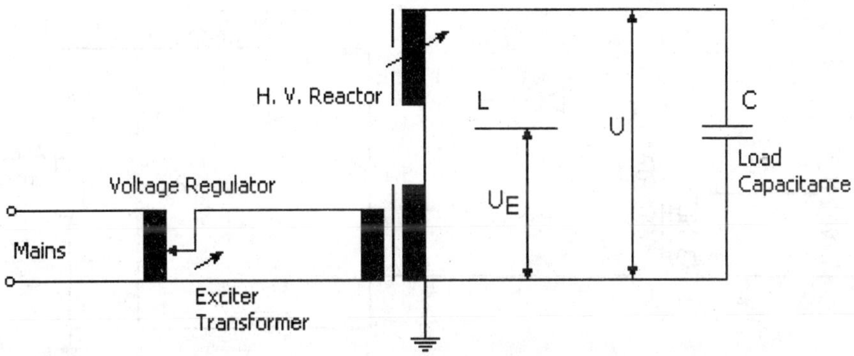

Fig. 2.20 (a): Schematic diagram of power frequency AC voltage test set..

The power frequency AC voltage test set consists of:
(a) Voltage regulating transformer: An air insulated autotransformer with remote controlled motor drive for increasing or decreasing the output voltage.
(b) Exciter transformer: The exciter transformer provides the input voltage and the input power to the series resonant circuit. The primary and secondary windings are galvanically separated. A copper foil shield between the two winding reduces the coupling capacitance between the primary and secondary windings.
(3) Variable H.V. Reactor.

Impulse voltage: An impulse voltage is a DC (un-directional) voltage, which rises rapidly from zero to maximum value and falls more slowly to zero, having a shape similar to the curve ABCD of Figure 2.20 (b). This curve is a full wave curve and the steeply rising portion AB being known as the wave front. The highest point B as the crest or peak and the remaining portion BD is called wave tail. This curve is similar to the lightning curve occurs during lightning discharge. The standard wave adopted is the 1.2/50wave. 1.2 microseconds refers the time required for the voltage to build-up from zero to the crest value. 50 microseconds represent the time taken for the tail voltage to drop down to half the peak value, counting from the start. Similarly, 1.2/60 waves means 1.2 microsecond for the voltage to build up to the peak value, and 60 microseconds for the voltage to drop to half the peak value.

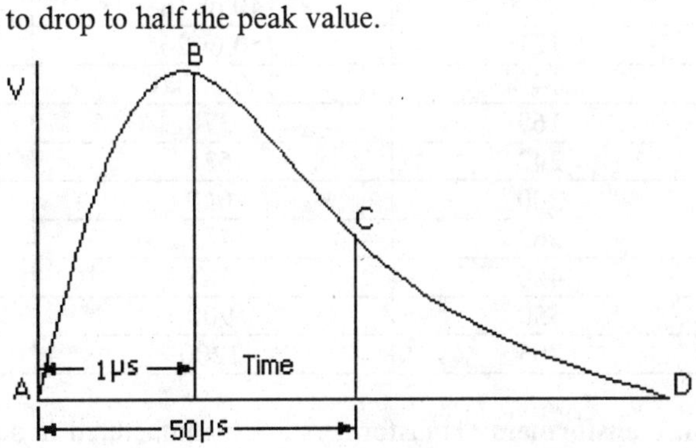

Fig. 2.20 (b): 1.2/50 impulse wave

Impulse generator: Figure 2.20 (c) shows the circuit diagram of a single stage impulse generator. It consists of a variable autotransformer, whose output is fed in to a step up transformer. The secondary is connected to a rectifier and a regulator. This charges a high capacity high voltage condenser C through a resistor R. If the switch S is closed one leg of the condenser C gets connected to earth and the full voltage on the other leg of the condenser is applied across the electrical apparatus under test. Because of the inductance L, a little time elapses before the voltage reaches the peak value. Inductance L therefore, determines the steepness of the wave front, i.e. it controls the interval of one microsecond in a 1/50 or 1/60 wave. After the peak value is reached, the voltage starts falling down as it gets discharged due to the leakage resistance R2, until it drop to zero. Hence R2 determines the slop of the wave tail and by adjusting it the time for half peak value of 50 microseconds in a 1/50 wave can be controlled. The purpose of resistor R1 is to prevent short-circuiting of the DC generator (rectifier) while switch S is closing. By employing a ladder network very high voltages (DC) can be developed.

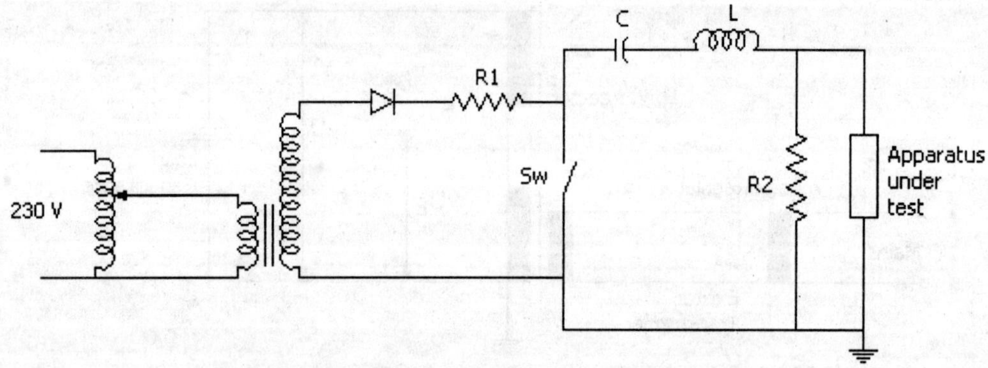

Fig. 2.20 (c): Single stage impulse generator test set

The impulse generator voltage can be measured by means of a sensitive high resistance type voltmeter. Checking the correctness of the voltage is by connecting a sphere-gap across the output terminals. Another method is by employing a voltage divider having a high resistance across the output terminals and connecting a cathode ray oscilloscope across a very small part of it at the earthed end. Cathode ray oscilloscope can be used for measuring the time interval in microseconds. During the test the impulse generator should be connected between earthed lead and live lead. Impulse withstand test voltages to be applied to the apparatus under test are given in Table 2.20 (1).

Table 2.20 (1): Power frequency and impulse withstand test voltages for high and extra high voltage electrical apparatus.

System voltage phase to phase (KV)	Maximum-system operating voltage Phase-to-phase (KV)	AC Power frequency with- stand voltage (One min) KV	DC Impulse withstand voltage (1.2/50μs) KV
60-66 or 69	72.5	140 or 165	325 or 350
110 or 115	121	250 or 265	525 or 550
132 or 138	145	300 or 320	625 or 650
150-161	169	370	750
230	242	525	1050
287	300	640	1300
345	362	785	1550
400	420	785	1550
500	550	900	1800
735	765	1200	2425

Over voltage protection on transformers: Transformers are manufactured in such a condition that it meets the requirements set by the standards. Transformer has certain power frequency withstand-voltage strength (Routine test) and certain impulse withstand voltage strength (Type test), which represents transformers endurance. Over-voltages are generally in a certain ratio to the rated net voltage and mostly below the power frequency voltage strength. On the other hand the external atmospheric over-voltages may in many case reach such values that not even a transformer with a impulse voltage strength in accordance with the standards, can withstand them. The transformer must be provided with protective devices against these over-voltages. In accordance with insulation coordination principles the protective levels determined by these devices shall be in a reasonable way below the endurance level of the transformer.

Either lightning arresters (Surge arresters) or spark gaps (Arcing horns) fastened to the bushings are used for over voltage protection. Lightning arresters provide a technically good protection, but in smaller transformers (Distribution transformers) spark gap may lead to a more economical total solution. Lightning arresters should be placed as close the transformer as possible, preferably between the transformer and the circuit breaker. Then they are able to protect better the transformer even against the steep surge waves coming from overhead lines. When lightning arresters are being used, the protective spark gaps need not be used simultaneously, on the contrary, this might be harmful, as their protection ranges partly overlap and the possible operation of the spark gap may cause a chopped wave, which stresses the transformer windings.

If transformer is expressed to a three-pole impulse voltage, the voltage of its insulated star point rises considerably (50% to 100%) higher than the voltage injecting line terminals. Therefore this voltage stresses has to be considered in various structural and operating conditions for transformer over-voltage strength. When the star point is brought out to the tank it has to be protected against impulse over-voltages except if the star point is directly earthed. The over-voltage protection is carried out by means of a lightning arrester connected to the star point. **Spark gaps must not be used for the purpose, because they will bring about a steep chopped wave, which may constitute a danger to the tap-windings if it is on the star point side.**

2.21 ON LINE MONITORING CONTROL SYSTEM FOR EHV POWER TRANSFORMERS.

Typical on-line transformer monitoring control system for a large power transformer is illustrated in Figure 2.21. TMCS equipment is mounted on or near the transformer to be monitored. Typical inputs include the values of dissolved gases and moisture content in the transformer oil, oil temperature (top, bottom and tap changer compartment), ambient air temperature, tap changer position, load currents and voltage, the status of both Buchholz relays, oil level, cooling fans and oil pumps. The system provides digital outputs for issuing set point limits and status alarms. The PLC (Programmable logic controller) performs data acquisition-monitoring, set point/status alarm generation, digital control output, remote client configuration and reporting, security access control and communications management. The measured data averages and subsequent computations of TMCS are summarized below.

(a) Apparent power (MVA): MVA output is calculated from the load current and voltage, and the maximum MVA is retained with a time tag. Warnings and alarms can be generated based on user-defined MVA limits.

(b) Winding hot spot temperatures: Temperature is analyzed by using the measured temperature input, a hot-spot increment calculated with the load current and computed from IEC loading guide.
(c) Insulation aging: Aging acceleration factor is derived from insulation moisture content and oil oxygen content. Aging is computed from IEC guidelines and display trend graph.

(d) Moisture Analysis: Amount of water in the oil, moisture contained in the insulation paper, water condensation temperature, bubbling temperature and bubbling safety margin etc computed for analyzing the moisture content.
(e) Cooling efficiency: Theoretical top oil temperature is computed and compared with actual measured top oil temperature. If the difference exceeds a user-defined set point, a warning or alarm is generated.

(f) Cooling system status and control: The second and third cooling stages of the transformer are monitored and controlled.
(g) Daily trending report: Certain analog measurements and calculated values are collected to present a daily summary in trend graph report for remote access.

.(h) OLTC temperature: Oil temperature in the tap changer compartment is compared with top oil temperature in the main tank. If the difference set point exceed, an alarm or trip command is generated.

(i) OLTC Tap position tracking: Actual tap position, cumulative transition count, transition count between resets and total number of tap changing operations are provided.

(J) Dissolved gas Analysis (DGA): Dissolved gas value obtained from the laboratory analyses should manually entered by the user. TMCS calculates gas ratios and compares them with acceptable user and IEEE limits to generate diagnostics and recommendations. Results are displayed in tables, histograms and trend graphs to show the evolution over time.

(k) Communications: TMCS system provides a wide range of connectivity and communication access methods including: * Direct access through RS-232 / 485 Port; *Dial-up access to a modem using a telephone line or mobile phone; * Communication links using industry-standard protocols through gateways to provide information to remote SCADA (Supervisory control and data acquisition system) or DCS (Distributed control system). *Access via an internet connection and through a router/firewall to a PC or PLC web server.

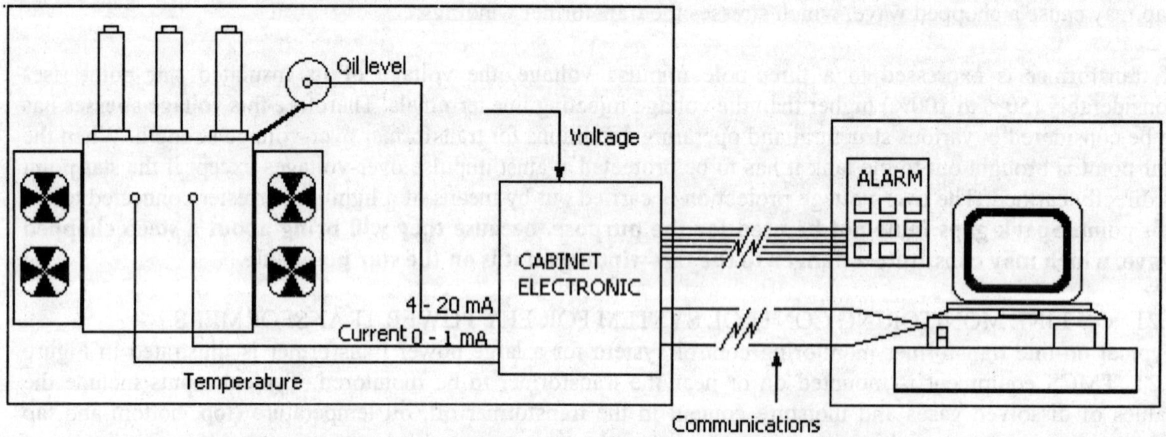

Fig. 2.21: Typical on-line monitoring system for power transformer.

2.22 TRANSFORMER TURNS RATIO AND VECTOR GROUP TESTER.

The test equipment introduced in this section is 'TETTEX' Transformer turns ratio tester, which can be used for testing transformer turns ratio, excitation current, phase displacement between the higher and lower voltage windings (vector group test), DC winding resistance, and transformer polarity. This instrument is ideal to use for determining the no load accuracy of CTs and PTs. Figure 2.22 shows the basic circuit diagram of the turns ratio tester.

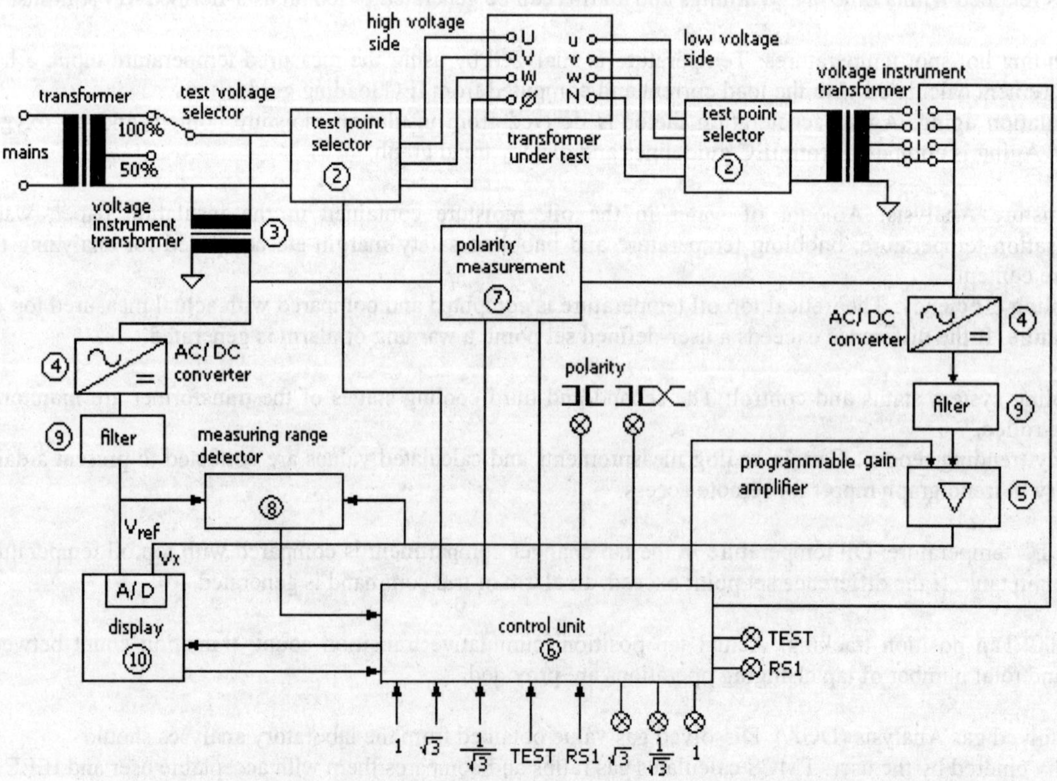

Fig. 2.22: Basic circuit diagram of a transformer turns ratio tester (Courtesy, Tettex).

1) Transformer turns ratio: Turns ratio test set can directly measure the turn ratio of single phase and three-phase transformers (phase-to-phase) and all-of its taps. The turn ratio can change due to faults, deteriorated insulation, contamination and physical damage or turn-to-turn short circuit in the windings. Deviations in the measurements will indicate problems in transformer windings or core.
2) Excitation current: TRT is capable of measuring exciting current (magnetizing current) by applying voltage to one of the winding. An accurate measurement of exciting current can provide information about the condition of a transformer core. Unwanted circulating currents or unintentional grounds can affect the exciting current and indicate a problem.
3) Phase angle deviation and vector group: The phase displacement between the high and low side of a transformer is generally very small. However the phase deviation can change significantly if there is deterioration or damage in the transformer core. TRT can measure this phase relationship (in minutes, degrees or radians) with the resolution necessary to detect a problem.
4) Winding resistance: TRT can be used for measuring the DC resistance of single and three phase transformer windings will aid in identifying problems such as shorted or open windings, as well as loose connections.
5) Transformer polarity: Polarity of a transformer becomes of interest in order to determine its proper connection within a power network. TRT can detect the correct polarity of a transformer.
Features of turns ratio tester

- Fully automatic; fast; easy to use; hand held operation.
- AC powered (single phase 230V).
- Alphanumeric keyboard and test leads.
- RS 232 for data transfer and printing and the data can be down loaded to a Personnel computer.
- Stores 200 test results and 100 user defined transformer test settings.
- Digital display and automatic self-calibration for each test.
- Records ratio errors of bushing current transformers.
- Report header information such as company name, transformer serial number temperature etc can be entered saved via keypad.

The ratio meter consists of the following functional elements as identified in the basic circuit diagram.

(1) Switch for selecting the excitation voltage in the test object.
(2) Switch for selecting the individual phases of three phase transformers.
(3) Highly accurate voltage transformer for transforming voltages to a value processable by the electronic circuits.
(4) AC/DC converter with high input impedance to prevent loading of the transformer under test.
(5) Ratio circuit (e.g.$\sqrt{3}$) to permit measurement of the actual turns ratio of different vector groups in three phase transformers.
(6) Logic for controlling the automatic range selection, the ratio circuit, and the measuring procedure.
(7) Polarity measuring for checking the direction of winding.
(8) Comparator for automatic range setting. Adjustable comparator (error limits) for go / no-go assessment of the test object.

2.23 PORTABLE TEST EQUIPMENTS FOR TRANSFORMER TESTING.

The testing and maintenance equipment covered in this section are for testing power transformers. Following precautions should be considered while selecting the test equipments.

(b) Supply lead length should be long enough for outdoor testing.
(c) Suitable for use in adverse ambient temperature and humidity.
(d) Yearly calibration facility and repair/service if required.
(e) Satisfactory performance under induced voltage/electrostatic interference conditions.
(f) Meet electromagnetic compatibility (EMC) directives.
(g) Suitable for use in system frequency 50 or 60 Hertz as appropriate.
(h) CE marked /UL (Under writers laboratory) listed preferred.
(i) Required carrying case and operation manual.

(1) Transformer winding resistance meter/kelvin double bridge:
Suitable for measuring winding resistance of single phase and three-phase star or delta connected transformers, generators, high voltage motors etc. Two independent displays read the resistance of both primary and secondary windings simultaneously. However, primary or secondary winding can also be measured separately. DC power source allows the selected current to flow through the winding(s) and the voltages developed across the windings are used for displaying the resistance value. (Display: 3 1/2 LED). Alternatively Kelvin double bridge can be used for accurate measurement of winding resistance.

(2) Tan-delta and resistivity tester for insulating oil (Loss factor meter):
Microprocessor controlled portable test set manufactured as per IEC 247 measures dielectric parameters like DC resistivity, dielectric constant and loss factor of the insulating oil of transformers, circuit breakers etc. Loss factor test set consists of: (1) Measuring unit for dielectric constant and dissipation factor (Tan δ) at 0 to 2000 V AC; (2) Resistivity unit with 500V DC power supply to measure the resistivity of the sample oil under test; (3) Three terminal stainless steel oil cell (Teflon insulation) for isolation of the H.T electrode, Guard electrode, and control electrode; (4) Heating chamber with temperature sensor to heat the test cell and sample oil under test up to desired temperature (maximum 120°C). (5) Test report printer (6) Curser key for changing parameters; (7) Display board with menu; (8) Protective cover with safety interlock.. Test method is described in section 2.18

(3) Transformer oil test set (Dielectric test set)
A portable fully automatic microprocessor based oil test set is used for determination of electric strength (breakdown value) of transformer oil up to 100 KV without external flashover. The oil test unit consists of: (1) High voltage transformer with control unit having zero-start interlock and HV chamber interlock; (2) Manual and motorized drive to increase voltage linearly; (3) Test cell, stirrer and gauge for adjusting the gap of 12.5 mm diameter electrodes. Figure 2.23 (a) illustrates the basic circuit of a fully automatic oil test set. Test method is described in section 2.18.

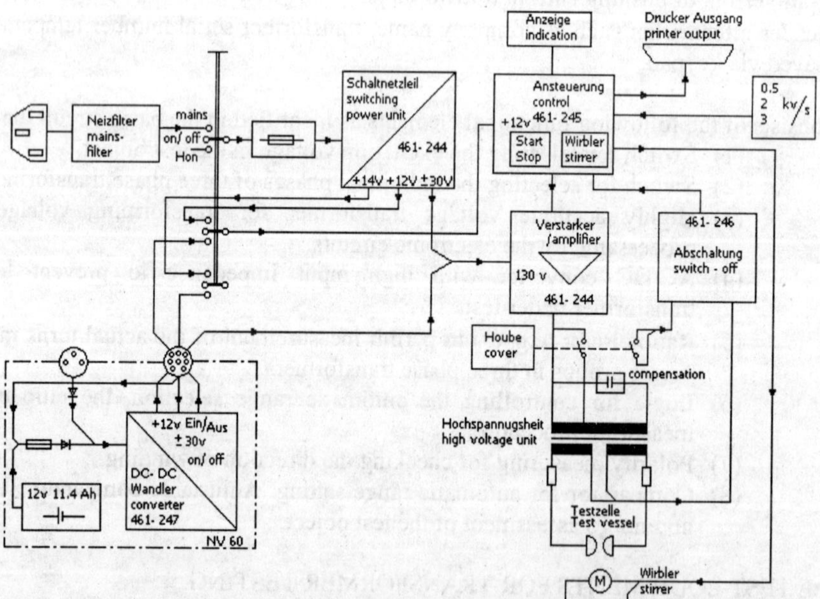

Fig. 2.23 (a): Basic circuit of a fully automatic portable oil test set

A portable fully automatic microprocessor controlled oil test set reduces the operators-task to preparing and loading the oil sample in to the test chamber and initiating the required test sequence. On completion of the test, the mean breakdown value of tests in the sequence is given and the value for each individual test may be recalled. Standard deviation calculations are automatically carried out in tests where specified. The test voltage is fully variable up to 60 or 100 KV. Oil test specifications have their 'stand times', 'stir times', 'rate of rise of voltage', and number of tests are pre-programmed in to the equipments memory. A quick 'five minutes' test sequence is available for rapid assessment of the condition of an oil sample. Also 'proof tests' in which the test voltage may be raised to a given value and retained there for one minute to see if breakdown occurs and then removed or increased until the sample does fail.

Figure 2.23 (b) shows the test vessel for insulating liquids based IEC 156 requirements. The unit assembly consists of: (1) Gauge for adjusting the electrode gap 2.5mm; (2) Vessel holder; (3) Glide bolt of test cell 0.4 litter; (4) Electrode holding bolt; (5) Collar, vessel; (6) O ring; (7) Glass vessel; (8) Pair of electrodes; (9) Magnetic stirring rod; (10) Lid for glass vessel; (11) Front hole nut; (12) Supporting part of test vessel; (13) Graduated collar; (14) O ring; (15) Counter sink screw; (16) Pressure spring; (17) Lifting magnetic rod.

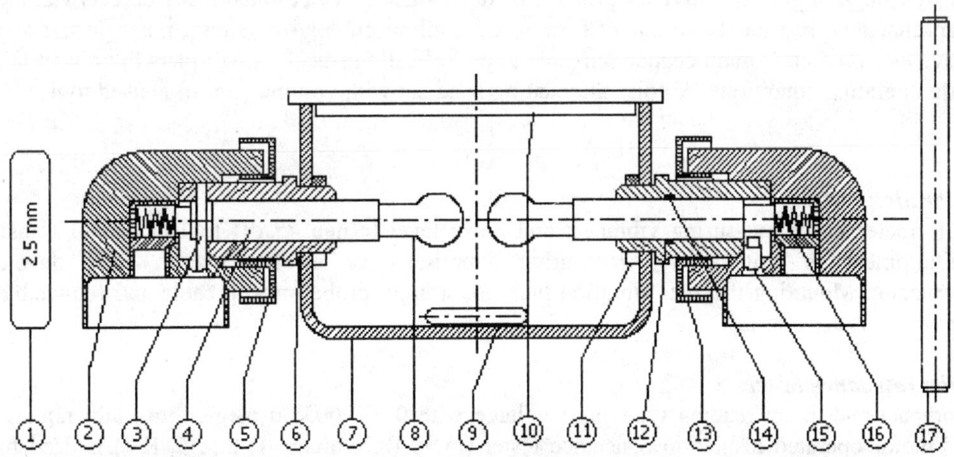

Fig. 2.23 (b): Typical test vessel for transformer oil testing (Courtesy BAUR)

The test set has a dot-matrix liquid crystal display, which shows a menu of test options, guides the operator simply through the set-up program, illustrates the correct test electrodes and gap to use, shows the progress of each individual test including the instantaneous voltage being applied and gives the results of the test sequence either numerically or as a sample pass/fail message. The covered oil test glass vessel, which contains the oil sample under test, is placed in the test chamber. The action of closing the chamber door submerses the high voltage electrodes (conforming to IEC 156) in the oil. The chamber door operates a safety interlock, which prevents access to the electrodes when they are "live". Oil stirring is achieved by a paddle magnetic stirrer, which is immersed in the oil at the same time as the electrodes. A self check program can be performed on the test sets controls and electronic circuits.

Portable oil test set is an ideal piece of equipment for carrying on to the site of transformers, switchgear and other electrical apparatus for the purpose of determining the dielectric strength of the insulating oils used in them. The test set is constructed in a sheet steel cabinet and is powered from an internal battery, rechargeable from the mains supply. A lead is available so that operation of the equipment may be maintained from a 12 volts vehicle battery.

(4) Karl Fischer moisture content measurement set (Aquameter):
Portable fully automatic microprocessor based PPM test set (Aquameter) measures the total amount of water contained in transformer oil. The results in PPM (Parts per million) directly correlate with the Kari Fischer colorimetric titration method. The automatic moisture content test set and a suitable syringe that has been flushed, inject a sample of the oil in to the test set. Depending upon the make of the test set the moisture content might be indicated by mg H20 i.e. the figure may be divided by weight of the sample injected in grams. This will display in PPM. The test method is described in section 2.18.
Range of measurement: 0 to 50 PPM (by weight)
Total analysis time: Should not exceed 25 minutes
Display: 3 ½ digits liquid crystal display
Rechargeable battery with charger unit and waste oil reservoir is provided.

(5) Portable dissolved gas analyzer:
Equipment is suitable for analyzing H_2 (Hydrogen) and CO2 (Carbon dioxide) in transformer oil. Analyzer consists of oil sampling device, oil-collecting bottles, sensing device, and display-unit etc. to carry out on the

spot dissolved gas analysis at site. The sensor is rated for oil temperature range from 10°C to 50°C and indicates dissolved gas concentration level in %. Test equipment is illustrated in figure 2.5 (c).

(6) Ultrasonic fault detector:

The fault detector will detect partial discharge, corona, and other ultrasonic activities happening inside the transformer by using a highly sensitive air probe. The detector will detect transformer defects viz. loose parts, defective tap changers, restricted / turbulent flow in oil cooling pumps by using a piezoelectric sensor. The detector provides a predictive maintenance schedule to periodically inspect transformers to prevent failures and maintain safe operating conditions. A noise attenuating head set with volume control is used to hear ultrasonic noise.

(7) Noise/vibration meter:

This portable meter is for measuring vibration and noise level (range 45 dB to 145 dB) of transformers / reactors. Equipment is suitable for measuring vibrations in electromagnetic field developed by transformer/reactor. Mounting magnet, vibration pick up, straight probe, pickup cable and retractable pick up cable are provided as accessories.

(8) Insulation resistance tester:

Portable, compact and direct reading type/multi voltage with 0 to 100,000 mega-ohm multi rated resistance ranges hand/motor operated insulation resistance tester (rated DC voltage 1, 2.5, 5, KV) is used for testing insulation resistance of HV/EHV equipments and cables. Digital types (push button operated) are available up to 10 KV, DC voltage ranges. Test leads are supplied with the megger for connecting to the equipment under test. For digital meters prior to the test the battery power is to be checked by pressing the battery test pushbutton.

Before carrying out the IR value maintenance test on Power transformers the HV and LV windings are to be isolated by opening the concerned circuit breakers and disconnectors (isolators). In case transformer is having a tertiary (TV) winding, ensure the isolation is essential prior to the commencement of the test.

Following precautions may be taken while conducting the IR value measurements:

(a) Porcelain bushings are to be cleaned by wiping with a clean dry cloth.
(b) When using a megger, connecting megger leads to the test source, the leads should not touch to the tank or each other. Joint should not be used in connecting leads.
(c) As the windings possess a substantial capacitance, the current carrying cords are to be touched only after discharging the current by shorting the leads with earth.
(d) During test the live terminal of the megger shall be connected to the winding under test and earth terminal of the megger is connected to transformer tank /earth point

IR measurements shall be taken (with out cable or bus bar /conductor) between each winding and earth, and all other windings connected together and the earthed tank and earth. IR values, varies with the type of insulation, winding temperature, duration of application of voltage, applied test voltage etc. Table 23.1 can be used for conversion of IR value in a different temperature.

Table 2.23 (1): IR value conversion factor. (Corrected to 20°C for oil filled transformers and reactors).

Temperature in degree Celsius:	0	5	10	15	20	25	30	35
Correction factor:	0.25	0.36	0.50	0.74	1.00	1.40	1.98	2.00
Temperature in degree Celsius:	40	45	50	55	60	65	70	75
Correction factor:	3.95	5.60	7.85	11.20	15.85	22.40	31.75	44.70

Assume that the IR reading obtained from a transformer at 40°C winding temperature is 600 mega-ohms, corresponding correction factor is 3.95 from table 2.23 (1). The IR value recorded in the test report is at 20°C. To convert the measured IR value in to 20°C: 600 x 3.95 = 2770 MΩ.

2.24: OPERATION AND MAINTENANCE OF TRANSFORMER COOLING SYSTEM.

The heat developed in the windings and core in an oil natural cooled transformer is transferred to the oil surrounding them and is then given off by oil to the tank walls, tank cover, and the radiators, all of which in turn dissipate the heat to the air surrounding the transformer. Heat transfer is facilitated by, the natural circulation of the oil setup in the tank. As the oil becomes heated, hot oil rises up to the cover, while at the tank walls and in the radiators, as it cools down and becomes more "dense" it sinks to the bottom of the tank. When a transformer is installed in a room (indoor type installation) adequate ventilation must be provided to allow the warmed air to escape and fresh air to enter in the room. The difference in temperature of inlet air and outlet air should not exceed 15°C when the transformer is fully loaded. If the oil temperature in an oil natural transformer is 80°C at the top layers of oil, the corresponding bottom temperature will be 30 – 35 degree Celsius.

Oil temperature is monitored by, using mercury type thermometers. A special pocket is provided in the transformer tank lid on the side where the low voltage bushings are arranged. This pocket is filled with transformer oil to lower the temperature gradient from the outside to the inside. Mercury thermometers are provided with bulb and capillary tube so that the thermometer can be mounted on the marshalling box. Oil natural forced air-cooled transformers use a series of small fans for cooling the radiators by blowing the air. These fans are mounted in pairs within every bank of radiator tubes. Fans will not operate if the oil temperature is less than 55°C. Second group of fans will start when the temperature exceeds 65°C or the set value.

Forced oil-cooled air-blast transformers are cooled by circulating the oil through air or water coolers with the aid of a centrifugal pump. The cooling surface of the tank in these transformers is rather limited and dissipates to the ambient atmosphere no more than 10% of the total heat loss. The reminder heat loss must be removed by, the coolers. Oil circulation must be started as soon as the transformer is switched ON. Air blast fan must be automatically ON when the temperature attains 50°C. When forced oil and water cooling is employed the hot oil is extracted from the top portion of the transformer tank by a pump, which circulates the oil through the water cooler and delivers it as cooled oil at the bottom part of the transformer tank. The off-take and intake pipes are arranged so that the oil enters the tank at one end and leaves it at the other end, attaining thus full circulation of the oil throughout the tank. The cooler is usually of the tube bank type in which the water is passed through the tubes and the oil is cooled as its flows over the surface of the tubes. The operation of the cooling system is checked by, determining the temperature of the oil inlet and oil outlet. At a maximum water temperature of 25°C the temperature difference in oil should not be less than 10°C.

When the oil pump is at a standstill, the static pressure of the oil should exceed the water pressure in the tubes by, 0.3 – 0.5 atm to prevent water from getting in to the oil on an emergency shutdown of the pump. This can be avoided by, placing the coolers and waterlines so as to provide necessary static head of the oil. If a pump is installed with the cooler on the suction side, it would setup a negative pressure differential and leads to the danger of water being sucked in to the oil circuit whenever leaks develop in the tubes. Special care should be taken to maintain the cooling system (piping, pumps and oil coolers) airtight especially the suction lines, thus preventing air from being sucked in to the system and getting in to the transformer.

For removing any air entered in to the oil, an air separator is placed in the oil feed line of the transformer. It consists of two concentric vertical cylinders so arranged, that the oil enters-at the bottom and thus allows the air to raise and escape from it. The oil is also discharged at the bottom, while the air gathers in the upper conical part, from which it is released to the atmosphere from time to time by means of an air release valve.

In a forced oil and water-cooled transformer when the transformer is switched ON, the oil pump and then the water pump should be started up immediately. In switching off the transformer, the water pump should be shutdown before the oil pump is switched off. In the event of failure in the cooling system during transformer operation (stoppage of fans, oil flow, water flow etc.) the temperature of the transformer will begin to rise rapidly. To warn against the failure in the cooling system alarm devices are furnished.

2.25 TRANSFORMER SWITCHING PROCEDURES AND SWITCHING SEQUENCE

Figure 2.25 (a) illustrates the switching sequence of a 400/765 KV step up transformer. To place a step up transformer in service, the lower voltage and higher voltage isolators are to be closed at first. Although interlocks are provided, while closing the isolators ensure that the respective circuit breakers are in open position. Now close the lower voltage side (incomer) breaker and subsequently close the higher voltage side (load) breaker. By this arrangement L.V breaker will make with transformer inrush current and H.V breaker will make with load current. In order to take the transformer out of service the H.V side breaker is opened at first to disconnect the load and then the L.V side breaker. If transformer isolator is installed in the circuit between power transformer and its H.V circuit breaker, it should be closed after closing the bus bar isolator when the transformer is to be switched ON. When switched off, first the transformer isolator and then the bus bar isolator should be opened. Usually, isolators are opened only if a shutdown (permit to work) is required.

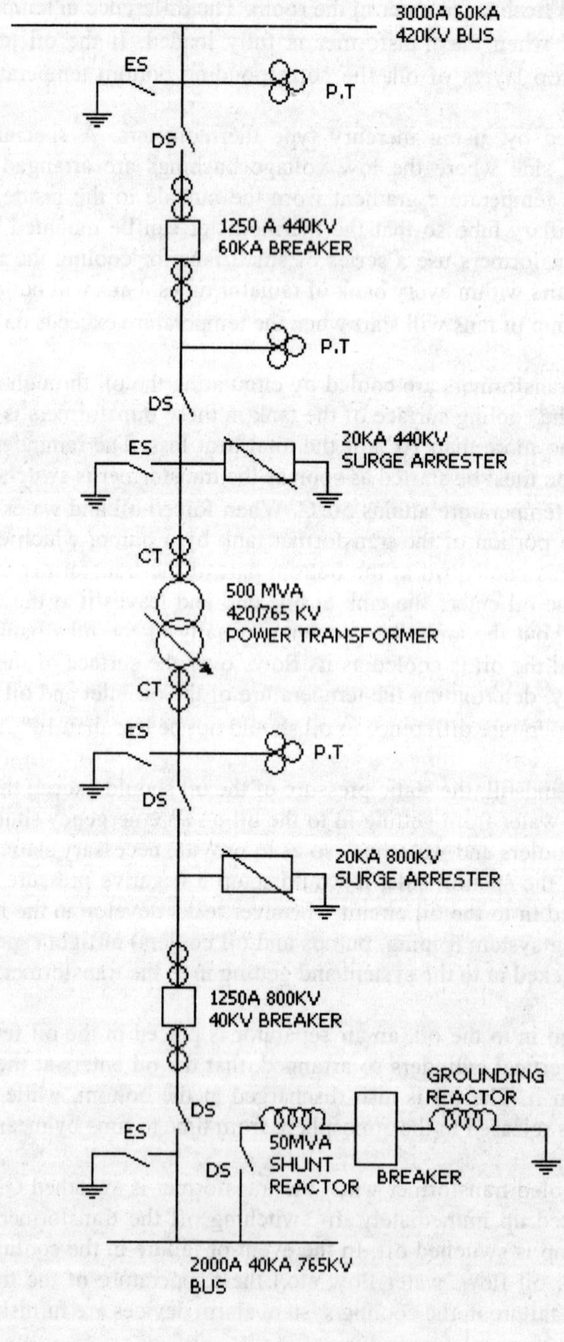

Fig. 2.25 (a): Single line diagram of a typical 420 / 765 KV, step up substation.

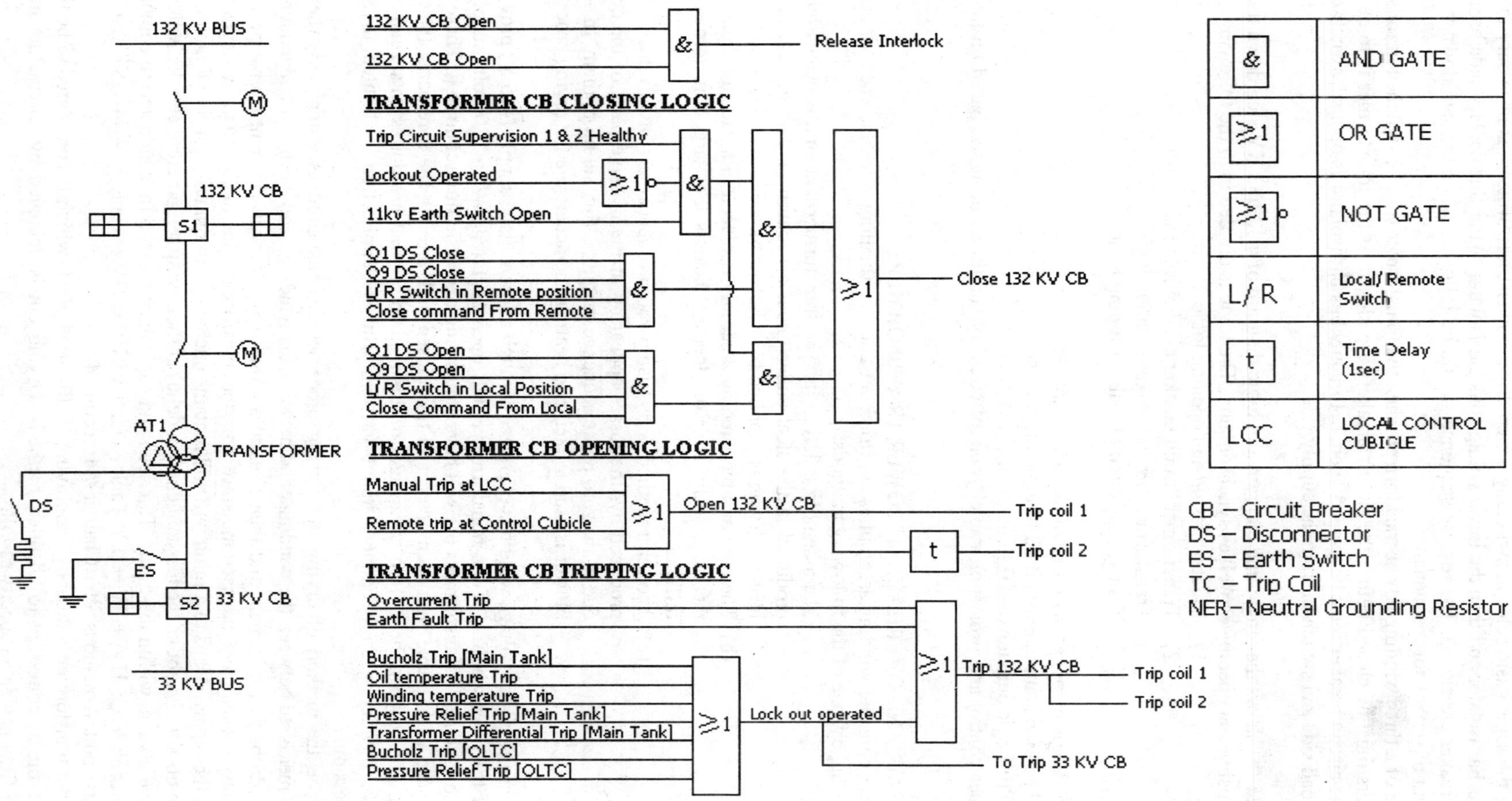

Fig. 2.25 (b): Logic diagram showing breaker closing and opening, and synchronizing of power transformer.

Observing the same basic rules in switching a step down power transformer it is necessary to close the higher voltage bus bar isolator and then the lower voltage bus bar isolator. After this the H.V side breaker and then the LV side breaker are closed. The reverse sequence should be followed when the step down transformer has to be taken out of service for maintenance.
In the case of a three winding power transformer when the transformer is to be switched in for service, the bus bar isolators must be closed before the circuit breakers are closed. If the transformer is to be switched out of service, the circuit breaker must be tripped open, before any bus bar isolator is opened, switch-out should begin from the load side and switch-in from the supply side.

Figure 2.25 (b) shows the single line diagram and logic diagram of a 132/33 KV step down transformer feeder breaker closing and opening as well as synchronizing. The logic is divided in to the following circuits:

1) Isolator closing and opening logic.
2) Transformer circuit breaker closing logic.
3) Transformer circuit breaker opening logic.
4) Transformer circuit breaker tripping logic.

OR GATE: Logic output exists if one or more logic inputs exists.
AND GATE: Logic output exists if all of logic input exists.
NOT GATE: Logic output exists if logic input does not exist.
Transformer control and protection cubicle control circuitry should be designed based on the approved logic diagram.

2.26 REPAIR AND OVERHAUL OF POWER TRANSFORMERS

Transformer core and winding assemblies are dried out after overhauling or replacement of one or more limbs of the winding by, one of the following methods:

(a) The assembly is left in its own transformer tank and is heated by, the heat losses produced in the steel either under a vacuum or with out vacuum. However the heat for drying is supplied by, a hot air blower.

(b) The core and the winding assembly is placed in a vacuum drying oven heated by means of steam coils or electrical heaters. For large transformers this method is difficult.

(c) The third method is by, using zero sequence currents. In this method, the heat is produced by, the losses appearing in the massive parts of the core and the tank due to the zero phase sequence magnetic flux set up in them. In addition a hot air blower is used to facilitate heating and accelerate the drying process.

The transformer higher voltage windings energized through a low voltage supply (415 V) provides the exciting current, if the other winding of the transformer is left open circuited. When 230 volts supply is applied per phase, each limb in the transformer core will have a pulsating magnetic flux set up in it. These fluxes are equal in magnitude, act in-phase with each other, and find closed path through the core parts, the transformer tank and the air gap between them. Two advantages of this method are that it requires no special exciting winding and allows the drying to be done without vacuum. But its application is limited to medium voltage transformers only.
Whatever be the method of drying, the drying processes is considered as completed when the insulation resistance measured between the windings and between the windings and earth at a temperature not lower than 80°C first drops to a minimum and then rises to a value which remain constant over a period of 6-8 hours. Another sign is when the condensed moisture from the transformer, due to certain air leakages through the tank joints and the piping, drops to a minimum and remains unchanged in quantity for 6 to 8 hours. For transformer rated from 66 KV and above the loss tangent (tan delta) at the drying temperature and the winding capacitances should have a value within the limits. Tan delta and capacitance test to be conducted in combination of HV + IV/LV + Tank + G; HV + IV + LV/Tank + G; LV/HV + IV + Tank + V in GST test mode. (For test equipments and test methods refer Chapter # 4, section 4.19).
Drying out a transformer is done by, employing oil filtration plant, which is considered to be the best practical method at site as compared to all other methods. Drying out is achieved by, circulating hot oil through a streamline filter having a capacity as follows.

Transformer oil capacity	Recommended capacity of filter plant
Up to 20,000 liter	2 Kiloliter per hour
>20,000 to 50,000 liter	4 Kiloliter per hour
Above 50,000 liter	6 Kiloliter per hour

Connect the inlet of the filter machine to the bottom of the transformer tank and the outlet to the top. Connect the vacuum pump to the top of the transformer tank after lowering the oil slightly to just above the winding. Run the oil filtration plant and vacuum pump so as to reach a vacuum of 5 torr. Now the main tank oil is circulated through the filtration plant and also getting heated up. Don't allow the oil temperature to go above 60 degree Celsius. The insulation resistance of winding between HT + LT to ground is measured at a fixed intervals.
The oil sample is taken at an interval of 12 hours and tested. The oil shall be circulated through vacuum filtration machine till the parameters are attained as per Table 2.26 (1) below.

Transformer HV side rated voltage	Break down voltage in KV (Minimum)	Moisture content in ppm (Maximum)	Resistivity at 90°C in Ω - cm (Minum)	Tan δ at 90°C (Maximum)
Medium voltage	40	25	$1 * 10_{12}$	0.05
High voltage	50	20	$1 * 10_{12}$	0.05
Extra high voltage	60	15	$1 * 10_{12}$	0.05

When the breakdown voltage is 60 KV and moisture content is less than 15 particles per million (ppm) for EHV transformers, the oil is considered to be dry.
After completing oil filtration before energizing the transformer following standing time should be allowed for all the trapped air to come out. Application of vacuum prior to oil filling is also given in Table 2.26 (2) below.

Transformer HV side rated voltage	Application of vacuum before oil filling (Hours)	Standing time after oil circulation and before energizing (Hours)
Medium voltage 3.3 to 33 KV	12	12
High voltage 66 KV to 220 KV	24	48
Extra high voltage 275 to 765 KV	36	120

2.27 PRACTICAL QUESTIONS AND ANSWERS ON POWER/DISTRIBUTION TRANSFORMERS

Q1: A transformer designed for 50Hertz power supply is connected to a 60Hertz power supply having same primary voltage. What will be the effect?
Ans: Flux density will be lower and the magnetizing current less. Noise and temperature will rise. Subsequently, the transformer will overheat and its life will considerably reduce.

Q2: Define the term impedance voltage? 1000 KVA 13.8 KV/220 V 60 Hz Delta / Star distribution transformer has a percentage impedance of 5.79. During short circuit test (Secondary terminals are shorted by copper bar) how much voltage is to be applied to the high voltage side (primary) to circulate full load current in the secondary?
Ans: Impedance voltage is the voltage required to be applied in the higher voltage side to drive rated current under short circuit condition in the lower voltage side. It is a vector sum of resistance voltage and reactance voltage. Impedance voltage is determined by conducting sustained short-circuit test.
Impedance voltage = (Higher voltage x Percentage impedance) / 100 = (13800 x 5.79) / 100 = 800Volts.

Q3: Explain the term, oil filtering or oil treatment in a transformer?
Ans: If the dielectric strength of the oil is below the specified value (Medium Voltage and high Voltage) the transformer oil shall be reconditioned after shutdown by using a filter machine. Filter machine has a oil circulating pump, heater and filter unit, inlet and outlet heat and oil resistant connecting hoses. Oil can be circulated through this machine for removing humidity and sludge's. Filtering processes may be continued until the dielectric strength of the oil improved up to the desired value. The colour of new transformer oil SHELL DAILA B is pale amber clear. (Refer section 2.14 and 2.26).

Q4: What are the possible causes that Buchholz relay operates and how to recognize?
Ans: (a) Loose air bubbles (Colourless and odorless).
(b) Short circuit (No gas bubbles will produce).
(c) Winding damage/burning (Coloured gas with bad smell).

Q5: What are the reasons for operating Buchholz relay?
Ans: (a) Inter turn faults or other winding faults.
(b) Loss of oil due to leakage.
(c) Core bolt or lamination insulation failure.
(d) Faulty joints/flash over.

Q6: What happens if the off load, tap-changer is operated when the transformer is energized?
Ans: Heavy sparking on tap-changer contacts and heavy flash over will take place. Even bursting of transformer is possible. It is safe to change the offload tap changer after switching off both primary and secondary.

Q7: Two numbers 500 KVA 11KV/415 V 50Hz transformers having same % impedance are paralleled. The off load tap-changer in the 11 KV side kept as follows: TR No: 1, No load output voltage 390 volts. TR No: 2, the no load output voltage 400 volts. What will be the load current in each transformer when it is paralleled?
Ans: When two or more transformers of different voltages (slight) are paralleled circulating current will pass through the paralleled winding. Ammeter connected to the transformer having highest voltage will indicate this circulating current plus actual load shared by that transformer. (Refer section 2.17).

Q8: What are the possible causes that operates differential relay?
Ans: (a) Internal short circuit or earth fault.
(b) Winding fault or turn-to-turn fault.
(c) Defective relay or current transformer failure.
(d) Prolonged inrush current.
(e) Connection current impulse.
Transformer differential protection is described in section 7.7 of Chapter # 7.

Q9: What are the disadvantages of transformer oil?
Ans: (a) Arc produced in the oil is inflammable (means flammable) and explosive. If arc is not extinguished the pressure in the tank may rise above the safe limit and explosion may occur.
(b) Oil absorbs moisture. Dielectric strength reduces by carbonization, which occurs during arcing.
(c) Oil is not suitable for those circuit breakers, which has to operate frequently. Example: Furnace, Motors, Railway traction services etc.
(d) Oil needs periodic testing and filtration and replacement. At lower ambient temperature the viscosity sharply rises and the speed of contact travel reduces in oil circuit breakers.
(e) The dust particles sludge formation can create flashover due to tracking.

Q10: Explain air cored current transformer known as Rowgowski Coil?
Ans: Rowgowski coil is essentially an air cored current transformer because it does not have a magnetic core unlike other current transformers. It has a linear response from zero current to very high values and will not saturate even very high value of short-circuit current. Rowgowski coil provide a voltage output directly related to the current passing through the primary (e.g. 1 Milli-volt / ampere).

This coil measures only the AC component of the current, not the DC component. Generally, the output of a Rowgowski coil is connected to an integrator circuit, which provides an output waveform.

Q11: What are the two types of surge arresters installed for lightning protection of transformers?
Ans: (a) Silicon carbide type with spark gaps.
(b) Zinc oxide surge arrester without spark gaps. Metal oxide surge arresters are widely used..

Q12: Assume that 1 MVA, 11KV/415 volts, distribution transformer has a percentage impedance of 6%. What will be the short circuit current at the low voltage Bus-bar which is very close to transformer?.

Ans: Transformer secondary current $Is = \frac{1 \times 1000000}{\sqrt{3} \times 415} = 1391$ Amps

Short circuit current Isc = (Is x 100) / %Z = (1391 x 100) / 6 = 23181 Amps = 23.181 KA

Q13: What is the absorbent used in a conventional transformer dehumidifier? How it behaves?
Ans: Silica gel is the absorbent used. Colour of silica gel is bright blue. When sufficiently moist, it changes to pink. Upon heating moisture will evaporate and colour will become blue again.

Q14: What is Askarel? What are the disadvantages comparing to Diala B transformer oil?
Ans: Askarel is a synthetic, cooling oil used instead of Shell Diala B, which is a mineral oil. Askarel is a special type of dielectric oil used to cool electrical equipment such as transformers. Some types of Askarel contain Polychlorinated biphenyl (PCB). Askaral produces poisonous gas and danger to life when it comes in to contact with air. Disposal of used Askaral is difficult.

Q15: Hermatically sealed distribution transformer's does not require a silica gel breather and no oil is taken as sample for testing. Why?
Ans: There is no contact with oil and air. Nitrogen gas cushion is provided to accommodate the contraction and expansion of oil at varying temperatures. Since the transformer oil cannot take-up any moisture the dielectric strength cannot deteriorate. If oil is drained for sample moisture will enter through the drain valve.

Q16: High and extra high voltage transformer has circuit breakers at both primary and secondary sides. Which circuit breaker will trip if Buchholz relay or differential relay operates?
Ans: Although primary side breaker is in priority, both the primary and secondary circuit breakers must trip simultaneously, when buchholz relay or differential relay operates. Most of the cases inter-trip facility is provided i.e. whenever one breaker trip due to fault, the other breaker will also trip. If breaker fails to open, breaker failure relay will operate to isolate the entire zone.

Q17: When 2 or more transformers of different MVA ratings are operating in parallel, which transformer will be heavily loaded?
Ans: Transformer with lowest percentage impedance will be heavily loaded.

Q18: Time over current and instantaneous over current relays are required on both primary and secondary of a step down power transformer. Explain its application?
Ans: (a) Primary side relays of a step down transformer will operate on internal and external faults.
(b) Secondary side relays will operate only on external fault..
Time over-current element operates overload and instantaneous over-current element operates on short circuit if the current exceeds the relay set value. [Refer Chapter # 7, section 7.6].

Q19: One end of the current transformer is always earthed. Why?
Ans: Preventing to induce a high voltage if an accidental open circuit occurs in the secondary circuit of the current transformer.

Q20: What is the relation between KVA, MVA and GVA?
Ans: 1 KVA (Kilovolt-ampere) = 1000 volt-ampere
1 MVA (Mega-volt-ampere) = 1000 KVA = 10^6 volt-ampere
1 GVA (Gega-volt-ampere) = 1000 MVA = 10^6 KVA = 10^9 volt-ampere

Q21: Explain the term's "dielectric" and "dielectric breakdown"?
Ans: Dielectric is an electrical insulating medium. Points at which, the insulating material separating two electrical charges permits current to flow between the two charges. Dielectric breakdown is often caused by, excessive voltage, excessive heat, or both.

Q22: What instrument is used for measuring moisture contents in transformer oil? What is the unit used to measure water contents?
Ans: Karl Fischer type analyzer is used for analyzing the water contents in transformer oil. The unit is "ppm" (Parts per million). A unit of measurement of the oil concentration particles in parts per million (ppm) of a

contaminant interspersed in a media. Commonly the concentrate of moisture found in transformer oil is measured in ppm. Maximum 35 ppm is acceptable value. More than that oil filtration is essential.

Q23: Explain the term "ferroresonance"?
Ans: In transformers an over-voltage condition, that can occur when the core is excited through capacitance in series with the inductor. This is especially prevents in transformers that have very low core losses. It can generally be prevented by, having a load connected to the transformer secondary

Q24: Describe the function and application of an off-load tap-changer in a distribution transformer?
Ans: The transformation ratio can be adjusted with an, off-load tap changer when the transformer is dead (de-energized). Usually the revolution quantity of the HV winding is regulated and there are normally five tap positions and the regulation range is ± 5%. The control shaft of the off-load tap changer is brought through the cover or the tank wall. The shaft end is provided with a handle, position indicator and locking device. When the tap changer is turned the locking device must be secured, because this ensures that the off-load tap changer has been set in operating position. It is recommended that the off-load tap changer is turned from one extreme position to another during annual maintenance. During service to prevent mishandling/mis-operation pad locks must be employed and keys are kept in a secured custody.

Q25: Explain the precautions to be taken while handling the gasket replacement in a transformer?
Ans: The gaskets in cover and flanges as well as between bushings and cover are usually made of oil resisting, vulcanized cork-sheet. If the gaskets are leaking, the leaks can be usually sealed by, tightening the screws. When the gasket has to be detached or replaced the sealing surface has to be carefully cleaned and gasket spread with a suitable sealing material. When jointing two gaskets, their ends should be beveled and glued by using sealing . Oil resisting rubber rings are used as gaskets for bushing bolts, shafts and spindles. Oil-resisting and heat-resisting plastic gaskets can also be used as shaft and spindle gaskets. All these gaskets can be tightened and replaced from outside the tank. When tightening the gaskets utmost care must be taken to prevent the breaking of screws/bolts or the gasket. In particular the stud nuts must be tightened very carefully by, using torque winch spanner.

Q26: Explain the performances and applications of an oil filter machine (Oil purifying equipment)?
Ans: The oil filtering/purifying equipment is a portable device used for filtering transformer oil and switchgear oil. The oil is circulated through filtering equipment for several hours till the desired dielectric strength of oil and polarization index value are achieved. The oil purifying equipment removes the following from the oil.

5) Dissolved moisture, free water.
6) Solid particles

The filter machine comprises the following components:

(d) Vacuum tank and vacuum pump;
(e) Centrifugal filter unit;
(f) Oil pump;
(g) Heater;
(h) Valves.

The oil is heated to temperature of about 70°C and is circulated through the filter unit. The filter plates in the filter unit remove the solid particles. The heated oil is passed through spray chamber and vacuum chamber to remove the water particles and the moisture. Heating of oil and application of vacuum accelerate the purification of oil. Oil filtering equipment should be available for commissioning, drying out and maintenance of transformers. Following are the applications of oil filtering equipment:

(e) Drying, degassing and deaerating transformer oil when treating transformers on site, either as new transformers or after repair.
(f) Drying out new or old transformers after prolonged period on off-load.
(g) The improvement of the insulation resistance of transformers in service.
(h) The bulk treatment of either new or used oil in storage or make-up tanks.

Q27: Define various applications of transformers in Nuclear power stations? What are the different types of test to be conducted on transformers designed for Nuclear power stations?
Ans: Following single phase or three phase transformers are required in a Nuclear power station:

(a) Step-up transformers for stepping up the generator voltage from medium voltage to extra high voltage. For example, 500MVA 24 KV/425 KV step-up transformer.
(b) Station service / Auxiliary transformers; for example 50/25/25 MVA 24/11/6.9 KV, 3 winding transformer.
(c) Autotransformers for fuel enrichment facility: Example 160/80/80 MVA, 220/11/6.9 KV autotransformer.
(d) Dry type transformers for indoor use; for example 1000 KVA 6600/380 volts transformer or 11000/415 volts transformer.
Nuclear transformers are subjected to various tests according to IEEE standards 323 and 344 and IEC 176 requirements as regards their electrical characteristics. The transformer satisfactorily passed the following tests; first the type tests, which included temperature-rise and seismic tests, and then a full program of tests such as:
a) Standard tests under normal operating conditions;
b) Tests under extreme conditions;
c) Ageing tests according to IEEE 74 standards;
d) Seismic shock and aircraft crash resistance tests.
e) Short-circuit withstand tests.

Q28: Current transformers to be installed for differential protection of the star connected winding of a power transformer shall be connected in delta. Similarly CTs installed in the delta-connected winding of the transformer is connected in star. What is the advantage for such an arrangement?
Ans: Assume that the power transformer is connected in delta / star. Balanced three-phase through current suffers a phase shift of 30 degrees. By connecting the current transformers secondary in star this problem can be solved. Further zero sequence current flowing in the star side of the power transformer will not produce current outside the delta on the other side. The zero sequence must therefore be eliminated from the star side by connecting the current transformers in delta. [Refer figures 7.7 (d) and (e) in Chapter # 7].

Q29: While selecting differential relays what are the points to be considered?
Ans: (1) Permit operation up on an internal fault during inrush current period; (2) Not to have excess restraint current resulting from the harmonic restrains of the secondary current due to current transformer saturation during internal fault; (3) Relay must operate during over excitation due to over-fluxing or over-voltages. Transformer differential relay (percentage and harmonic restraint) is demonstrated in section 7.7 of Chapter # 7

Q30: What are the errors caused in differential relay current transformers during short circuit?
Ans: (1) Inherent difference in CT characteristic arising out of difference in magnetic circuit, saturation condition etc. (2) Unequal DC components in the short-circuit currents. (3) Saturation of CT magnetic circuits during short circuit conditions. Due to these cause the relay may operate even for external faults.

Q31: What remedial measure is taken to avoid the operation of differential relay due to magnetizing current inrush in transformers?
Ans: To avoid this difficulty *harmonic restraint* is provided for the transformer differential relay. This relay filters the harmonic component from the inrush current (obtained through the CT) and feeds it to the restraining coil. The magnetizing current produced while energizing the transformer contains a large content of several harmonics. This harmonic content is used for obtaining restraining torque during switching in of transformer. The amount of restraint may be fixed, adjustable or variable. The variable percentage relay increases the restraint as the current increases.

Q32: During on-load tap changing process the transformation ratio will change. Thereby CT ratio will not match with the new tap settings. How this problem can overcome?
Ans: To overcome these difficulties '*percentage bias differential relay*' is being used. It is essentially a circulating current differential relay with additional restraining coil. The current flowing in restraining coil is proportional to $(I_1 - I_2) / 2$ and this restraining current prevents the operation during external faults. Because, with the rise in current due to external fault, the restraining torque increases and $I_1 - I_2$ arising out of difference in CT ratio is not enough to cause the relay operation.. Percentage characteristics of restraint slope are selected to accommodate error currents due to CT ratio imbalance and transformer ratio change during tap changing.

Q33: Why independent instantaneous over current unit is provided with harmonic restrained relays?

Ans: During saturation of current transformers, if the differential relay operation is restrained, instantaneous over-current unit will operate to isolate the system.

Q34: Gas sample collected from a Buchholz relay has neither any change in colour nor any sediment observed. What is the probable reason for accumulating gas and what precautions are to be taken?

Ans: Air in transformer tank due to (1) Oil level too low; (2) Air not completely released while commissioning; (3) Liquid filling separates air due to severe cooling and / or pressure release. Air can be removed by (1) Fill-up the liquid; (2) Air disappears with increased heating; (3) continue filtering oil for certain hours.

Q35: Gas sample collected from a Buchholz relay is milky white with black sediment. What will be the possible reasons?

Ans: Because of oil or askarel breakdown acetylene and hydrochloric acid is developed in the oil. Due to spark over in the winding or charred insulating material may produced carbon monoxide. Test listed in item (a) to (d) of Q36 is recommended to find the reasons of break down of oil.

Q36: Gas sample collected from a Buchholz relay is milky-white colour but no turbidity or sediment. What are the possible reasons?

Ans: Because of oil or askarel breakdown acetylene and hydrochloric acid is developed in the oil. To find the reasons for failure of oil, following tests are recommended:

(a) Check the insulation resistance and polarization index.
(b) Measure winding resistance. (If item (a) and (b) are satisfactory);
(c) Carryout open circuit test;
(d) If necessary conduct short circuit test.

Q37: Define the term 'Transformer bushing'?

Ans: An insulating structure, generally of porcelain and conical or cylindrical in shape, having a central conductor and provisions for mounting on a piece of equipment or a tank wall; insulates the conductor and permits carrying current through a ground barrier, such as a transformer tank, circuit breaker, reactor, high voltage capacitor etc. [Refer figure (d) of section 2.3].

Q38: Define the unit decibel? Which instrument is used for measuring the noise level of a transformer?

Ans: (a) Decibel (dB) is a unit used to describe the strength or intensity of wave-propagated phenomena such as sound or transmitted signals.

(b) One dB equals the least sound level detectable by the human ear, while 70 dB is equivalent to busy traffic and 150 dB is equal to a nearby jet taking off.

(c) Noise level meter is used for measuring transformer noise in decibels.

Q39: Define, the term 'on-load' and 'off load' tap changer? What are the factors to be considered while selecting an on-load tap-changer?

Ans: A mechanism on a power transformer that permits a tap connection to be changed to adjust the voltage ratio of the transformer. A tap changer can be on-load changer if it is designed to change taps with the transformer energized and loaded. Off-load tap changer requires deenergization of the transformer to change taps.

When assigning the rating of an OLTC it must be ascertained that:

(a) Breaking capacity, i.e. product of the relevant step voltage and the maximum through current which can be switched between two taps of a winding.
(b) Temperature rise, short-circuit current capability and thermal stability.
(c) Electrical and mechanical life expectancy of the tap-changer.
(d) Dielectric strength of the insulation of the OLTC.

Q40) Compare the terms 'BIL and BSL'?

Ans: (a) Basic lightning impulse insulation level (BIL): A reference impulse insulation strength expressed in terms of the crest value of the withstand voltage of a standard lightning impulse voltage wave. The standard lightning impulse wave rises to a crest value in 1.2 microseconds and drops to one-half crest value.

(b): Basic switching impulse insulation level (BSL): A reference switching impulse insulation strength expressed in terms of the crest value of the withstand voltage of a standard switching impulse voltage wave;

the standard switching impulse voltage wave rises to a crest value in 250 microseconds and drops to one-half of crest value in 2500 microseconds.

Q41: Demonstrate the conditions for mixing oils of two transformers?
Ans: Two transformer oils can be mixed, if they meet the following conditions:
(a) Comply with the same standard (e.g. IEC 296)
(b) Contain the same oxidation inhibitor or compatible oxidation inhibitors.
(c) Should have a neutralization value < 0.5 mgKOH/g of oil.
(d) Should have a water content < 20 μ g/g.
(e) Synthetic oil (Askaral) should never be mixed with mineral oil (Shell Diala B).

Q 42: Which colour is used for transformer painting? Why this colour is internationally accepted?
Ans: The standard colour internationally used is gray, shade RAL 7003. Oil and heat resistant dark gray paint is used for transformer surface coating. Minimum thickness of surface paint coating must be 80 microns. The use of gray colour is for reflection of sun radiation.

Q43: Define the terms "Two winding transformer", "Three winding transformer"?
Ans: The transformer whose cores carry two independent winding, i.e. HV and LV for each phase. Two winding transformer has two sets of windings identified as HV and LV windings. High Voltage winding refers to the winding of higher voltage class. Low Voltage winding refers to the winding of lower voltage class.

Three winding transformer refers to a transformer whose core carries three independent windings, HV, LV, MV for each phase. Three winding transformer has a third winding Medium voltage winding in addition to the primary and secondary. MV winding refers to intermediate voltage class between HV and LV. For example, 220/110/66 KV transformer: HV 220 KV; MV 110 KV; LV 66 KV.

Q44: Explain the technical term and application of Tertiary winding?
Ans: Tertiary winding is a winding in addition to the primary and secondary winding in a power transformer, which is provided for following purposes:

(a) To stabilize neutral in case of star/star transformer.
(b) To reduce third harmonics and control zero sequence impedance.
(c) To obtain additional voltage.

Q45: Transformer oil in service can be classified in to four groups. What are they?
Ans: Group 1: This group contains oils that are satisfactory for continued use.
Group 2: This group contains oil that requires only minor reconditioning to continue in service. Reconditioning is a process for removing water and solids using filters, centrifuges and vacuum dehydrators.
Group 3: This group contains oils that are in poor condition. These should be reclaimed. Reclaiming is a process for removing deterioration products such as sludge and organic acids using Fuller's earth and heat.

CHAPTER # 3

MEDIUM VOLTAGE SWITCHGEARS AND CIRCUIT BREAKERS

CONTENTS

3.1 MEDIUM VOLTAGE AIR INSULATED METAL CLAD SWITCHGEARS.

Switchgear is a general term, which covers switching and interrupting devices and their combination with associated control, metering, protective and regulating devices. Assemblies of these devices with their associated interconnections, accessories, enclosures and supporting structures used, primarily in connection with the generation, transmission, distribution and conversion of electric power.

IEC Publication 298 subdivides metal-enclosed switchgear and control-gear in to three types:

1. Metal clad switchgear and control-gear
2. Compartmented switchgear and control-gear
3. Cubicle switchgear and control-gear.

Metal-enclosed switchgear means a switchgear which is surrounded by a metal case or housing. Metal-clad switchgear is metal-enclosed switchgear having following features:

(a) Circuit breakers are usually withdrawable type, with a mechanism to move it between connected and disconnected positions, and equipped with self-aligning and self-coupling primary disconnecting device and plug-in control wiring system.

(b) Primary circuits are completely enclosed by grounded metal barriers that have no intentional openings between compartments. In the connected position, no, primary circuit components are exposed by the opening of a door.

(c) Automatic shutters that cover primary circuit elements when the removable element is in the disconnected, test or connected positions. Primary bus bars and connections are covered with insulating material throughout.

(d) Mechanical interlocks are provided for proper operating sequence under normal operating conditions. Instruments, meters, relays etc. and their wiring are isolated by, grounded metal barriers from all primary circuit elements.
(e) Truck type design of withdrawable circuit breaker is suitable for straight **roll-in / rollout** motion. Maintenance and trouble shooting and handling is easy. No lifting device is required.

Switchgear should be rodent, dust and vermin-proof metal clad indoor type extensible design. Panels are of robust construction and shall be unaffected by forces imposed by short circuit or other fault currents, vibration or changes in temperature. Degree of protection is IP 41 in compliance with IEC 529. Instruments, relays and control devices are flush mounted on the hinged door. All doors in the front, and removable covers on the back are gasketed all around with neoprene double lip gaskets. All louvers have screens with filters. Vents openings are covered with grills. The screens and grills are made of either brass or G.I wire-mesh. Figure 3.1 illustrates a 12 KV metal clad switchgear.

LEGENDS:

1. Circuit breaker chamber
2. Bus bar chamber
3. Cable connection chamber
4. Pressure relief chimney
5. Instrument chamber
6. Pressure relief
7. Bus bar
8. Bus bar branch
9. Low voltage multi-pin plug
10. Cladding partition walls
11. Sliding plate for covering fixed slide-in contacts
12. Slide-in contacts of the truck
13. Insulation pipe
14. Circuit breaker on truck
15. Current Transformer
16. Voltage Transformer
17. Space for cable end box
18. Earthing switch
19. Insulating hood

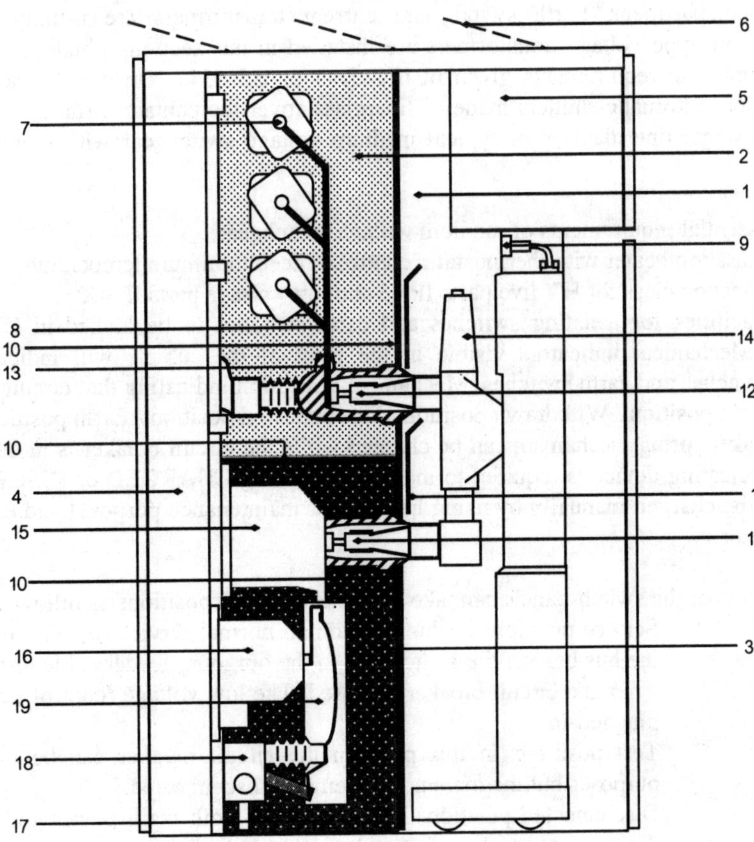

Fig. 3.1: Metal clad switchgear cubicle (Courtesy, BBC Brown Boveri).

The cubicle is of rigid sheet steel construction (Steel angle sections of high torsional strength bolted together and steel sheets of the enclosure are screwed to the frame.) with front doors for the instrument/relay box and the circuit breaker chamber. The rear of the cubicle is fitted with sections, which facilitate the installation of devices and post insulators. The rear of the cubicle is generally fitted with a steel sheet. The lower part of the rear of the cubicle (cable connection chamber) is fitted with pressure relief flap. At the front of the left-hand-side of the cubicle, inward folded steel strips reaching from top to bottom are welded in to the cubicle frame for laying the control cable running to the upper parts. At the bottom, the cubicle is provided with a ground plate in the area occupied by the truck. In order to permit unrestricted running of the control cable through the ground plate, appropriate cutouts are provided. The standard size of medium voltage metal clad switchgear is 800mm width, 2050mm height and 1650mm depth. Standard voltage ranges of medium voltage switchgears are 3.6 KV, 5 KV, 7.2 KV, 10 KV, 12 KV, 15 KV, 17.5 KV, 25 KV and 36 KV. Switchgear ratings are always given at its maximum voltages. As s standard practice all sheet steel is provided with an electro-coated and baked paint. The internationally accepted colour shade is RAL 7032.

Withdrawable switchgear has primarily been designed to provide a safe environment for maintenance work on circuit interrupters and instrument transformers. Fixed type switchgears are equipped with isolator switch to disconnect the power during maintenance. Interlocks are provided such that breaker closing is prevented in any intermediate position between service and isolated conditions. Mechanical interlocks ensure that breaker withdrawal or insertion is possible only when the breaker is off. Similarly, insertion of circuit breaker is not possible when the circuit is earthed. Breaker can be closed (without energizing the medium voltage power) in test position for maintenance check. Inside of a cell of metal clad switchgear, there are different and separate compartments used to segregate different components and functions from one another, to improve reliability and safety. Each compartment is separated by, a grounded metal barrier.

Standard compartments are: (1) LV compartment for mounting instruments and relays; (2) Bus bar compartment (Copper or aluminium bus bars representing R-Y-B phases); (3) Circuit breaker compartment: (4) cable termination compartment. Earth switch and current transformers are usually installed in cable compartment. Draw out type voltage transformers are installed in bus section cubicle. Draw out type circuit breaker has to comply, the requirements given in IEC 56-1 or BS 5311. On withdrawal of the truck from service to test position, automatic shutters made of fiberglass cover the contact surfaces. Figure (a) and (b) of section 3.13 shows single line diagram of typical medium voltage switchgear with longitudinal bus section coupling.

Following are the essential requirements of medium voltage switchgear:

1) Anti-condensation heater with thermostatic control to keep minimum temperature in the cubicle.
2) Ingress protection class for HV live parts IP 65 and low voltage parts IP 4X
3) Pad-lock facilities for isolating switches and earth switches to be locked in ON/OFF/EARTHED positions. Mechanical indicators visible in the front of the cubicle will indicate the position of isolating switches and earth switches. Mechanical indication indicating that circuit breaker on Service position / Test position / Withdrawn position / Disconnected position / Earth position.
4) Circuit breaker spring mechanism can be charged while the circuit breaker is in ON or OFF position. A visual indicating device is required to indicate the spring CHARGED or DISCHARGED position. Spring can be charged manually by using handle (for maintenance purpose) and electrically by using AC/DC motor.

The withdrawable parts of the switch-panels can take the three different positions as follows:

1. Service position: In this position all normal service (operation) connections from the bus bar via the switchgear to the outgoing feeder cable or bus ducts are made when the circuit breaker is closed. The low voltage (control circuit) connection is plugged-in.
2. Test position: In this position the circuit breaker can be operated for testing purposes but the main power remains disconnected.
3. Disconnected position: In this position both main power and control power are disconnected and earth switch can close if a work permit is to be issued.

(1) Electrical interlocks:

Following interlocks are required for operation of circuit breakers, disconnecting switches and earth switches.

(a) Circuit breaker could not be closed in service position if any of the following conditions are not satisfied: * All trip relays are reset; * Operating system (spring) is ready for tripping; * Associated earth switch is in open position; * For SF6 insulated circuit breakers SF6 gas pressure is adequate for safe operation.

(b) Disconnecting switch could not be operated if any of the following conditions are persisting:
*Relevant circuit breaker is in closed position; * Associated earth switches are closed.
*Disconnecting switch is required only when fixed type circuit breakers are employed.

(c) Earth switch could not be operated if any of the following conditions are persisting:
*Relevant circuit breaker is closed; * Associated disconnector is closed; * Breaker truck is inside the cubicle at the connected position.

(d) To prevent inserting relevant breaker truck while the grounding switch is ON.

(e) To prevent moving the breaker truck into or from the connected position while the breaker is in the on position.

(f) Breaker should not close when the truck not properly locked in to the service position or test position.

(g) To prevent disconnecting the control cable circuit (multiple pin plug-unit) when the breaker is ON.

(h) To prevent removing the breaker truck from the cubicle (beyond the test position) with out disconnecting the multiple plug-unit.

(i) To prevent inserting the breaker truck to service position (after the test position) without connecting the multiple plug-unit.

(j) The door cannot be open when the draw out type circuit breaker is in service position or intermediate position. Also low voltage multiple pin plug-unit cannot be disconnected.

(k) The draw out type circuit breaker can only be moved from the test position to the service position and vice versa if the circuit breaker is off and the door is closed.

(2) Key interlocks:

Keys are used for safety mechanical interlocking of switchgear. Following symbols are used to identify the system.

LO: Key absent: Key can be removed only when the device is open (OFF position).

LC: Unable to remove the key without closing the device (ON position only).

LOC: Key can be removed either the device is closed or open (both ON / OFF position).

(3) Current and voltage transformers:

Current transformers installed integral-to the switchgear should comply with the requirements of IEC 185 and IEC 60044. The maximum continuous primary current rating of the CT be not less than the equipment rating for which the switchgear is used. The CT is to be installed on the circuit side of the circuit breaker for both incoming and outgoing circuits. CT secondary is connected either in delta or in star depending on its applications. Accuracy class of the CT can be decided based on the individual applications. Current transformer for protection and metering is demonstrated in section 5.1 of Chapter # 5.

Draw out type voltage transformers installed integral-to-the switchgear comply with the requirements of IEC 186. They are three phase Delta/Star unit, primary connected through current limiting high voltage fuses which are capable of carrying circuit breaker short time withstand current. Standard secondary phase-to-phase voltage is 110 volts, when the rated nominal voltage is applied to the primary winding. Phase to neutral voltage will be $110/\sqrt{3}$ volts (63.5V). Secondary is protected through MCB or HRC fuses. Voltage transformer for protection and metering is demonstrated in section 5.2 of Chapter # 5. Single line diagram is given in figure 3.13 (e).

(4) Mimic diagram:

A single line diagram of the switchgear made of plastic symbols attached to the front door (preferably instrument chamber) for quick orientation of the operating personnel and to avoid switching mistakes. ON/OFF positions of the circuit breaker / earth switch / disconnecting devices can be identified through the semaphore relays incorporated in the mimic diagram. Coloured indication lamps red, green, amber and white are also used to indicate the ON/OFF/TRIP/ TRIP CIRCUIT HEALTHY indication of the breaker.

Semaphore indicators: These units are used on mimic diagrams to indicate to control room operators in power stations and substations whether remote switches and circuit breakers are open or closed. The semaphore, which usually takes the form of a line on a white background, is arranged to bridge the gap between adjacent lines in the mimic diagram when the associated circuit breaker or switch is closed. The indicators use attracted armature units without contacts, which give high operating torque and a very positive action. The semaphore units are available in 38 or 63 mm diameter in three models as follows:

a) Operation of one unit rotates the disc clockwise or counter-clockwise through 90°. The disc maintains the last indicated position when the control power fails.

b) Operation of one unit rotates the disc clockwise or counter-clockwise through 45°. Springs are fitted which holds the disc at neutral when both units are de-energized.

c) One unit only is fitted which, when energized, rotates the disc through 90°. A spring returns the disc to the original position when the coil is de-energized.

(4) Switchgear insulation:

The most common insulating medium has been air at atmospheric pressure, plus some solid dielectric materials. Under severe climatic conditions this requires precautions to be taken against internal contamination, condensation, corrosion, or reduced dielectric strength in high altitudes. Ribbed vacuum-potted epoxy resin insulators are used as structural supports for bus bars. Insulating sulphur-hexaflouride gas (SF6) at slight overpressure has also been used inside totally encapsulated medium voltage switchgears as insulating medium (refer section 3.19) for totally exclude these disturbing effects. In the gas insulated metal-clad switchgear all effects of the environment on high voltage carrying parts are eliminated.

(6) Fault level:

Recommended minimum fault level in a 3-phase medium voltage system as per BS requirements:

System nominal voltage (KV):	3.3	6.6	11	22	33
Fault level in MVA:	150	250	500	1000	1500
Short circuit current 3 sec. (KA):	21.5	21.5	21.5	25	25

Recommended minimum fault level in a 3-phase medium voltage system as per ANSI requirements:

System designated voltage (KV):	5	15	25	34.5
Fault level in MVA:	250	650	1100	1500
Short circuit current 3 sec. (KA):	25	25	25	25

Nominal system MVA = √3 x system nominal voltage in KV x Full load current in KA

Fault MVA = √3 x KV x 3-phase fault current in KA

KV = Line to line voltage / 1000 and KA = Line current in amps / 1000

Three phase fault current in KA = Fault level in MVA / (√3 x KV)

Two phase fault or double earth fault current in KA = Fault level in MVA / (2 x KV)

X/R value is a value determinant as to how long a short circuit current will remain on a circuit if uninterrupted by an over current device. X/R = Tan ϕ, X represents reactance in ohms and R represents resistance of the circuit in ohms.

Z = Impedance in ohms = $\sqrt{R^2 + X^2}$

3.2 MEDIUM VOLTAGE BUSBAR CONFIGURATION.

Electrical terms "bus bar" is a conductor or group of conductors that serves as a common connection (tapping points) for several circuits (branches), which is for interconnection of equipments of same voltage. Bus scheme is an arrangement of a conductor or group of conductors used to interconnect circuits and breakers in a substation. Bus bar schemes most often used are:-

1. Single bus bar system.
2. Main and transfer bus system
3. Double bus, single breaker.
4. Double bus, double breaker.
5. Breaker and a half system.
6. Ring bus system

Single bus bar system:
The single bus scheme is usually used in low voltage systems. Dependence on one main bus, serious outage may occur in the event of breaker or bus failure. Although the protective relaying is relatively simple, the single bus bar is considered inflexible and subject to complete power outage. Switchgear installations of normal service conditions having only one incoming source are preferably equipped with single bus bar systems as shown in Figure 3.2 (a). These switchgears are clear in their arrangement, simple to operate, require relatively little space, and are low in initial cost. Whereas switchgears with two incoming sources consists of single bus bar arrangement, having two bus sections and a bus coupler or bus tiebreaker as shown in Figure 3.2 (b). These switchgears are suitable for following types of operations depending on the requirements:

(a) Either of the one incoming source can feed the entire load, provided the tiebreaker is closed and the unused incomer breaker is open.
(b) Keeping the bus coupler open, either of the incomer feeders can feed their respective bus section.
(c) By closing both incomer breakers and tiebreaker the system can be synchronized to share the load by both incomer feeders.

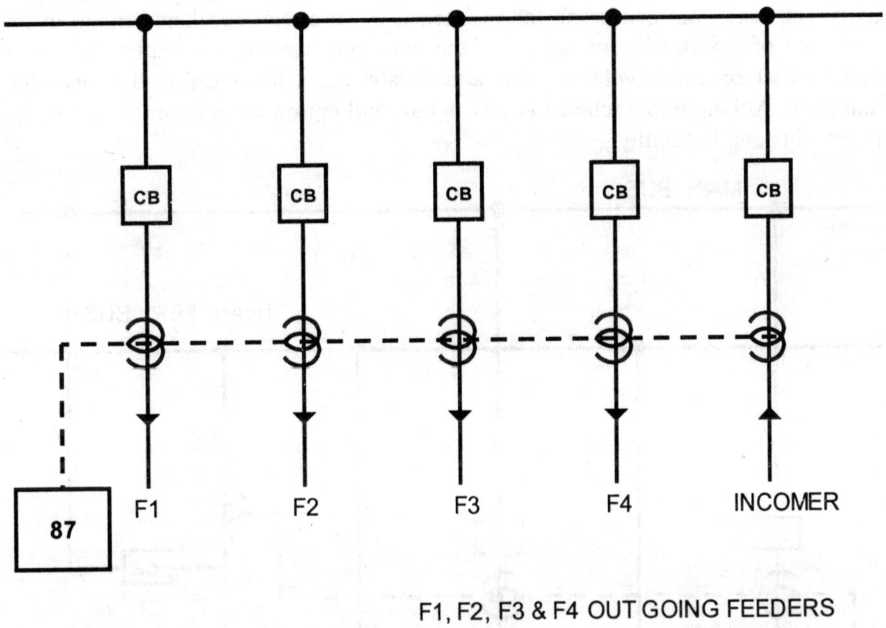

Fig. 3.2 (a): Single line diagram of single bus bar arrangement with withdrawable type breakers.

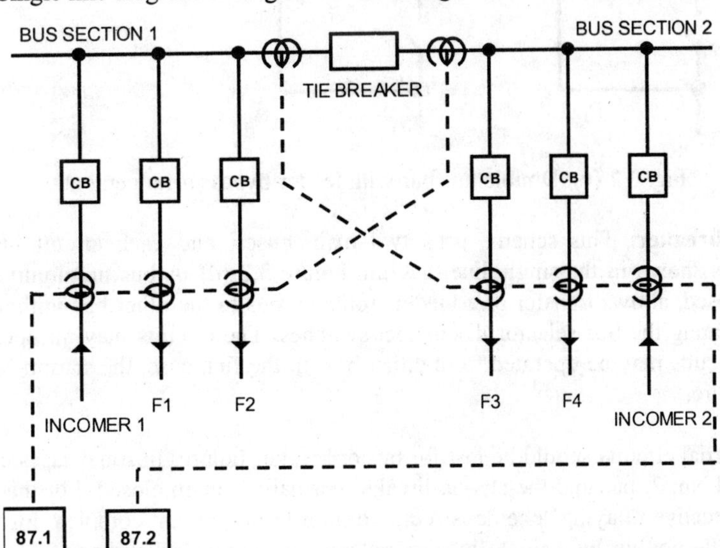

Fig. 3.2 (b): Single line diagram of single bus bar arrangement with bus section breaker.

In a single bus bar system disconnecting switches are not required provided draw out type circuit breakers are used. Bus differential protection scheme (Device No 87) for single bus, single incomer scheme and double incomer schemes are shown in the respective figures.

Main and transfer bus: The main and transfer bus scheme shown in Figure 3.2 (c) adds a double bus to a single bus scheme. An extra bus-tie circuit breaker is provided to tie the main transfer buses together. When a circuit breaker is removed from service for maintenance, the bus tie circuit breaker is used to keep that circuit energized. Unless the protective relays are also transferred, the bus tie relaying must be capable of protecting distribution feeders. This is considered unsatisfactory since relaying selectivity is poor. A satisfactory alternative is consists of connecting the line and bus relaying to current transformers located on the lines rather than on the breakers. For this arrangement line and bus relaying need not be transferred when a circuit breaker is taken out service for maintenance, then the bus-tie breaker used to keep the circuit energized. The bus differential protection scheme for main and transfer bus system is also shown in the figure.

If the main bus is ever taken out of service for maintenance, no circuit breakers remain to load any of the feeder circuits. Failure of any breaker or failure of the main bus can cause complete loss of service of the station. Disconnect switch operation with the main and transfer bus scheme can lead to operator error, injury, and possible shutdown. Although this scheme is low in cost and enjoys great security, it does not provide the high degree of reliability and flexibility.

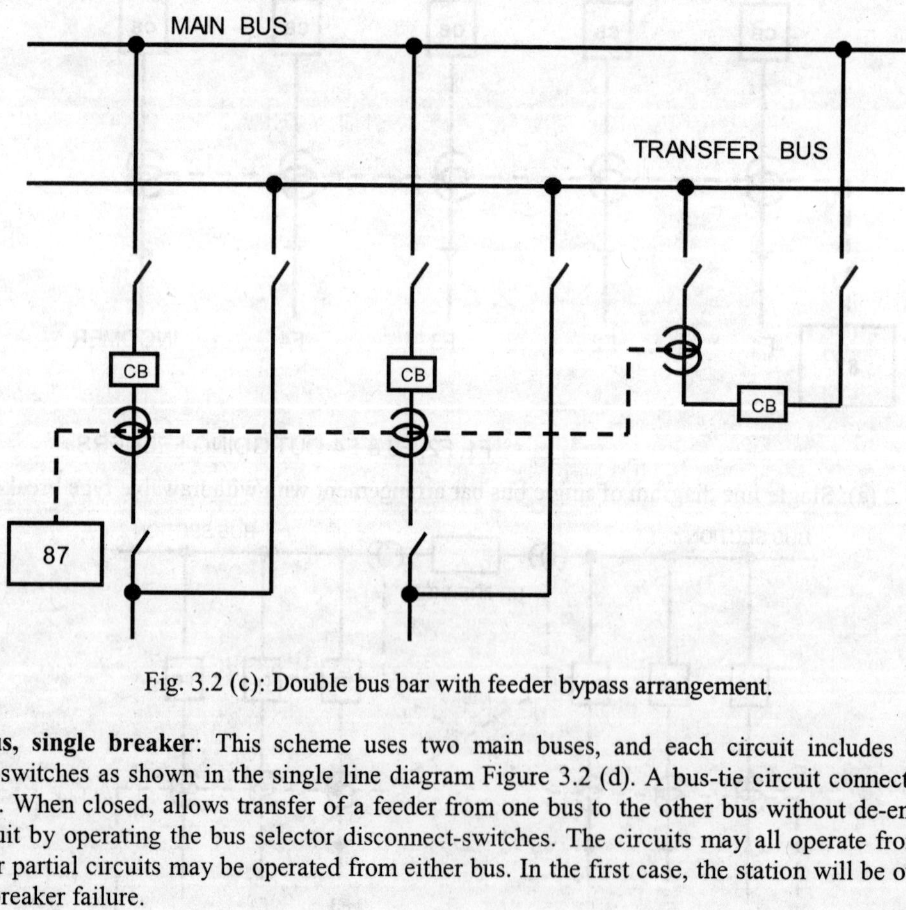

Fig. 3.2 (c): Double bus bar with feeder bypass arrangement.

Double bus, single breaker: This scheme uses two main buses, and each circuit includes bus selector disconnect-switches as shown in the single line diagram Figure 3.2 (d). A bus-tie circuit connects to the two main buses. When closed, allows transfer of a feeder from one bus to the other bus without de-energizing the feeder circuit by operating the bus selector disconnect-switches. The circuits may all operate from the No: 1 main bus or partial circuits may be operated from either bus. In the first case, the station will be out of service for bus or breaker failure.

In the second case, partial circuits should be lost for bus or breaker failure. In some cases circuits operate from both the no: 1 bus and No: 2, bus and the bus-tie-breaker normally remain closed. For this type of operation a very selective bus protective relaying scheme is required in order to prevent complete loss of the station for a fault on either bus. The double bus, single breaker scheme is poor in reliability and not normally used in modern substations. Bus differential scheme for double bus, single breaker system is also shown in the figure.

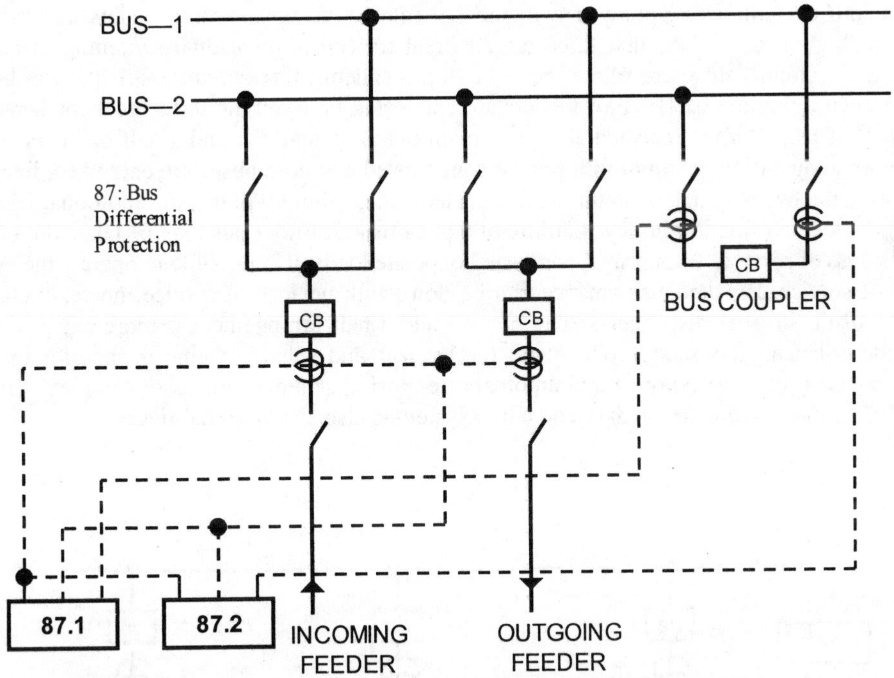

Fig. 3.2 (d): Double bus bar with single feeder breaker arrangement.

Double bus, double breaker: In this scheme two circuit breakers are provided for each feeder as shown in the single line diagram in Figure 3.2 (e). This scheme is usually employed SF6 gas insulated switchgears (GIS). Normally each feeder is connected to both buses. In some cases, partial circuits could operate on each bus. For these cases bus or breaker alone would cause the loss of partial circuits. The location of the main buses must be such as to prevent faults spreading to both buses. The use of two breakers per circuit makes this expensive. However, it represent a high order of reliability when all circuits are connected for operate on both buses. Bus differential scheme for double bus, double breaker system is also shown in the figure. Double bus bar arrangement facilitates: (1) Operation with asynchronous feeders; (2) Feeders with different degrees of importance to maintain operation during emergency conditions; (3) Isolation of consumers with shock loading from the normal network; (4) Balancing of feeders on two systems during operation; (5) Access to bus bars required during operation.

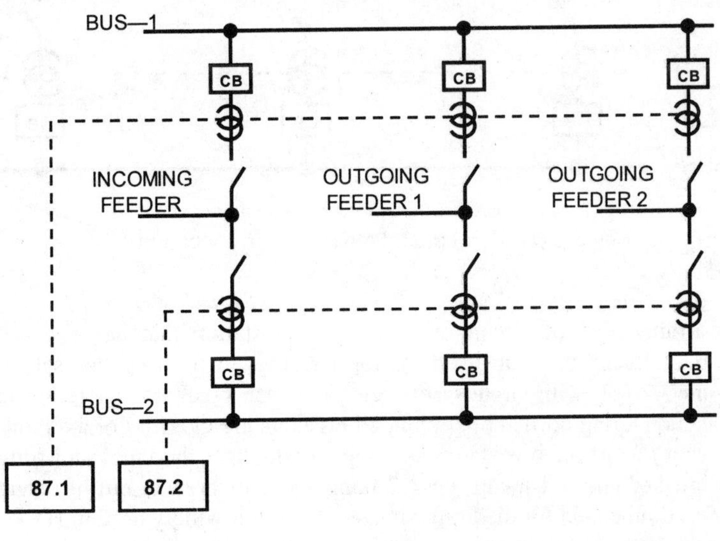

Fig. 3.2 (e): Double bus bar with double breaker arrangement.

Breaker and a half system: Descriptive of a method of interconnecting several feeders and breakers in a outdoor switching station or GIS so that three circuit breakers can provide dual switching to each of two circuits by having the circuits share one of the breakers. In this scheme, three breakers are in series between the main buses as shown in Figure 3.2 (f). Two feeders are connected between the three breakers, hence the term breaker and a half. This pattern is repeated along the main buses so that one and a half breakers are for each circuit. Under normal operating conditions all breakers are closed and both buses are energized. Each feeder is tripped by, opening the two associated circuit breakers. Tiebreaker failure will trip the additional feeder, but no additional feeder is lost if a line trip involves failure of a bus breaker. Either bus may be taken out of service at any time with no loss of service. With source connected opposite loads, it is possible to operate the system with both buses out of service. Breaker maintenance can be done with no loss of service, no relay changes, and simple operation of the breaker disconnects. The breaker and a half arrangement is more expensive than any other schemes described in this section. However, the breaker and a half scheme is superior in flexibility, reliability, and safety. Protective relaying and automatic re-closing schemes are more complex than for other schemes. Bus differential scheme for breaker and a half system is also shown in the figure.

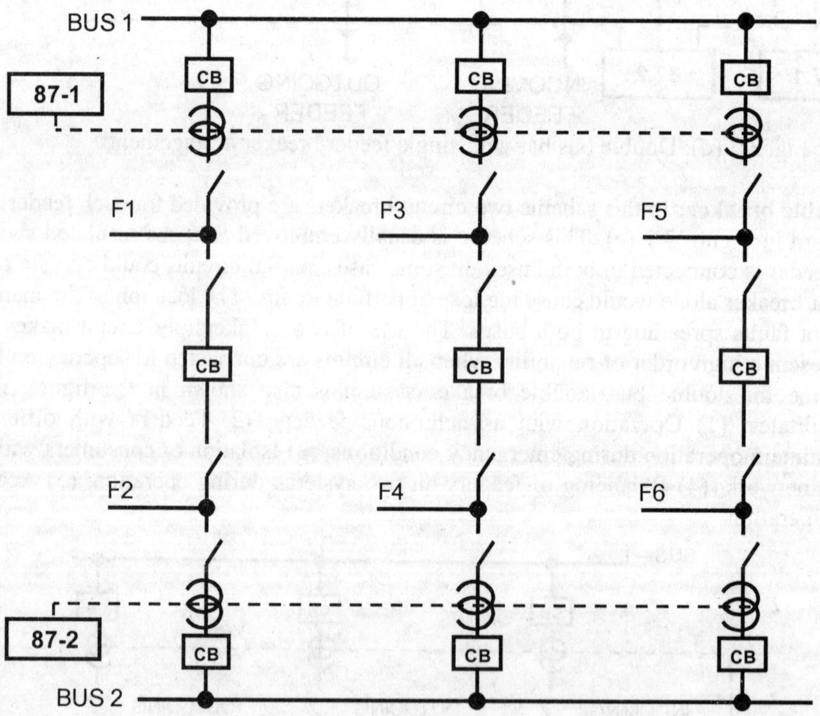

Fig. 3.2 (f): Breaker and a half bus arrangement.

Ring bus system: An arrangement of circuit breakers in a substation that has one breaker for each line position, with a single bus closing back on itself, to form a ring. In the ring bus scheme the breakers are arranged in a ring [Figure 3.2 (g)] with circuits connected between breakers. There are the same-number of feeders as there are breakers. During normal operation, all breakers are closed. For a circuit fault, two breakers are tripped, and in the event one of the breakers fails to operate to clear the fault, an additional circuit will be tripped by operation of breaker failure backup relay. Taking a line or breaker out of service requires opening the ring. Ring bus is not recommended for medium voltage system but widely used in HV outdoor systems.

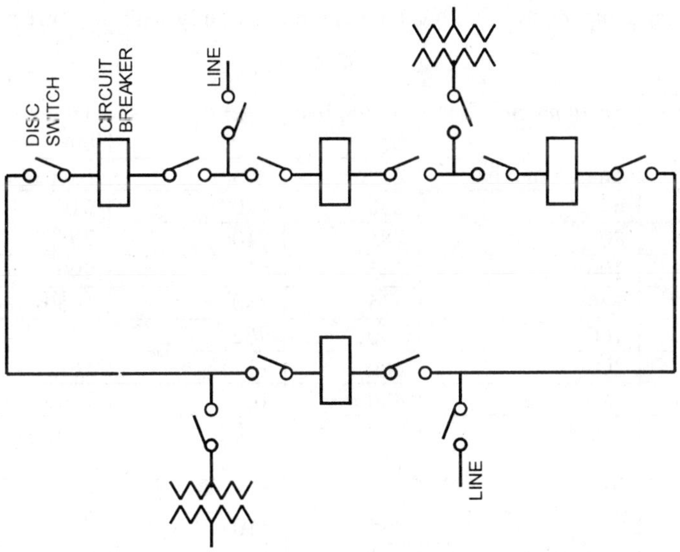

Fig. 3.2 (g): Ring bus arrangement.

During breaker maintenance, the ring is broken, but all lines remain in service. The circuits connected to the ring are arranged so that sources are alternated with loads. For an attended circuit outage, the line disconnect switch may be opened and the ring can be closed. No changes to protective relays are required for any of the operating conditions or during maintenance. The ring bus scheme is economical in cost, has good reliability, is safe for operation and flexible, but normally considered suitable for outdoor substations up to a limit of six feeders only. Protective relaying and automatic re-closing are more complex than for previous schemes described. It is common practice to build major outdoor substations initially as a ring bus; for more than five outgoing circuits, the ring bus is usually developed to the breaker and a half scheme.

3.3 SELECTION AND APPLICATION OF MEDIUM VOLTAGE BUS BARS.

In practice, "bus" refers to the main power bus in the switchgear. Bus made of copper, or aluminium, or cuponal rectangular bars are defined as bus bars.

Copper is malleable ductile, reddish metal, can be cast, forged, rolled, drawn, machined. Annealed copper is the best conductor for bus bars because of 100% conductivity at 20°C, higher operating temperature (softening temperature 180°C), low contact resistance and very high thermal conductivity (melting point 1083°C).
Other specifications of copper conductor bus bars are:

(1) Density 8.89 gram/cubic-cm.
(2) Tensile strength 20-28 Kgf/mm,
(3) Resistivity at 20°C: 1.724 μ Ω-cm.

Aluminium of high purity (99.5% pure electrical grade), which is greatly anticorrosive, fully spreading and hauling, and highly conductive (conductivity at 20°C: 61.5%) annealed aluminium is used as bus conductor.
Other specifications of aluminium conductor bus bars are:

(1) Melting point 660°C;
(2) Density 2.703 gram/cubic-cm;
(3) Specific gravity 2.703;
(4) Tensile strength: 9.2 Kgf/mm;
(5) Resistivity at 20°C: 2.803 μΩ-cm.

(1) Copper bus bar:

Table 3.3 (1) to (3) gives approximate AC ratings for rectangular copper, aluminium and cuponal bus bars respectively. BS 159 specifies that the temperature rise when carrying rated normal current at rated frequency shall not exceed 50°C and that this be based on an ambient temperature having a peak value not exceeding 40°C and an average value not exceeding 35°C measured over a 24 hour period.

Table 3.3 (1): Approximate AC ratings (at 50°C rise over 35°C ambient temperature) for rectangular copper bus bars. For other ambient temperatures and bus temperatures multiply with the correction factor 'K' given in Figure 3.3 (a).

Bar width	Bar thickness	Sectional area/bar	Single bar bus	Two bars bus	Three bars bus	Four bars bus
mm	Mm	Square mm/bar	Amps	Amps	Amps	Amps
16	4	64	250	440	610	780
20	4	80	285	510	705	900
25	4	100	365	650	900	1145
30	4	120	435	780	1050	1360
40	4	160	540	965	1325	1690
50	4	200	660	1175	1615	2065
60	4	240	800	1425	1965	2510
80	4	320	900	1600	2205	2815
100	4	400	1185	2110	2900	3710
12	6	72	215	385	530	675
16	6	96	290	510	705	900
20	6	120	360	640	880	1125
25	6	150	450	800	1100	1405
30	6	180	515	915	1265	1615
40	6	240	660	1175	1615	2065
50	6	300	790	1410	1940	2480
60	6	360	915	1630	2240	2865
80	6	480	1160	2065	2845	3635
100	6	600	1395	2400	3415	4185
125	6	720	1605	2760	3785	4815
160	6	960	2040	3515	4820	6129
40	10	400	850	1510	2080	2660
50	10	500	1060	1820	2595	3315
60	10	600	1225	2240	2975	3780
80	10	800	1525	2715	3600	4575
100	10	1000	1800	2970	4245	5400
125	10	1250	2150	3545	4815	6105
160	10	1600	2620	4320	5660	7075
200	10	2000	3140	5180	6780	8475
250	10	2500	3710	5750	7790	9645

Bus bar ratings are based on the expected surface temperature rise of the bus bar. This is a function of the thermal resistance of the bus bar and the power it dissipates. The thermal resistance of the bus bar is a function of the surface area of the bus bar, the orientation of the bus bar, the material from which it is made, and the movement of the air around it. The power loss of the bus bar is dependant on the square of the current passing through it, its length, and the AC resistance. Maximum bus bar ratings are not the temperature at which the bus bar is expected to fail, rather it is the maximum temperature at which the bus bar is considered safe to operate. Bus bars which are sleeved in an insulation material such as a heat shrink materials, may need to be de-rated because of the potential aging and premature failure of the insulation material.

The effects of short circuit on copper bus bars:

Short circuit current for copper bus bars in Kilo-amps = (0.122 x Cross sectional area in sq:mm)/√t, where t is the time in seconds. Minimum time will be 3 seconds. For example, the size of a copper bus bar is 100 x 6 mm 4 runs = 2400 mm^2 cross section will withstand a thermal short circuit of = (0.122 x 2400) / √3 = 169 KA for 3 seconds duration. Maximum fault level in MVA, for the above bus bar while use in a 33 KV system;

= √3 x KV x KA = 1.732 x 33 x 169 = 9660 MVA

KV: System phase-to-phase voltage in kilovolts; KA: System short-circuit current ratings in kilo-amps.

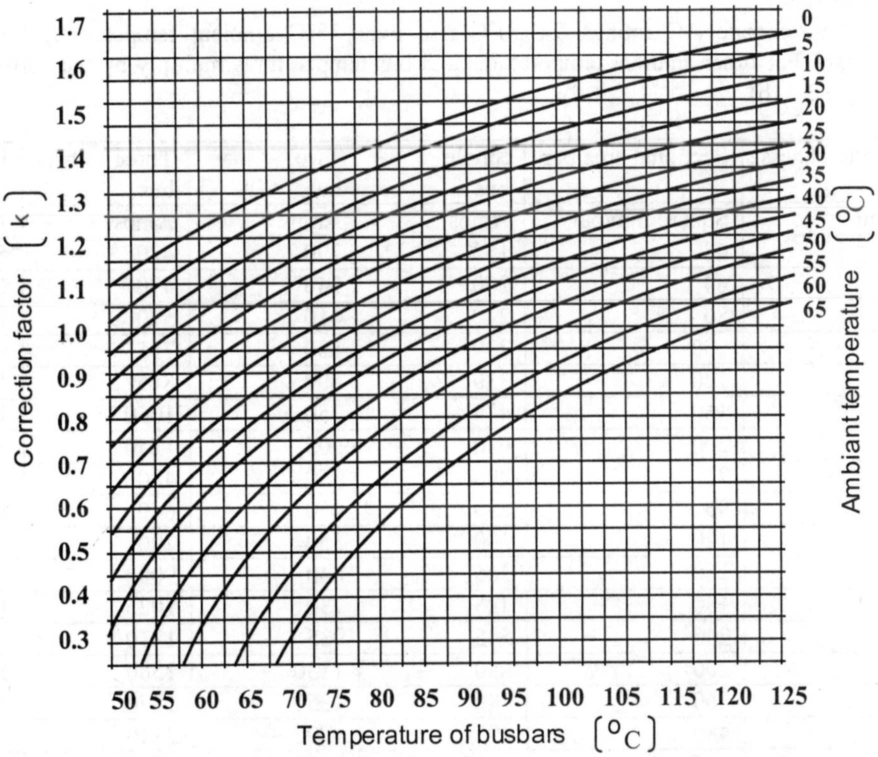

Fig. 3.3 (a): Correction factor for copper bus bar (Courtesy, ITE circuit breakers).

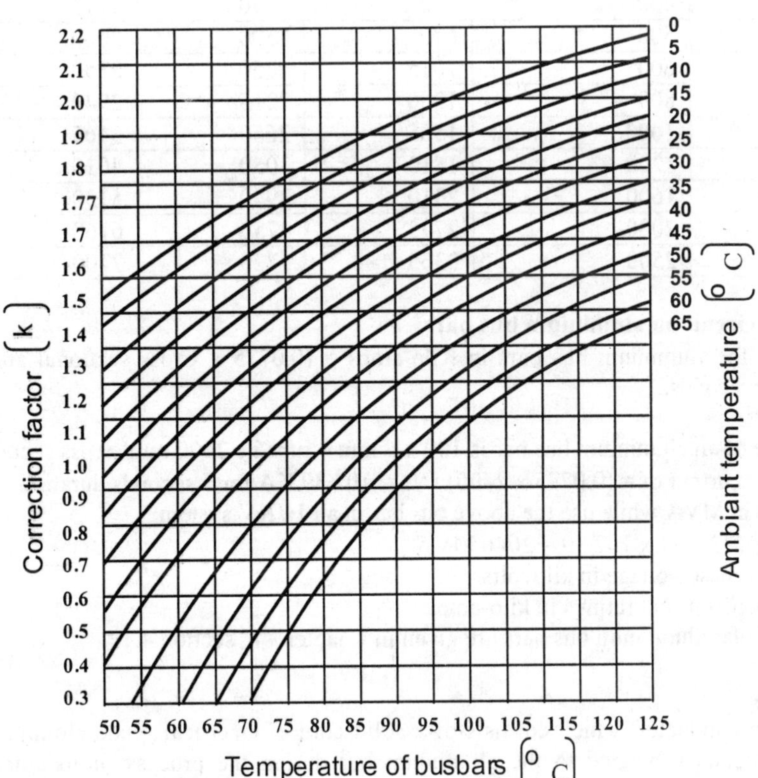

Fig. 3.3 (b): Correction factor for aluminium bus bar (Courtesy, ITE circuit breakers).

(2) Aluminium bus bar:

Table 3.3 (2): Approximate AC ratings (at 50°C rise over 35°C ambient temperature) for rectangular aluminium bus bars. For other ambient temperatures and bus temperatures multiply by the correction factors 'K' given in Figure 3.3 (b).

Bar width	Bar thickness	Sectional area/bar	Single bar bus	Two bars bus	Three bars bus	Four bars bus
Mm	Mm	Square mm/bar	Amps	Amps	Amps	Amps
12	4	48	155	290	420	535
16	4	64	200	340	470	600
20	4	80	240	410	570	720
25	4	100	290	530	755	950
30	4	120	330	600	845	1060
40	4	160	435	750	1050	1320
50	4	200	630	905	1250	1575
12	6	72	200	350	480	610
16	6	96	250	450	640	805
20	6	120	300	550	790	1000
25	6	150	365	640	900	1125
30	6	180	425	730	1025	1290
40	6	240	545	935	1310	1630
50	6	300	650	1130	1580	1950
60	6	360	780	1350	1870	2200
80	6	480	995	1700	2310	2745
100	6	600	1215	2030	2720	3190
120	6	720	1415	2415	3180	3640
160	6	960	1830	3100	4050	4600
40	10	400	720	1230	1713	2110
50	10	500	670	1500	2060	2505
60	10	600	1015	1750	2350	2795
80	10	800	1250	2215	2940	3355
100	10	1000	1565	2650	3465	3940
120	10	1200	1810	3050	4010	4560
160	10	1600	2310	3940	5130	5370
200	10	2000	2795	4750	6160	6710
250	10	2500	3365	5720	7700	8390

The effects of short circuit on aluminium bus bars:

Short circuit current for aluminium bus bars in Kilo-amps = (0.0775 x Cross sectional area in sq:mm) /√t, where t is the time in seconds.

For example, the size of an aluminium bus bar is 100 x 6 mm 4 runs i.e 2400 mm^2 cross section, will withstand a thermal short circuit current of = (0.0775 x 2400) / √3 = 107.39 KA for 3 seconds duration.

Maximum fault level in MVA while use the above bus bar in an 11 KV system;

= √3 x KV x KA = 1.732 x 11 x 107.39 = 2046 MVA

KV: System phase-to-phase voltage in kilovolts.

KA: System short circuit current ratings in kilo-amps.

Current ratings of tubular aluminium bus bars are given in Chapter # 4, section 4.12.

(3) Cuponal busbars

Cuponal is bimetallic conductor, which consists of a solid core of electrical grade aluminium with an outer layer of copper molecularly bonded to the aluminium bar during the process of manufacturing. Cuponal complies with BS 159 (Copper cladding to BS 1036). Table 3.3 (3), depict the current-ratings of cuponal bus bars.

Table 3.3 (3): Current ratings (50°C rise over 35°C ambient temperature) of rectangular cuponal bus bars

Bar dimension	Sectional area/bar	Single-bar (n=1)	Two nos bars (n=2)	Three-nos bars (n=3)	Four nos bars (n=4)
Width x thickness	Square mm/bar	Amps	Amps	Amps	Amps
25 x 6 mm	150	435	840	1250	1660
40 x 6 mm	240	635	1230	1810	2395
50 x 6 mm	300	780	1475	2165	2855
50 x 10mm	500	1000	1920	2840	3750
80 x 6 mm	480	1175	2185	3190	4195
80 x 8 mm	640	1320	2470	3610	4755
80 x 10 mm	800	1485	2790	4095	5395
100 x 6 mm	600	1425	2630	3825	5020
100 x 8 mm	800	1595	2955	4310	5665
100 x 10 mm	1000	1780	3315	4840	6370
100 x 12 mm	1200	1945	3645	5335	7025

Bus bar joints: The most widely used method of making a bus joint between two segments or unit lengths is of bolting or clamping, at a required torque. This method is simple and flexible and in which the joint can easily be dismantled if required. The efficiency of the joint depends on a few essential precautions, which are:

1) The contact pressure must be ample and be maintained.
2) The surfaces of the conductors must be clean.
3) With all conductors, the overlap should be equal to or greater than the width of the bus bars or 10 times the bar thickness, whichever is greater.
4) Joints between aluminium conductors must be treated to exclude moisture.
5) For joints between copper conductors, bolts of bronze or other copper alloy is preferable because these are resistant to corrosion, have higher electrical and thermal conductivities than steel and have a coefficient of thermal expansion closely approximating to that of copper.. By this means a more uniform pressure is maintained with changes in temperature.
6) Copper to copper joints may, with advantage, be tinned to give protection against corrosion or where high-current densities are unavoidable.
7) When a joint is made between dissimilar metals, (e.g. copper to aluminium, electrolytic action will occur if moisture is present so that the joint must be made moisture-proof by the application of grease or a joint compound. However bimetallic sheets are inserted in the contact surface.
8) Variations in temperature cause conductors to expand or contract and this may cause damage to the conductors or the supporting structure. With long runs expansion joint should be introduced at intervals of 12 to 15 metre depends on the bus bar length.
9) Number of bolts including size of bolts required for each joint is to be determined depending on the contact pressure to be maintained in normal service and during short circuit conditions.

3.4 MEDIUM VOLTAGE METAL-ENCLOSED BUS DUCTS.

Bus duct is an assembly of conductors with their associated connections, joints and insulating supports within a grounded metal enclosure. The conductors may be rigid or flexible. There are three types of metal-enclosed bus.

(a) Non-segregated-phase bus duct: Bus duct in which all phase-conductors are in a common sheet metal enclosure without barriers between phases. If associated with metal-clad switchgear, then the primary bus and connections shall be sleeved with heat shrinkable insulation material to the switchgear bus insulation system.

(b) Segregated-phase bus duct: Bus duct in which, all phase conductors are in a common metal enclosure (aluminium) but are segregated by metal barriers between phases.

(c) Isolated phase bus duct: Bus duct in which each phase conductor (tubular) is enclosed by, individual metal (aluminium) housing separated from adjacent conductor housings by an air space. The bus may be self cooled or may be forced cooled, using gas or liquid. Isolated phase bus ducts (Medium voltage) are demonstrated in section 1.11 of Chapter # 1. Similarly, HV/EHV isolated bus ducts are discussed in section 4.18 of Chapter # 4.

Bus bar arrangement

Figure 3.4 (a) and (b) shows the single and double bus orientation and inner and outer cubicle dimension for air insulated medium voltage bus bars up to 36 KV. Dimensional details of the metal enclosure cross sectional area of conductor (rectangular copper bar), current ratings, resistance, reactance and short circuit ratings etc for standard types are given in Table 3.4 (1).

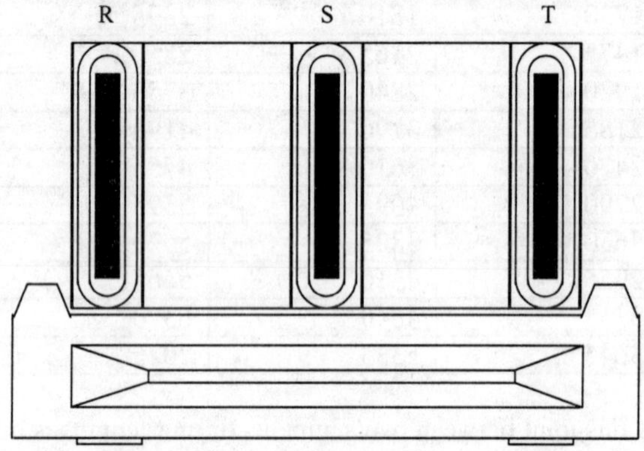

Fig. 3.4 (a): Single bar arrangement for bus duct.

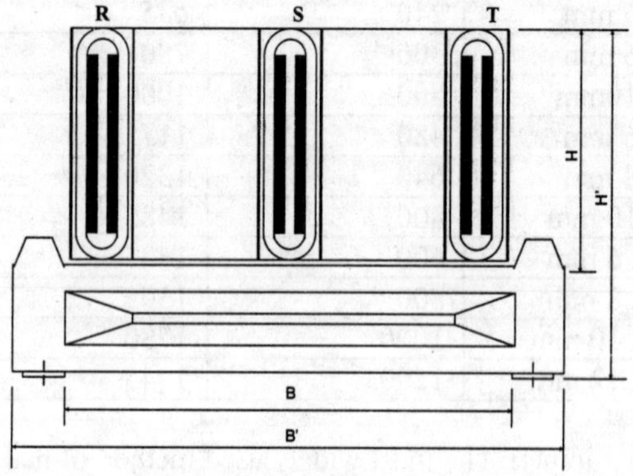

Fig. 3.4 (b): Multiple bar bus duct.

Table 3.4 (1): Technical data for medium voltage three-phase copper bus ducts.

Copper bar size	Sectional area	Current ratings	Inner dia-mension	Outer dia-mension	Resistance at 20°C	Resistance at 75°C	Reactance at 50Hz	1sec: S/C current
Mm	SQ: MM	Amps	Mm	Mm	μ Ω/m	μ Ω/m	μ Ω /m	KA
40 x 10	400	1690	300x140	390x215	45.9	55.3	124.7	38
050 x 10	500	1870	300x140	390x215	37.5	45.0	124.1	47
60 x 10	600	2030	300x140	390x215	32.1	38.4	123.5	57
80 x 10	800	2290	300x140	390x215	25.2	30.1	122.3	76
100 x 10	1000	2520	300x140	390x215	20.8	24.9	121.1	95
120 x 10	1200	2700	300x140	390x215	18.1	21.6	120.0	114
60x12x2	1440	3069	300x160	390x235	15.9	18.3	106.1	83
80x12x2	1920	3427	300x160	390x235	12.9	14.7	104.3	111
100x12x2	2400	3645	300x160	390x235	11.2	13.0	102.3	140
120x12x2	2880	3871	300x160	390x235	10.3	11.3	100.2	140
160x8x2	2560	3955	300x200	390x275	10.0	12.1	97.2	140
160x10x2	3200	4275	300x200	390x275	8.6	10.4	97.7	140
160x12x2	3840	4550	300x200	390x275	7.6	9.2	98.2	140

Figure 3.4 (c) illustrates a typical 4000 amps 36 KV metal enclosed air-insulated non-segregated bus duct with copper bars laid in flat formation. 150mm width, 12mm thick, 3 numbers rectangular copper bars are provided with 355 mm clearances between phases, and 225 mm clearances with respect to earth.

Mechanical forces on electrical bus bars under short circuit conditions:

As illustrated in Figure 3.4 (d), there is a force set up between parallel electrical conductors (bus bars) due to the magnetic field, which is directly proportional to the square of the current and inversely proportional to the distance between the conductors. Dotted lines show intensity of magnetic field. Cross sections through conductors have been shaded to illustrate the concentration of current in an alternating current circuit due to skin effect. The effect and direction of the mechanical force is caused by the reaction due to displacement of the magnetic field and the tendency for the centers of the concentration of current and the magnetic field to become coincident. The force involved may be expressed by the formula:-

Force in pounds, $F = \dfrac{5.4 \times I^2 \times L}{D \times 10^7}$

I = Instantaneous current in amperes
L = Length of parallel paths in feet
D = Distance between conductor centers in inches

An alternating current conductor when short-circuited produces an instantaneous peak value in amperes, which is dependent upon voltage, impedance and other factors. The maximum short-circuit condition on an AC system is usually expressed by the formula:-

Force in pounds, $F = \dfrac{43.2 \times I^2 \times L}{D \times 10^7}$

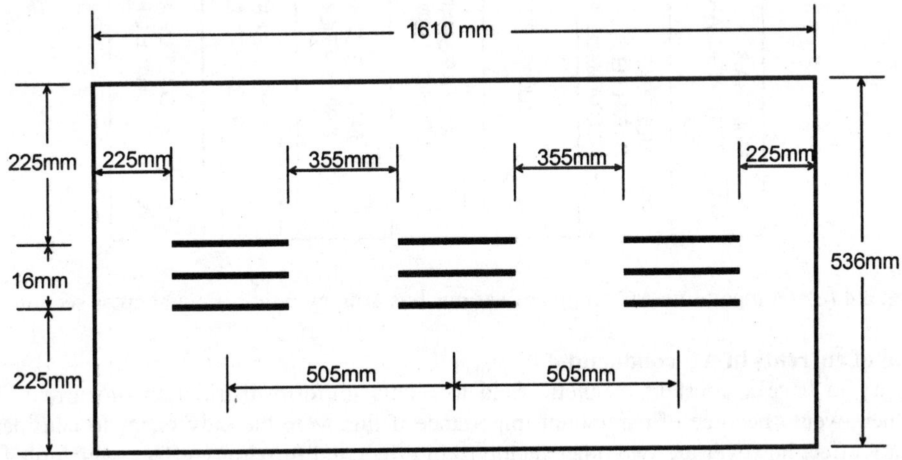

Fig. 3.4 (c): Typical 36 KV non-segregated bus duct arrangement

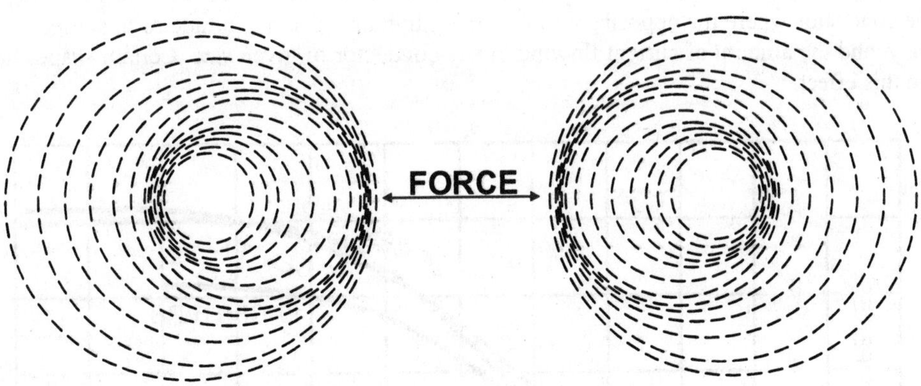

Fig. 3.4 (d): Force between two bus bar conductors.

Bus bar formations: The amount of heat generated in a conductor is proportional to its resistance and to the square of current it carries, while the temperature rise depends on the rate at which heat is dissipated, the latter taking place in varying degree by convection, radiation and conduction. Conductors completely surrounded by insulation will have the heat removed by conduction in the first stage, while those exposed to air will have the heat dissipated by convection and radiation. The maximum rate of heat dissipation with rectangular sections is given when the bar is thin, as this provides a long perimeter for a given cross-sectional area. When a number of rectangular bars are used in parallel, each bar is shielded by, an adjacent bar so that less heat is dissipated, and a point can be reached where further increase in the number of laminations does not sensibly increase the overall current rating. For this and other reasons, other formations are often used, such as those indicated in

Figure 3.4 (e), each formation shown being of equal cross-sectional area. The numerical figures compares the current ratings in different formations be regarded as an indication only.

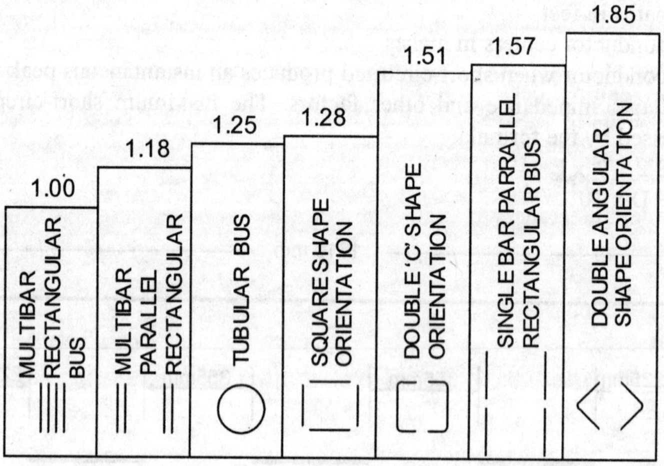

Fig. 3.4 (e): Comparative AC ratings of various bus arrangements of equal cross section.

Distribution of currents in AC conductors:
It is necessary to have a constant magnetic field to obtain uniform distribution of current. The shape of conductor then, would become of paramount importance if this were the only factor to consider. Skin effect and proximity effect however are two other factors skin effect and proximity effect, which play an important part in AC conductor efficiency, particularly when thousands of amperes are involved.

Skin effect: A conductor carrying alternating current is cut by the magnetic flux with every alternation, which produces a back e.m.f. The center portion of the conductor is cut by the greatest number of lines of force, which decrease in intensity towards the outer edges. Such being the case the current tends to crowd at the outer edges of the conductor where the opposing e.m.f. is at a minimum. The magnitude of this effect increases with the frequency, and the amount of current flowing in any conductor of given size. Certain shapes however tend to minimize this effect.

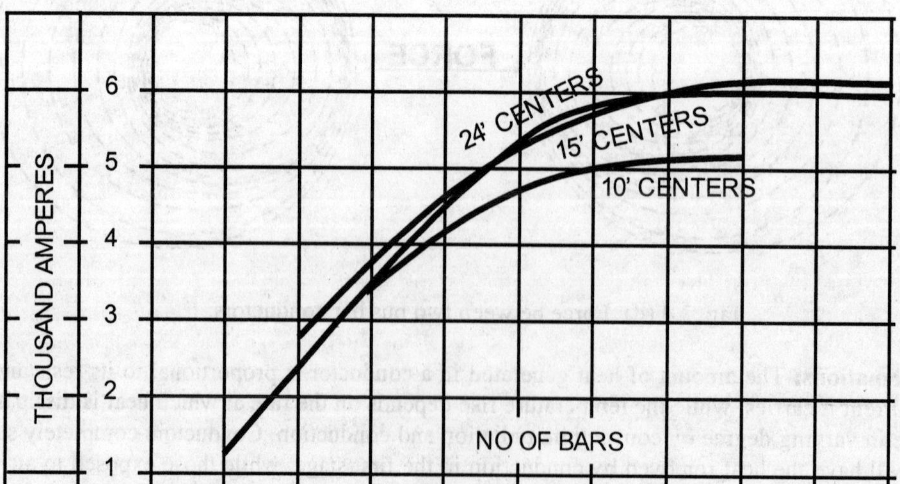

Fig. 3.4 (f): Variation in capacity for 10", 15" and 24" bus spacing of bus bars (Courtesy, ITE circuit breaker).

Proximity effect: This is a term given to the phenomena created between adjacent buses of different polarity. The interaction of the magnetic fields of adjacent conductors not in-phase with each other tends to crowd the current to one side of the conductors thereby increasing the apparent AC resistance and giving rise to additional losses. Adequate spacing between "go" and "return" conductors is the essential cure for losses due to proximity effect. Curve's in Figure 3.4 (f) shows variation in capacity, in 10", 15" and 24" bus spacings due to proximity effect.

Minimum clearances required between phases and phase to earth for metal clad air insulated low and medium voltage bus bars are given in Table 3.4 (2). Insulator creepage distance and power frequency test voltage after installation also furnished in this table. Impulse withstand test is not applicable for switchgears up to 17.5 KV.

Table 3.4 (2): Minimum clearances required for low and medium voltage air insulated enclosed bus bars and connections.

Rated voltage	Phase-to-phase clearance	Phase-to-earth clearance	Creepage distance	Power frequency withstand voltage (one minute)	Impulse withstand voltage level
415 V	20 mm	20 mm	20 mm	--	---
600 V	25 mm	25 mm	25 mm	2 KV	---
3.3 KV	50 mm	50 mm	50 mm	9.5 KV	---
6.6 KV	90 mm	65 mm	90 mm	17 KV	---
11 KV	130 mm	80 mm	140 mm	27 KV	---
15 KV	165 mm	105 mm	155 mm	36 KV	---
22 KV	245 mm	140 mm	205 mm	52 KV	150 KV
33 KV	355 mm	225 mm	305 mm	76 KV	200 KV

3.5 COMMON TERMS ON CIRCUIT BREAKERS AND SWITCHGEARS.

(1) Circuit breaker: A mechanical switching device, capable of making, carrying and breaking currents under normal circuit conditions and interrupting current under circuit fault conditions. MV Circuit breaker is essentially an assembly of parts on a rugged metal frame depending upon ratings and interrupting methods. The current, which a switching device is capable of breaking in an opening operation, is called breaking current. The magnitude of this current is of decisive importance for the life of the interrupter. The current, which flows during the process of closing or immediately after closing the breaker is called making current. It is equal to the inrush current or continuous current and equal to 2.5 times the breaking current. Medium Voltage fixed or withdrawable type circuit breakers (3.6 KV to 36 KV) are coming under the following categories: (1) Minimum oil circuit breaker; (2) Vacuum circuit breaker; (3) SF6 gas insulated circuit breaker. Low voltage circuit breakers are either air circuit breakers or oil circuit breakers.

(2) Breaking capacity: The root mean square (r.m.s) value of current at a certain power factor and a certain voltage, which a switching device or a circuit breaker is capable of breaking reliably in AC circuits, this is the r.m.s. value of the symmetrical component. Breaking capacity in MVA = $\sqrt{3}$ x System line to line voltage in KV x Three phase short circuit current in KA.

(3) Breaking currents: The value of currents, which a switching device or circuit breaker is capable of breaking in normal operation, is defined as "breaking current". The magnitude of this current is of decisive importance for the life of the contacts.

$$\text{Breaking current in KA} = \frac{\text{Fault level in MVA}}{\sqrt{3} \times \text{KV}}$$

Figure 3.5 (a) illustrates determination of breaking current.

AA' - BB' = Envelope of current wave.
BX = Normal zero axis of wave
CX = Displaced zero axis of wave

I_{AC} = Peak value of AC component at EE
I_{DC} = DC component of current at EE
EE = Instant of current separation

$$\frac{I_{DC} \times 100}{I_{AC}} = \text{Percentage of DC component at the instant of current separation.}$$

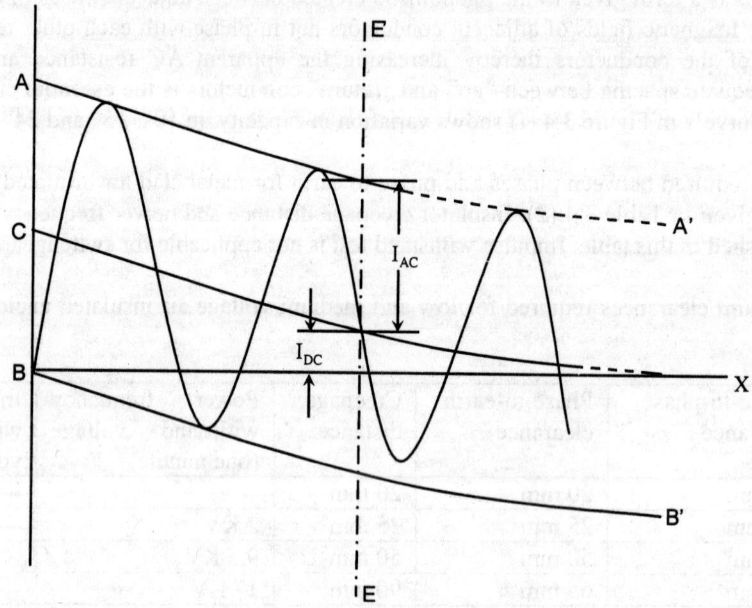

Fig. 3.5 (a): Determination of breaking current.

(4) Making capacity: RMS value of the symmetrical component of the making currents, which the switching device can handle safely, is defined as "making current". It is equal to the maximum instantaneous value of the terminal short-circuit current, i.e. the prospective peak withstand current.

Making capacity in MVA = 2.5 x Breaking capacity in MVA. = 2.5 x √3 x Line to line KV x KA

(5) Making-currents: The value of currents, which flows immediately after closing the breaker, is defined as "making-current". It is equal to the inrush current or continuous current.

Making current = 2.5 x Breaking current

Figure 3.5 (b) illustrates the determination of making current.

AA' – BB' = Envelope of current wave

BX = Normal zero axis

CC' = Displaced zero axis

I_{PK} = Peak making current

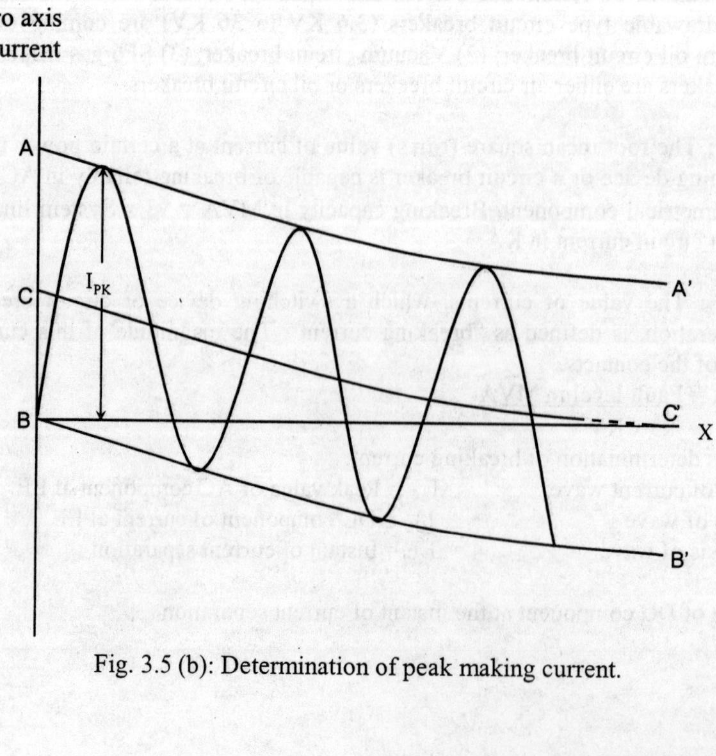

Fig. 3.5 (b): Determination of peak making current.

(6) Arc extinction: Arc is the discharge of electricity through air or other gas occurring across a gap. Arcing is a process of current flowing across a gap. To interrupt a circuit, not only the contacts must be opened but the arc drawn between them must be extinguished as well. An AC arc extinguishes automatically at current zero, but it must be prevented from re-striking at the voltage maximum by using Arcing chamber. A DC arc is extinguished by the fact that it is forced to require a higher voltage than the network is capable of supplying. This is affected by, extending it and cooling it intensively by using Blow out coil.

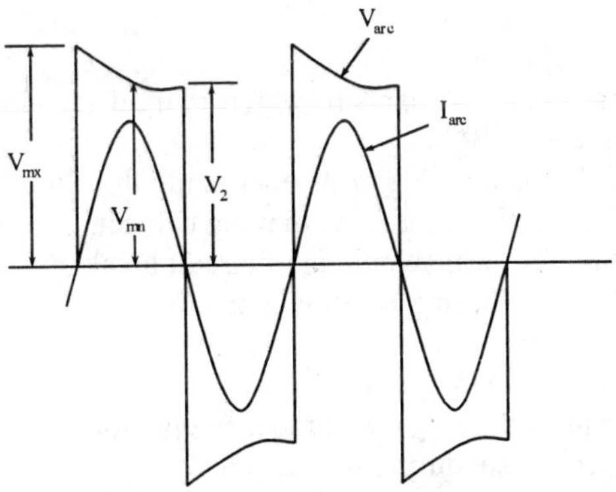

Fig. 3.5 (c): Waveform of AC arc (current and voltage verses time).

Figure 3.5 (c) illustrates the characteristics of AC arc current and voltage with respect to time. The voltage across the arc is in-phase with the arc current as arc is predominantly resistive. The voltage across the arc reverses with the current. At current zero, the voltage across the contacts is determined by, the voltage of the system. Actually the alternating current passes through zero two times per cycle, i.e, 100 times per second in a 50hertz system or 120 times per second in a 60hertz system. At every current zero the arc vanishes for a brief moment. However, the arc appears again with the rising current wave. (In AC systems, the current and voltage continuously change direction and magnitude and become zero at the instant of reversal).

The current zero is used for arc extinction i.e, in AC circuit breakers the arc is interrupted at a current zero. At current zero the space between contacts is de-ionized quickly by introducing fresh dielectric oil or gas or vacuum between the contacts. Hence the dielectric strength of the contact space increases to such an extent that the arc does not continue after current zero. A high voltage may appear across the contacts. This voltage may re-establish the arc if the dielectric strength of contact gap is less than the re-striking voltage. In that case the arc continues for another half cycle and may get extinguished at next current zero. After current zero, there exists a residual column of ionized gas. If the dielectric strength builds up rapidly, so that it is always greater than the re-striking voltage, the arc does not re-strike. If dielectric strength is less, the arc re-strikes. [See Figure 3.5 (d)]

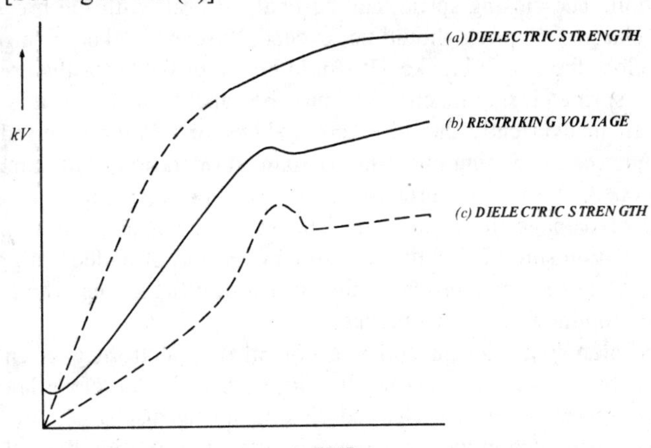

Fig. 3.5 (d): Growth of dielectric strength and transient recovery voltage.

(7) Interrupters: It is a sealed bottle type device in which the fixed and moving contact of a circuit breaker is embedded. Following types of interrupters are used with medium voltage (3.6 KV to 36 KV) circuit breakers:

1. Minimum oil type filled with transformer oil Shell Diala D or equivalent.
2. Vacuum interrupter create vacuum inside.
3. SF6 interrupter pressurized with sulphur hexaflouride gas.

Typically, the interruption device is designed so that the main fixed and moving contacts never see arcing themselves, that function being provided by arcing contacts specifically designed to do so.

(8) Circuit breaker components:

a) Operating mechanism: A mechanism, which is used for closing and opening of the circuit breaker [refer figure 3.7 (d)].
b) Contact assembly: For energizing or de-energizing the circuit. Stationary contact is known as fixed contact and separating contact as moving contact.
c) ON/OFF pushbutton for local switching of circuit breakers.
d) Mechanical ON/OFF and spring position indicator.
e) Closing solenoid (closing coil) and opening solenoid (tripping coil) for electrical as well as remote operation [refer figure 3.6 (c)].
f) Operation counter for indicating the number of operations
g) Device to block mechanism during maintenance
h) DC no volt release and / or AC under voltage release for generator circuit breakers..
i) Interrupter for R-Y-B phases. (Not applicable for low voltage circuit breakers.)
j) Anti-pump relay for trip free operation [refer figure 3.6 (c)].
k) Truck and Cradle for draw out type circuit breaker [refer figure 3.23 (a)].

(9) Stored energy mechanism: As illustrated in figure 3.7 (b), energy required for the tripping operation of the circuit breaker is stored in the breaker mechanism by the closing spring when the breaker is closed. Closing action keeps the wiping spring charged during closing operation. When the wiping spring is released breaker will trip. This is known as stored energy mechanism. Energy for closing the breaker is also stored in the breaker mechanism by the closing spring through the spring charging motor. A close coil and a trip coil are provided to release the spring. A manual pushbutton is also provided for any emergency trip. A set of auxiliary switches generally containing both 'NO' (Normally open) and 'NC' (Normally closed) contacts operated by the operating mechanism of a circuit breaker is provided. They are used to signal the current state and the change of state of the circuit breaker operating mechanism.

(1) Spring-charged mechanisms: The spring charging motor start/stop operation is controlled through a limit switch in the spring charging mechanism as shown in figure 3.7 (b). When the closing spring is released the limit switch will actuate to close its normally open contact to start the motor. When the spring is fully charged the limit switch will again actuate and open its contacts to disconnect the power supply to the spring charging motor. The mechanism will be charged automatically, for further operations, as soon as the circuit breaker has completed a closing operation. The closing spring can be charged both with the breaker in open and closed position. The time taken to charge the spring should not exceed 30 seconds. The spring could be fully charged before it can be released to close the circuit breaker. It would be not possible for the breaker to close whilst the spring is being charged. The spring closing mechanism must be capable such that it is not possible for a fully charged spring to be released inadvertently due to external shock or vibration caused by the breaker due to short circuit stress or any other cause. Spring charging by manual operation (with handle) may be carried out with doors of the cubicle opened. During their process no electrical or mechanical operation of the mechanism shall endanger the operator or damage the equipment. The spring mechanism is fitted with a local manual release, preferably by a pushbutton shrouded with a metallic cover and provided with means of padlocking to avoid inadvertent operation. Means are also provided for discharging the spring when the circuit breaker is in the open position, without attempting to close the breaker.

(11) Closing and tripping solenoids: Closing coil is a coil in the electromagnet energized by DC control power for closing the circuit breaker. By energizing the close solenoid, the close latch in the mechanism is rotated to release the closing spring. When the charged closing spring discharges, the breaker will close. By energizing the trip solenoid the trip latch in the mechanism is rotated permitting the linkage to collapse and the interrupter contacts open under the force of the wipe springs. Function check on closing and tripping solenoids, are described in section 3.12, figure (a) and (b) respectively.

(12) Trip-free operation: The capability of a switching device should have the moving contacts return to and remain in open position when the open operation is initiated after the initiation of a closing operation. Assume that a fault is persisting in the feeder or closing signal is initiated with out resetting the relay, the closing coil will energize to close the breaker. Before the main contact close the auxiliary NO contact of the breaker will close and the trip coil will energize and trip the breaker before its main contact closes. Trip free relay is an auxiliary relay whose function is to open the closing circuit of an electrically operated circuit breaker so that opening operation can prevail over the closing operation. Function test on circuit breaker trip free operation is described in section 3.12, figure (c).

(13) Anti-pump relay: An auxiliary relay used in association with a circuit breaker to prevent the circuit breaker from closing after an opening operation, as long as the device initiating the reclosing is maintained in the position for closing. Two normally closed (NC) contacts of the anti-pump relay (mounted on the breaker truck) is wired in series to the closing circuit of the breaker [refer wiring diagrams in figure 3.6 (c) or 3.8 (e)]. During a closing operation, cam rotation closes the LS contact, picking up the anti-pump relay coil thereby opening its contacts to interrupt the closing coil supply. Meanwhile, anti-pump relay seal-in through it's normally open contacts. If a sustained close command is being received anti-pump relay will prevent to energize closing coil. Assume that the closing signal is sustaining and the breaker is in tripped position, anti-pump relay will not allow-to-close the breaker. Function test on anti-pump relay is described in section 3.12, figure (a).

(14) Shunt release: A release, typically used to trip a circuit breaker. Shunt releases are energized from either the main circuit or from an independent source. Depending on its application, it is identified as:

(a) AC under-voltage release: A type of circuit breaker tripping release which is held energized during normal operation, with the tripping action being caused with the absence of the voltage. For a standby generator assume that a closing signal is initiated when the generator is out of service and mains power is ON, the breaker will not close as the under voltage release is de-energized. When the generator is running, the generator breaker can be closed only if the under voltage release is energized. Similarly if the generator voltage is lost due to any reason during operation, the breaker will automatically trip as the under voltage release is de-energized. Function test on under-voltage release is described in section 3.12, figure (d).

(b) DC No-volt release: Assume that a generator is loaded and the DC control power for break trip circuit fails, the DC no-volt release will de-energize and the breaker trips to safeguard the generator. DC no-volt release check is described in section 3.12, figure (e).

(c) Shunt-release: An electromagnet, which picks-up when its solenoid is energized and thus releases the breaker latching mechanism. This is used as an additional trip coil for remote tripping and interlocking circuit breakers. Application of additional trip coil is illustrated in Chapter # 4, figure 4.3 (d).

(15) Breaker truck and cradle: The mechanical structure, which supports the operating mechanism and the interrupters. Truck is supported on wheels or side rollers. Cradle is an assembly, which provides all the necessary mechanical and electrical interlocks, circuit breaker supports, shutter mechanism, racking mechanism, etc. required for a draw out type circuit breaker which, is intended to be installed inside a switchgear cell. Shutter is a device that is automatically operated to completely cover the stationary portion of the primary disconnecting devices when the removable element is either in the disconnected position, the test position, or has been completely removed. [Refer figure 3.23 (a)].

(16) Service, Test and Disconnected position: A withdrawable circuit breaker, in its service position (connected position) both primary and secondary control power is connected. In the test position the primary-disconnecting devices of the removable-elements is separated by a safe distance from the stationary contact element, and the plug-in type secondary control circuits are in operating contact. In the disconnected position, the primary (main power) and secondary (control power) disconnecting-device of the removable elements are separated by a safe distance. The process of moving a circuit breaker from the disconnected position to the test position and into the connected position or vice-versa is said to be "racking".

(17) Closing time and opening time: Closing time is the amount of time from the initiation of the closing operation and the instant when metallic continuity is established in all phases or poles. Permissive closing time for a medium voltage circuit breaker is usually 5 to 10 cycles (50 to 100 milli-seconds) after initiating close signal. Closing time = Breaker operating time + Bounce duration. Bounce duration is the time from the instant of the contacts touching until full contact is established. It determines the electrical service life and operational efficiency of a switching device (Circuit breaker). Terms related to the closing and opening of circuit breaker as per VDE 0660, part 1, is illustrated in section 3.5, figure (e) and (f) respectively.

Conventional method of measuring closing time and opening time of medium and low voltage circuit breakers are described in section 3.12, figure (a) and (b) respectively.

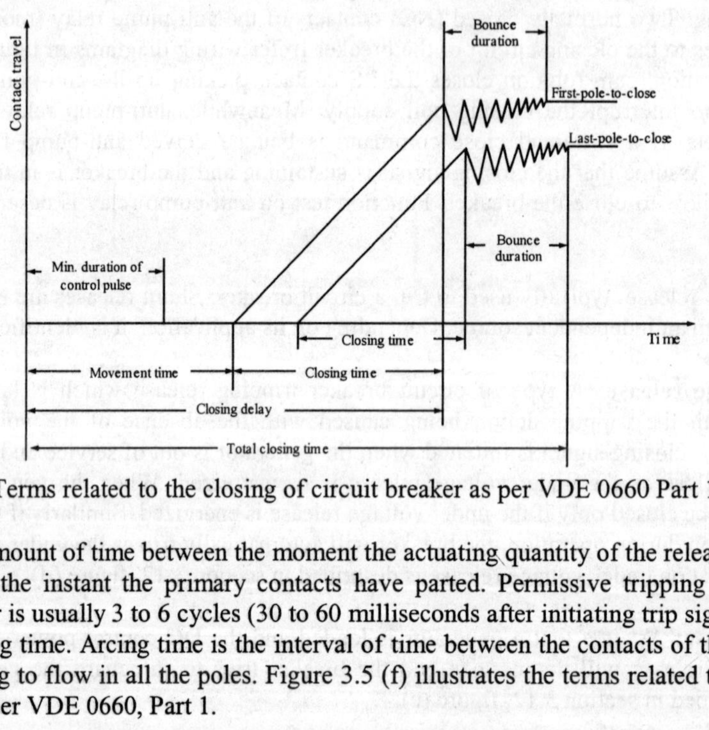

Fig. 3.5 (e): Terms related to the closing of circuit breaker as per VDE 0660 Part 1.

Opening time is the amount of time between the moment the actuating quantity of the release circuit reaches its operating value, and the instant the primary contacts have parted. Permissive tripping time for a medium voltage circuit breaker is usually 3 to 6 cycles (30 to 60 milliseconds after initiating trip signal. Tripping time = Opening time + Arcing time. Arcing time is the interval of time between the contacts of the first pole opening and the current ceasing to flow in all the poles. Figure 3.5 (f) illustrates the terms related to the opening of the switching devices as per VDE 0660, Part 1.

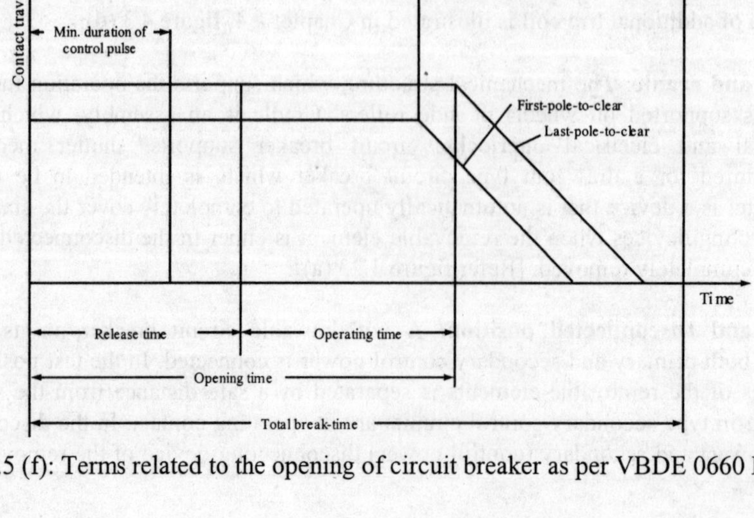

Fig. 3.5 (f): Terms related to the opening of circuit breaker as per VBDE 0660 Part 1.

Under IEC testing rules, there are three common rated operation sequences. The first is an open operation (O), followed by three minutes for cooling of the contacts, followed by a closing operation (CO), then 3 minutes, then a final closing operation **(O - 3min – CO - 3min - CO).**

The second sequence is **O – 0.3 sec – CO – 15sec – CO**.

The third sequence is **O – 0.3sec – CO – 3min – CO.**

O = opening operation; C = closing operation; CO = Closing followed by opening; T = Time

(18) Autoreclosing: Overhead line faults are caused by lightning or through birds, trees, animals etc. This results a momentary arcing faults and the arc in the fault can be extinguished by de-energizing the line by opening the circuit breaker. High speed tripping and high speed re-closing improves the stability of the power system. Hence the MV and HV/EHV circuit breakers used for distribution and transmission lines are provided with auto re-closing feature as illustrated in Figure 3.5 (g).

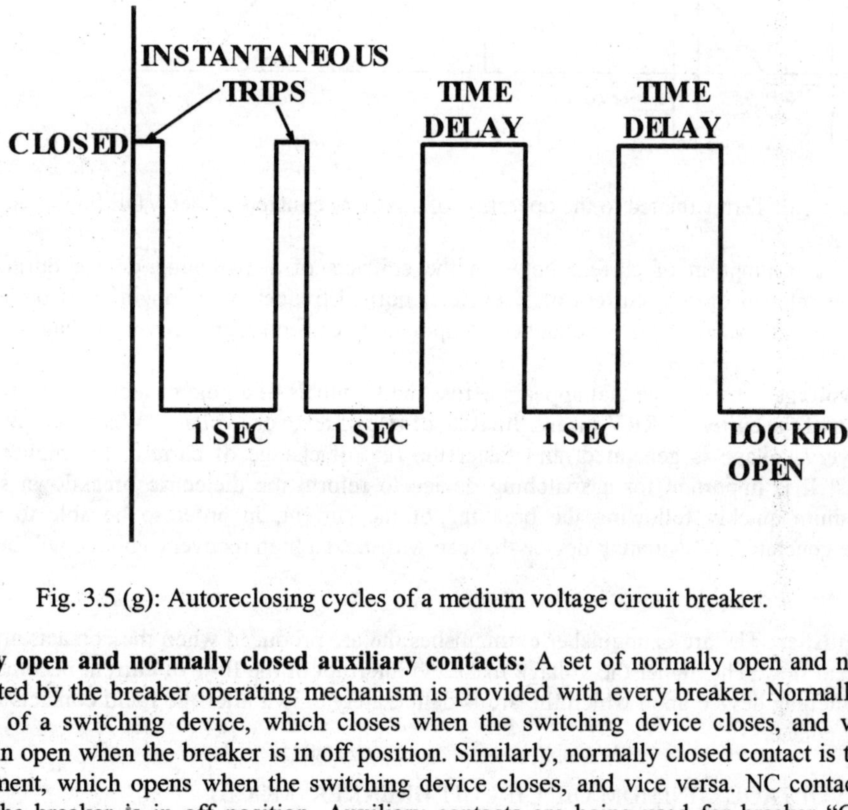

Fig. 3.5 (g): Autoreclosing cycles of a medium voltage circuit breaker.

(19) Normally open and normally closed auxiliary contacts: A set of normally open and normally closed contacts actuated by the breaker operating mechanism is provided with every breaker. Normally open contact is the contact of a switching device, which closes when the switching device closes, and vice versa. NO contacts remain open when the breaker is in off position. Similarly, normally closed contact is the contact of a switching element, which opens when the switching device closes, and vice versa. NC contacts will remain closed when the breaker is in off position. Auxiliary contacts are being used for breaker "ON/OFF" lamp indications, as well as interlocking purposes. Figure 3.5 (h) illustrates the terms related to the operation of auxiliary contacts as per VDE 0660, part 2.

LEGEND:

a = closing position of NC contact; b = open position of NC contact;

c = closing position of NO contact; d = open position of NO contact.

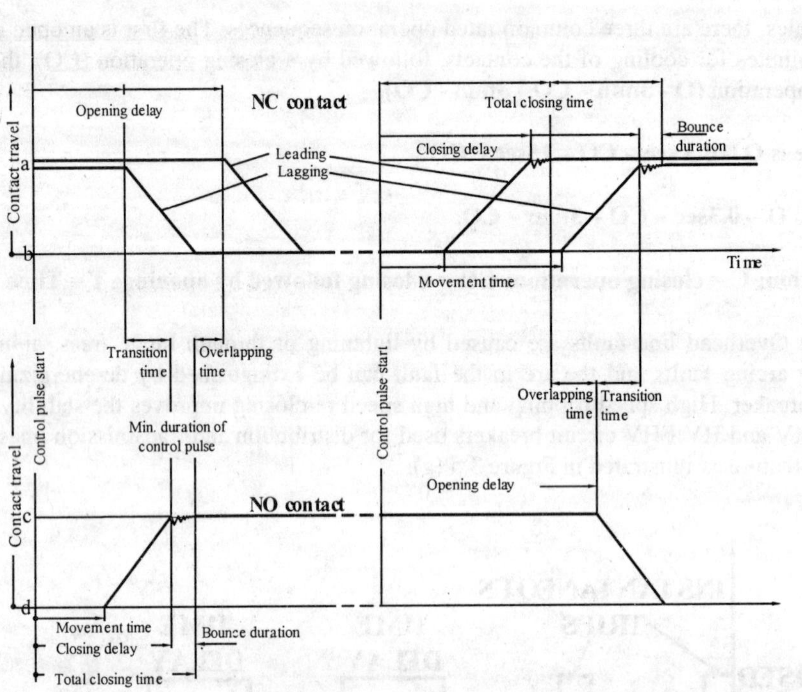

Fig. 3.5 (h): Terms related to the operation of auxiliary contacts as per VDE 0660 Part 2.

(20) Re-strike: A resumption of current between the contacts of a switching device during an opening operation after an interval of zero current of ¼ cycle at normal frequency or longer. It is preferable that re-strikes do not occur as they can stress the attached equipment by causing high recovery voltages.

(21) Recovery voltage: The voltage that appears across the terminals of a pole of a circuit-interrupting device upon interruption of the current. RRRV means the Rate of rise of recovery voltage. When current is interrupted quickly, a recovery voltage is generated, and faster the rate of change of current, the higher the recovery voltage becomes, It is important for a switching device to reform the dielectric breakdown strength of an interrupting medium quickly following the breaking of the current, in order to be able to withstand the recovery voltage generated. A switching device that can withstand a high recovery voltage will be less likely to re-strike.

(22) Arc extinguisher: The arc extinguisher extinguishes the arc produced when the contacts are pulled apart to interrupt current flow. The higher the voltage make the interrupt of the flow of current becomes harder. The contacts of a switching device upon which the arc is deliberately drawn after the main contacts have parted is said to be arcing contact

3.6 MEDIUM VOLTAGE MINIMUM OIL CIRCUIT BREAKER (MOCB).

Minimum oil circuit breaker is a switching device using a relatively small quantity (3 to 4 litters / pole) of mineral oil (Shell diala D) for its arc interruption. Indoor type MOCB's are intended for installation in the metal-clad cubicles. The circuit breaker pole consists of cross-vented interrupting chamber mounted in a fiberglass reinforced plastic tube. The insulating cylinder placed in the housing is of glass textile impregnated, with epoxy resin of a high mechanical endurance, which is completely filled with oil. The upper and lower current terminal, as well as oil level indicator are installed outside of the cylinder. In the upper part of the cylinder, above air **Cushion,** there is an expansion chamber with appropriate valves. All three poles have one common operating mechanism. Single pole medium voltage circuit breakers are used for Railway track electrification. Interrupter tube (housing) is designed to withstand the stresses generated during breaking operations. Figure 3.6 (a) illustrates the pole element (interrupter) of a medium voltage minimum oil circuit breaker.

LEGEND: 1. Gas exhaust vent;

2. Oil filling plug for filling oil;

3. Oil gauge / Oil level indicator

4. Tulip type spring-loaded contact.

5. Moving contact / Contact rod

6. Current carrying ferrule

7. Roller contacts

8. Insulating tube

9. Flange / Crank case

10. Oil draining plug.

11. Interrupting chamber

12. Terminal stud

13. Insulating rod.

14. Lever system/ Link

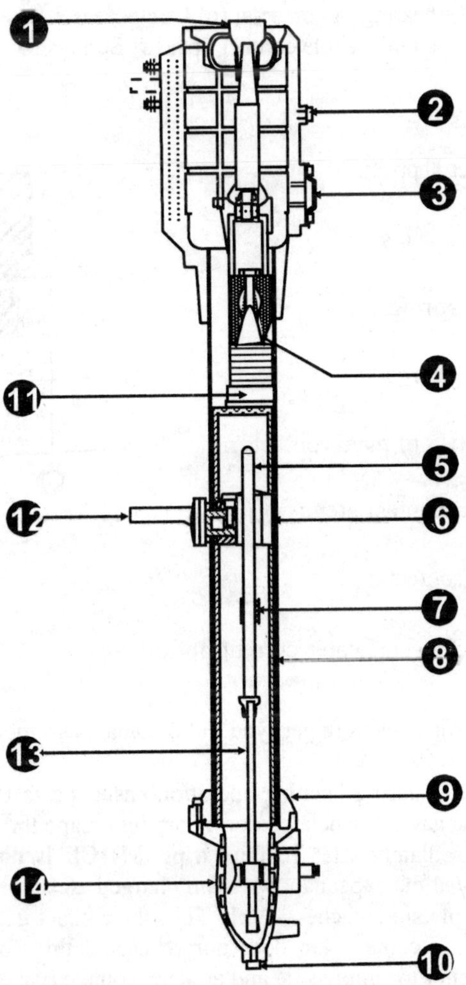

Fig. 3.6 (a): Pole element of minimum oil circuit breaker.

AC arcs are extinguished by utilizing the natural current zero. The main function of the arc-quenching device is to de-ionize the break during current zero in order to establish the dielectric strength of the contact gap as quickly as possible. During contact separation the arc decomposes the dielectric oil. The gases formed due to the decomposition of the oil causes increase in pressure within the chamber fitted in the interrupter. Arcing chamber accept and extinguish the arc. After the arc extinction, the contact space is filled with dielectric oil. Figure 3.6 (b) illustrates typical finger type Tulip contact assembly. The pole assembly houses the tulip type cup shaped contact provided with individually spring loaded contact fingers. Main contact is of electrolytic copper with tungsten copper tips. Coiled spring is of phosphor bronze. Moving contact stem is made of electrolytic copper. All contact surfaces of the current path are silver-plated or silver coated.

The spark gap and the contact rod tip are made as sinter-contacts on the copper tungsten basis to obtain a high thermal and electric conductivity. Contact design has following features: (a) Low contact resistance to minimize excessive heating of contacts; (b) Contact resistance is inversely proportional to the contact pressure; (c) Self cleaning type replaceable contact tips; (d) Springs having gradually rising characteristic.

LEGEND:

1. Contact support;
2. Main contacts;
3. Coiled spring;
4. Moving contact;
5. Arcing tip of main contact;
6. Moving contact stem;
7. Roller contacts;
8. Arrow (→) indicates current path.

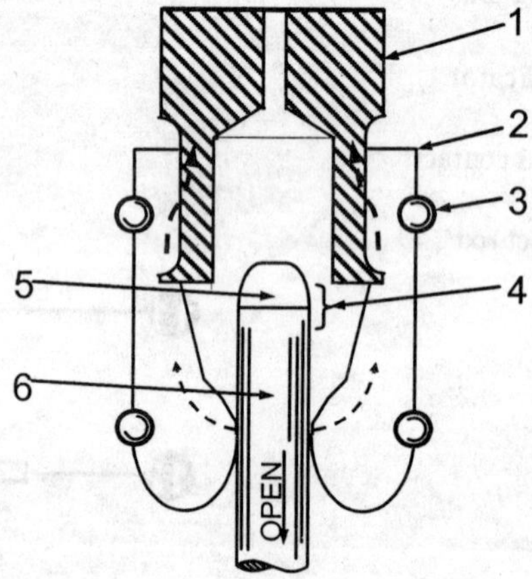

Fig. 3.6 (b): Typical finger type Tulip contact assembly for minimum oil circuit breakers.

The injected oil flow during opening operation ensures a fast dielectric recovery thereby making the breaker, free operation. The gasses associated during arcing escape through an exhaust vent. Oil shall be replaced once in 3 years or immediately after 10 fault trips. **MOCB is not suitable for capacitor switching.** When the current is interrupted the capacitance remain charged at + Vph (Phase voltage). After half a cycle, the voltage of contacts on supply side reaches – Vph. Thus the contact gap is subjected to a voltage of 2 Vph, half a cycle after current zero. If contact gap does not withstand this voltage, the breaker re-strikes causing release of energy from capacitor to supply side and another voltage rise after next current zero giving 4 Vph. The result is that the stress on the insulation and the contact gap due to this voltage is much higher than before the first re-strike. MOCB has a tendency to re-strike. Hence, MOCB is not suitable for capacitor switching. Other disadvantages are: (a) Arc produced in the oil is inflammable and if arc is not extinguished explosion may occur; (b) Oil absorbs moisture and dielectric strength reduces by carbonization; (c) MOCB is not suitable for those breakers which has to operate frequently (example furnace motor); (d) At lower ambient temperature the viscosity of switchgear oil sharply rises and the speed of contact travel reduces; (e) The dust particles and sludge formation can create flash over due to tracking. The operating mechanism is similar to the one illustrated in figure 3.7 (d).

Figure 3.6 (c) shows the control circuit diagram of a typical medium voltage circuit breaker. When the control power is switched on spring charging motor receives power at terminals 3 & 4, if the spring is in discharged position the motor starts to charge the spring. When the spring is fully charged, spring charging limit switch 52 SM/LS opens its NC contact to stop the spring charge motor. Closing latch monitoring switch 52CL/MS is closed only when latch is capable of blocking fully charged closing spring. This spring held open when the draw out type circuit breaker is between test and service position. 52 CL/MS is open momentarily during the process of closing or opening operations and it will not permit to charge the spring during the process of operation. The closing coil (terminals 6 & 7) is established through the normally closed (NC) contact of anti-pump relay (52Y). This relay prevents re-closing on a sustained closing command on a closed circuit breaker.

Trip latch checking switch 52 LCS is closed when latch is reset means breaker is fully open position. Normally closed auxiliary contact of the circuit breaker 52b, is connected in series with the closing coil 52X. This prevents the accidental energizing of closing coil when the breaker is already closed. Spring charge limit switch 52CHG (Contact closed when closing spring is fully charged) is wired in series to the closing coil to prevent an attempt to close the breaker when the spring is in discharged position. Spring will recharge automatically after every closing operation of the circuit breaker.

LEGEND:

1). 52CL/MS: Closing-latch monitoring switch;
2). 52SH/LS: Spring charge limit switch.
3). 52/CHG: Closing springs are fully charged;
4). 52CC: Closing coil or spring release coil.
5). 52Y: Anti-pump relay; 6) 52TC: Trip coil

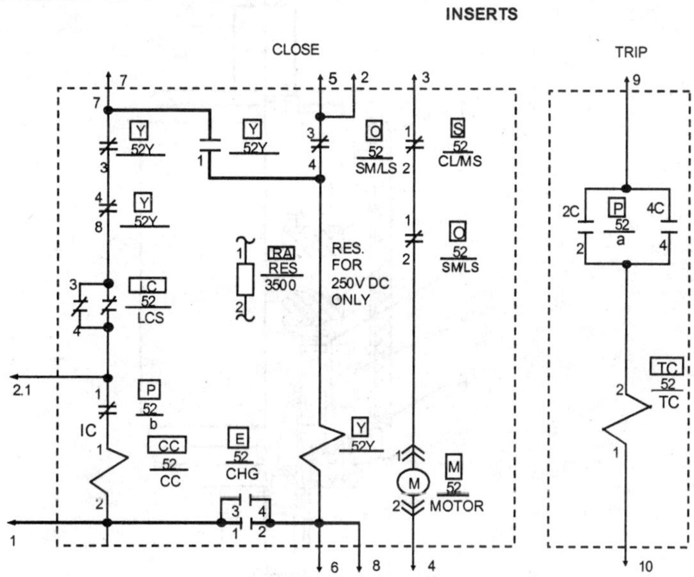

Fig. 3.6 (c): DC control circuit diagram of medium voltage MOCB / Vacuum circuit breaker.

During a close operation cam rotation switch 52CM/LS momentarily closes to energize anti-pump relay 52Y and the relay coil is sealed in through 52Y normally open contact. This relay will remain energized as long as DC control power is available at terminals 7 & 6. Anti-pump relay when energized opens its NC contacts to de-energize the spring release coil (closing coil). After closing operation, operator releases the spring-loaded pistol grip handle of the closing switch or releases the finger from the breaker close pushbutton. Then the control power to terminal 7 is disconnected and anti-pump relay de-energizes. Assume that during the process of closing operation a fault is persisting in the feeder, the protection relay will operates and energize the circuit breaker trip coil, which in turn open the circuit breaker and isolate the faulty feeder. Assume that the operator still not released the closing switch or a sustained closing command is being received anti-pump relay will prevent to energize closing coil. This is known as anti-pump feature.

Trip circuit is connected across terminals 9 & 10. Two numbers normally open auxiliary contacts are wired in series with the trip coil. This is for preventing the accidental energizing of trip coil when the breaker is in open position. Protective relay contact can initiate trip signal to energize the trip coil and it is not designed for breaking the supply to the trip coil. When a trip signal is applied the shunt trip coil will energize momentarily to open the breaker. When the breaker is opened trip coil is de-energized through 52a breaker auxiliary contacts. Hence the purpose of the auxiliary contact is breaking the supply to the trip coil too. Terminals 1 and 21 are for auto re-closing facility. Assume that the trip signal is persisting in the trip circuit of a breaker, which is tripped open (This condition persist before resetting the relay, which causes to trip the breaker.) and if a close signal is given the breaker is attempting to close but the trip circuit also simultaneously energizes to open the breaker. But during the process of closing operation the breaker auxiliary contacts closes before its primary contacts closes. This will permit the trip coil to energize before the breaker completes it's closing operation. The linkage in the breaker operating mechanism is mechanically trip free in any location on the closing stroke. By energizing the trip coil will rotate the trip latch and permit the circuit breaker to open fully. The linkage will reset as in a normal operation and the closing spring will recharge automatically. This is known as trip free operation.

3.7 MEDIUM VOLTAGE VACUUM CIRCUIT BREAKERS (VCB).

A circuit breaker in which, uses a vacuum bottle as its interrupter is called vacuum circuit breaker. Vacuum is a space that contains no air, gas or matter. VCB consists of motor or manual charged spring operated mechanism with individual vacuum interrupters actuated by common drive shaft arrangement. Medium voltage VCB's are ideally suitable for Arc furnace duties, capacitor bank switching and feeder switching. Partial section of a vacuum interrupter is shown in Figure 3.7 (a).

Legend

1. Insulator
2. Fixed contact
3. Movable contact
4. Metal bellows
5. Screen
6. Guide cylinder
7. Lid
8. Cover

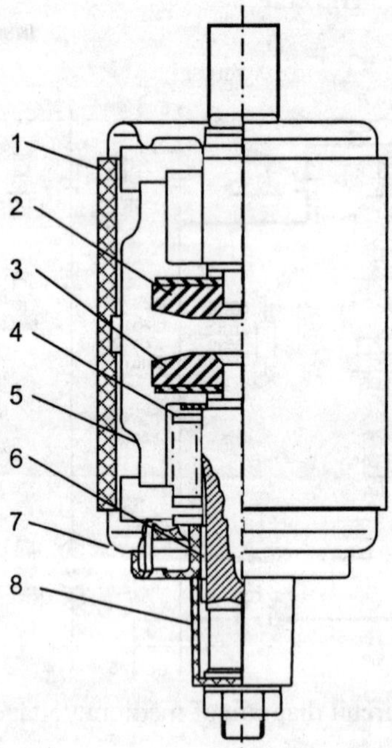

Fig. 3.7 (a): Partial section of a vacuum interrupter

In a Vacuum circuit breaker, vacuum interrupters are used for breaking and making load or fault currents. When the contacts in vacuum interrupter separate, the current to be interrupted initiates a metal vapour arc discharge and flows through the plasma until the next current zero. The arc is then extinguished and the conductive metal vapour condenses on the metal surfaces within a matter of microseconds. As a result the dielectric strength in the breaker builds up very rapidly.

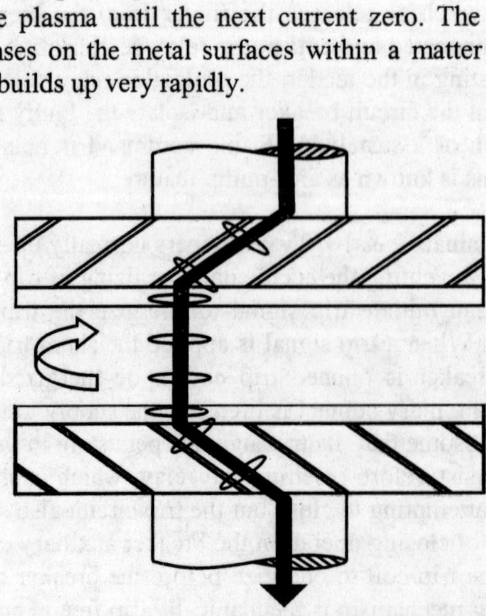

Fig. 3.7 (b): Arc rotating on the contact surfaces of Vacuum circuit breaker (Courtesy, Siemens Ag).

To prevent the contacts from overheating they are designed to ensure that the arc does not remain stationary. The magnetic field causes the arc to rotate on the contact surface due to the diagonal slots. Chopped current creates over-voltages in a network. These over-voltages have to be kept below the insulation level of the network.

The properties of a vacuum interrupter depend largely on the material and form of the contact. Oxygen free copper chromium alloy is the best material for medium voltage circuit breaker. In this alloy, chromium is distributed through copper in the form of fine grains. This material combines good arc extinguishing characteristic with a reduced tendency to contact welding and low chopping current when switching inductive load. Copper bismuth alloy or copper beryllium alloy are also used for manufacturing vacuum interrupter contacts. Figure 3.7 (c) illustrates the CrCu-alloy contact used in medium voltage Vacuum circuit breakers.

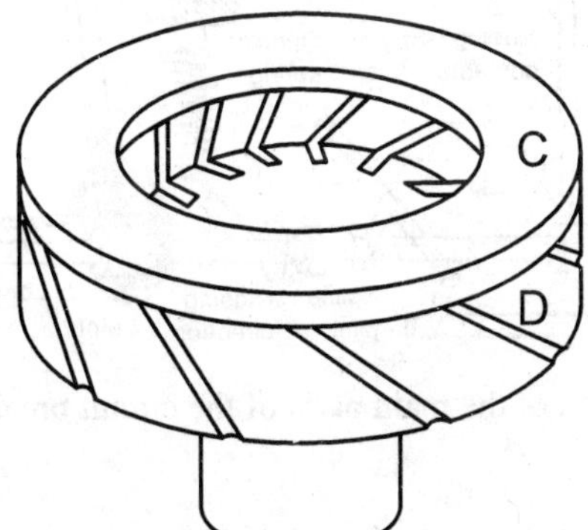

Fig. 3.7 (c): CrCu-alloy contact for vacuum circuit breaker (Courtesy, Siemens)

Due to the extremely low static interrupter chamber pressure of 10^{-4} to 10^{-8} bars, only a relatively small contact gap is required to achieve a high dielectric strength. In the opening process a vacuum arc is generated between the contacts, initiated by the current to be interrupted. The current continues to flow for a time through this plasma of electrons and metal vapour ions. Due to the spiral slotting of the contacts, the magnetic field generated causes the vacuum arc to rotate, and so local overheating. Contact gap varies from 6 to 20mm for medium voltage circuit breakers. The application of vacuum circuit breaker is limited to medium voltage level only, i.e, 3.6 KV, 7.2 KV, 12 KV, 15 KV, 25 KV, 35 KV.

Operating mechanism:
The operating mechanism is almost identical for medium voltage range minimum oil circuit breakers, vacuum circuit breakers and SF6 gas insulated circuit breakers. They are of the stored energy type, i.e. they are capable of performing OFF-ON-OFF cycle when their springs have been charged. The closing spring of the breaker is re-charged automatically after each operation. In case of a failure of the motor operating mechanism, the breaker can be operated manually by inserting a crank in the drive gearbox and the springs are charged. The control circuit of the drive motor is interrupted by insertion of the emergency crank. Figure 3.7 (d) is the schematic illustration of the main parts of the circuit breaker operating mechanism.

The circuit breaker closes or opens due to the action of various mechanical and electrical components known as operating mechanism. It consists of a spring and latching device, which holds the contact closed. As soon as the contact closes the spring become charged. The spring can be charged electrically by using spring charging motor, which will automatically operate on the action of a limit switch provided in the operating mechanism assembly. Breaker can be closed automatically through the use of solenoid known as closing coil. By discharging the spring the latch has moved to force the contact open. Breaker can be tripped electrically through the use of a solenoid known as tripping coil. Protection relays and trip devices senses the circuit problems and energize trip coil, which causes breaker contact to open and automatic isolation of faulted circuits.

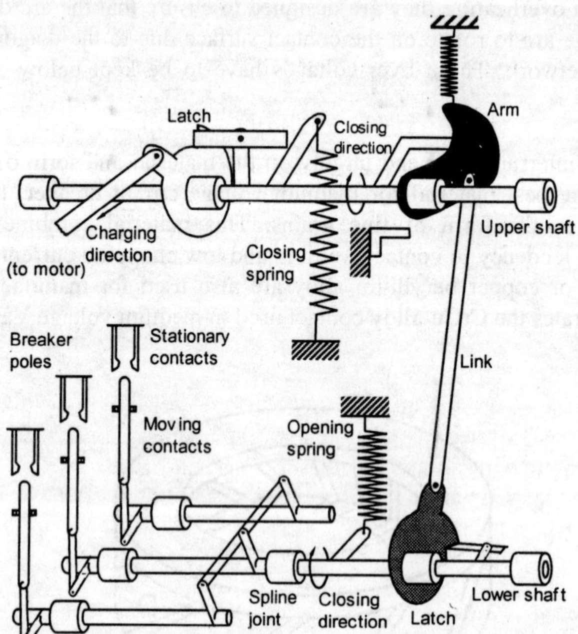

Fig. 3.7 (d): Schematic illustration of the main parts of the circuit breaker operating mechanism.

Contact-wipe and contact erosion:

(a) Wiping spring is used for applying force to the vacuum interrupter contact and to provide opening kick of force. An indicator is provided in the wipe spring assembly to indicate wipe. By using a filler gauge between the wipe indicator and erosion disc the difference in readings at the closed and open position of the breaker can be measured and adjusted if necessary.

(b) During long operation some parts of the contact tip will consume and accumulate in the erosion chamber in the form of powder. Contact erosion will decrease the wipe, which may be brought back to normal by performing wipe adjustment. Erosion indicator, (a visible white mark in the interrupter) will indicate the erosion, which can be examined in the de-energized and breaker closed position. Erosion indicator will indicate the erosion. Erosion rate is expressed in grams per column.

(3) The metal vapour plasma of an arc drawn in vacuum is highly conductive. As the arc voltage is only between 20 to 200 V, energy conversion in the break is also minimal. The high conductivity, in conjunction with the small energy conversion and short arcing times (bellow 15 milliseconds) are the reasons for the insignificant contact piece erosion and long electrical life of the vacuum interrupter. Figure 3.7 (e) illustrates the wipe indicator of a vacuum circuit breaker.

LEGEND:

1. Wipe spring
2. Operating rod insulator
3. Lock washer
4. Interrupter clamp
5. Wipe indicator
6. Clamp screw
7. Erosion disk
8. Lock nut
9. Hexagon projection

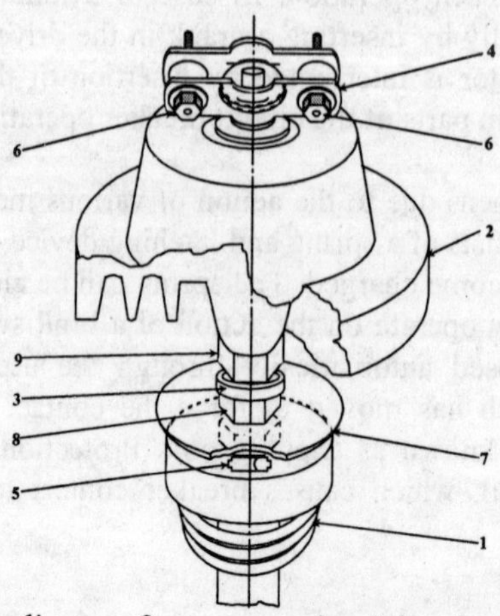

Fig. 3.7 (e): Wipe indicator of a vacuum circuit breaker.

Control circuit diagram of vacuum circuit breaker is shown in Figure 3.6 (c) of section 3.6.

Advantages and disadvantages of Vacuum circuit breakers:

Typical advantages of vacuum circuit breakers are:

1. Replaceable interrupter are sealed for life and no maintenance is required on the vacuum bottle.
2. No switching by-products i.e. cooling media and long switching life.
3. Constant quality of extinguishing medium
4. Suitable for capacitor bank switching where high rate of recovery of dielectric strength required.
5. Vacuum is non-flaming and non-poisonous.
6. Suitable for auto re-closing duty.
7. High summation current breaking capacity

Typical disadvantages of vacuum circuit breakers are:

1. Its use is limited up to 38KV system. Not suitable for high voltage applications.
2. Current chopping while breaking inductive current. This can be minimized by, using special contact material. This chopping current must be minimized in order to prevent unduly high over voltage building up while switching inductive load.
3. Re-striking while opening capacitor bank. Special re-strike-free interrupters are required for capacitor current breaking. For switching over voltage protection, surge arresters are being used.
4. R.C Surge suppressors are required for motor switching. It consists of a resistor (R) and capacitor (C) in series and connected between phase-to-ground near the rotating machine terminals. Capacitor connected to ground, absorbs the steep wave fronts of surge voltages.

Vacuum Integrity test:

Vacuum integrity test is performed, by using portable integrity test set 0 to 60 KV, direct current. The output is programmed to raise voltage (selectable raise time 500V/sec or 3000V/sec) at a preset rate to the desired test level. Once the unit reaches the preset voltage a dwell timer will hold the voltage at that level for the preset time duration. After the dwell time has elapsed, the unit will return to zero. Any failure during the test will be indicated on a " failure" lamp and the breakdown voltage will be indicated on the memory KV meter.

Test is to be performed on each pole with the circuit breaker in the open position by connecting the test leads between line terminal and load terminal of the vacuum circuit breaker. Following DC test voltages are recommended: (a) For 6.6 KV to 15 KV interrupters 40 KV, DC; (b) For 20 KV to 36 KV interrupters 60 KV, DC. Test duration is 5 second after attaining required test voltages. Condition of the interrupter is indicated in the test set it-self. If vacuum is lost, the open interrupter will flash over internally on application of test voltage. Figure 3.7 (f) shows the typical test circuit for vacuum integrity test.

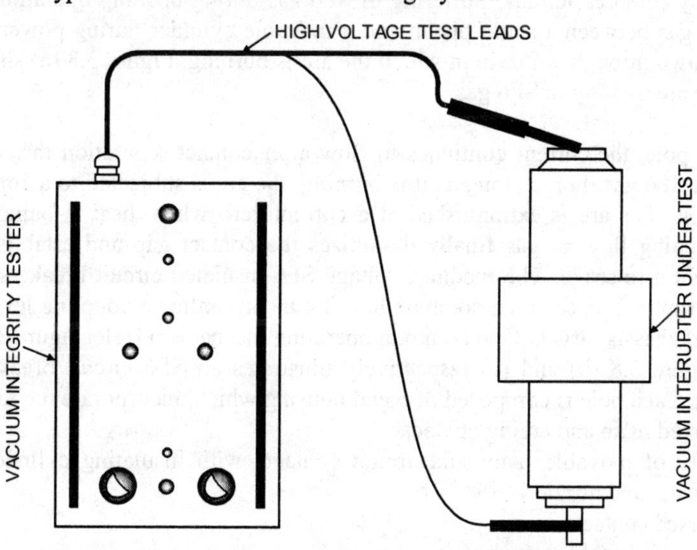

Fig. 3.7 (f): Vacuum integrity test on medium voltage vacuum circuit breaker.

Tests on vacuum circuit breakers: All tests shall be performed after pulling out the breaker from its cubicle.

(a) Simple method of checking vacuum in the interrupter at site is to check the force required for pulling the moving contact. If vacuum is higher, higher force is required to pull the moving contact. Simple hand held spring balance can be used to measure the pulling force. If vacuum is low the pulling force will be less and the interrupter may be subjected to vacuum integrity test.

(b) Over potential test by using AC or DC high-pressure test set: Test is to be performed for one minute on each pole with the circuit breaker in the open position: (a) Line to load; (b) Line to ground; (c) Load to ground. With the circuit breaker in closed position; (a) Phase-to-phase RY, YB, BR and (b) Phase to ground of each pole. Test voltage twice the value of rated voltage is applied gradually.

(c) Contact resistance measurement: Perform a milli-volt drop test or watt-loss test from line to load on each phase of a closed circuit breaker with the test leads at the line and load as demonstrated in section 3.10.

(d) Timing test: Perform a timing test on close/open operation as demonstrated in section 3.12 and compare the test result with pre-commissioning tests.

(d) Power factor or dissipation factor test: Tan delta tester (resistivity trster) described in figure 4.19 (f) of Chapter # 4 can be used for testing the degree of purity as well as aging conditions of the circuit breaker. Test procedure is described below.

Breaker should be in the open position with arc chutes installed. Power must be isolated or breaker is withdrawn if it is withdrawable type. Connect the high voltage test lead of the test set to the line side and low voltage test lead to the load side. Connect the ground test lead to the frame of the circuit breaker under test.

(a) Run a power factor/dissipation test in the "GUARD" mode (line side of phase to ground) and record the result of each phase.

(b) Run a power factor/dissipation factor test in the "UST" mode (Phase line to load terminals) and record the result of each phase.

Now connect the high voltage test lead of the test set to the load side and the low voltage test lead to the line side. (c) Run a power factor/ dissipation factor test in the "GUARD" mode (load side of Phase to ground) and record the result of each phase.

For all those tests correct for temperature, if necessary based on test set manufacturers guidelines.

3.8 MEDIUM VOLTAGE SF6 GAS INSULATED CIRCUIT BREAKERS

Medium voltage circuit breakers (3.3 KV to 36 KV) are intended for indoor installation and cubicle mounted draw out type design. Sulphur hexaflouride (SF6) gas is used as a medium for insulation and arc extinguishing. By operation principle they belong to a "PUFFER" type of SF6 circuit breakers, where gas stream for arc extinguishing is realized by compression and puffering of SF6 gas during opening operation. Puffer principle involves compressing the gas between a static piston and a movable cylinder during power interruption. The compressed gas is then blown through a nozzle in which the arc is burning. Figure 3.8 (a) shows the rotational breaking techniques of the arc rotating in SF6 gas.

In an SF6 circuit breaker pole, the current continues to flow after contact separation through the arc whose plasma consists of ionized SF6 gas. For, as long as it is burning, the arc is subjected to a constant flow of gas, which extracts heat from it. The arc is extinguished at a current zero when, heat is being extracted by the falling current. The continuing flow of gas finally de-ionizes the contact gap and establishes the dielectric strength required to prevent a re-strike. The medium voltage SF6 insulated circuit breakers are composed of three identical poles (interrupters) placed on a common housing incorporating a coupling leverage system. The housing is fixed on a metal chassis / truck. One common operating mechanism [refer figure 3.7 (b)] is fixed on the chassis front side. Figure 3.8 (b) and (c) respectively illustrates an SF6 circuit breaker pole in closed position and open position. Each pole is composed of metal housing which, incorporate the following:

1. Upper fixed main and arcing contacts
2. Assembly of movable main and arcing contacts with insulating cylinder, piston for gas compression and nozzle.
3. Lower fixed contacts
4. Bushing with suitable terminals.

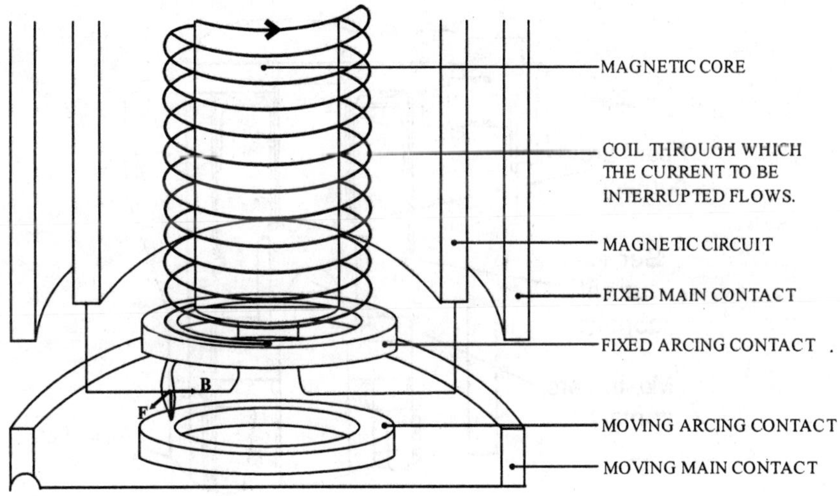

Fig. 3.8 (a): Rotational breaking techniques of the arc rotating in SF6 gas.

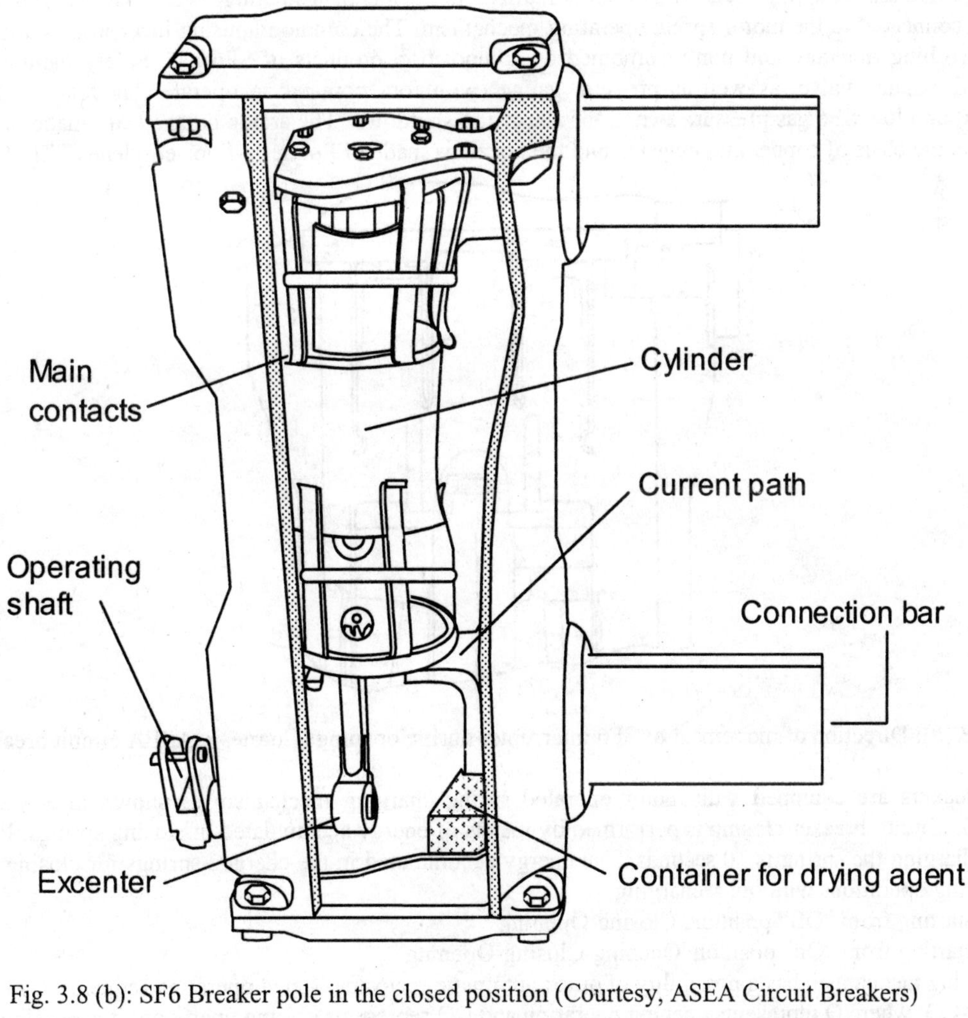

Fig. 3.8 (b): SF6 Breaker pole in the closed position (Courtesy, ASEA Circuit Breakers)

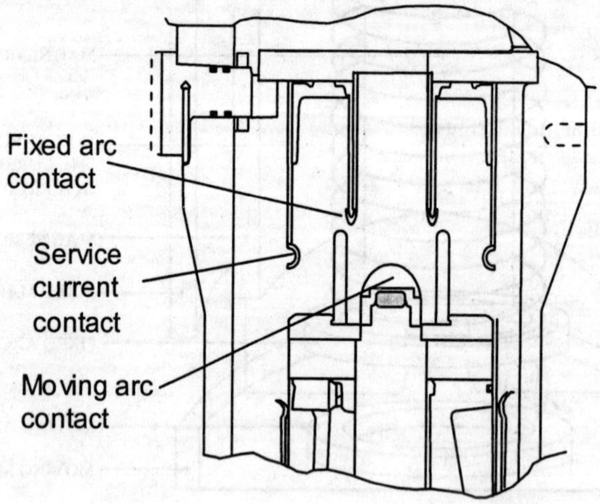

Fig. 3.8 (c): SF6 breaker pole in the open position (Courtesy, ASEA circuit breakers)

Figure 3.8 (d) illustrates the direction of movement of SF6 interrupter during opening. The connection between movable piston and coupling leverage system is realized by means of insulating lever. The coupling leverage system is connected to the motor spring operating mechanism. The common housing incorporates a molecular sleeve absorbing moisture and non-recombined de-composition products of SF6 gas. Safety membrane, gas filling and exhaust valve, as well as pressure gauge (with four contacts to operate flag relay and remote indication) and low SF6 gas pressure switch for alarm and shutdown. The arcing contacts are made of sintered material on the basis of copper and tungsten and the nozzle is made of Polytetra-fluor-ethylene (TEFLON).

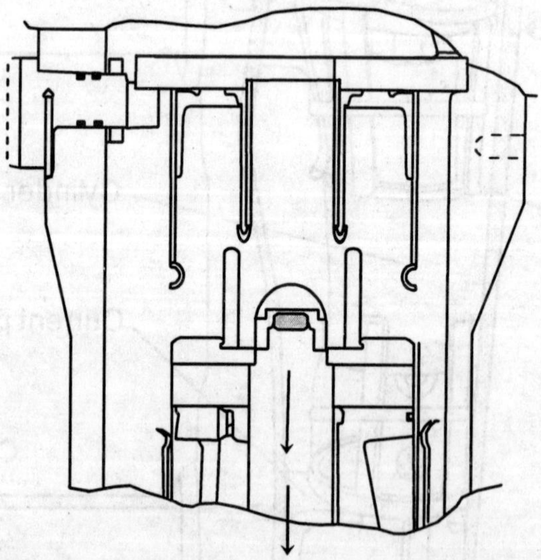

Fig. 3.8 (d): Direction of movement of SF6 interrupter during opening (Courtesy, ASEA circuit breakers)

Circuit breakers are equipped with motor operated spring charging mechanism as shown in figure (b) of section 3.7. Circuit breaker closing is performed by means of energy accumulated in closing springs. Required time for charging the spring is 10 seconds. The energy accumulated in the charged springs for closing enables the following operations with out recharging.

(1) Starting from "Off" position, Closing-Opening

(2) Starting from "On" position, Opening-Closing-Opening.

The operating mechanism has a possibility of quick automatic reclosing. Rated operating sequence O-0.3sec-CO-15sec-CO, where O represents opening operation and CO represents closing operation. It is possible to incorporate parallel opening release, under voltage release, operations counter, permanent anti condensation heater, mechanical interlock, anti-pump relay etc. It is also possible to include a condition indicator, which monitor and perform following activities:

- Records the number of interruptions
- Detect the current that interrupted
- Trigger an alarm if the gas pressure is low
- Opening speed is measured and an alarm is given if any abnormality
- Prevent the breaker to close if the gas pressure is low
- Blocking of close command when the gas pressure is low for subsequent tripping.

SF6 Circuit breaker characteristics (ASEA circuit breakers):

Item	Description	SF6 circuit breakers up to 24KV	36KV-SF6 circuit breaker
1	SF6 gas pressure at 20°C ambient temperature	2.5 bar	3.0 bar
2	Weight of SF6 gas per pole	1.0 Kg	2.0 Kg
3	Low gas pressure alarm (Pressure switch setting)	2.2 bar	2.7 bar
4	Low gas pressure tripping of breaker	1.8 bar	2.3 bar
5	Locking of closing circuit of breaker	1.8 bar	2.3 bar
6	Expected gas leakage per year	1%	1%
7	Closing time	< 100 milliseconds	< 100 milliseconds
8	Opening time	< 50 milliseconds	< 50 milliseconds
9	Operating duty cycle	CO-3 Min-CO	CO-3Min-CO

Possible refilling with SF6 gas is done by a simple connection of gas cylinder to the filling valve.

Advantages and disadvantages of SF6 circuit breaker:

Advantages: (1) Low level of current chopping and no excessive switching over voltage.

(2) No multiple re-ignition, no explosion because of SF6 is inert gas.

(3) Minimal contact erosion due to the inert gas and half cycle of the arc.

(4) Well suited for switching of transformers and reactors.

(5) Well suited for capacitor bank switching because: (a) Inrush current magnitude and frequency is negligible; (b) Re-strike free; (c) Re-ignition does not cause over-voltage.

Disadvantages: (1) Low summation current breaking capacity while comparing to Vacuum circuit breaker

Fig 3.8 (e) shows the schematic diagram of an SF6 insulated circuit breaker. Following devices are used to represent the circuit.

52: Circuit breaker
M: Spring charging motor
Y: Closing solenoid
M1 & M2: Charging contact
QF: Auxiliary contact of Breaker
KN: Anti-pumping relay
SE: Latched release contact
Y01 & Y02 shunt release
YM: Under voltage release
M3: Operating mechanism
Charged contact
SP: SF6 gas pressure switch
SM1: Closing push button
SM2: Opening push button
SM3: Opening push button
Under voltage release
Sn: Closing disabling contact

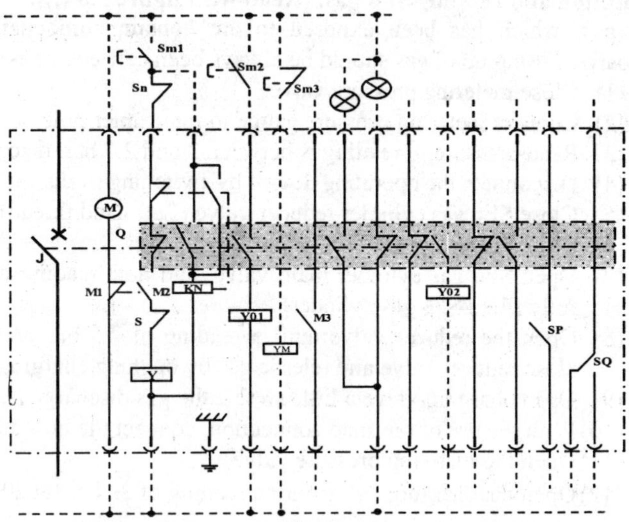

Fig: 3.8: (e): DC control circuit diagram of SF6 gas insulated circuit breaker (Courtesy, Merlin Gerin)

Operation sequence:
With the circuit breaker open, the closing springs uncharged, the control power source energized, and motor disconnect switch closed, operation occurs as follows:
(1) Immediately upon the availability of control power, the spring charging motor energizes and charges the closing springs. When the closing springs are fully charged, the limit-switch contact M1 is opened and M2 is closed.
(2) Operation of the breaker close switch (pushbutton SM1) energizes the latch release coil (closing solenoid Y) through the circuit breaker auxiliary contact 52b, the normally closed contact of anti-pump relay KN, the limit switch contact M2, closing disabling contact Sn, and SF6 gas pressure switch S. The latch release coil (Closing coil Y) release the closing latch. The springs then discharge to close the circuit breaker.
(3) When the spring discharge limit switch contact M1 is closed and M2 is opened and the spring charge motor energizes, and which in turn recharges the closing springs.
(4) When the circuit breaker closes, simultaneously the anti-pump relay (KN) energizes and opens its NC contact, which de-energizes the closing coil (Y). Anti-pump relay NO contact closes, which seals-in the anti-pump relay coil as long as the breaker close signal is maintained. The purpose of the anti-pump relay is to prevent pumping of the closing mechanism when closing a faulty power circuit.
(5) After the breaker has closed and when the 'close' switch (Pushbutton SM1) is released by, the operator the anti-pump relay de-energize.
(6) The circuit breaker can be opened or tripped by, operation of the trip control switch (Pushbutton SM2), which energizes the trip coil Y01 through the breaker auxiliary contact 52a.
(7) The under voltage device, if furnished, provides a direct acting AC under voltage tripping feature. The device must be energized to close the breaker and also to maintain the breaker in a closed position. During a fault trip protective relay will operate and which in turn energizes the lockout relay 86E to trip the circuit breaker.

Indication lamps:
White, amber, green and red indication lamps are used to indicate the status of a circuit breaker.
(a) White indication lamp lit through draw out type circuit breaker position switch NO contact when the breaker is in connected (service) position.
(b) Amber indication lamp lit through draw out type circuit breaker position switch NC contact when the circuit breaker is in test or disconnected position.
(c) Green indication lamp lit through breaker auxiliary contact 52b when the breaker is in open position.
(d) Red indication lamp lit through breaker auxiliary contact 52a when the breaker is in closed position.
(e) Trip circuit healthy indication (white indication lamp) is connected in series to the operating coil of lockout relay 86E. During a fault in the system, protective relay will operate which in turn energizes the lockout relay 86E and seal-in. Hence the lamp will go off and again lit when the lockout relay is rest.

Inspection and refilling SF6 gas: [Read with figure 3.8 (f)].
SF6 gas, which has been exposed to arc contain components, which combined with moisture become corrosive. Filling up of gas should be always been carried out as follows. [Refer Figure 3.8 (f)]

(1) Close metering pressure valve.
(2) Connect metering pressure gauge to interrupter pole.
(3) Read pressure, if reading is between 2 and 2.5 bar, disconnect gauge.
(4) Disconnect the operating device by switching of the motor, and operate by hand "close" and "open".
(5) Close SF6 gas cylinder reducer valve (Left hand thread).
(6) Close charging valve.
(7) Open SF6 gas cylinder main valve, and note reading on gauge (Should be approximately 70 bar for fully filled SF6 gas cylinder)
(8) Open the reducer valve until a reading of 2.5 bar pressure is registered. If the reading is too high, close reducer valve and release gas by opening charging valve with hose disconnected.
(9) Open charging-valve a little so that the gas discharge little bit, thereby emptying hose of any air.
(10) With the use of the snap connection, connect the hose to the metering tube.
(11) Open the metering pressure valve
(12) Open the charging-valve until a reading of 2.5bar (at 20°C) is registered on the metering gauge.

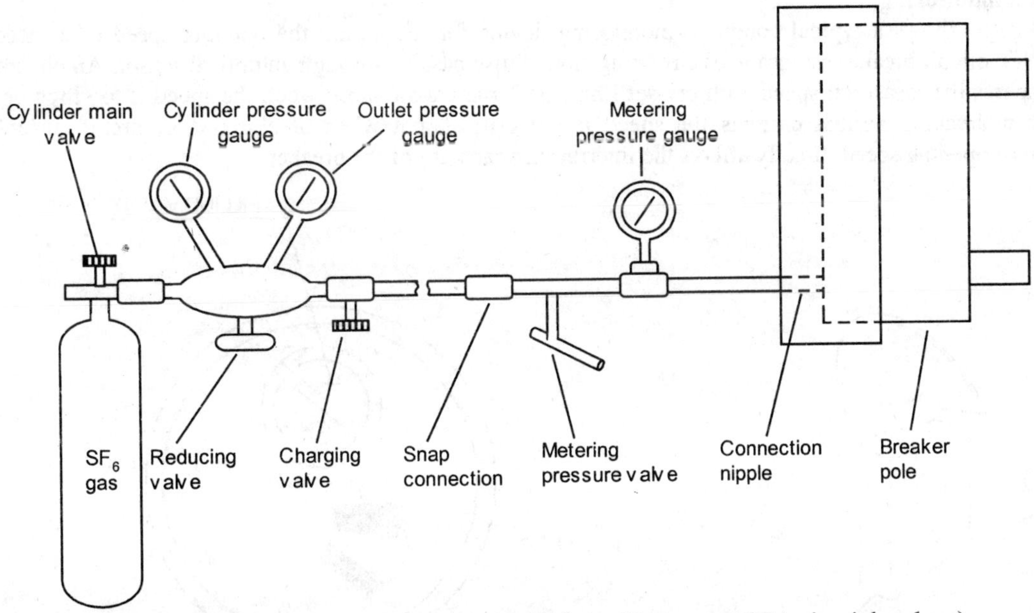

Fig. 3.8 (f): Filling of breaker pole with SF6 gas (Courtesy ASEA circuit breakers)

(13) Close the SF6 gas cylinder main valve.
(14) Close both charging and metering valves.
(15) Loosen the snap connection. (Note: The hose contains SF6 gas at a pressure of 2.5 bar and this will blow out.
(16) Loosen the metering unit until gas begins to escape, then open immediately the metering valve so that the back pressure valve in the interrupter pole automatically closes.
(17) Disconnect metering unit.
(18) Check the O-rings of the covers, if they are dry exchange with new once which have been greased. Mineral grease must not be used on EPDM O-rings. Replace the cover on the connection nipple.

Inspection of operating speed:
Inspection of operating speed can be made with a capacitive sensor. The sensor is connected to a conventional oscoilloscope. Typical speed measurement travel diagram of an ASEA brand SF6 insulated medium voltage circuit breaker is given in figure 3.8 (g).

Closing speed a/10:	Minimum 2.0 metre/second
Opening speed b/10:	3.7 to 4.0 metre/second
Closing time with nominal voltage:	Maximum 75 milliseconds
Opening time with nominal voltage:	33 to 38 milliseconds
Contact travel:	80 to 84 millimetres

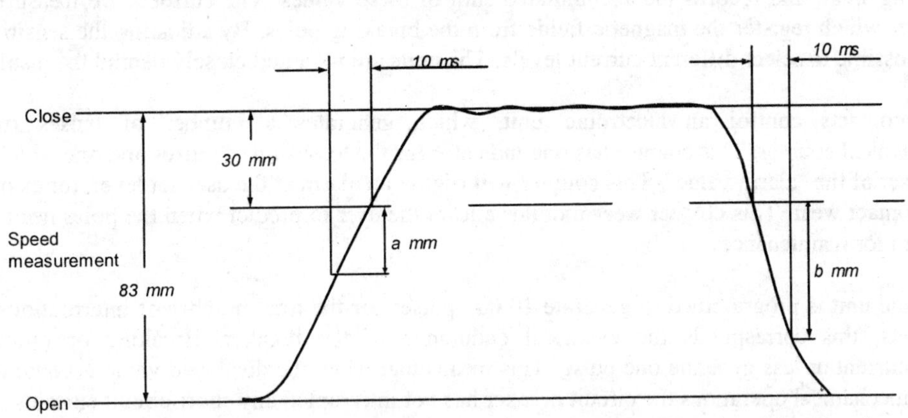

Fig. 3.8 (g): Speed measurement travel diagram (Courtesy, ASEA circuit breakers).

Condition monitoring:

Figure 3.8 (h) shows a typical condition-monitoring device for measuring the opening speed of a medium voltage SF6 circuit breaker by means of a rotating slotted disc passing through an optical sensor. An electronic unit compares the measured speed with pre-set limits and triggers an alarm when the speed is too high or too low. When breaking normal currents the speed is not critical, but when breaking short-circuit currents a reduction of opening speed directly affects the interrupting capacity of the breaker.

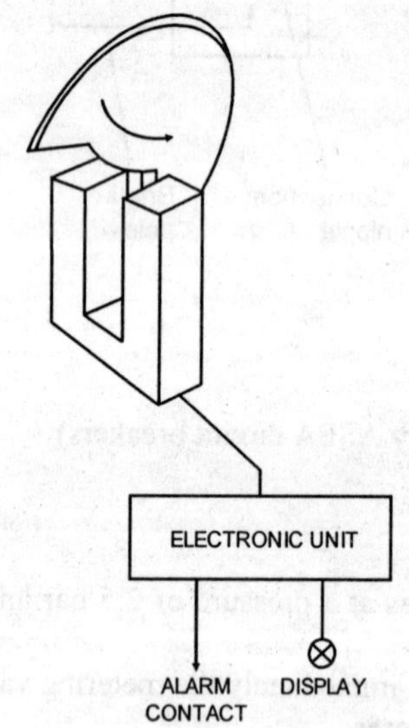

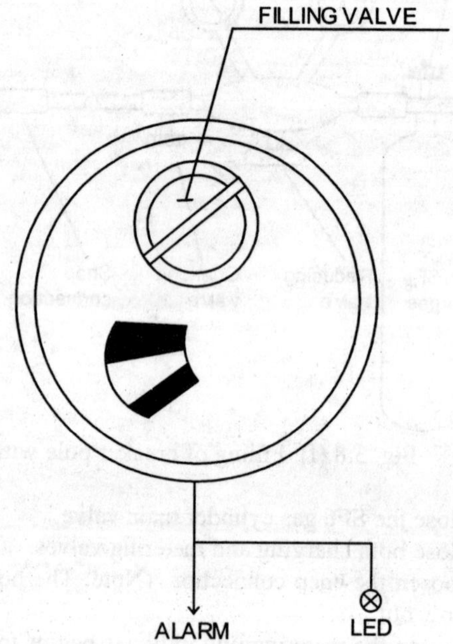

Fig. 3.8 (h): Contact speed monitor for SF6 breaker. Fig. 3.8 (i): SF6 gas density monitor with indicator.

The SF6 circuit breaker is very tolerant of a possible, though unlikely, loss of gas. The interrupting capability decreases very slowly as the pressure is reduced, and even at atmospheric pressure it is capable of breaking rated, continuous current. The condition monitor incorporates density (temperature compensated pressure) sensors to eliminate the need for necessary checks of the SF6 gas pressure.

Figure 3.8 (i) illustrates a density monitor, which has an indicator showing whether the breaker can break full short-circuit current (green area); at least rated, continuous current (Yellow area); or if there is risk for air leaking in (red area). The monitor will trigger both a visual indication (a red LED) and an alarm contact when the pressure approaches the lower limit at which a full short-circuit interruption may be completed successfully.

Contact-wear monitoring:

The monitoring system introduced in Figure 3.8 (j) measures the interrupted currents, calculates the corresponding wear, and records the accumulated sum of these values. The currents are measured with reed contact units, which register the magnetic fields from the breaking poles. By adjusting the sensitivity of these units, it is possible to select different current levels. The units are mounted closely behind the insulated breaker poles.

The reed contacts control an electronic unit, which generates a number of pulses triggering an electromechanical counter. This counter has one indicator for the total sum of pulses and one which can be pre-set by the user of the "alarm value". This counter will trigger an alarm at the user set level, for example 80% of permitted contact wear. This contact wear monitor allows the user to predict when the poles need replacement and thus plan for maintenance.

The electronic unit is programmed to generate 10,000 pulses for the total number of interruptions at different current levels, this corresponds the electrical endurance of the breaker. Breaking operations at rated, continuous current or less generate one pulse. This means that when the displayed value is equal to that of the counter for mechanical operations the circuit breaker has not interrupted any short-circuit currents.

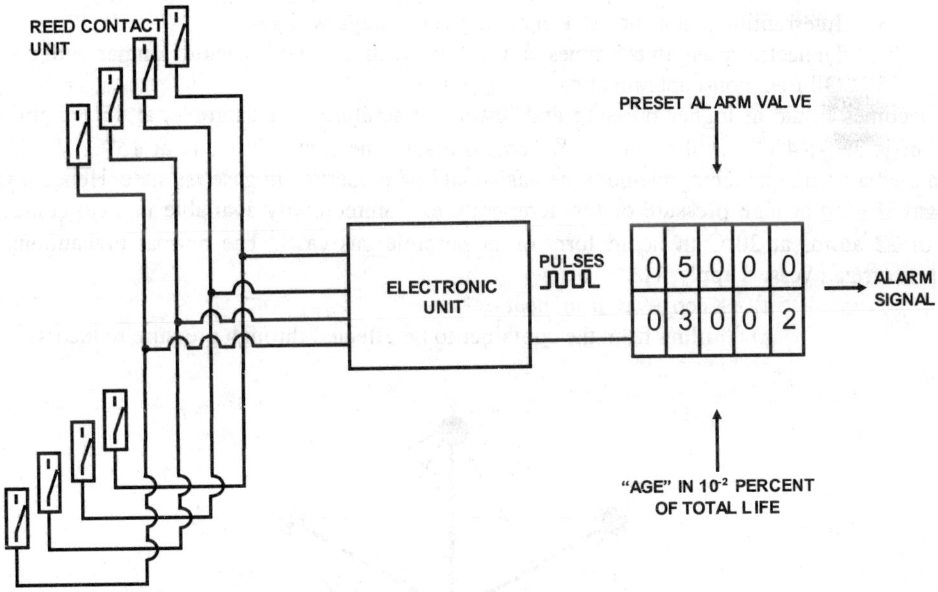

Fig. 3.8 (J): Principle for calculation of contact wear.

Medium voltage SF6 circuit breaker maintenance:

1. Periodic cleaning by using vacuum cleaner or lint free cloths.
2. Lubricating the operation mechanism as per manufacturers recommendations.
3. Measuring contact resistance with micro Ohm meter by injecting 100A 12 V DC supply across the interrupter poles after closing the breaker as demonstrated in section 3.10.
4. Measuring insulation resistance with 5 KV megger.
5. Inspect the carbon brushes of spring charging motor. Clean commutator if necessary.
6. Inspect the main disconnecting contact fingers and grounding contacts. Lubricate if necessary.
7. Check the shutter operation. Lubricate if necessary.
8. Inspect the multiple plug unit and auxiliary switches (NO/NC contacts)
9. Tight all control connections at the terminal blocks.
10. Verify the SF6 gas pressure inside the interrupter. If any doubt about the leakage of gas AC high pressure test may be conducted. Apply twice the value of system voltage for one minute duration between phase to earth after closing the breaker. Similarly apply 1.2 times the value of system voltage between the primary incoming and outgoing terminals of the interrupter when the breaker contact is opened.
11. Measuring resistances of closing coil, tripping coil etc.
12. Inspection of the operating mechanism by manual closing. Lubricate and adjust the mechanism if necessary.
13. Measure closing time and opening time and compare with factory test report. [Section 3.12].
14. Conduct trip free operation check as demonstrated in section 3.12 [figure (c)]
15. Conduct anti-pump relay function check as demonstrated in section 3.12 [figure (a)].

3.9 PROPORTIES OF SULPHUR HEXAFLOURIDE GAS.

Sulphur Hexaflouride is commonly known as SF6 gas. The highly stable 6-molecule consists of one central atom of sulphur (S) surrounded by six (6) atoms of fluorine. Figure 3.9 illustrates SF6 gas structure. SF6 gas is odorless, colourless, heavy gas that spreads slowly in the atmosphere, although non-toxic, will not sustain life. Its unique properties and characteristics make it an excellent insulating gas and gaseous dielectric within the electric utility industry. Commonly used in high voltage power applications. SF6 is used extensively in circuit breakers and other switchgear. It is also used in linear accelerators, high voltage transformers, switches, capacitors and coaxial cables. It is used as an insulator and/or arc-extinguishing medium (interrupting medium), for medium voltage, high and extra-high voltage circuit breakers because of:

1. .SF6 is neither combustible, nor toxic. Explosion proof and non poisonous gas.
2. Will not age with time, breaking capacity and dielectric is high.

3. Interruption is not forced. Hence no over voltage will generate.
4. Dielectric strength is 3 times above in par with air and is roughly on par with oil.
5. Oil free, non-contaminating

SF6 gas becomes liquid at higher pressure and lower temperature. For example, at 15 Kg/cm^2 pressure the liquification is at (-) 4°C. Similarly at 10 Kg/cm^2 pressure the liquification is at 15°C. While using as an insulation media or arc quenching medium the gas should be preserved in gaseous state. Hence it is essential to heat the gas if used at high pressure or low temperature. Commercially available in steel containers under a pressure of 22 atoms at 20°C in liquid form or in portable gas carts. The normal precautions of handling portable pressurized vessels apply, viz:

a) Keep away from heat
b) Filling from the container to be effected through pressure reducers.

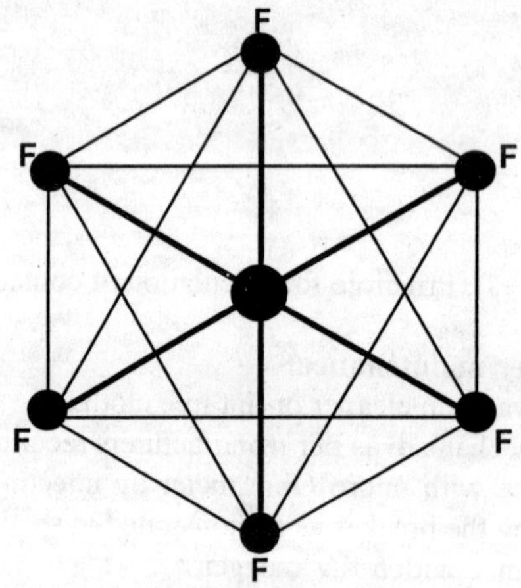

Fig. 3.9: Sulphur Hexafluoride gas structure

Inhalation of a small quantity of the gas is not harmful; in excessive quantities over long periods however, unconsciousness or even death may result from oxygen starvation. Decomposition or partial decomposition of the gas yields gaseous by-products (Sulphur flourides) and powdery solid residues (metallic fluorides and sulfides). Contact with these by-products on damp skin can cause severe irritation (especially eyes, mouth and respiratory tract). The gases by-product has a characteristic putrid smell similar to that of rotten eggs.

Following tests are conducted on SF6 gas.
(1) Condensation temperature (Dew point)
(2) Oxygen content (below 1% by volume)
(3) The acidity and the hydrolysable fluoride content

The due point is defined as the lower temperature to which air must be cooled in order for condensation to occur. The dew point is dependent on the concentration of water vapour present, and therefore on the relative humidity. Hygrometer is used for measuring dew point of gases. Battery powered intrinsically safe dew point hygrometer is designed for use at atmospheric pressure covering an overall range of (-) 110°C to (+) 20°C dew point with the display selectable in most common engineering units: degree C or F, ppm (part per million), gm/m^3 etc. The sensor is only exposed to the sample gas during a measurement and is never in contact with ambient air. Stainless steel quick connect swage-lock coupling is connecting the hygrometer to the equipment for making measurements [Refer figure 4.19 (a) and (b) of Chapter # 4]

Application of SF6 gas and recommended gas pressure

1. Circuit breakers up to 765 KV (5 Kg/cm^2)
2. Gas insulated substations up to 765 KV (3 Kg/cm^2)
3. Outdoor type current transformers up to 765 KV (5 Kg/cm^2)
4. Gas insulated extra high voltage cables up to 765 KV (5 Kg/cm^2)
5. Power Transformers (5 Kg/cm^2)
6. Hermetically sealed flame-proof switchgear (3 Kg/cm^2)

3.10 INSTALLATION, TESTING AND COMMISSIONING OF MV SWITCHGEARS.

Medium voltage switchgears are shipped in various segments and are assembled at site. Switchgears are installed on "U" type G.I channels (40 mm) grouted in the concrete floor in two or three rows to bolt at the switchgear base at the front, middle/back. Spring-loaded bolts and nuts ("T" shape) freely sliding in the channel slot is used to bolt the switchgear base to the channel. After proper alignment, segments are assembled as per manufacturers drawing. After completing the whole unit alignment, check the sliding in/sliding out alignment of each withdrawable circuit breaker. Then the bus bars are to be connected by using a torque wrench, at a defined torque. Control-circuit inter connection is to be carried out as per manufacturers wiring diagram. After completing the erection work, power and control cable termination is to be made as per the cable schedule.

Minimum clearance of 1000mm is required for all the four sides of the switchgear. If draw-out type circuit breakers are used the minimum clearance of 1500mm is required in the front. If two panels are placed face to face minimum 2000mm clearance is required between panels. Switchgear room must be vermin proof and there should be no leakage of roof or wall and roof sealing. Cable entries shall be properly sealed to prevent flooding the cable trench during rain. Spare UPVC cable ducts entering the switchgear room shall be plugged by using pipe-sealing duct. UPVC Pipes entering in the switchgear room shall be slightly lifted up the interior end to prevent sweeping of water inside the switch room. Pipes shall be properly sealed by, using suitable cable sealing compound.

The torque to be applied, on different types of bolts used for assembling bus bars are given in Table 3.10 (1). Vertical running medium voltage power cables shall be supported with suitable cable support assembly made of galvanized channel and clamped properly by using die-cast aluminium or moulded type insulated cable clamps. Pilot and control cables shall run through galvanized cable trays.

Table 3.10 (1): Torque to be applied on bolts for switchgear assembling.

Bolt size in mm	Bolt size in inch	Torque-(Newton metre)	Torque-(Footpounds force)	Torque-(Kilogram metre force)
12	½	70	52	7
16	5/8	180	133	18
20	3/4	258	190	26
24	1.0	445	325	45

Routine tests on assemblies of switchgear and control-gear (IEC 298 and IEC 439)

1. Effectiveness of mechanical actuating elements, interlocks, locks etc.
2. Check on conductors and cables that they are properly laid and terminated, cable-tags and ferrules are fitted, as per drawing and specification.
3. Visual inspection to determine degree of protection, creepage and clearance: distances are maintained.
4. Check on nameplates and markings of components and feeders.
5. Check on operation of shunt trip and under voltage release (if applicable), closing and tripping operation of all circuit breakers.
6. Electrical functional tests to check on wiring/interlocks.
7. Check on operation of protective devices with primary/secondary injection test.
8. Insulation-resistance check, on power and control circuits.
9. Power frequency dielectric test on power and control circuit

Following site tests are recommended to check the integrity of the circuit breakers, current and voltage transformers etc.

1. Leakage tests, gauge tests, stored energy system tests.
2. Electrical resistance of current path test (Contact resistance check by using ductor meter as demonstrated in section 3.10).
3. Clearance and mechanical adjustment check.
4. Closing and opening time check (Each trip coil is checked separately). Test procedures are given in section 3.12

5. Normal frequency voltage-withstand tests.
6. Functional check of circuit breaker, interlocks and indicators.
7. Ratio and polarity check of CT and PT as demonstrated in chapter # 5, section 5.4 & 5.5
8. Mechanical damage or failure/cracks/flashover spots etc.
9. Moisture accumulation, excessive rust, air circulation etc.
10. Function of space heaters and thermostats.
11. Insulation deterioration, cleaning of dust by using air blower.
12. Setting of protective relays.

Table 3.10 (2): Impulse withstand voltage tests on switchgears (1.2/60 Micro-second wave)

Switchgear rated voltage (60 Hz):	5 KV	8 KV	15KV	25 KV	38 KV	44 KV
Impulse withstand voltage:	50 KV	60 KV	95 KV	125 KV	150 KV	250 KV

Test voltages for 50 Hz system: (1.2/50 Microsecond wave) 22 KV- 150 KV and 33 KV- 200 KV.

Table 3.10 (3): One minute power frequency (50Hz) withstand voltage test on MV switchgears:

System voltage (KV)	Highest voltage (KV)	Power frequency with stand voltage (KV)	Factory routine test (KV)	New installation (KV)	Existing Installation (KV)
6.6	7.2	18	18	14.4	12.6
11	12	28	28	22.4	19.6
22	24	60	60	48	42
33	38	100	100	80	70

Table 3.10(4): One minute power frequency (60Hz) withstand voltage test on MV switchgears.

Switchgear rated voltage in KV:	3.6	7.2	13.8	17.5	24	36
AC Test voltage in KV:	16	22	34	38	50	70

Type tests on medium voltage switchgears:
Following tests are to be carried out in accordance to IEC standard 298:

(1) Short time current test on main circuits, earthing circuit, earthing switch.
(2) Making test on earthing switch.
(3) Mechanical operation test.
(4) Verification of degree of protection.
(5) Temperature rise test.

Destructive tests on medium voltage switchgears:
These tests are to be carried out by simulating an arc of 20KA RMS with a prospective peak of 2.5 x RMS for 0.5 and 1 sec in various compartments of the switchgear such as: cable compartment, common bus compartment, circuit breaker compartment, using arc monitors. Pressures and temperatures are recorded. Cotton indicators to measure degree of burn and intensity are used. This test reveals that the switchgear is safe from all hazards.

Testing and inspection of switchgear components:
Testing and inspection of medium voltage switchgear components such as current transformers, potential transformers, circuit breakers, earthing switches, busbar supporting insulators etc.
(1) Current transformers: To be tested in accordance with IEC Standard 185.
Routine tests:

Measurements of ratio and phase displacement error:

- One minute voltage test on the primary side and secondary side.
- Checks for terminal markings (Polarity test).
- Corona measurement test.

Type tests on current transformer:

- Impulse voltage test;
- Short-time and surge current test;
- Temperature rise test.

(2) Potential transformers: To be tested in accordance with IEC Standard 186.
Routine tests: (Refer Chapter # 5)

- One minute AC voltage tests on primary winding to earth, secondary winding to earth.
- Internal discharge test.
- Measurement of errors.
- Polarity check.
- Magnetizing current (Io) secondary winding at √3 x rated voltage.
- Sealing test.

(3) Breakers and earth switches: To be tested in accordance with IEC Standard 298.
(4) Bus bar insulators: To be tested for electrical and mechanical bracing characteristics and strengths to relevant IEC standards.

Contact resistance measurement:

The DC resistance of main circuit of each pole of a circuit breaker is of the order of micro Ohms. The resistance is measured by measuring DC milli volt drops across the contact. Micro Ohmmeter (Ductor meter) is the test instrument. Method of connecting the instrument is shown in Figure 3.10 (a). Minimum 100A DC (less than rated current of the circuit breaker) current is to be injected (with the breaker closed) at ambient air temperature. The reading obtained in the instrument is micro Ohm.

(1) Connect the micro Ohmmeter [both current and sensing cable].

(2) Set the DC current at 100A;

(3) Press the resistance push button;

(4) Observe the reading;

(5) Release the push button;

(5) Open the breaker;

(6) Repeat the test once more;

(7) Record average reading;

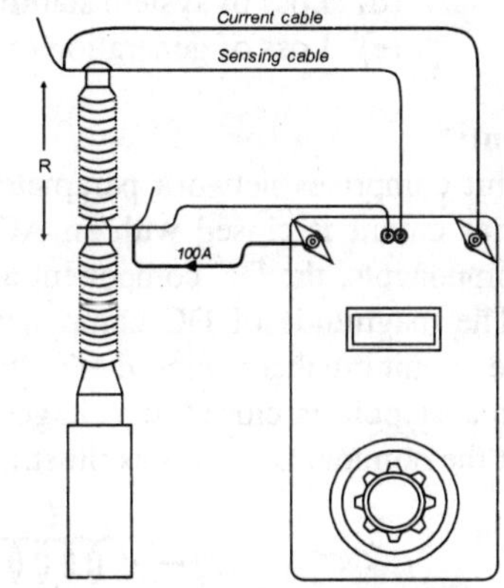

Fig. 3.10 (a): Measuring the contact resistance of an outdoor type breaker pole.

Figure 3.10 (b) shows the connection diagram for measuring the resistance of bus bar joints. Connect the micro Ohmmeter's current cable to the object being tested. Do not connect the sensing cables since measurements will be taken using an external movable voltmeter.

(1) Set the current at 100A (minimum);

(2) Connect an external milli-voltmeter to the joint;

(3) Read the voltmeter; say 0.1 mV

(4) R = V/I = (1/1000) ÷ 100 = 1/1000000 Ω

= 1 Micro Ohm.

(5) Switch off the instrument;

(6) Repeat the test on other joints also.

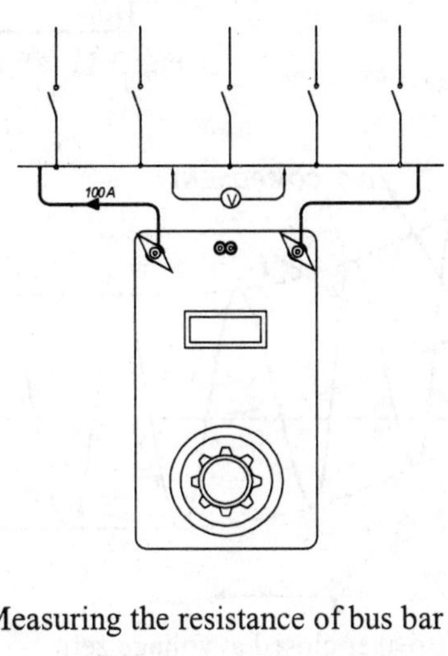

Fig. 3.10 (b): Measuring the resistance of bus bar joint.

3.11 SWITCHING PHENOMENA AND CIRCUIT BREAKER RATINGS.

1. Effect of voltage:

Over-voltage (switching surges) may occur in high voltage lines due the following reasons:

(a) Switching of line feeders;
(b) Auto re-closure of circuit breakers;
(c) Short circuit and line faults;
(d) Load shedding or tripping at receiving end of line;
(e) Disconnection of large inductive loads (Motor);
(f) Switching on large magnetizing currents (Transformers);
(g) Switching high voltage reactors,
(h) Single line to ground fault persisting in the line;
(i) Generator over-speed.
(j) Sudden loss of load;
(k) Shutting down generators without unloading.

Under-voltage may occur during the following situations:

(a) Power failure or system fault;
(b) Loose or corroded connections or jumper;
(c) Open circuit in one phase (breaking of line conductor);
(d) Loss of system stability or voltage dip due to starting of large motors;
(e) Loss of generation or generator overloading.

2. Effect of current:

An electrical circuit comprises network parameters like inductance (L), capacitance (C) and resistance (R). When an R-L series circuit is closed with an AC voltage source [See Figure 3.11 (a)] the resulting current consists of two components, the DC component and AC component. The AC component is superimposed on DC component. The magnitude of DC component depends up on the voltage at the instant of closing the breaker pole. If the circuit breaker is closed at voltage zero, the DC component is maximum as shown in Figure 3.11 (b). If the breaker pole is closed at voltage maximum the DC component is zero and the waveform is symmetrical about the nominal zero axis as illustrated in Figure 3.11 (c).

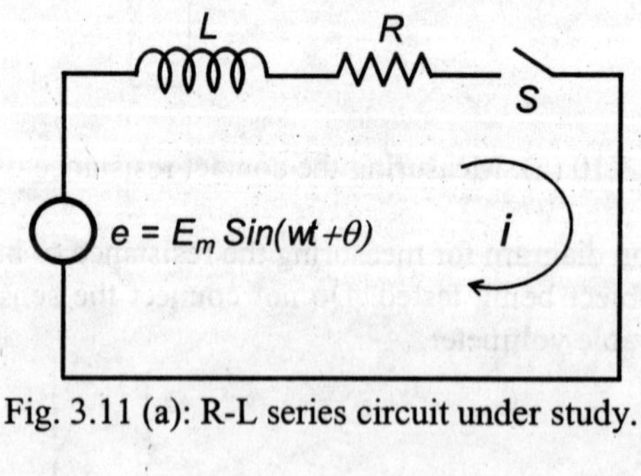

Fig. 3.11 (a): R-L series circuit under study.

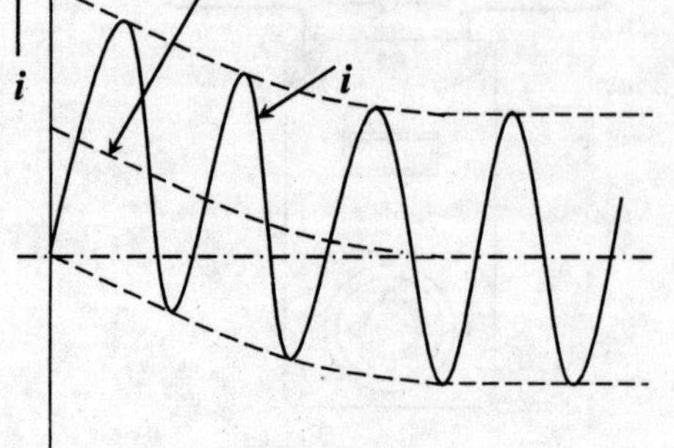

Fig. 3.11 (b): Breaker closed at voltage zero. (DC component maximum)

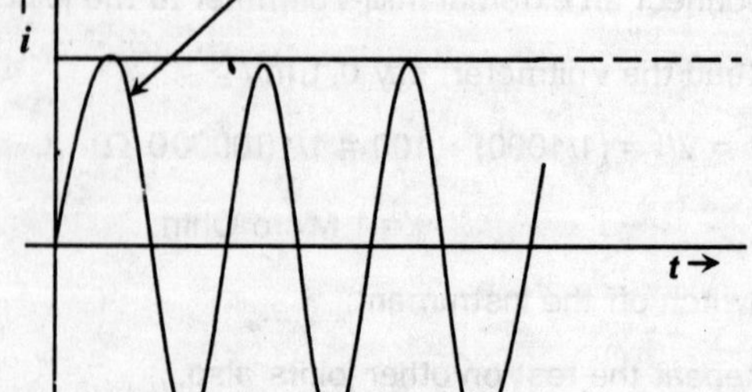

Fig. 3.11 (c): Breaker closed at voltage maximum: (No DC component).

3. Sub-transient, transient, and steady state conditions:

An oscillogram of three-phase short-circuit currents is shown in Figure 3.11 (d). When the alternator is short-circuited, the currents in all the three phases rise rapidly to a high value i.e. approximately 10 times to full load current during the first quarter cycle. The flux crossing the air-gap is large during a first couple of cycles. The reactance during these first 2 or 3 cycles is least and the short circuit current is high. This reactance is called sub transient reactance X'. The first few cycles come under sub-transient state. After a first few cycles, the decrement in r.m.s value of short circuit current is less rapid than the decrement during the first few cycles. This state is called the transient state and the reactance in this state is called transient reactance X". Breaker contacts separate in the transient state. Finally the transient dies out and the current reaches a steady sinusoidal state called the steady state. The reactance in this state is called steady state reactance (Xd). Since the short circuit current of the generator, lags behind the voltage by, 90 degrees. Hence the reactance involved, are direct-axis reactance.

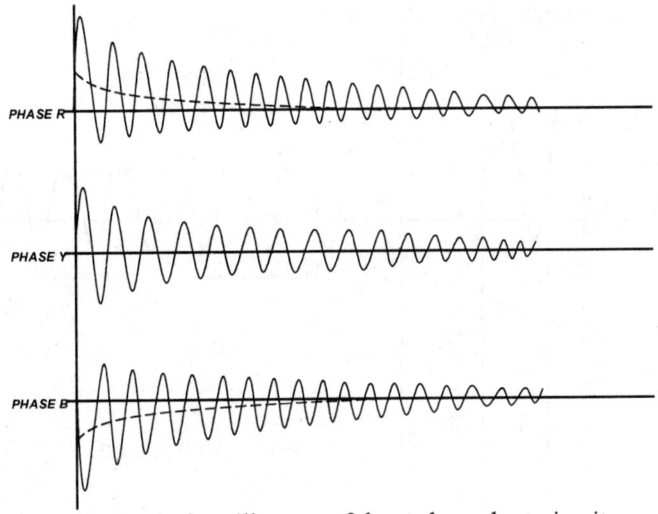

Fig. 3.11 (d): Typical oscillogram of three phase short-circuit current.

Consider Figure 3.11 (e), the DC components in the three phases are different; hence the waveform of the three phases are not identical. If voltage of phase Y is maximum; at the instant of short circuit, the AC component of the short circuit current is zero. Hence the waveform is symmetrical. NM is extended to meet the zero time ordinate at point A. Similarly ML is extended to meet the ordinate at B. LC meets the ordinate of zero time at C. Measure OC, OB, and OA. NM is a portion of envelope in steady state. LC is a portion of envelope in sub-transient state.

$$I = \text{Steady state current} = \underline{OA} = \frac{Ea}{\sqrt{2}\ Xd}$$

$$I' = \text{Transient current} = \underline{OB} = \frac{Ea}{\sqrt{2}\ Xd'}$$

$$I'' = \text{Sub-transient current} = \underline{OC} = \frac{Ea}{\sqrt{2}\ Xd''}$$

Ea = Induced e.m.f per phase;

Xd = Direct axis synchronous reactance;

Xd' = Direct axis transient reactance;

Xd" = Direct axis sub-transient reactance.

Transient current is the breaking current;

Sub-transient current is the making current;

Steady state current is the full load current.

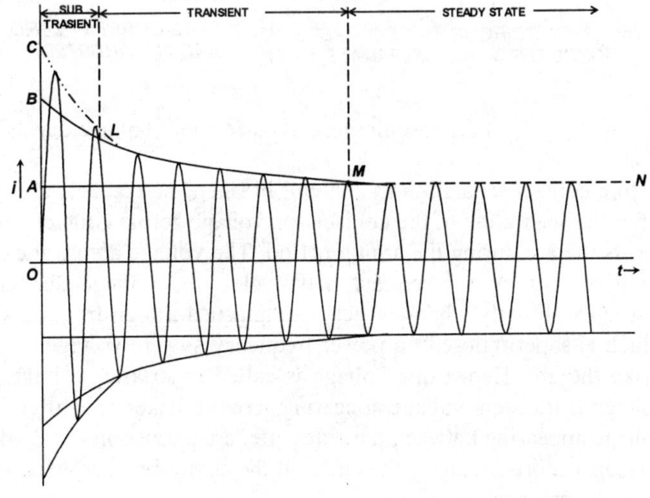

Fig 3.11 (e): Oscillogram of current in the phase having zero DC components.

4. Current interruption in AC circuit breakers:

Consider a circuit breaker connected to a generator on no load at rated terminal voltage. The circuit breaker is in open position and other side of the circuit breaker is shorted as shown in figure 1.13 (d) of Chapter # 1. Let the circuit breaker be closed at the instant when voltage of terminal B with respect to neutral is zero. In such case the short circuit in phase B will have maximum DC component as shown in Figure 3.11 (f). The current increases to a high value during the first quarter cycle. OM is the maximum instantaneous value of current during the short circuit. This is the making current. The circuit breaker opens after a few cycles when the protection relay operates. The r.m.s value of short circuit current at the instant of contact separation is the breaking current. During the separation of contacts of circuit breaker, an arc is drawn between the contacts. At current zero, this arc is extinguished and is interrupted.

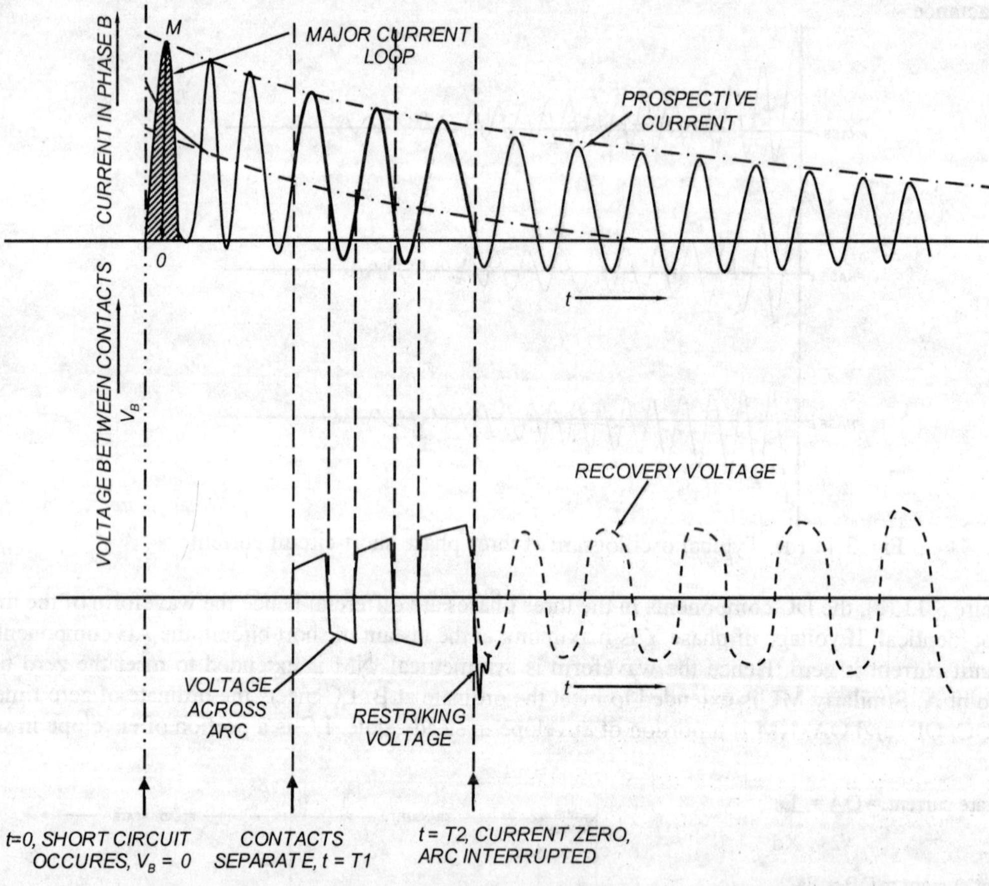

Fig. 3.11 (f): Oscillogram of current and voltage during fault clearing of a circuit.

Before contact separation in a circuit breaker, the contacts are closed and the voltage across a contact is zero. After the separation of the contact, the voltage across contacts increases. In fact this voltage is the voltage drop across the arc during the arcing period. The voltage across the arc is in-phase with the current since the arc is resistive. During sub-sequent half cycles, the voltage across the contact increases due to increased arc resistance. Finally when arc gets extinguished a high frequency voltage transient appears across the contacts, which is superimposed on power frequency system voltage. This high frequency transient voltage tries to re-strike the arc. Hence this voltage is called re-striking voltage or transient recovery voltage. The re-striking voltage is transient voltage appearing across breaker pole after final current zero. The power frequency system voltage appearing between the poles after arc extinction is called recovery voltage. The current that would flow (during a short-circuit) in the circuit if the circuit breaker were replaced by a solid conductor that current is said to be the prospective current.

5. Transient recovery voltage:

In AC circuit breakers the current interruption takes place at natural zero of the current wave. After a current zero, the arc gets extinguished if the rate of rise of transient recovery voltage between the contacts is less than the rate of gain of the dielectric strength. The voltage appearing between the breaker contacts at the moment of final current zero has profound influence on the arc extinction process. The voltage appearing across contacts after current zero is a transient voltage of higher natural frequency **(re-striking voltage)** superimposed on the power frequency system voltage (recovery voltage). Figure 3.11 (g) illustrates the waveform of the recovery voltage and re-striking voltage. After current zero, the voltage appearing across the contacts is composed of transient re-striking voltage and power frequency recovery voltage. **Recovery voltage** is the voltage, which appears across the terminals of a pole of a circuit breaker after the breaking current. Transient recovery voltage or re-striking voltage is the recovery voltage during the time in which it has a significant transient character. TRV lasts for a few hundreds of microseconds. It is the voltage across the first pole to clear because the same is generally higher than across the two poles, which clear later.

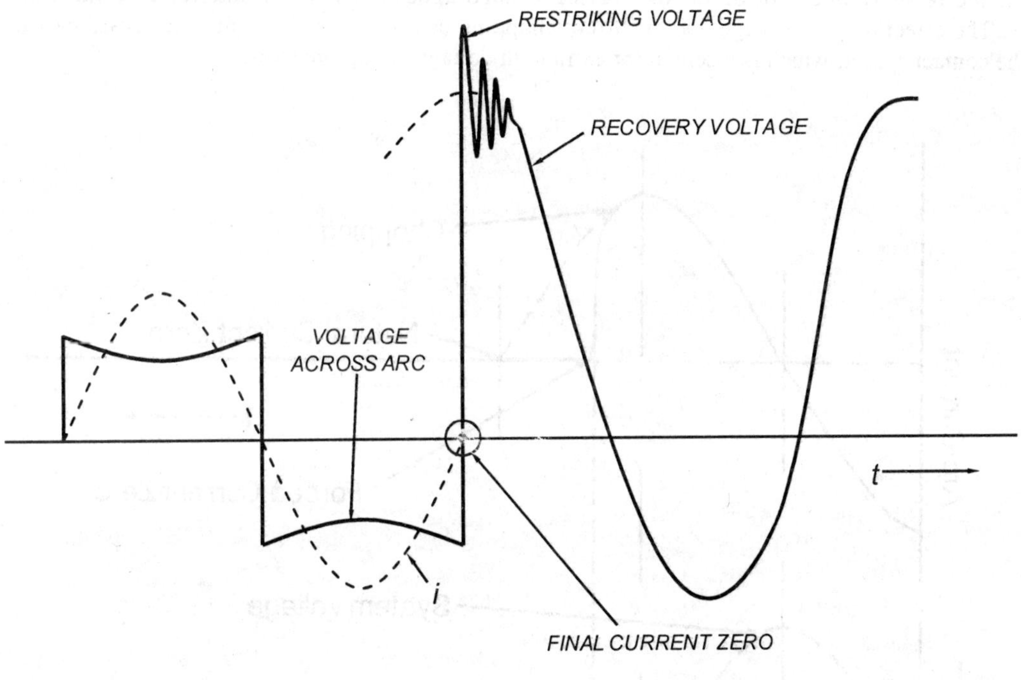

Fig. 3.11 (g): Oscillogram of transient recovery voltage after final current zero.

6. Interruption of small magnetizing current:

The necessity of interrupting small inductive currents arises while disconnecting transformers on no load. No load currents of transformer is magnetizing currents are almost at zero power factor lag. The current is smaller than nominal current ratings of the breaker. The breaking of such a low magnetizing current presents a severe duty on the circuit breaker. Figure 3.11 (h) illustrates a circuit interrupting low inductive current.

When interrupting low inductive currents such as magnetizing currents of transformer shunt reactor etc, the rapid de-ionization of interrupter contact space and blast effect may cause the current to be interrupted before its natural zero. This phenomenon of the interruption of the current before its natural zero is called **current chopping.** From the energy stored in inductance certain value of current is diverted to the capacitance at the moment of current interruption.

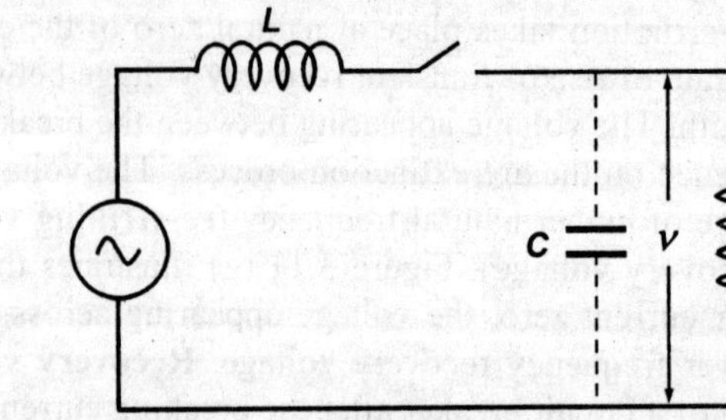

Fig. 3.11 (h): Typical representation of low magnetizing current circuit.

Figure 3.11 (1) illustrates interruption of low magnetizing current. Transient voltage having high recovery voltage appears across the contacts, unless the arc continuous. If it re-strikes a further, chop may occur or several chops may occur. Perhaps before the current is finally interrupted circuit breaker may fail to clear the fault. If the re-strike does not occur, the service voltage appears across the interrupter contact and on the system. The effect of over-voltage due to current chopping can overcome by connecting resistance in parallel with the contact spacer, which is essential for extra high voltage circuit breakers.

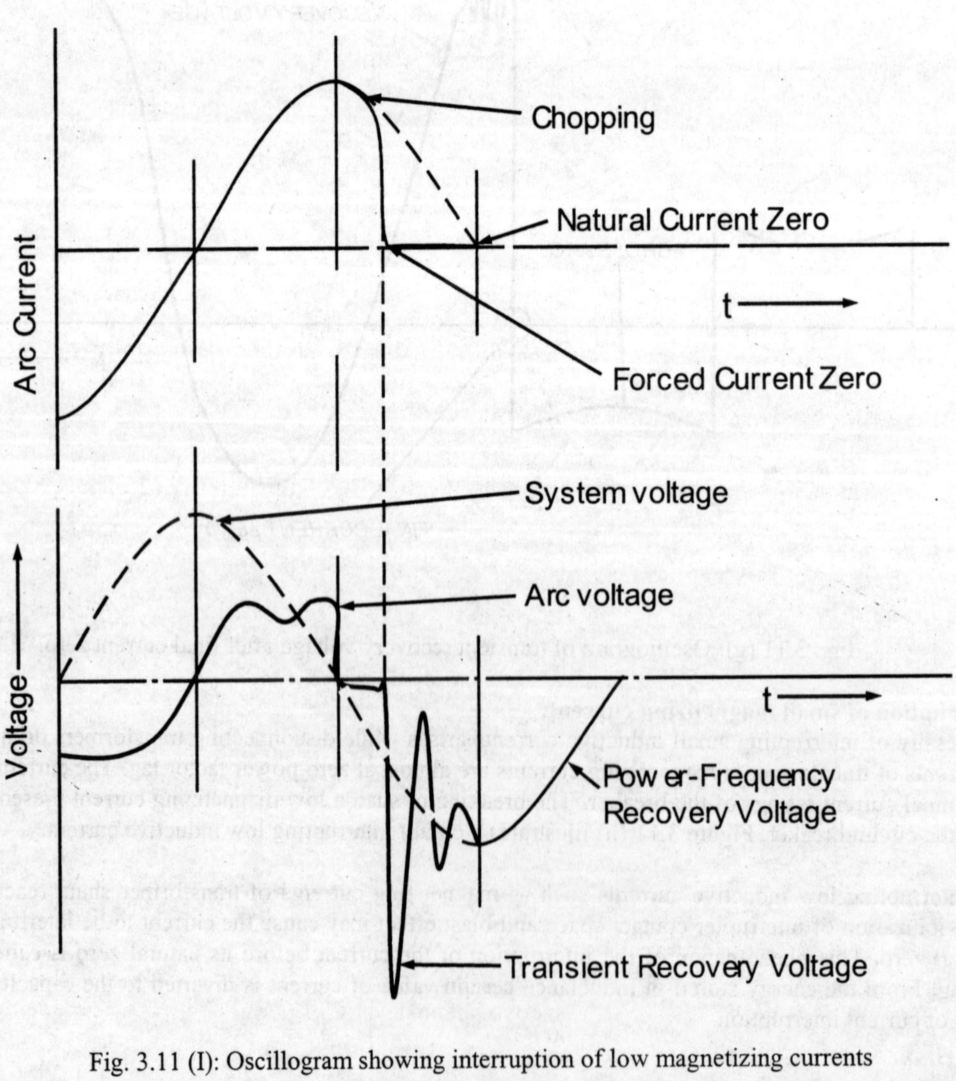

Fig. 3.11 (I): Oscillogram showing interruption of low magnetizing currents

7. Switching of capacitor bank:
While opening capacitor banks, the re-ignition and re-striking can occur in an interrupter. Capacitor banks are connected in the network to provide reactive power at leading power factor. The voltage across the capacitor cannot change instantaneously. Figure 3.11 (J) shows single-phase representation of star connected three-phase capacitor bank. Due to the 90° Phase difference, the voltage across the capacitor is at maximum value (Ec). At this instant (t_2) the capacitor remains charged. After half cycle (t_2) the recovery voltage of approximate magnitude of Emax appears across the circuit breaker and the total voltage across the circuit breaker is the sum of the two voltages. Figure 3.11 (k) shows typical waveform of clean interruption without re-strike (at t_1, current I interrupted).

Transient Recovery Voltage (TRV) = E_{Tmax} = Emax + Ec
Emax = Maximum value of power frequency voltage; Ec = Voltage across capacitor

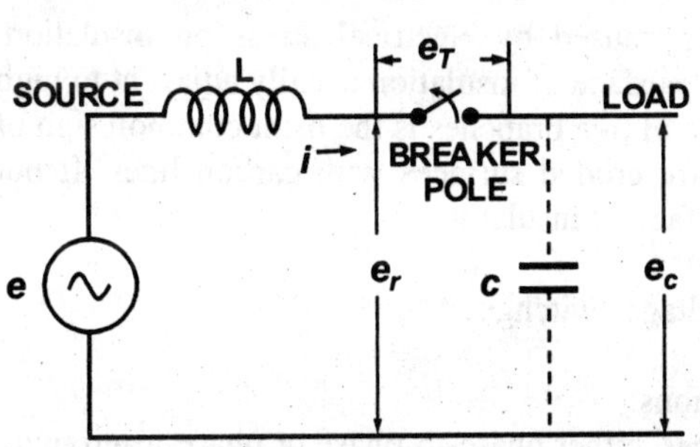

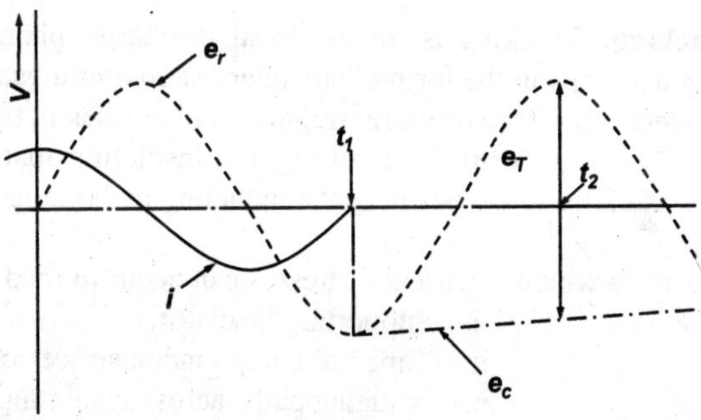

Fig. 3.11 (J): Representation of 3-phase capacitor bank. Fig. 3.11 (k): Waveform of current interruption.

If restrike occurs, the L-C circuit will oscillate. This current tries to maintain the arc. Hence the voltage across the interrupter rises up to 4 P.U. due to one strike and up to 6 P.U. with second strike. The energy to be dissipated during such arc is quite large and the interrupters may get damaged in the process after a restrike. Hence the circuit breakers used for capacitor duty must be **"restrike free"**. While closing the circuit breaker of parallel capacitor banks, the pre-arcing between contacts taken place before the contact touch. The energy in the arc is converted in to heat. While paralleling one capacitor bank with another, the frequency of inrush current is very high. To overcome this problem suitable reactor should be provided in series. Figure 3.11 (L) illustrates voltage and current waveforms after a restrike.

KEY: e_1 = Source side sinusoidal voltage; e_c = Voltage across capacitor C; e_r = Voltage across breaker pole

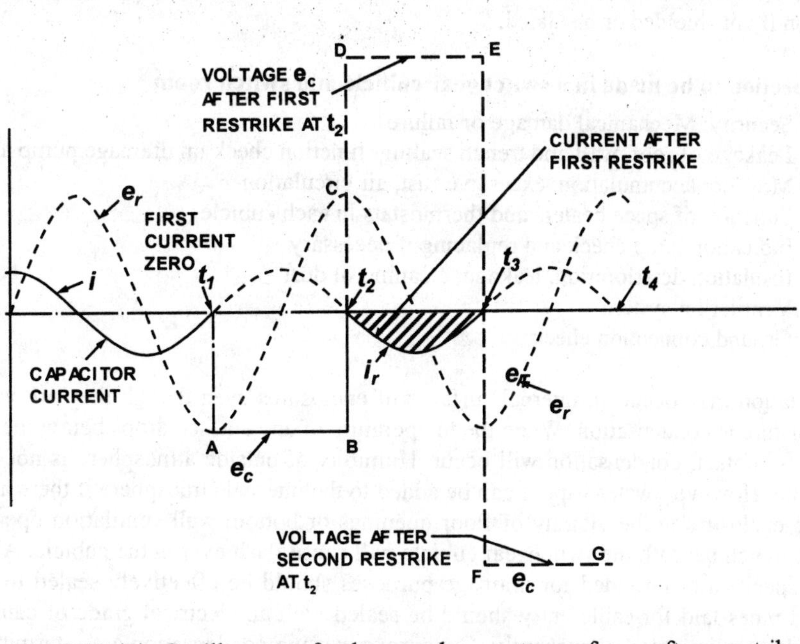

Fig. 3.11 (L): Oscillogram of voltage and current waveforms after a restrike.

3.12 PREVENTIVE MAINTENANCE OF SWITCHGEARS AND BREAKERS

Switchgear must be protected from extreme atmospheric conditions such as heat, cold, heavy dust, high winds, rain, snow, fog (thick cloud of water vapour), smog (mixture of fog and smoke), fumes, flash, salt, high humidity, lightning etc.

(1) Thermal effect: Temperature exposure for prolonged period can significantly shorten the electrical life of organic insulating materials. Heat damages (Thermal damages) can be observed from:

(a) Discoloration or darkening of material.
(b) Crazing, cracking, flaking of varnish.
(c) Embrittlement of tapes and cable insulation.
(d) Melting, oozing or excluding of substances.
(e) Carbonization of materials or finishes.

(2) Tracking: Tracking is an electrical discharge phenomenon caused by electrical stress on insulation. Tracking develops in the form of streamers or sputter areas on the surface of insulation usually adjacent to high voltage electrodes. One or more irregular carbon lines in the shape of tree branches is the most common sign of tracking. The sign of tracking on organic insulating materials are eroded surfaces with carbon lines. If not attended, tracking forms permanent conducting path along the surface of insulator.

Possible areas where electrical distresses can occur in medium voltage switchgear:

i. Supporting insulator.
ii. Taped or compounded splices or junctions.
iii. Bridging paths across insulating surfaces, either phase-to-phase or phase-to-ground..
iv. Edges of the insulation mounting hard wares either grounded to the metal structure or floating within the insulating member.
v. Hidden surfaces such as the adjacent edges between the upper and lower member of split-type bus supports or the edges of a slot through which a bus bar protrudes.

(3) Corona effect: Corona is an electrical discharge in air that only partially bridges the gap between two or more electrodes. Corona leads to power loss (although this is fairly minor at medium voltage) and causes radio interference, as well as leading to physical damage of the insulation if it is severe enough. Corona can be tested by, measuring the discharge magnitude using a radio receiver. The symptom for existence of corona in switchgear can be observed:

(a) In organic insulating materials, white powdery deposits on the surface or erosion of the surface of the insulating materials.
(b) Between two adjacent insulating members corona may form around bolt-heads or other sharp projection if not shielded or insulated.

(4) Physical inspection to be made in a switchgear cubicle and switch room

1. Security: Mechanical damage or failure
2. Leakage of roof, wall and trench sealing, function check on drainage pump and system.
3. Moisture accumulation, excessive rust, air circulation
4. Function of space heaters and thermostats in each cubicle
5. Indication lamp check and replacing if necessary
6. Insulation deterioration, leakage, cleaning of dust
7. Ventilation system
8. Ground connection check

Moisture accumulation may occur on internal surfaces of enclosures even though they are weatherproof. The source of this moisture is condensation. When the temperature of any surface drops below the dew point of the air with which it is contact, condensation will occur. Humidity of outside atmosphere is not controllable as it enters the enclosure. However, water vapour can be added to the internal atmosphere if there are pools of water at the base of the enclosure in the vicinity of floor openings or bottom wall ventilation openings. Storage of water in the cable trench beneath the switchgear cubicle will cause flash over in the cubicle. All floor openings, other than those specifically provided for drainage purposes should be effectively sealed to prevent entry of water. All unused pipes laid for cable entry should be sealed with an electrical grade of caulking compound. Water pools should be eliminated permanently. Conditions causing condensation are intermittent and may not be prevalent at the time of inspection. All internal surfaces should be examined for signs of previous moisture such as:

(a) Droplet depressions or craters on heavily dust-laden surfaces.
(b) Deposit patterns, such as might occur if a film of dirty water were left to evaporate on a flat surface.
(c) Excessive rust anywhere on the metal housing.

With proper maintenance the insulation of metal enclosed switchgear assemblies is expected to withstand more than 30 years. Moisture combined with dust is the greatest deteriorating factor for insulation. Perfectly dry dirt is mostly harmless, but even small amounts of moisture, such as condensation, will result in insulation leakage, which leads to eventual flash over if allowed to continue to accumulate. It is important in the maintenance of switchgear to know the condition of the insulation.

(5) Reasons for failure of medium voltage circuit breakers:

A circuit breaker is considered to have failed when the breaker fails to open or unable to interrupt power after a trip command is initiated. Modern high voltage switchgears are provided with breaker fail protection (refer section 7.11 of Chapter # 7), which is isolating the faulty zone. Major reasons for failure to trip open the breakers are:

- Mechanical failure of operating lever
- For MOCB, dielectric failure of oil or leakage of oil filled in the interrupter.
- For SF6 circuit breaker, dielectric failure inside interrupting chamber due to high moisture in SF6 gas.
- Insulation failure (Phase to earth) due to accumulation of moisture.
- Failure due to high transient recovery voltage (TRV)
- Trip coil open or short circuited

(6) Preventive maintenance on medium voltage circuit breakers

(a) Servicing operating mechanism and spring charging motor.
(b) Check closing time, opening time, anti-pump relay function check, and trip free operation check of medium voltage circuit breakers as illustrated below. Capacitive sensor for SF6 circuit breakers operation check is described in section 3.8. Tests on vacuum circuit breakers are described in section 3.7.
(c) Check oil level in MOCB interrupters and refill new Shell Daila D oil if necessary.
(d) Check contact erosion in vacuum circuit breakers and adjust wipe if necessary.
(e) Check SF6 gas pressure in SF6 circuit breakers. Refill gas if necessary.
(f) Apply Shell Vaseline 8420 or equivalent on terminals
(g) Apply Centoplex 24DL or equivalent on bearing and sliding surfaces
(h) Apply Ritzo 7/2 or equivalent on corroded areas or for corrosion protection

(7) Tests on medium voltage switchgears:

(1) Insulation resistance test
(2) Earth resistance measurement
(3) Primary and secondary injection test on protective relays.
(4) Power frequency withstand voltage test: (Test voltage for medium voltage switchgears are given in Table 3.10 (3) and (4). Test duration one minute.
(5) DC High pressure test on medium voltage cables by applying 2 to 2.5 times rated AC voltage for 10 to 15 minutes time depending on the ageing factor of the cable in service.

(8) Measurement of closing time of low voltage and medium voltage circuit breakers:

Circuit diagram for measuring the ***closing time*** of a medium voltage circuit breaker by conventional method is shown in Figure 3.12 (a). A triple pole MCB (Miniature circuit breaker), and a digital timer, which records time in millisecond is the only requirement for this test. Timer start/stop control is by using volt-free NO/NC contact. To select the available NO/NC contact to start or stop the timer, an in-built toggle switch is provided in the timer circuit. Withdraw the circuit breaker from the cubicle, charge the spring and connect the circuit as shown in Figure (a). While switching on the triple pole MCB;

(1) Closing solenoid energizes through the NC contacts of 52 (b), circuit breaker auxiliary contact and, 52Y/b anti-pump relay contact and LS spring charge limit switch (closed when the spring is fully charged position). When energized, which releases the closing spring and the circuit breaker closes. Anti-pump relay energizes and seal in through its NO contact.

(2) Timer start circuit connected through the third pole of the MCB activates and timer starts to measure the closing time.

(3) Closing solenoid de-energizes as the 52b (breaker auxiliary contact) and 52Y/b (anti-pump relay contact) in the closing circuit opens.

(4) When the breaker closes, through breaker main contacts (R-Y-B) the stop circuits of the timer activate and stop timing. Readout the time taken to close the breaker and compare with commissioning test report.

(5) The breaker will remain closed until the trip coil is energized or a mechanical trip is made.

For anti-pump relay function check switch off the triple pole MCB, the anti-pump relay drops off. Again switch on the MCB, the anti-pump relay will pick-up to prevent energizing the closing solenoid in a closed circuit breaker.

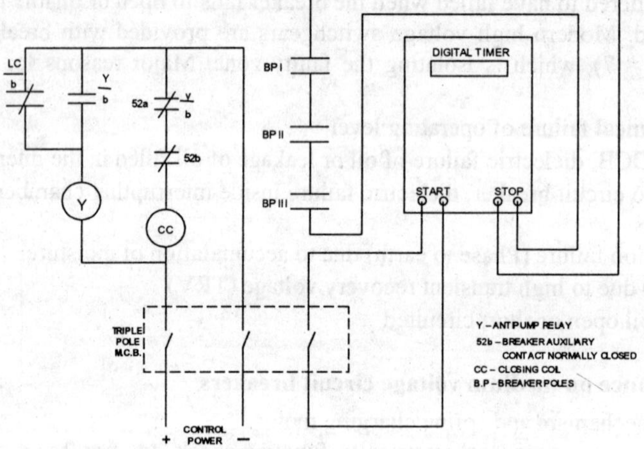

Fig. 3.12 (a): Circuit diagram for measuring closing time of a medium voltage circuit breaker.

(9) Measurement of opening time of low and medium voltage circuit breakers:

The circuit diagram for measuring the ***opening time*** of a closed medium voltage circuit breaker by conventional method is shown in Figure 3.12 (b). Assume that the circuit breaker under test is in closed position and the circuit is wired as shown in Figure (b). While switching on the triple pole MCB, the trip solenoid will energize through the auxiliary NO contact 52a and the breaker trips. Third pole of the MCB actuate the timer and timing start. When all the three breaker poles are opens, the stop circuit of the timer initiate and timer stops timing. Readout the time taken to opening the breaker poles, and compare with breaker commissioning test. Comparing to the previous test for closing time, in this test closed breaker contacts are connected in parallel to ensure the initiation of the stop signal to the timer when all the breaker poles are fully open. During the test, the toggle type selector switch in the timer should be placed in NC position. The test shall be conducted after withdrawing the circuit breaker from the switchgear cubicle..

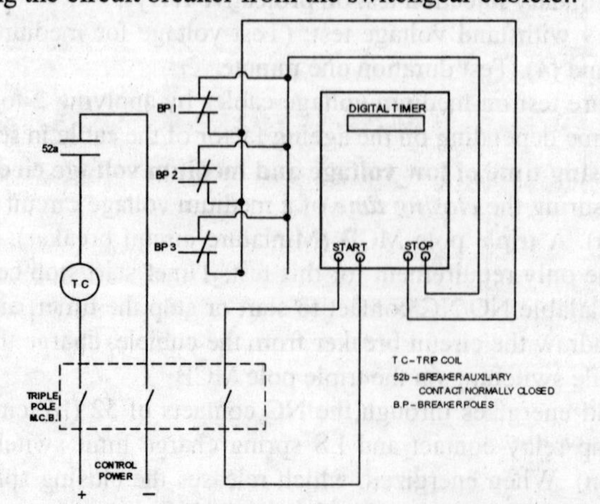

Fig: 3.12 (b): Circuit diagram for measuring opening time of a medium voltage circuit breaker.

(10) Trip-free operation check:

Circuit diagram for ***trip free operation*** check of circuit breaker is shown in Figure 3.12 (c). Assume that the breaker is in open position and the closing spring is charged. While closing the triple pole MCB, DC control power energizes the closing coil (CC). Breaker auxiliary contact closes before the breaker main contact start to close. Therefore, the trip coil (TC) will energize through the normally open contact 52a of the circuit breaker. Breaker moving contacts return to and remain in the open position when the open operation is initiated after the initiation of the closing operation. Both closing force and the opening command are simultaneously maintained. If the breaker fails to perform trip free operation as described above and perform closing operation the timer will stop timing through the breaker poles wired to the timer stop circuit.

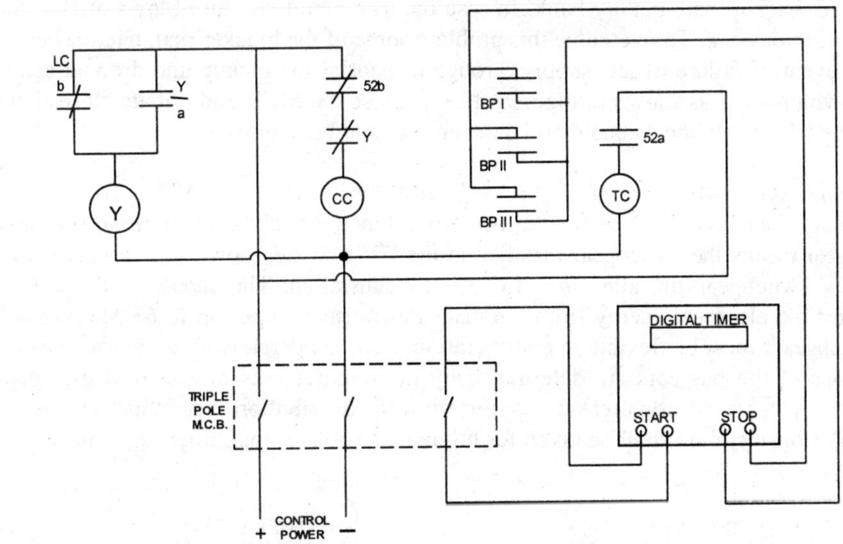

Fig. 3.12 (c): Circuit diagram for trip free operation check of a medium voltage circuit breaker

(11) Under-voltage release pickup – dropout check:

Low voltage and medium voltage consumers who receives power from electricity supply authorities has to provide three-phase voltage sensor [refer figure 1.3 (i) in Chapter # 1) with the incoming mains circuit breaker, provided they are using a standby generator. In the event of failure of mains power supply, voltage sensor will initiate trip signal to the mains power supply breaker and start signal to the standby generator. Generator breakers are equipped with AC under-voltage release, which permits to close the breaker only when the generator has build-up voltage. Similarly, in a running generator if the voltage drops below certain value, the under-voltage release drops and breaker trips.

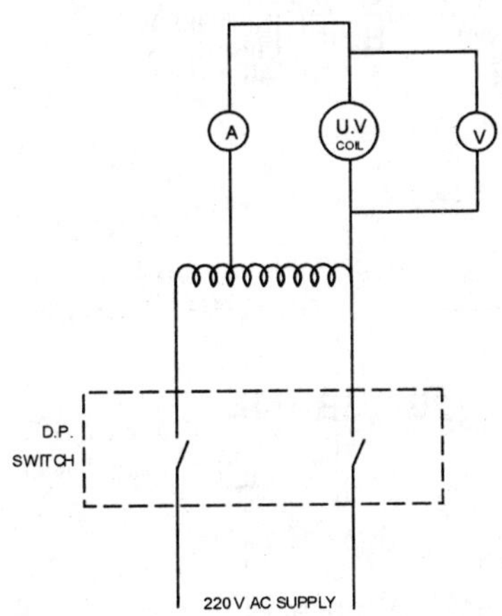

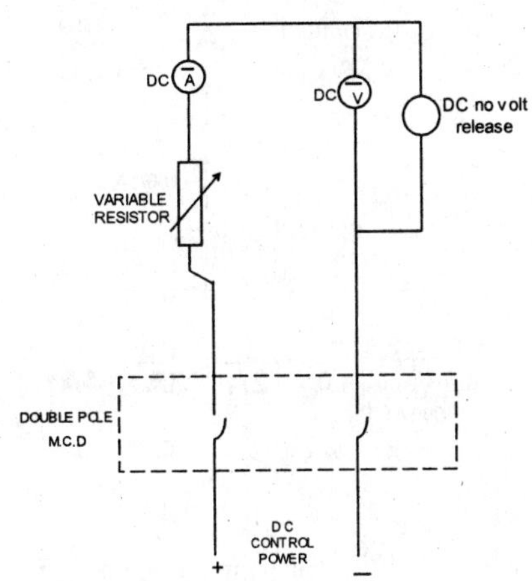

Fig: 3.12 (d): AC under-voltage release pickup and dropout check. Fig. 3.12 (e): DC no-volt release check.

By using a variable autotransformer under-voltage release can be tested at site by connecting as shown in Figure 3.12 (d). Increase the voltage gradually from zero to rated voltage. Record the pickup voltage, i.e. minimum AC voltage required to pickup the coil. Increase the voltage up to rated voltage. Measure the current drawn by the coil. Now decrease the voltage gradually from rated voltage to zero. Record the dropout voltage, i.e. voltage at which the coil dropout. For checking the breaker close/trip operation, energize under-voltage release by closing the DP switch and close the breaker. Open DP switch, under-voltage device de-energizes and breaker trips open.

(12) DC no-volt release check:
Assume that a generator is loaded and the breaker closing/tripping operation is by using DC power from the station battery charger backup with battery bank. In case the trip circuit DC fuse blows or DC source fail the protection -system will not work. To overcome this problem some of the breaker manufactures employ DC no-volt release. In the event of failure of DC supply through a rheostat the pickup and dropout can be checked. Connect the DC no volt release as shown in Figure 3.12 (e). Close the MCB and initiate close signal and close the breaker. Open the DP switch, the solenoid coil de-energizes and breaker trips.

3.13 MEDIUM VOLTAGE PRIMARY AND SECONDARY SWITCHING STATIONS

Primary and secondary distribution stands for the two basic functions of the medium voltage level. Primary distribution switchgear means the switchgear installed in the HV/MV step down transformer main substation. For example, 33 KV switchgears installed in a 132/33 KV substation. The capacity of equipment must be sufficient to transport the electrical energy from the main transformer (input up to 63 MVA) via bus duct or cable. Primary switchgears must be flexible in configuration, easy to operate with a minimum of maintenance. Design configurations of the bus bars are determined by the requirements of the local distribution system. Single bus bar system with bus section breaker is sufficient if the distribution system has adequate redundancy [refer figure 3.2 (b)]. Consideration shall be given for future extension or upgrading, spare feeders, and need of additional feeders.

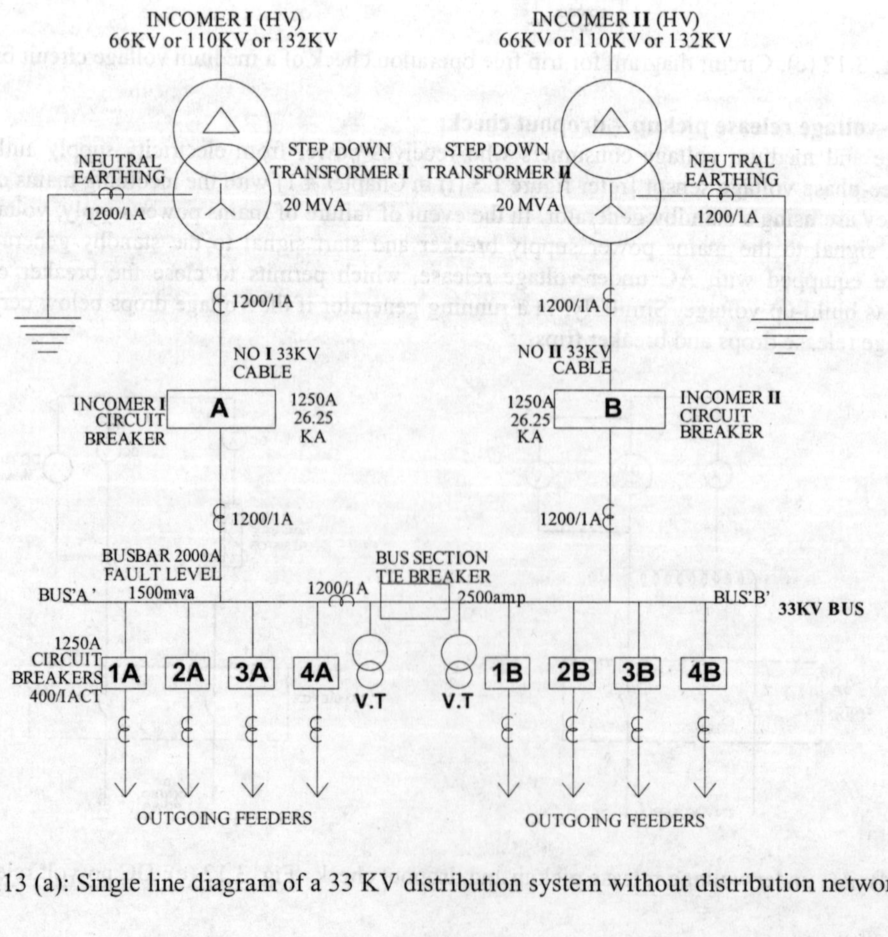

Fig. 3.13 (a): Single line diagram of a 33 KV distribution system without distribution network.

Fig. 3.13 (a) shows the single line diagram of a typical primary switching station, which consists of:

(a) 2 Nos 50/63 MVA ONAN/ONAF power-transformers: (50 MVA capacity while oil natural air natural cooling, and 63 MVA capacity when oil natural air forced cooling.) Incoming supply to the power transformer may be 132 KV or 110 KV or 66 KV, depending on the transmission network system. Transformer secondary is 33 KV.

(b) 33 KV switchgear consisting 2 Nos: Transformer panels with 1250 A withdrawable circuit breaker, 1 No: 2500 A bus tie breaker panel, and 8 Nos: 1250 A feeder breaker panels. Outgoing feeders are either radial feeders or ring feeders (Overhead line or underground cable).

Secondary distribution is the local area supply of the individual MV/LV distribution substations. Medium voltage system usually 13.8 KV, 11KV or 6.6 KV are considered as secondary distribution system. To reduce the network losses and voltage drops on the LV side, the distribution transformer substations should be installed directly at the load centers with its typical transformer ratings 50 KVA to 1600 KVA. The line configuration is mostly open ring / closed ring or radial feeders. Consumers with high power requirements have mostly their own distribution substation(s). Non extensible or extensible Ring Main Units (RMU) have been developed using SF6 gas as insulation and arc quenching medium in the case of load break systems.
Figure 3.13 (b) shows the single line diagram of a typical 11 KV intake switching station (secondary distribution system with out step down substation), which consists of:

(a) Incomer feeder Panel: 2 Numbers with 1250 A feeder breaker.
(b) Single bus bar system 2000 A 25 KA 3 seconds (Bus section 1 and Bus section 2)
(c) Bus coupler panel with two numbers draw out type three-phase potential transformers, and 2500 A bus tie breaker.
(d) Outgoing feeder breaker panels; 4 Numbers
(e) Outgoing spare feeder breaker panels; 2 Numbers
(f) Station service transformer feeder breaker panel: 1 Number
(g) Ring main unit 2R1T SF6 insulated (2 numbers 630 A and 1 number 200 A load break switches and earth switches): 6 units
(h) Distribution transformers 11KV/415 Volts: 7 Numbers.

All withdrawable circuit breakers in the switchgear except bus tiebreaker is rated for 1250 Amps, interchangeable from cubicle to cubicle. Bus section breaker is of 2500 Amps rating.

Following are common to all circuit breaker cubicles:

1. Withdrawable truck mounted circuit breaker with vacuum / SF6 / oil type interrupter.
2. Three-phase insulated copper or aluminium bus bar.
3. A set of automatic safety shutters covering the bus bar spouts painted in bright red colour.
4. Protection, control and instrument chamber located directly above the circuit breaker housing
5. Cable termination chamber at the back of the cubicle (except bus section cubicle)
6. Trip circuit supervision relay (This relay will not allow-to-close the circuit breaker if the trip circuit is unhealthy. Also connected to the red indication lamp in the front door of the panel.

Outgoing feeders: Feeders outgoing from the secondary switching stations are either radial or ring feeders as shown in the single line diagram. In the radial system, the overhead line or underground cable is run from the substation bus to distribution transformer. Several transformers are connected to one feeder. The voltage is stepped down to utilization level (3-phase 4-wire 415 or 3-phase 4-wire 220 volts) in several locations. In the underground system each transformer substation has a non-extensible ring-main unit (RMU) suitable for connecting one or two transformers. If more than 2 transformers in the same area, extensible type ring main units are being installed. Whereas for overhead lines outdoor type transformers (either pole mounted or ground mounted) are connected through expulsion fuses (Dropout fuses).

Overhead lines feeding indoor type transformers are connected through RMU (with out dropout fuses). Branches in radial lines of overhead lines are tapped through an isolator (disconnecting switch) or pole mounted circuit breakers. Since the entire load is served from a single source, full advantage can be taken of the diversity among the loads. This makes it possible to minimize the installed capacity. However the voltage regulation is poor because the entire load is fed from a single bus bar unit. A fault on the switchgear bus will interrupt service to all loads. Similarly, faults on the feeder circuit will interrupt service to all loads connected to that feeder. Since each transformer is located in a specific load area, it must have sufficient capacity to carry the peak load of that area.

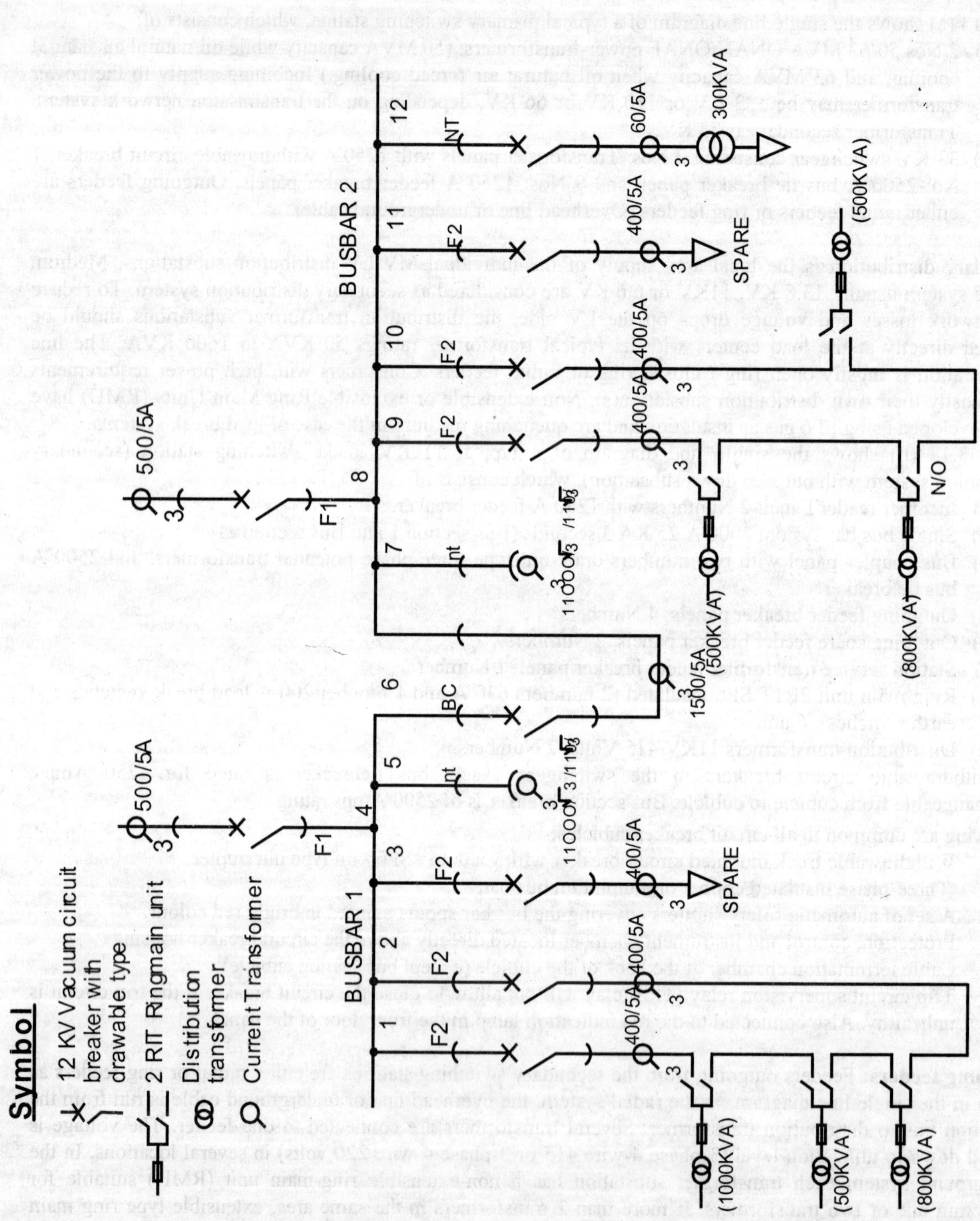

Fig. 3.13 (b): Single line diagram of an 11 KV intake switching station with distribution networks.

In ring type distribution feeders, the ring main circuit forms a complete loop and has isolating switches (for overhead lines) and ring main units (for underground cables) at strategic points for isolating a particular section in case of a fault For maintaining continuity of service ring main system described in section 3.14 is employed almost universally.

Since two identical feeders from different bus section supply power to the ring circuit the voltage drop is minimal. Assume that one transformer section is defective, the defective portion can be isolated and the power supply can be restored as two radial feeders. In normal service both feeders are ON and a loop is formed as a ring. If a fault is occurred in the ring circuit (other than individual transformer circuit) both feeder breakers will trip simultaneously. By isolating either side of the faulty section the power can be restored as radial feeders. The trouble-shooting is easy when comparing to radial feeders.

Protection co-ordination:

1) Primary loop system an n-1 outage condition shall be applied. Outage of each primary cable at the main source is to be considered. (For example 132/33 KV substation is the main source) Loading of primary transformers and outgoing cable should be within the limit of 80% of full load current in the load flow chart.

(2) The voltage drops at the primary (33KV) and secondary (11 KV) system bus bars should be within the limit of ± 6%.

3) Short circuit calculation (single phase and three phase) to be made on each primary (33 KV) and secondary (11 KV) circuit bus bars and ring main units. Value's that exceeds equipment rating is to be taken in to consideration.

(4) Protection settings may be calculated and protection co-ordination study carried out to derive the most efficient over current and earth fault protection-grading scheme for the equipment employed. Any violation less than 100milli seconds discrimination margin should be evaluated.

(5) All primary (33 KV) loop protection relays should be graded against the source substation using the standard international protection philosophy. Once the primary loop protection has been calculated, the secondary (11 KV) loop protection must be graded against it to ensure correct primary to secondary loop grading as well as secondary loop protection grading up to Ring main units.

(6) The main setting parameters (e.g. pickup and time multipliers) should be summarized. Protection setting sheets and grading diagrams are to be produced.

Incomer feeder panel (Figure 3.13 c).

The purpose of this 1250A switchgear panel is to control the incoming 3C 300 sq:mm feeder cable. Class 5P20 current transformers are provided for directional over current and earth fault protection and instrument using bay controller. High-speed current differential relays (Solkar RF) is provided at either ends of the incoming feeder for inter-tripping circuit breakers during a fault in the medium voltage feeder cable or line, and connected through pilot cable (10 or 20 pairs 2.5sq:mm) laid along with the main cable. C.T's at either ends (for current differential relays) must be similar type, for example 500/5 A, 10 VA, Class X, $Vk_P \supseteq 70$ volts.

Outgoing feeder Panel (Fig. 3.13 d)

Purpose of this 1250 A switchgear panel is to control the outgoing medium voltage feeder cable and/or overhead line. Current transformer Class 5P20 is provided for non-directional over current and earth fault protection. Outgoing feeder cable/overhead line can be connected as open ring or closed ring.

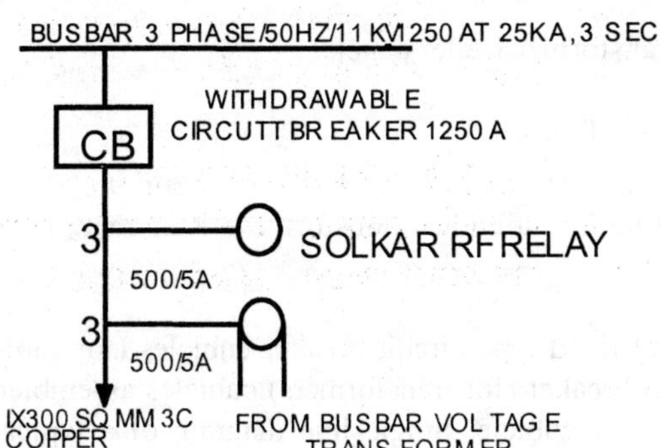

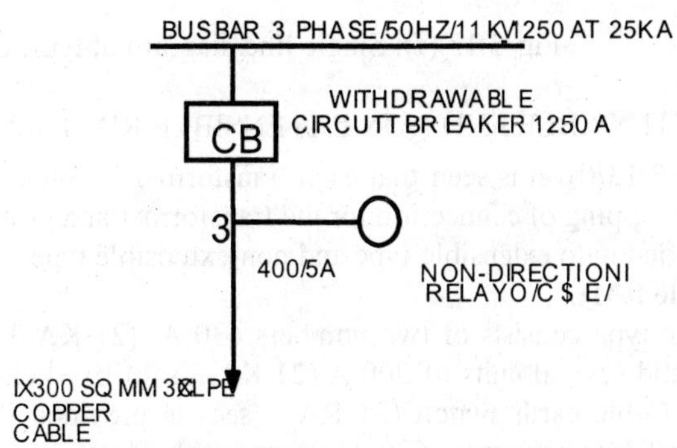

Fig. 3.13 (c): Single line diagram of incomer feeder. Fig. 3.13 (d): Single line diagram of outgoing feeder.

Bus coupler (Tie breaker) Panel (Figure 3.13e).

The purpose of this 2500 A switchgear panel is to sectionalize the two insulated bus bars. 1500/5A 10VA Class 5P20 C.T's are provided for over current and earth fault protection and instrument using bay controller. Either bus section have a draw out type design three-phase (11KV/√3): (110/√3), Class 3P, 5 limb cast resin insulated voltage transformer 100VA per phase, protected by HRC fuses for both HV and LV side of the voltage transformer. VT is capable of accurately reflecting ZPS voltage, i.e, segregated as single-phase or three-phase with suitable 5 limbs.

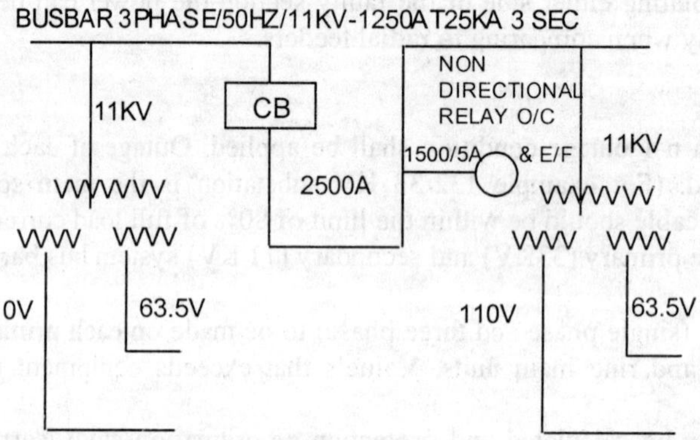

Fig. 3.13 (e): Single line diagram of typical bus coupler feeder panel with voltage transformers.

Transformer feeder Panel (Figure 3.13 f).

The purpose of this 1250 A switchgear panel is to control the outgoing feeder cable (3C 50 sq:mm) connected to Main distribution substation transformer, which also feed auxiliary supply to the intake station lighting, battery charger etc, in addition to the neighboring consumers and street lighting. 100/5A or 60/5 A, 10VA Class 5P20 C.T's are used for over current and earth fault protection, and instrument using bay controller.

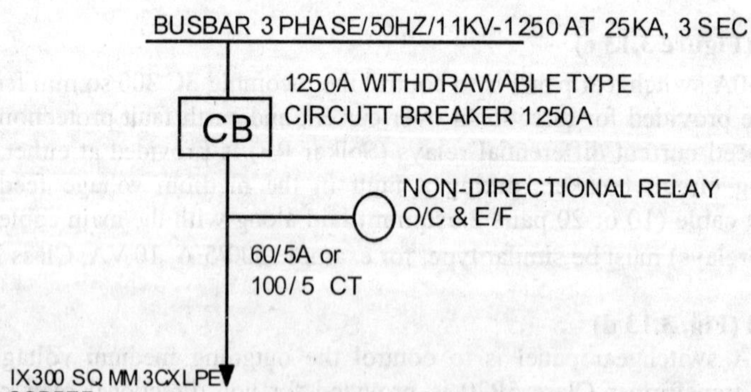

Fig. 3.13 (f): Single line diagram of typical transformer feeder panel.

3.14 EXTENSIBLE AND NON EXTENSIBLE RING MAIN UNITS

In Figure 3.13 (b) it is seen that each transformer is connected through an SF6 insulated ring main unit. This unit is for tapping of connection for the transformer and protection for individual transformers. Ring main units are classified in to extensible type and non-extensible type.

Extensible RMU

Extensible type consists of two numbers 630 A, (21 KA 3 sec) fixed type circuit breaker cubicles (for cable feeders) and several units of 200 A (21 KA 3 sec) fixed circuit breaker (for transformers) cubicles assembled together. Cable earth switch (21 KA 3 sec) is provided in every cubicle. Single line diagram of a typical extensible RMU consisting 630 A circuit breaker cubicle and Transformer circuit breaker cubicle is shown in Figure 3.14 (a). Other features of extensible ring main units are (1) 630 A 3-phase copper bus bar;(2)

Manometer for SF6 gas pressure indication (1.3 bar); (3) Neon voltage indication; (4) Degree of Protection IP 54; (5) normal rated BIL 95 KV for 11 KV RMU; (6) By adding new transformer units feature can be made.

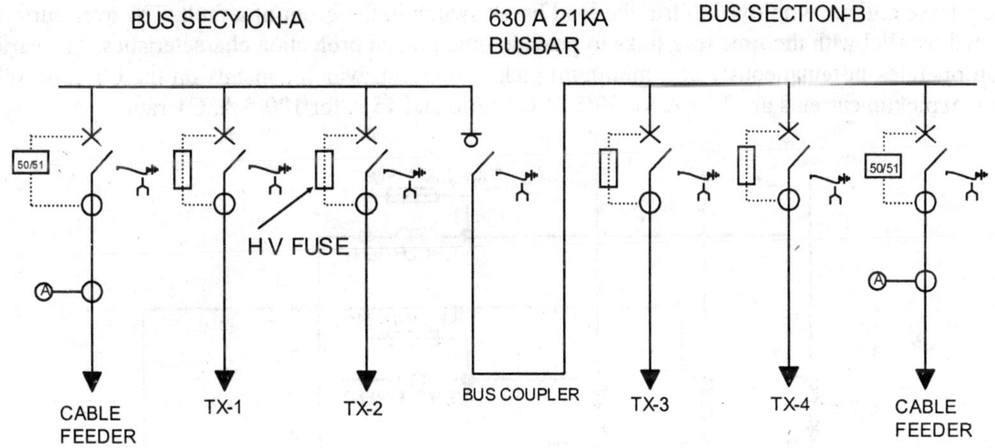

Fig. 3.14 (a): Single line diagram of extensible ring main unit cubicles (Courtesy, Merlin Gerin).

Non-extensible RMU

Non-extensible type RMU, 2R1T consists of two numbers 630 A (21 KA 3 sec) load break ring switches and a 200 A (21 KA 3 sec) load break transformer switch with high voltage HRC fuse. Similarly, 2R2T ring main unit consists of 2 numbers 630 A (21 KA 3 sec) load break ring switches and 2 numbers 200A (21 KA 3 sec) load break transformer switch with HRC fuses. Cable earth switches 21 KA 3 sec is provided with every load break switches. Typical layout diagram of a 2R1T non-extensible RMU is shown in Figure 3.14 (b). Other features are (1) 630 A nickel plated copper bus bar; (2) SF6 gas pressure 1.3 bar; (3) Hermetically welded tank, degree of Protcction IP 65; (4) Plug-in capacitor voltage indicator; (5) Pressure gauge: green indicates normal gas pressure and red indicate insufficient / low gas pressure; (6) HRC fuse (for transformer protection) with tripping linkage for the striker pin operation via a diaphragm; (7) Normal rated BIL 125 KV between phase and earth; (8) Rated power frequency-withstand voltage (1 minute) 50 KV; (9) Dual ratio current transformers with time limit fuses are used for over current protection and earth fault protection of transformers.

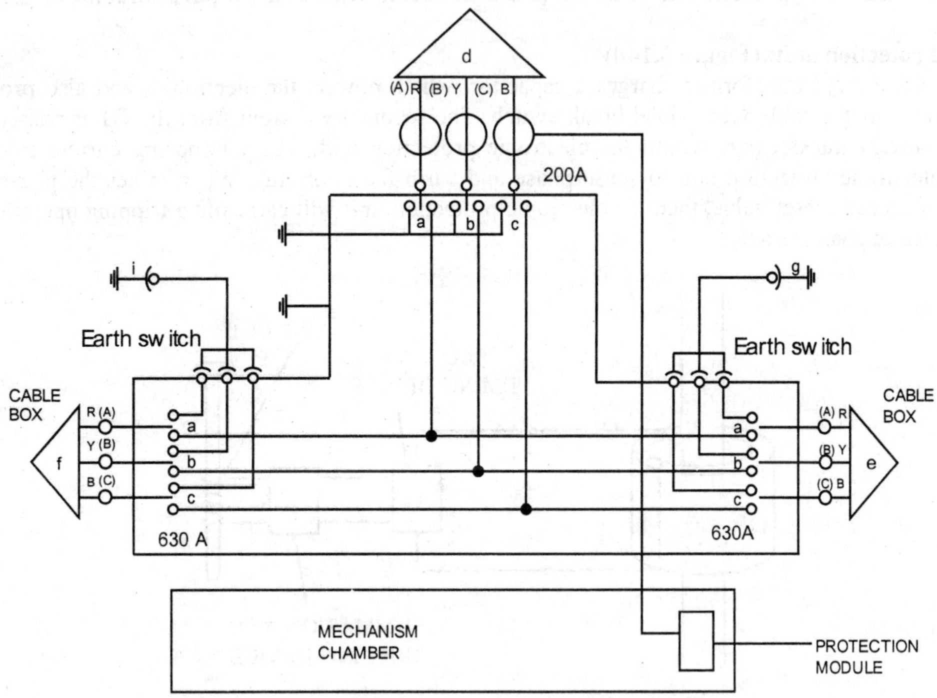

Fig. 3.14 (b): Typical layout diagram of non-extensible type 2R1T ring main unit

Typical circuit for 200 A transformer feeder and 630 A cable feeder (over current and earth fault protection) is shown in Figure 3.14 (c) and (d) respectively. In the transformer feeder two over-current release coils and one earth fault release coil are employed to trip the load break switch in the event of a fault. The over-current coils are connected parallel with the time fuse links to provide time graded protection characteristics. The earth fault release coil operates instantaneously at a minimum pick up current, which depends on the CT ratio selected. The minimum pickup currents are 27.5 A for 50/5 A, CT ratio and 45 A for 100/5 A, CT ratio.

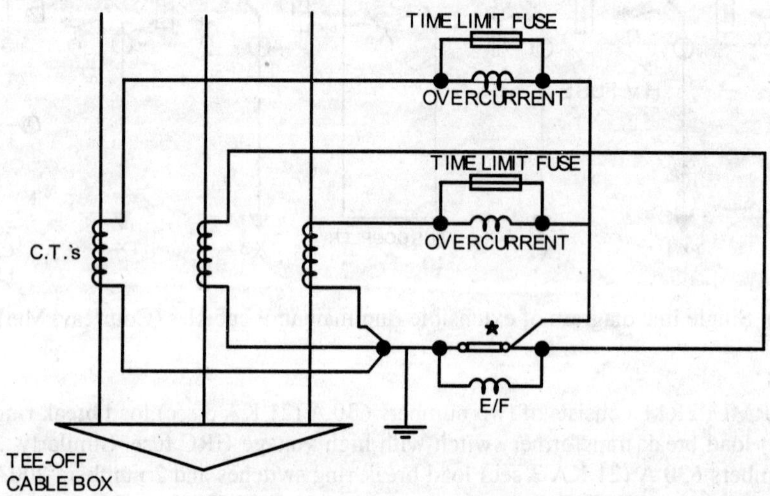

Fig 3.14 (c): Over current and earth fault protection for 200A Transformer feeder of non-extensible type RMU.

Safety interlocks for RMU: Interlocks prevents:
1) Direct switching from "ON" to "Earth" and "Earth" to "ON".
2) Switching to the "ON" position, when the test cover is open
3) Access for fuse renewal, with the switch in the "ON" position (only for transformer feeder with HV fuse).
4) Switching to the "ON" position when a blown fuse is in circuit with its striker pin protruding or CB tripped.

Electronic Protection unit: (Figure 3.14d)
The summation current transformer charges a capacitor, which powers the electronics and also provides the tripping energy for the cable feeder load break switch. The secondary current from the CT is passed through interposing current transformers within the electronic protection unit. The interposing current transformers enable the electronic protection unit to sense phase and earth fault currents. When either the phase or earth fault currents exceed preset value, then the electronic protection unit will carry out a tripping operation in line with its protection characteristics.

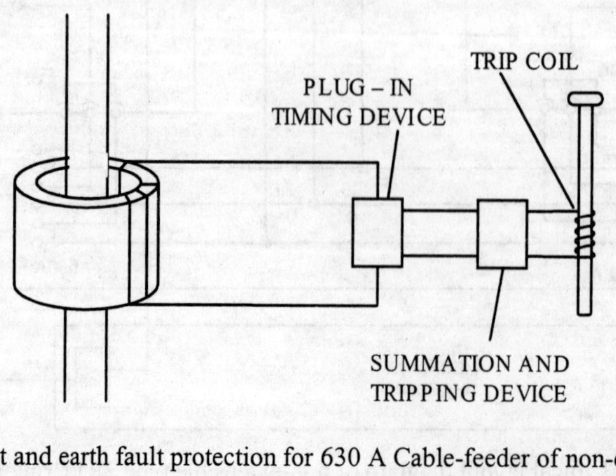

Fig. 3.14 (d): Over-current and earth fault protection for 630 A Cable-feeder of non-extensible type RMU.

3.15 BAY CONTROLLERS FOR CONTROL, MEASUREMENT AND PROTECTION

The bay controller is a microprocessor based feeder protection/metering equipment consists of a control / instruments section, and a protection section, each with its own microprocessor. The control section consists of the following:-

1. A local / remote switch with indicator.
2. A dynamic mimic diagram showing the position of circuit breaker, earthing switch etc.
3. An ON / OFF pushbutton to operate the circuit breaker.
4. A minimum of 6 digital inputs for external signals to be connected, e.g. low SF6 gas etc.
5. Software interlocking of circuit breaker with earthing switch, digital inputs etc.
6. Ammeter and voltmeter are integrated in to the control unit. Phase selection is through push buttons and the scale is software selectable. The active power Mega-volt-ampere (MVA), reactive power Reactive mega-volt-ampere (MVAR), and energy Megawatt hour (MWH) are also integrated in to the control unit and the scale is software selectable.
7. The bay controller indicates the maximum demand current value for the last 15 minutes and highest maximum demand value found since the unit was placed in service.

The protection section consists of the over-current, short circuit and earth fault protection. Numerical type relays with selectable characteristics of the definite time or IDMT (Inverse definite minimum time) which conforms to IEC 255-4 or BS 142 standards. The bay controller, have LED (light emitting diode) indicating a healthy auxiliary power supply.
Microprocessor controlled protection device is capable of record following values of the latest five operations of:

1. Phase fault currents on each phase with fault type.
2. Earth fault current and duration of fault.

The unit will memorize: Numerical display of the setting values, memorized fault value and relay operation.
Other features are:

1) Circuit breaker failure protection (CBFP) with a time setting of 0.1 to 1.0 second
2) Continuous self-supervision with auto-diagnosis for internal faults in the relay.
3) Plug in type power supply module.
4) Selectable output contact configuration with volt-free trip contacts.
5) Serial port for connection of the relay to the personal computer (PC). All setting of the relay could be possible to alter from the PC via the serial port.
6) Serial port for fiber optic SCADA (Supervisory control and data access) connection.
7) Terminal blocks for testing connections

3.16 CONTROL CUBICLE, CONTROL DESK, AND DUPLEX CONTROL BOARD.

For voltage levels up to 38 KV, the control and relays are usually mounted on the switchgear cubicles, whereas for high voltage (HV) feeders and extra high voltage (EHV) feeders (AC 60 KV to 800 KV), ultra high voltage (UHV) feeders (AC above 800 KV), high voltage direct current transmission (HVDC) feeders (400 KV and above) and electrical equipments for generation (Medium voltage generator), transmission lines, bus protection etc. the control and relay panel cubicles are used. Control and relay panel facilitate centralized control of the related controlled equipment in power stations, substations and other switching stations and industrial plants.

(1) Control cubicle:

Control board means a switchboard incorporating secondary switching devices such as indicating and operating devices and accessories for the remote control of switchgear. Control gear is the combination of switching devices with their associated equipments for control, measurements, protection and regulation of a feeder or equipment. Control board facilitates centralized control but it is the point at which all, vital information relating to the controlled equipment is received and assimilated. Unit panels are built of dimensions to suit mounted equipment, and composite boards are then formed from the unit panel. Figure 3.16 (a) illustrates the exploded view of a typical control cubicle.

The indoor type vermin-proof panels are bolted together to form complex-assemblies, which permit replacements, extensions, rearrangement and addition when necessary. The floor mounting type sheet steel panel "shell" is built up of a frame work cubicle consists of front panel, side panels, back panel, door-frame and roof providing rigidity and strength. The panel has a standard dimension of height 2250mm, width 600mm to 1000mm, and depth 600 or 800mm depending on the requirements. Knockouts are provided for flush mounting of instruments and control components. The relays are mounted in the cubicle on a swing frame which can be locked if do not require access from the front side. These frames are carried on hinges at the front of the cubicles. Alternatively, sheet steel cubicle construction can also be preferred for manufacturing control cubicles.

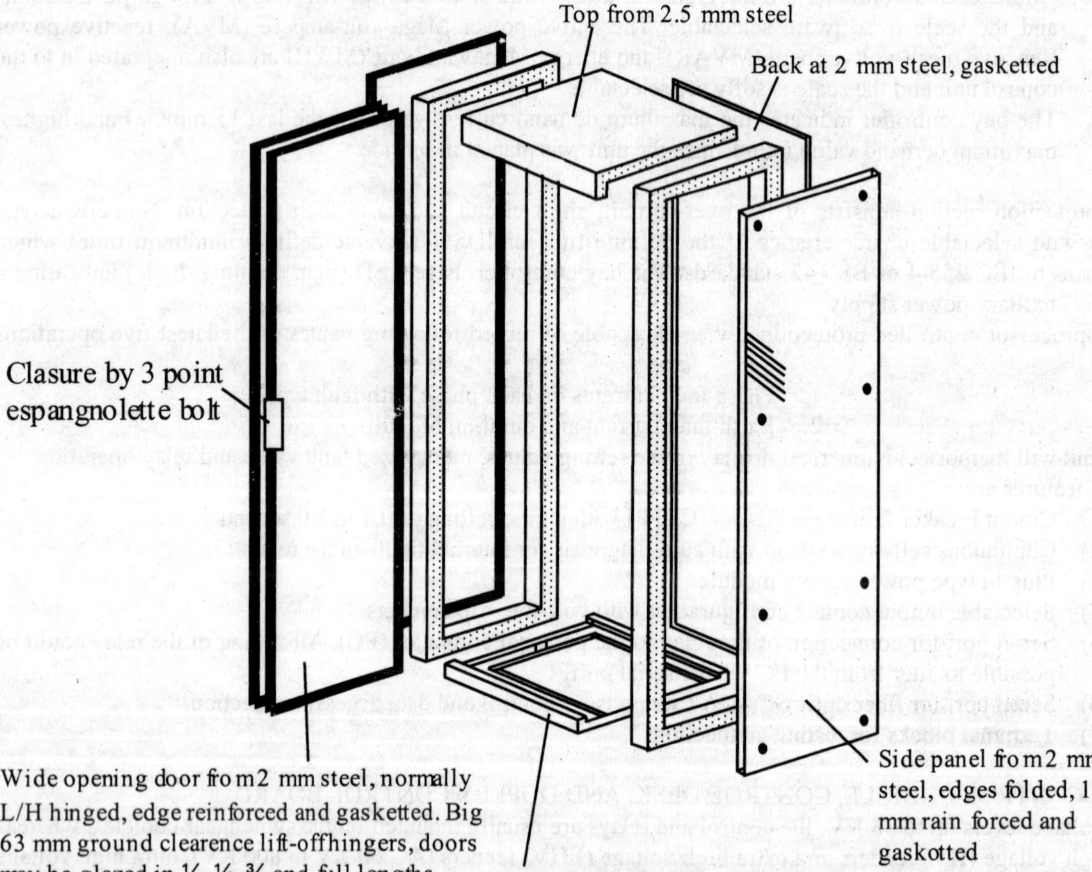

Fig. 3.16 (a): Exploded view of a typical control cubicle

The door at the front of the cubicle has a glass window (or glass doors) so that all the modules are visible when the door is lock. Doors which can be for right or left hand opening are hung-on, lift off hinges and have self locking handle, which locks automatically on closing. It requires tool or key to open. The cubicles are phosphated, painted with primer and finished with a topcoat of light gray (exterior) and matte white (interior) paint. Completed panels are equipped with earth bus, top and bottom ventilation facilities, interior lamp with door switch, and anti-condensation heater with thermostat.

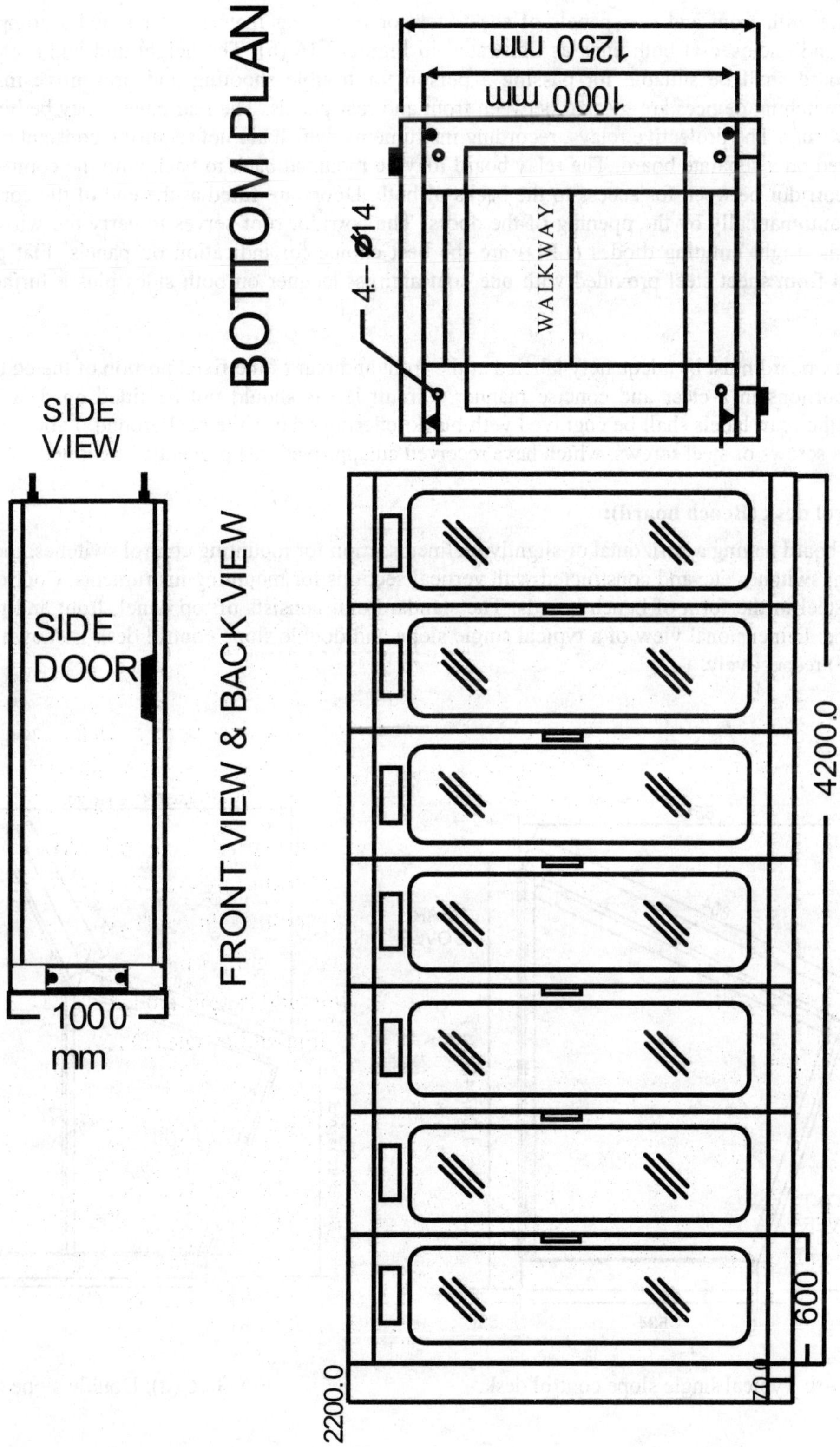

Fig. 3.16 (b): Duplex control board with front and rear panels.

(2) Duplex control board:

A structure with front and rear panels of sheet steel or insulating material, separated a comparatively short distance, and enclosed at both ends as illustrated in Figure 3.16 (b). The height and width of the assembled duplex board shall be suitable for passing a person for trouble shooting and preventive maintenance. No primary switching devices are located between front and rear panels. The rear panels may be hinged for access to panel wiring. The protective relays, recording instruments, which are not requiring constant observation, can be mounted on a separate board. The relay board may be mounted back to back with the control board, with a covered corridor between for access to the backs of both. Doors are fitted at the end of the corridor, which lit the light automatically by the opening of the doors. The corridor roof serves to carry the wiring between the two boards. Light emitting diodes (LED) are the best choice for indication on panels. Flat plate chassis is fabricated from sheet steel provided with one coat antirust lacquer on both sides plus a further coat enamel paint.

The duplex board must be adequately labeled at the front and rear of the fixed portion of the equipment, and on moving portions in a clear and concise manner. Circuit labels should not be fitted on detachable doors or covers. All circuit labels shall be engraved with black lettering on a white background. Labels shall be secured with brass screws or steel screws, which have received an approved rust preventive treatment.

(3) Control desk (Bench board):

A switch board having a horizontal or slightly inclined section for mounting control switches, indicating lamps, instrument switches etc, and constructed with vertical sections for mounting instruments. Control desk is made of sheet steel in the form of bench boards. The standard unit consists of top panel, front and rear covers and base frame. Dimensional view of a typical single slope and double slope control desk is shown in Figure 3.16 (c) and (d) respectively.

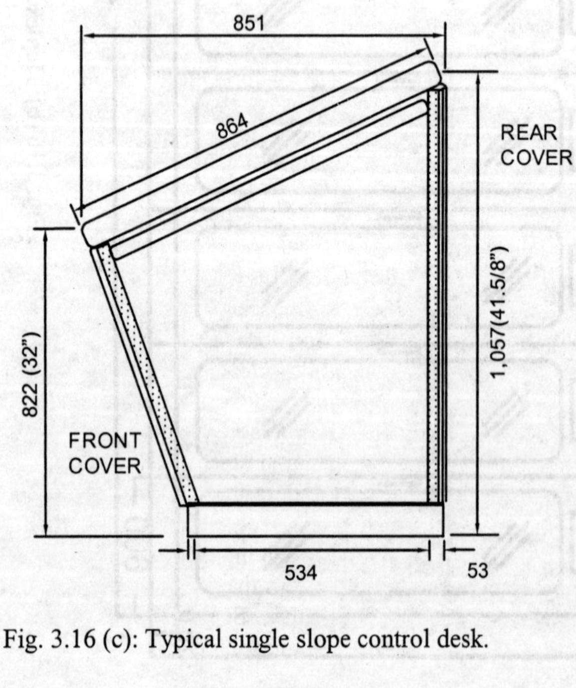

Fig. 3.16 (c): Typical single slope control desk.

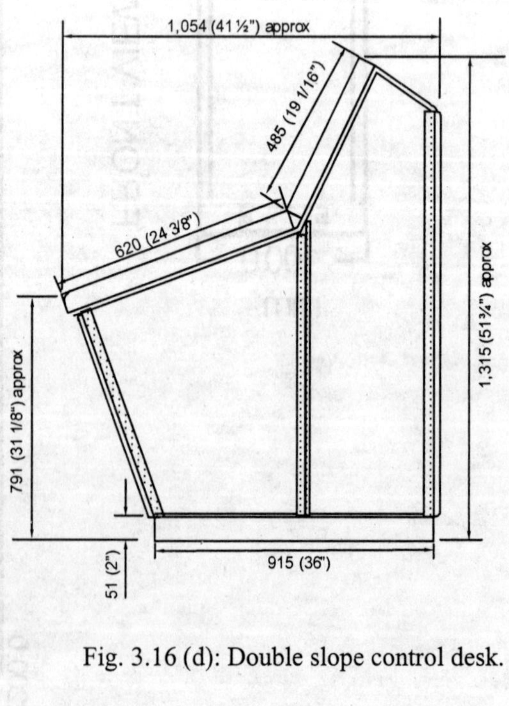

Fig. 3.16 (d): Double slope control desk.

Front door and rear cover on control desk are beaded with neoprene gaskets for dust proofing and positive sealing. Chases plate built from sheet steel is demountable, pivoted at base and top clamped. The desk shall be so constructed that it should not protrude so far as to hinder the easy reading of instruments and the operations of the controls. Floor plates should not be used as gland plates for control cable terminations but separate removable gland plates are required within the panel. Conductors of the incoming and outgoing control line are arranged in functional group and are connected through marshalling terminal rack, which has the following advantages:

(a) It collects all connections in one cable without regards to functional relationship. Simple planning and clear layout.

(b) It gives freedom in arranging units required in the control room.

(c) It facilitates extension of fault tracing of the control circuits.

(4) Control switches:

The panel incorporates local/remote selection switch, control switches, indicator lamps, fuses, links, miniature circuit breakers, terminal blocks etc. for control of controlled equipment. The control switches are divided in two types, namely; (1) Maintained contact type for use with all classes of electrical instruments, relays and performing various combinations; (2) Momentary contact type with spring return to original or off position, used for circuit breakers and start/stop control of electrical apparatus, etc. Handles made of insulating phenolic composition are available in three shapes oval, round, and pistol grip. Each handle fastened to the switch shaft has a recessed arrow moulded in to it, to aid in positioning.

The dial unit consists of three parts namely; dial plate, faceplate and faceplate cover. Selector switches are either "spring return, and make before break" or "Key selectors with key trapped positions". Control, reversing, selector and test switches are mounted, constructed and wired so as to facilitate the maintenance of contacts without the necessity for disconnecting wiring.

Shrouded pushbuttons must be of the non-retaining type made of non-hygroscopic material, non-swelling and fitted to avoid any possibility of sticking. The contacts of all switches and pushbuttons shall be strong and should have a positive wiping action when operated. Following locations are suggested for controlling the equipment.

(a) Local control: Located adjacent to the equipment to facilitate maintenance, inspection and emergency operation.

(b) Remote control: Located at control room, such as a power station or substation control room, where specified items of equipment are monitored and controlled by direct wire connection.

(c) Supervisory control: Located at a system control point, where principal items of equipment at a number of group control centers are remotely controlled.

Indication lamps conforming to IEC 529 are encapsulated lamp units with (1) The lens-bush assembly secured to the mounting panel by a locknut; (2) The lamp unit which screws-on to the lens-bush assembly. Replacement of the lens and access to the bulb are achieved by unscrewing the front bezel. Plastic or glass lenses are manufactured in red, green, blue, yellow, white, brown, gray and amber clear colours. Use of miniature circuit breakers complying with IEC 157 is permitted both on AC and DC circuits. Fuse shall incorporate H.R.C (High rupturing capacity) cartridges to IEC 269 or equivalent. Rewireable fuses should not be used. Carriers and bases for 6 amp fuses shall be coloured black and those for 16 amp fuses shall be green. Link-carriers and bases shall be white to identify fuse and link. Signaling devices are described in Chapter # 9, section 9.24.

(5) Terminal blocks: Terminal boards may be mounted in accessible positions and, when in enclosed cubicles, to be inclined towards the door. Spacing of adjacent terminal boards should not be less than 100mm and the bottom of each board may be not less than 200mm above the incoming cable gland plate. Separate studs must be provided on each terminal strip for the cores of incoming and outgoing cables including spare cores.

Standard types of terminals are:

1. Screw or stud type used with crimped ring type termination. Screws and studs are to be of not less than size M6. All studs are to be provided with nuts, washers and lock washers.

2. Insertion clamp type whereby the standard conductor or crimped termination is clamped between plates by a screw having a suitable locking device. Terminal entries shall be shrouded such that no current carrying metal is exposed.

Terminal assemblies are to be of the unit form suitable for mounting collectively on a standard assembly rail, secured from the front and giving the required number of ways plus sufficient spare ways. 415/240 Volts circuit terminals are to be segregated from other terminals and are to be fitted with nonflammable plastic covers to prevent contacts with any live parts. They are to have, warning labels, with red lettering, mounted thereon in a conspicuous position. The terminal blocks used for relay and control cubicle shall be removable, isolatable sliding link screw clamp type. The sliding link will facilitate in the testing and isolation purposes of all circuits during maintenance and trouble-shooting. Each terminal block have a test socket for the connection of a standard banana plug. Open-circuiting link are equipped with sleeved screws for connection of test plugs. Terminal blocks must be made of non-hygroscopic materials and shall be marked with clear and durable labels.

(6) Indicating lamps and fittings:
Indicating lamps to be fitted in to the fascias of switch and instrument cubicles or panels must be adequately ventilated. Lamps can be easily removed and replaced from the front of the panel by manual, means not requiring the use of extractors. The bezel of metal or other material holding the lamp-glass is of easily removable from the body of the fitting so as to permit access to the lamp and lamp glass. The lamps must be clear and fit in to an accepted standard form of lamp holder. The rated lamp voltage should be 10% in excess of the auxiliary supply voltage, whether AC or DC. Alternatively, low voltage (12 or 6 volts) lamp with series resistors can be used. The colour should be in the cap (glass) and not an applied coating and the different coloured glasses are to be interchangeable. Transparent synthetic materials can be used instead of glass, provided such materials have fast colours and are completely suitable for operating in tropical climates.

Few examples of indication lamp colours are given below:

- Red: Reserved only for the function mentioned; e.g. circuit breaker or contactor closed.
- Green: Reserved only for the function mentioned; e.g. circuit breaker or contactor open.
- White: Lamps normally alight; e.g. trip circuit healthy, equipment in normal service etc.
- Amber: Used where action is necessary; e.g. transformer high temperature, circuit breaker tripped due to faults, battery charger fail etc.
- Blue: Used for signal (with label); e.g. transformer tap change in progress, circuit breaker closing springs being charged etc.

(7) Metering and instruments: Bay controllers discussed in section 3.15 have in-built facility for reading.
Metering section could incorporate instruments and meters complying with IEC 51 and IEC 43 respectively and conforming industrial grade accuracy. Essential requirements are measurements of voltage (volt meter with selector switch), current (ammeter with selector switch), actual power (Kilowatt/Megawatt meter), active power (KVA/MVA meter), and reactive power (RKVA/RMVA meter), frequency, power factor, energy consumption (KWH/MWH meter), Hour meter etc as required. [Refer figure 5.3 (b) of Chapter # 5]

For measuring large quantities, voltage transducer, current transducer, combined var and watt transducer, frequency transducer etc (4-20 mA) connected through CT's and/or PT's are used in combination with the above instruments. Recording instruments for e.g, voltage, temperature etc are also incorporated in the metering section. Transducer circuit is illustrated in figure 5.3 (c) of Chapter # 5.

Most of the indicating and recording instruments are of flush-mounted pattern with dust and moisture proof housings. Where hinged covers (housings) are necessary, they are to be provided with locks. Standard dimension of indicating instrument is 100mm diameter. Instrument dials in general should be white with black markings and should be reversible where double scale instruments are specified. Dials shall be of such material that no pealing or discolouration will take place with age under humid tropical conditions. Instruments are usually provided with a readily accessible zero adjustment.

(8) Protection relays
The protection relays are equipped for to detect defective lines or apparatus, other power system conditions of an abnormal or dangerous nature and to initiate appropriate control circuit action. Protection relays are

designed and applied to provide maximum discrimination between faulty and healthy circuits. Equipment will remain inoperative during transient phenomena, which may arise during switching or other disturbance to the system. Protective relays are composed of plug in units placed in open racks. Plug in relays have generally individual transparent plastic covers and a target-resetting knob on the outside. The plug in system consists of electrical connections with plug-in sockets and pins. The relays are mounted on the terminal bases with screws. Protective relays for generators, transformers, transmission lines, and motor protection etc are demonstrated in Chapter # 6 to 9 respectively.

(9) Mimic diagrams

Strip mimic diagrams incorporating semaphore indication and discrepancy switch are provided on the control and relay panel to suit the system layout and switchgear status. The mimics are coloured suitably to distinguish with system voltages.

Following are the colour codes for mimic diagram in accordance with BS 381.

System voltage	Colour No:	Mimic diagram
<600 volts	557	Light orange
3.3 KV	439	Orange Brown
6.6 KV	166	French Blue
11 KV	537	Signal Red
22 KV	309	Yellow
33 KV	231	Green
66 KV	-----	Orange
132 KV	----	Black
220 KV	------	Red

Mosaic type tile system has the following advantages:

1. Mosaic mimic circuit diagram can be designed in every desired form, size and any required mounting position. Simple planning by using printed forms with grid.
2. The mosaic mimic diagram can be modified simply during installation and after commissioning without interruption of operation. Cutout or drilling work is not required. Clear layout because of small and uniform tiles, are being used.
3. Less wiring required by using plug and socket connections between the active tiles and the built-in plug strips. As such simple interchangeability is possible.

(10) Annunciation window panel:

A multi-window alarm fascia, with 'accept', 'cancel' audible-alarm, lamp test facilities mounted on the control and relay panel for specific fault indication. This remote audible-alarm will alert the control room operator of the operation of protection devices and mal-operation of equipments. All individual alarms have facility for selection to "urgent" or "non-urgent" classification. All alarms to have three conditions:

(1) Alarm operated; Bell or buzzer sounding, light flashing on corresponding annunciator window.
(2) Alarm accepted; Bell or buzzer silenced, steady light appears on the corresponding window.
(3) Alarm cancelled; Light extinguished on corresponding annunciator window, and ready to receive further alarm initiations.

All alarms grouped together on one annunciator display panel need common "lamp test", "accept", and "cancial" pushbuttons. Alarms must be capable of being "accepted" but not "cancelled" before the initiating relay or fault condition has been reset or cleared. Acceptance of one alarm in any group should not prevent the normal individual operation of any other alarm within the group. One potential free contact of each of the alarms is to be wired, either individually or connected in parallel with other alarms for the remote control applications. The alarm panel is to have its own "DC supply failure" alarm relay, to operate a separate annunciator to be installed on the same alarms panel, or other suitable location. The supply for this alarm shall be taken from station battery supply. Wiring diagram of a typical 10 points annunciator controller is shown in figure 3.16 (e).

Annunciator receives input signals from the protective or functional devices of the equipment for which, the annunciator is employed to alert the operator with flashing lights and horn. Annunciator modules works on 24, 48 or 110 volts DC supply. Those modules can be easily paralleled to accommodate any number of alarm inputs. The 10 points annunciator module have following control facilities:

1. Alarm acknowledgement pushbutton: This is for operator to acknowledge the alarm and changes the flashing light to steady light.
2. Horn silence pushbutton: Connecting silence input to positive power turns off the horn.
3. Reset pushbutton: This turns off each steady light whose corresponding alarm input is reset.
4. Lamp test pushbutton: This connects the test input and turns on all lights in the annunciation windows. Removing power from test input returns all lights to their previous state.

By inserting the option jumpers following additional facilities can be obtained.

(a) JUMPER 1: Any steady lights turn off automatically as soon as the corresponding alarm input is reset.
(b) JUMPER 2: Any flashing light will change in to steady light if the corresponding alarm input is off.
(c) JUMPER 3: Horn will be turned off whenever reset input is connected to input power.
(d) JUMPER 4: Horn will be turned off whenever flashing light changes to steady light.
(e) JUMPER 5: Horn will alternate ON for one second and OFF for one second until turned off.

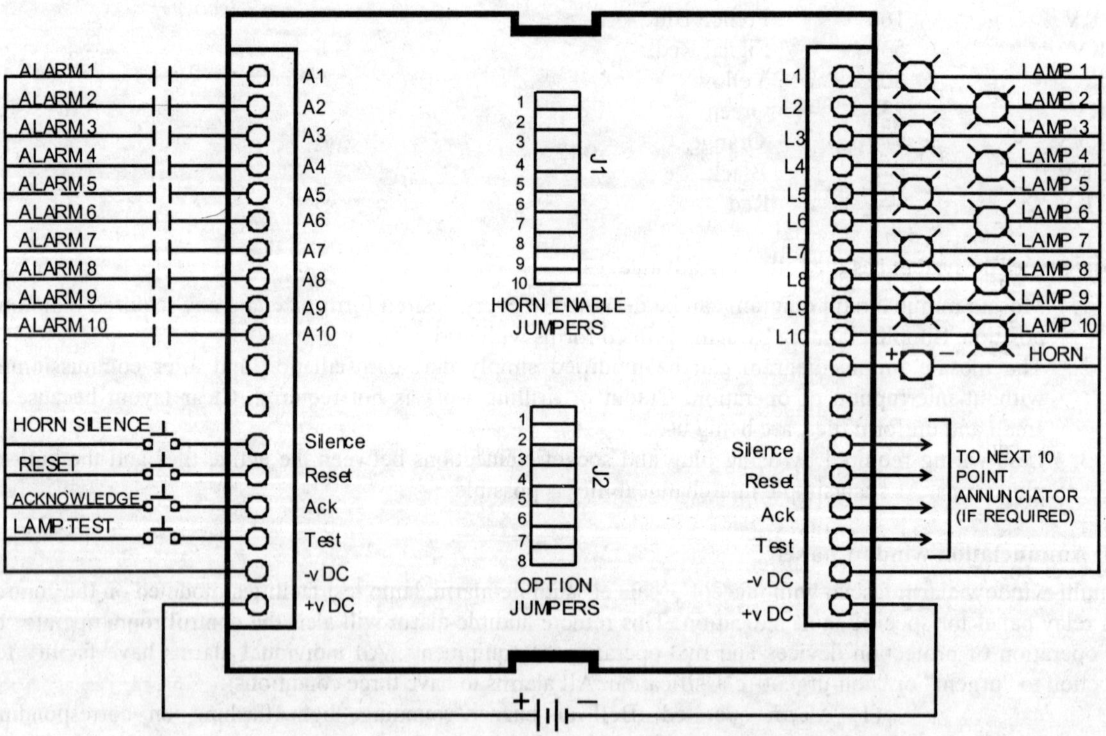

Fig. 3.16 (e): External wiring diagram of a 10 points annunciator module.

(11) Synchronizing system

Synchronizing section consists of synchroscope with polarity reversing voltage transformer for lamp bright at synchronism, synchroscope on/off switch, phase isolating transformer, frequency meter, voltmeter, synchronism check relay and indicating lamp for bright at synchronizing. Paralleling generators are discussed in section 1.7 of Chapter # 1. Similarly, paralleling transformers are discussed in section 2.17 of Chapter # 2.

(12) Control panel wiring:

The sequence of the wiring terminals may be such that the junction between multi-core cables and the terminals is affected without crossover. Claw washers or crimped connectors must be used to terminate all control wiring. Insulating bushes be provided where necessary to prevent the chafing of wiring. PVC insulated cables used for internal wiring of switch, control, metering, relay and instrument may conform to the requirements of BS 6231 type A or B as appropriate. The conductors should have a minimum cross section 2.5mm^2 (7/0.67mm or 1/1.78mm), but single stranded conductors should only be employed for rigid connections, which are not subject to movement or vibration during equipment operation. Flexible conductors 1.5mm^2 (30/0.25mm) or 2.5mm^2 (50/0.25mm) may be employed on indoor, independently mounted control and relay panels.

Wire colours should comply with British Standard 158, viz:-

a) Red, Yellow, Blue: Phase connections (R-Y-B) in current and voltage transformer circuits only

b) Black: AC neutral connections, CT and PT neutral connections, DC negative connections.

c) Gray: DC positive connections.

All wires should have numbered ferrules (Z type cable markers consists of numerical numbers and alphabets) at each termination, in accordance with BS 158. The same ferrule number should not be repeated on wires forming connections not directly in series or parallel in the same circuit. At points or interconnection between panels where a change of numbering cannot be avoided, double ferrules are to be provided. The ferrules on all wiring directly connected to circuit breaker trip coils and trip circuits must be of a colour different from that of the reminder, preferably red. No wires should be teed or jointed between terminal points. Bus wiring between control panels must be fully insulated and be completely segregated from the main panel wiring. All metallic cases of instruments, control switches, relays etc. mounted on control panels or in cubicles, must be connected by means of copper conductors of not less than 2.5mm^2 section to the nearest earth bar.

(13) Routine tests

1. A check of the mechanical design.
2. A check that all components are included.
3. A check on the function of all protective relays and apparatus from the cubicle terminals.

3.17 CURRENT LIMITING REACTORS AND STATIC VAR COMPENSATORS.

Inductive reactance stores magnetic energy and hinders the flow of alternating current. Capacitive reactance stores electric energy. Reactance is the component of impedance that does not dissipate energy. Reactor is a device used to introduce inductive reactance in to a circuit.

Current limiting reactors (Series reactors)

A reactor connected in series with a circuit or equipment, which is used to limit the current that can flow under fault conditions or switching conditions or otherwise to reduce the level of available short circuit current on the load side of the reactor. Current limiting reactors can be used to keep fault current magnitudes within the capability of the installed equipment. Another benefit of limiting fault current magnitude is smaller bus voltage drop during short circuit. Air cored or air gapped iron cored, dry type or mineral oil filled, (Temperature class 105/155/220°C) medium voltage reactors are suitable for motor starting or fault current limiting duty. Typical current limiting applications include:

1. Feeder reactors for limiting the current during surges, short circuit and fluctuations.
2. Motor starting reactors to limit the starting current of heavy motors.
3. Synchronizing or bus-tie reactors to limit the current during synchronizing, load sharing and fluctuating loads.
4. Smoothing reactors for smoothing the current wave form obtained from a rectified output.

A current limiting reactor is an inductive coil having a large inductive reactance (XL).

Short circuit current Isc = E/X if resistance R is negligible. Therefore, by increasing reactance X, the short circuit current will reduce. Figure 3.17 (a) shows the typical circuit arrangement of current limiting reactor with triggered current limiter. Under system loaded conditions, regulating voltage drops to below 95% are not uncommon. But this 5% voltage-drop can reduce the efficiency of connected equipment by nearly 10%. This is in addition to the direct energy loss in the reactor itself. It is a substantial reduction, which may not be tolerable and prevent start up of heavy motors. Bypassing the reactor with a triggered current limiter as shown in Figure 3.17 (a) can, however, mitigate these difficulties. It eliminates the continual energy losses related to the resistive portion of the reactor's impedance, and it eliminates the regulating voltage across the reactor since the impedance of the circuit is measured in micro-ohms. Assume that the symmetrical (rms) short circuit current in the bus bar is 15 KA when the reactor is in the circuit, 30 KA (rms) symmetrical with the reactor bypassed.

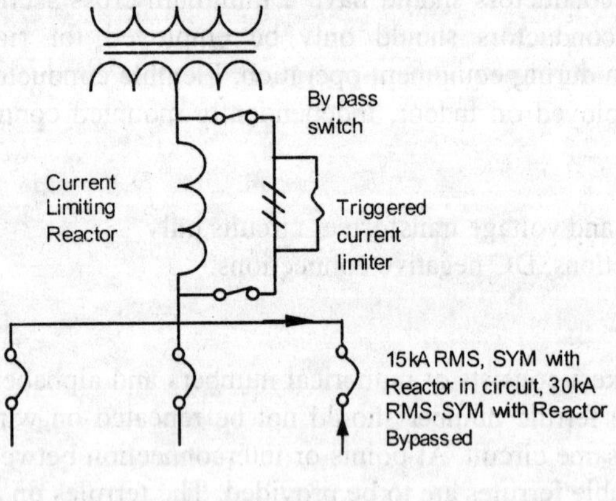

Fig. 3.17 (a): Current limiting reactor circuit

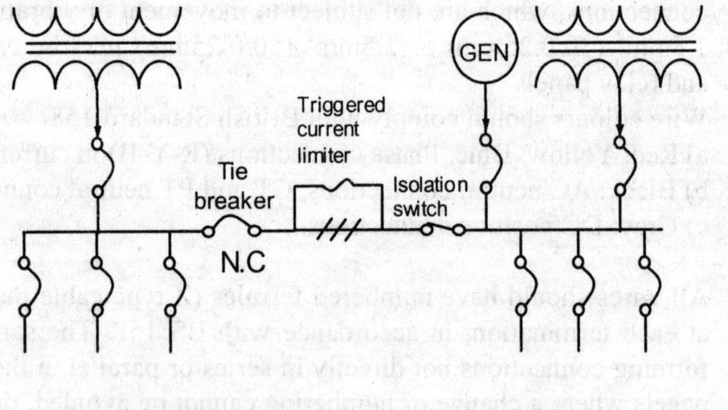

Fig. 3.17 (b): Bus tie closure reactor circuit.

Often the industrial power system Engineer is facing a dilemma. It may be a case of trying to start a large motor, or to better balance transformer loads, or to share the output of a generator with an adjacent bus. The overall system may posse's sufficient capacity to meet all of the needs if the tie(s) were closed. However, tie closure results in fault currents from both buses and these may exceed the fault ratings of the system. The best solution is the insertion of a triggered current limiter for bypassing the reactor as shown in Figure 3.17 (b). Upon occurrence of a fault, the reactor serves the tie in a current limiting fashion, whereby, that portion of fault current available through it is interrupted. The magnitude is thus reduced.

Consider the system depicted in Figure 3.17 (c). It has two facilities (buses) supplied from the same source. A fault at facility "A" will cause a temporary under-voltage situation at facility "B" that can cause motor starters, computers and lighting systems to shutdown. Triggered current limiter can also be used to bypass reactors in this application and maintain continuity to the other equipment while limiting the voltage drop at critical equipment. This is particularly essential in process industries where a momentary power disturbance can result in a costly shutdown.

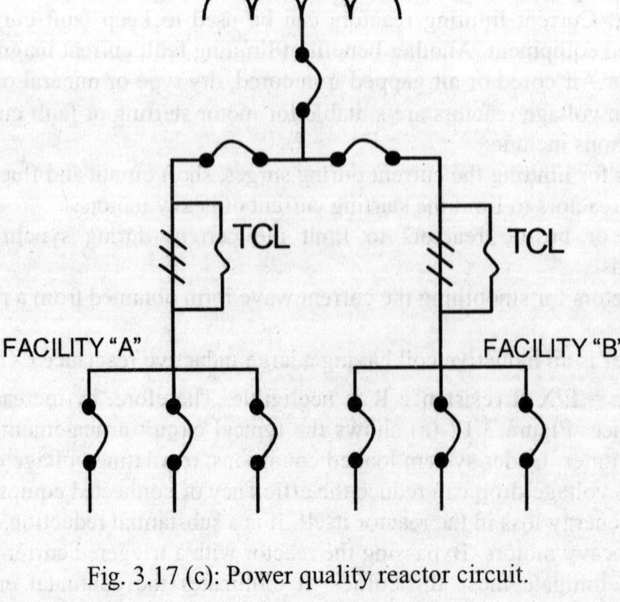

Fig. 3.17 (c): Power quality reactor circuit.

Shunt reactors

An electromagnetic device connected between phases or between phase and ground, used to introduce inductive reactance in a system. Shunt reactors can be connected to a bus or to a line and used to absorb reactive power and lower system voltage. Air core shunt reactors are used to compensate for capacitive VARs generated by lightly loaded underground transmission cables. Shunt reactors are normally connected to the transformer tertiary winding but can also be directly connected on high voltage systems. Air core, dry type construction (up to 10 MVAR) with epoxy impregnated, fiberglass encapsulated aluminium conductor windings. Reactors are provided with appropriate mounting pedestal made of non-magnetic material such as fiberglass, stainless steel, aluminium etc. Above 10 MVAR oil immersed types are used. Noise level of reactor is 60dB to 70dB throughout life. HV and EHV shunt reactors are demonstrated in Chapter # 4, section 4.13.

Static VAR compensator

Static VAR reactors are shunt reactors that are used with thyristor controls to manage power flow on the system and to provide dynamic voltage support. VAR reactors are used in conjunction with fixed or automatically switched shunt capacitors to provide a variable amount of reactive compensation (lagging or leading power factor) as required by the load of the system. The complete compensation system is referred to as a static VAR compensator (SVC). Static VAR compensator systems normally include the following reactor components:

1. Thyristor controlled shunt reactors (TCR).
2. Thyristor switched shunt reactors (TSR).
3. Filter Reactors (FR).

Power conversion Reactors

The application of power electronics and associated switching frequencies of up to 10 KHz in medium voltage distribution and industrial power-systems, has prompted the requirement for reactors capable of operating in such environments. Dry type air core reactors have the inherent advantages of linear inductance under all load conditions and low stray capacitance and specific Q-factors at predetermined frequencies. Power conversion reactors are used in inverters found in energy storage systems, motor drives, active filters, and real time VAR compensators. Power conversion reactors are installed as line / load reactors, DC link reactors or filter reactors to mitigate high frequency ripple components and to provide protection against potentially damaging power system disturbances. Power conversion reactors can use as current limiting reactors in application such as utility interface of wind turbines and other energy generation. Additional applications are found in AC load impedance for testing of power electronics equipment and cyclo-converters.

3.18 MEDIUM VOLTAGE CAPACITORS AND CAPACITOR BANK.

Capacitor is a device used to introduce capacitive reactance in to a circuit. Low voltage capacitors utilize a "self-healing" dielectric consisting of a very thin plastic film onto which metallised electrodes are deposited by vaporization. If a short circuit develops in the capacitor, the metal layer will vaporize in the area of the breakdown. This effectively cures the fault and the capacitor continues to function normally. Conversely, medium voltage and high voltage capacitors employ a different technique wherein the dielectric comprises several layers of polypropylene film impregnated with an insulating fluid (Jarylec C101). Electrodes are made from thin aluminium foils. A high voltage capacitor is made up of a number of such elements connected in a series-parallel arrangement. The total number of elements is determined by the capacitors power rating and operating voltage. Each element is fuse protected. After impregnation the completed assembly is hermetically sealed inside a steel container. The all-film dielectric used in high voltage capacitors is manufactured from the polypropylene film, which has following advantages:

- Reduced dielectric loss
- Decreased variation of capacitance with ambient temperature, to obtain a more constant output.
- Significantly improved capacitor performance at low ambient temperature.

Internal element fuse

Modern power capacitors manufactured in conformity with IEC 871-1 & 2 are designed to withstand high stresses where the electrical gradient in the dielectric is typically in excess of 65 volts per micron. The capacitors incorporate highly efficient backup protection so that, each individual element is safeguarded by a built-in, series connected fuse. In the event of a localized breakdown of the dielectric, only the faulty-element is to be disconnected by the fuse and any subsequent reduction in capacitor output is minimized. Figure 3.18 (a) and (b) shows the dimensional details of 300 KVAR single-phase (6350V) capacitor unit and 300 KVAR three-phase 6.6 KV capacitor unit respectively.

Discharge resistors: These are installed within the capacitor assembly to reduce residual voltage.

Capacitor bushing: One, two or three weld type porcelain bushings are fitted to the container. These have impulse withstand voltage of 75 to 150 KV.

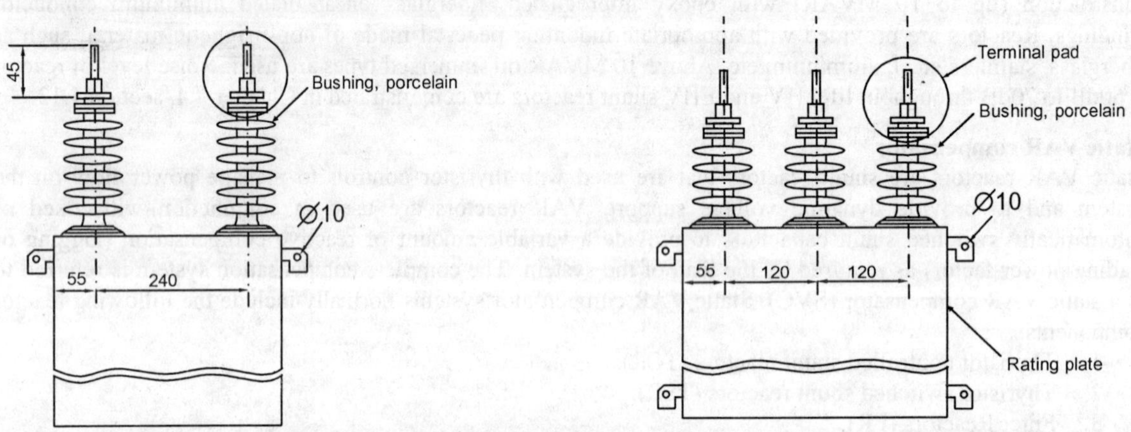

Fig. 3.18 (a): Single-phase 300 KVAR, 6350V capacitor. Fig. 3.18 (b): Three-phase 6.6 KV capacitor.

Capacitor bank

Capacitor units can be assembled in to a variety of configurations from a basic "top hat" arrangement to a large outdoor bank or multi-staged automatic bank. Typical capacitor bank connections one unit per phase in series and two units per phase in series are shown in Figure 3.18 (c) and (d) respectively. The capacitor bank size is expressed in KVAR or MVAR.

A capacitor can only be energized when the residual voltage is below 10% of the rated voltage. The energization of a capacitor bank by a re-strike-free circuit breaker can cause a transient over voltage, the first peak of which does not exceed √2 x 2 times the applied voltage (r.m.s value) for a maximum duration of ½ cycle. The peak value of the inrush currents must not exceed 100 times the rated current of the capacitor. In practice this value often needs to be limited to a lower figure dependent up on the switching device.

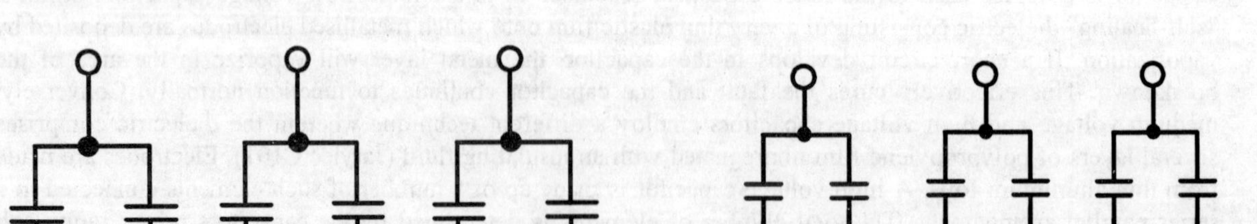

Fig. 3.18 (c): Capacitor bank connection (One unit per phase in series)

Fig. 3.18 (d): Capacitor bank connection (Two units per phase in series)

Capacitor bank protection:

1). Overload and over voltage protection: Protection should be designed to protect the capacitor bank against overloads created by both over voltage and over current. In the modern low loss capacitor, the risk of thermal breakdown is minimal and any failure more usually results from dielectric breakdown. This occurs as a result of over voltage, which in many cases, is caused by excessive harmonic current. Protection can be achieved by means of peak value voltage sensitive relays having characteristics designed to prevent over voltage.

2). Under voltage protection: Where capacitors are connected to a network fitted with fast autoreclosing breakers, they must be fitted with under voltage protection to ensure disconnection at a voltage dropout. They must not be re-connected until the residual voltage has fallen below 10% of the rated voltage.

3). External fuse protection: Fuse protection for medium voltage capacitor is for providing protection for individual capacitor units and the smaller capacitor bank. The selected fuse rating must take account of over voltages, over currents and switching transients such that spurious operation is avoided.

4) Unbalance protection: The purpose of unbalance protection is to disconnect a faulty bank before over voltage greater than 10% appear on remaining healthy units. To achieve this, the capacitor units are arranged in two parallel star connections as shown in Figure 3.18 (e), with the two star points being connected through a current transformer. Any fault occurring will result in current flow in the primary of the CT, and the secondary is connected to operate a current balance relay.

5) Damping reactors: While switching a capacitor bank, high current transients appear. These can be particularly high if the bank is connected in parallel with another bank, which is already energized. It may, therefore, be necessary to limit the inrush current by connecting a reactor in series with the capacitor bank. These transient current values can be calculated as follows:

(a) Switching of a single capacitor bank:

Crest of inrush bank current $Is = I_N \sqrt{2S/Q}$ Amps
I_N = Rated capacitor bank current expressed in amperes
S = Short circuit level in MVA at the point where the capacitor is to be connected
Q = The capacitor bank size expressed in MVAR

(b) Switching of a capacitor bank in parallel with an energized bank(s).

Crest of inrush current in amps $Is = Vn \sqrt{2/ Xc\, X_L}$
Vn = Phase to neutral voltage of the system and V = Phase to phase voltage of the system
Xc = Series connected capacitive reactance per phase expressed in ohms $Xc = V^2 (1/Q_1 + 1/Q_2) \times 10^{-6}$
Q_1 = The outputs of the bank to be switched in.
Q_2 = The sum of the already energized bank(s), expressed in megavars.
X_L = Inductive reactance per phase between the banks, expressed in ohms.

Figure 3.18 (e) shows the connection diagram for a 5 MVAR 33 KV double star capacitor bank installed in a 132/33 KV substation. 36 KV re-strike free vacuum circuit breakers are used for switching capacitor bank. Safety earth switch is provided on the cable side of the 33 KV switchgear panel in order to earth the outgoing cable (after racking out the circuit breaker) during maintenance or repair.
Following protective relays are employed for feeder protection and capacitor bank protection. **Automatic switching operations are performed by an under voltage relay connected to the secondary circuit of a potential transformer.**

1) Inverse definite minimum time (IDMT) over current relay for overload protection
2) Instantaneous over current relay for short circuit protection
3) IDMT earth fault relay for earth fault protection
4) Instantaneous earth fault relay for high current earth fault protection.
5) Current balance relay for capacitor unbalance protection

In the event of operation of any one of the associated protective relay the lockout relay (trip relay) will energize to trip the 33KV feeder circuit breaker.

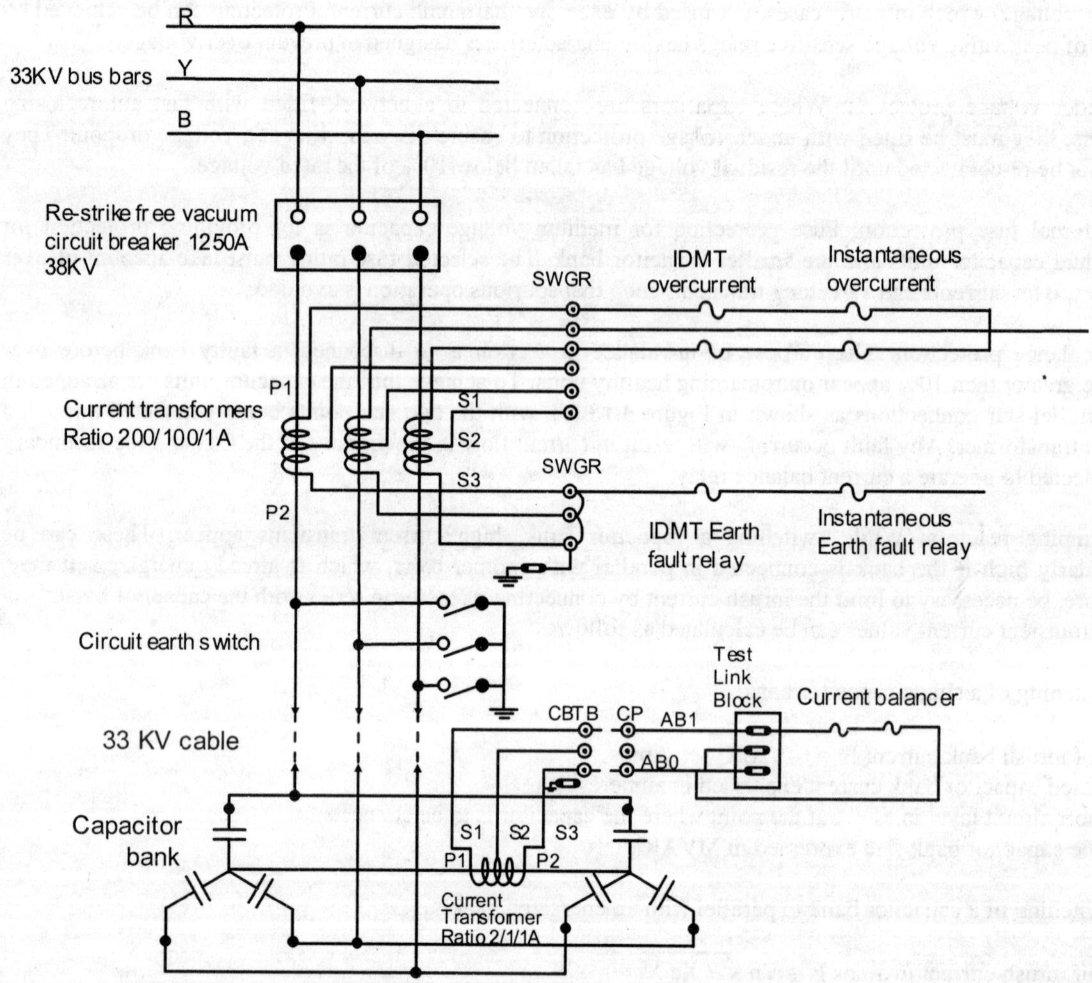

Fig. 3.18 (e): Typical connection diagram of a 5 MVAR 33 KV, double star capacitor bank.

3.19 MEDIUM VOLTAGE SF6 GAS INSULATED SWITCHGEARS.

This section describes *SIEMENS 8DA* medium voltage (7.2 to 36 KV) metal-clad SF6 switchgear with vacuum circuit breakers [Figure 3.19 (a) and (b)]. Six identical aluminium housings form the enclosure for the three poles of a switch panel and the three phase conductors of the single bus bars. The vertical poles are arranged in a line, as are the horizontal bus bar chambers on the top of the poles. The three pole columns are mounted on a base-frame whose supporting structures, carries the cable terminations. The design prevents (1) contamination and condensation effect; (2) Ingress of foreign matters, and ensures that an earth fault cannot become an inter-phase fault.

The bus bar housing for each phase is cast from a corrosion resistant aluminium alloy and is identical with the vacuum interrupter housing. The 2500 amps bus bars are of flat copper bar. In the chambers the bars are mounted on transverse insulators, which absorb the transverse forces arising from short-circuits but still allow movement in the longitudinal direction. The transverse insulator is supported at the side of the chamber in a sliding arrangement so as to permit thermal expansion. Bellows expansion pieces are fitted between approximately every 10 panels.

The bus bar housing also contains the three-position isolator. SF6 gas surrounding the tubes is simply for providing insulation to the earthed pole housing. Electronic plug-in modules provide for the display, protection, monitoring and operation of the switchgear. The isolator is operated with a removable handle through a shaft at the front, which is common to all the three poles. The switching positions are indicated thereby mechanically linked devices. Mechanical interlocking system prevents maloperation.
In addition to incoming and feeder panels, the switchgear covers bus sectionalizer, bus coupler and metering panels. The duplicate bus arrangement contains additional chambers for the bus isolators between the bus bars and the circuit breaker. Figure 3.19 (a) illustrates SF6 gas insulated medium voltage circuit breaker panel.

LEGEND: 1.Bus bar chamber; 2.Bus bars 1250 Amps, 25 KA, 3seconds; 3. Withdrawable type truck mounted circuit breaker; 4. Vacuum interrupter; 5. Circuit breaker operating mechanism with spring charge motor; 6. Current transformers; 7. Gas monitoring device; 8. Cable termination chamber; 9. Three position isolator; 10. Top and bottom bushings.

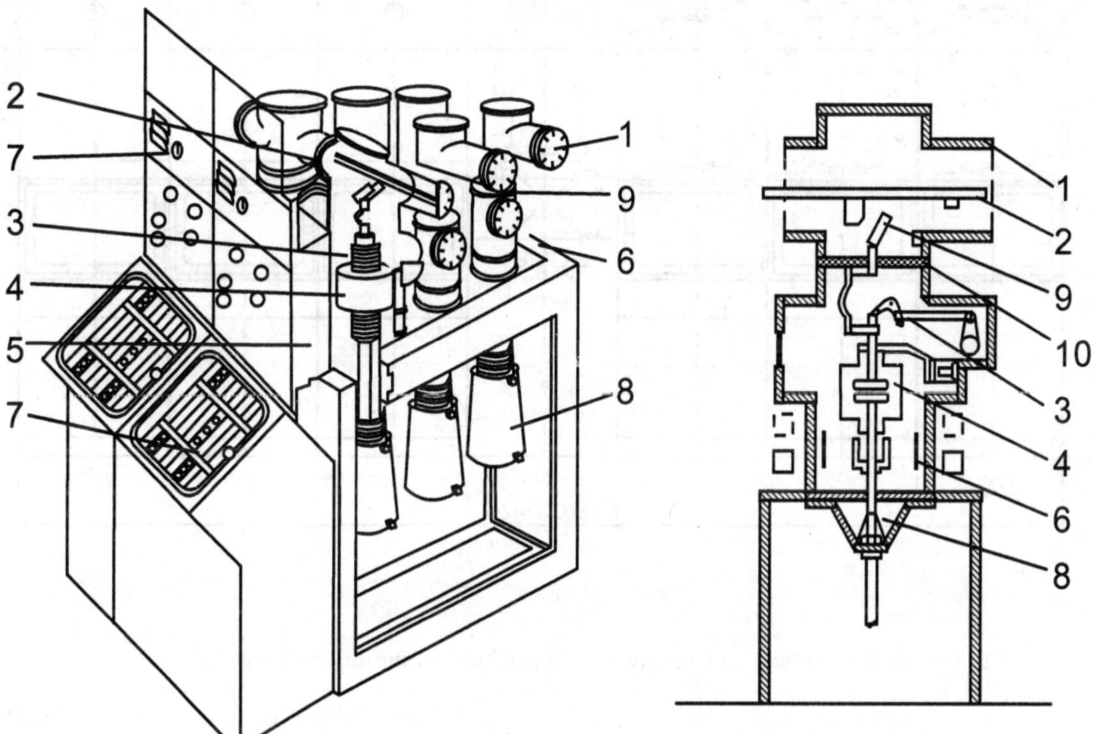

Fig. 3.19 (a): Medium voltage SF6 gas insulated switchgear; Circuit breaker panel (Courtesy, Siemens Ag).

In conjunction with the bus coupler, this arrangement makes it possible to change the bus on load. The technical data of *SIEMENS 8DA* medium voltage SF6 insulated switchgear is shown in the Table below.

Item	Technical data	Unit	7.2 / 10 KV	12 / 13.8 /15 KV	20/ 25 / 36 KV
1	Degree of protection	IP	IP65	IP 65	IP 65
2	Rated current of bus bar	A	2500	2500	2500
3	Rated current of feeders	A	2500	2500	2500
4	Rated power frequency withstand voltage	KV	28	36	70
5	Rated lightning impulse withstand voltage	KV	75	95	178
6	Rated short-circuit current	KA	31.5	31.5	25
7	Rated lightning impulse withstand current	KA	80	80	63

Figure 3.19 (b) illustrates the front view of a 7 panel medium voltage Sulphur Hexaflouride gas insulated switchgear assembly.

ALL DIMENSIONS IN MM

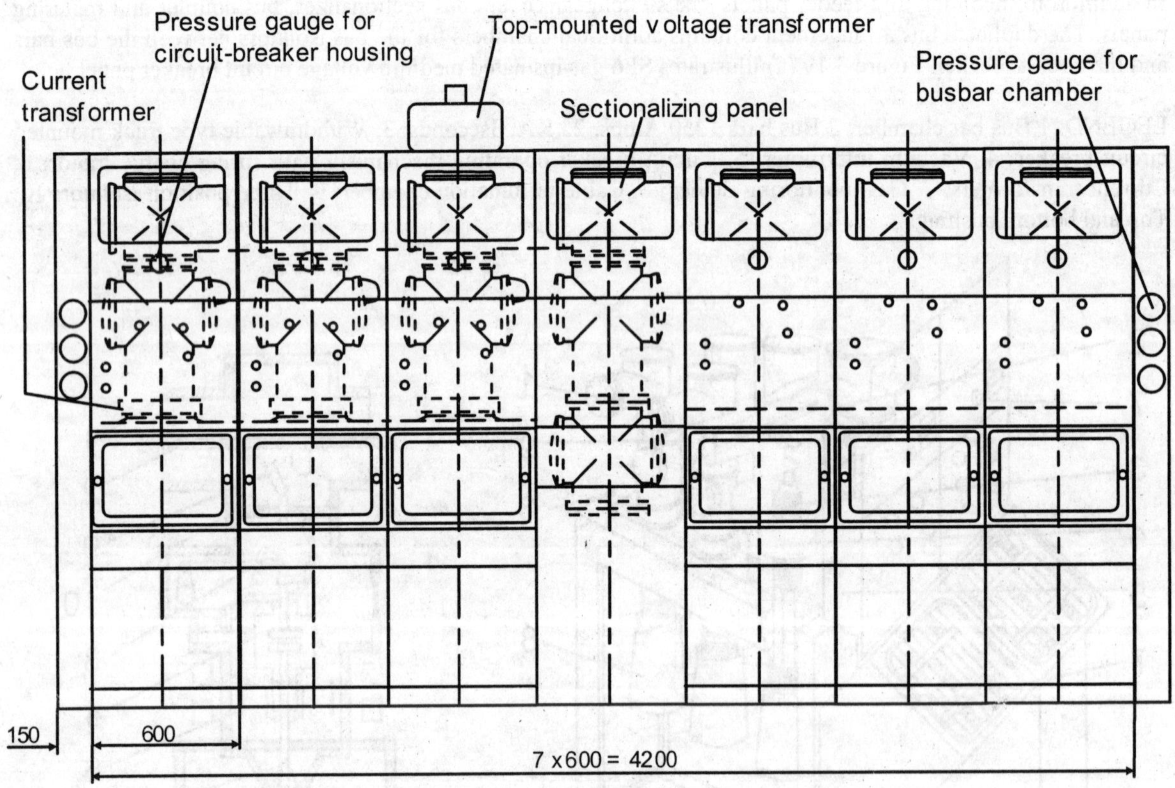

Fig. 3.19 (b): Medium voltage SF6 gas insulated switchgear (Courtesy Siemens Ag).

The chambers are filled with SF6 gas, which is maintained at a pressure of less than one bar above atmospheric pressure and insulates the normally live parts from the earthed encapsulation. The bus bar chambers are separated from the circuit breaker chambers by gas tight barriers. When panels have been joined together to form a switchgear unit, each bus bar phase has its own continuous, gas-filled compartment. The three circuit breaker chambers of each panel are interconnected by, a thin pipe. In this way the gas filling of the circuit breaker compartments can be monitored in each panel and that of the three bus bar compartments throughout the switchgear. All the gaskets are designed so that a leakage rate of 1% per annum, referred to each barriered compartment, is not exceeded. As this leakage rate, the test voltages are still held after a service period of more than 10 years without the SF6 having to be replenished. The cable termination point is outside the SF6 encapsulation. Screw-out links enable the cables to be disconnected from the switchgear. The secondary devices are mounted on a console below the circuit breaker mechanism. Similarly, relay box is mounted above the circuit breaker.

The main features of SF6 insulated switchgears are:

a) Non-aging SF6 insulating gas for insulating the high voltage equipment;
b) Slip-on and plug-in cable connection;
c) Static protection and shock proof;
d) Identical dimensions for rated voltage 7.2 KV to 36 KV switchgears;
c) Rated short-circuit breaking currents 16 to 31.5 KVA 3 seconds;
f) Feeder and bus-bar operating currents up to 2500 amps;
g) Dead tank design permitting the panels to be installed in any location;
h) Hermetically sealed enclosure housing the switching elements;
i) Impervious to climatic and environmental influences;
j) Construction: As single-phase earthed, metal-encapsulated units;
k) Three-position isolator and maintenance-free vacuum circuit breaker;
l) High operating safety, high reliability and high availability.

3.20 SUPERVISORY CONTROL AND DATA ACQUISITION SYSTEM.

SCADA is a centralized computer system that includes transmission of numerical quantities and alarms from substations to a control center. Communication of data is obviously vital to the performance of the systems and this is accomplished by a variety of means including radio, power line carrier, public telephone network, fiber optics or twisted pair pilot cables. While each system requires different combinations of equipment to provide the varying levels of sophistication, they also need different control structures depending on the precise nature and situation of the installation. Figure 3.20 illustrates the structure of telecontrol system implemented by, GEC measurements. The system is widely employed in 132/33 KV primary substations and associated medium voltage switching stations.

Master station: At the hub of a telecontrol system is the master station equipment. The master station has the capacity to handle several different communication lines with the ability to provide alternative routing in the event of line failure. To ensure continuity of operation in times of stress, the vital master station equipment is frequently duplicated and supported with battery backup supplies. Also concentrated at the master station is the global system database and besides organizing the regular monitoring of conditions at the outstations, its computer supports the operator interface. This can range from a single personal computer to a complete system with several colour VDU (Visual display unit) displays and keyboards with special function keys. From master station the operator can display alarm lists, schematic data and graphic formats, all regularly updated with current values to monitor the network and initiate control actions.

Communications: Tele-control can use normal voice or data channels of communications enabling the link between master and outstation to take one of several forms depending on specific economic and geographic considerations by, public telephone networks, which can provide either dedicated or dial up lines, by private twisted pair (pilot cable) lines or by radio for the more inaccessible outstations. Digital messages are signaled by modulating a carrier to indicate the 0 or 1 binary digits of the message. The modulation at the transmitting point and demodulation at the receiving end is done by the use of modems, with the interpretation of the message specified by the protocol, which is designed to include the vital elements of message security and error detection.

The signaling speed of a telecontrol system is governed by the time constant of the parameters being monitored. When faster update times are required they can be achieved by having more lines with fewer outstations per line or by choosing higher signaling speeds that are usually from the range of 50, 200, 600 or 1200 baud.

Outstations: Located closer to the plant being supervised, outstations are connected to the transducer and control devices. With simpler systems the outstations report back current parameter values on demand only, but when equipped with their own microprocessor they are able to report automatically on alarm status changes as well as undertaking other tasks such as the independent operation of control sequences.

Whilst catering for the primary functions of analogue or digital input and output signals the outstations also offer a range of facilities that cover pulse counting set point and other general requirements. There are other factors that also control the specification of outstations of equal importance to their practical performance and these include their proximity to high voltage machinery and switchgear, the availability and type of power supply and the severity of the environment.

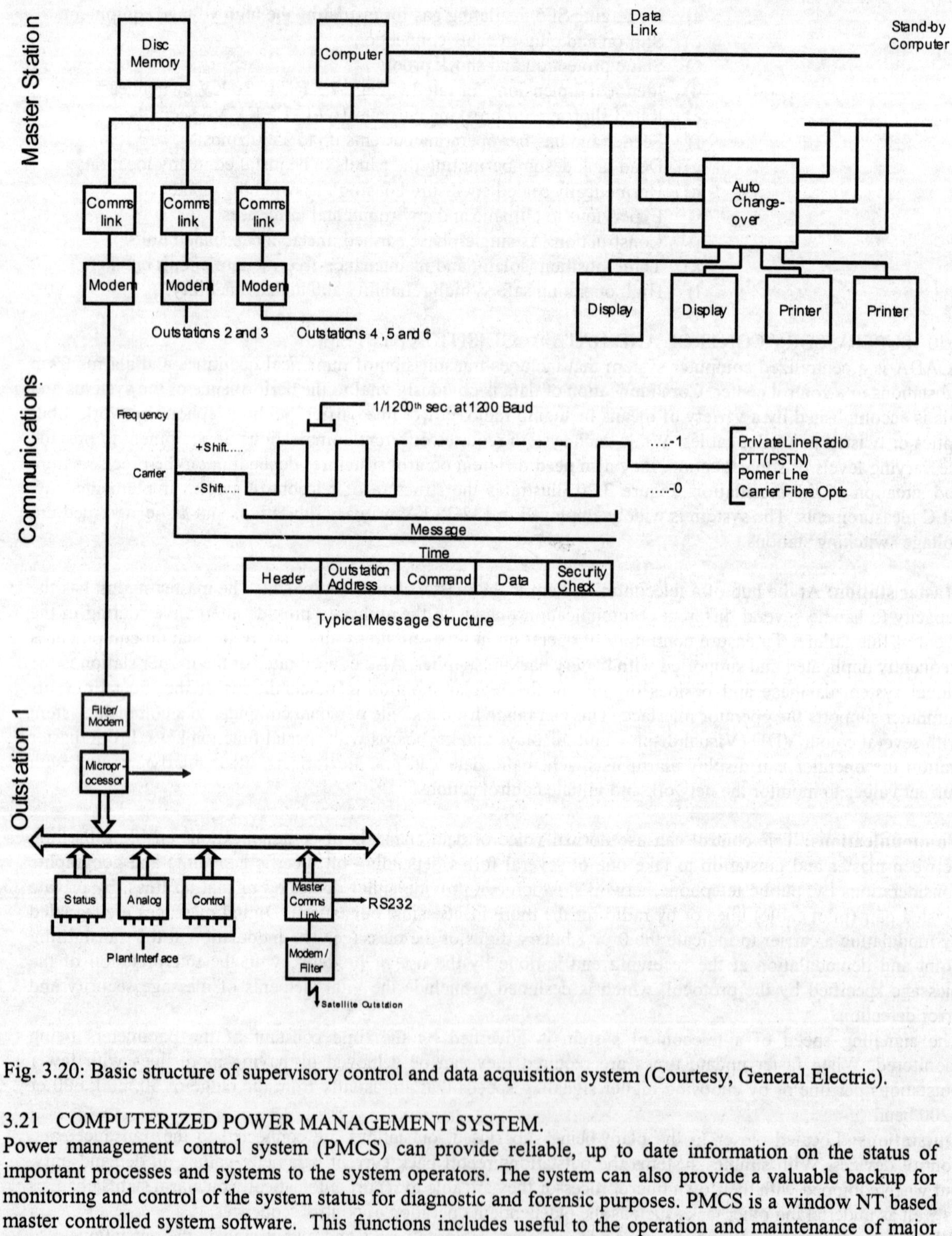

Fig. 3.20: Basic structure of supervisory control and data acquisition system (Courtesy, General Electric).

3.21 COMPUTERIZED POWER MANAGEMENT SYSTEM.

Power management control system (PMCS) can provide reliable, up to date information on the status of important processes and systems to the system operators. The system can also provide a valuable backup for monitoring and control of the system status for diagnostic and forensic purposes. PMCS is a window NT based master controlled system software. This functions includes useful to the operation and maintenance of major electrical systems in the data center facilities, including Uninterrupted power supplies, Generators, Auto-transfer switch, Static transfer switch, Paralleling switchgear, Power distribution system, motor control center, batteries and chargers etc. PMCS also includes predictive maintenance, power quality analysis, energy analysis etc. Figure 3.21 shows the network diagram of a typical power management system designed for a TV studio.

The system **Human Machine Interface** (HMI) is for the following functions:

1. Provide immediate analysis and report when a power quality problem occurs;
2. Provide monitoring data at each facility;
3. Provide a single data base for storing all disturbance monitoring and recording;
4. Evaluate performance of power conditioning equipment;
5. Requesting and receiving information from distributed facility **Intelligent Electronic devices** (IEDs) using MMS / UCA and modbus RTU - IED protocols;
6. Gathering and locally strong historical operation / fault events with original IED time stamping preserved;
7. Gathering and locally storing facility fault records and waveforms generated during the abnormal operation of facility devices;
8. Interfacing with Wide area network (WAN);
9. Providing access to individual IEDs from either the facility or dial-in remote locations, using specific IED protocols;
10. Provide an information service that can be offered to customers for evaluation of the system performance;
11. Identify internal power quality problems prior to catastrophic failure. An example is predicting the failure of a UPS based up on its output harmonics and unbalance;
12. Provide a platform to support the automated monitoring and maintenance of the data center facility;
13. Prioritize system maintenance and capital expenditure plans;
14. Produce summery graphs of CBEMA charts and time plots from the collected data.

Definitions and standards:

A. Modbus RTU **(Remote Terminal Unit)**: An industry standard, high performance network communications protocol developed by Modicon company.

B. Open protocol: A protocol which is published and used by other manufacturers and is, therefore, non-proprietary.

C. RS 485 / EIA 485: A physical wiring standard for high speed, noise tolerant network communication often used with the Modbus RTU protocol.

D. Ethernet: A high performance **local area network** (LAN) standard, providing the two lower levels of the ISO/OSI seven layer reference models, the physical layer and the data link layer.

E. Ethernet Gateway: A physical device that translates communications protocol to Ethernet communications protocol.

F. Communications protocol: A formal set of conventions governing the control of inputs and outputs within the communicating process.

G. Client / Server architecture: A network architecture in which each computer on the network is either a client or a server. **Servers are computers dedicated to acquiring, archiving, and displaying data. Clients are computers that present data from one or more servers to the end user.**

The communication network consists of a combination of RS-485 Modubus RTU and Ethernet TCP/IP technology. The system will support the following functions:

a) Customized graphic screens such as site plan, single line diagram, waveform capture for supported devices, control panel overview screen, PLC (Programmable logic controller) status screen, UPS tabular data screen, PDU tabular data screen, battery monitor status screen etc.

b) Remote dial-in capacity for remote diagnostics and trouble-shooting using a modem and appropriate communication software.

c) Automatic power analysis and report generation for power quality events. The system configuration is capable of operating from an alternate, hot standby computer with automatic changeover.

d) Capable for IRIG-B time synchronization. The system is capable of synchronizing the monitor clocks with a degree of accuracy dependent up on the communications topography using internet-based time synchronization services.

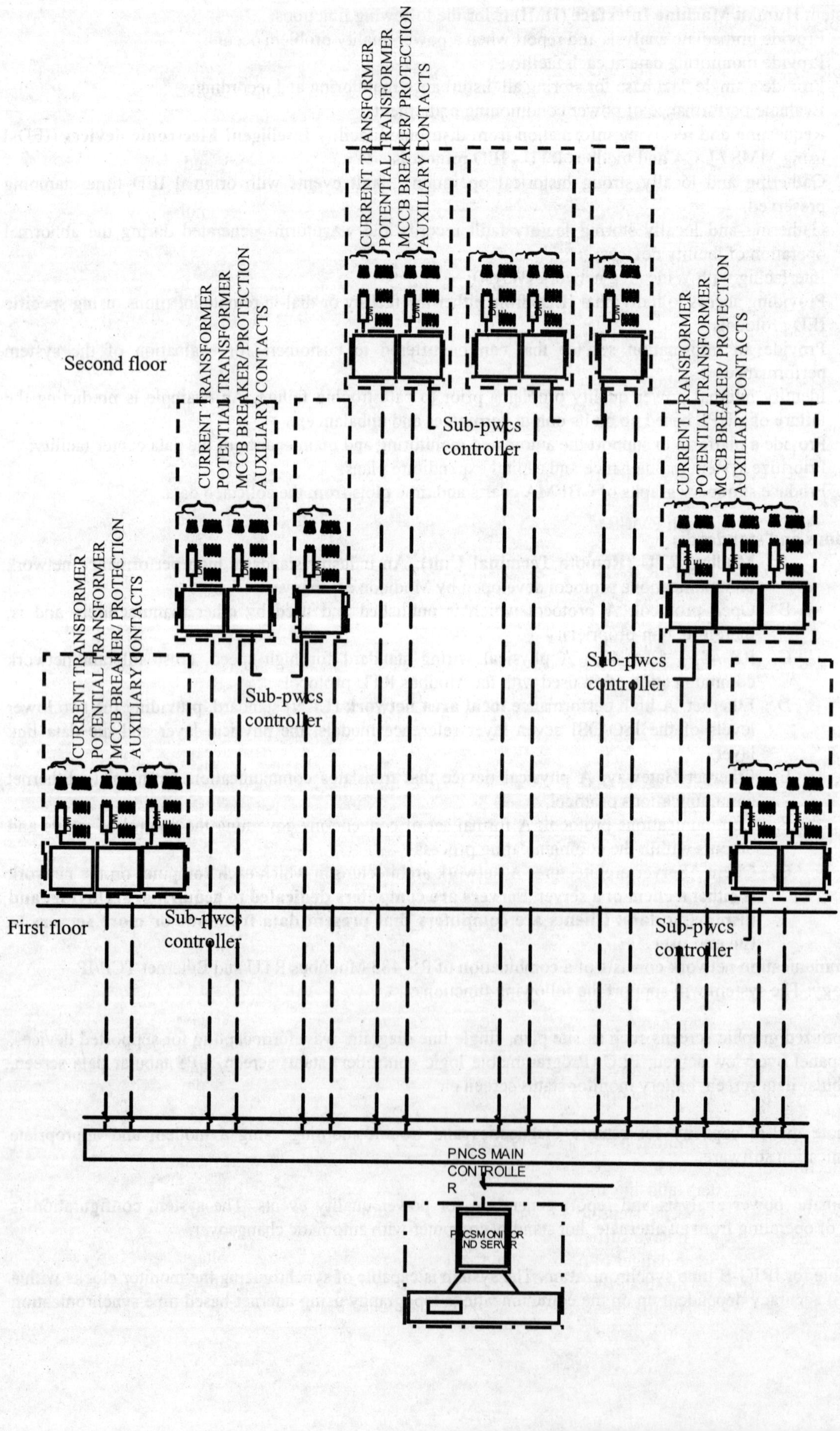
CURRENT TRANSFORMER
POTENTIAL TRANSFORMER
MCCB BREAKER/ PROTECTION
AUXILIARY CONTACTS
Second floor
Sub-pwcs controller
First floor
PNCS MAIN CONTROLLE R
PNCS MONITOR AND SERVER

Power quality meter (PQM): Power quality meter connected through instrument transformers (CT and PT) can monitor and record:

(1) Instantaneous readings such as frequency, load current per phase, minimum and maximum unbalanced 3-phase current with date and time, voltage (Phase to phase and neutral), minimum and maximum voltage unbalance with date and time, power factor (per phase and three-phase), real power, reactive power, apparent power, minimum and maximum power reading with date and time etc.

(2) Demand readings such as average and peak demand current per phase, average and predicted real power demand.

(3) Energy consumption readings such as accumulated energy (KWH) and accumulated reactive energy (RKWH)

(4) Waveform capture capability: Upon a user initiated command through a PMCS application software, the PQM will capture, and store in nonvolatile memory, 256 digitally sampled data points for each phase voltage and current. PQM will transmit the waveform samples over the network to the personal computer workstation for display, archival, and analysis.

(5) Harmonic analysis: PQM can complete harmonics analysis through 62nd harmonic THD and TIF.

Installation: As shown in figure 3.21 install all junction boxes repeaters and other appurtenances necessary for a complete, operational network to complete the PMCS. All power quality meters, electronic trip units of circuit breakers, transformer temperature monitors, motor protection devices etc should be installed as required in the design. All control-power, CT, PT, and data communications circuits shall be harnessed within the equipment enclosure. Where external circuit connections are required, terminal blocks should be provided. Install all HMI software, graphic screens, system configuration information and point databases on the host computer in accordance with PMCS users-guide.

3.22 DC CONTROL POWER AND DUAL BATTERY CHARGER UNIT.

Control power or operative source in a switchgear, is a current feeding the remote control circuits of circuit breakers, operative circuit of protective relay schemes, and various types of indication and alarm schemes. The basic requirement of a control power source is that in the event of a short circuit or abnormal operating conditions in the main power station or substation, the voltages of the control power should be high enough to activate the protection and control of every automatic device's associated with the switchgear and circuit breakers. To enhance reliability DC source from flooded electrolyte type storage battery cells (connected in series to form battery bank) is preferred for large power stations and substations. Dual battery chargers of suitable ratings with sealed battery banks of required back up time is employed for obtaining control power in small power station or substation.

AC can be used as control power provided if it is a reliable source other than mains power or from uninterruptible power supply (UPS). However for single unit tripping following methods are used in remote areas:

(a) AC power is applied direct to the trip coil of the circuit breaker through a current transformer secondary. During a short circuit in the feeder the breaker will trip, because the current and voltage across the terminals of the CT will grow. However it is not suitable for earth fault protection of an insulated neutral system, but suitable for earthed neutral system. Voltage transformers are unsuitable as the voltage will drop during a short circuit. Whereas combined CT and PT with rectified output is reliable.

(b) Charged capacitor can be used as control power in circuit breakers, which have to operate when the feeder is faulty. Capacitor can be charged through the rectified voltage from a voltage transformer. When the CT operated over-current relay operates, the relay contact closes and energize the trip coil through the capacitor to open the breaker. Thus the combined use of CT and PT through a capacitor is a reliable source.

Voltage and current regulated battery charger:

The selection of the battery charger is important for several reasons. Firstly, it could influence the life expectancy of the battery and the maintenance intervals. Secondly, the close tolerances of many electrical loads may necessitate special steps to minimize increases in the output voltage when the battery is being charged. The rectifier must have sufficient power to both recharge the battery and power the continues-load, on the system. To quantify the danger of poorly regulated battery chargers, a charger voltage 10 to 15 % above the recommended level can dissipate battery electrolyte within days, leaving the battery permanently useless. Conversely, a low float voltage means the battery will not recharge and, if the charger voltage is below the minimum float voltage, a slow discharging will result, even though all appears well.

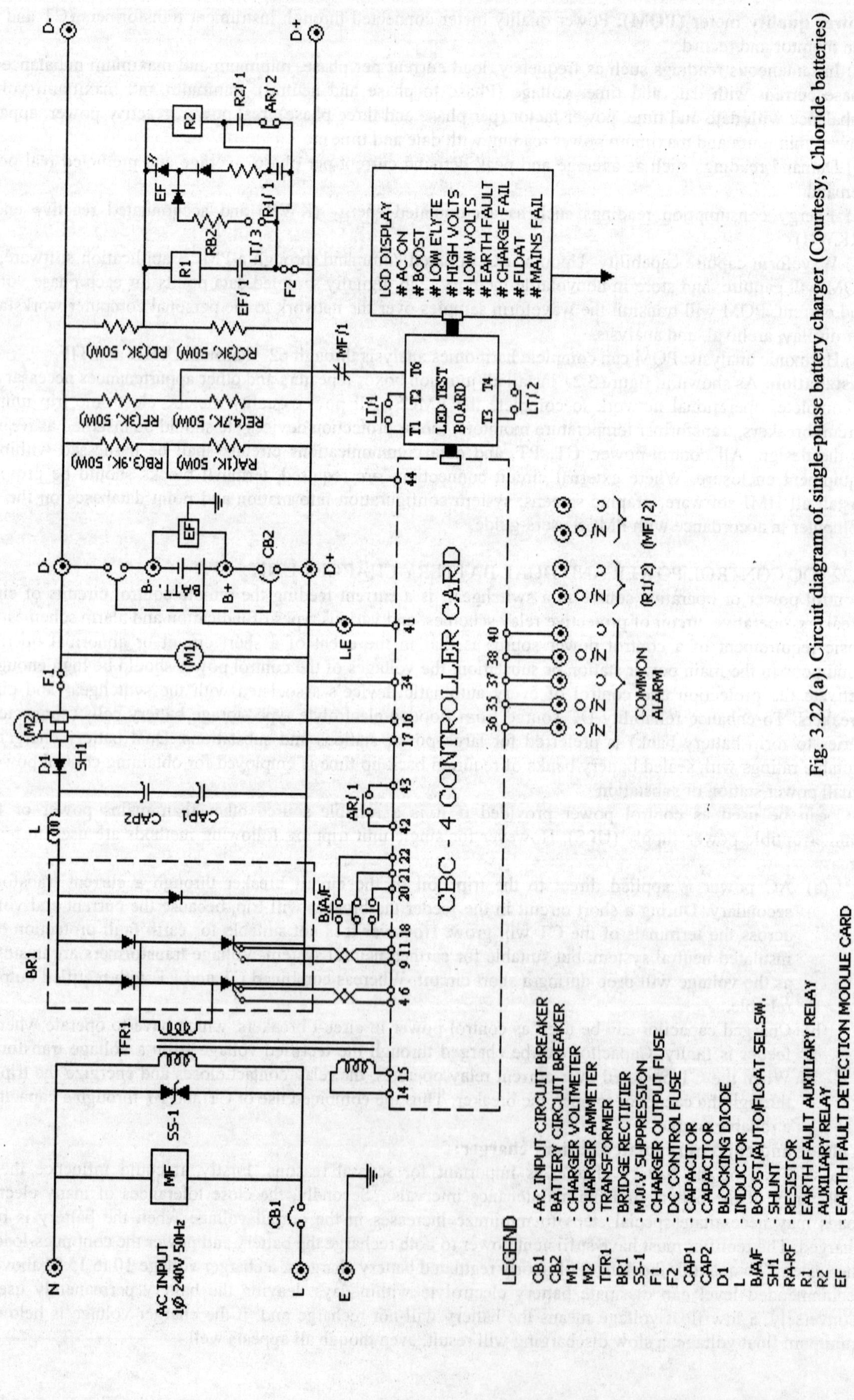

Fig. 3.22 (a): Circuit diagram of single-phase battery charger (Courtesy, Chloride batteries)

These problems can be avoided by the use of constant-voltage chargers, using thyristor technology. The output from the charger is controlled by the battery condition, and the cells draw just enough power to keep themselves in a high state of charge. Battery charger is built for charging both lead acid and nickel cadmium wet or sealed batteries and is available for single and three-phase AC input dependent on the power rating. Power stations and substations need either two independent units of chargers and battery banks or one dual unit with dual battery banks.

Figure 3.22 (a) shows the circuit diagram of a single-phase battery charger, which consists of:

1. Cubicle or 19 inches rack for accommodating the charger unit.
2. Low impedance leakage reactance transformer, which provides inherent short-circuit protection for the rectifier and reduces the peak current applied to the battery.
3. A phase controlled thyristor rectifier.
4. Solid-state circuitry, which constantly monitors the battery condition providing fully automatic boost and float charge functions.
5. AC input protection via miniature circuit breakers and DC output protection by fuse(s) ensuring protection against overload and short-circuit.
6. Power and control card: DC Voltage and current adjustment is on the control card. Easy for replacement and minimize down time.
7. Instruments such as AC/DC voltmeters and DC ammeter.
8. Labeled LED indicators to indicate individual faults and status of input power.
9. Audible alarm indication such as AC supply fail, charge fail, low or high battery voltage, low electrolyte level, boost charge, earth fault etc.

Both single-phase and three-phase charger circuits act as a constant voltage current limited regulator providing DC output current and voltage regulation in either the constant current or constant voltage modes. Usually charger will operate as a constant voltage charger at the float voltage level. This is adjusted to maintain the battery in a fully charged condition with minimal overcharge. Constant current boost charge is initiated automatically by the following conditions.

(a) Restoration of main AC supply;
(b) Battery voltage is less than 90% of float voltage.

Manual boost charge is possible by momentarily interrupting the incoming AC supply. Charger is automatically connected and float charge is initiated in the following two ways:

(a) The charged battery voltage rises in approximately 90% of the preset boost voltage level within a set time.
(b) Fully or partially discharged battery prior to boost initiation. If the battery voltage does not rise to the 90% level / within the set time, the boost continues under-voltage until the battery reaches the 90% level. At this point a timer is activated, which controls the boost for a preset time to complete the charge.

Operating and communication system for large units are provided with front-panel mimic diagram and detailed LED indications. Microprocessor controlled units have special features such as system logic with intelligent real time fault analysis, recording and memorization of the last 100 events, battery capacity test, and remote terminal unit (RTU) to communicate with substation management system (SMS) or power management control system (PMCS) or distributed control system (DCS) used in generating stations and HV/EHV/HVDC stations.

Figure 3.22 (b) shows the single line diagram of dual battery charger with DC distribution board. In the event of failure of one charger the changeover contactor will automatically transfer the load to the other charger. 20A double pole miniature circuit breakers are used for protection of distribution circuits. Battery banks are formed by, connecting cells or batteries in series and an isolator is used for disconnecting the battery bank. Battery bank will share the temporary load which is in excess of the charger capacity for example, simultaneous tripping of several circuit breakers. It serves as a stand by source control power for switchgears for a permissive backup time. When connected as a bank, the voltage across each series connected cell or battery will be more or less same. Surface contamination at the terminals of a battery will cause ground fault, voltage drop and leakage current.

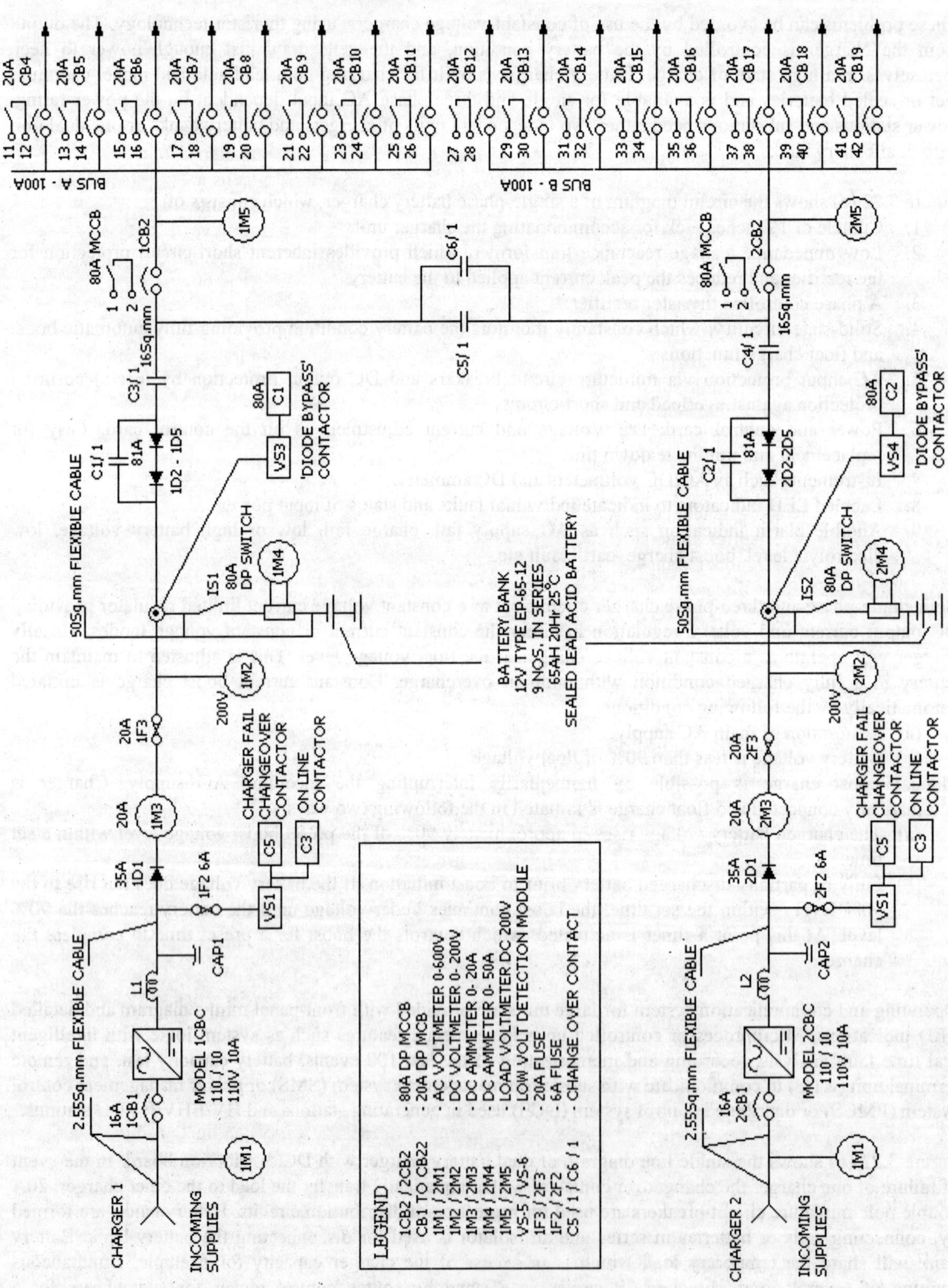

Fig. 3.22 (b): Single line diagram of a dual battery charger unit with battery banks and DC distribution board.

Sizing of rectifier and battery:
Whatever the category of electrical load, the sizing of the rechargeable battery installation will take in to account the rating of the load and the duration for which the batteries must provide power during an emergency. The choice of battery depends on the working life needed, and the maintenance considerations. Lead acid and nickel-cadmium cells offer the longest working life 15 to 20 years. Flat plate and tubular plate lead acid cells offer a working life of 10 years, and are often specified for computer installations, since the figure is in-line with the life expectancy of the computer. Sealed, recombination cells are designed for a 10 to 12 year life at an ambient temperature of 20 deg. C. Sealed cells require minimal maintenance, no gas is given off, and there is no risk of spillage and they are about half the size of equivalent rating vented lead acid cells.

Assume that the total estimated DC loads to be connected to the battery charger is 60 amps and the battery backup required is 12 hours. Overload capacity required 10%; Cell: Lead acid;
Battery ampere-hour capacity, C = 60 x 12 x 1.1 = 792 AH, say 800 AH.
Charging current = For lead acid cell, 15% of the battery ampere-hour capacity. = 800 x 0.15 = 120 Amps.
Total DC output current required from the charger = 60 + 6 + 120 = 186 A, say 200 A
The rectifier shall be suitable for 200 A loads. If the battery is required to provide full standby time at temperatures lower than 20°C, then increase this capacity by a further 10% for each 10°C below 20°C.
Number of 800 AH cells required to be connected in series to obtain 110 DC output:

(a) For Nickel cadmium cells (1.2 volts per cell) = 110 / 1.2 = 91 cells.
(b) For Lead acid cells (2 volts per cell) = 110 / 2 = 55 cells.

Nickel-cadmium cells offer some advantages, notable that their performance is less affected by extremes of temperature or by vibration. On the other hand, the capital cost is significantly higher than for lead acid cells of equivalent capacity
Table 3.22 (1): Comparison between Lead acid cell and Nickel cadmium cell:

Description	Lead acid cell (LA)	Nickel cadmium cell (NC)
Voltage per cell	Normal 2 V, and floating 2.15 V	Nominal 1.2 V, floating 1.40 to 1.46
Positive plate	Lead-antimony alloy (PBO2)	Nickel
Negative plate	Lead-antimony alloy (PB)	Cadmium
Electrolyte	Dilute sulphuric acid (2 H2 SO4)	Pottasium hydroxide
Specific gravity	1.215 at 20°C (Hydrometer reading)	1.20 at 20°C
Max: discharge current A	1.5 x Capacity in AH (one minute)	2 x Capacity in AH (one minute)
Max: Charging current A	0.15 x Capacity in AH (Max: 6 hrs)	0.2 x Capacity in AH (8 hours)
Container	Synthetic resin moulded	Polypropylene
Separator	Microporous rubber	Alkali-resistant synthetic
Capacity ratings	@ 10 hours	@ 5 hours

Note: Specific gravity: For each 1°C above 20°C, add 0.0007 and for each 1°C below 20°C, deduct 0.0007.

Sealed lead acid batteries (valve regulated batteries) are sealed except for a valve that opens when the internal gas pressure exceeds the design limits. These batteries can be used in confined areas and can be mounted in any orientation. It is widely used in switching stations, UPS, electronic and Information technology (IT) applications. A 10 A 110 V (DC) charger with 6 hour back up need 9 Nos 12 V 48 AH sealed LA battery

Storage battery maintenance: Storage batteries are either lead acid or nickel cadmium cells connected in series to form a battery bank. Battery is such an important item in switchgear operation that it must be given strict attention in the maintenance program. The battery charger plays a critical role since it supplies normal DC requirements to the station and maintains the batteries at a high level of charge. The batteries, in addition to supplying temporary heavy demands in excess of the charger capacity, serve as a standby source to trip breakers (if needed) upon loss of AC power. Failure of the charger or its AC supply transfers all DC load to the batteries.
Wet batteries should be inspected for proper level and proper specific gravity of the electrolyte. Low specific gravity readings indicate a low state of charge. If the reading between cells vary more than fifty points on the hydrometer scale, that battery probably has a bad cell and should be replaced. If all cells read consistently low (within 50 points), the battery bank should be fully charged, and the battery charger checked for proper

operation. Low electrolyte level may indicate too high a charging rate. In this case the "fault-voltage" setting of the charger should be checked against the specific gravity

The battery top surface should be clean. Surface contamination can produce leakage currents that present a drain on the charger and the battery. Battery terminal connectors should be tight and free of corrosion. If the terminal connectors are corroded they should be removed and cleaned thoroughly with bicarbonate of soda. Battery studs and cable ends should be cleaned thoroughly. If stranded cable is used it is advisable to cut off the corroded end. If this is not possible the strands should be separated and cleaned internally. Any dust accumulation on the battery charger should be blown or wiped clean. Ventilation openings should be clear of obstruction. Terminal connections should be checked for tightness. All relays, lights or horn's for indicating such abnormal conditions as grounds. Loss of AC power supply, and high or low voltage should be checked to ensure that they are operating properly.

While being charged, lead acid battery produces and emits a mixture of hydrogen and oxygen gases, which is very explosive. Open flames or sparks must not be permitted in close proximity to the batteries. The room or compartment in which batteries are located should be well ventilated. Smoking should be prohibited in these rooms or compartments. Explosion proof light fittings are only allowed in battery rooms. Battery charger incoming power should not be connected through earth leakage circuit breaker or residual current circuit breaker. This is to avoid power interruption during an earth fault on the other circuits. Charger cubicle must be properly and securely grounded. Charger shall be connected through a splash proof isolator. Connections to battery terminals must be re-torqued, cleaned properly and protective cover of the terminal is to be replaced.

Advantages and disadvantages of flooded electrolyte type batteries:

Advantages:

1. Lowest initial cost;
2. Highest cranking ampere;
3. Distilled water can be added if necessary;
4. Accepts higher recharge voltage.

Disadvantages

1. Spillable;
2. Operates upright;
3. Shorter shell life and shorter cycle life;
4. Cannot be installed near sensitive electronic-equipment;
5. Watering required.

Advantages of sealed batteries:

(1) Totally maintenance-free & Air transportable;
(2) Spill proof & leak proof, no corrosion;
(3) Deep cycle life install upright or on side;
(4) No gassing unless overcharged;
(5) Compatible with sensitive electronic equipment;
(6) Superior cell life and rechargeablility;
(7) Rugged and vibration resistant;
(8) Very safe at sea with no chlorine gas;
(9) Operates in wet environments;
(10) Will not freeze if fully charged;
(11) Suitable for unmanned remote stations.

3.23 LOW VOLTAGE AIR BREAK CIRCUIT BREAKERS:

All low voltage circuit breakers whether conventional Air break circuit breaker (ACB) or Moulded case circuit breaker (MCCB), are designed, manufactured and tested in conformity with IEE standard 157-1. Figure 3.23 (a) illustrates a withdrawable truck mounted type low voltage air circuit breaker. Breaker is assembled on a moulded base of high strength polyester glass compound supported by stainless steel frame. The use of stainless steel prevents magnetic heating. Closed-Open-Charged-Discharged position indicators are mounted on the breaker faceplate. Breakers have silver tungsten double break bridge type main contacts, with wedge contact surface. Main contact assembly is in two parts, namely fixed contact and moving contact. Each breaker pole has 2 sets of contacts; (1) Main contact; (2) Arcing contact. Arcing contacts are for absorbing arc during closing and opening operation, bolted to the main contacts and covered with arc chutes. The angular configurations of arcing contact minimizes the blow-off-forces produced by short-circuit currents. Two compression-springs per contact produce high contact pressure to ensure the breakdown of corrosive films and dirt.

Primary draw out contacts are provided with draw out type circuit breakers. Male and female units are made of silver plated copper. High pressure gripping action, along with a wiping action when contacts are first engaged, maintains low contact resistance and operating temperatures. Main draw out contacts utilize electro-magnetic force to create a "blown" effect to increase contact pressure as current flow increases. These contacts are pre-loaded with individual springs for each pair of contacts to provide a reliable self-aligning connection. Safety shutters are provided to cover the main plug-in contacts of the enclosure. When the breaker moves from the 'Test' to 'Connected' position shutter bolts mounted on the frame of the breaker lift the shutter to expose the main grounding contacts, which is provided to ground the breaker in its cabin. At first the grounding contact made of phosphor bronze to copper is engaged, which ensures a positive ground. Secondary contacts are of sliding type made of formed copper, cadmium plated and mounted in a polycarbonate moulding. The contacts are mounted such that the control circuit can be energized in the test position. Sliding contact unit consists of stationary contact mounted on the panel block and sliding contact mounted on the breaker frame. Auxiliary contacts are of either normally open (NO) or normally closed (NC). Every breaker have a multi-section rotary switch coupled directly to the closing shaft operated on a snap-action principle, which provides quick break switching. NO/NC switches 6 to 12 or 20 poles are available.

LEGEND:

1. Primary disconnecting contact;
2. Contact assembly; Arc chutes;
3. Operating mechanism;
4. Spring charging motor;
5. Trip coil / shunt trip / UV trip;
6. Current transformer (overload);
7. Sliding contacts;
8. Auxiliary contacts (NO/NC);
9. Breaker frame;
10. Handle for manual spring charging & manual operation.

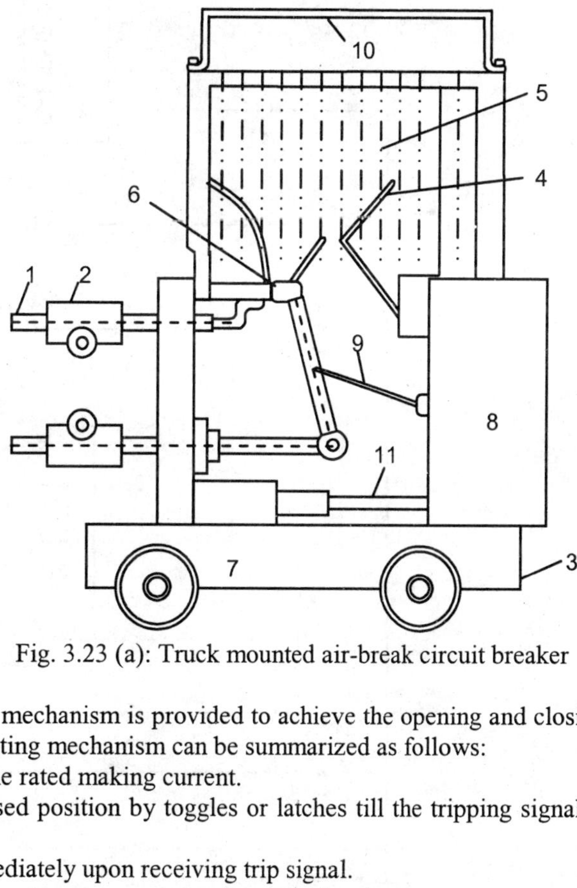

Fig. 3.23 (a): Truck mounted air-break circuit breaker

Circuit breaker operating mechanism: Operating mechanism is provided to achieve the opening and closing operations of the breaker. The functions of the operating mechanism can be summarized as follows:

b) Breaker can be closed rapidly at the rated making current.
c) To hold the circuit breaker in closed position by toggles or latches till the tripping signal is received.
d) To allow the breaker to open immediately upon receiving trip signal.
e) To perform trip free operation if an attempt is made to close a faulty circuit.
f) To perform the auto re-close cycle if desired.

While closing the circuit breaker, the operating mechanism should have enough power to overcome the following opposing forces:

1) Electromagnetic forces appear at the instant of contact touch, their magnitude being proportional to square of the current and the direction being opposite to the direction of closing. These forces are large if breaker is closing during a short-circuit.

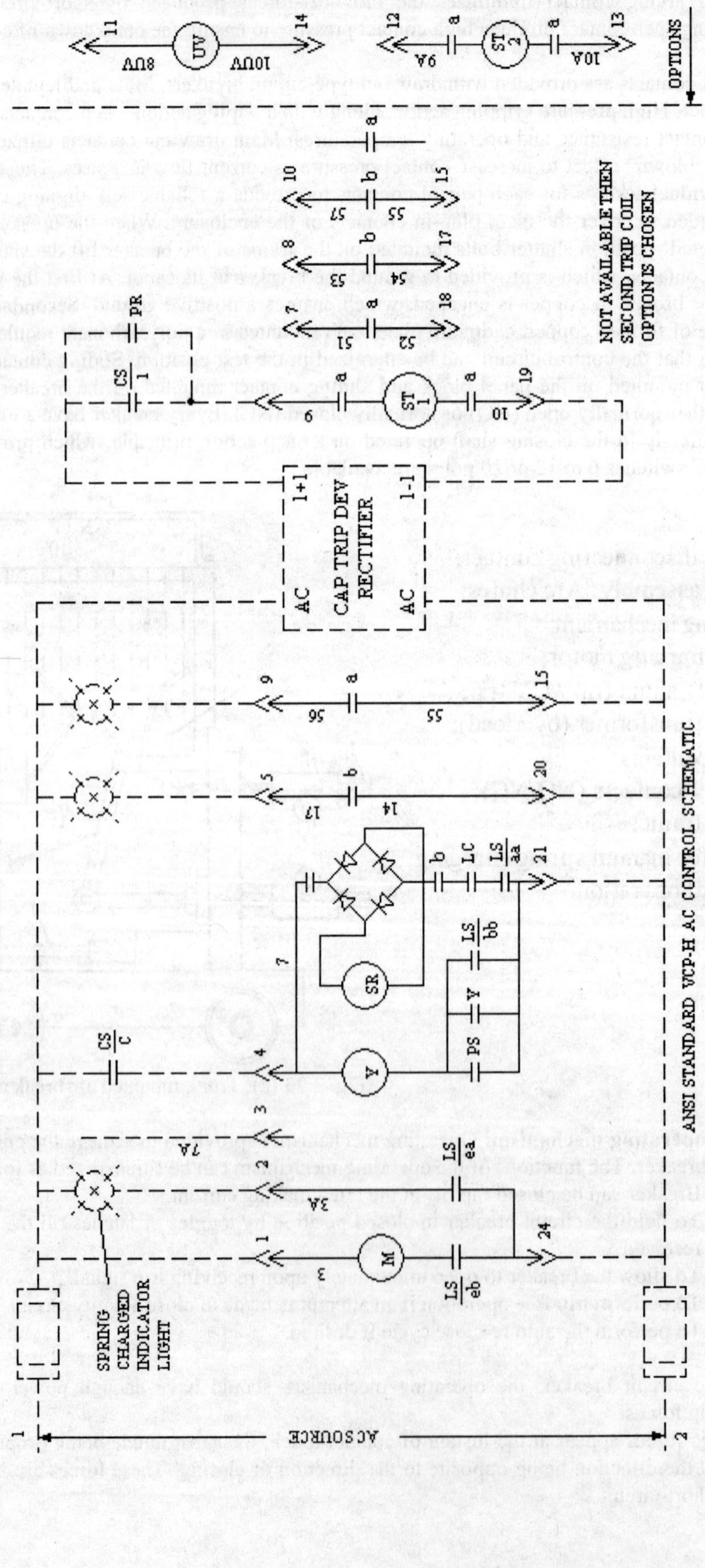

Fig. 3.23 (b): Typical AC or DC control-circuit schematic for a low voltage Air circuit breaker.

2) Breaker is closed by releasing the closing spring and opened by discharging the opening spring. Closing spring is charged either by charging handle or by motor. Opening-spring charge when the closing spring is released. While closing the breaker, these springs oppose the closure.
3) Inertia of movable sub assemblies of operating mechanism;
4) Opposing forces due to arc extinguishing medium.

Stored energy operating mechanisms are independent of the operator or power supply. The energy required for closing the breaker is stored in a charged spring. The breaker closing speed is independent of the operator. Figure 3.23 (b) shows the control circuit schematic of a low voltage Air circuit breaker (ACB). When closing coil (Y) is energized, closing spring is discharged to close the breaker. When the breaker is closed, it is held in latched position and the opening spring is held charged.

As soon as control power is restored, the spring charging motor automatically starts charging the closing spring. When the springs are charged, the motor cut off limit switch (LS) turns the motor OFF and the light "spring charging" becomes on. The breaker may be closed by, making up control switch closing contact (CS/C). Through the NC contact of 'LS' anti-pump relay 'Y' pickup through position switch (PS). This switch will remain closed when the circuit breaker is either in test position or in fully inserted position. It will remain open in intermediate positions and to prevent close the breaker. Closing coil (SR) will now picks up and the breaker will close and the circuit breaker 'off' light will goes off, and 'on' light will come in. The closing spring will now recharge the spring immediately. ST shows that the trip circuit is healthy. In case the protective relay (PR) operates or control switch (CS/T) turn to trip position, circuit breaker shunt trip coil will energize and trip the breaker.

When the tripping signal is initiated, shunt trip coil energizes. The latch is released and the breaker opens by spring action. Generally the low voltage circuit breakers have three positions 'Tripped-Reset-Closed'. After every closing operation or immediately after the availability of AC control power, spring charging motor starts automatically if the breaker closing spring is not fully charged. When the spring is fully charged, the spring charging limit switch opens its contact to stop the spring charge motor. When the charging cycle is complete the ratchet wheel is positioned so that a missing tooth is adjacent to the driving pawl and motor over-spin will not drive the ratchet wheel, thus preventing damage to the system.

Auxiliary contacts are either normally open (52a) or normally closed (52b). When the breaker is open all NO contacts remains open and when breaker is closed all NO contacts becomes closed. Similarly, all NC contacts remains closed when the breaker is open and opens when the breaker is closed. Breaker ON/OFF position is indicated in the panel by means of red and green indication lamps connected through NO/NC auxiliary contacts respectively. Electrical and mechanical interlocks are provided as a safety measure against erroneous operation of a switching device. Three types of interlocks are being used; (1) Electrical interlock; (2) Mechanical interlock; (3) Key interlock.

Control system is connected to the breaker either through slide-in contacts or multiple pin plug socket. Under-voltage trip unit provides protection against loss of system voltage. It prevents to close the breaker during the absence of system voltage. Anti-pump relay prevents to re-closing the breaker on a sustained close command, as the close signal must be removed to drop out this relay. The positive interlock prevents racking out of a closed breaker. Negative interlock prevents to close a breaker except it is in test or fully inserted position.

Arc chutes: The air in atmospheric pressure is used as an arc-extinguishing medium in air break circuit breakers. High resistance arc interruption principle is employed for arc extinguishers. When the breaker opens the main contacts part at first and the double break contacts quickly establish a wide air-gap. The current flow is transferred to the arcing contacts, through a heavy copper braid. The arcing contacts part and an arc is established and the magnetic field produced forces the arc up in to the arc chute. The arc chutes are made of fiber reinforced polyester and contains the steel arc chute plates and de-ionizing plates. The actions of the arc quenching and de-ionizing plates pulls the arc still further inside the arc chute where it is cooled and broken in to many small series arcs. Thus extended, cooled and quickly extinguished, without arcing on the main contacts. When the breaker closes, the arcing contacts touch first then the main contacts. Arc established in the arcing contact is being extinguished through the arc chutes.

Figure 3.23 (c) shows the arc chute of an air circuit breaker in contact closed and contact open position.

LEGENDS:

1. Main contacts
2. Arcing contacts
3. Arc rising direction
4. Arc getting split
5. Arc splitter plates
6. Terminal
7. Arc runners

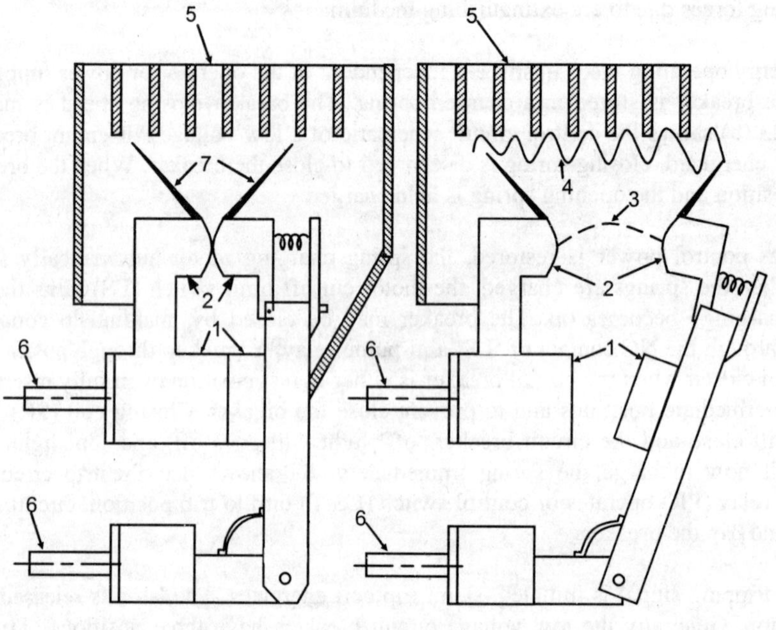

Fig. 3.23 (c): Arc extinction in air-break circuit breaker.

Series over-current tripping devices: Basic over-current tripping devices used on low voltage breakers are either electromagnetic or electronic tripping facilities. Figure 3.23 (d) shows the connection diagram of an electromagnetic trip circuit with earth fault release. Protection-CT's for over-current and short-circuit protection are mounted on the breaker poles and neutral CT for earth fault protection is mounted on the neutral bar.

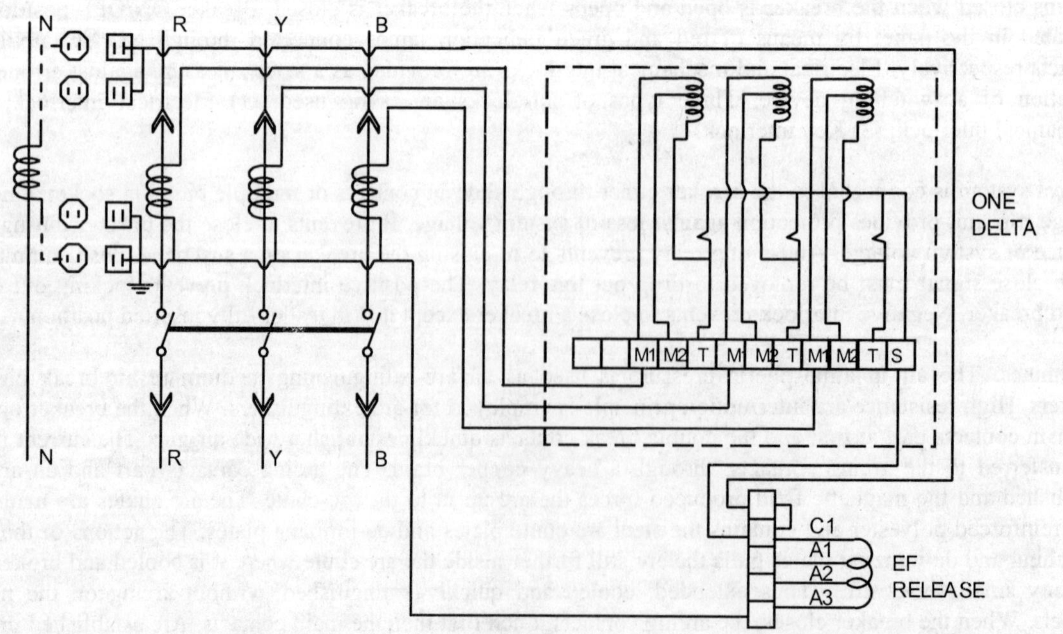

Fig. 3.23 (d): Electromagnetic over-current and earth fault release for ACB (Courtesy, Larsen & Tubro).

(a) Long delay characteristic: This is achieved by a magnetic element, which gives a delayed tripping in the order of seconds and minutes for values of over-current only in a few multiples of the trip coil rating. The time delay is obtained by means of adjustable valves that control the rate at which air enters in an expending air chamber. Its application is for overload protection.

(b) Short delay characteristic: This is obtained by the use of a magnetic element that gives a time delay in the order of cycles for heavy currents of fault current magnitude. The time delay is obtained by the application of valves similar to the long delay. But the valve orifice is larger which allows greater amount of air and hence gives a short time delay.

(c) Instantaneous electromagnetic release: This is obtained by the use of a magnetic instantaneous device with no intentional time delay. Its usual function is to give short-circuit protection. In the event of short-circuit, on the feeder or equipment, when the current equals to 10 times the setting a magnetic armature pickup releases the latching mechanism, causing the short-circuit current to be interrupted by opening the air circuit breaker. It is also used on breakers in cascade arrangements. Only pickup setting is required to define the instantaneous characteristics.

Solid-state protection: Current transformers mounted on the breaker poles provides, power input to the electronic circuit and current signal to the fault detection logic circuit shown in Figure 3.23 (e). The CT incorporated in the neutral is for ground fault protection. The solid-state protection is mounted on the breaker faceplate. Sensor tap setting is shown on the relay front plate by an adjustable rotatable disc or screen. A direct acting solenoid provides activation of the trip latch on the breaker and resetting after operation. Pickup levels and time delay settings are factory programmed. Once the breaker has been tripped on overload, short circuit or earth fault, lockout device prevent to close the breaker without resetting the trip devices. Following settings are to be made at site during commissioning:

1. Long time and short time curve on overload;
2. Instantaneous trip setting;
3. Backup protection.

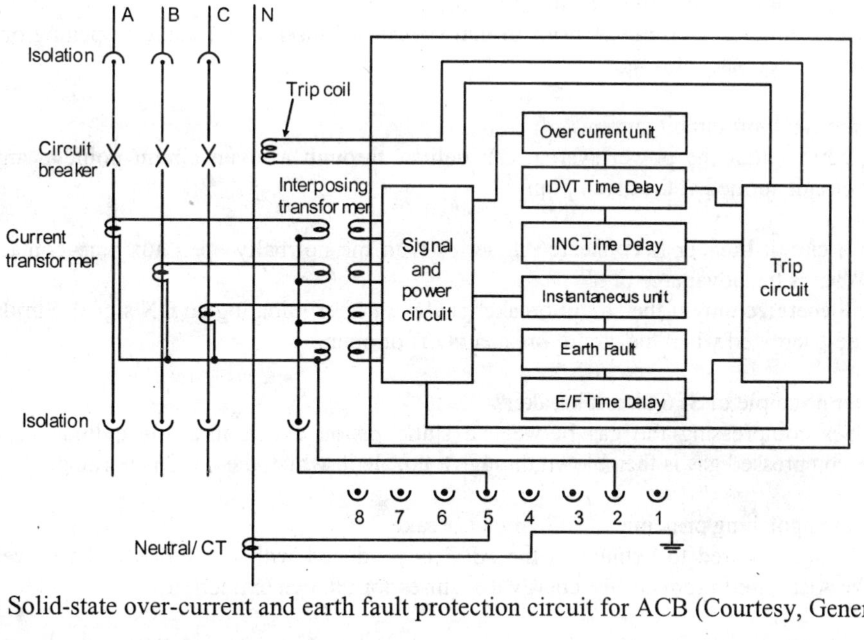

Fig. 3.23 (e): Solid-state over-current and earth fault protection circuit for ACB (Courtesy, General Electric).

Selecting circuit breakers for low voltage applications: While selecting circuit breakers for low voltage applications care shall be taken that the breaking capacity should not be less than the calculated fault level (Three-phase short-circuit current). Similarly the rated current of the breaker should not be less than 125% of the full load current. The short-circuit current in the secondary of a distribution transformer can be obtained by using the formula (Is x 100) / %Z. The value obtained is in amps.
Is = Transformer secondary current; Z = Transformer percentage impedance.

ACB maintenance: Following periodical maintenance checks are recommended in ACB or MCCB:

1. Connection of terminal lugs of main cables must be cleaned to secure solid connection between the stranded wires of the cable and terminal lug and then it's connection secured to the terminal bars of the ACB. The outer part of the terminal lug must be lubricated with petroleum jelly to prevent rust.
2. Main stationary and moving contacts must be clean with antirust solvent and traces of sparking and polished without using emery paper so that silvered surface will not be removed. Arc chutes shall be removed and arcing chamber is to be cleaned properly.
3. Spring and clearance between the moving and stationary contacts must be adjusted to be exactly identical for the three pairs of contacts.
4. The links of the operating tipping mechanism must be cleaned and any traces of rust removed by antirust solvent and lubricated to ensure free tripping and operation.
5. The thermal overload current heater element must be checked for any traces of overheating if applicable. The heater element should have good contact after cleaning. The tripping current for thermal overload must be 105% of the full load current. This can be verified by injecting current in the CT secondary circuit. If the heater element is not tripping at 105% current after a predetermined time, the element must be replaced.
6. Function-check of interlocking and protection circuits.

3.24 PRACTICAL QUESTIONS AND ANSWERS ON MV BREAKERS/SWITCHGEARS

Q1: Name the instrument used for testing the dielectric strength of vacuum chamber in a vacuum circuit breaker?
Ans: Vacuum integrity tester. The rate of recovery of dielectric strength in a medium voltage Vacuum interrupter is 50 KV/millisecond. [Refer figure 3.7 (f)].

Q2: Minimum Oil Circuit Breaker is not suitable for capacitor bank switching. Why?
Ans: MOCB has a tendency to restrike during switching or tripping operation, causing release of energy from capacitor bank. (Refer section 3.6).

Q3: What is break before make feature in a circuit breaker?
Ans: Normally Open contact (NO) closes prior to the Normally Closed (NC) contact opening or NC contact opening prior to the NO contact closing.

Q4: Define prospective short circuit current?
Ans: Maximum current that the power system can deliver through a given circuit point to any negligible impedance short circuit applied at the given point.

Q5: Trip coil of a circuit breaker is connected in series with the normally open auxiliary contact (52a) of a circuit breaker. What is the advantage of it?
Ans: Trip coil will energize only if the circuit breaker is ON, or after initiating an ON signal. Similarly, the trip coil will remain de-energized when the circuit breaker is off or open.

Q6: What is Puffer principle of SF6 circuit breaker?
Ans: This involves compressing the gas between a static piston and a movable cylinder during current interruption. The compressed gas is then blown through a nozzle in which the ARC is burning.

Q7: What is self-extinguishing principle of SF6 circuit breaker?
Ans: Sf6 gas pressure required to extinguish the ARC is produced with a piston via the movement of the contactor rod. The ARC itself produces the energy it requires for its own extinction.

Q8: Device used for sensing the closing and opening speed of a medium voltage SF6 circuit breaker? What is the approximate closing and opening speed of a medium voltage SF6 circuit breaker?
Ans: Capacity senser with oscilloscope is used for measuring the closing speed (2metre/second) and opening speed (4 metre/second) of a medium voltage SF6 circuit breaker [refer figure 3.8 (h)].

Q9: For switching on capacitor bank, why vacuum circuit breaker is preferred comparing to medium voltage Minimum oil circuit breaker and medium voltage sulphur hexaflouride gas insulated circuit breaker?

Ans: The Vacuum circuit breaker can indeed cause more intense re-striking and hence more acute over voltages than other MOCB or SF6 circuit breakers.

Q10: What is the minimum breakdown voltage of fresh oil prior filling in to medium voltage Minimum oil circuit breaker interrupter? Which oil is used for withdrawable type MOCB interrupter?
Ans: The oil used for filling MOCB interrupter is SHELL DIALA D. Minimum breakdown voltage at 2.5mm electrode gap is 50KV (20 KV per mm gap).

Q11: Name the instrument used for measuring the contact resistance of a Circuit breaker interrupter contact?
Ans: Ductor meter [Refer figure 3.10 (a)].

Q12: Is it possible to use an AC circuit breaker in DC circuit?
Ans: No, Alternating Current circuit breaker quenches ARC at current zero. Direct Current has no current zero. Hence AC circuit breakers cannot be used in DC. Also see answer to question Q42 and Q43.

Q13: Can a 50 Hertz circuit breaker is suitable for use in 60 Hertz system of same voltage?
Ans: The type tests of circuit breaker at 50 Hertz are not valued for 60 Hertz. Hence if circuit breakers are type tested for both 50 Hertz and 60 Hertz, then it can be used.

Q14: Circuit breakers for 6.6 KV, 11 KV, 33 KV, 66 KV etc are designated and identified as 7.2 KV, 12 KV, 36 KV, 72.5 KV circuit breakers. Why is it so?
Ans: Voltage ratings of circuit breakers manufactured in conformity with IEC 56 are designated and identified at their highest system voltage, not the nominal voltage.

Q15: Does a 36 KV circuit breaker could be used in 22 KV systems?
Ans: Yes, an AC circuit breaker can be used for any voltages up to its rated voltage provided the rated current, short circuit ratings, system frequency, breaking and making capacity etc must be within the limit.

Q16: What is the necessity of manufacturing medium voltage single pole circuit breakers?
Ans: For single-phase AC traction system, (Railways) eg. 25 KV r.m.s 12 KA or 16 KA breaking-current. Single pole breakers are also used in Neutral grounding resistor connection as illustrated in figure 1.5 (d) of Chapter # 1.

Q17: What is the maximum permissible operating time for circuit breakers, relays and fuses?
Ans: Time $t = \subseteq K (S/Isc)^2$ Seconds and short circuit current = $(A \times K) / \sqrt{t}$
S = Conductor cross sectional area
Isc = Short circuit current
K = Constant based on the cable or overhead lines as given below.
PVC insulated cables: Copper conductor K = 115, Aluminium conductor K = 76.
XLPE or EPR insulated cables: Copper conductor K = 143, Aluminium conductor K 94
Paper insulated cables: Copper conductor K = 127, Aluminium conductor K = 84
Overhead lines: Hard drawn copper conductor K = 108, Hard drawn aluminium conductor K = 70

Q18: How to determine the approximate minimum cross section of aluminium or copper bus bar required for a switchgear?
Ans: Minimum cross sectional area of electrolytic copper (99.9% purity) bus bar in sq:mm = Switchboard ratings in amps / 1.2, and for electrical grade aluminium bus bar the cross sectional area in sq:mm = Switch board current ratings / 0.75. The safe current carrying capacity of copper bus bar is 1.2 amps per sq:mm cross section. Similarly, the safe current carrying capacity of aluminium bus bar is 0.75 amps per sq:mm cross section.

Q19: Define the terms short circuit current, peak short circuit current, and symmetrical short circuit current?
Ans: Currents, which flows across the point of the fault for the duration of the short circuit is said to be short circuit current. Peak short circuit current is the maximum instantaneous value of the current after initiation of the short circuit. Power frequency component of the short circuit current is called the symmetrical short circuit current.

Q20: What is the definition of short time current?
Ans: According to International standards, the short time current is defined as the largest RMS (Root mean square) currents, which can be carried for a specified time without excessive temperature rise. That is without harmful electro-dynamic effects. Short time current is the peak short circuit current.

Q21: Describe the method for testing the bus bar phase identity in a medium voltage switchgear cubicle?
Ans: Connect a battery box to the bus bars as follows; R-phase 6volt battery, Y-phase 9volt battery, and B-phase 12volt battery, with negatives connected to the earth. Identify all points by measuring the voltage. P.T fuses (primary) must be removed while connecting the batteries.

Q22: What are the various safety interlocks provided in a draw out type low voltage air circuit breaker ?
Ans: (a) Interlock to ensure that the breaker is open and the closing spring is discharged before the breaker is pulled out from the connected position. (b) The breaker must be in open position and the closing spring is in discharged position before inserting the breaker in to the connected position. {When the handle is inserted to draw out or insert the breaker, breaker will trip if it is closed and also discharges the closing spring if it is charged.} (c) Prevents entry of any other brand breaker or any other frame size of same brand. (d) Closed breaker will trip if the compartment door is open.

Q23: What are the disadvantages of transformer oil?
Ans: (a) Arc produced in the oil is inflammable (easily set on fire) and explosive. If arc is not extinguished the pressure in the tank may rise above the safe limit and explosion may occur. (b) Oil absorbs moisture. Dielectric strength reduces by carbonization, which occurs during arcing. (c) Oil is not suitable for those breakers, which has to operate frequently. Typical examples are electric furnace, high voltage motor, Railway traction etc. (d) Oil needs periodic testing and replacement (except hermetically sealed transformers) even filtration. (e) In circuit breakers, at lower ambient temperature the viscosity of the oil sharply rises and the speed of contact travel reduces. (f) The dust particle and sludge can create flashover due to tracking.

Q24: What are the test voltages to be applied on medium voltage circuit breakers while conducting one minute AC high voltage test at site.
Ans: (a) Breaker closed and de-energized: Between breaker poles, 2.4 times the rated voltage and pole to earth $(V \times 2.4) / \sqrt{3}$ volts. (b) Breaker opened and de-energized: Across the pole element 1.2 times of rated voltage.

Q 25: Explain trip free operation of a circuit breaker with example?
Ans: The purpose of providing seal in unit in protective relay is for providing flag indication to identify that which relay is operated and what kind of fault is persisting. When the relay operates the breaker trips and the faulty area is isolated from the system. Meanwhile if a closing signal is attained, the breaker may probably close and the faulty line will re-energize and cause severe damage to the system. To prevent such an operation seal-in units are provided in electromagnetic relays. When the relay picks up seal in unit coil will energize and its NO contact will remain closed until the relay is reset. Hence the system can be charged only after resetting both protective relay and lockout relay. If a closing signal is attained without resetting those relays the breaker will attempt to close, but before the breaker poles (main contacts) closing, the auxiliary contact will close and the breaker will trip open. This operation is known as trip free operation and demonstrated in section 3.12.

Q26: What are the tests to be made in a potential transformer?
Ans: (a) Polarity check (b) Ratio check (c) Phasing check (refer section 5.5).

Q27: What are the tests to be made in a current transformer?
Ans: (a) Polarity check (b) Ratio check (c) Magnetization curve-check (refer section 5.4).

Q28: What are the three methods of connecting current transformers for ground fault protection?
Ans: (a) Residual sensing shown in figure 7.10 (a) of Chapter # 7; (b) Zero sequence sensing shown in figure 9.16 (a) and (b) of Chapter # 9; (c) Neutral sensing shown in figure 7.9 (a) of Chapter # 7.

Q29: What do you mean by "time current characteristics" of a relay? What are the different types of characteristics employed in relaying system?

Ans: Time current characteristics means the relation between time and current in a relay. (Refer section 5.17).

(a) Inverse definite minimum time characteristic (IDMT)
(b) Inverse time characteristics. (Very inverse / extremely inverse)
(c) Definite time characteristics.
(d) Instantaneous characteristics.

Q30: Specify the difference between device No: 51N and 51G?
Ans: Device No: 51N is an earth fault relay in which the relay coil is connected in series with the common return wire of the CT neutral as shown in figure 9.15 (a) of Chapter # 9. Device No: 51G is a ground fault relay connected to a C.T installed in the neutral earth of a transformer as shown in figure 7.9 (a) of Chapter # 7.

Q31: What do you mean by IP or let-through-current of a fuse?
Ans: Let-through-current (IP) is that current passed through a fuse while the fuse is interrupting during a fault within the fuse current limiting range.

Q32: What do you mean by I^2 t of a fuse?
Ans: I = Current (r.m.s); t = clearing time.
Two fuses can have the same let-through-current, but different clearing times. I^2t accounts for both 'I', and clearing time 't'. To achieve proper co-ordination between two fuses in series, it is necessary to ensure that total I^2 t taken by the smaller fuse is not greater than the I^2t value of the larger fuse.

Q33: What are the advantages of current limiting fuses?
Ans: Current limiting fuses are capable of isolating a faulted circuit before the fault current attains its peak value. This limits thermal and mechanical stresses created by the fault currents. Similarly, magnitude and duration of voltage drop produced by the fault current is reduced.

Q34: Define high rupturing capacity (HRC) fuses?
Ans: A fuse is a device for over-current protection with a circuit opening fusible member directly heated and destroyed by the passage of over-current through it. The part of a fuse, which melts when the current exceeds a predetermined value is called fuse element. High rupturing capacity fuses consist of porcelain shell housing or high strength ceramic tube or a fully insulated moulded plastic construction known as cartridge, the ends of which are closed by tightly screwed brass end caps with or without contact blades. Fusible elements are encapsulated with graded chemically inert sand and sealed within the housing. HRC fuse links incorporate non-deteriorating fine silver elements, which provides long trouble free life and have specially proportioned arcing zones, which satisfies the dual requirements of optimum performance under short-circuit.

Q35: Compare trickle charge and float charge in a battery system?
Ans: (a) Trickle charge is a method of ensuring that fully charged cells remain in that condition and this is affected by supplying a small charging current to just compensate for the internal cell losses. It is suitable for charging standby battery banks when it is idle (not connected to load).
(b) Float charge is a method of maintaining the battery in optimum condition while in use (connected to load). A constant potential charging source (2.25 volts / cell for lead acid batteries and 1.46 volts per cell for nickel cadmium batteries) is applied to the battery bank and load. This DC source having the ability to supply continuous and variable DC loads while ensuring that the battery is fully charged. Recharging can be achieved automatically with the boost facility.

Q36: What are the different types of cables used for medium voltage (3.6 to 36 KV) applications?
Ans: (a) PILC: Paper insulated lead sheathed cable (obsolete since 1960)

(b) XLPE: Cross-linked polyethylene insulated cables. For single core cables aluminium wire armoure (AWG) is being used. For three-core cables either steel wire armour (SWG) or double steel tape armour (DSTA) is used. Lead sheathed single-core as well as three-core cables are also available. In all cases the outer sheath is made of PVC (Poly vinual chloride) or HDPE (Heavy duty poly-ethylene).

(c) EPR: Ethylene Propylene Rubber insulated cable. It replaces XLPE insulation by EPR insulation. Armouring and outer sheath is similar to XLPE cables.

(d) PVC insulated armoured or unarmoured cables are widely used in low voltage systems and medium voltage up to 3600 Volts.

Q37: What are the factors to be considered for selecting a cable for MV networks?

Ans: (a) Maximum load current; (b) System fault level and short-circuit current. (c) Voltage rating (d) Method of laying; (e) Maximum ambient temperature (f) Route length. Refer appendices # 1 to 4 for more details.

Q38: Describe the method of calculating power KW, KVA and current in a three-phase load?

Ans: Three-phase power in watts = √3 x voltage between phases x Current per phase x power factor.

KVA = (√3 x voltage x current) / 1000; KW = KVA x Power factor

$$\text{Current in amps} = \frac{\text{Power in watts}}{\sqrt{3} \times \text{voltage} \times \text{PF}} \quad \text{or} \quad \frac{\text{KVA}}{\sqrt{3} \times \text{KV}}$$

Q39: Describe the formula for calculating voltage drop in a three-phase medium voltage cable?

Ans: Voltage drop = [√3 x Current in KA x Length in metre] x [R cosφ + X_L sin φ]

R = Effective resistance in ohm / KM

X_L = Inductive reactance ohm/KM

φ = Power factor

Q40: What are the safety precautions to be taken before switching on an earth switch in a medium voltage switchboard (ring system) prior to issue a work permit?

Ans: Since back feeding is possible in a ring system, following are the procedures for issuing work permit [refer figure 3.13 (b)]. Switch off the concerned circuit breakers. Disconnect secondary multiple plug unit. Rack out the circuit breaker.

(a) Switch off the ring main unit from which back feeding is possible.
(b) Check with high voltage probe to ensure that no power is available both incoming and outgoing side.
(c) Switch on the earth switch and lock it.
(d) Issue work-permit and demonstrate the area safe to work.

Q41: Explain the term power factor, lagging power factor and leading power factor?

Ans: Power factor is the ratio of active power to apparent power in alternating current system. The voltage varies between the maximum and the minimum in the form of sinusoidal curve, thus causing the current to constantly change direction. In circuits with purely resistive loads, the voltage and current attain their maxima simultaneously. Cos φ = Unity (Purely active power). In the case of inductive loads, the voltage leads the current, i.e, it attains its maximum ahead of the current (Lagging power factor). [Refer figure 1.4 (b) of Chapter # 1].

Where capacitive loads are connected, the current leads the voltage, i.e. it attains its maximum ahead of the voltage (Leading power factor): Cos φ = 0 (Purely reactive power). The greater the deviation from unity, the higher the stress set up in the switching device when switching the circuit. (Inductive load: Higher opening stress; Capacitive load: Higher closing stress). An inductive load can be balanced out by a capacitance, and vice versa. Optimum utilization of long distance medium voltage cables at unity power factor can produce Reactive power.

Q42: Define Arc-quenching medium and deionizing chamber in low voltage system?

Ans: (a) Arc-quenching medium which causes the arc to be extinguished. Air is the arc extinguishing medium used in low voltage switching devices such as ACB, MCCB (Moulded case circuit breakers) and MCB (Miniature circuit breakers) etc. In low voltage HRC fuses sand is the arc-quenching medium.

(b) Arc splitter chamber in the arc chute is the deionizing chamber. [Refer Figure 2.23 (c) above]. In this chamber, the arc is subdivided in to a number of small arcs by the arc-splitters, which it contains. An AC arc is extinguished at each → Current zero, but it must be prevented from re-striking. This is achieved by the fact that it travels away from the contacts and is driven in to the arc-splitters.

Q43: Explain arc-quenching method in Direct current circuit breakers?

Ans: For arc quenching in DC circuit breakers a special coil called blowout coil is used to extend the arc. It is fitted in the current path assembly or arcing chamber of DC switching devices and carries the arc current. The magnetic field due to this current "blows" the arc in to the chute, thus causing it to be extinguished rapidly and safely. DC circuit breakers are demonstrated in Chapter # 1, section 1.20.

Q44: Explain the term grading and trip discrimination in a power distribution network?
Ans: Power flowing from the secondary of a distribution transformer to the loads passes through a number fuses and circuit breakers (fitted with release or relays), which are connected from upstream to downstream in series. The operating times of the releases or relays and the rated currents are graded so that they decrease towards downstream load. Grading the protective devices in this way ensures trip discrimination.

Q45: Describe various types of protective releases used in low voltage system?
Ans: Protective releases are used in conjunction with automatic switches (Circuit breakers) and starters (for motors) to protect electrical equipment against the effects of overload, short-circuit, earth fault etc. A distinction is made between:
(a) Thermal releases: Bimetal strips used in the current path are heated by the currents flows through the load to be protected. The release is set to the rated current of that equipment to be protected. If the load current exceeds the preset value, the strips deflect and, by a mechanical device, cause the latching mechanism of the circuit breaker to be released and thus the low voltage air circuit breaker to trip. In case of low voltage starters, the NC contact of the thermal relay will open and de-energizes the holding coil of the contactor.
(b) Instantaneous electromagnetic releases are designed to trip an air-break circuit breaker by mechanical means in the event of a short circuit. If the current equals about 10 times the setting, a magnetic armature picks up and releases the latching mechanism of the air circuit breaker, causing the short-circuit current to be interrupted instantaneously.
(c) Delayed electromagnetic releases will provide trip discrimination (grading) between circuit breakers. Their time-delay is steplessly adjustable between zero and 500ms, but they will operate only if the fault is sustained until about 100ms prior to the preset delay expiring.

Q46: Define the term demand factor, diversity factor, and load factor?
Ans: (a) Demand factor: Ratio of maximum demand to the total connected load.
(b) Diversity factor: Ratio of the sum of individual maximum demands of the various sub-division of a system to the maximum demand of the whole system.
(c) Load factor: Ratio of the average load over a designated period of time to the peak load occurring in that period.

CHAPTER # 4

HIGH AND EXTRA HIGH VOLTAGE CIRCUIT BREAKERS AND SUBSTATIONS

CONTENTS:

4.1 AIR-INSULATED HV AND EHV OUTDOOR SWITCHING STATIONS

HV and EHV air insulated switching stations are designed for voltage levels from 60 KV to 800 KV, rated currents up to 8000 Amps, short circuit currents up to 100 Kilo-amps, Alternating current (50 or 60 hertz) and are popular wherever space restrictions as well as environmental circumstances do not have to be considered. Air-insulated out door substations of open design are directly exposed to the effects of weather and the environment. AIS is always set up in the form of a fenced-in electrical operating area, to which only authorized persons have access. Relevant IEC 60060 specifications apply to outdoor switchgear equipments. Minimum phase-to-phase and phase-to-ground clearances, is effected in accordance with IEC 60071. Outdoor switchgears must comply with following protective measures:

1. Interlocks for operation safety
2. Protective measures against voltage surges and lightning strike.
3. Protective measures against fire, water and noise etc.
4. Electrical stresses due to short circuit current, creepage distances and clearances.
5. Mechanical stresses due to weight, static and dynamic loads, ice, wind etc.

6. Mechanical stresses due to switching forces and short circuit forces.
7. Special stresses caused by earthquakes, altitudes (more than 1000M).
8. Fire precautions and environmental protection by using flame-retardant and non-flammable materials.
9. EMC grounding system for modern control and protection.

The design of an open switchyard determines its accessibility, availability, clarity and redundancy. Clarity and accessibility can be obtained by clear conductor routing, conductor levels, adequate protective clearances for installation, maintenance and transportation.

Basic substation design parameters: General requirements are (a) Nominal system voltage and frequency; (b) Ultimate substation capacity in MVA; (c) BIL requirements; (d) continuous/momentary/short circuit currents; (e) Electrical spacing and clearances.

Engineering designs: Following are the scope of Engineering designs: (1) System study and planning; (2) Site selection and survey; (3) Conceptual design and layout; (4) Equipment selection; (5) Grounding system and Lightning protection; (6) Control and protection system; (7) Communication system; (8) Fire protection and fire fighting system; (9) Civil and structural design (10) Computerized, substation management system; (11) Preparation of specification and tender drawings; (12) Yard lighting and fencing.

1) Types of substations: HV/ EHV/ UHV substations / switching stations are classified in to:

a) Transmission line switching stations or transformer substations to transform voltage levels between **High Voltage (60 KV to 372 KV), Extra High Voltage (400 KV to 800 KV) and Ultra High Voltage (above 800 KV).**
b) Step down Power transformer substations to medium voltage level of distribution (HV/MV), for example 132 KV/33 KV substations.
c) Step up Power transformer substation to step up from generation voltage level to high voltage system (MV/HV), for example 11KV to 132 KV.

Installations involving single bus bar arrangement require minimum investment, but they offer only limited flexibility for operation and maintenance. Designs involving 1 ½ or 2 circuit breaker arrangements and ring bus assure a high supply reliability and system redundancy. For bus and feeder lines, mostly aluminium conductors are used. Multiple conductors used as bus bars, causes higher mechanical stressing at the tension points. When short circuit currents are high, aluminium tubes are increasingly used as bus conductors. They are sized to handle rated current up to 8000 amps and short circuit current up to 100 KA.

Conventional air-insulated switch-bays consist of separately mounted disconnectors, earth switches, circuit breakers, lightning arrester, current and voltage transformers, which are connected to each other by conductors/tubes. Every device needs its own foundations, supporting steel structures, clamps and connectors etc. The bus disconnectors are of the pentograph, rotary and vertical-break type. Vertical-break disconnectors are preferred for the feeders. The bus bars located at the top (higher level) are single or double AAAC and the lower levels are of tubular types.

As an alternative to conventional substations an air-insulated modular switch bay can often be used for common layouts. In this case functions of several HV devices are combined with each other. This makes it possible to offer a standardized module. Modules consist of circuit breakers, motor operated disconnectors, current and voltage transformers, local control and relay cubicles etc.

Out door substation equipments

- Power transformer; * Substation bus (rigid or strain); * Disconnecting switches (Vertical/side/center/double break)
- Circuit breakers (Dead tank type or live tank type); * Surge arresters; * Bus support insulators; * Current transformers (external CT for live tank circuit breakers only) and potential transformers;
- Line traps and coupling capacitors **(Demonstrated in Chapter # 8, section 8.9)** or Teleprotection system * SCADA system (Refer Chapter # 3, section 3.20).

Table 4.1 (1): Ground and sectional clearances of outdoor type substations (switchyard)

Nominal system voltage (KV):	11 or 13.8	33	66	110 or132	220	400	500	765
Ground clearance (M):	2.75	3.70	4.0	4.60	5.50	6.0	6.50	6.5
Sectional clearance (M) (Phase-to-phase)	2.65	2.80	3.0	3.50	4.30	6.50	8	10

Figure 4.1 (a) and (b) respectively shows the single line diagram and layout drawing of one segment (Bus section A only) of a 110/11 KV outdoor type substation. The substation consists of 4 Nos 110 KV transmission line feeders (double circuit transmission lines by loop-in loop-out method), 2 Nos 110/11 KV Transformer feeders and sectionalized single bus bar system. Equipment legend indicates the ratings of primary equipments except transformer. 20 MVA, ONAN (Natural oil and air cooled) or 25 MVA ONAF (Natural oil and forced air cooled) three winding power transformer having vector group YNynd11 (Star connected primary, Star connected secondary, and delta connected tertiary winding). Transformer 11 KV neutral is grounded through a 10 ohm grounding resistor.

Technical information:

Outdoor type 2000 A 25 KA, 3-second tubular aluminium alloy bus supported on post insulator is being used as main bus. The branches are connected through 800 mm^2 AAAC (All aluminium alloy conductor).

Surge arresters with surge counters are provided on each feeder. Disconectors are provided on either side of each 110 KV circuit breakers. Provision for Voltage transformers, are kept on either bus section.

Following protective relays (numerical) are employed:

Line feeders:

(a) Device No: 21, Numerical distance relay (Refer Chapter # 8, section 8.4).

(b) Device No: 67/67N, Directional over current and earth fault relay (Refer Chapter # 7, section 7.10).

(c) Device No: 79, Auto-reclosing relay with synchronizing check (Refer Chapter # 8, section 8.15)

(d) Device No: 74, Trip circuit supervision relay (Refer Chapter # 7, section 7.12).

(e) Device No: 86, Tripping relay (refer Chapter # 5, section 5.12).

Transformer feeders:

(a) Device No: 87T, Biased-differential relay for power transformer (Refer Chapter # 7, section 7.7).

(b) Device No: 64, Restricted-earth fault relay (Refer Chapter # 7, section 7.14).

(c) Device No: 50 / 51, Inverse definite minimum time (IDMT) and instantaneous over current relay (Refer Chapter # 7, section 7.6).

(d) Device No: 74, Trip circuit supervision relay.

(e) Device No: 86, Tripping relay.

Bus section: (a) Over current and earth fault relay; (b) Trip circuit supervision relay; (c) Tripping relay; (d) Synchronism check relay.

11 KV switchgear: (a) Differential Protection C.T; (b) Over-current protection; (c) Bus zone protection.

Neutral earth bus for interchanging or paralleling the Neutral grounding resistors of the two transformers are established by introducing 11 KV single pole disconnecter switches. This will facilitate to avoid another neutral grounding resistor if a similar transformer is installed in the same switchyard.

All protection CTs are Class 5P20 and metering CTs are Class 1.0.

Following equipments are installed in the switchyard as shown in the layout drawing. (!) High level bus disconnectors; (2) Low level line disconnectors, (3) Low level transformer disconnectors; (4) Dead tank type SF6 circuit breaker for transformer feeders; (5) Dead tank type SF6 circuit breaker for Line feeders; (6) Dead tank type SF6 circuit breaker for bus section; (7) Potential transformers for bus section A; (8) Potential transformers for bus section B; (9) Surge arresters with surge counter for transformers; (10) Surge arresters with surge counter for line feeders; (11) Lightning masts with taper pointed air terminal; (12) Post insulators for supporting tubular aluminium bus bar.

In addition to the above equipments, supporting structures, tubular aluminium bus bars, AAAC (All aluminium alloy conductor) for jumpering, clamps and connectors, substation earth grid etc are required.

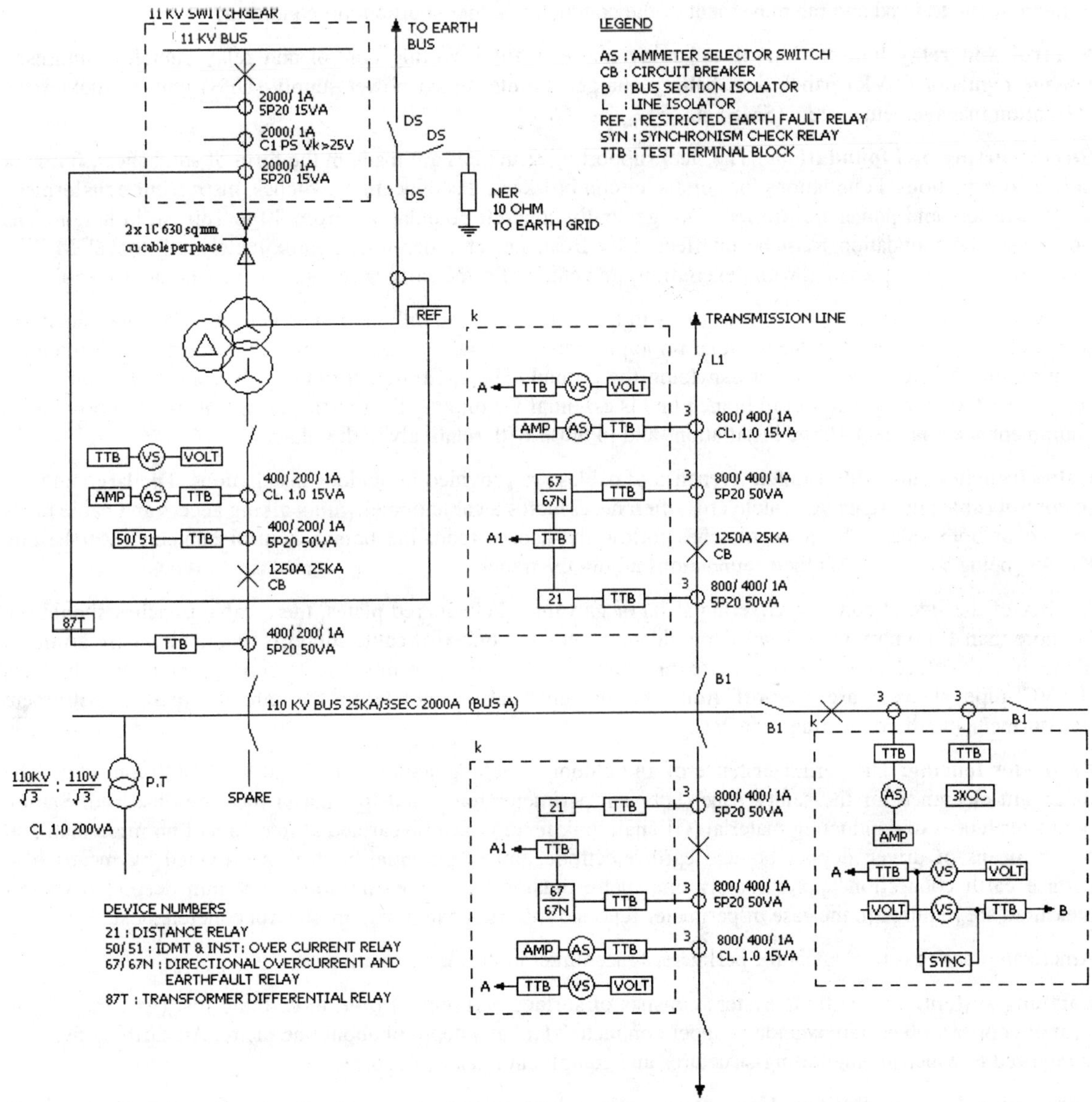

Fig. 4.1 (a): Single line diagram of one segment (bus section A) of a typical 110/11 KV outdoor substation.

A high voltage outdoor switchgear installation also includes transformers, medium and low voltage switchgear, and a variety of auxiliary services and other facilities. These must also be accounted in the station layout. Depending on the intended site, the construction of a switchgear installation must confirm IEC requirements or any relevant national standards. The minimum clearances and gangway width for different voltages are specified in IEC. If flexible conductors are used for bus bars and connections, allowance must be made for deflection due to wind and the movement of the conductors under short circuit conditions.

Control and relay house: Control and relay house is for installing control and relay cubicles, automatic voltage regulator (AVR) panel, dual battery charger, uninterrupted power supply (UPS) unit, Computerized substation management system (SMS) etc.

Steel structure and foundations: The steel supporting structures are made in the form of solid sheet, frame or lattice constructions. Foundations for portals, circuit breakers, disconnecting switches, instrument transformers, surge arresters and power transformers are generally concrete foundations from 30 to 180 cm in height. The bottom of the foundation must be unaffected by frost, i.e. at a depth of approximately 0.8 to 1.2 M. The foundations must be provided with penetrations and entries for the earth wires and, if appropriate, for cables.

Access roads and walk ways: Access roads in the usual sense are only laid in switchyards. The various items of switchgear, being built on the modular principle, can be brought by light means of transport to their intended position in the compound, without damaging the ground. The cable trench running in front of the equipment serves as a footpath. A read or rail branch line is essential for moving the transformers. It is usual to provide an equipment access route in large installations and in those with relatively high voltages.

Cable trenches and cable tunnel: Trenches of cables are provided in outdoor installations. The large number of control cables in extensive switchyards often necessitates a cable tunnel with walking access and cable racks on one or both sides. The main trenches follow the access road, the branch control cubicles (Marshalling Kiosks) being so placed that their foundations adjoin the trench.

In view of the size of concrete covering slabs or galvanized chequered plates, these cable trenches should not be more than 1000 mm wide. Their depth depends on the number of cable supports (cable trays) are arranged along the sides. A slope in the lengthwise direction and drain pipes ensure reliable drainage in the trench, ducts (UPVC pipe sleeves) are teed-off from the branch control cubicle to the circuit breaker, instrument transformers and disconnecting switches.

Perimeter fencing: The perimeter fence of an outdoor switching station must be at least 1800 mm high. The minimum clearance for the safety zone (between perimeter fence and live parts) must be observed. Station perimeter fences of conducting material (GI chain link fence) must be earthed at intervals of no more than 100 M by means of driven copper bonded earth electrode, unless potential control is provided by means of a surface earth connection approximately one metre outside the fence and about 500 mm deep. No special measured are required in the case of perimeter fences of plastic-coated wire mesh with concrete post.

American practice is to connect the perimeter fence direct to the station earth grid.

Earthing system: The earthing system consists of surface earthing strip or an earthing mat (galvanized iron strip or copper strip or bare stranded copper conductor) laid at a depth of about one metre. An earthing network is required to which all supporting-structures and equipment must be connected.

Conventional indoor stations: Conventional indoor high voltage substations are usually contained in single storey buildings, as these allow a straightforward plant layout. The circuit breakers and instrument transformers stand on the floor of the building. The bus bar isolators and feeder isolators are mounted on supporting steel work similar to outdoor switchyard. The bus bars are preferably tubular, supported on a frame or attached to the ceiling.

The bays are generally separated from each other by railings. If reduced clearances between bays have to be observed, solid partition walls of insulating material or armoured glass are placed between the branches. The control gear for each branch is contained in a cubicle, which incorporates a mimic display and is p0laced by the control gangway. The control and measuring cables need only shallow channels let in to the floor and covered with plates or slabs. Earthing wires can be laid in the concrete finishing layer. Earth wire should not be laid in the cable trench.

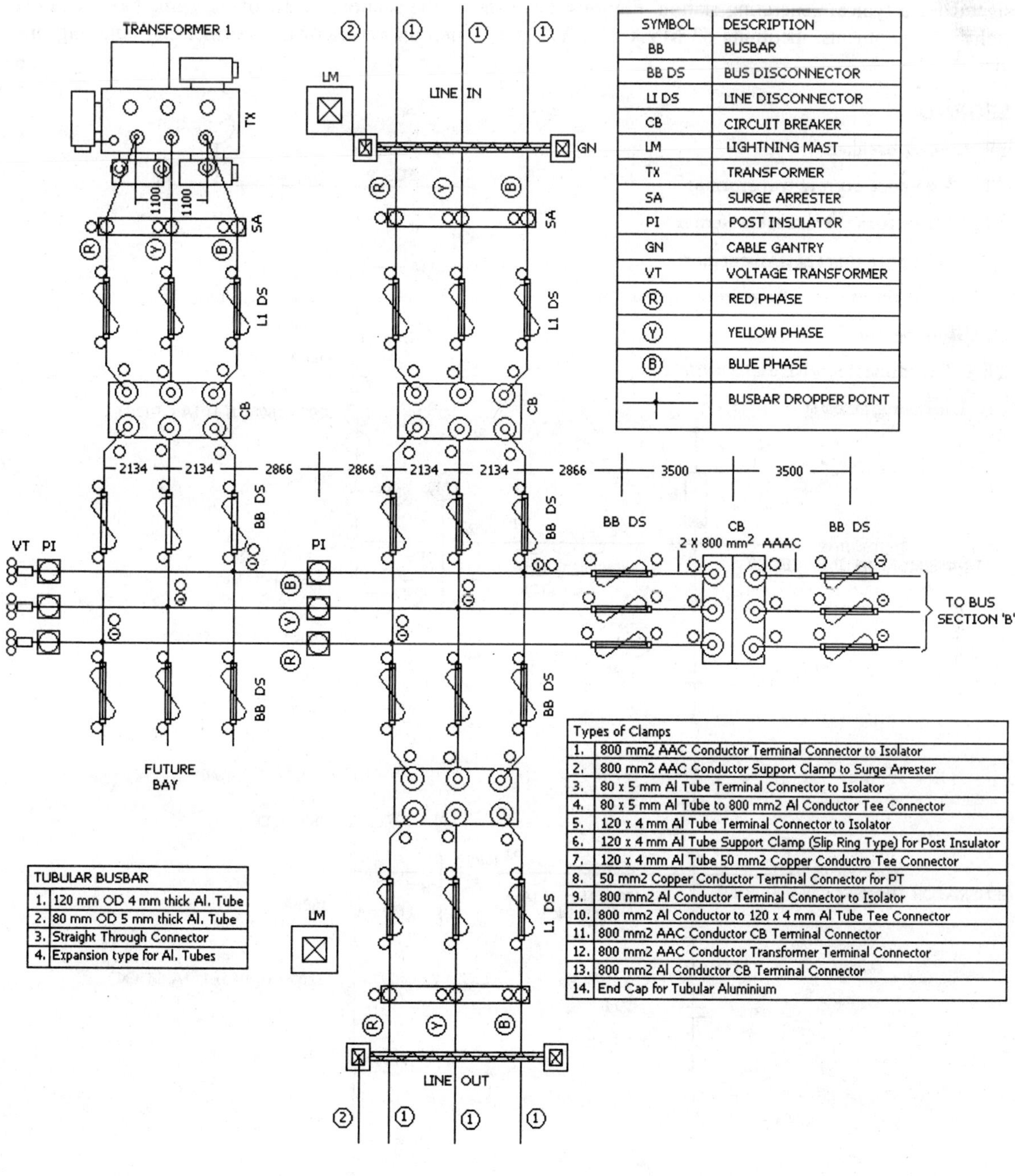

SYMBOL	DESCRIPTION
BB	BUSBAR
BB DS	BUS DISCONNECTOR
LI DS	LINE DISCONNECTOR
CB	CIRCUIT BREAKER
LM	LIGHTNING MAST
TX	TRANSFORMER
SA	SURGE ARRESTER
PI	POST INSULATOR
GN	CABLE GANTRY
VT	VOLTAGE TRANSFORMER
(R)	RED PHASE
(Y)	YELLOW PHASE
(B)	BLUE PHASE
—┼—	BUSBAR DROPPER POINT

Types of Clamps	
1.	800 mm2 AAC Conductor Terminal Connector to Isolator
2.	800 mm2 AAC Conductor Support Clamp to Surge Arrester
3.	80 x 5 mm Al Tube Terminal Connector to Isolator
4.	80 x 5 mm Al Tube to 800 mm2 Al Conductor Tee Connector
5.	120 x 4 mm Al Tube Terminal Connector to Isolator
6.	120 x 4 mm Al Tube Support Clamp (Slip Ring Type) for Post Insulator
7.	120 x 4 mm Al Tube 50 mm2 Copper Conductro Tee Connector
8.	50 mm2 Copper Conductor Terminal Connector for PT
9.	800 mm2 Al Conductor Terminal Connector to Isolator
10.	800 mm2 Al Conductor to 120 x 4 mm Al Tube Tee Connector
11.	800 mm2 AAC Conductor CB Terminal Connector
12.	800 mm2 AAC Conductor Transformer Terminal Connector
13.	800 mm2 Al Conductor CB Terminal Connector
14.	End Cap for Tubular Aluminium

TUBULAR BUSBAR	
1.	120 mm OD 4 mm thick Al. Tube
2.	80 mm OD 5 mm thick Al. Tube
3.	Straight Through Connector
4.	Expansion type for Al. Tubes

Fig. 4.1 (b): Typical layout drawing for one segment (bus section A) of a 110 KV outdoor substation.

Type of clamps required for installation of the aluminium tubular bus bar and AAA conducter for each location is indicated with numerical numbers. Clamp construction details are demonstrated in section 4.12.

Figure 4.1 (c) illustrates typical single line diagram of one bay of a 132 KV 1½ breaker switching station, designed for a typical generating station. Figure 4.1 (d) shows the sectional view of the same bay including switchyard equipments, incoming 63 MVA 11 KV/132 KV step up generator-transformer and outgoing line feeder.

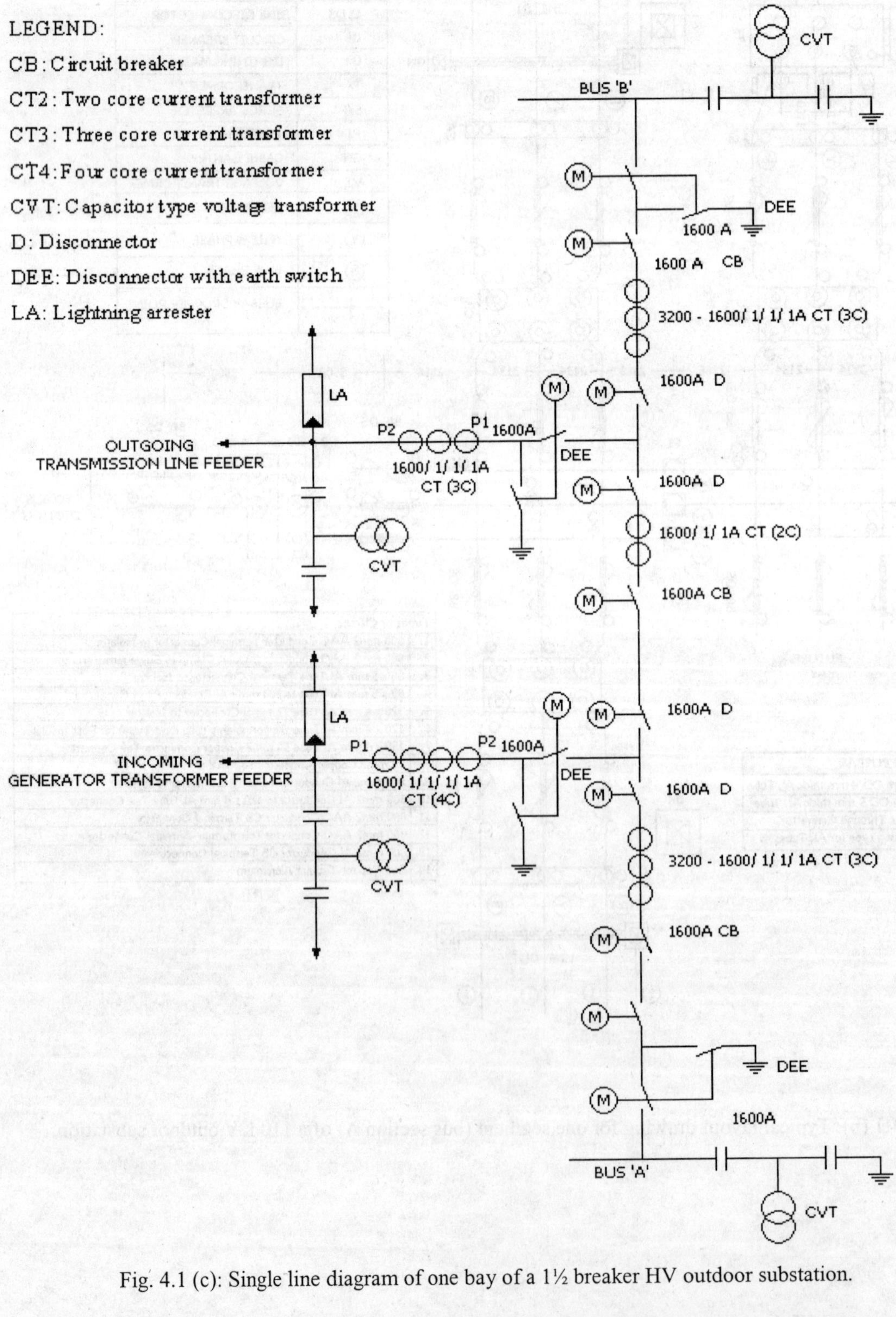

Fig. 4.1 (c): Single line diagram of one bay of a 1½ breaker HV outdoor substation.

The starting point for planning a switchgear installation is its one line diagram. This indicates the extent of the installation, such as the number of bus bars and feeders, and also their associated apparatus. Switching devices and insulators for outdoor type switching stations are built to insulation class N. For installations exposed to a normal climate, the porcelain is designed for a creepage distance of 23 to 26 mm/KV. In areas with heavily polluted air, such as in the vicinity of a power generating station or in industrial centers, and also in areas subject to much fog, the equipment (bushing and insulators etc) have a greater creepage distance of 31 mm per KV.

The bay discussed above has 2 feeders connected to the bus, 3 Nos 1600 A live tank circuit breakers, 2 Nos 3000 A tubular aluminium bus bars (Bus A and Bus B), one number outdoor type 2 core current transformer, 3 sets of 3 core CT's and one set 4 core CT, 4 sets of out door type capacitive potential transformers (CVT) and 2 sets of surge arrestors.

Live tank circuit breakers: Circuit breakers are for switching ON or switching OFF the generator or line during normal conditions. During abnormal conditions (during a fault) 2 breakers will simultaneously open to isolate the feeder. Circuit breakers have interlocking facilities to prevent closing the breaker if the disconnecting switch is open or earth switch is closed. SF6 live tank circuit breaker is demonstrated in section 4.5.

Current transformers: Outdoor post type current transformers are required, as the live tank circuit breakers cannot accept bushing type CT's. Secondary of post type current transformer cores are used for metering and relaying connections. Outdoor type current transformers are demonstrated in section 4.7.

Potential transformers: Capacitive voltage transformers (CVT) are employed (one per phase) in each feeder and bus. Secondary of the potential transformers are for metering and relaying connections, and for synchronizing application. CVT is demonstrated in section 4.8.

Disconnectors and earth switches: Motorized disconnectors are provided on either side of the breaker (Bus side and line or transformer side) so that by opening this isolator, breaker maintenance can be carried out easily. Solenoid type interlock is provided on the disconnecting switch to prevent remote closing of the breaker when the off load isolators are in off position. Earth switch is employed on each feeder side and bus side so as to enable to earth line or equipment or bus, during a shutdown prior to the issue of work-permit. This is an off load isolator in which one end is connected to the earth grid. During maintenance of line or equipment, this switch is placed 'ON' to ground the line. During normal service, the switch is kept opened. Key interlocks are provided so that circuit breaker cannot be switched 'ON' with out opening the earth switch. [Refer section 4.6].

Surge arresters: Surge arrester is connected between phase and earth (one per phase) on each feeder to protect the installation only against incoming atmospheric over-voltage. During normal power frequency voltages the surge arrester does not conduct. When a surge wave comes to the arrester, the gap breaks down and surge is diverted to the earth. The protection distance of a surge arrester is limited to maximum 20 M from the protected object for voltages 66 to 132 KV, and for 220 to 400 KV about 20 to 30 M. The required minimum distances from neighbouring equipment are specified by, the manufacturer. [Refer section 4.9].

Bus bar: All aluminium alloy conductors (AAAC) 400, 630, 800, 1000 sq:mm are used as bus bars and interconnection of equipments for current ratings up to 2000 A. Above that tubular aluminium bus 100 to 250 mm diameter (4 to 12 mm thick) are being used. AAA conductors single or multiple are strung between double dead-end string of disc insulators and supported on gantries. Tubular conductors can be mounted on post insulators in spans of up to 20 M. Rigid or flexible joints are allowed only near the post insulator support. Mid span joint will create sag on the tubular bus. An effective means of damping oscillation is to insert aluminium wires with sections of 400 to 630 sq:mm in to the tubes. Tubular conductors for busbars and equipment interconnections are sized according to both thermal and dynamic considerations. Installations in which both low-level and high-level bus bars are essential, AAAC conductors are strung for high-level bus, whereas tubular aluminium bus bars are used for low-level bus. For higher operating voltages parallel AAA conductors as a multiple conductor are employed in view of the maximum permissible surface voltage gradients. In the case spans carrying the stirrup contacts of single-column isolators, account must be taken of the difference in sag at temperature of -5°C to + 80°C. The change in sag can be reduced by means of springs located at one end of the span between the dead-end string and the portal structure.

Lightning protection: An outdoor switching station can be protected against lightning by providing aerial earth wires or lightning rods on the portals as illustrated in figure 4.2 (f)..

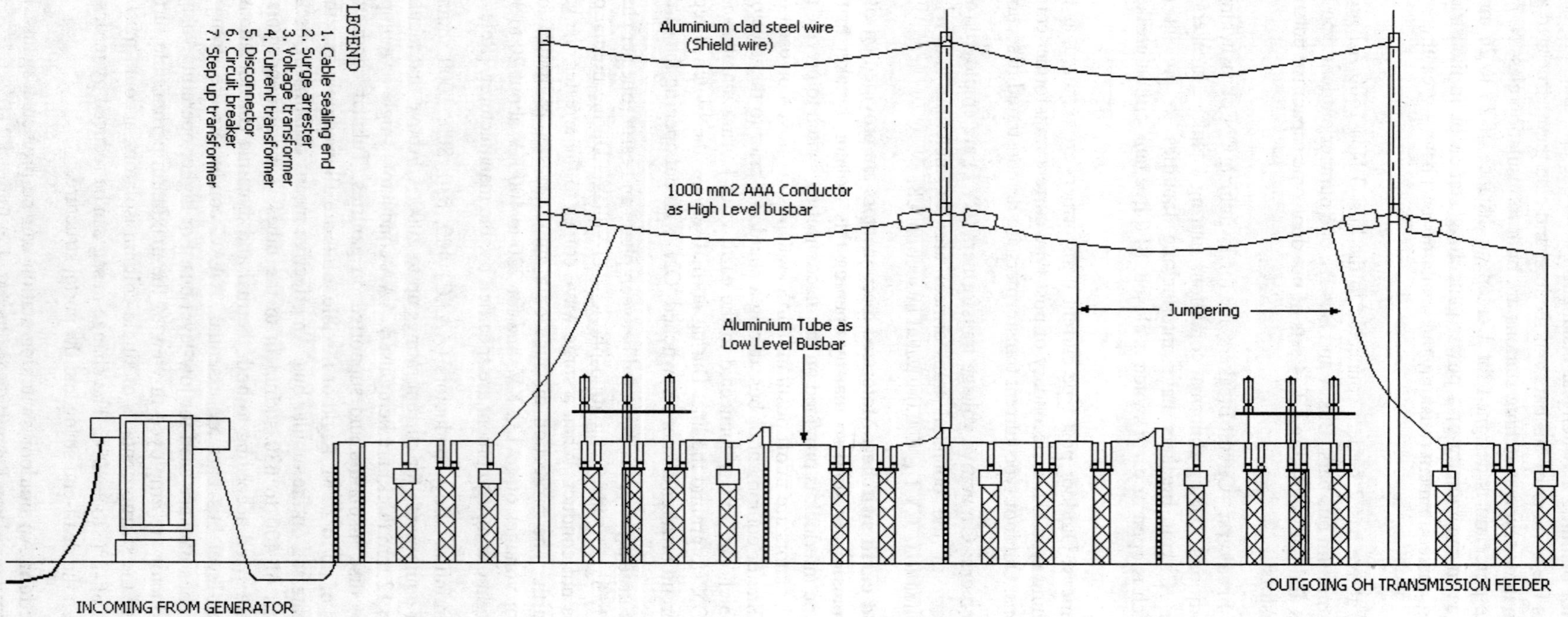

Fig 4.1 (d): Sectional view of a typical 1½ breaker high voltage outdoor 6 bay switching station.

Economical transmission voltages:

High voltage transmission requires conductors of smaller cross section, which results in economy of conductor material, but at the same time cost of high voltage line is high. A rough basis of determining the most economical transmission voltage is to use 650Volts per KM. For example, if the distance is 200 KM, then the most economical transmission voltage will be 200 x 650 = 132,000 Volts (132 KV). Loading of transmission line depends on the cross-section of the conductor and the voltage at the receiving end.

Following are the voltages internationally used for distribution and transmission of electrical Energy.

Low voltage: (3-phase/Single-phase): 220/127 V; 380/220 V; 400/230 V; 415/240 V; 440/254 V.

Medium voltage: (Nominal system voltages) 2.14 KV; 3.3 KV; 4.16 KV; 4.8 KV; 6.6 KV; 7.2 KV; 10 KV; 11 KV; 13.8 KV; 20 KV; 22 KV; 24 KV; 30 KV; 33 KV; 34.4 KV:

High Voltage: 60 KV, 66 KV; 110 KV; 132 KV; 150 KV, 220 KV; 230 KV; 330 KV, 380 KV;

Extra high voltage: 400 KV; 500 KV; 765 KV; 800 KV: Super tension: Above 800 KV up to 1200 KV.

High voltage direct current transmission (HVDC) system: 400 KV, 500 KV, 800 KV to 1500 KV.

High voltage network:

Network is a system of interconnected circuit components of generation, transmission and distribution lines operated so that any principal point has multiple source of power supply. Transmission grid is an interconnected network of transmission lines of various voltage ratings including associated equipment (Grid substations) for the transfer of electric energy in bulk between points of supply. Single line diagram of a typical network consists of generation, transmission and distribution is shown in Figure 4.1 (e). Generating station consists of two numbers 11 KV generators, which are directly connected to the respective step up delta / star power transformer (11 KV / 132 KV) by using bus ducts, to become a combined generator-transformer unit. For station auxiliary application 11 KV is tapped from the generator to the 11KV / 400 V station auxiliary transformer, through a medium voltage circuit breaker. Secondaries of the auxiliary transformers are tied together through low voltage bus tiebreakers for automatic transfer of station loads to the generator under operation. Following are the circuitry interlocks:

(a). Generator auxiliary breaker will close only if respective Main generator breaker is closed, and generator has build up proper voltage.

(b). When both generator L.V breakers are closed, the tiebreaker will remain open. Similarly when tiebreaker is closed either generator No:1 or generator No: 2, any one remains open..

(c) Assume that both G1 and G2 breakers are closed and tiebreaker is open, In the event of failure of L.V breakers G1 or G2, the tiebreaker will automatically close.

Power output from the generator-transformer unit is connected to the 132 KV outdoor bus through dead tank circuit breaker. 132 KV is sending out through double circuit transmission lines. At the receiving station, there are four different substations as follows.

(1) 132 / 220 KV step-up substation for transmitting 220 KV for distribution purposes.

(2) 132 / 400 KV step-up substation for transmitting 400 KV EHV for regional grid interconnection purposes.

(3) 132 / 33 KV step down substation for local primary distribution.

(4) 33 / 11 KV step down substation for local secondary distribution.

Further 220 KV is transmitted to another destination through double circuit transmission tower lines and connected to the receiving end 220 KV bus. 220 KV can step down to 132 or 110 or 66 KV depending on the requirements. Alternatively, Industrial consumers can utilize power from 220 KV bus to energize their primary distribution substation. Similarly, 400 KV is transmitted to another destination through double circuit transmission tower lines and connected to the receiving end 400 KV bus. 400 KV can interconnect with another power generation grid for export or import power as and when required. Alternatively, large industrial consumers can utilize power from 400 KV bus by stepping down to their process plant requirements.

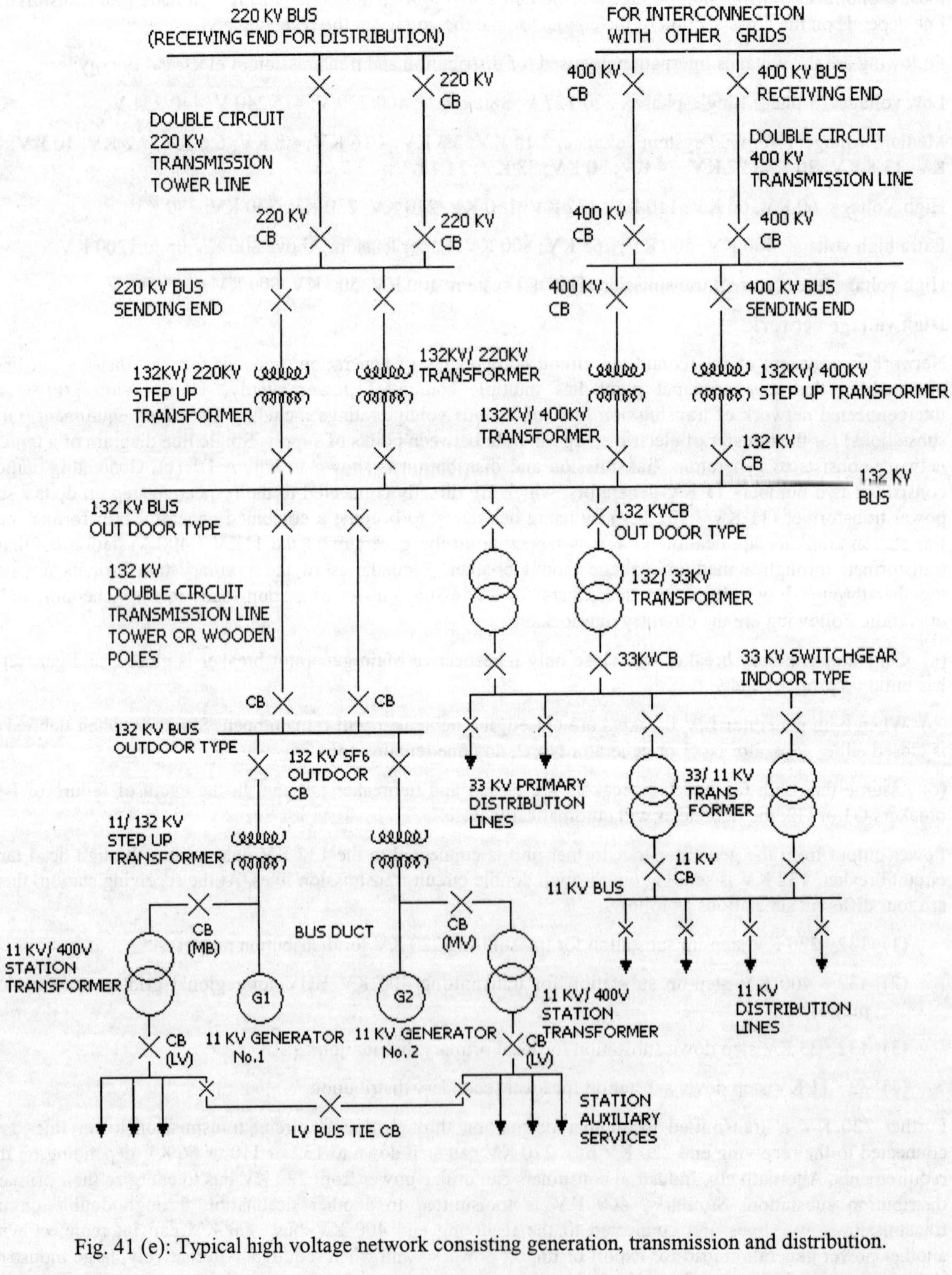

Fig. 41 (e): Typical high voltage network consisting generation, transmission and distribution.

Bus configurations for outdoor type AIS or indoor type GIS substations: Various types of bus arrangements for HV / EHV substations / switching stations and generating stations, its advantages and disadvantages are given below. The single line diagrams and bus protection schemes are discussed in Chapter # 3, section 3.2 and Chapter # 8, section 8.16.

Bus configuration	***Advantages***	***Disadvantages***
Single-bus **[Refer figure (a) of section 3.2]**	Lowest cost	Failure of bus or breaker results in shutdown Need complete shutdown for maintenance Can be used only where load can be interrupted
Two bus sections with tie breaker [Refer figure (b) of section 3.2]	Economical. Suitable for two incoming feeder system	Suitable for ring feeders. If one section is on maintenance or breakdown, the other section will feed the system. [Refer figure 4.1 (a)].
Double-bus, double breaker [Refer figure (e) of section 3.2]	Each circuit has two dedicated breakers. High reliability	Would lose half of the circuits for breaker failure if circuits are not connected to both buses.
	Any breaker can be taken out of service for maintenance	Most expensive. .
Main and transfer [Refer fig. 3.2 c]	Low initial and ultimate cost	Bus tiebreaker essential. Switching is somewhat complicated when maintain a breaker
	Any breaker can be taken out for service for maint:	Failure of bus or any circuit breaker results in shutdown of entire substation.
Double-bus single breaker	Either bus may be isolated for maintenance	Four isolating switches are required per circuit. One bus tie breaker also required
[Refer figure (d) of section 3.2]	Circuit can be transferred readily from one bus to the other by use of tie breaker	High exposure to bus fault. Bus protection scheme may cause loss of complete power when it operates.
Double-bus, single breaker		
		Bus tiebreaker failure takes entire substation out of service. Similarly, Line breaker failure takes all circuit connected to that bus out of service.
Breaker and a-half **scheme.**	Most flexible operation and high reliability.	One and a half breakers per feeder circuit [Refer figure 4.1 (c)]

[Refer figure (f) of section 3.2]	Breaker failure of bus side breakers removes only one feeder circuit from service	Middle breaker is responsive to either of the associated circuits.
	All switching is carried out via circuit breakers	Highly expensive
	No disconnect switching required for normal operation	
	Either main bus can be taken out of service at any time for maintenance	
	Bus failure does not remove any feeder circuit from service	
Ring bus [Refer figure (g) of section 3.2]	Low initial cost	If a fault occurs during a breaker maintenance period, the ring will be separated in to two sections.
	Flexible operation to breaker maintenance	Automatic reclosing and protective relaying-circuitry rather complex.
	Any breaker can be taken out for maintenance without interrupting load	Requires potential transformer in all feeder circuits since there is no definite potential reference point
	Requires only one breaker per circuit	Potential devices are essential in all cases for synchronizing line or voltage indication
	Does not use main bus	Breaker failure during fault in one of the circuit causes loss of one additional circuit owing to operation of breaker failure relaying.
	Each circuit is fed by two breakers	
	All switching is done via breakers	

4.2 STEEL STRUCTURES FOR HV AND EHV OUTDOOR SUBSTATIONS.

Switchyard equipments are supported by galvanized lattice frame design steel structures or fabricated channels to obtain minimum safety and electrical clearance to ground. No significant stresses are exerted on the equipment. The design of the structures shall be adequate for the mechanical loads subjected under fault conditions. Structures formed by mild steel angle, channels, flats, plates etc, are generally be hot-dip galvanized (after fabrication) to prevent corrosion or rusting and with combination of bolted or welded members. American Society of Civil Engineers (ASCE) Standard 10-97 describes design of lattice steel structures. Steel confirming to BS 4360 (or equivalent) Grade 43 is used for general purpose applications and Grade 50 for high tensile applications.

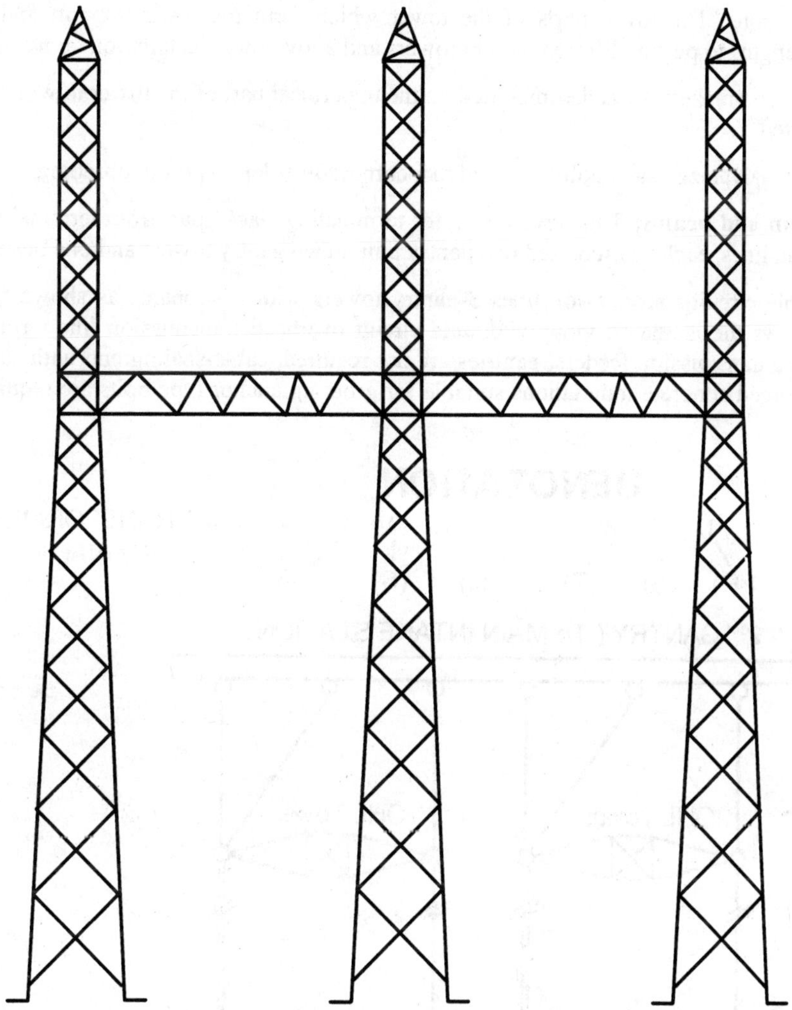

Fig. 4.2 (a): Lattice type double circuit gantry structure

Type of structure construction:

(a) Low profile/ high bay/ latticed;

(b) Structural shape: Wide flange, channel, angle, tubing and pipe;

(c) Tapered tubular-octagonal, multi-sided, round etc.

Different types of structures used in outdoor substations:

(1) Dead end tower (Terminal tower): Tower is a broad-base latticed steel support for stringing overhead transmission line. Dead end tower is a heavy tower designed for use where the transmission line loads the tower primarily in tension (pull) rather than compression (down push), such as in turning large angles along a line or bringing a line in to a substation. Terminal tower consists of:

(a) Tower body: The main or center part of the tower, designed in standard heights to which the leg extensions are attached.

(b) Cross arm or bridge: The arms of the structure to which the insulator strings are attached.

(c) Leg extensions: The lower parts of the tower which form the tower support and are designed in various lengths to permit different height towers and allow tower installation on non-level ground.

(d) Ground wire-bracket: A bracket mounted on the uppermost part of the tower to which the ground wire is supported.

(e) Step bolt: Galvanized steel bolts attached to a corner tower leg to permit climbing.

(2) Gantry column and beams: This structure is for terminating slack span from terminal tower. For single circuit transmission lines, each bay required one gantry unit. (Two gantry towers and one beam).

Whereas for double circuit transmission lines 3-gantry towers with two beams as shown in Figure 4.2 (a). Figure 4.2 (b) shows the isometric view of double circuit overhead transmission line termination to gantry structure. For cable transmission feeders, gantries are not required, cable-sealing end with support structure is being used. Reinforced concrete foundations suitable for grouting anchor type bolts are required for mounting gantries.

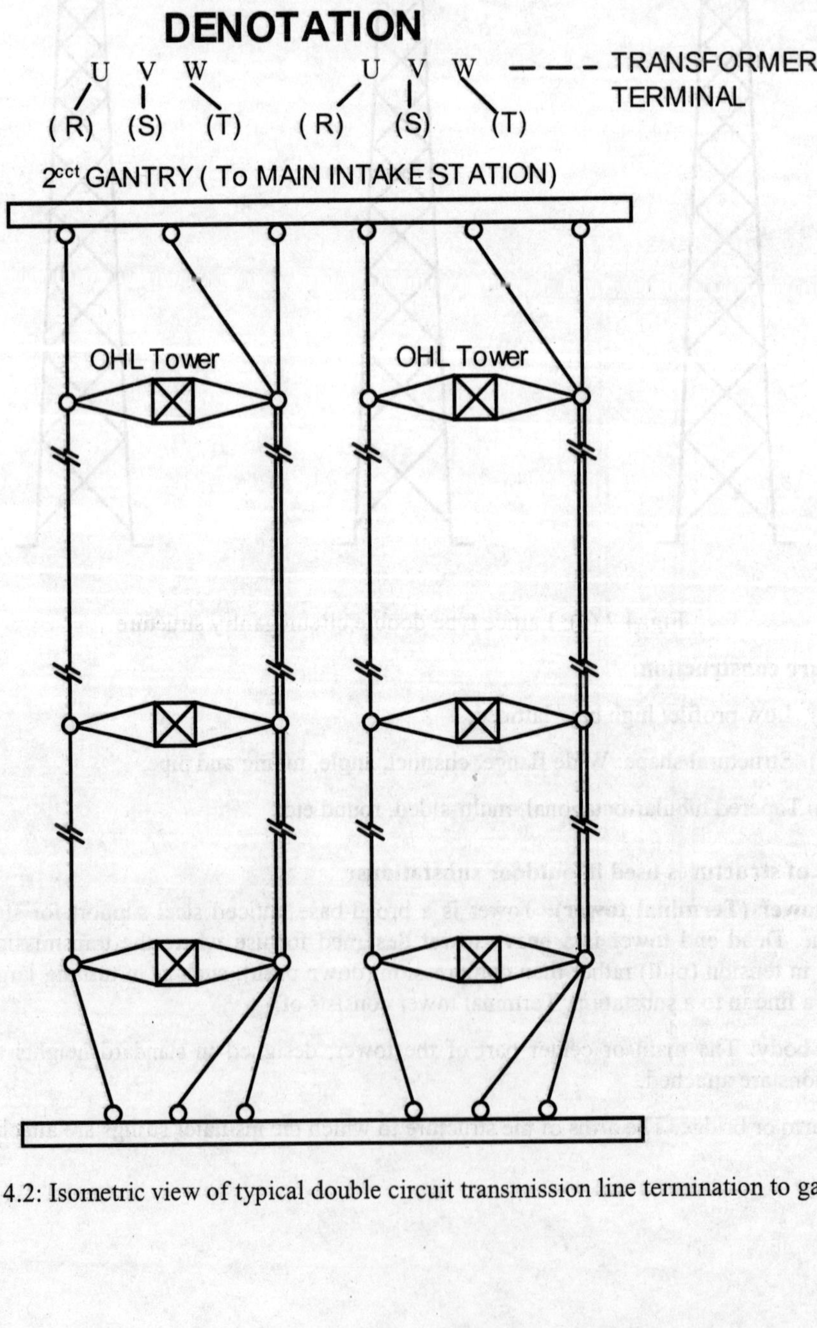

Fig. 4.2: Isometric view of typical double circuit transmission line termination to gantry.

For stringing conductors of a typical 132 KV line, following maximum tensions are recommended:

(a) Phase conductors 30,000 Newton per phase;

(b) Earth conductor 10,000 N per wire.

Tension and suspension sets (assembled with porcelain or toughened glass disc insulators and hardware) are used for stringing overhead conductors from terminal tower to the gantry. Typical tension string insulator assembly and suspnsion string insulator assembly are illustrated in Figure (c) and (e) of section 4.11.

(3) Equipment support structures: Structures for mounting outdoor type current transformer, potential transformer, surge-arrester, bus-support post insulator etc are of common design, only the difference is in the equipment mounting plates and overall height. The steel support structures are made in the form of solid frame or lattice constructions. A conductor tension of maximum 40 N/mm is specified for bus bar supporting structures. The strength of support structures, portals and foundations shall be calculated in accordance with relevant standards. Typical lattice structure elevation, base-plate and top plate arrangements are shown in Figure 4.2 (c). For high voltage substations (maximum up to 220 KV), the fabricated channel segments as shown in Figure 4.2 (d) can also be used. Substations with dead tank circuit breakers, the inbuilt bushing type, CTs are used and support structures for CTs are not required. Post insulator support structures are required only if tubular aluminium is used as bus bars. Concrete foundations for these types of structures are common, except the height and top plate mounting holes. Surge arrester support structures need provision for mounting surge counter with leakage current indicator.

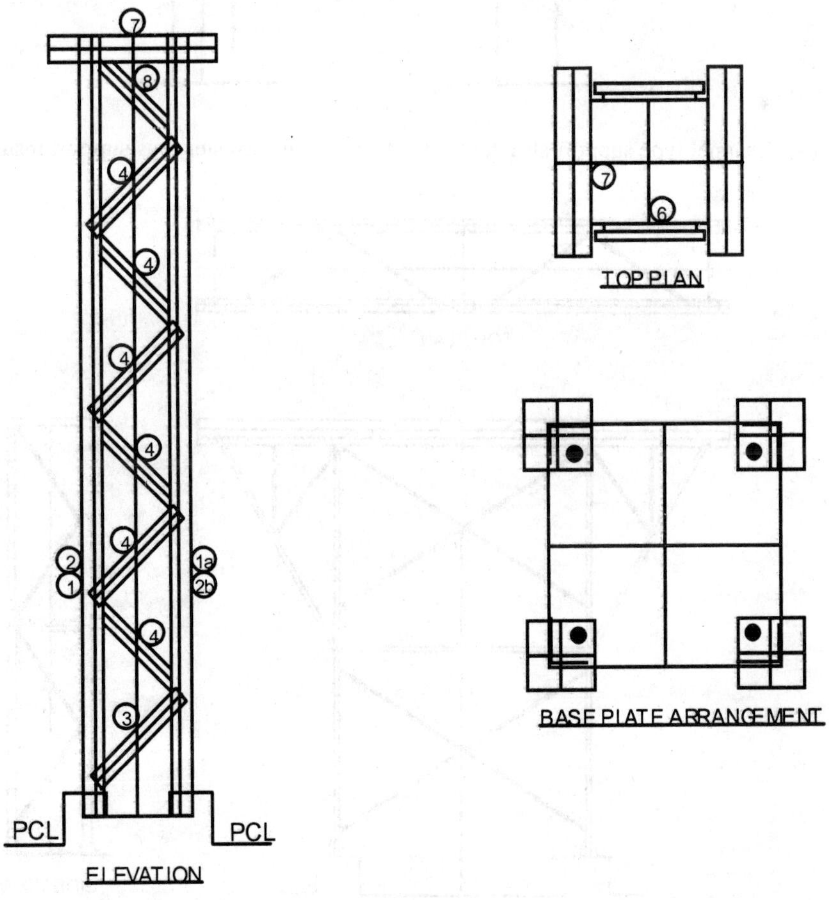

Fig. 4.2 (c): Lattice type support structure for CT, PT, surge arrester, bus support insulator etc.

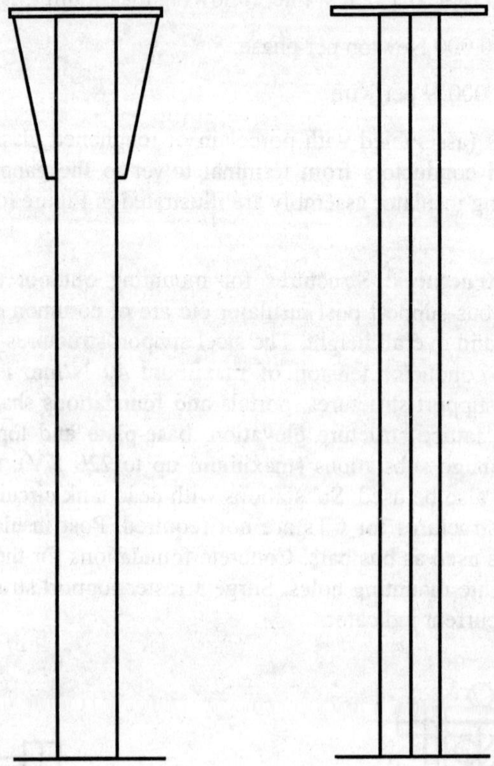

Fig. 4.2 (d): Channel type support structure for CT, PT, surge arrester, bus support insulator etc.

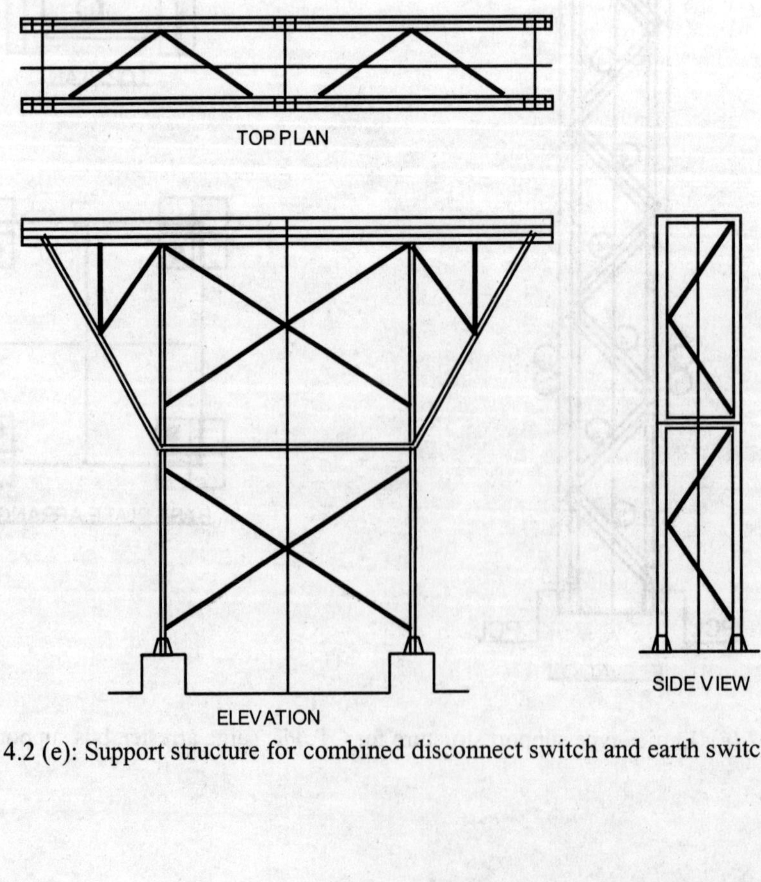

Fig. 4.2 (e): Support structure for combined disconnect switch and earth switch unit.

(4) Support structure for disconnect switch and/or earth switch: Figure 4.2 (e) shows the elevation, side view and top plan of a typical high voltage support structure for combined disconnect switch and earth switch unit. The structure shall be suitable for mounting the isolator base frame. Holes for fixing cable clip for earth conductor, earthing terminals suitable for double hole lug, R-Y-B phase identification plate, guide vanes for operating mechanism drive pipe, Handle mounting frame, Handle earthing facility etc shall be provided in the structure design. Provision for fixing motorized operating mechanism and guide vanes for supporting the operation drive pipes shall be provided based on manufacturers drawing. Operating handle shall be earthed by using minimum 120 sq:mm flexible tinned copper earth braids.

(5) Support structures for circuit breaker: Support structures for dead tank circuit breaker [Refer figure (a) of section 4.3] are supplied along with circuit breakers by the breaker manufacturers. For live tank circuit breakers [refer figure 4.5 (a) & (b)} structures are not required, but in both cases foundations are required.

(6) Lightning mast: Lightning masts are designed from 15 M to 30 M height depending on the design requirements of lightning system. During the past overhead shield wires are used to protect the substation equipments from lightning strike. The size of the conductor used for earthing screen is generally 7/9 SWG stranded GI wire. Alternatively aerial ground wire made of high tensile strength (12.7 mm diameter, 7strand) aluminium clad steel wire with breaking strength of 83.6 Newton's, conforming to IEC 1089 is being used. The shielding angle is 30° or 60°. Vibration dampers are provided at every end at a distance of 2M from every lightning mast. Shielding wire ends are to be terminated at the switchyard earth grid. Recent development in technology instead of shield wires air terminals are fitted at the top of the lightning mast and connected to the earth grid by using 25 x 3 mm bare copper strip or $70mm^2$ bare copper conductors as down conductor. The area to be protected from lightning strike is 50M radious of each air terminal. Overall switchyard coverage area is to be examined before deciding the total number of mast required. The number of mast required and the coverage area shall be calculated based on standards. Determining the protected zone in an open switchyard by universal method (adopted from the empirical curve by Wagner's method) is described in DIN-VDE Standard 0101. Figure 4.2 (f) shows a typical lightning mast structure and taper pointed air terminal.
Anchor bolts and templates are supplied with each type of structures. Anchor bolt is grouted in the open pockets of the reinforced foundation {refer figure 4.2 (f)}. Alignment of the bolt is made by, using template supplied with the structure. Structure is fastened to the foundation through anchor bolts. M20 size anchor bolts and nuts are used for structures up to 5M height. M32 size anchor bolts are used for tall structures such as gantry and lightning mast etc.

(7) Design loads for support structures:
Dead loads, line tensions, ice loads, wind loads, equipment operation loads, short circuit stress, construction loads, incoming line tensions, incoming ground wire tension, incoming line angles, incoming line span, high wind, heavy ice, seismic etc.

(8) Foundations
(a) Common type of foundations: (1) spread footings; (2) Drilled piers; (c) Slab-on-grade; (4) Pile foundations
(b) Foundation design parameters:
- Allowable soil bearing pressure and allowable passive lateral pressure
- Skin friction, frost depth, soil type, cohesion, unit weight etc
- Soil layers for drilled piers
- Angle of internal friction and modulus of sub-grade reaction
- Ultimate end bearing capacity and water table depth
- Ultimate skin resistance and ultimate pull-out skin resistance

Soil bearing capacity shall be obtained at 1 to 5 M depth (every 1 M intervals) derived or recommended by soil investigating laboratory based on Mackintosh or any penetration tests.

(9) Substation steel structure design parameters:
a) Maximum ratio of unsupported length of steel compression members to their least radius of gyration:

Main members	120
Bracings	200
Redundant	250
Bracings loading in tension	350

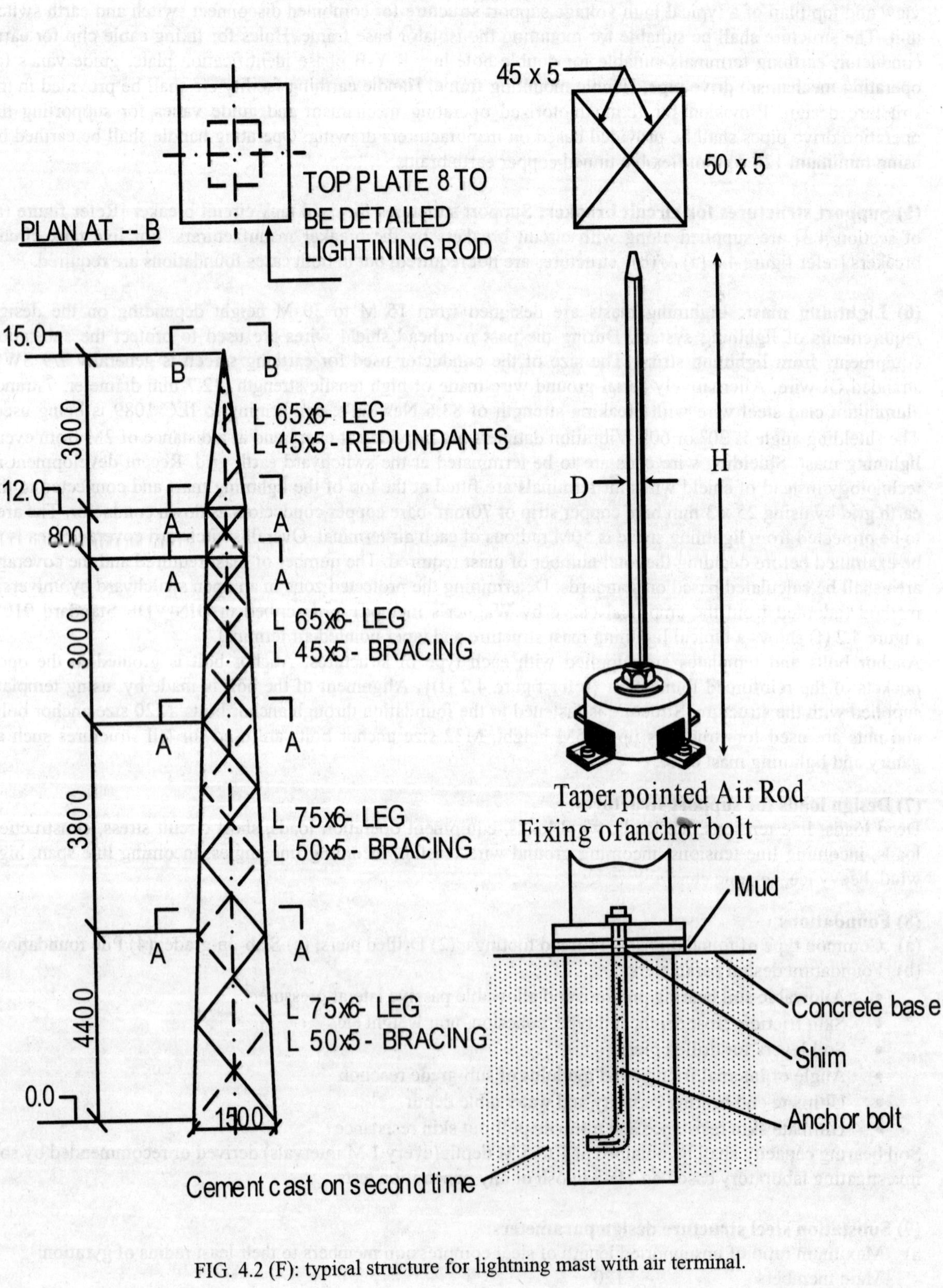

FIG. 4.2 (F): typical structure for lightning mast with air terminal.

b) Steel standard BS 4360 Grade 43A or equivalent
Elastic limit stress in tension members $255\ N/mm^2$

Ultimate stress in compression members in $N / mm^2 = Fa$ [Refer formula given in item (c) below]

c) Steel BS 4360 Grade 50C or equivalent
Elastic limit stress in tension members $410\ N/mm^2$

Ultimate stress in compression in $N / mm^2 = Fa = [1- 0.5 (K_L /r /Cc)^2]\ Fy$, where $\{K_L /r\} \leq Cc$

$Fa = \pi^2 E / (K_L /r)^2$ where $K_L /r \geq Cc$ and $Cc = \pi \sqrt{(2E / Fy)}$

d) Bolts Grade 5.8, Standard EN 20898-1 or equivalent
Ultimate shear stress $250\ N/mm^2$
Ultimate bearing stress $650\ N/mm^2$
Ultimate tensile strength $500\ N/mm^2$

4.3 SELECTION AND APPLICATION OF HV AND EHV CIRCUIT BREAKERS.

Mainly the following types of circuit breakers are used in HV and EHV applications:

1. Minimum oil circuit breakers (MOCB): A circuit breaker using a relatively a small quantity of mineral oil for its arc interruption method. Suitable for high voltage applications, but now it is an obsolete technology.
2. Bulk oil circuit breakers: A circuit breaker using huge quantity of mineral oil for insulation and arc extinction. Suitable for use in voltage range up to 400 KV, but now it is an obsolete technology.
3. Air blast circuit breaker: A circuit breaker using compressed air to force the extinction of the arc through an arc-chute system. Suitable for voltage range up to 800 KV, but now it is an obsolete technology.
4. SF6 insulated circuit breakers: A circuit breaker that uses Sulphur hexaflouride gas as its interrupting medium. Dead tank types are suitable for use in voltage range up to 550 KV and live tank types are available up to 1200 KV AC system voltages.

Circuit breakers are designed for outdoor on load operation, suitable for use in a tropical climate based on the meteorological, seismic and environmental data of the respective areas to be installed. The current carrying parts must be able to carry the rated current continuously without exceeding the temperatures specified in IEC standard 56. The breaker interrupter contact must be self-wiping and self-clearing type. The components that are part of the breaker assembly should be corona-free. Porcelain bushings shall be chocolate brown colour conforming to IEC 233 requirements. Creepage level of bushings to ground over insulation should be 20 to 31 mm per KV, depending on the degree of pollution.

Following are the accessories required with HV/EHV circuit breakers.

1. ON/OFF position indicator
2. Operation counter
3. Maintenance closing device and tools for slow opening and closing of breaker for maintenance check.
4. Under voltage relay for monitoring power supply to each compressor motor of circuit breakers having pneumatic tripping mechanism.
5. Anti-condensation heater and thermostatic control.
6. Auxiliary switches with NO and NC contacts.
7. Name plate indicating maximum system voltage and frequency, rated continuous current, short circuit ratings, year of manufacturing, brand name, type and model number etc.
8. For SF6 circuit breakers pressure gauge and pressure switches.
9. For oil circuit breakers oil level gauge

Interlocks to prevent closing the circuit breaker if any of the following conditions are not full-filled:

a) All trip relays are re-set
b) Operating system is adequate for safe operation (Spring or hydraulic/pneumatic system)
c) For SF6 circuit breakers, SF6 pressure is adequate for safe operation

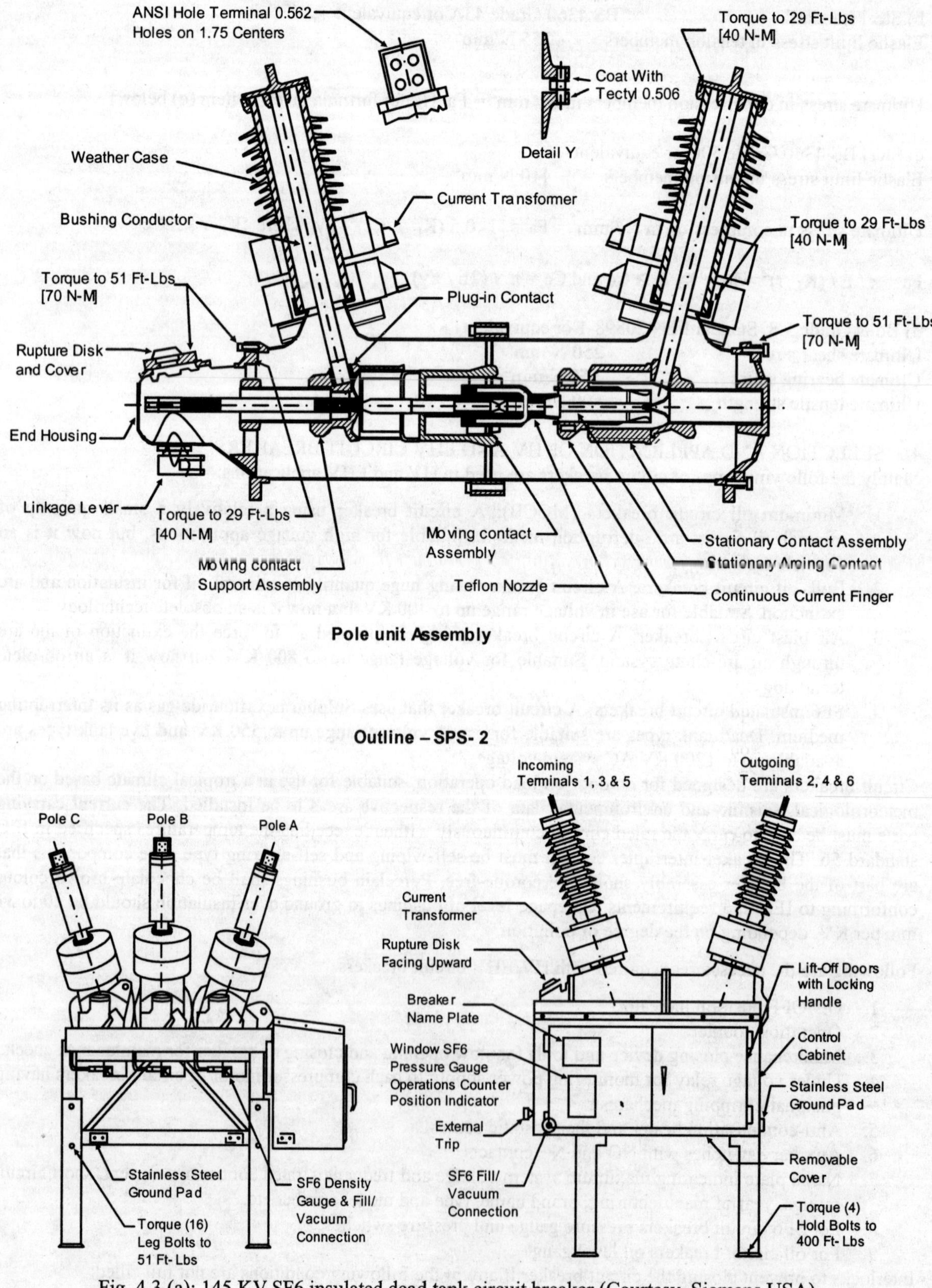

Fig. 4.3 (a): 145 KV SF6 insulated dead tank circuit breaker (Courtesy, Siemens USA).

Dead-tank circuit breakers

The distinguishing feature of dead-tank circuit breaker is that the interrupter chamber is provided in an earthed metal housing and the connection to the high voltage power is via an outdoor bushing. The current transformers are mounted directly on the bushing. Another added advantage is resistant to earthquakes because of their compact design and low center of gravity.

Figure 4.3 (a) illustrates the outline and pole unit of Siemens SPS2 model SF6 insulated dead-tank circuit breaker. Circuit breaker voltage ratings are always specified in the highest system voltage, i.e. a circuit breaker designed for 132 KV or 138 KV is specified as 145 KV, circuit breaker.

Live-tank circuit breakers

On live-tank circuit breakers, the interrupter chamber is located in the insulator, which can be either porcelain or of a composite material, and is at high potential, with the voltage level determining the length of the insulators for the interrupter chamber and the insulator column.

Figure 4.3 (b) shows one pole of a live tank type circuit breaker. Current transformers are installed separately outside the breaker. Another feature of SF6 insulated live tank breaker is comparatively small quantity of SF6 gas only required. To ensure the safe operation of live-tank circuit breakers in seismic regions, the breakers can be mounted on anti-friction surfaces.

LEGEND:
1. Supporting frame
2. Supporting insulator column
3. Interrupter
4. Control cabinet
5. Capacitor

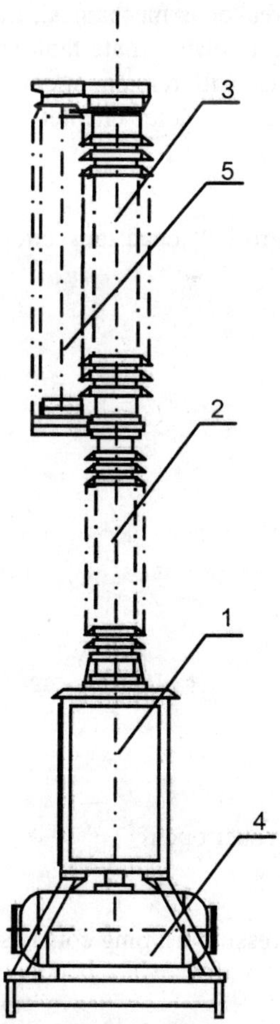

Fig. 4.3 (b): One pole of a live tank SF6 interrupter.

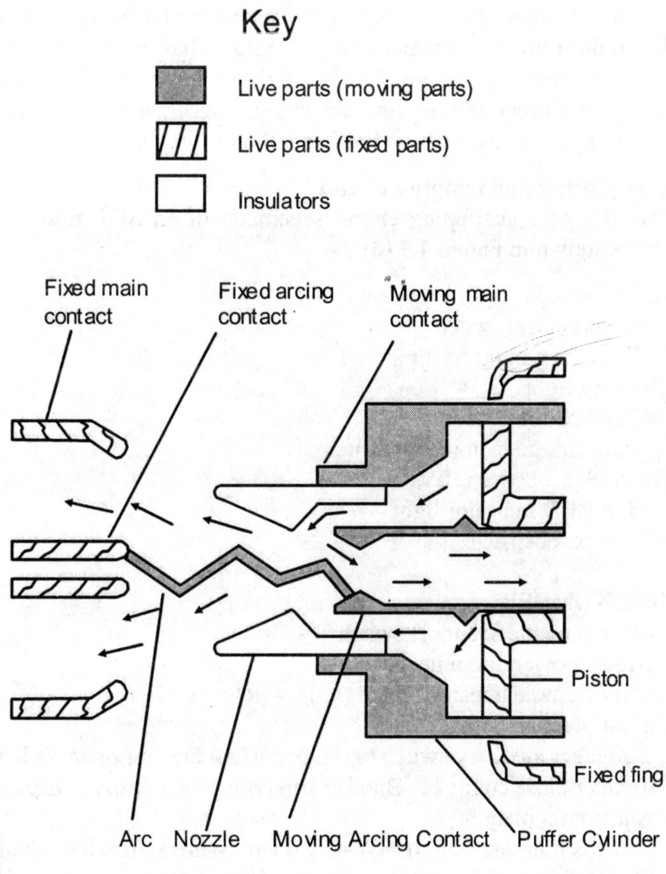

Fig. 4.3 (c): Puffer type interrupter.

Puffer type SF6 interrupter

The flow of quenching gas from puffer cylinder was made to flow in forward direction through nozzle and also through hollow contact tube in reverse direction. Double flow gives lengthening of arc through hollow contacts and removes heat of arc more efficiently. Figure 4.3 (c) shows inner construction of SF6 puffer type interrupter, which explains the flow pattern in double flow technique.

Quality control

1) Mechanical endurance tests on circuit breaker operating mechanism, tensile tests on operating levers and microstructure analysis of operating levers
2) Ultrasonic and radiography tests on all operating levers.
3) High voltage test on operating rod made as 100% customer inspection point (CIP).

Circuit breaker protection

Mechanical failure occurs when the breaker does not move following receipt of a trip command because of loss of DC trip circuit control power, trip coil failure, or trip linkage failure. Electrical failure occurs when the breaker moves in an attempt to clear a fault up on receipt of a trip command but fails to break the fault current because of miss-operation of the interrupter itself. In order to clear faults of these, electrical and mechanical failure, two different schemes of protection can be employed. The more conventional breaker failure scheme consists of using instantaneous current operated fault detectors, which pick up to start a timer when the fault relay operates. If the breaker fails to operate to clear the fault, the timer times out and send trip command to all necessary breakers to isolate the faulty zone. However, if the breaker operates correctly to clear the fault, enough time must be allowed in the timer setting to ensure reset of the fault detector relay.

For those faults where mechanical failure of the breaker occurs, an even faster scheme is in use. A normally open breaker auxiliary contact (52a) initiates a timer. This auxiliary switch is specially located to operate from breaker trip linkages to sense actual movement of the breaker mechanism. If the breaker is mechanical, this breaker failure timer is actuated through the auxiliary switch (52a) when the protective relay initiate fault trip signal to the breaker. If any breaker fails to clear the fault, the protective relays will remain operated, permitting the timer to time out and trip the necessary other breakers to clear the fault. Refer chapter # 7, section 7.11 for more details on breaker failure protection.

Breaker closing and tripping circuit

Typical closing and tripping circuit schematic of an SF6 insulated (three-pole controlled) dead tank circuit breaker is shown in Figure 4.3 (d).

LEGEND:
CS: Remote control switch
G: Remote green indicator light
LT: Housing light
LTSW: Switch for housing light
MS: Spring charge motor limit switch
PR: Remote protective relays
R: Remote RED indicator light
RCP: Duplex receptacle

DEVICE NUMBER:
08C: Close power disconnect switch
08M: Motor power disconnect switch
43: Local / Remote transfer switch (43L /43R)
52: Circuit breaker
52-1, 2 Breaker auxiliary switch (a = Open when breaker open, & b = Closed when breaker open)
52C: Breaker close coil; 52T: Breaker trip coil; 52T2: Breaker trip coil (Additional)
52Y: Anti-pump relay
63G: SF6 gas pressure switch (SW#1: Low pressure alarm; SW# 2 and SW#3: Low pressure tripping contacts).
63X: SF6 Low -pressure cutout auxiliary relay
69: Hand trip switch (Manual reset)
88: Spring charge motor Mechanism

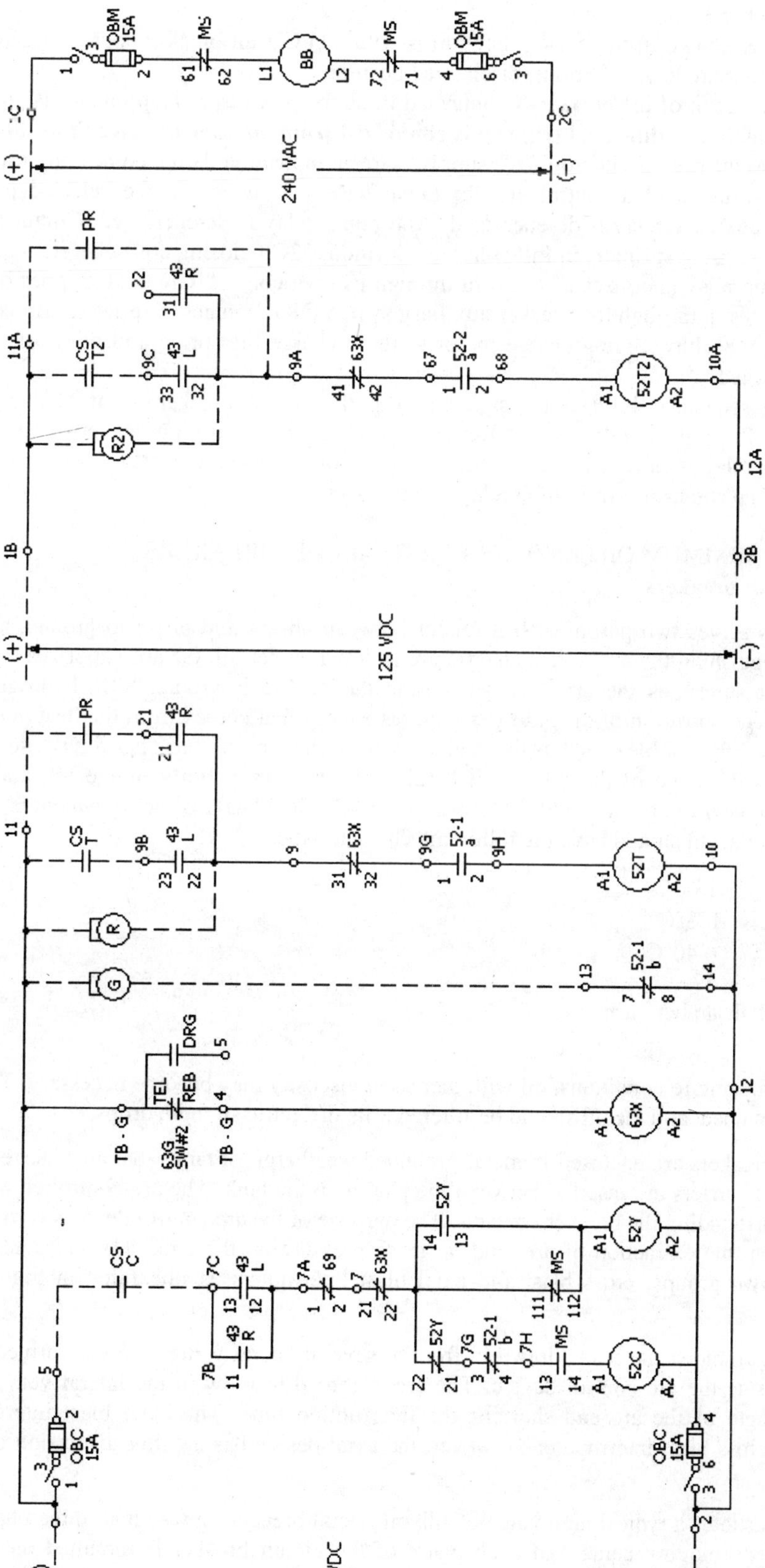

Fig. 4.3 (d): Control circuitry of an SF6 insulated three-pole dead tank circuit breaker. (Courtesy, Siemens Ag)

NOTE TO FIGURE 4.3 (d):

(a) All devices shown in the wiring diagram is with: (1) Circuit breaker open; (2) Circuit de-energized; (3) SF6 pressure low; (4) Spring-discharged position.

(b) DC close circuit of the breaker is connected through 15 A fuses. **Trip circuit is connected with out fuse protection. Additional trip coil is connected from another DC circuit of the same source.**

(c) Closing sequence: Switch-on DC supply; Green indication lamp comes in; Initiate close signal through spring loaded control switch; Local / Remote switch in the selected position. SF6 low-pressure auxiliary relay is de-energized; Anti-pump relay is de-energized. Circuit breaker is in open position; Closing spring is in fully charged position; 52C (Closing coil) energizes and breaker closes; Anti-pump relay energizes and seal-in through its own contact. Green lamp goes off; Red indication lamp comes in through the breaker auxiliary switch (NO) contact in series to trip coil and shows that trip coil is healthy. Spring charge motor starts to charge the spring and goes off when the spring is fully charged.

(d) Tripping sequence: Initiate trip signal to trip the circuit breaker or protective relay operates to energize the trip circuit; Local / Remote switch is in the appropriate position; SF6 low-pressure auxiliary relay is in de-energized position; Trip coil energize and breaker trips; Red lamp goes off; Green lamp comes in. Anti-pump relay de-energizes.

4.4 BULK OIL, MINIMUM OIL, AND AIR BLAST CIRCUIT BREAKERS.

(a) Bulk oil circuit breakers

The oil in OCB's serves two purposes. It insulates between phases and phase to ground, and it provides the medium for extinguishing the arc. When electric arc is drawn under oil, the arc vaporizes the oil and creates a large bubble that surrounds the arc. The gas inside the bubble is around 80% hydrogen, which impairs ionization. The decomposition of oil in to gas requires energy that comes from the heat generated by the arc. The oil surrounding the bubble conducts the heat away from the arc and thus also contributes to deionization of the arc. Main disadvantage of the oil circuit breakers is the flammability of the oil, and the maintenance necessary to keep the oil in good condition. Transformer oil (Shell Diala B) or equivalent is used in modern oil tight circuit breakers. Oil should have the following characteristics:

Flash point	133°C
Burning point	148°C
Freezing point	(-) 40°C
Viscosity	57s
Colour	Pale amber clear

For extra-low-temperature conditions, oil with increased viscosity may become necessary. The oil level should be carefully maintained, and the oil should be filtered if its dielectric strength drops.

Bulk oil circuit breakers are enclosed in metal-grounded weatherproof tanks that are referred to as dead tanks. Insulating fibrous barriers are inserted between the phases in the tank. The arc-controlled designs have an arc control device surrounding the breaker contacts. The purpose of the arc control devices is to improve operating capacity, speed up the extinction of arc, and decrease pressure on the tank. The arc control devices can be classified in to two groups: cross blast and axial blast interrupters as illustrated in Figure 4.4 (a) and (b) respectively.

In cross blast interrupters, the arc is drawn in front of several lateral vents. The gas formed by the arc causes high pressure inside the arc control device. The arc is forced to blow in the lateral vents in the pot, which increases the length of the arc and shortens the interruption time. The axial blast interrupters use similar principle as the cross blast interrupters. However, the axial design has a better dispersion of the gas from the interrupter.

Figure 4.4 (c) illustrates a typical high voltage bulk oil circuit breaker, in which all three phases are installed in the same tank. The moving contact of each phase of the circuit breaker is mounted on a lift rod made of insulating material. There are two breaks per phase during the breaker opening. The arc control pots (interrupters) are fitted over the fixed contacts. Resistors parallel to the breaker contacts are installed alongside the arc control pots. Current transformers are mounted on the breaker bushings.

Fig. 4.4 (a) Cross blast interrupter.

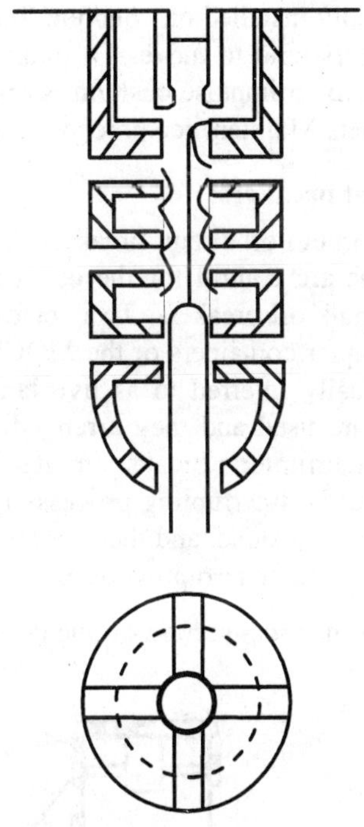

Fig. 4.4 (b): Axial blast interrupter.

LEGEND: 1.Bushing; 2.Oil level indicator; 3.Vent; 4.Current transformer; 5.Dashpot; 6.Plunger guide 7.Arc control device; 8.Resister; 9.Plunger bar

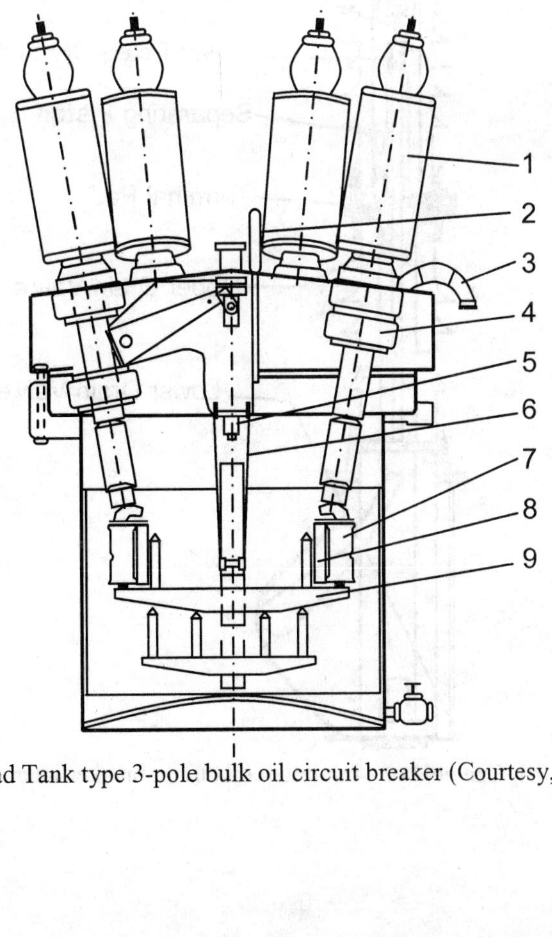

Fig. 4.4 (c): Dead Tank type 3-pole bulk oil circuit breaker (Courtesy, Allis Chalmers).

For high voltage system (above 275 KV, 40 KA), it is customary to use separate tank for each phase. The oil circuit breakers are usually installed on concrete foundations at the ground level. During interruption of heavy fault currents the breakers tend to move. To minimize the damage to the breakers, breakers with very high interrupting capacity have an impulse cushion is provided at the bottom of the breakers. The cushion is filled with an inert gas Nitrogen. Maintenance procedures of BOCB, is demonstrated in section 4.26.3.

(b) Minimum oil circuit breakers:

In the high voltage minimum oil circuit breakers the volume of transformer oil required is about 10% of bulk oil circuit breakers. The arc control for the outdoor type MOCB is based on the same principle as the arc control devices of the bulk oil breakers. To improve breaker performance, oil is injected in to the arc during interruption. The interrupter containers of the MOCBs are made of insulating materials and are insulated from the ground. This is usually referred to as live tank construction. Above 132 KV and up to 245 KV, two interrupters per phase are used and they arranged in series, so that each interrupter carries its share of the interruption duty. All interrupter's breaks simultaneously, and that the re-striking voltage is divided equally across the breaks during the interrupting process. The natural voltage division depends on stray capacitances between contacts and to the ground, and therefore is very uneven. This is corrected by connecting capacitances or resistors in parallel with the interrupting heads.

Figure 4.4 (d) illustrates the cross section of one pole of a high voltage minimum oil circuit breaker interrupter.

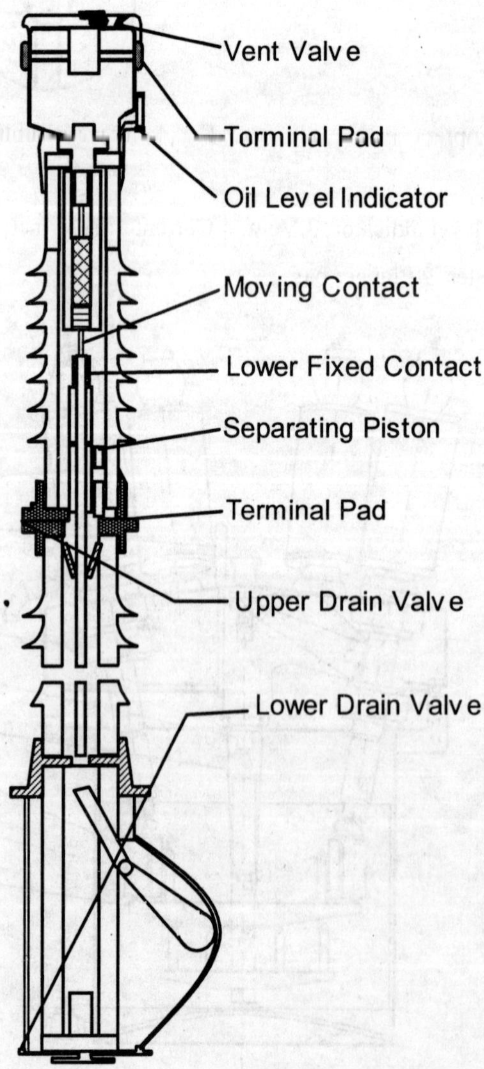

Fig. 4.4 (d): One pole of a minimum oil circuit breaker interrupter.

(c) Air blast circuit breakers:

In an air blast circuit breaker, air blowing across the parting contacts extinguishes the arc. High-pressure dry air at a pressure around 30 bar to 150 bar (for 60 KV to 800 KV ABCB) is stored in the air reservoir through air compressor. Figure 4.4 (e) shows one pole of an air blast circuit breaker. It consists of (1) Air receiver tank with pneumatic valve directly connected to the high-pressure air system: (2) Operating valve cubicle: (3) Hollow porcelain support insulator; (4) Series connected interrupters with **individual parallel pre-insertion resistor to minimize switching over voltages;** (5) Terminal for connecting IN/OUT phase bus to IPS tube. **EHV breakers are provided with parallel-connected capacitors (for each interrupter unit) to equalize the voltage distribution.**

Figure 4.4 (f) shows arc quenching in ABCBs. For opening operation the air is admitted in the arc extinction chamber. It pushes away the moving contact and the contacts are separated and the air blast takes away the ionized gaseous along with it and assists arc extinction. After a few cycles the arc is fully extinguished by the air blast and the arc extinction chamber is filled with high-pressure air. The high-pressure air has higher dielectric strength than that of atmospheric pressure. Hence minimum contact gap only required. The flow of air around contacts, are guided by the nozzle axial shaped contacts (axial). In axial blast type airflow, the air flows from high-pressure reservoir to the atmosphere through a convergent/divergent nozzle. The air flowing at a high speed axially along the arc causes removal of heat from the periphery of the arc and the diameter of the arc reduces to a low value at current zero.

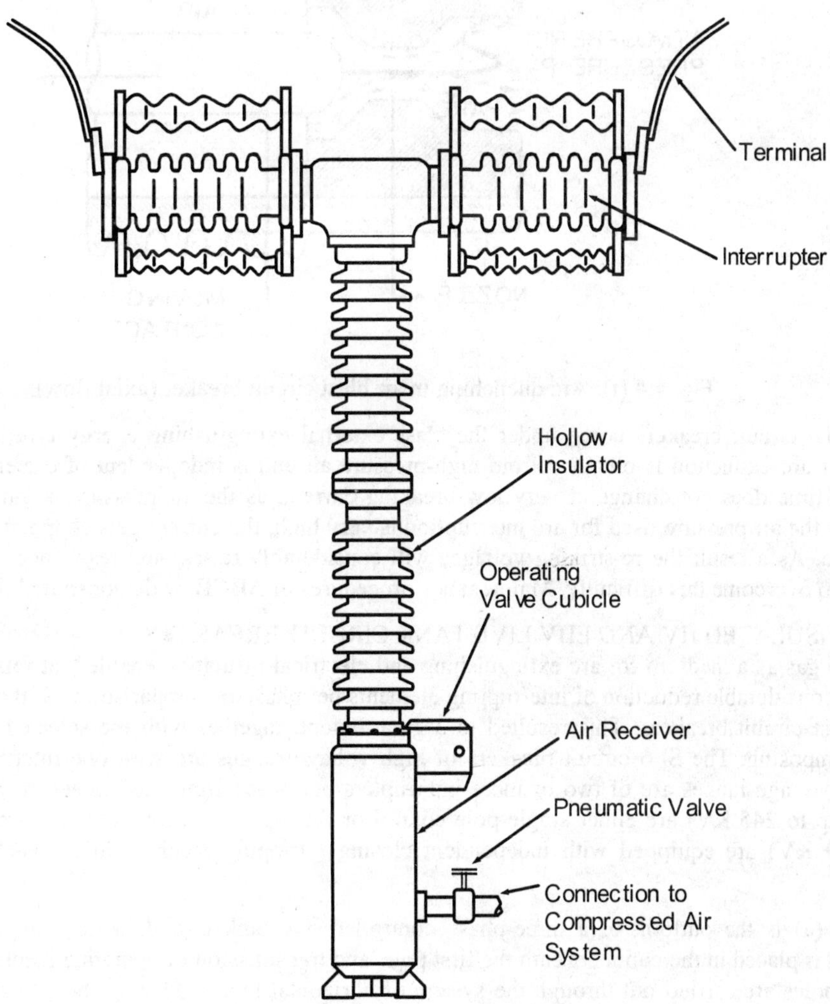

Fig. 4.4 (e): Air blast circuit breaker interrupter.

In an ABCB, the hollow porcelain support insulators house air pipes, which supply the opening air to the interrupters and the closing air to the make-switch air engine. Control is achieved with an air blast valve arranged in the base cabinet below the support column. At the top, the latter carries the metal box housing the air engine and the shaft on which the make-switch blade is mounted. When the circuit breaker is in its 'open' position, the internal spaces within the isolator remain filled with compressed air. If the circuit breaker is in the closed position, the interrupter and the isolator contacts are kept closed, and there is no compressed air in the isolator. To trip the circuit breaker, a stream of compressed air is injected in to the interrupters. Their contacts then separate to draw arcs that are extinguished by the airflow. After a short interval the compressed air is injected into the isolator spaces throwing the contacts apart and maintaining them in a separated position. As soon as the isolator contact is opened, the flow of air to the interrupters is cut off and their contacts recluse. To close the air circuit breaker, the compressed air is discharged from the spaces in the isolator. The latter then closes its contacts to make the circuit. Thus, the interrupters and the isolators of the circuit breaker operate in conjunction with each other only at the time of tripping. All other time the interrupter contacts remain closed.

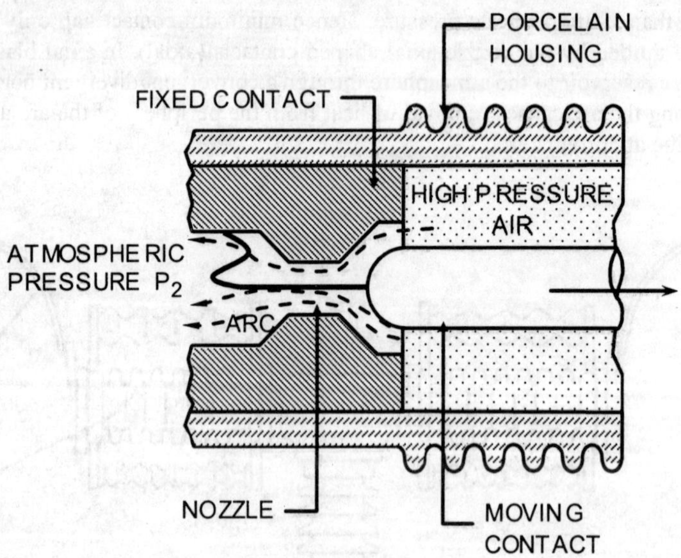

Fig. 4.4 (f): Arc quenching in air blast circuit breaker (axial flow).

The air blast circuit breakers come under the class external extinguishing energy type because the energy supplied for arc extinction is obtained from high-pressure air and is independent of current to be interrupted. The arcing time does not change at very low breaking current, as the air pressure is independent of the arc current, but the air pressure used for arc interruption is very high, the current gets chopped out before reaching natural zero. As a result the re-striking voltages will considerably raises, and resistance switching should be employed to overcome this difficulty. Maintenance procedures of ABCB, is demonstrated in section 4.26.4.

4.5 SF6 INSULATED HV AND EHV LIVE TANK CIRCUIT BREAKERS

Use of SF6 gas as a medium for arc extinguishing and electrical insulation enabled, at relatively low pressure (5 bars), a considerable reduction of interrupting elements per phase in comparison with the oil circuit breakers and air blast circuit breakers. This resulted to a great extent, together with the selected principle of circuit breaker composing. The SF6 circuit breakers of high voltage ranges are with one interrupter-per-phase and extra high voltage ranges are of two or more interrupters-per-phase connected in series. High voltage circuit breakers (up to 245 KV) are either single-pole control or three-pole control, whereas circuit breakers of 275 KV to 800 KV) are equipped with independent closing / tripping mechanism for each pole (single pole control).

Figure 4.5 (a) is the outlook of a three-phase controlled live tank circuit breaker in which the operating mechanism is placed in the cabin beneath the first pole, and transmission of operating mechanism energy to the other two poles are carried out through the system of horizontal levers. Placing the closing spring at the end pole, the horizontal levers, are subjected only to tensile strength. Capacitors in single interrupter breaker poles contribute to breaking of short-line fault currents.

LEGEND

1. Supporting frame with operating mechanism
2. Horizontal levers housing
3. Supporting frame
4. Closing spring
5. Interrupter
6. Insulator column
7. Capacitor
8. Control cabinet

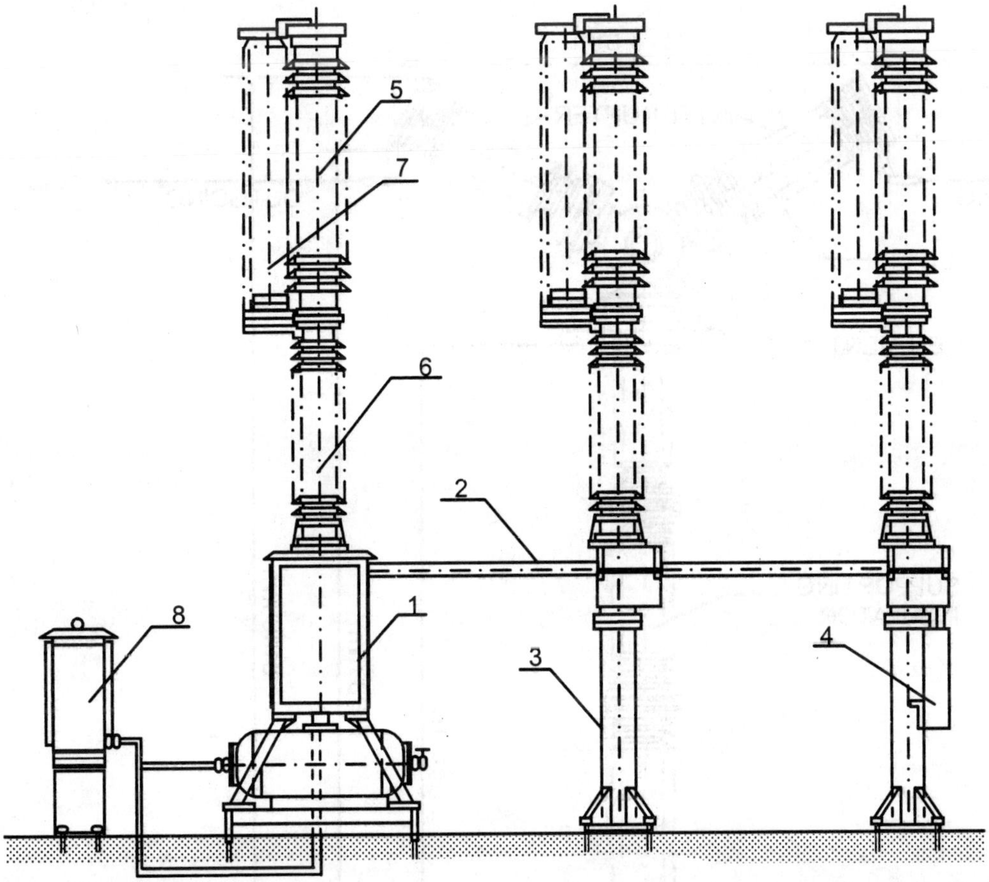

Fig. 4.5 (a): Outlook of high voltage SF6 insulated live tank 3-phase controlled HV circuit breaker. (Courtesy, Energoinvests)

Figure 4.5 (b) is the outlook of one pole of a live tank SF6 insulated single pole controlled 400 KV (EHV) circuit breaker, in which the pneumatic-spring operating mechanism and system of levers for transmission of the operating mechanism energy to the pulling insulating rod, which is placed in the insulator column of the circuit breaker pole, are accommodated in the supporting frame cabin of each pole. By means of the insulating rod and levers mechanism placed at the top of the porcelain column, in "Y" element (two interrupters per pole) the energy of the operating mechanism is transmitted to the movable parts of the interrupters.

Air reservoir, which serves the supply of the pneumatic operating mechanism, is placed below the cabin of each pole. The pneumatic operating mechanism takes compressed air as its driving power to carry out open operation and to perform close operation depends on spring force. Generally 245 KV and below SF6 high voltage circuit breakers are designed for 1 break per pole, not being equipped with parallel capacitors and pre-insertion resistors; whereas 275 KV and above (HV/EHV breakers) are designed in 2 break per pole but being equipped with parallel capacitors and pre-insertion resistors. The driving units of the close-resistors are operated at first, and some oscillating energy on the circuits is absorbed by the close-resistor to control the close over voltage. Owing to the use of hydraulic shock absorbers, the circuit breakers of this type are featured by high quality shock absorbing during closing and opening operations. At the circuit breaker with two or more interrupters per pole, the capacitor installed in parallel with each interrupter (the contact gaps) ensure an even voltage distribution control. The application of pre-insertion resistor is defined in Question number 3 of section 4.30. Protective bursting membrane is installed in each circuit breaker pole as a protection against an excessive pressure rise during possible appearance of the arc of uncontrolled duration.

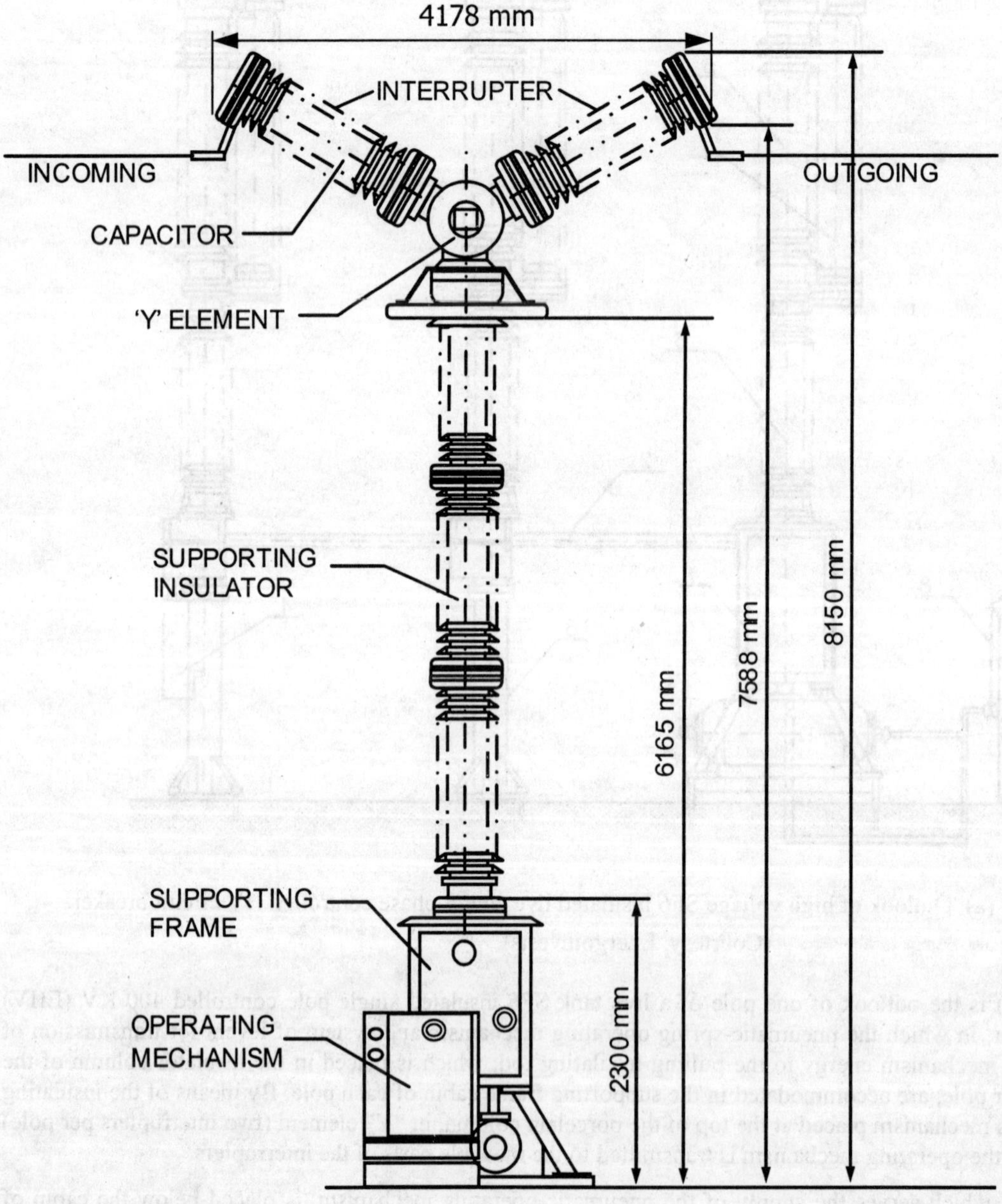

Fig. 4.5 (b): One pole of a 400 KV live-tank SF6 circuit breaker (Courtesy, Energonvests)

Type test should be performed on circuit breakers in order to prove their rated characteristics. Dielectric tests, temperature rise tests, rated peak and short time withstand current tests, mechanical operation tests etc. in any approved laboratories. Following conditions shall be fulfilled during the test:

1. Neither re-strikes nor over-voltage occur during line and cable charging current breaking
2. In case of small inductive current breaking and unloaded transformer current breaking, over- voltage factor does not exceed the permissible value, which resulted from the fact that they do not perform a direct current chopping.

4.6 HIGH AND EXTRA HIGH VOLTAGE DISCONNECTORS AND EARTH SWITCHES.

Disconnector or isolator is a mechanical switching device used for isolating a circuit or equipment from the power source. It is required to open or close circuits when power is interrupted. Disconnectors are for isolating a high voltage circuit during maintenance or breakdown of the equipment or line. Substation disconnect switches are designed for outdoor application and for use in a tropical climate based on the meteorological, seismic and environmental data of the respective areas to be installed. The main high voltage current carrying parts must be able to carry the rated current continuously with out exceeding the temperatures specified in IEC 129. Full contact and current carrying capacity should be maintained during over-travel or under-travel of the motor driven mechanism. Each blade individually counter-balanced to decrease operating effort and to prevent the blade from falling closed from any open operation. All the three blades are in positive continuous control through out the entire cycle of operation. The three poles should have angular synchronization during the closing operation. Each disconnector is equipped with hooks to permit attachment of portable safety grounding devices. Creepage level to ground over insulation should be 20 to 31 mm per KV, depending on the pollution level. No visual corona shall exist in either the open or closed position. Outdoor type disconnect switches are mounted on a lattice galvanized steel work support structure similar to the one illustrated in figure 4.2 (e).

Three-pole operating mechanism consists of shafting, coupling, crank-hanger etc to operate from ground level. Padlocking facility in ON/OFF position with position indicator located at the operating handle is required. Each rotating insulator stick is provided with a weatherproof type, greaseless, sealed ball or roller bearing. Similarly, operating rod is equipped with ball or roller bearings and brass bushings. Mechanism is designed for manual (1M height from ground level) as well as motor operation with interlock and auxiliary NO/NC contacts. Vertical operating shaft is provided with a flexible copper braid connection (120sq:mm) for grounding the operating mechanism. Provision is provided for uncoupling the motor whenever hand operation is required. Each earth switch must be mechanically interlocked to prevent its closing unless the respective disconnector is fully open. Similarly, each disconnect switch having an associated earth switch (combined unit) should be mechanically interlocked to prevent its closing unless the associated earth switch is fully open.

Figure 4.6 (a) illustrates one pole of a typical extra high voltage double break rotary diconnector switch. The fixed contacts are of the multi-finger reverse loop pattern. Contact pressure is applied to each individual finger by an insulated stainless steel spring. Contact fingers are of hard drawn copper, silver plated, and are bolted in to the aluminium alloy support housing. The disconnector blade is fitted with silver-plated extruded copper contact strips, which takes up contact pressure as the blade is rotated axially after entry into the fixed contacts. Electrolytic corrosion between the silver plated contact fingers and the aluminium alloy components of the fixed and moving contacts is inhibited by a general purpose electrical compound applied during manufacture. The disconnector blade is supported centrally in an actuator mechanism which is mounted on the rotating insulator column. The actuator housing supports the blade in bearings which are fitted with seals. A spring loaded linkage within the housing retains the blade in the position where the contacts can enter freely as the blade swings to the closed position.

Interlocks : A disconnector could not be operated (either closing or opening) if any of the following conditions are persisting.

1. Relevant circuit breaker is closed
2. Associated earth switch is closed

An earth switch could not be operated (either closing or opening) if any of the following conditions are persisting.

1. Relevant circuit breaker is closed

2. Associated disconnector is closed

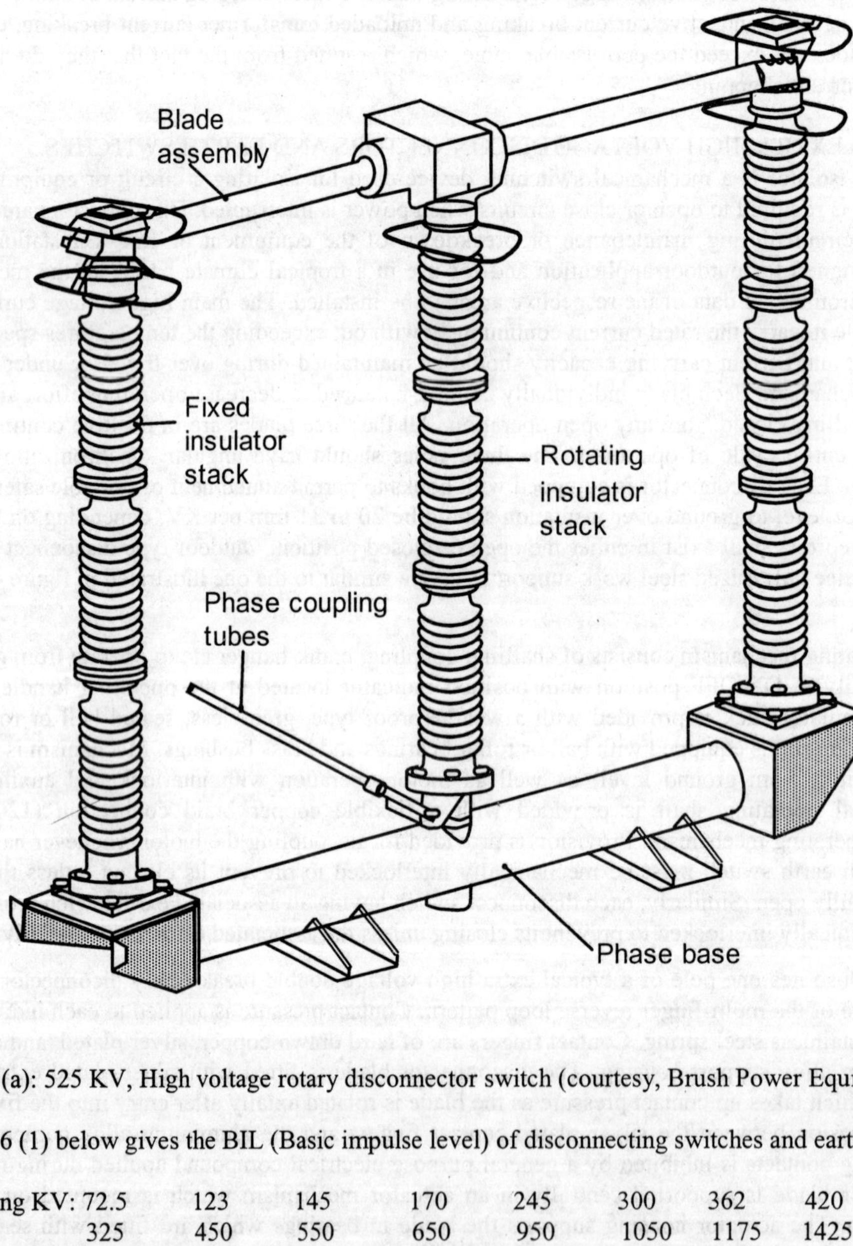

Fig. 4.6 (a): 525 KV, High voltage rotary disconnector switch (courtesy, Brush Power Equipments Ltd).

The table 4.6 (1) below gives the BIL (Basic impulse level) of disconnecting switches and earth switches.

Voltage rating KV:	72.5	123	145	170	245	300	362	420	525
BIL KV:	325	450	550	650	950	1050	1175	1425	1550

Figure 4.6 (b) illustrates one pole of a 525 KV earthing switch with geared winch mechanism for manual or electrical operation. The contacts of vertical break earthing switch comprise a fixed contact, which is a copper tube and aluminium alloy assembly mounted on the disconnector, and a multi-finger contact mounted on the earthing switch blade. The blade is aluminium alloy tubing, and is counterbalanced by a weight. Heavy laminated flexible conductor connects the earthing switch blade to the fixed structure and earthing terminal. The fixed contact assembly is heavy gauge hard drawn copper tube, electro tinned, mounted in an aluminium alloy casting, an inhibiting compound being applied during assembly to prevent electrolytic corrosion at the interface. Corona protection is provided by aluminium alloy 'buns' fitted at the inner and outer ends of the contact.

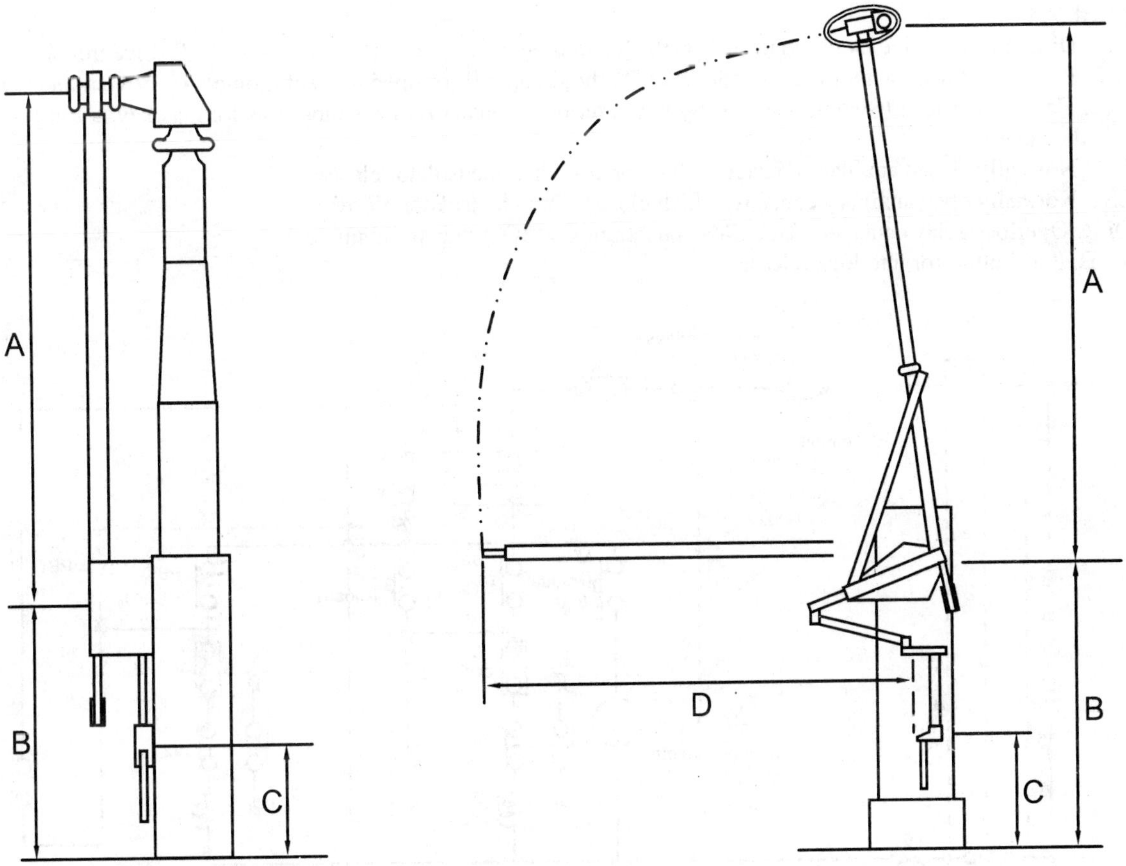

Fig. 4.6 (b): One pole of a typical 525 KV earthing switch (Courtesy, Brush Power Equipments Ltd).

Tests to be conducted on isolators as recommended in IEC 129.

1. Power frequency voltage dry test
2. Measurement of contact resistance of disconnect switch and earth switch (millivolt drop test)
3. Mechanical operation test (endurance test)
4. Corona existence check

To check the corona existence, the light shall be turned off in the test bay and visual corona start and stop voltages shall be recorded with the corresponding radio noise voltages on both ascending and descending voltage values. Preventive maintenance procedures of disconnectors and earth switches are discussed in section 4.28.1

Application of disconnect switches and earth switches:

1. Transformer feeder is equipped with, minimum, two disconnect switches and earth switches on each side of the transformer circuit breaker.
2. Line feeder is equipped with, not less than three disconnect switches and earth switches, two for maintenance on each side of the feeder circuit breaker, and one at the connection to the transmission line or cable.
3. Tiebreaker module is equipped with one maintenance earth switch between each disconnect switch and its associated circuit breaker.

Figure 4.6 (c) and (d) respectively, shows the schematic diagram of 110 volts DC control circuit for disconnect switch and earth switch having AC drive motors.

LEGEND

CC: Disconnector drive motor contactor (with DC holding coil) for closing operation of AC drive motor

OC: Disconnector drive motor contactor (with DC holding coil) for opening operation of AC drive motor

HIL: Handle interlock (Switch operated by key interlock, contact remains closed as long as key is trapped in the panel)

LS1: Normally closed auxiliary contacts, which opens when the isolator closes.

LS2: Normally open auxiliary contacts, which closes when the isolator closes.

OLR: Overload relay contacts; PBC: Close pushbutton; PBO: Open pushbutton:

MPB: Pushbutton for interlock release.

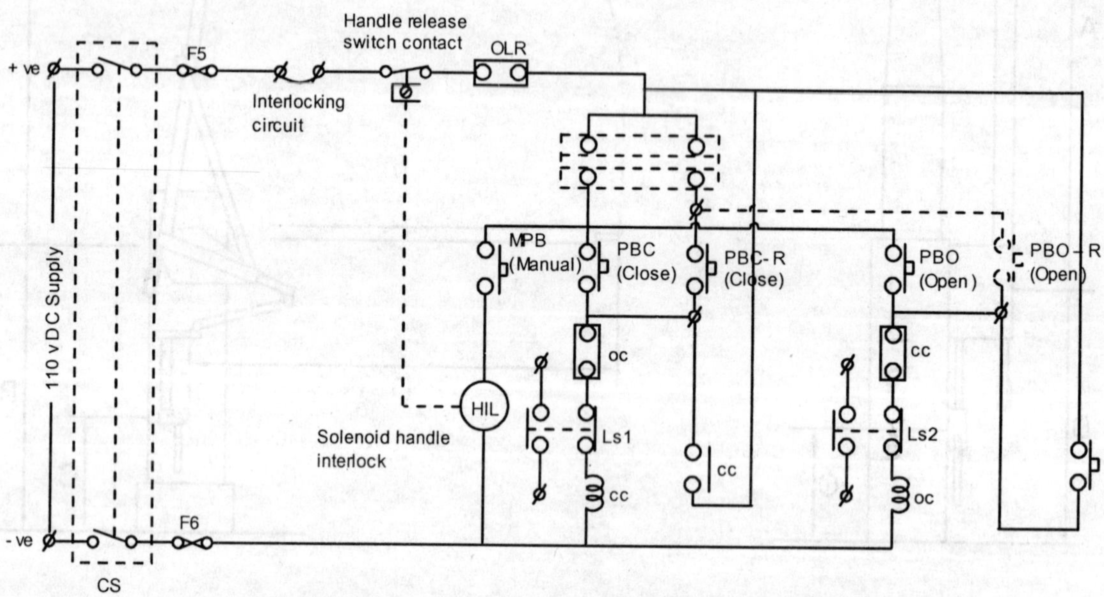

Fig. 4.6 (c): DC control circuit for disconnector drive AC motor

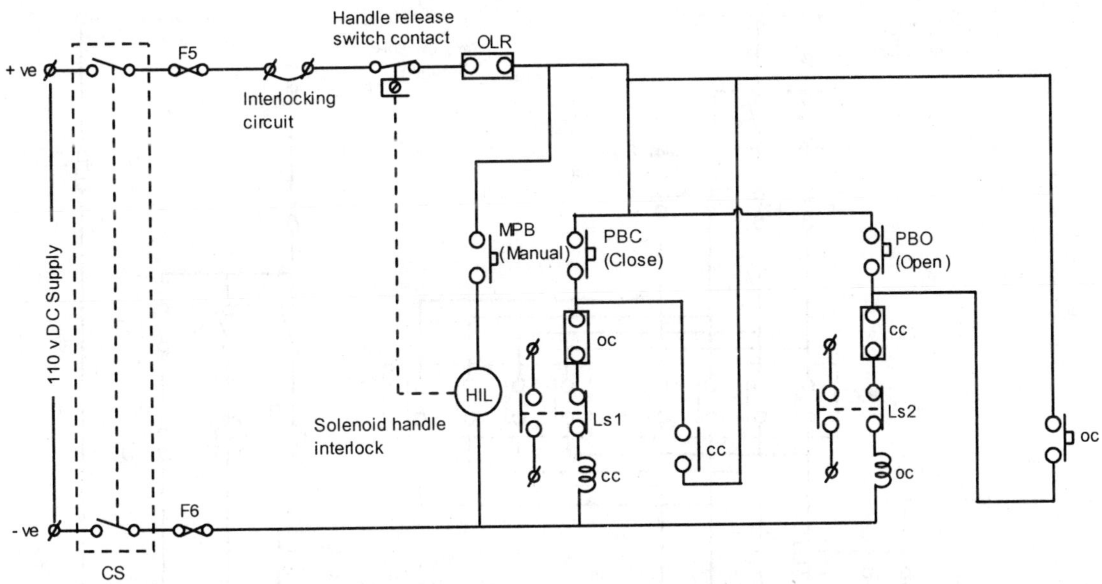

Fig: 4.6 (d): DC control circuit for Earth switch drive motor.

Figure 4.6 (e) illustrates the AC power circuit for the disconnector drive three-phase AC motor.

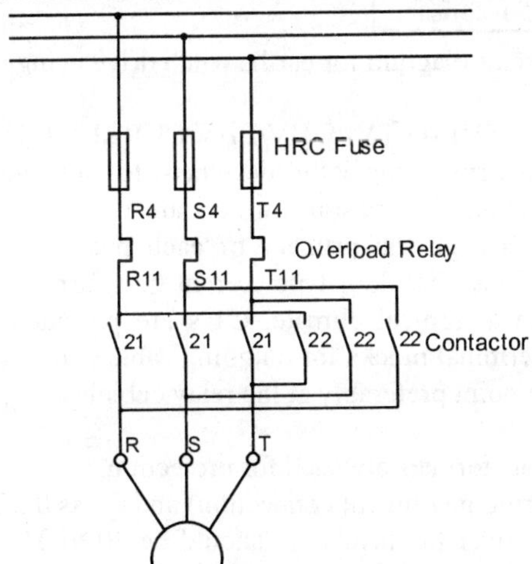

Fig. 4.6 (e): Connection diagram of disconnector drive three-phase AC motor.

Figure 4.6 (f) illustrates the AC power circuit for earth switch drive single-phase AC motor.

LEGEND:

CC, OC: Close or open contactors 110V, DC 7W.
CL: Cubicle lamp
CH: Cubicle Heater
CS: Control switch
F1, F2: Fuse for motor
F4: Fuse for heater
F5, F6: Control supply fuses
FL1: Fuse link
HS: Heater switch
HIL: Handle interlock coil
LS: Lamp switch
LS1: switch opens when the isolator close
LS2: Switch opens when the isolator opens
TH: Thermostat
OLR: Overload relay
PBC, PBO: Close and open push buttons
MPB: Pushbuttons for interlock recluse.
PS: Single-phase power socket.
SI: ON/OFF switch
PSS: Toggle switch for power socket
HIL: Handle interlock
M: Motor

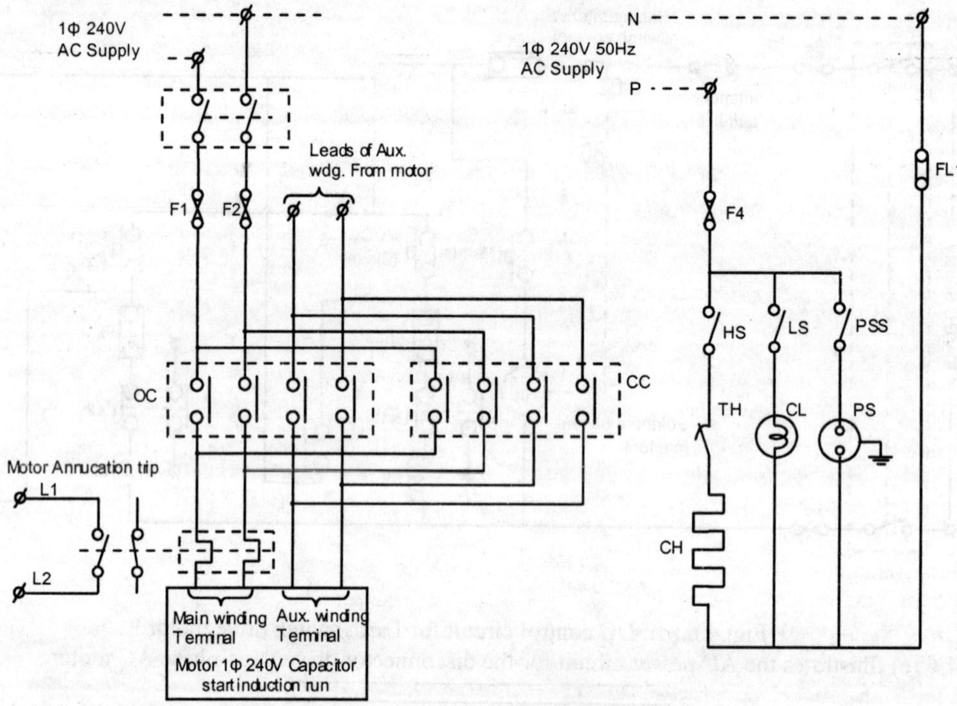

Fig. 4.6 (f): Circuit diagram for earth switch drive using single-phase motor.

4.7 OUT DOOR TYPE AND BUSHING TYPE HV/EHV CURRENT TRANSFORMERS.

Current transformer is a transformer specially designed to accurately represent the primary current proportionally in a secondary circuit. Current transformers are standardized to be 5 A or 1A in the secondary when rated current is passing through the primary of each phase. Current transformers are required for protection and metering applications. Out door type current transformers conforming to IEC 185 are suitable for outdoor operation located in a tropical climate. CT's are provided with a terminal box for secondary connections with shorting type terminal blocks for outgoing cable connections. The CT secondary (1A or 5 A) circuits are grounded at only one point preferably at the relay cubicle.

Class X or Class 5P20 current transformers are used for protection.
Class 1.0 is for metering (measuring instrument connection) and Class 0.2 is used for tariff metering.
Creepage distance to the ground over the insulation should be 20 to 31 mm/KV, depending on the pollution level.

Oil filled current transformer

Outdoor type CTs are of the bar single-turn primary and wire wound multi-turn secondary, filled with transformer oil and hermetically sealed. Oil level gauge is visible from ground. Oil drain valve with sampling means, automatic pressure relief device with alarm device for remote annunciation and two grounding terminal pads (diagonally opposite location) for connection to ground grid are provided. CT is designed for a minimum visible corona or brush discharge when it is completely assembled. Porcelain-insulator for CT is of chocolate brown colour and conforming to IEC 233. Nameplate clearly identifying individual winding classification for multiple tap winding (for example 800/400:1) or multi-core winding is provided. Outdoor type current transformers are installed on a lattice galvanized steel work support structure.

The primary winding consists of one or more turns of a flexible copper strip and is located inside the transformer head. The cores with secondary windings are housed in a light metal shell onto which the graded high voltage insulation is brought. The secondary connections are led through an earthed tube to the base of the transformer. In order to control the electric field strength the isolation is designed as a fine graded capacity bushing with metallic layers. Long transformer life is the drying and impregnation of the paper insulation carried out under vacuum. High- grade transformer oil is used as insulation oil. The insulator is brown glazed high quality electro-technical porcelain. To ensure high mechanical stability, the porcelain is fixed by means of a high grade Portland cement.

The transformer head manufactured from high-grade cast aluminium alloy contains the cores, the secondary and primary windings. The primary terminals are designed either as round or flat terminals. Transformer head permits an easy primary winding changeover in the ratio 1:2 or 1:2:4, externally by appropriate positioning of a copper link, this being easily accessible from outside. A hermetic and pressure free sealing of the current transformer is maintained through an oil-filled expansion chamber made of stainless steel. The oil expansion is shown by a visual indicator, which can bee viewable from outside. Because of hermetic sealing, the CT needs no maintenance except general cleaning of exterior parts. The base box is made of high-grade aluminium alloy and fitted with row-type or stud type terminals.

Figure 4.7 (a) shows the outlook of an HV out door type multi-core current transformer. Figure 4.7 (b) shows the circuit diagram of a multi-core single-phase current transformer.
Three secondary circuit can be connected either in star or delta depends on the protection application.
Class 5P20 core (50 VA burden) is suitable for protection applications. Class 1.0 core (15 VA burden) is suitable for metering applications. Preventive maintenance of outdoor type CT is discussed in section 4.28.2.

Tests required as per IEC 185

1. verification of terminal markings.
2. Power frequency tests on secondary windings.
3. Over-voltage inter-turn tests.
4. Determination of composite error.
5. Power frequency dry test on primary.
6. Partial discharge test.
7. Dielectric angle measurements.
8. Lightning impulse withstand voltage test.

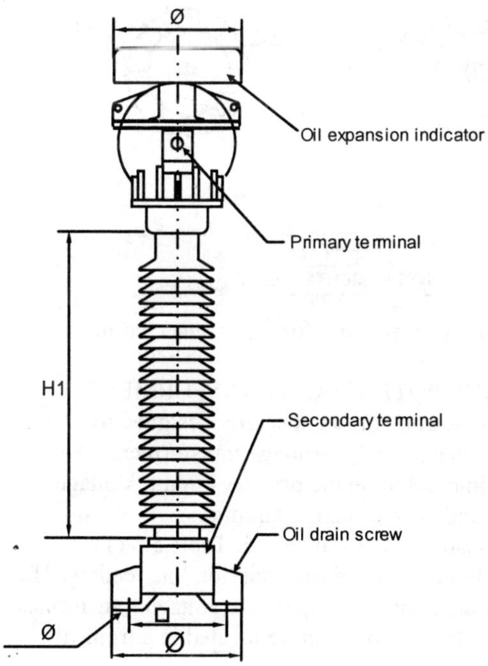

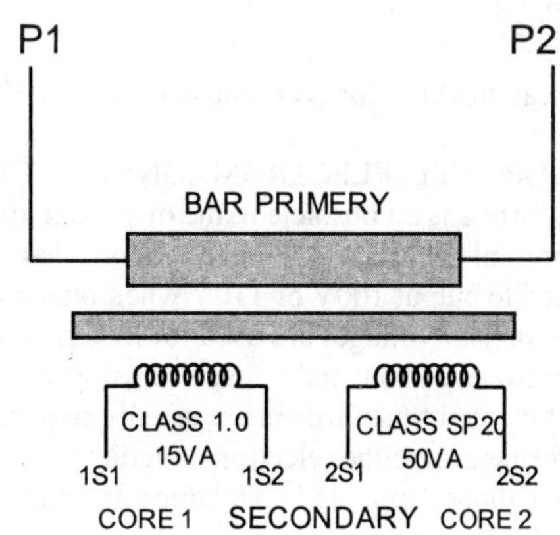

Fig. 4.7 (a): Outlook of outdoor type oil immersed CT. Fig. 4.7 (b): Circuit diagram of a multi-core CT.

Bushing type current transformers.

Dead tank circuit breakers are provided with multi-core current transformers in each bushing for protection and Metering application. Figure 4.7 (c) to (e) shows the polarity diagram and lead markings on the CT secondary. The polarity marks above the "X1" terminal indicates the like polarity for the marked primary (the end of the breaker terminal opposite the breaker contacts), and the marked secondary (terminal "X1") when intermediate taps are used. The tap numerically nearest "X1" has the same polarity as "X1".

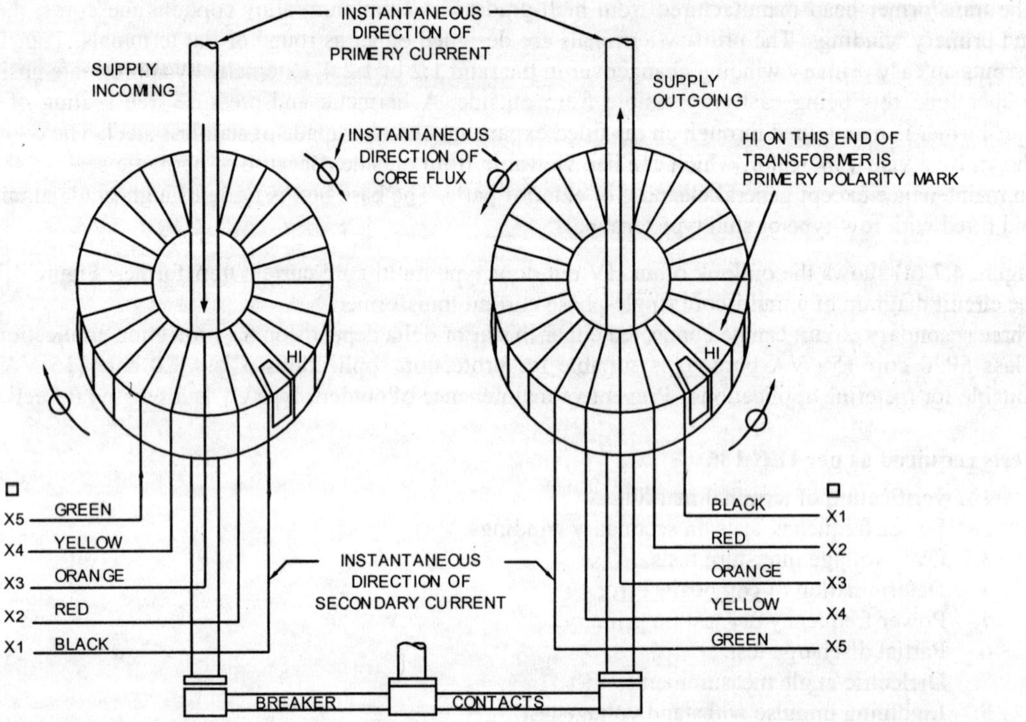

Fig. 4.7 (c): Polarity diagram of bushing type current transformer of dead tank breaker (Courtesy, Siemens).

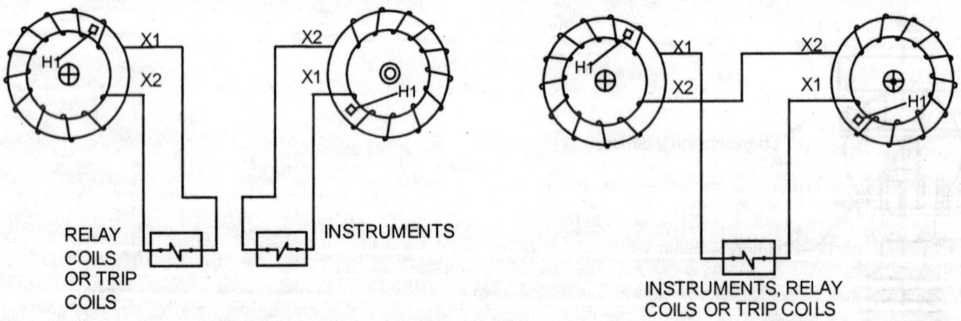

Fig. 4.7 (d): Lead marking for CTs connected direct. Fig. 4.7 (e): Lead marking for CTs connected in series.

4.8 OUT DOOR TYPE, ELECTROMAGNETIC / CAPACITIVE POTENTIAL TRANSFORMERS.

Potential transformer is an obsolete name of voltage transformer. A transformer specially designed to accurately represent the primary voltage proportionally in a secondary circuit. Voltage transformers are standardized to output 100V or 110V when rated voltage is impressed on the primary circuit. Voltage transformer secondary voltages are used for metering, relaying, and synchronizing circuits.
Comparison between current and voltage transformers are demonstrated in Chapter # 5, Table 5.3 (1).
Outdoor type potential transformers are usually required for each bus bars and transmission line feeders. The voltage transformers are either electromagnetic type (for H.V applications) or capacitive voltage transformer (for EHV applications), mounted on a lattice galvanized steel work support structure located in a tropical climate. The PT's are equipped with:

1. Ferro-resonance damping circuit, which is effective under all system conditions.
2. Two grounding terminal pads on diagonally opposite location, for earth connection to the substation earth grid. Each VT secondary circuit should be grounded at one location only, preferably at the first panel entry in the control-room.
3. Secondary fuses or miniature circuit breakers for each phase located such that they can be removed and replaced while the primary is energized. Where a PT is used for protective relay connection, which responds to a blown fuse, a protective switch or similar device should be provided, which shall

prevent the spurious relay operation due to a short circuit in the VT secondary circuit and simultaneously provide an alarm "PT failure"

4. Terminal box for secondary connections.
5. Nameplate clearly identifying individual winding classification especially for multiple secondary.

PT accuracy should not be affected by presence of pollution on the external surface. Creepage distance to ground over the insulation should be 20 to 31mm/KV depending on the pollution level.

Accuracy class: For relay and instruments is 3P, and for tariff metering 0.2.
Porcelain: Conforming to IEC 233 chocolate brown colour.
Insulating oil: Conforming to IEC 296 Shell Diala B or equivalent.
Accuracy requirements: According to IEC 186.

Special tests:

1) Radio influence voltage test along with corona test.
2) High frequency inert loss over the standard frequency range.

(1) Capacitive voltage transformer (CVT)

Figure 4.8 (a) shows the circuit diagram of a single-phase capacitive voltage transformer. Figure 4.8 (b) shows the outlook of a typical high voltage CVT.

LEGEND

1. Series reactor
2. Intermediate voltage transformer.
3. Harmonic suppression filter
4. Protective gap
5. Secondary terminal board
6. Faraday shield
7. Potential ground switch
8. Choke coil and gap assembly
9. Drain coil gap and carrier ground switch.

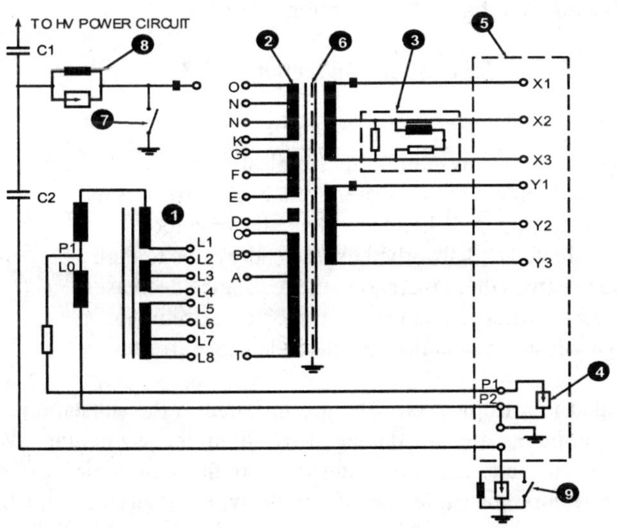

Fig. 4.8 (a): Circuit diagram of capacitive voltage transformer.

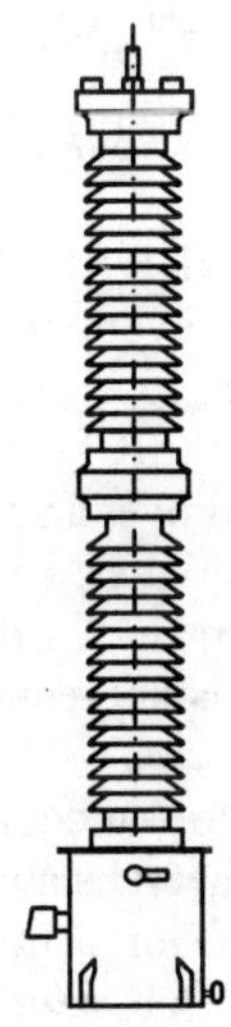

Fig. 4.8 (b) Outlook of a typical CVT

CVT unit consists of capacitor elements, housed in porcelain shells, each hermetically sealed and insulated with a high quality polypropylene film / paper dielectric and impregnated with highly processed synthetic fluid. Each capacitor section is equipped with a stainless steel expansion chamber, which will allow the synthetic fluid to expand and contract with changes in temperatures. Should there be excessive pressure build within a capacitor sections, the expansion chamber will engage a puncture pin, resulting in pressure release and visual indication of a problem. It is over these capacitor sections that most of the high voltage will be dropped. A tap voltage 5 - 10 KV is taken from the lower capacitor section and fed to an electromagnetic circuit in the cast aluminium base box.

The base box contains the intermediate transformer, which will provide the final output voltages via multiple tapped secondary windings, series compensating reactor and ferroresonance control circuitry. The base box is filled with dried mineral oil, protecting the components from environmental deterioration. Ferro-resonance is simply and effectively controlled by utilization of low flux density designed magnetic circuitry and a saturable reactor controlled damping circuit connected across the secondary winding. The ferro-resonance suppression circuit does not adversely affect transient response. Higher inherent capacitance values provide superior PLC (Power line carrier communication) coupling, better transient performance and improved stability.

(2) Electromagnetic type potential transformer.
Oil filled electromagnetic potential transformer consists of primary and multi-core secondary winding for each phase as shown in figure 4.8 (c).

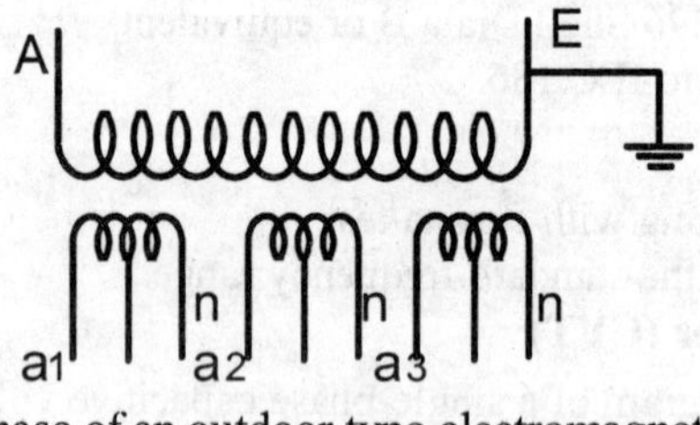

Fig. 4.8 (c): Circuit diagram of one phase of an outdoor type electromagnetic multi-core voltage transformer.

(3) Tests on voltage transformers as per ANSI C93.1

1. Capacitance and dissipation factor (before voltage test and after voltage test). Test equipment is illustrated in figure 4.19 (c) of section 4.19.
2. Power frequency voltage withstand test (dry and wet). Test voltage to be applied is given in Table 2.20 (1) of Chapter # 2.
3. Basic lightning insulation level voltage test (BIL). Test voltage to be applied is given in Table (1) of section 4.6.
4. Partial discharge test [Test equipment is illustrated in figure (f) of section 4.19].

Preventive maintenance procedures for outdoor type PT's are demonstrated in section 2.28.3.

4.9 GAPLESS ZINC OXIDE STATION CLASS HV/EHV SURGE ARRESTORS.
A device used to limit the severity of a voltage surge in a power system. In its simplest form, it could be a Spark gap, however a more repeatable and less stress inducing method is preferred. Surge arresters used earlier, was silicon carbide (SIC) discs in series with a spark gap. When the voltage become too high, the spark gap flashed over and the SIC discs conducted and absorbed excess energy due to their inverse resistance characteristics; i.e. when the voltage across them increases, the resistance decreases. In the early 1980's modern zinc oxide (ZnO) discs were introduced and as have such an extreme inverse characteristics (spark gap is not required). ZnO surge arresters are called metal-oxide surge arrester.

Surge arresters designed for outdoor operation located in a tropical climate, are installed in the substation, so that all components of the substation electrical equipments are not damaged by, lightning, switching over voltage or any other type of over voltages may occur, internally or externally to the boundaries of the substation. HV and EHV sub station class surge arresters are gapless metal-oxide type complying with the requirements of IEC 99-4. Porcelain used for the surge arrester must be in accordance with IEC 233 requirements and minimize the effects of pollution on the exterior porcelain. Lightning arresters are equipped with:

1. Pressure relief device for relieving internal gas pressure prior to porcelain rupture in the event of arrester failure.
2. Lightning surge counter and leakage current meter.
3. A link to bypass the surge counter when the surge counter is removed for maintenance.
4. Grading rings are used for corona discharge in 220 KV and above high / extra high voltage systems.

Surge arresters are designed for a minimum of visible corona or brush discharge. Creepage distance over insulation to ground should be 20 to 31 mm/KV, depending on the pollution level. Lightning arresters are mounted on a lattice steel structure. The ground conductor must be fully insulated from the structure and connected to the ground grid at a node of crossing conductors. Figure 4.9 (a) illustrates the cross sectional view of a typical high voltage gapless metal oxide surge arrester.

LEGEND

1. Container (Porcelain)
2. Clamping ring
3. Pressure sensitive diaphragm
4. Rubber gasket
5. Spring
6. ZnO Disc
7. Silicon Wedge
8. Silicon strip
9. Sulphur cement

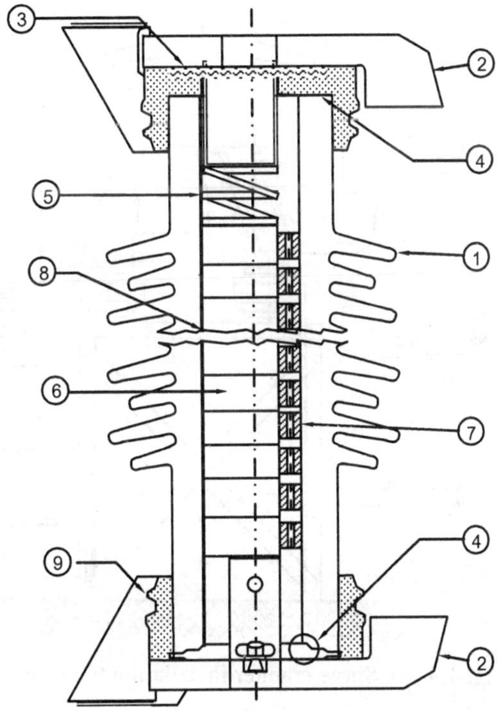

Fig. 4.9 (a): Cross sectional view of a gapless metal oxide surge arrester (Courtesy, Elpro International Ltd)

Lightning arrester consists of a series of zinc oxide disc. Silicon-rubber wedge is provided between the zinc oxide disc and internal porcelain wall. Heat generated in the discs from steady state or transient conditions is transferred through the silicon wedge and porcelain housing and then dissipated to the outside environment. A non-linear resistor is one whose resistance is not constant but inversely proportional to the applied voltage. Its resistance value decreases rapidly as the voltage across it is increased. It has an extremely low resistance value when the high surge voltage appears and thereby allows the flow of very heavy currents of the order of thousands of amperes and dissipates the energy quickly. What is the more important is that it recovers and presents a high resistance value to the normal line voltage as soon as the surge has disappeared, so that any tendency of the arc to continue is immediately disappeared. Standard discharge current ratings based on an 8/20 micro-second wave shape are 2.5 KA for medium voltage surge arresters, 10 KA for high voltage arresters and 20 KA for extra high voltage surge arresters.

The power frequency spark over voltage is the r.m.s value of the lowest power frequency voltage, applied between the line and earth terminals during the passage of the discharge current, which causes spark over of all the series gaps. The impulse spark over-voltage is the highest value of the voltage attained during an impulse of given wave shape and polarity applied between the line and earth terminals of the arresters prior to the flow of discharge current.

Voltage, which appears between line and earth terminals during the passage of discharge current, is called residual voltage. It is the voltage drop across the lightning arrester. For a lightning arrester, the residual voltage and the impulse spark over voltage should be the same so that there is no danger of the plant being subjected to sudden voltage variation when the arc caused by the spark over ceases.

Surge counters are devices intended to register the number of times a surge arrester has actually functioned and discharged a lightning surge. For this purpose the LA is mounted on an insulated base and the earth terminal of the arrester is connected through the non-resettable surge counter to the earth. A capacitor inductor circuit (with in built leakage current monitoring device) is used to count the number of discharges.

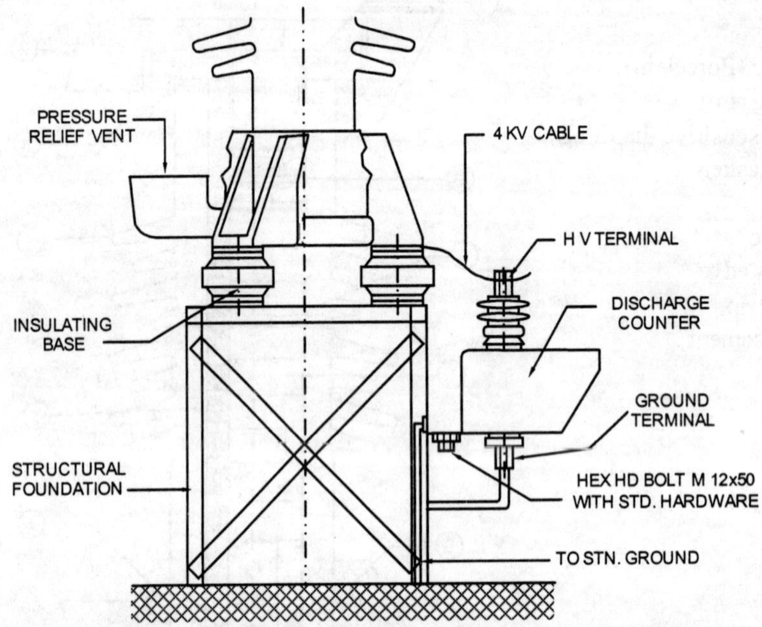

Fig. 4.9 (b): Surge counter installation (Courtesy, Elpro International Ltd)

Lightning arresters are mounted on a lattice galvanized steel support structure located close to the apparatus to be protected. The connection should be direct and solid by using suitable clamps. The earth connection to the station earth grid should be of 16 to 50 sq:mm insulated copper cable, even extremely heavy currents are likely to pass through it, for a few microseconds. For larger installations the earth connections are made direct to the earth grid through surge counter as shown in Figure 4.9 (b). For medium voltage distribution transformers, independent earth pit is being used for earth connection to lightning arrester, otherwise, over voltages on the line by back flashovers will be caused, because of the heavy voltage drop across earth, when discharge current is flowing.

Surge arresters should comply with the design tests outlined in ANSI/IEEE C.62-11 and IEC 99-4. The tests to be conducted are duty cycle test (operating duty test), high current short duration test, and low current long duration test (transmission line discharge test) with no loss in protective capability. Those tests verify that the surge arresters can dissipate lightning and switching surges while operating at rated voltages and thermally recover at maximum continues operating voltage (MCOV) at an elevated temperature. Gapless construction provide excellent contamination performance

4.10 CABLE SEALING END AND MARSHALLING KIOSKS.

Underground high and extra high voltage XLPE cables (up to 550 KV) and oil or gas insulated cables (up to 800 KV) entering/leaving an open outdoor type switchyard as incoming/outgoing power sources are terminated by using cable sealing end conforming to IEC 859, suitable for the appropriated voltage and current ratings. Sealing ends are mounted on a lattice galvanized steel work support structure. Three different types of hermetically sealed cable sealing ends are available:

1. Porcelain bush type for high voltage applications
2. Oil immersed type for voltage range up to 400 KV
3. SF6 gas insulated type suitable for 66 KV to 800 KV

Out door type cable sealing ends are designed and manufactured to use in a tropical climate and minimize the effects of pollution on the exterior porcelain, with minimum visible corona and brush discharge. Grading rings are used where necessary to reduce corona discharge. Creepage distance over insulation to ground should be 20 to 31mm/KV, depending on the degree of pollution. Porcelain used in cable sealing end is brown and glazed in conformity with IEC 233. Dedicated ground connection terminals are provided for earthing metallic cable sheath. Indoor type gas insulated HV/EHV switchgears and oil immersed power transformers have indoor type in-built cable sealing ends for terminating the incoming/outgoing cables.

Porcelain insulated high voltage cable sealing end: Figure 4.10 (a) illustrates the cut away view of a porcelain bush type cable-sealing end. Porcelain used is brown and glazed permanently marked for traceability by means that will not indent or affect porcelain surface and minimize the effect of pollution on the exterior porcelain. Porcelain bush type, high voltage cable sealing end consists of:

1. Connector
2. Connector support
3. Top metal fitting
4. Porcelain bushing
5. Pre-molded stress relief cone
6. Housing
7. Compression unit
8. Insulating compound
9. Bottom metal fitting
10. Corona shield
11. Gasket
12. Taping
13. Earth terminal
14. Mounting insulator

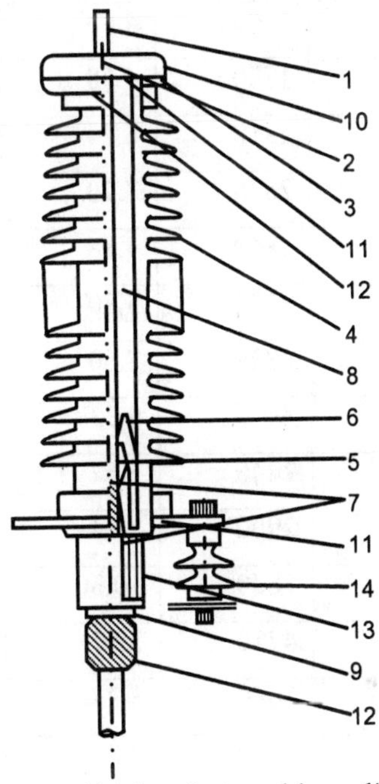

Fig. 4.10 (a): Typical porcelain insulated high voltage cable-sealing end

High voltage XLPE insulated single-core cables are terminated to the outdoor cable-sealing end mounted on galvanized lattice steel support structure. An insulated gland is provided in order to enable the cable sheath to be glanded and left unearthed in service. No significant stresses are exerted on the equipment. Galvanized ladder type steel cable trays are used for supporting the cables.

Oil immersed high voltage cable sealing end

Figure 4.10 (b) illustrates the cut away view of an oil immersed cable-sealing end. The synthetic oil used to fill the unit is Shell Diala B or equivalent (Transformer oil). Oil immersed type cable sealing end consists of:

80	5	1180	3.18	1770	1420	1780	1680
	6	1400	3.77	1920	1540	1930	1820
	8	1810	4.89	2200	1750	2200	2080
	10	2200	5.94	2410	1920	2420	2280
100	5	1490	4.03	2200	1750	2150	2020
	6	1770	4.78	2390	1900	2340	2200
	8	2310	6.24	2740	2170	2670	2510
	10	2826	7.70	3350	2650	3265	3070
120	5	1810	4.88	2620	2070	2500	2340
	6	2150	5.80	2860	2250	2730	2550
	8	2820	7.60	3270	2580	3120	2920
	10	3460	9.33	3590	2830	3420	3200
160	5	2440	6.57	3460	2710	3240	3010
	6	2900	7.84	3780	2950	3530	3290
	8	3820	10.30	4340	3390	4060	3780
	10	4710	12.7	4760	3720	4460	4140
200	5	3060	8.27	4290	3330	3960	3670
	6	3660	9.87	4690	3640	4320	4000
	8	4830	13.0	5390	4180	4970	4600
	10	5970	16.1	5920	4600	5460	5060
	12	7090	19.1	6330	4910	5830	5400
250	5	3850	10.4	5330	4100	4840	4460
	6	4600	12.4	5810	4480	5280	4670
	8	6080	16.4	6690	5160	6080	5610
	10	7540	20.4	7360	5680	6690	6170
	12	8970	24.2	7870	6070	7150	6600

The bus bar located at the top (high level bus) or tapping connections are usually AAAC (All aluminium alloy conductor) any of the following sizes. Depending on the continuous minimum rating (CMR) and short time rating (STR) requirements single or double conductor (Twin 'peach' arrangement) with spacers at every 2metre interval, are used as elevated bus bars.

(3) All aluminium alloy conductor: Aluminium is a metallic element, which comes from the ore Bauxite. Aluminium is a light metal, which can be given tremendous strength by alloying. Aluminium conducts heat and electricity, reflects light and radiant energy and resists corrosion. AAAC contains 97.28% aluminium, 0.5% magnesium and 0.5% silicon. AAAC is a nonmagnetic material. It does not exhibit the magnetic core loss found in ACSR (Aluminium conductor steel reinforced). AAAC's surface is significantly harder than AAC (All aluminium conductor). It is less liable to damage during installation. AAAC minimize corona effect, which is an important advantage in extra high voltage system. AAAC has high resistance to atmospheric corrosion and are suitable for use in coastal and industrially polluted areas. Strength of AAAC is twice that of AAC.

- Base plate with wiping gland and earth connection for bonding lead.
- Support insulators, seals and fixing materials, synthetic oil insulating medium etc.

Marshalling kiosk: Marshalling kiosks are installed in the switchyard for efficient interconnection of cabling between the various equipments of substation to control and relaying panels. The free standing floor mounted cubicle is provided for the marshalling of all ancillary equipment cabling associated with the circuit, i.e. circuit breakers, disconnectors, earth switches, current and voltage transformers etc. to be routed via trunk multi-core control cables to remote control and relay panels. Outdoor type cubicles made of electro-galvanized 2 mm thick sheet steel with degree of protection IP 41 to IEC 529. Figure 4.10 (d) shows the front/rear view, side view, and bottom plate. Typical outdoor type marshalling kiosk consists of

1. Vermin proof louvers comprising of brass gauze screen.
2. Rigid doors fitted with lock and weatherproof sealing material suitable for outdoor use.
3. Gland plate suitable for bottom cable entry.
4. Terminal block segregated by control, inter tripping, indication and analogue.
5. Anti-condensation heater and door switch operated light.

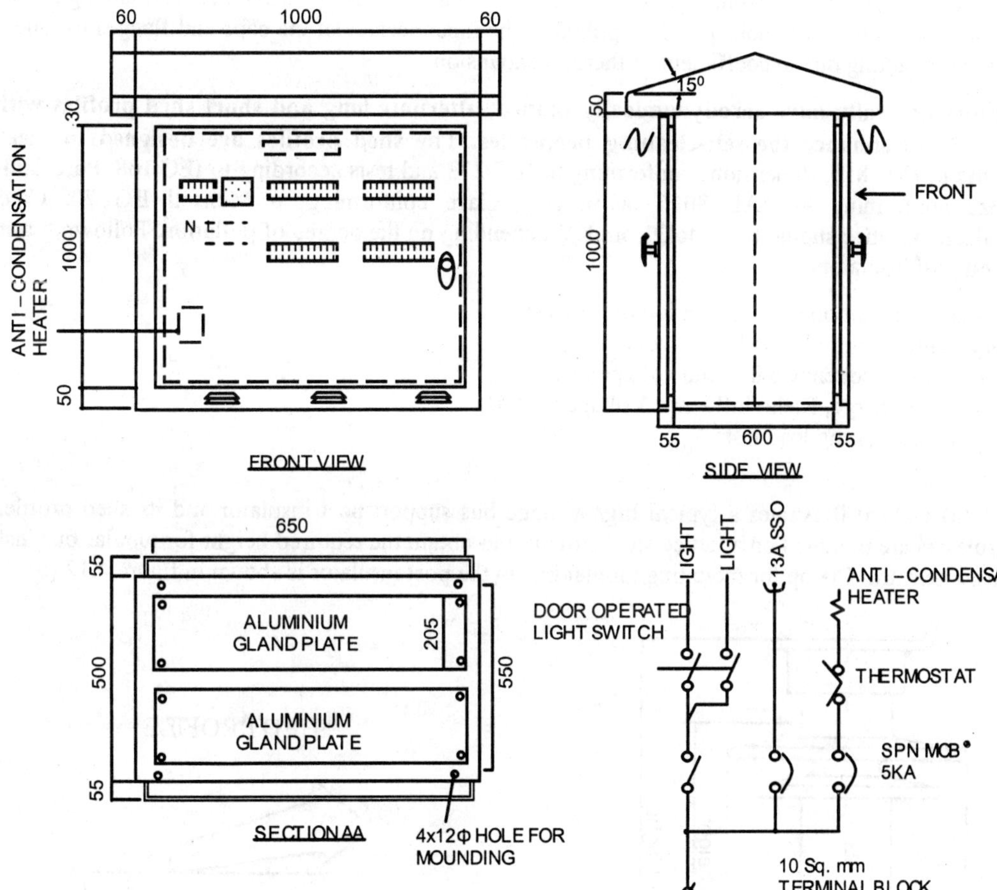

Fig. 4.10 (d): Typical interface marshalling kiosk for interconnection of cables.

4.11 BUS SUPPORT POST INSULATORS, STRING AND SUSPENSION INSULATORS.

Insulator is a device made of non-conducting material, used to give support to electrical conductors and shield them from ground or other conductors. An insulator inhibits the flow of current from the conductor to earth or another conductor. Post or disk insulators (Porcelain or toughened glass construction) require a high degree of safety and service reliability. Those insulators are subjected to high degree of static and dynamic loading such as bending, torsion, compression and short circuit forces through-out their life time. Insulators are subjected to various climatic conditions and high degrees of pollution, salt and snow accumulation.

Bus support post insulators: They are porcelain insulators, fully interchangeable units with slid core and cylindrical in shape, such that each unit can be used either upright or inverted position. Post insulators are designed such that the forces of combined short circuit and maximum wind loading and seismic forces should not exceed 50% of the declared strength of the insulators. Post insulators of solid core design have the following advantages:

- Outstanding service reliability, high degree of dynamic and static loading.
- Very low deflection at bending loads.
- High mechanical strength with respect to bending, torsion, tensile and compressive loads.
- Free from internal partial discharges, low radio interference voltage.

The metal parts are made of high-grade malleable cast iron/spheroidal graphite iron free from blowholes, rust and cracks. They are hot dip galvanized using zinc of very high purity. The mass of zinc coating is 610gm/sq:mm minimum. The bonding to porcelain is by using good quality Portland cement having a very low coefficient of expansion. Bituminous paint is applied to the inner surface of the caps and flanges to relieve the thermal stresses resulting due to coefficient of thermal expansion.

The insulators normally have aerodynamically shaped, alternate long and short shed profiles with the inclination 15° to enhance the self-cleaning properties. The shed profiles are designed to meet the requirements of IEC 815, dimensions conforming to IEC 273 and tests according to IEC 168. Porcelain is of brown glaze conforming to RAL 8016 or in gray glaze conforming to Munsell BG 70. Creepage distance/leakage distance should be 20 to 31mm/KV depending on the degree of pollution. Following tests are conducted on post insulators.

1. Visual examination and verification of dimensions.
2. Dry lightning impulse withstand voltage test.
3. Wet power frequency withstand voltage test.
4. Visible discharge, Radio influence Voltage (RIV).
5. Mechanical failing load tests.

Figure 4.11 (a) and (b) illustrates a typical high voltage bus support post insulator and its shed profile. Bus support insulators are mounted on a lattice steel structure to obtain the required height for tubular bus installed in the open switchyard. Clamp for mounting tubular bus to the post insulator is shown in figure 4.12 (o).

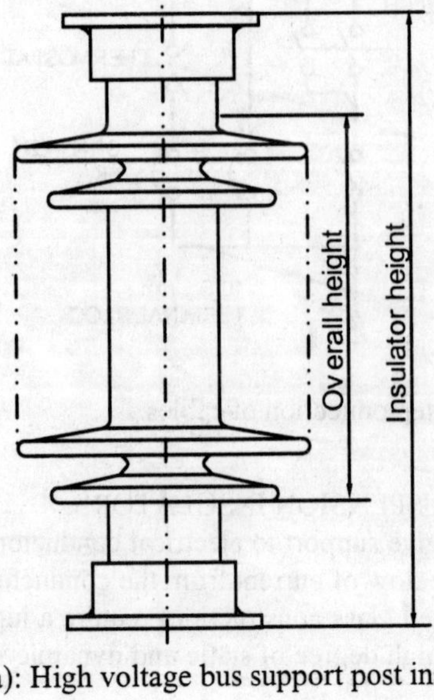

Fig. 4.11 (a): High voltage bus support post insulator:

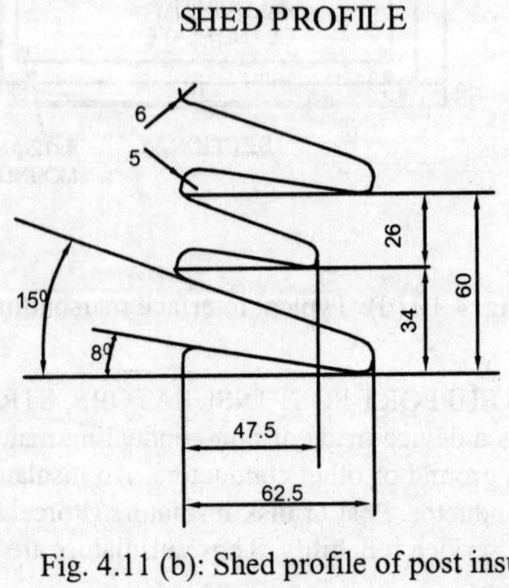

Fig. 4.11 (b): Shed profile of post insulator

String Insulator assembly: Porcelain disc insulator is an insulator with the skirt made by a ceramic processes. Toughened glass disc insulator is a fiberglass insulator most often covered with a white polymer compound resembling rubber. String insulator is an assembly of two or more disc insulators placed in series and are made in different lengths for different voltage levels. The higher the system voltage of a transmission line, the longer the insulator string. Table 4.11 (1) gives minimum number of disc insulator to be used per string.

Figure 4.11 (c) illustrates typical 210 KN string insulator assembly with bolted type tension clamp, consisting:

(1) Forged steel hot dip galvanized anchor shackle (Glalvanizing conforming to BS 729.)
(2) Forged steel hot dip galvanized 20mm ball link as per BS 3288.
(3) Mild steel hot dip galvanized arcing horn.
(4) Forged steel hot dip galvanized socket clevis with stainless steel R type security clip.
(5) Bolted type tension clamp (Slip strength of tension clamp 95% of the UTS of conductor)
(6) Disc insulators having ultimate tensile strength 210 Kilo Newton.

All bolts and nuts should be galvanized, whereas, spring washers shall be electro-galvanized.

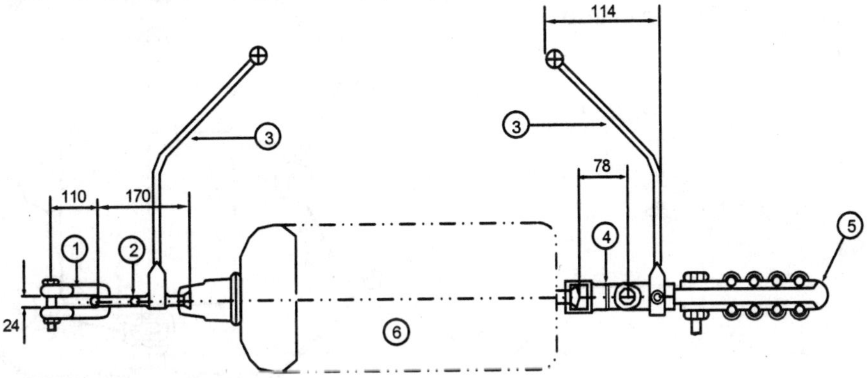

Fig. 4 11 (c): 210 KN string insulator assembly with bolted type tension clamp.

Table 4.11 (1): Number of disc insulator per string recommended for different voltage levels.

System voltage	Number of discs per tension or suspension string assembly	System voltage (EHV)	Number of discs per tension or suspension string assembly
66 KV	6 Nos 20mm 160KN	275 KV	16Nos 24mm 300 KN
110 KV	8 Nos 20mm 160 KN	330 KV	20Nos 24mm 300 KN
132 KV	10Nos 20mm 160 KN	400 KV	24Nos 28mm 400 KN
170 KV	12Nos 20mm 210 KN	500 KV	2 x 30Nos 28mm 400 KN(V-string)
220 KV	12Nos 20mm 210 KN	765 KV	4 x 40Nos 32mm 530 KN(V-string)

Figure 4.11 (d) illustrates the assembly of a typical 210 KN dual conductor string insulator assembly with compression type clamp per string.

LEGEND:

1. Anchor shackle (Steel)
2. Ball eye (20mm IEC standard)
3. Disc insulator (Porcelain)
4. Socket clevis (Ductile iron)
5. Yoke (Dual conductor)
6. Anchor shackle
7. Compression clamp (Aluminium alloy)

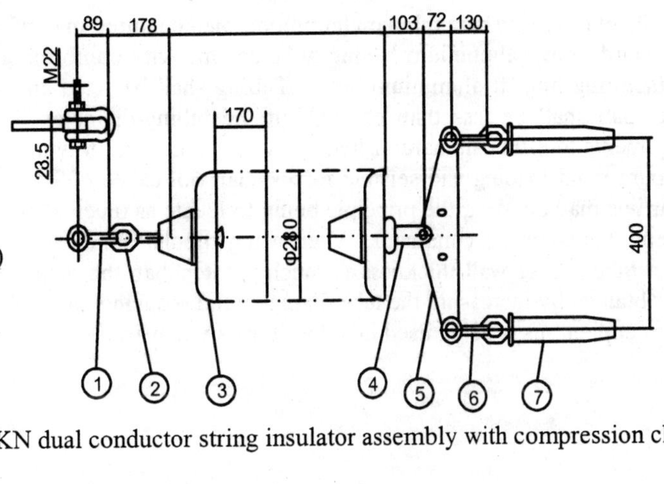

Fig. 4.11 (d): 210 KN dual conductor string insulator assembly with compression clamp.

Suspension insulator assembly: Suspension insulator is an insulator used to suspend the conductor from the structure; main part consist of the cap (upper part made of metal), the skirt (middle portion made of porcelain insulating material) and the ball stem lower metal portion (mallable iron). Suspension string is a string of disc insulators suspended from a tower-structure or a cross arm to support the conductor Suspension clamp attaches to an insulator string to hold the conductor. Figure 4.11 (e) illustrates single conductor suspension insulator assembly. Refer Table 4.11 (1) to select the number of disc insulators required per set. All hard wares are hot dip galvanized.

LEGEND:

1. Forged steel anchor shackle
2. Forged steel ball link
3. Mild steel arcing horn
4. Forged steel socket eye
5. Aluminium alloy suspension clamp
6. Armour rod
7. Disc insulator

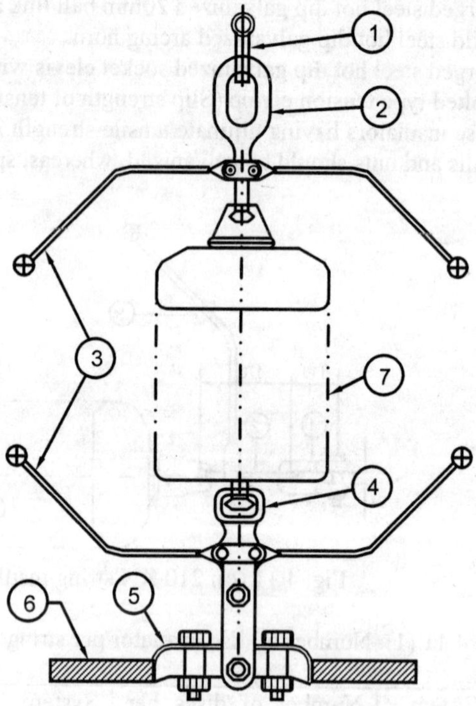

Fig. 4.11 (e): Suspension insulator assembly.

4.12 TUBULAR BUSBARS, CLAMPS AND CONNECTORS FOR SWITCHING STATIONS.

Air insulated bus bars are designed for conductor temperature 75°C, considering solar impingement, no wind and without any external or current thermal input. Safety factors for design shall be not less than 50% of the elastic limit to metal and 50% of the electromechanical test for porcelain. Due consideration must be given for the rated currents and 3 seconds short circuit currents. Large substations bus bars are required at lower level for tapping connections to equipments, and upper level bus bars for 'take-off' and 'take-in' incoming and outgoing feeders.

Lower level buses are bare tubular aluminium, manufactured in conformity with International Piping Standards (IPS). Hard drawn aluminium having 56% conductivity conforming to IEC 105 standard is widely used for manufacturing tubular aluminium buses. Tubing shall be sized and supported such that maximum sag of the tubing span shall be less than one-half of the tubing-diameter. Tubing should be provided with damping arrangements to eliminate natural frequency resonance due to wind. The forces of combined short circuit and maximum wind loading and seismic forces shall not exceed 50% of the published strength of the tubing. A tubular bus may be ideal, the principle being to locate as much as of the metal as possible equidistant from the magnetic center of the conductor. When using tubular conductors, there is little advantage to be gained by using a tube whose wall thickness is much greater than the depth of the penetration, the greatest advantage being obtained by increasing the tube diameter and reducing the wall thickness, the skin effect will be reduced. Tubular copper bus is being used in indoor type switchyard.

(1) Skin effect and proximity effect

When an alternating flux exists, a back e.m.f is induced by virtue of this flux cutting the conductor. The e.m.f is produced in the conductor by its own magnetic flux, and while the internal parts of the conductor are cut by the alternating flux from all parts of the conductor, the outlying parts are not, the line linkages decreasing as the edges of the conductor are reached. Thus, the conductor elements possess more and more reactance the nearer they get to the interior of the conductor so that uneven current distribution occurs through the cross section. **The current tending to 'crowed' in to the 'skin' and outer edges** of a single bar conductor and in the outer terminations of a multiple bar conductor. The effects of this phenomena, is known as **'skin effect'.**

Due to mutual induction between two conductors carrying current in opposite directions or of different phases, and this is known as **'Proximity effect'.** The condition here is that each conductor is cut by the flux from its neighbour and this leads to the current concentrating in those portions of each conductor nearest to the other. Here again, the effect can be minimized by choosing the best configuration to each conductor and more particularly, by adopting a wide spacing between conductors.

(2) Current carrying capacities of tubular aluminium bus:

Aluminium tubes are more economical than stranded conductors with bus bar currents of more than 1000 A. Tubes are available from 50mm to 250mm internal diameter, with wall thickness from 3 to 12mm. For the same conductor cross-section area, a tube of larger diameter has greater dynamic strength than one of smaller diameter. Tubular conductors can be mounted on post insulators in spans of up to 20 metres. To avoid costly expansion type joints they are welded at site in lengths of up to 60 metres. Dampers of various makes are available for supporting any oscillation of the tubes. Tubular conductors for bus and equipment interconnections are sized according to both thermal and dynamic considerations given in Table 4.12 (1).

Current carrying capacities of bare tubular aluminium bus (GR 610176) having 56% conductivity, at 40°C ambient temperature, is given in Table 4.12 (1). To find the current ratings of copper tubular bus of similar sizes, multiply the current ratings given against the corresponding sizes in the said Table by, 1.28.

The aluminium tubes should be handled carefully during transit and installation in order to insure no scratches or cracks to the finish of tubing. Cross sectional area of aluminium tube in sq:mm = 3.14 ($R^2 - r^2$) where R= outer radious in mm, and r = inner radious in mm. Assume that overall diameter (OD) of an aluminium tube is 90mm and inner diameter (ID) is 79mm, the cross sectional area = 3.14 ($45^2 - 39.5^2$)

$$= 3.14 \times (2025 - 1560.25) = 1459.3 \text{sq:mm.}$$

Short circuit ratings in KA = (0.0775 x 1459.3) / $\sqrt{t}$, where 0.0775 is a constant for aluminium and t is the duration of short circuit. Isc, for 3 sec = 113/1.732 = 65.25 KA. To find the short circuit ratings of copper tubular bus, the constant for copper bus is 0.122.

Table 4.12 (1): Current carrying capacity of Tubular aluminium bus at 35°C ambient temperature and 65°C operating temperature.

Outside diameter	Wall thickness	Cross section	Weight per metre	Current AC / DC	Current AC / DC	Current AC / DC	Current AC / DC
Mm	Mm	mm^2	Kg	Indoor painted A	Indoor bare A	Outdoor painted A	Outdoor bare A
50	5	707	1.91	1120	909	1190	1140
	6	829	2.24	1210	983	1290	1230
	8	1060	2.85	1370	1110	1460	1390
	10	1260	3.39	1490	1210	1500	1510
63	5	911	2.46	1400	1130	1450	1380
	6	1070	2.90	1520	1230	1570	1490
	8	1380	3.73	1730	1390	1790	1700
	10	1664	4.56	2086	1660	2150	2040

1. Connector
2. Connector support
3. Top metal fitting
4. Bushing
5. Pre-molded stress relief cone
6. lower corona shield
7. Compression pipe
8. Compression unit
9. Insulator
10. Bottom metal fitting
11. Corona shield
12. Gasket
13. Gasket for bottom plate
14. Taping
15. Earth terminal
16. Bottom plate

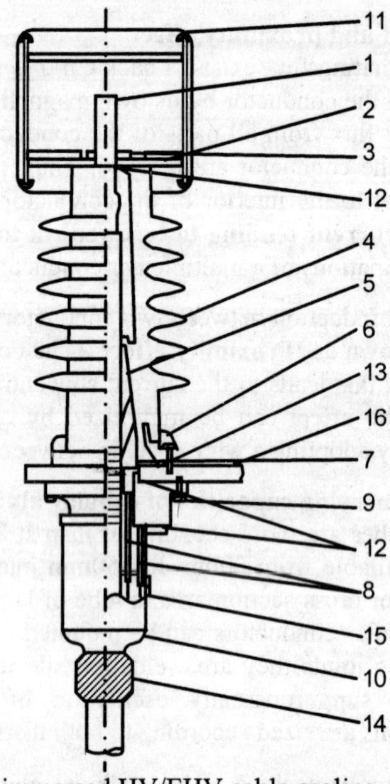

Fig. 4.10 (b): Typical oil immersed HV/EHV cable-sealing end

SF6 insulated high/extra high voltage cable sealing end

Figure 4. 10 (c) illustrates the cut away view of a typical Sulphur hexaflouride insulated cable sealing end. SF6 insulated cable sealing end consists of:

1. Connector
2. Connector support
3. Top metal fitting
4. Bushing
5. Pre-molded stress relief cone
6. lower corona shield
7. Compression pipe
8. Compression unit
9. Insulator
10. Bottom metal fitting
11. Corona shield
12. Gasket
13. Gasket for bottom plate
14. Taping
15. Earth terminal
16. Bottom plate

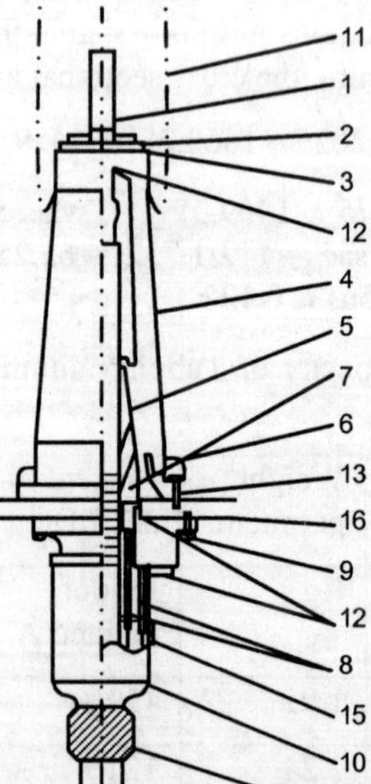

Fig.4.10 (c): Typical SF6 insulated HV/EHV/UHV cable sealing end

Basic outdoor termination kit for single core XLPE (Cross-linked polyethylene) insulated cable consists of:

- Composite type insulator with glass fiber reinforced epoxy resin tube and silicon rubber sheds.
- Top and bottom flanges glued and sealed to the composite insulator.
- Corona shield integrated in top flange.
- Pre-moulded stress cone.
- Solid rod top connector.

Table 4.12 (2) gives the technical data and current ratings of AAAC conductors used for bus applications.

Table 4.12 (2): Current carrying capacity of All aluminium alloy bus conductor.

Conductor size sq:mm	No:of wire and diameter (mm)	Overall diameter (mm)	Weight (Kg/Km)	Resistance at 20°C (Ω/km)	Current ratings at 75°C (A)
400	37/4.06	28.4	1320	0.0698	750
630	37/4.66	32.62	1730	0.0531	1200
800	91/3.35	36.9	2233	0.0415	1600
1000	91/3.74	41.1	2770	0.0336	2000

(4) Clamps and connectors: Clamps and connectors for tubular aluminium bus are made of high strength aluminium alloy (grade 356-T6) casting and have galvanized steel bolts. Similarly connectors and clamps for tubular copper bus (BS 2784) are made of high strength copper alloy casting and have silicon bronze bolts. Connectors are of sufficient size to minimize corona and radio influence voltage. Fittings should be designed with rigid, slip, or expansion design to eliminate thermal expansion forces from being applied to insulators and equipment bushings. Following are the recommended tightening torque of bolts:

Bolt size	Galvanized steel bolts	Silicone Bronze bolts	Stainless steel bolts
M10	19.2 NM	14.7 Newton-Metre	35 NM
M12	45.2 NM	33.9 Newton-Metre	48 NM
M16	90.4 NM	67.8 Newton-Metre	80 NM

Different types of clamps and connecters for switchyard equipments and tubular aluminium bus / tubular copper bus are illustrated in Figure 4.12 (a) to (P). Typical example for accessing the quantity and type of clamps are indicated in figure 4.1 (b) of section 4.1. Factors to be considered for design of clamps and connectors are: Conductor tension 1000Kg; Wind load 560Kg; Forces due to short circuit 1600Kg; Short circuit current 40 KA, 3 second. Hexagonal headed bolts (Stainless steel Grade 304) with flat and bell eville washers are used for tightening the clamps.

Tests on clamps and connecters: Clamps and connectors are subjected to following tests:

(1) STC (Short time current) test: Inject 40 KA rms current 3 seconds duration through connector to check its performance during a short circuit or a fault.
(2) Temperature rise test.
(3) Corona test similar to the test on aluminium tube.
(4) RIV test: Radio interference voltage test for extra high voltage and ultra high voltage connectors to detect radio interference applicable to communication circuits.

Configuration of clamps and connectors:

(1) Expansion type straight connector for jointing tubular buses of similar outer dimensions [Figure 4.12 (a)].
(2) Straight connector for joining of two tubular buses of similar outer dimensions [Figure 4.12 (b)].
(3) Tee connector for connecting tubular buses of similar outer dimensions [Figure 4.12 (c)].
(4) Tap connector for tapping connection from tube to AAAC or ACSR conductor [Figure 4.12 (d)].
(5) Tee connector for connecting conductor-to-conductor [Figure 4.12 (e)].
(6) Tee connector for connecting tubular buses of dissimilar outer dimensions [Figure 4.12 (f)].
(7) Pad type terminal connector for twin AAAC conductor [Figure 4.12 (g)].
(8) Right angled terminal pad for 90degree connection for equipments [Figure 4.12 (h)].
(9) Compression type terminal connector for AAAC/ACSR conductor [Figure 4.12 (*I*)].

(10) Braided connector for ground connection to equipments/Flexible earth bond [Figure 4.12 (*j*)].
(11) Parallel groove connectors for connecting 2 AAAC or ACSR bus conductors in parallel [Figure 4.12 (*k*)]
(12) Pad type Tee connector for AAAC bus conductor (for surge arrester connection); [Figure 4.12 (L)].
(13) Corona bell for fitting on tubular bus ends [Figure 4.12 (*m*)]
(14) End cap for plugging the ends of tubular bus [Figure 4.12 (n)].
(14) Fixed or sliding type post insulator clamp for mounting tubular bus [Figure 4.12 (o)].
(15) Single bolt holding clamp for twin AAAC bus conductor [Figure 4.12 (p)].

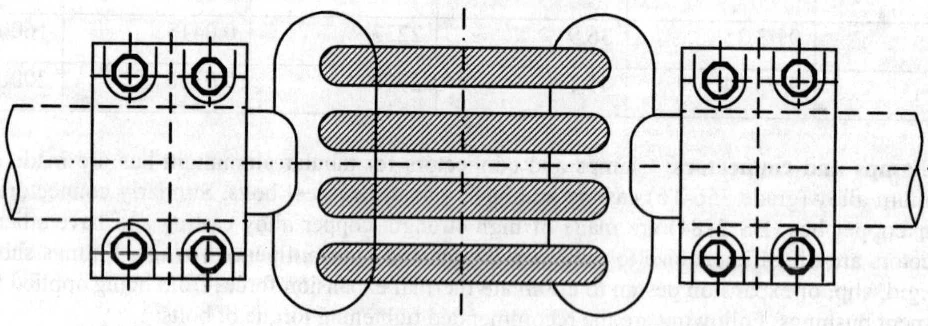

Fig. 4.12 (a): Expansion type straight connector for joining tubular buses.

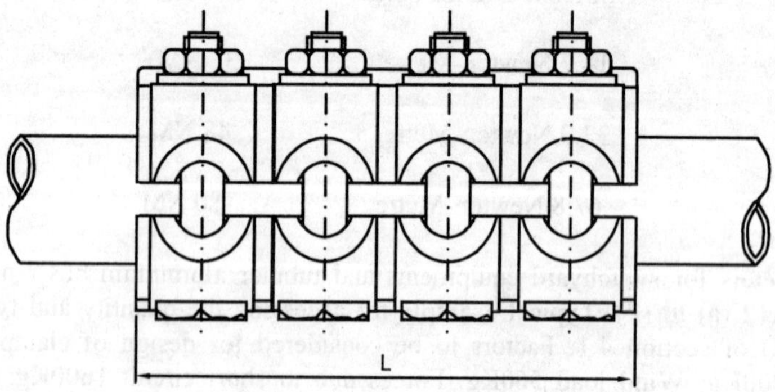

Fig. 4.12 (b): Straight connector for joining tubular buses.

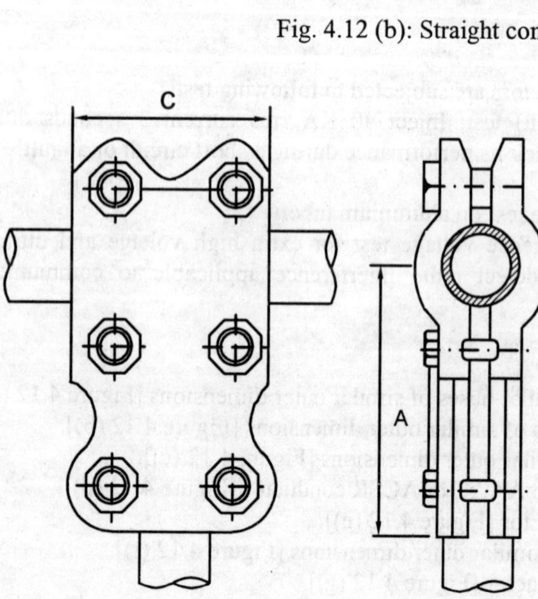

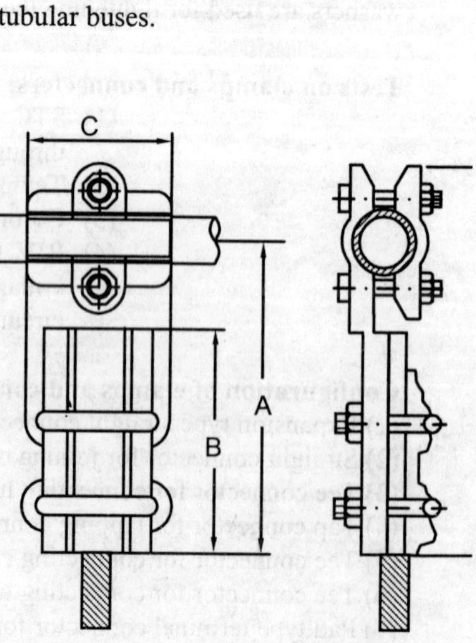

Fig. 4.12 (c): Tee connector, tube-to-tube connection. Fig. 4.12 (d): Tap connection tube to AAAC conductor.

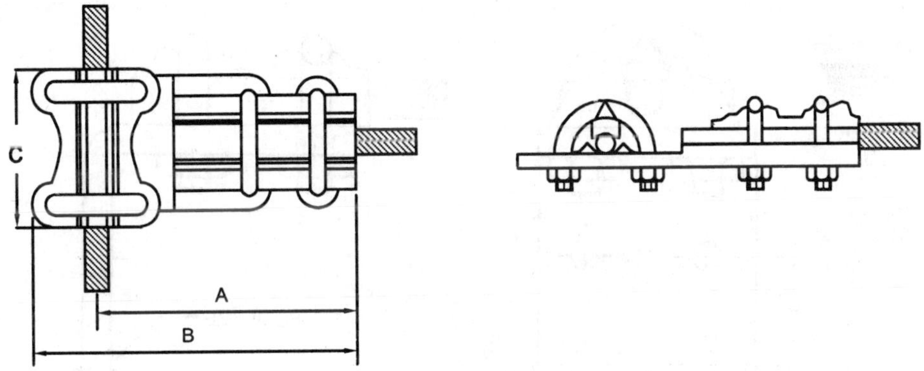

Fig. 4.12 (e): Tee connector conductor-to-conductor.

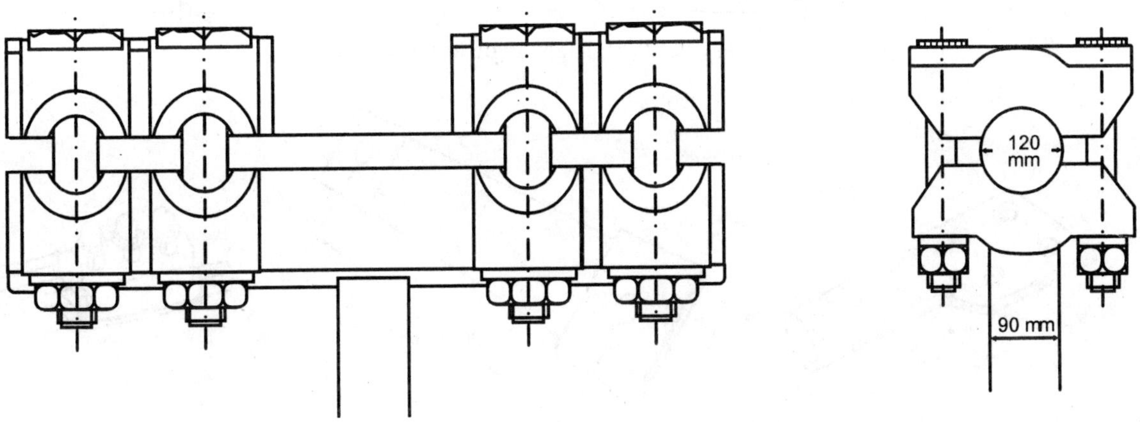

Fig. 4.12 (f): Tee connector for connecting tubular buses of dissimilar outer dimensions.

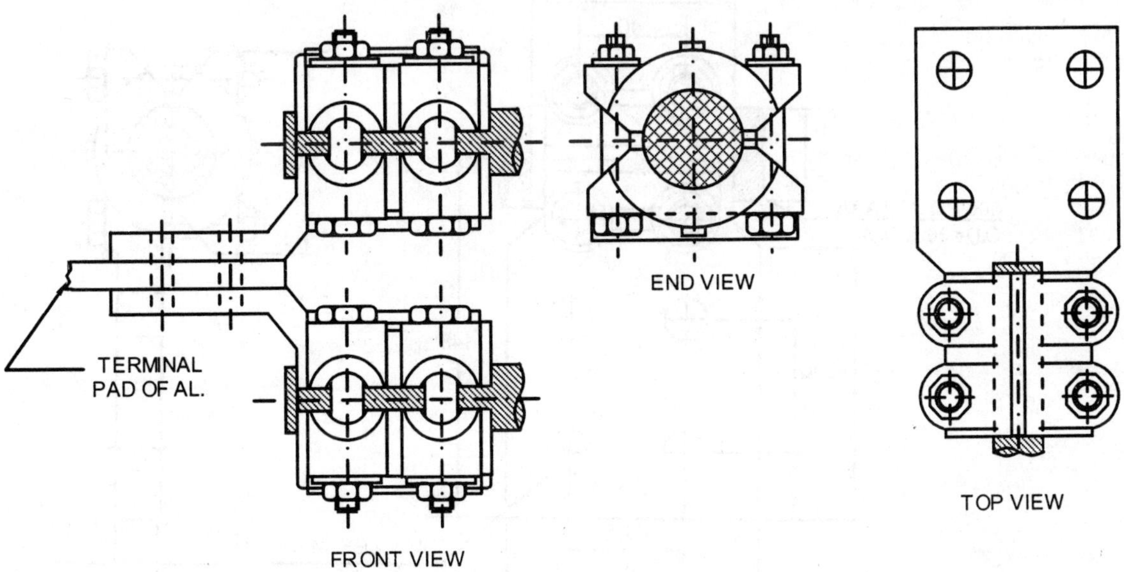

4.12 (g): Pad type terminal connector for twin AAAC conductor.

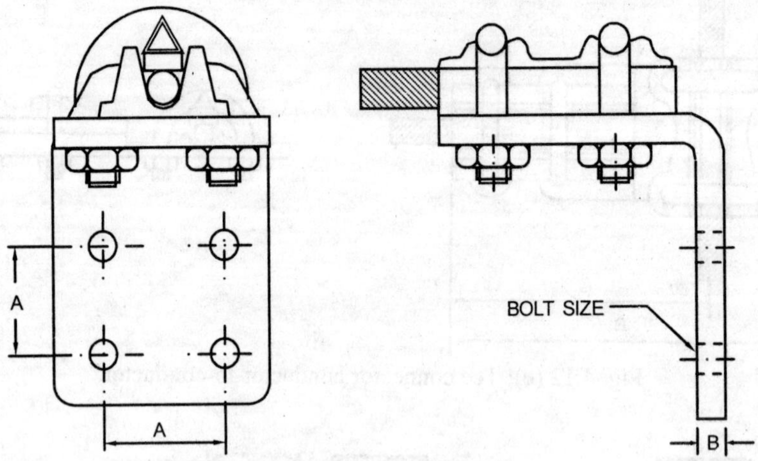

Fig. 4.12 (h): Right angle terminal pad.

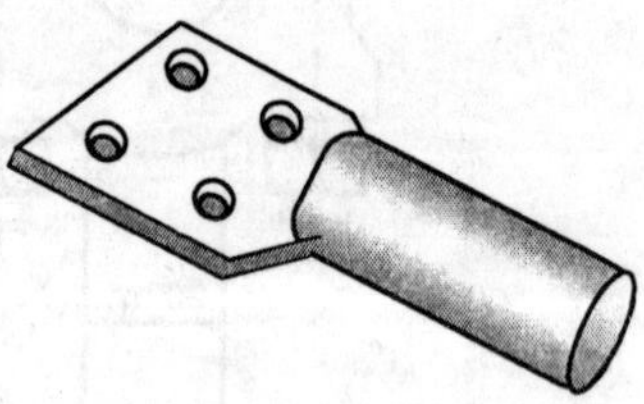

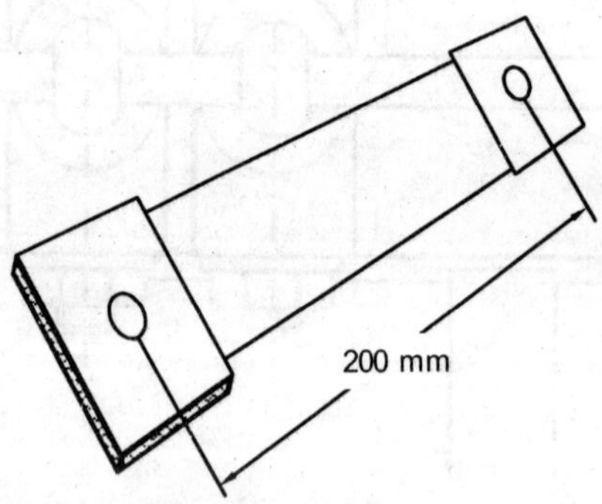

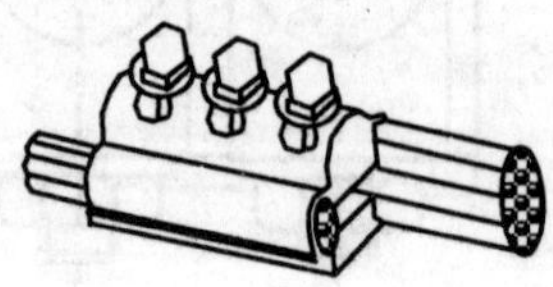

Fig. 4.12 (i): Terminal lug compression type. Fig. 4.12 (j): Flexible earth bond. Fig. 4.12 (k) P.G. Clamp

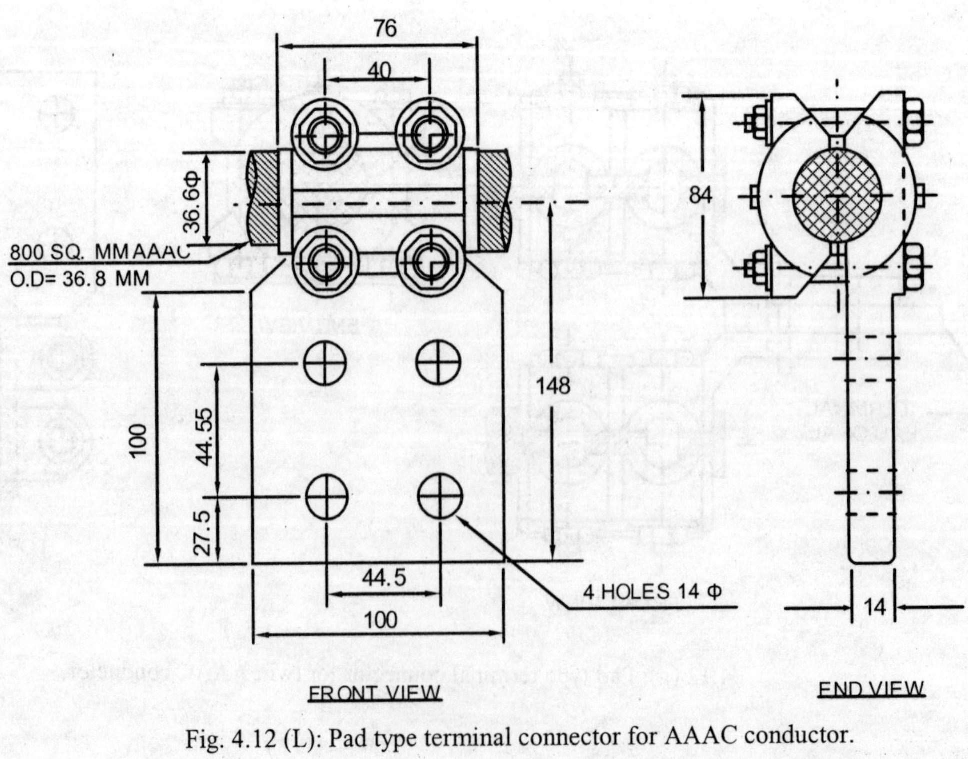

Fig. 4.12 (L): Pad type terminal connector for AAAC conductor.

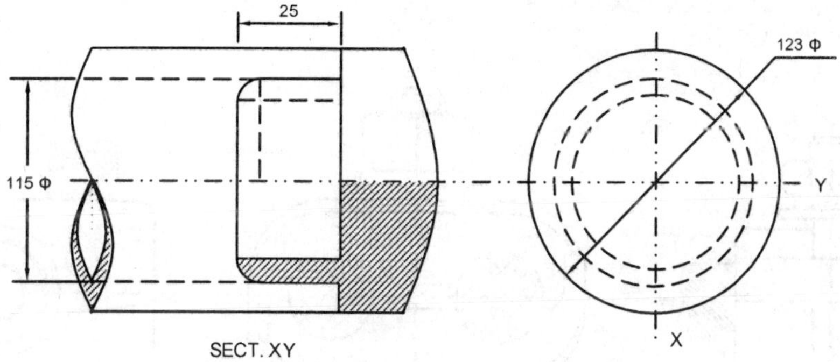

Fig. 4.12 (m): Corona bell for tubular bus.

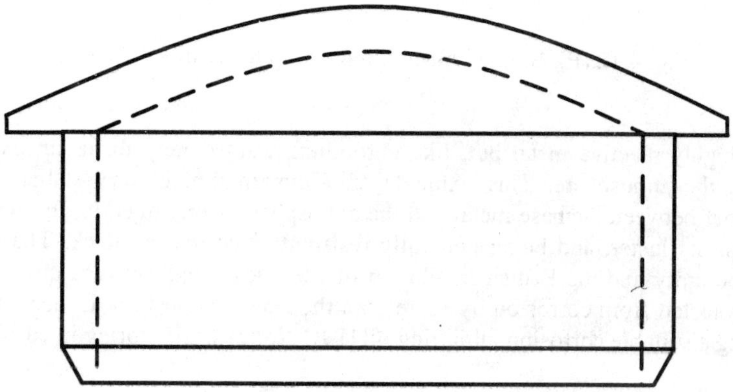

Fig. 4.12 (n): End cap for tubular bus.

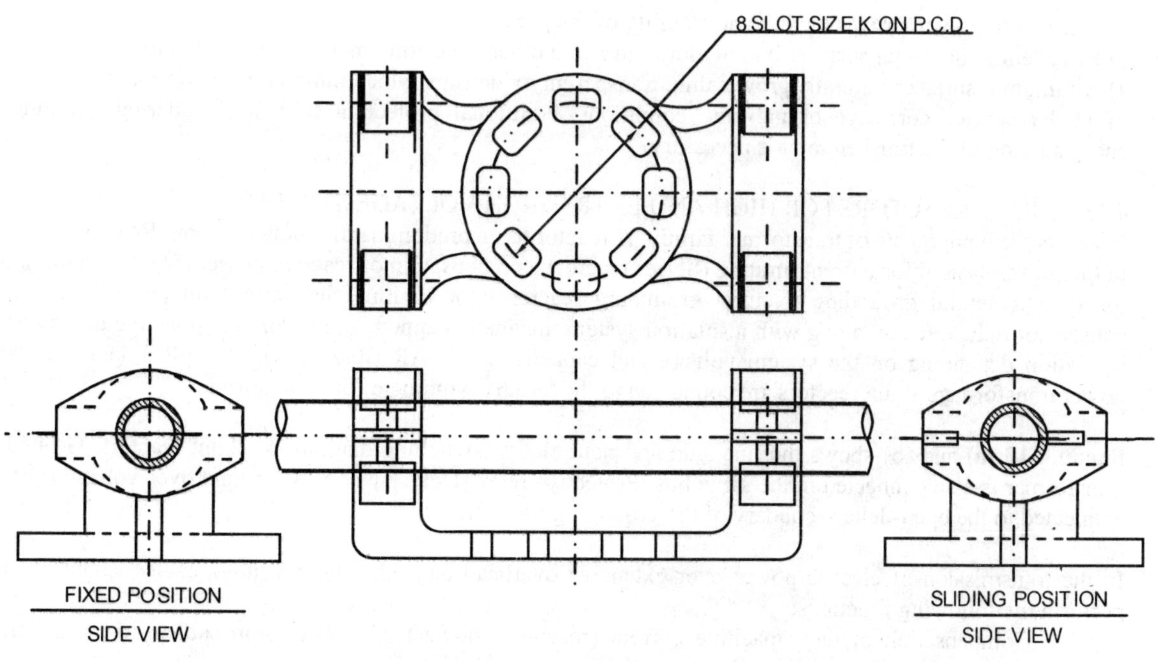

Fig. 4.12 (o): Fixed or sliding type post insulator clamp for mounting tubular bus.

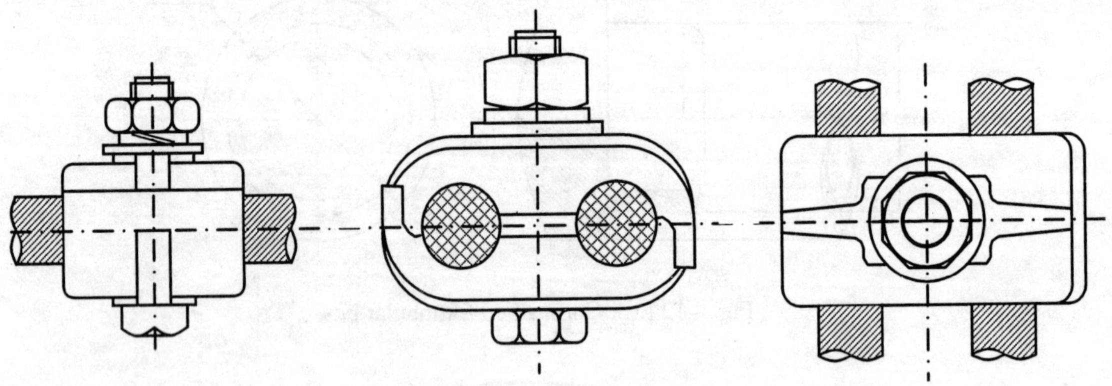

Fig. 4.12 (P): Single bolt-holding clamp for twin AAAC conductor.

Aluminium is a highly reactive metal but, like chromium, immediately forms an oxide layer on its surface when exposed to the atmosphere. This oxide layer, although thin is very stable and acts as a total and impermeable barrier between the base metal and the atmosphere. Consequently, further oxidation is prevented, the metal retaining its luster, and being generally resistant to corrosive attack. The requirements of the US Underwriters Laboratory and the British Institution of Electrical Engineers are quite specific that aluminium connectors, be protected from corrosion by more than their own oxide film. Hence aluminium connectors are protected by, using a suitable corrosion inhibiting oil (EJC No: 2) while storing in corroded atmosphere.

Following are the advantages of using aluminium tubular bus and aluminium connector for open switchyard:

1) Excellent electrical contact can be achieved with bare aluminium surfaces in contact with aluminium connectors.

2) Petroleum jelly improves the life and stability of the joint.

3) Roughening the metal surfaces and of aluminium and other contacting metal improves the joint.

4) Aluminium surfaces naturally grow a thin, transparent oxide film, which inhibits most corrosion.

5) Under service corrosive or galvanic conditions, additional protection such as lacquering, painting or encapsulation of the finished joint is necessary.

4.13 SHUNT REACTORS FOR HIGH AND EXTRA HIGH VOLTAGE SYSTEM.

Reactors are equipments of transformer family. A reactor has a predominantly inductive coil. Reactors are used in the power system for current limiting (Series reactor), compensation of reactive power (Shunt reactors), and for system neutral grounding (Neutral grounding reactors) for limiting the earth fault current. A reactor consists of inductive coil along with insulation system, magnetic gapped core or air core, bushing etc. oil or air insulation depending on the system voltage and capacity in MVAR (Reactive mega-volt amps). For large power transformers shunt reactors are connected to the tertiary winding of the transformer.

Figure 4.13 (a) and (b) shows the line side and neutral side switching diagram of shunt reactors. Grounding transformer is also connected in the same bus. Protective relay (Device No: 59N, ground over-voltage relay) is connected to the open-delta secondary of the grounding transformer.

In the transmission of electric power over extensive overhead and other high voltage cables, shunt reactors perform the following functions:

1. Compensation of the capacitive current (reactance power) of transmission cables, in particular, in networks with low or no load.

2. Reduction of mains-frequency over voltages when a sudden-load-drop or load rejection (no load) occurs.
3. Improvement of the stability and efficiency of energy transmission.

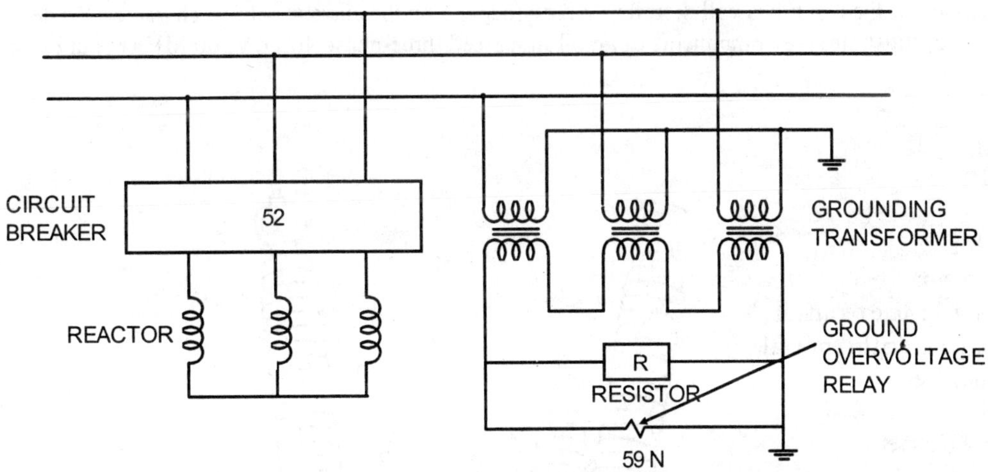

Fig. 4.13 (a): Shunt reactor connection with three pole supply side switching.

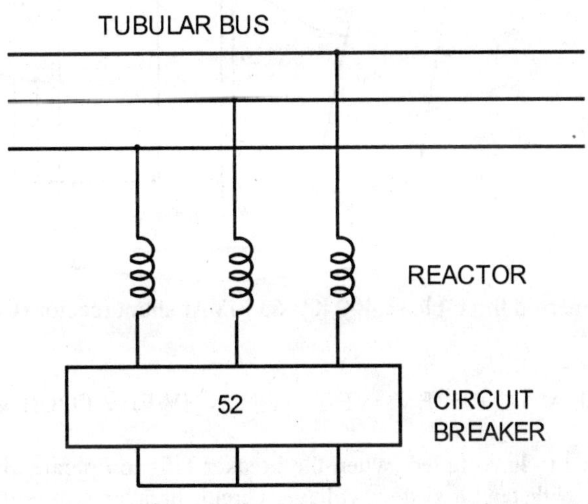

Fig. 4.13 (b): Shunt reactor connection with three-pole neutral side switching.

There are two types of oil-filled shunt reactors:

(1) With iron core divided by an air gap; in which the current voltage characteristic is practically linear only up to 1.2 to 1.3 times the rated voltage. In this type, the air gaps are formed by shims of magnetically neutral material with a very high coefficient of elasticity. Between the air gaps there are iron packages, which are made of transformer laminations glued together in parallel or radial layers. The iron packages on the air gap shims are also glued to one another. The induction in the iron core of the reactors can, as in transformers, be selected as relatively high. Hence high-density magnetic energy occurs in the air gaps. In order to reduce the eddy current losses in the windings and iron packages, which are caused by the quadrature components of magnetic flow occurring in the vicinity of the air gap, the latter must be kept small enough.

(2) Without iron core with external magnetic return; in which the current voltage characteristic is practically linear up to 1.5 to 1.6 times the rated voltage. With this type the magnetic return of induction and density of magnetic energy is consequently low too. Consequently this type has comparatively large dimensions, weights

and losses. However, the windings of these reactors behave well when impulse voltage occurs. Because there is no iron core in the winding, the earth capacitance of the winding, and also the ratio of the earth capacitance to the in-phase capacitance of the winding is very small and the initial distribution is therefore approximately linear.

The application of the two types will therefore largely depend on the current voltage characteristic desired. Figure 4.13 (c) illustrates the components of an oil immersed three-phase 400 KV, 60 MVAr shunt reactor.

LEGEND:
1. Tank
2. Radiator
3. Conservator
4. Bushing for line terminals
5. Bushing for earth terminal
6. Buchholz relay
7. Turret
8. Control cabinet

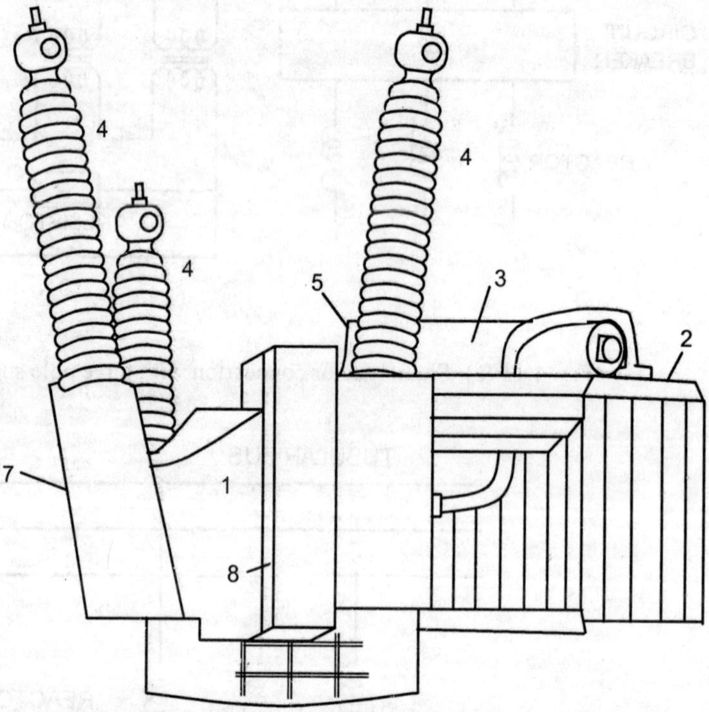

Fig. 4.13 (c): Oil immersed three-phase 400 KV 63 MVAr shunt reactor (Courtesy, Trafo Union).

4.14 CAUSES OF FAILURE AND PREVENTIVE TESTS ON HV/EHV EQUIPMENTS.

(1) Circuit breakers

A circuit breaker is considered to have failed, when the breaker fails to operate after a command is given or unable to interrupt the arc or withstand a system voltage. Circuit breaker failure during a load break or fault trip have resulted in blasting of interrupting chambers, pre-insertion resistor chambers, grading capacitors, tie operating rods etc. Besides above, the failure of breakers could also be attributed due to following reasons:

1. Mechanical failure: Damage of operating lever, shearing of the locking pin of the pull rod, Failure of mechanical coupling between tie rod and operating mechanism, Failure of actuating valve in operating mechanism etc.
2. Interrupter failure: Dielectric failure inside interrupting chamber due to high moisture in SF6 gas (for SF6 circuit breakers) high moisture in oil (for oil circuit breakers). Dielectric failure in air blast circuit breakers due to leakage of compressed air system. Failure due to foreign particles (eye pieces) inside interrupter.
3. Insulation failure: Poor insulation (Phase to earth) due to accumulation of moisture on tie rod during storage.
4. Failure due to high TRV: In case of circuit breakers switching HVDC filter banks, may cause high transient recovery voltage and leading to internal breakdown in grading capacitor or interrupter.
5. Electrical failure: Grading capacitor failure, pre-insertion resistor failure, Trip coil open circuit or short circuit etc.

6. Gasket failure: Gaskets can sometime fail by forming a gas or liquid seal. Care should be taken against unevenly applied greasing of the gasket and positioning of the gasket.
7. SF6 gas leakage: Possible origins and causes for SF6 gas leakage are (a) Corrosion near a seal due to moisture content in SF6 gas; (b) Damage of seal; (c) Impurity under a seal; (d) Porosity of metal component (casting, brazing etc)
8. In air blast circuit breaker, O-rings are used for sealing the static parts. The good quality neoprene rubber O-rings and properly designed grooves for O-rings reduce the chances of air leakage.

Circuit breaker failure could be identified at the incipient stage and corrective actions can be taken accordingly. However following areas are suggested for preventive maintenance: Test equipments are introduced in section 4.19

(a) SF6 gas cylinder to be tested for due point, air content etc as per IEC 376. Hygrometer is used for due point measurement.
(b) Minimum time for PIR (Pre-insertion resistor) contacts open prior to opening of main contacts should be 5milli-seconds. (Refer Question No:13 in section 4.30)
(c) Routine tests shall include measurement of dynamic contact resistance measurement and tan delta measurement of grading capacitor in order to have base values.
(d) Contact travel measurement, closing and tripping timings, trip/close coil current-check etc by using circuit breaker operation analyzer.
(e) SF6 gas leakage, air pressure leakage, hydraulic oil leakage monitoring

(2) Current transformers:
Most of the CTs have failed due to pre-mature aging of insulation. Besides, other probable reasons of failure have been attributed to high system parameters i.e. voltage and frequency, switching over voltages, lightning over voltages. To minimize the failure of CTs following yearly tests are suggested to carryout at site:

1. Measurement of tangent delta and capacitance.
2. Recovery voltage measurement.
3. DGA monitoring, Furan analysis.
4. Dielectric test on insulating / cooling oil.

(3) Potential transformers:
Main reasons for CVT failure are high value of tan delta, abnormal secondary voltage, High value of capacitance, oil leakage, abnormal noise etc. Besides the above following problems may occur:

- Snapping of bellow connection.
- Burning of damping resistor.
- Failure of lightning arrester in the system.
- Failure of CVT capacitor stacks.
- Blackening of insulating/cooling oil in EMU tank.

(4) Metal oxide surge arresters:
Main reasons for failure of surge arresters are premature degradation of ZnO (Zinc oxide) discs. To minimize the failure of lightning arresters, they are monitored for the presence of third harmonic resistive current in the leakage current flowing through surge arresters. Leakage current is indicated in the surge counter and this value should be within the limit of 500 micro-amps.

(5) Disconnect switch and earth switches:
Following are the reasons for failure of isolating / grounding switches:

a) Accumulation of dirt, snow, salt and other foreign particles on the insulator surface.
b) Failure or bypassing interlock may cause accidental operation.
c) Sparking or flashover due to mis-operation.
d) Lacks of attention or periodic maintenance as per manufactures instruction.

(6) Outdoor tubular bus:
Insulation resistances of various segments are to be measured by using 5 KV megger. Minimum acceptable insulation value at the end of one-minute test (between phase to phase and phase to earth) should not be less than 1000 Mega-ohms. Continuity and resistance check to verify the effectiveness of bus joints and terminations. The test shall be carried out at a current of 10 to 20 amps DC by using a digital precision

voltmeter and ammeter. Resistance R = V/I ohms. Periodic tightening of all bolted connections of clamps and connectors to the equipments including straight joints and taping connections in order to avoid spark-over due to loose connection.

4.15 SF6 GAS INSULATED HV AND EHV INDOOR SWITCHGEARS.

GIS compact dimensions and design make it possible to install HV and EHV substations up to 800 KV, right in the middle of load centers of urban or industrial areas and highly polluted areas. Each incoming/outgoing feeder-bay is factory assembled and includes the full compliment of isolating switches / grounding switches, instrument transformers etc. The earthed metal (alluminium alloy) enclosures of GIS assure not only insensitivity to contamination but also safety from electric shock. By using GIS the danger of fire and explosion is eliminated, there is no pollution due to oil leakage, no noise and radio interference. GIS switchgears 66 KV and above are manufactured in conformity with IEC standard 60517. Properties of SF6 gas is demonstrated in Chapter # 3, section 3.9.

Essential requirements for Gas insulated substations:

1. Medium and high voltage switchgears are of three-phase non-magnetic-metal enclosed construction, and extra high voltage switchgears are of single-phase segregated metal enclosed type. Cast aluminium alloy or wrought aluminium alloy are used as enclosures as per CENELEC codes EN 50052 and EN 0064. Minimum safety clearances between live parts to earth and between phases are in accordance with BS 7354. The design of the metal enclosure are such that to minimize losses and heating due to circulating currents and withstand overpressure caused by internal faults corresponding to maximum fault levels for a minimum time of 500milli-seconds. Bursting disc with suitable vents (including indication lamp and alarm) shall be provided, and directed away from operating zones to avoid injury to the personals.
2. Vertical and horizontal access for inspection, maintenance and cleaning of equipment and insulators etc are by using fixed aluminium ladders and/or catwalk structure fitted with handrails.
3. Switchgears are divided up in to separate gas compartments by each bay, by use of gas tight barriers i.e, each bay for the switchgear, which has to be isolated and detain out of service as a result of gas leakage, internal fault or preventive maintenance. Each gas compartment have facilities for routine checking of gas moisture, contact and purity. Position indicators are provided for all circuit breakers, disconnectors and earthing switches to indicate open, closed positions. Labels for identifying the equipments also required.
4. Gas compartments are fitted with connection point for gas filling and gas treatment. Bus bar enclosures are segregated in to gas tight compartment and have facility for quick discharging of gas, vacuum treatment and gas filling. In order to prevent absorption of moisture each gas compartment is fitted with gas filters. Filter element can be replaced without taking the live equipment out of service.
5. Sulphur hexaflouride gas for use in the switchgear has to comply with IEC 376. Low-pressure gas system is employed to minimize leakages and eliminate any possibility of liquefaction of the lowest ambient temperatures. As a rule the minimum dew point temperature in SF6 gas filled equipment should not exceed minus 20°C at the working pressure. Temperature compensated gas density or gas pressure monitors are provided for each gas section. SF6 gas monitors are fitted with alarm and tripping contacts, which operates at the set value.
6. Bus bar connections and enclosures must be suitable for absorbing the effects of thermal expansion and contraction. Switchgear expansion joints are of flexible connections. Connections between switchgear and transformer are capable of withstanding the maximum amplitude and frequency range of vibration emanating from the transformers. A flexible connection is recommended at the coupling point.
7. Earthing of each gas chamber enclosure that are separated by insulation flanges should be interconnected by means of physical earthing strips to reduce the safe touch potential. Main earthing connection to the switchgear consists of minimum 50mm x 6 mm copper strips.
8. Facilities for measurement of circuit breaker contact resistance and closing/opening timing test without removal of covers has to provide.
9. GIS is to be designed in such a way to have minimum EMC (Electromagnetic compatibility) disturbance on both directions (from inside or out side enclosures and vice versa). This is achieved to the insulators, which are surrounded by aluminium ring. All operating mechanisms are sealed inside steel boxes, which give them natural electromagnetic protection.

10. Control and relay cubicles are to be designed for full compliance to all actual EMC requirements such as digital bay controller and digital protection relays in all respect to the good functioning of the equipment. Control and relay cubicles are made of steel sheets, which give them natural electromagnetic protection. Low voltage cables should be shielded types.

Gas Insulated Switchgears:

Figure 4.15 (a) and (b) shows the single line diagram and outlook of two bays of a typical 132 KV GIS having one and-a-half breaker arrangement. The metal enclosures are made of aluminium alloy. Each gas compartment (gas zone) is entirely independent as illustrated in figure (b). Electrical connection to bus bar is automatically achieved when bolting one section to another. Each gas zone is equipped with: terminal for manipulation with gas, pressure vacuum gauge for control and signalization of gas state and safety membrane. SF6 gas leak detectors (gas monitoring and pressure monitoring device) are provided for each gas compartment. Static sealing is applied between two fixed parts, usually the flanges of enclosure. The gaskets are of a round cross-section made of ethylene propylene. The correct selection of duct dimensions towards the gasket, avoids the permanent deformations of gaskets and thus of rapid aging, loss of flexibility and so of the sealing quality. Dynamic sealing is applied on all axis. For the rates of motion up to 5 m/s a simple solution with rings, made of ethylene propylene, having a round cross section, is used For higher rates of motion and high gas pressure, the gaskets of a ring type, made of Polytetrafluorate (PTFE), i.e. Teflon with built-in metal springs, are used.

LEGEND:
QD: Disconnector switch.
QE: Earth switch.
QF: Circuit breaker.
TA: Current transformer
TV: Voltage transformer
W: Cable end box.

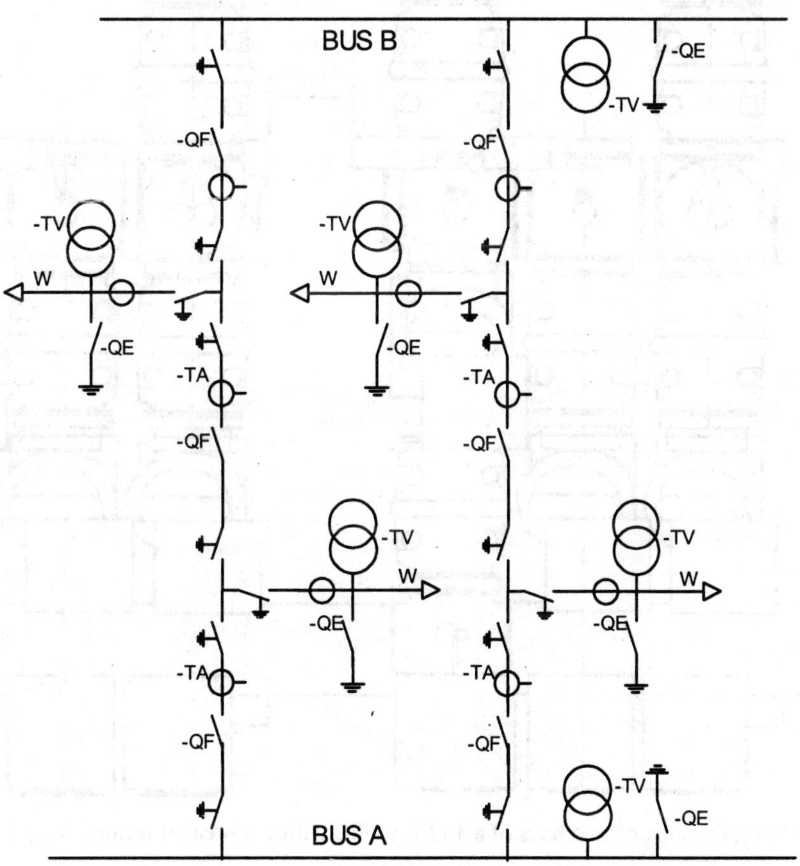

Fig. 4.15 (a): Single line diagram of two bays of a 132 KV GIS with 1½ breaker arrangement (Courtesy, Schneider Electric).

To prevent incorrect switching sequences fail safe design safety interlocks are employed. Mechanical interlocks are key type or padlock type. "Viewing windows" are provided to confirm the correct operation of disconnectors and earth switches. Mechanical devices are provided to indicate whether the switching devices are in open/closed/earthed position. Stored energy spring operated mechanism of the puffer type circuit breaker will indicate the charged/discharged condition of the spring. Current transformers are located at the cable side of the respective breakers. Indoor cable sealing ends are provided for termination of HV cables. Surge arrester and electromagnetic voltage transformers are enclosed with separate enclosures. The apparatus in the switchgear are so designed that there is no need for a special maintenance, even after longer service period. Extension of switchgear can be performed without longer pause of operation of the existing switchgear. An electrical overhead traveling crane is required for erection, replacement or extension.

A metal enclosed local control panel is used for control and indication purposes of each bay with following features: (a) Mimic diagram incorporating position indicators; (b) Annunciation windows with lamp test facilities; (c) Protective relays with test plugs; (d) Measuring instruments; (e) control switches, fuses, miniature circuit breakers, contactors, indicators, push buttons etc. Terminals for terminating control cables for connecting remote control of apparatus, auxiliary switches (NO/NC contacts), SF6 density switches, Voltage and current transformer secondary connection terminals are incorporated in the control cubicles.

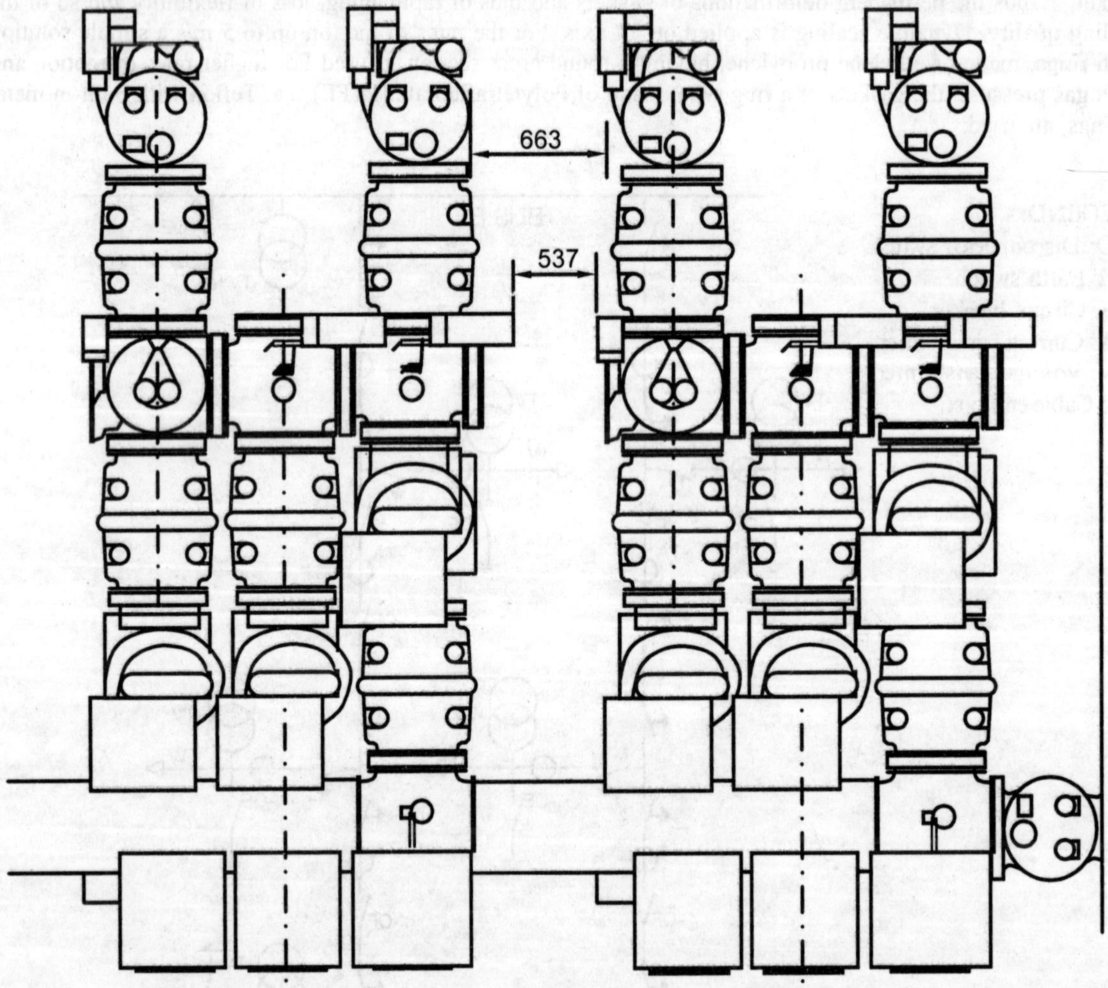

Fig. 4.15 (b): Outlook of two bays of a 132 KV GIS with 1½ breaker arrangement (Courtesy, Schneider Ele).

The majority of SF6 substations are indoor type, but the outdoor type also available. The outdoor execution includes the following special measures:

- Sealed operating mechanism housings;
- Projection of the flanges outside the seals to prevent the entry of moisture and corrosion;

- Rust protection of bolts and supporting structures;
- The use of a special paint for reflection of sun radiation;
- Roof for sun shading if high normal currents are involved;
- The paint may have to be inspected periodically, touched up or renewed.

Figure 4.15 (c) shows the single line diagram of a 420 KV GIS with double bus bar arrangement.
LEGEND:
CB: Circuit breaker; CT: Current transformer; DS: Disconnector; ES: Earth switch; PT: Potential transformer.

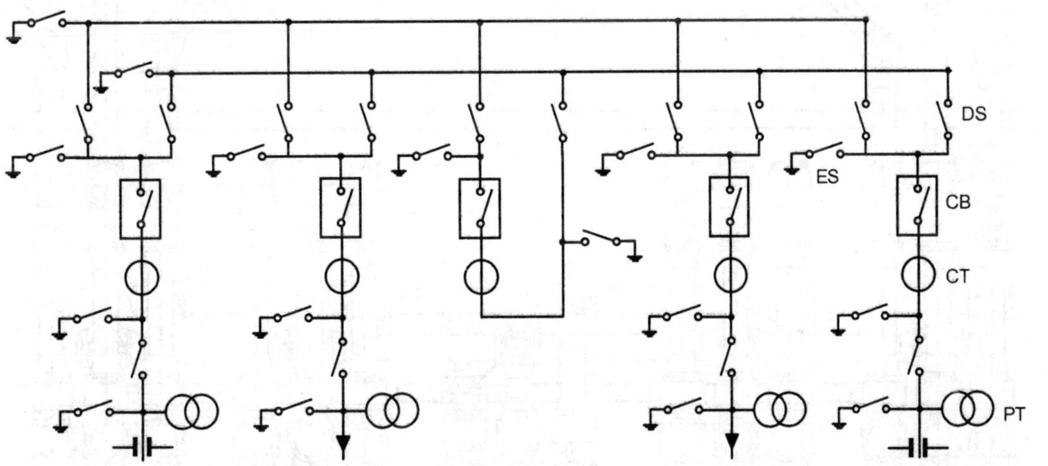

Fig. 4.15 (c): Single line diagram of a 420 KV GIS with double bus bar arrangement (Courtesy, BBC).

When deciding whether the switchgear should be installed indoors or outdoors, it is necessary to consider such aspects as protection against ambient conditions, environmental considerations in a built-up area, reduced costs of maintenance and the advantages of carrying out overhauls indoors, independent of weather conditions, etc. Figure 4.15 (d) illustrates the sectional view of a 420 KV GIS feeder bays with overhead line and cable feeder terminations.

LEGEND:
1. Circuit breaker
2. Disconnector
3. Earthing switch
4. Current transformer
5. Voltage transformer
6. SF6 / Air bushing
7. SF6/oil cable end box
8. Local control cabinet
9. Bus bar

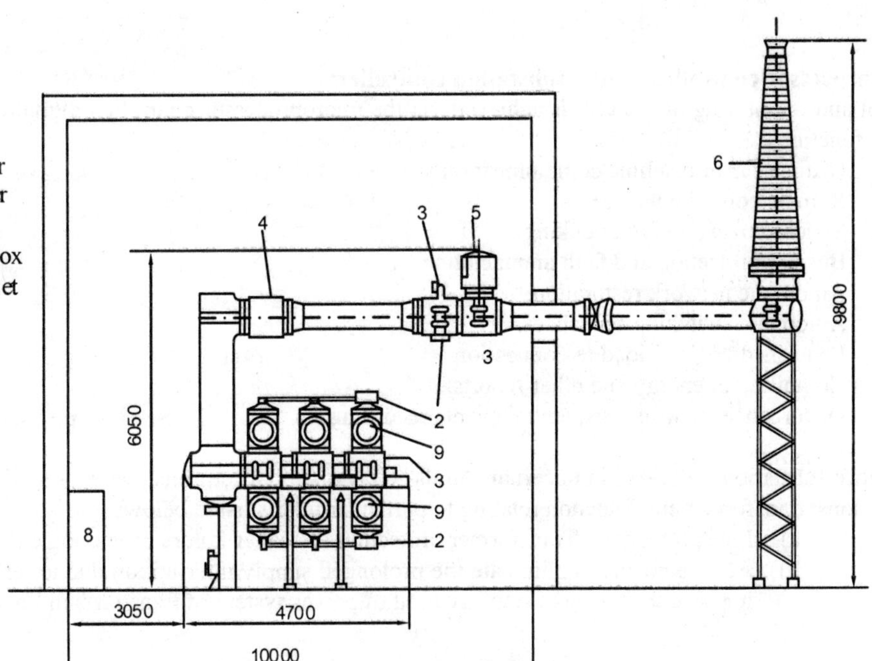

Fig. 4.15 (d): Sectional view of a double bus 420 KV GIS with outdoor bushings (Courtesy, BBC).

Figure 4.15 (e) illustrates the outlook of a double bus bar 420 KV Gas insulated switchgear.
LEGEND: **1: Circuit breaker; 4: Current transformer; 5: Voltage transformer; 6: Bushing; 8: Cabinet; 9: Bus**

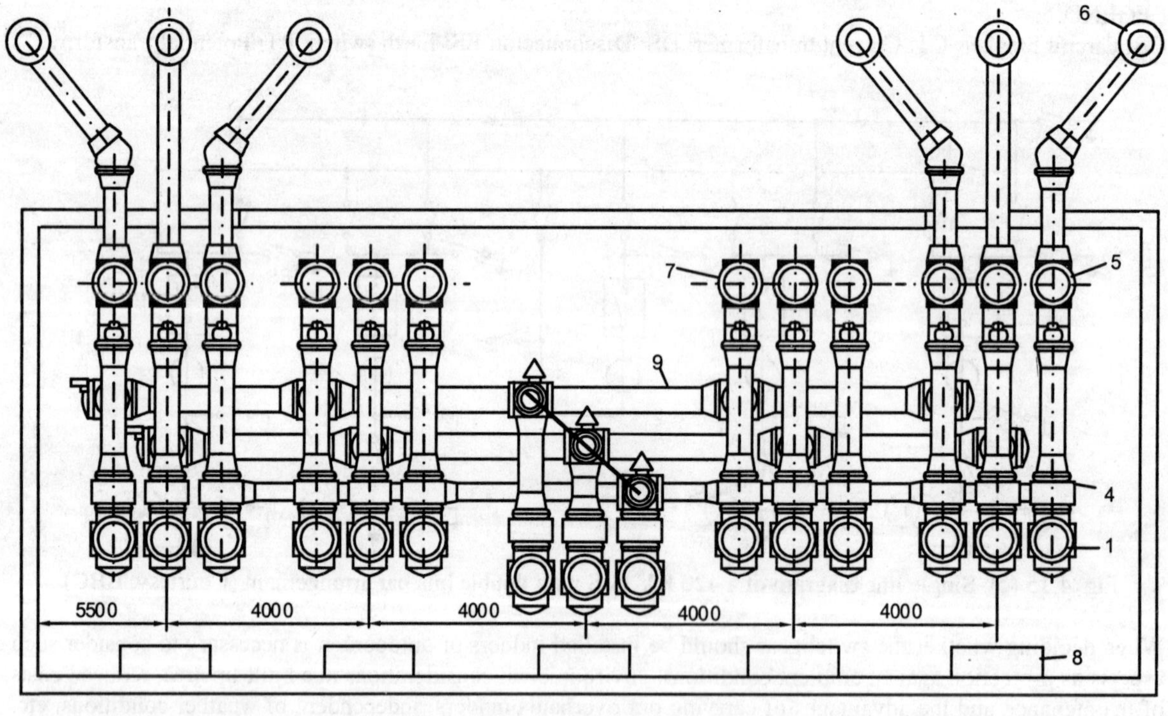

Fig. 4.15 (e): Outlook of a double bus bar 420 KV GIS (Courtesy, BBC Brown Boveri).

Microprocessor controlled digital substation controller:
Control and monitoring of the GIS is achieved via the microprocessor controlled digital controller. Following are the functions:

1. Ordinary man-machine communication system.
2. Remote control interface.
3. Synchronizing and interlocking.
4. Bus bar protection and fault annunciation.
5. Automatic network restoration.
6. Automatic switching sequences.
7. Load shedding and load re-connection.
8. Compiling of energy and other reports.
9. Disturbance recording/sequential events recording.

The entire substation is divided in to certain "units" (Bays) similar to protective zones, which include line, bus bar sections, transformer etc. Function relating to particular unit is listed below:

a) Line protection / Transformer protection / Breaker failure protection etc.
b) Auto-reclosing to eliminate the prolonged supply interruption due to temporary faults and to improve the transient stability limit of power system of transmission lines.

c) Synchronizing check.
d) Energy metering.
e) Acquisition and time logging of events.
f) Acquisition of position indication and measured values.
g) Execution of commands from substation level computer.
h) Back-up control.
i) Fault detection, minimize damage, disconnect faulty line.

4.16 HV AND EHV APPARATUS INSTALLED INTEGRAL TO GIS.

SF6 Switchgears (GIS), like any other switchgear, incorporates all elements necessary for switchgear designs such as circuit breaker, disconnector, earth switches, CT, PT, etc.

(1) Circuit breakers for GIS

High voltage circuit breakers are designed with one interrupter per pole and extra high voltage breakers minimum 3 interrupters per pole. The operating mechanism is of electro-pneumatic type, (one per pole or one for all the 3 poles) built-in for high voltage applications. One operating mechanism per pole is exclusively built-in for extra high voltage applications. The circuit breaker is of an auto-pneumatic puffer type, i.e. there is a piston, which provides necessary pressure of SF6 gas during tripping operation in each interrupter. Good qualities of this gas enable the realization of circuit breaker with the least number of interrupters. Figure 4.16 (a) illustrates one pole of an extra high voltage GIS circuit breaker.

LEGEND:
1. Interrupter
2. Terminal
3. Enclosure
4. Voltage stress shield
5. Grading capacitor
6. Operating rod
7. Support insulator
8. Hydraulic operating mechanism

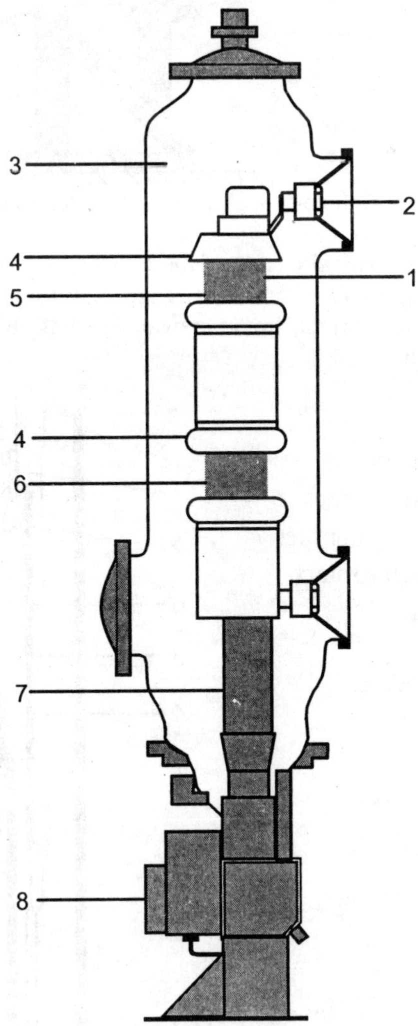

Fig. 4.16 (a): One pole of an EHV GIS circuit breaker with two interrupters (Courtesy, BBC Brown Boveri)

GIS circuit breaker unit comprises three metal-clad breaker poles. Each pole consists of the operating mechanism, the interrupter column and the enclosure with the basic supporting structure. Depending on the rated voltage and breaking current, the breaker column is provided with one or more interrupters. Capacitors in parallel with the contact gaps assure an even distribution of the voltage in multi-interrupter breakers. All interrupters inside the same enclosure are mechanically interconnected and are therefore operated simultaneously.

In extra high and extra high voltage networks, closing on to overhead transmission lines on no-load causes transient over-voltages. These over-voltages can be limited to a permissible level by closing resistors. The resistors are accommodated in a separate unit as shown in Figure 4.16 (b). The lead-time of the resistor contact is assured by hydraulic coupling with the operating mechanism of the circuit breaker.

LEGEND:
1. Interrupter
2. Closing resistor
3. Contact ofresistor unit
4. Hydraulic coupling

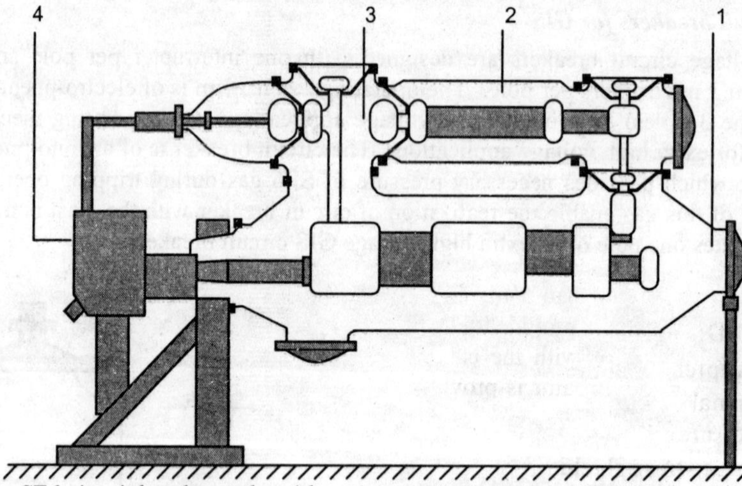

Fig. 4.16 (b): Extra high voltage SF6 circuit breaker pole with resistor unit (Courtesy, BBC Brown Boveri).

The compact symmetrical design of the GIS breaker interrupting chambers is illustrated in Figure 4.16 (c). Main and arcing contacts are so arrange that to protect the main contact from burning. Arcing after commutation of the current, from the main contacts always take place in the arc-extinguishing zone between the arcing contacts.

LEGEND:
1. Fixed main contact
2. Fixed arcing contact
3. Moving arcing contact
4. Moving main contact
5. Blast nozzle
6. Insulator
7. Metal enclosure

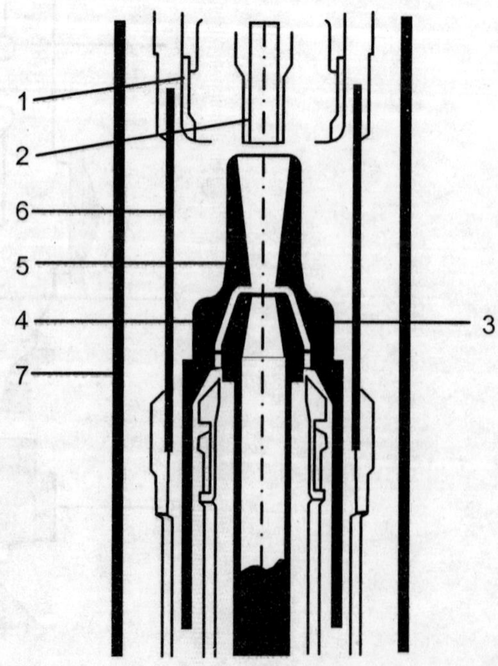

Fig. 4.16 (c): Cut away view of an EHV single pressure puffer type interrupter (courtesy, BBC Brown Boveri).

Operating mechanism: The operating system consists of the following components:-

(a) Operating unit with operating cylinder, control valves, high-pressure accumulator and low-pressure reservoir.
(b) High-pressure pump, motor-operated and emergency manual pump.
(c) Filter, monitoring and control circuits.
(d) Auxiliary switches.

Single-interrupter breakers are provided with a single-pole or three-pole operating mechanism. Circuit breakers with several interrupters per pole are equipped with a separate operating mechanism for each pole. Circuit breakers are equipped with an operation counter to record the number of operations. Circuit breakers are capable of:

(a) Out of phase switching
(b) Auto-reclosing duty cycle
(c) Switching of capacitive currents and magnetizing currents without generating transient over voltage.
(d) Transmission line breakers are for single pole and/or triple pole operation and reclosing the specified number of times with the dead times specified.

Circuit breakers operating mechanisms (Spring or hydraulic type) are fitted with two trip coils either for independent or for simultaneous operation. Anti-pumping relays are provided to prevent reclosing if the closing coil remains energized and the circuit breaker fails to latch in the closed position or is tripped during the process of closing (trip free operation). In the event of any one phase failing to complete a closing or tripping operation, the breaker will automatically trip open and alarm will be initiated. Permissible pole discrimination is less than 5 ms on closing and less than 10 ms on reclosing. For non-electrical tripping a shrouded pushbutton is provided. Facilities for manual slow closing and slow opening of the circuit breaker for maintenance purpose (with the cubicles closed) is incorporated in the operating mechanism. Mechanically operated ON/OFF indicator is provided. Mechanisms capable of storing energy for 2 operations are operated by DC control power.

(2) Disconnect switch / Isolators for GIS

There are two main designs of isolators: (1) Angular isolator has the connections under angle of 90°; (2) Line isolator has the connections in one plane. Both are in one isolating distance. Disconnector is able to switch charging currents and closed loop currents (bus bar changeovers). Operating mechanism of all types of the isolators is of three-pole electromotor type with a possibility of manual operation. The isolators are equipped with a position indicator indicating the service condition. Isolators comply with IEC 129, IEC 265 and IEC 517 with pad locking facility. Mechanical and electrical interlocking facility with associated circuit breakers and earthing switches are provided. Automatic means are provided for electrically, isolating the faulty disconnector in the event of gas leakage in the disconnector chamber. The sectional view of one pole of a switch disconnector is shown in Figure 4.16 (d), which employs puffer principle for arc extinction.

LEGEND:
1. Enclosure
2. Moving contact
3. Operating rod
4. Crank drive
5. Operating mechanism
6. Compression piston
7. Interrupter
8. Fixed contact

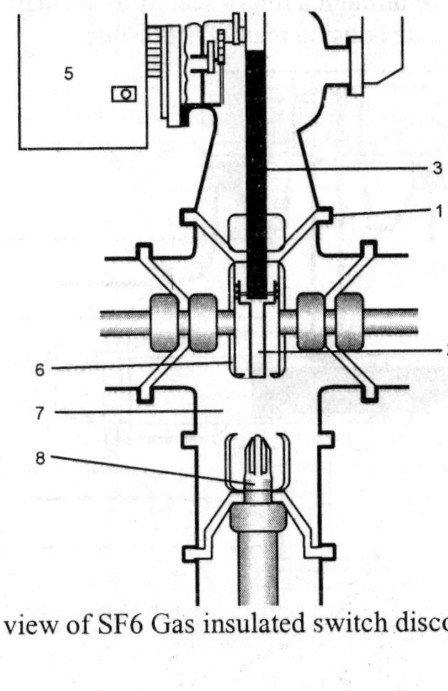

Fig. 4.16 (d): Sectional view of SF6 Gas insulated switch disconnector (Courtesy, BBC Brown Boveri)

The switch disconnector in Figure (d) is equipped with a spring-operated mechanism with charging motor (5). The moving contact (2), which is permanently linked with the operating rod, is opened and closed via a crank-drive (4). Each pole has its own spring-operated mechanism in which sufficient energy for two operations can be stored. When opening, the piston (6) generates the gas blast required for extinction of the arc. Separate arcing contacts prevent the load current path from being affected by the switching arc. The gas blast immediately cools the gap between contacts. The switch disconnector can be installed in Tee-off version or L version with or without earth switch. Viewing glass is provided for checking the position and wear of the contacts.

LEGEND:
1. Enclosure
2. Barrier insulator
3. Fixed contact
4. Shield for fixed contact
5. Moving contact
6. Spindle drive
7. Contact support
8. Insulated drive shaft
9. Driving motor

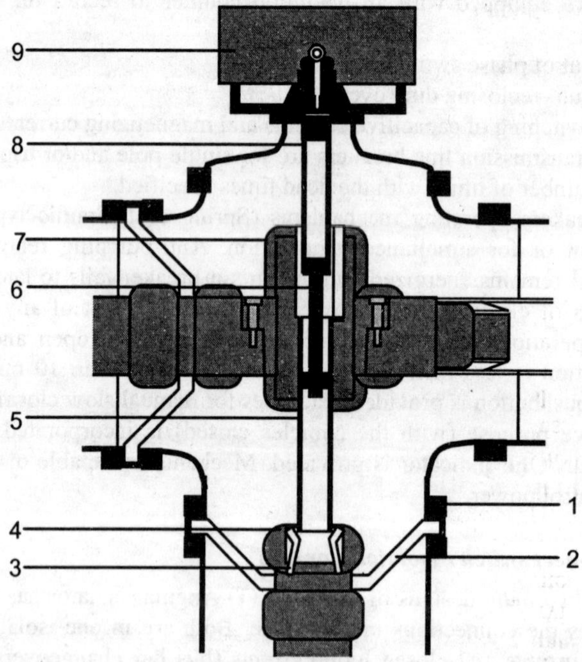

Fig. 4.16 (e): SF6 Gas insulated Tee-off disconnect switch (Courtesy, BBC Brown Boveri)

Disconnectors are available either as Tee-off disconnect or as an inline disconnect as shown in Figure 4.16 (e) and (f) respectively. The Tee-off disconnect integrated in the bus bars, greatly simplifies the layout of the installation. The active part consists of the fixed contact with contact fingers and the contact support carrying the tubular moving contact. Shielding for fixed contact assures an even distribution of the electric field. The moving contact is operated from a motor gear drive through a rotary seal by an insulated shaft. The motor drive is mounted outside the gas compartment in a separate housing readily accessible.

LEGEND:
1. Enclosure
2. Barrier insulator
3. Fixed contact
4. Shielding for fixed contact
5. Moving contact
6. Rack-and-pinion drive
7. Contact support
8. Insulated drive shaft
9. Driving motor

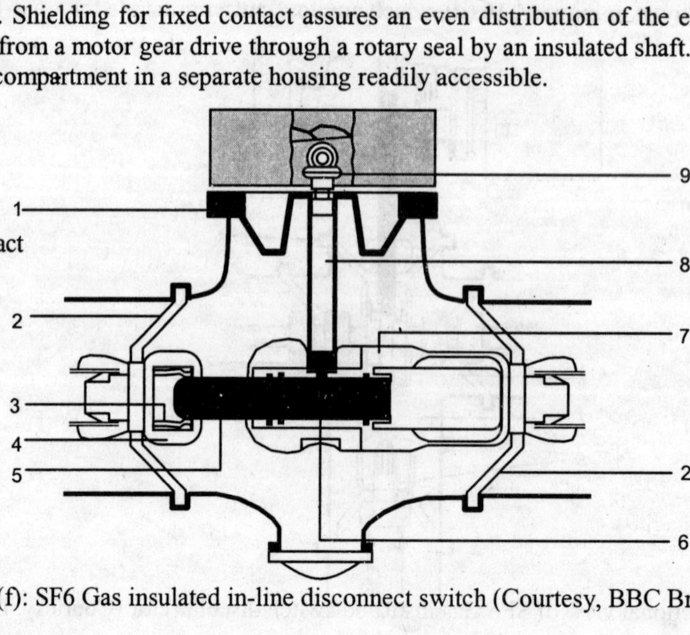

Fig. 4.16 (f): SF6 Gas insulated in-line disconnect switch (Courtesy, BBC Brown Boveri).

(3) Maintenance earth switch and high- speed earth switch

Upon normal and special interventions there is no possibility of provisory earthing in metal enclosed GIS. For that reason all-important groups of apparatus are permanently equipped with earthing switch. The earthing switch is used in order to earth the apparatus, from both sides, on which the operation are carried out especially for protection of personnel during maintenance and overhaul or erection, and in order to discharge static electricity that exists in the apparatus separated from the system. Service earth switches are equipped with electromotor operating mechanism with a possibility of manual operation.

High-speed earthing switches are installed in to switchgear at the places where dead state cannot be determined with a certainty or for earthing higher capacitance overhead feeder lines or underground cable feeders. High-speed earthing switches are so designed that it can be connected at rated voltage withstanding short circuit current without damages. For high voltage system one electromotor-operated mechanism is used for all the three poles. Earthing switches are mechanically and electrically interlocked with associated disconnectors and circuit breakers to prevent closing the earth switch on to a live circuit or to make the circuit alive when the earthing switch is closed. Provision for direct visual verification of the earthing switch ON/OFF position and pad locking is provided. To check whether a point to be earthed really is dead, the earthing switch is provided with a capacitive tap for connecting a voltage test devices, this will reduces the risk for closing on to a live conductor. Section of an earthing switch on a Tee unit is shown in Figure 4.16 (g).

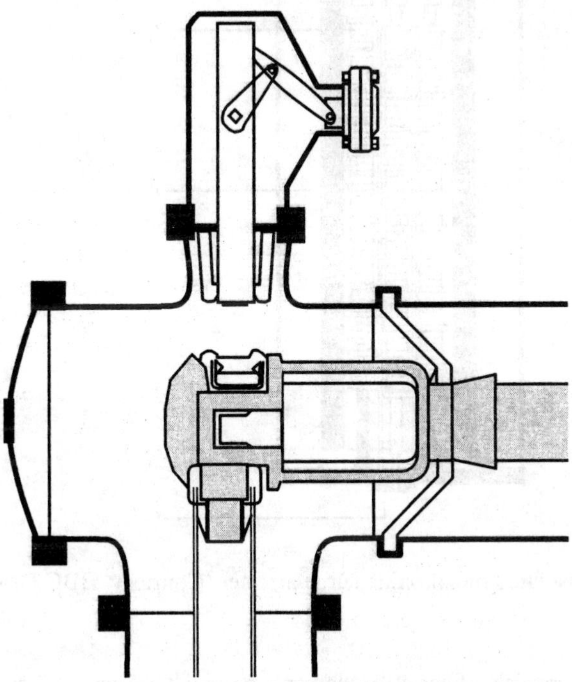

Fig. 4.16 (g): SF6 Gas insulated earthing switch on a Tee bus (Courtesy BBC Brown Boveri).

(4) Surge arrester

Surge arresters of the metal oxide SF6 gas insulated types are employed to protect the GIS equipments against switching and lightning surge voltages. Surge arresters are provided with operation counter, gas pressure monitors, shielding for voltage distribution control, pressure devices, insulated earthing terminal, gas filling and drain valve etc. Surge arresters are of high thermal capacity, capable of withstanding the maximum power frequency operating voltages due to continuous and temporary over-voltage conditions. For incorporation in SF6 switchgear, two types of surge arresters are recommended:

(1) Arresters with magnetically blown spark gap, and non-linear silicon carbide resistors in series;

(2) Arresters with metal oxide resistors (without spark gaps). The protective characteristic is similar for both types of arresters. In the case of high energy switching surges, arresters with metal oxide resisters are preferred

as they have a high- energy absorption capability. The cut away view of a SF6 gas insulated metal oxide arrester designed for use in GIS unit is illustrated in Figure 4.16 (h). The active part consists of series resistors, arranged in three double columns. A cylinder with capacitive grading surrounds the resistors and ensures an even voltage distribution over the columns. The active part is mounted concentrically in the metal enclosure and insulated with SF6 gas.

LEGEND:

1. High voltage connection
2. Metal enclosure
3. Metal oxide resistors
4. Grading cylinder
5. Earth terminal

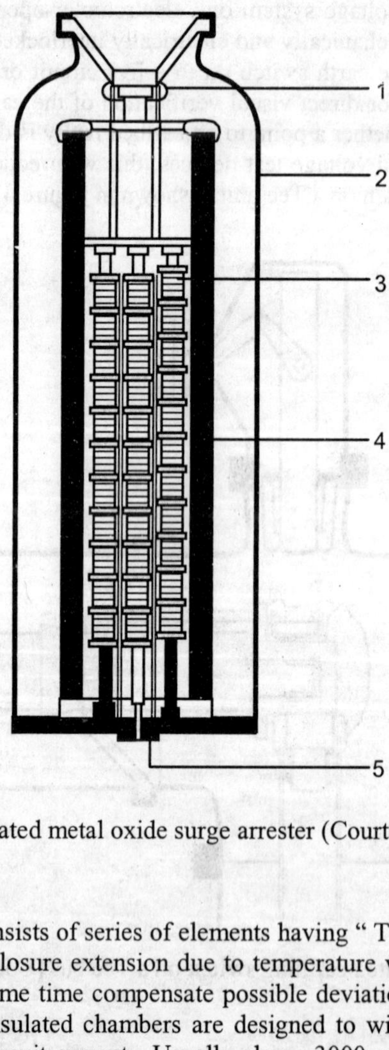

Fig. 4.16 (h): SF6 gas insulated metal oxide surge arrester (Courtesy, BBC Brown Boveri).

(5) Bus bars

Bus bars up to 3000 amps rating consists of series of elements having " T " or " I " or " C " shape. In order to neutralize the forces, caused by enclosure extension due to temperature variation, bus bars are equipped with axial compensators, which at the same time compensate possible deviations during production. Either copper or aluminium bus bars, with gas-insulated chambers are designed to withstand required rated current, short time current and 3 seconds short circuit current. Usually above 3000 amps rating, phase segregated tubular aluminium are used. The tubular conductors are supported at each end by an insulator. The conductors are plugged to silver-plated finger contacts on the supporting insulator. These sliding contacts permit the tubular conductors to expand axially on a temperature rise, without imposing any mechanical stresses on the supporting insulators. The enclosure consists of welded aluminium sheet to which flange portions of cast aluminium are welded. Longitudinal expansion is taken-up by metal bellow compensators. The enclosure is dimensioned to the full return current. Compensators are bypassed by, copper straps. The bus bars are sectionalized by, barrier insulators in to separate gas compartments in accordance with the functional and operational requirements. For interconnecting the individual switchgear compartments, for changes in direction, elongations and branching off, the design, with enclosure, tubular conductor and barrier or supporting insulator with integrated conductor connecting plate is used.

(6) Current Transformers

CTs installed in GIS is of a bus type. Bus conductor in the switchgear serves as a primary winding while secondary winding is formed on ring magnetic cores. It can be equipped with several protection and metering cores with necessary characteristics. Current transformers conforming to IEC 185 and IEC 60044 are being used. Facilities are to be provided for primary injection whether CTs are installed inside or outside the SF6 filled chambers or cable termination chamber. The metal clad current transformers with ring core are located in the switchgear in accordance with the protection and metering requirements. The base flange and core carrier surround the primary conductor carried by support insulators as shown in Figure 4.16 (i). The ring cores, impregnated with moulded resin, are protected against external influences by a metal cover. A terminal box mounted on the cover contains the secondary connections.

LEGEND:
1. Base flange
2. Terminal box
3. Cores
4. core carrier
5. H.V. Conductor
6. Enclosure
7. Insulation

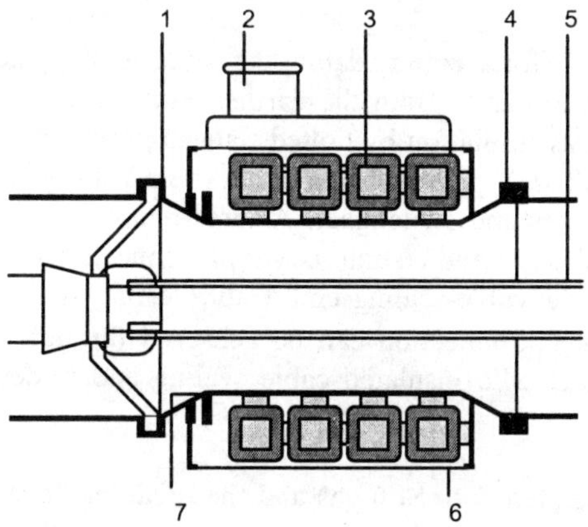

Fig. 4.16 (i): Current transformer installation in gas insulated switchgear (Courtesy, BBC Brown Boveri).

(7) Voltage transformers

Voltage transformer for use in high voltage switchgear (GIS) is of inductive type conforming to IEC 186. Main insulation being SF6 gas, synthetic foils impregnated with SF6 gas are used as inter-turn insulation. VTs are made with two secondary windings for protection and metering and one tertiary winding for earth fault protection. Figure 4.16 (j) illustrates a single-phase inductive type voltage transformer designed for GIS. They are connected to the switchgear with the standardized connecting flange via a barrier insulator. The primary winding is insulated with SF6 gas and connected to the HV terminal (7) by a flexible connection. The primary winding (5) surrounds the core on which the secondary windings (4) are also wound. The connection between the secondary winding and the terminals in the external terminal box is made through a gas tight multiple bushing.

LEGEND:
1. Enclosure
2. Cover with pressure release disc
3. Core
4. Secondary winding
5. Primary winding
6. High voltage shielding
7. High voltage connection
8. Barrier insulator

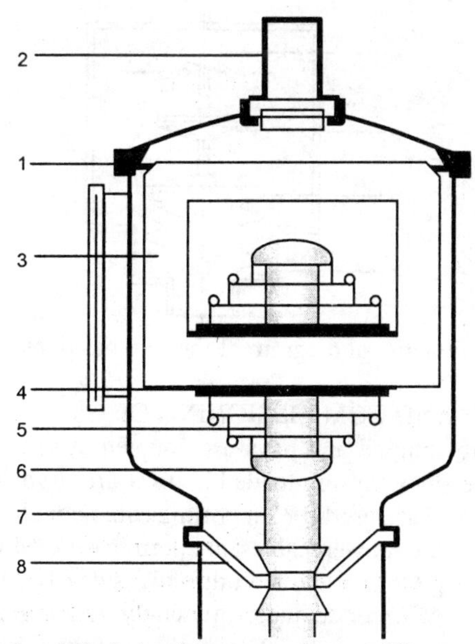

Fig. 4.16 (J): Gas insulated metal clad voltage transformer (Courtesy BBC Brown Boveri)

Capacitive voltage transformers are always employed in extra high voltage switchgears. Two systems are available:

(a) Transformers with high capacitance connected to an intermediate transformer. The oil-insulated capacitor of conventional design is accommodated in an enclosure filled with SF6 gas. The high voltage connection to the GIS is made through a barrier insulator. The low voltage choke and the intermediate voltage transformer are housed separately in a cabinet on the earth potential side.

(b) Transformers with a low capacitance accommodated in the current transformer or in a separate housing, connected to an electronic power amplifier.

(8) Cable sealing chambers

The metal enclosed cable sealing end chamber, (for accommodating the cable-sealing ends), which are suitable for termination of single core HV/EHV power cable. Both the earthed and high voltage ends of the cable sealing ends are adequately sealed off. SF6 gas insulation by bolted flanges provided with multiple rings and gaskets to prevent SF6 gas penetration in to the HV power cables. Each cable sealing end chamber has testing flanges for HV withstand testing of main cables and switchgear. A three-phase set of test bushings together with plug-in connections are provided for HV withstand testing. Dry type connections according to IEC 60859 are used for terminating HV/EHV cables to the cable-sealing end. Cable testing shall be in accordance with IEC 60859 standard i.e 24 hours Un/√3 volts. Connection can be achieved through SF6 bus ducts having expansion joint, by assembling flange on GIS. SF6 insulated cable sealing end is depicted in figure (c) of section 4.10.

(9) SF6 gas density monitors:

The dielectric strength of the switchgear insulated with SF6 gas and the breaking capacity of the SF6 circuit breaker depend on the density of the gas. Since the pressure varies with temperature, it is the gas density, which is monitored. For this, a density monitor is employed. Figure 4.16 (k) shows the schematic arrangement of a density monitor. The gas pressure acts on metal bellows (2), the movement of which is transferred to a bimetal plate (3) for compensation of the temperature. In the event of gas leakage a micro-switch (4) is actuated. The gas compartments separated by barrior insulators are each monitored by their own density monitor. They are fitted with non-return valve connectors for mounting density monitors, evacuation and for filling gas from a mobile storage container.

LEGEND:

1. Enclosure
2. Metal bellows
3. Bimetal plate
4. Micro-switch

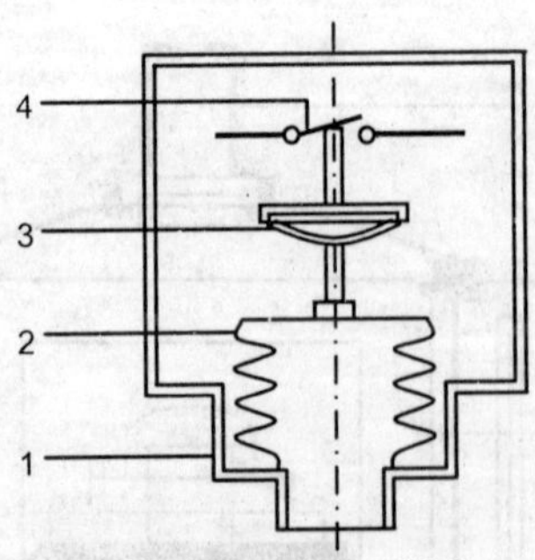

Fig. 4.16 (k): Functional diagram of the SF6 gas density monitor.

4.17 INSTALLATION, TESTING AND COMMISSIONING OF GIS.

Factory assembled bays of GIS are shipped and bays are coupled at site. GIS is installed on 'U' type steel channels embedded in the concrete floor. Spring-loaded T bolts are used for fastening the switchgear to the channel. Separate supporting structures are used for supporting cable box, bus duct and other heavy parts. After assembling and alignment, control and power cables are terminated. Minimum clearance of 1500 mm is required in the front, cable box side 1000 mm and the other two sides 1200 mm. Terminal pads are located at several points of the GIS structure in order to meet the safety requirements in accordance with IEEE 80 standard concerning the grounding and safety rules. The earthing of the GIS shall be made through copper bus bars running along or below the GIS. In order to achieve the interlocking functions, protection relays, control switches instruments and AC/DC supply, control cables are laid between GIS and control and relay panels. SF6 gas containers are provided to fill the gas before commissioning.

Tests on GIS (Test equipments are introduced in section 4.19)

Factory routine tests are performed on each completed bays as per recommendation of IEC 60694. After erection following tests are being performed:

(1) Insulation resistance test of the completed unit;
(2) Measurement of the resistance of the main circuit;
(3) Tightness test of each compartment sealed at site;
(4) Function test of all equipments to confirm the operation;
(5) Primary and secondary injection tests on protection relays and verification of relay settings;
(6) Checks and verifications of the interlocking between bays when control and monitoring functions are achieved in the local control cubicle;
(7) Checks and verification of the gas supervision system;
(8) High voltage dielectric tests as per procedure/recommendation of IEC 60517;
(9) DC voltage High-pressure test on HV/EHV XLPE cables;
(10) Tests on SF6 gas (a) Condensation temperature; (b) Oxygen content (below 1% by volume); (c) The acidity and hydrolysable fluoride content; (d) Verification of gas pressure in each bay (3 kg/cm^2).

Test voltages to be applied to GIS are given in Table 4.17 (1). Tests to be conducted are:

(a) BIL (Rated lightning impulse withstand voltage);
(b) SIL (Rated switching impulse withstand voltage);
(c) Power-frequency withstand voltage.

Impulse withstand test set is described in figure 2.20 (c) of Chapter # 2. Similarly, power frequency with stand test set is shown in figure (f) of section 4.19.

Table 4.17 (1): High voltage test on gas insulated EHV switchgears

Rated system voltage (Umax)	Rated power frequency with stand voltage (One minute)	Rated lightning impulse withstand voltage (Peak value)		Rated switching impulse withstand voltage (Peak value)		Combined voltage test value
KV	KV	Phase-to Earth: KV	Across the contact gap	Phase-to Earth: KV	Across the contact gap	KV
300	460	950	950 (170)	750	650	700 (245)
362	500	1050	1050 (205)	850	950	800 (295)
420	680	1300	1300 (240)	950	1050	900 (345)
525	740	1425	1425 (300)	1050	1175	900 (430)
765	960	1800	1800 (435)	1300	1550	1100 (625)

Note: The values in bracket correspond to the peak value of the AC voltage in KV at the opposite terminal.

SF6 insulated, metal enclosed HV switchgear is much more compact than conventional switchgear which makes use of air as the insulating medium. The clearance required is only 5 to 10% of the value required for outdoor switchgears. This is due to the fact that the dielectric strength of sulphur hexaflouride (SF6) at a pressure of one bar is approximately 2.5 times that of air at the same pressure. In metal clad GIS, SF6 is under a pressure of 2 to 6 bar. This increases the dielectric strength. The dielectric strength must then, be proved by AC, lightning impulse and switching impulse voltage and/or a combination of these voltages. The most complicated test is the combined voltage test. Its purpose is to prove that a flashover does not occur across the open contact gap even with the rated peak impulse voltage being applied to one terminal and the normal operating voltage being applied to the second terminal (-180° out of phase). The voltage across the contact gap is then the sum of the two individual voltages.

Testing cast resin insulators: The test specification lays down that no measurable partial discharge should occur at 1.1 Umax. (Corresponding to approximately twice the phase to earth voltage), is far above the IEC recommendation which, for example, permits a partial discharge rate of up to 20 pC at 1.1 Umax / √3 for cast resin insulators. During the test, the mounting of the insulator corresponds to the type of mounting in the final assembly. The SF6 gas pressure is also adjusted to the same value as the operating pressure in the final equipment.

Testing of modular assemblies: A high voltage test is the last operation carried out on a completed modular assembly in the factory. The SF6 pressure is adjusted to the minimum operating pressure and a test voltage applied as recommended by IEC. [Refer table 4.17 (1)]

Site test on completely assembled switchgear: A further quality control measure is a megger test (by using a 5/10 KV megger) as well as high voltage test (One minute power frequency withstand voltage) at site after final assembly to verify damages to components or the presence of any foreign particles in the switchgear, which could give rise to a fault during operation. The test on the complete GIS substation assembly is carried out on each phase, the other phases being earthed. Thus, in a three-phase totally enclosed system, the insulation between phases also cover under the test. In general, only 80% of the rated withstand voltage given in the GIS nameplate is a applied during the tests.

4.18 SF6 INSULATED HV AND EHV TRANSMISSION BUS-DUCTS.

SF6 insulated bus-duct has many applications beyond its use in GIS installations. Few major applications are substation optimization, line crossing, underground services, tunnel, environment solutions etc. The basic system consists of three parallel isolated phases of coaxial transmission line. Each phase consists of a grounded aluminium alloy tube, which encloses a concentric tubular aluminium alloy conductor. The inner conductor is supported within the outer enclosure by solid dielectric insulators. The interior of the bus is filled with SF6 gas to provide electrical insulation between the inner tubular conductor and outer enclosure. The various components of the bus assembly including straight sections, elbows, tees and crosses are factory assembled (Figure 4.18) in shipping units up to 60 feet (18M) long sections. Each section is shipped with dry nitrogen at 5 PSI (35KPag) to keep the interior of the bus clean and dry.

In the field, center conductors are joined together using plug-in contacts. The outer enclosure is either welded or bolted together using flanges with double O-ring seals. The joints are then leak checked after complete assembly. Supports are provided at every one, metre interval. In the case of underground installation a coating of corrosion protection material is applied. After filling SF6 gas at the required pressure the bus can be energized. The support insulator may be either a Tripost or a conical epoxy insulator. These insulators are attached to the conductor and are allowed to move within the enclosure to compensate the thermal expansion. HM type finger contacts are used throughout the system to provide a low resistance and compact current transfer path. Technical particulars of SF6 insulted bus ducts are given in Table 4.18 (1).

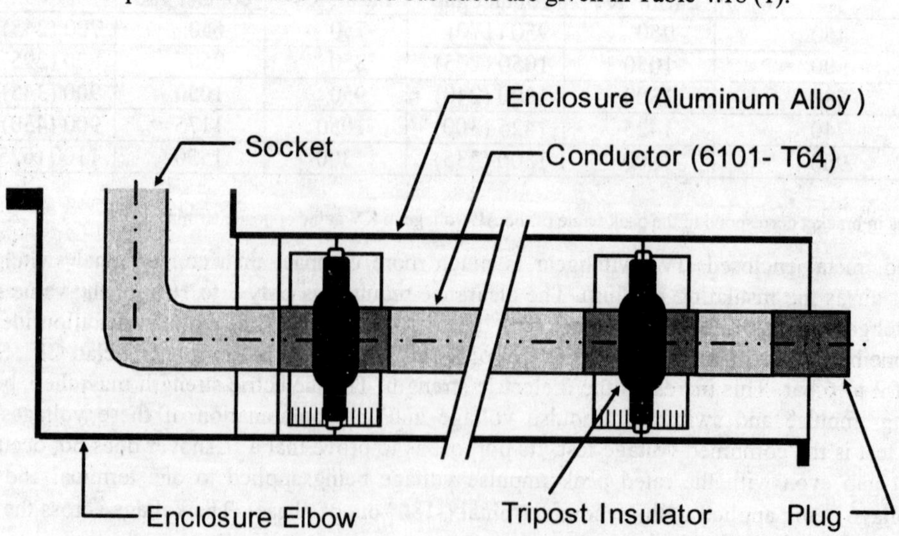

Fig. 4.18: SF6 insulated phase segregated HV/EHV bus duct.

Table 4.18 (1): Characteristics of various voltage classes of bus-ducts.

Voltage class	Unit	121/145kv	169kv	242kv	300kv	362kv	440kv	550kv	800kv
Rated voltage	KV	110/132	150	220	272	330	400	500	765
1minute Power frequency with stand Voltage	KV	215	365	425	460	500	680	740	960
Lightning impulse withstand voltage	KV	550	750	900	1050	1300	1425	1550	1800
Switching surge insulation level	KV	N/A	N/A	720	750	950	1050	1175	1425
Current rating	A	2500	2500	3000	3000	3500	4500	4500	5000
Single-phase Power loss/metre	W	117	117	150	150	170	232	232	261
Short-circuit ratings	KA	63	63	80	80	80	80	80	100
Single-phase capacitance/metre	Pico farads	59.5	59.5	52.6	52.6	53.1	54.2	54.2	45.1
Surge impedance	Ohms	56	56	63.4	63.4	62.8	61.5	61.5	73.9
Single-phase inductance/metre	Micro henry	0.187	0.187	0.211	0.211	0.210	0.205	0.205	0.247
Internal diameter of enclosure	Mm	226.1	226.1	292.1	292.1	362	495.3	495.3	609.6
Tubular bus outer diameter	Mm	88.9	88.9	101.6	101.6	127	177.8	177.8	190.8
SF6 gas density	Kg/m^3	30.76	30.76	30.76	33	33	30.76	30.76	30.76

4.19 PORTABLE TEST EQUIPMENTS FOR TESTING HV/EHV EQUIPMENTS.

Portable test instruments for power transformer testing, is described in section 2.23 of Chapter # 2.

(1) Acoustic monitoring of the insulation system of GIS: Acoustic monitoring of SF6 gas can be performed during service, with externally mounted sensors and a portable diagnosis instrument. It is a non-invasive, self supported technique which offers several benefits such as detection of defects in GIS, immunity to external noise, defects can be localized and recognized, risk assessment based on source characterization. The signals from the defects may vary widely from continuous signals from internal corona to pulse shaped signals from moving particles.

Continuous signals

- Peak signal over one cycle
- RMS signal over one cycle
- Degree of modulation with the power cycle
- Degree of modulation with twice the power frequency

Pulse shaped signals

- Peak value of impulse signal
- Phase angle of pulse occurrence
- Time since last pulse

A portable instrument that supports all those features can operate either in continues mode or in pulse mode. The instrument is also equipped with a loud speaker that allows a technician can observe and recognize signals. The instrument performs a measurement automatically. Results may together with instrument settings, afterwards be down-loaded to a personnel computer (PC) for further analyses and transfer to databases. The instrument can be powered either from the mains power supply of design frequency or from a rechargeable battery.

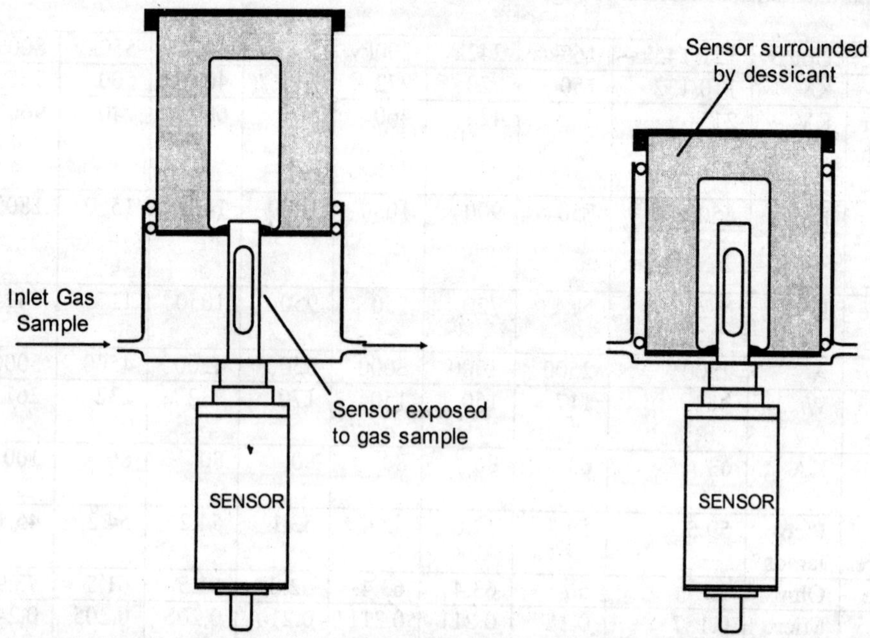

Fig. 4.19 (a): Read position of hygrometer sensor Fig. 4.19 (b): Dry down position of hygrometer sensor

(2) SF6 gas leak detector: It is a hand held portable instrument provided with a detachable sensing probe to detect the presence of gas leaks in high voltage switchgear. Instrument displays in cc/sec, gm/yr and ppm (Particles per million) selectable units. Provided with data storage and printing features.

(3) Dew point meter: Hygrometer is used for measuring the condensation temperature of SF6 gas .in gas insulated circuit breakers and nitrogen gas in transformers. Instrument is provided with suitable couplings/valves and connecting tube to connect with SF6 gas sampling point. Figure 4.19 (a) and (b) illustrates the read position and dry down position of a typical aluminium oxide ultra high capacitance sensor provided with dew point meter. Meter will display dew point temperature corresponding to pressure at which the dew point is measured. It is battery operated with rechargeable 9V battery.

Technical data: Range 5 to 60°C; Display LCD 2 line 20 character adjustable contrast; Operating pressure 0 to 0.5 bar;

(4) Micro-ohm meter:

(a) Digital micro-ohm meter: A microprocessor controlled instrument for measuring the contact resistance of circuit breaker and bus bar joints/connections. This portable unit, have built-in software to carry out different tests and store the results and provision for connecting a PC. Equipment should enable quick demagnetization of CT after testing circuit breaker contact resistance. Measurement range 0 to 200 micro-ohm; Test current output 0 to 600 A maximum 15 seconds (full wave rectified). Results are displayed on LCD display. Information about current generation or memory location is also available.

(b) **Digital DUCTOR Ohmmeter:** This instrument is suitable for resistance measurements down to 1μ Ω to 20 ohm over five ranges using the four terminal measurement system. It is ideal for measuring circuit breaker contact resistance, earth-bonding resistance, transformer winding resistance, bus bar joints, welded connections, rail bonds etc. The sample under test is connected to the C1, C2, P1 and P2 terminals of the instrument by using the leads provided with the instrument. Test current (up to 100 A) is passed through terminals C1 and C2, the resistance measurement is made between terminals P1 and P2. Range selection is by a rotary switch and an ON/OFF switch is provided, which includes a momentary 'ON' position to conserve battery power and avoid overhearing the sample when testing at high current and a lock 'ON' position for continuous operation. A reverse switch interchanges the P1 and P2 connections to enable forward and reverse readings to be averaged when a zero-off set is suspected.

(5) Circuit breaker operation analyzer: The instrument is suitable for testing of HV/EHV circuit breakers (up to 800 KV). Test data is stored and analyzed on PC with software supplied with the instrument. The unit is suitable for measuring circuit breaker contact movement during closing, opening and autoreclosing and make/break operation. Contact speed at various stages of operation, opening and closing time, make and break time and closing resistor pre-insertion time etc. Other features of the circuit breaker Analyser is as follows:

(a) Compatible to EMC/EMI environment; (b) Provided with all accessories and connecting leads; (c) Capable of storing data at temperature from 10 to 50°C and humidity 10 to 99%; (d) The notebook PC Pentium 166 MHz with software are provided with facility for display and generate reports in graphical and numerical formats and compare results obtained at different times; (e) Direct print facility; (f) Travel adapters and transducers

(7) Gas filling and evacuating equipment: The unit have a minimum storing capacity of 105 Kg provided with all the necessary pipes, couplings, flexible tubes and valves for coupling to the equipment for the filling or evacuating SF6 gas.

(8) Surge arrester leakage current Analyzer: Suitable for measuring various components of surge arrester leakage current such as resistive current, capacitive current, and third harmonic current. Instrument will indicate total leakage current within the range of 0 to 5 milliamps. Suitable to measure and analyze leakage current of surge arrester up to 800 KV, AC in energized condition without removing surge monitor and earth connection. Battery operated (Rechargeable Nickel- Cadmium cell) with facility to produce printout or leakage or leakage current wave.

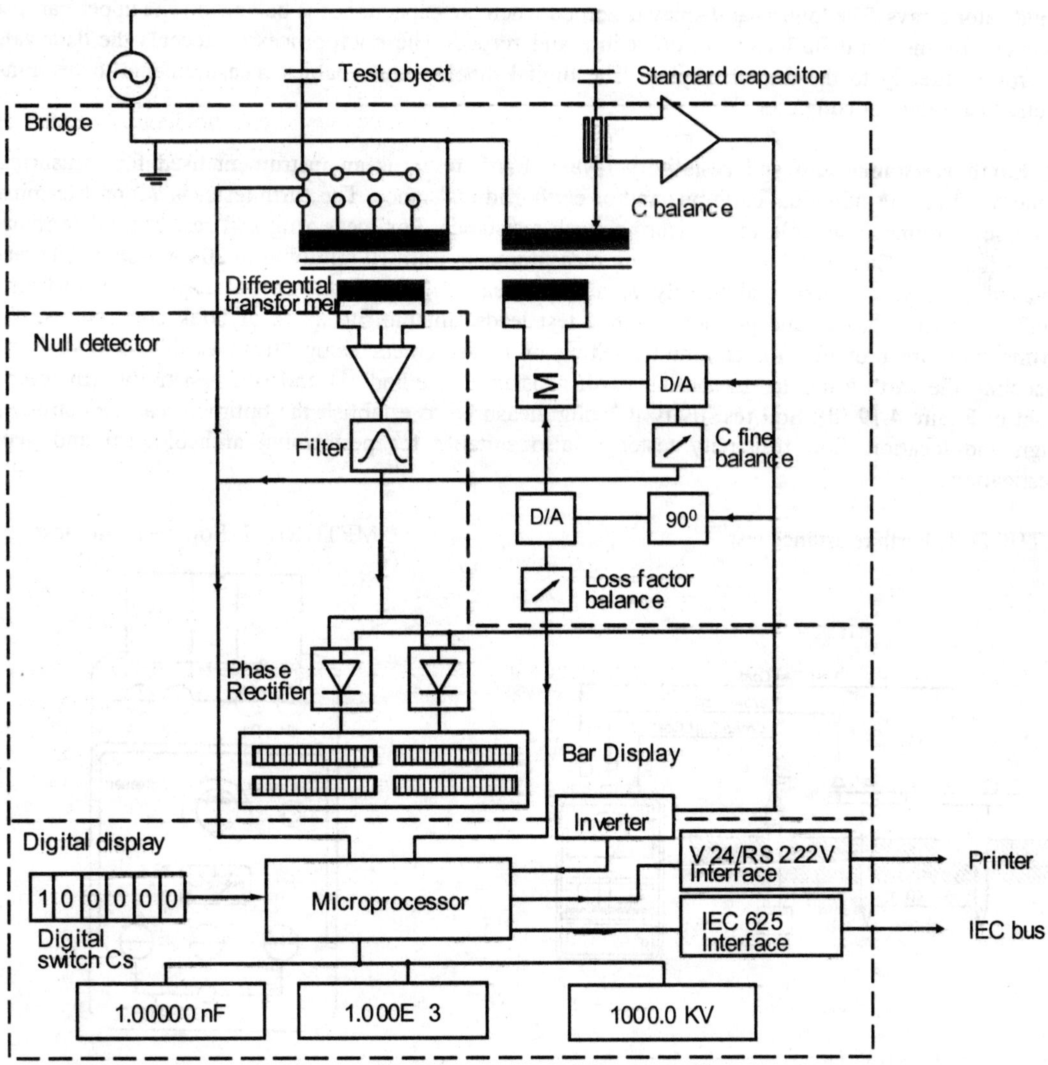

Fig. 4.19 (c): Schematic diagram of a capacitor and Tan delta measuring bridge (Courtesy, ASEA Hafely).

(9) Capacitance and Tan delta test set: This equipment consists of Capacitance and tan delta measuring bridge, high voltage AC power supply transformer unit, control unit and a standard capacitor. Unit is for testing H.V bushings, Capacitive-voltage transformers, Power capacitors etc. Periodic measurement of dissipation factor and capacitance of solid insulating components, the set is ideal to conduct routine diagnostic tests on electrical equipments. Special shielding arrangement is provided to suppress external interference. This enables accurate measurements even in electrically noisy environment particularly in energized switchyards up to 800 KV, AC.
The tan delta measuring bridge depicted in Figure 4.19 (c) consists of a measuring bridge, a null detector and a standard capacitor. The maximum test voltage is limited only by, the rated voltage of the standard capacitor and can exceed 1000 KV. For capacitor balancing, the number of turns of the differential transformer is changed until the flux in the core has reached a minimum value. The digital module will automatically compute the capacitance of the test object and provide a direct digital display of the value. For tan delta balancing, the standard capacitor current is routed via a current transformer and an amplifier. The tan delta switches directly indicate the value of the dielectric dissipation factor tan δ.

The differential transformer is provided with a detector winding to enable a measurement of its core flux. The null detector is connected to the output of the detector winding. A flux in the core induces a current in the detector winding. This current is amplified in a low-noise amplifier, filtered in an digital band-pass filter and then routed to a phase selective rectifier, which rectifies the current and displays it logarithmically on the two bar indicator arrays. The lower bar display is zeroed when the capacitance is balanced. The upper bar display is influenced by the tan delta balancing procedure and zeroed. The microprocessor accepts the data value and forwards it directly to the digital display. The digital display unit enables measurements to be transferred directly to a printer or computer.

(10) Earth resistance and soil resistivity tester: Earth tester is an instrument used for measuring earth resistance values of individual earth pits and/or earth grid resistance. The earth tester is a 3 or 4 terminal fully automatic instrument, suitable for measuring earth resistance. For measuring soil resistivity 4 terminal earth tester is required. There are 4 ranges covering measurements from 10 milliohm to 20 Kilo-ohm. The reading is displayed quickly, accurately and directly, on a large, clear 31/2digit liquid crystal display. The instrument has a built in battery charger and provided with 4 test leads suitable for spade or hook connections. Terminal shorting bars are provided for continuity testing or measurement using "dead earth" method. Method of connecting the earth tester for measuring earth resistance (method: 1) and soil resistivity (method: 2) are shown in Figure 4.19 (d). Soil resistivity is being measured to establish the optimum earth electrode system design and location. Soil resistivity tester is also suitable for performing archeological and geological investigations.

METHOD: 1, Earth resistance test

METHOD: 2, Soil resistivity test

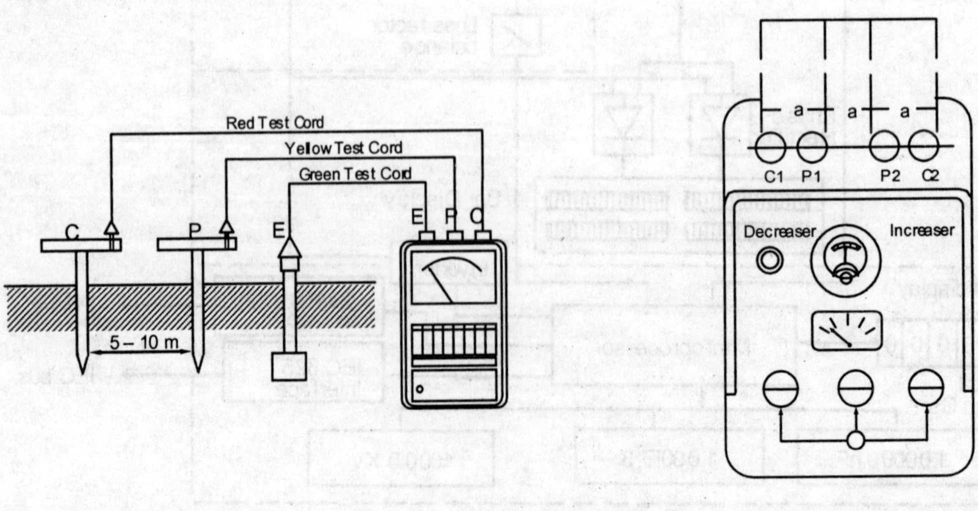

Fig. 4.19 (d): Test connections for measuring earth resistance and soil resistivity test.

The conventional null balance (Central zero) earth tester contains a battery driven oscillator, which passes current through the resistance under test from terminals C1 to C2 and the consequent potential difference across this resistance is applied to terminals P1 and P2 of the galvanometer. This potential difference is balanced by an equal and opposite potential difference produced across an adjustable resistance through the knobs in the instrument with the result that, at balance (needle exactly at zero position), no current flows in the circuit. Read the resistance value directly from the three knob position and multiply by range selector switch position to obtain the test result in ohm.. Following method is used to determine the profile of the soil resistivity for the location where earth grid is to be built.

(a) The Wenner four spike measurement method as shown in the figure (d) above is used
(b) Connect the P1-P2 potential spikes at a distance of 'a' and C1-C2 current spikes on either side at a distance of 3a, from P1 and P2 in the same line as shown in figure. Maintain the center point as reference for each measurement.
(c) Ensure that the depth "d" of the test spikes is not more than a/20 in each test.
(d) Take 6 resistivity readings at various locations within the effective area as follows:

Test No:	Spacing P1 & P2	Spacing C1-C2	Depth "d" of each spike	Resistance in ohm
1	1000 mm	3000 mm	1000/20 = 50 mm	
2	2000 mm	6000 mm	2000/20 = 100 mm	
3	3000 mm	9000 mm	3000/20 = 150 mm	
4	4000 mm	12,000 mm	4000/20 = 200 mm	
5	5000 mm	15,000 mm	5000/20 = 250 mm	
6	6000 mm	18,000 mm	6000/20 = 300 mm	

For large substation areas record similar readings at various locations. Take average value of the 6 resistivity readings or 18 readings and apply the formula given in IEEE guide for safety in substation grounding (ANSI / IEEE Standard 80) to obtain the required touch potential and step voltage.

11) DC high-pressure test set: DC high voltage test sets are for checking the quality of insulation in electrical power cables, transformers, switchgears and insulators. Test sets are available in the voltage range of 0 to 70 KV, 0 to 120 KV or 160 KV. Figure 4.19 (e) shows a typical test set. An air insulated design, which generates the DC high voltage that is delivered to the load under test. Tests are performed by applying controlled high voltages to the unit under test at a value specified in IEC Standard 502. Measuring the leakage current (in micro-amps) helps determine unit under test's ability to withstand over-voltages such as lightning strikes and switching surges. Proof testing is used for acceptance testing of aged and or repaired cable. For the proof test, the unit under-test will, either withstand the test voltage or it will "break down".

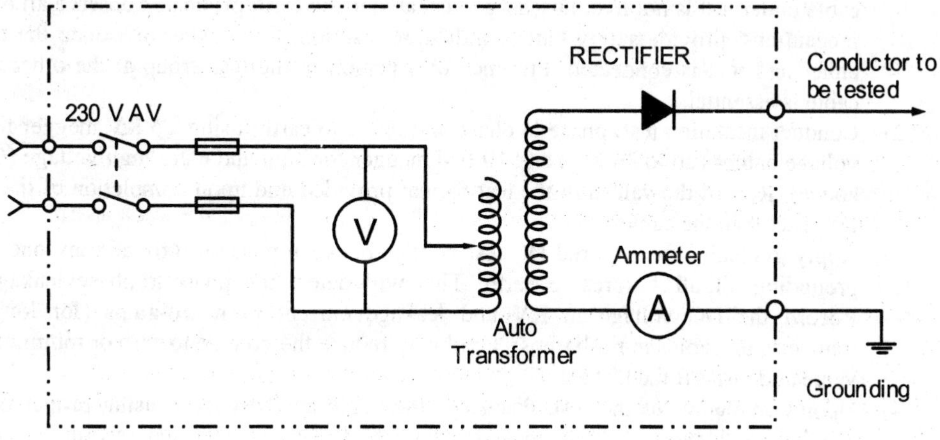

Fig. 4.19 (e): DC high-pressure test set (Hi-pot test set)

Acceptance test is a test made after installation, but before the cable is placed in normal service. This test is intended to detect shipping/handling or installation damages and to show any gross defects or errors in workmanship on splicing and termination. Maintenance test is test made during the operating life of cable. It is intended to detect deterioration of the system and to check the entire workmanship so that suitable maintenance schedule can be initiated. If there is any deterioration, the leakage current will increase. In the event of failure of cable within the specified test voltage the test equipment will trip automatically. Following are the environmental influences applicable for cable in service:

(a) Temperature: The dielectric strength of some cable insulations is reduced at elevated temperatures. This necessitates a reduction of the test voltages at higher temperatures. **Temperature gradients in the cable insulation, caused by heat dissipation from the conductor can result in usual potential hazard upon application of DC high voltage.**

(b) Atmospheric conditions: High humidity and conditions favoring condensation on exposed surfaces can affect test results to a marked degree. Contamination of termination surfaces can greatly increase conduction current and reduce flashover levels. Relative air density affects the measurement of test voltage by gaps or similar means and the flashover at terminations. At elevations higher than 1000m, over-insulation of termination is required to withstand both working voltages and prescribed test voltages. Wind can cause erroneous current readings.

(c) Extraneous electric fields: Although field tests on cable are often made in the vicinity of energized equipment, extraneous electrical fields will have little influence on direct voltage test results. Due to the stress and ionization of air between the circuit on test and nearby energized circuits, it is possible that flashover may occur. When spacing is marginal, usual precautions may be required to prevent this. Such precautions may include insertion of grounded shielding to protect adjacent circuits in service.

The conversion factor for AC to DC will be 2.4, as recommended by IEC 502. Hence DC voltage to be applied = 2.4 x AC system phase-to-phase voltage (for new cables as acceptance test). The test will be carried out only between conductor of one core and the grounded screen. All other cores (conductors) are connected to the ground during the test. For multi-core cables repeat the test in all other cores also. For maintenance test or test after repair of cable, the DC test voltage to be applied is 2.4 x system voltage phase to ground. Duration of test is 15 minutes for shielded (Armoured) cable and 5 minutes for non-shielded cable. In maintenance testing, it is more important that potential weaknesses be found out without actually causing breakdown. It is important that the test be carried at least 10% above the normal operating voltage level to ensure relatively safe continuous operation. Test sets are provided with zero interlock i.e, the start from zero volts. The rate of increase from zero to the specified test voltage shall be uniform. The time to reach the full voltage level shall not be less than 10 seconds and not more than 60 seconds. After the full test voltage is applied, leakage current measured in micro-amps is recorded initially and at every one-minute interval thereafter. Following are the test procedures:

1) Obtain work permit if the switchgears at either end is already energized. Ensure that the cable under test is not live. Discharge the cable using earth probe and observe all other safety precautions; provide safety barrier indicating caution. Disconnect or isolate the cable from either end if it is connected. Presence of a person in the test group at the other end of the cable is essential.
2) Conduct insulation test (phase to phase and phase to earth) using a 5 KV megger for medium voltage cables (up to 36 KV) and 10 KV megger for high and extra high voltage (66 KV and above). Record the values in the test format provided and upon completion of the insulation test discharge the cable.
3) Apply gradually the required DC test voltage between phase-to-ground (any one core) after grounding all other cores to earth. This will detect the phase-to-phase leakage current. Record the DC voltage in KV and leakage current in micro-amps (for long distance transmission cables in milliamps). Gradually reduce the voltage to zero or minimum possible value and turn off the test set.
4) Upon completion of the test, discharge the cable and test leads using proper earth probe supplied with the test set. Repeat the test on all other cores and record the voltage and leakage current.
5) After completing the hypot test, measure and record the insulation resistance. Discharge the cable and connect back to the switchgear. Return the work permit after clearing the site.

6) Plot the curves for leakage current verses time and leakage current verses applied voltage.

12) Power frequency withstand voltage test set:
Figure 4.19 (f) shows the simplified schematic diagram of a series resonant Power frequency test set. It consists of a variable voltage transformer, an high voltage exciter transformer and an HV reactor. The regulator provides a variable voltage to the exciter transformer. The secondary winding of the exciter is connected in series to the HV reactor L and the load capacitor C. The inductance of the reactor can be varied in a range of about 1:30 by changing the air gap of the iron core in the reactor. The load capacitance C consists of the capacitance of the test sample, the capacitance of the voltage divider and of the stray capacitances of all components in the high voltage system. For testing, the reactor is adjusted so that the impedance of L corresponds to impedance of C. This means that C and L are tuned to series resonance. In case of flashover during testing on the H.V. side the resonant circuit is detuned and the test voltage collapses immediately. The short circuit current is limited to the impedance of the H.V. reactor. A remote controlled motor drive is provided for increasing and decreasing the output voltage of the voltage regulating-transformer. The input circuit breaker and the main contactor with primary overload circuit are integrated in to the regulator cabinet.

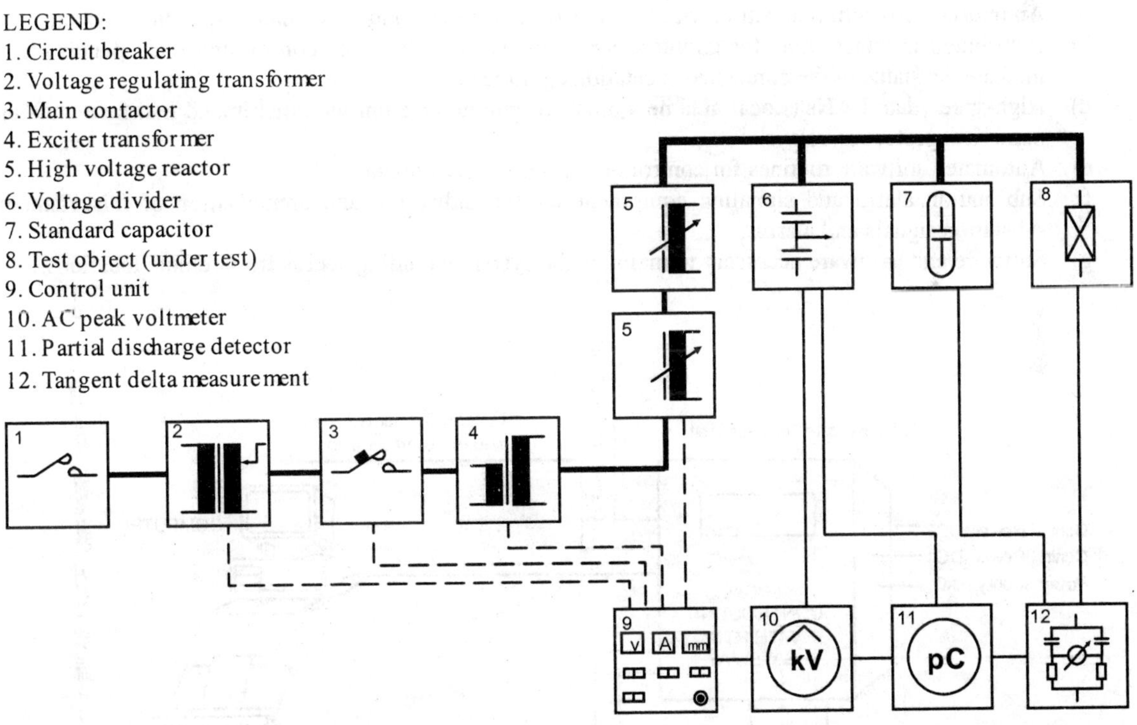

Fig. 4.19 (f): Schematic diagram of series resonant power frequency test set (Courtesy, ASEA Hafely).

The oil insulated exciter transformer provides the input voltage and the input power to the series resonant circuit. The primary and secondary winding are galvanically separated. A copper foil shield between the two winding reduces the coupling capacitance between the primary and secondary winding which allows to-reduce common mode interference from the mains power. The equipment provides a power frequency test voltage of 400 KV per module with output current ratings of 1, 2 and 4 amps. Up to 3 modules can be cascaded to reach an output voltage of up to 1200 KV. The unit is suitable for conducting power frequency tests on electrical equipments Gas insulated switchgears, EHV outdoor switchgears, EHV cables etc.

4.20 COMPUTIRIZED SUBSTATION MANAGEMENT SYSTEM.

Sub station and transformers are most important elements in the transmission and distribution networks of power system. Modern digital control technology enables to control and monitor the substation equipments and increases power quality and availability. Robust, modular bay control devices are integrated in the high voltage bays, and directly interface the processes signals. The high level of integration continues self-monitoring of primary and secondary devices. A comprehensive range of functions such as distributed integrated interlocking and checked command output ensure a high level of operational reliability. A modern compact computerized control system provides an overview of the status of the whole substation and supports the operator even under unusual conditions. Protective devices can be integrated in the system by means of data exchange and common overall functionality.

(1) SMS for high voltage substations: SMS is the primary point of control and providing controlled operation of all high voltage switchgears and monitor all electrical parameters on all feeders and bus bars on high voltage switchyard. AC Power distribution board, UPS and DC control board can also be monitored. SMS sketched in Figure 4.20 (a) consists of:

a) An operator console comprising VDU (Visual display unit) and operator keyboard (with mouse and printer) to control the operation of the substation and selection of the displays. When the VDU is energized a display will remain on the screen, which enables the operator to select and move between screens. Electrically operated switchgear and other control functions are controlled via the operator console. Controls are based on a select before operate procedure, so that the operator may execute or cancel the control. If execute is selected the control will be carried out.

b) An interface for communication with SCADA (Supervisory control and data acquisition) system.

c) Distributed interface units for circuit breakers, power transformers, control and relay panels etc. to indicate the status of the connected substation equipments.

d) High-speed data LANs (Local area networks) for communication with distributed interface units and numerical protection relays.

e) Automated software routines for control the substation equipments.

f) Sub station alarm and signaling equipment for the indication and annunciation of miscellaneous substation signals and alarms.

g) Software and hardware necessary to maintain the system including access from remote locations.

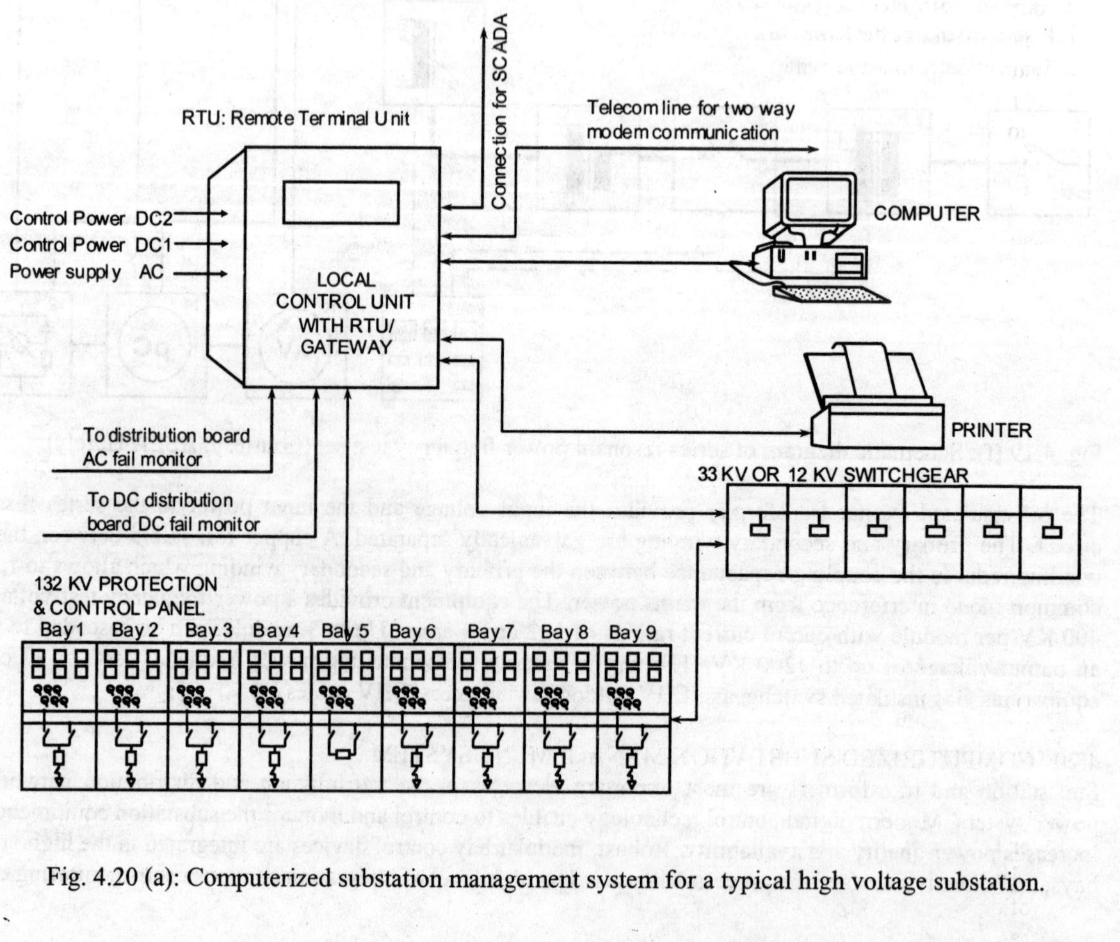

Fig. 4.20 (a): Computerized substation management system for a typical high voltage substation.

SMS performs automated substation functions such as circuit breaker autoreclose, feed imbalance calculation, transformer parallel operation and voltage regulation. The system shall include RTU (Remote terminal unit) facilities for communication of control, alarms and indications to the load dispatch center. Every event occurring in the sub station may cause an alarm. Each alarm is logged on the printer and displayed on the control screen.

2) Substation control and monitoring system for EHV substation: Substation control system in larger stations (EHV substations or HV switching station associated with power generating stations) is capable of providing following functions:

(a) Time logging of events: The central computers will continuously printout on logging prints of all events.
(b) Centralized local control: The configured operating mimic diagram is presented in accordance with physical status and validity. The control device will send the control command depend on the confirmation.
(c) Alarm/event processing and historical data storage in the computer hard disc for a minimum period of one year on on-line basis.
(d) Synchronizing with GPS (Global positioning system) clock for the high precision timing.
(e) Communication with remote control center: Offer functions for control and monitoring system diagnosis help.
(f) Communication with power station DCS: Only passage of information from SCS to DCS (Distributed control system)
(g) Communication with remote load dispatch center through RTU (Remote terminal unit).

Substation control and monitoring system depicted in Figure 4.20 (b) consists of standard hardware subassemblies such as:

(a) Site supervisor on PC (Personal computer) base;
(b) Substation controller on industrial PLC (Programmable logic controller) base;
(c) Communication network on fiber optic and copper medium;
(d) Protection supervision; (e) Fiber optic star coupler; (g) Redundant station computers;
(h) GPS (Global Positioning system); (I) Redundant LAN (TCP/IP) system.

Input to the substation control and monitoring system is being obtained from the following:

- BCU (Bay control units for feeders (One BCU per feeder); * Protection relays;

Out going communication interface systems are: (1) Load dispatch centre;
(2) Power station DCS (Distributed control system).

Input/output modules

Modules are designed to mount directly on switchgears/protection panels etc. and directly connected to the SCS without any interposing device. They have the following functions:

STATUS	CONTROLS / COUNTERS	MEASUREMENTS
Circuit breaker positions: closed/ open	Breaker closing / opening	Phase currents R, Y, B
Disconnector-positions: closed/ open	Disconnector closing/opening	Phase-to-phase voltage RY, YB, BR
Earth switch positions: closed / open	Earth switch closing /opening	Phase-to-phase voltage V_{RY}, V_{YB}, V_{BR}
Control circuit failure	Trip relay resetting	Frequency
Circuit breaker lock-out	Reclosers enable/disable	Active and reactive power
SF6 pressure low 1st threshold	Protection scenario switching order	Trip current
Circuit breaker failure		
Trip circuit failure	Operation-counters / tripping counters	Power factor
Battery and charger /UPS alarms	+ve and –ve active and reactive energies	Capacity loading of feeders
Tripping by protection system	Reclosing cycle counters	Capacity loading of bus bars

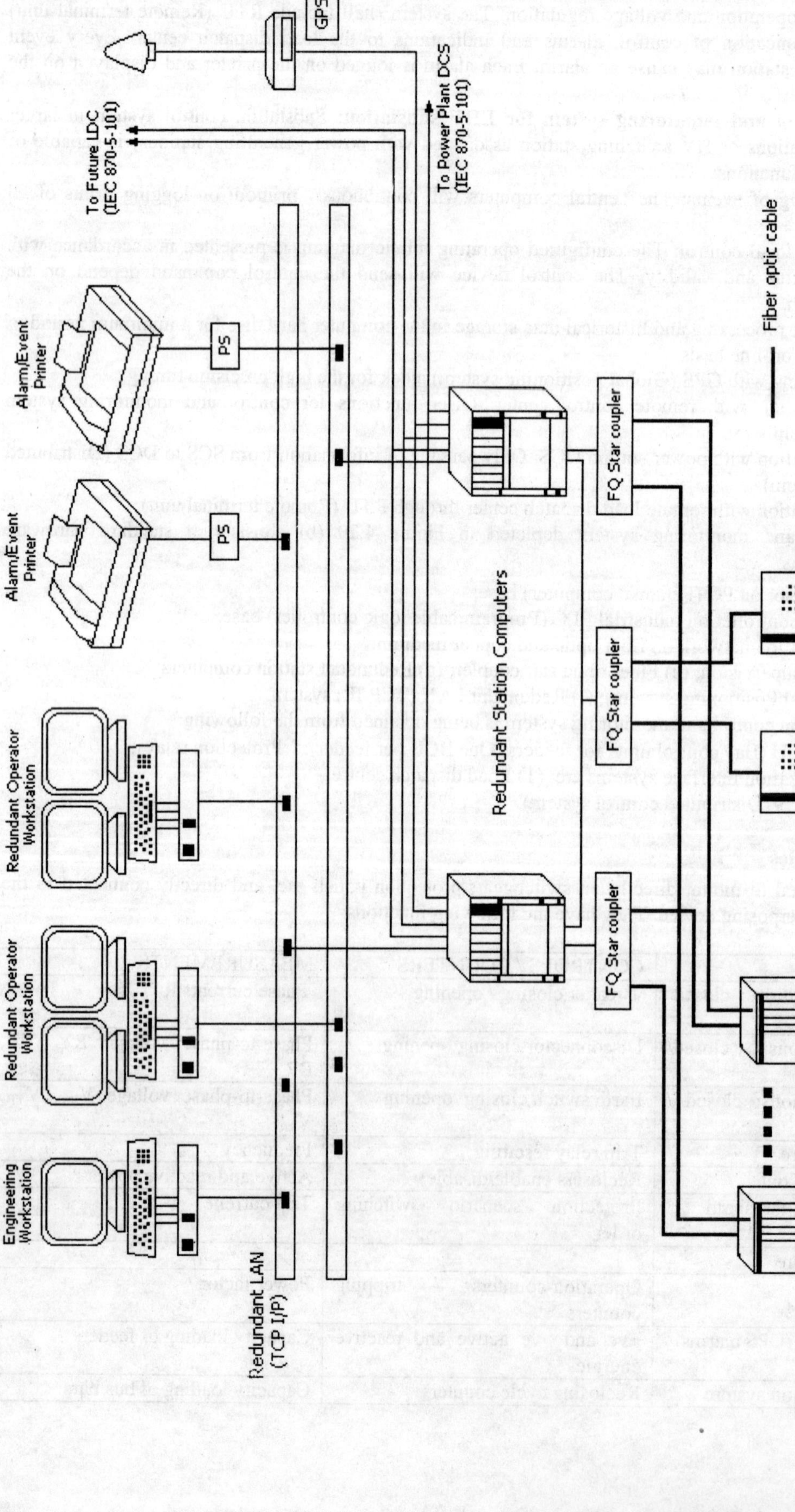

Fig. 4.20 (b): Substation control system for EHV substation or HV switching stations of Power plant.

4.21 HIGH VOLTAGE DIRECT CURRENT TRANSMISSION SYSTEM.

A high voltage direct current system consists basically of two converter stations at either end connected by a DC overhead line or DC submarine cable. The voltage of the converter can be changed very rapidly by, altering the delay angle of the thyristor valves. In steady state operation, only the resistance of the line and the equivalent resistance of the two terminal stations are effective in the DC circuit. Hence no reactive power problem occurs in the overhead or underground DC transmission system. The transmission distance is limited only by economic efficiency of the project. HVDC can be used to couple systems of different rated frequency. The short circuit current is limited to 2 to 3 times the rated current. Hence the contribution made by the HVDC system to the short circuit current in the in-feeding AC system is negligible.

Figure 4.21 (a) shows four important types of HVDC transmission systems.

(a) Long distance overhead transmission: Station cost of DC transmission are higher than AC transmission, but the line costs are lower because of lighter and lower height tower and simple two conductor transmission. In DC transmission, neither any reactive power is transmitted nor any skin effect is present. The economical transmission distance is 300 to 1400 KM.

(b) Long distance cable transmission: The conditions obtaining with overhead lines also apply in a similar way to a cable transmission system. In addition to that the dielectric losses in DC cables are negligible. Reactive power compensation is required in AC cable transmission. In the case of submarine cables with which intermediate stations for reactive power compensation is not possible. Hence HVDC cable is the only solution for long distance submarine transmission. The economical transmission distance is 10 to 800 KM.

(c) Interconnected system: HVDC can also be used to interconnect AC system operating at 50 Hertz and 60 Hertz power system. In such cases HVDC is the only technical solution to import or export power. One of the most important advantages of interconnected system operation is the saving in installed generator capacity. If the systems to be interconnected have different power generating structures, i.e, thermal generating plants and hydroelectric generating plants, interconnected system operation permits utilization of the most favorable form of generation in each case. If there is a surplus of hydropower available, this low cost power can be transmitted to the other system through HVDC transmission. On the other hand, if there is a shortage of water reserves, power required to cover the base load can be obtained from the thermal generating plants in the other system.

(d) Integrating HVDC transmission into the AC system: In the development of AC systems, load flow problem often occurs. These must be solved by, installing additional lines and/or quadrature regulating transformers. In such cases, HVDC is an alternative solution, which may offer additional advantages because of the control facilities it provides. When feeding HVDC into an AC system, (through inverters) both capital costs and losses can be reduced by, bypassing voltage levels and feeding the HVDC supply direct in to the load center. HVDC can favorably influence the performance of the AC system. By improving the transient stability of the AC system, it can make possible an increase in the transmission power in the AC system without any additional investment.

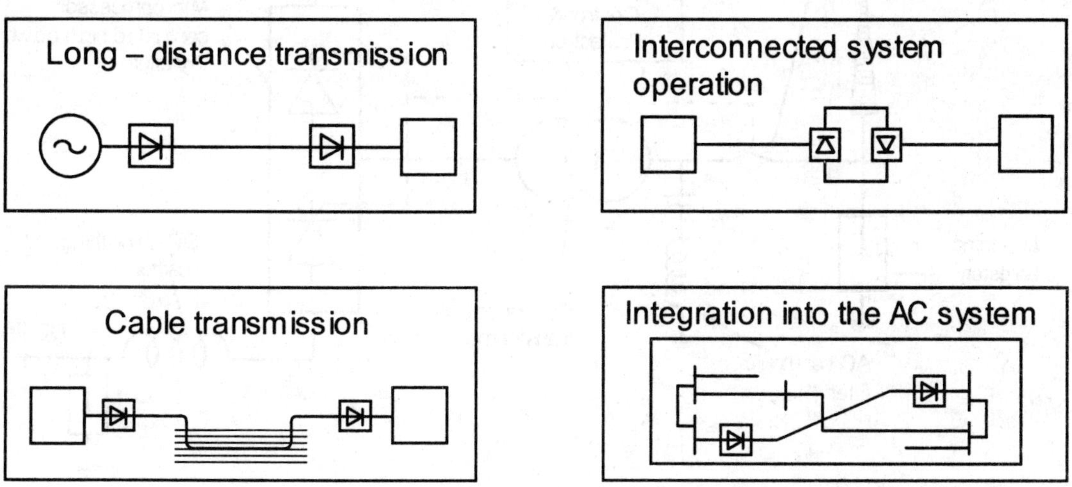

Fig. 4.21 (a): Four methods of transmission for high voltage direct current system.

Figure 4.21 (b) shows typical towers for 800 KV AC Transmission and ± 500 KV DC. Both lines are designed for the same transmission capacity. HVDC lines have a much higher transmission capacity than HV/EHV lines for the same right-of-way width. Overall cost of HVDC transmission is much lower than AC system.

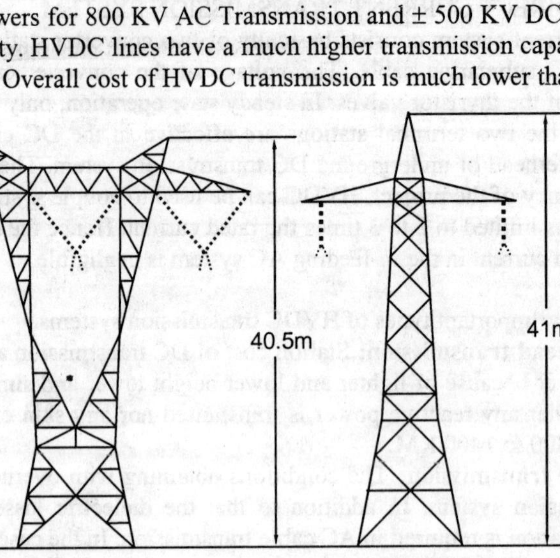

Fig. 4.21 (b): Comparison of towers for an 800 KV AC line and ± 500 KV DC line.

Figure 4.21 (c) illustrates the basic circuit of an HVDC converter station. It consists of SF6 Gas insulated Extra High Voltage switch gear, EHV circuit breaker, Surge arrester, AC filter, Converter transformer, 12 pulse thyristor module, Dc filter etc. During conversion of the current harmonics are produced on the AC side, which are kept away from the AC system by filter circuits. At the same time, AC filter provide part of the reactive power requirements of the HVDC station. The voltage on the DC side of the converter bridge also contains harmonics, which are smoothened by the smoothing reactor and, where necessary by, DC filter circuits. The AC circuit breaker shall be capable of disconnecting capacitive currents of three-phase filter circuits and compensating capacitors.

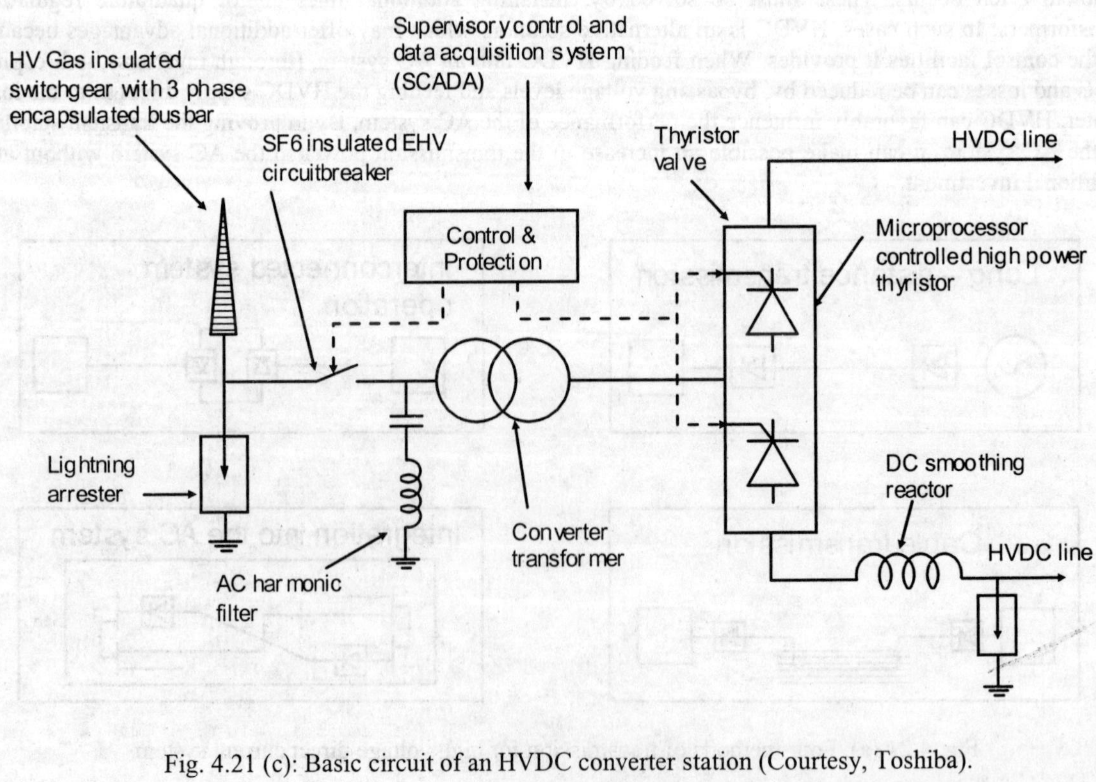

Fig. 4.21 (c): Basic circuit of an HVDC converter station (Courtesy, Toshiba).

Converter transformers: Converter transformers connect the AC network to the thyristor valve bridge, and adjust the voltage on the valve side to a suitable level based on the DC voltage used for the transmission. Converter transformers for HVDC are built with 2 or 3 windings in single phase or three-phase units. When the converter valves turn on, the windings on the valve side are galvanically connected to a high DC potential, and the dielectric strength of their main insulation therefore has to be designed for high DC voltage. Windings and iron parts are specially dimensioned owing to the high harmonic currents and the consequent leakage flux.

AC filter circuits: Filter circuits absorb current harmonics generated by the converter, and reduce distortion of the system voltage. Twelve-pulse converter groups are used to reduce the harmonic content of the system voltage by eliminating particularly the 5th and 7th harmonics. Filter circuits also provide some fundamental frequency reactive power needed by the converters.

Smoothing reactors: DC reactors are used in HVDC stations to smooth the direct current and limit the short-circuit current in the event of DC line faults. They are usually built in the form of coreless, oil-insulated reactors with an iron return path.

Thyristor valve: For the construction of the valves, a tower design is preferred. This permits a higher degree of compactness and reduces cost. The adoption of the modular system permits high design flexibility, quick replacement of modules. Series connected thyristors tiers are completely independent of one another. Neutron irradiation of the silicon has made it possible to produce thyristors with larger diameter. The introduction of water-cooling has led to a compact design, better utilization of the thyristors, high current conduction, lower losses and the elimination of noise problems. **Static compensators are employed to suppress over-voltages.** The thyristor is a solid-state semiconductor device similar to diode, but with an extra control terminal that is used to switch the device on at a particular instant during the AC cycle. The insulated-gate bipolar transistor (IGBT) is also used. Because the voltage in HVDC systems, around 500 KV to 1200 KV, exceed the breakdown voltages of the semiconductor devices, HVDC converters are built using large numbers of semiconductors in series. The low voltage control circuits used to switch the thyristors on and off need to be isolated from the high voltages present on the transmission lines. This is usually done optically, in a hybrid control systems, the low voltage control electronics sends light pulses along optical fibers to the high-side control electronics. Another system, called direct light triggering, dispenses with the high-side electronics, instead using light pulses from the control electronics to switch light-triggered thyristors (LTTS). A complete switching element is commonly referred to as a 'valve', irrespective of its construction. Figure 4.21 (d) shows typical light energy triggered thyristor valve and protective gate pulse

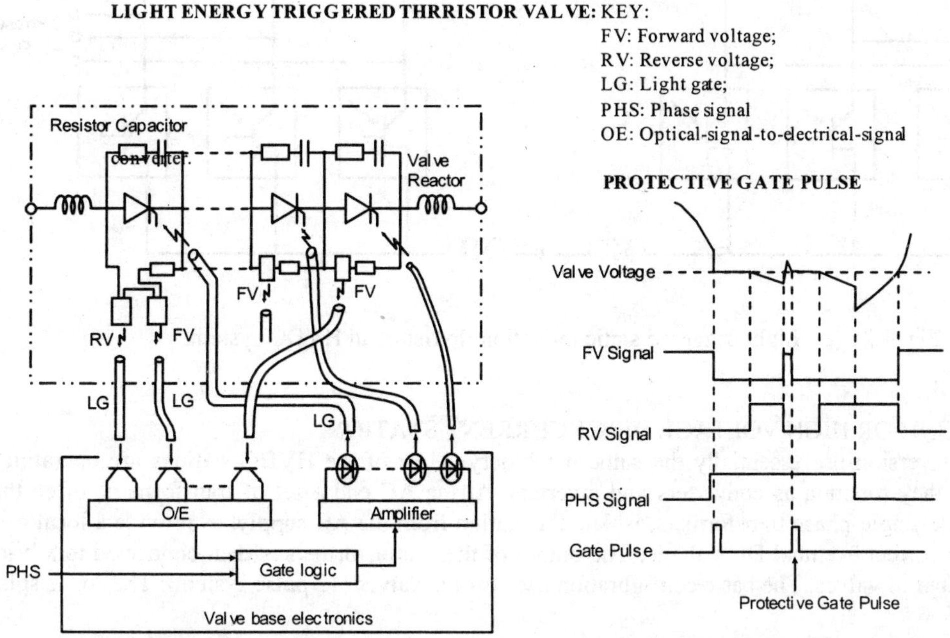

Fig. 4.21 (d): Light energy triggered thyristor valve and protective gate pulse (Courtesy, Toshiba).

There are two causes of over-voltages:
(1) From outside the valve due to switching or lightning surge. To overcome this problem, valve arrester directly connected across each valve.
(2) From inside the series string of thyristors due to dynamic voltage unbalance among series connected thyristors caused by partial turn-off etc. To prevent over-voltage, protection firing provided to all thyristors connected in series simultaneously, when forward voltage appears during thyristors are turned on.
Light energy triggered thyristor (LTT) valve can start to operate immediately after it is energized, since it does not have any thyristor level electronics to be changed. This valve also can be fired when the AC system voltage drops. A triggering signal is send to the LTT in the form of light energy. The thyristor module can be easily removed and replaced by using the module replacement filter. The self-sealing cooling water coupler, used to connect the cooling water piping to the thyristor module enable easy disconnection and re-connection between the module and piping without spilling cooling water.

Figure 4.21 (e) shows light triggered static induction thyristor having conversion efficiency of 99.9% at the commercial frequency of 50-60 hertz, together with a very low-loss capability. Compared with the electrically triggered p-n-p-n thyristor and electrically triggered gate-turn-off thyristor (g.t.o), the outstanding features of the SI thyristors include; low forward voltage drop; high speed switching; high blocking gain; high turn-on and turn-off current gain; high di/dt and dv/dt capability; and high gate to cathode breakdown at times of over-current break.

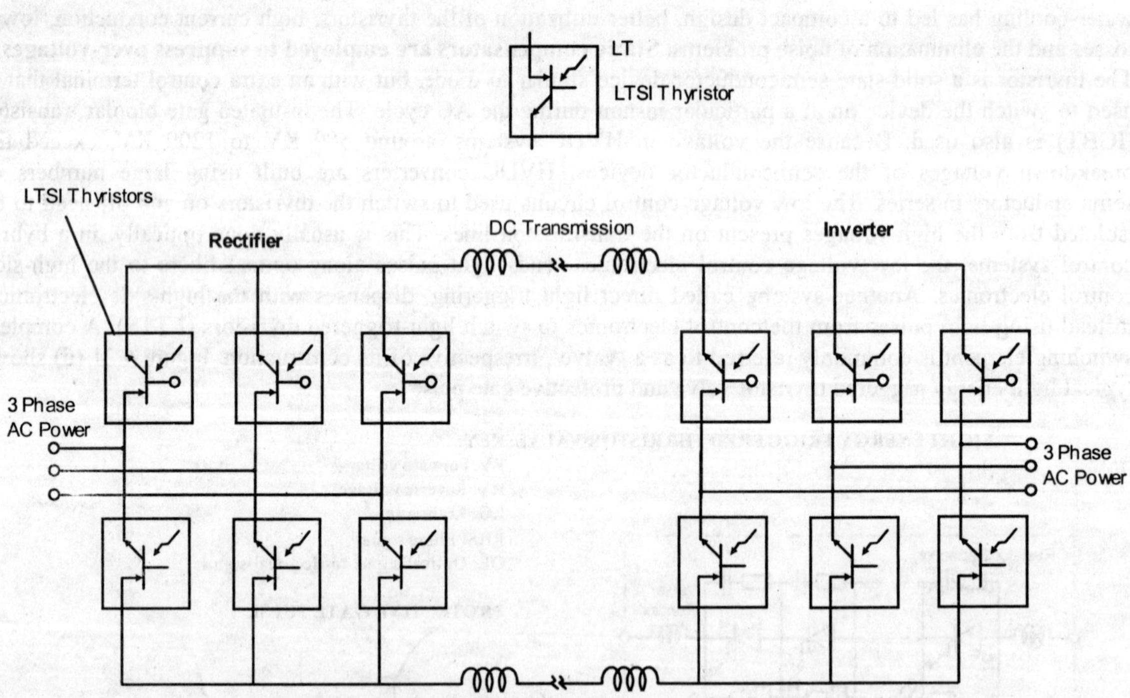

Fig. 4.21 (e): Light triggered static induction thyristors in HVDC system.

4.22 APPARATUS FOR HIGH VOLTAGE DIRCT CURRENT STATION.

Conversion and inversion use essentially the same machinery. Most of the HVDC stations are operating in such a way, that they function as converters and inverters. At the AC end a set of transformers, often three physically separate single-phase transformers, isolate the station from the AC supply, to provide a local earth, and to ensure the correct eventual DC voltage. The output of these transformers is then connected to a bridge rectifier of a number of valves. The basic configuration uses twelve valves (12 pulse system). The AC is split in to two separate three phase supplies before transmission. One of the sets of supplies is then configured to have a gamma secondary, the other delta secondary, establishing a 30°, phase difference between each of the sets of three phases. With twelve valves connecting each of the two sets of three phases to the two DC rails, there is a phase change every thirty degrees, and harmonics are considerably reduced. In addition to the above, various passive resistive and reactive components help eliminate harmonics on the DC rails.

Once the DC has been generated, a constant potential difference exists between two rails. One of the rail is earthed, establishing it at earth potential, the other rail is connected to a transmission line (monopolar transmission). Without an accompanying earth the potential is equalized by, an earth current (known as telluric currents and other extremely low frequency waves) between the earth electrodes at the two stations. There are many areas where such an earth current is not permissible, for example, metal pipe lines, where earth electrodes is in seashore, where sea water is an earth return path (navigational compasses) etc. Hence a second conductor is laid in the monopole transmission lines as an earth return. An alternative to monopolar transmission is bipolar transmission in which a pair of conductors is used, each at a high potential with respect to ground, in opposite polarity.

The advantages of bipolar systems are:

1. Under normal load, negligible earth current flows.
2. When a fault develops in line, current can continue flow under these fault conditions using the earth as a return path, operating in monopolar mode.
3. As, for a given power, bipolar lines carry only half the current of monopolar lines.
4. The monopolar system, carry typically 1500 MW, whereas the bipolar system carry typically 3000 MW with the same size of transmission line conductors.

Figure 4.22 (a) shows the principal components of an HVDC station. The bipolar arrangement has the advantage that if one pole fails, transmission can continue at half power with the current return via earth. The reactive power needed for the converters, amounting to about 55% of the active power is usually compensated with capacitor banks. Some of these incorporate filter circuits so that the harmonic is not affected by current harmonics and so as to keep distortion of the system voltage within acceptable bounds. The direct current is smoothened with a reactor. Especially in the case of overhead links, the DC voltage is also filtered to prevent telephone interference.

LEGEND:

1. AC switchgear
2. AC filter and reactive power compensation
3. Converter transformers
4. Converter groups
5. DC switchgear
6. Smoothing reactor and DC filter
7. DC transmission line Pole 1 & 2

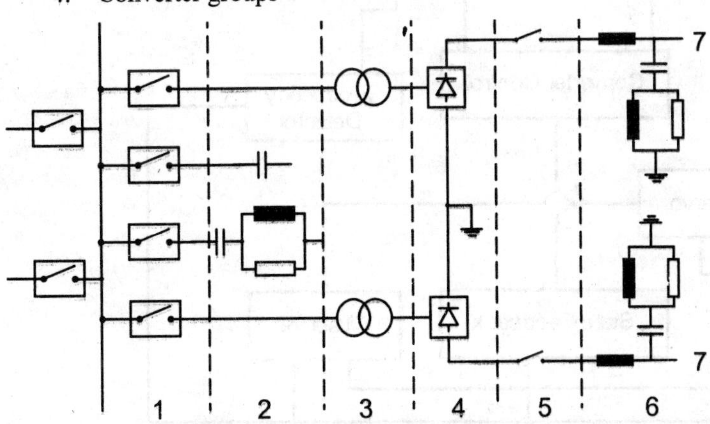

Fig. 4.22 (a): Principal components of an HVDC station:

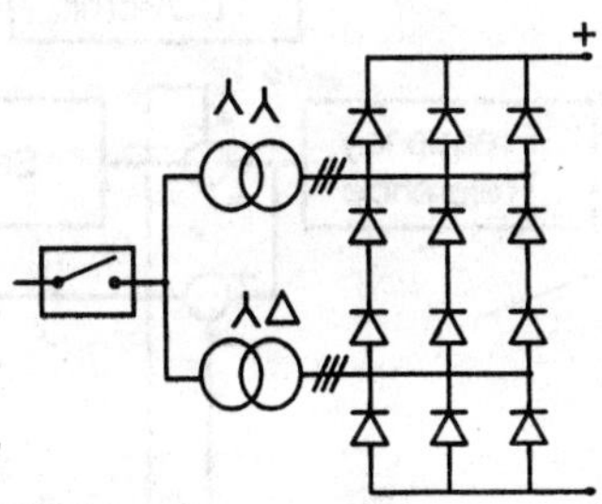

Fig. 2.22 (b): Twelve pulse converter

The converters used are three phase bridge arrangements, as in Figure 4.22 (b). On the DC side, pairs of bridges are connected in series. The respective transformers, one of which is in Yy0 vector group connection, and the other on Yd5 connection, on the three phase side are brought to a common circuit breaker to form a 12 pulse group. Twelve pulse groups are connected in series or parallel as in Figure 2.22 (c) and (d) respectively.

The purpose of the bypass switch in parallel with the twelve-pulse group is to connect or disconnect the station direct current when the group is put in to, or taken out of, operation. The shunt isolator enables the direct current to be diverted round a disconnected group.

LEGEND:

1. 12-pulse-converter; 2. Bypass breaker; 3. Group isolator; 4. Shunt isolator; 5.Line isolator

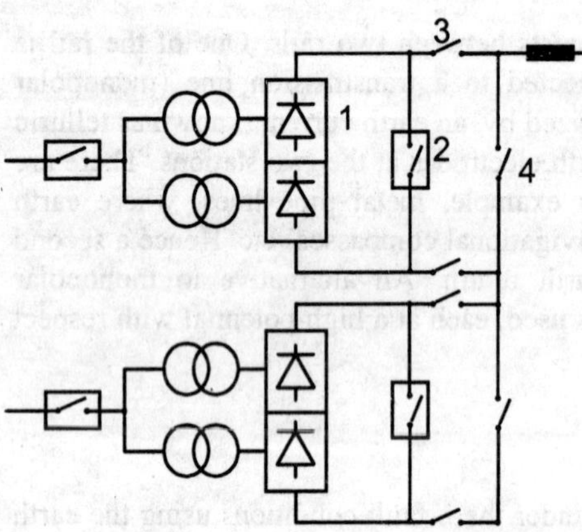

Fig. 4.22 (c): Series connected 12 pulse group:

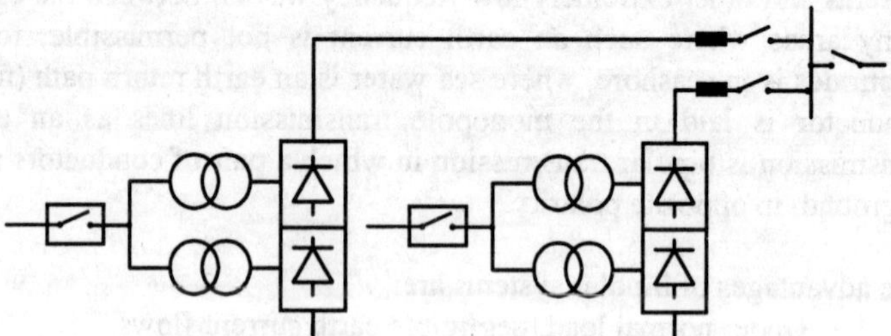

Fig. 4.22 (d): Parallel connected 12 pulse group

Automatic frequency control: When it is required to improve frequency deviation in normal operation or after a disturbance in the system, automatic frequency control (AFC) function is required. Basic AFC executes proportional control by taking in to account frequency differences between two systems, which are connected via an HVDC transmission link. The multi-variable AFC, based on modern control theories shown in Figure 4.22 (e) has many advantages. It produces better control response because it contains the observer, which feedback to the converter control. This system is essential for the HVDC systems linking 50 Hertz and 60 Hertz.

Fig. 4.22 (e): Automatic frequency control (Courtesy, Toshiba).

Power swing damping control: The modulation control of the DC power improves power swing stability and effectively damps power oscillations. Figure 4.22 (f) shows the block diagram of power swing modulation control, and power oscillation with and without damping control.

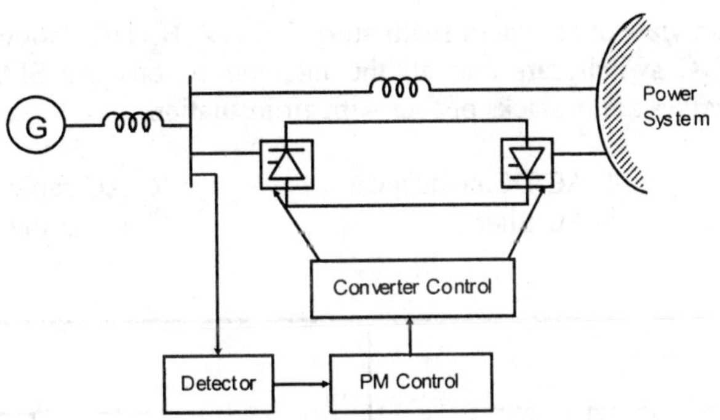

Fig. 4.22 (f): Power swing modulation control Courtesy, Toshiba).

Starting up the generator: When an HVDC system is feeding from an isolated generator, at the sending end the system has to be started up in coordination with the governor action of the generator. When bipolar operation is available, overall transmitted power can be built up smoothly from zero to the rated value by having two poles transmit power [Figure 4.22 (g)] in opposite directions.

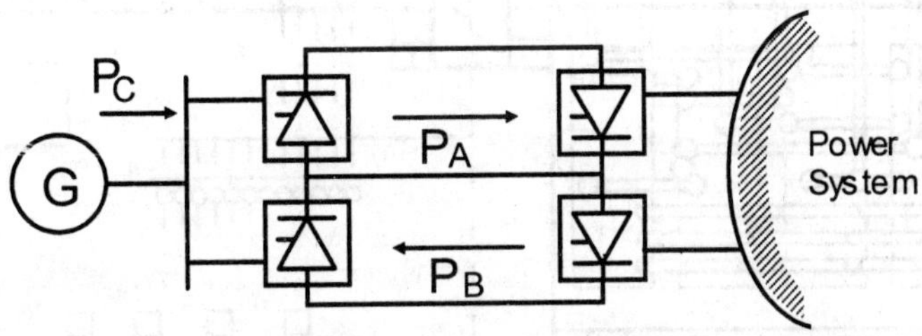

Fig. 4.22 (g): Two pole power transmission (Courtesy, Toshiba).

HVDC stations are built as purely outdoor installations or with parts of the station indoors. The layout of a 500 KV (DC) outdoor station designed for two-pole transmission is depicted in Figure 4.22 (h). For each pole of the station there are four series connected three-phase bridges, each with a rating of 240 MW at 500 KV nominal DC voltages. The thyristor valves are contained in pairs in common oil filled tank mounted on an insulated platform.

LEGEND:
1. AC in-feed
2. AC switchgear
3. AC filter circuit
4. Converter transformers
5. Thyristor valve
6. DC switchgear
7. Smoothing reactors
8. Surge capacitors/ DC filters
9. Outgoing DC line
10. Earth electrode line
11. Heat exchanger
12. Control room
13. Station services
14. Workshop
15. Compensating Capacitors

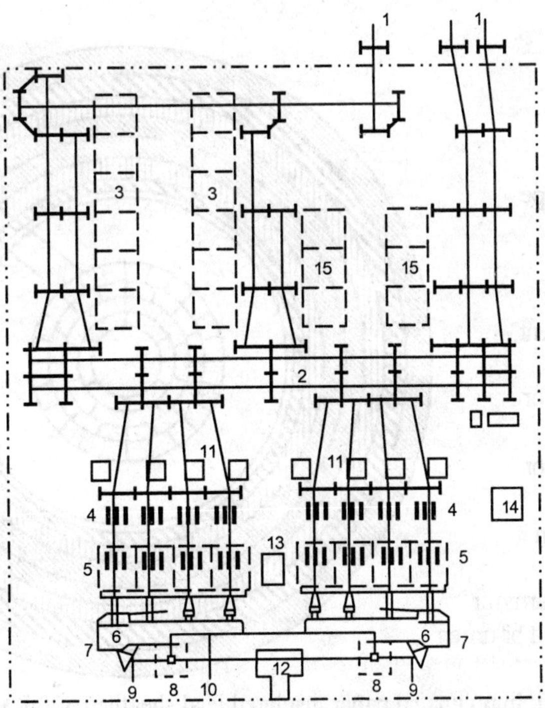

Fig. 4.22 (h): Typical layout of a 500 KV, HVDC station (Courtesy, BBC Brown Boveri)

Figure 4.22 (i) shows the plan view of an indoor multi-story 500 KV, HVDC station for both AC and DC cable connection. The AC and DC switchgears and all the interconnections are SF6 gas insulated metal-clad construction. The thyristor valves are in stacks of four with air insulation.

LEGEND:

1. Transformer
2. Smoothing reactor
3. Converter
4. AC/DC switchgear
5. AC filter
6. AC cable feeders
7. Outgoing DC cables

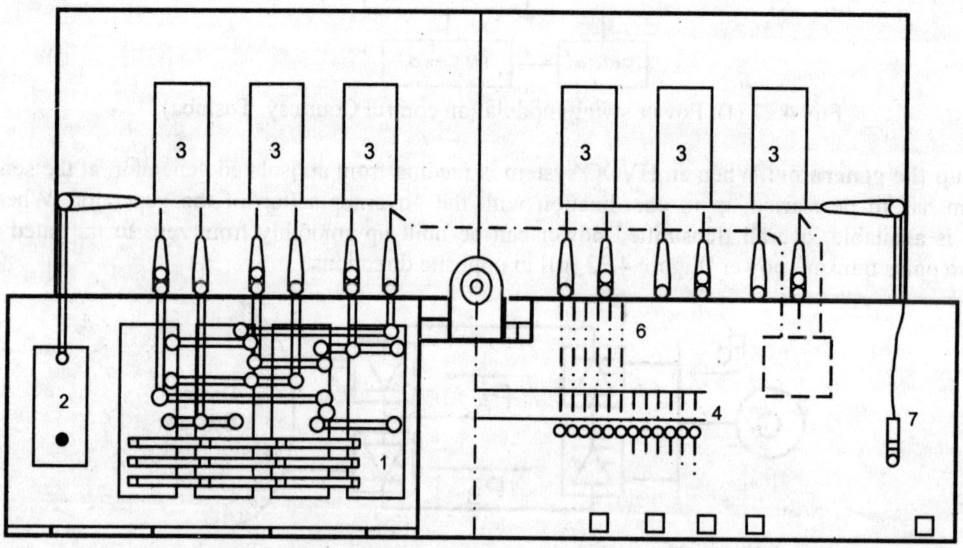

Fig. 4.22 (i): Plan view of an indoor 500 KV, HVDC station (Courtesy, BBC Brown Boveri)

HVDC submarine cable: The cross section of an impregnated paper insulated lead sheathed 800 KV, HVDC submarine cable with return conductor is illustrated in Figure 4.22 (J). This cable is solid state containing copper core wrapped in insulation and is hermetically sealed inside a rubber sheath. It consists of:

1. Copper conductor
2. Conductor screen
3. Impregnated paper tape
4. Insulation screen
5. Copper woven fabric tape
6. Lead sheath
7. Polyethylene sheath
8. Bedding
9. Transversal reinforcement
10. Bedding
11. Copper return conductor
12. Bedding
13. Copper return conductor
14. Bedding
15. Polyethylene insulation
16. Bedding
17. Galvanized steel wire armour
18. Polypropylene yarn and bitumen

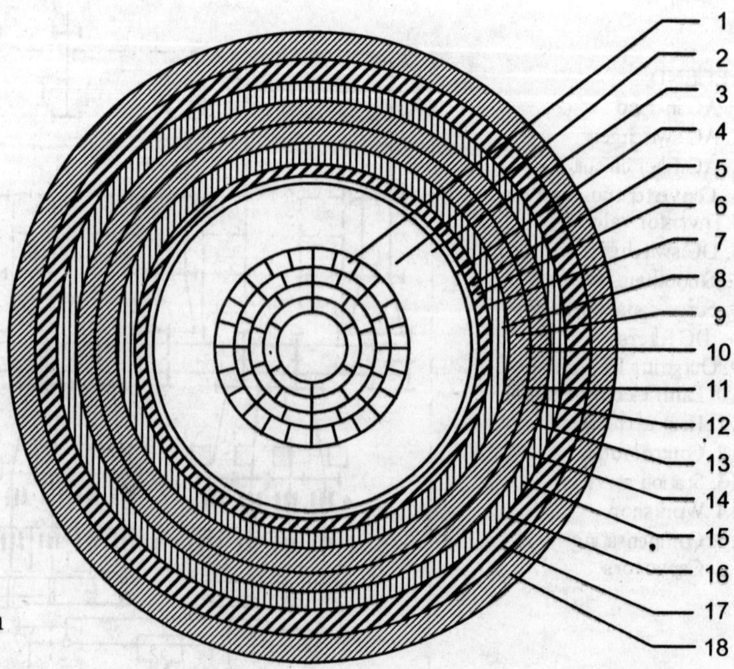

Fig. 4.22 (J): Impregnated paper insulated lead sheathed 800 KV, HVDC submarine cable.

4.23 COMPARISON BETWEEN HVAC AND HVDC TRANSMISSION

Table 4.23 (1) describes the advantages and disadvantages of high voltage or extra high voltage alternating current (HVAC) transmission system in comparison with high voltage direct current (HVDC) transmission system.

Table 4.23 (1): Comparison between HVAC and HVDC transmission systems.

Item	High voltage AC transmission	High voltage DC transmission
1	Transmitting 3-phase AC voltage 66 KV to 1500 KV (50 Hertz or 60 Hertz).	Transmitting high voltage DC 300 KV to 1200 KV.
2	Transmission loss approximately 0.6% of the transmitted power.	Transmission losses are lower. For the same capacity, the loss will be 50% of HVAC transmission losses..
3	HVAC system, need 3 live conductors and 1 earth conductor.	HVDC system, need either one conductor or two conductors.
4	1200 sq: mm 400 KV double circuit EHV transmission is equivalent to →	1620 sq: mm 400 KV single conductor + Earth HVDC transmission.
5	AC systems running in synchronism (same frequency) can only link.	HVDC links AC systems of two different frequencies (50 hertz and 60 hertz).
6	AC cable transmission length is limited due to reactive power produced by cable capacitances.	With DC cable no such reactive power is produced. Hence suitable for long distance sub-sea transmission system.
7	Power varies on load conditions	Very easy to control the active power in HVDC system, depending on the application and network requirements.
8	Power swings can occur.	Damping of power swings in the AC network is possible by automatic control.
9	Frequency varies on load conditions	Constant frequency control and redistribution of power flow in the AC network is possible.
10	In HVAC system control is limited	Unlimited possibilities for the control of the HVDC system by means of analogue and digital simulation of the power system.
11	HVAC have system stability problem.	HVDC does not have system stability problem.
12	HVAC need switching stations on either side of the transmission line	HVDC need converter stations on either side, which is very expensive.
13	HVAC contributes short circuit current to the interconnected network system. Hence short circuit current will increase in the receiving station.	HVDC does not contribute any short circuit current to the interconnected AC system.
14	Suspected electromagnetic field is a health hazard for nearby residents of HVAC transmission lines.	HVDC does not produce low frequency electromagnetic field. It a possible health advantage for nearby residents.
15	Corona discharge is the creation of ions in a fluid. In strong electromagnetic field electrons are torn from unionized air, and either the positive ions or else the electrons are attracted to the conductor, whilst the charged particles drift. This effect can cause considerable power loss, creates audible and radio frequency interference, generates toxic compounds such as oxides, nitrogen and ozone and lead to arcing.	Due to the space charge formed around the conductors, an HVDC system may have about half the loss per unit length of an HVAC system carrying the same amount of power.

4.24 EMERGENCIES AND TROUBLES ON HV/EHV CIRCUIT BREAKERS.

Circuit breakers, as is known are designed and selected to break the electric circuit while carrying the normal load currents or fault currents. When a breaker is opened, the arc that is drawn between the fixed and moving contacts is extinguished in oil/SF6 gas/compressed air or by other means. The breaking capacity is generally expressed in Megavolt ampere (MVA), this is the maximum permissible power flow the circuit breaker can safely interrupt.

Breaking Capacity in MVA = $\sqrt{3}$ x Phase-to-Phase voltage in KV x Short-circuit current in KA.

Damage of circuit breakers and even their destruction can result from a failure to extinguish the arcs drawn between the contacts, faults in the contact systems such as overheating and melting of the contact, flashover across the internal and external insulating parts, malfunctioning of the operating and actuating mechanisms, breakage of insulating links and failure of closing or tripping coils etc. Circuit breaker should not be closed after blocking the relay (with out opening the isolators on both side) when a persistent short-circuit existing on the line. Low oil content circuit breakers should be provided with arc resistant contacts and be controlled by three spring operating mechanism to obtain a better velocity characteristic. The best choice for circuit breaker is the SF6 insulated breakers. In the bulk oil circuit breakers failure to extinguish the arcs, burning of the contacts, and deterioration of oil may be resulted from lack of attention.

Air blast circuit breaker troubles most frequently arise from:

(a) Lowered capacity during the interruption of a short-circuit current or the switch-off of a lightly loaded power line/power transformer.

(b) A flashover down the support insulator column or insulation of a blast air pipe.

(c) Breakage of a support insulator, interrupter chamber or blast air-pipe.

(d) Faults in the contact system or actuating parts or worn out rubber gasket.

(e) Faults in the control circuitry.

4.25 SWITCHING PROCEDURES, SEQUENCE, AND OPERATION OF BREAKERS.

As a rule the routine closing and opening of circuit breaking is carried out from the control room by means of hand operated control switches or automatic closing through DCS (Distributed control systems in power stations) or SCMS (Substation control and monitoring system) or by autorecloser for transmission feeders. The circuit breaker can be closed or opened from the control panel or control desk electrically but manually by using either spring-loaded pistol grip type switch or pushbutton. In performing a breaker switching operation, the operator firmly, but smoothly turns the pistol grip handle to the right for breaker closing and release the handle and the 'ON' red lamp lights up. When released the handle, the switch automatically turn back to the neutral position under the force of the return spring. While switching-off the circuit breaker a reverse action will take place and the 'OFF' green light will lights up. A circuit breaker may also be closed or opened by means of pushbuttons. In this case the operator has to depress the 'CLOSE' pushbutton for initiating closing action and 'OFF' pushbutton for opening action meanwhile the requisite signal lamps lights up.

Indicating lamps are not always sure signs but operator can watch the indicating instruments to make sure that the breaker is closed unless DCS or SCMS are not employed. Closing time of breaker is 100 to 150 milliseconds. If the closing action is not initiated within this time, operator has to check the reasons for not closing. If a fault is persisting or the closing signal is initiated without resetting the relay after a fault trip, if the operator attempt to close the breaker a trip-free operation will take place i.e. before energizing the main circuit, the breaker will trip open. Most of the generator circuit breakers are equipped with AC under voltage release and DC no volt release mechanism. If the DC control power (which is used for opening the breaker during a fault) fails the breaker will trip-open automatically. Similarly, on a generator circuit breaker if proper AC voltage is not buildup AC under voltage relay will prevent to close the breaker even if a closing signal is initiated. It is dangerous to block those releases.

Figure 4.25 illustrates the simplified logic diagram of a transmission line feeder duly supported with single line diagram of a triple pole operated circuit breaker (no provision for single pole tripping) with potential transformers installed in the transmission line feeder. The logic is classified in to 5 different groups as follows:

(1) Isolator closing and opening logic (NOT GATE);

(2) Feeder circuit breaker closing logic (AND GATE & OR GATE) ;

(3) Feeder circuit breaker opening logic (OR GATE);

(4) Feeder circuit breaker tripping logic (OR GATE);

(5) Feeder synchronizing logic (AND GATE & OR GATE).

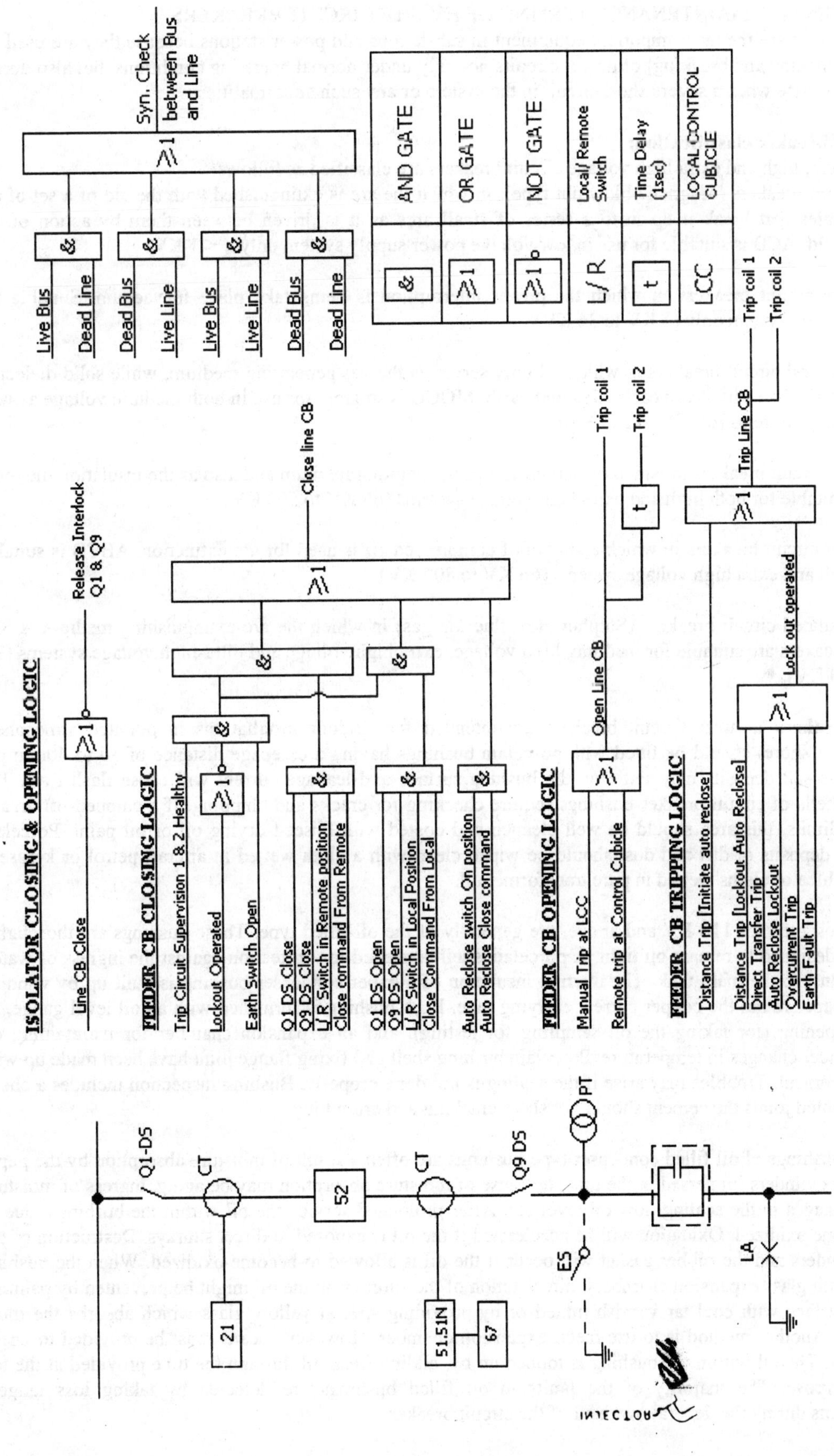

Fig. 4.25: Simplified logic diagram for a transmission line feeder..

4.26 PREVENTIVE MAINTENANCE TESTING OF HV/EHV CIRCUIT BREAKERS.

Circuit breakers are the most important equipment in substations and power stations because they are used for switching (making and breaking) of power circuits not only under normal operating conditions, but also during emergencies arise when a severe short circuit in the system or any such abnormalities.

(1) Circuit breaker classification:

Low, medium, high and extra high voltage circuit breakers are classified as follows:

(a) Air circuit breakers (Magnetic blow out type), in which the arc is extinguished with the aid of a set of arc resistant plates that break it up in to a series of small arcs as it is driven between them by action of the magnetic field. ACB is suitable for use in low voltage power supply system only. (< 1 KV)

(b) Vacuum circuit breakers in which the power interruption is being take place in vacuum. Suitable for medium voltage system only (1 KV to 36 KV)

(c) Minimum oil circuit breakers in which oil only serves as the gas generating medium, while solid dielectric parts isolate the live parts from each other and earth. MOCB is suitable for use in both medium voltage as well as high voltage systems (66 KV to 245 KV).

(d) Bulk oil circuit breakers in which oil serves as a gas-generating medium and also as the insulation medium. BOCB is suitable for both high and extra high voltage systems (66 KV to 500 KV).

(e) Air blast circuit breakers in which a stream of compressed air is used for arc extinction. ABCB is suitable for both high and extra high voltage systems (66 KV to 800 KV).

(f) SF6 insulated circuit breakers (Sulphur Hexafluoride gas) in which the arc-extinguishing medium is SF6 gas. SF6 breakers are suitable for medium, high voltage, extra high voltage and ultra-high voltage systems (3.3 KV to 1500 KV).

Circuit breakers failure: Circuit breakers are intended for outdoor installations in polluted atmosphere (example sea shore) should be fitted with porcelain bushings having a creepage distance of 30 to 40mm per KV, because salt deposits may settle on the bushing surface and leakage current will cause flash over. The porcelain shells of circuit breaker bushings require checking for cracks and chipping. If a chipped-off area is within the limits, this area should be well cleaned and coated with linseed drying oil or oil paint. Porcelain shells with deposits of dirt and dust should be wiped clean with a cloth wetted in aircraft petrol or kerosene solvent naphtha or cloths wetted in pure transformer oil.

Bushings designed for 110 KV and above, are generally of the oil-filled type. These bushings are thoroughly sealed and designed to remain oil tight. A porcelain shell is needed for protection against the ingress of water, snow and dust to the main tank. The internal insulation of a paper condenser bushing is built up by winding bakelized paper round the copper current carrying tube. Each bushing is furnished with an oil level gauge, an oil drain opening (for taking the oil sampling for testing), and an expansion chamber for maintaining oil tightness under changes in temperature. Porcelain bushing shell and fixing flange joint have been made up with magnesite cement. Troubles may arise if the sealing is not done properly. Bushing inspection includes a check of the cemented joints the cement should not show cracking and crumbling.

Failure in bushings of oil filled condenser type bushings are often a result of moisture absorption by the paper tube barrier cylinders immersed in the oil. The cause of moisture absorption may be aging, ingress of moisture through leakages in the sealing, low oil level etc. After prolonged service the oil within the bushings, due to aging become oxidized. Oxidation will be accelerated if the oil is exposed to direct sunrays. Destruction of the barrier cylinders and the rubber gasket will occur if the oil is allowed-to-become oxidized. When the bushing are fitted with glass expansion chambers, direct action of the sunrays on the oil might be prevented by painting the glass surface with coal tar varnish mixed or by providing special yellow glass which absorbs the more active rays. Another method is to use metal expansion chamber. However, means must be provided to check the oil level. The oil within the bushing is topped up by, adding fresh oil through the tube provided at the top for this purpose. The majority of the faults in oil filled bushings are detected by taking loss tangent measurements during the general overhaul of the circuit breaker.

(3) Bulk oil circuit breaker maintenance: If oil circuit breakers are installed where the ambient temperature drops below – 5 degree C, the viscosity of the oil rises, thereby lowering the velocity of the moving contacts when the breaker tripped or closed. Hence oil circuit breakers are furnished with heaters to warm the oil in the tank during winter. During a routine preventive maintenance repair the arc control devices [Refer figure 4.4 (c)] should be wiped clean and the accessible parts of the liners and gaskets, plates and other insulating parts closely inspected after draining the oil. If an arc control chamber accumulated carbon deposits, it should be washed in clean dry transformer oil. Any of the arcing chamber parts that shows, signs of burning it should be replaced.

To check the condition of the insulation of the moving parts within a circuit breaker, insulation resistance measurements are taken with an insulation tester (5 KV megger for HV breaker and 10 KV megger for EHV breaker) and compared with previous test results. The insulation of the arc control devices, barriers enclosing them, and other parts associated with a bushing in a circuit breaker is checked together with a given bushing when the loss tangent is measured. If the values are within the prescribed limiting figure then the insulation is satisfactory.

To dry out the internal insulation it is not necessary to dismantle the breaker. This is done by blowing hot air at a temperature of 90 degree C, through the tank for 30 to 40 hours. Heating the oil in the tank to a temperature of 70 to 90 degree C may serve the same purpose. Another method used for drying is to hang 2 or 3 numbers 1000 W incandescent lamp inside each empty tank. The heat emitted by these lamps (when it is lit) is used to maintain the same temperature conditions as with a hot air blower. The drying being carried out 12 to 15 hours. When the drying period elapses the tank is filled with dry transformer oil having a dielectric strength of 50 KV at 2.5 mm electrode gap.

The condition of the contact assembly in a bulk oil circuit breaker is checked at every time, the breaker is given a general overhaul and also after every 5 short-circuit fault trips. Mechanical means are used for checking contact pressure. Finger contacts can be checked for proper pressure by means of a loading weight. Cluster contacts can be checked by, using a dynamometer to measure the force required to pullout the contact rod. Point contact systems are checked by, measuring the amount of compression of the contact backup spring. The force required to pullout the contact rod is measured.

In butt type contact systems, the contact pressure is measured indirectly by determining the deflection undergone by the springs or the distance of travel of the moving contacts. In a brush contact system the gap between the contact parts is checked with a feeler gauge. It should not penetrate more than 4 mm at any place between the brush and solid contact face. A dynamometer is used to measure the pressure of the brush on the solid contact part.

For checking the electrical condition of the contacts in a circuit breaker, measurements of the contact resistance are taken by using a micro-ohmmeter in the voltage drop method by injecting 400 A DC to the contacts when the breaker is closed. If the measurements show that the contact resistance of any given contact pair has increased by more than twice the value obtained during the commissioning test, it is necessary to improve the condition of the contacts. Circuit breaker contacts require checking for their simultaneity of closing and opening whenever they are adjusted, this being accomplished with the three lamps or six lamps method. Three-lamp 6 or 12 volts method is used for checking a circuit breaker when its contacts are enclosed within the tank. The six-lamp circuit serves to check the contacts after the tank has been lowered.

The most common problem met with the operating mechanism of oil circuit breaker is:-

(a) Circuit breaker fail to close: The probable cause is a burnt-out closing-coil, a blown DC fuse, failure of an auxiliary contact or relay. Other causes may be a break in the closing circuit, seizure of the solenoid plunger, defective auxiliary contacts, interlocks associated with the tripping circuit has not closed. Control supply voltage has dropped below minimum value etc.

(b) Circuit breaker fails to open (trip): The probable causes may be burnt-out trip coil, only one-half of the trip coil is operative, the trip circuit remains broken, the trip free links have moved too far beyond the dead centre line, dirt or rust prevents the trip coil plunger to move freely, a break in the control power, station battery voltage is very low, a short-circuit exists somewhere in the control circuitry.

(4) Air blast circuit breaker maintenance:
Each air blast circuit breaker should be checked daily while it remains in service. During daily inspection following points are to be inspected.
(a) The pressure in the air receiver (by pressure gauge reading) should be within the limits permissible for a given circuit breaker. Check oil leaks if any.

(b) The piston of the make-switch arm, in the closed position its end should be fully home between the fixed contact jaws.

(c) Signs of heating, seen by the presence of temper colours on the make-switch blade, the fixed contact and the line terminals.

(d) The condition of the porcelain parts, especially the support insulators, check for cracks that may develop at a fixing point during a sudden drop in the ambient temperature or during the operation of the breaker.

(e) Oil shock absorber leak.

(f) Air supply valve operation, checked by a look at the flow indicator to see that the float remains at or higher than the mid point of the gauge glass.

During air blast circuit breaker preventive maintenance (monthly schedule) the interrupter chambers, the make switch actuating mechanism, moving and fixed contacts, and the devices in the control cabinet are inspected. The porcelain parts are inspected after they have been wiped clean. Before starting the work the stop valve on the breaker air supply line should be closed and the air in the receiver discharged by unscrewing the plug at the bottom. If the contact resistance is found too high the interrupter chamber is removed and the contacts are to be reconditioned or replaced.

The make switch is serviced paying attention to the condition of the piston stop, the seat of the indexing ball in the cylinder, the welded seams of the levers on the actuating shaft, the bronze bearing of the oil shock absorber shaft, and the gaskets at the separator as well as cover joints etc. In checking the travel of the actuating mechanism and oil shock absorber pistons, the make switch is manually closed and opened. If the inspection of the make-switch sliding contact reveals that some of the plates show signs of fusion, the surfaces should be smoothed with a fine cut file. Any of the backup springs, which have lost their temper or are rusty, should be replaced. Following this, the plates should be lightly coated with petroleum jelly and the sliding contact reassembled. The make switch fixed contact and ball joint also require checking. All the contact surfaces are wiped with a cloth and then washed with aircraft petrol if necessary.

When the circuit breaker is given a general overhaul, all its units and parts are inspected and if necessary reconditioned or replaced. These are mainly the interrupter, main porcelain support column, pneumatic breaker operating devices, make-switch contacts and actuating mechanism, and air receiver etc. When the breaker has been made ready for operation, it is subjected to mechanical tests according to its operating instructions.

To guard against air circuit contamination each circuit breaker is connected to the supply airline through an air filter. These units are furnished with valves, so that they can be cleaned without shutting off the air supply. While ABCB remains in service all the air supply lines should be blown out at regular intervals, using high-pressure air taken from the main line coming from the compressor. Receivers are connected to the compressor line through a non-return valve, which prevents the receivers from losing their air if a break occurs in the air supply line. To guard against operation of the breaker at a pressure below normal, the control system includes an under pressure switch whose contact will open and break the tripping control circuit as soon as pressure drops too low.

An airflow indication is provided in the supply line coming from the pressure-reducing valve. The case with a sight window, when the airflow is sufficient, the aluminium ball within the glass tube will remain suspended in the air stream and be seen in the window. If the air flow stops, the ball drops out at sight.

Following are the test to be conducted during annual maintenance.

(1) The contact resistance measurements are taken using either a double bridge micro-ohm meter or milli-voltmeter method by injecting DC current. Contract resistance R = V/I ohm. The total resistance of the current carrying circuit should not exceed 500 Micro-ohms for interrupter and 250 Micro-ohms for make-switch. If exceeds repair or replacement is required.

(2) Simultaneous closing of contacts in any given phase is checked by means of an oscillograph. Same instrument can be used for checking the closing time and opening time of the circuit breaker.

(3) Simultaneous opening of the contacts are to be checked. When the contact systems are adjusted, measurements are taken of the contact travel and spring pressure. Their value should agree, within the limits of permissible tolerance, with the figures given in the test certificate. The spring pressure is checked with the aid of a small pneumatic press.

(4) Measurements are made to determine the amount of air taken by the breaker during closing and opening operation, for conditioning the internal support column space, and for covering the leakage loss. This is done with the aid of a precise pressure gauge, (with a 25 kg/cm^2 scale) connected to the air receiver or to the line coming from the stop valve at the air supply main line.

(5) A check should be made of the air control valve solenoid voltage. The voltage must be between 80 to 120 percentage of the rated voltage and the valve should operate at this voltage at the air pressure of 20-21 kg/cm^2

(6) Flow of conditioning air cut off: Before carrying out tests of the circuit breaker insulation or putting the breaker in to service after an overhaul, it is necessary to dry out the insulation in the interrupter chambers and the internal parts of the porcelain support column by passing compressed air through them for 2 to 3 hours.

(7) The action of the remote control circuit is checked by performing three-phase and per phase closings and openings from the control room.

(8) By means of a DC high-pressure test set, a measurement is taken of the leakage current of the porcelain support column at 40 KV voltages. An insulation resistance measurement is to be taken with a 5 KV megger.

(9) To check the distribution of the voltage between the stacked support-insulators carrying to make switch fixed contact, use is made of a live line voltage tester with testing stick.

4.27 SWITCHING PROCEDURES, SEQUENCE, AND OPERATION OF SUBSTATIONS.

Switching operations in substation should only be entrusted to specially trained personnel having the necessary technical knowledge, practical experience and trained in safety regulations and procedures. To guard against any mistakes, various warning, operating instructions, should be displayed through out the substations to alert the operator. Therefore the bus bar systems, the switch houses and their individual cells, the bays in outdoor stations, the various units of high voltage equipments and apparatus, the operating mechanism of the circuit breakers and disconnecting switches etc. should be clearly named, numbered and also marks to identify the purpose they belongs to. This is very important because the cells of indoor substations and bays of outdoor substations are quite similar in appearance and the equipment they contain. To prevent wrong operation of the switchgear, primarily of the isolators, systems of mechanical interlocking direct and indirect, should be incorporated wherever possible so that no isolator can be opened when it carries load current.

Isolators/Disconnectors

In switch houses it is frequent practice to use electromagnetic interlocking by means of which no operation may be carried out on a given equipment until the requisite key has been fully inserted in to the lock on the operating mechanism. This interlocking does not allow the isolator to be opened or closed if the respective circuit breakers remain closed. It prevents such an operation because the circuit breaker auxiliary switch contact break the circuit supplying current to the locks on the isolator operating mechanisms. Since the lock remains de-energized, the key cannot fully enter the lock, and the latch pin prevents the isolator from being operated.

In figure (b) of section 4.1, the isolators connected to the main bus bars (MB) by Tee-off conductors are called bus bar isolators (BB-DS). The isolator connected between the circuit breaker and the outgoing line, is denoted by, the letters 'LI-DS'. The correct sequence of operation is as follows:
The bus bar isolator is closed first, then the line isolator. Only after closing both isolators the breaker is switched on. Failing which if a fault is persisting in the line or due to load current if the breaker energized while closing the isolator, heavy arc will develop, flash over will take place which in turn lead to a trip out and perhaps personnel injury. When it is required to disconnect the circuit at first trip the breaker, then open the line isolator, and finally the bus bar isolator. Same sequence is observed in substations with a double bus bar system.
Recent development of substation management system left the choice for high and extra high voltage unmanned substations.

Although isolators are operated on off load, closing of an isolator in a charged line should be done quickly and firmly and in all cases operation should be continued to the end even if the arcing develops. The closing should occur without shock between the moving blades and the fixed contacts. If arcing begins and the operator has not completed the closing operation, but discontinues it and starts retract the blades, the arc not only continue to burn but even burn still more intensely because the air becomes ionized as soon as the arcs are drawn.

Three-pole isolators fitted with a lever operating mechanism should be opened quickly and in one movement until the blades reach their extreme open position. Isolators with worm gear operating mechanism, is the best choice for HV/EHV substations. Such units are equipped with motor driven mechanisms designed for remote operation from control room. During the absence of control power isolator can be operated by, rotating the wheel type handle. When an operator has to switch an isolator, at first look for any signs of broken support insulator or bent or faulty linkage and tie rod members. Operator should make sure that all three blades fully enter their fixed contact jaws accurately and tightly while closing a three-pole isolator. If the isolator blades seize, brute force should not be used to overcome the resistance to movement. At-first, look carefully over the operating mechanism and the interlocks. For example, suppose the circuit breaker failed to trip and the operator try to open the associated isolator the mechanical interlock will prevent to open the isolator. It is quite possible that a fault may be developed due to malfunctioning of the operating mechanism or the isolator actuating parts.

Isolators are not proof against self-opening on passage of short circuit currents even if a normal contact pressure is ensured. Therefore isolators are provided with an electromagnetic latch. This comprises two steel bands superimposed on the copper bars of the knife blades at the point of their contact with the fixed contacts of the isolator. During the flow of heavy currents through the blades the steel bands will be attached to each other and press against the blade bars, thus increasing the contact pressure. When making repairs, see that the latches are in good order

Earth switch:
The most reliable means of earthing provided in substations are the permanently installed earthing switches, which are connected to the substation earth grid. These switches are mechanically interlocked with the isolators. These earthing switches are operated in the same way as the isolators. To avoid making a mistake in operation, the operating handle of the earthing switch mechanism is painted in green colour, or a colour differing from isolator handle.

In small substations where there is no earth switch provision, a portable substation earthing device with C clamp as illustrated in Figure 4.27 is being used for earth connection to earth grid. The portable earth set should be applied by first attaching the earth conductor to convenient and safe point to the earth grid bus, then, the other end is attached with the aid of a tipped insulating stick to the conductor to be earthed. Only then should be the remaining conductors of the set to be attached in the same way to the required parts. Earthing method described above ensure that any charge remaining on a conductor will be drained to earth at the first touch. During issuing work permit, the area permitted to work is earthed by using the portable earthing device.

Before any circuit may be earthed, whether by means of a stationary earthing switch or a portable set of safety earthing conductors, a check should be made with a portable voltage indicator to make sure the conductors of the circuit concerned are not live. If a voltage indicator is not available an insulating rod of the same voltage level can serve the same purpose. Absence of a cracking sound or signs of sparkings as the metal head of the insulating rod is brought near the conductors indicates that the circuit is not live. This method can only apply during dry weather.

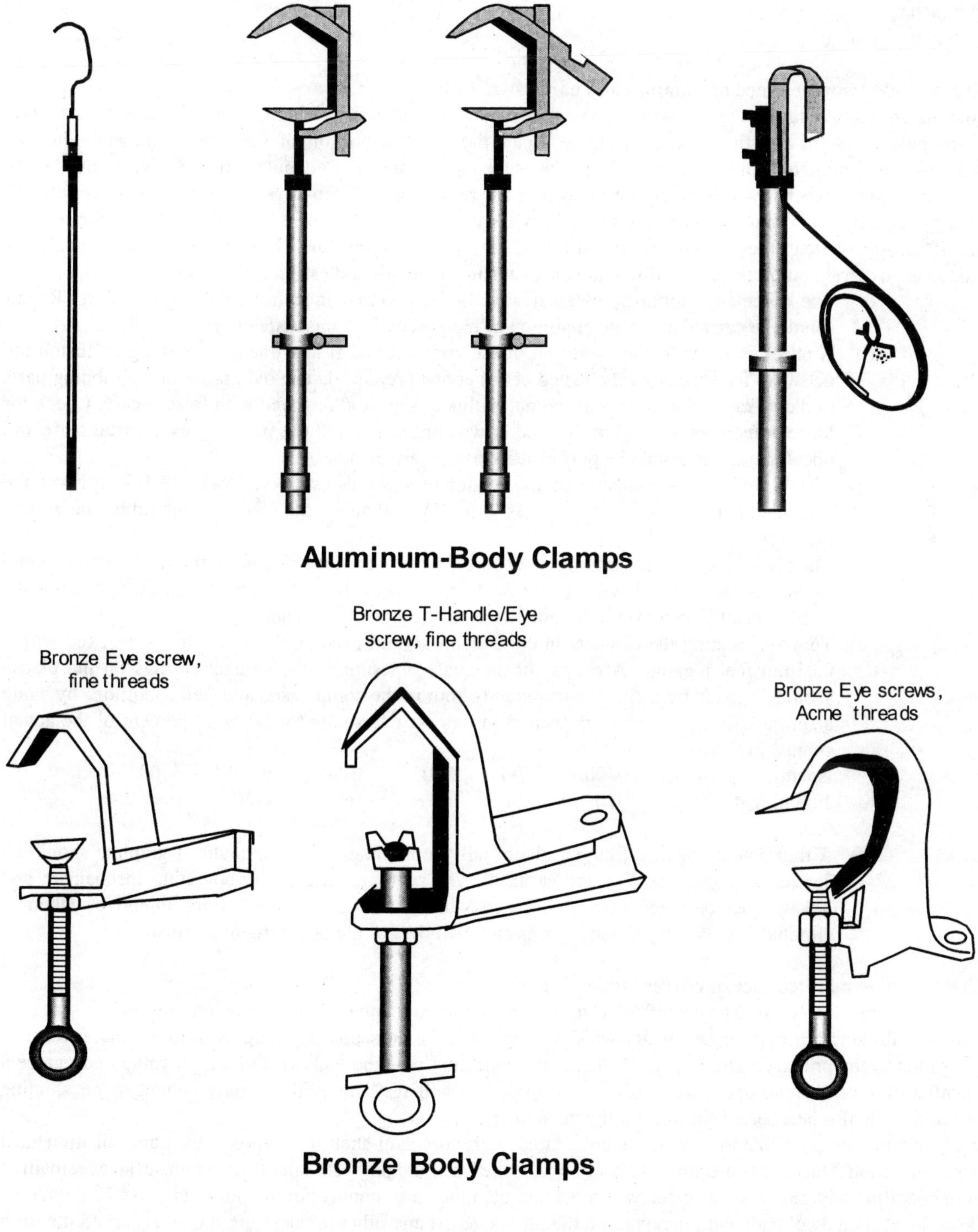

Fig. 4.27: Portable substation earthing device with C clamp (Courtesy, A B Chance co).

4.28 PREVENTIVE MAINTENANCE OF HV/EHV SUBSTATION EQUIPMENTS

Preventive maintenance of following outdoor type HV/EHV substation equipments are discussed below.

(a) Isolator / disconnector;
(b) Earth switch / shorting switch;
(c) Current transformer;
(d) Potential transformer;
(e) Surge arrestor;
(f) Reactor;
(g) Bus bar system;

(1) Preventive maintenance of isolators and earth switches:

Isolators are high voltage switches, which serve to provide an open and visible break in a de-energized section of the power system and thus make it safe to repair the isolated portion of the line equipment. Shorting switches are similar to isolators but the outgoing side phases are shorted out at the receiving end of the transmission line, where there is no circuit breaker at the receiving end step down substation. This switch will remain closed during a shut down (permit to work) will cause the operation of the circuit breaker at the sending end if an inadvertent (accidental) energization of the transmission line. Following are the preventive maintenance carried out in isolators / disconnectors, shorting switches and earthing switches.

(a) The porcelain should be cleaned with lintless wetted in petrol or methyl hydrate. Repair should be carried out if the condition of the porcelain is unsatisfactory.

(b) A check is made to the condition of the contacts and if any traces of burning or fusion are detected, the surfaces are cleaned or the contact replaced. The old grease in the rubbing parts of the linkages should be washed out with kerosene and renewed with fresh grease. Check for loose bolts, nuts, springs at the lead down connection and the fixings. Several trial close and open operations should be performed during maintenance.

(c) Check simultaneous closing of the blades in a 3-pole isolator. Up to 33 KV systems the permitted blade lag is 3mm, whereas in 66 KV and above the blade lag should not be greater than 5mm.

(d) The blades require checking to make sure that they do not strike in on the fixed contact while closing because they have become bent or over-travel. Each blade should directly enter the fixed contact jaws and stop within 3 to 5mm from the blind end.

(e) To avoid heating the contacts in the isolator should make a close fit. This is checked with a 0.05mm feeler gauge. A check for adequate pressure of the contact springs on the blades should be made by taking measurements both in the compressed and free conditions by using a spring balance. The pull measured in this way accounts for 30 to 40 percent of the actual contact pressure.

Isolator rating in Amps:	400	600	800	1000	2000	3000
Pull in Kgf:	10	20	40	60	80	100

(f) A thin coating of acid free petroleum jelly containing a slight amount of graphite should be applied to the surfaces of the contacts. The rubbing parts in the operating mechanism and linkage members should be lubricated with non-freezing grease. Care should be taken to eliminate excess play in the tie rods and members of the operating mechanism.

(2) Preventive maintenance of current transformers:

No current transformer should be left with its secondary circuit open. If opened while energized, since no current is flowing through the secondary winding, there will be no secondary magneto-motive force to act in opposition to the primary m.m.f. As a result the magnetic flux will suddenly rise to a high value and induce a potential of several thousand volts across the secondary terminals. This will not only endanger the winding insulation, but also be a serious hazard for the personnel.

Outdoor type current transformers are manufactured with porcelain shell, cast epoxy resin and oil immersed paper insulation. During maintenance it should be checked that the porcelain and the contact surfaces remain in good condition and the oil is in the correct level and also the earth connection remain intact. At 20 degree C, the oil level should coincide with the mark on the oil gauge. At any other temperature the level should not drop below the bottom minimum level marking at the expansion chamber head. The dielectric test of the oil and the

loss tangent should be measured during annual maintenance and compare the value with the previous test results. If the values dropped below normal the current transformer should be dried out after draining the oil. Current transformer insulation may be dried out by, shorting the secondary and injecting current to the primary or current is injected to the secondary and the primary is shorted. In both case current should not exceed more than 10% of its rated value and the process can be continued 15 to 18 hours but the temperature may be within the limits of 75-80 degree C. The insulation is considered to be dry when the insulation resistance remains constant for 3 – 4 hours. Built-in primary or secondary injection test set should not be used for injecting current as they are short time rated equipments.
The polarity checking consists in making sure that the leads have been connected to primary terminals P_1 and P_2 and the secondary terminals S_1 and S_2, so that the terminals actually correspond, respectively, to the start and finish of each winding.

(3) Preventive maintenance of potential transformers:
During service electromagnetic voltage transformers require checking for correct oil level, condition of the porcelain shell, current limiting resistors, protective secondary fuse etc. Besides this they require the regular checking of the HV connecting terminal pad, porcelain surfaces and sampling of oil for dielectric test. Care should be taken to maintain the oil level at the gauge mark corresponding to the ambient temperature at the time of inspection. In addition to the above outdoor type voltage transformer require regular checking for satisfactory conditions of the porcelain shell, the oil expansion chamber, and the moisture absorbers serving to prevent ingress of moisture to the oil.

The winding may require a dry-out if it is found that the insulation resistance of the winding and the dielectric strength of the oil is considerably reduced. If some oil leak has reduced the oil level in such an extend that a portion of the core and winding left uncovered, the winding will likewise required a dry-out. Dry-out procedures shall be similar to power transformer one by blowing hot air or circulating hot oil. When a voltage transformer is taken out for an overhaul, a measurement of the magnetizing current should be taken with the secondary voltage maintained at the rated value and the primary left open circuited. If this no load current is greater than the value mentioned in the test certificate, it is necessary to open the transformer and inspect the internal parts. The condition of the high voltage winding insulation is judged by the value of several measurements namely loss tangent of the oil type bushing or porcelain shell, insulation resistance absorption ratio (R60 / R15 = > 1.2). A drop in value greater than 30% of the test report value indicates that the insulation should be dried out. Voltage transformer secondary can be subjected to high voltage test up to 1000 volt AC for 1minute duration.

(4) Preventive maintenance of surge arrester:
To protect substation equipments against waves of over voltage that may arise on overhead transmission lines and protection against induced surges due to lightning discharges near the affected overhead lines, use is made of metal oxide surge arresters for each line feeders and transformer feeders. In order to prevent lightning arresters from operating on the occurrence of an earth fault in the circuit, and avoid the risk of damage this involves, these arresters have grading rings, which make metal connections with the covers (shunting the resistors in the ring holders).

The condition of the lightning arrester insulation is checked by, applying a rectified DC voltage to it and determining the leakage current. Test voltage and leakage current are in accordance with manufacturers test certificate. The insulation resistance can be checked by using an insulation tester and compare with test certificate values. Spark gap breakdown voltage is to be conducted by applying AC high voltage to the surge arrester in accordance with the recommendations of the manufacturer.

(5) Preventive maintenance of reactors:
When inspecting an air-cooled indoor reactor, the parts supporting the coils and the porcelain insulator should be checked for cracks, the insulator fixing for tightness, and the metal caps and bases for intact joints. Measurements are taken of the insulation resistance of the parts between the turns and the fixing bolts and compared with the previous measurements. Reactors should be dried out if it is found that a large portion of the varnished surface has become unsatisfactory or the insulation resistance has sharply dropped below the values given in the manufacturers test certificate.

Following are the preventive maintenance to be conducted on an outdoor type high/extra high voltage oil immersed reactor.

(1) Dielectric strength of oil, moisture content in oil, sulpher content in oil, tan delta, colour of oil. (Shell diala 'B' Pale amber clear)
(2) Insulation resistance and continuity check.
(3) Loss tangent of the oil type bushings.
(4) Oil level in the main tank and bushing.
(5) Cleaning the bushing, tank, attending oil leak if any.

(6) Preventive maintenance of bus bar system:
Frequency with which the insulators of the outdoor type substations required cleaning depends on the kind and amount of deposits that settle on them (snow, salt, dust etc). Usually dry rags, rags wetted with water, methyl hydrate, kerosene etc. are used for cleaning. Water spray through nozzle can be used. For live washing use insulated water hose with earthed nozzle. Chipped-off edge (not greater than 60 mm and depth 10 mm) if any on the porcelain insulators, it is permissible to apply 2 coats of alkyd-resin varnish to the bared area and dry the coating for 2 hours at 50 degree C (use 1000 watt incandescent lamp). Multi-shed insulators should not have more than two chipped areas in any vertical line. Unsatisfactory cemented joints may lead turning of the porcelain in the cap or base fitting. If such joints are detected, the insulators should have its fittings re-cemented.

Bushings in the bus bar systems require checking for a shaky current carrying bar or rod, traces of moisture on the internal bakalized paper insulation, scratches on the surface of the paper insulation, and disintegration of the varnish coating. Substation string and post insulators are subjected to the following tests:

(a) Insulation resistance measurements with 5 KV megger. IR value should not be less than 300 Mega-ohms for each set.
(b) Check for equal voltage across each unit of stacked post or tension string set with the aid of a hot stick and KV meter. Test should not be done during foggy or rainy weather or wet snow. When working with hot stick following minimum clearance may be maintained.

System voltage in KV:	6.6 to 36	66 to 110	132 to150	220	400 to 500
Clearance in metre:	1.00	1.50	2.00	3.00	5.00

(c) For corrosion protection of bolted copper bus bar joints the contacting surface should be prepared with a rough cut file, cleaned with a steel wire brush with a coating of petroleum jelly applied to the surface. A similar procedure is followed for aluminium bus bars. In outdoor substations the bolted joints can be made more airtight and weather proof by coating them with red lead and linseed oil paint or synthetic resin varnish. This also applies to all welded joints.
(d) High voltage testing of each single element insulator according to its standard testing procedures.

4.29 EARTH GRID INSTALLATIONS IN POWER STATIONS AND SUBSTATIONS.

The two primary functions of a safe earthing system are:

(6) To ensure that a person who is in the vicinity of earthed facilities during a fault is not exposed to the possibility of a fatal electric shock.
(7) To provide a low impedance path to earth for currents occurring under normal and fault conditions.
(8) Provide ground connection for the neutral for transformers, reactors, and capacitors etc.
(9) Provide the discharge path for surge arresters, lightning rods and similar devices.
(10) Grounding of equipments and lines during repair and maintenance.

Substation and generating station safety requirements calls for the grounding of all exposed metal parts of switchgears, structures, transformer tanks, fences, steel work of buildings, switchboards, secondaries of instrument transformers etc. so that a person touching or nearby of any of this cannot receive a dangerous shock.

There are variety of international standards available, which provide empirical formulae for the calculation of earthing design parameters and shock potential safety limits. The standards, which are widely referred to, are:

IEEE Standard 80, IEEE guide to safety in substation grounding.
IEC Standard 479, Earthing design for high voltage substations and power stations.
BS 7354, Code of practice for design of high-voltage open terminal stations.

- Electricity Association Technical specification 41 – 24. Guidelines for the design, installation, testing and maintenance of main earthing systems in substations.

In order to ensure safety of people at a substation, it is necessary to ensure that step and touch potentials in and around the switchyard earth grid coverage area during earth fault conditions are kept below set limits.

(1) Step potential: The step potential is defined as the potential difference between a persons outstretched feet, normally one metre apart, without the person touching any earthed structure. **(Step potential is the voltage across the two points on the ground level in the substation during an earth fault).** In accordance with IEEE Standard 80, permissible step voltage is 1,024 volts. Permissible step voltage in accordance with IEC standard 479-1 is 1494 volts.

(2) Touch potential: The touch potential is defined as the potential difference between a person's outstretched hand, touching an earthed structure, and his foot. A person's maximum reach is normally assumed to be one metre. **(Touch potential is the potential between finger of a raised hand touching a substation structure and the persons feet during an earth fault).** In accordance with IEEE standard permissible touch voltage is 351 volts. Permissible touch voltage in accordance with IEC Standard 479-1 is 430 volts.

(3) Mesh potential: The mesh potential is defined as the potential difference between the centre of an earthing grid mesh and a structure earth connected to the buried grid conductors. This is effectively a worst-case touch potential. For a grid consisting of equal size meshes, it is the meshes at the corner of the grid that will have the highest mesh potential. For earth grid formed with bare stranded annealed high conductivity copper conductor or copper/Aluminium flat, copper quoted earth rods (Minimum 20 mm diameter 1.8 metre long 4 Nos jointed with heavy duty coupling, per earth pit) are to be installed by driving with power generated hammer unit. (Where Galvanized iron flat is used as earth grid conductor, fabricated G.I. Pipe or G.I. plate is being used as earth electrode).

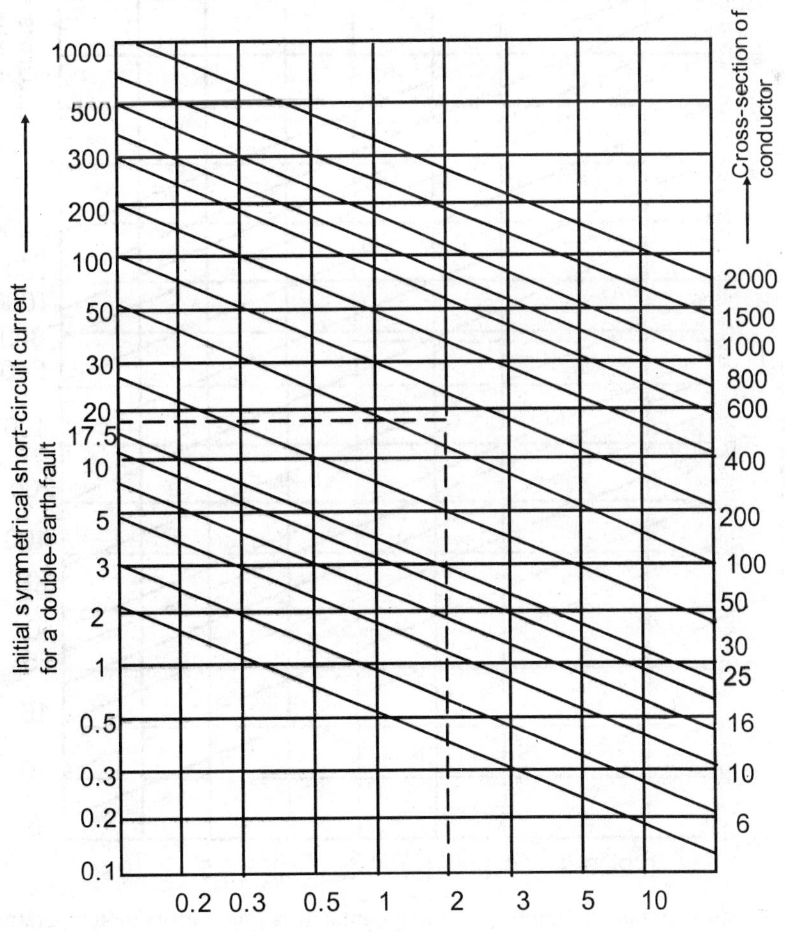

Fig. 4.29 (a): Rating of bare copper earthing conductors for an ultimate temperature at 200C
(Initial temperature 20C. Conversion for an ulti: temp: 300C: $q_{300\ deg\ C} = q_{200\ deg\ C}$ x 0.8)

Earthing design considerations:

The earthing conductors, composing the grid and connections to all equipment and structure, must possess sufficient thermal capacity to pass the highest fault current for the required time. Also, the earthing conductors must have sufficient mechanical strength and corrosion resistance. The design safety criteria installing earthing grid is to be based upon earth fault current equal to main bus bar fault level. Assume that the main bus bar of a substation is designed for 17.5 KA 5 second duration fault level, the earth grid conductor dimensioning current for earth fault must be 17.5 KA magnitude and 3 second duration. Figure 9.29 (a), (b) and (c) respectively illustrates the short circuit rating of bare copper earthing conductors, bare aluminium earthing conductors and galvanized iron mild steel earthing conductors for an ultimate temperature at 200 degree Celsius (initial temperature 20 degree Celsius). The dotted line in the curves shows that at 17.5 KA, 3 seconds fault-ratings, the cross section of copper is 185 mm^2, aluminium 240 mm^2, and mild steel 400 mm^2 at 200 degree Celsius ultimate temperature. At 300 degree Celsius conversion factor 0.8 is to be applied. Hence the revised equivalent size will be copper 185 /0.8 = 231.25 (the standard size is 240 mm^2) , aluminium 300 mm^2 and galvanized mild steel 500 mm^2.

The earthing of metallic fences around a substation / power station is a vital importance because dangerous touch potentials can be involved and the fence is often accessible to the public. Fence earthing can be accomplished in two different ways. The common practice in the UK is to erect the fence away from the grid sides, typically 2 metres, and to earth the fence independently. In USA, the common practice is to extend the grid sides to one metre beyond the fence line and connect the fence to the substation earth grid..

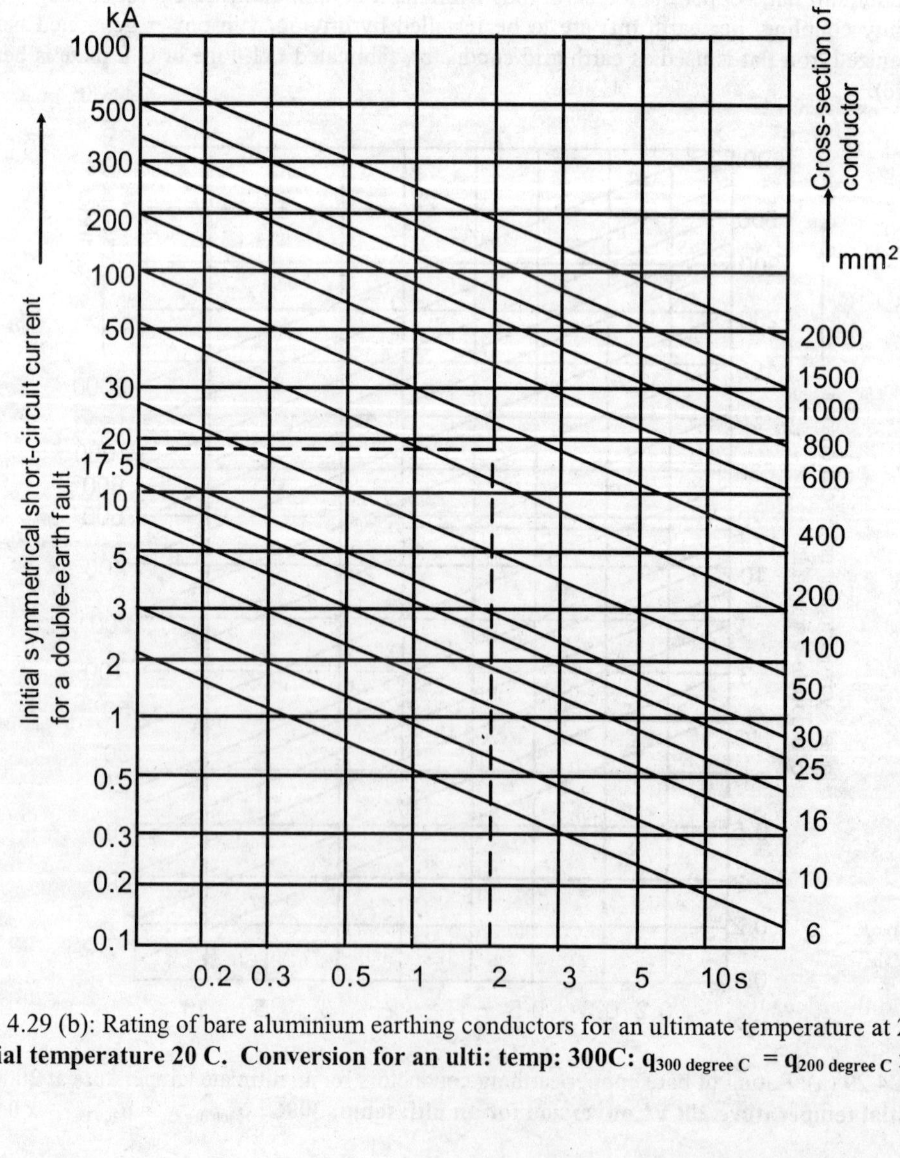

Fig. 4.29 (b): Rating of bare aluminium earthing conductors for an ultimate temperature at 200C

(Initial temperature 20 C. Conversion for an ulti: temp: 300C: $q_{300\ degree\ C} = q_{200\ degree\ C} \times 0.8$)

Earthing requirements for power stations and substations:

Earth grid should be provided for the outdoor switchyard, transformer yard and buildings where GIS, large HV motors etc. are installed. The earth grid for power station should cover machine hall, water treatment plant, workshop etc. An earth grid of buried G.I. flat or copper flat / aluminium flat / stranded copper conductor designed for specified earth fault current (25 to 50 KA, 3 seconds) within the permissible step and touch voltage, assuming a crushed stone surface with a resistivity of 3000 Ω-metre and a maximum exposure time of 0.5 seconds. Earth wires of overhead transmission lines terminated to the gantry should be connected to the earth grid by using copper conductors. Terminal tower footing earthing and 4 corners of shield wires above the switchyard (if applicable) should be connected to the earth grid. Copper conductor connections to the earth rod and cross-junctions of earth grid (all copper to copper joints) in the buried earth grid are to be by using cad weld technique or by using exothermic connections. For aluminium-conductors brazed technique is being used. For G.I flat earthing electric welding is being used but apply bituminous compound to prevent corrosion. Each connection to the earth grid must be at a link chamber adjacent to the grid with two conductors from the grid connected to one terminal.

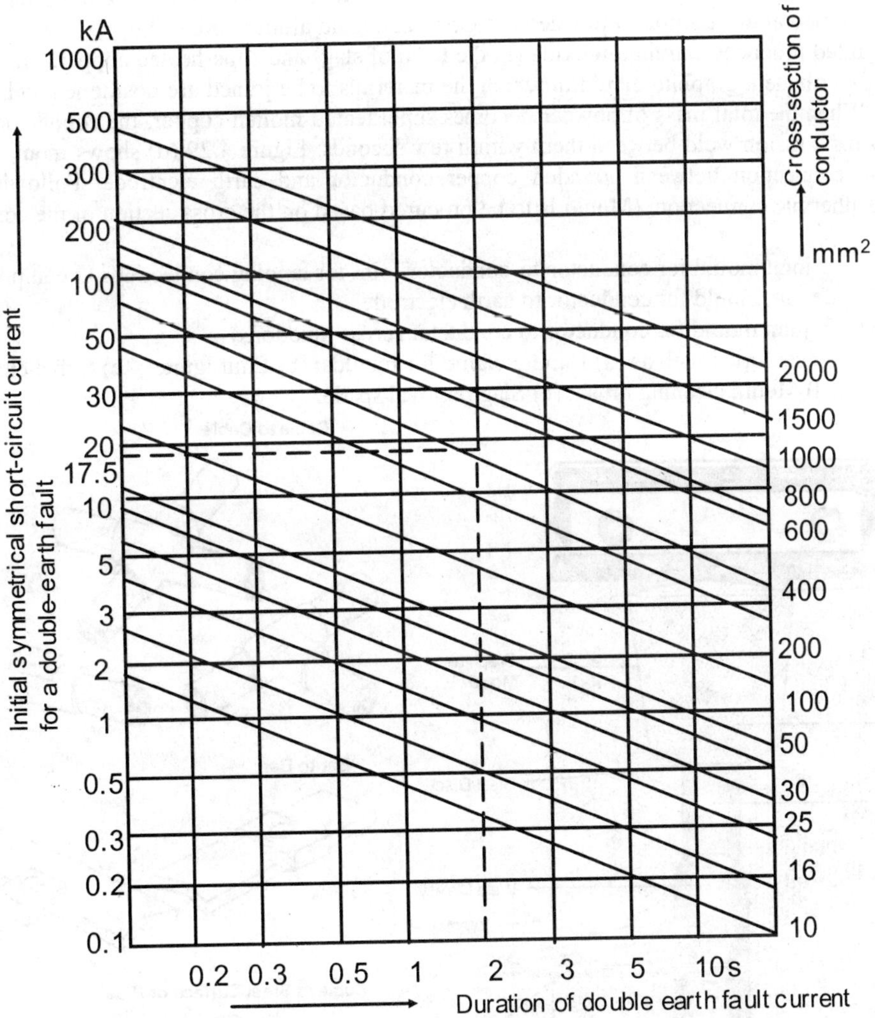

Fig. 4.29 (c): Rating of galvanized steel earthing conductors for an ultimate temperature at 200C

(Initial temperature 20C. Conversion for an ulti: temp: 300C: $q_{300\ deg\ C} = q_{200\ deg\ C} \times 0.8$)

Earthing of equipments at power stations and substations:
The frames of all electrical apparatus and the bases of all steel work should be connected to by conductors of the same cross sectional area of the earth or subsidiary branches running to a group of equipment or conductor which is capable of withstanding earth grid fault current for 3 second duration. All generators, transformers, circuit breakers, auxiliary equipments, disconnectors, earth switches, surge arresters, cable sealing end bases etc must be connected to the earth grid. Surge arresters installed for the protection of transformers should be connected by, direct low reactance paths both to the transformer tank and to the earth grid. Where station fences are of non-insulated metallic material, it should be connected to the power station / substation earth grid at 30 metre intervals to a 35 sq:mm copper conductor (by using cadweld method i.e. exothermic connection) buried one metre outside the fence at a depth of 750 mm. Earth strip run within buildings, steel structures or above ground level on apparatus should be neatly supported in non-ferrous clamps. Stranded earthing conductors are to be terminated with sweated or crimped cable lugs. **Earth conductor should not be laid with control or power cables**. Metallic cable trays installed in cable trenches shall be connected to earth bus.

Exothermic connection
Exothermic connection processes is a simple, portable, efficient method of welding copper-to-copper (flat or stranded conductor) or copper to steel without the use of an external power source. Exothermic connections utilize the high temperature reaction of powdered copper oxide and aluminium. ($2A_1 + 3CuO - Al_2O_3 + 3Cu$), which when ignited produces aluminium oxide (in the form of slag) and superheated copper. The reaction take place in a semi-permanent graphite mould in which the materials to be joined are positioned and ignited using a flint igniter. When the total mass of powder becomes superheated molten copper, the conductors or surfaces to melt and forms a fusion weld between them within few seconds. Figure 4.29 (d) shows mould arrangement for exothermic connection between stranded copper conductor and earth electrode. Following tools are required for exothermic connection. (Mould is to be procured based on the cross section of the conductor to be installed).

1) T joint mould for conductor-to-conductor joint for tapping connections to equipments.
2) T joint mould for conductor to earth electrode.
3) X joint mould for conductor to conductor (cross junctions)
4) Accessories such as (a) Handle clamp for moulds; (b) Flint igniter; (c) Cable cleaning brush; (d) Mould cleaning brush; (e) Slag removal spade.

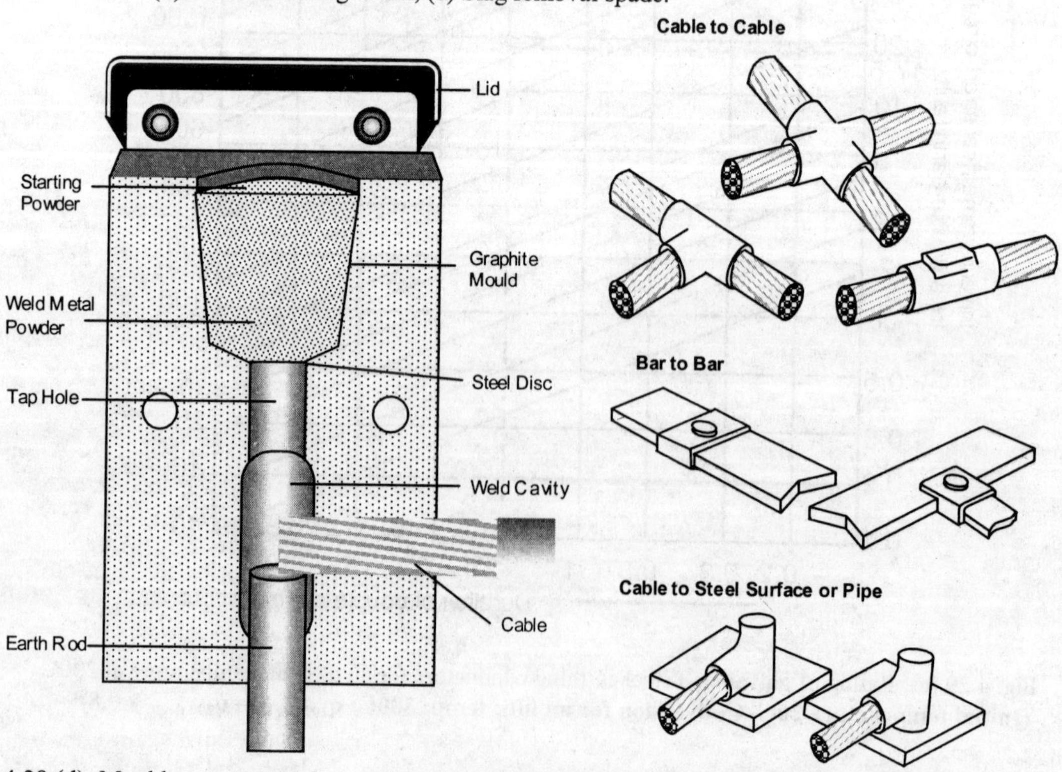

Fig. 4.29 (d): Mould arrangement for exothermic connection, cable to earth electrode (Courtesy, W.S.Furse).

Following are the advantages of using exothermic connectors:

(1) Will not be affected by high current surges.
(2) Will not loosen or corrode at the point of exothermic weld.
(3) Current carrying capacity equal to or greater than that of the conductors welded.
(4) Earth pit chambers are not required.

Inspection and testing of earthing system:
Earthing system require regular inspection, periodic checking and testing to detect any signs of damage and broken connections. The earth resistance is also measured at regular intervals. Each time a routine repair or overhaul is carried out on some unit in a power station or a substation, its earthing connection should be checked for continuity up to the main earthing bus. Two other things requiring checking in service are continuity of the earthing circuit branches and reliability of the contact joints at the point of connection. Tests for this purpose are carried out by, using a rheostat and 500 VA 12 V step down transformer. Connect the 12 V phase lead of the transformer to the earth lead or earth rod under test through a rheostat in series. The other lead (neutral) is connected to earth through a test prob. Lack of current flow in the circuit branch under test, fluctuations of the ammeter pointer during the test or a low value of current in the circuit are a sign of break or a poor contact in the earth connection. At a point where a poor contact exists, either sparking or heating to even a red hot-temperature can be detected.

4.30 PRACTICAL QUESTIONS AND ANSWERS ON HV/EHV BREAKERS/SUBSTATIONS.

Q1: Define step potential and touch potential in a substation earthing system?
Ans: Two primary functions of a safe earthing system are: (1) to ensure that a person who is in the vicinity of earthed facilities during a fault is not exposed to possibility of a fatal electric shock; (2) to provide a low impedance path to earth for currents occurring under normal and fault conditions. The substation earth grid is used as an electrical connection to earth at zero potential reference. This connection however, is not ideal due to the resistivity of the soil within which the earth grid is buried. During typical earth fault conditions, the flow of current via the grid to earth will therefore result in the grid rising in potential relative to remote earth to which other system neutrals are also connected. This produces potential gradients within and around the substation ground and is defined as GPR (Ground potential rise). GPR of the substation under earth fault conditions must be limited so that step and touch potential limits are not exceeded, and is controlled by keeping the earth grid resistance as low as possible. (Refer section 4.29).
Step potential is the voltage across any two points on the floor level.

The touch potential is defined as the potential between finger of raised hand touching a substation structure and the feet.

Q2: What do you mean by creepage distance of an insulator or bushing? How it is measured? Describe IEC recommendation for creepage distance?.
Ans: Creepage distance is the shortest distance between two conducting parts or conducting part to earth along the surface of the insulation material. For example the post insulator shown in Figure (a) of section 4.11, assume that few drops of water is falling at the extreme top (conducting part close to porcelain insulator) and observe how the water drops reach at the bottom mounting plate (earthing point), the actual distance covered for reaching the water is the creepage distance. It can be measured by using a thread.

Creepage distance is calculated on the basis of phase to ground voltage and the degree of atmospheric pollution as listed below.

a) Clean areas:	16mm/KV
b) Moderately polluted areas:	20mm/KV
c) Industrial areas:	25mm/KV
d) Highly polluted area (sea shore):	31mm/KV

Q3: What are the methods adopted for protecting the HV/EHV equipments from lightning surges?
Ans: (a) Surge arrester (b) Shielding wire (c) Lightning mast with air terminal.

Surge arresters (Lightning arresters) serve in general to protect the equipments only against incoming atmospheric and switching over-voltages. An outdoor switching station/substation can be protected against lighting by stringing earth wires (earth wire shielding) or by providing taper pointed) air terminal on the portals for the bus bars and overhead lines. Lightning masts are designed and installed to support the air terminal at a particular height. The protected zone must include the gantry towers all switchgears and transformers installed in the switchyard.

Q4: What are the causes of developing switching surges while closing or opening of HV/EHV circuit breakers?
Ans: (a) While closing circuit breakers switching surge may develop due to: (a) Unloaded, long distance transmission line; (b) Unloaded underground transmission cables; (c) Autoreclosing.
(b) While opening circuit breakers switching surge may develop due to: (a) Transient recovery voltage; (b) Current chopping; (c) Inrush current of transformers and reactors; (d) Re-strike while opening capacitive current [Refer section 3/5 of Chapter # 3]

Q5: What are the reasons for developing momentary over-voltage / sustained over-voltage in power system?
Ans: (1) Momentary over voltage may occur due to: (a) Sudden-rejection of load; (b) Switching on large capacitive load; (c) Earth fault.
(2) Sustained over voltage may occur due to: (a) Reactive power flow; (b) Tap changing in progress.

Q6: What are the reasons for voltage dip in power system?
Ans: (1) Starting heavy motors (2) Switching on large inductive load (3) Momentary line faults (4) Rejection of load by any one parallel running generator:

Q7: Explain various methods of load frequency control of power system?
Ans: Load dispatch center performs the duty of load frequency control in a utility system containing generation, transmission and distribution. Load frequency control is achieved by continuous matching of generation of power with prevailing load conditions. There are two methods:
(a) Primary control: Frequency control by the action of the turbine governor is called primary control. Governor controls the turbine speed by admitting more steam-to steam turbines or more water in hydro turbines. Thereby the power output of the generator is also increased up to the set value. Another method is to start additional unit if available.
(b) Secondary control: Frequency control by introducing load shedding is the secondary load frequency control. Load shedding is automatically performed by the frequency relay. Time of operation of the relay is a function of the difference between the actual frequency and the set frequency. The load is disconnected in steps depending on the priority of the load when the frequency falls below a predetermined value. Similarly the load is reconnected when the frequency exceeds the high set value.

Q8: What are the various methods of voltage control in HV/EHV system?
Ans: (a) By using of on-load automatic tap changing power transformers.
(b) Switching in shunt reactors during low loads or while energizing long distance transmission lines (Sending end and receiving end only) to cancel ferranti effect. Ferranti effect means the receiving end voltage is higher than the sending end voltage of a transmission line.
(c) Switching in shunt capacitors at receiving end at high loads or poor power factor.
(d) Use of series capacitors on either ends of long distance transmission lines to compensate reactive power.
(e) Use of synchronous condensers (unloaded synchronous motors) in receiving stations for reactive power compensation.
(f) Use of shunt reactors while starting medium voltage motors in order to overcome voltage dip
(g) Use of thyristor controlled static shunt compensators.

Q9: Define the term tracking of insulators? What are the reasons for tracking? How it can be overcome?
Ans: Tracking is formation of permanent conducting path along the surface of the insulator. Following are the causes:
(a) Degradation of surface glaze of porcelain insulator due to sparking.
(b) Presence of conduction film along the surface of porcelain insulator due to accumulation of moisture and dirt, salt layer, snow etc.
(c) Cracks on insulator due to mechanical stress.
(d) Leakage current along the insulator surface

To prevent tracking, the insulators should be cleaned regularly. Water bath by spraying water keep the insulator dry and clean.

Q10: Define the term corona and critical disruptive voltage?
Ans: An electrical discharge in air that only partially bridges the gap between two or more electrodes. Corona leads to power loss and causes radio interference, as well as leading to physical damage of the insulation. Corona can be tested by measuring the discharge magnitude using a radio receiver, and this is then referred to Radio influence voltage (RIV) test.

Corona due to dirt, snow, rain, moisture, fog, humidity, temperature and pressure effect are considered as critical disruptive voltage.

Q11: What are the main features of a metal oxide surge arrester used in HV/EHV system?
Ans: (a) Arrester diverts lightning surge current to ground in a controlled manner without power interruption.
(b) Reduce lightning interruptions caused by insulation flashovers in transmission/distribution lines.
(c) Effective protection for unshielded and supplemental protection for shielded transmission and distribution lines.
(d) Metal oxide arrester works in parallel with line insulator. During a surge, the arrester limits voltage across the insulation to a value below the insulator flashover voltage.

Q12: Compare the difference between an HV disconnector (used in open switchyard) and HV load break switch (used in Gas or air insulated metal clad switch gear)?
Ans: Disconnector is used for isolate a equipment when the power is de-energized, usually for maintenance purposes. It is an isolating switch with out load breaking capacity. Whereas, load break switch is designed for on load operation, i.e. to break the load if necessary. Usually load break switch is used for energizing off load (unloaded lines), for example, magnetize and de-magnetize transformers and for medium duty fault interruption. In HV/EHV system load breaking is carried out through circuit breakers only.

Q13: Define pre-insertion resistance and its application on extra high voltage breakers?
Ans: Circuit breakers are bi-stable devices (stable in both open and closed positions). When loaded, their contacts are closed and carrying load current. A circuit breaker without resisters has two states, closed (means zero impedance across the main contact) and open (infinite impedance across the contact means ∞). In the closing operation, resisters are used as the intermediate state (between open and close position). These resisters might be closing in a three step process i.e. **OPEN- RESISTER LEVEL-CLOSED.** The resistors ease the impedance change from an open circuit to a closed circuit.

During a fault, a disturbance, or normal switching off, the circuit breaker must open and isolate the circuit. This circuit interruption happens very quickly (2 cycles). It is this rapid transition that can cause a buildup of very high voltage in the circuit. The rate of change of circuit impedance is the cause of this voltage buildup. Switched resistors that bridge the main contacts can alleviate the dangerously high voltage buildup by making the interruption a three-step process instead of a two-step process. As such a resistor will limit the build up of voltage that could exceed the BIL (Basic insulation level) of substation equipments.

Q14: Explain the term "Arc interruption" in a circuit breaker?
Ans: The arc is a discharge of electricity through gas. It is an ionized path of particles that conducts electricity. It may be considered a conductor during the time the arc is established. The basic conception of arc interruption is to stretch out the arc and cool it. Twice the cycle the current is zero, if there is sufficient dielectric strength buildup between the contacts as the voltage rises the arc will not be re-established.

Q15: What are the two different arc-extinguishing methods employed in SF6 insulated circuit breakers?
Ans: (a) Single pressure system: The puffer type breaker uses a moving piston or cylinder to compress the sulfur Hexaflouride gas that is forced across the parting contacts during the contact opening sequence.
(b) Two pressure system: A high-pressure reservoir stores the sulfur Hexaflouride gas under a high pressure for quenching the arc during the contact opening sequence.

Q16: Explain the term "flashover" in high voltage system?

Ans: A disruptive discharge around or over the surface of an insulating member, between parts of different potential or polarity, produced by the application of voltage wherein the breakdown path becomes sufficiently ionized to maintain an electric arc. In high voltage testing the term "flashover" is used when a disruptive discharge occurs over the surface of a solid dielectric in a gaseous or liquid medium.

Q17: Define the term Hi-pot test on high voltage cables?
Ans: High potential test is short named as Hi-pot test. A test performed by applying a high voltage for a specified time to two isolated points (core to earth of a cable or between cores) in a device to determine adequacy of insulating materials. DC high-pressure test sets are used for testing XLPE insulated HV/EHV cables. [Refer figure (e) of section 4.19, DC high-pressure test].

Q18: What is distributed control system? Where it is used?
Ans: These systems provide "real-time" monitoring and control of a given "process" within a plant. These are also referred to as "in-plant" systems. All major components of the system are usually confined to one or several close by facilities. The communications media consists of primarily coax or fiber cable. Wireless medium may be used within a plant (at low bandwidth/speed) or between buildings through microwave point-to-point connections (at higher bandwidth/speed). Examples of places where a DCS would be used include a power plant, a refinery etc. [Refer Chapter # 1, section 1.1, figure (L), Distributed control system].

Q19: Describe ferroresonance effect on high/extra high voltage potential transformers?
Ans: Apart from lightning surge and overload (by exceeding its rated burden) an HV/EHV, PT may get destroyed due to "ferroresonance". This may occurs, when the only path to ground on a three-phase ungrounded system or single phase grounded system is through the PT, and magnetizing reactance of the PT happens to be of such a value as to resonate with the line capacitance. Under this condition, the PT will be subject to a voltage far in excess of its normal value and the PT is liable to get burnout. Another possible cause for a PT burnt-out is due to the discharge of the energy stored in line capacitance, provided an unloaded line disconnected from the source leaving only the PT in the line circuit.

Q20: Discriminate switching surge and surge withstand capability?
Ans: (1) Switching surge:
High voltage spikes, can occur when current flowing in a highly inductive circuit or a long transmission line, is suddenly interrupted. As the magnetic field about the inductive conductor collapses, a brief by very-high voltage can be generated at the terminal point of the circuit.
(2) Surge withstand capability:
Surge withstand capability is a measure of an electrical device's ability to withstand high voltages or high frequency transients of short duration without being any damages. Surge withstand capability can be tested in an equipment by applying an oscillatory wave, (Frequency range of 1 to 1.5 MHz, voltage range of 2.5 to 3 KV) crest value of the first peak, envelope decaying to 50% of the crest value of the first peak in not less than 6 microseconds from the start of the wave. The source impedance is from 150 to 200. The wave is to be applied to a test specimen at a repetition rate of not less than 50 tests per second for a period of not less than two seconds.

Q21: Describe perimeter fencing in an outdoor open switchyard? Specify material list for a typical HV/EHV substation fence and gate?.
Ans: The perimeter fence of an outdoor switching station must be at least 1800 mm high. The minimum clearance between perimeter fence and live parts (safety zone) must be provided based on the system voltage. Station perimeter fences made of conducting materials must be earthed at intervals of no more than 100 M by means of driven earth rods, unless potential control is provided by means of a surface earth connection approximately 1 M outside the fence and about 0.5 M deep. No special measures are required in the case of perimeter fences made of plastic-coated wire mesh with plastic coated or concrete post.

Following are the list of items to be procured for a typical substation fence.

1) G.I. Fence post made of 65 x 65 x 8 mm angle iron, 2.9 M height.
2) 8 SWG GI / PVC insulated chain link mesh 50 x 50 mm, 2.4 m height.
3) Straining wire (barbed wire) 3 runs (above wire mesh at 100mm intervals.
4) Gateposts made of 150 mm diameter 4mm thick pipe, 2.7 M height.

5) Swing type lockable double door gate 3 M width, 2.4 M height.

Q22: Describe earthing system in an HV/EHV/HVDC substation?

Ans: Earth grids are designed in accordance with relevant IEC or IEEE standards, based on the soil resistivity measurement at site. Usually bare copper strip or stranded conductors (240 or 300 sq:mm) or galvanized iron earth strips (240 or 400 sq: mm) is being laid at every 5 M interval (longitudinally and transversely), 1 M below the finished surface level of the switching area. In case of G.I. flat is used as earth conductor cross-junctions of strips are welded and bitumen compound is applied in order to prevent corrosion. Where as copper conductor is used as earth conductor every cross junctions, tapping points and earth rod connection to the grid must be made by exothermic connection using cadweld powder and die set. Sufficient number of earth pits (deep buried earth plates or G.I pipe or copper coated high carbon steel earth rods) based on the design requirements shall be provided and connected to the grid. The earth resistance shall be less than one ohm.

All supporting structures and equipments must be connected to the earthing network by using conductors having cross section similar to the earth grid. In the case of networks with solidly earthed neutral, particular attention must be paid to the supplementary requirements in view of the high earth-fault current occurring in the event of an earth fault. Certain ground conditions make it difficult to obtain a reliable earth resistance, whilst particular installations may require a very low resistance. In such cases, Marconite (a product of Furse) provides a convenient and permanent solution. By adding it in place of sand and aggregate, to cement, a conductive concrete is formed around the buried earth electrodes. The copper coated earth electrode shall be minimum 20 mm diameter and overall length 5.4 metre. For GI earth electrode salt and coal mixture is used.

Q23: Describe cable trench, cable support system, and cable routing in an open switchyard?

Ans: The switchyard main concrete trench 1 to 1.2 M width and 1 to 1.5 M depth (covered with concrete slabs or galvanized steel chequered plates) are provided in outdoor installations. The main trenches follow the access road and the branches adjoin to the equipments. A fall in the lengthwise direction and the drain holes ensure reliable drainage. In each branch, UPVC ducts are teed off for the control cables following the equipments. Cable supports (Heavy duty galvanized perforated or ladder cable tray as required) are arranged along the sides together with 2 or 3 tier support brackets at every 1.5 M intervals.

Cable support accessories such as fish plates, cross- junction, bend, Tee, reducer and riser etc are to be provided as required in the layout drawing. Cables are laid as per the cable schedule and care shall be taken to prevent crossing of cables. Single core power cables are laid (only ladder type cable trays) in tri-foil formation and clamped with tri-foil clamps (of required short circuit withstand capacity) at every 3 M intervals. Separate trays are to be used for control cables. Cable identification tags following cable numbers as per cable schedule are required for each cable at every 50 M intervals in straight lines, both ends and every turning points. Control and power cables shall be fastened to the tray in an approved manner. Earth conductor should not be laid with control or power cables. AC and DC power cables are segregated and laid separately.

Q24: Describe AAAC conductors and IPS aluminium tubes used for outdoor bus bar installation?

Ans: All aluminium alloy conductors not less than 400 mm^2 or two parallel wires as a multiple conductor are employed for jumpering purposes in view of the maximum permissible surface voltage gradients. Tensioned AAAC conductors of suitable cross section can be used as bus bar for nominal current ratings below 2000 A. For higher ratings or to meet the required short-circuit ratings IPS (International Piping Standards) aluminium tubes having wall thickness from 3 to 12 mm are being used. Tubular conductors are mounted on post insulators in spans of up to 20 M. Dampers of various types are available for suppressing any oscillation of the aluminium tubes. An effective means of damping oscillation is to insert aluminium wires with cross-sections of 300 to 600 mm^2 in to the tubes. Current ratings of tubular aluminium conductors and AAAC are given in section 4.12 (1) and (2) respectively.

Q25: Describe portable earthing equipment used in outdoor HV/EHV substations?

Ans: Portable earthing equipment is used for temporary earthing of outdoor high voltage substations or overhead / underground transmission lines where maintenance is to be carried out (refer figure 4.27). It has been designed to provide safe and sure clamping where certain connections are to be made on dirty or heavily oxidized copper / aluminium tubular bus bars or stubs or conductors. The clamps, sockets, insulated operating pole and cables are designed to suit their respective applications. They are safely withstood mechanical type tests and or short time current type tests specified in ESI 41-21, section 5. In accordance with ESI (Engineering Standards Institution) specification, PVC insulated flexible aluminium conductor 150 mm^2 cross-section are being used as earth lead. Number of leads to be used is based on the system short circuit current. Up to 17.5 KA 1 lead is sufficient. (31.5 KA 2 leads, 47.5 KA 3 leads and 63 KA 4 leads).

Q26: What are the different types of XLPE cables used in HV/EHV system and its current ratings?
Ans: XLPE (Cross-linked polyethylene) cables single core up to 2500 mm^2 cross-section and up to 550 KV voltage ranges are manufactured in the following construction features:

(a) Copper tape shielded cables: Suitable only for small earth fault current capacity circuits.

(b) Copper wire shielded cables: Suitable for large earth fault current capacity circuits.

(c) Corrugated aluminium sheathed cables: Used for direct burying applications.

(d) Stainless steel sheathed cables: To increase protection from an earth fault current, copper wire shielding is applied underneath the sheath.

(e) Lead sheathed cables: Lead, a material possessing good anti-chemical characteristics, protects cable insulation completely from water and damaging substances, but not resistant to mechanical shocks. Water blocking tape is applied over the core providing longitudinal water barrier between core and lead sheath. Lead alloy sheath provides radial water barrier and carries the short-circuit currents. Cables with a waterproof layer formed from laminated lead under the outer sheath to avoid water penetrating in to the cable insulation through the PVC outer sheath. Extruded black MDPE compound provides anti-corrosion protection.
Technical data and current ratings are given in Appendix # 1 to 4.

Q27: Describe AC power frequency voltage test on HV/EHV XLPE insulated cables?
Ans: The power frequency voltage test on XLPE insulated HV/EHV cables are to be made at ambient temperature using an AC test voltage at power frequency. The test voltage shall be raised gradually to the specified value, which may then be hold for the given time between conductor and metallic screen.

Rated nominal voltage (Phase to phase)	Test voltage to be applied (Times of phase to neutral voltage)	Duration of test (Hours)
66 to 220 KV	2.5	0.5
275 to 345 KV	2.3	1.0
400 to 550 KV	1.9	1.0

Q28: What are the different types of oil-filled cables used in HV/EHV transmission systems.
Ans: Paper insulated oil-filled power cables (invented in 1924), having a long history of wide application, since 1935 to 1985. Due to the introduction of XLPE insulated HV/EHV cables (in 1985) the application of oil-filled cables up to 550 KV is limited. Between 550 KV and 765 KV, high-pressure oil-filled cables are used. Due to introduction of long transmission (reactance free) HVDC cables, again the application of oil-filled cable is obsolete.

Following types of single core oil-filled cables were used for HV/EHV transmission.

(a) Aluminium sheathed oil filled cables: Having large earth fault current rating capacity.
(b) Lead sheathed oil filled cables: Used in heavy-duty environments requiring good anti-chemical characteristics, protects cable insulation from water and other damaging substances. Lead sheath is not resistant to mechanical shocks. Armoured oil filled cables are used for underground applications.
(c) Oil filled submarine cables: For submarine HV/EHV power transmission.

Oil-filled cables are classified, in to low-pressure, medium-pressure, and high-pressure cables depending on the permissible pressure range between normal operating position and transient operation. Following are the permissible pressure ranges:

(a) 3 to 6 Kg /sq:cm for low-pressure cables.
(b) 6 to 11 Kg / sq:cm for medium pressure cables..
(c) 18 to 26 Kg / sq:cm for high-pressure cables.

Q29: Why mass impregnated paper insulated cables are preferred for HVDC submarine applications? Explain the method of laying cable in deep-sea area?
Ans: HVDC cable consists of main conductor, conductor screen, impregnated paper insulation, insulation screen, copper woven fabric tape, lead sheath, polyethylene sheath, bedding and transversal reinforcement as well as bedding for the return conductor. Return copper conductor is laid up around the main cable similar to armour wire and insulated with polyethylene insulation [refer figure 4.22 (J)].
Above that galvanized steel wire armour, then outer sheath made of polyethylene yarn and bitumen. During manufacturing process immediately after paper wrapping over the conductor the cable must be placed in to a suitable impregnation tank, where the paper has dried under vacuum before the impregnation itself with oil took place.

Installation and burial of the submarine cable in deep sea is by using a low impact, hydraulic jet-plow called a cap-jet. The cap-jet will create a very narrow trench and the fluidized sediments quickly settle around the cable after the plow has passed. The trench will normally be fully reinstated within a few current or tide cycles

Q30: Explain the terms 'transmission', 'transmission line' and 'transmission tower'?
Ans: (a) Transmission: The bulk transport of electricity from large generating stations over significant distances to interchanges with large industries and distribution networks of utilities.
(b): Transmission line: A high voltage or extra high voltage or ultra high voltage power line (overhead or underground) used to transmit electric power efficiently over long distances.
(c): Transmission tower: A broad-base latticed hot dip galvanized steel support for line and earth conductors.

Q31: What are the different types of lattice-towers used for single or double circuit transmission lines?
Ans: (a) Tangent suspension tower, which can be used for normal spans where no angle in the line occur.
(b) Angle suspension tower, which can be used for normal spans with a very small angle turn in the line or with longer spans on tangents.
(c) An angle tower, which can be used for normal spans with a large angle turn in the line. Insulators are in the strain position.
(d) Dead end tower, which can be used at either ends of the transmission lines. Anchored or guyed towers are used in long spans.
(e) Transposition towers are special towers used for changing the relative position of conductors in an overhead line. For example, take off tower, EHV line crossing tower, long span river-crossing tower, Anti-wind tower used for reinforce anchor section of transmission lines.
(f) Terminal tower, which can be used near the switchyard for taking of overhead transmission line to the gantry structure.

Q32: What are the different types of foundations used for erecting towers of overhead transmission lines?
Ans: (a) RCC foundation: Steel reinforced concrete construction (tied up with steel rod).
(b) Pile foundation: Concrete foundation supported by, steel pipe piling or bore hole concrete piling.
(c) Rock foundation: Pits are made by, boring holes in the rock. Tower leg stub is placed in the pit and concrete is poured in the pit.
(d) Steel grillage foundation: Rectangular or square grillage base are used for each base leg of the tower. The grill is buried in the leg stub of the tower without concrete. Tower footing is welded to the grillage base.

Q33: What are the different configurations employed while designing lattice steel towers?
Ans: (a) Single circuit horizontal configuration: A single circuit tower designed with horizontal cross arm in which all insulator strings ('I' string or 'V' string) are attached in a horizontal plane.
(b) Single circuit delta configuration: A tower with the two outside insulator strings in the same horizontal plane and the center string supported at a higher level.
(c) Double circuit vertical configuration: A tower with three cross arms, each supporting two circuit conductors; all three phases of one circuit usually vertically located in one side of the tower.

Q34: What are the different types of footings employed for tower structures?
Ans: (a) Concrete footing: A footing designed for special conditions and consists buried reinforced conrete.
(b) Rock footing: Footing consisting of stub angles cemented in to a hole drilled in solid rock..

(c) Pressed plate footing: Footing consisting of galvanized steel plate, ranging in size 600 sq: mm to 1500 sq: mm, single or multiple.
(d) Grillage footing: Footing made of framework of galvanized steel with wide-flange beams and channels; attached to footing stub angle and attaching lug extension.

Q35: Give details of fire fighting equipments to be located in an HV/EHV sub stations, according to NFPA recommendations? (NFPA: National fire protection association)

Ans: Table 4.24 (1) below shows NFPA recommendation for fire protection and detection systems to be employed in HV/EHV substations. (NFPA: National fire protection authorities)

Location and equipment name	Recommended fire protection system	Recommended fire detection system
Power-Transformer Station transformer	Automatic fixed spray water deluge systems (NFPA 15)	Quartzoid-bulb-detectors (NFPA 72 specification)
Cable trenches and cable floors	Nil	Smoke detectors
Electronic and computer rooms	FM-200 Clean agent fire extinguisher (NFPA-2001) & Hand-held Portable fire extinguishers (NFPA 10)	Smoke detectors/Heat detectors and alarm system (NFPA 72)
Control-room and Medium voltage switchgear room	Fire hose reel with cabin (NFPA 14) & Hand held portable fire extinguisher	Smoke/Heat detector and alarm system (NFPA 72)
Outdoor area	Nil	Break glass manual call points

CHAPTER # 5

CURRENT AND VOLTAGE TRANSFORMERS, RELAYS AND TESTING APPARATUS

CONTENTS:

5.1 CURRENT TRANSFORMERS FOR PROTECTION AND METERING.

Current transformer is a transformer specially designed to accurately represent the primary current in the secondary circuit. Current transformers are standardized for a secondary current of 1 ampere or 5ampers, when rated current is passed through the primary circuit, although other values are possible. Current transformer is used to measure the amount of current flowing in a circuit such as metering devices or protective relays. Its primary winding is rated in excess of the expected continues current of the circuit and the secondary will be normally being proportional to normal primary current. Current transformer is transforming heavy currents in to very low values for protection and metering.

Based on its construction, the following types of CT's are available.

(a) Bar primary [Figure 5.1 (a)] in which the primary is the single or multi-bar rectangular bus bar.
(b) Ring type [Figure 5.1 (b)] in which the primary is a single core cable or one core of a multi-core cable.
(c) Window type [Figure 5.1 (c)] in which the primary is the square or angular bus bar.
(d) Bushing type [refer figure 4.7 (c) of Chapter # 4] in which bushing draw out lead of circuit breaker/transformer/reactor etc is the primary.
(e) Outdoor type [refer figure 4.7 (a) of Chapter # 4] in which tubular bus bar is the primary
(f) Split core type or Toroidal type [Figure 5.1 (d)] in which multi-core cable is the primary.

Different types of connections employed for current transformer secondary winding in a three-phase system and its advantages and disadvantages are demonstrated below.

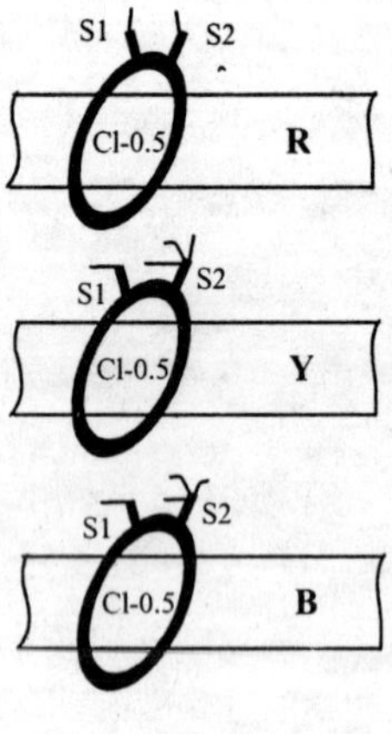

Fig. 5.1 (a): Bar primary current transformer.

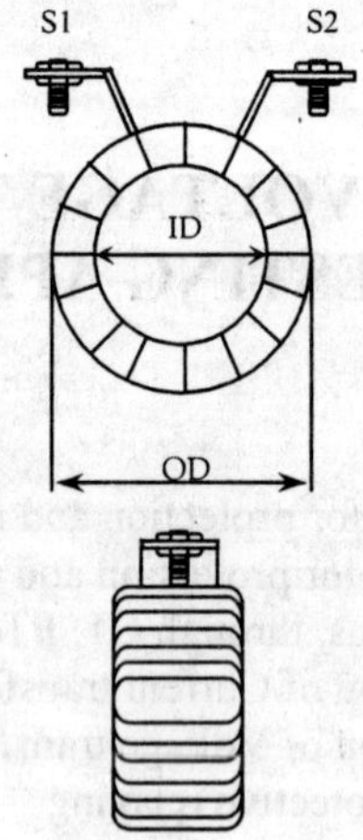

Fig. 5.1 (b): Ring type current transformer.

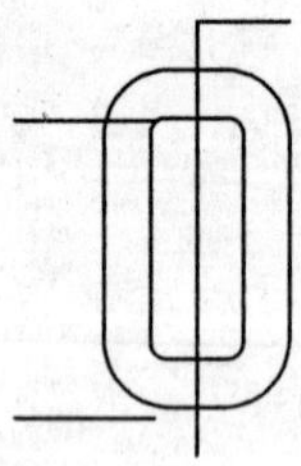

Fig. 5.1 (c): Window type current transformer.

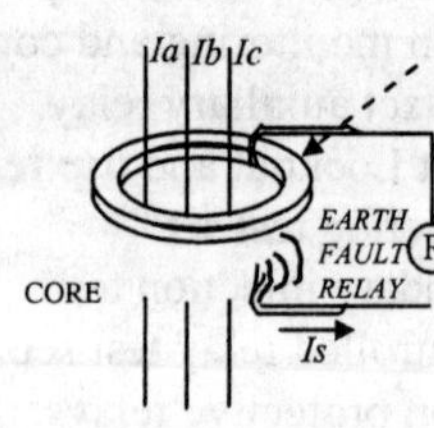

Fig. 5.1 (d): Toroidal / split type current transformer.

(1) Star connection: In the star connection the secondary of current transformers of the three phases have their terminals having negative polarities connected together as shown in Figure 5.1 (e) to form the neutral wire. Secondary current is directly proportional to the primary current. Assume that the ratio of the current transformers in a three phase system are 500/5 amps and if the primary current is 500 amps per phase the secondary current in the CT output will be 5 amps per phase. Hence, except for special cases CT output is always connected in star.

(2) Incomplete star connection: In this scheme current transformers are provided only in two phases of a three-phase system and the secondary windings are joined together as in the star connection scheme [Figure 5.1(f)] and the return wire (Neutral) carries a current equal to the vector sum of two phases.

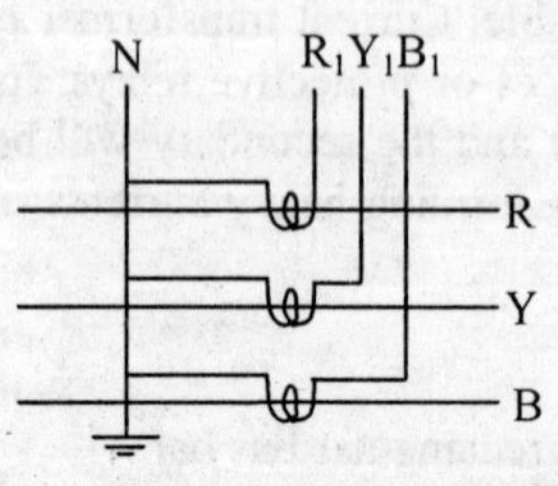

Fig. 5.1(e): Star connected current transformers.

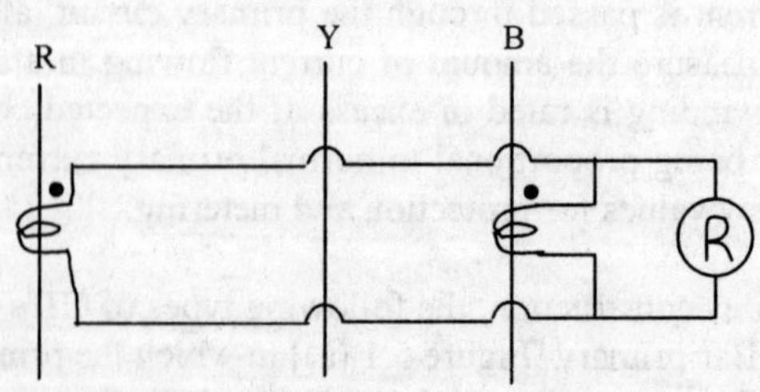

Fig. 5.1 (f) Incomplete star connection

(3) Delta connection: In the delta connection the secondary windings of current transformers of the three phases have their unlike terminals connected in series as shown in Figure 5.1 (g). In a delta-connected secondary the CT output will be $\sqrt{3}$ x phase current. For example assume that in a delta-connected system the CT ratio is 500/5 amps and 500 amps is the current in the primary, the secondary phase-current will be 5 amps, whereas the secondary CT output currents will be $\sqrt{3}$ x5 amps.

(4) Incomplete delta connection (Vector difference connection): In this scheme the current transformers are provided only in any two phases and the unlike terminals are joined together as in the delta connection. Figure 5.1(h) illustrates the Incomplete-delta connection.

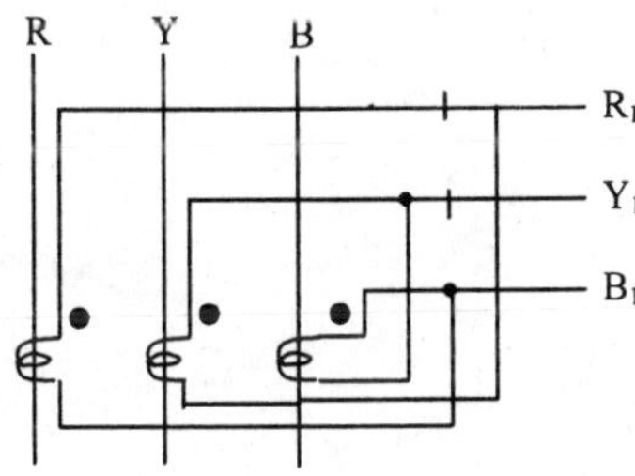

Fig. 5.1 (g): Delta connected current transformers.

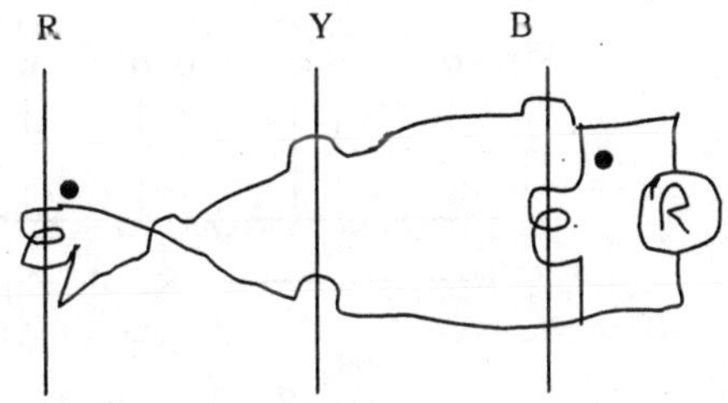

Fig. 5.1 (h): Incomplete delta connection.

(5) Zero sequence connection: In these schemes the current transformers are provided in all the three phases and the secondary terminals having identical polarities are connected together and the relay connected across them as shown in Figure 5.1 (i). In this zero sequence current filter scheme the current flowing in the relay is equal to the vector sum of the CT secondary currents of the three-phases. Ir = Ia + Ib + Ic = 3 x I_o, and consequently this current is actually zero sequence current. This scheme is suitable for earth fault protection because the current flows through the relay only in the event of single phase or two-phase earth fault.

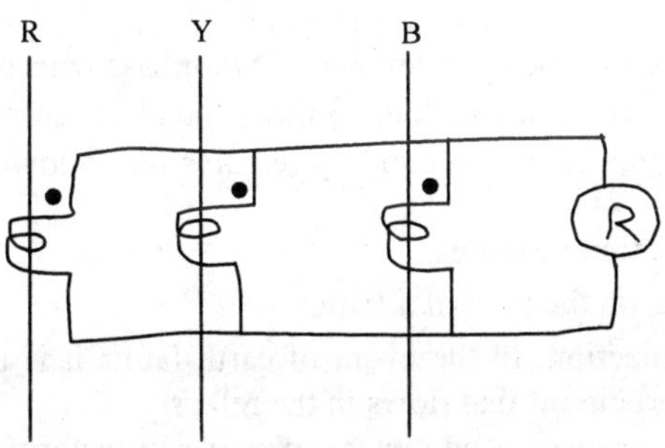

Fig. 5.1 (1): Zero sequence connection.

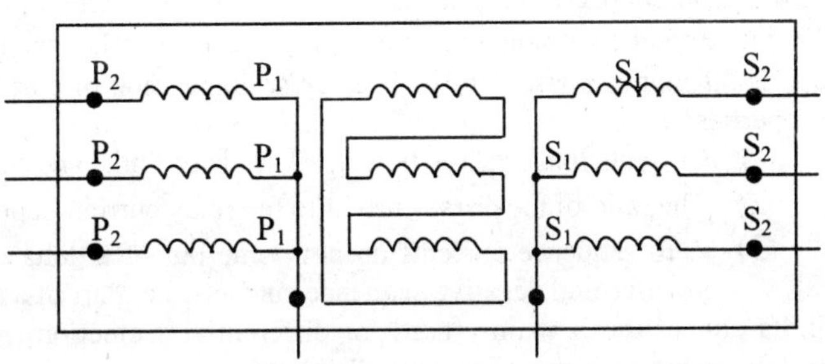

Fig. 5.1 (J): Interposing current transformer.

(6) Interposing current transformer: With the winding of the power transformer being connected in delta/star or star/delta, the current in amps supplied by the CT connected in to delta equals $\sqrt{3}\ I_1/N_1$, while the current in amps supplied from the star connected CT is I_2/N_2. Conditions will meet when $\sqrt{3}\ I_1/N_1 = I_2/N_2$.
I_1 = Primary current; I_2 = Secondary current; N_1 = Primary side CT ratio, and N_2 = secondary side CT ratio. To compensate this error, interposing current transformers are used with electromechanical relays. Typical interposing current transformer diagram is shown in Figure 5.1(J).

(7) **Summation current transformer**: A multi-terminal current transformer to which each of the three phase currents is connected and having a different number of turns associated with each phase so that a single phase output current results from any combination of single phase or poly-phase input currents. The primary is usually an autotransformer arrangement and the secondary is usually, but not necessarily, a separate winding.

The summation current transformers are also built with a common secondary, which is connected to the burden. It is essential that summation CT's are used on currents of same frequency and phase. During ratio and phase angle error measurement primary windings are connected in series. Figure 5.1 (k) shows a summation CT having six winding primary which is fed from 6 feeder CT's of the same phase. Copper bar is the common secondary which gives an output equivalent to the total current of the corresponding phase of the six feeders. If it is required the total current in all the three phases to be measured additional two similar units are required for connecting the remaining phases.

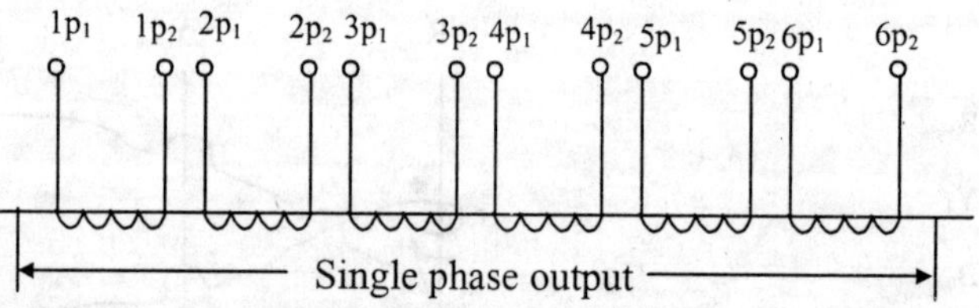

Fig. 5.1 (k): Summation current transformer circuit.

(8) Comparison between star and delta connection of CT secondary:
When current transformers and corresponding relays are connected in ***star*** the neutral wire carries a current to their vector sum. $I_N = I_A + I_B + I_C =$ zero, where I_A, I_B, I_C are the current in three phases and I_N is the neutral current in the star connected secondary of the CT's under normal operating conditions. In the event of a three-phase fault in the main line, the CT neutral current remains zero. In a two phase fault (short circuit) the current in the faulty phases are de-phased by 180°. These are equal in value and opposite in phase and no current exist in the CT neutral. For this reason **earth fault relay connected in to the neutral wire will not respond during phase-to-phase fault, which is an important feature of star connection**. After the occurrence of two-phase to earth faults, the current in the neutral wire is equal to the vector sum of the currents in the two faulty phases, which is a value other than zero and the earth fault relay operates. When the secondary circuit of one of the CT is open the neutral wire develops a current equal to the phase current, which will cause unexpected operation of the relay connected in to the neutral wire.
In the delta-connected scheme each relay carries a current equal to the vector difference of two-phase currents. During normal operation and a three phase fault the relay carries a current, which is √3 times the phase current and is 30° out of phase with it. Thus ***delta*** connection of current transformer secondary features the following properties:

1) Currents in the relays flow at all kinds of faults and protection responds.
2) The ratio of the phase current to the relay current depends on the kind of a fault.
3) Zero sequence currents do not come out of a delta connection. In the event of earth faults it is the positive and negative sequence currents, i.e, Part of a short circuit that flows in the relays.

Delta connection is mainly used for differential protection (star connected windings) of power tıansformers and distance protection of transmission lines.

(9) Comparison between Incomplete-star connection and Incomplete-delta connection:
Incomplete star connection scheme [figure 5.1 (f)] the return wire carries currents equal to the vector sum of the corresponding two phases. $I_N = (-)\ (I_A + I_C) = I_B$, i.e, equals the currents of the phase (CT) lacking in the secondary circuit. When a two-phase fault occurs between phases in which CT's are provided the current in the return wire will be zero. When an earth fault occurs in the phase in which CT is not provided, protective relay connected in this circuit will not operate. Hence the incomplete star connection scheme does not respond to any single phase to earth faults and is therefore used with short-circuit protection only.
Incomplete delta connection scheme [figure 5.1(h)] is known as vector difference connection. Under symmetrical loading and three-phase fault conditions relay current Ir = √3 x phase current. When a two-phase fault occurs between phase A and C, Ir = 2 x Iph. If the fault is between A and B, or B and C, Ir = Iph where Iph is the phase current. Hence this scheme is not suitable for phase to ground fault but suitable for phase-to-phase fault.

(10) Secondary circuits of current transformers:
A CT is designed to operate at a low flux density, with a closed secondary circuit, i.e, with the secondary current flowing continuously and having a demagnetizing action on the flux produced by the primary current. In a CT, the leakage flux is of the same order as the working flux. A peculiar feature of a CT is that the voltage developed across the secondary is directly related to the value of the impedance of the burden across it. Since

the current ratio is fixed, if the load impedance is more the voltage developed is more. As the load impedance across the secondary becomes high approaching open circuit condition, the voltage across the terminals becomes very high and the magnetic flux approaches the saturation value for the core and the exciting current increases very rapidly. Under this condition the CT overheats. During short-circuit in the primary (worst condition as shown in figure 8.15 (b) of Chapter # 8) side if the secondary is open circuited the CT secondary will develop very high voltage. Similarly, during a fault, the primary of the CT is heavily loaded and if the secondary is open-circuited, the primary temperature rapidly increases and the core gets saturated. Hence the core, get overheated and the CT may be burnout. For this reason unused CT terminals should be left short-circuited.

Instrument transformers (current or voltage), neutral wire should be connected to the ground only at one point because (1) to prevent differences of potential in the instrument transformer secondary circuit and (2) to facilitate the removal and re-establishment of the ground connection, in order to make periodic tests for deterioration of insulation and accidental ground, in the instrument transformer secondary circuit. Differences of potentials between different points in the station ground grid, is not equal due to the flow of fault current through the ground grid. Such differences of potential can result in the flow of current through the relays, instruments and meter coils and cause possible incorrect performance of the relay and in-accuracies in the readings of the instruments.

If the CT secondary ground connection is disconnected or removed while the CT is energized, dangerous voltage may result in the secondary side due to electrostatic coupling. Current transformer secondary is grounded (except delta connected CT) to prevent inducing dangerous voltage in the CT secondary. For verifying the effectiveness of the ground connection of the CT, connect the neutral lead of the secondary injection test set to the ground terminal (earth bar) and inject a test current at the neutral terminal (star point) of the CT, if the test set is loaded, the neutral ground connection is intact.

(11) Current transformer burden, percentage error and knee point voltage:

The load connected to the secondary of a current transformer is expressed in volt-amps or burden. $VA = Is^2 Z$, where Z is the impedance in ohm and, Is = Rated CT secondary current in amps. Assume that the output of a 1000/5 amps CT is 100 volt-amps. $Z = 100/5 \times 5 = 4\ \Omega$. It means the resistance of connecting leads and relay coils should not exceed 4 ohms. Provided the CT ratio is 1000/1 amps and the burden is 100 VA, the impedance will be $100/1 \times 1 = 100\Omega$.

Current-Transformer output in volt-amps	Impedance in ohms for 1 A, secondary CTs	Impedance in ohms for 5 A, secondary C Ts
5	5	0.2
10	10	0.4
15	15	0.6
30	30	1.2
60	60	2.4

CT's are connected in series to increase burden.

$$\text{CT percentage error} = \frac{(Kn\ Is - Ip) \times 100}{Ip}$$

Kn = Rated transformer ratio I_1 / I_2

Ip = Actual primary current

Is = Actual secondary current

Knee point voltage of a CT is defined as the point on the magnetization curve where a 10% increase in voltage produces a 30% increase in magnetizing current.

(12) Accuracy classes of current transformers:

In an instrument CT, accuracy is important only within the normal load range up to 120%. Whereas in a protection CT, accuracy is not important below rated current but is most important for overloads and short circuits up to primary saturation current, since the relay has to function properly under abnormal conditions. The standard saturation factors adopted are 5, 10, 15 and 20. Saturation factor is partly related to the "burden" and the product of the two should not exceed 150. When a CT is used to energize a protective relay, it must maintain its characteristic ratio up to some multiple of its rated current. Standard multiples are 5, 10, 15, 20, and is known as the "Accuracy Limit Factor" (ALF). Therefore, the selection of protective current transformers in relation to accuracy class and ALF require a close examination of relay characteristic and circuit conditions, which includes the relay burden and the pilot wire lead burden.

Accuracy class at 100% load fòr measuring CT and protection CT, and its characteristics are given in Table 5.1 (1) below.

Accuracy class for metering current transformers			Accuracy class for protection current transformers			
Accuracy	Current error	Phase displacement	Accuracy	Current error	Phase displacement	Composite error
0.1	± 0.1%	± 5 minutes	5P5	± 1%	± 60°	5%
0.2	± 0.2%	± 10 minutes	5P10	± 3%	± 60°	10%
0.5	± 0.5%	± 30 minutes	5P15	± 5%	± 60°	15%
1	± 1%	± 60 minutes	5P20	± 10%	± 60°	20%

Note:
(1) Accuracy class 5P10 means at 10 times rated current CT having 5% error.
(2) Accuracy class X or class PS or class 5P20 current transformer means magnetizing current at √K/4 ratio, where K = Knee point voltage of the CT. These types of CT's are used for transformer and transmission line protection.
(3) One minute phase angle error refers 1/60 th part of one degree.

(13) Measuring current transformers: Class 0.1 for Precision testing or standard for testing other CT's, Class 0.2 for Precision metering and Tariff metering, Class 0.5 for energy meter, Class 1 non revenue measurement, Class 3 for general industrial meters, Class 5 for approximate measurements.

(14) Current transformer ratio:
The ratio of primary amps divided by secondary amps, i.e. 500/5 amps CT would have a CT ratio 100:1, means when 100 amps passing through the primary, the secondary current will be 1 ampere..

Example 1: An ammeter designed to connect with an 800/5 ampere CT is connected to 800/5 A CT. If the ammeter reads 600 amps what will be the actual primary current and secondary current passing through the ammeter.
CT design ratio = 5/800 = 0.00625
Since the ammeter reads primary current 600 amps, actual CT secondary current = 0.00625 x 600 = 3.75 amps.
Alternate method: CT ratio = 800/5 = 160.
Since ammeter reads 600 amps (as primary currents) the CT secondary current = 600/160 = 3.75 amps.

Example 2: An ammeter designed (dial marked) for connecting to a 100/5 ampere CT is connected to 200/5 ampere CT. If ammeter reads 25 amps what will be the actual primary current.
Ammeter design CT ratio = 5/100 = 0.05
Actual CT design ratio = 5/200 = 0.025
Multiplication factor = 0.05/0.025 = 2
Actual ammeter reading = 25 x 2 = 50 amps. Similarly if a 100/5 A ammeter has dial calibrated/scaled for 200/5 A, ammeter will read full reading but indicate only half the actual reading.

5.2 VOLTAGE TRANSFORMERS FOR PROTECTION AND METERING.

Voltage transformer (Potential transformer) is a transformer, with its primary winding connected in shunt with the voltage that is to be measured, which gives an accurate low voltage proportional to the high/extra high voltage system it is measuring. Potential transformer used to accurately scale AC voltages up or down, and to provide isolation between primary and secondary. The voltage transformer ratio is of primary volts divided by the secondary volts. Generally voltage transformer is transforming higher voltages in to lower values (120 volts between phases) for protection and metering applications. Based on its primary and secondary connection Potential Transformers are designated as follows:

(1) Delta/star connection: A three-phase transformer having delta connected primary and star connected secondary as shown in Figure 5.2 (a).

(2) Star / star connection: In this design as shown in Figure 5.2 (b), both primary and secondary are connected in star. The potential transformer can use with or without primary neutral earthing. With the primary neutral grounded, the phase voltages on the secondary side correspond to phase voltages of the primary side to earth. If the primary neutral is unearthed, its potential will be other than earth potential.

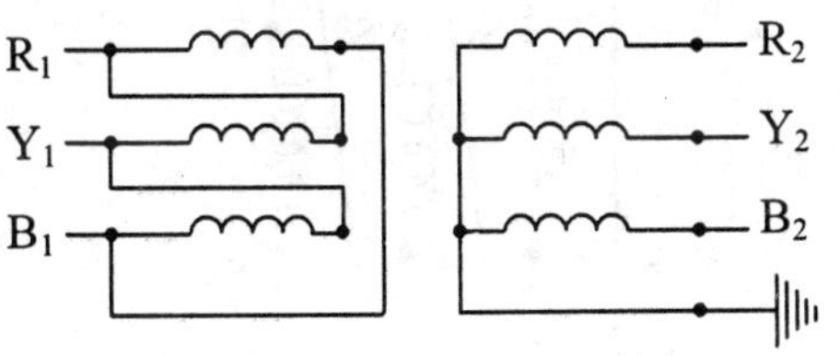

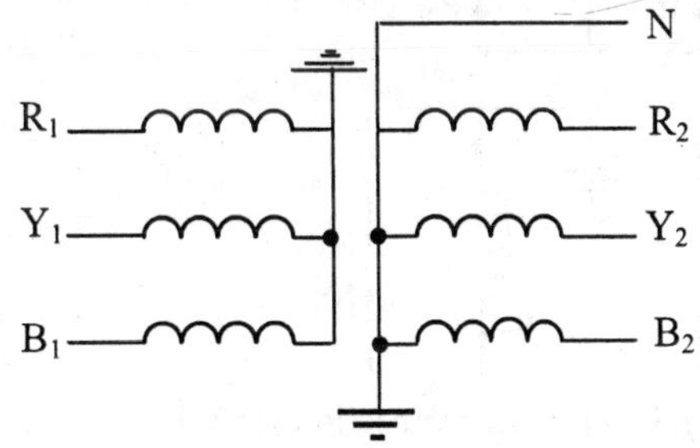

Fig. 5.2 (a): Delta/star connected voltage transformer. Fig. 5.2 (b): Star/star connected voltage transformer.

(3) Zigzag connection: Figure 5.2 (c) shows the diagram of Zigzag or interconnected star voltage transformer. In this connection line-to-line voltage is equal to $\sqrt{3}/2$ times the star voltage. Alphabets, R-Y-B represents primary terminals and alphabets r-y-b represents secondary circuit terminals.

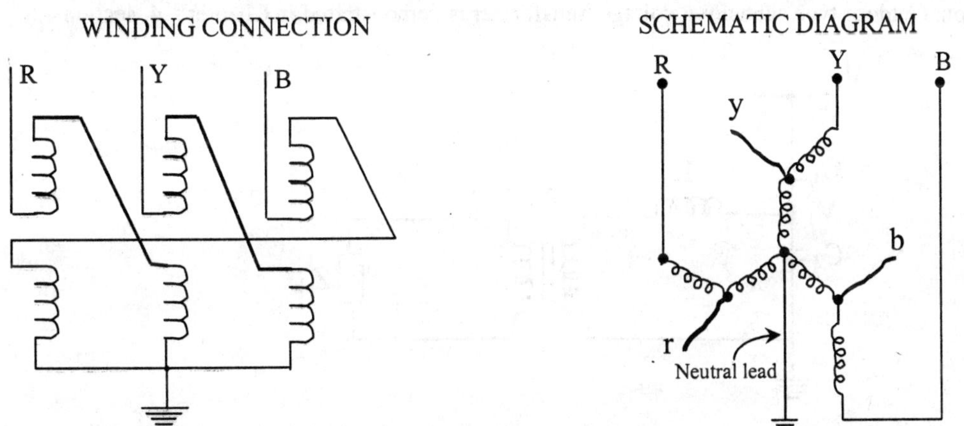

Fig. 5.2 (c): Zigzag connected voltage transformer (Interconnected star connection).

(4) Open delta connection: Open delta is formed by two single-phase transformers connected across, three-phase line voltage. Secondary is also connected to obtain a 3 phase 120 volts supply. Both the primary and secondary sides one side being absent as shown in Figure 5.2 (d). Typical application diagram is shown in figure 8.12 (a) of Chapter # 8.

(5) Broken delta connection: Broken Delta is formed by means of 3 single-phase voltage transformers. The primary windings are connected in star with earthed neutral and series connected secondary (Zero sequence voltage filter) as shown in Figure 5.2 (e). Relays are connected to the broken apex of the delta. Secondary residual voltage at normal working condition is zero. Resultant voltage $V_R = 3Vo/N$ where Vo = Zero sequence voltage and N = Transformation ratio. Under imbalance condition or up on earth fault in the primary residual voltage will be developed (equal to the faulted phase voltage) and the relay will operate. Typical application diagram is shown in figure 8.12 (g).

In systems where open delta or broken delta voltage transformer is essential for connecting relays, but not provided, suitable interposing voltage transformers can be used. Star connected primary and open delta or broken delta secondary as appropriate is employed.

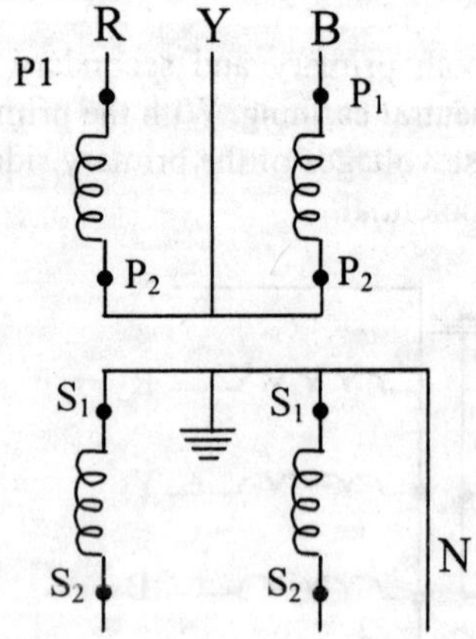

Fig. 5.2 (d): Open delta connection for VT.

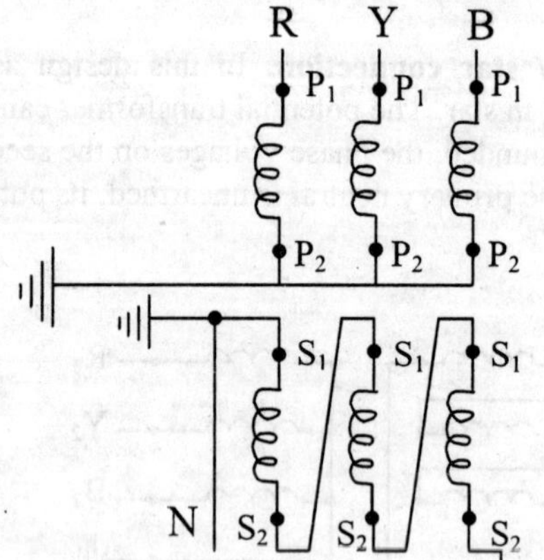

Fig. 5.2 (e): Broken delta connection for VT.

(6) Capacitive voltage transformer: Capacitive voltage dividers are used for outdoor high and extra high voltage system to supply potential source to protection and metering devices associated with the system. They consists of a number of series connected capacitors placed between the phase conductor and earth. The load is connected across capacitor C_2 via a step down transformer as shown in Figure 5.2 (f). To minimize the error a reactor Xc and capacitor C_3 is used in the circuit. If a short-circuit occurs in the system the primary voltage drops to zero but due to capacitance C and inductance X voltage will remain in the secondary approximately 10 second duration. Outdoor type capacitive voltage transformer is demonstrated in Chapter # 4, section 4.8.

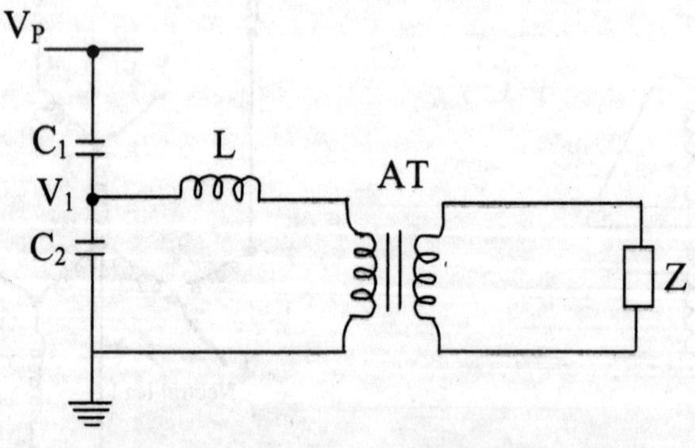

Fig. (f): Capacitive voltage transformer.

If voltage transformer primary neutral is not earthed, the zero sequence component of voltage due to an earth fault cannot flow through primary windings. Hence phase to earth voltages of system, which contain zero sequence component do not get truly transformed. As such the earth fault on the system cannot be sensed on the secondary side of the voltage transformer. Hence the neutral of star connected primary should be earthed.

Accuracy class and percentage error for potential transformers:

Measuring instruments: Class 1
Energy meters: Class 0.5
Tariff meter: Class 0.2
Protection: Class 3P

$$\text{Percentage error of a PT} = \frac{(Kn\ Vs - Vp) \times 100}{Vp}$$

Kn = PT ratio Vp/Vs; Vp = primary voltage; and Vs = secondary voltage.

5.3 INSTRUMENT CONNECTIONS THROUGH CT, PT AND TRANSDUCER.

Instrument transformer is defined as a transformer designed to reduce current or voltage from a primary value to a proportional standard low-level value. Instrument transformers are either current transformer or voltage transformer. Instrument transformer serves three main purposes:

a). To insulate the instruments, especially if they are high tension.

b). To transform heavy current and higher voltages to lower standard values.

c). To achieve standardization of voltage and current ratings of instruments and relays.

The standard secondary side ratings internationally approved for current transformer is 1 amp or 5 amps. Similarly the standard secondary phase to phase voltage ratings for potential transformer is 100 volts or 120 volts. Table 5.3 (1) compares the function and application of CT and VT.

Table 5.3 (1): Comparison between Current transformer and Potential transformer:

	Current transformer	Potential transformer
1	Steps down higher currents to lower currents	Steps down higher voltages to lower voltages
2	A CT primary is connected in series with the supply line or inserted in the supply phase conductor	A PT is connected across the supply line or to the power source
3	Primary Ampere-turns are nearly equal to the secondary Ampere-turns	Turns per volt in the primary is nearly equal to the turns per volt in the secondary
4	Primary has one or few turns, whereas the secondary has large number of turns	The primary has large number of turns, whereas the secondary has very less number of turns
5	The number of turns is inversely proportional to the current	The number of turns are directly proportional to the voltage
6	The secondary of a CT should never be left open circuited while energized and always connected to the burden or short-circuited. No fuse should be inserted	In a PT the secondary should never be short-circuited and protected by employing fuses both in the primary and secondary
7	If the burden load is increased the primary current will not increase	If the secondary load is increased the primary current will increase
8	If current is injected in the secondary no current will produce in the primary	If voltage is injected in the secondary high voltage will produce in the primary

Energy meter connection through CT and PT:

Energy meter is a device that measures the total kilowatt-hour of energy that a consumer uses. Figure 5.3 (a) shows the schematic diagram of a energy (KWH) meter connected through CT and PT. Current coils and voltage coils are connected from the same phase. CT is connected in forward polarity. CT ratio in all the three phases must be same for 3-phase metering. Connections to the three-phase meter may be effected in the forward phase sequence. Rated CT ratio is printed in the meter nameplate. If the CT ratio is not the same as the ratio mentioned in the meter, multiplication factor may be used for conventional type KWH meters to obtain the correct reading. Multiplication Factor = (Actual CT ratio x Dial factor) / Rated CT ratio given on meter

Example: Assume that 100/5 amps CT (Ratio 5/100 = 0.05) is used with 300/5 amps (Ratio 5/300 = 0.01667) energy meter and the dial factor given in the meter nameplate is 1,

MF = 0.05/0.01667 = 3

In case of current and potential transformer, both are not the same as the ratio mentioned in the meter.

MF = (Actual CTR x Actual PTR x DF) / (Rated CTR in meter x Rated PTR in meter)

CTR: CT ratio; PTR: PT ratio; DF: Dial factor

For modern 5 A rated digital KWH meters can set for use with CT having 5 A secondary, and can obtain direct reading without multiplication factor.

LEGEND:
CC: Current coil
PC: Pressure coil
PT: Potential transformer
CT: Current transformer

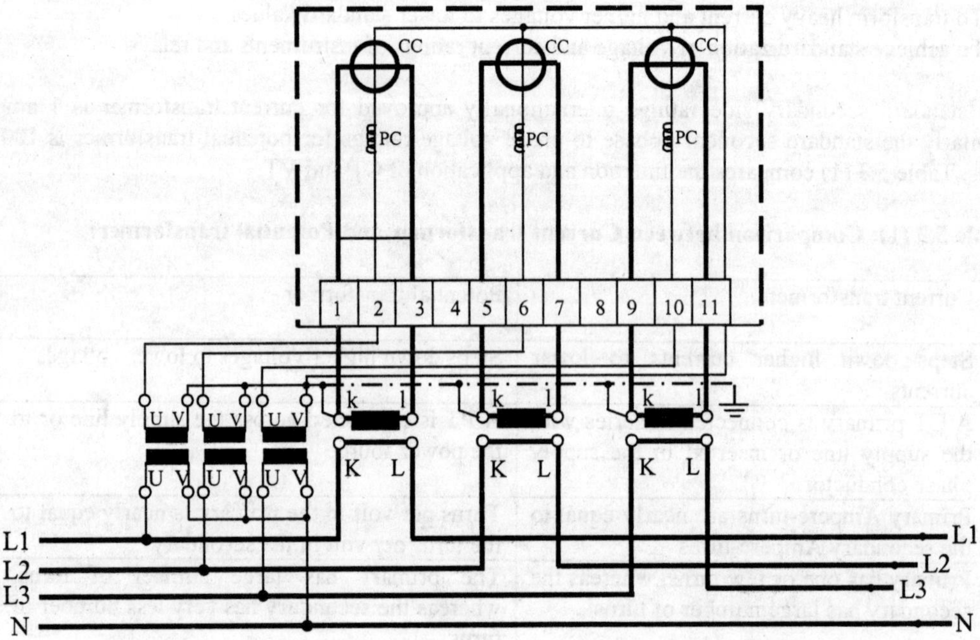

Fig. 5.3 (a): Energy meter connection through current and potential transformers.

Switchboard instruments:
Figure 5.3 (b) shows the schematic diagram for connecting the following measuring instruments:

1. Voltmeter with selector switch to indicate voltage between phases and /or phase to neutral. Voltmeter is connected to the potential transformer circuit.
2. Ammeter for all the three phases to indicate the actual current in each phase. Alternatively, ammeter can connect to the CT circuit through selector switch.
3. Frequency meter connected through frequency transducer to indicate the supply frequency in Hertz. It is connected to the voltage transformer secondary circuit
4. Power factor meter (with central unity scale) indicates lagging / leading power factor. It consists of one current coil and three pressure coils connected through a selector switch to measure the power factor in all the three phases.
5. KVA or MVA meter indicates apparent power in Kilovolt amps or Mega-volt amps. It consists of 1 pressure coil and 1 current coil per phase. KVA = $(\sqrt{3} \times V \times I) / 10^3$.and MVA = $(\sqrt{3} \times V \times I) / 10^6$.
6. KVAR or MVAR meter indicates reactive power in Reactive Kilovolt amps or Reactive Mega-volt amps. It is similar to KVA/MVA meter but connected through phase shifting transformer to measure the reactive power. KVAR = $(\sqrt{3} \times V \times I \times \sin\phi) / 1000$ and MVAR = $(\sqrt{3} \times V \times I \times \sin\phi) / 10^6$
7. .KW or MW meter indicates active power in Kilowatts or Mega-watts in a source. It consists of 1 current coil and one pressure coil per phase. KW = $(\sqrt{3} \times V \times I \times \cos\phi) / 1000$ and MW = $(\sqrt{3} \times V \times I \times \cos\phi) / 10^6$
8. Kilowatt-hour meter or Megawatt hour meter measures the energy consumption.

Microprocessor controlled Instrument calibration set capable of calibrating multi-meters, wattmeter, ammeters, volt meters, frequency meters, thermo-meters, strip chart recorders, clip on ammeters etc. are used for calibration of instruments to meet the requirements of ISO 9001 calibration certificate.

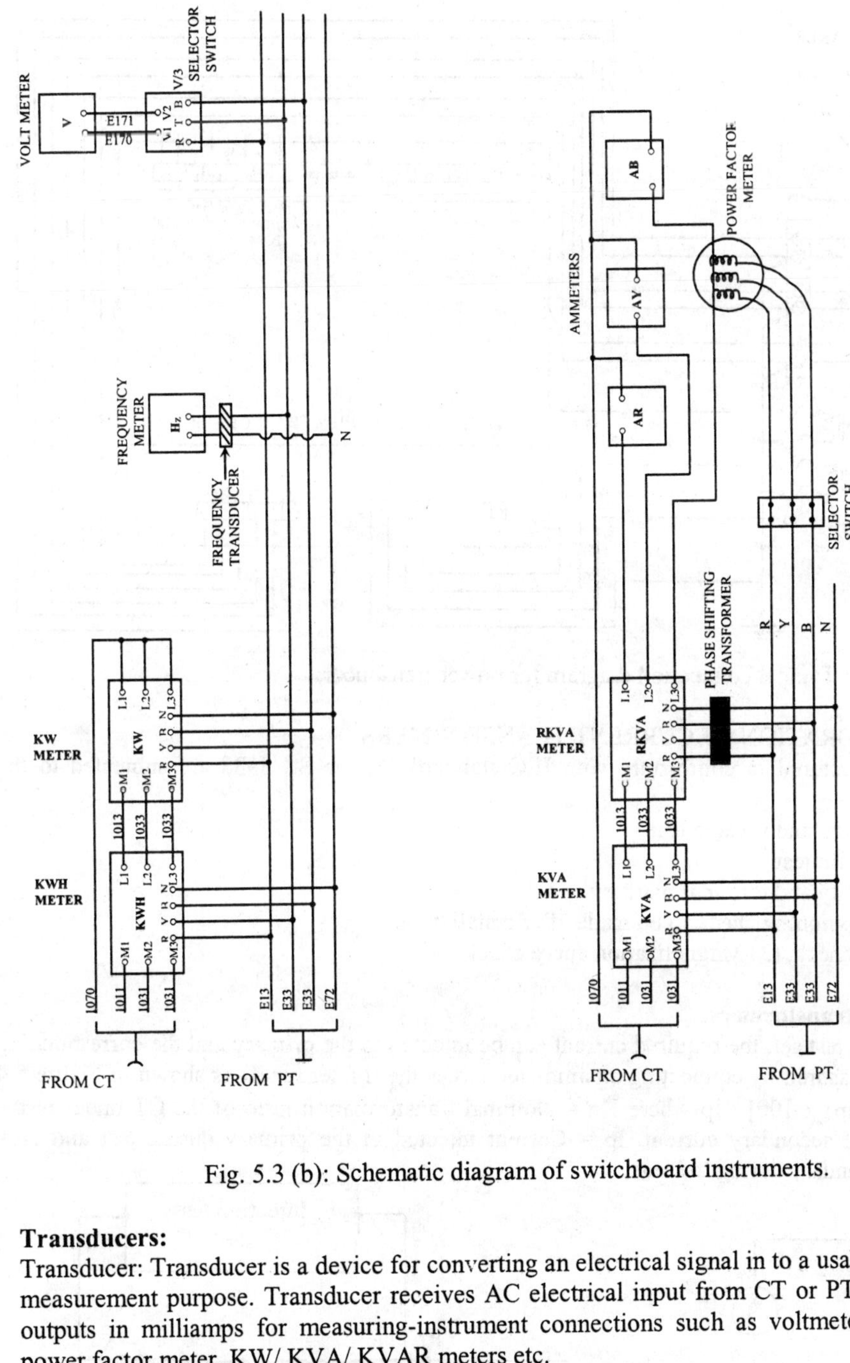

Fig. 5.3 (b): Schematic diagram of switchboard instruments.

Transducers:

Transducer: Transducer is a device for converting an electrical signal in to a usable direct current or voltage for measurement purpose. Transducer receives AC electrical input from CT or PT and produce proportional DC outputs in milliamps for measuring-instrument connections such as voltmeter, ammeter, frequency meter, power factor meter, KW/ KVA/ KVAR meters etc.

Following types of transducers are widely used:

1. Voltage transducer: For voltage measurement
2. Current transducer: For current measurement
3. Frequency transducer: For frequency measurement
4. Var transducer: For KVAR or MVAR measurement
5. Watt transducer: For KW or MW measurement
6. Energy totalizer transducer: For KWH or MWH measurement
7. Power factor meter transducer: For power factor measurement

Typical connection diagram of a three-phase power transducer connected through CT and PT is shown in Figure 5.3 (c).

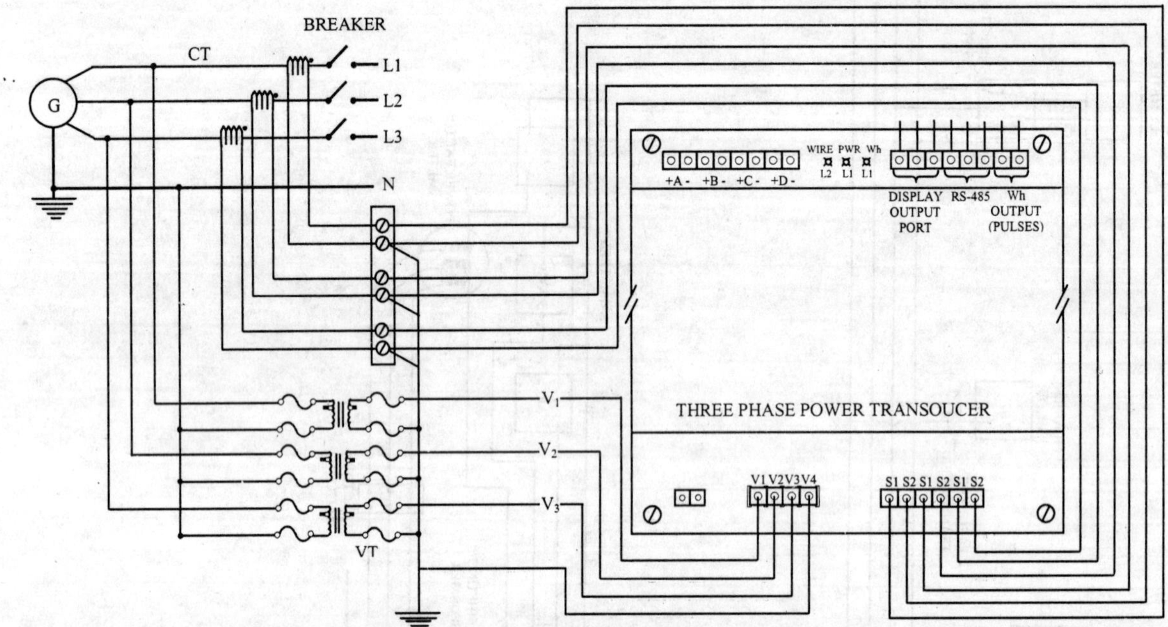

Fig. 5.3 (c): Typical connection diagram for power transducer.

5.4 TESTING AND CALIBRATION OF CURRENT TRANSFORMERS.

Current transformers manufactured in conformity with IEC standard 185 or BS 3938 are subjected to the following tests:

1. Power frequency withstand voltage test
2. Over-voltage inter-turn test
3. Verification of polarity and terminal marking

Following are the pre-commissioning check to be made after installation:
(1) Ratio check, (2) Polarity check, (3) Magnetization curve check

(1) Ratio check on current transformers:

By using a primary injection test set, the required current can be injected to the primary and the corresponding secondary current can be measured by connecting an ammeter across the CT terminals as shown in Figure 5.4 (a). Ratio error = [(kn Is – Ip) x 100] / Ip where Kn = Nominal transformation ratio of the CT under test = Rated primary current/Rated secondary current. Ip = Current injected in the primary during test and Is = Current measured in the secondary during the test.

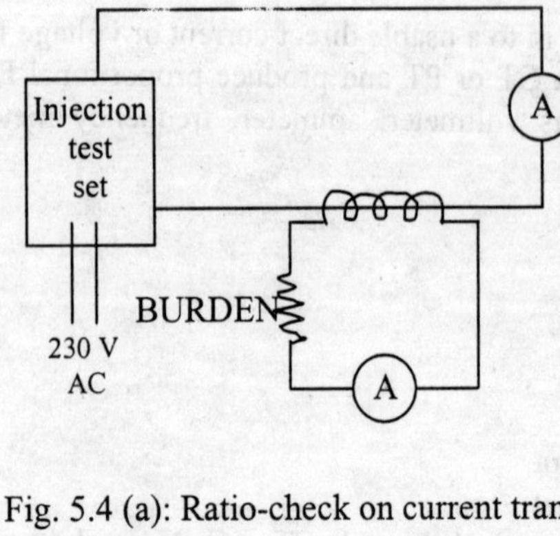

Fig. 5.4 (a): Ratio-check on current transformer.

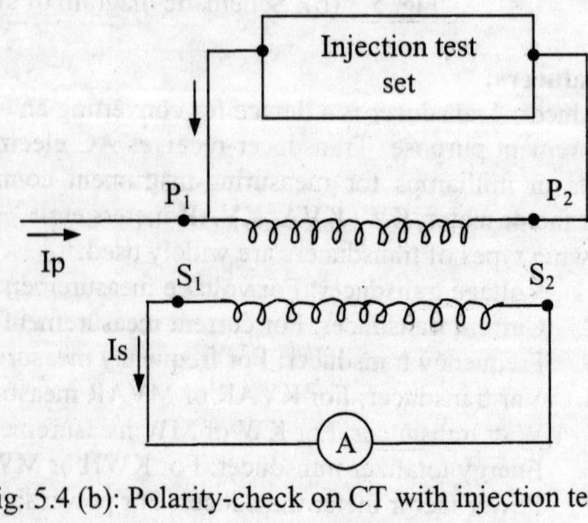

Fig. 5.4 (b): Polarity-check on CT with injection test set.

(2) Polarity check on current transformer:

In instrument transformers, Polarity is the indication of the direction of the current flow through the primary terminals with respect to the direction through the secondary terminal. In a current transformer primary side polarity is marked P1 (power-in) & P2 (power-out), whereas the secondary terminals of the CT is marked S1 & S2, i.e. the current flows from S_1 to S_2 as shown in figure (b).

Following are the different methods employed for testing the polarity of a current transformer:

1) By using primary or secondary injection test set.
2) By using battery and centre zero DC moving coil voltmeter
3) By using Polarity test set

The circuit for checking the CT polarity with a single-phase primary/secondary injection test set is shown in Figure 5.4 (b). If instantaneous current flows from P_1 to P_2 as marked by the arrow Ip, the instantaneous current will flow from S_1 to S_2 through ammeter as shown by arrow Is.

The circuit for testing the CT polarity by using a battery and center zero DC moving coil voltmeter is shown in Figure 5.4 (c). When the key switch is pressed, current from the 6 volts battery enters the primary through terminal P_1. Central zero DC moving coil voltmeter connected across the secondary will give a positive kick provided the polarity setup is correct.

The circuit for testing the CT polarity by using the CT polarity tester is shown in Figure 5.4 (d). Polarity can be conveniently checked by paralleling the reference current transformer secondary with test transformer secondary through two ammeters A_1 and A_2, connected as shown in figure (d). If A_2 ammeter is reading higher than A_1, the polarity is in accordance with terminal markings. Test diagram is shown in figure 5.14 (n).

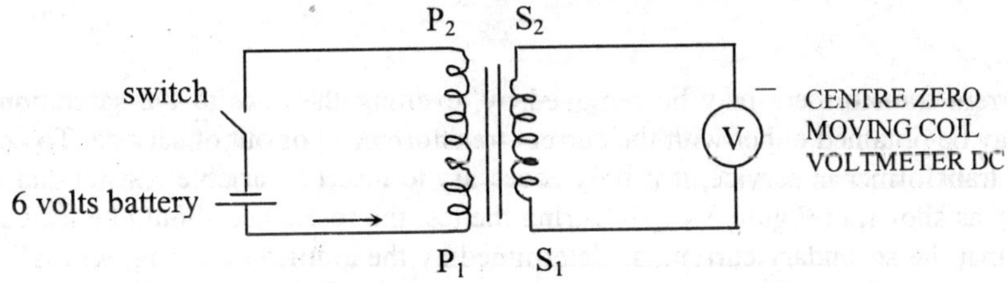

Fig. 5.4 (c): Current transformer polarity test by using battery and center zero DC voltmeter.

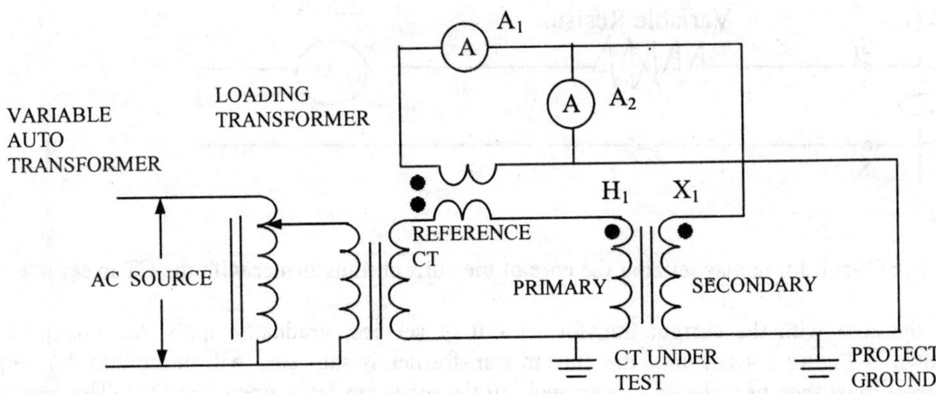

Fig. 5.4 (d): Current transformer polarity test by using polarity test set.

(3) Magnetization curve check on current transformer:

Figure 5.4 (e) shows the test diagram for the magnetization characteristic test of a CT. With the primary open circuited and after disconnecting secondary outgoing connection, connect a voltmeter across the secondary. An autotransformer (0 to 230 volts) is used to inject voltage to the CT secondary through an ammeter. Increase the voltage gradually and observe the ammeter reading at every 10% increase. Knee point is defined as where a 10% increase in voltage cause 50% increase in exciting ampere-turns or 30% increase in current.

Figure 5.4 (f) illustrates a typical excitation characteristics curve of a CT. Current transformer saturation curve is generally plotted in secondary voltages verses exciting current measured in secondary. During short-circuit, upon reaching saturation, magnetizing inductance become low and the total primary current is utilized in exciting the core alone and therefore the secondary output of the CT disappears.

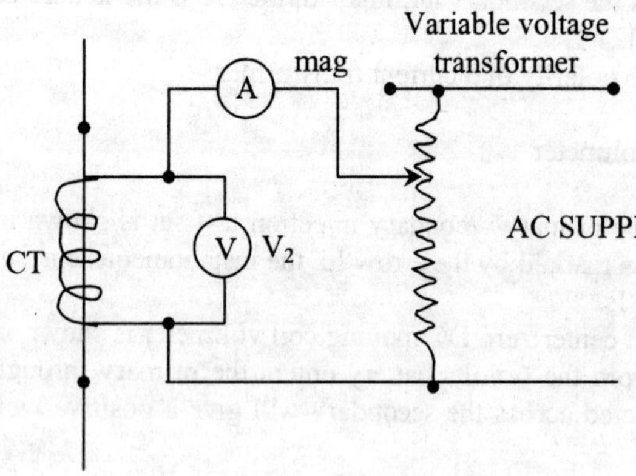

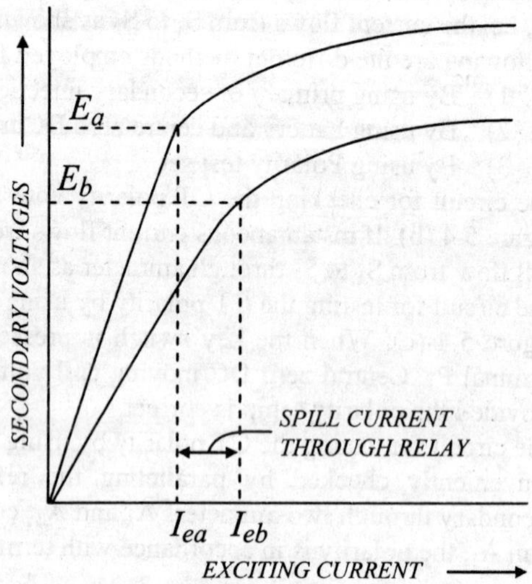

Fig. 5.4 (e): Magnetization characteristics test. Fig. 5.4 (f): Magnetization curves of current transformers.

Magnetization of current transformers may be removed by, exciting the core to the saturation voltage. The point of excitation may be obtained either with the current transformer in or out of service. To demagnetize the core with the current transformer in service, it is only necessary to insert a variable resister and an ammeter in series with the burden as shown in Figure 5.4 (g). During the test the resistance should be increased from zero to such a magnitude that the secondary current, as determined by the ammeter reading, will fall to one-half its original value or less. The resistance is then slowly reduced to zero and the resister and ammeter removed from the circuit.

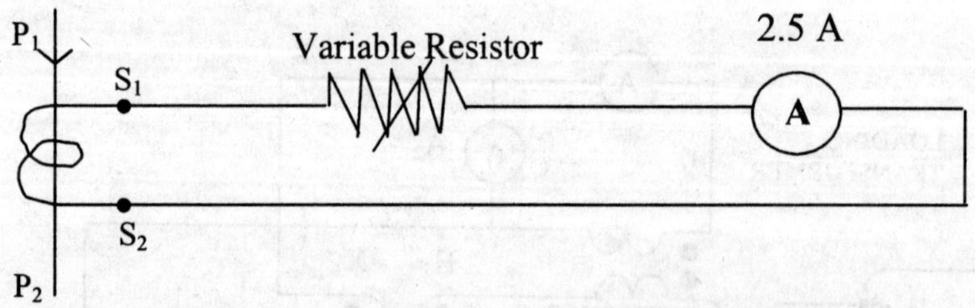

Fig. 5.4 (g): Circuit for demagnetizing the core of the current transformer with the CT in service.

To demagnetize the core with the current transformer out of service, gradually apply AC voltage to the secondary as shown in Figure 5.4 (h) until the current transformer is saturated with minimum 2.5 amperes flowing. This current must then be reduced to zero with all the other tap leads open-circuited. This process of gradually reducing the amperes to zero from the saturation level will demagnetize the CT.

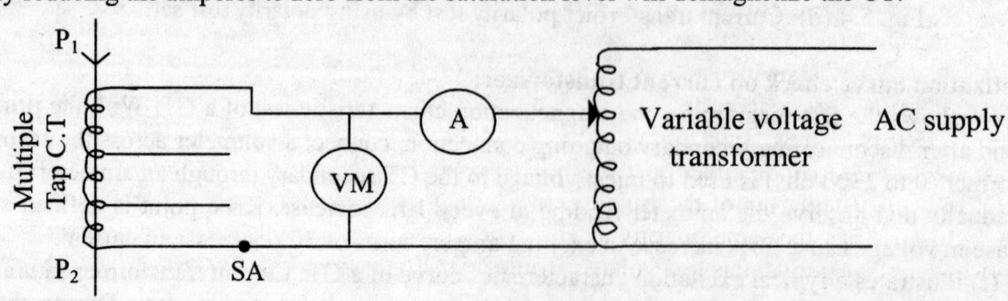

Fig. 5.4 (h) Circuit for demagnetizing the core of the current transformer while the CT is out of service.

(4) Calibration of current transformer: Current transformers would be calibrated against standard transformers or similar devices. The primary windings of the two transformers are connected in series. (For bar primary CT insert both CT in the loading cable). The small difference between the secondary currents can be measured by using compensating current comparator, which provides the reading for ratios and phase angle deviations of the transformer under test. [Refer figure 5.4 (i)].

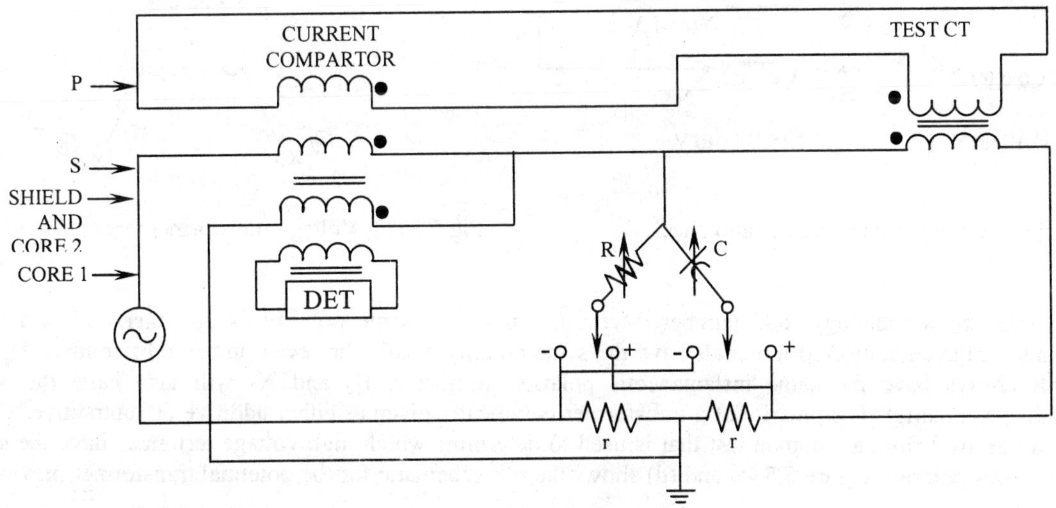

Fig. 5.4 (I): Calibration of current transformer by using compensated current comparator.

5.5 TESTING AND CALIBRATION OF VOLTAGE TRANSFORMERS

Voltage transformers manufactured in conformity with IEC standard 186 A or BS 3941 describe voltage and phase error test. Following tests are conducted as pre-commissioning tests on potential transformers:
(1) Ratio check; (2) Phasing check; (3) Polarity check;

Ratio check: This test can be conducted by applying a low voltage equivalent to PT secondary voltage applied to the primary. Then the AC voltmeter connected to the secondary as shown in Figure 5.5 (a) will indicate the available secondary voltage.
Percentage error can be calculated by using the formulae, [(Kn Vs – Vp) x 100] / Vp
Kn = Rated transformation ratio of the PT under test = Rated primary voltage/ Rated secondary voltage given in the PT nameplate.
Vp = Test voltage applied in the primary.
Vs = Voltage measured in the secondary during the test.

Phasing check: With the primary (all the 3 phases) alive, the secondary phase sequence can be checked by, using a phase sequence meter connected across the three phases. This test can be conducted during commissioning stage only.

Polarity check: When dealing with AC systems, polarity can sometimes be a deceptive term. Unlike DC equipment, AC components do not have terminals designated positive and negative: instead, each terminal changes from positive to negative and back again in every cycle. The polarity of transformer terminals is, therefore, a question of instantaneous polarity. Figure 5.5 (b) illustrates the concept for an instant of time when the voltage applied to H_1 is at its peak positive value. When terminal H_1 is positive, terminal H_2 will always be negative. On the low voltage side, however, there are two distinct possibilities: The low voltage terminal directly across from H_1 may be either positive or negative at this given instant, depending on the way that the terminals have been brought out of the winding. In the diagram shown in Figure 5.5 (b), low voltage terminal diagonally across H_1 has the same polarity as H_1: When H_1 is positive, this low voltage terminal is positive. Similarly, when H_1 is negative, this low voltage terminal is also negative.

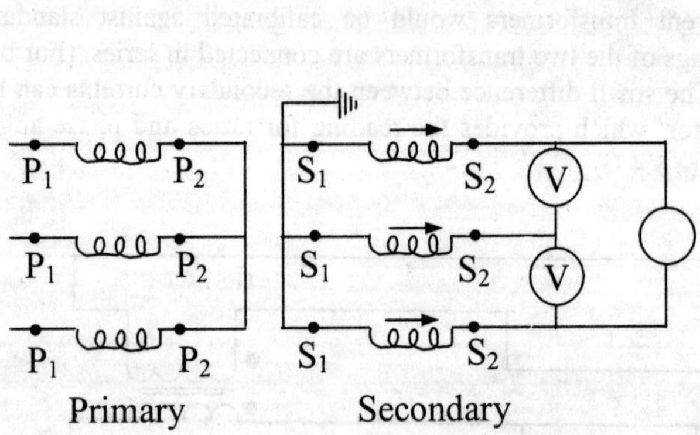

Fig. 5.5 (a): Potential transformer ratio check.

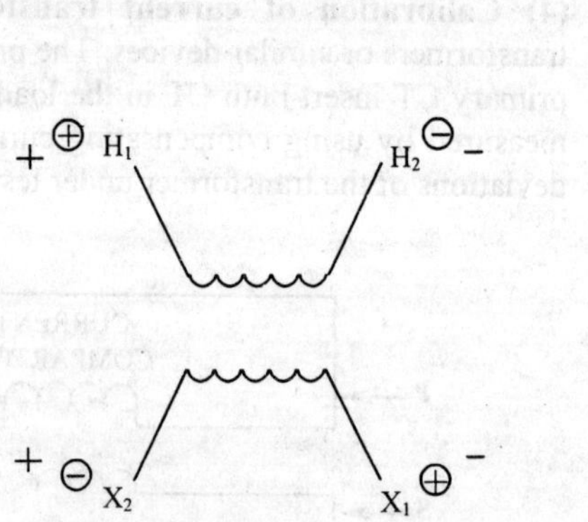

Fig 5.5 (b): Voltage transformer terminal marking.

In the standard terminology, odd numbered-terminals have the same polarity as all other odd numbered terminals, and even numbered terminals have the same polarity as all other even numbered terminals. H_1 and X_1 will always have the same instantaneous polarity. Similarly, H_2 and X_2 will also have the same instantaneous polarity. The polarity of a transformer is typically given as either additive or subtractive. These terms are derived from a common test that is used to determine which high voltage terminals have the same instantaneous polarity. Figure 5.5 (c) and (d) shows the test schematic for the potential transformer previously discussed.

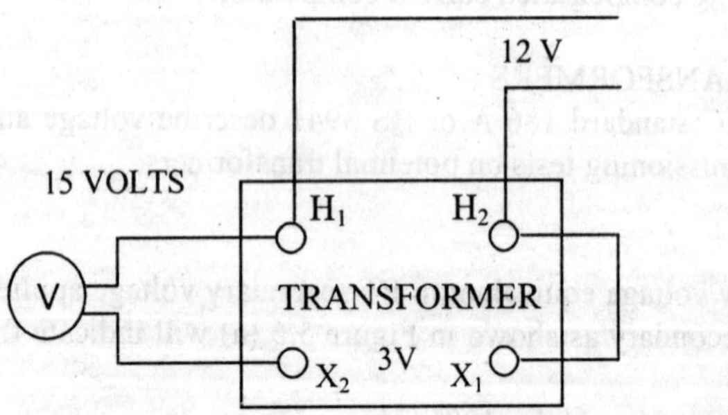

Fig. 5.5 (c): Polarity test on VT (additive polarity).

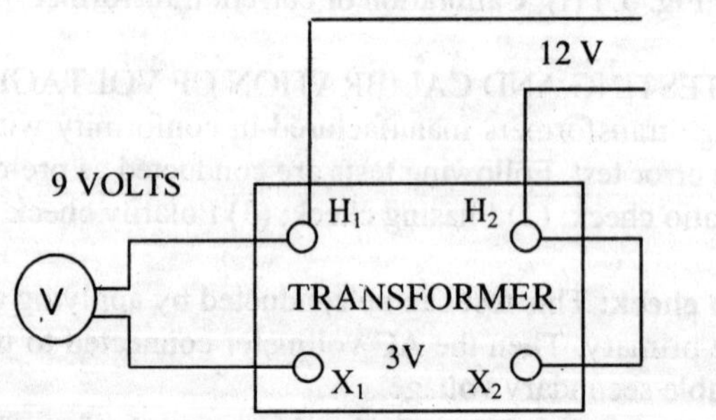

Fig. 5.5 (d): Polarity test on VT (subtractive polarity).

The test connection for polarity check of PT is as follows:
One of the high voltage terminals is connected to the low voltage terminal directly opposite with a jumper. A voltmeter is connected across the other high voltage terminal and it's opposite low voltage terminal. The high voltage winding is energized with low voltage AC. (12 volt AC is used in this example) Assume that the transformer shown in Figure 5.5 (c) has a 4:1 step down ratio. If 12 volts applied across the primary, 3 volts will present in the secondary. If more than 12 volts is present in the voltmeter, X_2 must have an instantaneous polarity opposite that of H_1 and the difference in potential between the two terminals is 12 + 3 = 15 volts. This arrangement is known as additive polarity.

The opposite case is shown in Figure 5.5 (d). If less than 12 volts, is present in the voltmeter H_1 and its opposite low voltage terminals have the same instantaneous polarity. The difference in potential across the two terminals is 12 – 3 = 9 volts. This arrangement is known as subtractive polarity.

Calibration of voltage transformer: A voltage transformer would be calibrated against a standard transformer or a capacitive divider having the same nominal ratio as the transformer under calibration. In the case of a standard transformer method, the primary windings of the two transformers are connected in parallel to the power source. The small differences between the secondary voltages are measured with a voltage comparator circuit [Figure 5.5 (e)] that provides the readings of transformer ratio and phase angle corrections.

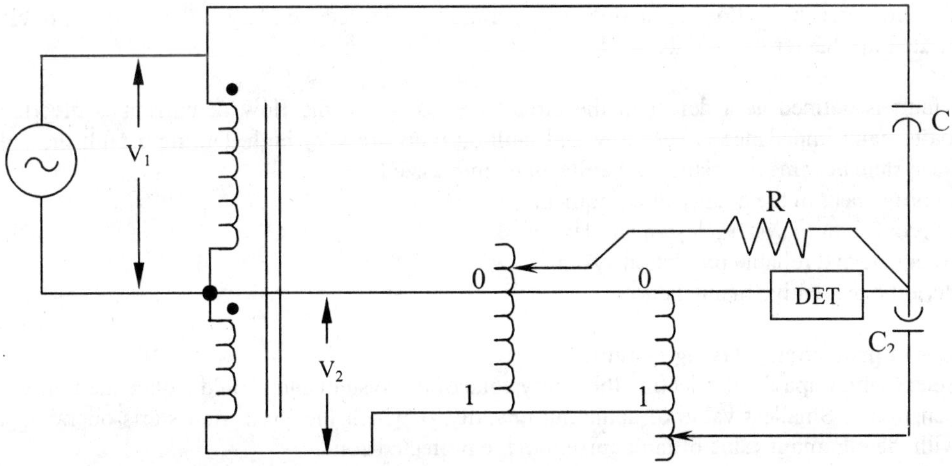

Fig. 5.5 (e): Calibration of voltage transformer by capacitive divider method

5.6 COMMON TERMS ON PROTECTIVE RELAYING

Relay is an electrical device that is designed to respond to specific input conditions by closing contacts or making a similar abrupt change in a control circuit. Inputs are electrical or mechanical or thermal. Protective relay means a relay whose function is to detect defective equipment or other power system faults and to initiate appropriate control, such as tripping circuit breakers to isolate the faulty area. Common types on a power system include over-current relay, under/over voltage relay, high/low frequency relay, ground fault relay, differential relay, directional relay, distance relay and reverse power relay etc.

Relay, which place an important role in minimizing the faults and also in minimizing the damages in the event of fault by, tripping the circuit breaker of the faulty system. By disconnecting the faulty system so quickly improves the system stability, service continuity and system performance. Localize effect of fault and minimize the damage and prevent insulation failure and fire. Relay system means an assembly, usually consisting of measuring units, relay logic, communications interfaces, and necessary power supplies. A permissive relay system is one in which the functional cooperation of two or more relays is required before a control action can become effective.

(1) Relay classification: Relays are classified in to following groups.

1) Main relays: Protective relays whose main function is to detect defect in the system or apparatus, and to initiate appropriate control circuit action and serve to isolate the protected area. Over-current and earth fault relay are demonstrated in section 5.17.

2) Auxiliary relays: A relay whose function is to assist another relay or control device by supplying supplementary actions, some specific functions are: (1) Providing circuit seal-in functions (2) Increasing available number of independent NO or NC contacts (3) Providing contacts for electrical circuits interlocking.

3) Signal relays/annunciator relays: A device that visually indicates that a relay or some other device has operated. Its primary importance is to indicate some abnormality on the power system, whose function is to register the operation of some protection and control light (warning) and audible alarm signals. Annunciator system is demonstrated in Chapter # 3, section 3.16.

4) Back-up relays: Back up protection that operates independently of specific components in the primary protective system and is intended to operate if the primary protection fails or is temporarily out of service. Typical back-up relay is demonstrated in Chapter # 6, section 6.19.

5) Re-closing relays: A programming relay whose function is to initiate the sequence of actions leading to automatic re-closing of a circuit breaker after certain type of fault tripping. Re-close means the automatic closing of a circuit breaker following an opening operation via protective relay action. Typical re-closing relay is demonstrated in Chapter # 8, section 8.15.

Electrical fault is defined as a defect in the circuit due to which the flow of current is diverted from the indented path. Fault impedance is very low and fault currents are very high. During a fault the voltages of a three-phase system become unbalanced. Fault can be minimized by:

1. Improvement in the quality of equipments.
2. Improvement in system design and layout
3. Adequate and reliable protection system
4. Periodic preventive maintenance

(2) Qualities of protection relaying system:

1. Selectivity: Capable of selecting the faulty zone of the system and should isolate the faulty circuit
2. Sensitivity: Smallest value of actuating quantity at which the Protection starts operating in relation with the minimum value of fault current in the protected zone.
3. Stability: Quality of protective system by the virtue of which the protection remains inoperative and stable under certain specified conditions such as system disturbance, through and transient faults etc. In a relay system stability is a measure of the degree of certainty of correct performance. Denotes certainty of correct operation together with assurance against incorrect operation from all extraneous causes.
4. Reliability: Protection should not fail to operate in the events of faults in the protected zone. Protection system should not operate un-necessarily. Rapid fault clearing improves power system reliability.
5. Discrimination: Enable to distinguish between normal condition and abnormal condition. Abnormal condition means short-circuit, earth fault, under/over voltage, under/over frequency, unbalanced load, reverse power, high temperature etc.
6. Speed and time: Fault clearing time means relay time and circuit breaker time. Relay time means instant of fault to closing of relay contact. Circuit breaker time means from closing of relay contact to final arc extinction in circuit breaker.
7. Adequateness: Protection provided for any equipment is judged by considering: rating, location, probability of abnormal condition, continuity of supply, cost of machine etc.
8. Redundancy: Duplicated elements in a system for the purpose of enhancing the reliability of continuity of operating the system.

(3) Relay characteristics:

Inverse time characteristic: The operation time of a relay is a function of current and time. Operating time is inversely proportional to the square of the operating current. Such a characteristic of the relay is called inverse time characteristic. A relay whose characteristics is such that the time lag is not fixed, but varies inversely as the current, i.e larger the current, lesser the time as shown in Figure 5.6. Two settings have to be made on the relay, i.e, time and the current. The advantage of inverse time characteristic is that the equipment such as a transformer or a generator can be utilized to the best advantage so that it can safely take heavy overloads for short periods and lesser overloads for longer periods, without tripping. On systems in which there is large variation in fault currents between the two ends of the feeder, because faster operating times can be achieved by the relays nearest to the source, where the fault level is the highest.

Inverse definite minimum time characteristic: Relays with inverse definite minimum time (IDMT) curve has a characteristic, which is inverse up to a certain value of current and then become substantially independent as shown in Figure 5.6. IDMT characteristics conforming to IEC 255-4 and the BS 142 standards are classified in to 4 groups.

1. Inverse characteristic
2. Very inverse characteristic
3. Extremely inverse characteristic
4. Long time inverse characteristics

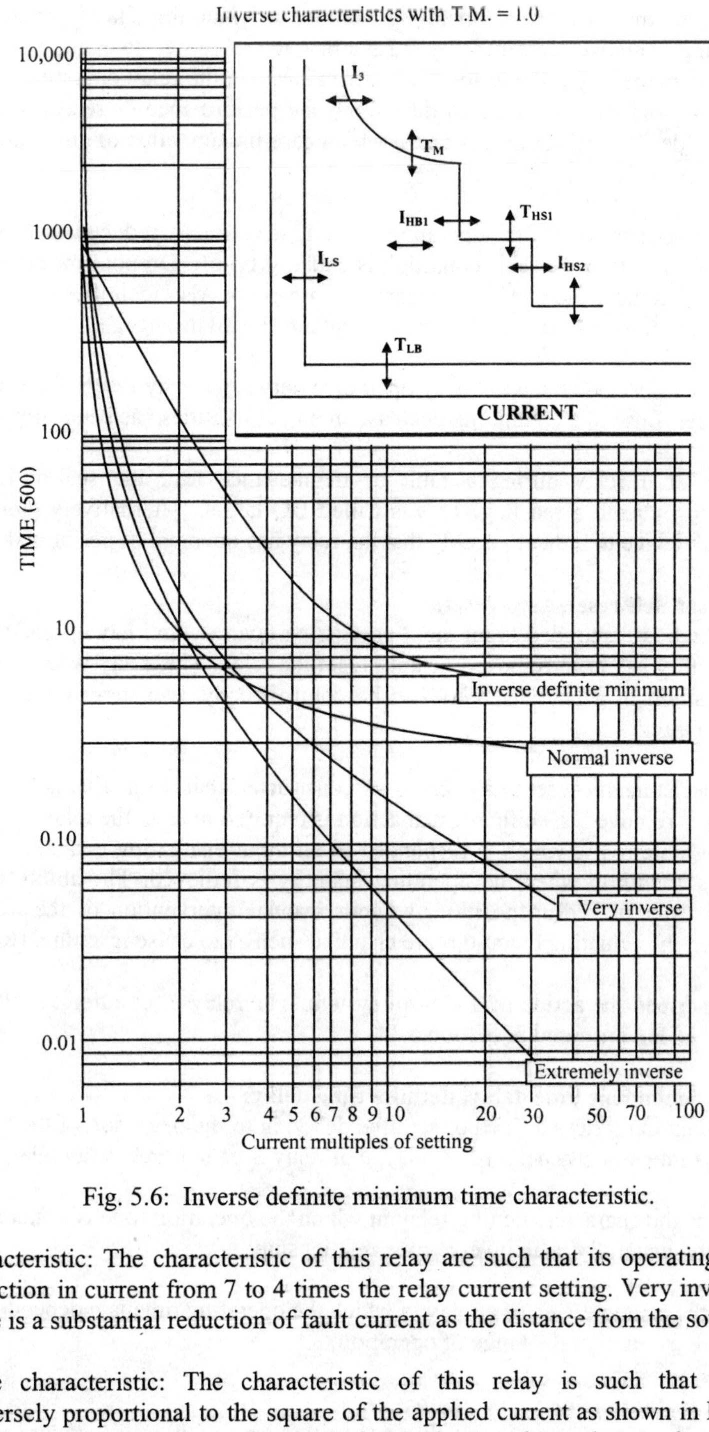

Fig. 5.6: Inverse definite minimum time characteristic.

Very inverse characteristic: The characteristic of this relay are such that its operating time is approximately doubled for a reduction in current from 7 to 4 times the relay current setting. Very inverse over current relays are suitable if there is a substantial reduction of fault current as the distance from the source increases.

Extremely inverse characteristic: The characteristic of this relay is such that the operation time is approximately inversely proportional to the square of the applied current as shown in Figure 5.6. Suitable for protection of distribution feeder circuits in which the feeder is subjected to peak current on switching in, example: Large motor starting

Protective relays are grouped on the basis of measurements of following operating quantities:

1. Magnitude measurement: Eg; over-current, over-voltage etc

2. Product measurement: Eg; power (VI cos ϕ)
3. Ratio measurement: Eg; impedance (V/I)
4. Comparison between similar electrical quantities: Eg; Vector difference between currents.

(4) Pickup, drop off, reset and DC target:
The pickup value is the minimum value of operating quantity at which the relay is on the verse of operation. For example if the setting of an over current relay is 2.5 amps, the relay start to operate a current slightly above 2.5 amps. Plug setting is made to get the desired number of turns in the relay operating-coil. Whatever be the plug setting the ampere turns will be same. In describing the performance of relays having multiple inputs, pickup has been used to denote contact operation, in which case pickup value of any input is meaningful only when related to all other inputs.

Assume that the relay is operated and if the operating quantity is gradually reduced, at a certain value the relay contact, which is closed, tend to open. This condition is called drop off. Dropout means the change in contact position of a relay at the moment the relay just departs from pickup. Also identifies the maximum value of an input quantity, which will allow the relay to depart from pickup (i.e. to disengage).

Relay is said to-be reset when the contact is fully open or otherwise a relay resets when it re-attains an initial condition, in which all response to a continuing decrease in input quantities has been completed.

To confirm operation of a relay during a fault or maintenance test, the seal-in unit energizes in an electromagnetic relay to indicate a red flag. This is called DC target. Alternatively target is a supplemental mechanical or electrical device to indicate visibly that the relay has operated or performed its function.

(5) Latching, hand reset, self reset, auto-reset:
An electrical relay, which is responded to an input energizing quantity and having picked-up remains in that condition after the quantity has been removed or until reset the relay. This relay is said to be latching relay or bistable relay. The position of a latching relay can be controlled by, two input circuits or two methods of connection of one input circuit.

Hand reset relay: A mechanically reset relay that is so constructed that it remains in the picked-up condition after the input quantity is removed, specific manual action is required to reset the relay.
Self-reset relay: Monostable relay, which is responded to an input energizing quantity and having picked-up returns to its, previous condition when the operating quantity is removed. The ability of a relay contact or target to reset from a fully picked-up position, without manual intervention or the need for supplemental electrical resetting when the actuating quantities are changed such as to cause resetting. [Refer figure 5.12]

Auto-reset: A term described the action of a control system. The relay reset automatically after an operation. Typical self reset relay is demonstrated in section 5.11.

(6) Time delay relay, dependent time delay, definite time delay:
A time delay relay, which introduces a fixed or set time delay, in to the operation of the relay or a relay whose operation or resetting is intentionally delayed. This type of relay is called time delay relay.

Dependent time delay is the characteristic of a relay in which the operation time is a function of the magnitude of the actuating quantity, generally in an inverse-time relationship.

Definite time delay is the characteristic of a relay in which the operating time is independent of the value of the actuating quantity, once it is within the range of operation.

(7) High-speed relay, Instantaneous:
High-speed relay is a relay that operates in less than a specified time of 50 milliseconds.

Instantaneous: A qualifying term indicating that no delay is purposely designed in to the device. The relay operating time is about 17 to 25 milliseconds.

(8) NO/NC and Zero contact, Make before break:
NO- Normally open contact: A contact, which closes a circuit when the relay picks up.
NC- Normally closed contact: A contact, which opens a circuit when the relay picks-up
Zero contact: Contact is closed when the switch is in off position e.g. ammeter selector switch.
Make before break contact: Before breaking NC contact, the NO contact will open

(9) Sensitivity, stability:
Sensitivity: With respect to burden, an inverse measure of the signal volt-amperes required for operation. With respect to signal level, an inverse measure of the magnitude required for operation.

Stability: An inverse measure of variations in actual performance, to changes in any influencing quantity such as auxiliary voltage, temperature etc.

(10) Device numbers:
The devices in switching equipments are referred to by numbers with appropriate suffix letters according to functions performed by them. These numbers are based on a system, which has been adopted as standard. The definitions and functions of ANSI device numbers which is internationally accepted are listed in section 5.24

5.7 ELECTROMAGNETIC TYPE PROTECTION RELAYS.
Based on the principle of operation and construction, electromagnetic relays are classified as follows:
1. Attracted armature type; 2. Balanced beam type; 3. Induction disc type; 4. Induction cup type;
5. Moving coil type; 6. Moving iron type;.

The most widely used one is the induction disc or cup type. Induction pattern relays operate on the same principle as induction motor. Torque is produced by subjecting the moving conductor (disc or cup) to two alternating field. The two fields can be derived from one quantity by arranging to energize two electromagnets with an appropriate phase shift between them or by separate quantities. The addition of a capacitor and resistor components in series with the voltage coil, produces a leading phase shift, which can easily be made more than 90°. Reversal of coil connections gives the effect of a lagging phase shift.

Attracted armature type electromagnetic relays energized by AC supply will tend to vibrate because the flux must pass through zero at every half cycle and at these points the armature will be released slightly from the magnetic pole. To eliminate this effect it is usual to split the magnetic pole and surround one half with a low resistance copper band. The eddy currents induced in this loop cause a phase delay in the flux passing through the loop as compared with that in the other half of the pole. Hence the flux does not come in to zero on the whole face of the magnet pole at any instant. So that a hold on force is always present.

(1) Series sealing circuit for normally open relay contact:
Figure 5.7 (a) shows the circuit diagram of an electromagnetic over current relay having normally open (NO) contact used for tripping the associated circuit breaker. Assume that the circuit breaker (device No: 52) is "ON", its auxiliary contact (52a) is closed. During an over-current or short circuit in the outgoing feeder (after the breaker), the over-current relay (device No: 50) pick-up, when the current exceed the set value. The circuit breaker trip coil energizes through the relay contacts and the circuit breaker trips open to isolate the faulty area and the relay is "sealed in", through the momentarily energized seal in unit and indicate a red flag. Breaker auxiliary contact (52a) opens to isolate the trip coil supply. If it is required to switch-on the breaker, the relay has to reset by pushing the reset latch. If an attempt is accidentally made to close the breaker prior to reset the relay, the trip circuit will energize through the seal-in contact and a trip free operation will take place because the breaker auxiliary contact closes before the main contact close.

(2) Series sealing circuit for normally closed relay contact:
Figure 5.7 (b) shows the schematic diagram of a series sealing circuit for an under-voltage electromagnetic relay having normally closed relay contact. Relay is connected to the incoming feeder circuit through a voltage transformer. During the presence of power supply, the under-voltage relay (device No: 27) contact remains open. During under-voltage or no-volt condition, assume that the breaker is "ON" the relay contact closes and the breaker trips open and the relay contact is sealed-in through the seal in unit. Before re-closing the breaker the relay has to reset.

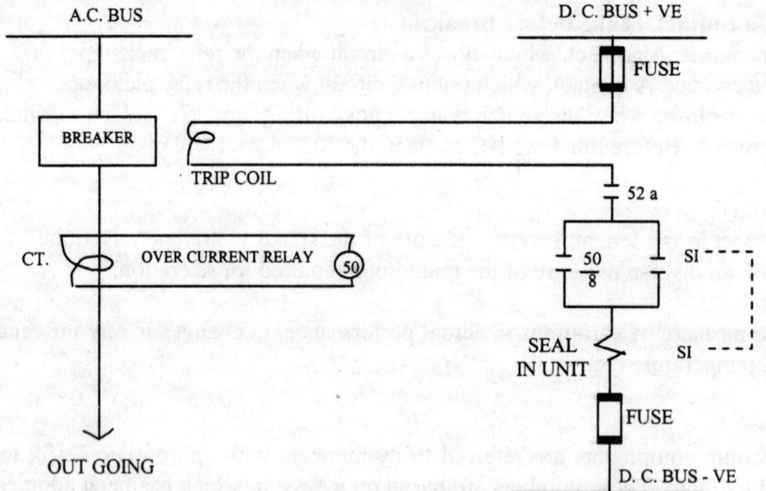

Fig. 5.7 (a): Series sealing circuit for normally open relay contact.

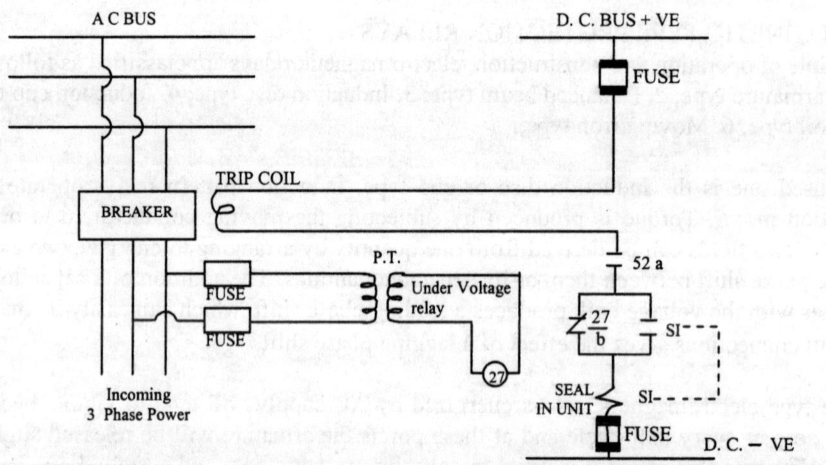

Fig. 5.7 (b): Series sealing circuit for normally closed relay contact.

(3) Shunt sealing circuit for electro-mechanical relays:

In Figure 5.7 (c), assume that the circuit breaker is closed, the auxiliary contact (device No: 52a) remain closed. During the occurrence of a fault in the protected zone, over-current relay (device No: 50) picks-up if the current exceed the set value. Then circuit breaker trip coil energizes to trips open the circuit breaker. Seal-in unit which is connected in parallel to the trip coil will energize and seal-in to prevent re-closing the breaker without resetting the relay. When the circuit breaker is tripped, its auxiliary contact (device No: 52a) opens and the trip coil and seal-in unit coil de-energizes.

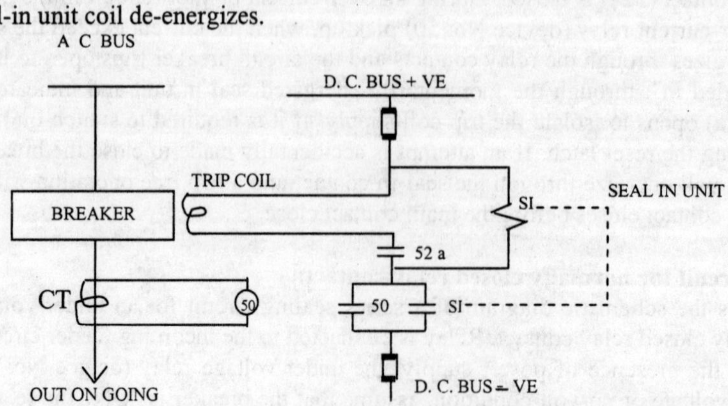

Fig. 5.7 (c): Shunt sealing circuit for electro-mechanical relays.

5.8 SINGLE AND DOUBLE ACTUATING QUANTITY STATIC RELAYS.

Static relay is an electrical relay in which the response is developed by electronic, magnetic, optical or other components without mechanical motion. Static relays are classified in to (1) Single actuating quantity type, and (2) Double actuating quantity type.

Single actuating quantity static relays:

These types of relay having only one input source either current or voltage. For example: Over-current relay, Under-voltage relay, Frequency relay Etc. Figure 5.8 (a) shows the synoptic diagram of a single actuating quantity frequency relay. Input from the PT is supplied to the squaring amplifier through low pass filter. The output is fed to a measuring element.. If time delay is required, a timing circuit is to be introduced. External circuit diagram of a static frequency relay used for over/under frequency protection is given in figure 6.18 (a) of Chapter # 6.

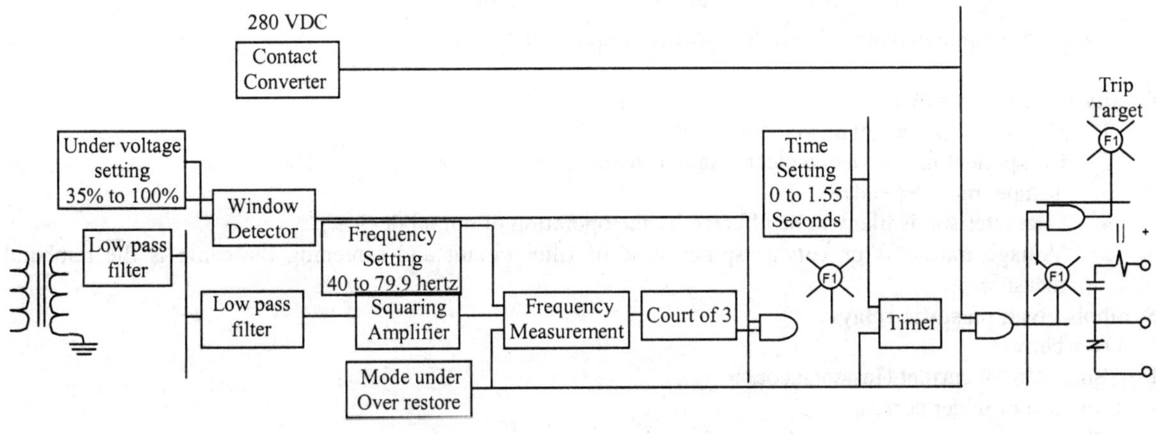

Fig. 5.8 (a): Synoptic diagram of double actuating quantity static relay.

Double actuating quantity static relays:

These types of static relays have double input source either current from two different sources or both current and voltage. For example: Directional relay, Distance relay, Differential relay etc. Figure 5.8 (b) shows the Synoptic diagram of a double actuating quantity static distance relay. The input from P.T and CT are fed in to the distance-measuring element and the input from PT is fed in to direction measuring element. The outputs of distance element and direction element are fed in to logic circuit. When the quantity exceeds the set value the tripping and alarm relays and remote trip relay will energize. Typical external connection of distance relay is shown in figure 8.4 (f) of Chapter # 8.

Advantages of static relays:

1. Less burden on CT and PT
2. No moving contact except auxiliary relay in the output circuit.
3. Single unit with several functional blocks for various protections.
4. Superior characteristics and accuracy.
5. Logic gates (Complex protection scheme).
6. Programmable operation.
7. Self-supervision facility.
8. Simplified testing and servicing.
9. Improved selectivity by reducing resetting time and overshoot time.
10. Interface with supervisory control and data acquisition system (SCADA).
11. Transducers for conversion of electrical or non-electrical quantities.
12. Compact and free from vibration.

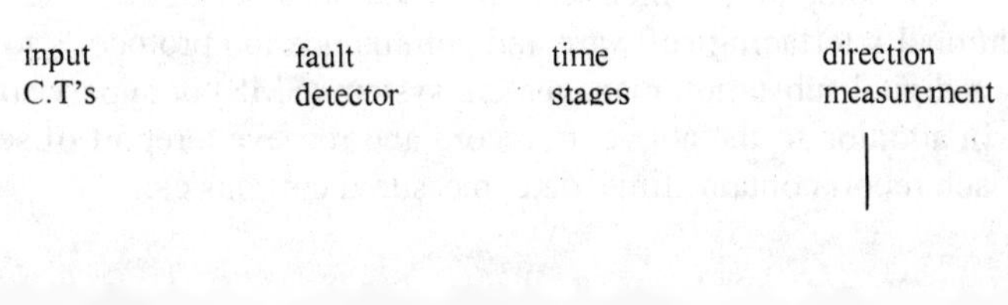

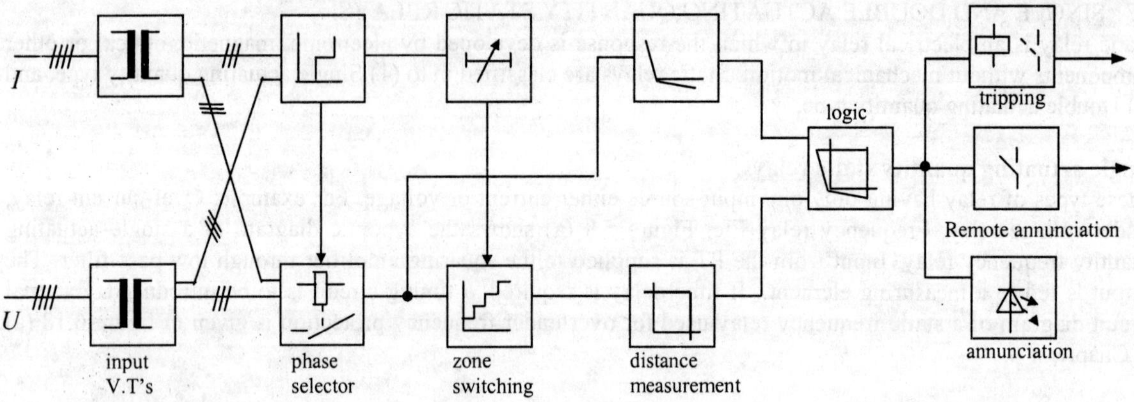

Fig. 5.8 (b): Synoptic diagram of double actuating quantity static relay.

Disadvantages of static relays:

1. DC auxiliary control power is essential.
2. Component failure due to electrostatic discharge.
3. Temperature dependent.
4. Characteristic is likely to be affected by the operation of output device.
5. Voltage transients or voltage spikes. Use of filter circuit and screening the cable is the remedial measure.

Symbols given on static relays:

I > Over-current

I >> Short-circuit current (Instantaneous)

I < Low load or under current

I_0 Earth fault current

θ Thermal overload

5.9 MICRO PROCESSOR CONTROLLED NUMERICAL PROTECTION RELAYS.

The digital system generally operates groups of 8 or 16 or 32 bits of information at once. Some digital relays are with 16 digit microprocessor. The information to be processed might be:

1. Textual: eg; normal or emergency state
2. Numerical: eg; value of current, voltage, power etc
3. Logical: logical condition imposed on a relay to operate.

This form of information is represented in a digital system by codes of binary digits.

Advantages of microprocessor based protective relays:

1. Single relay having large number of protective and monitoring functions.
2. Programmable feature: Measured values of variables are processed digitally by microprocessor.
3. High level of flexibility: The relay meets the most complex protective and monitoring requirements.
4. The memory of the relay enables to retain the value of variables responsible for tripping and time taken the relay to operate etc.
5. Precise measurement: Digitally display the value of current, voltage, active and reactive power, Power factor etc.
6. Comprehensive self-monitoring and self-checking feature.
7. Increased communication ability: Data interface access.
8. Easy to install, operate, set and use.
9. Easy to access stored data and easy to input new data.
10. Provides fault designation. Information can be hooked to fault recorder and fault location indicator.
11. High speed: 12 to 32milli-seconds tripping time.

Programs suitable for use on a personnel computer, which can be used to interrogates the relay and communicate settings to the relay. Additional interfacing software and communication protocol's to allow the relay to be controlled and integrated by a digital substation management system (SMS) or supervisory control and data acquisition system (SCADA). In addition to the above, to record and retrieve a report of several past fault trips in order of their occurrence. Each report contains time, date, measured currents etc.

Figure 5.9 shows the synoptic diagram of a numerical relay.

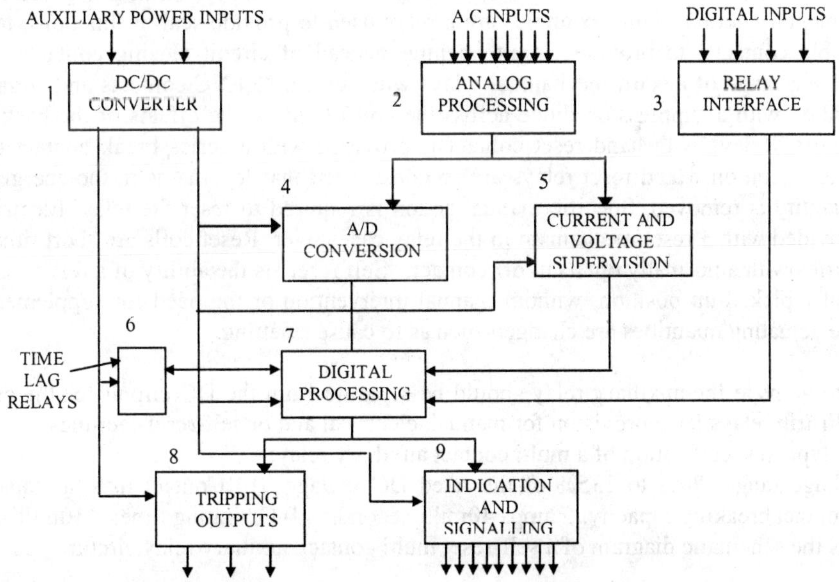

Fig. 5.9: Synoptic diagram of a typical numerical relay.

5.10 INTEGRATED PROTECTION MONITORING AND CONTROL SYSTEM.

Programmable protection and control system has a microprocessor or microcomputer in its circuit. An integrated protection monitoring and control system (IPMC) can perform functions: data acquisition, data processing, data transmission, protection and control. Types of electronic circuit in protection system include:

1. Analogue circuits
2. Digital circuits
3. Hybrid circuits

Data transmission channels: Power line carrier communication (PLCC), Fiber optic cables (Teleprotection), Microwave (Radio link) and pilot cables discussed in Chapter # 8, section 8.9, 8.8 and 8.11 respectively.
Following protective and monitoring functions can be introduced through microprocessor system:

1. Backup protection
2. Auto re-closing sequence
3. Sequential tripping of load
4. Load shedding
5. Remote signaling

Microprocessor based system can be utilized for the following control functions:

1. Load management
2. Frequency control
3. Planning operation
4. Economic loading
5. Emergency and post emergency actions

Power system is managed by:

1. SCADA: Supervisory control and data acquisition. (Refer Chapter # 3, section 3.20)
2. EMS: Energy Management System. (Refer Chapter # 3, section 3.21)
3. AGC: Automatic generation control system. (Refer Chapter # 1, section 1.8)
4. SMS: Substation management system (Refer Chapter # 4, section 4.20).
5. DCS: Distributed control system (Refer Chapter # 1, figure 1.1 *(l)*

IPMC is employed in modern diesel power stations for automatic priority starting/stopping, synchronizing and loading of diesel generator sets.

5.11 SELF RESET MULTI CONTACT AUXILIARY RELAY.

A relay, whose function is to assist another relay or control devices in performing a general function, by supplying supplementary action. Some examples are a relay used to provide seal-in functions, to increase the number of available contacts, to provide circuit opening instead of circuit closing contacts or vice-versa. Auxiliary relays are a range of electro-mechanical relays with several NO/NC contacts and complying to B S 142. Relays are fitted with a suppression diode across the coil to reduce the effects of the back e.m.f, which occurs on switch off. Relays with hand reset contact is provided with a series break contact to cut off the operating coil after operation. Hand reset relays are so constructed that it remains in the energized condition after the input quantity is removed. Specific manual action is required to reset the relay. Electrical and hand reset units are provided with a reset mechanism in the relay case cover. Reset coils are short time rated which is connected in series with a normally open cut off contact. "Self reset" is the ability of a relay contact or target to reset from a fully picked-up position, without manual intervention or the need for supplemental electrical resetting when the actuating quantities are changed such as to cause resetting.

DC circuit used to activate the auxiliary relay should be separate from the DC circuit for the circuit breaker tripping coil. Multi-trip relays have provision for manual, electrical and/or self-reset-facilities.
Following are the typical specification of a multi contact auxiliary relay:
(a) Operative voltage range: 80% to 135% of the rated DC voltage; (b) Contact making capacity: 5 amps continuous; (c) Contact breaking capacity: 5 amps 40milli-seconds; (d) Operating time: < 10milli-seconds.
Figure 5.11 shows the schematic diagram of a self-reset multi contact auxiliary relay circuit.

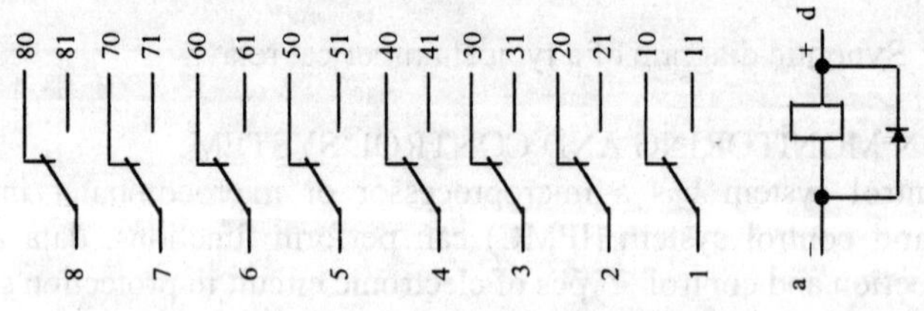

Fig. 5.11: Schematic diagram of multi contact auxiliary relay (Courtesy, Siemens Ag).

5.12 ELECTRICAL/HAND RESET LOCKOUT AND TRIP RELAY.

Lockout relay is an electrically reset or hand-reset auxiliary relay whose function is to hold associated devices inoperative until it is reset. Lock out relay is a high-speed mechanically latched control relay with electric trip and manual or electric reset provision. These relays are used in conjunction with other protective relays. When energized, the circuit breaker trip coil will be de-energized through its own normally closed (NC) contact. Manual reset means the unit will stay locked out in the trip position until manually reset. Electrically reset means reset coil can be energized through a remote control switch. DC circuit used for connecting the circuit breaker trip circuit is used for energizing lockout relays. Figure 5.12 shows the schematic diagram of a fast acting lockout relay having 8 changeover contacts and DC 110 volts operating and reset coils. Latching type relays have hand or electrically reset contacts and hand reset red coloured flag indicators. Lockout relay picks up whenever the associated protective relay operates as indicated in figure 1.2 (g) of Chapter # 1.
Following are the typical specification of a multi-contact lockout relay:
(a) Contact rating: 10 amps, Pickup time < 10 ms; (b) Instantaneous current: 80 A/200 ms or 150 A/10 ms; (c) Making capacity: 40A/0.5 sec 110 V DC; (d) Device number is 86 for lockout relay

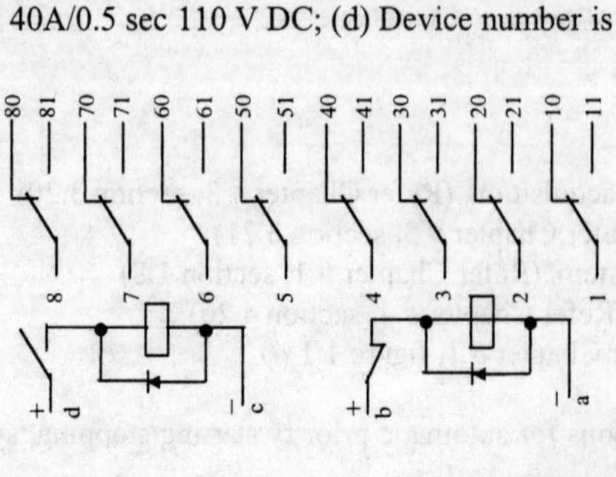

Fig. 5.12: Schematic diagram of lockout relay (Courtesy, Siemens Ag).

5.13 PRIMARY CURRENT INJECTION TEST SET.

The philosophy of primary current injection testing is directly related to the tester's desire to simulate the actual working conditions of the protective equipment as closely as physically possible under non-laboratory conditions. The primary concern of the tester is the availability and portability of the test set. There is little possibility that ever have needs to calibrate a relay while applying primary current. Primary injection is used in providing the integrity and polarity of various protection schemes including differential relay and complicated line protection circuitry and is usually the final test before energization and in-service testing at work site. Current transformers, low voltage circuit breakers and current operated relays should be subjected to primary injection test to verify the correctness of the connection and the reliability of its operation. Primary current injection test set is a loading transformer designed to take supply at 230 volts (primary) and ranging from 5 to 15 KVA (500, 1000, 1500, 2000, 3000, 4000, 5000 amps range) at a secondary voltage of 3 to 15 V, by connecting the secondary windings in series or parallel or series-parallel.

Figure 5.13 (a) and (b) respectively shows the external connection diagram and circuit diagram of a typical primary injection test set. The output current can be varied by a built-in autotransformer. While testing the thermal or magnetic protection or solid-state built-in protection of Moulded case circuit breakers / Air circuit breakers etc. an external timer can be connected for measuring the tripping time. By injecting current to the CT primary (bus bar) or slipping test lead through the CT, the effectiveness of connection and the operation of relays can be verified. This unit is not designed for continuous duty and maximum permissible loading time is usually 15 minutes depending on the design parameters.

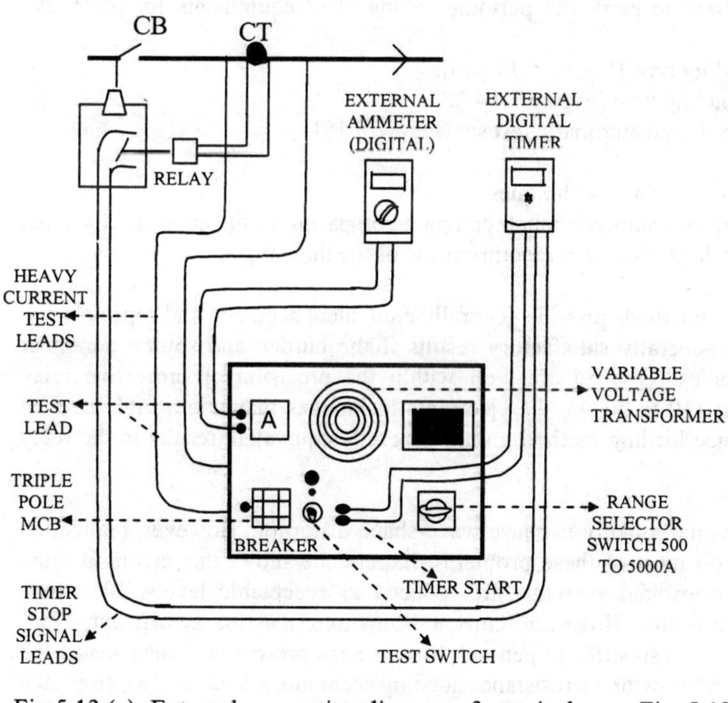

Fig.5.13 (a): External connection diagram of a typical. Primary injection test set.

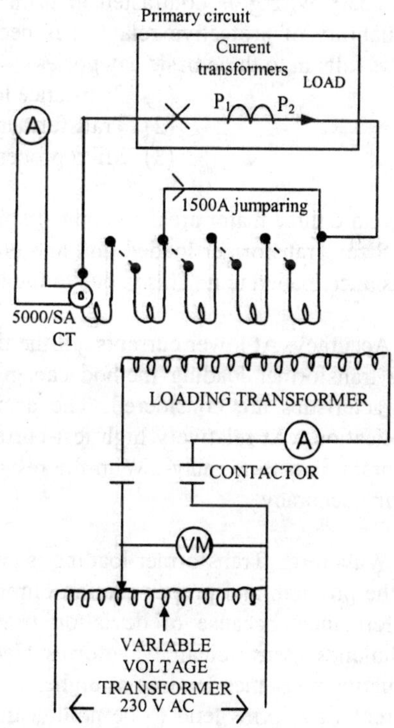

Fig. 5.13 (b): Internal power circuit diagram of a Primary injection test set.

Test method:

a) Isolate the switchgear and observe a work-permit without earthing the area to be tested. Verify the presence of voltage in the switchgear by, using a voltage tester.

b) Select required current to be injected and connect the secondary as required. Bolt the test leads (current source) of the primary injection test set for adjusting the current to be injected.

c) Ensure that variable voltage transformer knob is in zero position and range selector switch is in off position.

d) Switch on the test set by switching on the triple pole MCB and select the approximate test current in the range selector switch.

e) Observe ammeter reading and adjust the exact value of test current by, changing the position of variable voltage transformer knob.

f) Now switch off the test set and connect the test leads to the primary of the C.T under test, i.e connect to either side of the C.T on the bus bar (with correct polarity) or slip-in the lead through the CT and bolt the test leads.

g) Connect the timer start signal leads to one pole of the MCB, so that when the breaker is switched on timer will start. Connect the timer stop lead to the relay contact so that when the relay operates the timer will stop.

h) Switch on the test set and observe reading of ammeter, and timer. Repeat the test for other phases also. Remove the test set and restore the disturbed connections.

If the ratio of the CT under test is 1000/5 amps, a primary current of 1000 ampere is to be injected to obtain a secondary current of 5 amps. Assume that the relay connected to the said CT is set at 3 amps, the currents to be injected in the primary is (1000 x 3)/5 = 600 amps. If a current slightly above 600 A is injected in the primary, the relay will operate after elapsing the set time. From the readings of the ammeter (connected through a multi-ratio CT) in the secondary circuit, it is possible to judge whether the circuit connections are intact, and if not, determine the nature of the mistake.

5.14 APPARATUS FOR SECONDARY INJECTION TESTS.

Secondary injection is a descriptive term used to indicate that relay test voltages and currents are applied to the secondary wiring as contrasted to primary injection methods. In order to ensure healthiness and maximum availability of protective relays it is necessary to carry out periodic testing. Test equipments for protective relays falls in to three basic categories.

(1) Resistance loading type [Figure 5.14 (m)].
(2) Transformer loading type [Figure 5.14 (a)].
(3) Microprocessor-based automatic test set (Figure 5.15].

There are three major areas of comparison for the three techniques:

(1) Size: Transformer loaded unit and electronic units are much compact comparing to the equivalently rated resistance loaded unit. This is due to the low heat dissipation requirements of the three types.

(2) Accuracy: At lower currents, all the three methods provide generally equivalent accuracy and repeatability. The transformer loading method can give generally satisfactory results if the burden and source nonlinear characteristics are considered. The accuracies provided are well within the precision of protective relay applications. At relatively high test-currents (10 to 30 A), the electronic techniques maintain a high level of accuracy in setting relays. With the resistance loading method giving generally equivalent results in the relay setting accuracy.

(3) Waveform: Transformer loading is particularly likely to cause wave-shape distortion. However, realization of the problem and proper caution eliminates most of these problems. Experience shows that errors in relay performance, because of deviation from sinusoidal currents, are reduced to acceptable levels. Electronic techniques assure clean waveforms electronically. However, current limitations may be significant. Non-inductive resistance loading at higher currents is superior in general. Since relays present nonlinear loads, the current waveforms tend to be nonlinear. The resistor in resistance loading techniques tends to "swamp" the load's non-linearity and thus, a relatively sinusoidal waveform is assured.

Following apparatus are employed for secondary injection test:

1) Transformer loading type secondary test set: This type of secondary injection test set derives its test voltage and or currents from a variable autotransformer. This technique is specially, useful in high current testing since the currents are developed at lower voltage, thus reducing the power requirements for the testing source. For secondary injection test, 0 to 100 ampere variable current set is sufficient. Transformer loading type relay test set circuit illustrated in Figure 5.14 (a) consists of variable transformer, buck-boost transformer, medium and coarse control reactors, injection transformer, in-built time counter, ammeter etc. Set is designed for short-term duty (not for continuous duty) and suitable for (select 50 or 60 Hertz supply) testing over-current relays and earth fault relays etc.

The current is controlled by means of tapped reactors in the primary circuit of the injection transformer. The injection transformer is provided with secondary tapings chosen to correspond with the current setting of the relay under test. This ensures that the relay impedance is small when reflected back in to the primary circuit of the injection transformer and reduces the harmonics in the test current that are due to saturation of the magnetic circuit of the relay under test. The test set incorporates a digital timer 0.1ms to 999.99 seconds. When using the set, test current should be set approximately with the test leads shorted out to prevent unnecessary heating. The relay coil can then be connected for the final adjustment prior to test.

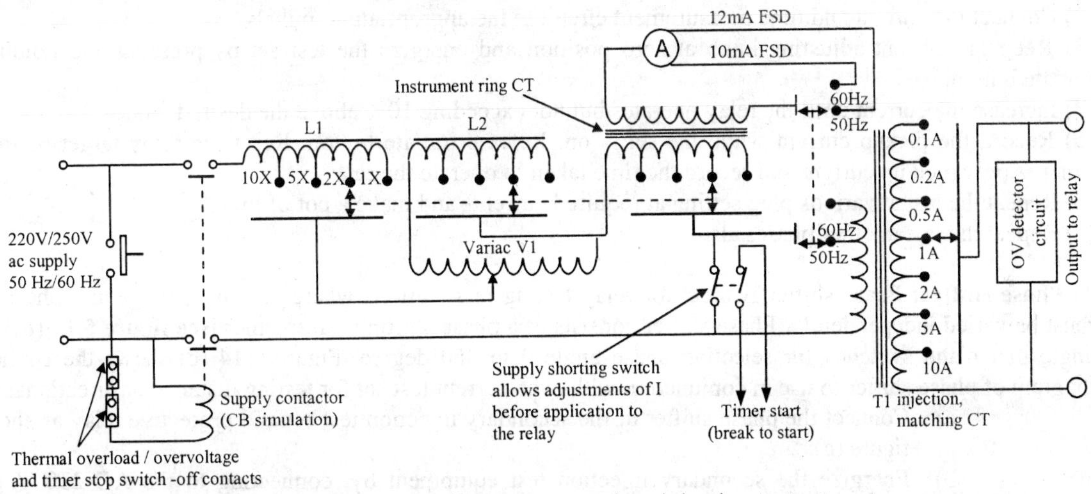

Fig. 5.14 (a): Transformer loading type secondary injection test set.

The test set is provided with following facilities:

1. Provision for current output ranges 0 to 10 A, 0 to 40 A and 0 to 100 A.
2. AC variable voltage output 0 to 250 V and 0 to 350V single phase 1 A
3. Fixed DC 110 volts output 1 A for using as auxiliary supply to electronic relays.
4. Variable DC output 20 to 220 V 1 A
5. 10 Microfarad 450 V, capacitor provides phase shift while testing directional protection.
6. Resister 0.5, 1.0, 25, 100, 500, 1000 and 2500 ohm with tapping facility for the test of low impedance relays. Resistors can be used for divide the voltage.
7. Tripping circuit is provided with signal lamp to indicate operated position.
8. Digital timer to indicate the time taken for relay operation.

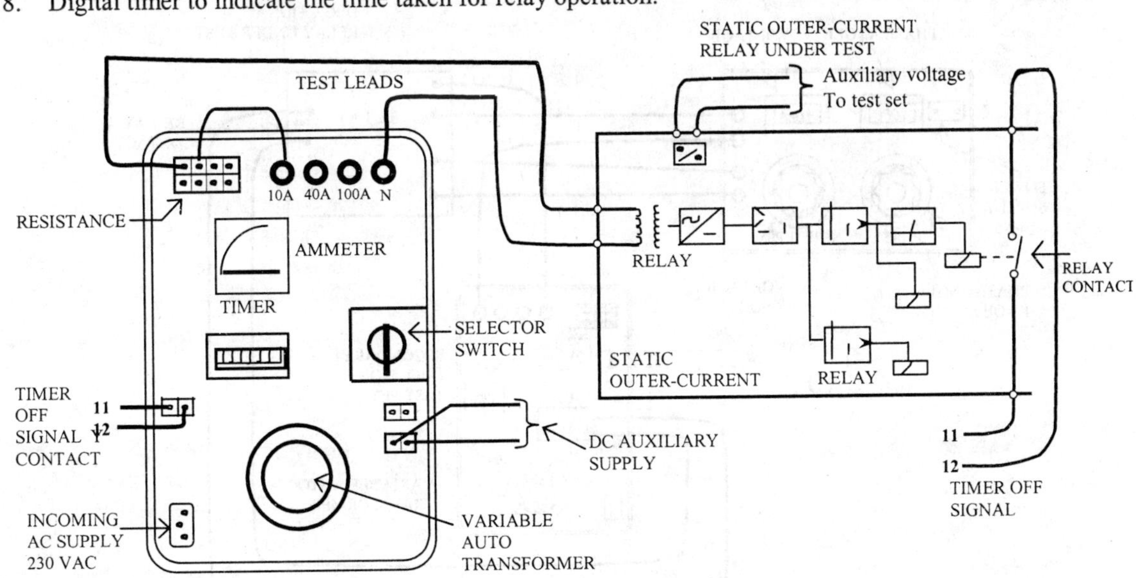

Fig. 5.14 (b): Typical test connection of secondary injection test set.

Secondary injection test checks the operation of the protective relay at its settings and the time required for operation. For pre-commissioning check and routine annual maintenance check secondary injection test is acceptable. Figure 5.14 (b) shows typical test connection for a solid-state over-current relay.

Test procedure for over-current relay is as follows:
(1) Connect the desired auxiliary voltage to the solid-state relay under test. Auxiliary voltage is not required for electromagnetic relays and digital relays.
(2) Connect the current and time measurement circuit in the appropriate terminals.
(3) Keep the current adjusting knob at zero position and energize the test set by pressing and holding the initiate button.
(4) Increase the current until the relay operates but not exceeding 10% above the desired value.
(5) Record the pickup current while the set is on. Release initiate button. Reset the relay target button and timer. Apply pick up current and record the time taken to operate the relay.
(6) Repeat the test at various plug setting at required currents and make a not of time.
(7) Repeat the test in other phases also.

2) Phase shifter: Phase shifter **is** ideal for relay testing in situations where current, voltage and phase angle must be varied independently. Phase shifter consists of a phase shifting transformer **[see figure 5.14 (h)]** phase angle meter and switches for selecting phase angle 0 to 360 degree. Figure 5.14 (c) shows the connection diagram of phase shifter to use in conjunction with over-current test set for testing distance or directional relay.

a) Connect the phase shifter to the secondary injection test set and protective relay as shown in figure (c).
b) Energize the secondary injection test equipment by, connecting to the AC 230 V power supply. 'U' terminal represents voltage leads and 'I' terminal represents the current leads.
c) Set the voltage to a low value by turning phase shifter voltage knob.
d) Set the current obtained from secondary injection test set to a low value.
e) Set the phase angle approximately by, using the phase shifter knob.
f) Adjust the current by using secondary injection test set.
g) Vary the voltage and phase angle using the respective knobs on the phase shifter. **(Always set the phase angle first and then change the voltage. This is because varying the phase angle affects the amplitude of the voltage, but the phase angle is not affected when the voltage is varied).**
h) Repeat the test and record the current, voltage and phase angle and time during relay operation.

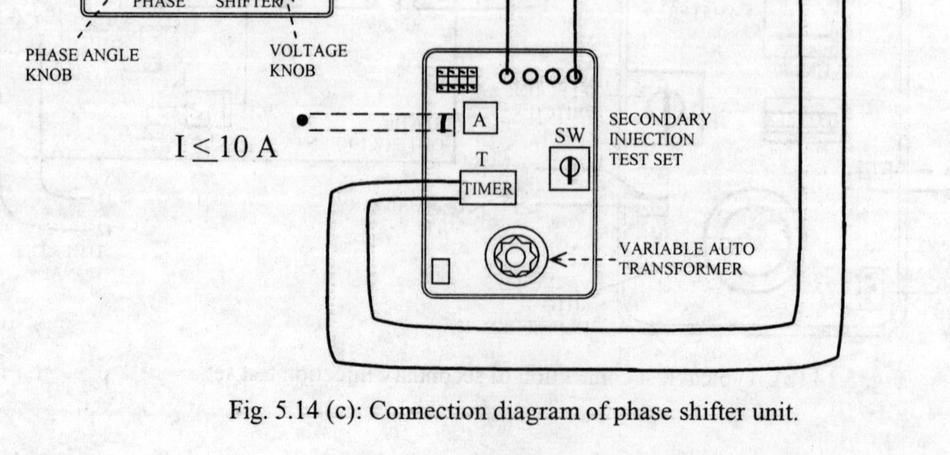

Fig. 5.14 (c): Connection diagram of phase shifter unit.

(3) Variable voltage transformer: Variable voltage transformer is an autotransformer in which the secondary voltage can be varied from zero to a specified value. It consists of single layer of copper wire wound on a toroidal core and a carbon brush, which traverses this winding. The brush track is made by, removing a portion of the insulation from each turn of the winding. The brush is always in contact with one or more wires and continuously taps off any desired fraction of the winding. Brush is fitted on an arm, which can be driven on load by, rotating a wheel or knob by hand. Electric motor can also be used for driving the shaft in which the arm is fitted.

Since most of the single-phase voltage relays are working at 120 or 220 V, AC 0 to 250 volts 15 A single phase variable voltage ransformer is sufficient for testing single phase relays. For testing various 3-phase relays 3-phase 120 V and 3-phase 415 V supply is required. AC 3-phase, 4-wire 0 to 500 V 15 A variable autotransformer is sufficient. Typical circuit diagram for single phase and 3-phase variable transformers are shown in Figure 5.14 (d) and (e) respectively.

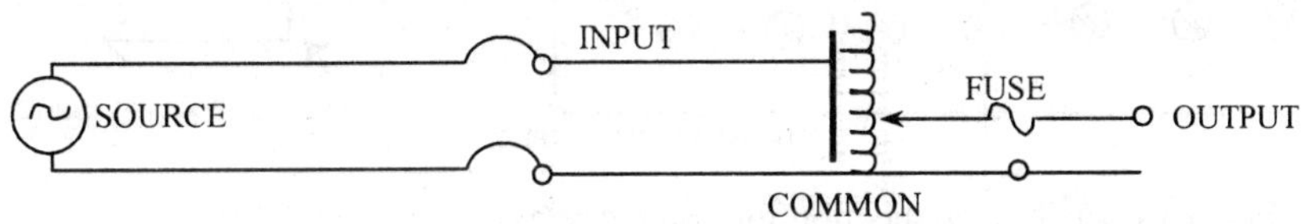

Fig. 5.14 (d): Single-phase variable voltage transformer.

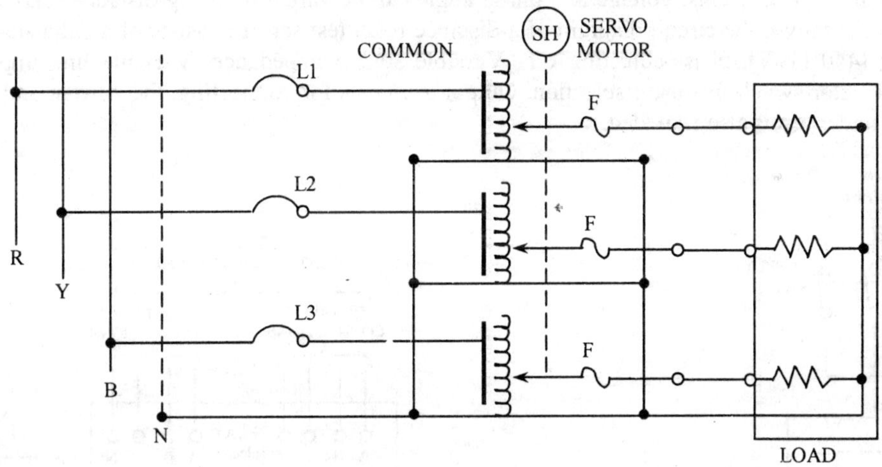

Fig. 5.14 (e): Three-phase variable voltage transformer

(4) Voltage relay test source:

Figure 5.14 (f) shows a typical AC test source for testing voltage relay. T_1 and T_2 are variable autotransformers for coarse and fine adjustments. T_3 is a filament transformer and its output is used for voltage relay pickup and dropout tests. The test set has 3 output terminals in which Z is common neutral, between terminals X and Z 230 V AC supply can be obtained. Precision test voltage can be availed from terminals Y and Z.

LEGEND: T1 and T2: Variable voltage transformer; T3: Filament transformer; V: Voltmeter.

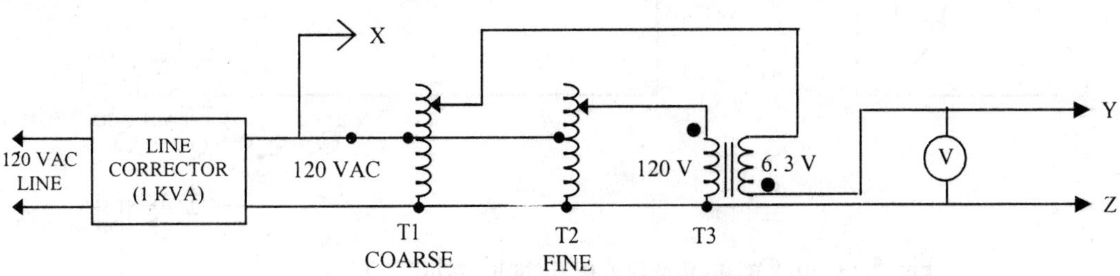

Fig. 5.14 (f): AC test source for testing voltage relay

Figure 5.14 (g) illustrates the test connection for typical under-voltage relay. Terminals X, Y and Z are to be connected to the respective terminals of the test source [Figure 5.14 (f)]. When the test switch is closed filament transformer secondary (6.3 V) is in series to the relay coil. When the test switch is open full voltage is applied to the relay coil through terminal X and Z.

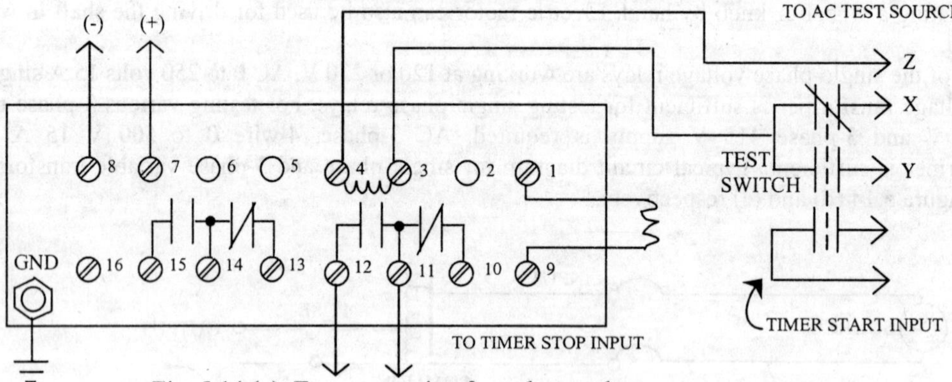

Fig. 5.14 (g): Test connection for voltage relay.

5) Distance relay test set: For testing distance relays it is necessary to vary the current, voltage and phase angle independently. Currents, voltage and phase angle can be varied by using distance relay test equipment. Figure 5.14 (h) shows, the circuit diagram of a distance relay test set. It consists of a delta/star phase shifting transformer (440/110V), phase-adjusting CT, Variable source impedance, Variable line impedance, digital timer and selector switch for phase selection. Output terminals for connecting, the current and voltage source to the relay under test is also provided.

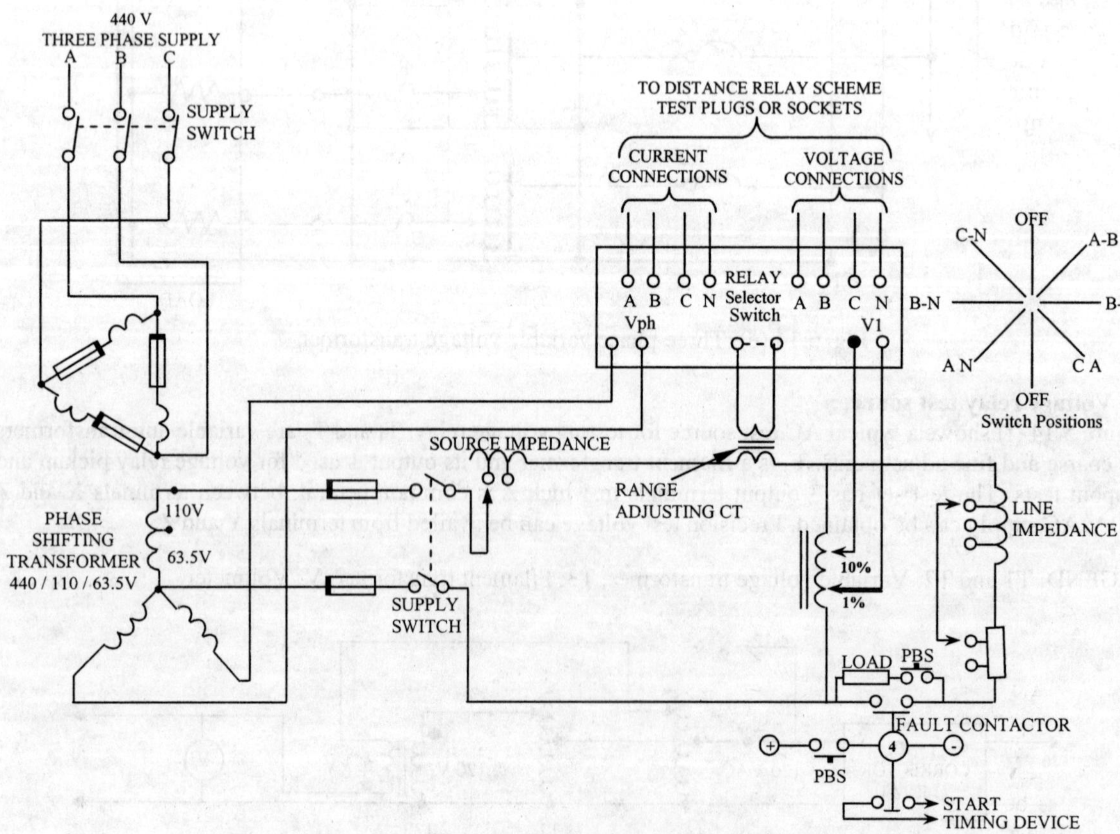

Fig. 5.14 (h): Circuit diagram of distance relay test set

When a fault occurs on the system being protected, the relay voltage falls immediately from the nominal value to the fault voltage depending on the ratio, while the current instantaneously rises from load value to the fault value. Both these sudden changes in magnitude are accompanied by changes in phase angle. The test equipment is connected so as to represent actual system conditions. With the supply switch closed and the fault contactor in the un-operated condition the normal working voltage is applied to the relay under test via the variable voltage transformer. When the fault contactor is closed, fault current is applied to the relay via the range adjusting current transformer. At the same instant the voltage applied to the relay collapses to the fault voltage V_1, the magnitude of V_1 depending on the ratio of the source impedance to the line impedance. The variable voltage transformer has 1% and 10% tapings to allow the line impedance to be matched to the relay ohmic setting. By varying the source impedance the relay ohmic setting can be checked over a wide range of voltage and current magnitudes.

6) Test block: Figure 5.14 (i) shows the connection diagram of a typical test plug and test socket. Test block housed within an Epsilon enclosure, have facilities for monitoring and secondary injection testing of protection relays in conjunction with single fingered or multi fingered test plug. Test block has 14 pairs of spring-loaded contacts, which are linked to a terminal block positioned in the rear of its enclosure. Each pair of contacts is normally closed completing the circuit through the test block when the associated protection equipment is in use.

When the cover is removed a yellow fascia is revealed which is attached to the test block this gives a visual indication and warning that the protection scheme or relay is not in service. The insertion of the test-plug to the test-socket open circuits the 14 contact pairs. It is recommended that the relay is wired to the even numbered terminals in the test module. The connections to other equipment such as CT's, VT's, and DC supplies should be made to the odd numbered terminals. This will ensure that the connection of the test plug, the sockets on the even numbered side of the test plug are the isolated relay circuits and the sockets on the odd numbered side are connected to the potentially live supplies. It is important that the sockets in the test plug, which correspond to the CT secondary windings, are linked prior to the test plug being inserted in to the test block. This will ensure that the CT secondary windings are short-circuited prior to disconnection from the protection relay.

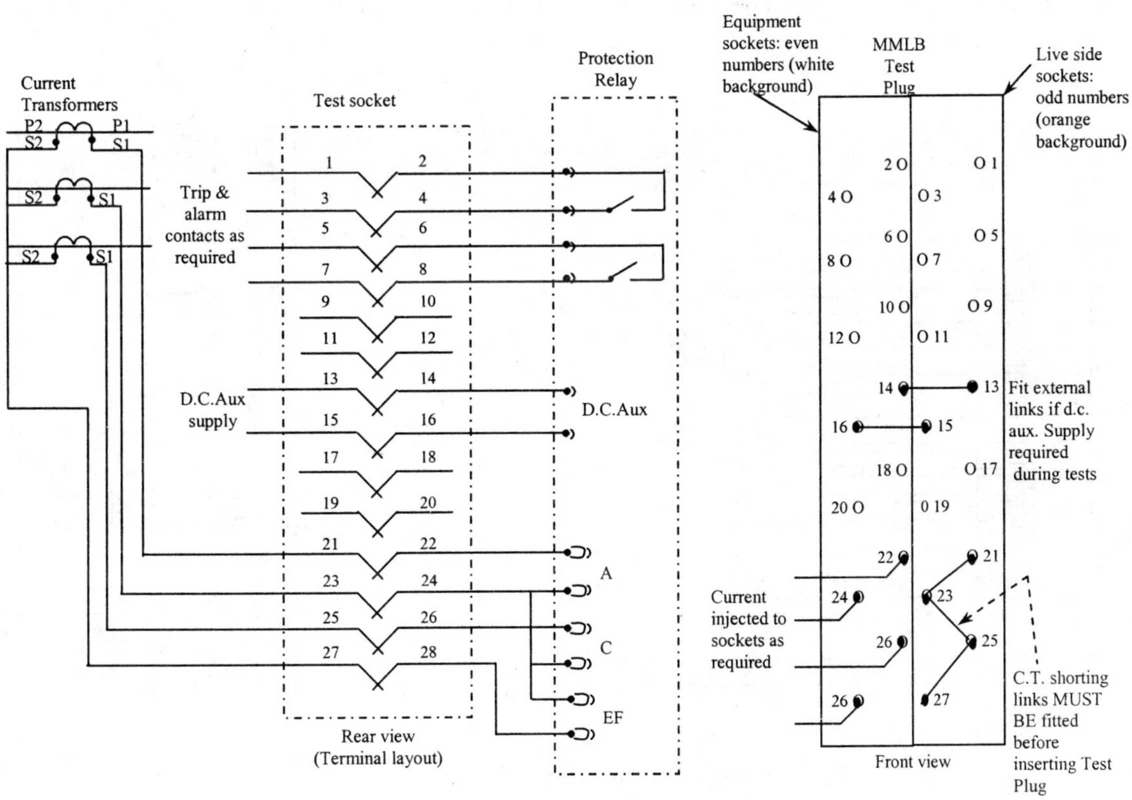

Fig. 5.14 (I): Test plug and test socket for relay test connection (Courtesy, Vatech Reyrolle)

Test switch illustrated in Figure 5.14 (J) consists of a test jack and current-shorting elements placed in CT circuits to facilitate checkout, trouble shooting, calibration and periodic testing of relays, meters, transducers, and instrumentation. These switches permit testing to take place without de-energizing the primary circuit and may be separate or built in to a protective-relay case.

Test probe illustrated in Figure 5.14 (J) can be used to provide convenient, standard banana jack connections to both relay and case terminals in point pairs. It is equipped with a red CT shorting plug, which can be inserted in to the two case side banana jacks before the probe is inserted into a relay CT circuit so that the required short circuit is maintained on the CT. Several of these two point probes can be used into a relay at the same time. They are keyed to prevent accidental inversion and incorrect point selection.

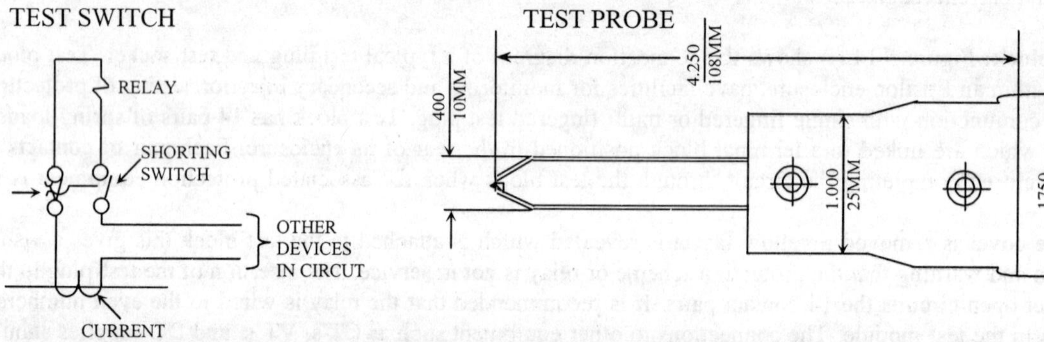

Fig. 5.14 (J): Typical test switch and test probe

Routine testing of 14 or 28 point, moulded case, draw out relays can be accomplished by removing the relay cover at the back and substituting the desired test plug for the connection plug. Before any of the test probe or test plug are inserted in to a relay, they should be carefully inspected to insure that proper connections are made to them and that these connections are tight. It is specially, important that relays, which receive current from CT secondary circuit shall have these case side test terminals short circuited before the test plug is inserted.

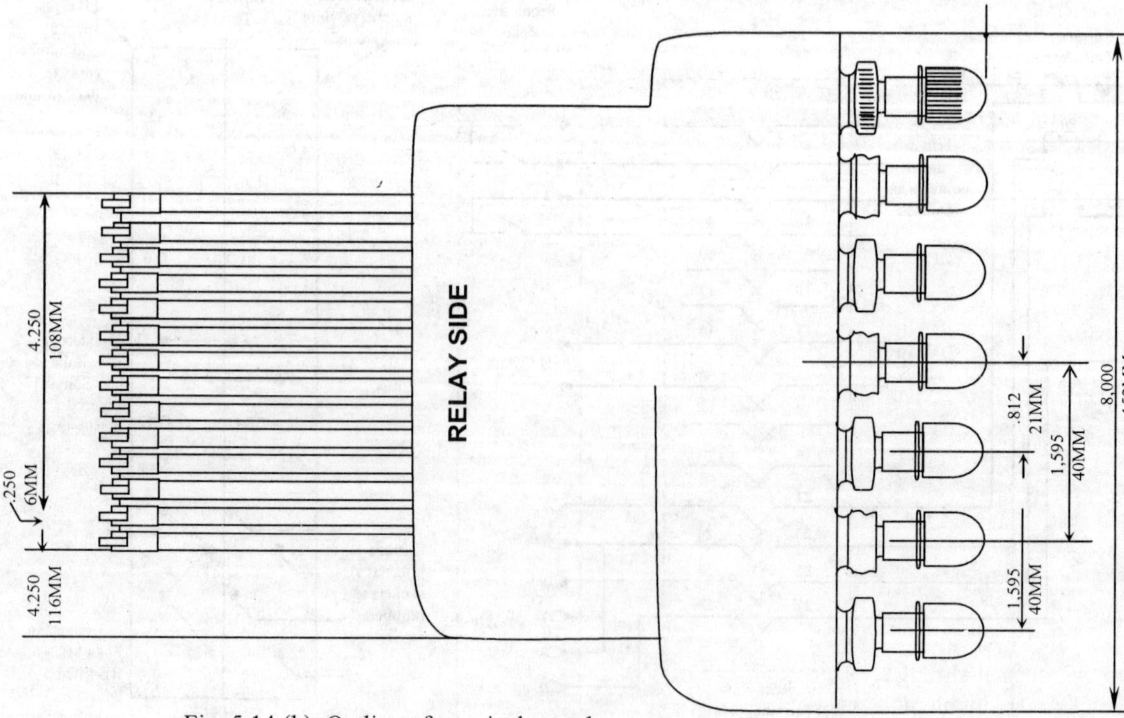

Fig. 5.14 (k): Outline of a typical test plug.

Outline of a 14-point test plug is depicted in Figure 5.14 (k). It can be inserted in to any 14 or 28 point moulded case, draw out relay after the relay connection plug has been removed. The test plug construction is keyed to prevent accidental inverted insertion. The terminals of the test plug consist of 14 concentric binding posts. The larger, outside, red terminals provide access to the case terminal points while the smaller, black terminals provide connection to the relay connection points. In addition, the center of the black terminals contains a standard size banana jack. The concentric binding post are numbered on the nameplate so that number 1 through 14 are right side up and apply when the plug is used in the bottom of the relay case. If the relay has a connection system in the top of the case, inversion of the test plug will be required before it can be inserted. In this case, nameplate terminal numbers 15 through 28 will appear upright are applicable. Accessory links are furnished with each test plug and include through connection and shorting link, test clips etc.

Test plug is a bolted assembly the 28 brush strips are insulated from each other and terminate via internal wiring on one of the 14 concentric binding posts. All the brush strips on the relay side of the plug terminate on the inner binding posts (black thumb nuts). All the brushes on the case side of the plug terminate on the outer binding posts (red thumb nuts).

7) DC Relay test set (Power supply unit)
DC relay test set illustrated in Figure 5.14 (L) is a power supply unit suitable for testing DC under-voltage and over-voltage relays, DC over-current relays, DC under-voltage releases, closing and tripping coils of circuit breakers etc. It is a power supply unit, which provides a triple free variable DC voltage up to 250 V that can easily accommodate a high variable load. Since there is a separate output for connecting spring charging motors, this set is ideal for testing circuit breakers. The best way to ascertain whether or not solenoids and protective mechanisms are sluggish or set improperly is to supply the system with the minimum pickup-up and drop-off voltages.

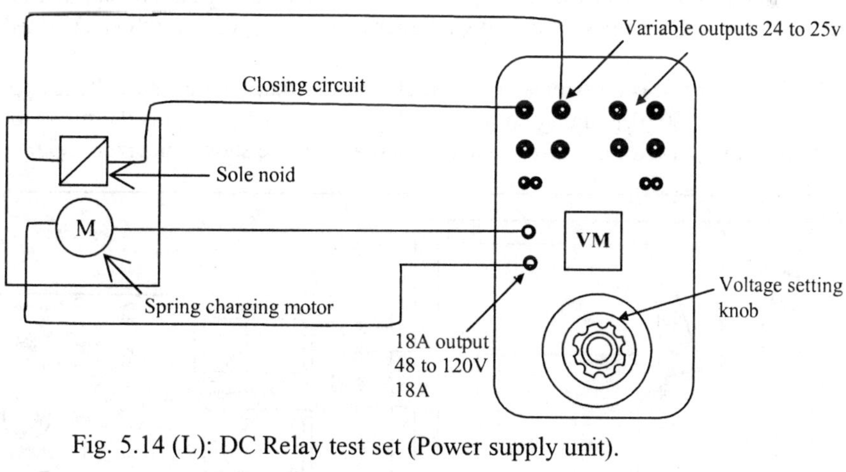

Fig. 5.14 (L): DC Relay test set (Power supply unit).

8) Resistance loading type secondary injection test: This is the "classical" technique for developing test values. A variable resistance is placed in series with the test specimen and the assembly is connected to a voltage source. Current control is then affected by varying the resistance. The assembly consists of a variable autotransformer, rheostat (load box) serving to adjust the current fed to a relay for conducting secondary injection test, provided with double pole switch, Ammeter, Voltmeter, time counter actuated by an external NO/NC contact etc. The basic method of connecting them to test a static over-current relay is shown in Figure 5.14 (m). Current through the relay coil can be adjusted by varying the rheostat, which is connected in series to the relay coil and the assembly is connected to a voltage source.

Test method:

1) Keep the rheostat-sliding knob at the minimum possible level.

2) Switch ON the double pole switch and adjust the rheostat until the relay pick-up and then switch off the DP switch and reset the timer. Detain the rheostat at the relay pick-up position.

3) Switch ON the double pole switch. Timer starts counting time and after elapsing the set time the relay picks up. When the relay operates the relay contact closes and the timer times out.

4) Note down the timer reading and ammeter reading and compare with the set values of current and time. Repeat the test by changing the plug setting and time setting.
5) Repeat the test on other phases also.

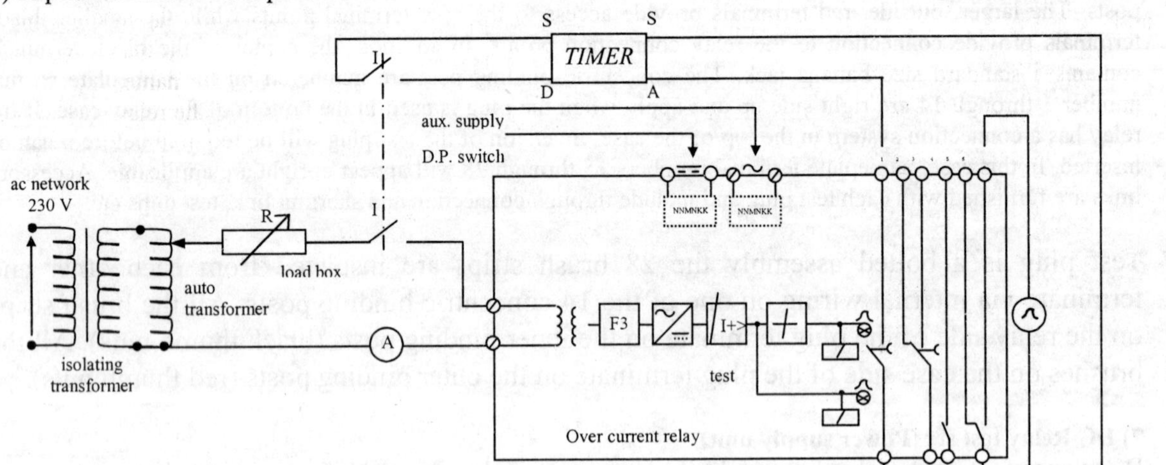

Fig. 5.14 (m): Test connections of resistance loading type relay testing equipments.

9) C.T magnetization, ratio and polarity test set: Test set provides a variable voltage output and digital instrumentation for testing single and multi-ratio CTs using the voltage comparison method. Figure 5.14 (n) shows the test connection for performing saturation and polarity of bushing type CT of a dead tank type circuit breaker. While conducting magnetization characteristic test voltage is gradually applied to the secondary of the CT under test. When the CT begins to saturate, a larger increase in current will be detected for a small increase in voltage.
Polarity of the CT under test is determined by special circuitry that divides the voltage applied to the secondary winding by either 10 or 100 (depending on the switch position) and then adds the result to the primary voltage. An increase in magnitude indicates correct polarity, and a decrease shows incorrect polarity.

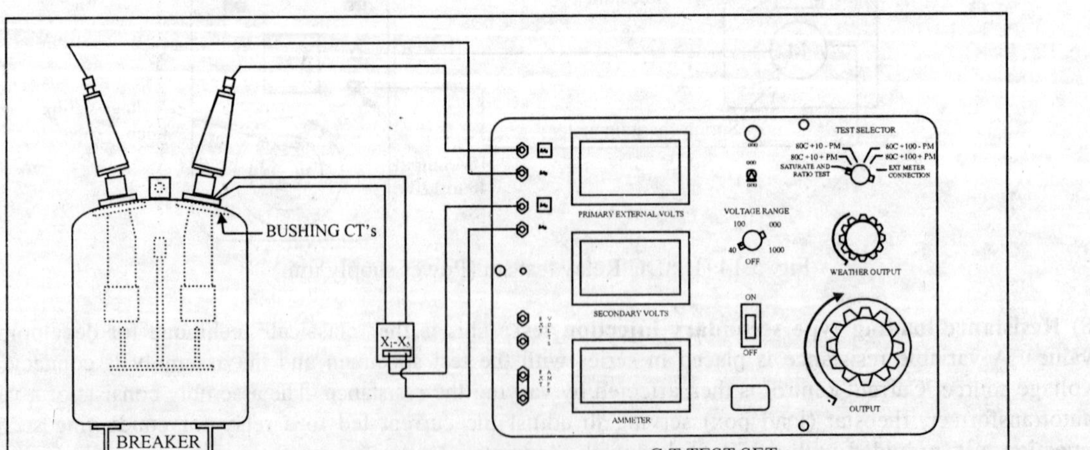

Fig. 5.14 (n): Connection for performing saturation, ratio and polarity test of bushing type current transformer

The ratio test is performed by comparing a voltage applied to the secondary winding to the resulting voltage produced on the primary winding. As an example, if one volt per turn is applied in the secondary winding, the voltage present on the primary winding would be one volt. More specifically, if 120 volts were applied to the secondary of a 600/5 A, current transformer (120:1 ratio), one volt would be present on the primary winding.

Figure 5.14 (o) illustrates the test connection for verifying ratios of a multi-ratio current transformer.

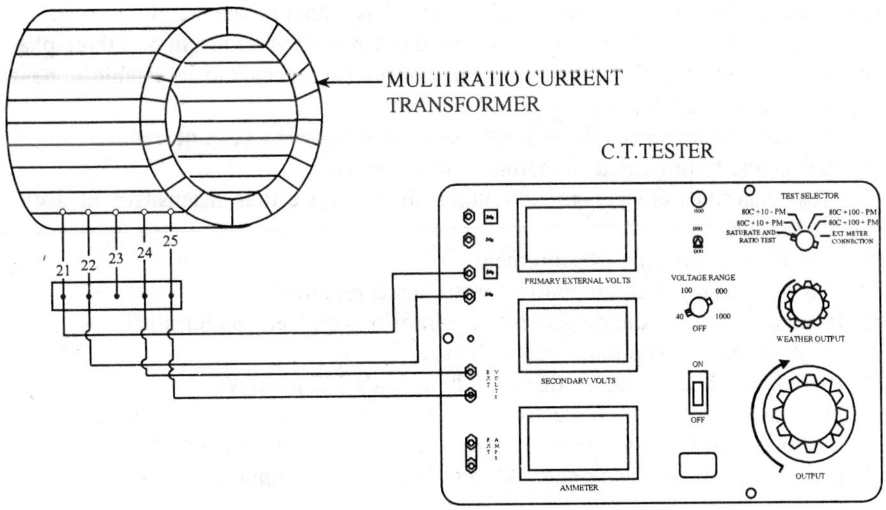

Fig. 5.14 (o): Connection for verifying ratio of multi-core current transformer (Courtesy Avo International).

10) Phase angle meter: Phase angle meter is ideal to test directional relays and to conduct directional test on instrument transformers. Directional element is an element of protection that determines the relative phase relation of a current with respect to another current or voltage to establish, whether a relay operation should be completed. Figure 5.14 (p) shows typical test connection for directional relay by using secondary injection test set and phase angle meter. Select the desired current and voltage based on the set values of the directional relay under test. Use the testing unit to operate the protective relay under test. Check that the relay operates within the specified angle range by reading the phase angle on the meter display screen. Direction of current flow is indicated in the single line diagram.

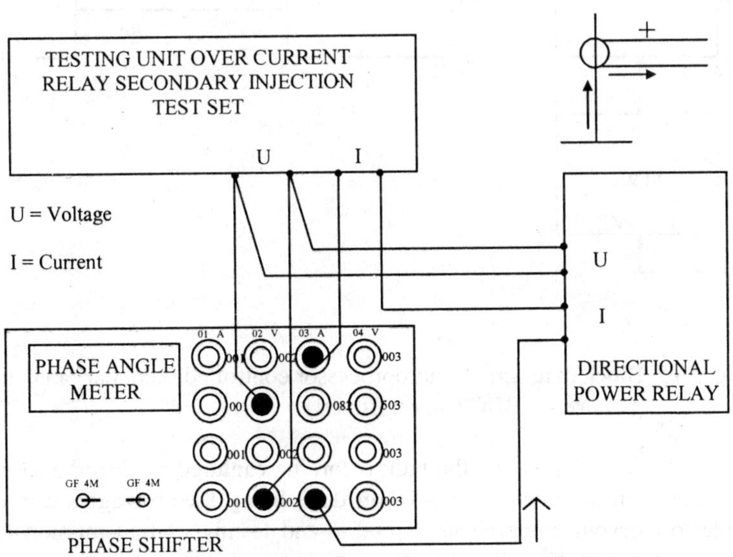

Fig. 5.14 (p): Phase angle meter connection for directional relay testing.

5.15 MICROPROCESSOR CONTROLLED RELAY TEST SET.

The test set described in Figure 5.15 is BBC Brown Boveri, type XS 92a, which is suitable for testing the function and as an aid to recording the operating characteristics of all kinds of protective relays, especially distance relay, directional relay, and frequency relays etc. It contains a 16-bit microprocessor, which permits dynamic and static testing within wide ranges, whilst selecting current, voltage, phase-angle and impedance as parameters.

Following are the main features of microprocessor controlled relay test set:

(1) Suitable for both 50 Hz and 60 Hz single phase input power supply.
(2) Exact simulation of the three-phase voltages and a phase current of a three-phase system.
(3) Voltage output with variable frequency of high accuracy and adjustable slope df/dt.
(4) Phase angle settable from 0 to 360 degrees.
(5) System characteristics (kind of fault and impedance etc.) can be entered.
(6) Selectable testing mode: dynamic or incremental.
(7) Test quantities are generated synthetically and are thus insensitive to disturbances in the power supply.
(8) Accurate quartz time measurement.
(9) No additional test equipments or instruments required.
(10) Convenient entry and display of the parameters on the hand terminal.
(11) Testing sequences programmable by user.
(12) Serial interface for connecting peripherals. RS 232 interface.
(13) Two possibilities for connecting test set and relay: (a) Universal connector i.e. test cable and test plug; (b) By test jumpers to the banana sockets on the front.
(14) Provision for variable voltage AC and DC auxiliary supply.

LEGEND:

1. NF92 Auxiliary supply for the electronic circuits.
2. AU92 Three-phase voltage amplifier.
3. XC92 Control-unit.
4. YS92 Program storage cards.
5. EX92 Power supply input unit
6. NX91 DC/DC Converter for amplifier
7. AL92 Single-phase current amplifier
8. AX91 Output unit with switching logic

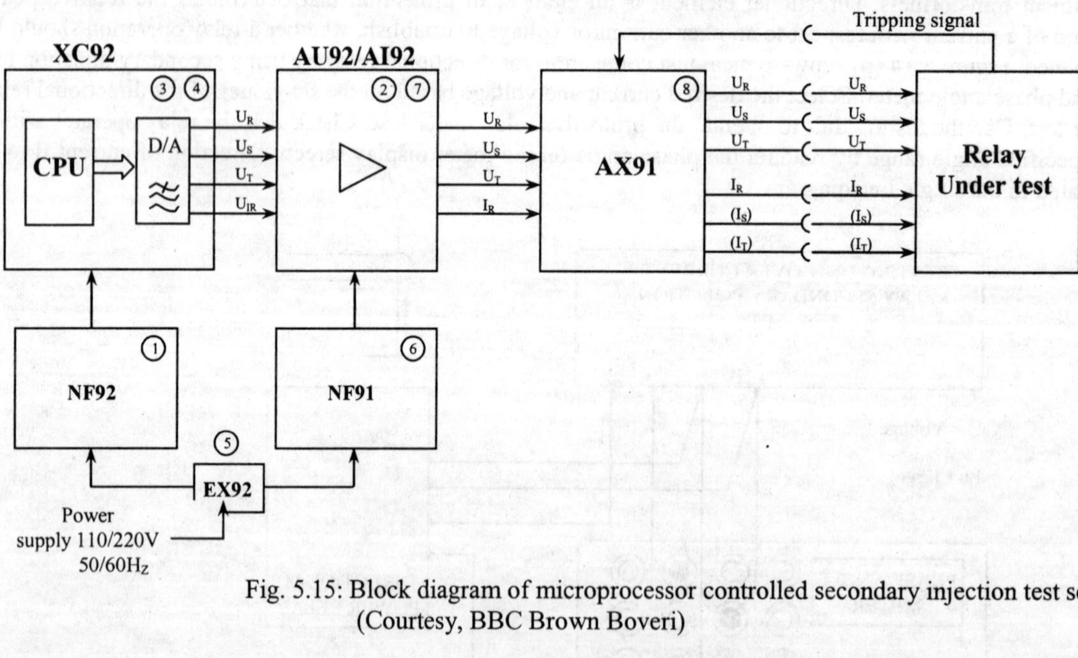

Fig. 5.15: Block diagram of microprocessor controlled secondary injection test set. (Courtesy, BBC Brown Boveri)

Automatic relay test sets are capable of displaying the fault recording captured by disturbance recorders (used in transmission line feeders) as well as transient simulation done using Electromagnetic transient program (EMTP). Also it is possible to carryout comprehensive end-to-end testing of transmission line protections including protection signaling in conjunction with time synchronizing equipment.

This instrument contains four separate static generators as follows:

1) AC current generator: AC current for testing the relay: (Range 10, 40, 100 A)
2) AC voltage generator: Phase shiftable AC, range 0 to 360° adjustments via the multi-function knob
3) DC voltage generator: DC voltage for relay under test: 130 V, 0.9 amps, continuous duty.
4) Auxiliary voltage generator: AC auxiliary voltage up to 250 V, 30 VA continuous duty, software driven.
5) Frequency generation 40 Hz to 500 Hz, frequency adjustment: 1milli-hertz.

All outputs are adjustable and metered at the meantime on the large graphic LCD display. Manual and semiautomatic testing capabilities, with the possibility to transfer test results to a Personal computer (PC) via RS 232 interface.

These results can be recorded, displayed and analysis by the software that operates with Windows 98. Test settings can be stored and recalled up to 10 settings from the local memory. Up to 500 test results can be saved in to a permanent memory.

The electronic digital timer has a fully automatic start and stop (both for make and break) input that can be either a volt-free contact or a contact having voltage. Set of resistors, (range 0.5, 1.0, 22, 470, 1000 and 2200) for the test of low impedance relays are provided. AC 230 V 5A 50/60 Hz incoming power is required. Set is suitable for testing relays and transducers (except distance relays which required 3-phase unit or 3 single phase units). The unit can measure and display voltage, current, impedance, power factor, phase angle and time via an easy to read liquid crystal display. Indication is provided to show status of timer start-stop inputs and NO/NC timer contacts.

Simulators for 3phase relay testing:

This unit will generate 4 independent voltages (0 to 150V) and 3 independent currents (0 to 15A) with facilities for controlling their amplitudes and phase angle independently. Input 230 V 50 or 60 Hertz. The unit is provided with df/dt facility, i.e. frequency variation with respect to time. The unit will provide 3-phase output power for testing 3-phase relays.

5.16 MAINTENANCE TESTS ON PROTECTIVE RELAYS.

The commissioning and maintenance of protection equipment should only be carried out by, skilled personnel trained in protective relay operation and capable of observing all the necessary safety precautions and regulations appropriate to the equipment and also the associated primary plant.

As a rule, maintenance testing is carried out during the periods of overhaul and routine maintenance repair of the equipments or feeders. Post-emergency testing should be carried out after each occurrence of an emergency or false operation of the protection or control system. Testing can also be carried out whenever it is suspected that the equipment is not operating properly.

The scope of complete maintenance testing is as follows.

1) The protective relay and automatic control equipment should be physically checked to make sure that they are in a mechanically fit condition. The equipment must be free from dirt or dust and foreign particles.

2) A check should be made of the electrical performance characteristic of the relay, making sure that the relays operate in compliance with their settings. Relays have been correctly set and the contacts are intact.

3) The magnetization curve of each of the main current transformers should be measured and plotted. All the current and voltage transformers checked for their transformation ratio, polarity and ohmic resistance of the winding.

4) Each circuit should be measured for its insulation resistance to earth (except electronic devices) by using a 500 V megger. Tightness of connection screws should be checked.

5) All the fuses and circuit breakers in the control circuitry should be checked for fit condition and the fuse element ring and tripping current setting adequate for selective action.

6) Sequences of operation of the protection and control circuit to be checked for reliable operation.

7) The tripping and closing circuits of the circuit breakers and other apparatus should be checked for reliable operation.

8) By primary injection of the working current, the relay operation and automatic control circuits should be subjected to an overall test for current response and proper sequence of action.

9) Function check of the trip device or trip relay should be verified by shorting the trip contact of the relay immediately after major maintenance.

5.17 TESTING AND SETTING OF OVERCURRENT/EARTH FAULT RELAYS

Figure 5.17 (a) and (b) respectively shows the AC schematic diagrams of a typical three-phase electromagnetic and static over-current relay. Device No: 52 designate the circuit breaker, which is for isolating the feeder. 52a is the normally open auxiliary contact of the circuit breaker. 52a will remain closed when the circuit breaker is in closed position. Relay contact will closes if the current and time exceeds the set value. In the event of closing the contact due to over-current or short circuit, the circuit breaker trip coil will get energized and the breaker trips. Circuit breaker trip coil will de-energize as the CB auxiliary contact 52a opens. When the circuit breaker opened out, the fault current is disappeared because the protected zone is isolated. Once the relay is operated it is locked out, and it is required to reset the relay before switching on the breaker.

LEGEND:
CO: Time over-current unit; IIT: Instantaneous over-current unit; TDEF: Time delay earth fault unit; IEF: Instantaneous earth fault unit; ICS/L & ICS/T: Indicating contactor switches; T: Auxiliary time delay unit; 52: Circuit breaker; TC: Trip coil;

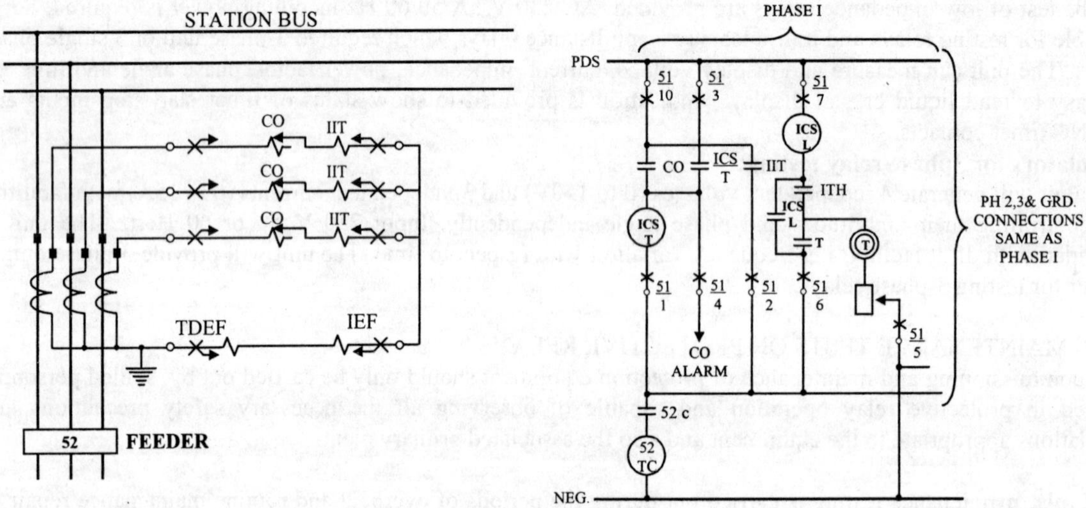

Fig. 5.17 (a): AC/DC schematic diagram for electromagnetic type over-current and earth fault relay.

Care should be taken in selecting the relay instantaneous element setting to ensure that the relay will not be operated by the initial high off set current caused by a fault beyond the protected section. This relay limitation is known as transient over reach. False tripping due to high inrush current during switching operation also taken in to consideration while setting high-set element

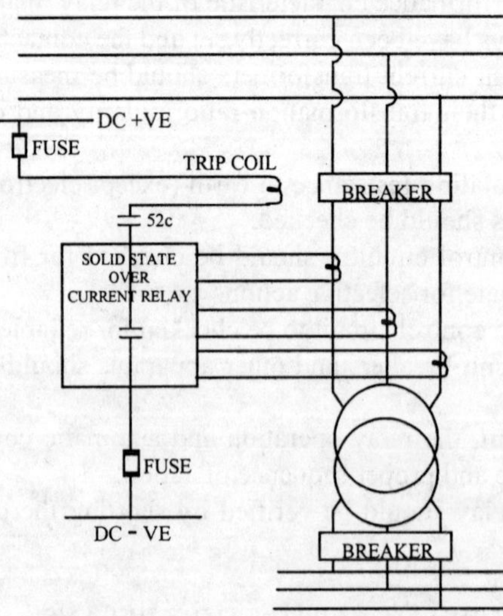

Fig. 5.17 (b): AC and DC schematic diagram of static over-current relay.

Inverse definite minimum time (IDMT) relays: IDMT relay has characteristics in accordance with BS 142. Over-current relays with IDMT characteristics are suitable for radial feeders. Minimum permissible time grading interval between the over-current relays at successive breakers is approximately 0.5 second. This interval is usually too long to obtain fast clearance times at the power source where fault levels are highest.

Combined IDMT and Instantaneous relays: For long lines of transformer feeders where the source impedance is high in comparison with circuit impedance, a high set instantaneous element is combined with a standard inverse time over-current relay to reduce circuit breaker tripping times under short circuit conditions. Under these conditions the time grading intervals between successive breakers with the combined relays are also reduced.

Very inverse definite minimum time relays: A very inverse time over-current relay is suitable for systems where the fault current decreases appreciably as the distance from the power source increases. The very inverse time relay give longer time grading intervals and so give better discrimination in the above application.

Extremely inverse definite minimum time relays: An extremely inverse time over current relay has characteristics for which the operating time is approximately inversely proportional to the square of the operating current. These relays are suitable for the protection of distribution circuits feeding chiller units, pumps etc, which are subject to peak current on switching in and remain connected after prolonged interruption of the power supply.

Figure 5.17 (c) shows the test diagram of the over-current relay for pick up and timing test. Current slightly above the set value is injected to the relay-operating coil by using a secondary current injection test set. Relay contact is connected to the timer circuit of the test set. Adjust the current in the ammeter by shorting the current leads. Switch of the set and connect the leads to the relay operating coil. Switch on the set, ammeter shows the current injected and the timer reads the operating time in seconds/milliseconds. Repeat the test on other two phases and earth fault coil. Every operation the relay target will indicate that the relay is operated.

Figure 5.17 (d) shows the functional check. Here circuit breaker trip coil is replaced by a lockout relay (Device No: 86). Timer starts, when the required current is injected to the relay coil. When the over-current relay operates the lock out relay pick up and lock out. Hence the timer stops.

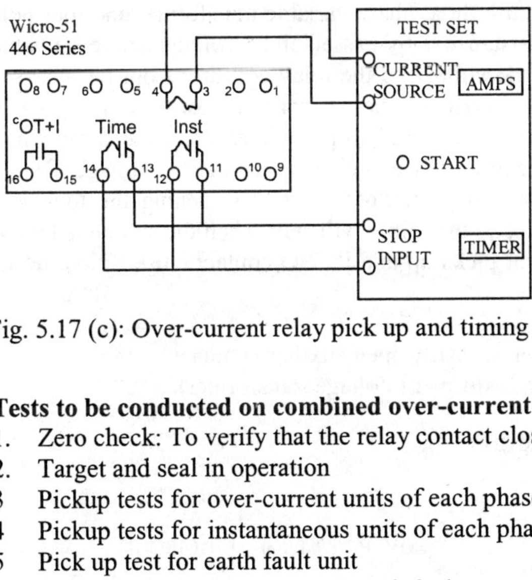

Fig. 5.17 (c): Over-current relay pick up and timing test.

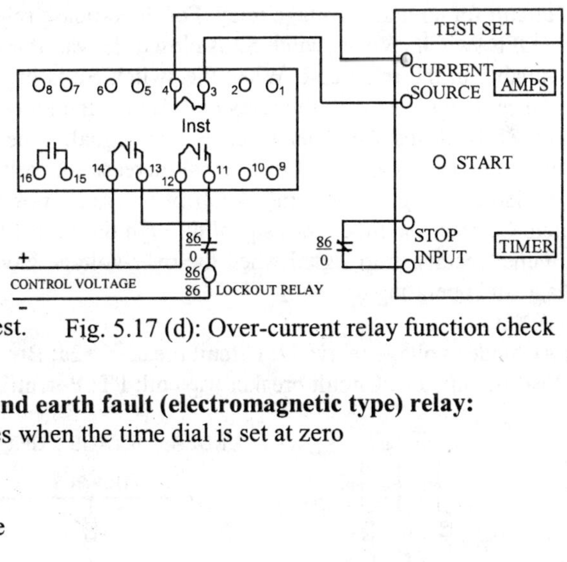

Fig. 5.17 (d): Over-current relay function check

Tests to be conducted on combined over-current and earth fault (electromagnetic type) relay:

1. Zero check: To verify that the relay contact closes when the time dial is set at zero
2. Target and seal in operation
3 Pickup tests for over-current units of each phase
4 Pickup tests for instantaneous units of each phase
5 Pick up test for earth fault unit
6 Pick up test for instantaneous earth fault
7 Timing test against item 3 to 6 above

Over-current relay setting:

Plug setting refers to the magnitude of current at which the relay, start to operate.

Plug setting multiplier (PSM) is the ratio between anticipated secondary current of the connected current transformer to the set value of the relay setting plug. PSM = Anticipated CT secondary current in amps/Plug setting.

Assume that an 11 KV 3-phase Diesel Generator, the full load current is 90 A/phase.

CT ratio = 150/5 = 30

Anticipated current in the CT secondary = 90/30 = 3 A

Assume that the plug setting is set at 2, PSM = CT secondary current/plug setting = 3/2 =1.5

Current multiplier value of an over-current relay = Pickup current/Tap setting value

Similarly time setting can increase or reduce the relay operation time. **Time setting multiplier (TSM) is the ratio between the desired operation time and time taken to operate the relay when TSM is set at 1. TSM = t/s = Desired operation time in seconds/ Time in seconds taken to complete the operation of the relay when TSM is set at 1. Assume that the relay takes 4 seconds when TSM is set at 1, and actual time required is 2 seconds the TSM setting will be 2/4 = 0.5**

Suggested setting of an over-current time delay element is 100% of the rated full load current of the equipment to be protected. Set value may be derived based on the CT ratio. Instantaneous element is to be set 10 to 12 times of the full load current, depending on the system fault level. Suggested setting of an earth fault time delay element is based on the earth resistance value measured at site. Assume that the touch potential of the earthing system is 50 volts and the measured value of earth resistance is 0.8 ohm, current setting = 50/0.8 = 62.5 A. Assume that the protection CT ratio is 100/5 (say 20), the plug setting = 62.5/20 = 3.125 (set at 3).

Plug setting range for over-current and earth fault relay:

Device	Relay element	Current setting range (PSM)	Time setting range
51	Over-current/overload	50% to 250 % of rated secondary current	0.05 tol (TSM)
50	Instantaneous/high set	50% to 400% (o.5 In to 40 In)	Instantaneous
51N	Earth fault	10% to 80% of the rated secondary current	0.05 to 1 (TSM)
50N	High set earth fault	10% to 100% (o.1 In to 10 In)	Instantaneous

5.18 TESTING AND SETTING OF UNDER/OVER VOLTAGE RELAYS.

Figure 5.18 (a) shows the AC and DC schematic diagrams of a typical under/over voltage relay. Over voltage relay operates when the system voltage raise above the set value. Under voltage contacts remain closed during the absence of power or when the voltage drops below the set value. Figure 5.18 (b) illustrates the conventional test circuit for an under voltage relay. For three-phase relay, use three-phase variable transformer and four pole ON / OFF switch. When switch S2 is closed the variable resistance is by-passed and a voltage above set value is available in the relay coil. When the switch S2 is open the voltage to the relay coil drops out because the resistance is in series with the relay coil. Hence the relay drops out and the NC contact closes. Similarly when switch S2 is closed the timer receives stop signal. When the switch S2 is open, timer starts but meanwhile, relay contact closes and the timer stops. Increase the voltage gradually and observe the pickup voltage. Detain the variable voltage transformer knob in the same position and switch off power by opening the four-pole switch. Connect the timer start signal through the fourth pole, so that timer will start when the switch is turned on. Timer receive stop signal when the over-voltage element picks up and its NO contact closes. Note down voltage and operating time.

LEGEND:

27: AC under-voltage relay; 52: Circuit breaker; 52a: Breaker normally open auxiliary contact;
SI: Seal-in unit; TC: Circuit breaker trip coil; PT: Potential transformer (Voltage transformer).

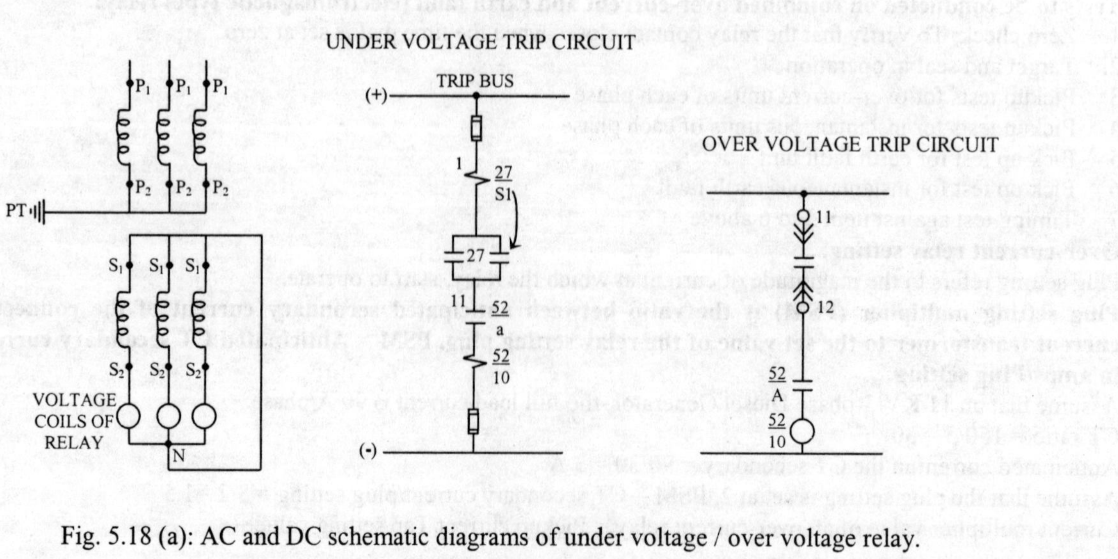

Fig. 5.18 (a): AC and DC schematic diagrams of under voltage / over voltage relay.

For testing drop off level, the initial voltage will be slightly higher than the set value and gradually reduce the voltage to verify at what voltage the relay dropout. Typical relay characteristic shown in Figure 5.18 (c) discriminates the pick up voltage level and dropout voltage level.

Tests to be conducted on all the three-phase of under / over voltage relay:

1. Pickup voltage and dropout voltage of over-voltage element (device No: 59).
2. Pickup voltage and dropout voltage of under-voltage element (device No: 27).
3. Timing checks on item 1 and 2 above.
4. DC Target and seal-in test on electromagnetic relay.

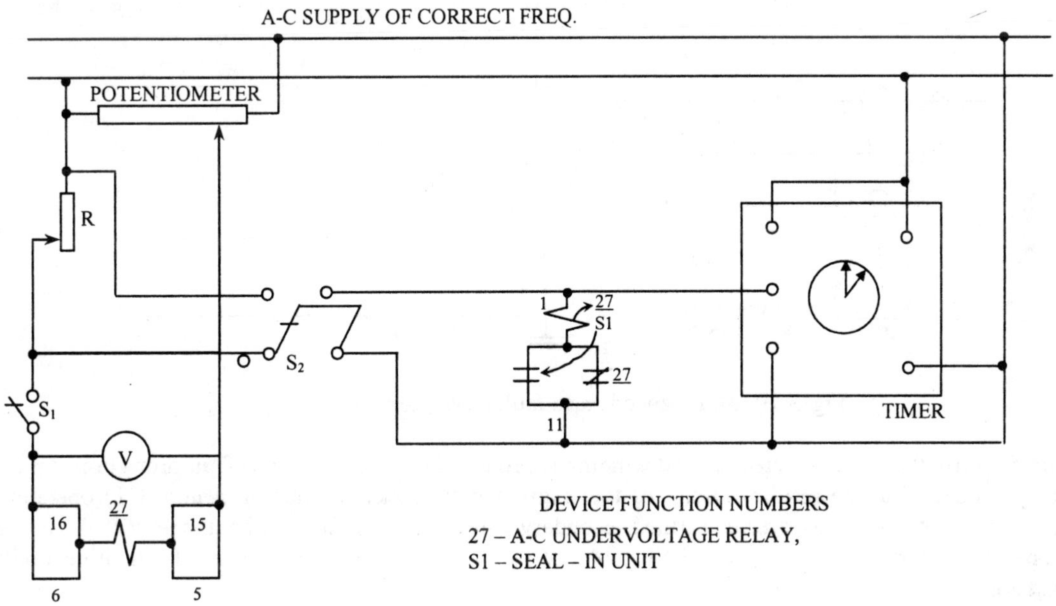

Fig. 5.18 (b): Test connection for under-voltage relay.

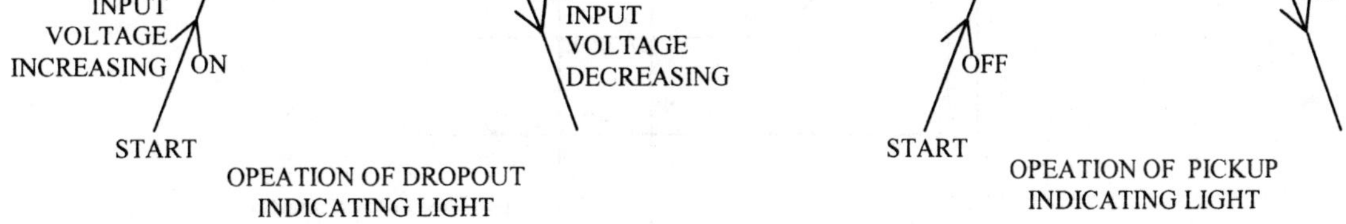

Fig. 5.18 (c): Operation of Pickup and drop out light emitting diode indication.

5.19 RESTRICTED EARTH FAULT PROTECTION RELAY (64).

Restricted protection means a protective system that is restricted to specific type of fault or abnormal condition within a specific zone of protection. Restricted Earth Fault (REF) protection relay is an instantaneous relay used with generator, transformer, reactor, having solidly grounded neutral. Equipments with resistance or reactance grounded neutral are protected by, employing ground fault differential protection described in

Chapter # 6, section 6.15. Earth fault relay connected in residual circuit of current transformers give protection against earth faults on the delta connected or unearthed star connected windings of transformers. A current or voltage proportional to the zero-sequence component of a set of poly-phase currents / voltages is defined as the residual current / voltage. It is equal to the phasor sum of the three-phase currents/voltages. Figure 5.19 (a) shows a delta/star transformer with earth fault relay connected in residual circuit (Balanced earth fault protection) in the delta side, which operates on internal earth faults on primary delta windings only. Earth fault on secondary side do not produce Zero sequence currents on the primary side. Hence separate REF protection is required for high speed tripping for faults on star connected earthed secondary windings.

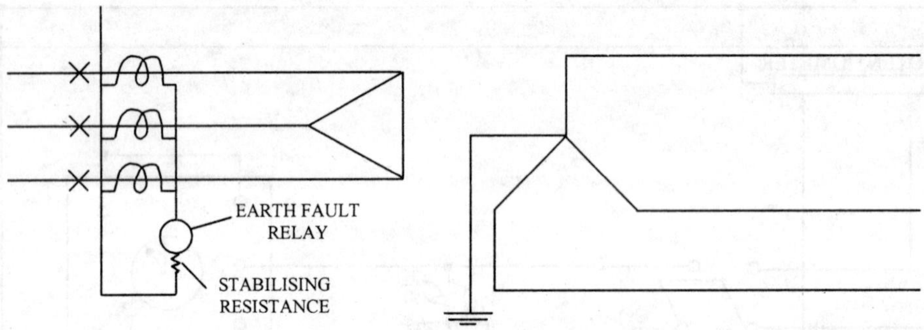

Fig. 5.19 (a): Balanced earth fault protection

In Figure 5.19 (b), the star connected earthed winding is protected by restricted earth fault protection. An earth fault relay connected to the residual circuit of four current transformers (including neutral CT) operates on internal earth fault in the star connected earthed secondary windings. Earth fault within the protected zone only flows through the earth fault relay. Thus REF protection will not respond on the event of a fault beyond the protected zone.

When fault occurs very near to the neutral point of the transformer, the voltage available for driving earth fault current is very small. Hence fault current would be very low. If the relay is to sense the fault near the neutral point it has to be too sensitive and would therefore operate for external faults and switching surges. Hence the practice is to set the relay such that it operates for earth fault current of the order of 15% of rated fault currents. Such setting protects only restricted portion of the winding. Hence the name restricted earth fault protection. **Series or shunt sealing is not provided with REF relay.**

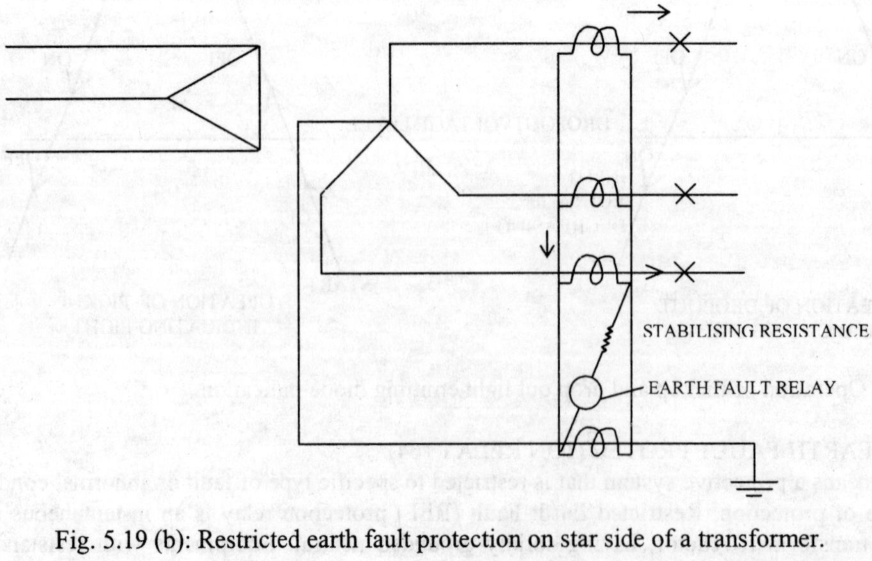

Fig. 5.19 (b): Restricted earth fault protection on star side of a transformer.

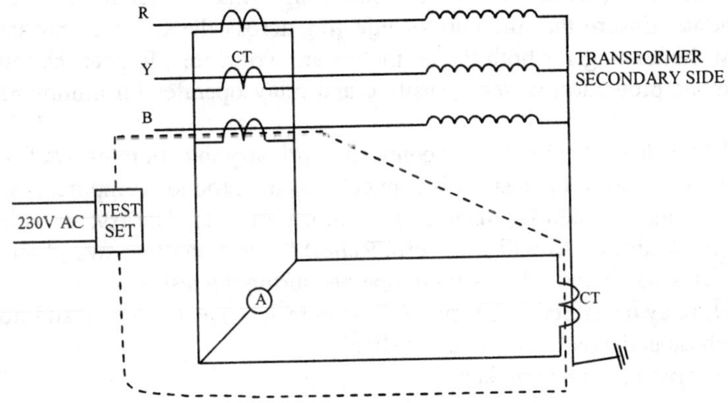

Fig. 5.19 (c): Polarity-check on current transformers used for restricted earth fault protection.

A stabilizing resistor is connected in series with the operating coil of REF relay for adjusting the desired current setting of the relay. Usually 50 ohm resister is enough with 5A, CT and 200 ohm resistor with 1A, CT. Exact value of stabilizing resistor can be calculated by using the formula $Sr = \frac{(V/2) - (Vr)}{Ir}$

V = Knee point voltage = 2 I_f (Rs + Rp) for balanced protection and machine differential protection. For residual applications 2I_f (Rs + Rc) where Rc = Lead resistance/phase taking in to account the burden of all other connected devices.

Rp = Maximum lead resistance between the relay circuit and the CT.

I_f = Equivalent secondary pilot current at maximum fault current

Rs = CT secondary winding resistance

Rp – Maximum lead resistance between the relay circuit and any CT

Vr = Relay operating voltage

I_r = Relay operating current

Following tests are to be conducted on REF protection scheme:

1). Polarity check: Polarity of CT can be checked by connecting the test set as shown in Figure 5.19 (c). Relay is to be pulled out and an ammeter to be connected across the CT. While injecting the current through any one phase CT and neutral CT, the ammeter will read zero if the polarity is correct. Repeat the test for the other two phases also. During the test, test leads are either slip-in through the CT or connect on either side of the primary of the bus / cable in which the CT is inserted.

2). Secondary injection test to verify pickup and timing: Connect the secondary injection test set as shown in Figure 5.19 (d) for injecting the currents to the relay coil through stabilizing resistor. Record the reading of Ammeters A_1 and A_2 as well as voltmeter V. Test set will indicate the operating time if the relay contact is connected to the timing circuit. Ammeter A_1 reads the relay pickup currents.

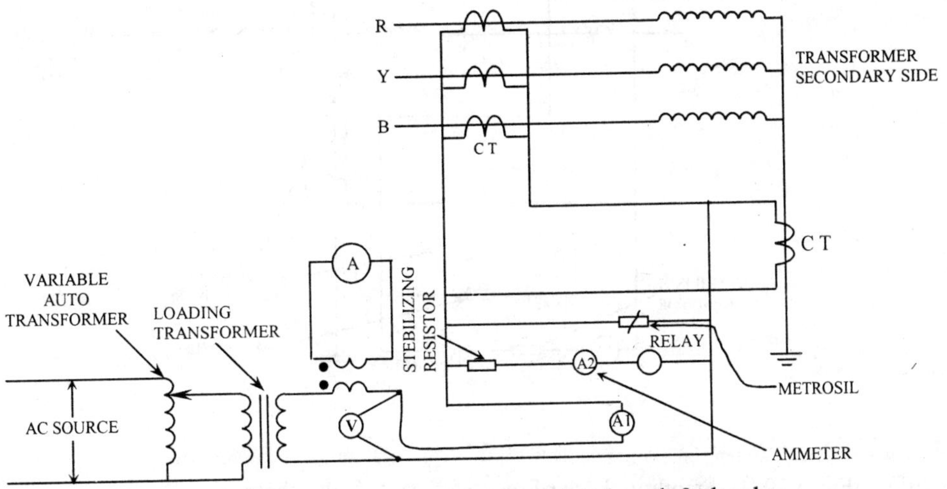

Fig. 5.19 (d): Secondary injection test on restricted earth fault relay.

3) Sensitivity check: Figure 5.19 (e) shows the method of connecting primary injection test set for sensitivity check of REF protection scheme. Ensure that the current injecting across the CT, will not pass through the transformer windings. Record the reading for both the ammeters and voltmeter. Repeat the test for other two phases also. Test reveals that the protection is very sensitive and relay operates on minimum value of fault current.

4). Stability check: Figure 5.19 (f) shows the method of connecting primary injection test set for stability check of REF protection scheme. One test lead of the test set is connected to the ground. Temporary connection at the winding terminals and relay terminals should be made as shown in figure (f). The test set is loading through neutral earth. At correct polarity Ammeter A_2 will read zero. Repeat the test on other two phases also. The test reveals that the protection remains stable and relay will not operate during the test.

Numerical restricted earth fault relay described in Chapter # 7, section 7.14 has following additional features:

1. Time delayed three-phase under-voltage characteristic.
2. Adjustable residual polarizing voltage pickup.
3. Easy to access stored data and easy to input new data.
4. The relay provides high level of flexibility and high-speed operation.

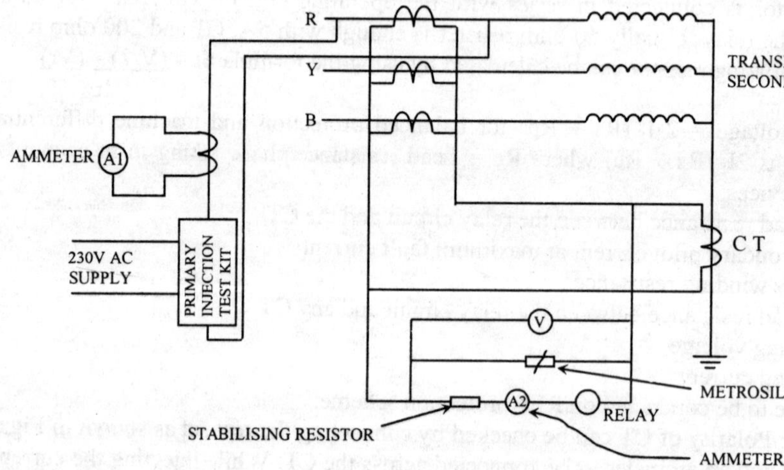

Fig. 5.19 (e): Sensitivity-check on restricted earth fault scheme.

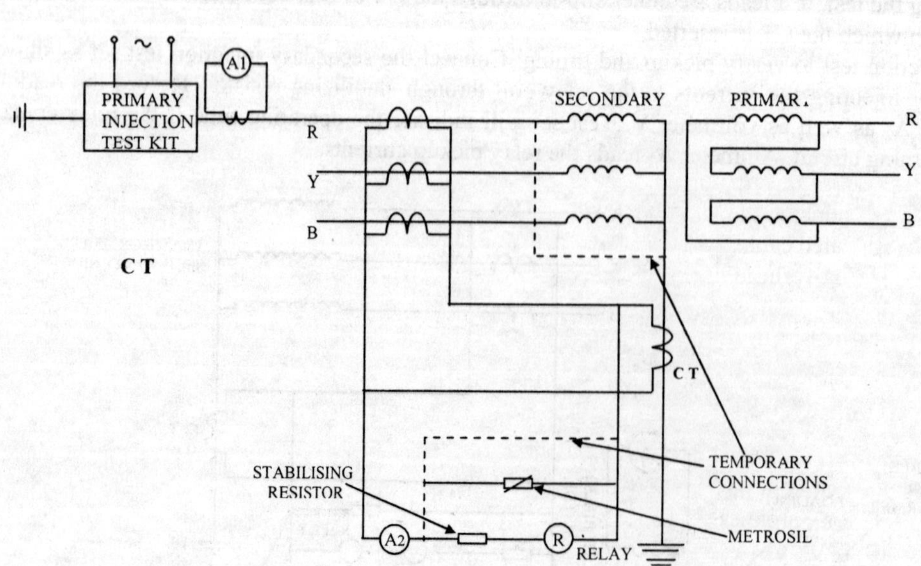

Fig. 5.19 (f): Stability-check of restricted earth fault scheme.

5.20 GRADING MARGIN AND RELAY COORDINATION

When a relay is de-energized operation may continue for a little longer time because:

a) For induction disc relay has stored kinetic energy in the motion of the disc.
b) For electronic circuit may have energy stored in capacitors.

Overshoot time is the time required by the relay if still energized to achieve the some amount of operational advance. Since the current transformers has ratio error due to the exciting current required to magnetize their cores, the relay characteristics may have positive or negative error. Hence provision for positive error time is necessary.

Grading margin: It is the time margin between the operation of two adjacent relays (upstream and downstream) depends on:

1. Circuit breaker tripping time;
2. Relay overshoot time;
3. Operation error;
4. Safety margin.

For medium voltage system minimum 0.4 second whereas for high voltage system computerized relay setting software technology is to be applied.

Recommended grading margin for distribution systems:

$$\text{Time setting} = t \times \frac{(2Er + Ect)}{100} + (t_{cb} + t_o + t_s) \text{ seconds}$$

Er = Relay timing error as per IEC standard 255-4. (7.5% for induction disc relay, and 5% for electronic relay)
Ect = CT ratio error
t = Normal operating time of relay nearer to the fault in sec:
t_{cb} = Circuit breaker interrupting time in sec: (0.1 sec: for oil and SF6 gas insulated CB's. For vacuum CB 0.06 sec)
t_o = Overshoot time of relay in sec: (Electromagnetic relay 0.05 sec: and Electronic relay 0.03 sec)
t_s = Safety margin
Grading margin allowed between fuse and over current relay 0.04t + 0.15 sec: where t = Normal operating time of fuse in sec. For comparing the characteristics of fuse and over-current relay when it is used for grading, plot the characteristic curves of both the fuse and relay in one graph sheet and compare the curve for safe operation for proper grading.

Maximum permissible tripping time: For clearing a fault in a circuit protected with circuit breaker, relay or fuse, tripping time $t \leq k \times (S/Isc)^{2}$ seconds
S = conductor cross-section in mm^2
Isc = Short-circuit current
K = Short-circuit constant

i) PVC (Polyvinyl chloride) insulated cable: Copper conductor 115, aluminium conductor 76.
j) XLPE (Cross-linked polyethylene) or EPR (Ethyline propylene rubber) insulated cable: Copper conductor 143, aluminium conductor 94.
k) Paper insulated cable: Copper conductor 127, aluminium conductor 84.
l) Hard drawn overhead line: Copper conductor 108, aluminium conductor 70.

Fault current in Transformers: For distribution transformers connected in delta/star, transformer secondary short circuit current, Isc = (secondary full load current/Percentage impedance) x 100 amps. Assume that an 11 KV/433 V 1000 KVA DYN 11, three-phase transformer, the secondary current and % impedance given in the nameplate is as follows; I_2 = 1333 amps, %Z = 6, short circuit current (three-phase fault current) in the secondary side terminals Isc = (1333/6) x 100 = 22,216 amps.

Three-phase fault current affected in the primary = Isc x (Vs/Vp) x 1 amps, where Vp = primary voltage, and Vs = secondary voltage between phases.

Earth fault current I_{EF} = Isc x (Vs/Vp) x 0.58

In a delta/star transformer, phase-to-phase fault in the star side: Star side over-current relay sees $\sqrt{3}/2 = 0.866$ times of three-phase fault current. Delta side relay sees full three-phase fault current. Maximum duration of over-current = 0.5 x %Z of the transformer.

In a delta/star transformer, phase to earth fault in the star side: Star side relay sees full earth fault current. Delta side earth fault relay sees 1/√3 = 0.58 times of the phase to earth fault currents.

$$I_{EF} = \frac{\text{Secondary full load current x 100}}{\sqrt{3} \text{ x } \%Z}$$

When two or more similar capacity transformers are paralleled;

$$\text{Fault MVA} = \frac{\text{Transformer MVA x No: of transformers in parallel}}{\text{Percentage-impedance}}$$

Per unit reactance = % Reactance/100

Fault current for three-phase transformers connected in delta/star or star/delta:

$$\text{Maximum short circuit current on primary side of a transformer} = \frac{\text{Transformer Kilovolt ampere x 100}}{\sqrt{3} \text{ x } \%Z \text{ x Phase to phase primary voltage}}$$

$$\text{Maximum short circuit current on secondary side of a transformer} = \frac{\text{Transformer Kilovolt ampere x 100}}{\sqrt{3} \text{ x } \%Z \text{ x Phase-to-phase secondary voltage}}$$

5.21 PROTECTIVE RELAYS FOR MV EQUIPMENTS AND FEEDERS.

Protective relays for medium voltage (3.3 KV to 33 KV) capacitor bank, rectifier, autotransformer and furnace transformer are listed in Table 5.21 (1) to (3) respectively. Similarly protective relays for medium voltage bus bar protection, overhead line feeder and underground cable feeder are listed in Table 5.21 (4) to (6) respectively.

Table 5.21 (1): Protective relays used for protection of medium voltage capacitor bank. [Refer section 3.18]

Device #	Relay title	Type of protection
50/51	Instantaneous/IDMT over current relay	Short circuit and overload protection
51N	IDMT earth fault relay	Time delayed earth fault protection
27/59	Under/over voltage relay	Under/over voltage detention
60	Capacitor current balance relay	Unbalanced current protection
55	Power factor relay	Automatic switching-control of capacitor

Table 5.21 (2): Protective relays for rectifier, and rectifier transformer protection [Refer section 8.19 & 20]

Device #	Relay title	Type of protection
50	Instantaneous over-current relay	Short circuit protection
51	Inverse /very inverse time over-current relay	Overload protection
64N	Restricted earth fault relay	For rectifier transformer earth fault
61	Frame leakage relay	High resistance earth fault
58	Rectification failure relay	Supervision of rectifier circuit

Table 5.21 (3): Protective relays for autotransformer / furnace transformer protection. [Refer section 7.6 & 7]

Device #	Relay title	Type of protection
50/51	Instantaneous/IDMT over-current relay	Short circuit and overload protection
50/51N	Instantaneous/IDMT earth fault relay	Earth fault protection
87	Differential relay	Internal phase and earth fault
99	Impedance relay	Backup protection for autotransformer

Table 5.21 (4): Protective relays for medium voltage bus-bar protection. [Refer section 8.16]

Device #	Relay title	Type of protection
87	Biased differential relay	Phase fault and earth fault
67N	Directional earth fault relay	Residual connection for earth fault
50BF	Breaker failure protection	For isolating protected bus-bar zone
61	Frame leakage relay / insulated switchgears	High resistance earth fault protection

Differential protection (Device No: 87) schemes for bus bars are designed depending on the different types of bus bar arrangements. Single line diagram showing bus differential protection for different types of bus bar arrangements are shown in Chapter # 3, section 3.2.

Table 5.21 (5): Protective relays for medium voltage overhead line radial feeders.

Device #	Relay title	Type of protection
50/51	Instantaneous/IDMT over-current relay	Short circuit and overload protection
51N	Inverse time earth fault relay	Earth fault protection
27	Under voltage relay	Under voltage protection
81	Under frequency relay	Under frequency protection
79	Auto-reclosure relay	For auto-reclosing of feeder breaker

Table 5.21 (6): Protective relays for medium voltage underground cable ring and radial feeders.

Device #	Relay title	Type of protection
50/51	Instantaneous/inverse time O/C relay	Short circuit and overload protection
64G	Ground fault relay	Earth fault protection
46	Phase balance current relay	Current balance protection
67/67N	Directional over-current and earth fault relay	Directional protection for ring feeders

5.22 TESTS ON MCCB AND MOTOR CIRCUIT PROTECTORS.

Moulded case circuit breakers (MCCB) have moulded cases with non-accessible contacts for inspection and maintenance. Motor circuit protectors and adjustable magnetic-trip-only circuit breakers have no thermal or electronic sensing elements to cause them to trip at small multiples of their current rating. They are limited to use in combination starters that contain motor starters with overload relays. These overload relays protect the branch circuit against low-level over-currents. Inverse time circuit breakers, however, contain an over current-sensing element and a time delay mechanism. The time delay is inversely proportional to the magnitude of the current. This function can be checked by the following procedures:

1. Isolate the breaker from power and inspect the breaker against damage or overheating.
2. Perform several mechanical ON/OFF operations.
3. Apply 300% of the breaker's rated continuous current to each pole (through a primary injection test set) to determine that the circuit breaker will trip on an overload.
4. When installing the breaker after test, make sure all connections are tightened properly.

Table 5.22 (1): MCCB overload trip test; tripping time, in seconds, at 3 times of rated continuous current of breaker.

Rated continuous current (Amps)	Minimum time for electronic sensing breakers (seconds)	Minimum tripping time for thermal / magnetic breakers (seconds)	Maximum tripping time for normal protection (seconds)	Rated voltage (volts)
15-45	3	-	50	240
50-100	5	-	70	240
110-225	10	5	200	240
15-45	5	-	80	600
50-100	5	-	150	600
110-225	10	5	200	600
250-450	25	10	250	600
500-600	25	10	250	600
700-1200	25	10	450	600
1400-2500	25	10	600	600

5.23 ESSENTIAL REQUIREMENTS FOR PROTECTION SYSTEMS.

1. Protective relays of the withdrawable types conforming to IEC 255 or BS 142 or ANSI standard is recommended for protection of equipments and power system networks.
2. Hand reset relays should have provision for resetting without opening the cover.
3. Those circuits, subject to remote supervisory control need electrically reset tripping relays.
4. Relay contacts must be capable, make firmly without bounce and the whole of the relay mechanisms unaffected by vibration or external magnetic fields. **[Bounce time is the interval from the initial make (or break) of a contact to the instant of sustained closure (or opening)].** Operating time does not include bounce time.
5. Relays, where appropriate, might be provided with operation indicators. Separate coloured light emitting diode (LED) indicators are required for each phase.
6. Relays, which rely for their operation on an external DC supply, the trip supply of the associated circuit breaker is being used. This supply should be monitored and an alarm provided in event of failure.
7. Microprocessor based numerical relays shall have serial communications facilities for connection to the substation control system for remote diagnostic and parameter setting.
8. For solid-state relays need protection for static circuitry from transient voltages which could reach the circuitry via connections to instrument transformers or the station battery. The routing of cables should be such as to limit interference to a minimum. Any auxiliary supplies necessary to power solid-state relays are from the station main battery bank.
9. Relay designs should be suitable to meet the site climatic conditions and control room is to be air conditioned in order to prevent overheating the components.
10. To minimize the effect of electrolysis, relay coils operating on DC supply, is to be connected such that the coils are not continuously energized from the positive pole of the battery.
11. Auxiliary relays suitable for continuous operation at 110 volts DC nominal, 120 volts float without the use of a voltage dropping resistors or diodes are preferred.
12. Labels describing the application, ANSI device number and title of the relay must be provided with each relay.
13. Relays shall be designed for operation under the system frequency (50 or 60 Hertz) adopted by the supply authorities.
14. For bus bar and short zone schemes, the rated stability limit must be not less than the three phase symmetrical breaking capacity of the associated switchgear.
15. For transformer and generator protection schemes, the rated stability limit should not be less than the maximum through fault level as limited by the impedance of the protected equipment.
16. The fault setting of any type of fault should not exceed 10% of the CT rated secondary current.
17. Current transformer knee point voltages should not be less than twice the relay circuit setting voltage.
18. The maximum peak voltage across current transformer secondary wiring should not exceed 3000 volts under maximum internal fault conditions.
19. All protection current transformers shall be Class X, or PS or 5P, low-reactance type in accordance with BS 3938, section K2, Appendix K.
20. Compilation and acquisition of data's of existing network, system load flow and short-circuit analysis studies, and protection co-ordination studies shall be conducted in accordance with ERACS (Electrical Research Association) power system simulation analysis software. Relay setting parameters are derived on the basis of these studies.
21. Whenever the relay module is withdrawn from the housing, provision is required for automatic shorting of the CT terminals to prevent opening the continuity of CT circuits.

5.24 ANSI STANDARD DEVICE NUMBERS AND SUFFIX LETTERS.

Defined in ANSI standard (American National Standards Institute) C37.2, the device function numbers are a world wide standardized system for describing the devices in switching equipments referred in numbers with appropriate suffix letters according to functions performed by them. They are commonly used to describe the type of protection applied to a circuit. For example, the most common form of protection is over current, usually designated as 50/51, Device 50 designate instantaneous over current (short circuit protection), and Device 51 designate time over current (overload protection). The definitions and functions described by American Institute of Electrical Engineers (AIEE) are described below.

Device No	Definition and function **(Courtesy, ANSI & AIEE)**

1. **Master element:** An initiating device such as a control switch, float switch etc.
2. **Time delay starting or closing relay:** A device whose function is to give a desired amount of time delay before or after any point of operation in a switching sequence.
3. **Checking or interlocking relay:** A device, which operates in response to the position of a number of other devices or to a number of predetermined conditions in a equipment.
4. **Master contactor:** A device generally controlled by device No: 1(Master element).
5. **Stopping device:** A device used to place and hold a equipment out of function.
6. **Starting circuit breaker:** A device whose principal function is to connect a machine to its source of starting voltage.
7. **Anode circuit breaker:** Circuit breaker used in the anode circuits of a power rectifier.
8. **Control power disconnecting device:** A disconnecting device such as a pull out fuse, MCCB/MCB used for the purpose of connecting/disconnecting a control circuit.
9. **Reversing device:** A device used for the purpose of reversing functions.
10. **Unit sequence switch:** A device used to change the sequence in which unit may be placed in and out of service in multiple unit equipments.
11. **Reserved for future applications.**
12. **Over-speed device:** A speed-switch, which functions on over-speed.
13. **Centrifugal speed-switch:** A slip-frequency relay or any device operates at approximately synchronous speed of a machine.
14. **Under-speed device:** A speed-switch, which functions when the speed of a machine falls below a predetermined value.
15. **Speed or frequency matching device:** A device functions to match and hold the speed or the frequency of a machine or of a system equal to that of another machine or system.
16. **For future applications.**
17. **Shunting or discharge switch:** A device serves to open or to close a shunting circuit.
18. **Accelerating or decelerating device:** A device used to close or to cause the closing of circuits, which are used to increase or decrease the speed of a machine.
19. **Starting to running transition contactor:** A device which operates to initiate or cause the automatic transfer of a machine from the starting to the running power connection.
20. **Electrically operated valve:** A solenoid or motor operated valve, which is used in vacuum, air, gas, oil, water or similar lines. Following suffix letters are used to designate applications: **20BD:** Blow down valve; **20BL:** Block valve; **20BP:** Bypass valve; **20CH:** Check valve; **20D:** Discharge valve; **20EP:** Electro pneumatic instrumentation valve; **20IS:** Isolation valve; **20MA:** Manifold valve; **20PR:** Pressurizing valve; **20R:** Recycling valve; **20RF:** Relief valve; **20S:** Suction valve; **20TT:** throttling control valve; **20VT:** Vent valve. Following suffix letters are used to indicate the operation of mechanically actuated auxiliary switches on valves: **20ac:** Open only when valve is fully closed; **20ao:** Open except when valve is fully opened; **20bc:** Closed only when valve is fully closed; **20bo:** Closed except when valve is fully opened; **20to:** Opened by torque-responsive mechanism, to stop valve opening; **20tc:** Closed by torque-responsive mechanism, to stop valve closing.
21. **Distance relay:** A relay, which functions when the circuit admittance, impedance, or reactance increases or decreases beyond pre-determined value. **(Distance relay is being used for phase and ground fault protection of transmission lines).**
22. **Equalizer circuit breaker:** A circuit breaker, which serves to control or make and break the equalizer.
23. **Temperature control device:** A device functions to raise or to lower the temperature of a machine or other apparatus when its temperature varies beyond a predetermined value.
24. **For future application:** (This device number is widely used for designating **Volts/hertz protection** of generators)..
25. **Synchronizing or synchronism check device:** A device operates when two AC circuits are within the desired limits of frequency, phase angle, or voltage to permit the paralleling of these two AC circuits.
26. **Apparatus thermal device:** A device functions when the temperature exceeds/decreases a predetermined value. Following suffix letters are used to designate applications: **26F: Field winding**

(Rotor) over temperature; 26O: Transformer oil over temperature; 26W: Transformer winding over temperature.

27. **Under-voltage relay:** A device, which functions on a given value of under-voltage. (Device number **27/50** is used for designating **inadvertent energization protection** of alternators. Similarly, **27/59** is used for designating **under/over voltage protection** of equipments.
28. **For future applications.**
29. **Isolating contactor:** An isolator used expressly for disconnecting one circuit from another for the purpose of emergency operation.
30. **Annunciator relay:** A non-automatically reset relay which gives a number of separate visual indications up on the functioning of protective devices.
31. **Separate excitation device:** A device connects a circuit such as the shunt field of a synchronous converter to a source of separate excitation during the starting sequence.
32. **Directional power relay (Reverse power relay):** A relay which functions on a desired value of power flow in a given direction.
33. **Position switch:** A device used for makes and breaks contacts when the main device or apparatus, which has no device function number, reaches a given position.
34. **Motor operated sequence switch:** A multi-contact switch, which fixes the operating sequences of major devices during starting and stopping or during other sequential switching operations.
35. **Brush operating or slip ring short circuiting device:** A device used for raising, lowering or shifting the brushes of a machine, or for short-circuiting slip rings.
36. **Polarity device:** A device operates or permits the operation of another device on a predetermined polarity only.
37. **Under-current or under-power relay:** A device, which functions when the current or power flow decreases below a predetermined value.
38. **Bearing protective device:** A device, which functions on excessive bearing temperature or on other abnormal mechanical conditions such as undue wear, which may eventually result in excessive bearing temperature. Protected bearings are identified as follows; **38M1:** Motor bearing, inboard; **38M2**: Motor bearing, outboard; **38P1:** Pump bearing, inboard; **38P2:** Pump bearing, outboard; **38C1:** Compressor bearing, inboard; **38C2:** Compressor bearing, outboard; **38L1:** Gear bearing, low speed, inboard; **38L2:** Gear bearing, low speed, outboard; **38H1:** Gear bearing, high speed, inboard; **38H2**: Gear bearing, high speed, outboard Where more than two bearings are employed in the same axial line they are numbered consecutively from the **inboard or drive end.**
39. **Mechanical condition monitor:** A device, which functions upon the occurrence of an abnormal mechanical condition such as vibration, or seal failure. Specific types are designated by suffix as follows: **39VB:** Vibration monitor; **39SF:** Seal failure monitor.
40. **Field failure relay:** A relay, which functions on failure of machine field current or on an excessive value of the reactive component of armature current in AC machine. (Device number 40 is used to designate Loss of field relay / Exciter failure relay / reactive power relay).
41. **Field circuit breaker:** A device, which functions to apply or remove the field excitation of a machine. (Typically DC circuit breaker).
42. **Running circuit breaker:** A device whose principal function is to connect a machine to its source of running voltage after having been brought up to the desired speed on the starting connection.
43. **Manual transfer or selector device:** A device transfers the control circuits so as to modify the plan of operation of the switching equipment or of some of the devices.
44. **Unit sequence starting relay:** A device, which functions to start the next available unit in a multiple, unit equipment on the failure or on the non-availability of the normally preceding unit.
45. **Atmospheric condition monitor:** A device, which functions upon the occurrence of a predetermined atmospheric condition such as hazardous explosive atmosphere, smoke or fire. Specific types are designated by suffixes as follows; 45HA: Explosive atmosphere monitor; 45SM: Smoke monitor; 45FR: Fire monitor.
46. **Reverse phase or phase balance current relay:** A relay, which functions when the poly-phase currents are of reverse phase sequence or contains negative phase sequence due to unbalanced load. This device number is used for designating Negative phase sequence relay.
47. **Phase-sequence voltage relay (Phase reversal voltage relay):** A device, which functions upon a predetermined value of poly-phase voltage in the desired phase sequence.

48. **Incomplete sequence relay:** A device, which returns the equipment to the normal or off position and locks it out if the normal starting or stopping sequence is not properly completed within a predetermined time. Specific types are designated by suffixes as follows: **48L:** Locked rotor current.
49. **Machine or transformer thermal relay:** A device, which functions when the temperature of an AC machine armature or other load carrying winding exceeds a predetermined value. (Generator or motor stator **winding temperature protection**).
50. **Instantaneous over-current or rate-of rise relay (High set phase over-current relay):** A relay, which functions instantaneously on an excessive value of current or an excessive rate of current rise. Specific types are designated by suffixes as follows; **50BF:** Instantaneous over current breaker failure protection; **50G:** Instantaneous over-current ground fault relay connected to neutral CT; **50N:** Instantaneous over-current earth fault relay; **50/51VR:** Voltage restraint, instantaneous and time over-current relay.
51. **AC time over-current relay:** A relay with either a definite or inverse time characteristics, which functions, when current in an AC circuit exceeds a preset value. Specific types are designated by suffixes as follows; **51G:** Time delayed ground fault over-current relay (Standby earth fault relay) connected to neutral CT; **51LR:** Excessive starting time, **51N:** Time delayed earth fault over-current relay.
52. **AC circuit breaker:** A circuit breaker, which is used to close and interrupt an AC power circuit under normal conditions or to interrupt this circuit under fault or emergency conditions. Auxiliary contacts for circuit breakers are designated as follows; **52a:** Auxiliary switch closed when the circuit breaker is closed; **52b:** Auxiliary switch closed when the circuit breaker is open; **52aa:** Auxiliary switch closed when the operating mechanism of circuit breaker is in operated position; **52bb:** Auxiliary switch closed when the operating mechanism of the circuit breaker is in the non-operated position; **52LC:** Latch checking switch, closed when the circuit breaker mechanism linkage is latched after an opening operation; **52LS:** Circuit breaker spring charging limit switch.
53. **Exciter or DC generator relay:** A device, which forces the DC machine field excitation to buildup during starting or which functions when the machine voltage has built up to a given value.
54. **Reserved for future applications** (Used for designating **frame leakage relay**).
55. **Power factor relay:** A relay, which operates when the power factor in an AC circuits becomes above or below a set value. Also used for automatic switching control of capacitor banks.
56. **Field application relay:** A relay, which automatically controls the application of the field excitation to a synchronous motor at some predetermined point in the slip cycle.
57. **Short-circuiting or grounding device:** A power or stored energy operated device, which functions to short circuit or to ground a circuit in response to automatic or manual means.
58. **Power rectifier misfire relay:** A device, which functions if one or more of the power rectifier anodes fails to fire.
59. **Over-voltage relay:** A relay, which operates on a given value of over-voltage. Specific types are designated by suffixes as follows; **59N**: Neutral displacement relay (over-voltage); **59G/27TN:** 100% Stator ground fault protection.
60. **Voltage or current balance relay:** A voltage balance relay, which operates on a given difference in voltage between two circuits. Current balance relay operates on a given difference in current input or output in a circuit. Specific types are designated by suffixes as follows; **60FL:** voltage transformer fuse failure relay
61. **For future applications.**
62. **Time delay stopping or opening relay:** A time delay device, which serves in conjunction with the device, which initiates the shutdown stopping or opening operation in an automatic sequence.
63. **Liquid or gas pressure switch:** A device, which operates on given values of liquid or gas pressure or on a given rate of change of these values. Specific types are designated with suffix letters as follows: **63MT:** Transformer main tank Buchholz relay; **63TC**: Transformer tap changer protection relay.
64. **Ground protective relay:** A device, which functions on failure of the insulation of a machine, transformer or other apparatus to ground. Specific types are designated with suffix letters as follows. **64G:** Restricted earth fault relay; **64N**: Differential Earth fault protection; **64R:** Rotor earth fault protection.
65. **Governor:** A equipment which controls the gate or valve opening of a prime mover.

66. **Notching or jogging device:** A device, which functions to allow only a specified number of operations of a given device or equipment. It also functions to energize a circuit or to permit intermittent acceleration or jogging of a machine at low speeds for mechanical positioning.
67. **AC directional over-current relay:** A device, which functions on a desired value of AC over-current flowing in a predetermined direction. Specific types are designated by suffixes as follows; **67P:** Directional phase fault relay; **67N:** Ground directional relay.
68. **Blocking relay:** A device which initiates a pilot signal for blocking or tripping on external faults in a transmission line or operate with other devices to block reclosing on an out-of-step condition or on power swings. This device number is also used for designating **out-of-step protection.**
69. **Permissive control device:** A two position manually operated switch, which in one position permits the closing of a circuit breaker or placing of a equipment in operation and in the other position prevents the circuit breaker or the equipment from being operated.
70. **Electrically operated rheostat:** A rheostat, which is used to vary the resistance of a circuit in response to some means of electrical control.
71. **Level switch:** A switch, which operates on given values or on a given rate of change of level. The following designations are used for specific applications; **71SB:** Switch response level in scrubber; **71SO:** Switch response to level in seal oil tank; **71ST:** Switch response to level in storage tank. (71L: Low oil level; 71H: High oil level)
72. **DC circuit breaker:** A circuit breaker used to close and interrupt a DC power circuit under normal conditions or to interrupt this circuit under fault or emergency conditions.
73. **Load resistor contactor:** A contactor used to shunt or insert a step of load limiting, shifting or indicating resistance in a power circuit.
74. **Alarm relay or Trip circuit supervision relay:** A relay other than the annunciator, which is covered under device no: 30, which used to operate or to operate in connection with visual or audible alarm.
75. **Position changing mechanism:** A mechanism, which is used for moving a removable circuit breaker unit to and from the connected, disconnected and test positions.
76. **DC over-current relay:** A relay, which functions when the current in a DC circuit exceeds a given value.
77. **Pulse transmitter:** This unit is used to generate and transmit pulses over a telemetering or pilot wire circuit to the remote indicating or receiving device.
78. **Phase angle measuring, or out of step protection relay:** A relay, which functions at a predetermined phase angle between two voltages or between two currents or between voltage and current.
79. **AC reclosing relay:** A relay, which controls the automatic reclosing and locking out of an AC circuit breaker.
80. **Flow switch:** A switch operates on a given values or on given rate of change of flow. The following designations are used for specific applications; **80AR:** Switch responsive to flow of room ventilation air; **80AM:** Switch responsive to flow of air to force ventilated motor; **80LO:** Switch responsive to flow of lubricating oil; **80SO:** Switch responsive to flow of seal oil; **80W:** Switch responsive to flow of water.
81. **Frequency relay:** A relay, which functions on a predetermined value of frequency either under or over or on normal system frequency or rate of change of frequency.
82. **DC reclosing relay:** A device, which control the automatic closing and reclosing of a DC circuit breaker generally in response to load circuit conditions.
83. **Automatic selective control or transfer relay:** A device, which operates to select automatically between certain sources of conditions in an equipment or performs a transfer operation automatically.
84. **Operating mechanism:** Complete electrical mechanism or servomechanism, including the operating motor, solenoids, position switches etc, for a tap changer, induction regulator or any piece of apparatus, which has no device function numbers.
85. **Carrier or pilot wire receiver relay:** A device, which is operated or restrained by a signal used in connection with carrier-current or DC pilot wire fault directional relaying. Specific types are designated by suffixes as follows; 85PLCC: Carrier or pilot wire relay phase comparison via power line carrier communication; 85TP: Tele protection equipment via OPGW fiber optic cable.
86. **Locking-out relay:** An electrically operated, hand or electrically reset relay, which functions to shutdown and hold an equipment out of service on the occurrence of abnormal conditions. If it is **electrically reset, device number 86E** is being used.

87. **Differential protection relay:** A protective relay, which functions on a percentage of phase angle or other quantitative difference of two currents or of some other electrical quantities. Specific types are designated by suffixes as follows; **87B:** Bus differential protection; **87BFP**: Breaker failure differential protection; **87CD:** Phase segregated current differential protection for transmission feeders; **87G:** Generator differential protection; **87G(SP):** Differential protection for split phase winding generators (turn-to-turn short circuit): **87M:** Motor differential protection; **87N:** 100% Restricted earth fault differential protection; **87T:** Transformer differential protection; **87TEED:** Teed feeder differential protection; **87TG:** Combined generator-transformer differential protection.
88. **Auxiliary-motor or motor-generator:** One equipment used for operating auxiliary equipments such as pumps, blowers, exciters, rotating magnetic amplifiers etc. The following designations are used for specific applications; **88:** Spring charge motor of circuit breaker; **88C:** Compressor; **88CA:** Compressor, instrument air; **88F:** Fan; **88FR:** Ventilation fan (delivering air to room); **88FE:** Exhaust fan; **88FSC:** Fan as space cooling unit; **88FSH:** Fan on space heating unit; **88FM:** Fan serving forced ventilated air; **88FMC:** Fan serving forced air cooler; **88L:** Lubricator; **88P:** Pump; **88PLO**: Pump, lube oil; **88PSO:** Pump, seal oil; **88PSU:** Sump pump; **88PW:** Water pump.
89. **Line switch:** A device used as a disconnecting or isolating switch in an AC or DC circuit.
90. **Regulating device:** A device whose function is to regulate a quantity or quantities such as voltage, current, power, speed, frequency, temperature and load at a certain value.
91. **Voltage directional relay:** A relay, which operates when the voltage across an open circuit breaker or contactor exceeds a given value in a given direction.
92. **Voltage and power directional relay:** A relay, which permits or causes the connection of two circuits when the voltage differences between them exceeds a given value in a predetermined direction and causes these two circuits to be disconnected from each other when the power flowing, between them exceeds a given value in the opposite direction.
93. **Field changing contactor:** A device functions to increase or decrease in one-step the values of field excitation in a machine.
94. **Tripping or trip free relay:** A device, which function to trip a circuit breaker, contactor or equipment or to permit immediate tripping by other device or to prevent immediate reclosure of a circuit interrupter in case it should open automatically even through its closing circuit is maintained in closed condition.

Device number 95 to 99 used only for specific applications on individual installations. For example, Device number 95 is widely used for designating Generator backup protection impedance relay. Similarly Device number 96 is used for designating Auto-loading relay and device number 97 is used for designating Trip circuit supervision relay.

SUFIX NUMBERS AND SUFIX LETTERS FOR DEVICES:

(a) **Suffix numbers for devices controlled directly:** A similar series of numbers starting with 201 instead of 1, be used for those devices which function in a machine, feeder or other equipment when these are controlled directly from the supervisory system. Typical examples for such device numbers are 201, 205, 294, etc.

(b) **Devices performing more than one function:** If one device performs two relatively important functions in a equipment, it is desirable to identify both of these functions, by using a double function number and name such as 27/59 under/over voltage protection, 50/51 Instantaneous and time delayed over current relay.

(c) **Suffix numbers used with device numbers:** If two or more devices with function number suffix letter are present in the same equipment, they may be distinguished by numbered suffixes, Eg: 52X-1, 52X-2 etc.

(d) **Suffix letters used with device numbers:** Suffix letters are used with device numbers for various purposes. They may be distinguished by, letters. Eg: 20/LS

CHAPTER # 6

GENERATOR PROTECTION RELAYS

CONTENTS:

6.1 SELECTION AND APPLICATION OF GENERATOR PROTECTION RELAYS.

Generators are a vital part of power system, and their protection deserves critical consideration. For the larger machines, a consistent pattern of protection has evolved. For the smaller machines below 5 MW, simple protection is employed. In addition to low voltage generators (maximum up to 1 MW), the standard generation voltages are 3.3KV, 6.6KV, 10KV, 11KV, 22 KV at 50 Hz, and 5 KV, 7.2KV, 13.8 KV 22.8 KV at 60 Hz. The design KVA or MVA capacity of the individual generator depends up on its prime mover which drives the generator.

System stability study:

A system stability study is appropriate for systems interconnected with other utility generating stations. This study determines the ability of the local generation to stay in synchronization with the remainder of the power system during a system disturbance. Station auxiliary services emergency generators are not considered for stability studies. The stability study may evaluate the relay settings and/or modifications to the protection scheme associated with the generators and utility. The analysis will determine relay settings that will allow the generator out-of-step protection to clear the faulty condition before stability is lost.

Harmonic study:

A harmonic study can determine whether harmonic currents (High frequency currents) will cause problems. Variable frequency drives (VFD), Uninterruptible power supply (UPS), and any power semi-conducting equipment produce high frequency currents (harmonic currents) and have an inherently poor power factors, sometimes are adversely affected by the harmonic currents that flow in a power system when VFD or rectifiers are used. The harmonics can overexcite the capacitors and the systems inductances under certain conditions. The net result could be failure of electrical equipment due to overheating or over-voltage, as well as noise in communication circuits. From a harmonic study, recommendations can be made concerning the needs to install power line filters or to rearrange equipment in order to separate harmonic sources.

Generator protection:

The hazards against which protective devices guard on faults or abnormal operating conditions such as short-circuit, unbalanced currents, loss of field, over-excitation, reverse power, abnormal frequencies etc are listed in Table 6.1 (1), along with its technical requirements.

Table 6.1 (1): Protective relays recommended for generator protection.

Device No:	Relay title	Relay application	Technical requirements
87G	Differential protection relay	For generator internal protection	Protection against generator winding faults
87TD	Transverse differential relay	Inter turn fault protection i.e. turn to turn fault	Only for generators with split-phase winding
50/51V	Voltage-restrained over-current relay	Over-current and short circuit protection	Relay operates even if the sustained fault current is lower than full load current
26F	Rotor-winding temperature protection	Protection against rotor winding overheating	Applicable only for separately-excited generators
50/51G	Neutral ground fault relay	Earth fault protection. Relay connected to the neutral CT.	Inverse time delay relay for NGR earthing
59N	Neutral-displacement relay (over voltage relay)	Relay connected to the secondary of earthing transformer	Generator-neutral-earthed via grounding-transformer. Used for combined GT unit
46	Negative-phase sequence relay	Protection-against unbalanced load	Time lag over current relay with negative sequence filter.
32	Reverse power relay	Protection-against motoring (prime mover / drive failure)	Inverse time relay for DG set. Definite time relay for turbine generators.
40	Field failure / loss of excitation relay	Protection against loss of excitation	Mho or reactance relay
64F	Field ground relay / Rotor earth fault relay	Protection against rotor earth fault	DC shunt excitation or thyristor excitation system
81	Low / high frequency relay	Protection against low or high frequency	Measuring single phase voltage
27/59	Under/over-voltage relay	Protection against low or high voltage	Measuring three phase voltage
49	Winding temperature protection	Protection against over heating generator stator	RTD embedded in the stator winding detects temperature
95	Back up impedance relay	For back up protection of GT unit	Additional protection for GT combined unit
78	Out of step protection relay	Pole slip protection	Measuring phase angle
38	Bearing-temperature protection	Protection-against bearing over heating	For turbo/hydro generators. Not for diesel generators.
12	Over-speed protection	Protection against over speed	For diesel generator sets and hydro generators
25	Synchronism check and synchronizing relay	For auto synchronizing generators	Compare bus voltage, frequency and phase angle with generator
87TG	Biased differential-relay	For overall protection of combined generator transformer unit	Additional protection for combined generator transformer unit.
24	Volts/hertz relay (Over fluxing relay)	To detect voltage-regulator malfunction	Protection against over excitation, over fluxing of GT unit.
14	Under speed protection	To detect governor failure	Protection against under speed

6.2 PROTECTIVE RELAYS FOR HYDROELECTRIC GENERATORS.

Figure 6.2 illustrates the single line diagram representing protection system for a 43 MVA, 11 KV, 50 Hz separately excited hydroelectric generator with 43 MVA 11 KV/132 KV delta/star step-up transformer and 11 KV/440 V 1000 KVA step down auxiliary transformer. Relays employed for the generator protection and transformer protection are listed in Table 6.2 (1). No circuit breaker is provided between generator and main or auxiliary transformers. Generator neutral is grounded through grounding transformer. Main and auxiliary transformer neutral is solidly grounded.

LEGEND:

Device numbers used with figure 6.2 is listed in Table 6.2 (1) below.

ACB: Air circuit breaker; SCB: SF6 circuit breaker.

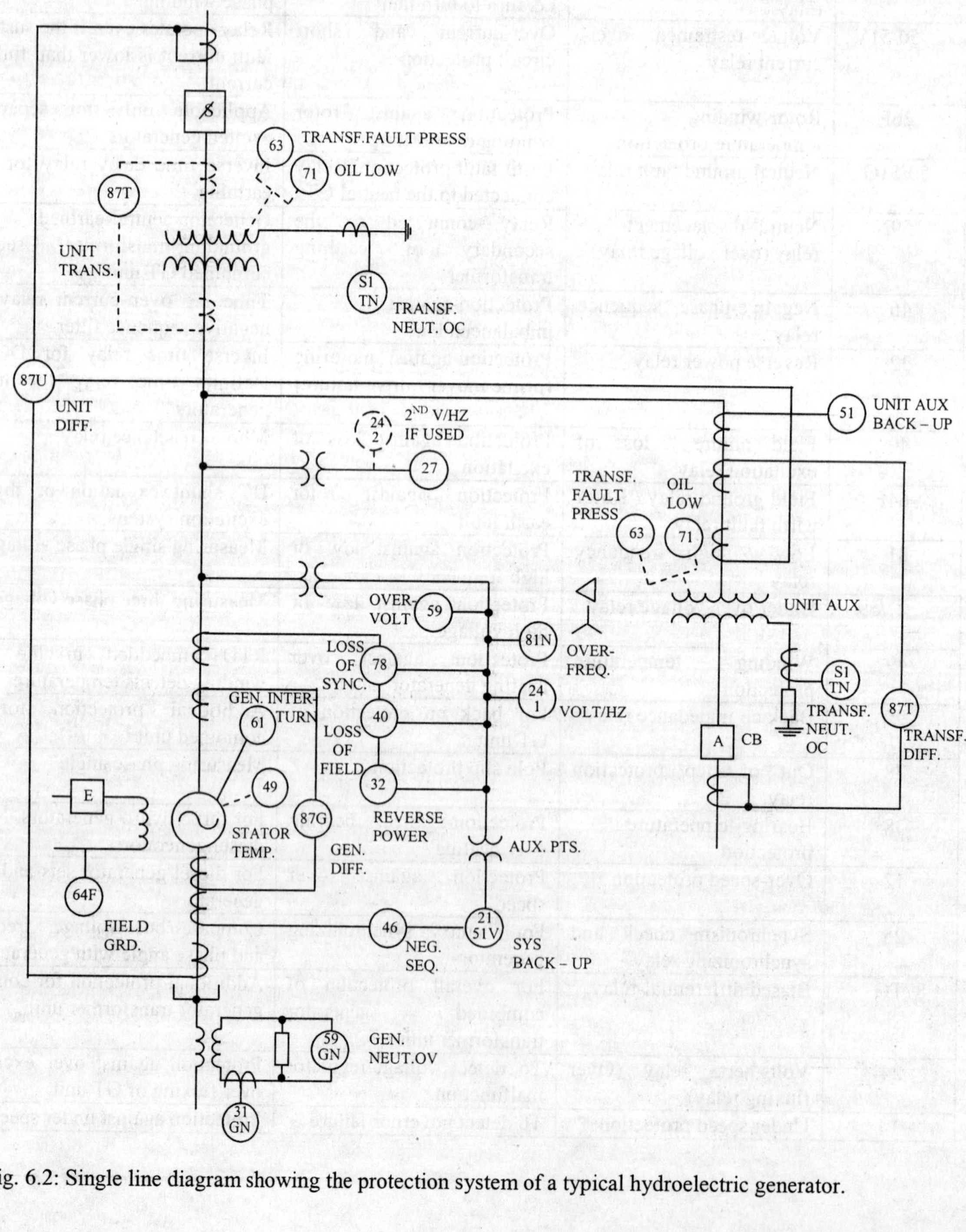

Fig. 6.2: Single line diagram showing the protection system of a typical hydroelectric generator.

Table 6.2 (1): Protective relays used for a combined hydroelectric generator-transformer unit.

Device No:	Relay title	Relay application
27	Under voltage relay	Under voltage protection
40	Loss of field relay	Protection against loss of excitation
46	Negative phase sequence relay	Protection against unbalanced load
51V	Voltage restraint over-current relay	Generator overload protection
51TN	Transformer neutral over current relay	Transformer earth fault protection
59GN	Neutral displacement relay /voltage relay	Earth fault protection connected on earthing transformer secondary
61	Inter-turn fault relay	Generator winding turn to turn fault protection
64F	Field ground relay	Rotor earth fault protection
81	High / low frequency relay	Protection against low / high frequency
87G	High speed biased differential relay (% restraint)	Generator internal phase and earth fault
87T	Harmonic restraint differential relay	Transformer differential protection
87U	Generator-Transformer differential relay	Generator-Transformer differential protection
78	Loss of synchronism relay	Out of step protection of GT unit
49	Stator temperature protection	Protection against overloading of generator
12	Over-speed	Over-speed due to sudden rejection of load
14	Under-speed	Under-speed due to Governor failure
38T	Bearing temperature high	Bearing over-temperature.
63	Buchholz or Gas pressure relay	Transformer winding fault
71	Oil level switch	Low oil level tripping
24	Voltage / hertz relay	Over excitation over fluxing protection
21/51V	Synchronism back up relay	Back-up protection for synchronism

6.3 PROTECTIVE RELAYS FOR GAS AND STEAM TURBINE GENERATORS.

Figure 6.3 illustrates the single line diagram representing protection and metering of a typical 63 MVA, 11 KV 50 Hz Steam turbine generator / Gas turbine generator with 63 MVA 11 KV/132 KV step-up power transformer. Relays used for the protection of generator, generator-transformer unit and back up protection for generator, are listed in Table 6.3 (1). Although generator circuit breaker is provided, the unit is operating as a combined unit because provision for paralleling is between combined units (132KV side). Generator neutral is grounded through a distribution transformer primary and transformer neutral is grounded through a neutral grounding resistor.

Protective devices such as stator temperature, cooling medium temperature, automatic voltage regulator control and over-speed protection etc are incorporated in generating units because of the stored rotating energy of the generator need fast clearing protection. Phase fault protection is provided by a primary current differential relay with independent current transformers. Stator ground fault protection is provided with two independent relay schemes, employing independent current transformers. As a minimum one of this schemes should provide protection for 100% of the stator winding i.e. restricted earth fault protection. In both internal phase fault and ground fault (differential relay) operation, simultaneous trip of the generator breaker, excitation system and initiate closing signal to turbine valve or shut down of prime-mover. Back-up impedance protection is also essential.

A poorly coordinated relaying system will result in nuisance outages and greater damages to equipments when a system fault does occur. Proper coordination usually means the proper settings of protective relays. Device coordination also means choosing the correct type of device to begin with, or the replacement of the correct device if the provided device cannot be set for the proper result. Function check and setting of the relays must be verified by conducting primary and secondary injection tests.

Mechanical devices employed for the protection of turbo-generators are demonstrated in section 6.20.

LEGEND:

A: Ammeter
AVR: Automatic
EX: Exciter
G: Generator
GT: Gas turbine unit.
H: Running hour meter
Hz: Frequency meter
KVARh: Reactive kilovolt ampere-hour meter
KWh: Kilowatt-hour meter
MW: Megawatt meter
MVAR: Mega volt-ampere meter
PF: Power factor meter
PMG: Permanent magnet Generator.
V: Voltmeter

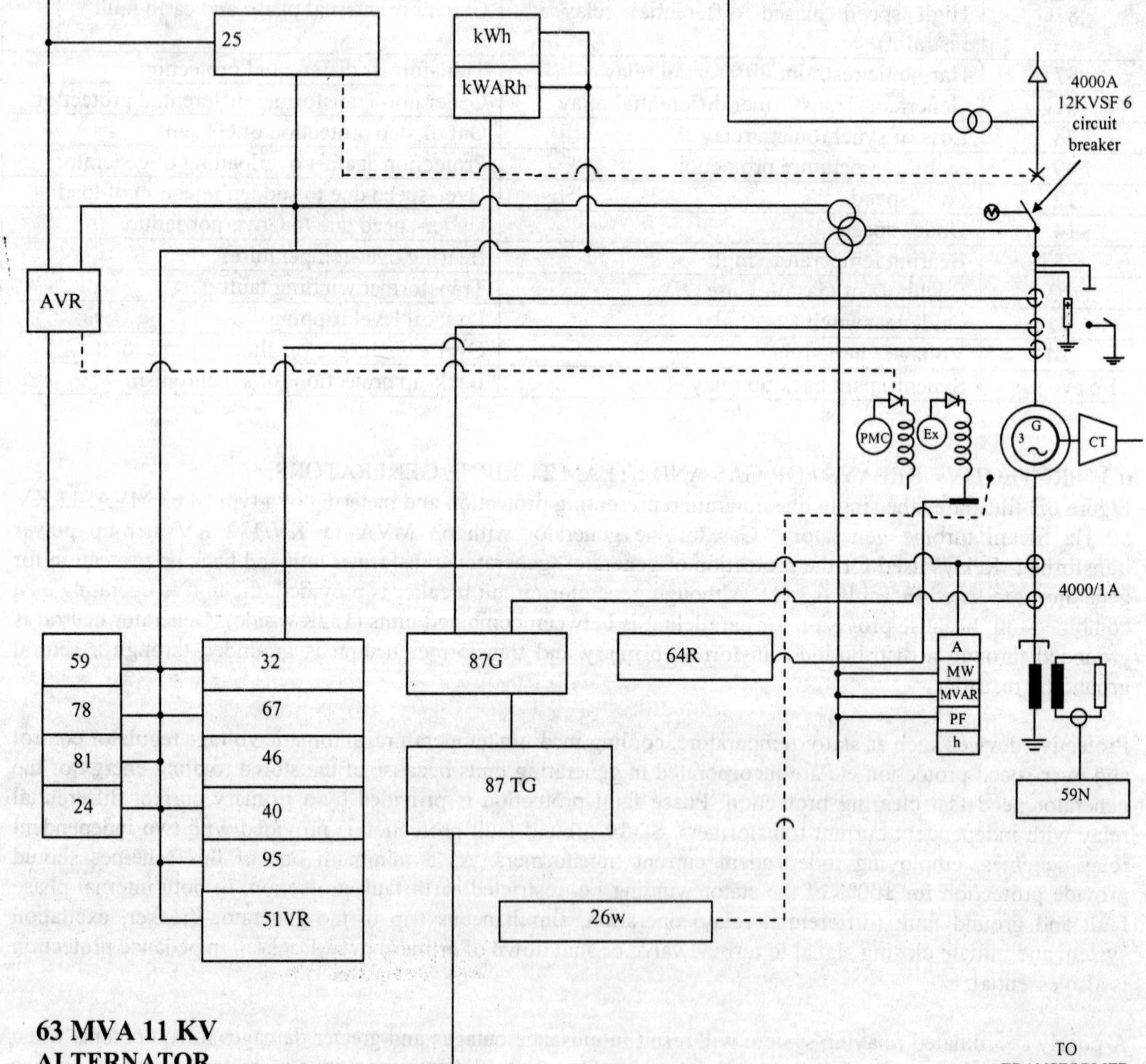

Fig. 6.3: Single line diagram showing the protection and metering system of a typical turbo-generator.

Table 6.3 (1): Protective relays recommended for gas or steam turbine medium voltage generators.

Device No:	Relay title	Relay application
24	Volts/hertz protection / over-fluxing protection	Protection against voltage regulator malfunction.
25	Synchronism-check-relay/Auto synchronizing relay	Check differences in voltage / phase angle / frequencies
49	Overload protection	Protection against over loading of generator
32	Reverse power relay	To prevent motoring paralleled generators
46	Negative phase sequence relay	Protection against unbalanced load
50/51V	Voltage restraint over-current relay	Overload and short circuit protection
59	Over-voltage relay	Over-voltage protection
64R	Rotor earth fault relay	Rotor earth fault protection
59N	Neutral displacement relay/Voltage relay	Protection against earth fault
67	Directional over-current relay	Directional protection of generators
78	Pole slip protection/out of step protection	Out of step protection of paralleled generators
81	High / low frequency relay	Protection against high / low frequency
87G	High speed biased differential relay (% restraint)	Generator internal phase and earth fault protection
87TG	Harmonic restraint biased differential relay for generator-transformer unit	Additional protection for generator-transformer and unit auxiliary transformer if provided.
95	Back up impedance relay for GT unit	Additional protection for GT unit
40	Loss of excitation/Field failure relay	Protection against loss of excitation of rotor

6.4 PROTECTIVE RELAYS FOR DIESEL ENGINE DRIVEN GENERATORS.

Figure 6.4 illustrates the single line diagram representing the protection and metering system of a typical self-excited, 5 MVA, 13.8 KV, 60 Hz diesel generator set. Relays used for the protection of the Diesel engine driven generator set is listed in Table 6.4 (1). Generator control and protection is designed for running in parallel with other generators or with utility supply including auto-start/auto-synchronizing facility. Generator neutral is grounded through neutral grounding resistor.

Table 6.4 (1): Protective relays used for a typical medium voltage diesel engine driven generator.

Device No:	Relay title	Relay application
25	Synchronism check relay	Check differences in bus and generator voltage/phase angle/frequencies
49	Generator stator winding temperature	Protection against overheating stator winding
32	Reverse power relay	Protection against motoring
50/51V	Voltage restraint over-current relay	Overload and short circuit protection
51N	Standby earth fault relay	Earth fault protection
59	Over-voltage relay	Over-voltage protection
64G	Restricted earth fault relay	Earth fault protection of stator winding
67	Directional over current relay	Directional protection of paralleled generator
81	High /low frequency relay	High/low frequency protection
87G	High-speed percentage-differential relay	Protection against internal phase faults and earth faults.
12	Over-speed switch	Shuts down the engine if the engine speed exceeds the set value or 110 %
14	Low oil pressure switch	Shuts down the engine if the lube oil pressure reduces below the set value.
15	High engine temperature switch	Shuts down the engine if the engine temperature exceeds the set value.

LEGEND: A: Ammeter; Ex: Exciter; G: Generator; h: Running hour meter; Hz: Frequency meter; KVARh: Reactive Kilovolt ampere-hour meter; KWh: Kilowatt-hour meter; MVAR: Reactive mega-volt ampere; MW: Megawatt meter; NGR: Neutral grounding resistor; PMG: Permanent magnet generator; V: Voltmeter; V/S: Voltmeter selector switch. (Device numbers are given in Table 6.4 (1) above.

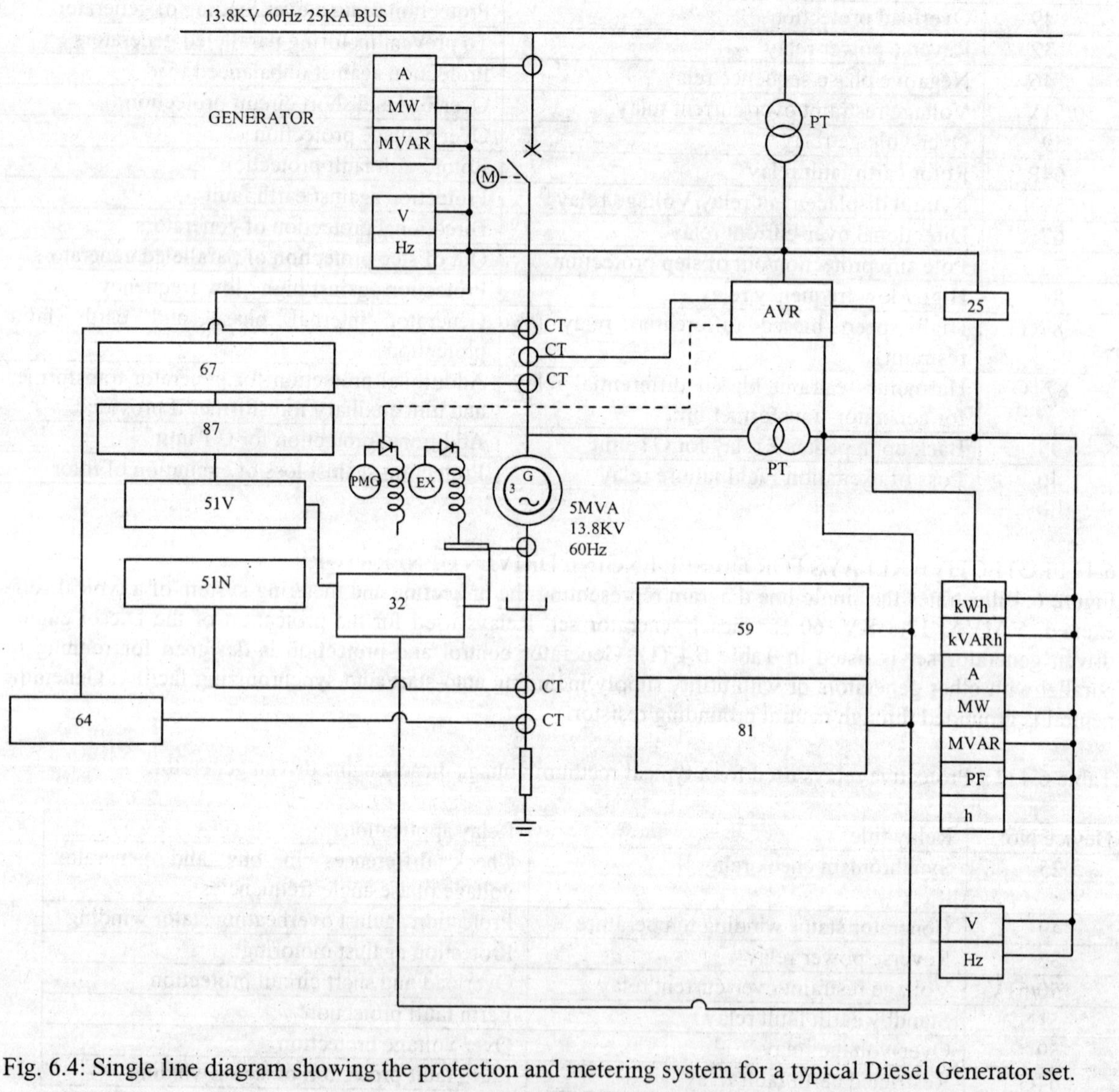

Fig. 6.4: Single line diagram showing the protection and metering system for a typical Diesel Generator set.

6.5 DIFFERENTIAL RELAY FOR GENERATOR PROTECTION (87G).

Differential connection is a connection of current transformer secondary circuits whereby a relay receives the phasor difference of the respective currents entering and leaving the protective apparatus, the C.T polarities being such that the difference of current entering and leaving is zero under normal conditions. Differential current is the phasor difference of CT secondary current resulting from a differential connection. Differential relay responds the difference between incoming and outgoing electrical quantities associated with the protective equipment. In an alternator, differential relay measure the difference of current in the starting end and finishing end of the stator windings.

A high-speed percentage restraint differential relay is used for generator stator winding phase-to-phase faults, phase to earth faults, phase-to-phase and phase to earth fault protection. Relay is biased to prevent mal-operation during an external fault, designed for differential protection of rotating machines and have a percentage bias slope of approximately 10%. Operation of the relay will trip the generator circuit breaker(s), field circuit breaker and shut down the generator prime mover. For low voltage generators unbiased differential relay and for high voltage generators biased differential relay is employed. Saturation of CT magnetic circuit during short-circuit, the differential relay may loss its stability for through faults (external faults). To overcome this difficulty the percentage differential or biased differential relay is used with additional restraining coil. This restraining current prevents the operation during through fault conditions. Harmonic restraint is not required for generator protection. "Restraint" is defined as the action of an input quantity when its presence results in an increase in the threshold value of another input quantity or otherwise limits the operation of the relay. Figure 6.5 (a) illustrates the AC/DC circuit for a typical conventional differential relay suitable for a star connected alternator with six leads brought out.

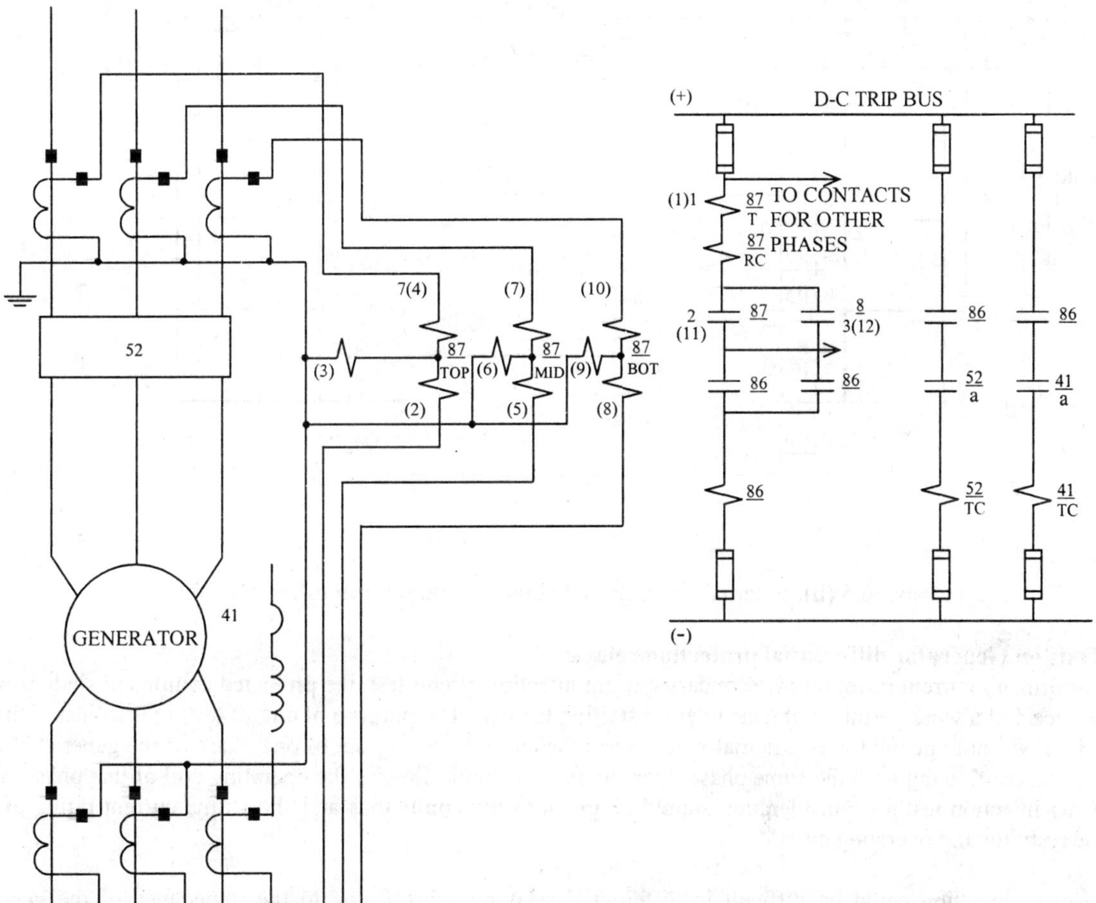

52: Circuit breaker
86: Lockout relay
87: Differential relay
SI: Seal-in unit
T: Target
41: Field circuit breaker

Fig. 6.5 (a): AC/DC circuit of an induction disc type differential relay.

This relay provides protection for rotating electrical machines against transverse faults or longitudinal faults. Upon existence of an internal fault in the protected generator or motor the relay issues a trip command to the circuit breaker connecting the machine to the network and also suppresses the excitation. Percentage restraint permits accurate determination between internal and external faults at high currents. The operating coil of the percentage differential relay operates when the difference between the current in two bias coils exceed above the set value of the relay. When the relay operates lockout relay energizes to trip the circuit breaker.

Figure 6.5 (b) illustrates the external connection diagram of a numerical generator differential relay. Features of numerical protection relays are described in section 5.9 of Chapter # 5. Numerical relays can record and retrieve a report of several past fault trips in order of their occurrence. Each report contains date, time and measured values etc. Programs suitable for use on a personal computer can be used to interrogate the relay and communicate settings to the relay. Additional interfacing software and communication protocols allow a relay to be controlled and interrogated by a digital substation management system and / or SCADA system.

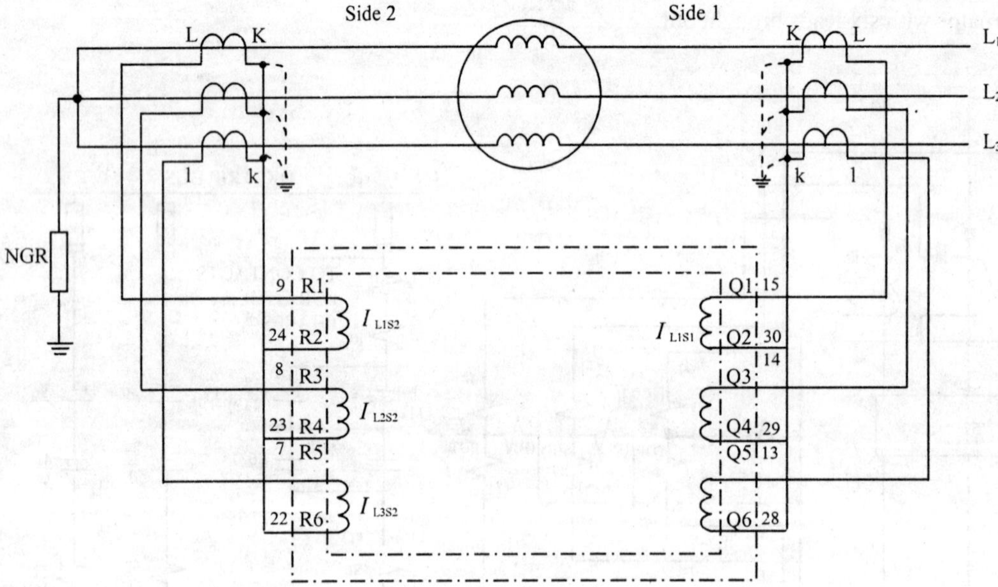

Fig. 6.5 (b): External connection diagram of a numerical differential relay.

Tests on Generator differential protection relays:

For primary current injection or secondary current injection circuit test, the protected equipment shall not be in service and a work permit is obtained before starting the test. The purpose of circuit testing is to insure that the relays will not operate for an external fault. When the current flowing out of one phase of the generator equals the current flowing in to the same phase, then no current should flow in the operating coil of this phase. When using injection testing, consideration should be given to the continuous and short time current rating of both the restraint and operating coils.

Primary injection could be difficult in differential relaying scheme due to the impedance of the generator winding. Most test sets could not inject enough primary current through the generator winding to make the test. However on small generators the test leads can slip-in through the CT to conduct the tests. For large units, circuit test on the secondary of the CT is the best alternative method. Following tests are recommended:

(1) **Pickup and timing test:** Connect the secondary injection test equipments as shown in Figure 6.5 (c). Inject current to the operating coil through restraining coil of any one side (any one phase at a time). Record the pick up current and time. Repeat the test on the other side of the same phase. Repeat the test on the other two CT's also.

(2): **Through fault test:** With the secondary injection test set connected as shown in Figure 6.5 (d), secondary current flowing in the restraint windings and non in the operating coil would ascertain correct connections to the restraint windings. Inject equal current on either sides (same phase) of the restraining coil. Relay could not pickup. Record the current and time observed during the test. Repeat the test on the other two phases also.

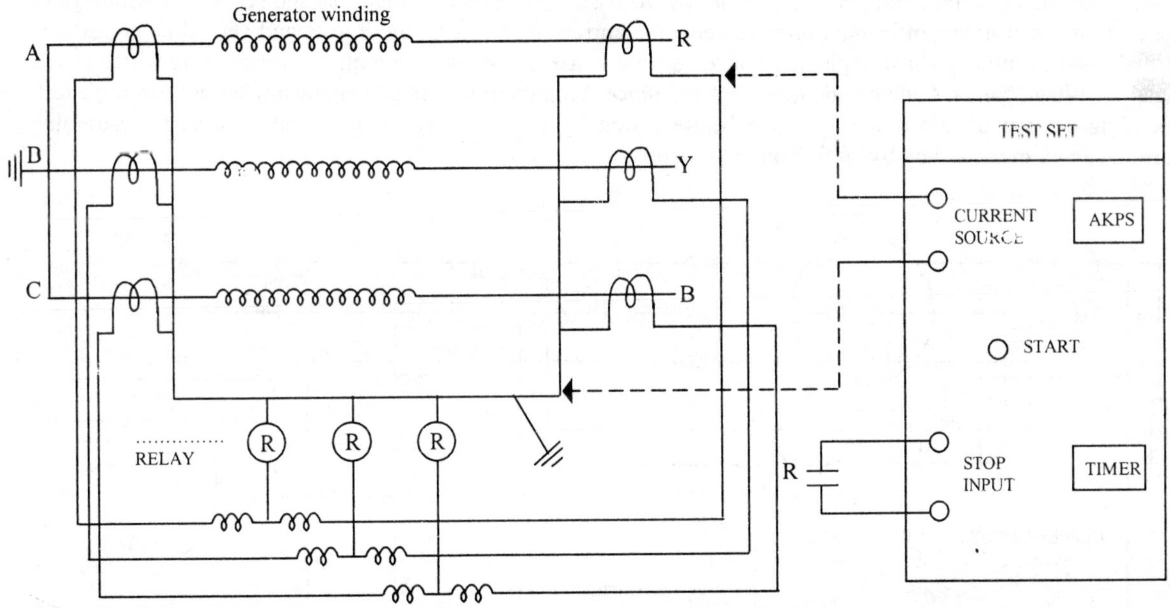

Fig. 6.5 (c): Pickup and timing tests on differential relay.

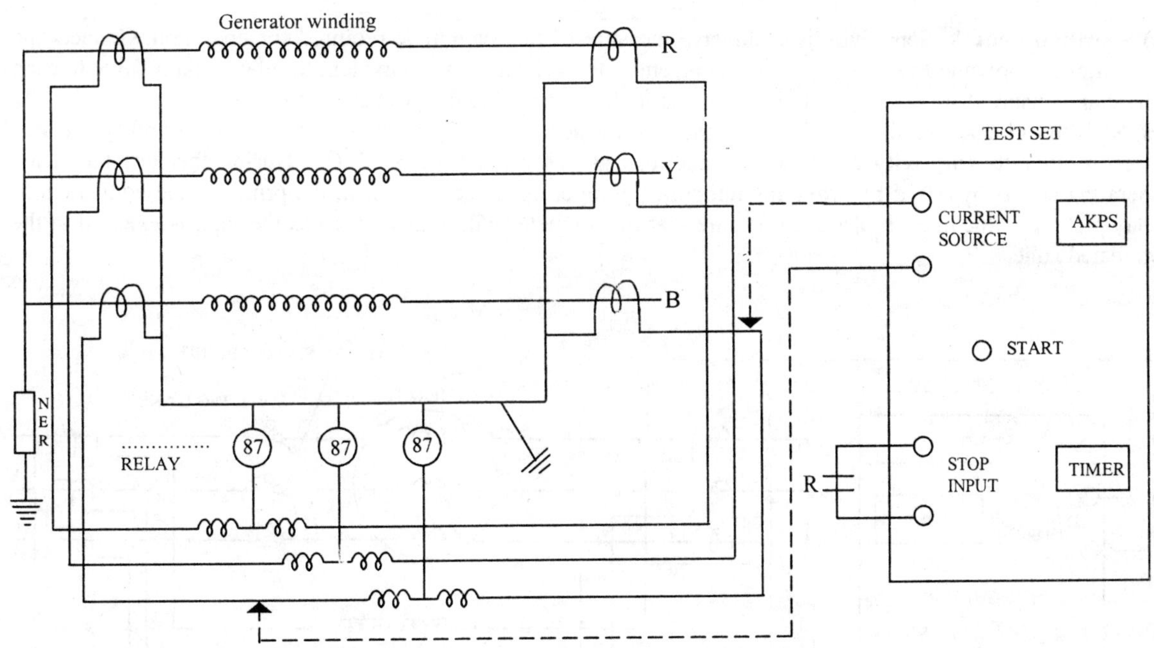

Fig. 6.5 (d): Through fault test on differential relay.

(3) **Slope measurement test:** Slope is the ratio of the threshold operating value to the restraining quantities in a differential relaying scheme. Slope = Operating current / Restraining current. Apply the AC current source to the terminals of the current transformer as shown in Figure 6.5 (e). For each application of current, an ammeter would be used to verify the presence or absence of the current in each current path of the differential scheme, and all values should be recorded in an orderly manner. Discrepancies in readings will indicate improper wiring of the circuit. For each connection of the current source, current flow is being detected only in discrete paths. For each phase-to-neutral connection, the current should be present only in one operate and one restraint

winding of the corresponding phase differential unit. It should be remembered that the secondary windings of the current transformers offer high impedance to the current flow during these tests and should be considered virtual open circuits. A phase angle meter is suggested to use in conjunction with the ammeter, in which case a suitable voltage can be selected and used as a reference throughout the tests. While carrying out the slope test, operating current of differential coil can be measured by bypassing restraining coil. Similarly, restraining current can be measured by bypassing operating coil.

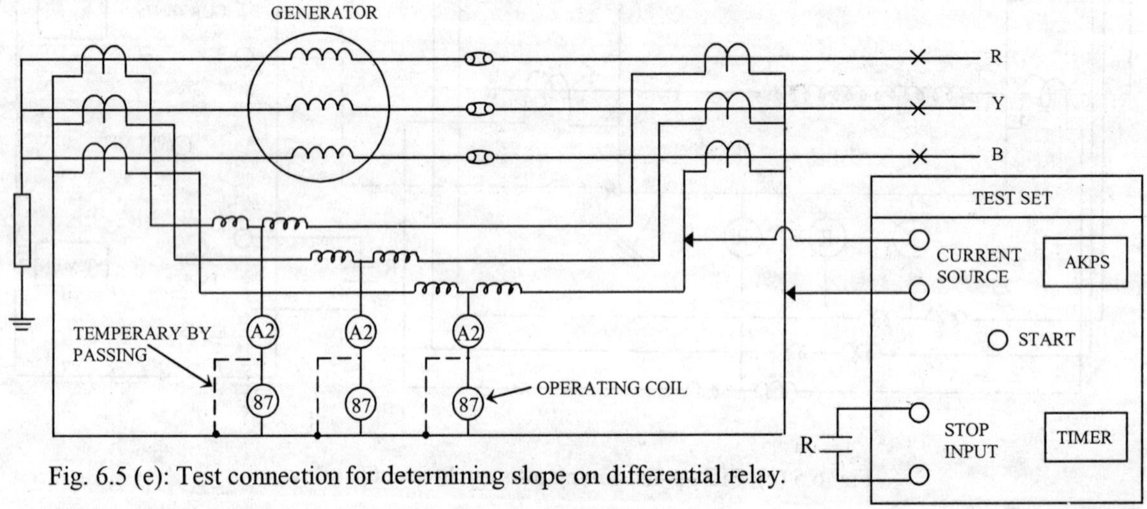

Fig. 6.5 (e): Test connection for determining slope on differential relay.

4) Sensitivity check: Sensitivity is an inverse measure of the magnitude required for operation. Connect the generator as shown in Figure 6.5 (f). Inject current in the primary side equivalent to relay pickup value in each phase and ensure that the relay will pickup as the fault is internal to the protected zone.

(5) Stability check: Stability check is a measure of the security of a protective relay system. Stability check is a test similar to sensitivity check but connections as shown in Figure 6.5 (g). During this test the relay, operating coil is bypassed by providing temporary jumpering. Inject current in the primary side equivalent to relay pick up value in each phase and ensure that the ammeter will indicate zero as the fault is external to the protected zone.

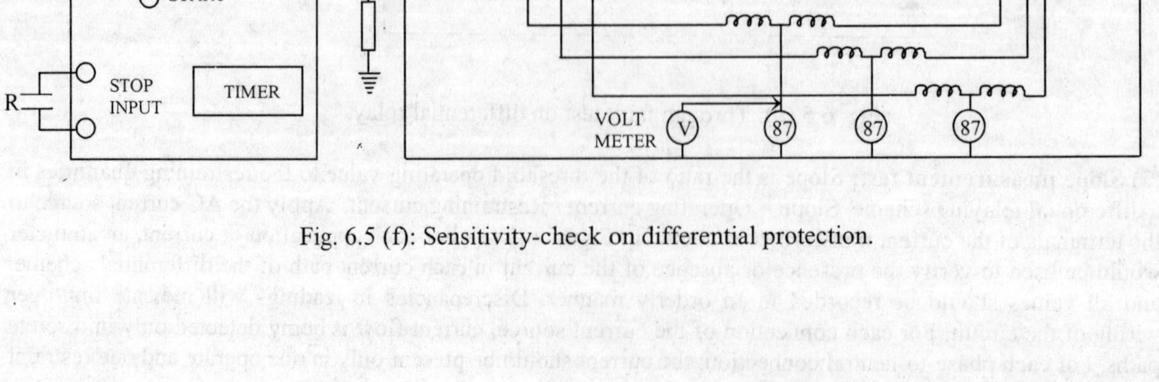

Fig. 6.5 (f): Sensitivity-check on differential protection.

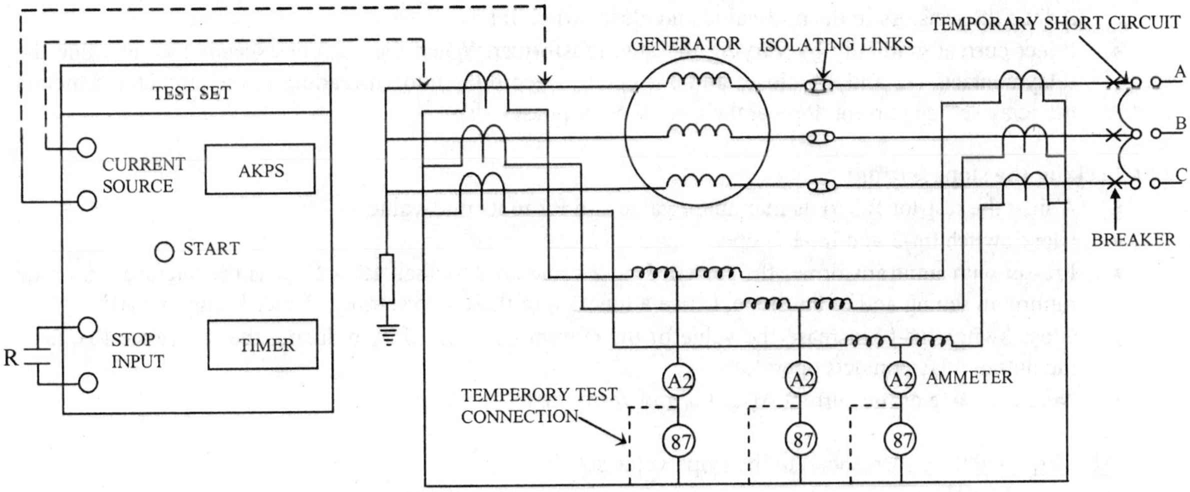

Fig. 6.5 (g): Stability-check on differential protection.

Secondary injection tests on static or digital differential relay:

Figure 6.5 (h) illustrates the test circuit of a typical three-phase static or numerical differential relay by using resistance loading type test materials. Following are the list of items required for this test:
(1) 220 V single phase isolating transformer; (2) Adjustable single phase autotransformer; (3) Two numbers digital AC ammeters; (4) Variable resistors RΔ (470 Ω for 1 A version relay and 100 Ω for 5 A relay); (5) Variable resistor R2 (47 Ω for 1 A version relay and 10 Ω for 5 A relay); (6) DC auxiliary supply for static relay; (7) Ohmmeter (8) Switches Int-1 and Int-2.

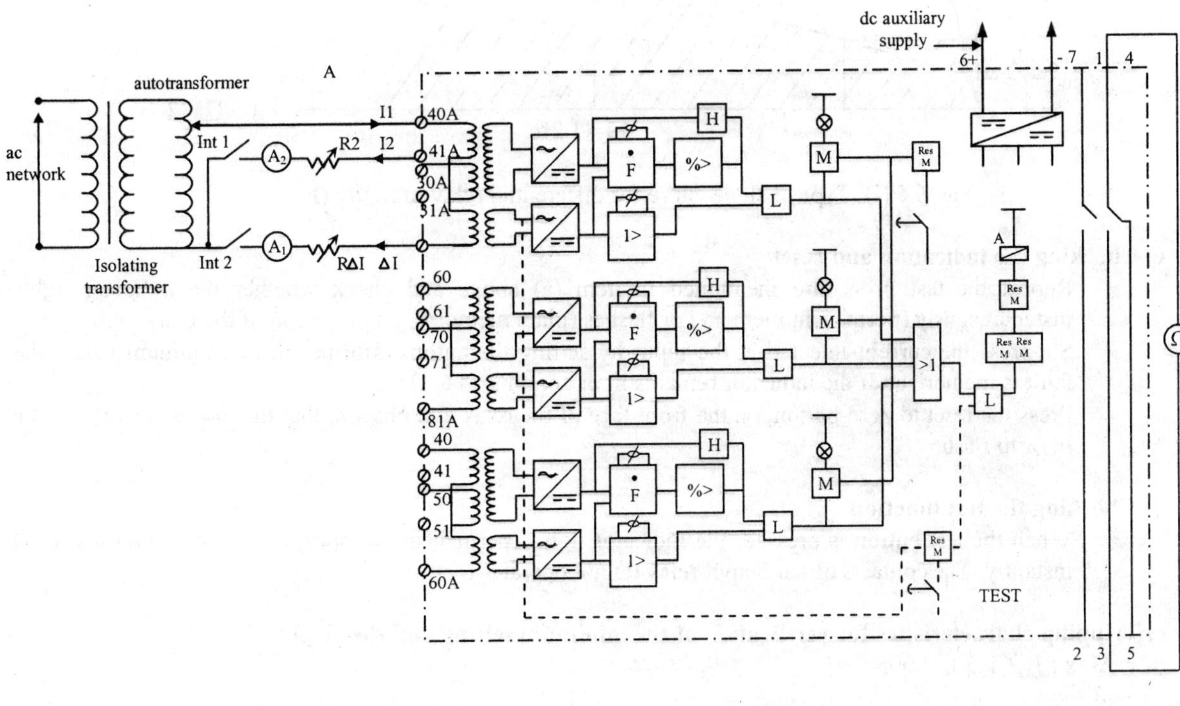

Fig. 6.5 (h): Test connection for a typical static differential relay (Courtesy, Stromberg).

a) Checking the minimum setting and operation of the relay contacts:

- Connect the relay as shown in figure (h) and switch on the power supply with both switches open. Adjust the resistors in the mid-value and close switch Int-1.
- Inject current gradually by varying the autotransformer. When the current exceeds the set value the relay contacts 1-2 and 4-5 closes and 3-4 opens. Record the current reading in the ammeter, which is the relay setting current. Repeat the test on other phases also.

b) Checking the slope setting:

- Adjust the resistor RΔ to its maximum value and R2 to its mid-value.
- Close switch Int-2 and Int-1 is open.
- Pre-set with autotransformer the current I_2 to a value not less than 1.2 x I_0. I_0 is the intersection of the minimum setting and of the slope, hence a function of these two settings [Refer Figure 6.5 (i)].
- Close switch Int-1. Increase the value of the current ΔI injected by reducing the resistance RΔ, until the output relay contacts operate.
- Note the value of the current ΔI and I_2 and verify that:

$$\frac{\Delta I}{I} = \frac{2\,(\Delta I - 0.005)}{2\,I_2 + \Delta I}$$ correspond to the slope value set.

Perform the same test for other two phases also

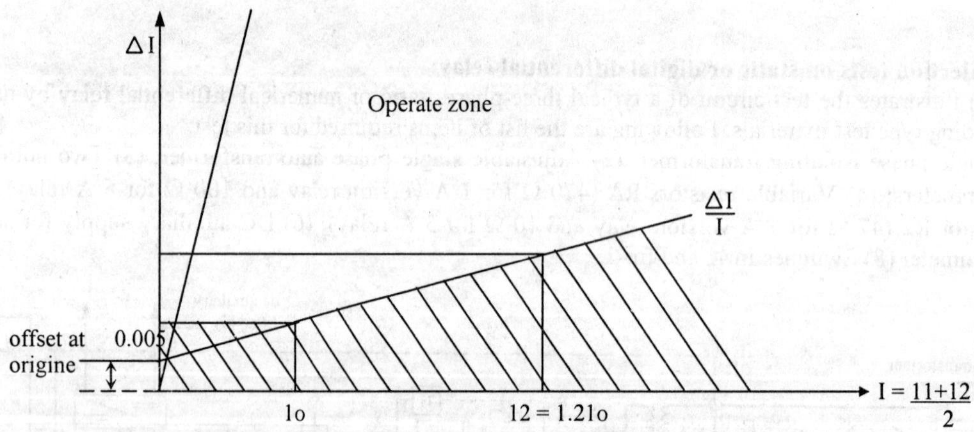

Fig. 6.5 (i): Typical slope curve for differential relay in figure (h).

c) Checking the indication and reset:

- Repeat the test procedure mentioned in item (a) above and check whether the indicator lights instantaneously (permanent memory) or flashes (plain memory), on operation of the relay.
- Suppress the current injected at the input by setting the autotransformer to its minimum value; the fault is memorized if the indicator remains lit or continuous to flash.
- Press the reset to zero-button, on the front face of the relay and observe that the indicator ceases to be lit or to flash.

d) Checking the test function:

- When the test button is pressed: the indicator lights (permanent memory) or flashes (plain memory) instantly. The contacts of the output relay do not operate.

e) Tripping characteristics for verification of the minimum setting and the slope:

$$\Delta I = \frac{\Delta I}{I} \times \left[\frac{I_1 + I_2}{2}\right] + 0.005$$

$$\frac{\Delta I}{I} = \frac{I - 0.005}{(I_1 + I_2)/2} = \frac{2\,(\Delta I - 0.005)}{I_1 + I_2}$$

Secondary injection tests on induction disc type differential relay.

Figure 6.5 (J) shows the internal connection diagram of an induction disc type single-phase differential relay (General Electric type CFD). Terminals 5 and 7 are the CT inputs and terminal 6 is the common wire connected to the CT. Secondary injection test connection is illustrated in Figure 6.5 (k). S1 and S2 are the two independent switches; R1 and R2 are adjustable resistors; I_1, I_2 and I_0 are digital ammeters.

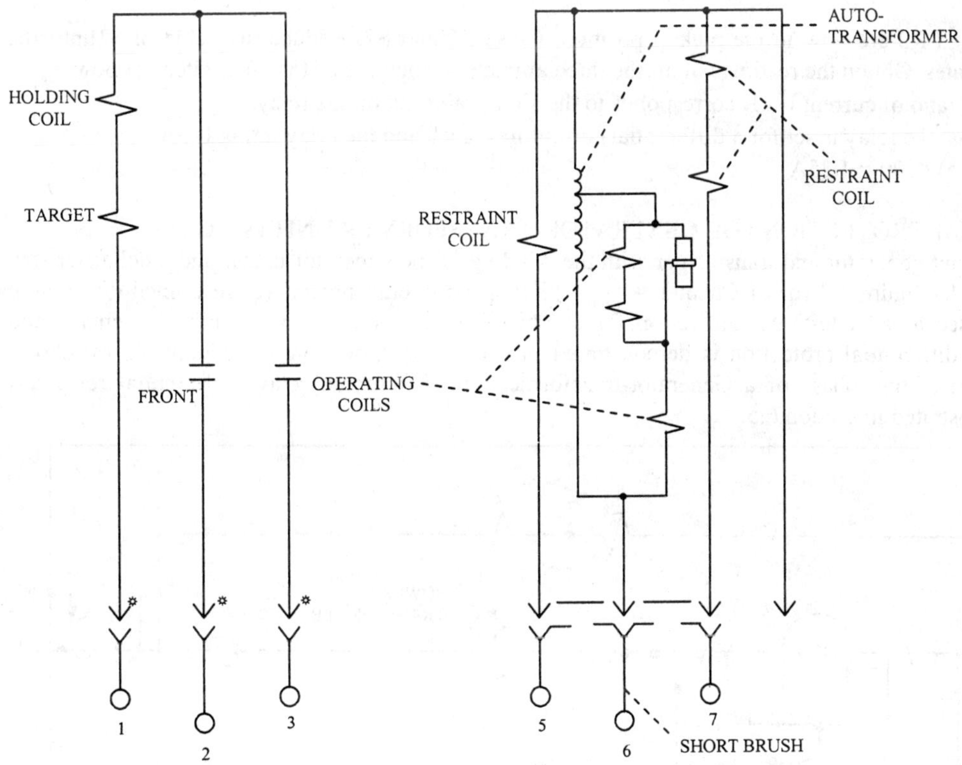

Fig. 6.5 (J): Internal circuit diagram of induction disc type differential relay (Courtesy, General Electric).

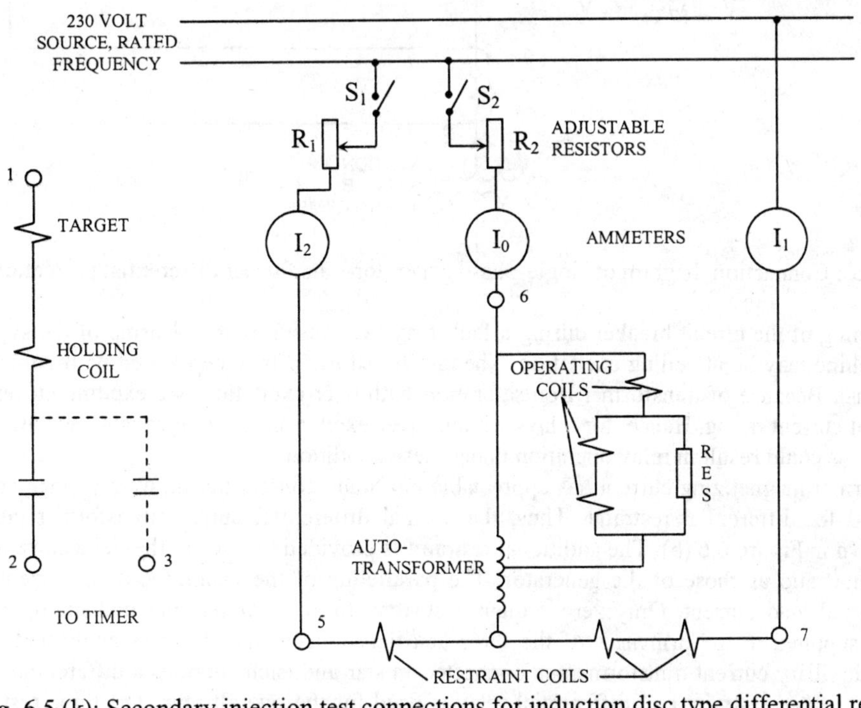

Fig. 6.5 (k): Secondary injection test connections for induction disc type differential relay

a) Checking pickup:

- Close-switch S1 and adjust variable resistor R1 until the relay pickup. Observe the target element dropped during pickup. Keep R1 in the same position and open switch S1. Reset the target.
- Close-switch S2 and adjust variable resistor R2 until the relay pickup. Observe the target element dropped during pickup. Keep R2 in the same position and switch off S2. Reset the target.

b) Slope check.

- Both RI and R2 are now in the pickup position. Close S1 and S2. Reduce the value of S1until the relay operates. Obtain the readings of all the three ammeters when the test is on. Switch off power.
- Verify the ratio of current I_1 / I_2 corresponds to the slope value set on the relay.
- Assume that the relay is set for a differential current Id = 25% and the relay rating I=5A
- Id = (25 x 5) / 100 = 1.25A

6.6 DIFFERENTIAL PROTECTION FOR GENERATOR-TRANSFORMER UNIT (87TG).

This consists of a unit generator and transformer with the winding of the generator in star and a delta star step up transformer [Refer figure 1.2 (q) of Chapter # 1]. A high speed overall percentage restrained differential protection relay used as an additional protection for combined generator transformer unit. Percentage and harmonic restraint differential protection is demonstrated in Chapter # 7, section 7.7. Figure 6.6 (a) shows connection diagram of one phase of a Generator-transformer unit differential relay. Differential relay test methods are demonstrated in section 6.5.

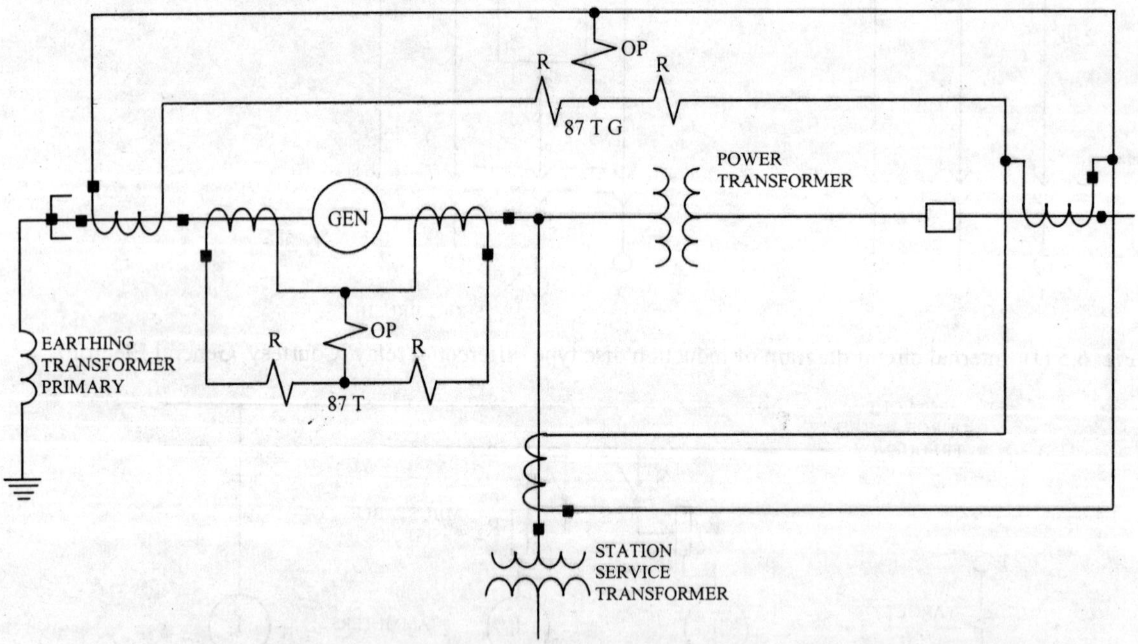

Fig. 6.6 (a): Connection diagram of single-phase generator-transformer differential protection.

A sudden tripping of the circuit breaker during a fault may be, caused by the clearing of the system fault and hence the machine may be at ceiling excitation. The unit transformer may be excited with voltages exceeding 130% of normal. Because of transformer iron saturation with over-excitation, the exciting current can exceed 25% of the unit current rating. Hence, for relays without over-excitation restraint capability, normal differential relay connections could result in relay operation under these conditions.

As the transformer magnetizing current has appreciable harmonic content during over-voltage conditions, this current is used for differential restraint. Thus, the normal differential current transformer connections are altered as shown in Figure 6.6 (b). The additional restraint is provided by, inside-the-delta current transformers having the same ratio as those of the generator. The paralleling of the inside-the-delta current transformers eliminates normal load current. Only zero sequence current, third harmonic and odd multiples of the third harmonic are supplied to the primaries of the three auxiliary current transformers connected in series. The output of the auxiliary current transformers is connected in star and each supplies a differential relay restraint coil. Normally a three-restraint coil differential relay is used for the overall unit. The three restraint coils are supplied from generator, main transformer high voltage side and station service transformer CT's. To provide separate relay restraint from the inside delta current transformers, the station service transformer differential current CT's are now paralleled with the generator current transformers.

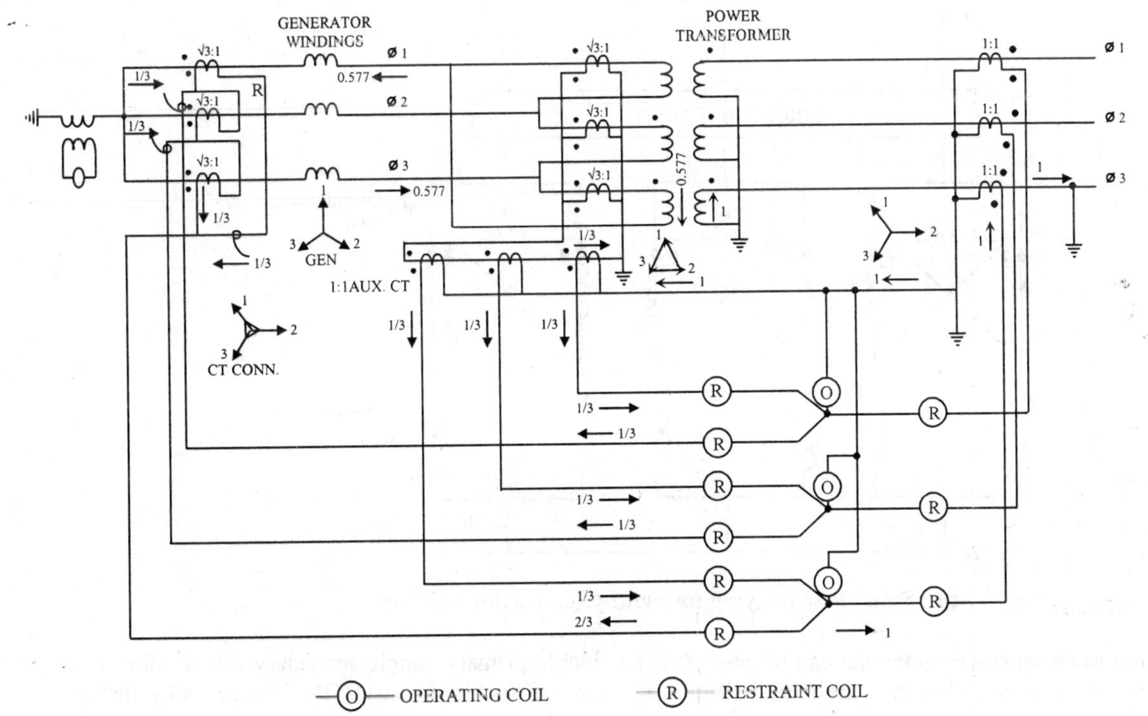

Fig. 6.6 (b): Differential restraint scheme for overall protection of unit generator-transformer.

The conventional differential connections have star connected current transformers on the delta winding side and delta connected current transformers in the star winding side of the power transformer. Thus the delta current transformers on the higher voltage side normally act as zero sequence filters. However, the zero-sequence current is now inserted in the lower voltage side connections and it also shall be introduced in the higher voltage connections. This is done by, connecting the high side current transformers in star. Then for proper phasing relationship, the lower voltage side current transformers are connected in delta.

6.7 TRANSVERSE DIFFERENTIAL PROTECTION FOR TURN-TO-TURN FAULT (87TD).

Differential relaying demonstrated in section 6.5 and 6.6 will not respond to faults between turns because there is no difference in the currents at the ends of a winding with shorted turns; a turn fault would have to burn through the major insulation to ground or to another phase before it could be detected. Transverse differential relays are used for generator stator winding inter-turn (turn-to-turn) fault protection. Turn fault protection has been devised for multi-circuit generators [two circuits (windings) per phase connected in parallel], and is used quite extensively in large low speed hydroelectric generators because the coils of high speed steam-turbine generators usually have one circuit per phase, which does not require turn-fault protection. The conventional method for providing turn fault protection is called "split phase relaying" and is illustrated in Figure 6.7 (a). Transverse differential relay operates on cross differential principle. The current transformer primaries are inserted in the parallel winding paths and the secondary circuits are cross connected. During inter-turn fault in the phase winding, the out of balance current of CT secondary circuits flows through the relay. Such a protection is extremely sensitive.

If there are more than two circuits per phase, they are divided in to two equal groups of parallel circuits with a CT for each group. Split phase relaying will operate for any type of short circuit in the generator windings, although it does not provide as good protection as differential relaying for some faults. An inverse-time over-current relay is used for split-phase relaying rather than an instantaneous percentage differential relay, in order to get the required sensitivity. For its use to be justified, split phase relaying must respond when a single turn is short-circuited. Moreover; the relay should not respond to any transient unbalance occurred during an external fault. If percentage restraint were used to prevent such undesired operation, the restraint caused by load current would make the relay too insensitive at full load. Consequently, time is relied on to prevent operation on transients.

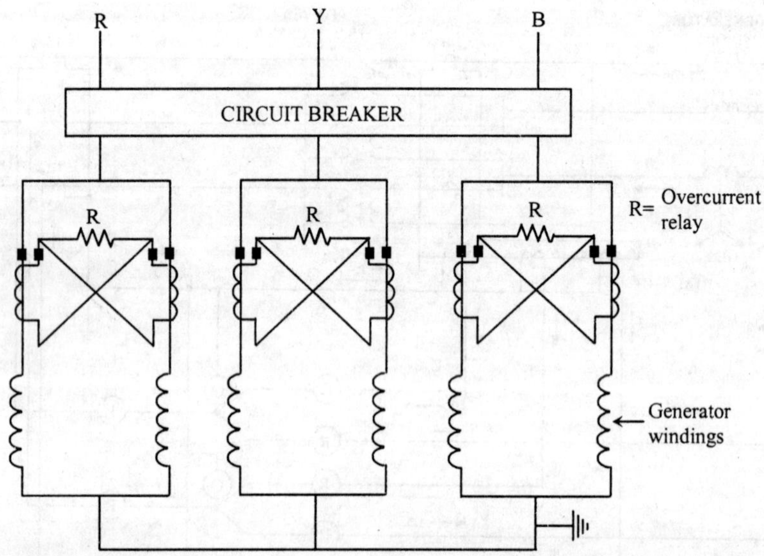

Fig. 6.7 (a): Split phase relaying for multi-circuit stator winding.

Faster and more sensitive protection can be provided if a double-primary, single secondary CT, as shown in Figure 6.7 (b) is used rather than the two separate CT's. Such a double-primary CT eliminates all transient unbalances except those existing in the primary currents themselves. With such CT's and with close attention in the generator winding design to minimize normal unbalance, very sensitive instantaneous protection is possible.

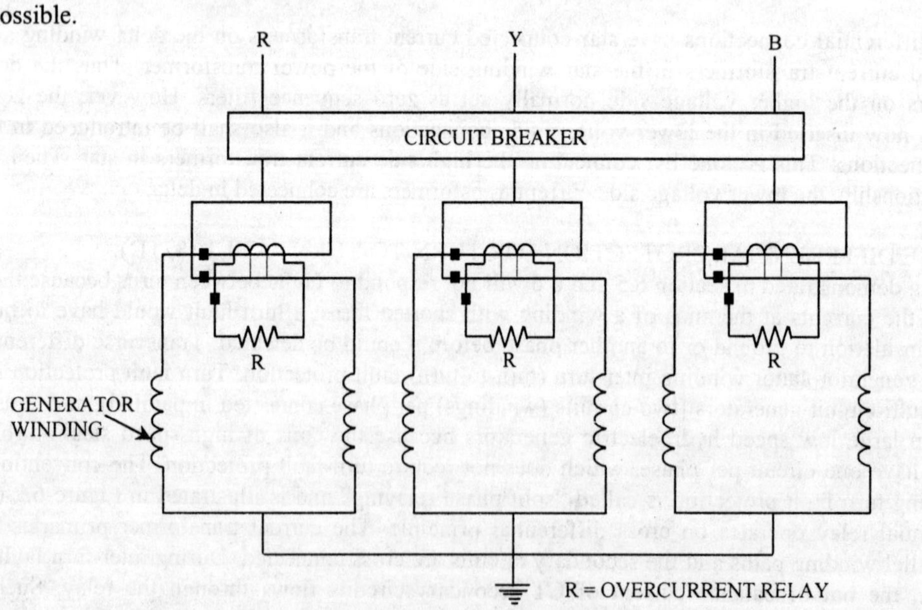

Fig. 6.7 (b): Split phase relaying with double primary current transformers.

6.8 GENERATOR MANAGEMENT RELAY FOR OVERALL GENERATOR PROTECTION

Generator management relay demonstrated in this section is **General Electric 489 relay**. This microprocessor controlled numerical relay provides overall protection, metering, and monitoring functions. This relay can be used as primary or backup protection on synchronous or induction generators of 25, 50 or 60 Hertz alternating current.

Monitoring functions.

Relay display following metering functions:

1. Current R, Y, B phases
2. Voltage RY, YB, BR
3. Power KVA, KVAr, KW
4. Energy MWh and MVArh
5. Power factor
6. Frequency
7. Demand and maximum demand functions include display current, power (KW, KVA and KVAr)

Figure 6.8 (a) illustrates the functional block diagram of Generator overall protection. Following are the protection incorporated.

ANSI device number and protection:

12: Over-speed
21: Distance
24: Volts per hertz
27: Under-voltage
27/50: Inadvertent energization
32: Reverse power/Low forward
38: Bearing over-temperature
39: Bearing vibration (analog inputs)
40: Loss of excitation (impedance)
40Q: Loss of field (reactive power)
46: Negative sequence over-current
47: Voltage phase reversal
49: Stator thermal protection (RTD)
50: High set phase over-current
50BF: Breaker failure detection
50/51 G: Ground over-current
51VR: Voltage restrained over-current
59: Over voltage protection
59G/27TN: 100% stator ground
60 FL: VT fuses failure
67G: Ground directional relay
76: Over excitation (analog input)
81: Over/under frequency
86: Electrical lockout
87G: Percentage differential
STL: Sequential tripping logic
TCS: Trip coil supervision

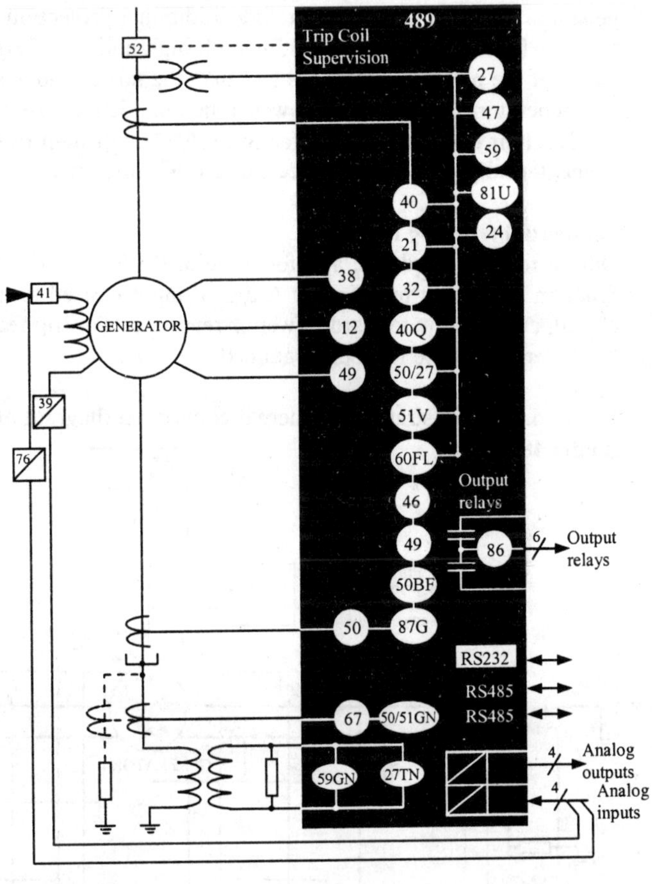

Fig. 6.8 (a): Functional block diagram of Generator management relay (Courtesy, General Electric)

Machine fault protection:

Percentage differential element (87G) is the primary protection against machine faults. Instantaneous over-current element (50) protects the machine from system faults. In addition to a ground over-current element (51G), a VT input is provided to monitor the machine neutral voltage. The generator management relay can detect ground directional (67G) by comparing the angle between neutral voltage and ground current to determine whether a ground fault is within the generator. 100% stator ground fault protection is provided through an over-voltage element (59G) that operates on fundamental neutral voltage only and an adaptive element (27TN) that operates on third harmonic voltage ratio at the generator terminals and the generator neutral. Monitoring of stator RTD's provides thermal protection (49) to stator windings. RTD inputs can be configured to monitor and protect against bearing over temperature (38) conditions. The programmable analog inputs can be configured to monitor bearing vibration transducers. Alarm or trip functions may be configured for vibration protection (39).

Protection elements associated with the operation of the excitation includes over excitation (24) measuring volts/Hertz, under voltage (27), and over voltage (59) Definite time or inverse time curves may used to activate alarm or trip functions. Loss of field protection is accommodated using loss of excitation (40) and reactive power (40Q). Rotor heating in generators due to negative sequence current is a well-defined concept. A generator should have a rating for both continuous and also short time operation when negative sequence current components are present as defined by the equation $K = I^2 t$. Three voltage restrained over current elements (51V) provides backup protection for system faults. The pickup levels for the inverse-time curves are adjusted in a fixed relationship with the measured phase-to-phase voltage. High set phase over current (50) also provides backup protection to other elements.

Distance protection (21) implements two zone of Mho phase-to- phase protection (total of six elements), which is intended to backup for primary line protection. The elements make use of the neutral end currents and the generator terminal voltage to provide additional protection for internal and unit transformer faults. Alarm and tripping functions are provided for both high and low frequency (81). On a total or partial loss of the prime mover if the power generated is less than the no-load losses of the machine real power will start flowing in to the generator. The reverse power function (32) is used to trip the generator when it begins motoring. **Inadvertent energization protection (50/27) will help to limit the damage that can occur if the generator is accidentally placed in service while it is shutdown.**

Sequential tripping logic:
During routine shutdown, and for some of the less critical trips, it may be desirable to use the sequential trip function to prevent over speed. A digital input is used to monitor the turbine valve status. When the valve is closed, either a low forward power or reverse power trip feature will trip the breaker once the generator output has fallen below the level programmed.

Figure 6.8 (b) illustrates the external connection diagram of **General Electric Generator management relay model 489)**

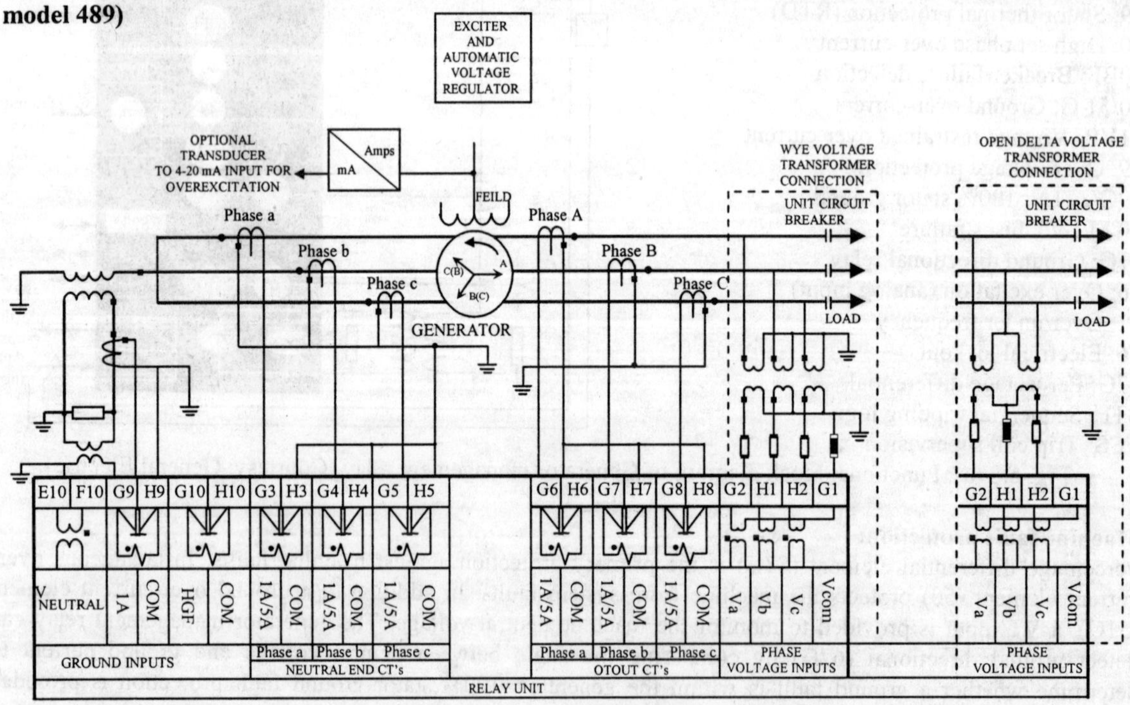

Fig. 6.8 (b): External connection diagram of Generator management relay (Courtesy, General Electric).

6.9 VOLTAGE RESTRAINT OVER-CURRENT RELAY FOR GENERATOR PROTECTION (50/51V).

In this relay the over-current unit operating value is a function of the applied voltage. The relay is set so that maximum load current will not cause operation with the minimum expected system operating voltage. During fault conditions, the reduced voltage causes less restraint and the relay will operate at a lower current, which varies with the voltage magnitude. There may be an application problem with this relay if the system voltage during a limited fault is not reduced substantially.

Conventional voltage restraint over current relay contains an induction disc, which is influenced by the magnetic fields of two electromagnets. The current actuated electromagnet produces torque on the disc to close the relay contact and is known as the operating coil. The potential actuated electromagnet produces torque on the disc to open the relay contact and is known as the restraint coil. When the voltage applied to the restraint coil reduces, a smaller amount of current is required to pickup the relay. Relay is used for over-current protection of generators. Voltage restrained over-current relays distinguish between an un-cleared system fault and a generator fault.

In many instances the generator synchronous reactance's causes the sustained fault current to be lower than full load current, depends on the load condition before the fault or the performance of the automatic voltage regulator. By providing a voltage restraint over current relay, this problem can be solved. This relay operates on one curve under overload conditions when the system voltage is normal. The relay operates on another curve under fault conditions, when the system voltage falls below a predetermined value. The characteristics of the relay behave on the basis of the voltage and current at the generator terminals. Relay operates even if the sustained fault current is lower than the full load current. Voltage restrained over-current relay connection diagram and trip circuit is illustrated in Figure 6.9 (a).

Regardless of the amount of current passing through the operating coil of the over-current unit, no operation takes place unless the under voltage unit has "dropped out". This means that the over-current unit may be set to operate less than full load current when the voltage falls below a predetermined value. Conversely, the over current unit will not operate as long as the voltage is above the predetermined value.

LEGEND

52: Circuit breaker
OC: Current operated coil
VC: Voltage restraint coil
SI: Seal-in with target
TC: Trip coil
86: Lockout relay
41: Field breaker
51: Voltage restraint over current relay

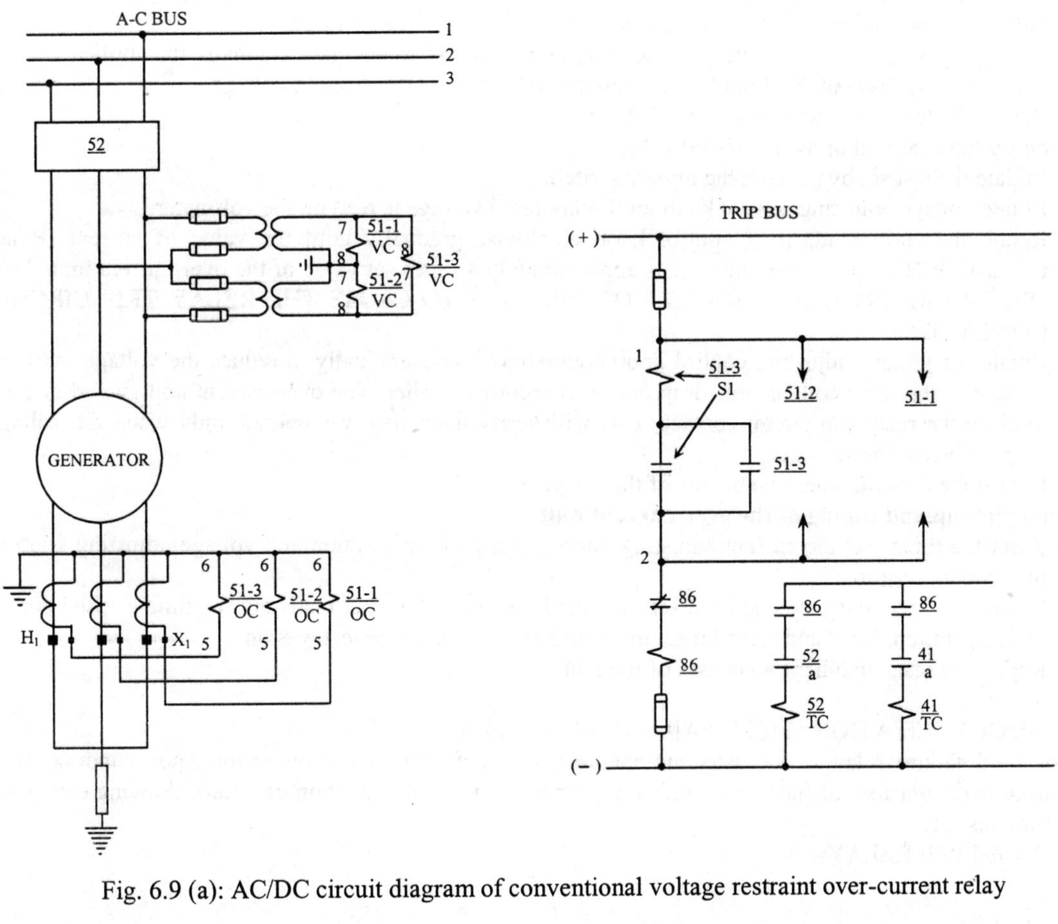

Fig. 6.9 (a): AC/DC circuit diagram of conventional voltage restraint over-current relay

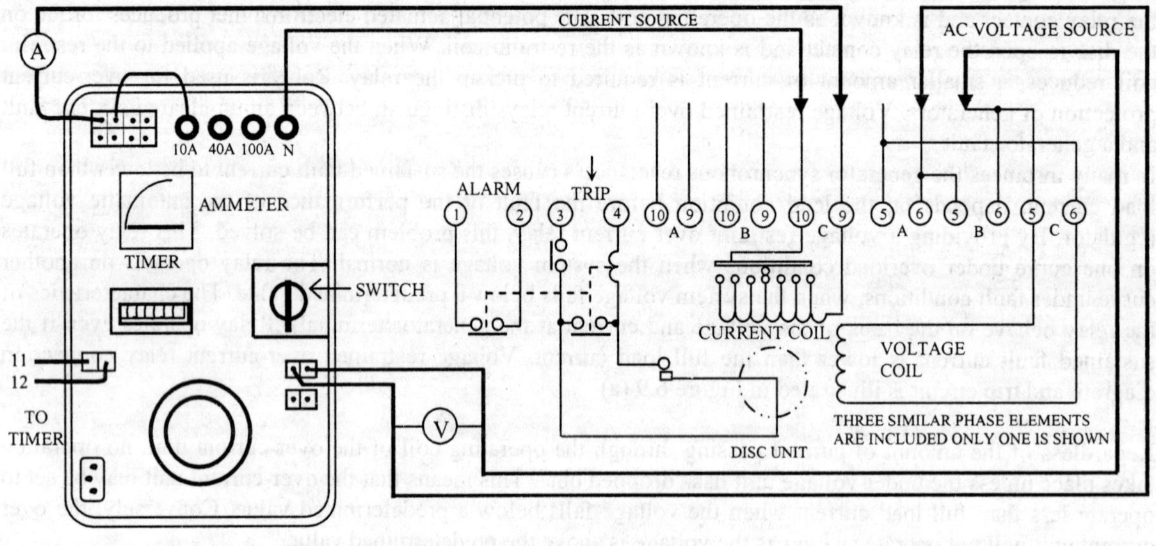

Fig. 6.9 (b): Test diagram for induction disc type voltage restraint over-current relay.

Test procedure: Connect the secondary injection test set as illustrated in Figure 6.9 (b).

(1) Testing pick-up and dropout of under voltage unit:

a) Initiate the test set by pushing the initiate switch.

b) Rotate the AC voltage adjusting control knob clockwise to increase gradually the voltage applied to the voltage unit of the relay (Relay terminals 5-6) until the relay operate (slightly above the set voltage). Read and record this value of the voltage as the pick-up voltage.

c) Rotate the AC voltage adjusting control knob anticlockwise to decrease gradually the applied voltage until the relay dropout. Read and record this voltage value as the dropout voltage.

d) Repeat the tests on other two phases of the relay.

(2) Testing voltage control of over-current relay:

a) Initiate the test set by pushing the initiate switch.

b) Rotate voltage adjusting control knob until relay rated voltage is read on the voltmeter.

c) Rotate the current adjusting control knob clockwise gradually until the value of current (Relay terminals 9-10) read on the ammeter is approximately 4 times set value of the over-current unit. THE OVER-CURRENT UNIT SHOULD NOT OPERATE TO CLOSE THE RELAY TRIP CIRCUIT CONTACT.

d) Rotate the voltage adjusting control knob counterclockwise gradually to reduce the voltage until the voltage to the relay coil become drop out level recorded earlier. The over-current unit should operate to close the relay trip circuit contact. This will verify that relay will operate only when the voltage dropout below the set value.

e) Repeat the tests on other two phases of the relay.

(3) Testing pick-up and timing of the over-current unit:

a) Reset the timer; set the current adjusting knob in the pick-up position and voltage-adjusting knob in the dropout position.

b) Initiate the secondary injection test set, the relay operates and timer reads out the time elapsed during relay operation. Read and record the current and voltage when the test was on.

c) Repeat the tests on other two phases of the relay.

6.10 LOSS OF EXCITATION / FIELD FAILURE RELAY (40).

Generator field failure relay is for detecting the loss of excitation to the generator rotor winding. In a synchronized generator loss of field may cause the generator to run as induction generator drawing excitation current from bus bar.

IMPEDANCE TYPE RELAY:

The Loss of excitation relay [Alsthom type TZG] shown in Figure 6.10 (a) is a capacitive impedance relay designed for the protection of synchronous machines against field failure. The relay supervises the ratio V/I of the voltage of a winding to the current, which it delivers. The input quantities are a compound voltage and two-phase current. This type of connection gives better insensitivity of the relay to phenomena other than field failure (for example, oscillations of the machine). Field failure in a synchronous machine due to poor excitation or a fault in the field winding or circuit, can lead rapidly to harmful overheating of the rotor.

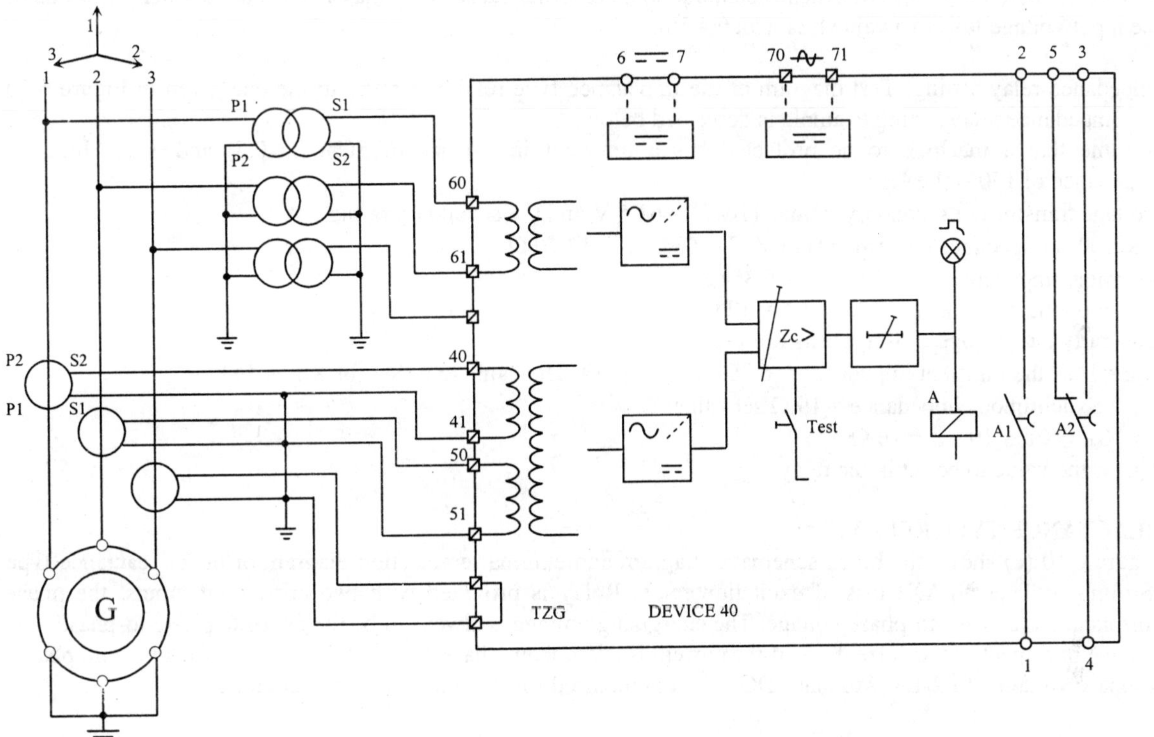

Fig. 6.10 (a): Block schematic diagram of impedance type loss of excitation relay (Courtesy, Alsthom).

The voltage provides electrical isolation and converts the voltage to that required for the electronics that voltage is caused to lag by 90° by a phase-shift circuit. The current transformer delivers the difference between the phase currents. The image of the resistance's which will delimit the tripping area of the impedance diagram. The voltages V and I are added to obtain the image of the vector CM, where C represents the center of the tripping circle. The signal is rectified and compared with the rectified signal. If the synchronous machine operating point is within the tripping circle shown in figure 6.10 (b), a start command is issued to the timing equipment. On expiry of the preset time the relay contact will close and initiate trip signal to the circuit breaker.

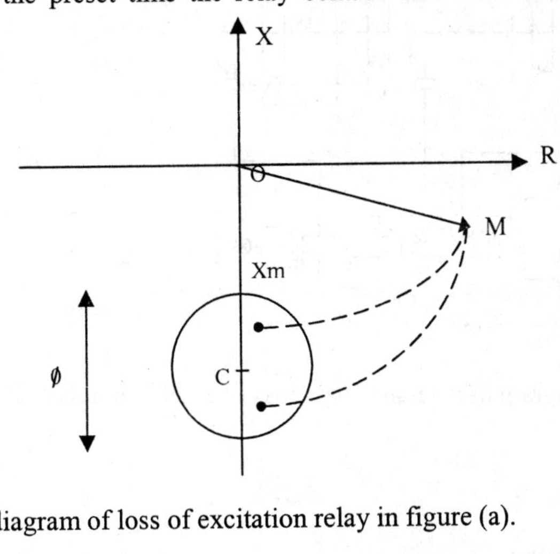

Fig. 6.10 (b): Impedance diagram of loss of excitation relay in figure (a).

Operating characteristic: The impedance of a synchronous machine winding can be represented by a vector, which is an image of the ratio V / I. In the event of field failure, the alternator functions as a synchronous generator and takes reactive power from the network. The end of the vector moves towards the X-axis following a trajectory, which is a function of the manner in which the field failure occurs. The boundary of the operating area is a circle centered on the X axis; it must enclose the ends of all possible trajectories. When the characteristic has been well selected, the relay remains insensitive to all phenomena other than field failure (loss of excitation) i.e. loss of synchronism due to an external cause. The relay is locked out when the value of the input voltage falls to a value less than 0.4 Vn.

Impedance relay setting: Test diagram of the impedance type relay is similar to the one given in Figure 6.10 (e). Impedance relay setting example is described below.
Assume that a machine to be protected has a transient impedance of 50% (i.e.0.5) and a synchronous impedance of 150% (i.e.1.5).
Voltage transformer secondary rating: $110/\sqrt{3} = 63.5$ V and CT secondary rating 5 A.
The 100% impedance corresponds to $V / I = 63.5 / 5 = 12.70\ \Omega$
Transient impedance = $12.70 \times 0.5 = 6.35\ \Omega$
Synchronous impedance = $12.7 \times 1.5 = 19.05$
Generally the settings chosen are as follows:
Xm = Half the transient impedance = $6.35 / 2 = 3.175\ \Omega$. The value to be set for Xm is $3\ \Omega$
X_M = Synchronous impedance = $19\ \Omega$ set value.
$\phi = X_M - Xm = 19 - 3 = 16\ \Omega$
This is the value to be set in the relay.

REACTANCE TYPE RELAY:
Figure 6.10 (c) shows the block schematic diagram and external connection diagram of under reactance type (Stromberg Type SPAX) loss of excitation relay. Relay is provided with two energizing inputs, the phase current and the phase-to-phase voltage. The energizing voltage is always to be the opposite phase-to-phase voltage in respect of the current, i.e. if the current is taken from phase-L1 the voltage is to be taken from phase-to-phase voltage of L2-L3. Auxiliary DC power is required for the relay electronic circuits.

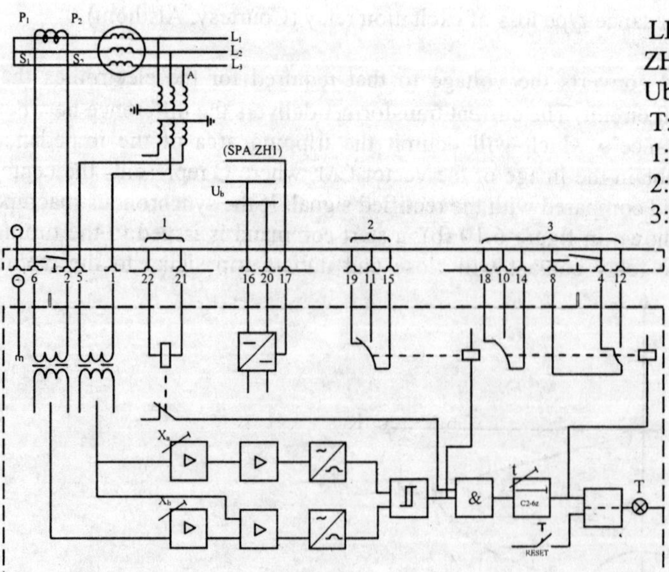

LEGEND:
ZH1: Electronic voltage supervision relay.
Ub: Auxiliary DC supply for Electronics.
T: Operation indicator
1: Blocking input
2: Starting output
3: Delayed trip and alarm output

Fig. 6.10 (c): Block schematic diagram of reactance type loss of excitation relay (Courtesy, Stromberg)

The area of operation of the relay is the area inside the periphery of the circle shown in Figure 6.10 (d). The circle itself is defined by the settings Xa and Xb, which are the points of intersection between the periphery of the circle and the negative X-axis. The setting Xa defines the offset of the circle from its locus and setting Xb defines the diameter of the circle after Xa being set.

The diameter of the characteristic circle is D = 2r = Xb – Xa.

The locus of the circle is located along the negative X-axis in a point defined $P = Xa + \frac{(Xb - Xa)}{2}$

During loss of field supply of a synchronous machine, the reactance locus of the machine rapidly moves in to the circle, depending on the settings of the relay. When the relay starts, the starting output relay picks-up and after the set time the relay contact closes provided the fault is persists. The operation of the relay can be prohibited during power swing or short circuit by means of an external control signal fed to the relay blocking input.

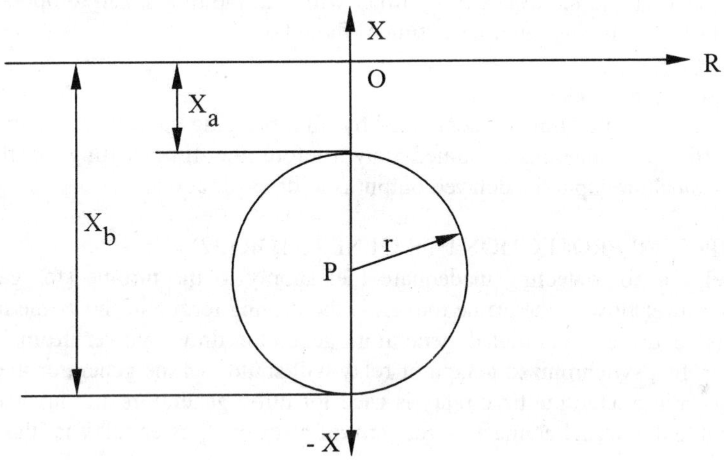

Fig. 6.10 (d): Operation characteristic of reactance type loss of excitation relay illustrate in figure (c).

Typical test connection for loss of excitation relay is shown in Figure 6.10 (e). An accurate measurement of the relay-operating characteristic should require a test set with adjustable phase angle between voltage and current. Phase shifter is being used for adjusting the phase angle during the test. Test procedure for under reactance relay is as follows.

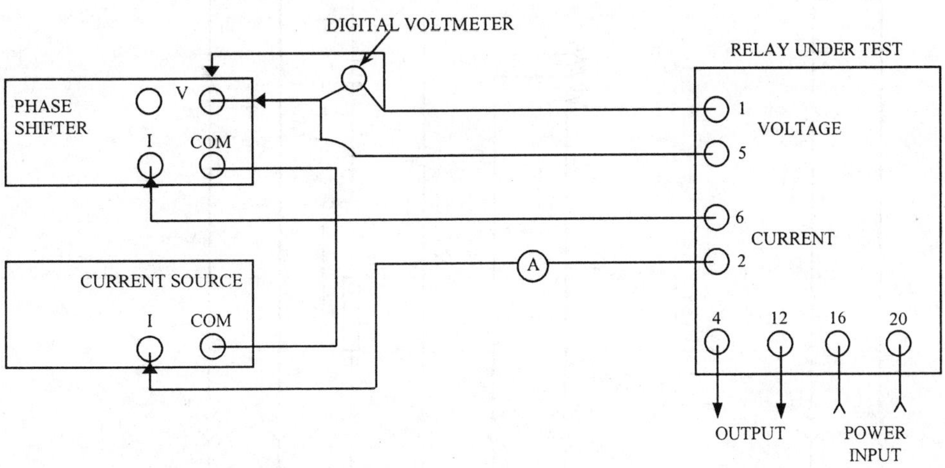

Fig. 6.10 (e): Test connection for loss of excitation relay illustrated in figure (c).

Drop-off, pick-up ratio-check.
Apply test voltage to the relay approximately 50 volts. The test current is slowly raised from zero by, regulating the current supply transformer. At a certain level corresponding to the level Xb the relay starts and remains in its operated state, until the current is raised to a level corresponding to the setting Xa. At this current level the relay resets and the current is recorded.
The reactance X = V / I Ω, while the phase angle between voltage and current is zero. At the setting Xa = zero, the relay is not permitted to reset as the current is raised.. It does not reset, until the current is lowered under the level corresponding to the setting Xb. Repeat the tests by changing the value of Xb and record the test results.
Relay operating time-lag check:
Connect the timing circuit such that the timer would start when the test set is initiated and stop when the contact of the relay under test is operated. The relay is brought to operate by connecting the voltage circuit and raising the current. Switch off the test set. Detain the pickup value of current and voltage adjustments in the test set. Switch on and initiate the test set. The timer will read the time taken to operate the relay at its pre-set value. Repeat the test by changing the time setting of the relay.

Blocking input operation check:
The blocking input and its operation are controlled by, first bringing the relay to operate and then the blocking input (terminals 16-20) is energized immediately (before the time setting of the relay elapse). Upon energization of the blocking input the delayed output is to drop-off at once.

6.11 REVERSE POWER PROTECTION FOR GENERATOR (32).

Reverse power relay is for detecting inadequate fuel supply to the turbine (for gas turbine generator) by measuring reverse power flow to the prime mover. If the driving torque of the prime mover is reduced and the prime mover fails to drive a paralleled generator, generator draws power from bus bars and runs as a synchronous motor. In a synchronized generator relay will shutdown the generator in the event of motoring or prime mover drive-failure. Definite time relay is used for turbo-generators and inverse time relay is for diesel generators. Internal and external connection diagram of a reverse power relay is illustrated in Figure 6.11 (a) and (b) respectively.
Current transformer secondary is connected to terminals 5-6 with provision for automatic shorting of the terminals 5-6 when the relay is withdrawn from its housing. Relay current coil have tap setting facility to set the current at the desired value. Voltage transformer secondary (phase-to-phase) is connected to terminals 7-8. Terminals 1and 2 is volt-free normally open (NO) contact. Terminals, 9 and 10 is volt-free normally closed (NC) contact.

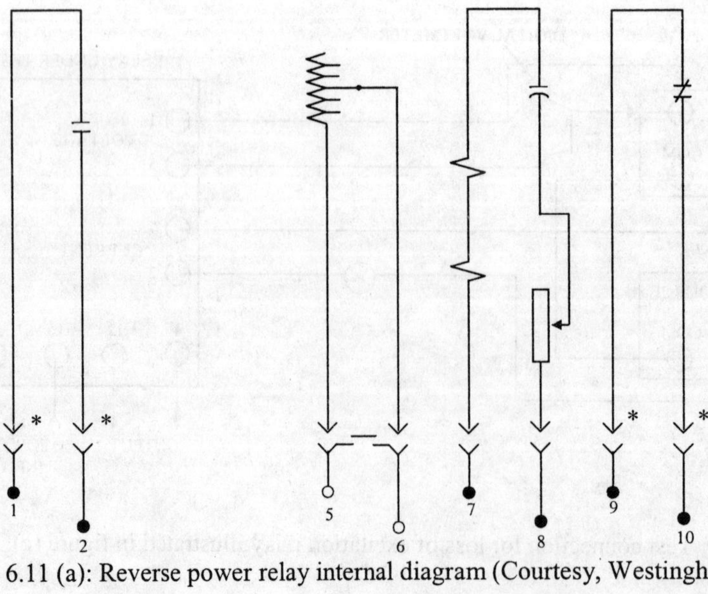

Fig. 6.11 (a): Reverse power relay internal diagram (Courtesy, Westinghouse):

Reverse power relay must be sensitive enough to detect power levels lower than those required to motor the generator. Sensitive is much more important on steam and hydro turbines than on reciprocating engines and gas turbines. The following table represents the reverse power requirements to motor a generator when the prime mover is rotating at synchronous speed with no input power supplied by the prime mover.

Prime mover type	Percent of rated KW
Hydro-turbines	0.2 to 2.0
Steam turbines	3.0 (Condensing / Non-condensing)
Diesel engines	25 (No cylinders firing)
Gas turbines	50 (Due to compressor load)

Reverse power or under power interlock:

When a turbine generator is shutdown in emergency, to avoid the risk of over-speed due to delayed or imperfect closing of a steam valve, it is desirable to delay the opening of the circuit breaker; steam trapped in the casing of a large turbine is often sufficient to cause over-speed. A centrifugally operated mechanical over-speed device is normally fitted and arranged to close the stop valves if the speed increases by more than 5 to 10%. The sensitive reverse power relay retains the generator on load until the onset of 'motoring' and then operates to open the circuit breaker.

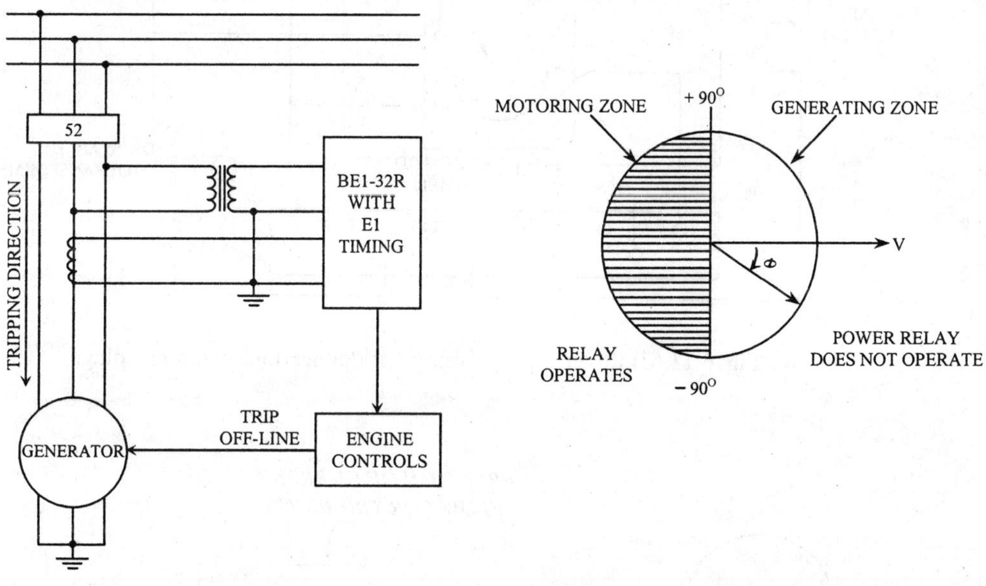

Fig. 6.11 (b): Reverse power relay external connection diagram.

The reverse power relay is generally set for levels as low as possible with steam turbines typically being set not higher than 3% and diesels and gas turbines slightly below 10%. Time delays are usually utilized to avoid nuisance tripping caused by reverse power transient surges, which may result from synchronizing or other system disturbances. These time delays are typically set from 2 to 10 seconds. Following tests are to be conducted on reverse power relay.

*Pick up and timing: Relay will not operate on correct phasing. Relay will operate only if test leads are reversed.

Test connections are given in Figure 6.11 (c). Figure 6.11 (d) shows test connections when test plug is used. During testing current is injected to terminals 5-6 and voltage is applied to terminals 7-8. Timer is for recording the pickup time.

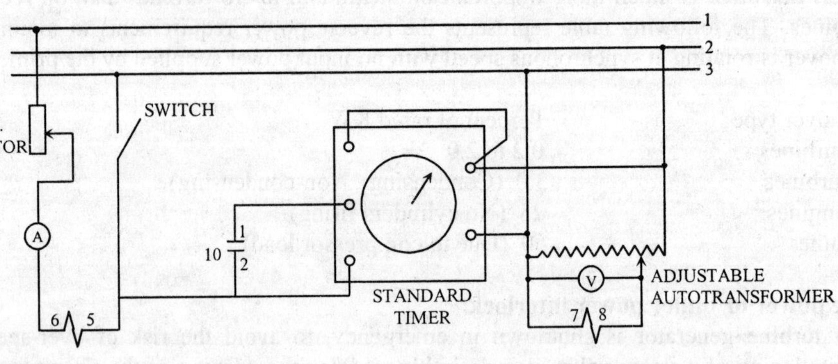

Fig. 6.11 (c): Test connections for reverse power relay.

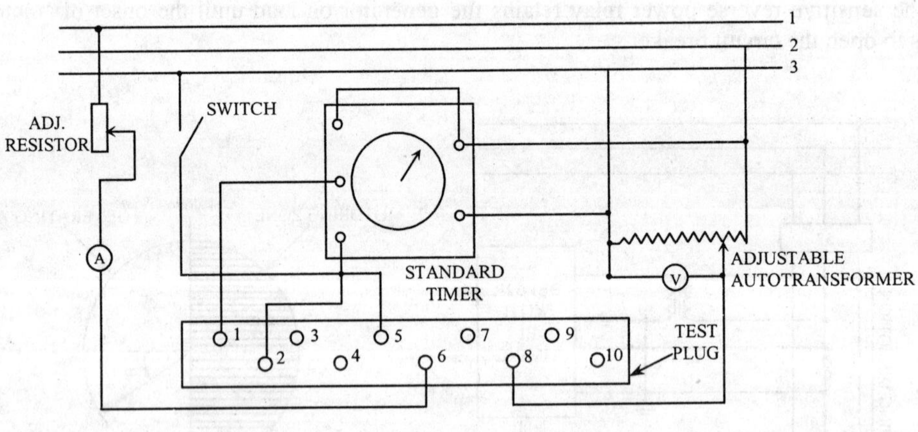

Fig. 6.11 (d) Reverse power relay test connections using test plug.

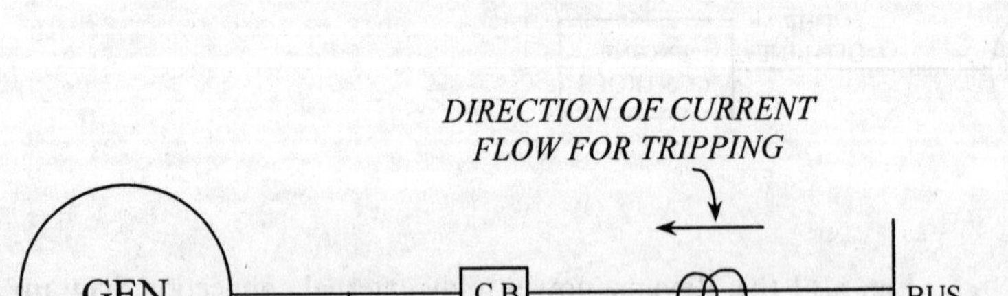

Fig. 6.11 (e): Reverse power protection representing motoring action of a paralleled generator.

Reverse power relay operating zone:

Reverse power relay should have directional stability for the entire relay operating-zone. 90 to 270° phase angle is the motoring zone. The active power flowing through the relay is given by, P=VI cos φ, whereas φ is the phase angle between voltage and current.

P is positive when phase angle is - 90° to + 90° (270 to 360° and 0 to 90°)

P is zero when phase angle is 90°, and 180°

P is negative when phase angle is + 90° to - 90° (90 to 270°)

This can by verified by using a phase shifter and connecting the test circuit similar to the one shown in figure 6.11 (e).

Example for setting reverse power relay:

Assume that an 11 KV, 1400 KW diesel generator set having following parameters.

Current transformer ratio = 150/5 A = 30

Voltage transformer ratio = 12000/120 V = 100

Relay setting = 0.42 Amps (CT secondary current for relay pickup)

Primary current required for picking up the relay = 0.42 x 30 = >12.6 A

Relay is set to trip for a reverse power of $\sqrt{3}$ x 12.6 x 11 = 240 KW which corresponds to 17% of the generator ratings.

Time delay 4 seconds is acceptable.

6.12 NEGATIVE PHASE SEQUENCE PROTECTION FOR GENERATOR (46).

There are a number of system conditions that may cause unbalanced three-phase currents in a generator. The most common causes are system asymmetries (un-transposed lines), unbalanced loads, unbalanced system faults and open circuits. These system conditions produce negative phase sequence components of current which induce a double frequency current in the surface of the rotor, the retaining rings, the slot wedges, and to a smaller degree in the field winding. These rotor currents may cause high and possibility dangerous temperatures in a very short time. Two types of relays are introduced here for this protection: (1) Electro-mechanical (induction disc type) time over-current relay with an extremely inverse characteristic; (2) Static relay with a time over-current characteristic, which matches the "$I^2 t$" capability curves for generators.

Negative sequence current, time-over current relay will provide protection against sustained unbalanced faults or severely unbalanced loads appearing in the generator terminals and protection from all negative sequence current conditions that might damage the machine. The characteristics and setting of this relay is based on the negative sequence capability of the generator to be protected. Operation of this relay will disconnect the generator from the network system i.e. load disconnection by tripping the breaker. This relay compares the three phase currents in the system.

LEGEND: 46: Negative sequence relay; 52: Circuit breaker; OC: Operating coil;
RC: Restraining coil; TC: Trip coil; T&SI: Target and seal-in.

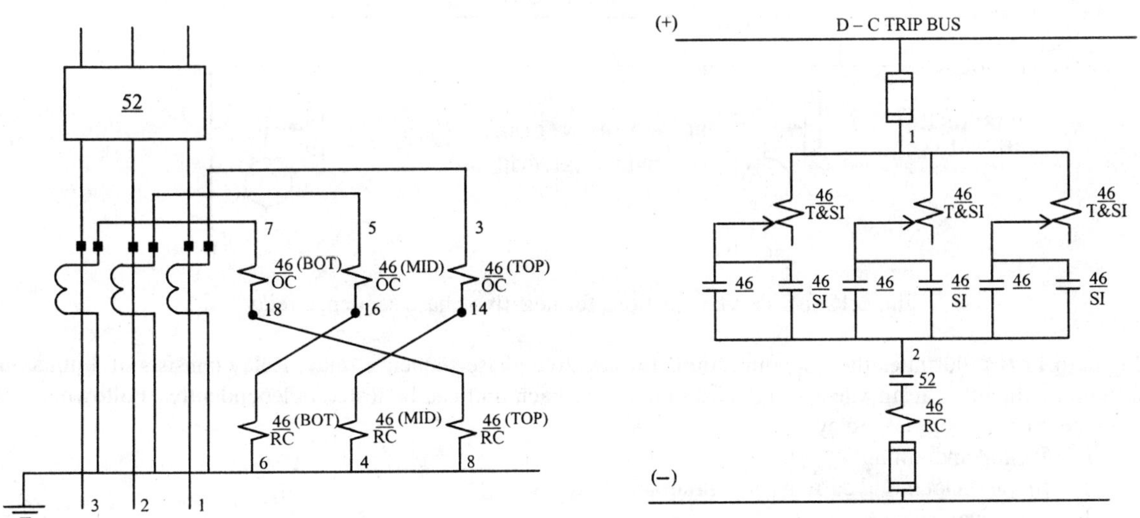

Fig. 6.12 (a): AC/DC circuits of conventional type negative phase sequence relay.

CONVENTIONAL RELAY

The conventional type relay is composed of three individual induction discs with two coils per disc connected as illustrated in Figure 6.12 (a). One-coil produces a contact closing torque on the disc and is called operating coil. The second coil produces a contact opening torque on the disc and is called a restraint coil. These two coils are currents from different phases of the circuit and the relay will operate when the phase currents become sufficiently unbalanced. The trip circuit contacts associated with all three induction discs are connected in parallel. Schematic diagram of DC trip circuit is also shown in figure (a). When the negative sequence relay (46) pickup, the circuit breaker trip coil (52/TC) will energize and trip the circuit breaker (via 52a breaker auxiliary contact) provided, the circuit breaker is in closed position

Generator negative phase sequence protection comprises a two stage setting; Stage 1: (alarm): Adjustable setting to match the generator continuous negative phase sequence capability (definite time delay less than 3 second).

Stage 2: (tripping): An adjustable thermal characteristic capable of being set to match generator short time negative phase sequence current equal to the generator continuous capability while closely matching the generator $I^2 t$ capability

Relay setting guidelines: Assume that 1400 KW, 11 KV generator; CT Ratio 150/5 = 30

Generator full load current = 1400 / (√3 x 11 x 0.8) =91.85 A

CT Secondary current = 91.85 / 30 = 3.06 A; set over current unit at 3.1 amps; set negative sequence pickup at 15% of tap.

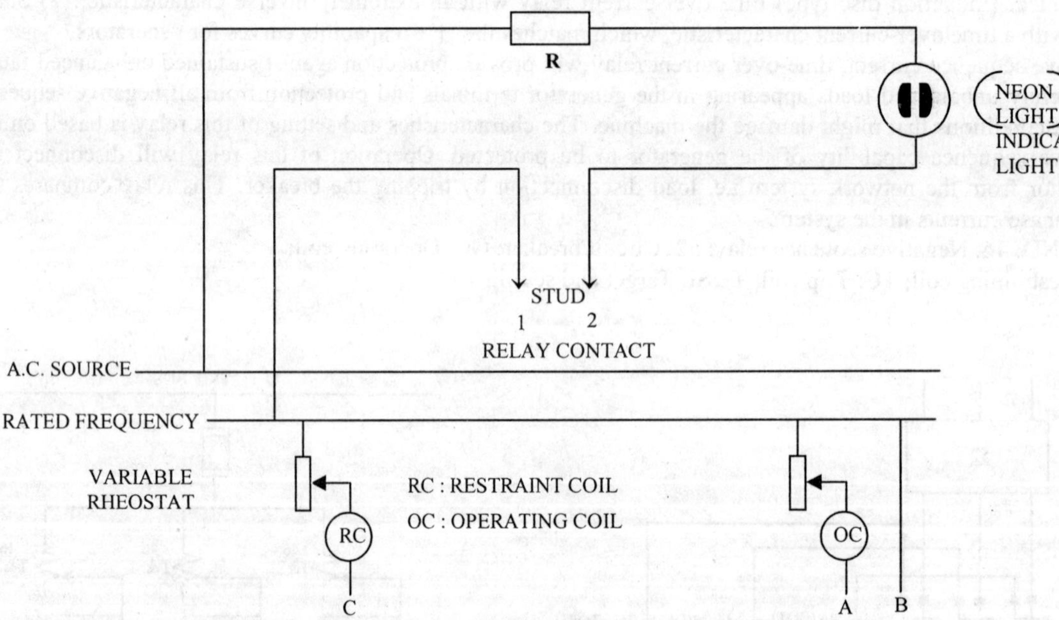

Fig. 6.12 (b): Test connections for negative phase sequence relay

Figure 6.12 (b) illustrates the test connections for negative phase sequence relay. Relay consists of 3 units one at bottom, the other at middle and the third unit at top. Each unit can be tested ındependently. Following tests are recommended on NPS relay.

1. Pickup and timing
2. Slope = Operating current / Restraining current.
3. Electrical balance
4. Target and seal-in

Testing pick-up, target and seal-in:

(a) Connect the relay and testing devices as shown in figure. Be sure the ON/OFF switch is off. Connect the relay trip circuit to a neon-indicating lamp. Connect the relay-operating coil (terminals 3-14) by looping terminals A and B in the test circuit.

(b) Turn power ON/OFF switch to ON. Slowly increase current by adjusting the variable rheostat until the relay contact close. See that neon lamp lights. Record this value of current as pick-up current. Decrease current until the disc return its original position.

(c) When the relay operates the target and seal in unit activate. Repeat the test for other two relay units (terminals 5-16 & 7-18) operating coils. Return rheostat to zero position and switch off power.

Testing timing:

(a) Connect the timer on circuit through the power on switch and timer stop circuit through the relay contact. Switch on power and set the test current by, adjusting the rheostat until the ammeter indicates the desired test current. Switch off the power.

(b) Reset digital timer by depressing the reset button. Switch on power the unit will energize and the timer will begin to run. When the relay contacts close, the timer will stop. Record the timing. De-energize the power.

Repeat the test for operating coils of other 2 units also.

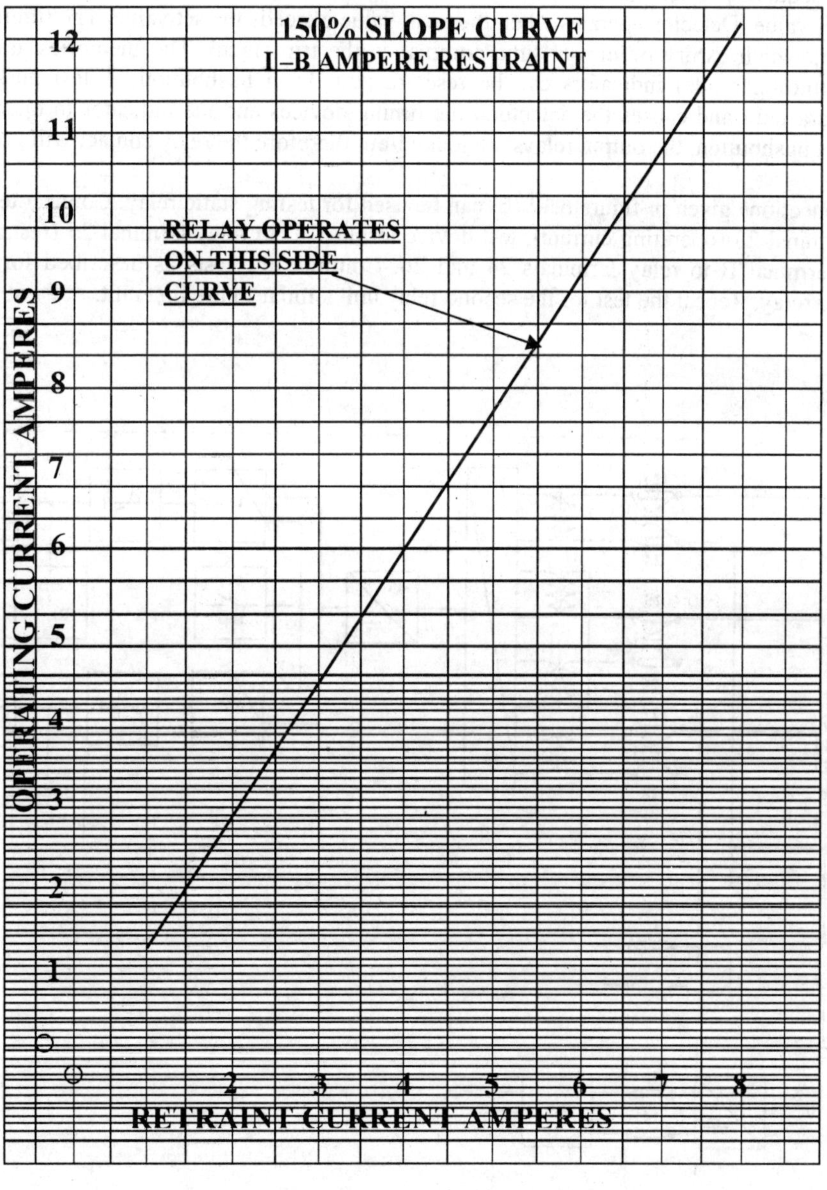

Fig. 6.12 (c): Typical slope curve for 150% slope at one to eight ampere restraints.

Testing slope:
Connect operating coil (top) and restraint coil (top) for slope test. Energize restraining coil by looping terminals B-C adjust current to pick-up value and observe ammeter reading. Connect timer circuit also. Loop terminals A-B-C, switch on power and adjust corresponding variable rheostats to regulate the currents of operating coil and restraint coil until the disc of the relay under test is stopped about half way between full open position and trip position. Record both values of current and calculate slope [See Figure 6.12 (c)]. Repeat tests on mid and bottom relay unit also.

STATIC RELAY

Figure 6.12 (d) illustrates the block diagram and external connection diagram of a static negative sequence over current relay (GE type MCND). Two current transformers provide electrical isolation and enable a voltage image of the current to be obtained. Phase shift circuit (the third current transformer) provides the negative sequence component. The image of the negative sequence component is then rectified and compared with a set value. Detector operates when the peak value exceeds the set value. The timing device consists of an oscillator, which expiry of the set time commands the trip signal. The memories associated with the LED (Light emitting diode) indicators can be reset to zero by a pushbutton. A test pushbutton is provided to simulates a fault and causes the detectors, the timing devices and the indicator to operate. During the test by using test pushbutton, the output relays are locked-out therefore the relay contact will not activate.

Test connections given in figure 6.12 (b) can be used for testing static relay. Connect test device terminal A to relay terminal 23 (operating current), test device terminal C to relay terminal 25 (restraining current) and test device terminal B to relay terminals 24 and 26. Continue the tests as described for conventional negative sequence relay. Repeat the test for the second relay unit similar to the first unit.

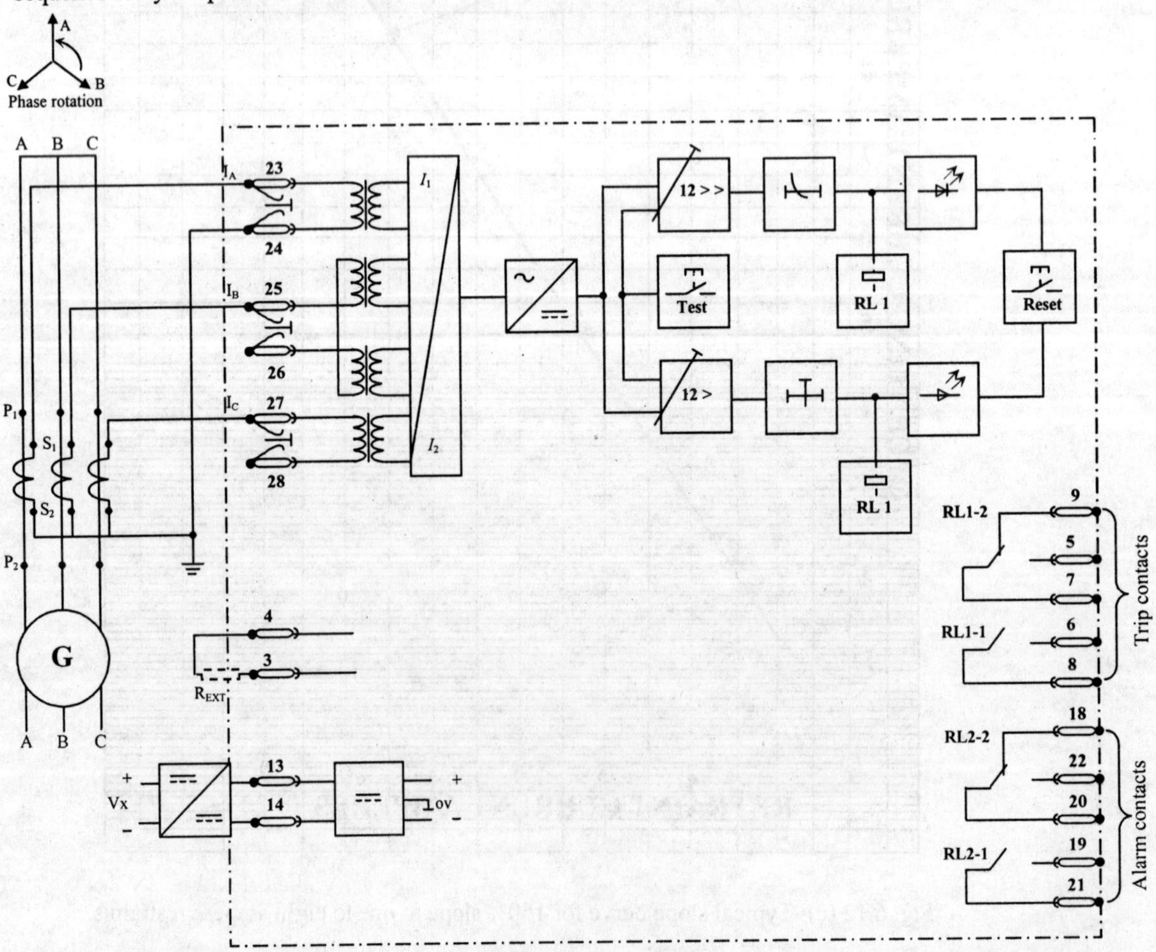

Fig. 6.12 (d): Block schematic diagram of static negative sequence relay (Courtesy, General Electric).

Principles of symmetrical components:

The principles of symmetrical components allow an unbalanced system to be considered as three separate balanced systems. These balanced subsystems may then be analyzed as single-phase quantities. These quantities are the positive, negative and zero sequence components of current and voltage.

The positive sequence component of current (I_1) represents the portion of the total current which has normal phase rotation and produces no adverse effect on the system. An ideally balanced system contains only positive sequence phase current and voltages as shown in Figure 6.12 (e).

Principles of symmetrical components:

The principles of symmetrical components allow an unbalanced system to be considered as three separate balanced systems. These balanced subsystems may then be analyzed as single-phase quantities. These quantities are the positive, negative and zero sequence components of current and voltage.

The positive sequence component of current (I_1) represents the portion of the total current which has normal phase rotation and produces no adverse effect on the system. An ideally balanced system contains only positive sequence phase current and voltages as shown in Figure 6.12 (e).

The zero sequence component of current (I_0) also has no adverse effect on a three-phase medium voltage system because it produces no appreciable magnetic flux and causes no excessive heating in the generator rotor or winding [refer Figure 6.12 (f)].

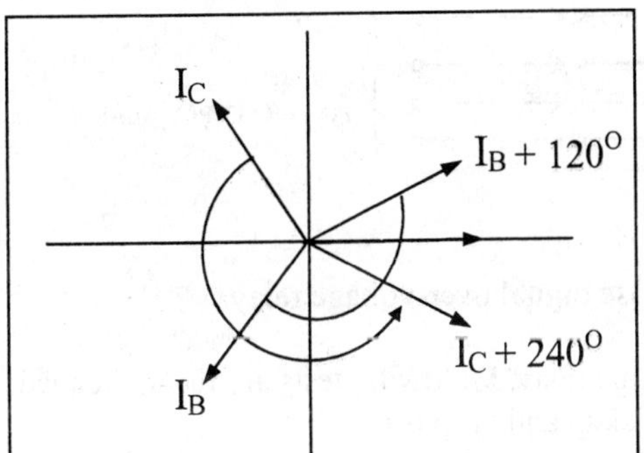

Fig. 6.12 (e): Positive sequence currents.

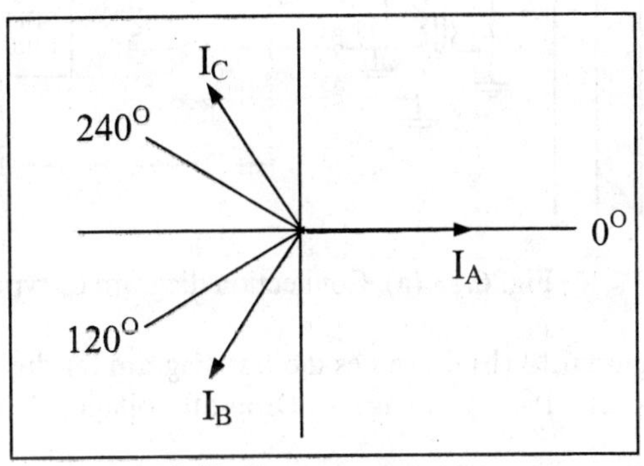

Fig. 6.12 (f): Zero sequence currents

The negative sequence component of the current (I_2) produces a magnetic flux in the stator that has the same rotational speed as the rotor flux, but in the opposite direction. This causes the stator magnetic flux to rotate at twice the system frequency and induce eddy currents into the rotor. These eddy currents create excessive heat in the rotor iron and windings, and, if allowed to persist, could result in severe damage to the system. Figure 6.12 (g) represents negative sequence currents in a generator.

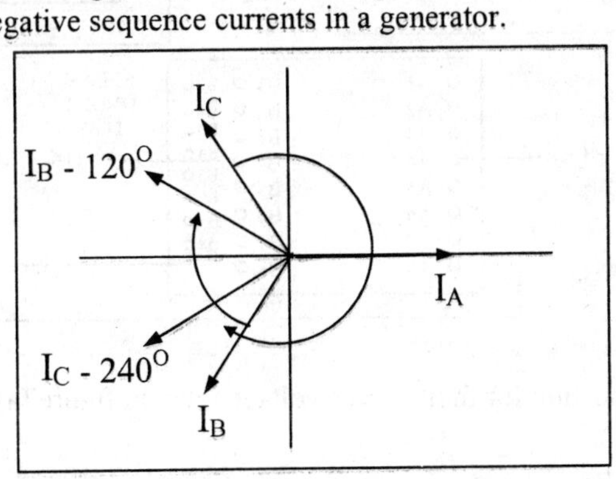

Fig. 6.12 (g): Negative sequence currents in a generator.

6.13 NUMERICAL OVER-VOLTAGE PROTECTION (59).

Voltage relay responds to voltage, may be an under-voltage relay or over-voltage relay or a combination of both. Generator over voltage will cause failure of insulation and damage of equipments. Over voltage relay described here-in is an inverse or definite time digital relay measuring three-phase voltages, set to trip quickly for voltage in excess of those expected following full load rejection of the generator and to trip for sustained voltages in excess of + 10%. Relay consists of four independent voltage elements, (three single phase elements and one positive sequence element), which can be configured as either under voltage or over voltage and set for single or three-phase operation, with independent definite time delay for each element. The advantages of digital over-voltage relay are programmable output contacts, status inputs, user friendly settings and indications, facility for storage of 500 time-tagged event records, storage of five waveform records, communications with fiber optic interface, self monitoring capability etc. Figure 6.13 (a) illustrates the connection diagram of a typical three-phase digital over-voltage relay.

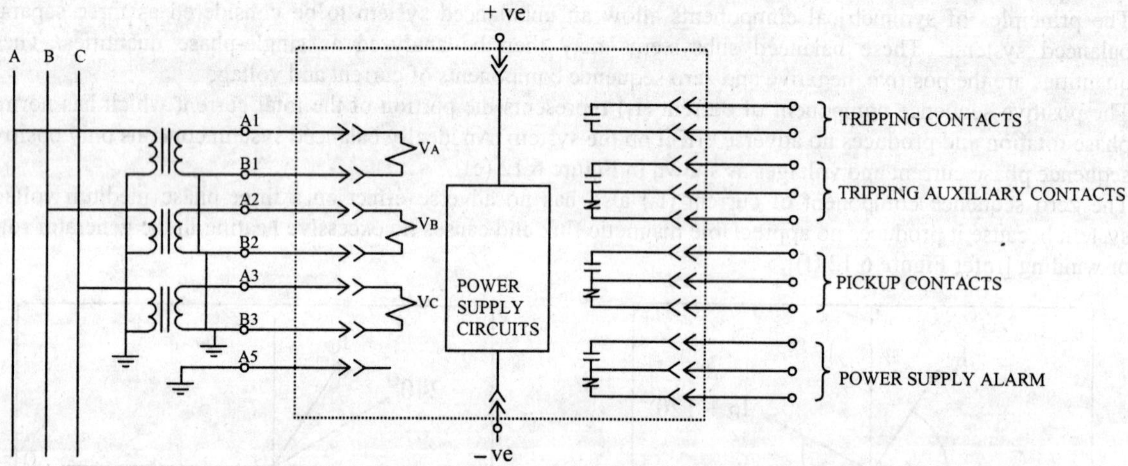

Fig. 6.13 (a): Connection diagram of typical three-phase digital over-voltage relay.

Figure 6.13 (b) illustrates the test diagram for digital over voltage relay. Following tests are recommended:
a) Pickup voltage; b) Drop-off voltage; C) Timing for pickup and drop off.

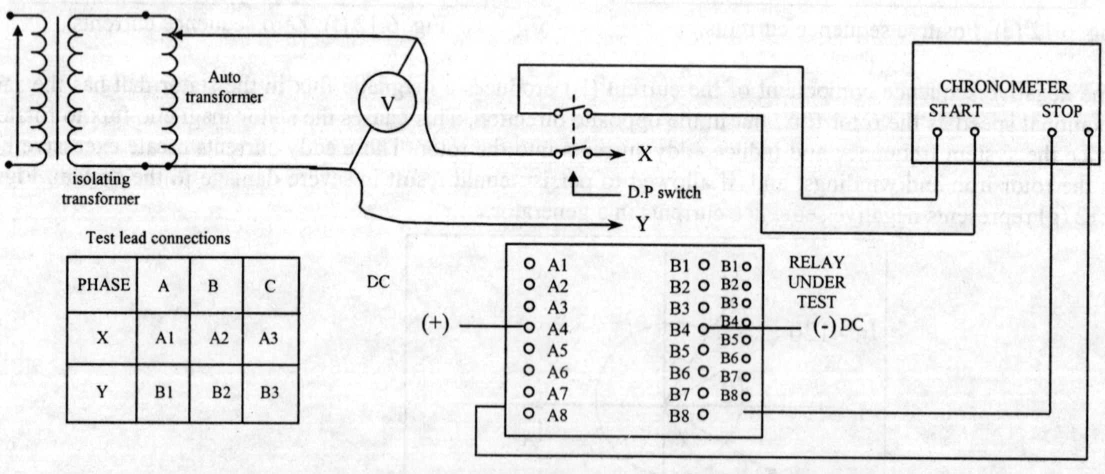

PHASE	A	B	C
X	A1	A2	A3
Y	B1	B2	B3

Fig. 6.13 (b): Test connection for digital over-voltage relay in figure (a).

Test procedure:

(a) Connect isolating transformer, (which is essential for testing static and numerical relay tests) variable voltage transformer for regulating the output voltages and chronometer (Timer) for registering the relay operating time.

(b) For testing phase element, connect the test leads to relay terminals A1 – B1 as indicated in the test lead connection table or figure (b). Switch on the double pole switch and slowly rotate the variable voltage transformer knob to raise the voltage until the relay pick up. Record the pick up voltage.

(c) Switch off power and reset the timer. Switch on power with the desired pick up voltage. Relay operates and timer shows the elapsed time. Record the operating time.
(d) Slowly reduce the voltage until the relay drop off and record the drop off voltage. Switch off the DP switch. Reset the timer.
(e) Rcpcat similar tcst on all other relay elements.

6.14 OVER-FLUXING PROTECTION FOR GENERATOR-TRANSFOPMER UNIT (24).

The over excitation (over-fluxing) is protected by employing volt/hertz relay connected in the PT circuit of generator. This relay will detect over-fluxing condition and protect the generator-transformer units from over-excitation. Over-fluxing of generator main transformer and / or associated auxiliary transformer cause overheating of transformer cores. Over-excitation of a generator or power transformer may occur during start-up, shutdown, or as a result of remote load rejection. **This relay detects the ratio of voltage to frequency and pickup when the ratio of voltage to frequency is greater than set value**. Relay initiate an alarm and eventually trip the unit after an adjustable time delay. The setting of the over-fluxing protection relay shall be coordinated with the excitation limiter of AVR because it acts as a primary protection in case of voltage regulator failure.

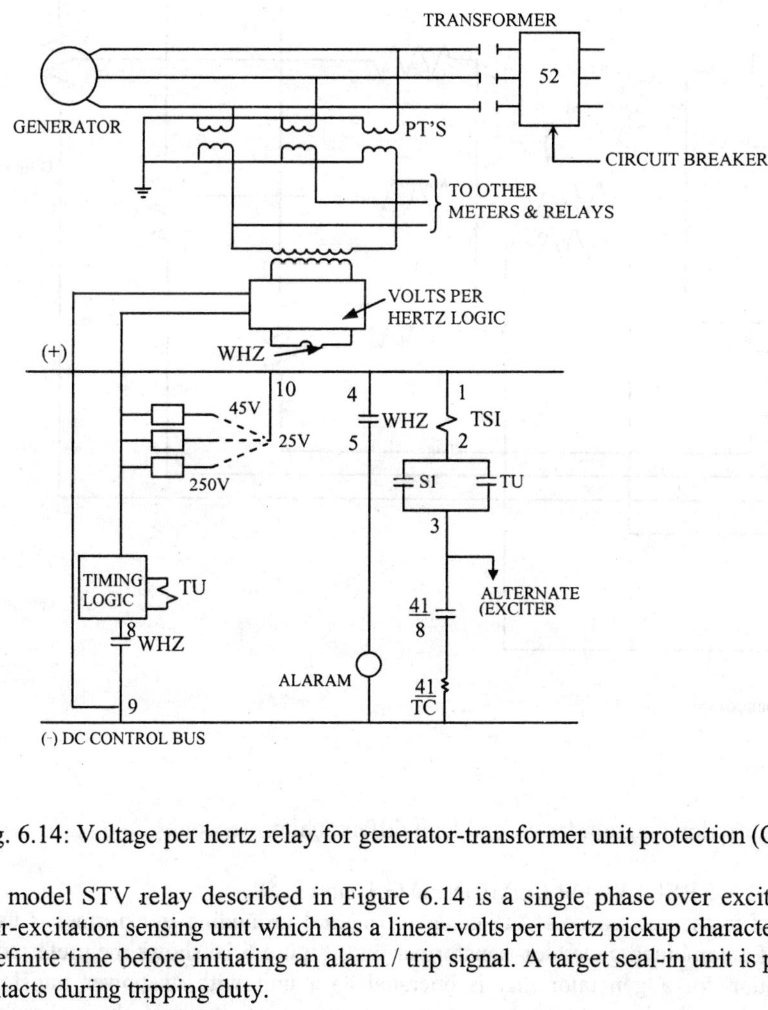

Fig. 6.14: Voltage per hertz relay for generator-transformer unit protection (Courtesy, General Electric).

GE model STV relay described in Figure 6.14 is a single phase over excitation relay, which consists of an over-excitation sensing unit which has a linear-volts per hertz pickup characteristic and a timing unit to provide a definite time before initiating an alarm / trip signal. A target seal-in unit is provided to protect the timing unit contacts during tripping duty.

6.15 GENERATOR GROUND FAULT DIFFERENTIAL PROTECTION (64G).

Earth fault relay responds to system earth faults; may be over current with or without directional discrimination. A time delayed or inverse time over current relay for monitoring the current in the generator neutral resistor to detect ground fault in the generator. The relay is connected to a current transformer inserted in the connections to the grounding resistor. Generators with solidly grounded neutral (low voltage generators), instantaneous earth fault relays (restricted earth fault relay described in Chapter # 5, section 5.19) are used. . Stator ground fault protection has to respond the generator design frequency, must be sensitive enough to protect the whole stator winding. The problem is to get the required sensitivity and at the same time to avoid the possibility of undesired operation because of CT errors with large external fault currents. Figure 6.15 shows the connection diagram of a typical differential relay whose operating coil is inserted in the neutral of the differential relaying circuit and polarizing coil is energized from a CT in the generator neutral. A polarized relay provides greater sensitivity without excessive operating-coil burden; the polarizing CT may have a low enough ratio so that the polarizing coil will be "soaked" for the short dimension of the fault. For resistance or reactance earthed generator ground fault protection, ground fault differential protection depicted in figure 6.15 can be used. Test methods are similar to restricted earth fault relay demonstrated in Chapter # 5, section 5.19.

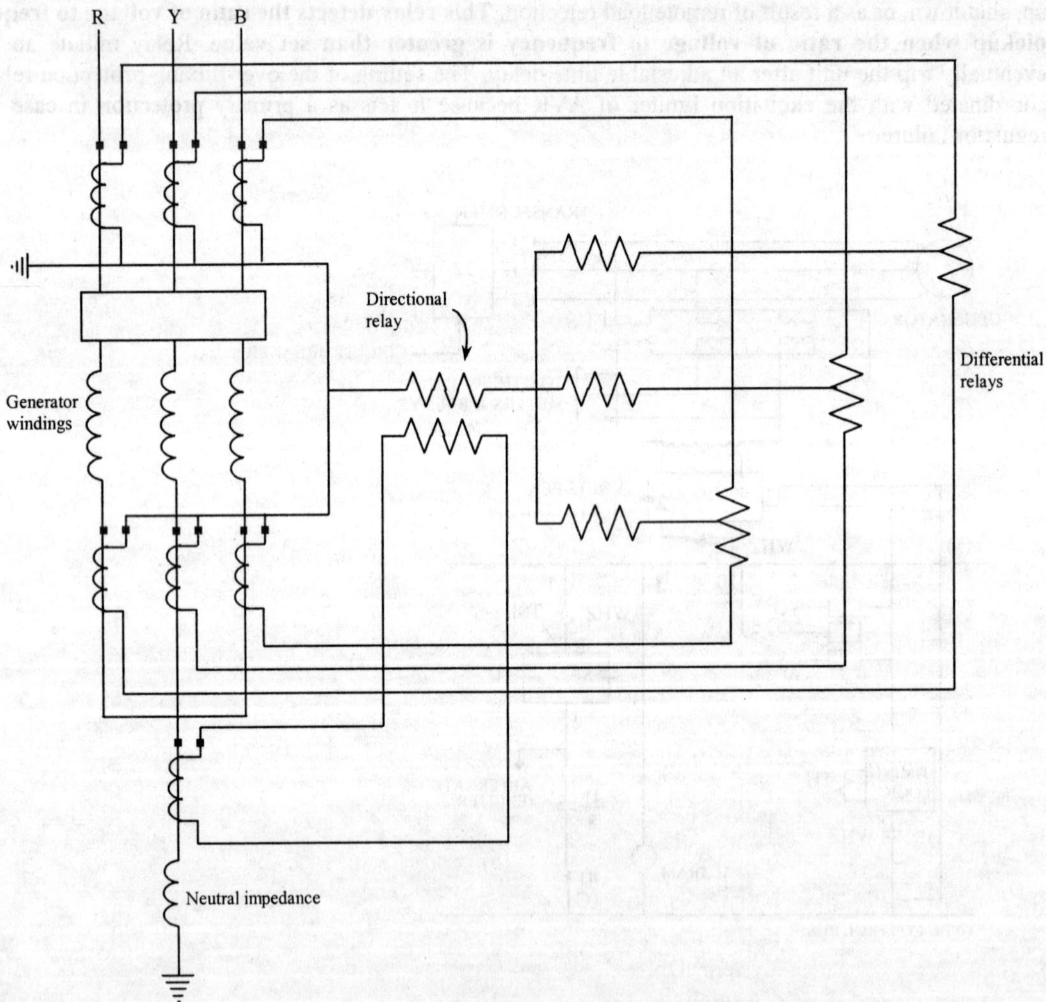

Fig. 6.15: Connection diagram for ground fault differential protection

6.16: NEUTRAL DISPLACEMENT RELAY FOR COMBINED G.T UNIT (59N).

An over voltage relay connected to the secondary of the generator neutral grounding transformer is usually used for earth fault protection of a combined generator-transformer unit. Figure 6.16 shows the preferred way to provide ground fault protection for a generator that is operated as a unit with its power transformer. Generator neutral is grounded through the primary high voltage winding of a single-phase distribution transformer. A resistor and an over voltage relay are connected across the low voltage winding. The relay measures the neutral voltage. The relay is set to operate during an abnormal internal ground fault and shutdown the self-excited unit. For separately excited generators tripping of mains circuit breaker and field breaker is sufficient. Even though the fault current is very low, some welding type damages of the stator laminations may occur if the generator is permitted to continue operating with a ground fault in the winding.

The over voltage relay must be sensitive to fundamental-frequency voltages and insensitive to the third-harmonic and its multiples. The relay may require adjustable time delay so as to be selective with other relays for ground faults on the high-voltage side of the main power transformer for which there may be a tendency to operate owing to capacitance coupling between the power transformer windings particularly if the high voltage winding of the power transformer does not have its neutral solidly grounded.

The reason for providing reactance earthing to a combined generator transformer unit is because the generator windings and the transformer primary windings can be treated as an isolated system, which is not influenced by the transmission line earthing system. Hence the common practice is to earth the generator neutral through the primary winding of a reactance transformer. The secondary of the reactance transformer is connected to a resistor to prevent high transient over voltage. Neutral displacement relay connected in the secondary of the reactance transformer will isolate the generator transformer unit during the occurrence of an earth fault in the protected zone.

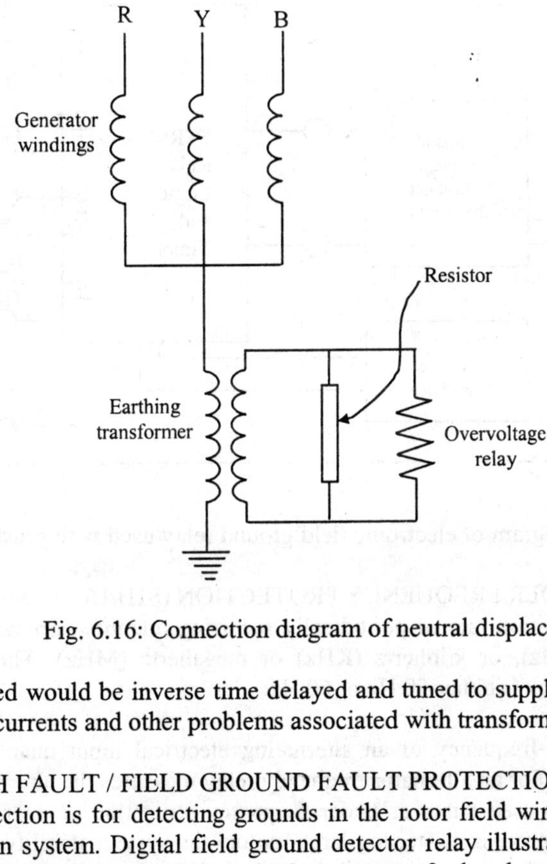

Fig. 6.16: Connection diagram of neutral displacement relay

The relay recommended would be inverse time delayed and tuned to supply frequency to avoid mal-operation due to third harmonic currents and other problems associated with transformer inter-winding capacities.

6.17 ROTOR EARTH FAULT / FIELD GROUND FAULT PROTECTION (64F).

Rotor earth fault protection is for detecting grounds in the rotor field winding and preventing possible short circuit in the excitation system. Digital field ground detector relay illustrated in Figure 6.17 is for detecting failures in the main field insulation of DC excitation system of a brush type synchronous machine. The relay will provide alarm when single earth fault in the rotor. Single earth fault does not harm but a second fault causes unbalanced magnetic forces causing damage to shaft, bearings etc. The relay is connected to Generator field excitation system through a field voltage transducer. Similarly, generator voltage transformer secondary (120 volts) also connected to the relay through a voltage transducer. 110 Volts DC is used as auxiliary power for the electronic circuit.

To ensure that this protection will function for a ground in the field winding, it is necessary that the rotor iron be grounded without depending on a path through the bearings, since the oil film may withstand the voltage applied by the relay, and thus prevent the relay from operating when required. Grounding means must not be stalled where it will bypass the bearing insulation, which is provided for prevention of shaft currents. The ground detector unit will respond to grounds in the negative field lead of up to 500 ohms at 80% of AC relay voltage. The relay may be used for instantaneous or time delayed operation.

Field ground relay for brushless alternator is illustrated / described in figure 1.2 (p) of Chapter # 1. The conventional type relays using the potentiometer method detection comprises a resistor across the field winding, with a center tap connected via a sensitive voltage relay to earth. This system is most sensitive to faults at the extremities of the winding whilst faults in the center could remain undetected. These types of relays are obsolete due to the development of electronic relays.

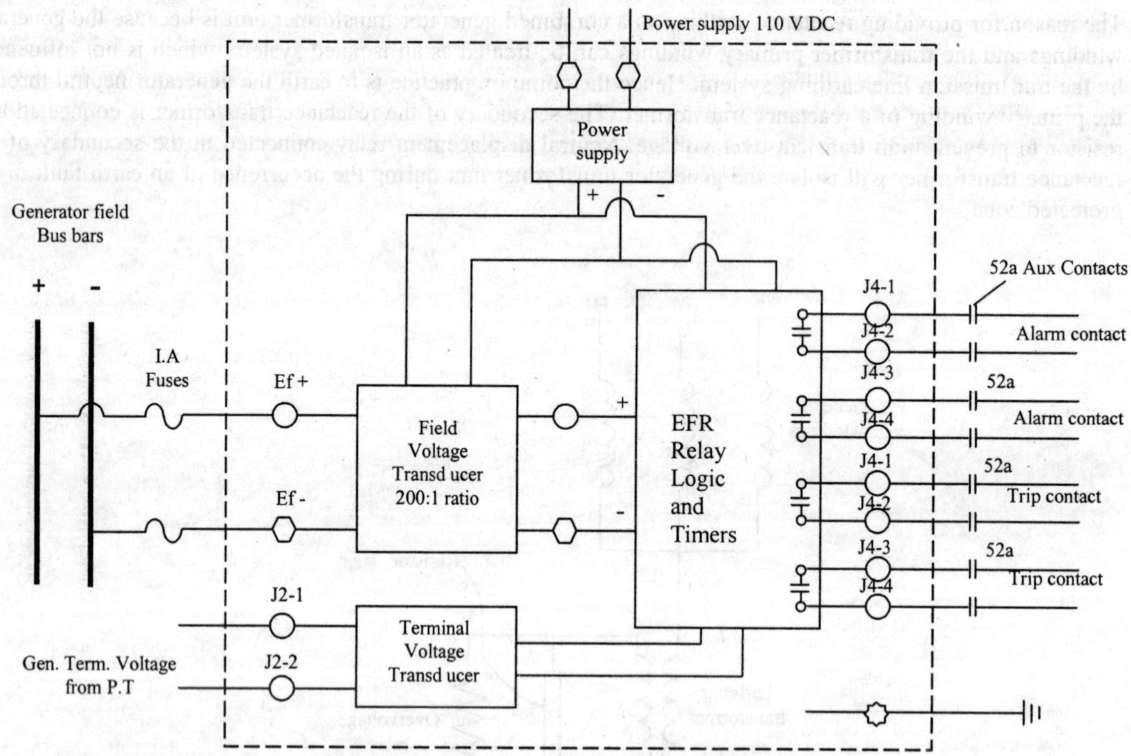

Fig. 6.17: Connection diagram of electronic field ground relay used with brush type generator.

6.18 GENERATOR OVER/UNDER FREQUENCY PROTECTION (81H/L).

Frequency is defined as the repetition rate of periodically recurring quantity commonly stated in cycles per second, and the unit is hertz (Hz), or kilohertz (KHz) or megahertz (MHz). The standard frequency of alternating current power generation is either 50 Hz or 60 Hz.

Frequency relay responds to the frequency of an alternating electrical input quantity; may respond to an increase or decrease in frequency. For an alternator frequency relay measures the alternator frequency or speed. Frequency relays are (Device 81) used either as under frequency protection or over frequency protection of generators or motors. During the process of starting large motors the system stability will be disturbed due to high starting current the frequency may probably fall down and under-frequency relay will operate to isolate the circuit breaker. Similarly if a heavy loaded generator rejects the load due to failure of the system or a fault, the frequency may probably increase due to failure of governor. Over frequency relay then operate to shutdown the prime mover and breaker.

Frequency relays employed for generator protection has high and low time delay settings for alarm and tripping of circuit breakers. Under frequency causes failure of blades of steam turbines. Frequency relays are generally connected to the secondary of voltage transformer as illustrated in Figure 6.18 (a). It has two pairs of coils, which are connected in parallel through impedances. The impedances vary with frequency of supply. At rated frequency no torque is exerted. When the frequency is higher or lower than the set value then the relay operates. Block schematic diagram of the frequency relay is described in figure 5.8 (a) of Chapter # 5.

The potential source connected to the relay is stepped down, filtered and converted to a square wave. It is this square wave that is measured by the frequency element. The frequency measuring circuit compares the period of the incoming square wave against a crystal reference. If the source frequency differs from the set point for more than three consecutive periods or cycles the circuit gives an output. If the under-voltage supervision has not operated this output starts a time delay (which can be set to zero), which in turn drives the output contact. The rate of change feature if selected will bypass the time delay if the next lower frequency element has operated.

Numerical relays have four independent frequency elements, each of which can be configured as either under or over frequency. Frequency setting ranges 47 Hz to 62 Hz.

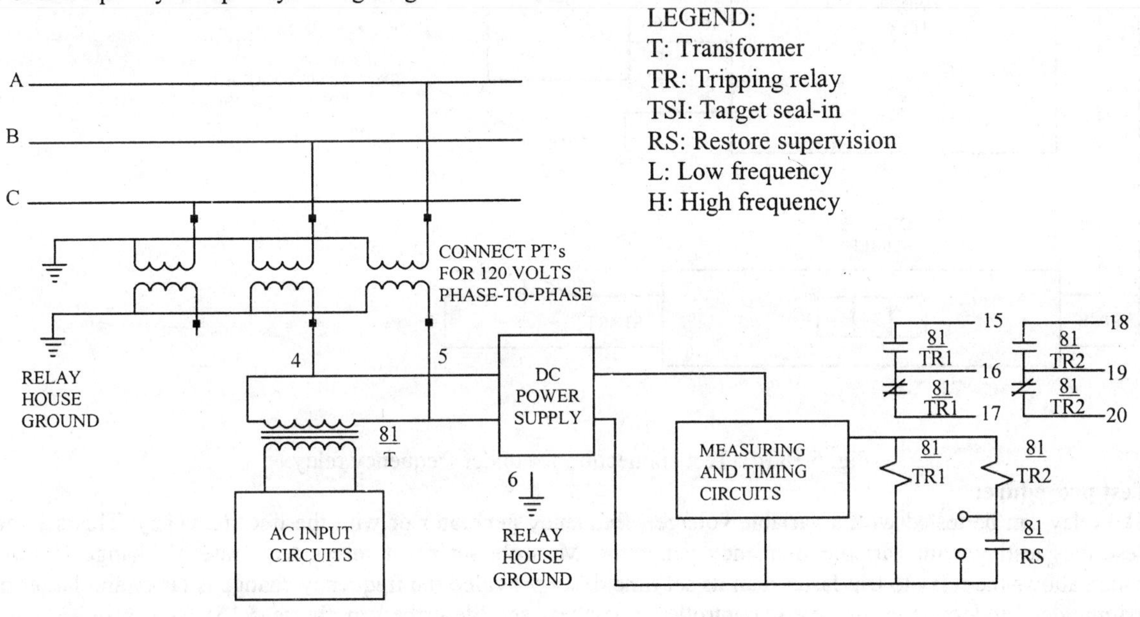

Fig. 6.18 (a): Frequency relay external connection diagram.

Figure 6.18 (b) shows the trip-circuit wiring diagram for frequency relay shown in figure (a) above.

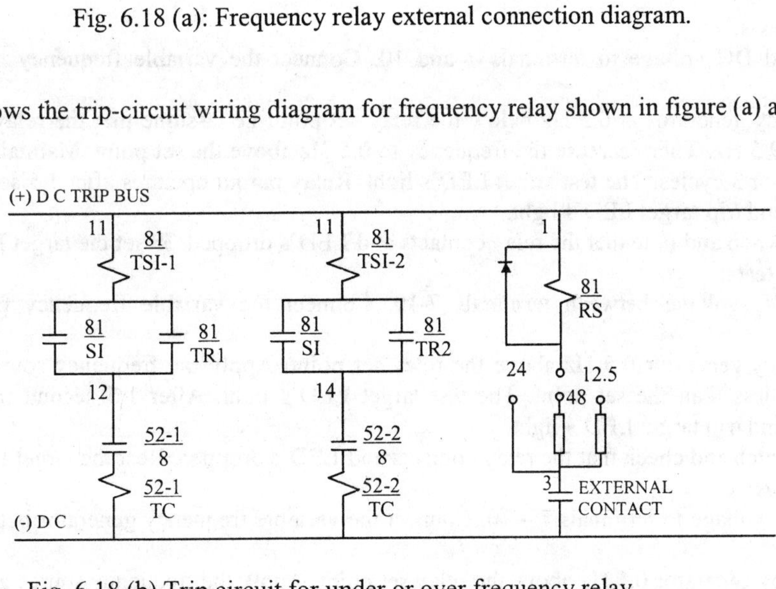

Fig. 6.18 (b) Trip circuit for under or over frequency relay.

Figure 6.18 (c) shows the typical test connections of an under-frequency relay. Variable with frequency drop control, digital timer and a double pole single throw (DPST) switch, DC voltage source is required for test connections. For digital frequency relay testing, an automatic relay test set with transient simulator is sufficient.

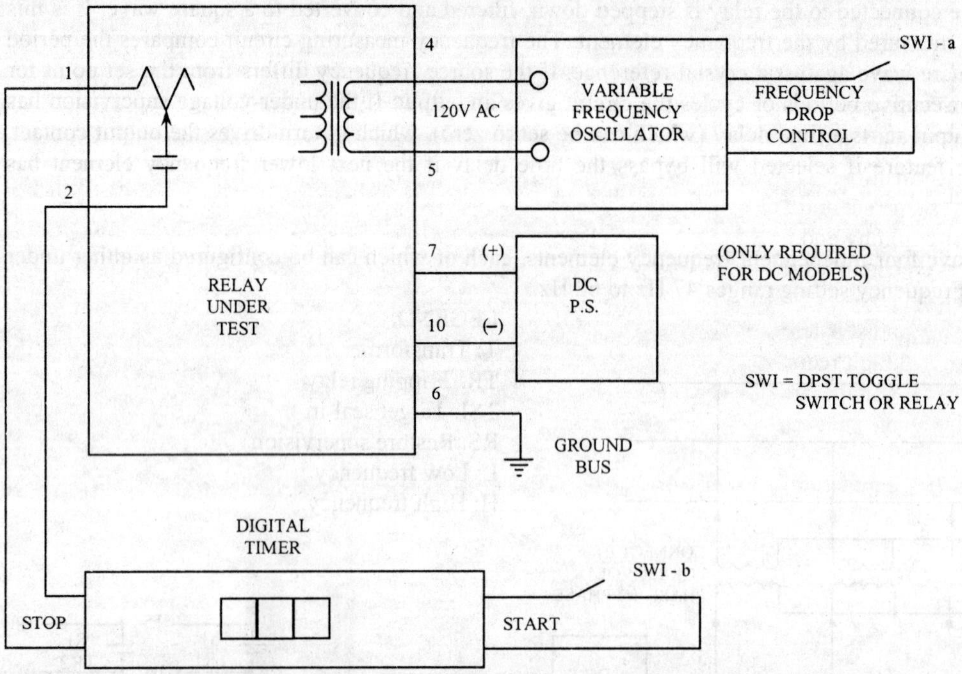

Fig. 6.18 (c): Test connection for under frequency relay.

Test procedure:

The relay can be tested with a variable voltage / frequency generator or with the line frequency. This section describes testing with variable frequency generator. Multiple set point relays have rate of change feature, which allows the relay to trip faster than its set time delay provided the frequency change is faster and larger in magnitude. Modern microprocessor controlled relay test set (described in figure 5.15) have provision for testing frequency relays.

Over frequency tests:

1) Apply the rated DC voltage to terminals 7 and 10. Connect the variable frequency generator between terminals 4 – 5.

2) Set the frequency generator at 0.5 Hz below the relay set point i.e. assume that the relay is set for 50 Hz, apply voltage at 49.5 Hz. Then increase the frequency to 0.5 Hz above the set point. Maintain the frequency at the higher setting for 3 cycles. The test target LED's light. Relay output operates after 1.5 seconds and the trip contacts operates and trip target LED's light.

3) Open the DP switch and note that the relay contacts and LED's dropped. Reset the target LED.

Under frequency tests:

1) Apply rated DC voltage between terminals 7-10. Connect the variable frequency generator between terminals 4-5.

2) Set the frequency generator 0.5 Hz above the relay set point. Apply the frequency source and reduce the frequency 0.5 Hz less than the set point. The test target LED's light. After 1.5 second time delay the trip contacts operates and trip target LED's light.

3) Open the DP switch and check that the relay contacts and LED's dropped. Rest the target LED.

Rate of change tests:

1) Apply rated DC voltage to terminals 7 – 10. Connect the variable frequency generator between terminals 4-5.

2) Set the frequency generator 0.5 Hz above the relay set point. Apply the frequency source and quickly reduce the frequency 0.5 Hz below set value. The test target LED's light. The rate of change has overridden the set time delays on the output. The trip contacts operates and trip target LED's lights at once. After 1.5 seconds all LED's should be lit.

3) Open the DP switch and note that trip contacts and all LED's dropped. Reset the target LED.

6.19 GENERATOR BACKUP IMPEDANCE PROTECTION RELAY (95)

Backup impedance protection is provided to detect faults both in generator and in the networks including transformers. The relay demonstrated in this section is General Electric model LPS which has four zones of phase and ground mho distance functions. This relay is designed for phase and ground over-current instantaneous backup, ground time over-current backup, over / under voltage backup protection, out of step blocking and tripping applications. Other advantages of generator backup protection digital relays are:

1.Waveform sampling of current and voltage inputs
2. High-resolution oscillography and playback
3. Users-configurable I/Os (input / output)
4. Integrated RMS metering
5. Trip circuit monitoring and self-test diagnostics
6. Fault location, event and fault recording (minimum 150}
7. Measurements: Current, voltage, frequency, KW & KVAR
8. LCD indication and manual breaker control
9. RS 232 and RS 485 serial ports

Functional block diagram of generator back up impedance relay (GE type LPS) is shown in Figure 6.19 (a).

LEGEND:
50P: Instantaneous phase over-current protection
21P: Phase and ground Mho distance protection
78: Out-of step protection (swing condition)
67N: Directional ground fault protection
67P: Directional phase fault protection
50/51G: High set and time delayed earth fault
27/59: Under / over voltage protection

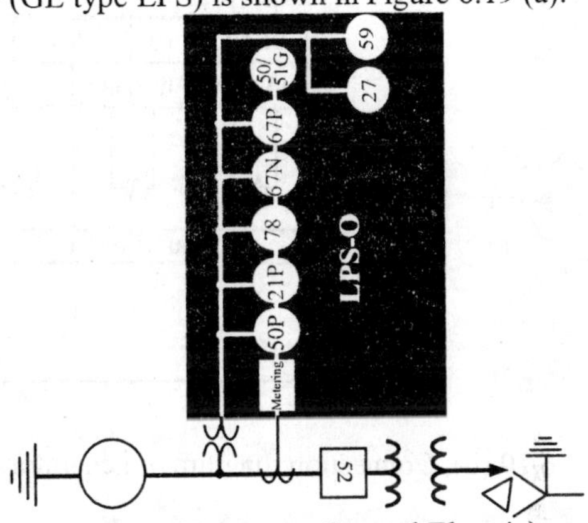

Fig. 6.19 (a): Functional block diagram of generator backup protection relay (Courtesy, General Electric)

Distance protection:

Four-zone time delayed distance protection with positive sequence voltage polarized Mho characteristics, are provided. The reach of the three forward-looking zones can be compensated for a delta-star transformer. Out-of step blocking monitors swing condition and block tripping. Out-of step tripping logic is provided with a choice of two or three Mho type characteristics with adjustable shapes. Loss of synchronism or a power swing between two areas of the power system is detected by measuring the positive sequence impedance seen by the relay over a period of time as the power swing develops.

Non-directional over-current backup:

The relay provides instantaneous phase over-current (IOC) and instantaneous ground over-current, as well as time over-current (TOC) functions. Both IOC and TOC functions can be set as non-directional or directional.

Directional ground over-current:

The ground directional functions are forward and reverse negative sequence current and voltage operated. The ground instantaneous and time delay functions can be independently set with directional control.

Over / under voltage, and fuse failure backup protection:

Three single-phase over/under voltage detectors and a positive sequence over-voltage detector are provided. Fuse failure logic detects a full or partial loss of AC potential and blocks tripping of distance and directional functions.

DC trip circuit monitor:

DC battery voltage is monitored across each open trip contact. An alarm triggers when the voltage becomes virtually zero. A current sensor in series with each trip contact is provided, to log an event message on the DC trip current status following the trip.

Connection diagram of typical generator backup protection relay is shown in Figure 6.19 (b) below.

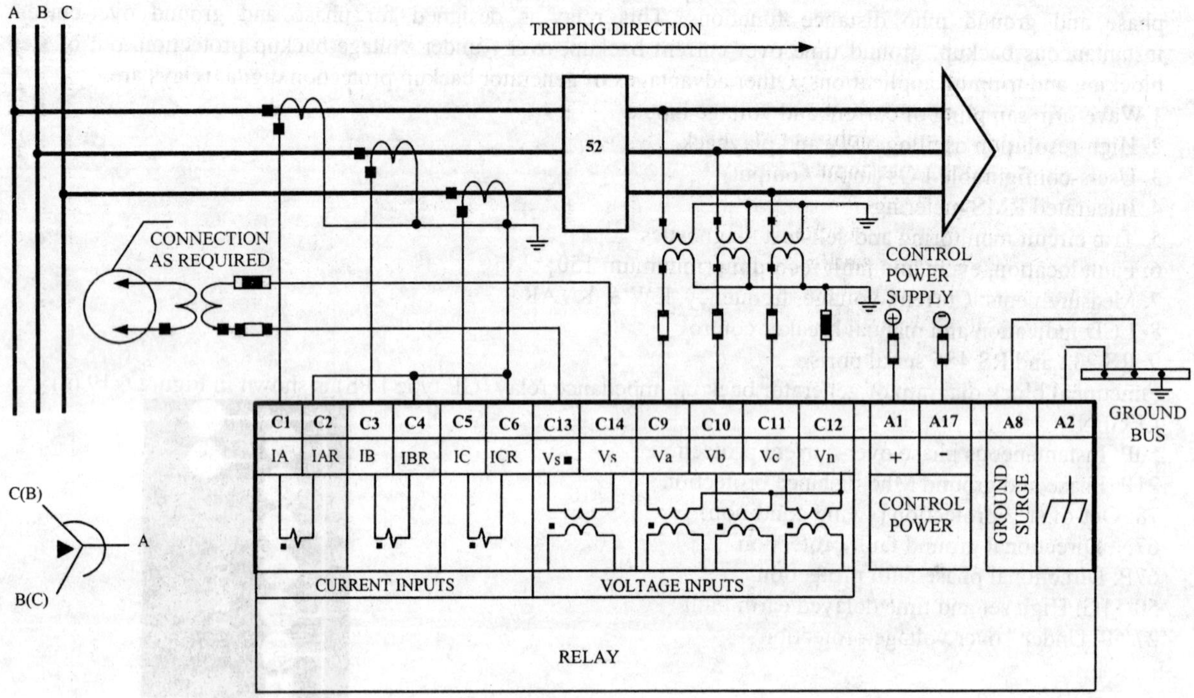

Fig. 6.19 (b): Connection diagram of generator backup protection relay Type LPS (Courtesy, General Electric)

6.20 NON-ELECTRICAL LOCKOUT TRIPPING FOR GENERATORS.

Electro-mechanical protection means protection against overheating of stator winding, Excessive bearing temperature, over-speed, low forward power interlock, pole slip protection etc.

1. Stator winding temperature protection: (49)

Resistance temperature detectors are embedded in the stator winding for monitoring the internal air temperature and core temperature. The resistance of the RTD proportionally increases when the temperature increase. These RTD's are connected to a measuring circuit (refer section 7.16, Chapter # 7), which will operate when the temperature exceeds the set value and initiate an alarm. Overheating of stator winding (due to the failure of cooling system) will cause failure of winding insulation. Stator winding temperature protection is employed for all types of generators above one MVA capacity.

2. Bearing temperature protection: (38)

This protection is mainly used for turbo-generators and hydro-generators; not applicable for diesel generators. Excessive bearing temperature may arise due to mechanical defects, impurities in the lubricating oil or failure of oil circulating system. Excessive bearing temperature is being detected by employing temperature-monitoring device. An induced e.m.f of some volts may be developed in shaft of large generators owing to certain magnetic dissimilarities in the armature field. Bearing currents can overcome by earthing the bearing pedestals of each side of the generator.

3. **Over-speed protection: (12)**

Over speed protection is required to detect a failure of the governor system. The characteristics should ensure that the relay should not respond on full load rejection of generator. Operation of the over speed device or switch, will shutdown the unit. The speed is monitored by, mounting an inductive proximity-probe, or Hall-effect sensor, near the shaft key or keyway as shown in Figure 6.20. The output of the sensor sends a pulse to an assignable digital input, which has been configured as a tachometer.

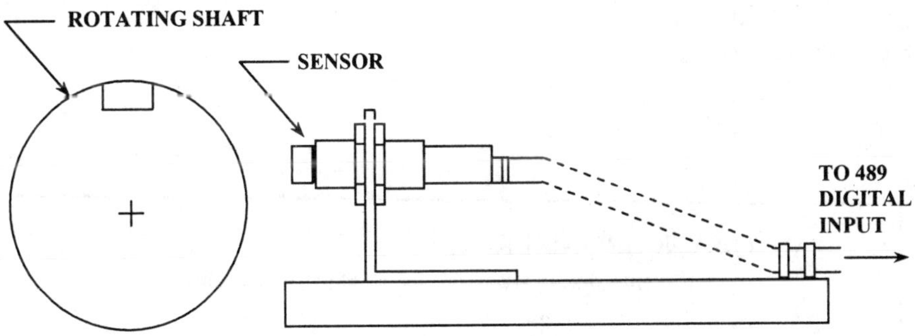

Fig. 6.20: Monitoring generator speed by using inductive proximity probe

4. Vibration protection: (39)
Vibration transducers protect the machine from excessive bearing vibration. Alarm or trip functions can be configured for vibration protection.

5. Low forward power protection for steam turbine generators:
A sensitive low forward power interlock scheme, which will prevent tripping of the generator circuit breaker until the steam flow through the steam turbine has stopped or fallen to a value which would not cause a dangerous over speed when the circuit breaker trip. The normal recommended setting of low forward power protection might be 0.5% of generator rating.

6. Pole slip protection for gas turbine generators:
Generator pole slip protection **(Out of step protection)** is for giving trip output if one pole slip occurs, but have a variable setting so that the number of pole slips required to cause tripping be present. The protection will detect pole slipping in either direction but provision for selecting any one, slip direction.

6.21 SYNCHRONISM CHECK / AUTO SYNCHRONIZING RELAY (25).
Combined synchronism check and system synchronizing relay can automatically select check synchronizing and /or system synchronizing by measuring the relative phase angles between lines and bus voltages. The relay will prevent closure of the circuit breaker if either the phase angle, slip frequency or the voltage magnitude of the incoming and running voltages fall outside prescribed and preset limits.

An electronic measuring relay which is monitoring, the voltage, phase angle and frequency difference between two voltages, primarily when synchronizing two generators or a generator and mains supply. When both systems are within pre-determined limits, a relay contact will close/pulse to allow synchronization. Dead bus breaker closing can also be selected. When the auxiliary voltage is applied to the relay and the generator and bus voltages are nominal, the green LED's bus and generator become "ON" and the relay will begin monitoring the voltage difference ΔV. If the incoming generator voltage is high or low the appropriate contact in the relay will close and initiate the voltage regulator to raise or lower the voltage. Figure 6.21 illustrates the connection diagram of a check-synchronism / auto synchronizer relay.

When the difference between the two voltages within the level set on the relay, the relay will monitor phase angle ($\Delta\theta$). If the phase angle is not matching or the frequency is not matching the relay will give signal to the governor to raise or lower the incoming generator speed/frequency/phase angle to match with the bus frequency/phase angle within the level pre-set on the relay. When voltage, frequency and phase angle are continuously within limits for the period set, SYNC: LCD will light and the output relay contact will close to energize the incoming generator breaker. On a dead bus if the generator voltage, frequency and phase angle are within the set value, the relay will energize to close the breaker. Generator synchronizing circuit is demonstrated in Chapter # 1, section 1.7.
Relay setting ranges:
Frequency range: 35 to 70
Voltage differential: 2 to 10%
Phase angle differential: 4 to 20° (adjustable)

Synchronization pulse 100ms (selectable)
Delay: 0.2 to 1 second (adjustable).
LEGEND: CB: Circuit breaker;
G: Generator;
M: Prime mover or governor;
S: Servomotor

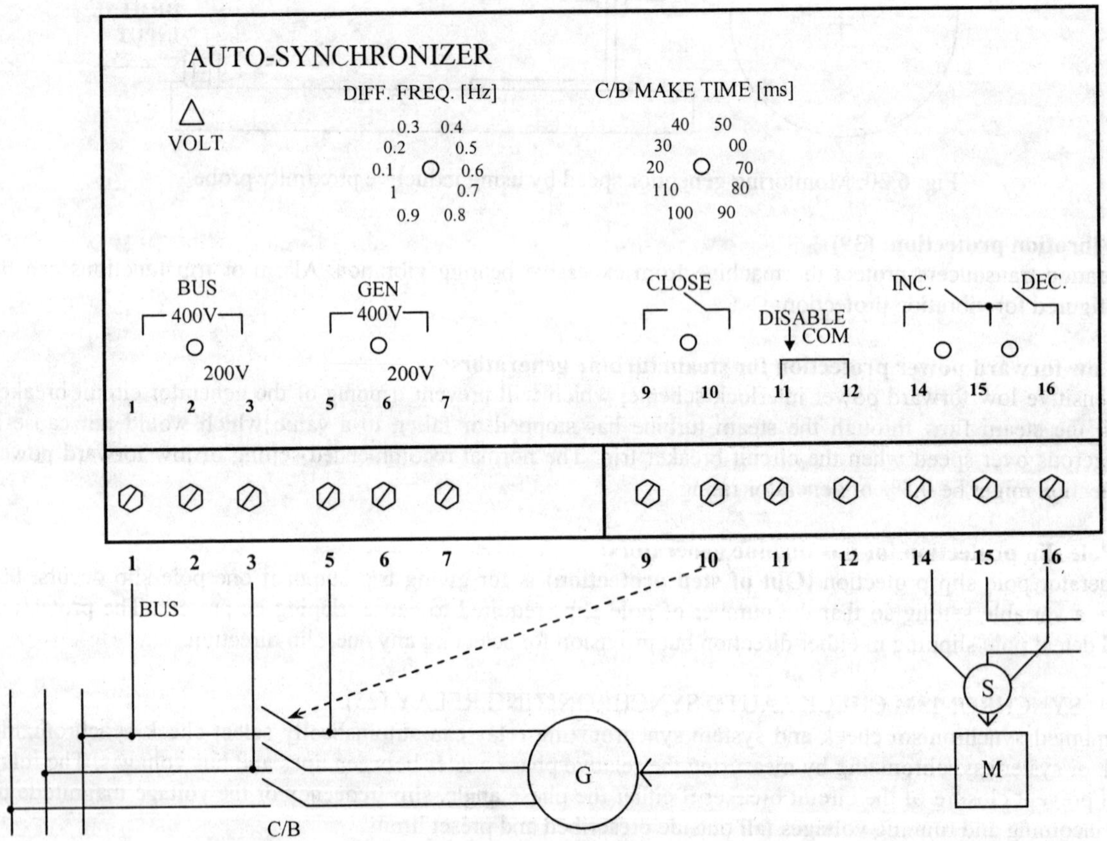

Fig. 6.21: Connection diagram of a typical auto-synchronizing relay.

Advantages of digital auto synchronizing relay:

1. Independent check synchronizing and system synchronizing setting.
2. Adjustable slip frequency, phase angle and time delay.
3. Under-voltage and differential blocking.
4. Split system detection
5. Configurable dead bus and/or deadline charging.
6. Self reset, hand reset or delayed reset contacts.
7. Integrated manual close guard feature.
8. Several time tagged events and few waveform records.

CHAPTER # 7

TRANSFORMER PROTECTION RELAYS

CONTENTS:

7.1 SELECTION AND APPLICATION OF TRANSFORMER PROTECTION RELAYS.

The substation employs many types of transformers, the most important of which are step up transformers, step down transformers, distribution transformers etc. Transformer may be subjected to short circuit between phase and ground, open circuit, turn to turn short circuit, and overheating. Faults usually begin as turn to turn failures and frequently develop in to faults involving internal ground fault. It is highly desirable to isolate transformers with faulty winding as quickly as possible to reduce the possibility of oil fires.

A feasibility study determines whether the system upgrades, future provision and existing equipment will meet the present and future system requirements. A short circuit study is performed to determine the maximum fault currents that would be present in the power system during a system disturbance. As plant expansion occurs, loads may be moved and larger one added, leading to increased levels of available short circuits currents. In addition, the power company supplying the plant may have increased the available fault capacity due to the enlargement of its own system. The possibility of increasing the amount of short circuits current available in to a fault by these changes is the major reason for a periodic system study. If the short circuit capacity of the system exceeds the design capacity of the switchgear, a dangerous situation exists for both plant personnel and system equipment. Under fault conditions, the protective devices would attempt to interrupts the fault current, which could cause a violent failure. Therefore, the need and importance of determining the short circuit capabilities of a system cannot be stressed enough.

Proper coordination of protective devices should be a built in feature of a system design. Protective device coordination, also known as selectivity, is the ability of the closet upstream protective device to detect and clear the system fault with out the operation of another protective device further upstream in the power system. As backup protection, if the nearest device fails to operate for some reason, the next set of protective devices should be coordinated so they will operate before extensive damage result. Many cases of unexplained outages or heavily damaged equipment are accepted with out question or knowledge that the real reason may be improper coordination of protective devices. A poorly coordinated system will result in nuisance outages and greater damage to equipments when a system fault does occur. Proper coordination usually means the proper setting for protective relays. Device coordination also means choosing the correct type of device to begin with, or the substation of the actual device if the existing device cannot be set for the proper result.

Chart given in Table 7.1 (1) describes the electrical and mechanical protections required for large power transformers.

Table 7.1 (1): Relays required for the protection of power transformers.

Device No.	Relay Title	Relay Application	Technical Requirements
50	Instantaneous phase over current relay	Short Circuit protection	Relay operates due to short circuit faults
50G	Instantaneous earth fault relay.	Zero sequence current protection	Relay is connected to the CT provided in the neutral bushing / neutral earthing.
50N	Instantaneous phase over current relay fault relay.	Earth fault protection	Relay operates due to earth fault in primary, secondary and tap changer.
51	IDMT phase over current relay	Over load protection	For two winding transformer relay is required in the primary only, but for three winding transformer relay is required in all the three windings.
51G	Stand by earth fault relay	For back up protection of neutral grounding resistor.	Relay is connected to the CT installed before the neutral grounding resistor.
51N	IDMT phase over current earth fault relay.	Earth fault protection	Inverse Definite Minimum Time (IDMT) characteristic.
50 BF	Breaker failure protection relay.	Breaker failure protection	If the primary protection fails to trip the CB relay will initiate a trip of all of the CB associated with the same bus section
59.	Over Voltage relay	Over voltage / over fluxing protection	Relay operate due to over voltage or due to saturation of magnetic circuit.
64G	Restricted earth fault relay	Internal- earth fault protection	For delta connected or un earthed star winding, relay is connected to the residual circuit of the CT.
67N/ 87N	Directional / differential earth fault relay.	Directional / differential connection for earth fault protection.	Earth fault protection
87T	High speed based transformer differential relay.	Internal protection (short circuit, earth fault, fault in tap changer).	Star connected winding, CT's are connected in delta and delta connected winding CT's are connected in star.
64N	High impedance relay.	Differential ground fault protection	For transformers grounded through grounding resistor.
74	Protection-supervision relay.	Protection circuit supervision	Relay operates if CT circuit wiring becomes open circuited.
26 - W	Winding over temperature	Winding over heating protection	Dial type winding thermometer
26-O	Oil over temperature.	Cooling system control	Dial type oil thermometer.
63MT	Main tank Buchholz relay	Short circuit / winding damages.	Operates due to oil surge or gas.
63TC	Tap changer protection relay (Buchholz type)	Flash over / Fault in tap changer.	Oil surge in the tap changer tank.
20	Tank over pressure relief valve	Incipient faults	Excessive oil pressure in the main tank.

7.2 STEP UP SUBSTATION AND POWER TRANSFORMER PROTECTION.

Figure 7.2 illustrates the single line diagram of a typical 63 MVA, 11/132KV, Ynd1 Delta / star transformer, use as step up transformer designed for a generating station. The 132 KV star connected secondary neutral is grounded through a neutral grounding resistor. Circuit breakers with double trip coils are provided at the down stream (11KV) and upstream (132KV). Following are the protective relays employed.

1. Overload protection (device # 49)
2. Phase over current relay with instantaneous and time delay over current elements (device #50/51)
3. Earth fault relay Inverse definite minimum time (device #51N)
4. Restricted earth fault differential relay (device #64)
5. Percentage and harmonic restraint high speed biased transformer differential relay (device #87T)
6. Non electrical protections listed in section 7.18

Operation of the transformer primary side over current relay and earth fault relay incorporated in the primary neutral earthing will cause operation of trip relay to energize the 11KV circuit breaker trip coil No. 2. Inter trip facility provided in the trip circuit will trip both upstream and downstream breakers simultaneously. Operation of high speed biased transformer differential relay or restricted earth fault relay will cause operation of high speed trip relay. This relay will initiate tripping of both primary and secondary side circuit breakers through trip coil No. 1, (primary protection) and isolate the unit. Arrow mark on the transformer secondary indicates that on load tap changer is on the high voltage winding.. Transformer vector group is Yn d1, i.e, high voltage side (132 KV) star connected with neutral brought out and lower voltage side (11 KV) delta connected.

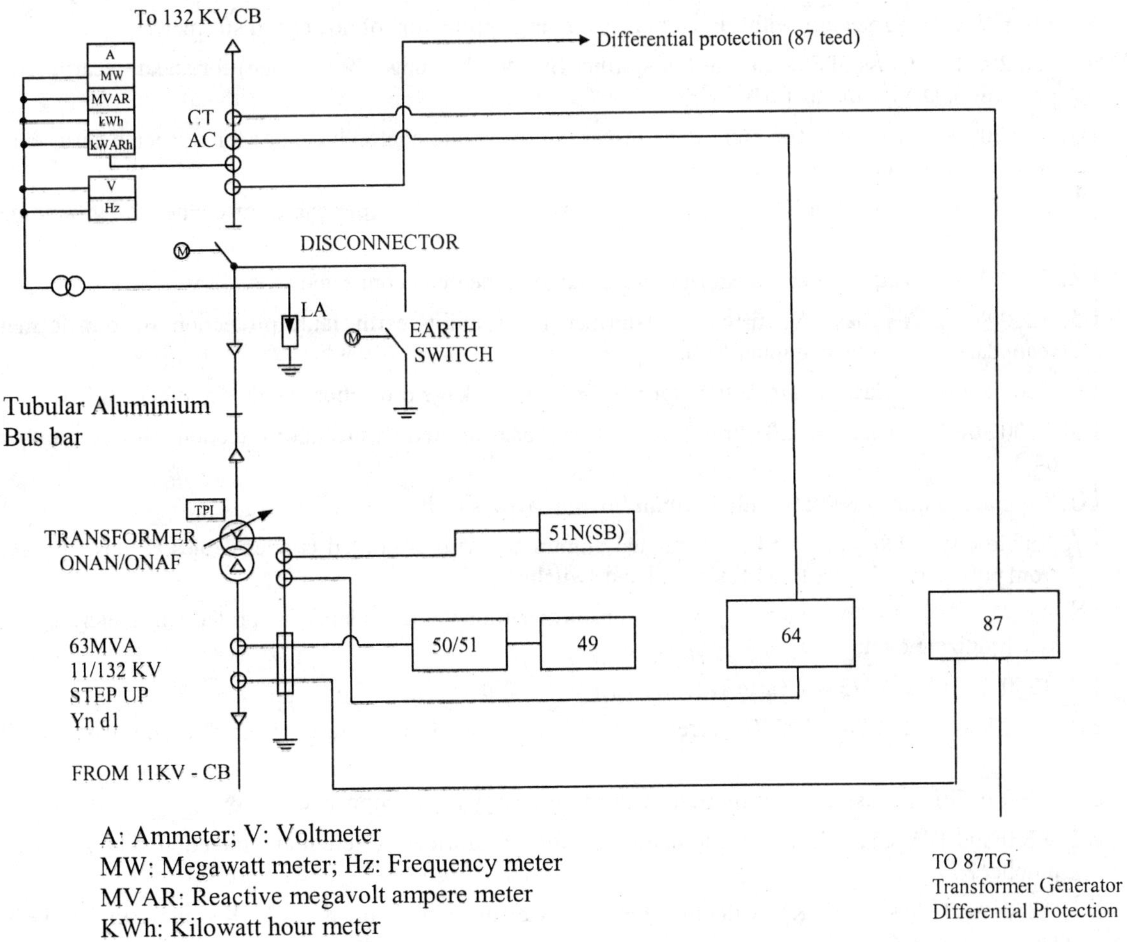

Fig: 7.2: Single line diagram of a typical 63MVA 11/132KV step up Power transformer

7.3 STEP DOWN SUBSTATION AND POWER TRANSFORMER PROTECTION.

Figure 7.3 illustrates the AC schematic diagram of a 63 MVA, 132/33 KV star/delta (YNd11) step down power transformer, in a receiving station. In the star connected primary, the star point is solidly grounded to earth by using 500 sq: mm bare stranded copper conductor. Zigzag grounding transformer is connected to the delta connected secondary. 200 KVA grounding transformer have a star connected 3-phase 4 wire 415 V secondary, which can be used for substation auxiliary services such as battery charger, light and power circuits, air conditioning system, computerized substation management system etc. Zigzag grounding transformer neutral is connected to a 19 Ohm neutral grounding resistor through a disconnecting switch and grounded to the substation earth grid as shown in the figure. Bypass disconnecting switch also employed for solid grounding of the Zigzag grounding transformer neutral. Equipments installed in the substation are listed below.

1. 138 KV Surge arresters with surge counter for lightning protection of substation.
2. 132 KV/√3: 120/√3 V capacitor type potential transformer for protection and metering.
3. Wave trap and coupling capacitor for power line carrier communication system.
4. Earth switch (Shorting switch) for shorting and earthing the overhead line during maintenance / repair
5. 800 A Triple pole motor operated disconnector switch for off-load disconnection of line.
6. 300/200/1 A, Class X current transformers for connecting transformer differential protection relay; Device number 87T.
7. 300/200/1 A, Class 5P10 current transformers for over-current and earth fault protection (50/50N) instantaneous and (51/51N) time delayed.
8. 138 KV Surge protectors with surge counter for surge protection of power transformer.
9. 300/200/1 A, Class 5PS20 current transformer (Neutral bushing 132 KV side) for standby earth fault protection: Device number 51G.
10. 300/200/1A Class 5PS20 current transformer (132 KV side neutral bushing) for restricted earth fault protection; Device number 64G.
11. 33 KV 3C 120 sq: mm XLPE insulated steel wire armoured copper cable for connecting grounding transformer.
12. 200 KVA Zigzag earthing transformer for grounding the delta connected secondary.
13. 1200/800/1 A, Class X current transformer for standby earth fault protection of transformer secondary side; Device number 51G.
14. 1200/800/1 A, Class X current transformer for frame leakage protection; Device number 54G.
15. 1200/800/1 A, Class 5Ps20 current transformer for restricted earth fault protection; Device number 64G.
16. Neutral grounding resistor with disconnector and bypass switch.
17. Single core 1000 sq:mm XLPE insulated aluminium wire armoured copper cables (2 nos / phase) from power transformer to 33 KV metalclad switchgear.
18. 33 KV/√3: 120/√3 V, star/star voltage transformer (double secondary) for protection, metering and synchronizing circuit.
19. 1250 A, 31.5 KA, 33 KV earth switch.
20. 1200/800/1 A Class 10P10 current transformers for directional over-current and earth fault protection.
21. 1200/.800/1 A Class 0.2, current transformers for energy meter connection.
22. 1200/800/1 A Class X current transformers for transformer differential protection relay; Device number 87T.
23. 1250 A, 31.5 KA, 33 KV withdrawable type Vaccum circuit breaker (33 KV incomer breaker); Device number 52..
24. 1250 A, 31.5 KA, 33 KV metal-clad switchgear with incoming and outgoing feeders.
25. Synchronism check relay 33 KV paralleling: Device number 25.

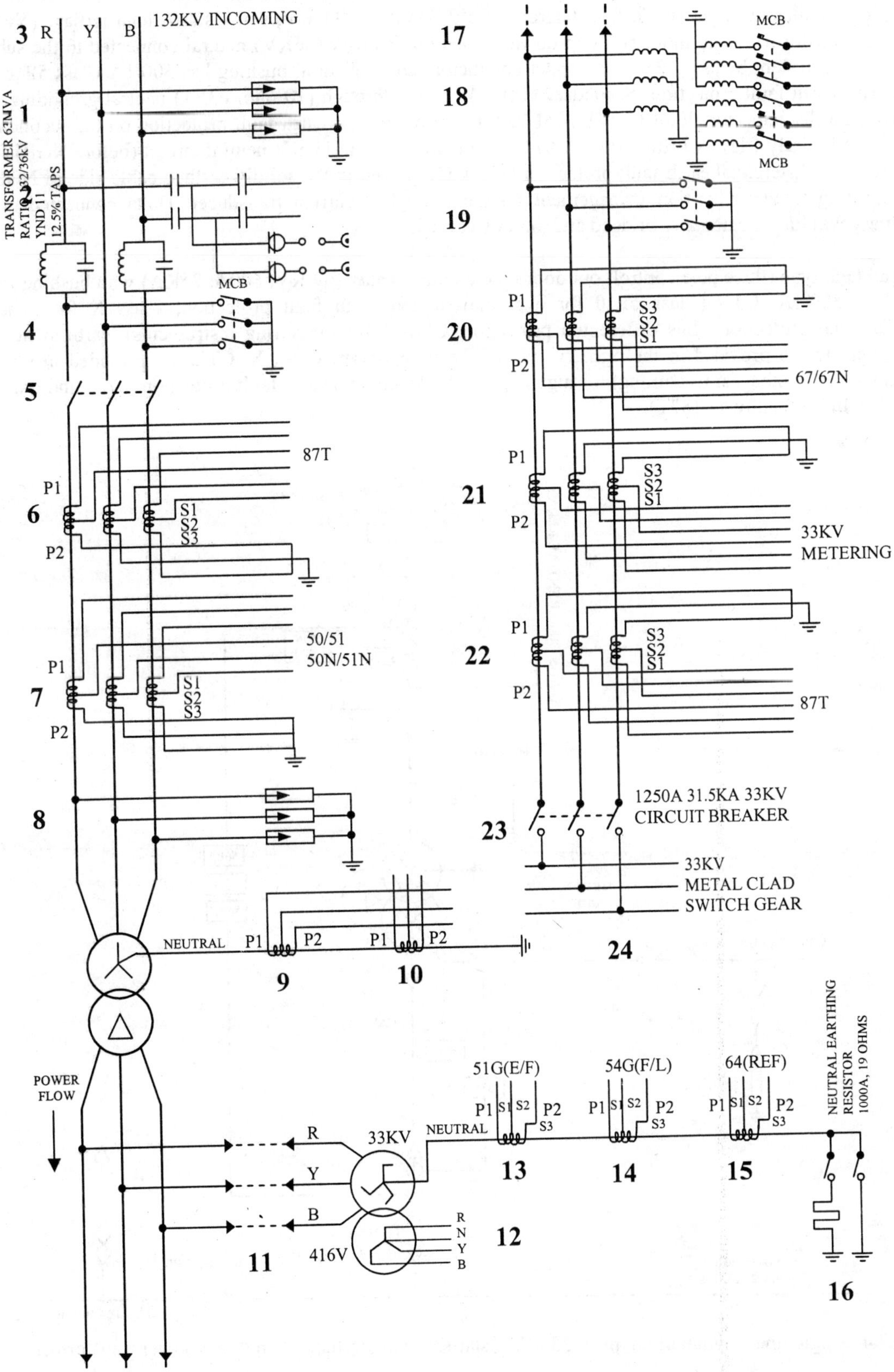

Fig. 7.3: AC schematic diagram of a typical 132/33 KV outdoor type step down transformer substation.

7.4 INDUSTRIAL SUBSTATION AND POWER TRANSFORMERPROTECTION.

Figure 7.4 illustrates the single line diagram of a 25MVA, 66/11 KV, star / star / delta tertiary (YnYnd11) power transformer in an Industrial step down substation. Primary (66KV) neutral connected to the substation grounding system by using 630mm^2 copper conductor cables. Neutral bushing has 300/1A Class 5P10 CT for primary earth fault protection. Secondary (11KV) earthed through (10 ohm 635A) neutral grounding resistor through a disconnector. 2000/1A, Class 5P20 CT is provided for earth fault protection on the secondary side (50N). Similarly Class X (ratio 2000/ 1 A) CT is provided in the 11 KV neutral circuit (before NGR) for high impedance differential earth fault protection (87N). CT placed in the solidly earthed cable side of NGR is for connecting to the substation management system through a current transducer. Delta connected unloaded tertiary winding is externally bridged and directly earthed.

Dead tank type (three pole control) out door type circuit breaker (69 KV, 800A, 25KA) with bushing mounted 4 core 300/1A, CT's (Class 5P10 for over current and earth fault protection, Class X for transformer differential protection / bus differential protection, Class 1 for measuring instruments), earth switch, surge arrester etc are provided in the primary side of the transformer. Class X, CT's are provided inside 12KV, mental clad switchgear (Incoming) for high impedance differential earth fault protection (87N) and transformer biased differential relay. (87T).

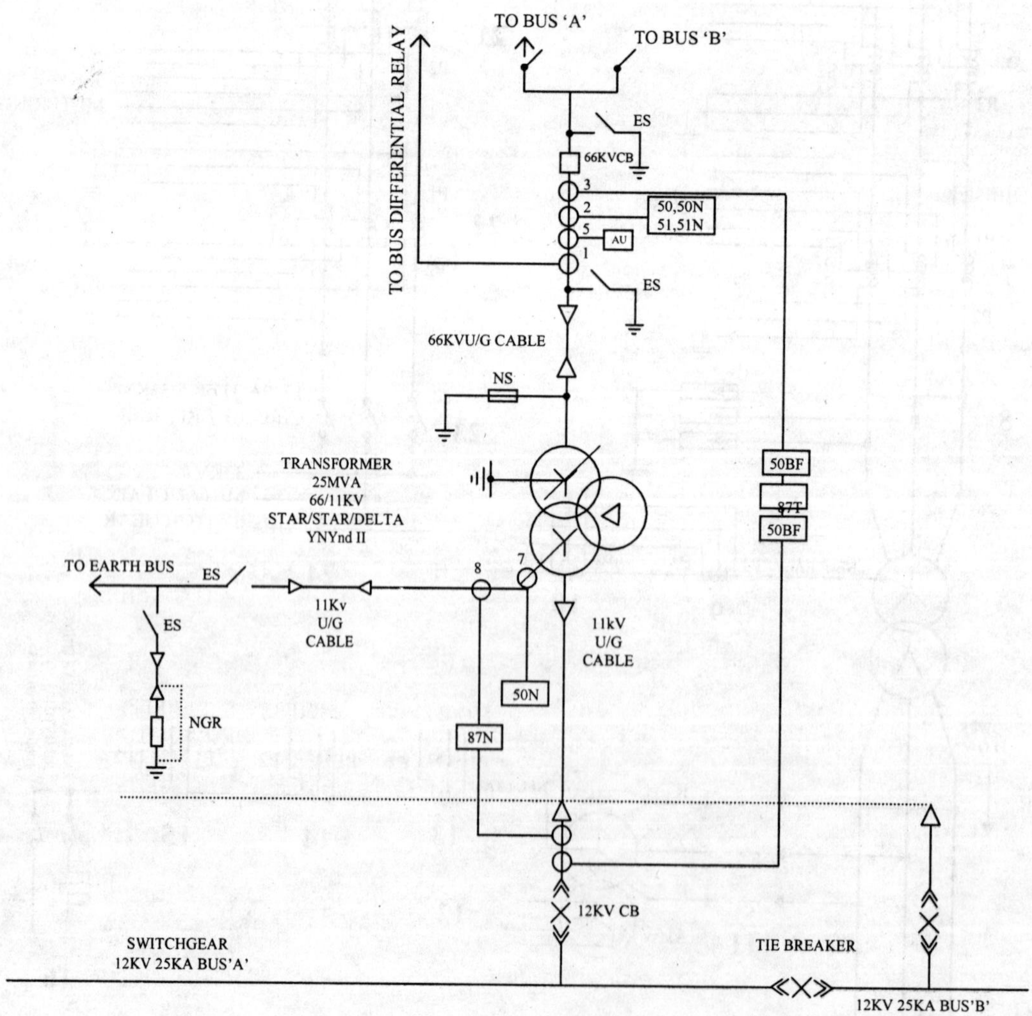

Fig.7.4: Single line diagram of a typical 25 MVA star/star/delta tertiary, step down power transformer.

Following are the protection employed for the transformer.

1. Transformer high speed biased differential protection (87T)
2. Transformer high impedance differential earth fault protection (87N)
3. Time delay Phase over current and earth fault protection (51/51N)
4. Instantaneous over current and earth fault protection (50/50N)
5. Breaker fail protection, instantaneous over current (50BF)
6. Instantaneous earth fault relay, neutral CT, 11KV side (50G)
7. Non Electrical protection as listed in section 7.18

Operation of the transformer primary (66KV) side over current and earth fault protection will cause operation of high speed latching multi trip auxiliary relay. This will initiate trip signal to the transformer 66KV circuit breaker via inter trip provision. Transformer (11KV side) neutral differential earth fault protection (87N) will provide instantaneous tripping of transformer primary and secondary circuit breakers. If the neutral earthing resistor is bypassed due to any reason, CT installed in the secondary neutral bushing is being utilized for energizing the earth fault relay and initiate tripping of both primary and secondary breakers.

Operation of transformer high speed biased differential relay (87T) and high impedance differential earth fault relay (87N) will cause operation of multi tripe auxiliary relay. This relay will initiate trip signal to trip 66KV and 11KV, circuit breakers simultaneously and activate circuit breaker fail protection (50BF). Successful tripping of transformer primary and secondary circuit breakers shall cause the CB fail protection relay to automatic reset. If the breaker's fails to trip and the fault current continuous to flow the CB fail protection relay will operate and initiate trip signal to all the breakers associated with the 66KV bus section to trip and isolate the concerned bus section. In the 66KV side breaker trip coil No. 1 is used for primary protection.

7.5 DISTRIBUTION SUBSTATION AND TRANSFORMER PROTECTION.

Figure 7.5 illustrates the single line diagram of 1600 KVA 11000/415 V, Delta / star (DYn 11) Distribution transformer substation with provision for synchronizing the low voltage side.

Following protection relays are employed in this scheme.

1. Synchronism check relay (25)
2. Under voltage relay (27)
3. Over-current protection (49)
4. Instantaneous over current relay (50)
5. Time delay over current relay (51)
6. IDMT Earth fault relay (51N)
7. Buchholz relay (63B)
8. Winding temperature high (26WT)

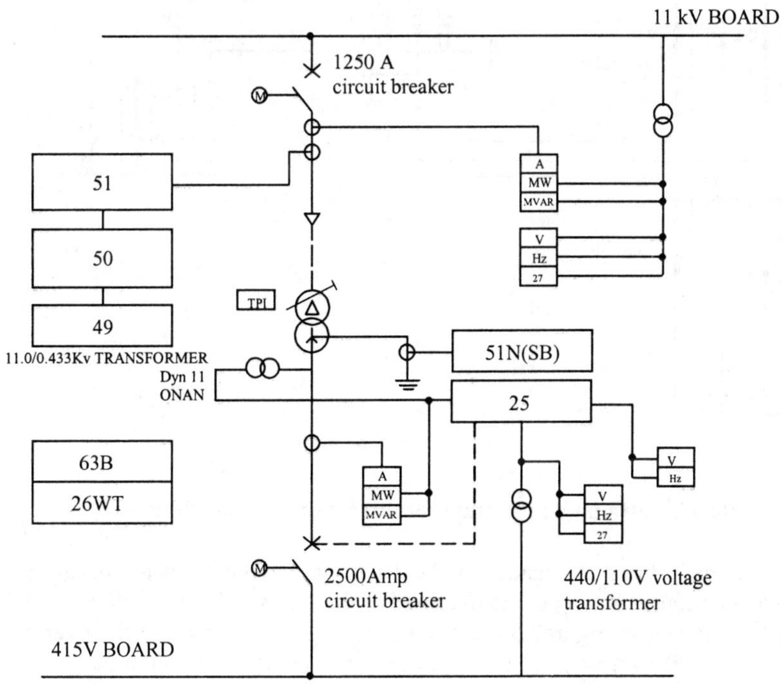

Fig: 7.5: Single line diagram of a typical 1600 KVA 11 KV/415 V delta/star distribution transformer.

7.6 OVER CURRENT AND EARTH FAULT PROTECTION FOR TRANSFORMERS.

Over current relays are located in the primary winding of a two winding transformers as shown in Figure 7.6 (a). Relays in the secondary windings will operate in the event of a fault in the secondary bus bar or outgoing feeders. Over current relay in the primary side when operated, it should trip both the primary and secondary circuit breakers. Transformers with on load tap changer, both time delay and high set instantaneous elements are required for protection.

Overload protection on three winding transformers must be installed in all the three windings as shown in figure 7.6 (b) to ensure reliable operation of the transformer with one winding de-energized.

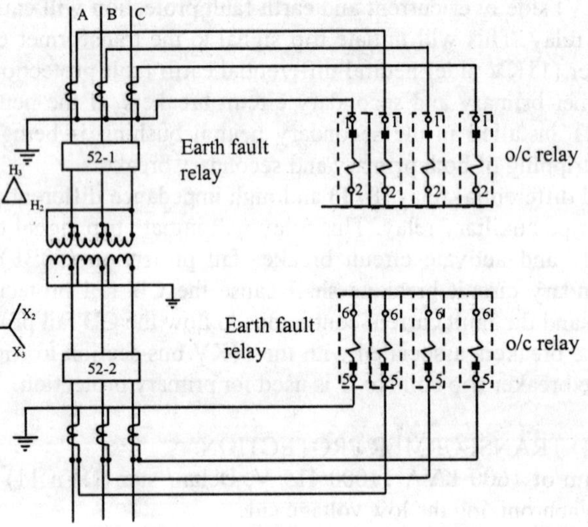

Fig.7.6 (a): Over-current and earth fault protection for two winding transformer

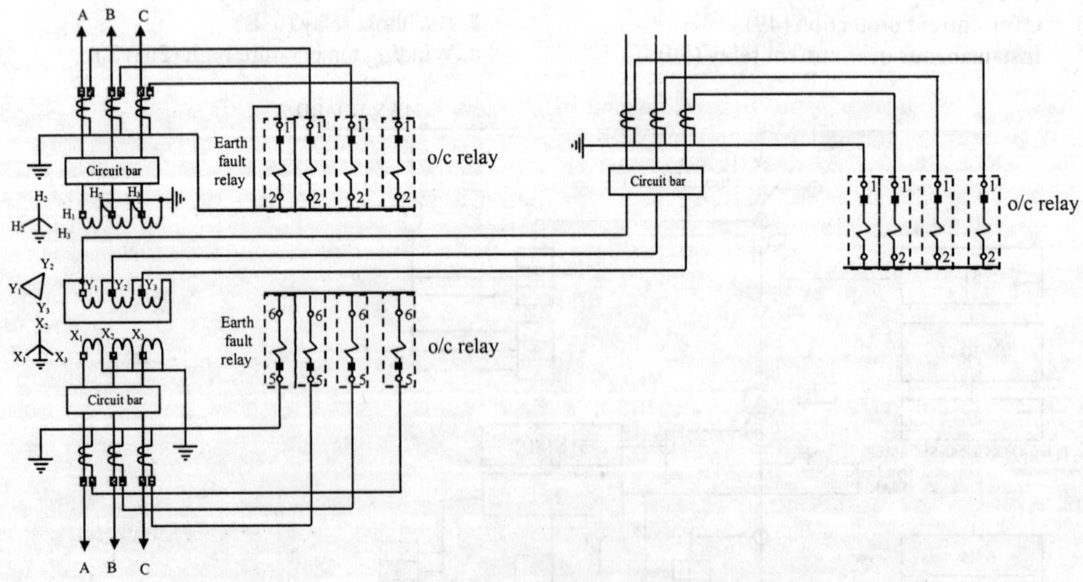

Fig.7.6 (b): Over-current and earth fault protection for three winding transformer

Over current protection of autotransformers are made on the basis of the requirements of three winding transformer. The overload protection must respond to the overload of the series winding, common winding and auxiliary winding (if provided) as shown in Figure7.6 (c). Over current relay monitoring the overload of the common winding must be installed on the zero taps of the auto transformer. The overload of the series winding is determined by, the currents in the leads of the high and low voltage respectively. Auxiliary winding if provided also need separate protection in the load side. Instantaneous over current relays are provided to isolate the transformer on heavy fault currents and its operation zone embraces only a part of the transformer. Although the current cut off is basically a protection against internal faults, it must deenergize the transformer from all sides having power sources.

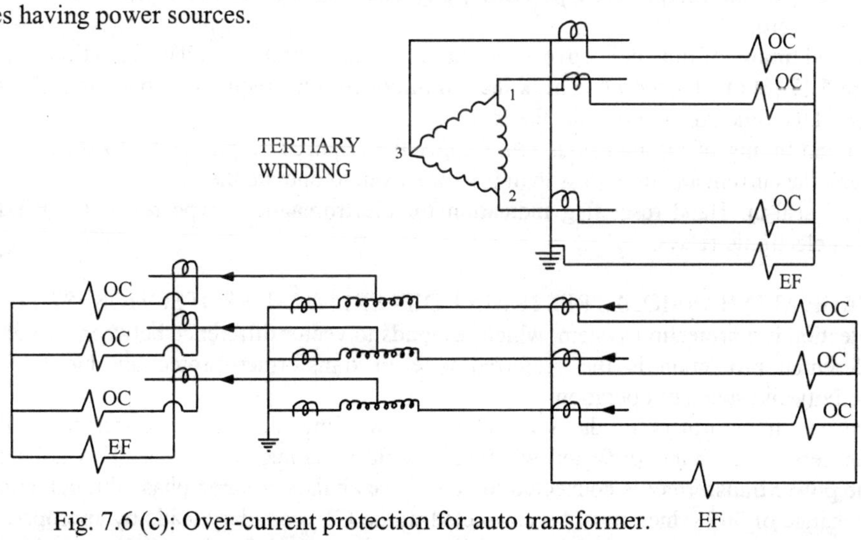

Fig. 7.6 (c): Over-current protection for auto transformer.

Tertiary winding protection: The tertiary winding of a three winding transformer or an auto transformer is usually of much smaller kilovolt ampere rating than the main windings. Therefore over current relays employed for the protection of main windings offer almost no protection to such tertiary windings. During external system ground faults, these tertiary windings may carry heavy currents. In the event of failure of the primary protection for external ground faults separate tertiary over-current protection may be desirable. If the tertiary is used to carry the load, partial protection can be provided by a single over-current relay connected to the parallel connected secondary of three current transformers (one in each winding) of the delta connected tertiary winding. This connection (figure 5.1 (I) of Chapter #5) provides only zero sequence overload protection and does not operate for positive and negative sequence overload current. In this case, the relay will operate for system ground faults but will not operate for phase faults in the tertiary or its leads. If necessary, differential relay shall be provided for protection against phase faults.

Grounding Transformer protection: Grounding transformer can be either a zigzag or a star delta connected transformer. Over current relay connected to delta connected current transformers as shown in Figure 7.6 (d) is the protection usually employed for grounding transformers used for main transformer grounding. If the grounding transformer is of the zigzag variety (refer figure 7.3) internal faults, such as turn to turn faults, may be limited by the magnetizing impedance of an un-faulted phase. Hence, Buchholz relay is essential in such Zigzag transformers. Grounding transformers are seldom switched by, themselves. However, when they are switched, they are subject to magnetizing inrush current as such harmonic restrained over current relays are used to prevent inadvertent tripping upon energizing.

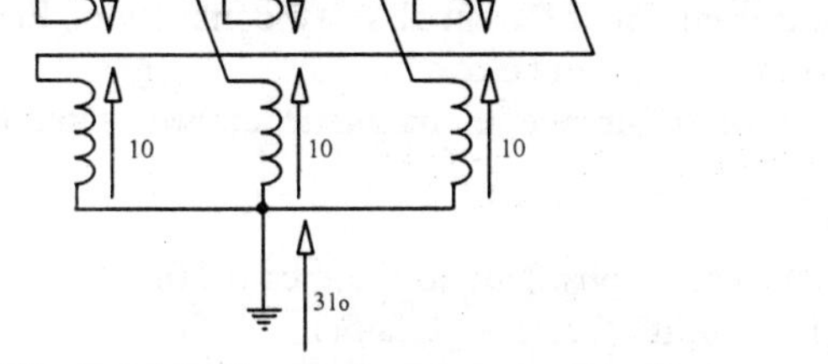

Fig. 7.6 (d): Over-current protection for Zigzag grounding transformer.

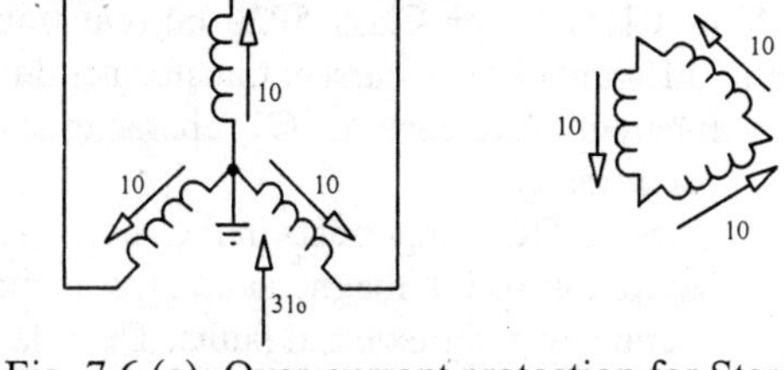

Fig. 7.6 (e): Over-current protection for Star/delta grounding transformer.

Test on over-current and earth fault relay:

1. Zero-check: For indication disk type relays, physically verify that the contact closes when the time dial is set at zero.
2. Pick up and timing of time delay over–current unit: Connect the secondary injection test set as shown in figure 5.17 (c) of Chapter # 6. Check the minimum currents required to pick up at the required plug setting and the time taken to operate the relay.
3. Pick up and timing of instantaneous unit: Apply the required current (8 to 10 times normal current) and check the current and time (less than 0.1 sec) taken to operate the relay.
4. Target ad seal-in: Hand reset flag indication for electromagnetic type relay. LED indications will appear in electronic relays.

7.7 PERCENTAGE AND HARMONIC RESTRAINT DIFFERENTIAL PROTECTION (87 T)

Differential protection is a protection system, which responds to vector difference between two or more similar quantities. Differential protection is the preferred type of transformer protection due to its simplicity, sensitivity, selectivity and speed of operation.

1. The current transformers in the star connected winding should be connected in delta; current transformers in the delta connected windings should be connected in star. This is because (assume that the power transformer is connected in delta / star) balanced three phase through current suffers a phase change of 30^0, which must be connected in the CT secondary leads by appropriate connection of the CT secondary windings. Further zero sequence current flowing in the star side of the power transformer will not produce current out side the delta on the other side. The zero sequence must there fore be eliminated from the star side by connecting the current transformers in delta, from which it follows that the current transformers on the delta side of the power transformer must be connected in star in order to give the 30° phase shift.
2. The delta connection of the current transformers should be replica of the delta connection of the power transformers; the star connection of the current transformers should be a replica of the star connection of the power transformers.
3. If the primary and secondary current transformer ratios are not exactly matched, taking in to account of the voltage ratio of the transformer, interposing current transformers are required in the current transformer secondary circuits to match the units properly so that no appreciable current will flow in the relay operating coil, expect for transformer internal fault conditions.
4. Power transformers with on load tap changer the differential protection current transformers should be matched at the midpoint of the tap changing range so that the current transformer error will then be a minimum for the maximum tap position in either direction.
5. Whenever, the transformer is energized transformer exciting inrush current, which may flow only in the primary winding. To avoid this difficulty harmonic restraint is essential for the relay. This relay filters the harmonic component from the inrush current and feeds it in to the restrained coil.
6. For transformer and generator transformer differential protection schemes, the rated stability limit should not be less than the maximum through fault level as limited by the impedance of the protected equipments only.

While selecting differential relays following points are to be considered.

a. Permit operation up on an internal fault during inrush current period.
b. Not to have excess restraining current resulting from harmonic restraints of the secondary current due to current transformer saturation during internal fault.
c. Relay must operate during over excitation due to over fluxing or over voltage.

Differential relay current transformer:

Class X or Class PS or Class 5P20 current transformers are used for differential relay connection. Errors caused in differential relay current transformer during a short circuit is given below.

1. Inherent difference in CT characteristic arising out of difference in magnetic circuit, saturation condition etc.
2. Unequal DC components in the short circuit currents.
3. Saturation of CT magnetic circuits during short-circuit conditions. Due to these cause the relay may operate even for external faults. The relay may lose its stability for through faults.

On-load tap changing of transformers.

During on load tap changing process, the transformation ratio will change. Thereby CT ratio do not match with the new tap settings. To overcome these difficulties "Percentage differential relay" or "Bias differential relay" is used. The current flowing in restraining coil is proportional to $(I_1 - I_2) / 2$ and this restraining current prevents the operation of the relay because, with the rise in current the restraining torque increases and $I_1 - I_2$ arising out of difference in CT ratio is not enough to cause the relay operation.

Magnetizing current inrush:

To prevent the operation of differential relay due to magnetizing current inrush occurred during energizing or switching-in a transformer, harmonic restraint is provided for the differential relay. This relay filters the harmonic component from the inrush current and feeds it to the restraining coil. The magnetizing current contains a large content of several harmonics. This harmonic content is used for obtaining restraining torque during switching-in of transformer. The amount of restraint may be fixed, adjustable or variable. The variable percentage relay increases the restraint as the current increases. Independent instantaneous over-current units are provided with harmonic restrained relays in order to isolate the system when the differential relay operation is restrained during saturation of current transformer.

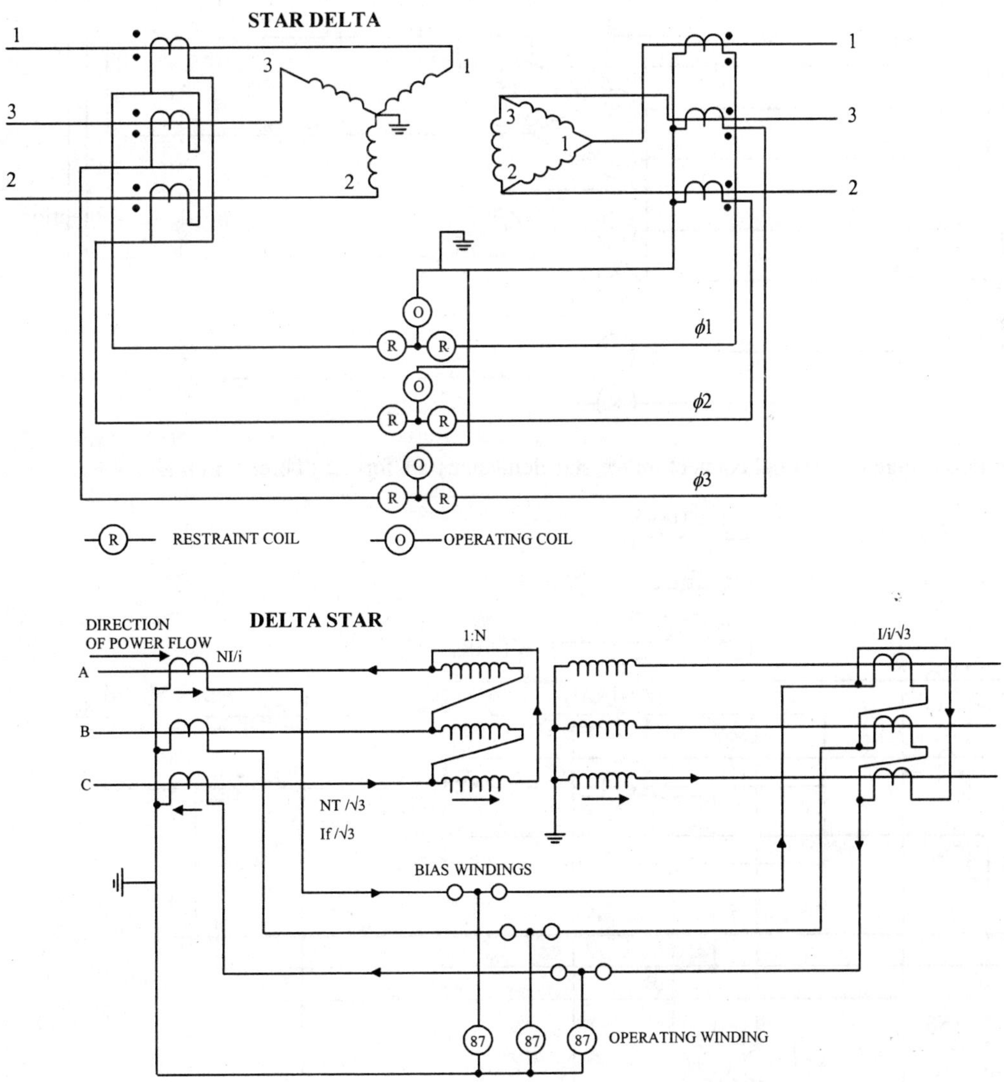

Fig. 7.7 (a): Percentage differential relay connection for star/delta and delta/star transformer (Two winding).

Differential protection (Device 87T) protects transformers against internal short circuits earth faults, and inter-turn faults. Current transformers are installed on either side of the transformer windings. Differential relays used for the protection of two windings power transformers have two through current restraint coils and one differential (operating) coil as illustrated in Figure 7.7 (a). Differential relay used with three windings power transformers [(Figure 7.7(b)] have three through current restraint coils and one differential current coils/phase.

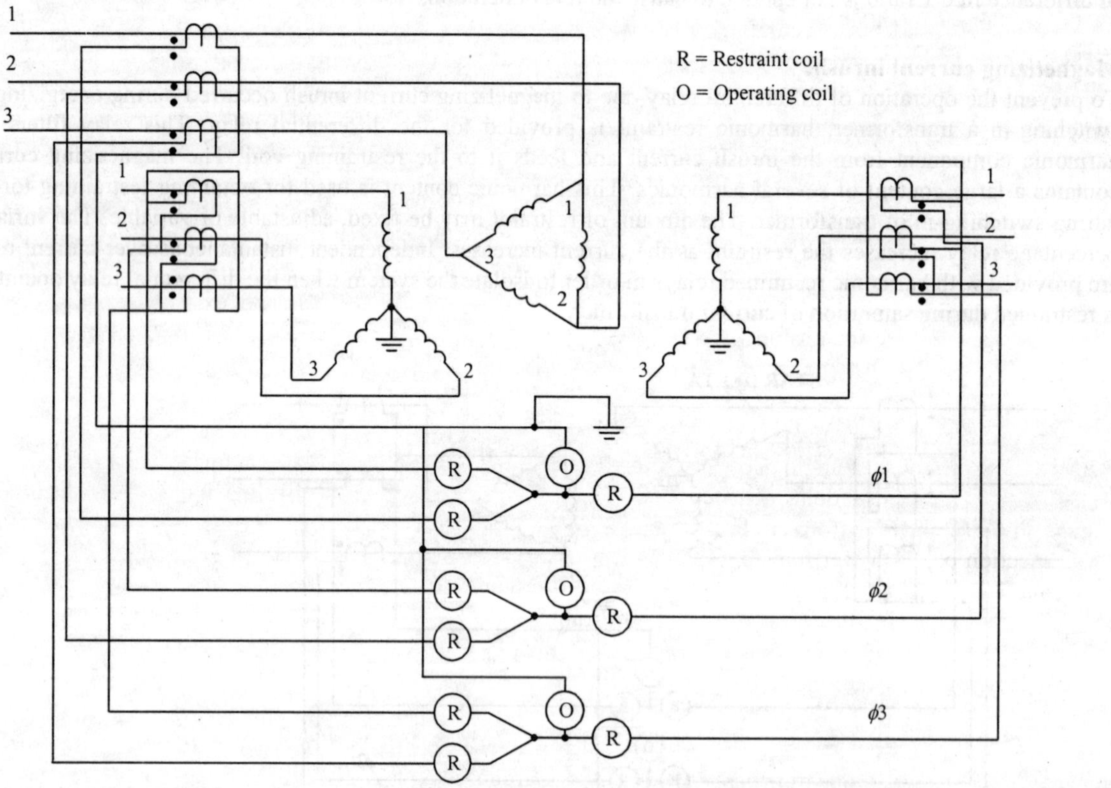

Fig. 7.7(b): Percentage differential connection for star/delta/star transformer (Three windings).

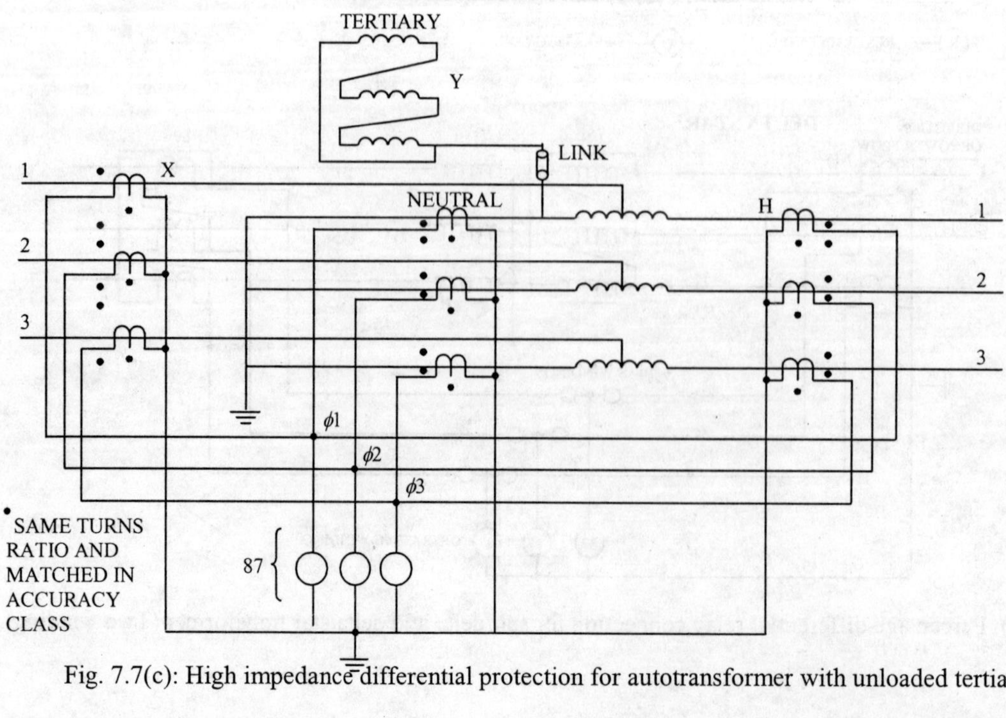

Fig. 7.7(c): High impedance differential protection for autotransformer with unloaded tertiary.

Differential protection employed for three-phase autotransformers have three sets of current transformers connected in star and three sets of restrained coils and one operating coil connected similar to three windings transformer. Relays used for autotransformer protection does not require bias windings. It is common practice to provide high impedance differential protection for large HV and EHV autotransformers. Typical differential relay connection for 3-phase auto transformer is shown in figure 7.7 (c). This arrangement provides protection against all type of phase faults and ground faults but not turn to turn faults. This protection is immune to the effects of magnetizing inrush currents, because inrush currents remain cancelled by the neutral current transformer. Also there is no imbalance current in the relay circuit due to the load tap changing equipment. Thus a high impedance differential relay can be applied with out any harmonic restraint, load bias, or time delay. Auto transformers are often provided with a tertiary delta winding and connected as shown in figure (c). The differential relay does not provide protection against phase faults or turn to turn faults in the tertiary windings but the relay would sense ground fault.

The percentage and harmonic restraint differential relay is a transformer differential protection relay provided with the features of percentage and harmonic restraint and has a sensitive polarized relay as the operating element. Percentage restraint permits accurate determination between internal and external faults at high currents. Harmonic restraint enables the relay to distinguish, by the difference in waveform, between the differential current caused by an internal fault and that caused by transformer magnetizing inrush.

The primary and secondary currents of star/ delta transformer always differ not only by their values but also by their phase. The phase shift angle depends on the vector group of the transformer windings. The phase shift is compensated by means of delta connection of the secondary of the CT's installed in the star connected windings of the power transformer. The delta connection of the CT windings must exactly correspond to the delta connection of the power transformer windings. The current transformers located in the delta side of the power transformer are star connected as illustrated in the figure.7.7 (a). It follows from the vector diagram 7.7 (d) that the current in the line wires of the current transformers connected in delta I_{AB}, I_{BC} and I_{CA} are shifted through 30^0 .Currents in the wire of the second group of current transformers lab, Ibc and Ica coincides in phase with their primary currents and are, therefore shifted through 30° relative to the primary as shown in the vector diagram 7.7 (e).

The method of connecting one of the current transformer groups in to star, and the other group in delta, ensures phase shift compensation of primary currents of positive and negative sequence. The zero sequence currents occur in case of an earth faults they can from a closed loop only via the transformer winding, which is connected in to star, provided its neutral is earthed. Then the zero sequence currents are transformed in to delta connected windings. It means that in a differential protection of transformers with star/ delta connected windings the zero sequence currents flow only through the current transformers, which are installed in the star side of the power transformer. By this arrangement such flow of primary currents in similar to the current distribution present in the event of a fault inside the transformer. It may cause incorrect operation of the protection and this can be overcome by delta connecting the CT's installed on the star side of the power transformer.

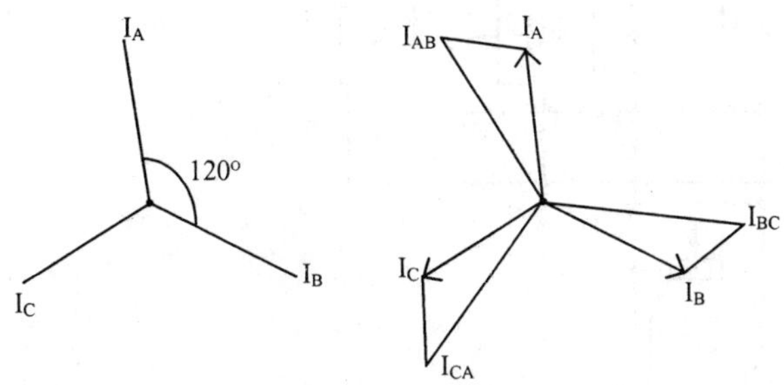

Fig. 7.7 (d): Star-delta vector diagram

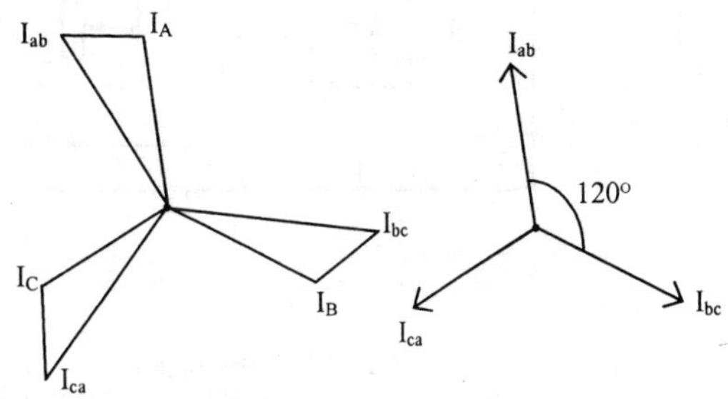

Fig. 7.7 (e): Delta-star vector diagram

Transformation ratio of the CT's in the primary and secondary sides are selected in such a way that the, currents in the protection arms of equal value in normal running and external fault condition. With the windings star/ delta connected, the current in the arm supplied by the CT's connected in delta is equal to $\surd 3I_1$ / n_1, while that in the arm supplied fro the star connected CT's is equal to I_2 / n_2 and the condition will meet when $\surd 3I_1/ n_1 = I_2 / n_2$

I_1 = Rated primary current; I_2 = Rated secondary current; n_1 = Primary CT ratio; n_2 = secondary CT ratio.

To compensate this ratio error with electromechanical relays an interposing current transformer (refer figure 5.1 (j) of chapter #5) is being used. This does not require for electronic relays. While switching on a transformer the inrush current flows only through the primary windings, and as five times full load current and persists nearly one second. It has the same effect as an internal fault as far as the differential relay is concerned. This inrush current is essentially a pulsating direct current, which rapidly decays. It contains a large percentage of harmonic components. This facts is utilized to block the operation of the differential relay during the current inrush period by providing restraining coils and harmonic restraint comprising series and parallel turned filter circuits. This makes the differential relay inoperative during the current inrush. Usually differential relays are required only for transformers 1500KVA and above.

Saturation of CT magnetic circuit is possible during an external short circuit in this condition the relay may loose its stability for through (external) faults. To overcome this difficulty the percentage differential relay or biased differential relay is used with additional restraining coils.

Numerical differential relay:

Figure 7.7 (f) shows a simplified schematic diagram of a transformer differential relay with harmonic restraint. The operating current is the phasor sum of the currents entering the protected transformer. A through current transformer having two primary circuits forms the restraint current for two winding transformers. Each of the through current transformer primary circuits is connected to the main current transformer circuits. The resulting restraint current is the phasor difference of the currents entering the transformer. The relay has three independent through current transformers for three winding transformer applications. The relay rectifies each of the secondary currents of the through current transformers independently and then sums them to form a restraint current. The main operating unit of the transformer differential relay is a polarized relay. This unit performs an amplitude comparison of the rectified currents applied to the operating, O, and restraint, R, coils. The unit trips when the current in the operating coil exceeds the current in the restrained coil. During transformer magnetizing inrush conditions the unfiltered operating current may contain, in addition to harmonic, a DC offset component. The band pass filter, L_1, C_1 blocks the DC component, but the notch filter, L_2, C_2 passes the DC component, thus providing an additional temporary restraint that increases relay security of inrush. Figure 7.7 (g) shows the connection diagram of a numerical transformer differential protection relay.

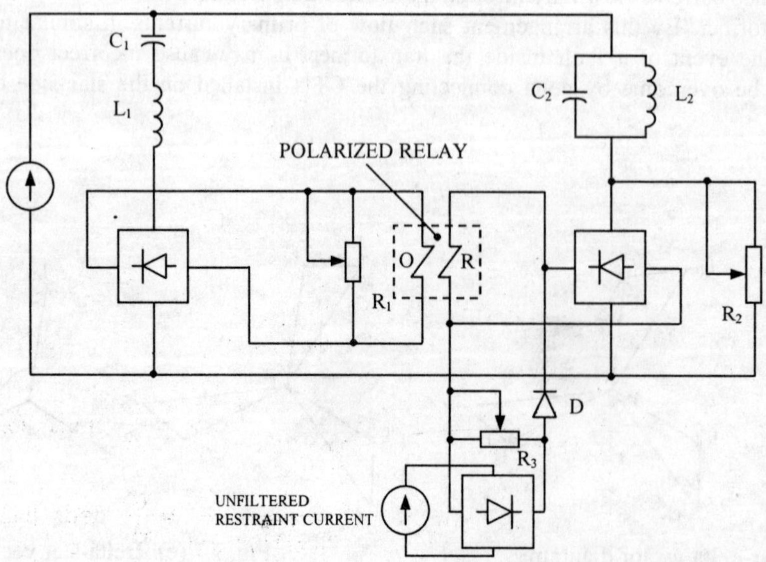

Fig. 7.7 (f): Schematic diagram of Transformer differential relay with harmonic restraint

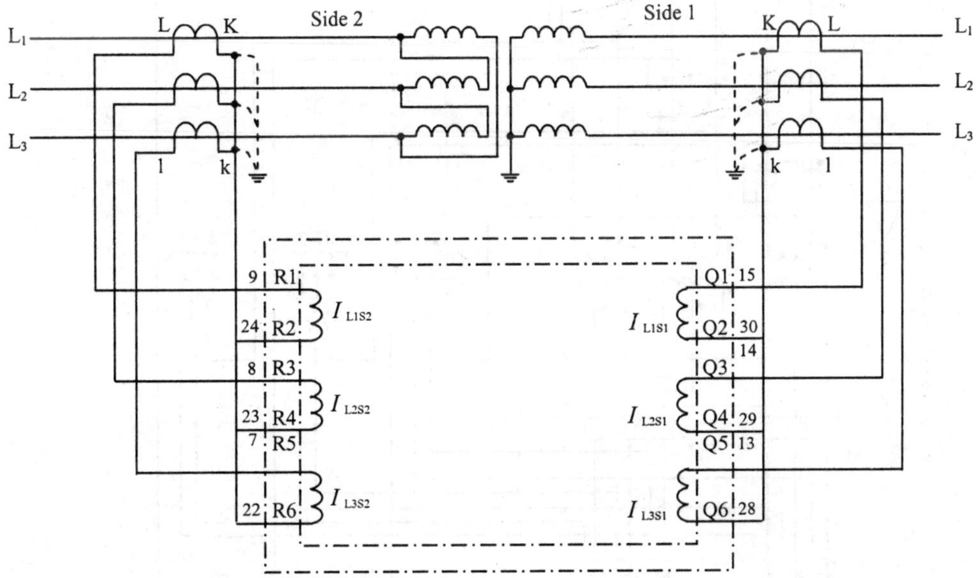

Fig. 7.7 (g): Typical schematic connection diagram of numerical differential protection.

The electronic differential relay has ratio matching taps and incorporates a second harmonic restraint function where large transformer magnetizing inrush is present. The proportion of second harmonic to fundamental, for restraint, is set at minimum 15% and this value is easily adjusted as the application may require. The percentage differential operating characteristic prevents operation until the differential current is greater than a certain percentage of the through current. The characteristic accommodates current transformer errors, particularly those resulting from CT saturation at high current faults external to the protected zones. The adjustability of the percentage characteristic to other requirements of the application such as load tap changer variations. Minimum pickup is also adjustable, and in some applications allows sensitivity as low as 13% of tap.

Differential protection of single – phase transformers in a three phase bank.
Single phase HV and EHV transformers are widely used in three phase banks (e.g. HVDC substations) with or without spare transformers. Differential relay connections are dependent to some extent on transformer connections, location of current transformers, and whether or not the spare power transformer remain energized continuously. If the differential zone extends to circuit breakers on both sides of a transformer, then changing the current transformer secondary circuit is not required to place the spare transformer in service.

Figure 7.7 (h) shows the connection diagram of differential protection scheme for a three phase transformer bank consisting three single phase transformers. Star connected primary can feed either higher voltage source by closing 52H circuit breaker or lower voltage source by closing 52 L circuit breaker. Secondary is connected in delta. Electrical and mechanical interlocks are provided to prevent closing both the breakers together. Primary side current transformers are located at the circuit breaker. Secondary side current transformers are of bushing type installed on the transformer and its secondary circuit is connected identical to the primary connections. In this case CT secondary circuit has to be switched or re-wired if a spare transformer to be included in the system. This scheme requires additional relaying to provide protection on the tertiary make up bus.

METHOD # 1

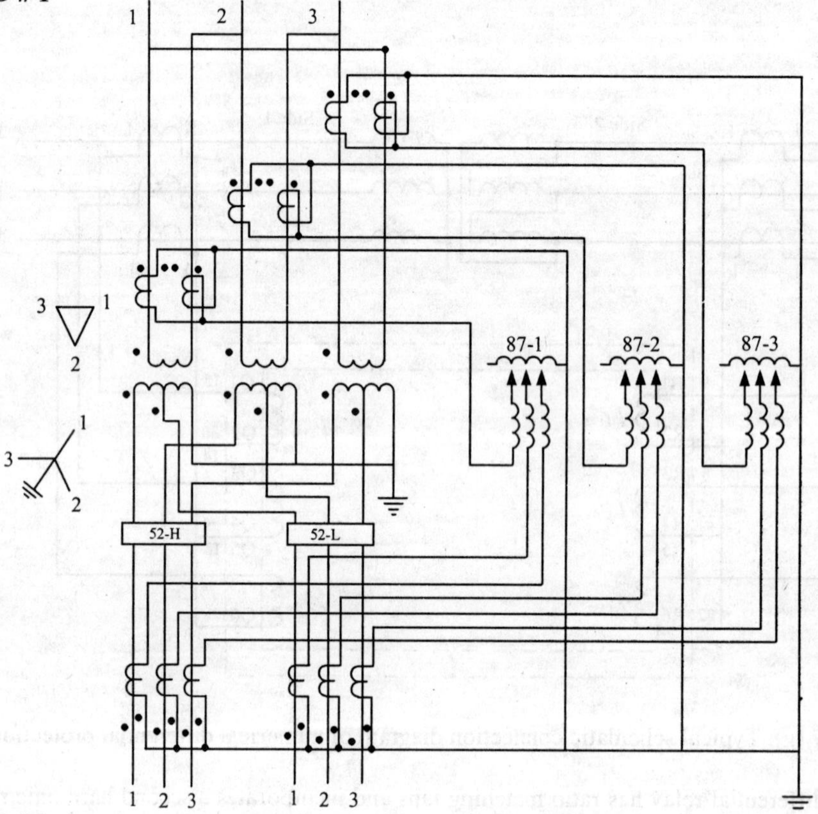

METHOD # 2

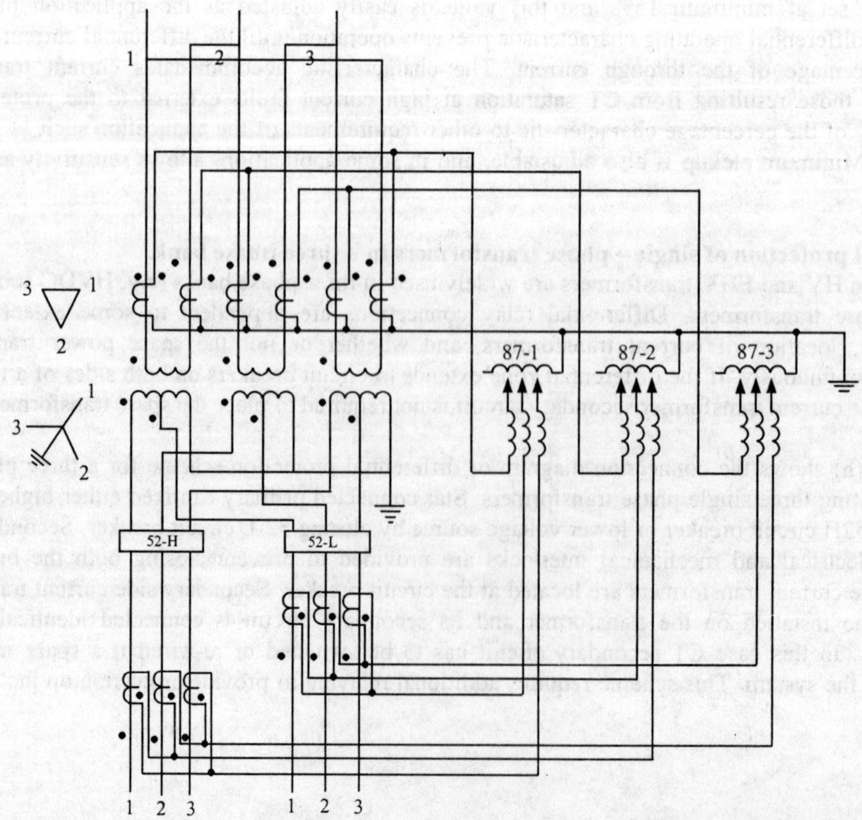

Fig. 7.7(h): Differential protection of single-phase transformers connected in three-phase banks.

Differential relay primary current injection testing:

Prior to transformer energization, transformer differential relay wiring should be tested by primary injection or secondary injection. A combination of these tests may be required to verify all restraints and operate circuits. In addition to these tests, an-service test should be made. The differential relays should be in-service when the transformer is energized. As far as possible a final test should be made with 10% load. The currents in the restraint circuits and the operate circuits should be checked. The ratio of the measured currents should be nearly the same as the ratio of the relay settings.

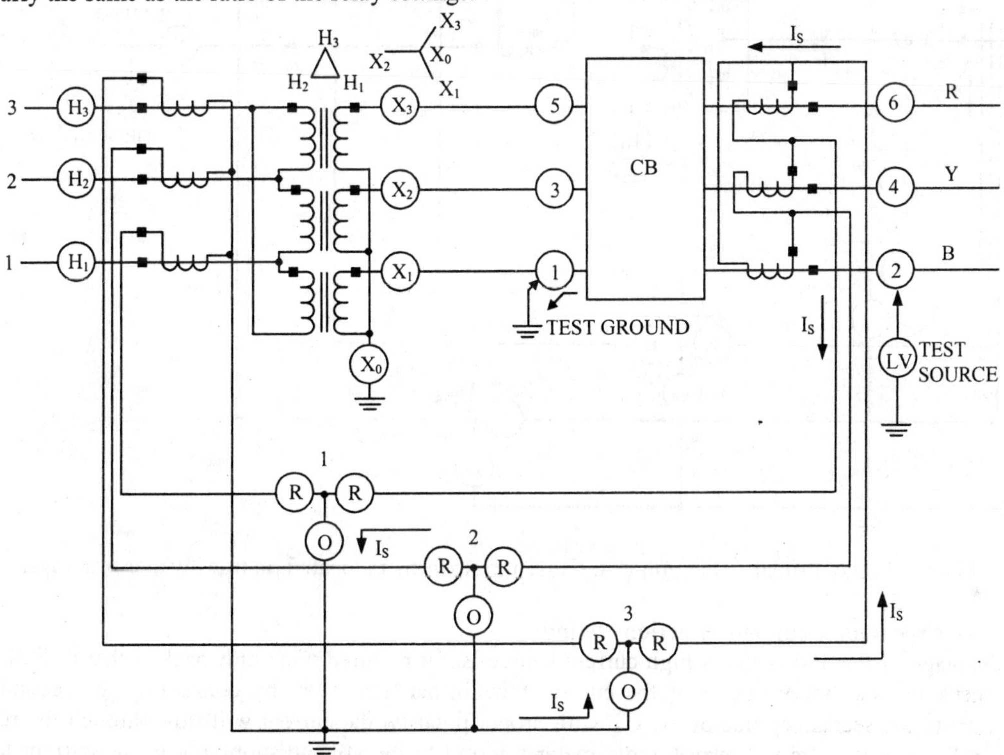

Fig. 7.7(I): Differential relay Primary current injection: Current transformers located in circuit breaker.

(a) Current transformers located in circuit breakers. Figure 7.7 (I) shows the primary injection test connections for CT's installed in circuit breaker. The current source should be injected to phase B on the breaker bushing. Breaker shall be closed with a ground on the phase B bushing next to the transformer. If the current transformer secondaries are connected in delta, the primary current divided by the CT ratio can be seen in the phase B relay operating coil, as well as the phase R relay operating coil. If the current transformer secondaries are connected in star, the current would flow only in phase B relay operating coil. In order to verify the current direction (polarity) through the relay coil a phase angle meter to be connected in the current transformer secondary. The other phases can be checked in a similar manner.

(b) Current transformer located in the transformer: Figure 7.7 (J) shows the primary injection test connection for CT's installed in transformer bushing. The current source should be connected to the bushing to be checked with other side bushings tied together and grounded to create a three phase to ground fault. A phase angle meter shoúld be connected to the CT secondary to verity polarity in each restraint coil. As stated in the previous test, measure the current in the restraint coil and operating coil by allowing sufficient current to flow to make the test.

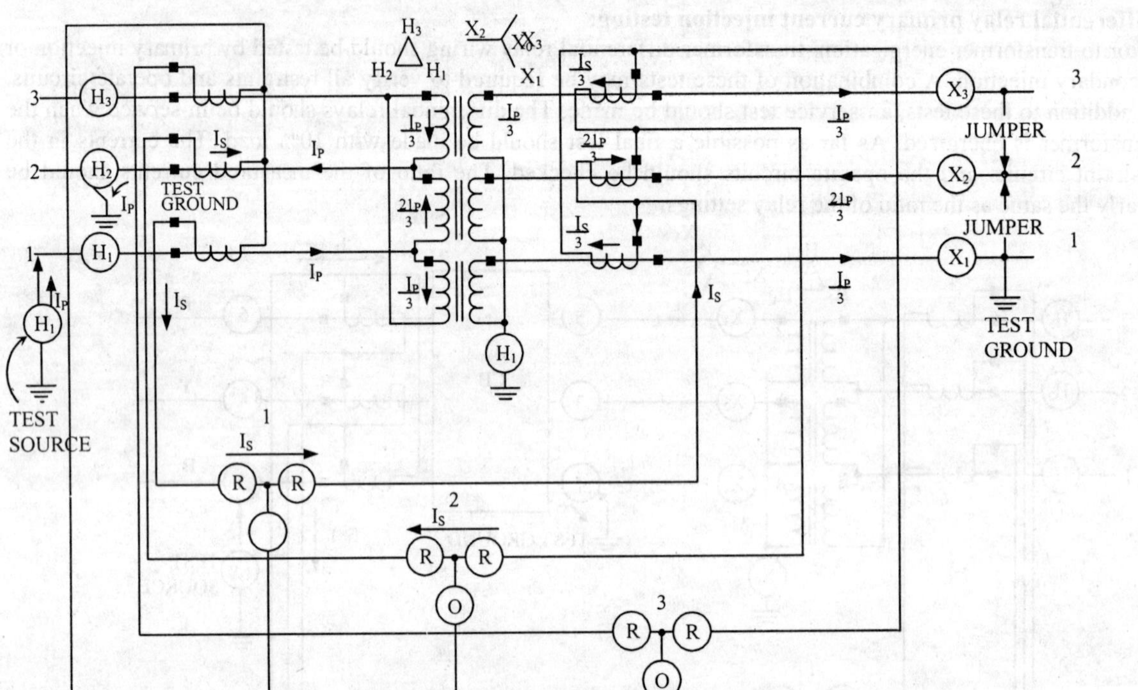

Fig. 7.7(j): Differential relay Primary injection test: Current transformers located on transformer bushings.

Differential relay secondary current injection testing:

The main advantage of this test is that a high current source is not required. One drawback is that it does not completely check the secondary circuit of the current transformer. However, by connecting the secondary injection test set to the secondary side of the CT with proper polarity, the current will flow through the relay restraint and relay operating coil. A phase angle meter referred to the voltage supplying to the current tests source will verify the wiring from the current transformer to the relay. This check should be made on either side of the power transformer for all the phases. Figure 7.7 (K) and (L) respectively shows the secondary injection test connection on delta and star connected current transformers.

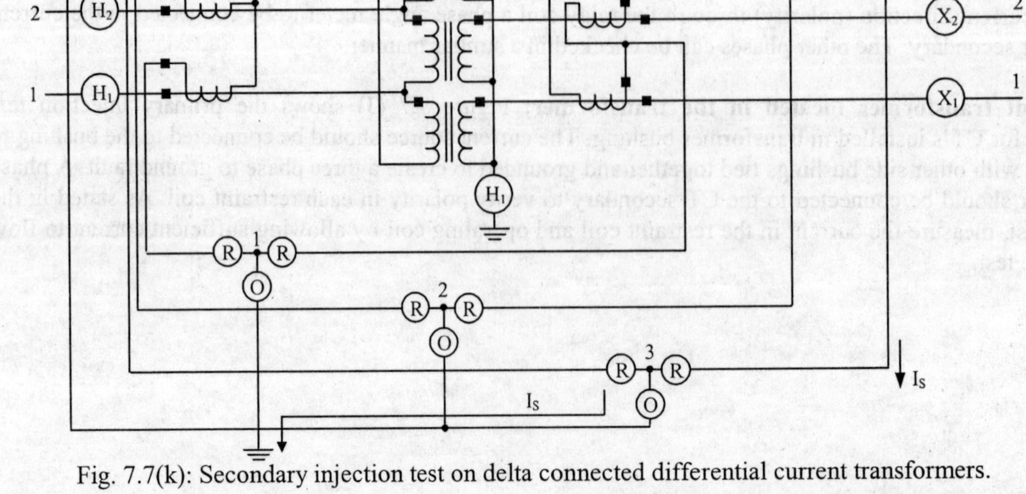

Fig. 7.7(k): Secondary injection test on delta connected differential current transformers.

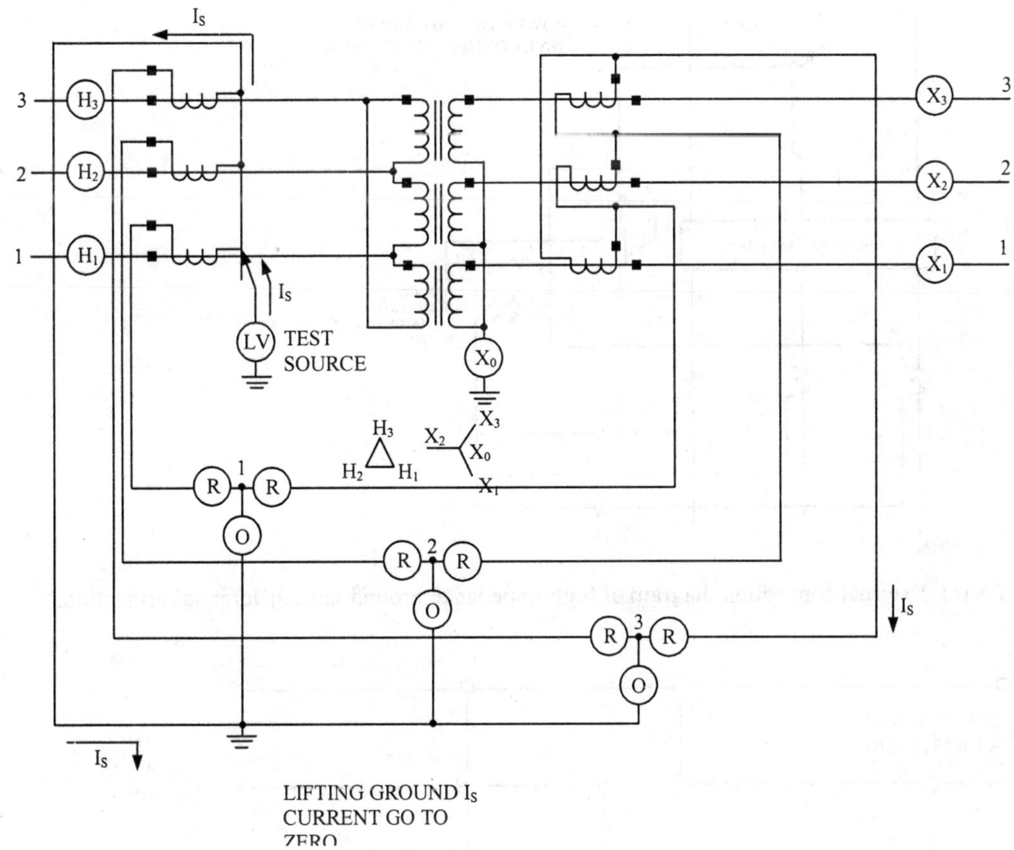

Fig. 7.7(L): Secondary injection test on star connected differential current transformers

Test to be conducted on percentage and harmonic restraint differential relay:

1. Pick up of differential harmonic restraint (DHR) unit.
2. Slop check: Operating current divided by restraining current.
3. Harmonic restraint or through fault check.
4. Pickup of instantaneous unit.
5. Target and seal in for electromechanical relay; LED indication on electronic relays.
6. Time current characteristics check.

Test method is similar to generator differential relay demonstrated in Chapter # 6, section 6.5

7.8 HIGH IMPEDANCE DIFFERENTIAL GROUND FAULT PROTECTION (64G)

A widely used scheme for protecting a why (star) winding of a resistance grounded transformer against ground faults is shown Figure 7.8 (a). Internal faults produce a reversal in the operating current direction with respect to the polarizing current direction causing the relay to operate. Where differential relays are used, the primary function of this high impedance neutral ground relay is to back up other earth fault protections employed.

A neutral ground relay may accomplish a primary relaying function where low resistance grounding is used. The auxiliary transformer is carefully chosen with a ratio that will minimize the effect of CT error for external faults and to force a restraint condition to exist. The auxiliary current transformer is necessary if the phase and neutral current transformers are of different ratios.

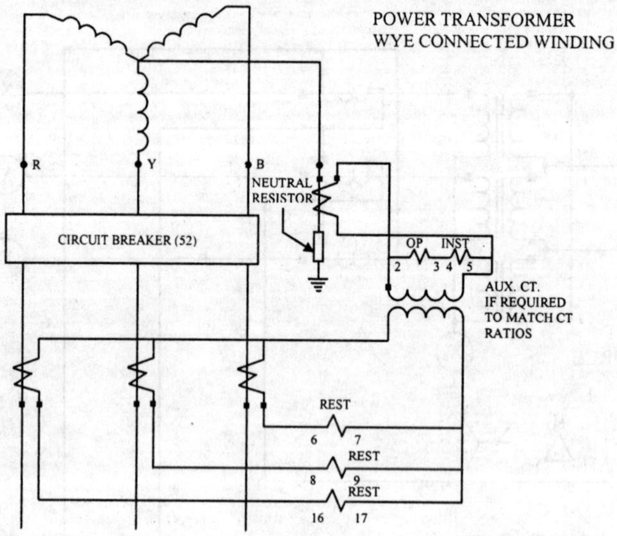

Fig. 7.8 (a): External connection diagram of high impedance ground fault differential protection.

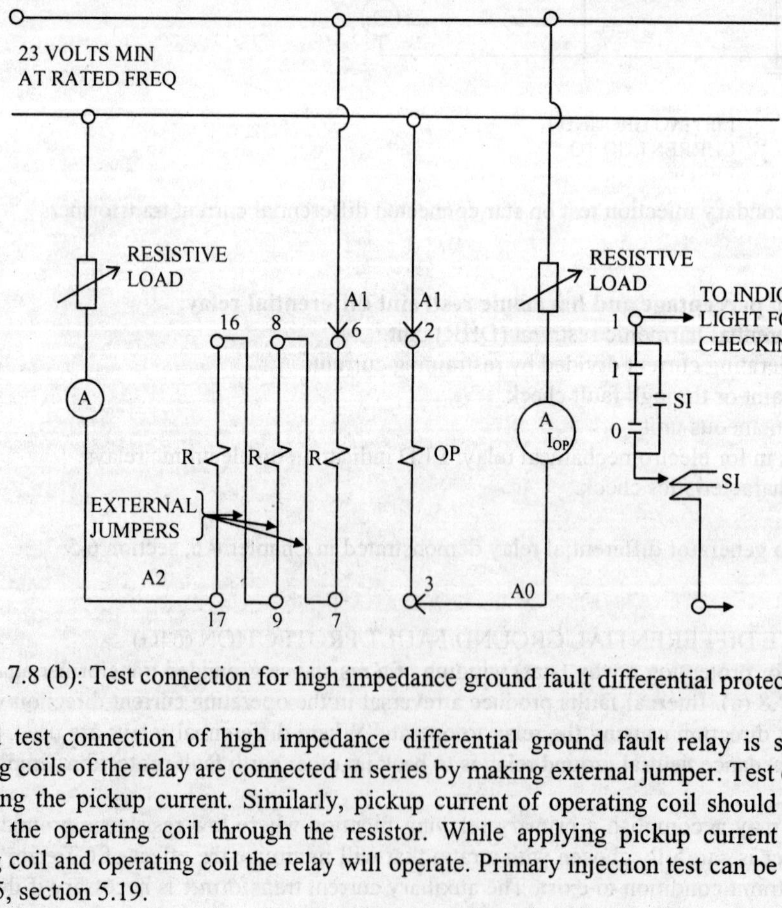

Fig. 7.8 (b): Test connection for high impedance ground fault differential protection relay.

Simplified test connection of high impedance differential ground fault relay is shown in figure 7.8 (b). Restraining coils of the relay are connected in series by making external jumper. Test current should be applied for checking the pickup current. Similarly, pickup current of operating coil should be adjusted by applying current to the operating coil through the resistor. While applying pickup current simultaneously on both restraining coil and operating coil the relay will operate. Primary injection test can be made as demonstrated in Chapter #5, section 5.19.

7.9 STANDBY EARTH FAULT PROTECTION FOR TRANSFORMER (51G)

Restricted earth fault protection (64N) protects the transformer winding against earth faults. Phase over current and earth fault relay (50/51 & 50/51N) protects the transformer against external overload, short circuit and earth faults. The primary advantages of ground relays over phase relays, is their sensitivity. Ground relays can normally be applied with sensitivities of 10% or less at full load current. Stand by earth fault relay (50G) shown in Figure 7.9 (a), provides back up protection for solidly grounded (SG) system. Relay is connected to the secondary of a CT, Class 5P20, which is inserted usually in the neutral bushing. The earth fault current find its return path through the earth and then flows through the neutral-to-earth connection.

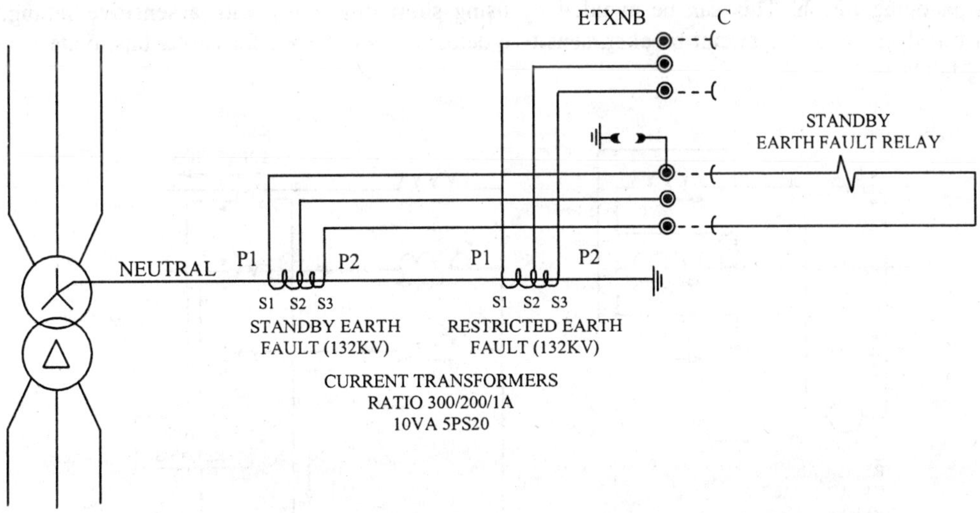

Fig. 7.9 (a): Standby earth fault protection for solidly grounded system.

Standby earth fault relay (51G) shown in Figure 7.9 (b) is for back up protection of resistance grounded systems. Relay is connected through a Class X current transformer provided in the transformer neutral bushing. Transformer differential relays may not be sensitive enough to operate on ground faults where the transformer bank or system is grounded through impedance. In these cases, it may be necessary to apply a sensitive time over current relay in the transformer impedance grounded neutral or a time over voltage relay connected across the neutral impedance. These relays shall be co coordinated with feeder and line protection relays, which they may overlap. It is possible to provide high speed protection and to avoid the need for coordination by using sensitive relays, which are connected to trip only for ground in the protected zone.

The magnitude of earth fault current is dependent on the type of neutral earthing (solid earthing, resistance earthing, reactance earthing or through Zigzag earthing transformer) and location of fault. In a resistance earthed system earth fault relay will provide instantaneous tripping (during an earth fault) if the neutral earth resistance is bypassed due to any reason. Method of testing earth fault relay is similar to over current relay testing demonstrated in section 7.6

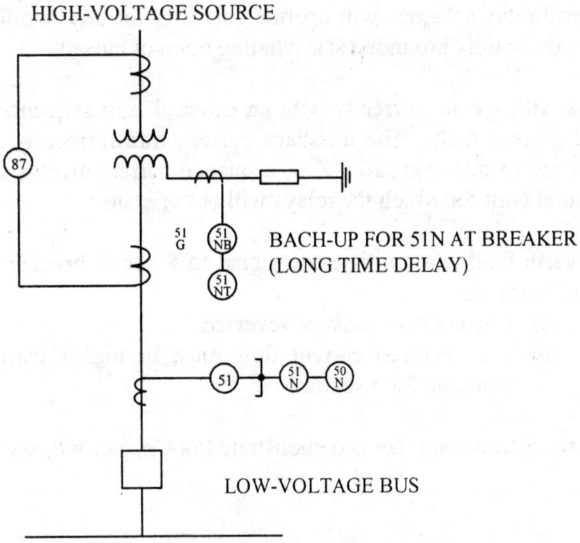

Fig: 7.9 (b): Standby earth fault relay for backup protection of resistance grounded system.

7.10. RESIDUAL AND DIRECTIONAL GROUND FAULT PROTECTION.

A residual relay, device 51G as shown in Figure 7.10 (a) or (b) can detect ground faults with in the delta winding of the transformer and in the phase conductors between the current transformers and the winding, when an external source of zero sequence current is available. Instantaneous over current relays can be used but sensitive settings will probably result in incorrect operations from dissimilar current transformer saturation and magnetizing inrush. This can be avoided by using short time relay with a sensitive setting. By using current transformers at the circuit breaker, sensitive detection is obtained for cable, bus, delta windings, and bushing faults.

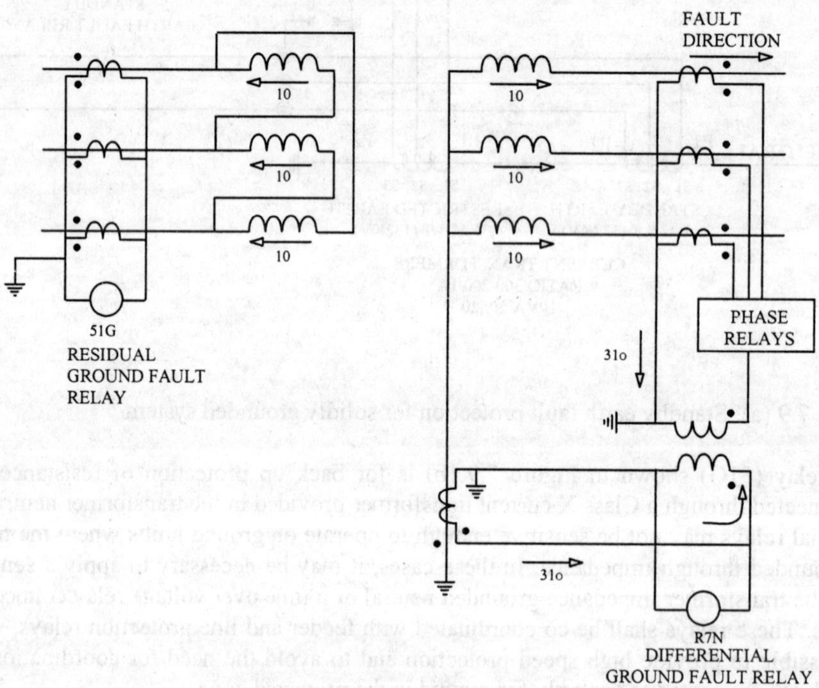

Fig. 7.10 (a): Differential ground fault protection and residual ground fault protection.

To successfully detect faults in grounded star connected transformer windings, the relay system shall discriminate between faults internal and external to the protection zone. The ground differential relay 87N in figure 7.10 (a) or the directional relay 67N connected as shown in figure 7.10 (b) is sufficient. Both differential and directional relay schemes will operate correctly for any internal ground faults with the circuit breaker in the circuit to the solidly grounded star winding open or closed.

Those relays will operate correctly with an external zero sequence current sources, and they will not operate for external ground faults. The auxiliary current transformer is necessary if the phase and neutral current transformers are of different ratio. Zero sequence current arrows shown on both figure (a) and (b) are for an external ground fault for which the relays will not operate.

Directional earth fault relay initiate trip signal to a circuit breaker when it senses two abnormal conditions in the following sequence.

(a) Current flow must be reversed.

(b) The reversed current flow must be higher than the set value, and the current flow must continue for a set time.

Test circuit for directional relay is demonstrated in Chapter # 8, section 8.11.

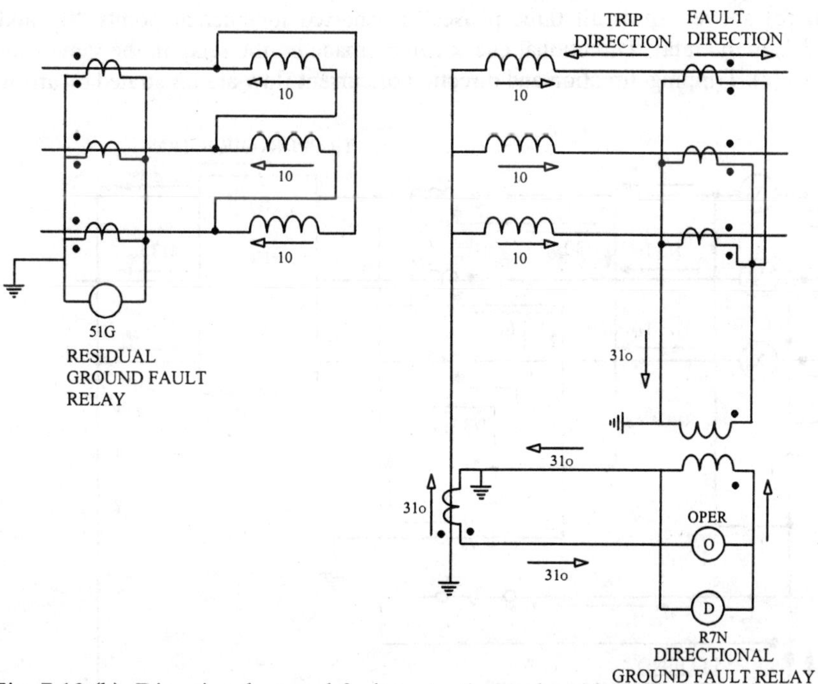

Fig. 7.10 (b): Directional ground fault protection and residual over-current protection.

Test on current polarized ground directional relays.

Phase directional and ground directional relays and test methods are demonstrated in Chapter # 8, section 8.12 (figure 8.12 (a) to (q)). This section introduces the primary and secondary injection techniques used for verifying current circuits of transformer neutral current.

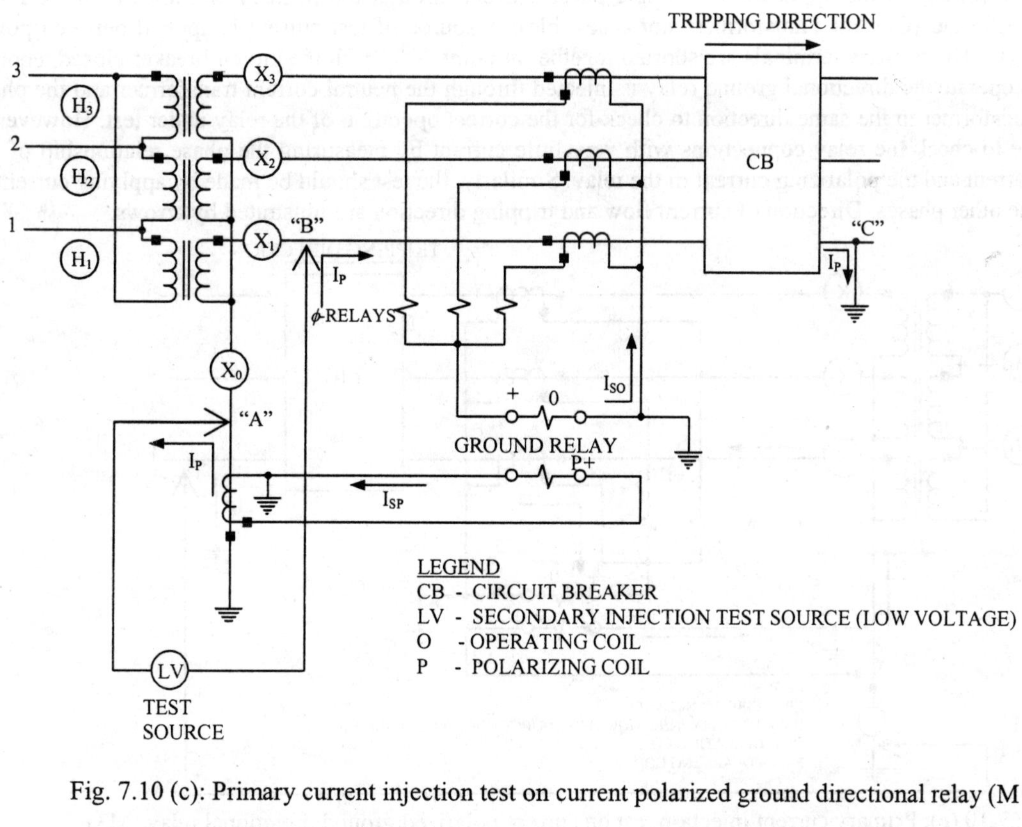

Fig. 7.10 (c): Primary current injection test on current polarized ground directional relay (M1).

Figure 7.10 (d) shows the application of single phase current through all the three phases. Test connections are similar to figure 7.10 (c) above expect all three phases are shorted together at points "B" and "C". This connection simulates 3 I_0 in the relay. Directional check can be made on the relay in the same manner as with the circuit of figure 7.10 (c). Tripping direction and direction of current flow are illustrated by arrows.

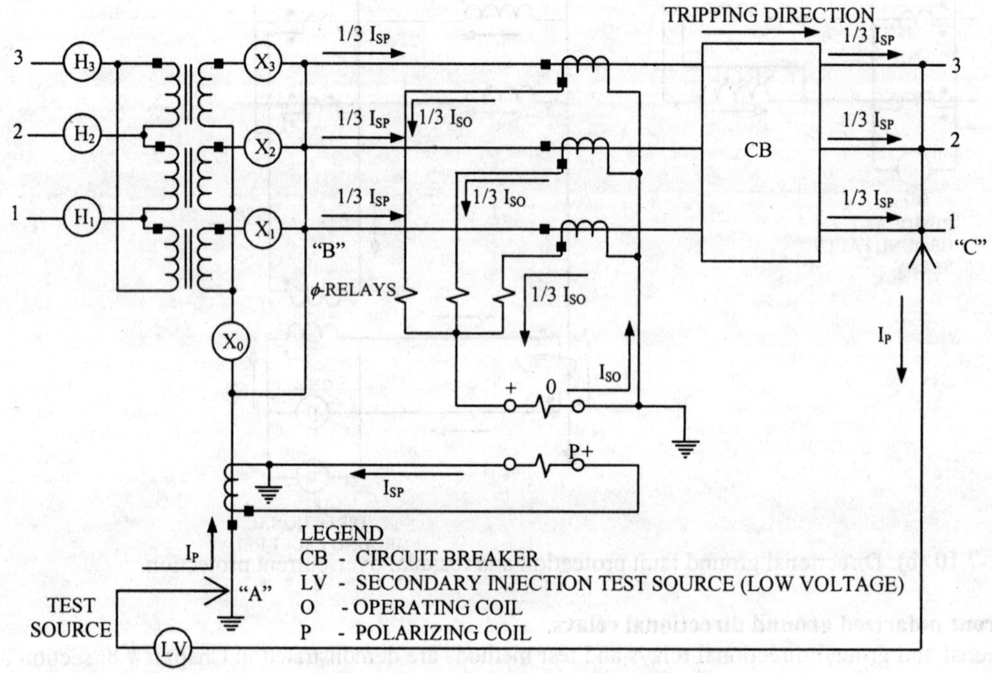

Fig. 7.10 (d): Primary current injection test on current polarized ground directional relay (M2).

Figure 7.10 (e) shows the application of single phase current through the primary windings of the CT and power transformer (Current Transformers not accessible). A source of test current is applied between points "A" and "B". The primary terminals are shorted together at point "C". With the circuit breaker closed, enough current to operate the directional ground relay is injected through the neutral current transformer and the phase current transformer in the same direction to check for the correct operation of the relay under test. However, it is possible to check the relay connections with very little current by measuring the phase relationship of the operate current and the polarizing current in the relay. Similarly, the test should be made by applying current to each of the other phases. Direction of current flow and tripping direction are illustrated by arrows.

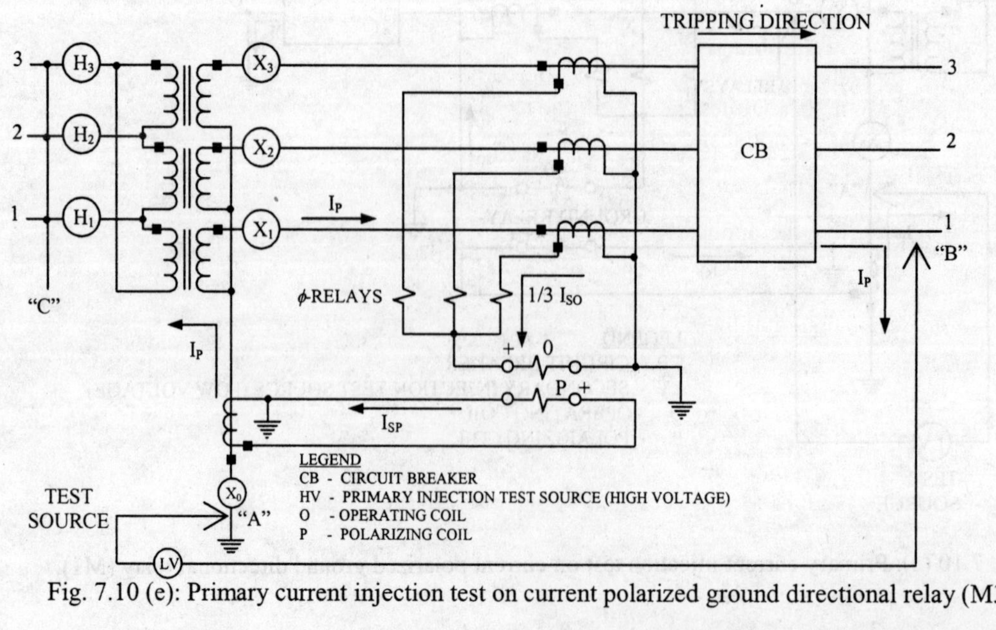

Fig. 7.10 (e): Primary current injection test on current polarized ground directional relay (M3).

Figure 7.10 (f) shows the application of single phase current through the primary winding of all current transformers to simulate zero sequence current. A source of test current is applied between points "A"and "B". All three phases are shorted together at points "B" and "C". With the circuit breaker is closed the same current is injected into all three phases which simulates 3 I_0 in the ground relay circuit. Proper operation of the relay can be verified by observing operation of the relay and / or measuring the phase relationship (phase angle) of the "operate" and "polarizing" currents. Tripping direction and current flow directions are indicated by arrows.

(DURING TEST SHORT TERMINAL 1-2-3 AFTER THE CIRCUIT BREAKER)

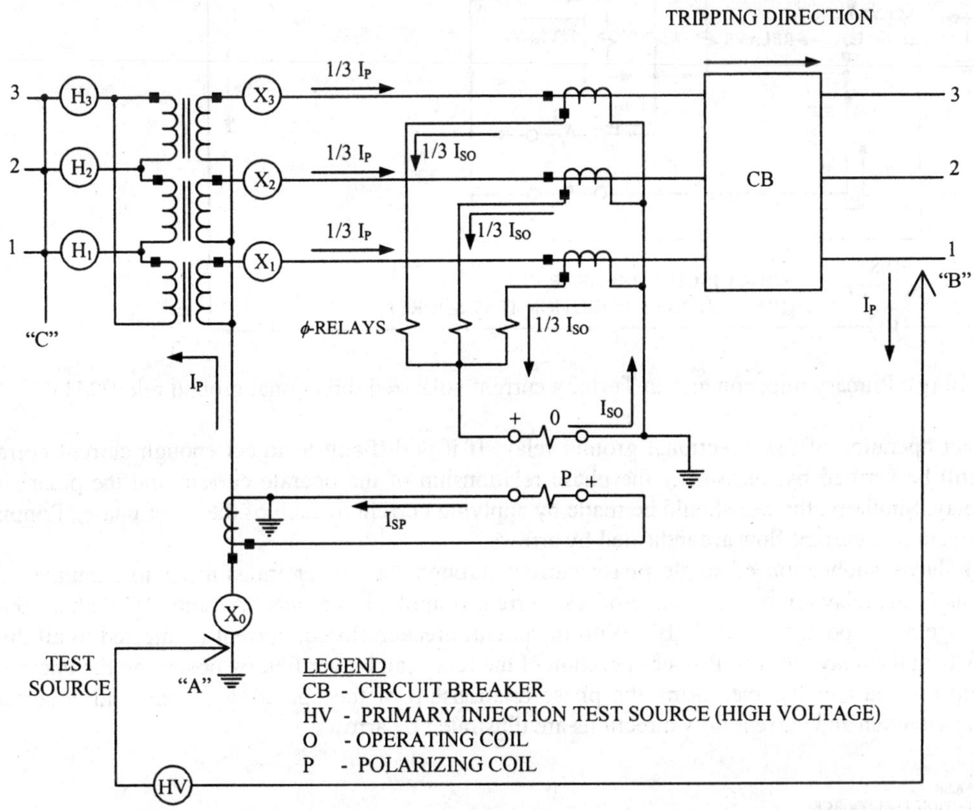

Fig. 7.10 (f): Primary current injection test on current polarized ground directional relay (M4).

Test on Tertiary current polarized ground directional relays.

Primary injection techniques are used for verifying tertiary current circuits. If the tertiary current transformer primary is not accessible, a DC test for polarity is usually required. Two methods of Primary injection (M1 and M2) for a three phase autotransformer with ground relay polarized from the delta tertiary CT winding is explained below.

Figure 7.10 (g) shows the application of single phase current through the primary windings of the current transformer and the power transformer A source of test current is applied between points "A" and "B". All three phases are shorted together at point "B" to allow current to flow in the delta winding. With the circuit breaker closed, enough current to operate the ground directional relay is injected through the power transformer and the circuit breaker current transformers causing a current flow in the delta winding.

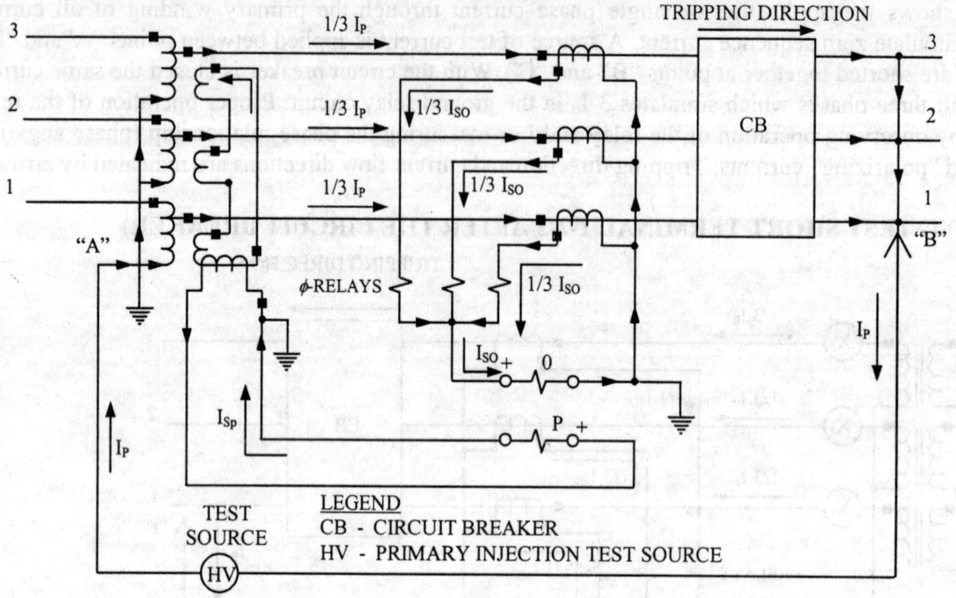

Fig. 7.10 (g): Primary injection test on Tertiary current polarized directional ground relay (M1).

Check for correct operation of the directional ground relay. If it is difficult to inject enough current correct operation can still be verified by, measuring the phase relationship of the operate current and the polarizing current in the relay. Similarly, the test should be made by applying current to each of the other phase. Tripping direction and direction of current flow are indicated by arrows.

Figure 7.10 (h) shows application of single phase current through the power transformer to simulate zero sequence currents in the relay circuits. A source of test current is applied to points "A" and "B" with all three phases shorted together at points "A" and "B". With the circuit breaker closed, current is injected to all three phases, which 3 1_0 in the relay circuits. Proper operation of the relay can be verified by observing the operation of the relay contacts and / or by, measuring the phase relationship of the operating current and polarizing current. Tripping direction and current flow directions are illustrated by arrows.

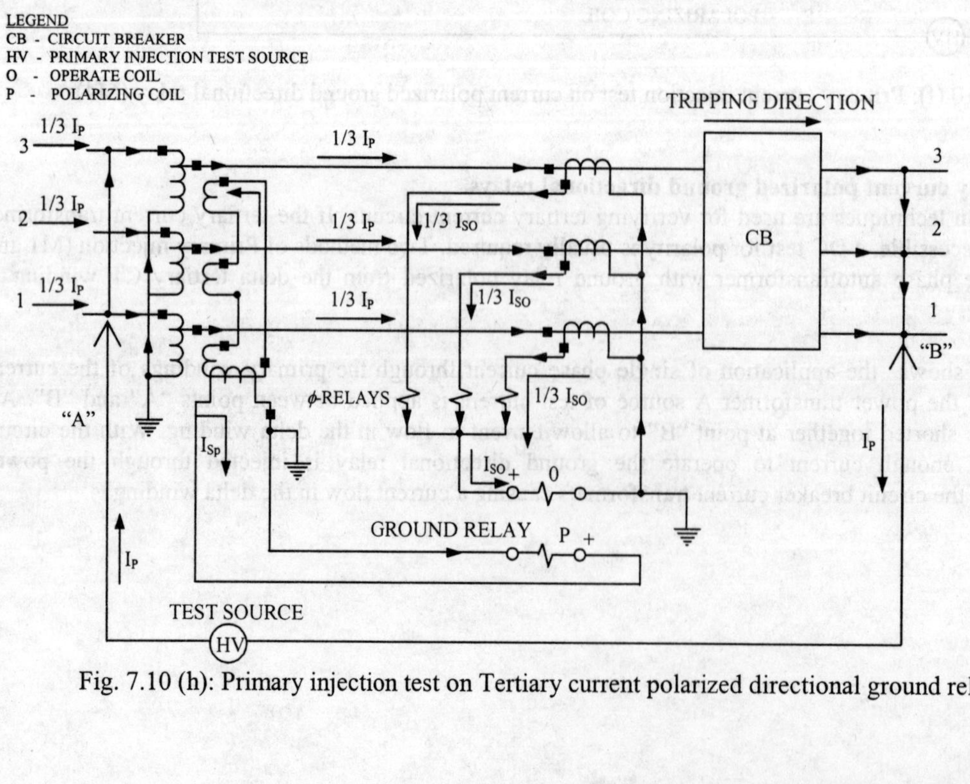

Fig. 7.10 (h): Primary injection test on Tertiary current polarized directional ground relay (M2).

7.11 CIRCUIT BREAKER FAILURE PROTECTION RELAY (50BF)

A breaker failure occurs when the circuit breaker fails to correctly open and isolate the faulty circuit after trip commands have been issued by the protection system. It is then necessary to isolate the breaker bus bar zone to ensure fault clearance. This relay is an instantaneous over current relay which provides rapid backup fault clearance in case the circuit breaker nearest to the fault fails to respond to a trip command. It is suitable for power systems of all voltage levels with single and or three pole circuit breaker operation.

The initiation signal can be issued from any protection or supervision equipment. Information from the breaker auxiliary contact is only required for the breaker failure protection during faults which produce little or no fault current flow. Figure 7.11 shows the application and function diagram of a breaker failure protection relay. Assume that a fault is developed at location F (bus section A) and breaker 5 fails to trip, breaker 1A, 2A, 3A & bus coupler breaker 4 will simultaneously trips to isolate the bus section A.

Operation of other transformer primary protection relays will activate the breaker failure relay. After tripping the circuit breaker by the primary protection shall cause the circuit breaker fail protection to reset. If the primary protection fails to trip the current breaker of the faulty circuit and isolate the faulty portion, breaker failure relay employed for the breaker failure protection will initiate a trip signal to all of the circuit breaker associated with the same bus section. Bus tie breaker (No. 4) will trip during a breaker failure fault in bus zone A or B.

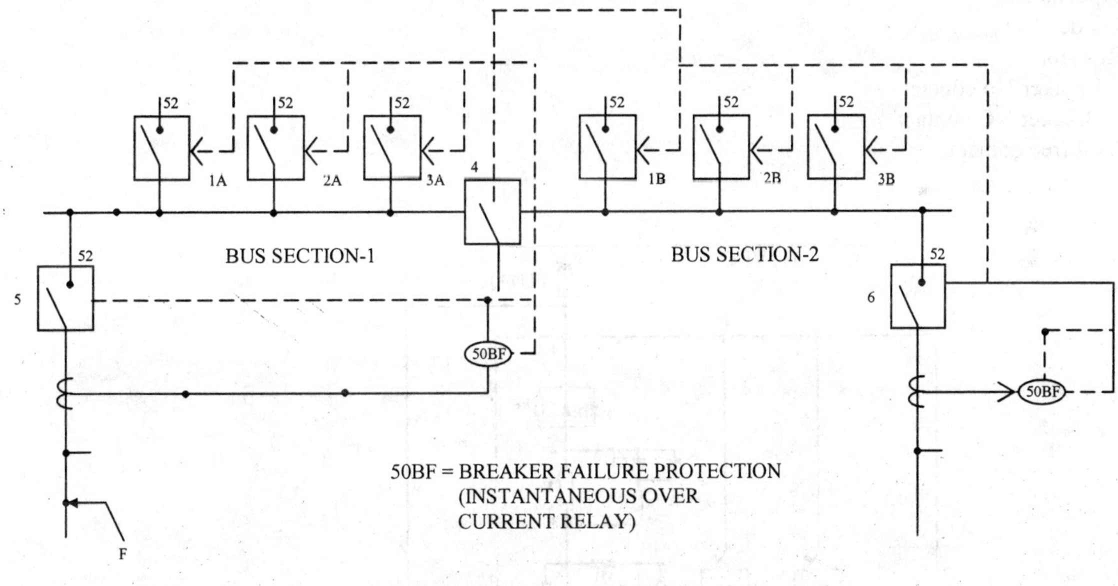

Fig. 7.11: Application and function of circuit breaker failure protection.

7.12. TRIP CIRCUIT AND PROTECTION FAILURE SUPERVISION (74)

These relays are for continuous supervision of the trip coil circuits of the circuit breaker in either the open or closed position and independent of local or remote operating mode or selector switch position. Its voltage free contacts can be used for:

1. Blocking the breaker
2. Giving trip signal to another upstream breaker or a second trip coil of the same breaker.
3. Local or tele-control signal code.
4. Alarm

In normal conditions, the relay cannot produce a false trip due to high resistance offered in the operating coil circuit. Relay elements are delayed on drop off to prevent false alarms during faults on DC wiring on adjacent circuits or due to operation of any trip relay contact of the breaker. Figure 7.12 shows the schematic diagram of a typical trip circuit supervision relay. Relay alarm elements are provided with self resetting flag indications.

There are differing requirements for monitoring a trip circuit:

1. Supervision of the trip circuit with the circuit breaker closed.
2. Supervision with the circuit breaker open and closed.
3. Pre closing supervision, where a circuit breaker is prevented from being closed if trip relays have been not reset after a fault trip.
4. Alarm circuit supervision.

Circuit breaker closed supervision: Will initiate an alarm and provide indication if the following conditions persist.

- Failure of the trip supply (110V, DC)
- As open circuit in the trip coil winding
- An open circuit in the trip circuit wiring and if the trip coil should fail to respond to a trip command.

Trip circuit supervision relay is usually employed for every high and extra high voltage circuit breakers. For medium voltage circuit breakers individual "trip circuit healthy" (white) indication lamps are employed for monitoring the trip circuit. All digital relays have self supervision feature i.e. respond on failure of auxiliary power supply, open circuited CT or open / short circuited PT.

LEGEND
C =Capacitance
D = Diode
R = Resistor
52a = Breaker No contact
52b = Breaker NC contact
V = Volt free contact.

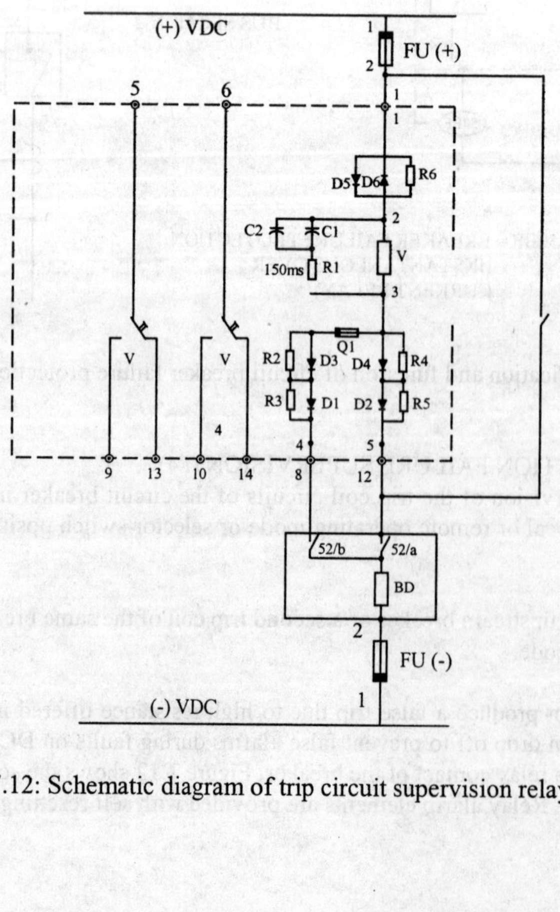

Fig. 7.12: Schematic diagram of trip circuit supervision relay (Courtesy, Siemens Ag).

7.13 NUMERICAL RELAY FOR TRANSFORMER OVERALL PROTECTION

Microprocessor controlled numerical transformer protection relays are capable of providing following protection and alarm functions for a power transformer or autotransformer. Single line diagram in Figure 7.13(a) shows the summary of protection function of Siemens 7UT612 numerical relay.

<u>Device number and protection function</u>

87	Differential protection
50/51	Over-current protection
50/51N	Earth fault protection (calculated neutral)
50/51G	Ground fault protection (measured ground)
49	Overload protection (IDMT)
26	Thermal protection (minimum 12RTD's)
48	Negative sequence over current protection
87N	Restricted earth fault protection (100%)
50BF	Breaker failure protection
86	Lockout protection

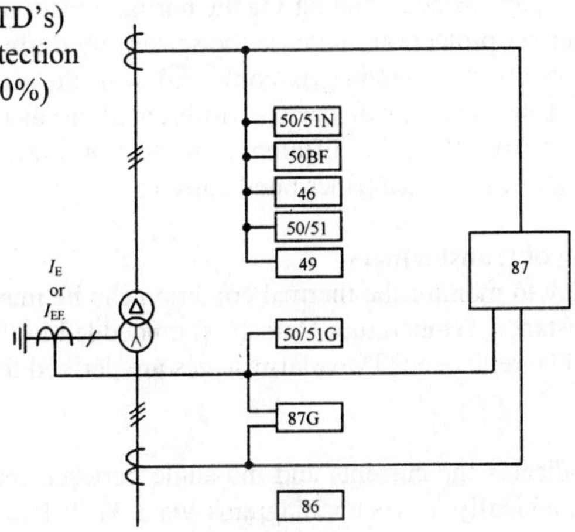

Fig. 7.13(a): Summary of protection function of transformer overall protection relay. (Courtesy, Siemens Ag)

Figure 7.13 (b) shows the standard connection of numerical transformer protection relay to a two winding transformer with neutral consideration for obtaining sensitivity on single phase faults.

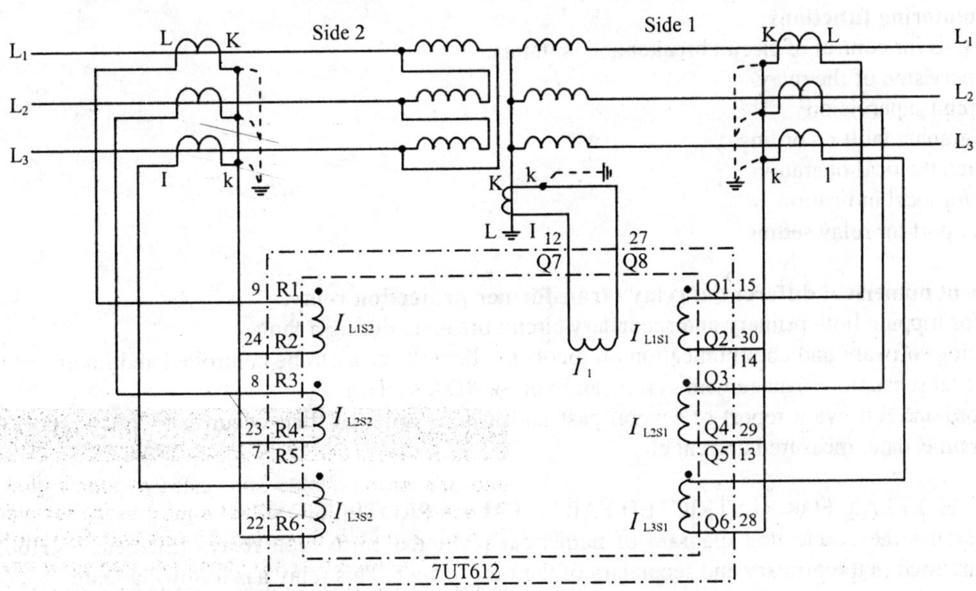

Fig. 7.13 (b): Transformer overall protection relay with neutral current measurement (Courtesy Siemens Ag).

Differential Protection

1. Fast clearance of internal fault with high set differential elements.
2. Restrain of inrush current with 2nd harmonic
3. Restrain against over fluxing with 3rd or 5th harmonic.
4. Additional restrain for an external fault (CT saturation detector)
5. Insensitivity to current transformer errors due to the freely programmable tripping characteristic
6. Differential protection function can be blocked externally by means of a binary input.
7. No need to employ interposing current transformer.

Restricted earth fault protection

This relay contains a normal sensitivity I_E and a high sensitivity I_{EE} current measuring input. Measurement of the star point current of an earthed winding via the normal sensitivity measuring input, and consideration of the current by the differential protection, increase the sensitivity during internal single phase faults by 33%. If the sum of the phase currents of a winding is compared with the star point currents measured with the normal sensitivity input I_E, a sensitive earth current differential protection can be implemented. This function is substantially more sensitive than the differential protection during earth faults in a winding detecting fault current as small as 10% of the transformer rated current.

Thermal monitoring of transformers.

The ability of the relay to monitor the thermal condition can be improved by serial connection of a temperature measuring unit (Resistance Temperature Detectors) embedded in the transformer winding. Maximum up to 12 measuring points can be registered. Two alarm stages are derived for each measuring point.

Measurements:

The measurement indicates the currents and the angle between the currents (e.g vector group). These values may be displayed graphically as vector diagrams via a Web Browser, and are therefore independent of the configuration software provided with the relay. The fault records of the relay contain the phase and earth currents as well as the calculated differential and restraint currents.

System interface:

1. The PC interface allows rapid accesses to the parameters, status and fault event data
2. The service and system communication interfaces ensures that the requirements for different (electrical and optical) communication interfaces and protocols.

Control and monitoring functions:

1. Commands for control of circuit breaker and isolators.
2. Self supervision of the relay
3. Trip circuit supervision
4. Oscillographic fault recording
5. User friendly local operation
6. LED's for local indication
7. PC front port for relay setting.

General feature of numerical differential relay / transformer protection relay.

1. Logic for tripping both primary and secondary circuit breakers during a fault
2. Interfacing software and communication protocols to allow the relay to be controlled and interrogated by a digital substation management system and / or SCADA system.
3. To record and retrieve a report of several past fault trip in order of their occurrence. Each report to contain time, date, measured current etc.

7.14 NUMERICAL RELAY FOR RESTRICTED EARTH FAULT PROTECTION

Figure 7.14 illustrates the connection diagram of numerical restricted earth fault relays (Siemens 7VH60). Separate relays are used in the primary and secondary of the transformer. This relay has following features.

- Acquisition and evaluation of measured values
- Operation and LED display
- Auxiliary voltage supply

- Single pole sensitive current relay with instantaneous / time delayed characteristic
- The AC input impedance of the relay is adjusted by means of a series of high wattage resistors
- Adjustable residual polarizing voltage pickup.

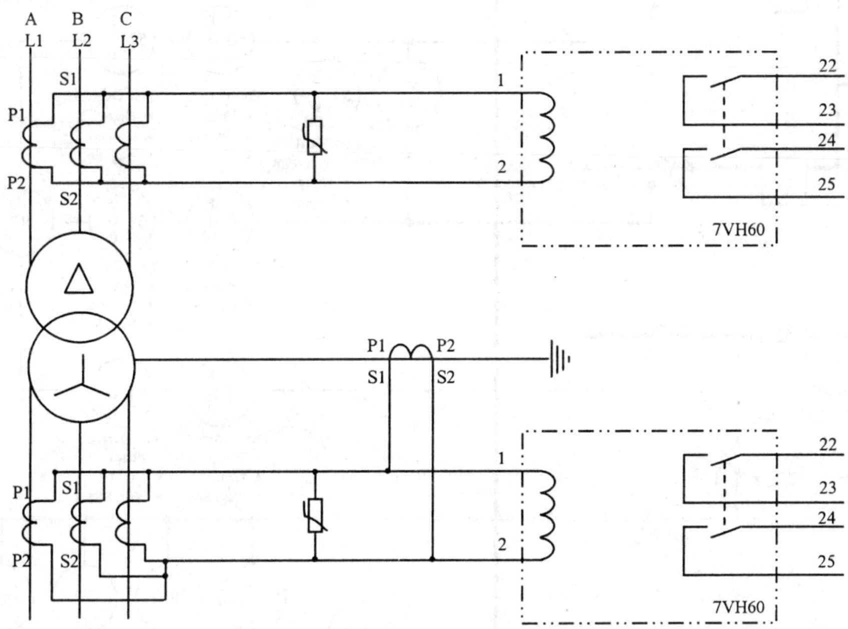

Fig. 7.14: Connection diagram of numerical restricted earth fault relay (Courtesy Siemens Ag).

The sensitive relay input from the CT, galvanically isolates the relay static measuring circuit. The AC measured current is band pass filtered and rectified to a proportional DC voltage. This voltage is monitored by, a Schmidt trigger circuit. If the set DC voltage, equivalent to the relay rated operating current is exceeded, then the trigger operates to energize the command output relay as well as the operation indicator. An auxiliary DC supply monitoring circuit consisting of a green LED and an NO / NC relay contact is provided to indicate the status of the DC supply.
Test method for restricted earth fault relay is demonstrated in Chapter # 5, section 5.19.

7.15 NUMERICAL RELAY FOR AUTOTRANSFORMER OVERALL PROTECTION

The numerical protection relay introduced in this section is SEL (Switchgear Engineering Laboratories) model 387E relay is suitable for overall protection of all type of two windings and three winding transformers. Figure 7.15 (a) illustrates the functional overview of the relay along with circuit diagram when applied to autotransformer.

Differential protection (87T)

Relay has three differential elements. These elements use operate and restraint quantities calculate from the two or three winding input currents. Set the differential elements with either a single or dual slope percentage differential characteristic, as shown in figure 7.15 (b). Relay provides security against conditions that may result in relay mal-operation, resulting from both system and transformer events. Use the fifth harmonic element to prevent relay mal operation during allowable over excitation conditions. Second and forth harmonic elements provide security against inrush currents during transformer energization, complimented by the DC element, which measures the DC offset. The even harmonic elements offer the choice between harmonic blocking and harmonic restraint, in the blocking mode. Select either blocking on an independent phase basis or on a common basis, as per application and philosophy.

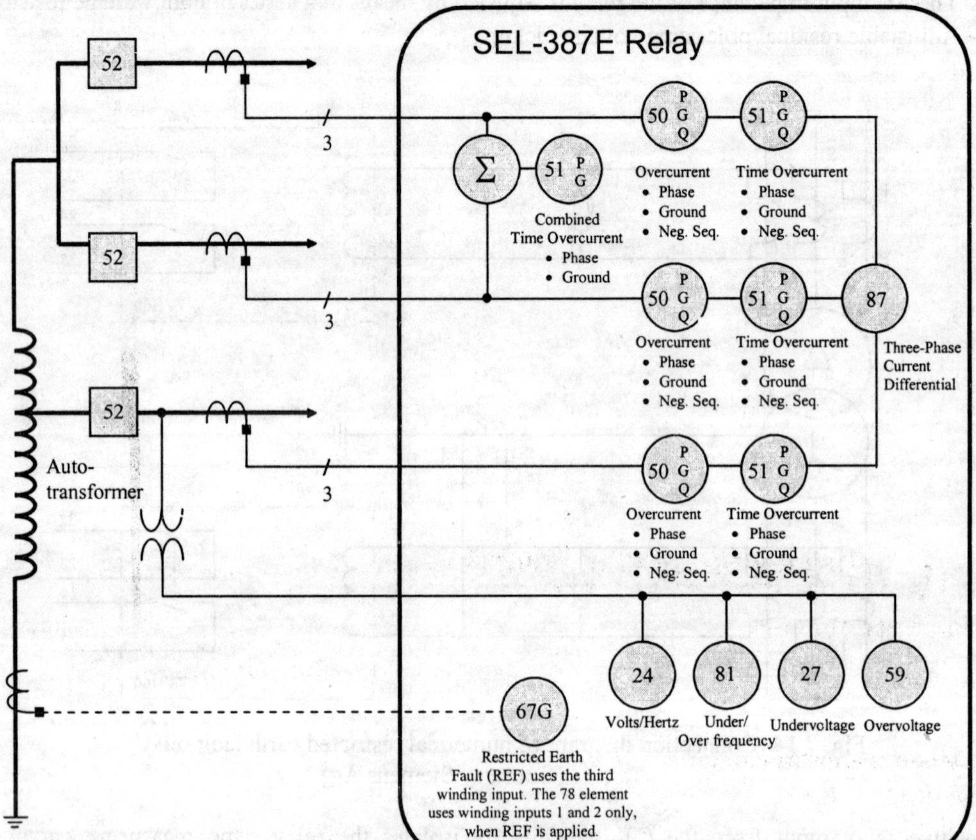

Fig. 7.15 (a): Functional over-view of Autotransformer overall protection relay (Courtesy, SEL)

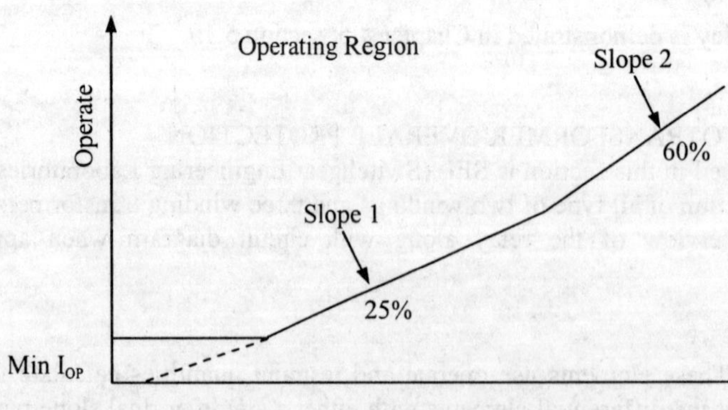

Fig. 7.15(b): Dual slope percentage differential characteristics

Over current protection (50/ 51)

Each of the three numbers 3 phase current input terminals has a total of eleven over current elements, nine of which are torque controlled. For backup over current protection in Ring-bus or breaker and a-half configurations, two combined over current elements operate on the sum of the currents of the secondary windings. The combined currents from two separate breaker CTs emulate the current as if from a single bushing CT applied on the power transformer.

Restricted earth fault protection (directional 67G)
The REF function compares the directions of neutral current and winding residual current, for sensitive ground fault detection in ground-wye or autotransformer connected windings.

Volts per hertz protection (24)
Over excitation occurs when the magnetic core of a power apparatus becomes saturated. When this happens, higher harmonic frequencies become more prominent, which results in overheating and consequent reduction of apparatus life. Over-excitation conditions are detected by a volts-per-hertz element and the relay output can be used for alarm or trip function.

Relay characteristics
Relay provides sensitive, instantaneous definite time elements plus a settable composite inverse time / definite time characteristic. The inverse time element has a percent travel operating characteristic. This characteristic coincides well with the heating effect that over excitation has on transformer components.

Metering functions:
Measured quantities include.

1. Three phase voltage and current from all inputs
2. Three phase and per phase MW, MVA and MVARh
3. Three phase and per phase MWh and MWARh
4. Differential currents, volts per hertz, system frequency, harmonics
5. Station battery (four settable alarm levels)

Intelligent breaker monitor.
Relay keeps track of the number of breaker operations, total interrupted current by pole, and contact wear by pole. Schedule timely breaker maintenance based on actual breaker wear that is related to the breaker manufactures maintenance curves.

Other features: Under / Over voltage protection, Sequential events recorder, enhanced automation elements.

7.16 DIGITAL TEMPERATURE CONTROLLER AND MONITOR.
Digital temperature controller with RTD (Resistance temperature detector) or thermostat is for monitoring temperature of six different measuring points simultaneously. This instrument is especially suitable for monitoring core temperature of transformers, motors, generators, bearings etc. Wiring diagram of ZIEHL TR 600 unit is shown in Figure 7.16.

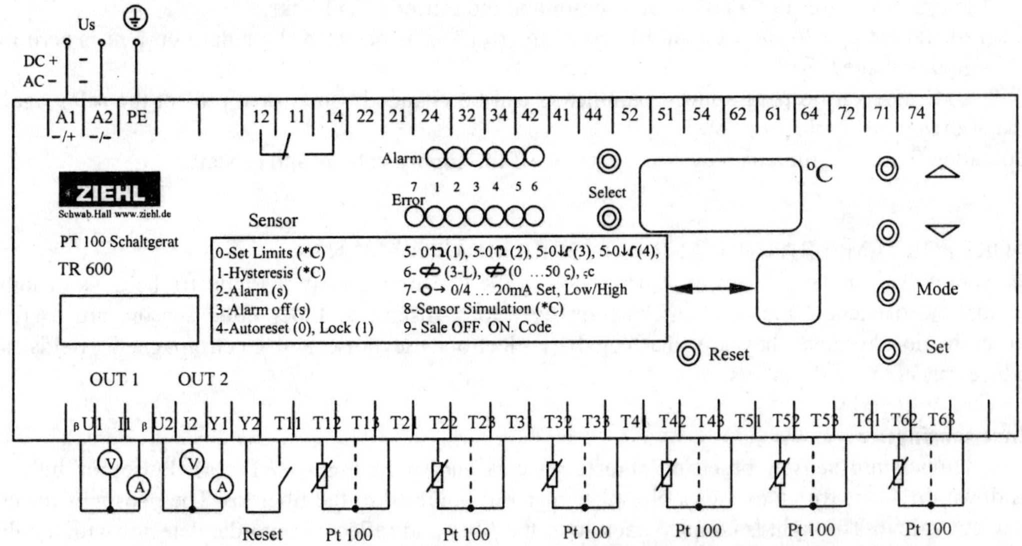

Fig. 7.16: Wring diagram of digital temperature controller/monitor (Courtesy, Ziehl)

Temperature sensors are connected to the plug in terminals, for example T11, T12, T13 etc. AC 230V or DC 110V power supply shall be connected to the appropriate terminals. Terminals Y1-Y2 is for connecting remote reset pushbutton.

Function over view.

- Measuring and monitoring range – 199 to + 800^{0}C
- 6 sensor inputs with 2 or 3 wire connection
- 6 relay outputs K1 to K6 with change over contact
- Sensor error relay monitors sensor break or short as well as power supply failure
- 2 Analog out put 4 ----- 20m A, and 2 -----10V, with individual scaling.

Displays:

** Built-in 3 digit, temperature display and 1 digit program-mode display.
** LED alarm showing the state of alarm relays.
** LED sensor-error blinking at sensor short-circuit or sensor interruption.
** Stored valves of minimum and maximum temperature can be displayed.
** "Sensor select" display showing temperatures of different sensors.
** "Alarm select" display showing switching points.

LED's alarm:

Off:	Temperature below switching point.
ON:	Temperature beyond switching point.
Blinking: (1x on 4x off)	Alarm relay delay time is running.
Blinking: (4x on 1x off)	Alarm relay delay time off is running.
Blinking: (1x on 1x off)	Relay locked, ready for reset.

Alarm relay can reset with reset pushbutton. The operating delay time (measuring time) of the relay depends on the number of sensors connected and the measuring function. With continuous change of temperature the measuring time is about 3 – 4 seconds. With sensor short-circuit the measuring time increases.

In relay locked mode the relay can switch ON when all the following parameters are fulfilled.

(1) The temperature decreases below the switching back limit.
(2) The alarm relay delay-time off has overrun.
(3) A reset signal is initiated. In the ready to rest status the alarm LED will be blinking 1x on 1x off.

Trouble shooting:

a) LED sensor error indicates a failure at a sensor and the sensor LED blinks.
b) If sensor failure due to short-circuit or sensor interruption is detected the output current is zero mA, and output voltage 0 Volt.
c) With code save on no programmed parameters can be changed. Code save protect the relay against unauthorized manipulations.
d) Operation failure: Failure display "E0", Switch off the supply voltage and re-start.

7.17 SENSORS FOR TEMPERATURE AND PRESSURE MEASUREMENTS

Fiber optics is now the standard means of transmission in the telecommunications industry because of light's enormous capacity to encode and send information over long distances. Fiber optic sensors are used for transformer protection because they are unaffected by electro-static noise and electromagnetic fields, and cannot produce sparks or short circuits.

Temperature sensing:

A fiber optic temperature sensor, based on fluorescence is shown in Figure 7.17 (a). Pulses of light are transmitted down the fiber, which excites a phosphor material bounded to the fiber tip. The phosphor material glows a different colour. The light is coupled back in to the fiber and reflected onto the detector with a colour separation filter. The persistence of the fluorescent afterglow depends on the temperature of the phosphor. A relay converts the time-varying optical intensity in to a 4 to 20 mA signal. A direct accurate temperature reading can then be displayed locally and / or remotely up to 100 M. Alarm and trip functions can be incorporated. Glass fibers installed in transformers are protected with several layers of reinforcing materials. This makes relatively thin fiber optic cables very strong. They have a tensile strength of 500N and a minimum bending radious of 30mm. The dielectric strength of temperature probe made of such cables far exceeds that of transformer oil. Method of connecting fiber optic temperature sensor for winding hot spot measurements is shown in Figure 7.17(b)

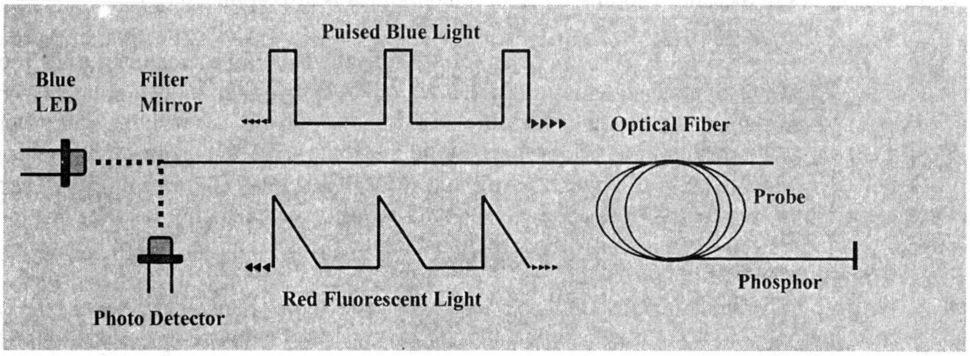

Fig. 7.17(a): Fiber optic temperature sensor.

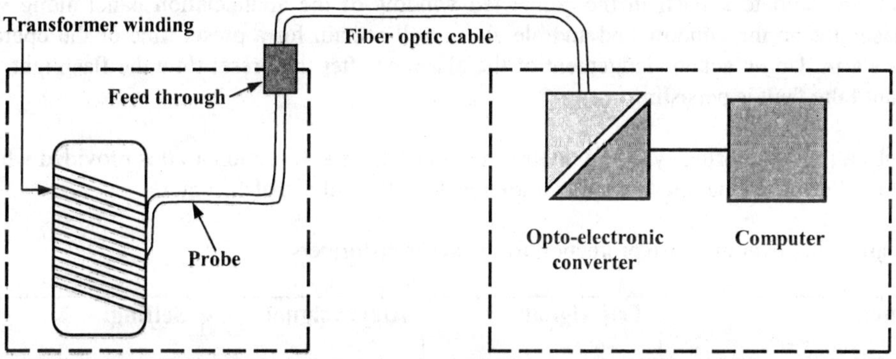

Fig. 7.17(b): Winding hot spot measurement by using fiber optic sensor.

Pressure sensor:

Pressure sensors are used for internal pressure monitoring of transformer bushings interferometer shown in Figure 7.17 (c) is a light source, such as an incandescent lamp or light emitting diode (LED), is used to illuminate the fiber. Sensing transducer at fiber tip consists of miniature sandwich of two partially reflecting optical surfaces with a microscopic gap between them. The colour spectrum that is reflected from the sensor tip is modulated because of optical interference from the reflections of the two optical surfaces. An optical wavelength analyzer is used to analyze the spectrum of the reflected light, and the gap spacing can be determined to within a fraction of average wave length of light used. Fiber optic pressure sensor are immune to electrical interference and can withstand a very high temperature without measurement drift.

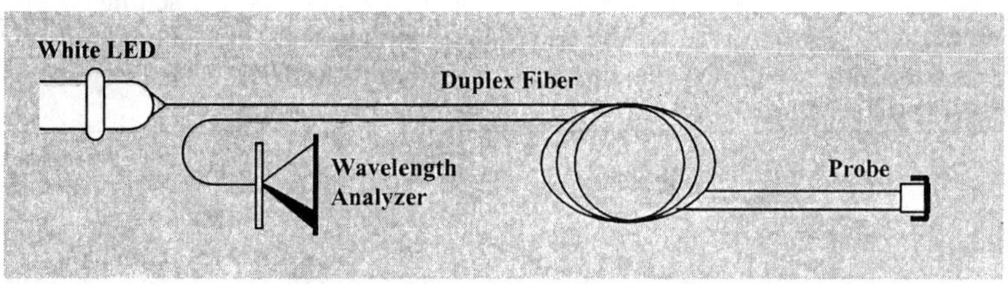

Fig. 7.17(c): Fiber optic pressure sensor

7.18 NON-ELECTRICAL PROTECTIONS FOR POWER TRANSFORMERS

Transformer overheating protection is provided to give an indication of over temperature, to trip the circuit breakers if the temperature exceeds a predetermined value. Overload relays are connected in the current transformer circuits to detect overloading. Others operate direct on top-oil temperature indicator (figure 2.6 (a) of Chapter # 2) with capillary tube or top-oil temperature supplemented with heat from an adjacent resistor connected to a current transformer in the circuit. A sensor using a glass chip sensitive to temperature changes employ's fiber optics techniques to measure winding hot spot temperatures is also applicable.

Gas-oil pressure relays (Buchholz relay figure 2.5 (a) of chapter # 2) are available for attachment to the top of transformer tanks having conservator to indicate windings faults, which produce gas or sudden pressure waves in the oil. Rapid collection of gas or pressure waves in the oil, due to short circuits in the winding will produce fast operation. Possible causes of operation (1) loose air bubbles (colourless) (2) short-circuit (no gas bubbles)(3) Winding damage (coloured gas will appear). Tap changer Buchholz relay (figure 2.8 (c) of Chapter # 2) will operate in the event of flash over on diverter switch or fault in tap changer. Incipient faults due to the composition of oil and short-circuit in the winding will develop excessive pressure in the tank. Pressure relief devices with alarm and tripping contacts are provided.
Pressure relief valve (figure 2.7 of Chapter # 2) is employed to prevent brusting of transformer tank in the case of sudden rise of the tank internal pressure. Over heating and over pressure protections employed for a power transformer is listed in Table 7.15 (1) below.

In the event of a trip signal, the lockout relay (Device No: 86) will energizes to trip circuit breakers on either primary and secondary and initiate a flash in the connected window of the annunciation panel along with audible alarm. The flashlight on the window and audible alarm will remain for a preset time or the operator may acknowledge the alarm. Up on acknowledgement of the alarm or after the preset time the flashlight will become steady light, until the fault is persisting.

If the computerized substation monitoring system demonstrated in Chapter # 4, section 4.20 is provided which, can control and monitor all electrical parameters and communicate with load dispatch center.

Table 7.15(1): Overheating and over pressure protection for power transformers.

Device No:	**Description**	**Trip signal**	**Alarm signal**	**Setting**
63B/MT	Main tank Buchholz relay	Surge trip	Gas alarm	Factory set
63B/TC	Tap changer Buchholz relay	Surge trip	Gas alarm	Factory set
63B/ET	Earthing-transformer Buchholz relay	Surge trip	Gas alarm	Factory set
26/WT	Main-transformer winding temperature high	High-temperat: trip	High temperat: alarm	Alarm 95°C, trip 120°C
26/OT	Main-transformer oil temperature high	High-temperat: trip	High temperat: alarm	Alarm 90°C, trip 120°C
71L	Main tank oil level low		Low-level alarm	Float switch
71L	Tap changer oil level low		Low-level alarm	Float switch
	Cooling fan failure		Alarm	Fan failure circuit
80	Oil flow indicator		Alarm	Pressure-switch setting
	Oil pump failure		Alarm	Pump-failure circuit
20	Tank over pressure / Excessive oil pressure	Oil-pressure trip	High-pressure alarm	Factory set

CHAPTER # 8

RELAYS FOR TRANSMISSION LINE AND BUS PROTECTION.

CONTENTS:

8.1 SELECTION OF RELAYS FOR TRANSMISSION LINE PROTECTION.

The substation/switching stations employs many protective-relaying systems in order to protect the equipment associated with the station, the most important of which are:

1. Transmission lines emanating from the substation.
2. Power transformers
3. Station buses

Restrictions and limitations on building new transmission lines necessitate optimization of transmission networks. This optimization imposes challenges on distance relay based transmission line protection. Network optimization increases transmission line loading and requires fast fault clearing times because of reduced stability margins. In many cases series compensation, Single-pole tripping (SPT), or the combination of both is necessary to optimize transmission network. Series compensation generates sub-harmonics that can cause distance element overreach. SPT adds complexity to the ability of the distance element to track the power system frequency during single-pole open (SPO) conditions when the line protection uses line side potentials. Shunt compensation can corrupt the distance element polarization because of the presence of transient voltages during three-pole open conditions when the line protection uses line-side potentials. Single-pole tripping applications without arc extinction methods can jeopardize power system operation if the fault condition has not disappeared before the re-closing attempt; that is, the breaker closes under fault condition, making the power system prone to instability.

Primary protection:

The primary protection should provide high-speed simultaneous tripping of all line terminals. However, high-speed sequential tripping of three terminal lines may be necessary to prevent imposing load limitations due to overly sensitive relay settings.

Back-up protection:

The back-up protection should have independent current transformer. For dead tank type circuit breakers, both primary and back-up relays should be connected to independent CTs located on the "bus" side of the breaker so that breaker faults will be detected by the primary and back-up relays of both zones adjacent to the breaker. An independent voltage transformer or independent secondary winding of same voltage transformer is acceptable for back-up protection. DC control circuit shall be independently protected and connected to the second trip coil of the circuit breaker. Non-pilot tripping must be provided.

Out-of-step protection:

Out-of-step protection is sometimes used in the following applications:

(a) To block automatic re-closing in the event, tripping is caused by instability.

(b) To block tripping of phase distance relays during power swings

(c) To block tripping at selected locations and permit tripping at others during unstable conditions so that load and generation in each of the separated systems will be in balance.

Bus protection:

Primary protection should be current or voltage differential relays. Independent back-up protection preferably differential protection is required.

Protective relays recommended for transmission line protection and substation bus protection and their applications are given in Table 8.1 (1).

Table 8.1 (1): Transmission line (overhead / underground) and bus protection relays.

Device No:	Relay Title	Relay application	Technical requirements
87CD	Phase segregated current differential protection	Phase and earth fault protection	Phase segregated relay for I pole and 3 pole operation
87TEED	High-speed biased-differential relay	Phase fault and earth fault protection of Teed feeder Bus bar	Protection for one-and-half circuit-breaker bus bar arrangement.
87BFP	Breaker failure protection	Breaker-failure protection	Tripping the circuit breakers associated with faulty zone
51/51N	Non-directional over-current and earth fault relay	Back-up over-current and earth fault protection	IDMT characteristic, plain over-current relay
85P	Pilot wire relay	Phase fault protection for Teed feeder lines	Suitable for 3 ended short distance lines or cable feeders
67	Directional over-current relay	Phase fault protection	For double circuit feeders
67N	Directional ground fault relay	Earth fault protection	For double circuit feeders
21	Distance relay	Phase and earth fault protection	3 zone transmission lines
85PLCC	Power-line carrier relaying-scheme.(carrier-current protection)	Inter tripping circuit breaker on the other end of the line	Phase comparison via power line carrier communication
85TP	Teleprotection equipment for power network.	Inter tripping circuit breaker on the other end of the line.	Via OPGW fiber optic cable
54FL	Frame leakage relay	Earth fault protection	For Gas Insulated stations
79	Autoreclosing relay	Autoreclosing circuit breakers after a fault trip	With provision for dead end closing/synchronism check
87B	High-impedance circulating current bus differential relay	Phase fault and earth fault protection in the bus zone	High impedance circulating current relay
87B	Percentage restraint bus differential relay	Instantaneous over-current relay	Low impedance voltage relay
21	Switched 3 or 4 zone distance-relay	Phase fault and earth fault protection	Applicable only for under ground cable transmission
F/D	Fault locator / Disturbance recorder	Measuring location of transient /persistent faults	Record-graphically the fault voltage and current.

Remote tripping of the breaker at the other end of the line is employed for the following protections:

1. Distance relays
2. Current differential protection (for 2 or 3 end feeders).
3. Pilot wire relaying scheme (for short distance transmission lines/cables)

Breaker failure protection:

In addition to local breaker failure protection, it is required that local breaker failure initiate direct transfer trip when one or more of the following conditions exist:

(a) Speed is required to assure system stability.

(b) Remote back-up protection is unacceptable because the number of circuits and area affected.

(c) Sensitivity of remote relay schemes is inadequate due to connected transformers, generators or line and faults or because of strong in-feed from parallel sources.

8.2 RELAYING SCHEMES FOR HV/EHV TRANSMISSION LINES.

Transmission line relays are located at the substation relay panel and comprise following types of relaying schemes:

1. Direct under-reaching
2. Permissive under-reaching
3. Permissive over-reaching
4. Directional comparison
5. Pilot wire/teleprotection/microwave/power line carrier communication

(1) Direct under-reaching (DUR) relays:

These relays at each bus terminal of the protected line sense fault power flow in to the line. Their zones of operation must overlap but not over reach as shown in Figure 8.2 (a). The operation of the relays at any terminal initiates both the opening of the local breaker and the transmission of a continuous remote tripping signal to effect instantaneous operation of all remote breakers. In Figure (a), for a line fault near bus A, the relays at A initiate trip signal to trip the breaker at A, and send a transfer trip signal to B via power line carrier or Tele-protection scheme. The reception of the trip signal at B trips breaker B.

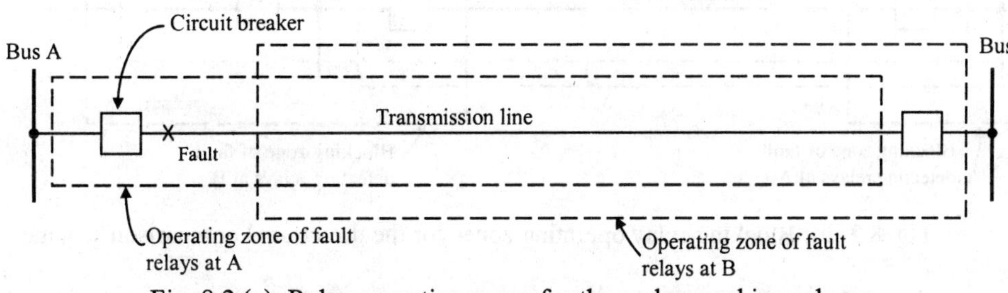

Fig. 8.2 (a): Relay operating zones for the under-reaching scheme

(2) Permissive under-reaching (PUR) relays:

The operation and equipment for this scheme are the same as that of the direct under-reaching system (Figure 8.2a), with the addition of fault detector units at each bus terminal. The fault detectors must over-reach all remote terminals. They are used to provide added security by supervising remote tripping. For a fault at A, relays at A trip breaker A directly and send a transfer trip signal to B. The reception of the trip signal plus the operation of the fault detector at B trips breaker B.

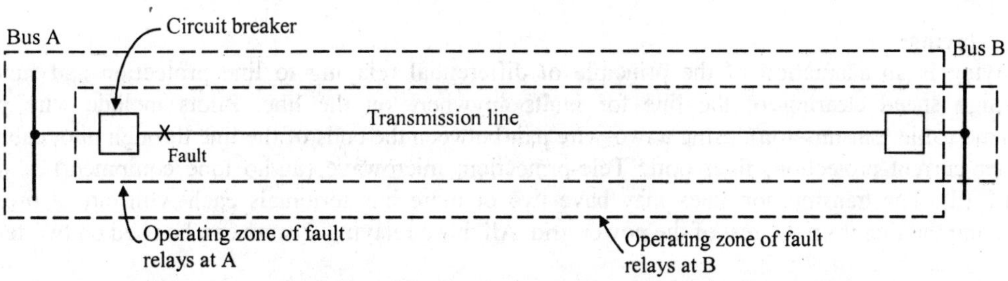

Fig. 8.2 (b): Relay operating zones for the over-reaching scheme

(3) Permissive over-reaching (POR) relays:

In this scheme fault relays at each bus terminal of the protected line sense fault power flow in to the line, with their zones of operation over-reaching as shown in Figure 8.2 (b). Both the operation of the local relays and a transfer trip signal from the remote terminals are required to trip any breaker. Thus, in the example of Figure (b) for the line fault near A, fault relays at A operate and transmit a trip signal to B. Similarly the relays at B operate and transmit a trip signal to A. Breaker A is tripped by the operation of the fault relay A plus the remote trip signal from B. Likewise, breaker B is tripped by the operation of fault relay B plus the remote trip signal from A.

(4) Directional comparison relays:

The channel signal in the system shown in Figure 8.2 (c) is used to block tripping in contrast to its use to initiate tripping in the previous DUR, PUR and POR schemes. Relays at each bus terminal of the protected line section sense fault power flow in to the line. Their zones of operation must over-reach all remote terminals. Additional fault detecting units are required at each terminal to initiate the channel-blocking signal. Their operating zones must extend further or be set more sensitively than the fault relays at the far terminals. The blocking zone at B is extended further behind breaker B than the operating zone of relays at A. Correspondingly, the blocking zone at A is extended further out in to the system than the operating zone of the relays at B.

For an internal fault in line AB, no channel signal is transmitted from any bus terminal. In the absence of any channel signal, relays at A, initiate instantly trip breaker A, and relays at B instantly trip breaker B. For the external fault outside AB as shown in Figure (c), the blocking zone relays at B transmit a blocking channel signal to prevent the relays at A from tripping breaker A. Breaker B will not trip because the B operating zone does not see this fault.

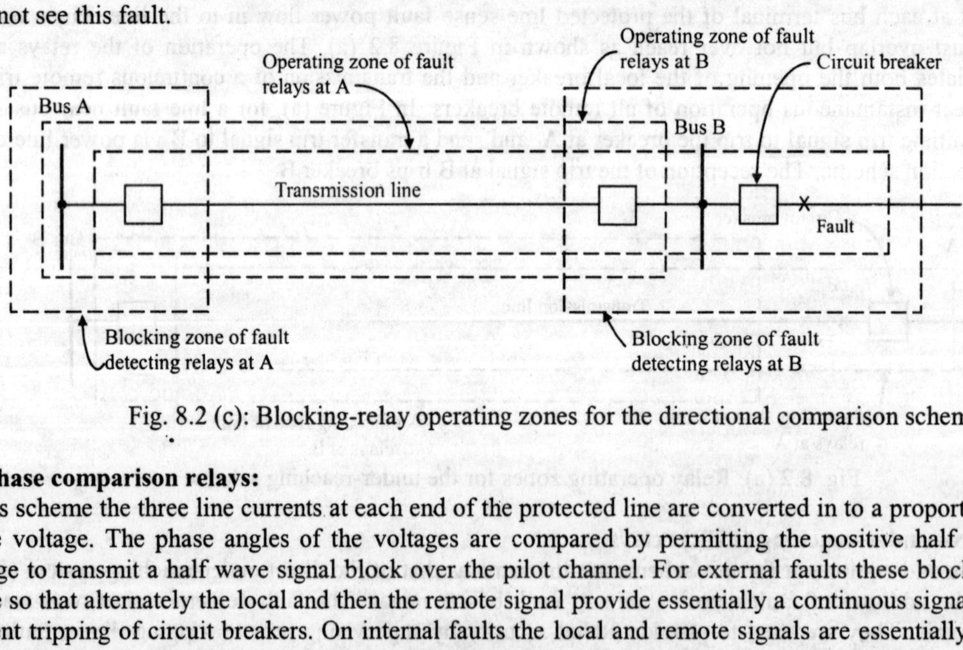

Fig. 8.2 (c): Blocking-relay operating zones for the directional comparison scheme

(5) Phase comparison relays:

In this scheme the three line currents at each end of the protected line are converted in to a proportional single-phase voltage. The phase angles of the voltages are compared by permitting the positive half cycle of the voltage to transmit a half wave signal block over the pilot channel. For external faults these blocks are out of phase so that alternately the local and then the remote signal provide essentially a continuous signal to block or prevent tripping of circuit breakers. On internal faults the local and remote signals are essentially in phase so that approximately a half cycle of no channel signal exists. This is used to permit the fault relays at each terminal to trip their respective breakers.

(6) Pilot relaying:

Pilot relaying is an adaptation of the principle of differential relaying to line protection and functions to provide high speed clearing of the line for faults anywhere on the line. Pilots include wire pilot (for underground cable transmission), using a two-wire pair between the ends of the line through pilot cable; Power line carrier current protection; fiber optic Tele-protection; microwave (audio tone equipment) as shown in Figure 8.2 (d). The transmission lines may have two or more bus terminals each with circuit breakers for disconnecting the line from the rest of the power grid. All those relaying system can be used on two terminal or multi-terminal lines. The relaying systems program the automatic operation of the circuit breakers during power system faults.

(7) Communication media for remote tripping of circuit breakers:

(a) Power line carrier communication:

(b) Microwave /Radio link:

(c) Fiber optic /Tele-protection:

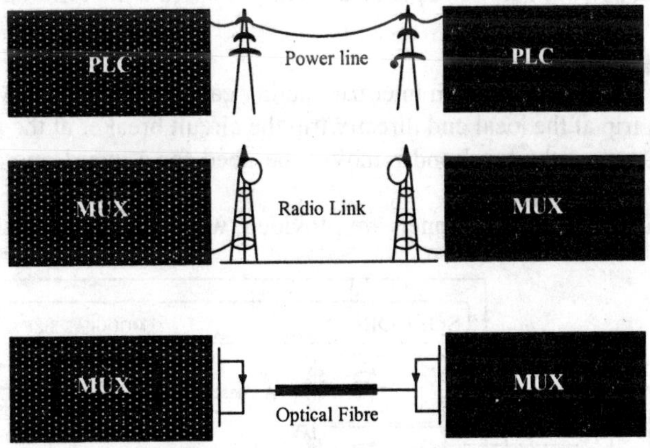

Fig. 8.2 (d): Communication media for remote tripping of transmission line breakers.

8.3 PHASE SEGREGATED CURRENT DIFFERENTIAL PROTECTION (87CD).

The phase segregated current differential relays are employed for all types of phase and earth fault protection in HV and EHV transmission lines. This protection is suitable for single-pole and three-pole circuit breaker tripping and autoreclosing scheme. The sensitivity of protection meets definite operation under minimum plant and single outage conditions and stable for external faults. The operating time is substantially independent of fault current magnitude. The current differential relay will operate over fiber optical circuits laid in the overhead shield wires of the transmission lines. Interfaces to the optical fiber communications system is provided by using fiber optic multiplex on either end of the transmission line substations. The relays are incorporated with indicators to indicate the phase and earth fault in operated position. Indication must not be lost in event of a supply failure. In addition to tripping contacts are provided for initiating single pole and three-pole autoreclosing, energizing fault locators and disturbance recorders, remote signaling and alarms.

A self-monitoring feature is incorporated in the numerical relay to detect hardware and software faults and hence to guard against spurious operation of the relay. In the event of component failure the self-monitoring facility will lockout the relay and report the defect to the computerized substation management system. Power on diagnostic test facility is included. In addition to the general features for numerical relays, the system has facility for oscillographic recording of analogue and binary signals, when abnormal system conditions are detected. Suitable for use with optical fiber cable for transmission line end-to-end communication for inter-tripping commands up on fault detection. Specification for fiber optic cable (OPGW) used in the overhead shield wire is given below.

Fibers: glass 10/125μm; Wave length: 1300 nm; Attenuation: 0.5 dB/KM.

Connection diagram of current differential relay (Va Tech Reyrolle, model Solkor-N) is illustrated in Figure 8.3. Microprocessor controlled current differential relay is used for differential feeder protection, providing complete protection against short-circuits and earth faults, for overhead transmission/distribution lines and underground cable feeders. The relay compare the current at the sending end and receiving end of the protected feeder.

Current differential protection:

The current differential protection will perform magnitude and phase angle comparison of currents, on a phase-by-phase basis, although tripping will be three-phase. The protection is capable of compensating of different CT's at each end of the feeder. The protection is stable for through faults at high fault levels when the line CT's saturate.

Backup over-current protection:
In the event of a communication link failure, the 3 pole DTL (definite time logic)/IDMTL backup three-phase over-current protection will provide backup protection against phase faults and earth faults for the faulty line.

Guard relays:
An over-current guard is added to the differential protection for the security of the scheme. This over-current element can be configured to operate as guard to operate the differential element to trip.

Inter-tripping:
The protection will provide an inter trip facility capable of the following, as selected on the relay:

(1) A trip at the local end directly trip the circuit breaker at the remote end, or
(2) A trip at the local end removes the need for a guard operation at the remote end, allowing tripping with a weak in-feed.

Two additional inter-trip channels are provided, which allow external devices to directly trip remote breaker.

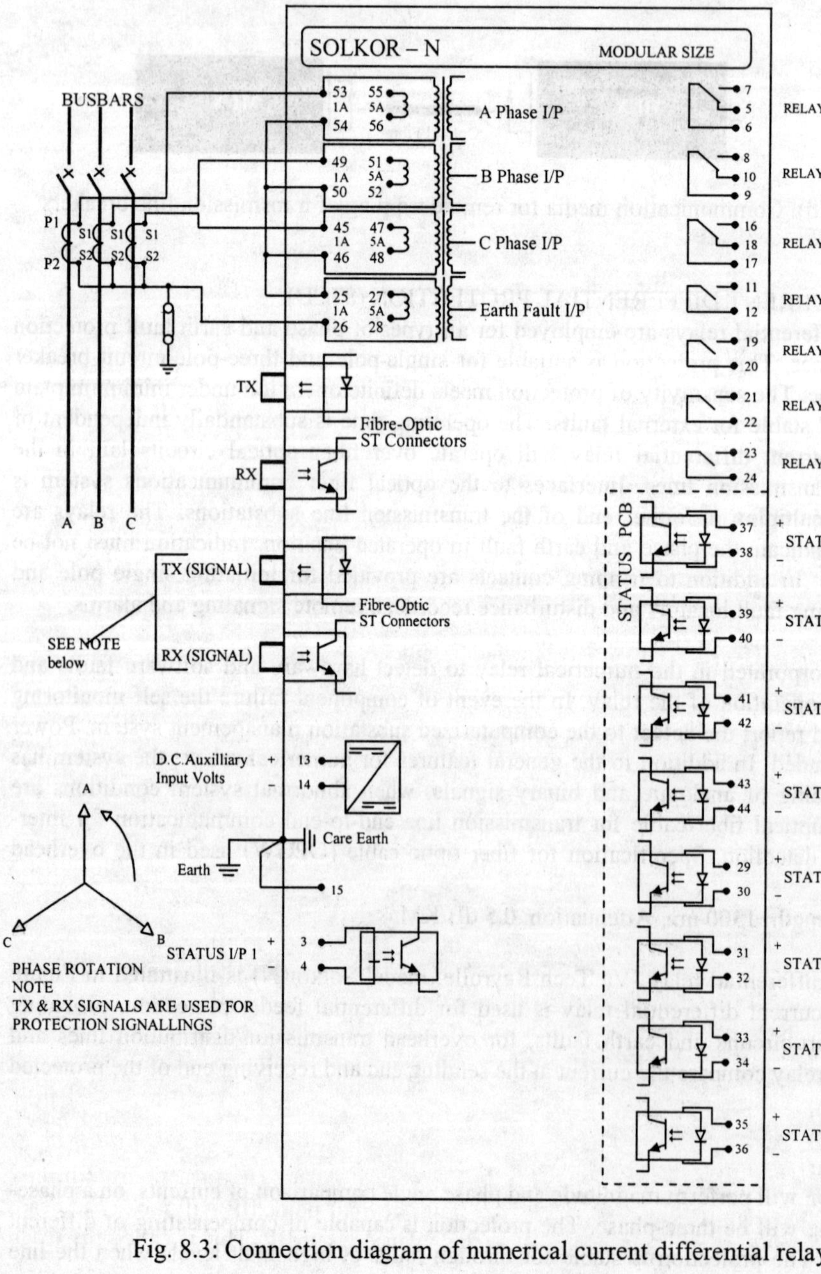

Fig. 8.3: Connection diagram of numerical current differential relay (Courtesy, Vatech Reyrolle)

Testing:

Testing facilities are provided that allow tests as follows:

(a) A single end to be tested in isolation.
(b) Both ends to be tested together to ensure integrity of the communication link, and,
(c) Both ends to be tested together to prove the directionality of the CT's at either ends.

Signaling channel:

Protection must select any one of the following signaling methods.

- RS 485 electrical link using twisted-pair cable
- Optical fiber link at 820nm or 1300nm
- Laser optical link

Trip circuit supervision:

The trip circuit is monitored by a status input with the circuit breaker is in both the open and closed position. This is linked to an alarm and configured to operate an output relay.

Circuit breaker fail protection:

The circuit breaker fail function is triggered by a trip signal from the relay or from an external device. It operates by monitoring the current following a trip signal and issues an alarm, if the current does not stop within a specified time interval. The alarm can be used to operate an output contact to backup an upstream circuit breaker. A further time delay enables another backup stage.

Metering and indications:

The device is capable of displaying the following measurements:
+ The local and remote ends primary currents and secondary currents
+ Differential primary currents

The device will indicate; protection healthy, inter-trip received, breaker trip, protection operating and signaling channel healthy. In the event of a fault trip, the device will record a disturbance record of the local end currents, in primary amps, for a minimum of 1 second.

8.4 DISTANCE PROTECTION FOR TRANSMISSION LINES (21).

A relay, which functions when the circuit admittance, impedance or reactance increases or decreases beyond predetermined limits. Its application is limited to high and extra high voltage transmission lines. Since the impedance of a transmission line is proportional to its length, for distance measurement it is appropriate to use a relay capable of measuring the impedance of a line up to a predetermined point. Such a relay is described as a distance relay and is designed to operate only for faults occurring between the relay location and the selected reach point, thus giving discrimination for faults that may occur between different line sections.

If the relay is designed so that its operating torque is proportional to the current and its restraining torque proportional to the voltage, then according to the relative number of ampere-turns applied to each coils, there will be a definite ratio of V/I at which the torque will be equal. This is termed as reach point setting of the relay.

The operating principle of distance relaying can be illustrated by the beam element and transmission line representation shown in Figure 8.4 (a) and (b) respectively. In figure (a), if equal magnetic forces are produced by voltage E and current I, the beam will be balanced; that is it will neither tilt toward the "E" nor "I" magnet. If the current and voltage coils are designed or adjusted such that, for a solid fault on the line at the point BP in figure (b), the voltage Em just balances the fault current I on the beam element, then the relationship is:

$E_m / I = (I Z_n) / I = Z_n$ which is the impedance of the line to the balanced point BP.

Since Zn is a setting made on coils of the beam element, any fault located less than Zn, distance from bus BI will move the beam toward the operate coil, and conversely, any fault beyond point BP will move the beam toward the restraint coil. The operate zone is from the bus BI to the balance point BP. This is called the reach of the relay.

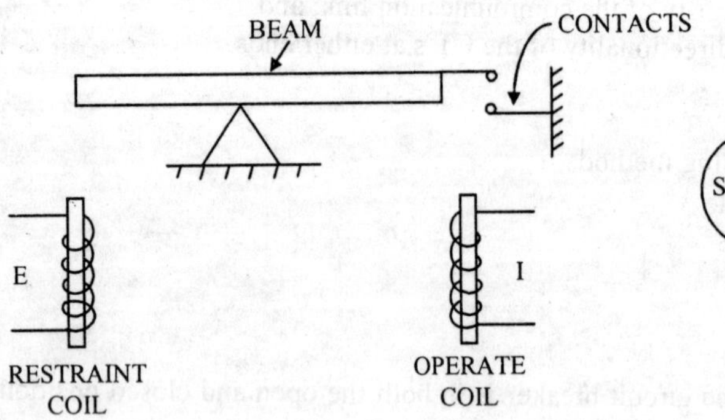

Fig. 8.4 (a): Representation of distance relay.

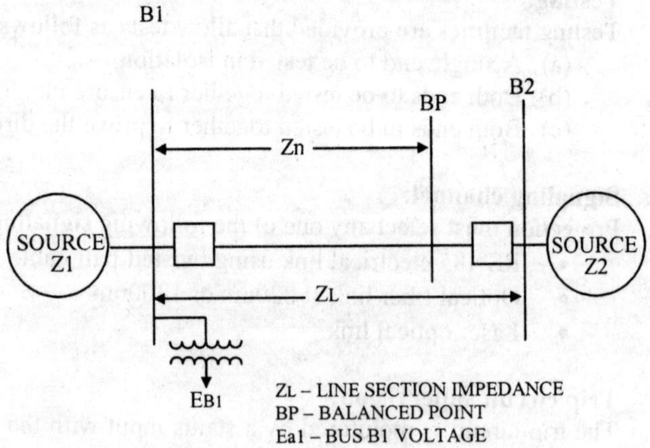

Fig. 8.4 (b): Transmission line representation.

Or otherwise, any increase in the current coil ampere-turns without a corresponding increase in the voltage coil will make the relay unbalanced. So that below a given ratio of E/I the operating torque will become larger than the restraining torque and the relay will close its contacts. It is possible to adjust their ohmic reach setting by changing the relationship of the ampere-turns of the operating coil-to those on the restraining coil making it possible to select a setting suitable for the length of the line to be protected.. A distance protection will comprise an instantaneous directional Zone 1 protection and one or more time delayed zones. The remaining part of the line, which is not covered by Zone 1 is protected by a time delayed directional zone of protection referred as Zone 2. Remote backup protection for all faults on the adjacent line is usually provided by a third zone of protection, which is further time delayed to discriminate with Zone 2 protection plus circuit breaker trip time.

Connection diagram of a conventional type differential relay is illustrated in figure 9.13 (c) of Chapter # 9.

From the application standpoint, the following points should be noted.

1. The relay is directional, so as to operate only for faults on the protected line;
2. Relay reach for faults within the protected line section is essentially independent of generation level, system configuration and the impedance behind the relay and is a function of the line impedance;
3. Operation is instantaneous unless intentional time delay is added.

This relay is used for protection of transmission lines in which the relay measurements is based on measuring impedance (V/I ratio) or reactance or admittance at relaying point, which gives a measure of distance between relay location and fault location. Ring or radial feeders feeding from several sources of power supply (power network) need fast and sensitive protection system to disconnect the circuit breakers provided to isolate the faulty portion of the line. Distance scheme is adequate and quick acting providing selectivity and sensitivity in circuits of any configuration. The time delay of distance protection varies with distance between the protection and the point of fault. The main component of distance protection is a distance element (measuring element), which measures the distance from the protection to the fault location.

Following types of distance relays are employed for three-zone transmission line phase fault and earth fault protection.

(1) Impedance type distance relay: A non-directional relay measuring impedance. It is sensitive to power swings. **Operating characteristic of an impedance relay is by means of R-X diagram [Impedance diagram shown in Figure 8.4 (c)] a circle of radius Z.** Relay operates for a value below the set value of impedance. The impedance relay takes no account of the phase angle between the current and the voltage applied to it. For this reason its impedance characteristic when plotted on an R-X diagram is a circle with its center at the origin of the co-ordinates and of radius equal to its setting in ohms. **The relay operates for all impedance values less than the setting that is for all points within the circle.**

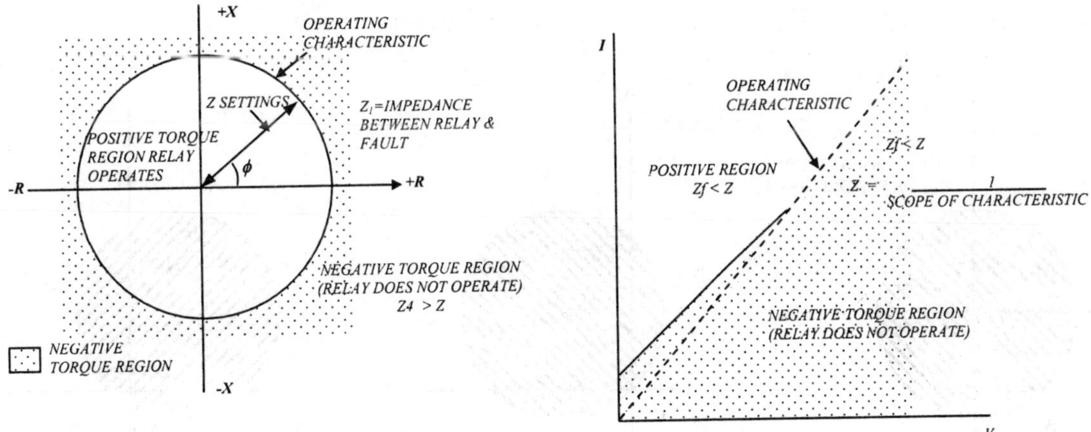

R-X diagram of Impedance Relay

Operating characteristic of an impedance relay

Fig. 8.4 (c): R-X diagram and operating characteristic of impedance type distance relay.

(2) Reactance type distance relay: Reactance type relay has reactance (X), measuring unit. It is an over-current relay with directional restraint. **Relay is suitable for short lines in which arc resistance is important. Reactance relays are designed to measure the reactive component of the protected transmission line.** Any increase in the resistance component of the fault impedance will have no effect up on the relay reach. However, when the fault resistance is of such a high value that load and fault current magnitudes are of the same order, the reach of the relay is modified by the value of the load and its power factor and may either over reach (leading source angle) or under reach (lagging source angle). Reactance relay characteristic (Mho starter characteristic) and operating characteristic is shown in Figure 8.4 (d).

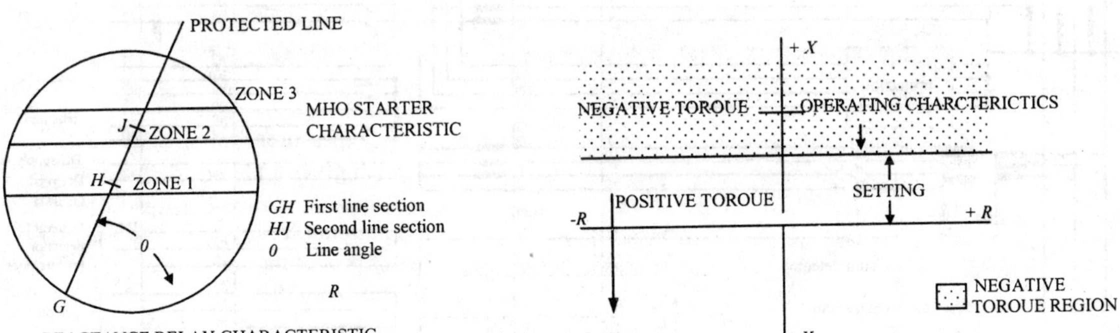

REACTANCE RELAY CHARACTERISTIC

Ideal characteristic of reactance type distance relays

Fig. 8.4 (d): Mho starter and ideal characteristic of Reactance type distance relay.

(3) Mho type distance relay: Mho type relay measures a component of admittance (Y), which is the reciprocal of impedance. Mho is the unit of admittance. It has directional three step three-zone characteristic as shown in Figure 8.4 (e). Reactive reach of the relay goes on changing for various ratios of resistance/reactance (R-X). **Suitable for power swings and zone 1 and zone 2 applications of long distance transmission lines. Least affected by arc resistance. Off set mho relays are used for zone 3 applications, backup protection of bus bars and for blocking main relay during power swings.** In mho relay its characteristic is a straight line on an admittance diagram. The characteristic of this relay when plotted on an R-X diagram is a circle whose circumstance passes through the origin. The relay is inherently directional and will operate only for faults in the forward direction.

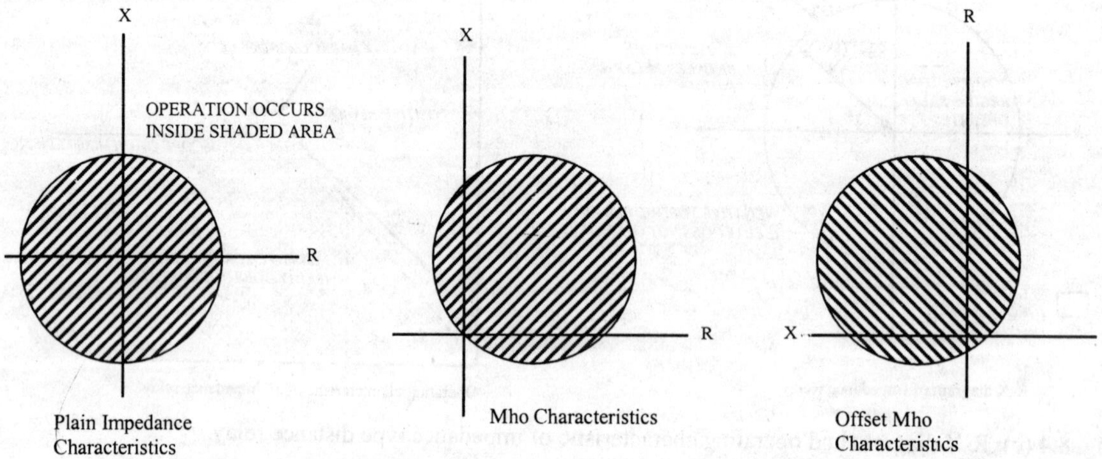

Fig. 8.4 (e): Plain impedance, Mho/offset Mho characteristics of admittance type distance relay.

Block schematic diagram of a typical distance relay is depicted in figure 5.8 (c) of Chapter # 5. Schematic diagram of Siemens model 7SL27 distance relay is illustrated in Figure 8.4 (f). When a fault occurs on a system being protected, the relay voltage falls immediately from the normal value to the fault voltage, while the current instantaneously rises from some load value or zero to the fault value. Both these sudden changes in magnitude are accompanied by changes in phase angle.

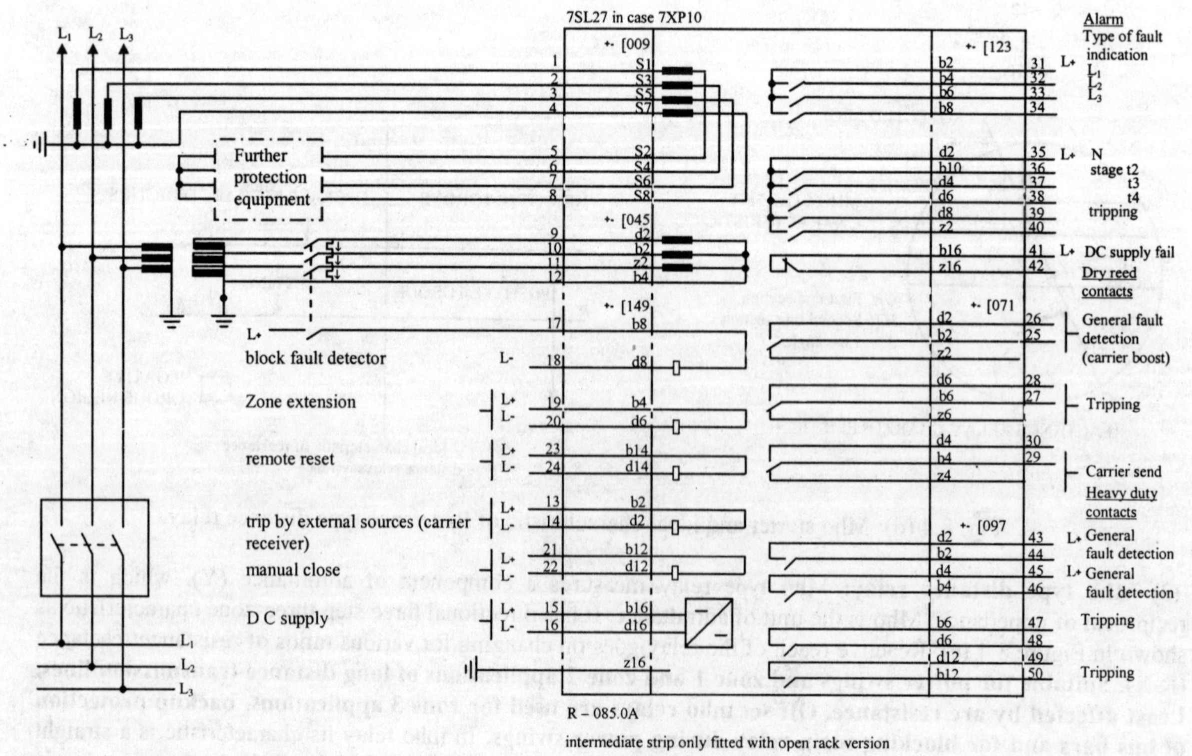

Fig. 8.4 (f): Schematic diagram of numerical distance relay (Courtesy, Siemens Ag)

Two types of fault detection elements are available for phase selection.

(a) Over-current fault detectors:

For use in systems where the minimum fault currents are greater than full load currents. The increased currents in the sound phases should not exceed the actual current settings of the fault detector. One over-current fault detector per phase and one earth fault detector (residual current) is provided. This fault detector can be applied in all systems independent of the method of system earthing. The setting range of over-current element is 1 to 4 times full load current and 0.2 to 0.8 times full load for the residual current element.

(b) Under impedance fault detector:

For use in systems where the minimum fault currents are below full load currents. These are applicable for solidly or resistance earthed systems. Each unit consists of one minimum and one high set over-current detector as well as one under-voltage detector. Setting range is 0.25 to 1 times full load current.

Quadrilateral tripping characteristic:

This provides a high degree of arc tolerance up to eight times the line reactance setting with earth faults. Thus, the characteristic can be adjusted to the requirements of long as well as short lines. Even relatively short overhead lines can be protected within the first distance zone. This ability to accept a high arc resistance has an even, more favorable effect when the relay is used to protect short cables. Arc fault resistance at the cable-sealing end can be covered by appropriate R/X settings.

The relay provides three settable directional distance zones Ia, II and III and a fourth zone Ib which can be controlled by, external sources e.g. autoreclose relay for zone extension or zone reduction and permissive under-reach transfer tripping. [Refer Figure 8.4 (g)].

Stage t_4 is a further back-up zone for faults within the distance reach of the unidirectional fault detector. It can be set for forward faults, reverse faults or unidirectional. .

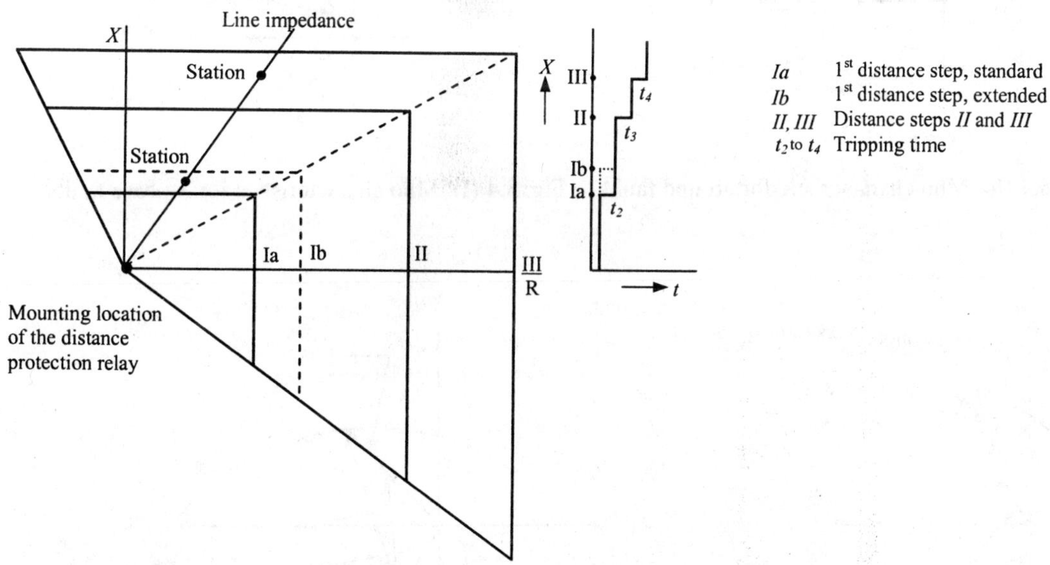

Fig. 8.4 (g): Mounting location of the distance protection relay (Courtesy, Siemens Ag).

Distance relay operation characteristic is a boundary curve, which determines the operating conditions of the relay. Various characteristic curves and its performances are described below.

1. Plain impedance characteristic for non-directional impedance relays.
2. Mho characteristic for directional impedance relays.
3. Offset mho characteristic (relays with offset circular curve).
4. Elliptical characteristic (in the form of an ellipsis).
5. Reactance characteristic (straight line parallel to axis representing resistance).
6. Polygon characteristic for directional relays.

Advantages of employing distance protection for transmission lines:

a) Selectivity of operation in networks involved any number of supply sources.
b) First zone covers 85 to 90% of the protected line. It maintains stability in the event of a close-up fault.
c) High sensitivity to short circuit and earth faults.
d) Better protection and adjustments against loads and power swings.
e) Backup protection against phase-to-phase short circuit to the adjacent sections.
f) Improved reliability of measuring elements.

Mho characteristics for phase to ground faults and three-phase faults (no load flow) are shown in Figure 8.4 (h) and (I) respectively. Figure 8.4 (J) shows Mho characteristics for phase to phase and two phase to ground faults (No load flow).

LEGEND:

Zc = Setting impedance	Z_{IL} = Positive sequence line impedance
Zs = Source impedance	$Z\alpha$ = Zero sequence line impedance
K_1 = Positive sequence Current distribution factor	I_L = Pre-fault load current
K_0 = Zero sequence current distribution factor	I_F = Fault current

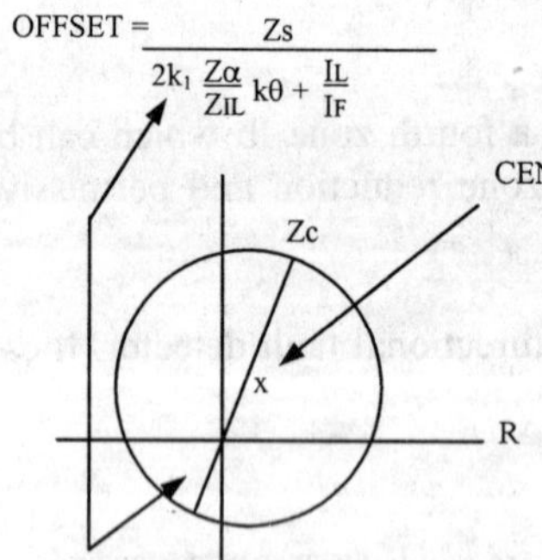

Fig. 8.4 (h): Mho characteristic for ground faults.

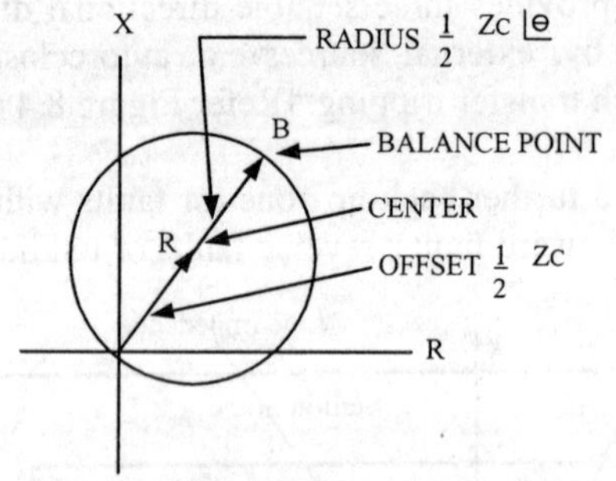

Fig. 8.4 (I): Mho characteristics for 3-phase faults.

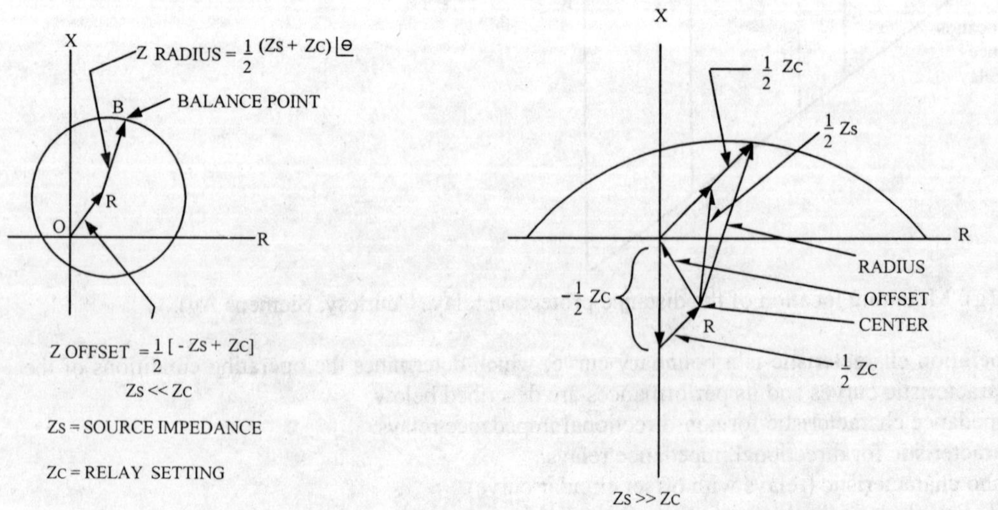

Fig. 8.4 (J): Mho characteristics for phase-to-phase and two phase-to-ground faults (No load flow)

Distance relay testing:
Either conventional method by using secondary injection test set and phase shifter unit as described in figure 5.14 (c) or Microprocessor controlled test set described in figure 5.15, (Chapter # 5) can be used for testing distance relays. Typical test set that gives a more realistic simulation of fault conditions is shown in Figure 5.14 (h) of Chapter # 5. The equipment is connected so as to represent actual system conditions and the test procedure is also demonstrated there-in. Distance relay are required to measure impedance of the protected line accurately over wide range of voltage and current. The impedance measurement of these relays can be checked by, using this test equipment. The equipment checks the measuring accuracy of the relay under static conditions only i.e, is the current is increased slowly or voltage is decreased slowly until the relay operates.

It is usual to check the relay ohmic setting at the actual line angle. The choke and resistance tapings of the line impedance Z_l are provided for this purpose. In order to check the characteristic of the mho or reactance relays, angles other than the line impedance angle may be chosen. The points usually checked on mho and reactance relay characteristics are shown in Figure 8.4 (k) and (L) respectively.

Referring the test equipment connection in figure 5.14 (h) of Chapter # 5, load current can be applied to the relay, by operating the load pushbutton just before operating the fault contactor. Operation of the fault contactor short-circuits the load resistance and presents only the line the line impedance Z_l to the relay. The use of a relay selector switch avoids any human error that might otherwise occur when changing the voltage and current connections from one measuring element in the relay under test to the other. By injecting in to the scheme through the secondary voltage and current connections, the whole distance scheme is made to perform, the secondary wiring to the relay is checked, and all associated auxiliary relays are made to operate.
LEGEND: Z_l: Line impedance; θ: Relay characteristic angle; φ: Line angle

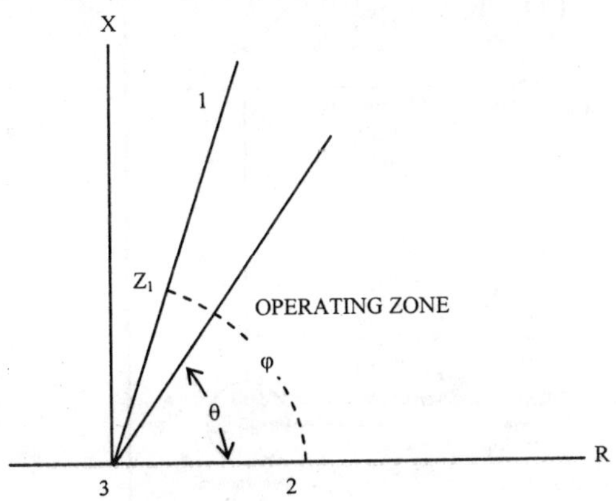

Fig. 8.4 (k): Operating zone of Mho relay

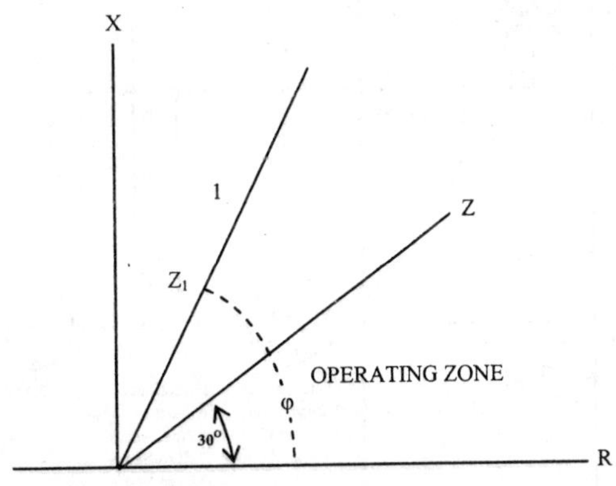

Fig. 8.4 (L): Operating zone of reactance relay

8.5 MICROPROCESSOR CONTROLLED NUMERICAL LINE PROTECTION RELAY.
Numerical transmission line protection combines the power and flexibility of microprocessor technology for continuous monitoring all fault loops and zones. The reach of the zone is set independently of the other zones with separate settings for phase and earth fault protection. Time delays can be set separately for phase and earth fault for all zones. Where appropriate the signaling schemes include current reversal detection, circuit breaker echo and weak in-feed detection to ensure correct operation of the relay.
Functional diagram of a typical line protection relay **(SEL-311, Schweitzer Engineering Laboratories)** is illustrated in Figure 8.5 (a).

Numerical distance relays have following facilities:
1. Three-zone phase and earth fault sensing (3 zone distance/time characteristic) with 12 or 18 measuring elements.
2. The ability to stop both the principal settings and an alternative set of settings in the memory of the relay.
3. Inclusion of logic to perform communicating type distance scheme such as: (a) zone 1 extension scheme initiated by an external input; (b) over/under reach scheme; (c) blocking scheme; (d)

interrogation by substation automation equipment (e) single shot autoreclose (f) circuit breaker fail protection.

4. Capacity to monitor 3-phase voltage, current, real and reactive power for the feeder locally or remotely.
5. Provision for directional earth fault element and voltage transformer supervision.
6. The accuracy of the fault location independent of the line loading prior to the fault, the magnitude of the fault resistance, and actual fault current in-feed from the remote line end.
7. Switch on to fault (SOTF) protection provides fast tripping, if the breaker is re-closed with earthing clamp left in place.
8. Fault records: Last 10 fault records are available in the memory with time and date of trip and nature of fault.
9. Over/under voltage, over/under frequency, Backup IDMTL over current protection (if required).

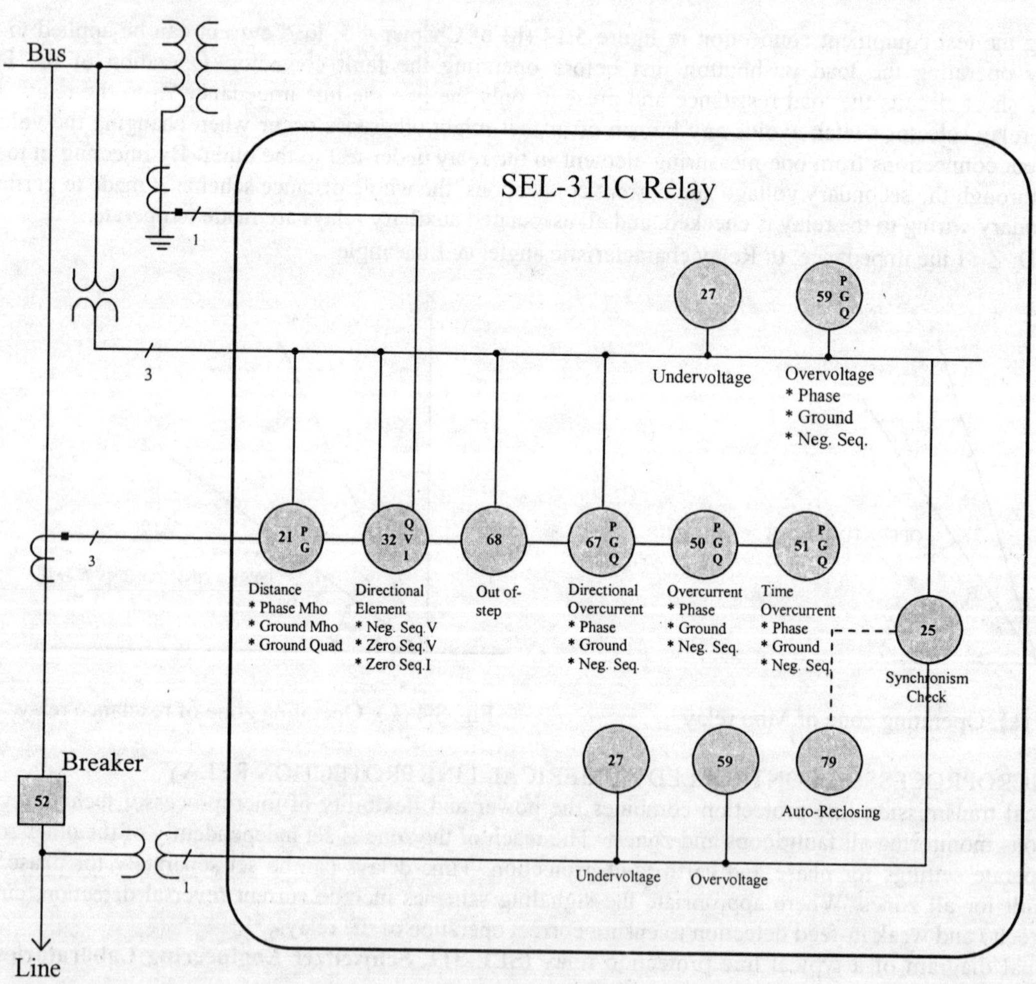

Fig. 8.5 (a): Functional block diagram of numerical overall line protection relay (Courtesy, Schweitzer)

Following volt free output contacts are provided for numerical distance relays:

1. Tripping contact for direct or indirect breaker tripping
2. Autoreclosing for single phase and 2 phase faults.
3. Zone 2-timer contact to initiate breaker tripping on zone 2 faults.
4. Zone 3-timer contact to initiate breaker tripping on external fault.

5. Self-supervision: defective relay or failure of auxiliary DC power to the relay; self reset contact to initiate alarm.
6. Carrier-send: Communicating protection schemes to the remote end circuit breaker.
7. Earth fault signal: To indicate or annunciate that the relay start operation due to an earth fault.
8. PT supervision: For signaling potential transformer supervision logic (self-reset) and blocking of relay operation.
9. Start signal to fault locator and disturbance recorder (self-reset) during phase and ground fault.

LED (light emitting diode) indications are provided on the front of the relay to identify the faulty phase or phases and the zone for which tripping occurred. Indication must not be lost in the event of supply failure. Overall fault clearing times, i.e. from fault initiation to arc extinction is limited as follows.

1. Zone 1 setting: Up to 72% of the total protected line length, i.e. 90% of a distance relay zone 1 reach assuming 80% zone 1 setting: 100 milliseconds
2. From 72% to 100% of total protected line length: 140 milliseconds.

The operating characteristic for each zone is variable mho characteristics for all type of faults. Fault monitoring systems are being incorporated along with distance relays. It provides for on-line fault recording, which means that oscillagrams are printed out on occurrence of a fault. Fault-locators installed with distance relay measures and indicate accurately the distance between the substation and the point of fault. Since the distance relay, fault recorder and fault locators are connected to the secondary of line CT and PT, the calculation of distance is based on the principle of distance relay. The fault distance is shown on % of total line length based on the calculated line impedance.

Communication aided schemes:
Relay is suitable following types of pilot schemes:
a). Direct under-reach transfer trip
b). Permissive under-reach transfer trip
c). Permissive over-reach transfer trip
d). Hybrid permissive over-reach transfer trip
(e) Directional comparison blocking scheme
(f) Out-of step tripping and power swing blocking

A line pickup (switch on to a fault) function provides tripping if the breaker is closed in to a zero voltage bolted fault when line side potential is used. Blocking function restrains selected protection elements during power swing conditions. Tripping can be set as instantaneous or delayed. Under the delayed option, the trip occurs when the current is low, to avoid over-stressing the circuit breaker.

Figure 8.5 (b) shows the relay operating zones with communication assisted tripping. Four zone phase and ground distance elements plus directional ground elements provide a convenient array of line protection solutions. Permissive overreaching/under-reaching and directional comparison blocking/unblocking schemes are supported. The built-in, four-shot re-closer provides greater flexibility in protection and control of transmission lines.

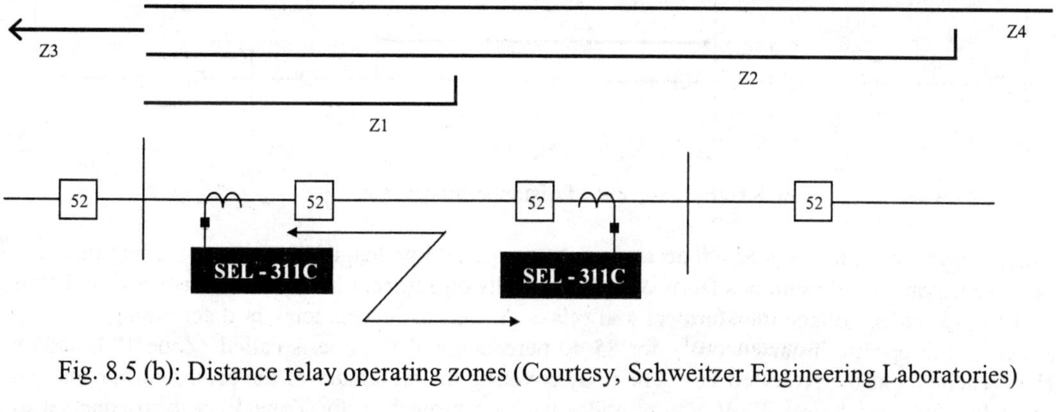

Fig. 8.5 (b): Distance relay operating zones (Courtesy, Schweitzer Engineering Laboratories)

8.6 CONCEPT OF DISTANCE RELAY ZONES IN TRANSMISSION LINES

Distance relays respond to the voltage and current applied to them and are usually more highly responsive at some lagging current angle. Figure 8.6 (a) shows a typical R-X diagram (impedance diagram) that describes the behavior of these devices. Most distance relays have a characteristic similar to curve 1 or 2 as indicated in the R-X diagram. Faults producing an apparent-impedance at the relay location that falls inside the characteristic circle will cause the relay to operate.

Reach, over-reach and under-reach of distance protection:

Reach: Reach is the limiting distance of the protection. The faults beyond which are not within the reach of the protection (say 100%).

Over-reach: Operation of a distance relay for a fault beyond its set protected distance (say 115%).

Under-reach: Failure of distance relay to operate within the set protected distance (say 70%).

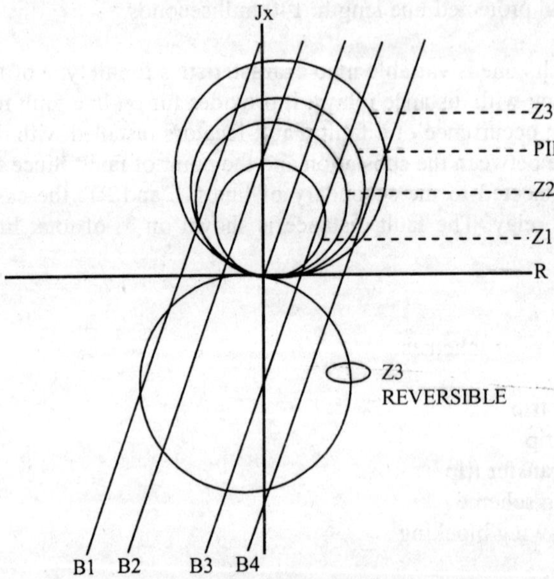

Fig. 8.6 (a): R-X diagram of distance relay

Since a distance relay has a distinct ":reach" irrespective of source impedance and is directional, it is for protecting a zone. Concept of distance relay zone is shown in Figure 8.6 (b). Zone 1 relays cover a portion such as 80 to 90% of a transmission line. Zone 2 relays respond to faults at all locations on the line and also to others in proximity of the line end. Zone 3 relays are also often used and may be directional in the same sense or opposite senses as the zone 1 and zone 2 relays, or in some applications may be non-directional.

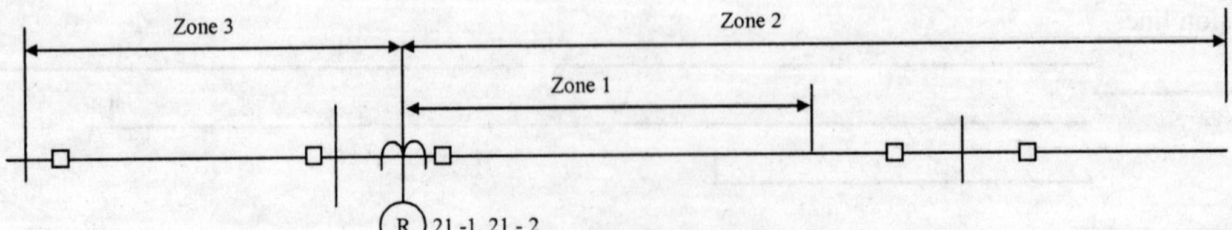

Fig. 8.6 (b): Concept of distance relay zones

Distance relays are set to reach 85-90 percent of the protected line length. Settings exceeding this range could cause false tripping for far-end bus faults or close-in faults on adjacent lines due to performance differences of current transformers, voltage transformers and relays as well as inaccuracies in determining line impedance. The relay set to operate instantaneously for 85-90 percentage of the line is called "Zone 1" based on a 90% reach on each end of the protected line. The relay covering the remainder of the protected line and part of the adjacent line is called "Zone 2". It also provides back-up protection for Zone 1. A third zone set to extend beyond the adjacent line section, can be added to provide additional back-up protection. It must have a longer time delay setting than Zone 2 in order to coordinate properly. At least two zones of protection are necessary to protect a line section. Figure 8.6 (c) illustrates zone distance relaying.

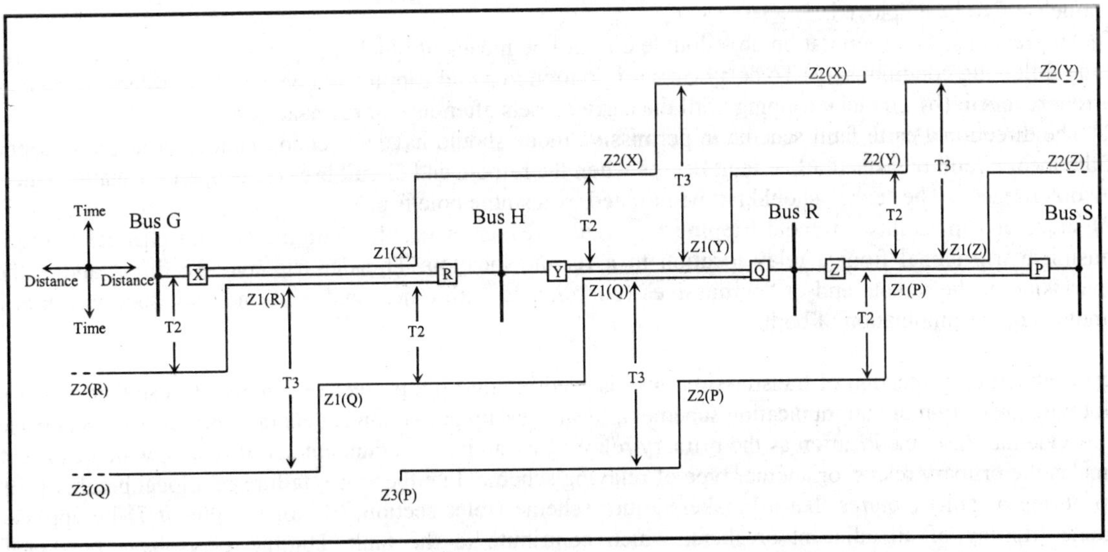

Fig. 8.6 (c): Step time zones of distance relay protection.

Zone 2 is set for 100% of the protected line plus 25-50% of the adjacent line, with typical delay of 0.2 to 0.3 second. Similarly, zone 3 is set for 100% of the protected line, plus 100% of the next line section plus approximately 25% of the third line. The zone 3, time delay setting is typically from 0.5 second to 3 seconds. The preceding reach settings apply to the shortest adjacent line sections when line sections of different length emanate from the protected line far end bus.

8.7 DISTINCTIVE FEATURE OF DISTANCE RELAYING SCHEME.

Application of a distance relay is for the protection of HV and EHV overhead transmission lines from all type of phase fault and earth faults. Phase and earth fault compensation feature is provided for accurate distance measurements and to allow for variation in the path of earth faults on the system. While implementing the distance protection scheme, distinctive features described below are to be considered.

1) Zones 1 and 2 will operate only for faults in the protected direction. Relays should not operate on reverse faults even if the voltage supplied to the relay falls zero on all the three-phases. Zone 2 have a time delay setting facility.

2) Zone 3 must be non-directional and are capable of being independently offset in both directions. Zone 3, have a time delay setting facility

3) Starting must be by impedance relays. The relay characteristic should cover the protected line plus the longest line emanating from the remote station taking current in-feed in to account. The starting relays are usually employed as zone 3.

4) The operating time of each zone might be substantially independent of fault current magnitude. In a previously de-energized line if the circuit breaker is closed in to a fault, instantaneous tripping of CB is essential.

5) Power swing blocking is essential to ensure no mal-operation of the distance relays due to power swings between the several power sources in the transmission network.

6) Voltage transformer supply to the distance relay is to be monitored. In the event of loss of one or more phases, the supervising system should inhibit relay operation and initiate an alarm.

7) Contacts for initiating trip and/or autoreclose signals for single pole and 3-pole breakers, starting fault locators, distribution recorders, signaling and alarm as required.

8) All measuring and starting elements in the healthy phases of the faulted transmission feeder line and all measuring elements on the parallel line reset and are unaffected by the currents which flow in the healthy circuit during the single phase re-closer dead time.
9) To achieve discriminative clearance of high resistance earth faults, directional earth fault (DEF) relays (polarized by zero-sequence) operating in conjunction with Tele-protection channels or power line carrier channels are to be employed.
10) To prevent spurious operation on a double circuit line means of blocking operation should be incorporated in the following conditions; (a) To delay carrier initiation to avoid tripping at one end of a protected line due to current reversal; (b) To block tripping until the carrier resets after current reversal.
11) The directional earth fault scheme in permissive mode should have an "echo" facility to facilitate tripping of the local circuit breaker if a line fault occurs when the remote end circuit breaker is open for maintenance or any other reason. The "echo" should not be initiated by a single pole trip.
12) Transfer trip facility / remote tripping of circuit breaker in which a communication channel is used to transmit a trip signal from a relay location to a remote location. Transfer trip may be direct and without supervision at the remote end or "permissive" (coordinated with a near end trip) and with supervision at the remote end, or combination of both.

Remote back-up protection of transmission lines is used in non-pilot protective schemes (those that do not use pilot wire protection or communication schemes), local back-up protection is generally preferred. Local backup is provided at the same location as the primary relaying by adding a redundant set of relays, which can be the same as the primary relays, or another type of relaying scheme. In either case, failure of a local breaker (fail to trip during a fault) requires that a breaker failure scheme (refer section 7.11 of Chapter # 7) be applied to initiate tripping of all adjacent breakers, which contribute to the fault. Digital relays have breaker fail protection unit, which can be programmed as required.

The parallel transmission lines shown in Figure 8.7 (a) between buses G and H illustrate a coordination problem for faults in the end zone at F_1 or F_2. Failure of Zone 1 relays at bus H to trip for these faults can cause all zone 2 relays on all lines connected to bus H to trip, since zone 2 time settings are set the same for all lines. Otherwise, the Zone 2 with the shortest time setting would always trip first for end zone faults)

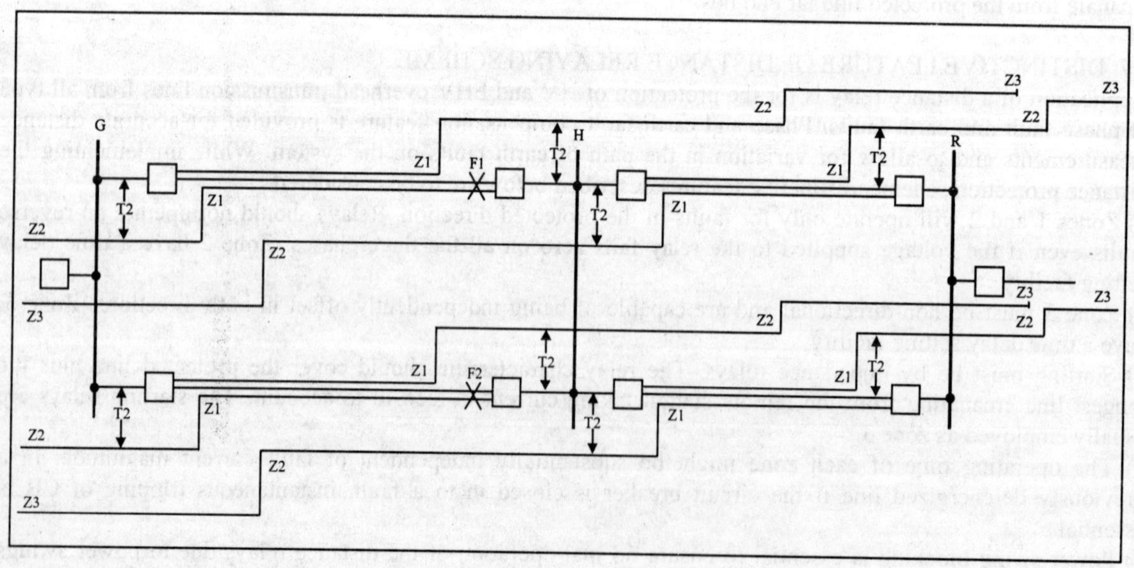

Fig. 8.7 (a): Distance relay scheme on parallel lines.

A line terminating in a transformer [Figure 8.7 (b)] permits setting the Zone 1 reach at bus H, part-way in to the transformer so that the entire line is protected. Any relaying applied for the protection of the transformer must initiate tripping of the local breaker and the remote breaker, at bus H typically by a transfer tripping scheme. If Zone 2 or Zone 3 relays are applied, they are set to reach through the transformer bank into the adjacent line sections.

Single-phase distance relays have variable reach for different type of faults if the transformer has delta-star or star-delta connected windings. Three-phase type distance relays "see" the transformer as impedance that does not change with the type of fault. A distance relay measures impedance from the voltage transformer location, and direction from the location of the CT. From a relaying standpoint, (at bus G) measuring line voltage and current is preferred, since reach is then a function of the line only. Using Line voltage V_L and the current at the bus end of the line I_L also measures only line-impedance. However, faults in the transformer would be recognized by the distance relay as an apparent impedance. The line voltage V_H is a function of the remote end current from bus H, while the relay current is from the nearest end bus G in the tripping direction. When bus G voltages and currents are used, the transformer is included in the reach of the relay. Care must be taken to include the effect of the transformer turns ratio and the ratio change due to transformer taps.

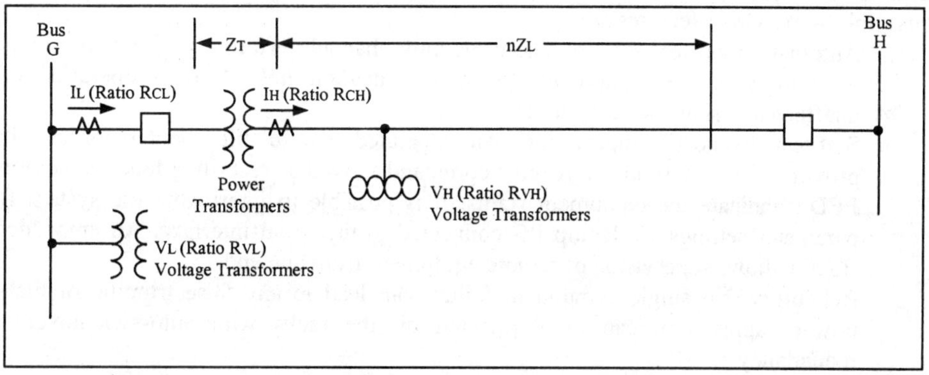

Fig. 8.7 (b): Distance protection for line terminating on a transformer bank.

Zone 1 must be set for the minimum transformer ohms for any tap position in order to prevent over-reaching. Conversely, Zone 2 must be set for more than 100 percent of the maximum transformer ohms plus line ohms to ensure full end-zone coverage. To account for errors for calculation of impedances, the zone 1 relay is typically set equal to $0.99Z_T + 0.90Z_L$. Note that if the transformer impedance is actually Z_T, and is much larger than Z_L, the percentage of line protected by Zone 1 is limited.

8.8 DIGITAL TELEPROTECTION SYSTEM FOR POWER NETWORKS.

Transfer-trip relay is a relaying scheme for remote tripping of a circuit breaker in which a communications channel is used to transmit a trip signal from a relay location to a remote location. Transfer-trip may be direct and without supervision at the remote end or permissive (that is, coordinated with a near-end trip) and with supervision at the remote end, or combinations of both.

Teleprotection equipment operating on a frequency shift principle is employed for direct tripping and permissive tripping on the transmission lines with the following protection features.

a) Permissive inter-tripping channels initiated by the distance relays.
b) Permissive inter-tripping channels for use with the zone protection
c) Direct inter-tripping channels initiated by bus bar and breaker failure protection.

The Teleprotection equipment signaling for a command output should be less than:

1. Direct tripping 45 milliseconds.
2. Permissive tripping 25 milliseconds

Fiber optic system:

The increasing demand for transmitting voice, data processing and line protection over long distances was the reason to replace ground wires used for lightning protection of transmission lines by, optical power ground wire (OPGW) with steel tube. The central element of the OPGW tube is made of aluminium clad steel or aluminium alloy. Various numbers of coloured fibers are integrated in this steel tube. The steel loose buffer is filled with jelly in order to uncouple the fibers from transversal strain when the cable is subjected to mechanical stresses. Optical time domain reflectometer (OTDR) is an instrument that measures transmission characteristics of fiber by sending a pulse of light down the fiber and measuring the light scattered across the length and reflected back from the end as a function of time.

Composite overhead ground wire (OPT-CW) with optical fiber cable (single mode 48 core) provided on the transmission line is used for Teleprotection data transmission. Fiber optic cable is being laid from nearest terminal tower to substation Teleprotection panel. Fusion splicing of fiber optic cable, installation of junction box and patch panel, termination of fiber optic cable from patch panel to relay panel is the other scope of work in the fiber optic system.

Teleprotection equipment:

ABB model NSD 570 Teleprotection equipment is described here. This equipment is designed for transmission of 4 simultaneous commands in analogue mode and up to 8 independent commands in digital mode of operation. The system will automatically choose the shortest transmission times i.e. analogue links 6 ms and digital links 4 ms. Other features are:

1. Automatic loop test feature: The protection channel performs an automatic loop test to monitor the healthiness of the equipment and communication link. Normal operation of the equipment is unaffected during such loop tests.
2. Self-test diagnostics/supervision: An integrated non-volatile event recorder with time stamping is provided for each send and receive command as well as recording link and equipment status changes. LED's indicate the equipment status. It is possible to interrogate the system for faults and verify parameter settings via laptop PC connected to the serial interface. An embedded operation channel (EOC) allows supervision of remote equipment from one end.
3. Reliability: No single component failure can lead to any false tripping or mal-operation. Modular power supply unit can be duplicated on the racks with auto-switchover, to further enhance redundancy.
4. Interfacing with protection relays: The command interface can directly interface with the protection relays. Interfaces are programmable for both normal as well as heavy duty switching applications. Each command is individually configurable for blocking, permissible for direct tripping.

Signal transmission:

Typical representation channel of a digital Teleprotection system is shown in Figure 8.8 (a). Signaling commands from the protection relay scheme enter the signaling equipment via optoisolators. Each of the live commands is coded as two data input bits. The encoded data is used to key an enhanced LED transmitter, which is coupled to an optical fiber. At the receiving end the light signals are detected as pulses, which are decoded and the data is reformed. Decoding the status of the two bits associated with each Teleprotection command provides the control for high-speed output reed relays. Typical Teleprotection message format is shown in Figure 8.8 (b).

The optical components operate at a wavelength of 850 nanometers, using multi-mode graded index optical fibers having core and cladding diameters of 50 and 125 micrometers respectively with an assumed loss of just below 4 dB per kilometre. The optical fiber medium forms an interference free data transmission link.

Protection relays in conjunction with communication links provide the best possible means of selectively for isolating faults on transmission lines and other important items of electrical plants. Tele-protection system selectively disconnects the faulty part by transferring command signals within the shortest possible time. Depending on the protection scheme in use, the command signals trip the remote line end breaker either directly (direct tripping) or are first enabled by the local protection device (permissive tripping). Other protection schemes involve tripping prevention by the local protection device (blocking).

A fundamental requirement in all these applications is that command signals are communicated reliably at the highest possible speed even if the channel is disturbed by the faults (dependability). On the other hand, interference on the communication channel must never cause unwanted operation of the protection by simulating a tripping signal when there is no fault on the power system (security). From the communications-engineering point of view, the bandwidth a Teleprotection equipment occupies must also be taken in to account. The most important features of a Teleprotection system are therefore transmission time, dependability and security.

LEGEND:
DB: Distribution box (Telecommunication)
MDF: Main distribution frame (telecommunication)
PDF: Plant distribution frame.
TDB: Telecommunication distribution box.
OPT-GW: Composite overhead ground wire with optical power cable.
UG-OPT: Underground composite control and optical fiber cable.

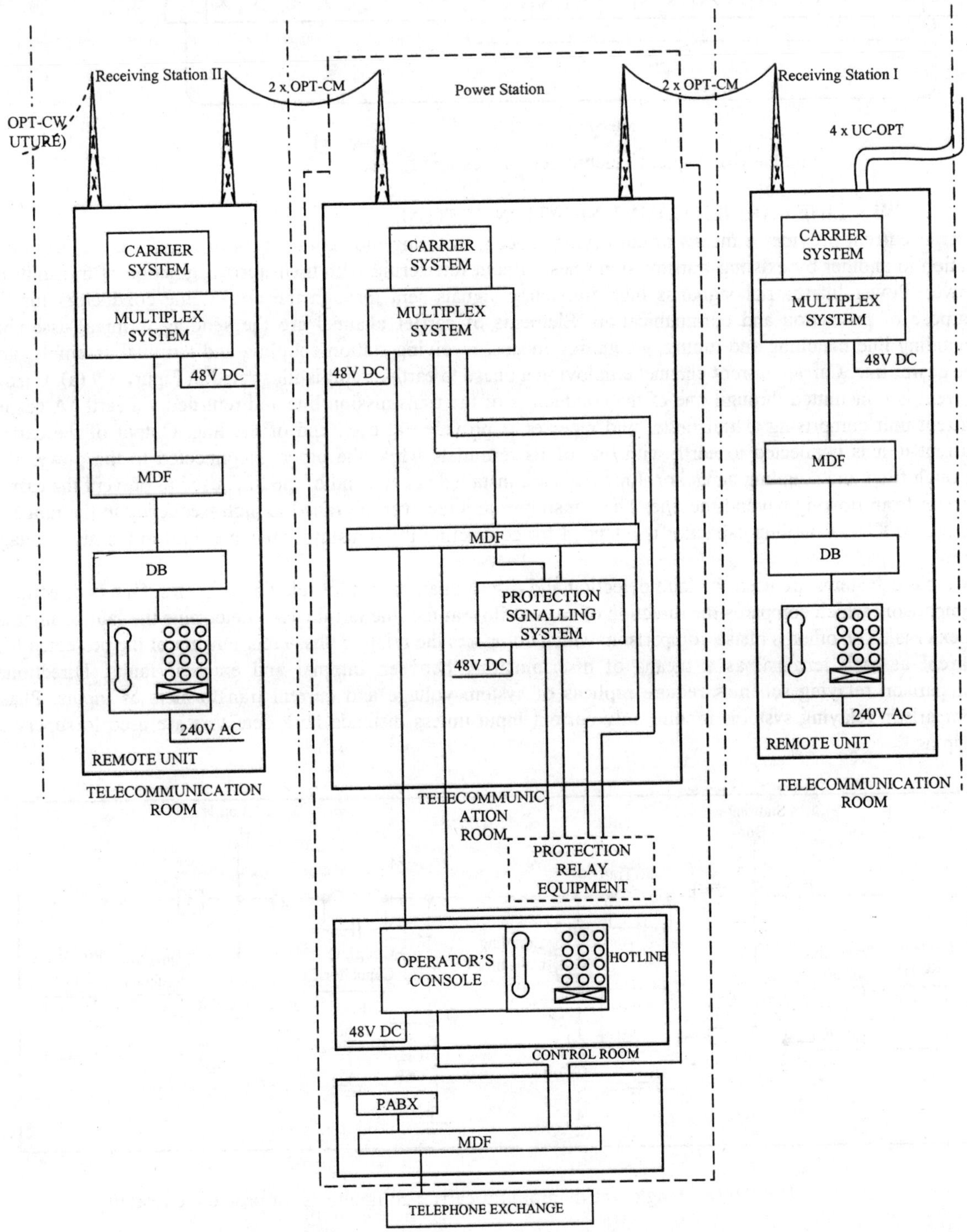

Fig. 8.8: Typical representation channel of a digital Teleprotection system.

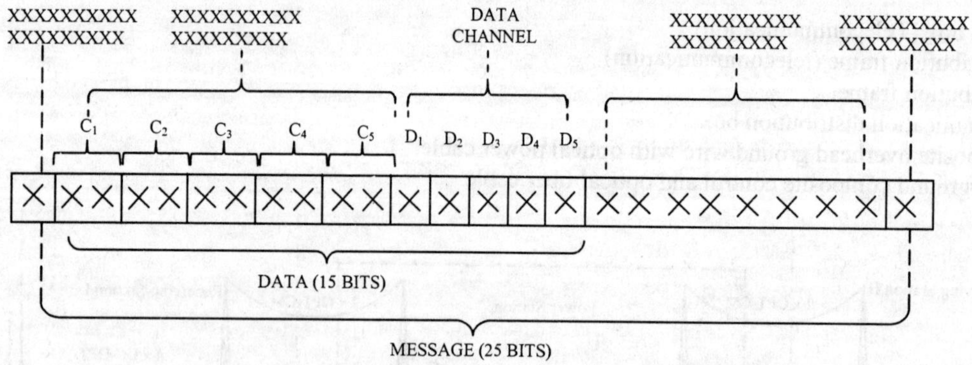

Fig. 8.8 (b): Typical Teleprotection message format.

8.9 POWER LINE CARRIER COMMUNICATION SYSTEM.

Carrier current provides a means of conveying speech, metering indications, control impulses, etc, from one station to another by existing transmission lines without interfering with their normal function of transmitting power. Power line carrier signal is high frequency signals sent through the power line conductors for the purpose of protection and communication. Elements of carrier channel are the sending terminal assembly including line matching and tuning, a coupling means, receiving station coupling and terminal assembly, and the power line. Carrier current channel employing a phase to earth circuit is illustrated in Figure 8.9 (a). Carrier current is transmitted through one of the conductors of the transmission line and returned via earth. A carrier current unit comprising a transmitter and receiver is provided at each end of the line. Output of the carrier current unit is connected to earth with one of its terminals while the other is connected to the power line through filter and coupling capacitor. Line traps are installed at each end of the line, used to prevent the carrier current from flowing beyond the line. The transmitter and receiver are tuned to high frequency in the range of 30 to 300 KHz. Coupling capacitor is intended for connecting the transmitter/receiver unit to the high voltage line.

Two basic systems are used for fault detection and discrimination in pilot relaying schemes. One is directional comparison, which compares the direction of current flow at the line terminals to determine the fault is internal or external. The other is phase comparison, which compares the relative phase relationship of the protected line current at each terminal as a means of discriminating between internal and external faults. Directional comparison relaying schemes require replicas of system voltage and current transformers as inputs. Phase comparison relaying systems require only current input unless distance fault detectors are used to supervise tripping.

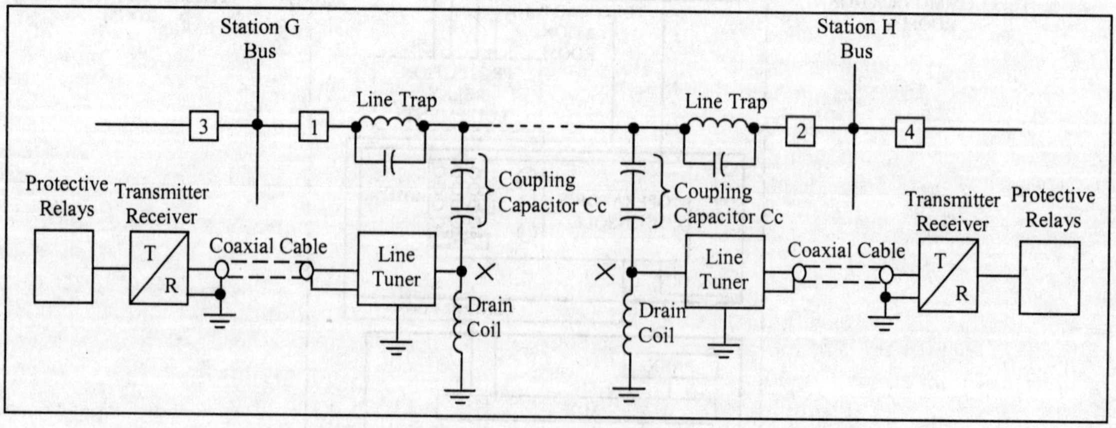

Fig. 8.9 (a): Single line diagram for carrier components for protective relaying.

Coupling capacitor:

Figure 8.9 (b) illustrates a typical paper capacitor, the standard carrier-coupling device made up of a large number of sections of connected in series to obtain the proper voltage. They are stacked mechanically to provide units in the higher voltage insulation classes. Typical units range in voltage and capacitance from 66 KV to 765 KV is from 0.015 μF to 0.004 μF. The capacitor is mounted on a metal base as illustrated in Figure 8.9 (c) to provide convenient installation and space for connection to its terminal. The unit contains main capacitor (C), 50 or 60 Hz drain coil (L_1), protective gap (G), grounding switch (S), tuning coil (L_2), impedance matching transformer (IMT).

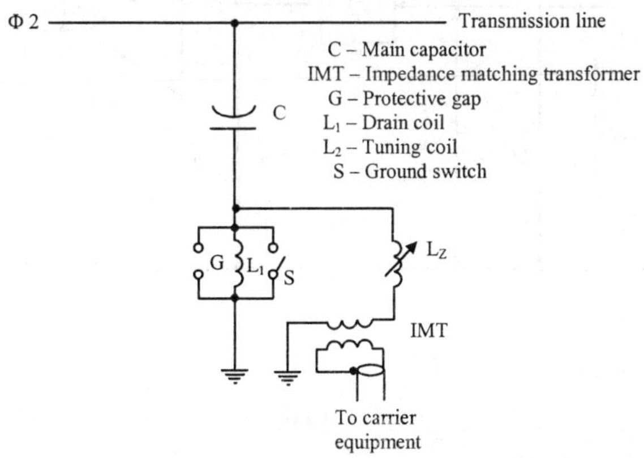

Fig. 8.9 (b): Single line diagram of coupling capacitor

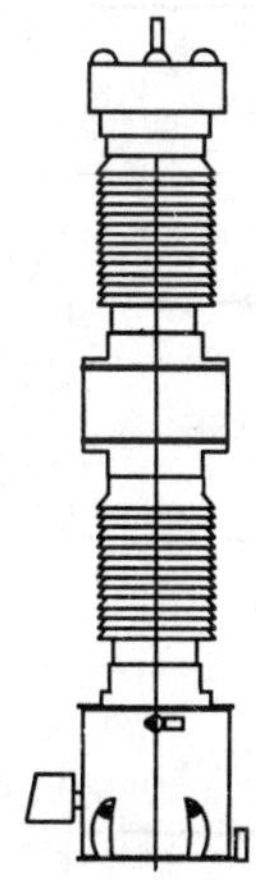

Fig. 8.9 (c): Outlook of a coupling capacitor

Wave trap/Line trap:

Wave trap or Line trap is intended to block high frequency currents preventing them from spreading beyond the line. Line trap impedance Z is a function of frequency f. The line trap is essentially a resonance circuit tuned to a certain frequency of the carrier current unit. It comprises a power induction coil and a variable capacitor C. Discharge D is a resonance resistor installed to protect capacitor C from over voltage. Power coil of the line trap is designed to carry load current as well as short circuit current of the line. Single core, braided, lead sheathed, steel tape armoured high frequency cable is used for connecting the equipment. The input impedance of this cable is 100 ohm/KM at 100 KHz. Filter units are intended to match the input impedance of the cable with the line input impedance and connect the bottom plate of the coupling capacitor to earth, forming a closed loop for high frequency currents.

Phase comparison carrier protection:

A phase comparison scheme consists of: (1) High frequency transmitters and receivers for two-way communication between the ends of a line; (2) Starting units for controlling the transmitters in accordance with the primary system current; (3) Output stages operating under the control of the starting units and the high frequency signal. The relay described herein is General Electric type Contraphase P10 static relay designed for transmission line unit protection scheme, which compares the phase angle of the fault current at both ends of a transmission line by, modulating a high frequency signal transmitted over the line. Figure 8.9 (d) and (e) respectively shows the block diagram of phase sequence network and starting unit of the relay. Secondary current from the line current transformers enters the sequence network and starting unit. The positive and negative phase sequence components [refer figure 8.9 (f) and (g)] are extracted and applied to separate fault detectors, which have two threshold levels – low set and high set. Low set controls the high frequency transmitter and high set enables the phase angle measurement associated with the 'hf' transmissions to proceed. The margin between low set and high set ensures that both ends are transmitting 'hf' correctly when high set has only just operated at one line end, for a marginal fault.

Phase comparison schemes respond to any phase shifts from the reference conditions, but tripping is usually permitted only when the phase shift exceeds an angle of typically 30 to 90 degrees, determined by the time delay setting of the measurement circuit, and this angle is usually referred to as the stability angle. The detector produces a logic output corresponding to the gap in the high frequency transmissions in accordance with phase angle information produced from the CT secondary currents via the modulators. Hence, the duration of the detected gap is proportional to the phase shift between the primary currents at the two ends of the transmission line (assuming both transmitters are transmitting). If the high set is operated, the detected gap is fed in to the discriminator. When the gap setting is exceeded, an output pulse having the supply period is produced, setting

the output bi-stable and operating the trip contacts and protection operated alarm. The trip contacts reset when the output bi-stable, is reset by high set resetting.

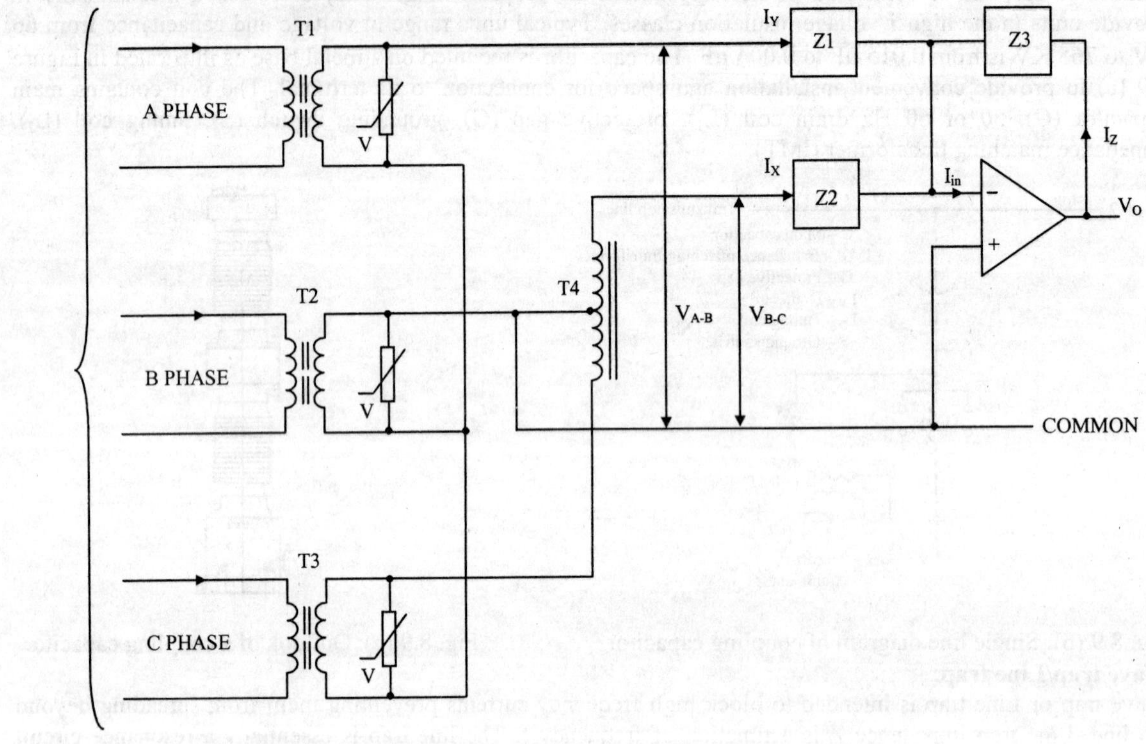

Fig. 8.9 (d): Block diagram of carrier protection phase sequence network (Courtesy, General Electric).

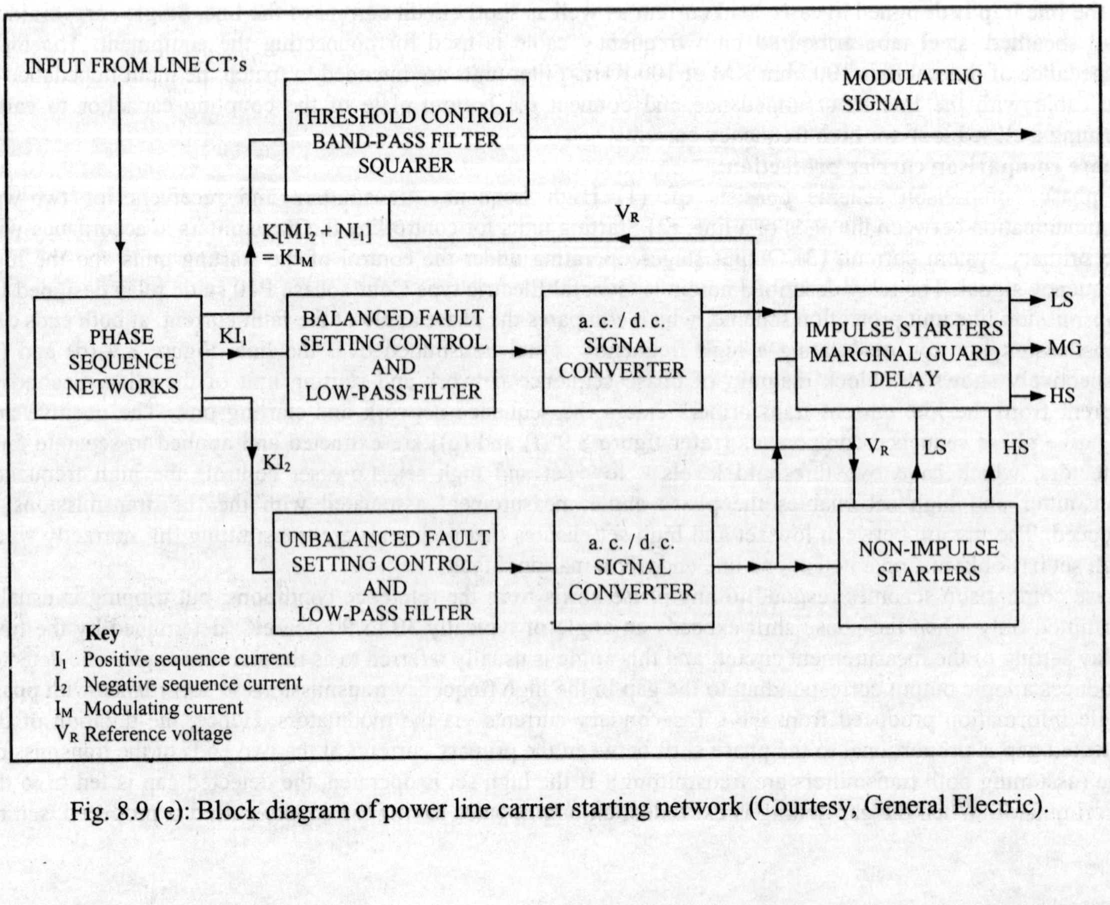

Fig. 8.9 (e): Block diagram of power line carrier starting network (Courtesy, General Electric).

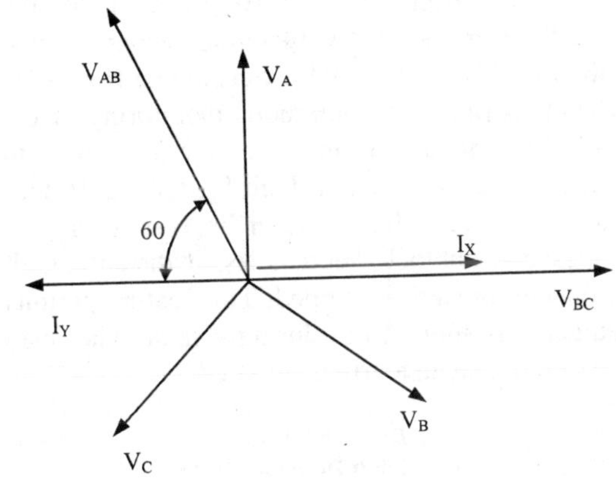

$I_X + I_Y = I_Z = O$

Fig. 8.9 (f): Network with positive sequence current.

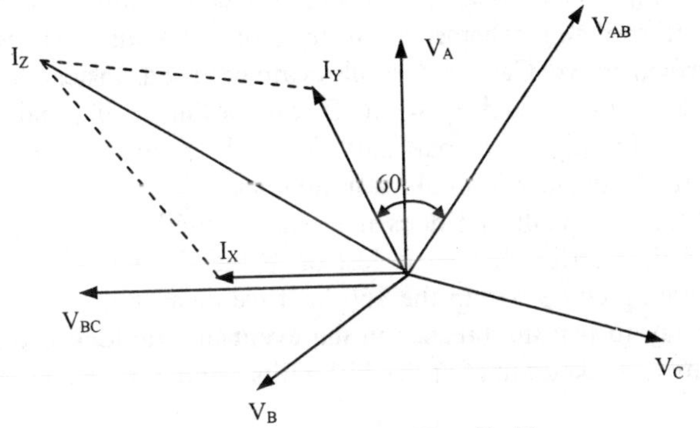

$V_O = I_Z\, Z_3$

$I_X + I_Y = I_Z = \sqrt{3}\, I_Y$

Fig. 8.9 (g): Network with negative sequence current.

8.10 PILOT RELAYING FOR CARRIER CURRENT PROTECTION.

High speed clearing of faults is universally required on transmission systems in the interests of maintaining stability, minimizing shock to wide areas of the power system, and decreasing fault damage. Pilot relaying is an important ingredient in this process. Pilot relaying entails the use of information obtained from one or more remote terminals as well as local information to establish the need to trip or refrain from tripping a breaker. Carrier signals sent from one end to the other end of the transmission line to trip the remote circuit breaker is called carrier transfer (inter tripping). Carrier signals sent from one end to the other end of the transmission line to prevent the tripping of the circuit breaker is called carrier blocking. Carrier signals sent to other end of the transmission line so as to reduce the relay time at that end by shunting the step timer is said to be carrier acceleration. Distance protection relays are used for fault detection in these schemes. Carrier current protections are classified in to (1) Directional comparison with carrier current blocking; (2) Differential comparison carrier current protection.

Directional comparison carrier current protection:

Relay operation is based on the comparison of the fault power flow directions at the ends of the protected line. Figure 8.10 (a) illustrates the operation of directional comparison blocking system. At bus A, a distance type relay (21A1) is set to overreach the remote terminal, set for about 120 to 150 percent of the protected line impedance. Another distance relay (21A2) is connected to reach in the reverse direction and set to reach farther than the distance relay (21B1) at the remote terminal bus B. The distance relays at bus B are set in the same manner but "look" in to the opposite direction. For the internal fault F_I, both distance relays 21A1 and 21B1 "see" the fault, but relays 21A2 and 21B2 do not, so carrier is not transmitted. Pickup of 21A1 and 21B1 at both ends trips breaker 52-1 and 52-2. For the external fault F_E, relays 21A1 and 21B2 operate. At bus A, receipt of the blocking carrier signal prevents tripping of breaker 52-1. At bus B, relay 21B1 did not operate to trip breaker 52-2. No carrier signal is transmitted during normal conditions. Failure of carrier channel will cause false tripping for external faults. Blocking systems are normally used with off-on type power line carrier.

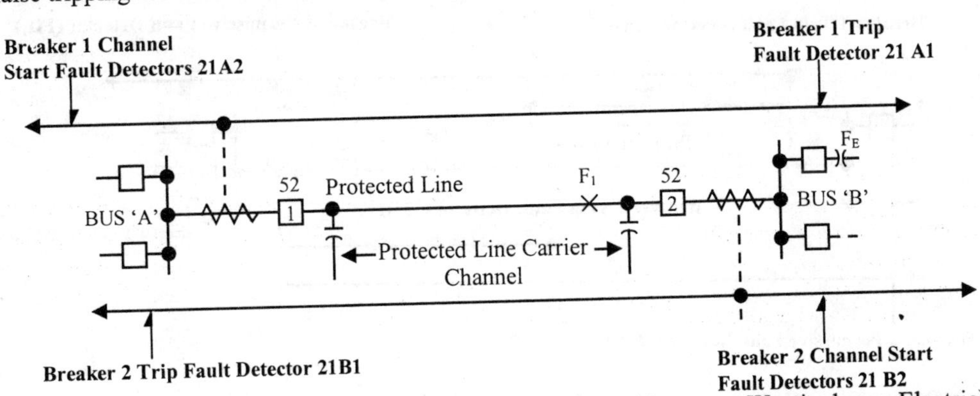

Fig. 8.10 (a): Directional comparison blocking system. (Courtesy, Westinghouse Electric)

Unblocking systems are used with frequency shift type power line carrier. Figure 8.10 (b) illustrates the operation of this scheme. Fault detectors 21A and 21B are set the same as in the blocking carrier scheme described above. Carrier start relays are not used. Instead a continuous blocking signal is transmitted from each end, F_1 at bus A and F_2 at bus B, except during internal faults. This provides continuous monitoring of the channel. During an internal fault F_I, the distance relays (21A and 21B) at each terminal key the transmitter to shift the frequency from block to unblock, completing the trip circuit. For the external fault F_E, relay 21B does not "see" the fault and does not send an unblocking signal to bus A. Therefore, neither breaker is tripped. When the carrier channel is lost or in the absence of both block and unblock frequencies, if distance fault detectors pick up within the 150 ms time-delay period, the associated breaker is tripped. This feature permits the relay to trip the breaker in the event the unblock trip frequency is shorted out during a fault. The relay scheme is locked out after the 150 milliseconds time delay has expired, and an alarm is initiated.

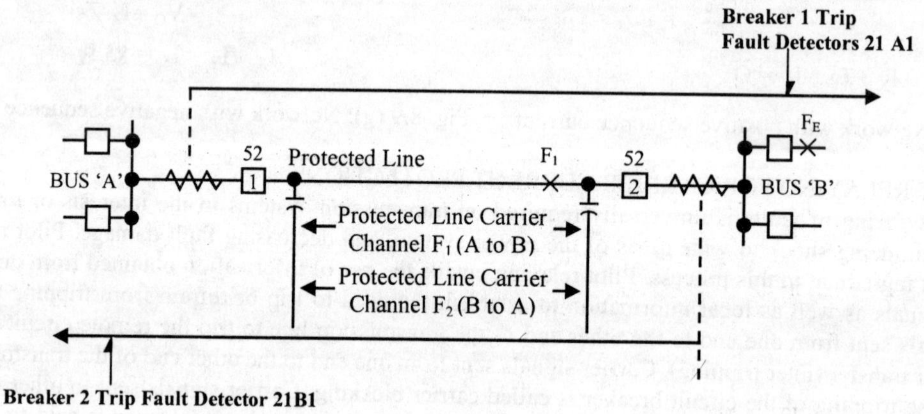

Fig 8.10 (b): Directional comparison unblocking system. (Courtesy, Westinghouse Electric)

Overreaching transfer trip schemes are used with telephone circuits and microwave but not suitable for power line carrier system. Frequency-shift audio tones are used for the signals. A guard-state frequency is transmitted continuously during normal power system conditions. When an internal fault occurs in the protected line, the tone shifts to the trip state at each terminal, permitting the relay to trip its associated breaker. For an external fault relay does not pickup and no transfer trip signal is transmitted.

Under-reaching transfer trip systems are used with power line carrier scheme, and can be applied either permissive or non-permissive schemes. Figure 8.10 (c) illustrates the operation of this scheme. The distance type fault detector 21A and 21B has a Zone 1 type of setting: that is, it under-reaches the length of the protected line. Without the fault detector FD, the scheme is non-permissive. Either the relay 21A / 21B or a tone signal from the remote end can trip breaker. A false output from the channel would cause incorrect tripping of its associated breaker. To improve security, the system is made permissive by adding the FD fault detector relays, set to over reach the line. This relay supervises the transfer trip circuit.

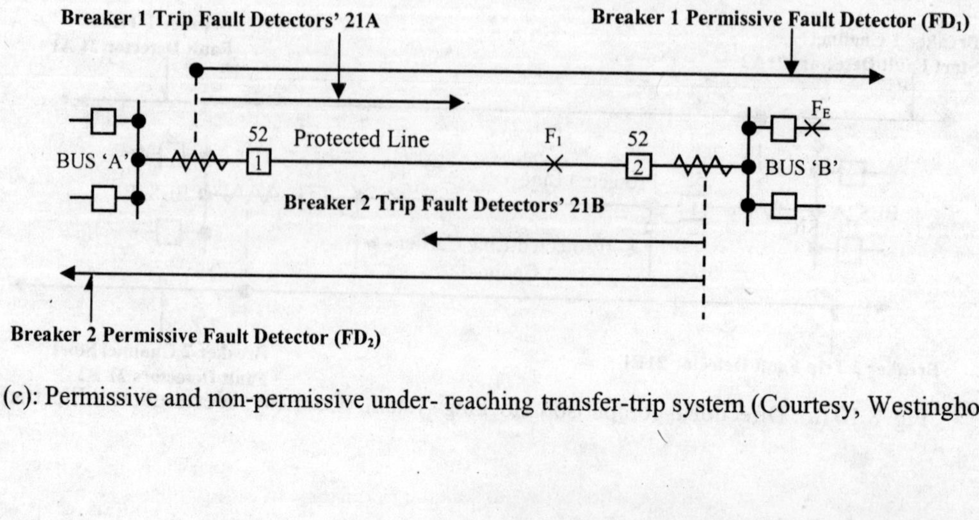

Fig. 8.10 (c): Permissive and non-permissive under- reaching transfer-trip system (Courtesy, Westinghouse)

Phase comparison:

Phase comparison relaying schemes are grouped in to categories called "single-phase comparison blocking," "dual-phase comparison un-blocking," "dual-phase comparison transfer-trip" and "segregated phase comparison." Except for the latter, all systems are a composite sequence current network whose output is a single-phase voltage proportional to the positive, negative and zero sequence current input. The sequence network filter output voltage is converted to a square wave. The positive voltage magnitude corresponds to the positive half-cycle of the filter voltage, and the zero magnitude corresponds to the negative half cycle. The local and remote square waves are compared at each terminal to determine if the fault is internal or external to the protected line. The local square wave is delayed by, an amount equal to the absolute channel delay time to make the comparison valid. Current or distance type fault detectors are used to supervise tripping, for security.

A single-phase comparison blocking system is normally used with an off-on power line carrier channel. Figure 8.10 (d) illustrates the basic operation of this system. Two over-current fault detectors (at either end of the line), are used in the current only system. The carrier start unit FD1 permits keying of the transmitter by the local square wave. FD2 has a higher pickup setting than FD1 and is used to arm the pickup circuit. These fault detectors coordinate the keying of the carrier square wave with the comparison of the local and remote square waves.

For an internal fault, when both the local input and receiver input to the AND are coincident for 4 ms or more, a trip output occurs, provided FD2 is picked up. For an external fault, the AND output exists for less than 4 ms, and no trip output occurs, even if both fault detectors are picked up. If the minimum internal three-phase fault current is less than twice the maximum load current, supervision by distance type fault detectors, responsive only to three-phase faults, should be used to supplement the over current fault detectors. This scheme makes a comparison on every other half-cycle of the power frequency. If an internal fault occurs just before the next half cycle, tripping is delayed by an additional half cycle.

The dual phase comparison unblocking system compares conditions during both half-cycles of the power system current wave. This eliminates the additional half-cycle delay, which can occur in the preceding scheme. Frequency-shift power line carrier is used for the unblocking system, so as carrier signal is continuously transmitted. This provides channel monitoring and eliminates the need for the carrier-start fault detector FD1. This system requires one frequency at each terminal. FD2 is applied to arm the trip circuit.

In the basic operation of the dual compare, as in the single comparer scheme, a square wave is generated from the power system current wave. The transmitter is keyed to its mark frequency when the square wave goes to a positive magnitude, and is keyed to its space frequency when the square wave goes to zero. The receiver has two outputs corresponding to the mark and space frequencies. A comparison is made every half-cycle.
two outputs corresponding to the mark and space frequencies. A comparison is made every half-cycle.

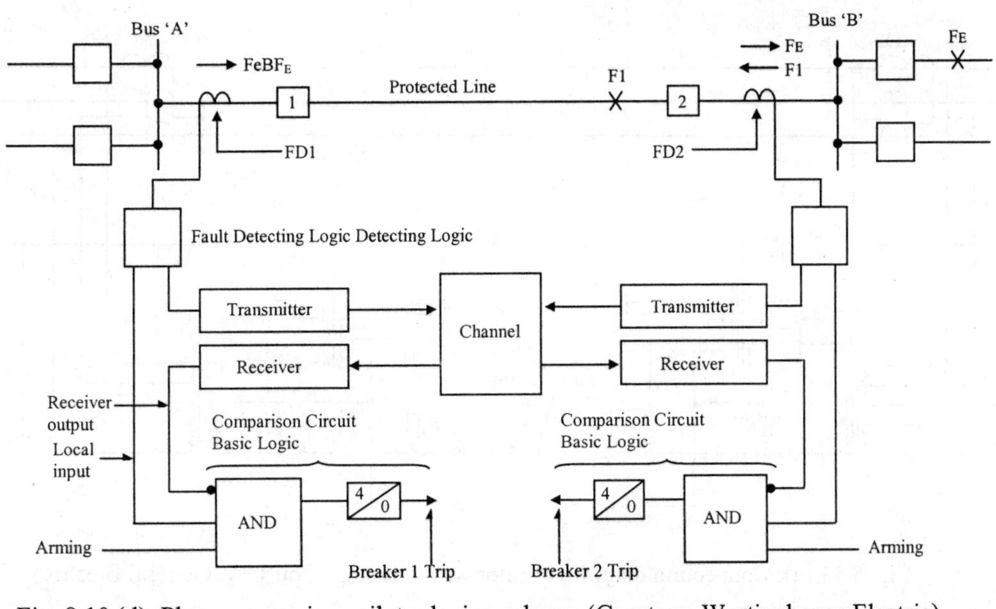

Fig. 8.10 (d): Phase comparison pilot relaying scheme (Courtesy, Westinghouse Electric).

Differential comparison carrier current protection:
Relay operation is based on the comparison of instantaneous direction of currents at each phase at the line end over a communication channel. To allow the use of a single channel, some such systems use a combination of the individual phase currents to generate a single quantity for comparison. Others use a combination of the symmetrical components (positive, negative, and zero sequence) of the phase currents, and by adding the combination a single-phase sinusoidal voltage is produced and converted to a square wave for comparison at the two line end terminals.

The concept of the scheme is that external faults will cause the local and received remote quantities to be essentially equal in magnitude and opposite in direction, while internal faults will cause them to be possibly different in magnitude but essentially in phase. In the comparison, the local quantity is delayed by an amount equal to the inherent channel delay; providing near perfect coincidence for external faults.

Segregated phase comparison system:
This system compares the instantaneous direction of currents at the two ends of the transmission line for each phase rather than utilizing their symmetrical components. Each phase requires a separate channel. A local sinusoidal voltage proportional to phase current is converted, for each phase, to a square wave delayed by an amount dependent on channel delay and compared to the received remote quantity for the corresponding phase. Internal faults will produce essentially in-phase comparisons. External faults will produce comparisons essentially 180° out of phase. Considerable angular variation in these comparisons will still provide precise information regarding fault location.

8.11 PILOT WIRE RELAY FOR SHORT DISTANCE TRANSMISSION SCHEME (85)

Pilot wire relay is a three-phase high-speed relay designed for simultaneous tripping at the terminals of an under ground or overhead medium voltage or high voltage Power line. The power line three-phase currents energize the relay operating circuits through current transformers and are converted by a combination positive and zero sequence filters in to a single-phase output voltage. The relays, which are located at each power line terminal, normally have polarity to cause a circulating current through the pilot wire. When a fault occurs between the terminals of the power line, polarity of the single phase output voltage from one of the relay (very near to the fault) will reverse, causing the two single-phase output voltages to oppose each other in the pilot wire. Therefore, the output voltage of each relay is bypassed through the relay-operating coil causing relay trip circuit contact closure. Figure 6.11 (a) illustrates the connection diagram of a pilot wire relay.

LEGEND:

Pr: Pilot padding resistor	T1: Summation transformer
Pc: Phase comparator	T2: Auxiliary transformer
Ro: Linear resistor	To: Operating coil
RVO: Nonlinear resistor	Tr: Restraining coil

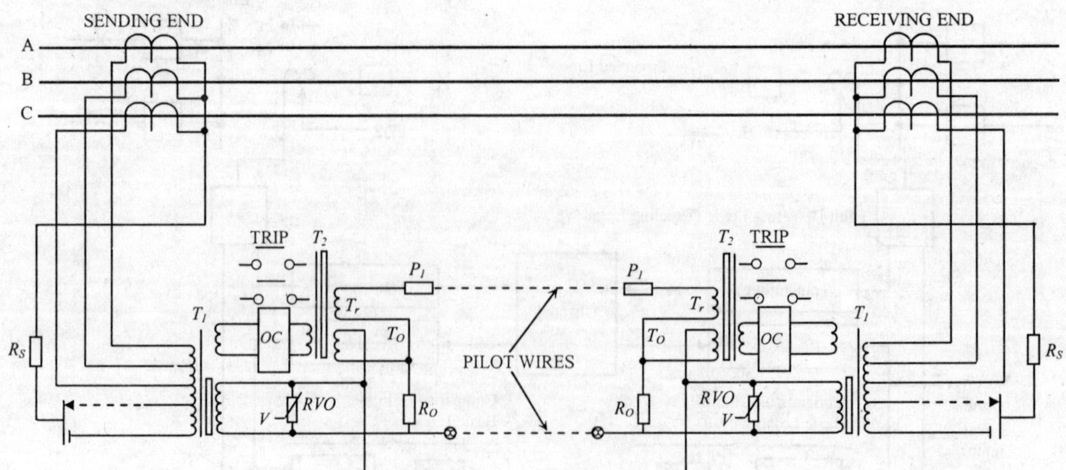

Fig: 8.11 (a): Connection diagram of pilot wire relaying (Courtesy, General Electric).

Pilot wire relay operates on the circulating current principle, and uses summation transformer with a neutral section, which is tapped to provide alternate earth fault sensitivities. Phase comparators are used for measurement and a restraint circuit gives a high level of stability for through faults. High-speed operation is obtained with moderately sized current transformers. The comparators are tuned to the power frequency, so desensitizing the relay to the transient high frequency charging currents, which may flow in to a feeder when it is energized. The tuning also improves the CT output ensuring high-speed operation under adverse conditions of CT saturation. Internal faults give simultaneous tripping of breakers at both ends. A padding resistance is provided in the relay so that the pilot wire loop resistance may be adjusted to the designated value of 1000 ohms. When a pilot isolation transformer is used an insulation barrier capable of withstanding 15 KV can be obtained and the isolation transformer enables operation with pilot loop resistance up to 2500 ohms.

Pilot wire scheme is a logical complement to distance schemes, particularly in the case of very short lines for which correct distance measurement is difficult or impossible. The cost of the pilot wires themselves limits the economic application of pilot wire protection to distances of up to about 20 KM. By appropriately compensating the vector group, power transformers can be included in the zone of protection as illustrated in Figure 8.11 (b).

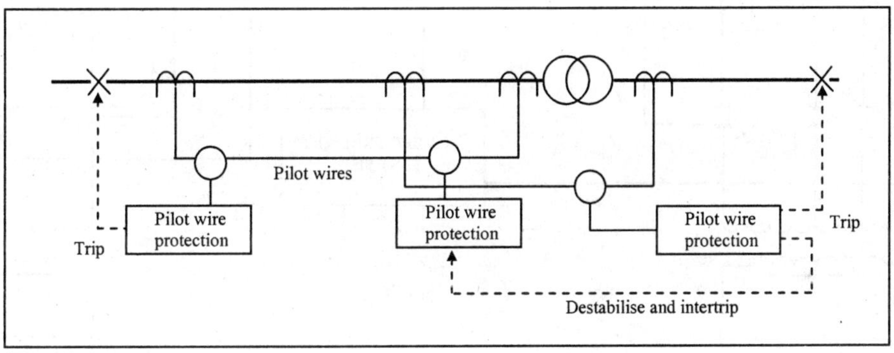

Fig. 8.11 (b): Application of pilot relay for protection of transformer feeder (Courtesy, General Electric).

The various current settings for pilot wire relay can be checked using the over current test set. To obtain the correct settings, the pilot wires must be connected to the relays (at each end of the line) and the correct pilot compensation must be set on the relays. The current setting of the relays may then be checked by injection in to each phase in turn as shown in Figure 8.11 (c). The results obtained should tally with the manufacturers declared current setting for the length and type of pilots in use. This verifies the sensitivity of the relay under test.

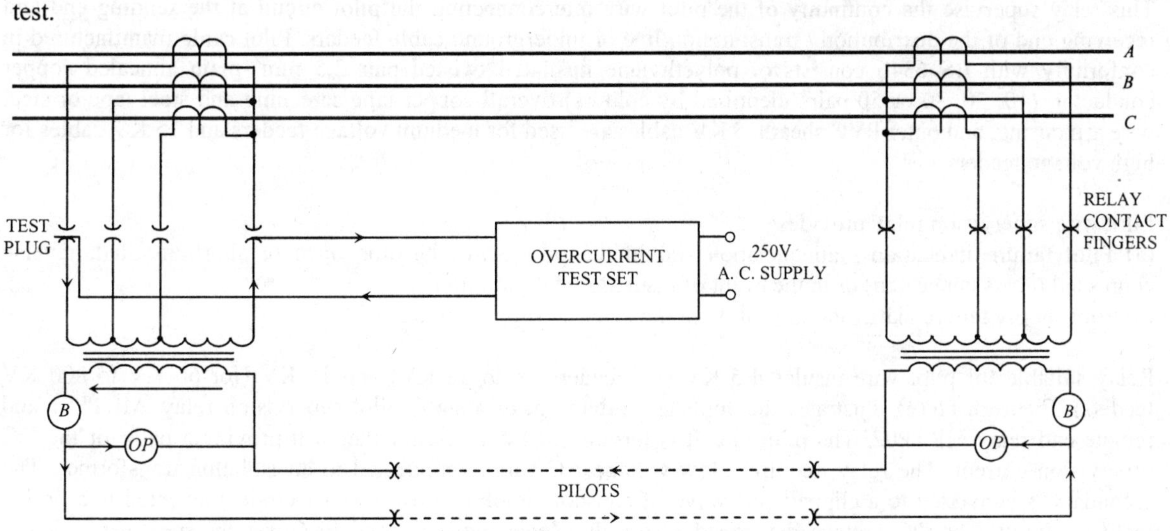

Fig. 8.11 (c): Sensitivity-check on pilot wire relay by using secondary injection test set.

The stability of the pilot wire protection can be checked by, using the feeder conductors to connect the summation current transformers at each end of the feeder in series. Secondary injection can then be made by, using the secondary injection test set as shown in Figure 8.11 (d), the current circulating through the feeder conductors, summation transformers and pilot wires. Several times the relay rated current can be made to circulate through the summation transformer primaries: a corresponding current circulates through the pilots. This test is very useful, as it is practically impossible to produce the same magnitude of circulating current in the pilots when carrying out the test.

During secondary injection test following functional tests are recommended:

1. Phase to neutral pickup by permitting the current to pass through phase to neutral as shown in figure (c) above. Repeat the test on other phases also and observe the pickup current..
2. Phase to phase pickup by injecting the current between any two phases of the summation transformer. Repeat the test on other phases also and observe the pickup current.
3. Target indication during each operation.

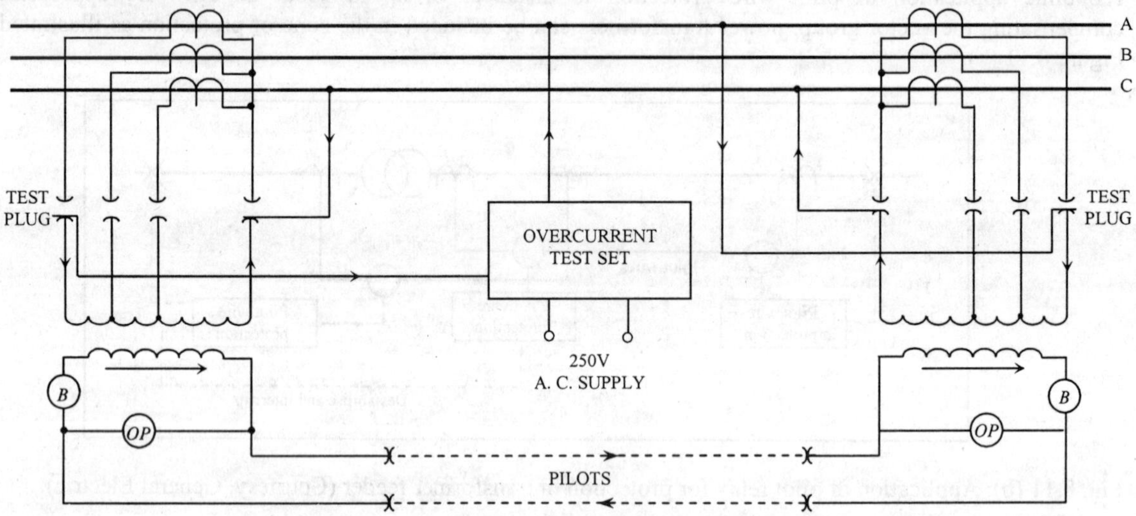

Fig. 8.11 (d): Stability check on pilot wire relay by using secondary injection test set.

Pilot circuit supervision relay:

This relay supervise the continuity of the pilot wire interconnecting the pilot circuit at the sending end and receiving end of the distribution / transmission line or underground cable feeders. Pilot cable manufactured in conformity with BS 6346 consists of polyethylene insulated twisted pair 2.5 mm^2 plain annealed copper conductor, (10, 20, 30 or 50 pairs identified by colours) overall copper tape screening and steel tape or steel wire armouring, and outer PVC sheath. 5 KV cables are used for medium voltage feeders and 15 KV cables for high voltage feeders.

Pilot wire supervision relay provides:

(a) Pilot failure indication / annunciation should the pilot wires become open or short-circuited, reverse connected (cross connected) or in the event of insulation deterioration.

(b) Pilot supply failure alarm and indication in the event of supply failure.

Relay suitable for pilot wire insulated 5 KV (for feeders up to 36 KV) and 15 KV (for 66 KV to 800 KV feeders). Figure 8.11 (e) illustrates the application diagram of a static pilot supervision relay. MRTP01 and remote end relay MRTP02. The pilot circuit is terminated by, a resistor that will provide a path for the DC supervision current. The relay, require a low voltage AC supply connected to an isolation transformer. The secondary is converted to a clipped sine wave of constant amplitude by, a Zener diode connected in a bridge rectifier circuit. The DC voltage developed across the Zener diode is used to power the measuring circuit, which in turn measures the current flowing in to the injection filter.

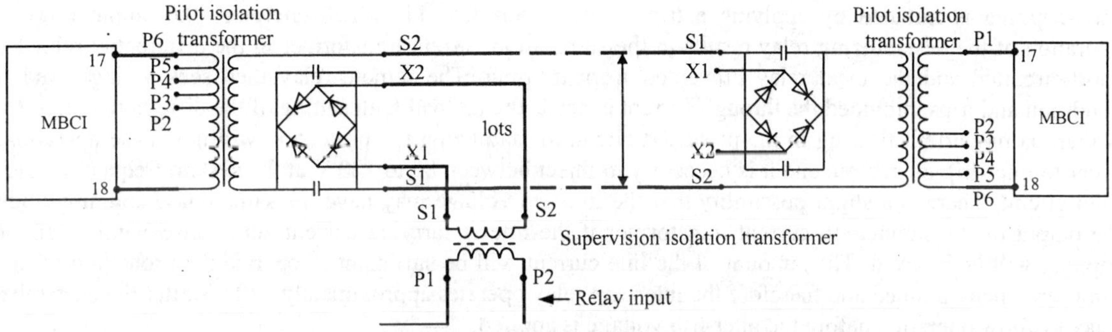

Fig. 8.11 (e): Application diagram: Pilot wire supervision relay (Courtesy, General Electric)

The clipped sine wave voltage is rectified in the injection filter and a capacitor is charged to the peak value to produce a constant level DC voltage. A capacitor connected in the pilot circuit between terminals 17 and 18 bypasses the AC pilot current and directs a DC current from the supervision circuit to the pilot circuit. To enable crossed pilots to be detected and ensure correct indication for pilots which become short circuited at the remote end, a second injection filter is included at the remote end of the pilot circuit. The AC supervision supply is also monitored and, in the event of a failure a time delayed alarm is initiated.

Destabilizing and inter tripping relay:

Under certain circumstances it is necessary to cause the operation of a pilot wire protection scheme when the protected feeder is subjected to, what appears to the protection scheme as a through fault (external fault). This relay is designed for: (1) Use with pilot wire relay (Translay system); (2) Destabilizes the feeder protection so that tripping occurs at remote end when feeder is carrying current; (3) Inter-trip by injecting AC current through pilot so that tripping occurs at remote end when feeder is carrying no current. A circuit diagram for the relay, which depicts the destabilizing and inter-trip facility, is shown in figurc 8.11 (f). The relay incorporates an inverter and is powered by DC only. On energizing the relay RL1 open to indicate the supply is healthy and the inverter is operating. The relay incorporates a full bridge inverter, which receives a complementary square wave signals from the oscillator circuit.

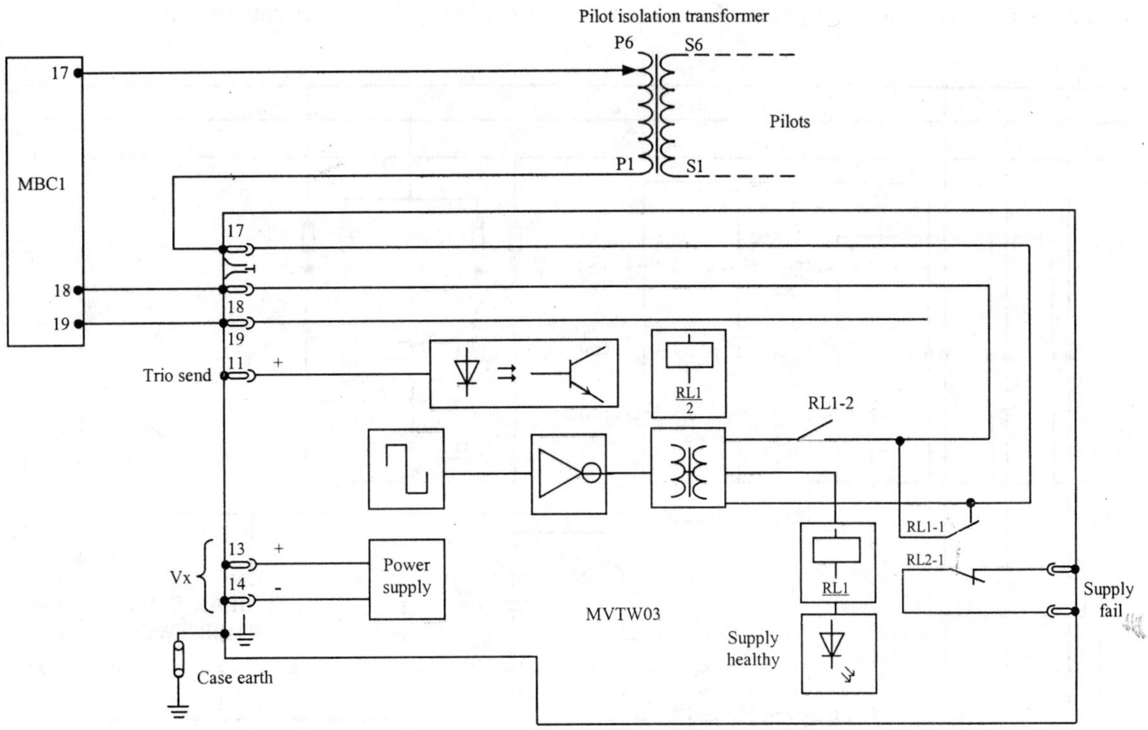

Fig 8.11 (f): Application diagram: Destabilizing and inter-tripping relay. (Courtesy, General Electric)

Inter-tripping is initiated by applying a trip signal to terminal 11, which energizes the output relay. The operation of the destabilizing relay results in the summation current transformer in the differential relay being short-circuited and the local relay prevented from tripping. The remote relay then sees a single and feed condition and trips, provided the through current exceeds the no load fault setting of the differential relay.

If there is no current flowing in the protected circuit, destabilizing the protection will not cause operation. In order to inter-trip the remote end it is necessary to inject between 80 to 120 V at the system frequency in to the pilot circuit. There is a slight possibility that the injected voltage may have the same phase and amplitude as the output of the summation current transformer if the line is carrying current, and consequently a risk that tripping will be blocked. This amount of the line current will be sufficient to operate the protection when the pilots are open-circuited and therefore the inter-trip relay operates approximately 120 ms after the destabilizing relay to allow operation before the inter-trip voltage is applied.

8.12 DIRECTIONAL OVER CURRENT AND EARTH FAULT RELAY (67).

Directional relay responds to the relative phase position (direction) of a current with respect to another current or reference voltage. Directional protection responds to flow of power in a definite direction based on CT and PT locations. Directional relays respond to the magnitude and direction of power applied to the relay terminals. Both directional power relays and directional over-current relays, directional earth fault relays come under the group "Directional relays". When fault current can flow in both directions through the relay location it is necessary to make the response of the relay directional by the introduction of directional control element. It is a power-measuring device in which the system voltage is used as reference for establishing the relative direction of the fault current.

Directional over-current relay:

Figure 8.12 (a) shows the connection diagram of a phase directional induction disc over-current relay (GE type JBC). It trips a circuit when it senses two abnormal conditions in the following sequence:

(a) Current flow must be reversed;

(b) The reversed current flow must be higher than a prescribed amount (relay set value), and the flow must continue for a predetermined time.

Relay operates for faults in direction of arrow shown in figure 8.12 (a).

LEGEND:

D: Directional unit; DOC: Directional unit operating coil; DPC: Directional unit polarizing coil; IOC: Instantaneous over-current unit; 52TC: Circuit breaker trip coil; TOC: Time over-current unit.

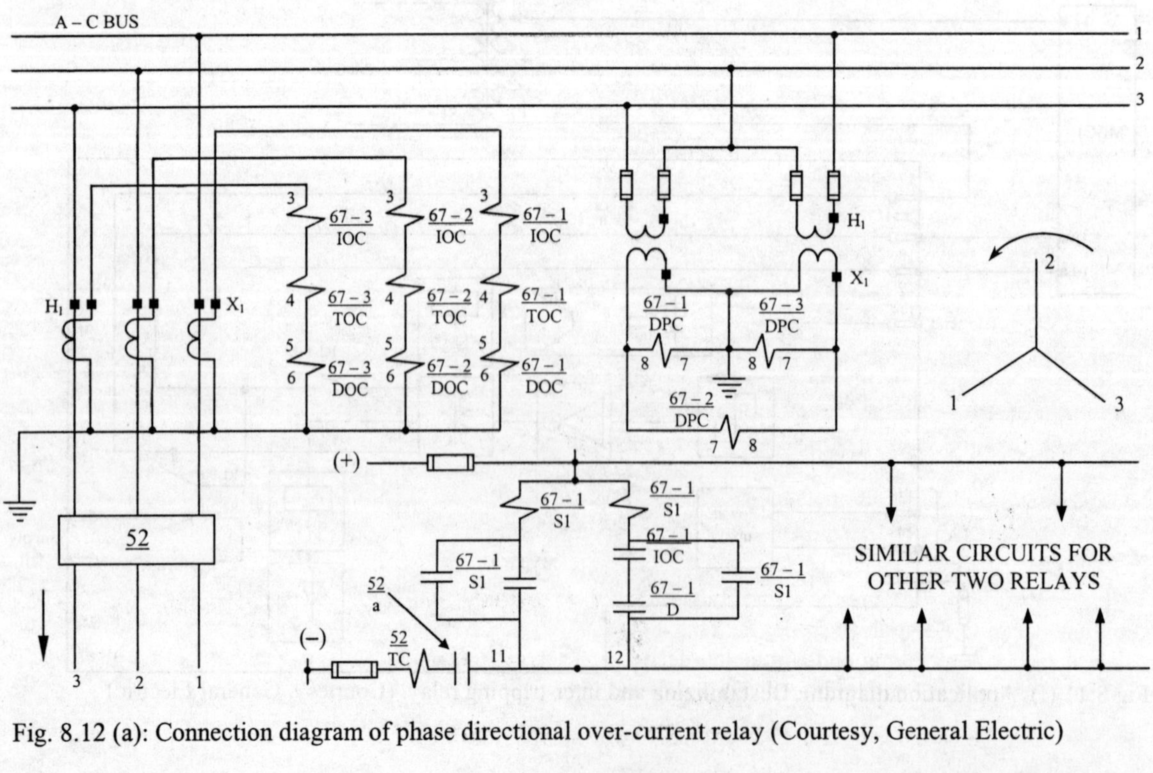

Fig. 8.12 (a): Connection diagram of phase directional over-current relay (Courtesy, General Electric)

This relay is composed of two units, a directional unit and an over-current unit. The directional unit is similar to a single-phase wattmeter. It contains a voltage actuated and current actuated coil, and when these two coils are energized, a torque is produced on the unit's disc. A 180° shift in phase relationship between the voltage and current produces a reverse torque on the disc. Normally, the torque produced holds the directional unit contacts open. When the current flow in the circuit reverses, and exceeds the preset value of current and time, the directional unit contact will close. The over current unit of the relay is instantaneous type. The directional unit contact must be closed before operating torque will be produced on the induction disc of the over-current unit. DC trip circuit is also shown in the figure. Contacts of instantaneous unit and directional unit are connected in series. Relay operates for faults in direction of arrow shown in figure (a).

Application of directional relay:
Consider a 110 KV feeder SR [sending end (s) and receiving end (R)] passing through substation A as indicated in Figure 8.12 (b). Circuit breaker CB3 in feeder section AR is provided with a phase directional relay R which will trip the CB3 if fault power flow is in direction AR alone. If there is a fault in feeder section AS, the circuit breaker CB3 does not trip. However for faults in feeder AS circuit breaker CB1 will trip because the protective relay is set with a directional feature to act in direction AS.

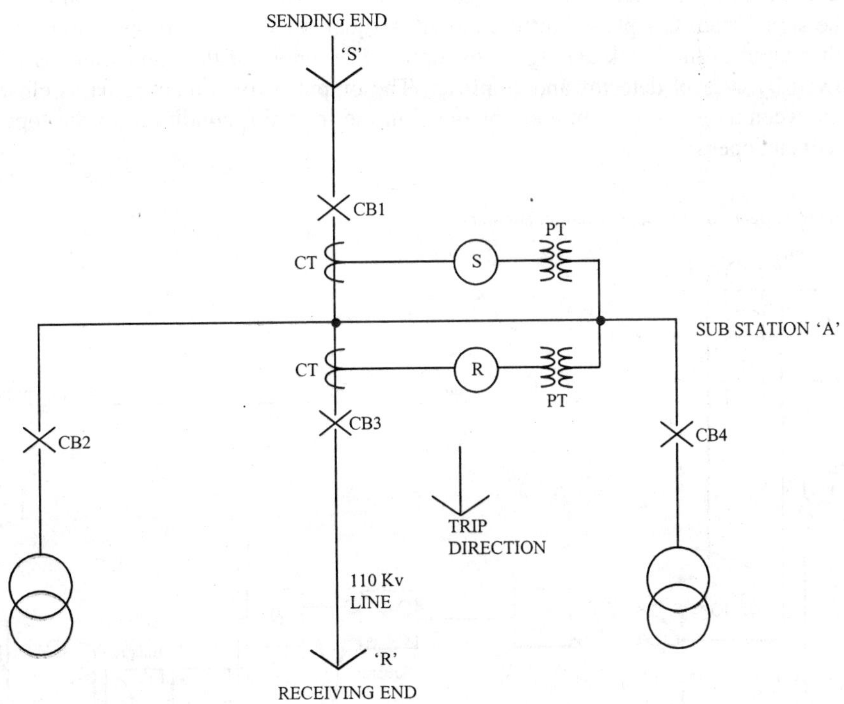

Fig: 8.12 (b): Application of directional relay.

Ring and radial feeders having supply from both ends:
Ring or radial feeders with both end supply is protected, by using power directional relays at either ends. A plain over-current protection will not respond to the power direction. Therefore the selective clearance faults in circuits with two-end supply cannot be obtained with out employing power directional relays at either end. Time delays for the protections acting in the same direction of the power flow are selected on the step grading principle. Minimum pickup of directional unit and time current characteristic is to be checked. In Figure 8.12 (c), there are two parallel feeders with overload relay at the sending end and reverse power relay at the receiving end. In the event of a fault in feeder A, fault current will flow in two ways; (1) directly in to fault location through feeder A, and the circuit breaker CB-1 will trip; (2) indirectly through feeder B and receiving station bus bar in to the fault in feeder A. This would cause the reverse power relay to operate and trip circuit breaker at feeder A receiving end and isolate feeder A. In the absence of reverse power relay the fault current would have tripped CB3 and both feeder A and B would have been tripped.

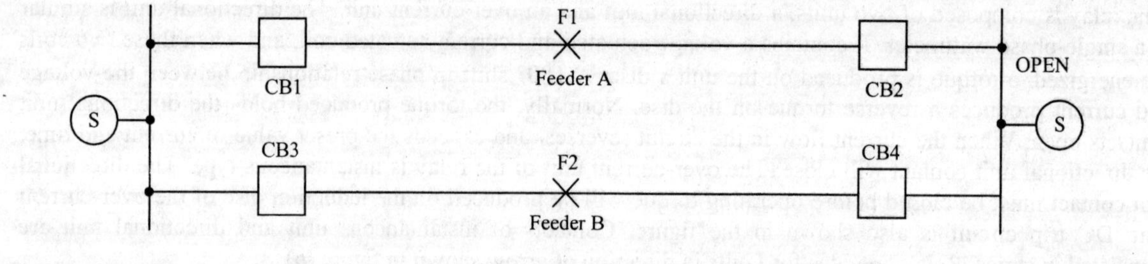

Fig. 8.12 (c): Reverse power protection for parallel feeders

The electronic relay (GE type MET1) illustrated in Figure 8.12 (d) is a directional relay suitable for protection of parallel feeders, ring feeders, parallel operating transformers, generators earthed through neutral grounding resistor etc. The polarizing voltage input is isolated by, an interposing voltage transformer, the output of which is connected to a phase shifting circuit. The phase shift is determined by, a switch on the module front plate. The signal obtained from this circuit is squared by, an operational amplifier circuit and fed to one input of a block average comparator. The current input to the relay is isolated by, an interposing current transformer. This output is phase shifted by, a fixed amount to make the overall range of adjustment on the voltage input easier to obtain. The signal from this phase shifting circuit is squared by, a second operational amplifier circuit and fed to the other input of the block average comparator. The output of the comparator is fed to an integrating circuit, followed by, a level detector and amplifier. The output relay contact remains closed when the phase relationship between the input current and voltage is in the 'restrain' condition. In the 'operate' condition the output relay contact opens.

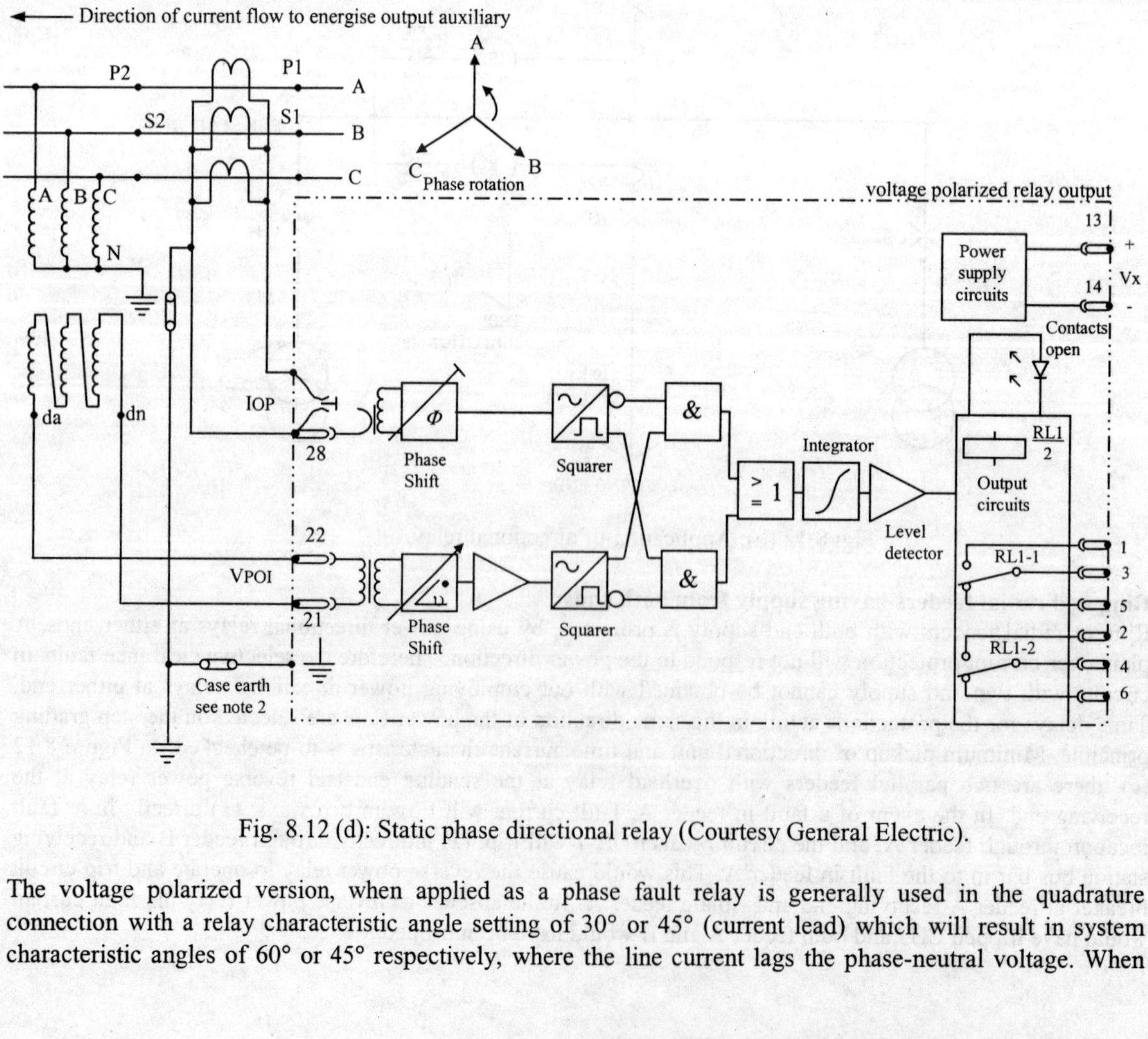

Fig. 8.12 (d): Static phase directional relay (Courtesy General Electric).

The voltage polarized version, when applied as a phase fault relay is generally used in the quadrature connection with a relay characteristic angle setting of 30° or 45° (current lead) which will result in system characteristic angles of 60° or 45° respectively, where the line current lags the phase-neutral voltage. When used for earth fault applications, the polarizing voltage is supplied by a three-phase voltage transformer tertiary winding and a relay characteristic angle of 45° or 60° (current lag) is used for solidly earthed systems and zero degree for resistive earthed system.

Numerical directional relay for over-current and earth fault protection:
Figure 8.12 (e) illustrates the hardware structure of a numerical directional over-current relay (Siemens 7SJ64). Polarity of current transformers for incoming (towards bus bar) and outgoing (towards line) are illustrated in Figure 8.12 (f). This connection determines the measuring direction of the device (forward = line direction).

Voltage inputs can either be used to measure the three phase-to-ground voltages, or two phase-to-phase voltages and the displacement voltage (e-n voltage). It is also possible to connect two phase-to-phase voltages in open-delta connection.

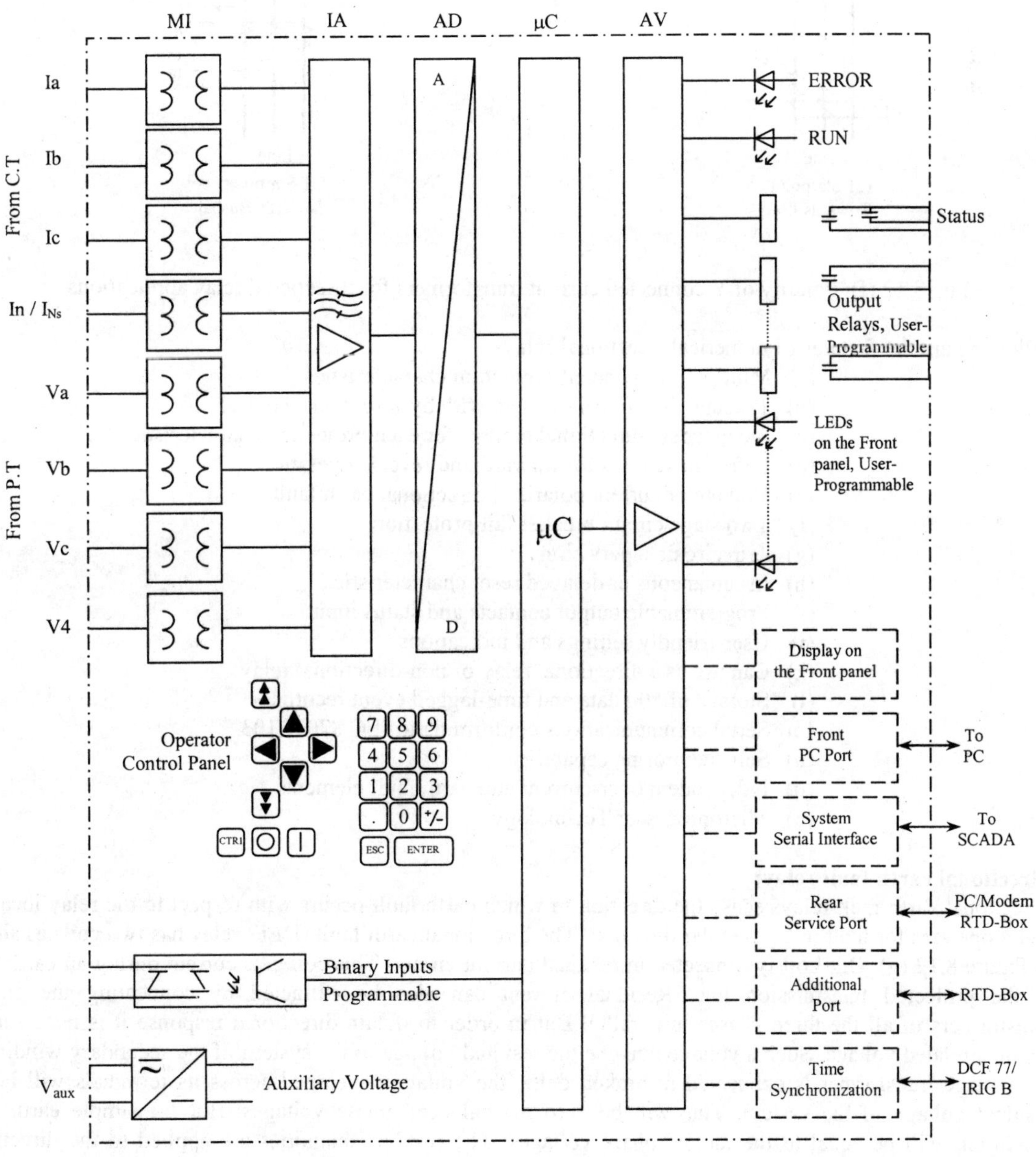

Fig. 8.12 (e): Hardware structure for directional over-current and earth fault relay (Courtesy, Siemens Ag)

The analogue input quantities are passed on to the input amplifiers (IA). The input amplifier IA stage provides high-resistance terminations for the analog input quantities. It consists of filters that are optimized for measured-value processing with regard to bandwidth and processing speed. The analog-to-digital (AD) stage consists of a multiplexor, an analog to digital A/D converter and of memory components for the transmission of digital signals to the microcomputer system.

The phase sequence of the three-phase secondary voltages should be checked when the voltage transformers are first energized. Final acceptance of the potential polarized phase relay should be made with protected transmission line energized and carrying load. The best means to establish power flow direction is to arrange to have the transmission line carry load radially by opening down stream breaker. Long overhead transmission lines or cable feeders can be checked with charging current only.

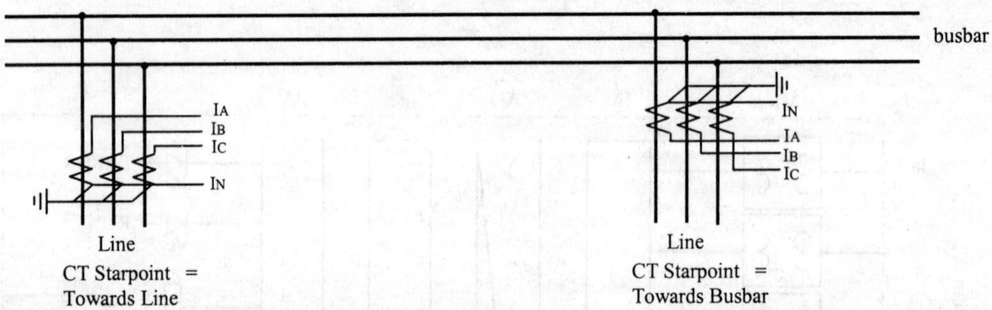

Fig. 8.12 (f): Polarity of Y connected current transformers for directional relay applications

Following are the features of numerical directional relays:

(a) Multiple independent protection characteristics
(b) Tri-state directional element with by-directional control
(c) Independent directional control for each protection characteristic
(d) Different settings for forward and reverse operation
(e) Voltage or current polarized directional earth fault
(f) Two stage circuit breaker fail protection
(g) Trip circuit supervision
(h) Instantaneous or delayed reset characteristic
(i) Programmable output contacts and status input
(j) User-friendly settings and indications
(k) Can use as a directional relay or non-directional relay
(l) Storage of 500 data and time-lagged event records
(m) Serial communications conforming to IEC 870-5-103
(n) Self-monitoring capability.
(o) Independent over-current and earth fault elements
(p) Microprocessor Technology

Directional earth fault relay:
Directional earth fault relays sense the direction in which earth fault occurs with respect to the relay location; and it operates for fault in a particular direction. The directional earth fault (DEF) relay has two coils as shown in Figure 8.12 (g). One coil is connected in residual current circuit. This coil gets current during an earth fault in the protected transmission line. Residual current can also be extracted by connecting the current transformers of all the three phases in parallel. But in order to obtain directional response it is necessary to obtain a related voltage. Such a voltage must be the residual voltage of the system. If the secondary winding of the voltage transformer is connected in broken delta, the voltage developed across its terminals will be the residual voltage of the system. This will be zero for balanced phase voltages. But for simple earth fault conditions will be equal to the faulted phase voltages. The residual quantities are applied to the directional element of the earth fault relay. If broken delta voltage transformer is not available an interposing voltage transformer (primary star and secondary broken delta) can be used.

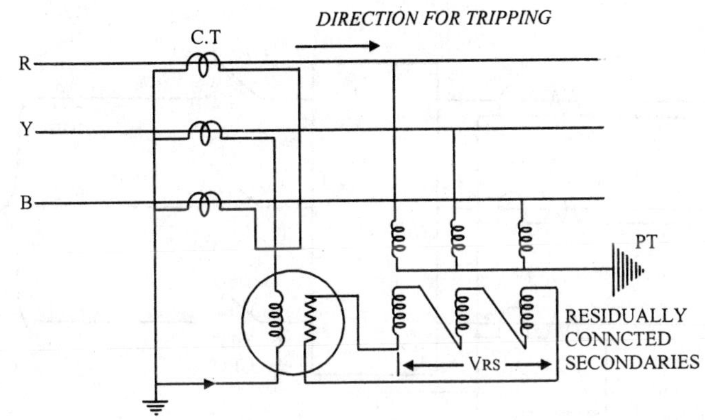

Fig. 8.12 (g): Connection diagram of directional earth fault relay.

Test connection for phase directional relay is shown in Figure 8.12 (h). The directional unit contacts should close when the relay is energized with the above connections. Following are the tests to be conducted:
(a) Directional unit – Minimum pickup: Refer figure 8.12 (a), terminals 5-6 is the directional unit operating coil, which is connected to the CT circuit, and terminal 7-8 is directional unit polarizing coil connected to the PT circuit. Connect the test circuit with correct polarity as shown in figure (h). By adjusting variable resistor increase output until directional unit contacts close. Reduce output just until the contacts start open. Read and record the pickup value of current. Reverse leads of potential polarizing coil and apply current slightly above pickup value the directional unit contact will not close. Repeat the test on other phases also.

(b) Testing pickup and timing of over-current unit: Over-current element is connected to terminals 3-4. Inject current through variable resistor or secondary injection test unit and observe the pickup values of instantaneous element and time delay element. Observe operating time and record it. Repeat the test on other phases also.

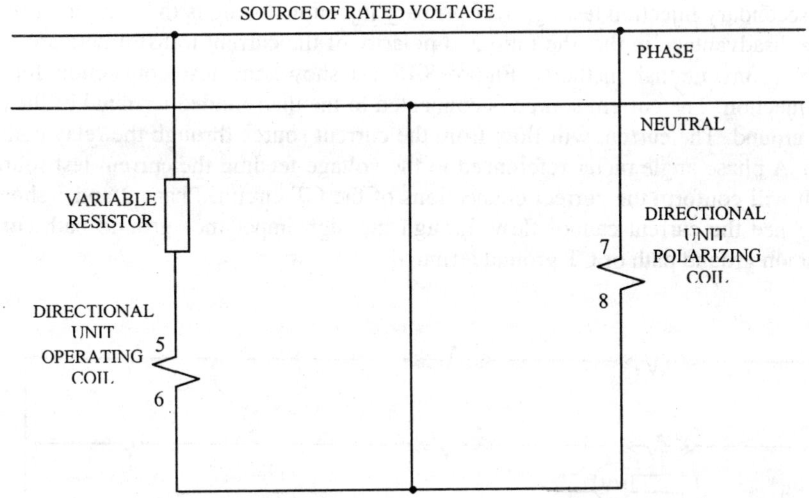

Fig. 8.12 (h): Test connections for phase directional over-current relay.

Primary injection test on phase directional relay:
Typical test circuit for current source is shown in Figure 8.12 (i). The current source should be tied to phase 1 on the current transformer primary away from the protected line section. A ground must be placed on the phase 1, terminal next to the line section. Sufficient secondary current must be provided so that a phase angle meter can be used to check the polarity at the relay. The reference should be the voltage at the test source. Phase 2 and 3 should be tested in the same manner. Where more than one set of current transformers serve the relays, it would be necessary to test all the sources. Configurations such as ring bus, breaker-and-a–half and double breaker schemes usually have more than one set of current transformers.

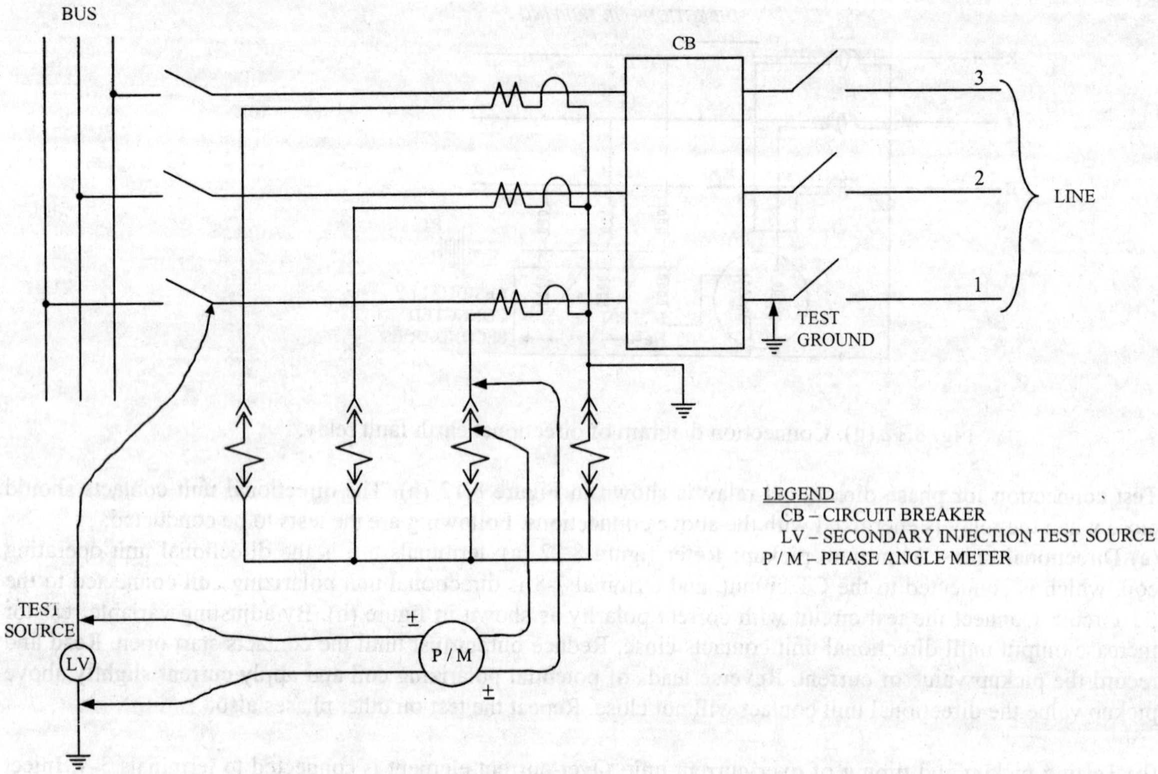

Fig. 8.12 (i): Primary injection test on phase directional over-current relay by current injection method.

Secondary injection test on phase directional over-current relay:

The advantages of secondary injection testing, over primary injection testing is that a high-current source is not required. There is a disadvantage in that the ratio and polarity of the current transformers are not checked and must be verified by, conventional methods. Figure 8.12 (J) shows the test connection for current circuit secondary current injection. The current source is connected to the ungrounded terminal of the phase 1 current transformer and to ground. The current will flow from the current source through the relay coils to the current transformer ground. A phase angle meter referenced to the voltage feeding the current test source can be used to test the circuit. It will conform the correct connections of the CT circuit. Phase 2 and 3 should be tested in the same manner. Since the current cannot flow through the high impedance ground path current should be injected to the common ground path or CT ground terminal.

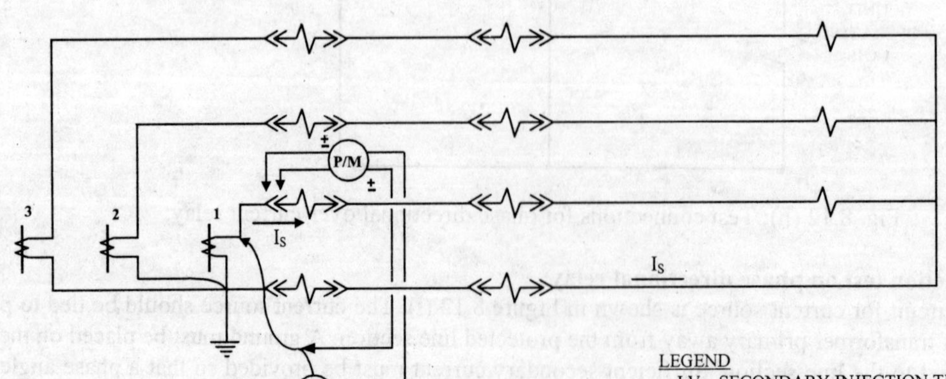

Fig. 8.12 (J): Secondary current injection test on phase directional relay by current injection method.

Current circuit, voltage injection test on phase directional relay:

An alternate method of testing correctness of wiring in current circuits is shown in Figure 8.12 (k). Resistance voltage divider (A series connection of 5 low wattage 120 V bulbs) is used to inject current in to each phase and neutral branch of the current circuit. CT normal ground connection must be disconnected during this test since the test voltage source is referenced to ground. A voltmeter referenced to ground can be used to check for proper voltages at every device terminal in the phase 1 circuit (96 V), phase 2 circuit (72 V), phase 3 circuit (48 V), and the neutral circuit (24 V). Correct polarity of connections can be determined by, opening the relay circuit, and reading the voltages on each terminal. Correct polarity in this example would be indicated with 96 V on "N" and 24 V on "M". Any wiring errors that might exist should cause no damage to devices because of the current limiting effect of the least two bulbs in series.

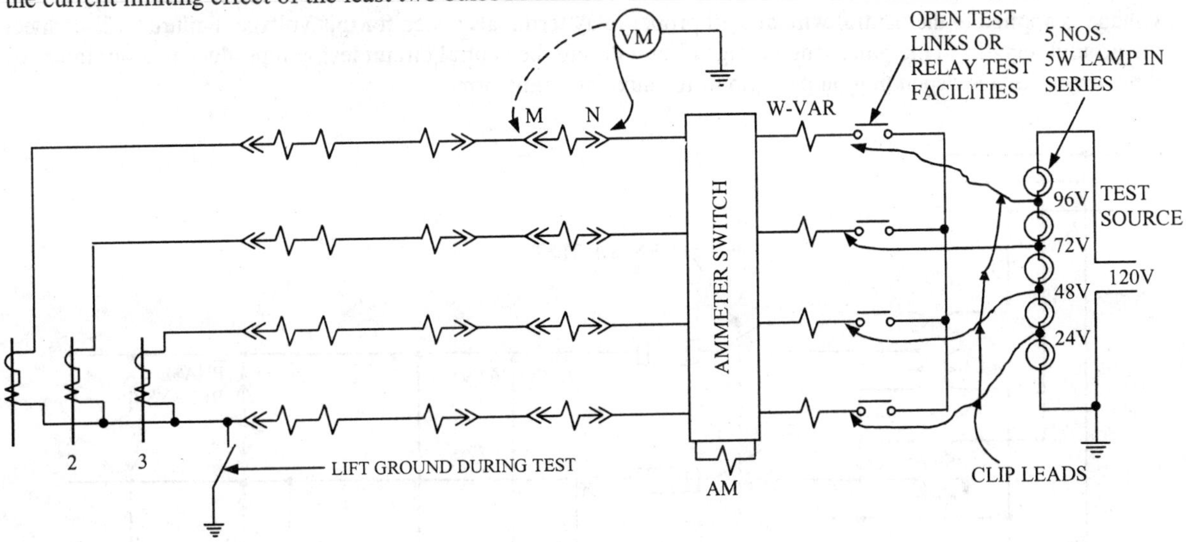

Fig. 8.12 (k): Secondary voltage injection on phase directional relay by current circuit.

Voltage circuit, voltage injection testing on phase directional relay:

Voltage circuit secondary wiring can be tested for correctness in a similar manner to that described in the current circuits (voltage divider test) in figure 8.12 (k). In Figure 8.12 (L) to prevent back-feed of voltage transformers and sustained secondary output voltages from the star-broken delta circuit. Correct connections to all terminals of all voltage circuit devices may be verified by, voltmeter check of the presence of the proper injected voltage for that branch of the circuit, including the neutral

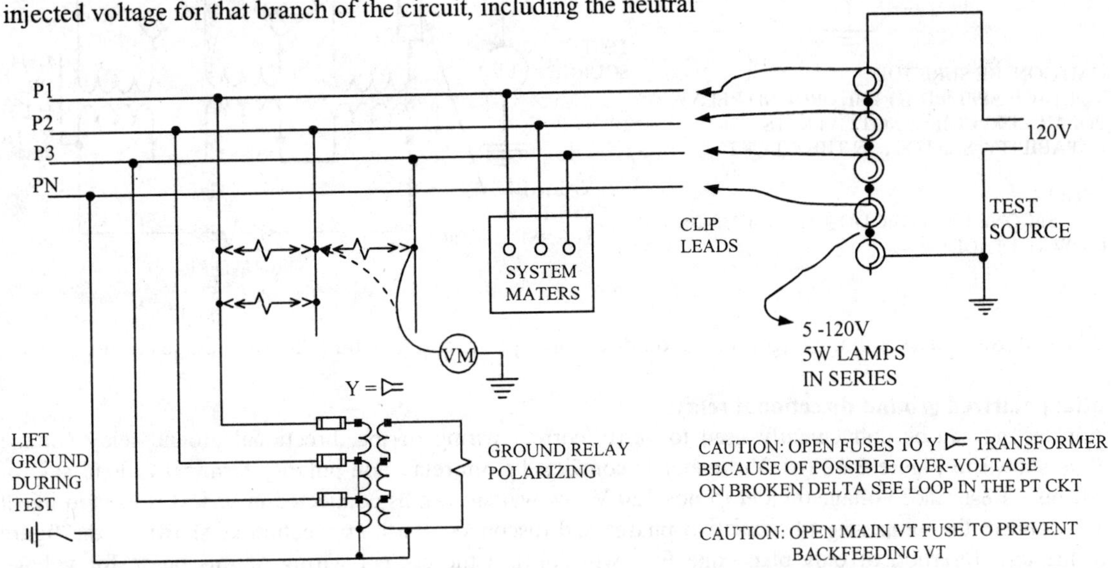

Fig. 8.12 (L): Secondary voltage injection on phase directional relay by voltage circuit.

Figure 8.12 (m) shows the method of testing the voltage circuit of combined directional phase and ground fault relays. The circuit to be tested must be disconnected from the source devices by opening the fuses. Temporary grounds are placed on phase 2 and 3 to eliminate back-feed through delta-connected loads. A voltage of operating value (normally 67 V) is applied between phase 1 and ground, through a variable voltage transformer. Phase 1 connections can be verified by, reading the voltage on all terminals, which is connected to phase 1. Zero voltage should be checked on phase 2 and 3 device terminals. Each phase can be tested in turn by, grounding the other two phases and repeating the above procedure.

The neutral circuit can be tested in a similar manner, after removing all the three fuses of the ground relay circuits. The three-phase wires should be grounded and the ground removed from the neutral wire, the test voltage is applied to the neutral wire and all proper relay terminals tested for this voltage. Failure to disconnect the ground relay from the polarizing voltage circuit during the neutral circuit test will produce in a minimum of three times voltage depending on the ratio of the auxiliary transformer.

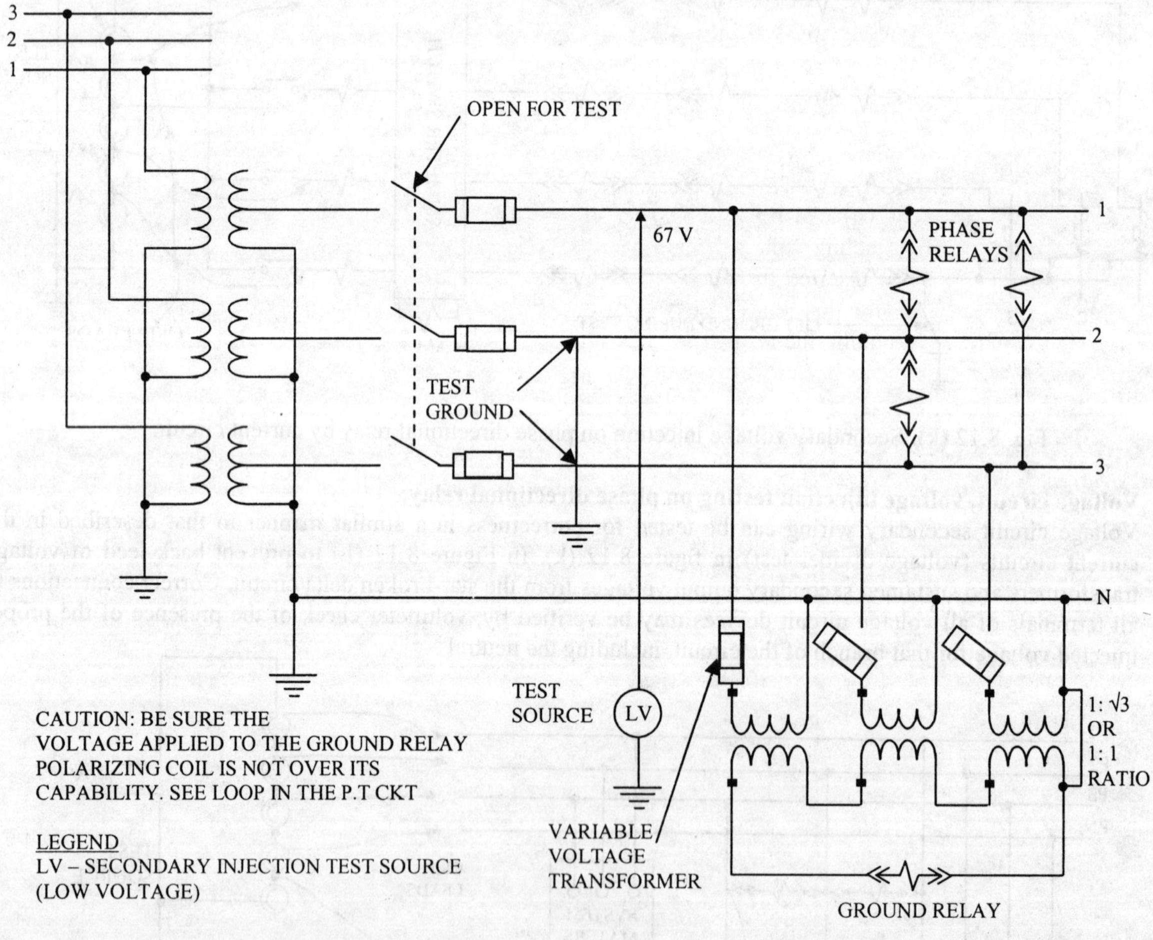

Fig. 8.12 (m): Secondary voltage injection test on directional phase and ground relay by voltage circuit.

Potential polarized ground directional relay:
Injection testing can be conveniently used to verify correct wiring of the directional ground relay voltage circuit as shown in Figure 8.12 (n). Voltmeter is connected from relay non-polarity terminal to load side of inserted fuse. Resistance voltage divider (5 nos 120 V low wattage lamps connected in series) is used to inject current. Connect the jumpering of other two phases and disconnect earth connection as shown in the figure during the test. Insertion of only phase-one fuse will confirm the correct wiring of this phase for voltage measurements (1:√3 ratio) 96/1.732 = 53 V. Insertion of only phase 2 fuse after changing the jumpering should give 72/1.732 = 35 V, and for phase 3 should give 48/1.732 = 18 V.

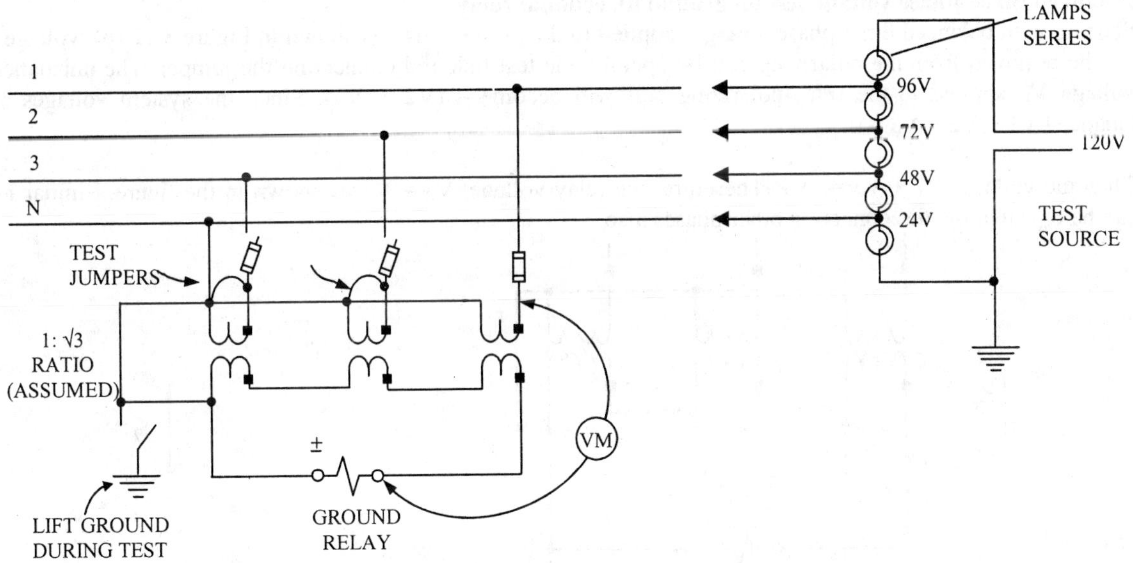

Fig. 8.12 (n): Secondary voltage injection test on ground directional relay by voltage circuit.

Circuit in Figure 8.12 (o) can be conveniently used to verify correct wiring of the ground relay voltage polarizing circuit by injecting voltage (115 V) to each phase. Voltmeter is connected from relay non-polarity terminal to load side of inserted fuse. Insertion of only the phase 1 fuse after making the test jumpering will confirm correct wiring of this phase for voltage measurements (1:√3 ratio 67 V). Similar measurements of phase 2 and 3 after changing the test jumpering will yield the same results. If an auxiliary voltage transformer 1:1 ratio were used, the voltmeter would read essentially zero

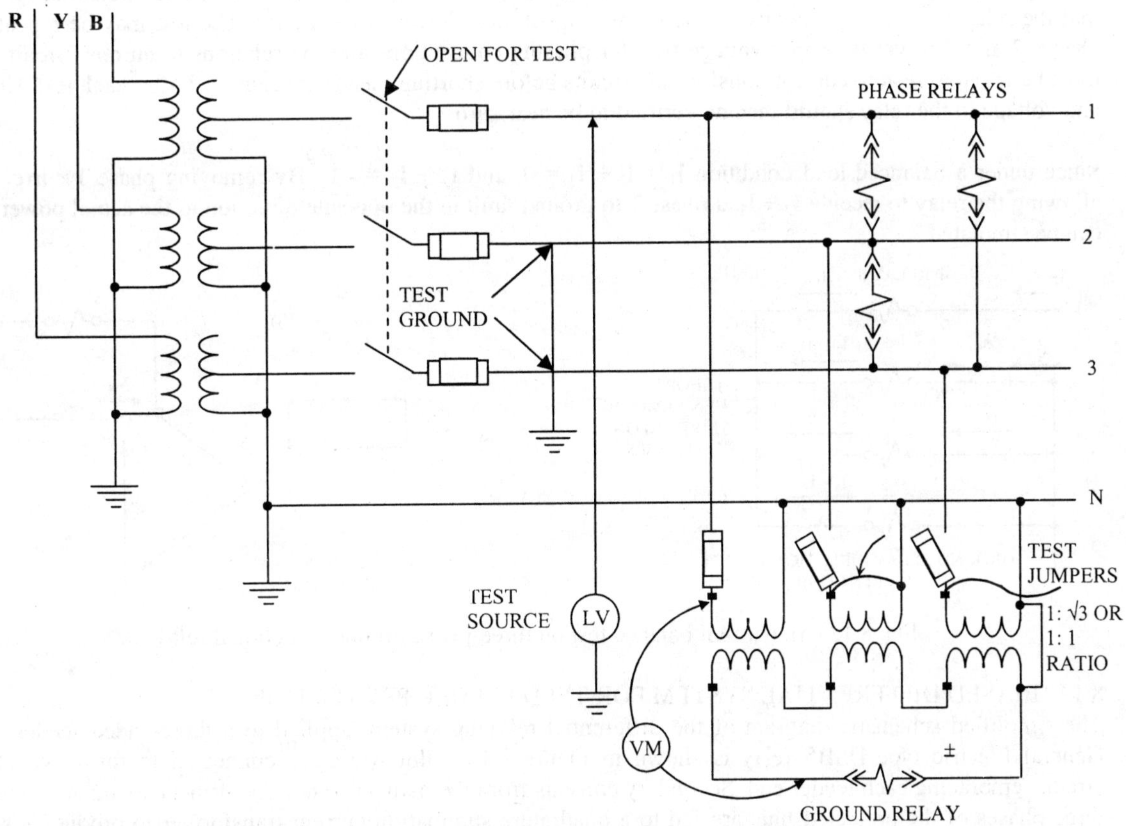

Fig. 8.12 (o): Secondary voltage injection test on ground directional relay by voltage circuit.

Balanced three-phase voltage test on ground directional relay:
Starting with balanced three-phase voltages applied to the ground relay as shown in Figure 8.12 (p), voltage V can be removed from the polarizing coil by opening the test link and connecting the jumper. The unbalanced voltage V_R applied to the relay-polarizing coil will become – (V2 + V3). Since the system voltages are balanced V1 + V2 + V3 = 0.

Then the voltage, V2 + V3 = -V1. Therefore, the relay voltage, V_R = V1 as shown in the figure. Similar test can be repeated by, disconnecting other phases also.

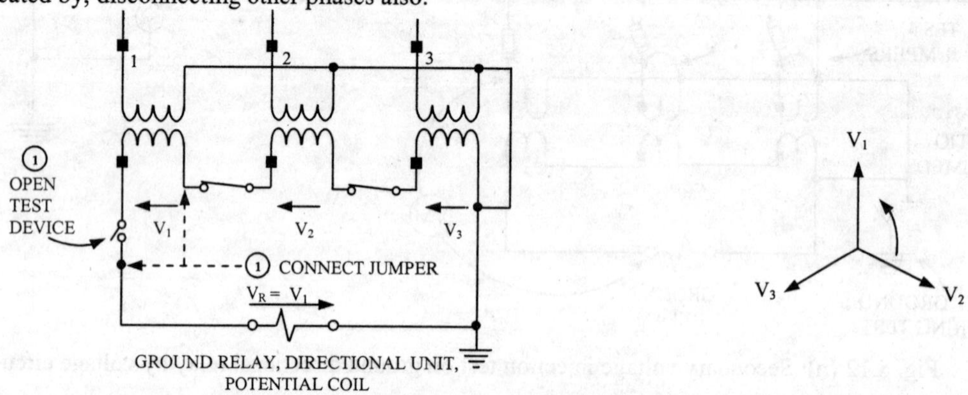

Fig. 8.12 (p): Balanced voltage test on ground relay

Current balance test on three-phase ground directional relay:
As shown in figure 8.12 (q), phase 2 and phase 3 are shorted to neutral and the relay current paths opened at a convenient point in the phase 2 and phase, 3 relay current circuits. The ground directional relay under test is receiving currents and voltages that simulate a phase 1 to ground fault. Secondary current and phase angle readings should be taken in the ground relay using V_R as the phase angle meter reference potential to verify that the relay is receiving effectively the phase 1 quantities shown in the figure. The test may be repeated to phases 2 and 3 to verify proper voltage transfer phasing connections and the relations to current circuit. Care must be taken to restore current transformer circuits before shorting means are removed after each test. Current and voltage to the relay should then be verified to be near zero.

Since under a balanced load condition $I_1 + I_2 + I_3 = 0$, and $I_2 + I_3 = -I_1$. By removing phase 1 current and allowing the relay to receive $I_2 + I_3$, a phase 1 to ground fault in the opposite direction to the actual power flow can be simulated.

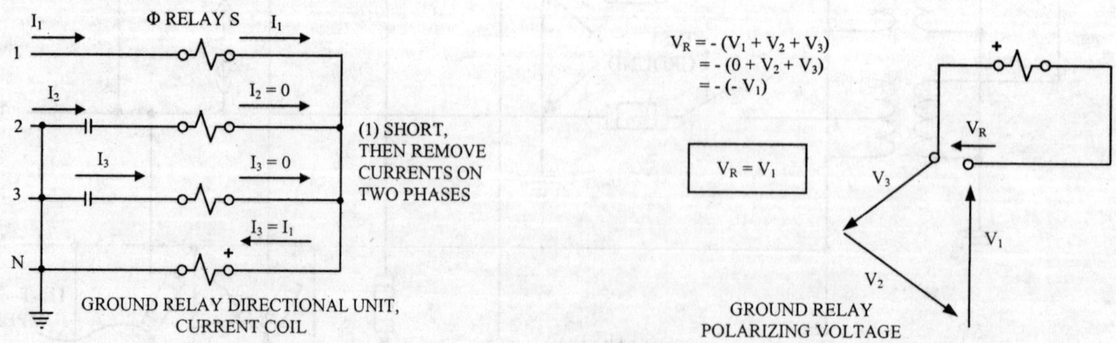

Fig. 8.12 (q): Current balance test on three-phase ground directional relay.

8.13 BIASED DIFFERENTIAL SYSTEM FOR TEED FEEDER PROTECTION.

The simplified schematic diagram of the differential relaying system, applied to a three-ended feeder using General Electric type DSB5 relay is shown in Figure 8.13. Pilot wires are connected to form two closed circuits embracing each feeder end. Secondary currents from the main current transformers, associated with the three phases of the protected line, are fed to a quadrature summation current transformer to produce a single relaying quantity, which is a definite function of the three line currents at each line-end.

Refer symbols for figure 8.13 given in the next page.

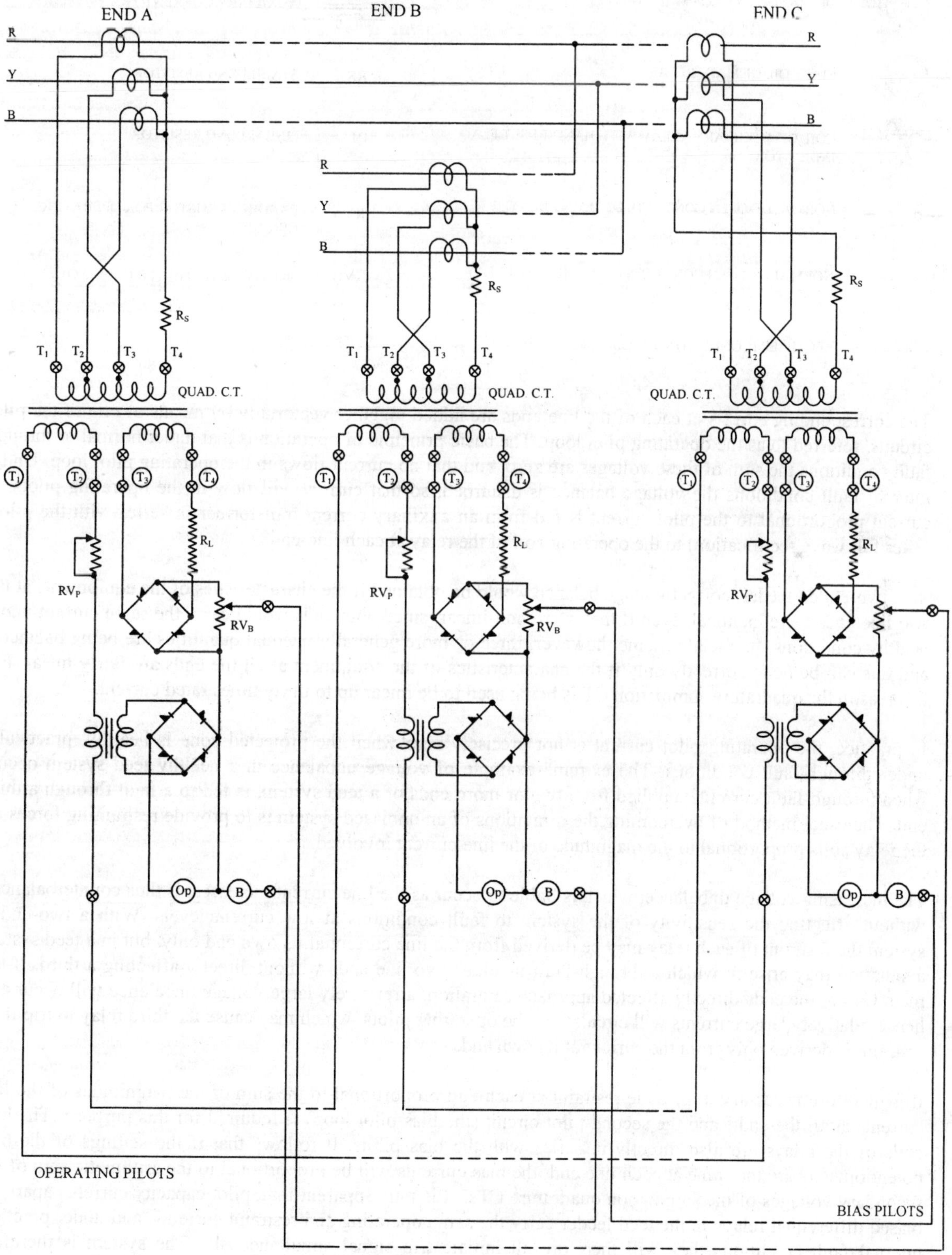

Fig. 8.13: Simplified schematic diagram for differential protection to a three ended feeder (Courtesy, GE)

KEY FOR FIGURE 8.13:

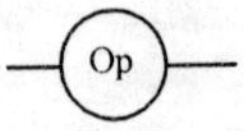	OPERATING COIL OF MAIN RELAY	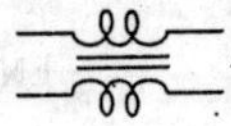	AUXILIARY CURRENT TRANSFORMER
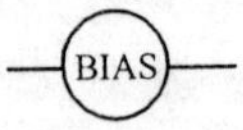	BIAS COIL OF MAIN RELAY	RS	STABILIZING RESISTOR
	COIL OF AUXILIARY RELAY WITH HAND-RESET FLAG INDICATOR	RL	LINEARIZING RESISTOR
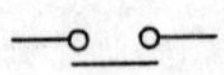	NORMALLY-OPEN CONTACTS OF MAIN RELAY	RVp	PADDING RESISTOR FOR OPERATING CIRCUIT (0 – 250 Ω)
	NORMALLY-OPEN CONTACTS OF AUXILIARY RELAY	RVB	BIAS POTENTIOMETER (0 – 100 Ω)
	RECTIFIER (CONDUCTING FROM LEFT TO RIGHT)	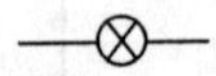	TERMINAL

The corresponding e.m.f's at each of the line ends are added together vectorially by means of one of the pilot circuits, referred to as the operating pilot loop. The basic principle of operation is that under normal or through fault conditions the sum of these voltages are zero, and that no current flows in the operating pilot loop. Under internal fault conditions the voltage balance is disturbed, so that current will flow in the operating pilots. A current proportional to the pilot current is fed from an auxiliary current transformer in series with the pilots (after full wave rectification) to the operating coil of the relay at each line-end.

In a two-ended feeder, correct voltage balance would be obtained if the characteristics of the equipments at the two line ends were identical, even if they were non-linear, since both ends would carry the same current under healthy conditions. In a teed scheme, however, three or more generally unequal quantities are being balanced, and this can be done correctly only if the characteristics of the equipment at all the ends are fairly linear. For this reason the quadrature summation CT is being used to be linear up to thirty times rated current.

In practice, the operating pilot current is not precisely zero when the protected zone is healthy, practically under through-fault conditions. The extreme example of voltage unbalance in a healthy teed system occurs when through-fault current, supplied from two or more ends of a teed system, is fed to a fault through a third end. The usual method of overcoming the limitations of an unbiased system is to provide restraining forces on the relay coils proportional to the magnitude of the line current involved.

The increasing voltage unbalance, which is liable to occur as the line current increases, is thus counterbalanced without affecting the sensitivity of the system to fault conditions at low current levels. With a two-ended system the restraint of each relay may be derived from the line current at its own end only, but in a teed system a situation may arise in which a through-fault involves two line ends without directly affecting a third. If the main CTs at the ends directly affected approach saturation, a relatively large voltage unbalance will occur and hence relatively large currents will circulate in the operating pilots, which may cause the third relay to trip if its restraint is derived only from the current at its own end.

It is therefore necessary to provide restraint at each end proportional to the sum of the magnitudes of the line currents at all the ends, and the second pilot circuit (the bias pilot loop) is required for this purpose. The bias coils of the relays are also directly in series with the bias pilots. It follows that if the settings of the bias potentiometers are the same at each line end, the bias currents will be proportional to the arithmetic sum of the secondary voltages of the summation quadrature CTs. It is thus apparent that, pilot capacity currents apart, all biased differential relays in the teed feeder carry the same operating and restraint currents, and under practical internal fault conditions they will therefore all initiate trip signal simultaneously. The system is therefore inherently inter-tripping.

8.14 FUNCTION AND APPLICATION OF AUTO-RECLOSING SYSTEM.

The process of automatic closing of a transmission or distribution line circuit breaker after a fault trip is called autoreclosing. The aim of autoreclosing is to eliminate the supply interruption due to temporary (momentary) faults and to improve transient stability limit of power system of overhead transmission lines. Single-pole and/or three-pole shot repetitive autoreclosing relays are employed for re-closing circuit breakers after an earth fault or phase-to-phase fault (except three-phase faults). These relays have deadline closing and check synchronizing facilities. Lockout is a feature in autoreclosing system, which prevents closing of the circuit breaker after certain tripping operation. The following modes of operations are selectable by means of a autoreclosure mode selector switch(s) and over the substation computerized control system (SCS).

1. Single-pole, high speed, autoreclose: Autoreclose is only be initiated in the event of a single phase to earth fault.
2. Three-pole delayed re-closing: Delayed re-closing is only be initiated in the event of a single phase or two phase fault.
3. Single-phase high speed and /or three-phase delayed autoreclosing as appropriate.
4. Without autoreclosing: Three phase faults tripping without autoreclose will take place for any type of fault/inter tripping.

Following requirements are to be introduced in the autoreclosing systems:

a) If a second earth fault occurs or a fault is persisting in the line during the single-pole autoreclose dead time, three-pole tripping with subsequent delayed autoreclosing is recommended. If the autoreclosing selector switch is in the single-pole reclose mode, three-phase tripping with lockout should follow.
b) The high speed and delayed autoreclosing dead times have to be coordinated with the remote station circuit breaker autoreclose relay settings.
c) Reclaim time is the time period following the automatic re-closing of the circuit breaker might be chosen to match the duty cycle of the circuit breakers, assuming the shortest available dead time. Usually the duty cycle for HV and EHV transmission line breakers are O – 0.3 sec – CO – 180 sec. – CO. The reclaim time commences at the instant the re-close command is given to the circuit breaker and, therefore, includes the CB closing time. The closing command should be limited to 2 seconds, after which the re-closing relay will automatically reset without resetting the reclaim timer. The re-closing relay will also reset if deadline check or synchronism check conditions are not satisfied within the predetermined time of the check relays being energized.
d) Re-closing equipment is provided with operation counter to record the number of re-closures and lockout has been reached.

Varities of autoreclosing schemes:

a) Rapid autoreclosing to prevent loss of synchronism: In cases where there is danger of lossing synchronism, non-repetitive rapid autoreclosing is used. Single shot operation, re-closed within 0.3 sec.
b) Delayed autoreclosing for meshed network: Before systems can be interconnected, it should be synchronized. The automatic synchronizer is used in conjunction with autoreclosing, and re-closes more than 1 second after tripping.
c) Autoreclosing scheme with desired switching sequence (Ring buses): In case a circuit breaker interrupts several lines the autoreclosing scheme must ensure that the switching sequence follows a correct pattern.
d) Programmed autoreclosing/interruption: Central monitoring system, which involves not only programmed autoreclosure but also programmed interruptions.
e) Multi shot autoreclosing for distribution lines: Not suitable for cables, only for overhead distribution lines.

Sequence of delayed autoreclosing (DAR):

t = 0	Fault occurred
t = 0.1 sec.	Circuit breakers of either end opened and make the line dead
t = 6 sec	Voltage monitoring relay at sending end check whether line is dead and then reclose breaker
t = 16 sec	Synchronism monitor at the receiving end, between the charged line and bus and permit breaker closing

Typical application of autoreclosing schemes:

When applying relays to re-closing schemes the general requirement is one relay per circuit breaker. Digital autoreclosing and synchronizing relays can cover all requirements for autoreclosing in single or double busbar, one-and-a-half breaker and mesh substations. Following systems are adopted in the autoreclosing scheme:

(1) Re-closing radial distribution system where no synchronizing is required: This scheme is applied either single-pole high-speed autoreclosing or three-pole delayed autoreclosing.

(2) Autoreclose with integral check and system synchronizing. Suitable for both single-pole high-speed autoreclosing and three pole delayed autoreclosing.

(3) Integrates the autoreclose and synchronizing functionality in to a distance protection relay to provide high-speed single-pole and three-pole tripping and re-closing. Ideally suited to sub-transmission overhead lines.

(4) Auto-isolation for teed feeders, single or double bus bar: Typically used when a transformer is Teed off a feeder from a single or double bus bar. For a fault on a feeder, if it is an overhead line, the sequence is: trip, re-close; and if another trip occurs, isolate the line, re-close. If it is a cable feeder, the sequence is trip, isolate the cable, re-close. For a fault on the transformer the circuit breaker trips, the transformer isolator is operated, then the circuit breaker is closed again. [Figure 8.14 (a)]

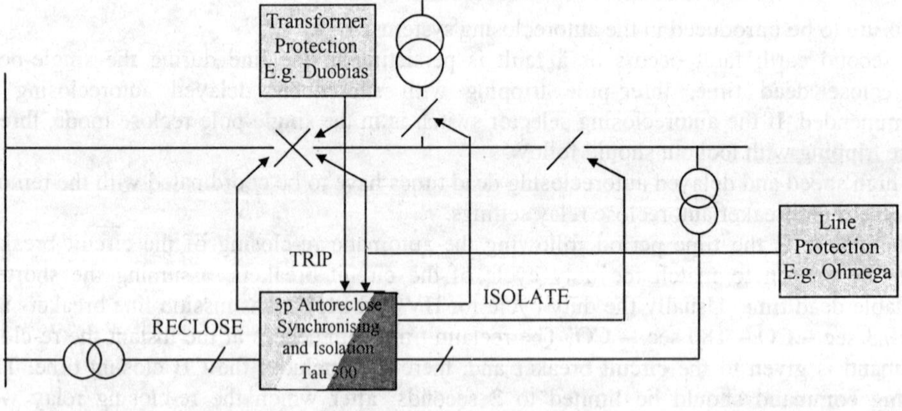

Fig. 8.14 (a): Autoisolation for Teed overhead feeder

(5) Auto-isolation for Teed cable feeders: Figure 8.14 (b) shows 2 cable feeders and a transformer. For a fault on either of the cables the autoreclosure will isolate the cable, then re-close the transformer circuit breaker. For a fault on the transformer the autoreclosure will isolate the transformer and lockout. In each case the remote ends are re-closed by their own re-closing relay when the inter-trips are removed.

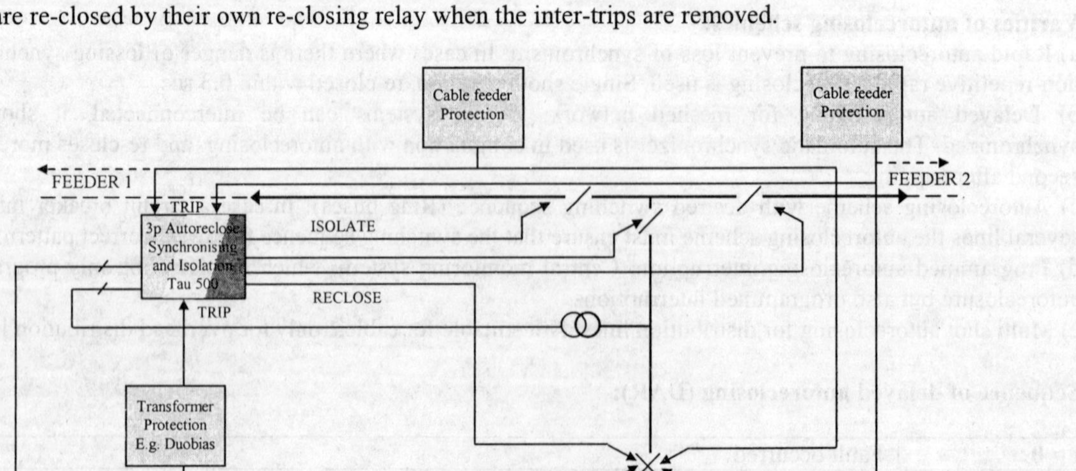

Fig. 8.14 (b): Autoisolation for Teed cable feeder

(6) Switch-and-a-half and mesh substations: As shown in Figure 8.14 (c), one autoreclosure can be used with the entire circuit breaker, while another one is used for the circuit breakers at the outsides of the diameter. The re-closing relay can control up to 2 isolators on each side of the circuit breaker.

Re-closing in a mesh substation is similar to a teed feeder, except there is a need for isolator control on both sides of the circuit breaker. If all breakers are closed prior to a fault, blocking logic creates a priority to such that one relay will ensure the correct circuits are isolated before closing its circuit breaker, thus releasing the next.

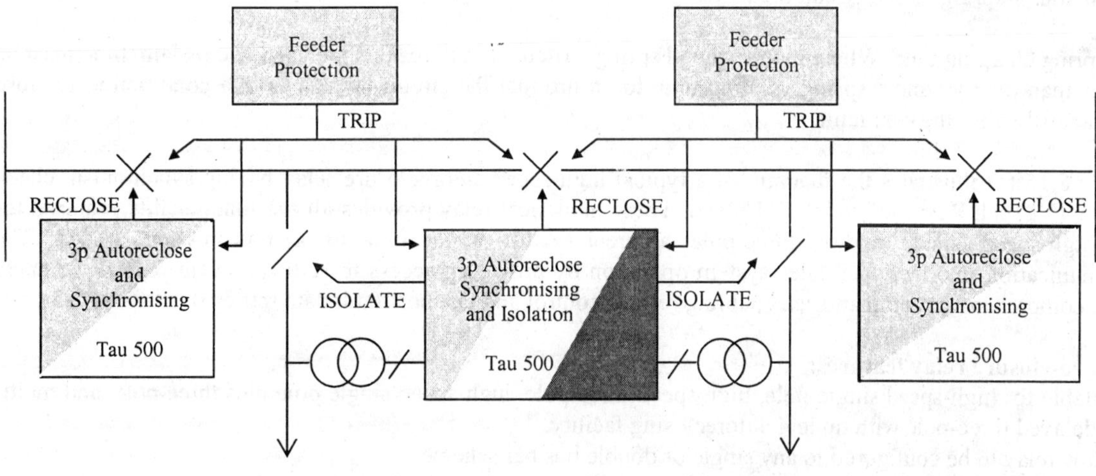

Fig. 8.14 (c): Switch-and-a-half re-closing

8.15 NUMERICAL AUTO-RECLOSE AND SYNCHRONISM CHECK RELAY (79)..

Most fault leading to power system disturbances are attributable to weather conditions, primarily lightning. The voltage wave arising in connection with a lightning stroke can result in over voltage, over-current and flashovers to earth or between phases. Voltage waves with peak values in the order of 100 KV are propagated with the velocity of light in to the substation and may destroy the equipment, if the over-voltage cannot be limited. Reliable surge arresters constitute the first link in the protective chain providing reliable protection against over-voltages, if they are correctly selected, properly located and coordinated with other equipment. A flashover gives rise to fault currents 10-40 KA, which may destroy the equipment, if they are not disconnected rapidly and effectively. Protective relays and circuit breakers constitute the second link in the protective chain. If they are correctly selected and coordinated they provide fast and reliable fault clearance.

We cannot protect overhead lines in the same way against over-voltages, but the faulted line section must be rapidly and selectively tripped. Instrument transformers, protective relays and circuit breakers form the fault clearing system, which must guarantee a high reliability. Line faults are by far the most usual type of fault occurring. Reliable clearing of line faults followed by high-speed autoreclosing is a necessity for a high level of availability performance. Circuit breakers and protection system must have a design and mode of operation permitting fast and selective clearing of faults as well as high-speed autoreclosing after the arc has been extinguished. Faults in sub-transmission and distribution network account for the largest share of power failures affecting consumers, in terms of both quantity and accumulated energy.

Following are the terms related to autoreclosing:

(1) De-ionization of fault path: After the fault current has been interrupted, a certain time must be allowed for ionized air to disperse so that the arc does not re-strike when the supply is restored. This time will depend on the system voltage, cause of fault, weather conditions etc.

(2) Protective relay resetting time: Where time delayed protection is used it is essential that the timing device completely resets during the dead time so that correct discrimination will be maintained after re-close on a persistent fault.

(3) Reclaim time: The reclaim time must be long enough to allow the protective relays to operate when the circuit breaker is reclosed on to a persistent fault. Sensitive definite time earth fault relay is often used to detect high resistance earth faults caused by broken conductors falling on to dry ground. It is impractical to make this protection stable during through faults. It is usually assumed that such high resistance earth faults are persistent and dangerous. Hence contacts on the sensitive earth fault relay, is used to block autoreclosing and lockout the circuit breaker.

(4) Circuit breaker re-closing impulse: A re-closing impulse of 0.1second duration is usually adequate foe pneumatic or spring closed circuit breakers.

(5) Spring charging time: Where motor wound spring closed circuit breakers are used, the reclaim time must be longer than the maximum spring winding time to ensure that the circuit breaker is in a condition to re-close satisfactorily after the next fault.

Figure 8.15 (a) illustrates the diagram of a typical high-speed autoreclosure relay having synchronism check facility (VaTech Reyrolle model TAU 100). These numerical relay provides all the functionality required for the high-speed single and/or three-pole autoreclose for application to a transmission feeder. The communication interface facilitates system operation by providing access to settings, event reports, counters and a comprehensive command set, enabling remote control and fast post fault data retrieval.

Auto-re-closure relay features:
* Suitable for high-speed single-pole, high-speed three-pole, high-speed single pole plus three-pole, and multi-shot delayed three-pole with up to 4 autoreclosing facility.
* Allow relay to be configured to any single or double bus bar scheme.
* Built in check and system synchronizing facility, external check and system synchronizing facility automatic isolation, and system reconfiguration.
* Pole discrepancy protection for circuit breaker, isolators and earth switch (alarm and trip)
* Failed to close/failed to open annunciation for circuit breaker, isolators and earth switch.
* Ferro-resonance suppression through isolation or earthing.
* Programmable LED's for annunciation of autoreclose outputs.
* Event recording of 500 time tagged records.
* Fiber optic communication ports and RS 232 port for relay interrogation.
* V.T failure alarm and blocking (Voltage transformer fuse failure).
* Fully programmable 27 digital inputs and 29 output relays.
* Built-in logic eliminates the need for external auxiliary relays and associated wiring.
* Industry standard IEC 60870-5-103 protocol.

Settings for autoreclosure relay
* Close mode: OFF, 1 Pole, 3 Pole, 1P/3P, 3P/3P, 1P/1P, 1P1P/3P3P, 1P3P/3P
* Deadline and dead bar charge/close : Enabled/Disabled
* Check synchronism close/unconditional close: Enabled/Disabled
* 1P dead time: Range 0.05 to 100s
* 3P dead time: Range 0.1 to 900s
* Close-pulse: Range 0.2 to 20s
* Reclaim time: Range 1 to 600s
* Synchronism close delay: Range 0 to 60s
* Permissive close delay: Range 0 to 600s
* Sequence initiate time: Range 0 to 120s
* Persistent inter-trip: Range 1 to 120s
* CB fail to open delay: Range 50 to 200ms
* CB memory timer: Range 0 to 5s
* CB indeterminate Range 50 to 200ms
* Minimum lockout timer: Range 0 to 60s

Check synchronism Settings:
* Dead bus/Dead line: Range 5 to 150%
* Live bus/Live line: Range 10 to 155%

LEGEND:
AR: Autoreclosing unit
CB: Circuit breaker
CMS: Control and monitoring system
D: Disconnector (Isolator)
VT: Voltage transformer

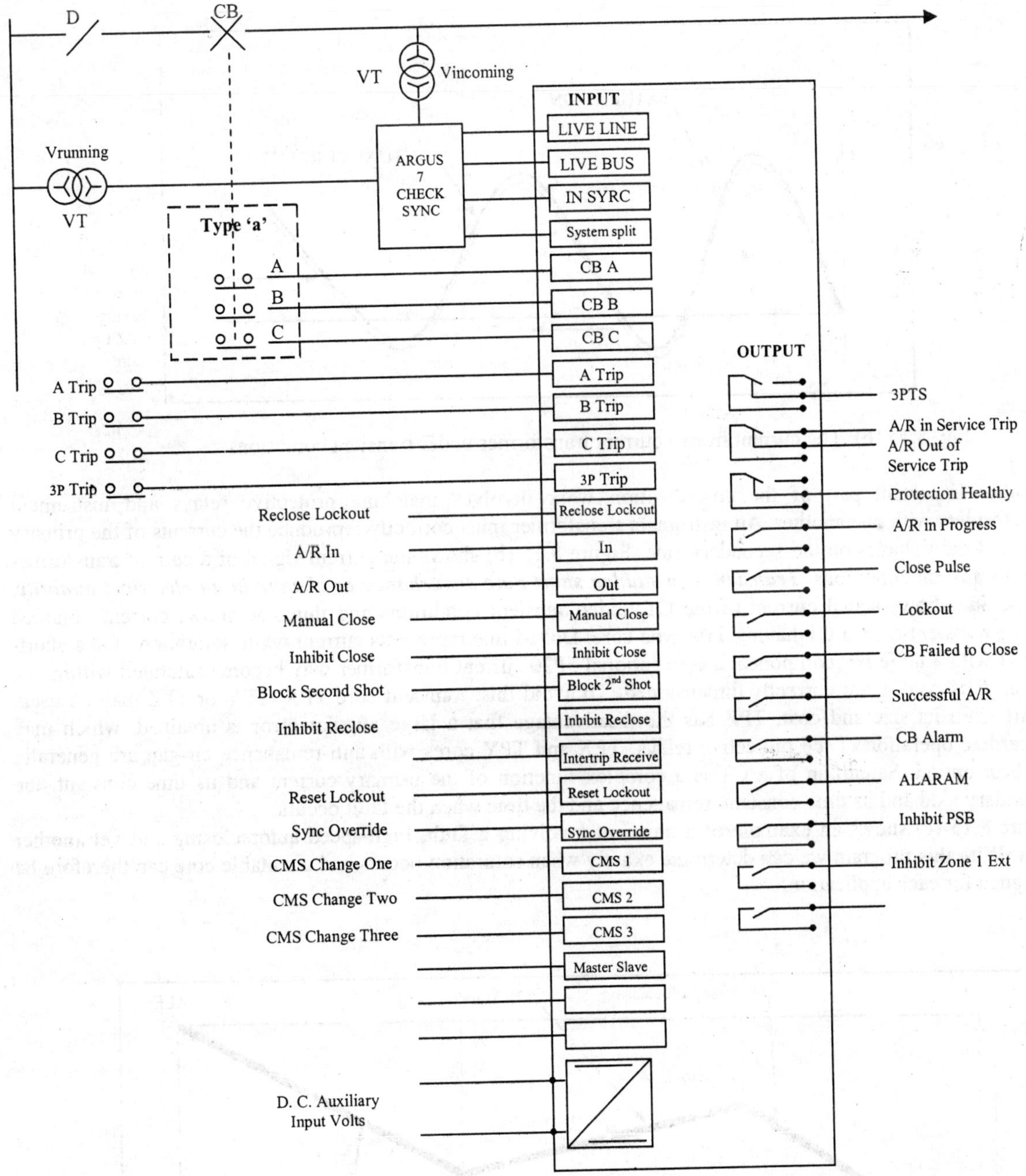

Fig. 8.15 (a): Digital high-speed autoreclose relay with synchronism check facility (Courtesy, Reyrolle).

Clearing of faults:

The fault clearing system comprises current transformers, voltage transformers, protective relays autoreclosing equipment and circuit breakers. It is necessary to take in to account short-circuit currents, stability requirements and network configuration. Selectivity plans must be made to co-ordinate the protection schemes in different substations. This is just as an important factor as the modern protective relays themselves, for achieving a reliable fault clearing system. For example distance relays with separate setting of the reactance and resistance make it easier to co-ordinate different substations and obtain selectivity between load and fault impedance.

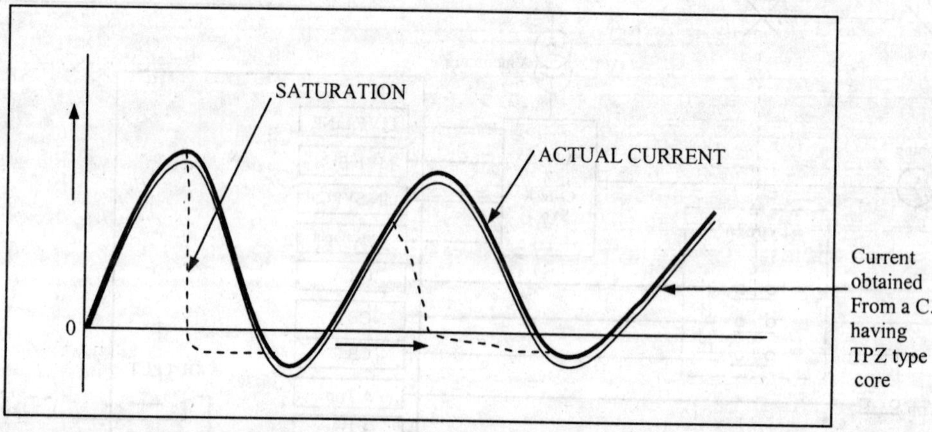

Fig. 8.15 (b): The current from a current transformer under transient conditions.

Another important part of the co-ordination work involves matching protective relays and instrument transformers with one another. An instrument transformer must correctly reproduce the currents of the primary side and the voltages on the secondary side. Figure 8.15 (b) shows the current signal of a current transformer under transient conditions. ***Transient is a sudden short time disturbance or change in an electrical quantity.*** Thick line shows actual current of the CT under transient conditions and thin line shows current obtained during transient from a CT having TPZ type core. Dotted line represents current while saturation. On a short-circuit with a large DC component a conventional 5P20 current transformer may become saturated within one cycle, if its core is not correctly dimensioned. To avoid this, transient core TPX, TPY or TPZ may be used. Apart from its size and cost, TPZ has the disadvantage that a large angular error is obtained, which may jeopardize operation of the protective relays. TPX and TPY cores with anti-remanence air-gap are generally the best option. Saturation of a CT is a complex function of the primary current and its time constant, the secondary load and its time constant, remanence and the time when the fault occurs.

Figure 8.15 (c) shows an example of a transient involving a fault, high-speed autoreclosing and yet another fault. With this program we can determine exactly when saturation occurs and a suitable core can therefore be designed for each application.

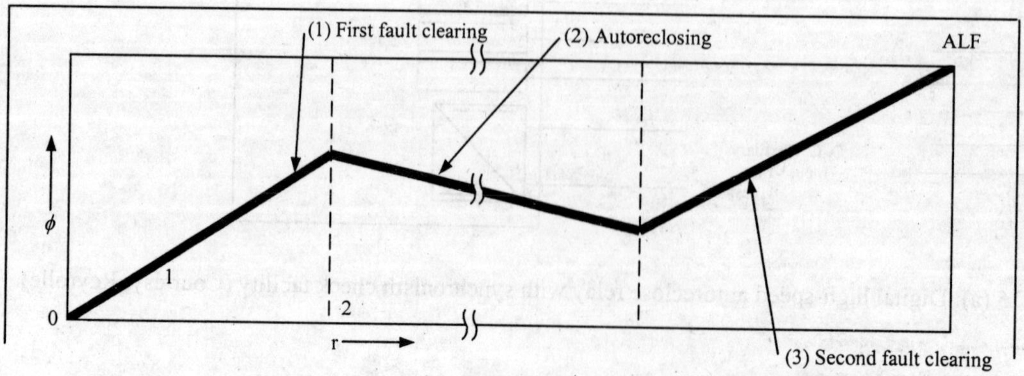

Fig. 8.15 (c): Magnetizing characteristic of a current transformer on fault clearing.

Capacitive voltage transformers are frequently used together with distance relays. Figure 8.15 (d) shows voltage transients from capacitive voltage transformers for a nearby fault on a line. A highly capacitive voltage transformer gives here a substantially lower transient than a low capacitive one. IEC standards state that the transient after one cycle must not exceed 10%.

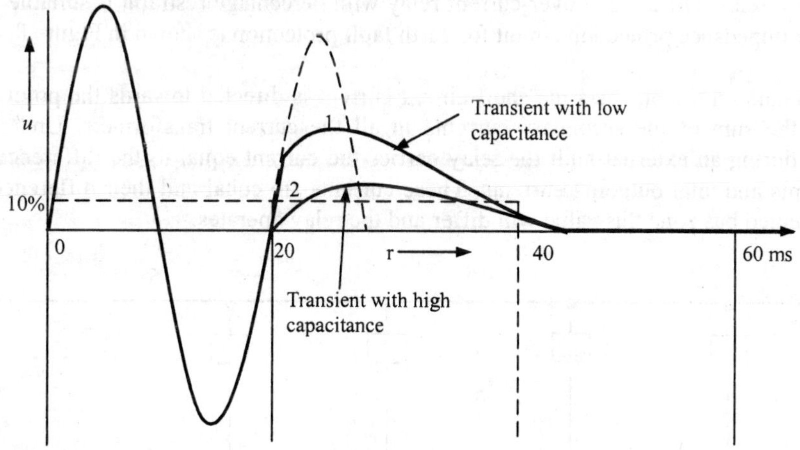

Fig. 8.15 (d): Voltage transients from capacitive voltage transformers.

8.16 PERCENTAGE DIFFERENTIAL RELAY FOR BUSBAR PROTECTION (87B).

Station bus protection deserves very careful attention, since bus faults are, as a rule, the most serious fault that can occur in an electrical system. Many methods are employed to protect the station buses. Among them are, the use of over-current relays, backup protection, directional-comparison schemes, etc. By far the most effective and preferred method used to protect the buses consists of percentage differential relaying, using either current or voltage differential relays. The differential relaying is preferred because it is fast, selective, and sensitive. For stability reasons, it is essential that phase faults on bus bars be cleared instantly. On such occasions, protections capable of high speed clearing of faults become a necessity on the bus bars. Conventional bus differential relay connection for different types of bus arrangements are shown in Chapter # 3, section 3.2.

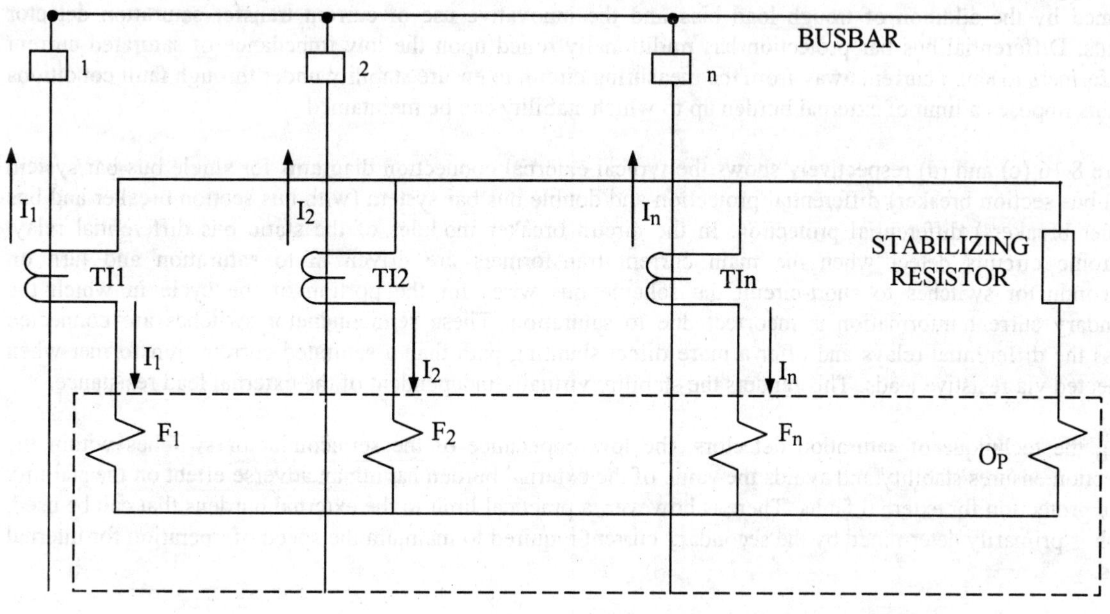

Fig. 8.16 (a): Bus zone differential protection for both phase fault and earth fault protection.

Principle of differential bus bar protection is based on the comparison of magnitude and phase of current incoming to the bus and outgoings from the bus / protected zone. All the incoming and outgoing feeders of the bus bar incorporate current transformers of appropriate ratings but equal ratio and the relay is connected as shown in Figure 8.16 (a) for phase fault and earth fault protections. All the three, phases can be co⁻ .cted by using a 3-element relay. Differential over-current relay with percentage restraint is suitable for bus differential protection. Low impedance protection circuit for earth fault protection is shown in Figure 8.16 (b).

When a fault occurs on the bus bars the short-circuit current is directed towards the point of fault. The relay current equals the sum of the secondary currents in all the current transformers. Under normal operating conditions and during an external fault the relay carries the current equal to the difference between the total incoming currents and total outgoing currents. These currents are equal and their difference is zero. During a fault in the protected bus zone this value will differ and the relay operates.

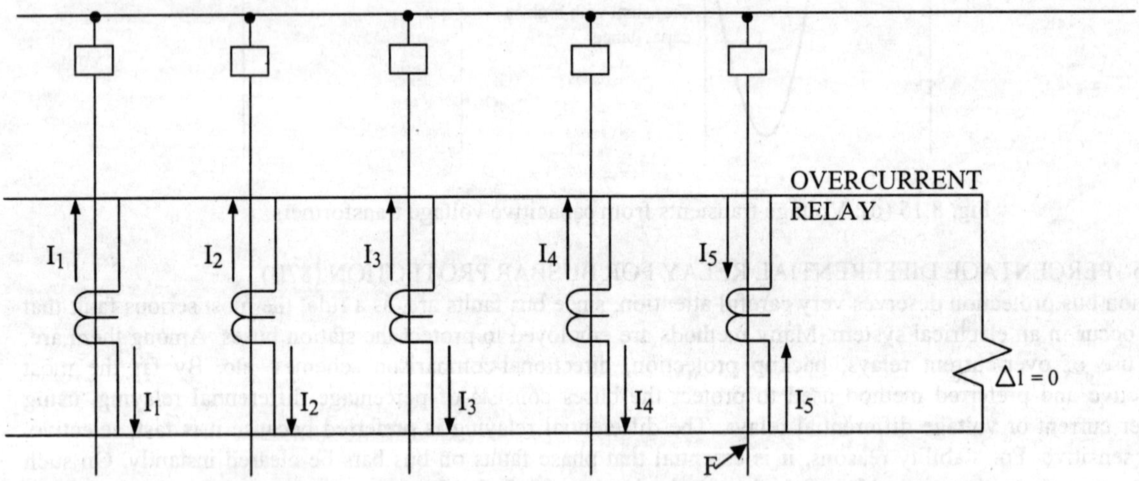

Fig. 8.16 (b): Single line diagram for bus zone differential earth fault protection.

The design is based on the well-known Merz-Prize circulating current principle. Through fault stability is assumed by the addition of trough load bias and the innovative use of current transfer saturation detector circuits. Differential bus bar protection has traditionally relied upon the low impedance of saturated current transformers to shunt current away from the measuring circuit to ensure stability under through fault conditions and this imposes a limit of external burden up to which stability can be maintained.

Figure 8.16 (c) and (d) respectively shows the typical external connection diagrams for single bus bar system (with bus section breaker) differential protection and double bus bar system (with bus section breaker and bus coupler breakers) differential protection. In the circuit breaker modules of the static bus differential relay, electronic circuits detect when the main current transformers are driven in to saturation and turn on semiconductor switches to short-circuit the scheme bus wires for the portion of the cycle in which the secondary current information is incorrect due to saturation. These semiconductor switches are connected across the differential relays and offer a more direct shunting path than a saturated current transformer when connected via resistive leads. This renders the stability virtually independent of the external lead resistance.

Using the technique of saturation detectors, the low impedance of the semiconductor switches within the protection ensures stability and avoids the value of the external burden having an adverse effect on the stability of the protection for external faults. There is however, a practical limit to the external burdens that can be used, which is primarily determined by the secondary current required to maintain the speed of operation for internal faults.

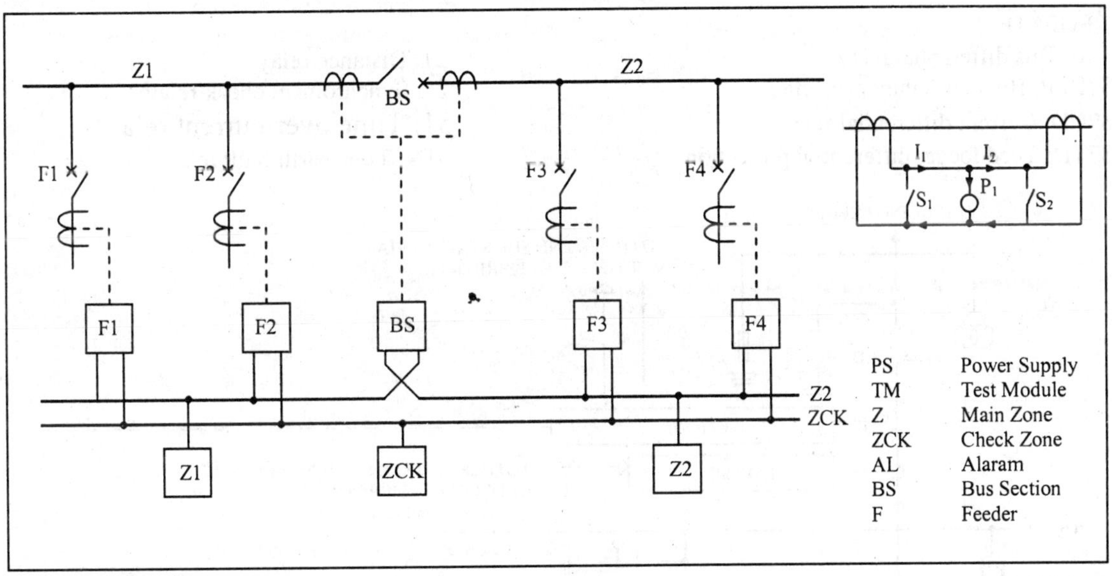

Fig. 8.16 (c): Static bus differential protection circuit for single bus bar arrangement.

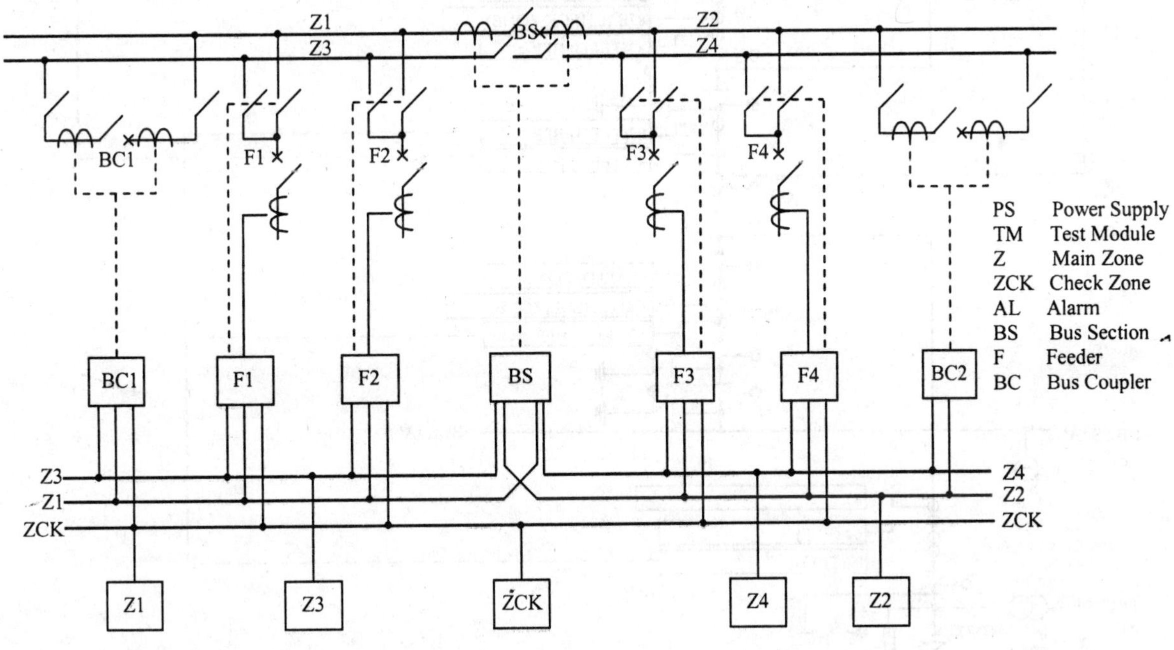

Fig 8.16 (d): Static bus differential protection circuit for double bus bar arrangement.

Bus differential protection for 1½ breaker configuration.

The single line diagram given in Figure 8.16 (e) shows the circuit arrangement of one diameter of a 1½ breaker configuration in an air insulated high voltage switchgear, which consists of one incoming feeder and one outgoing feeder, three circuit breakers, 2 disconnectors per breaker and 5 numbers earth switches. Two separate bus differential schemes are provided for each diameter in order to avoid protection blind zones and improve selectivity. A high-speed percentage restraint relay is used for short circuit and earth fault protection in the protected bus zone areas. Harmonic restraint is not required for bus differential protection. The protection of each circuit breaker is monitored by two sets of relays fed from the protection current transformers. During an internal bus fault, operation of this relay will initiate a trip signal to the respective circuit breakers. The relay outputs are connected in series in a "two out of two" arrangement. The relay has an operating time 10 ms and a consistent reset time less than 15 ms.

LEGEND:
87B: Bus differential relay
87BFP: Breaker failure protection
87CD: Current differential relay
87TD: Teed feeder differential protection
21: Distance relay
25: Synchronism check relay
51: Time over-current relay
51N: Time earth fault relay

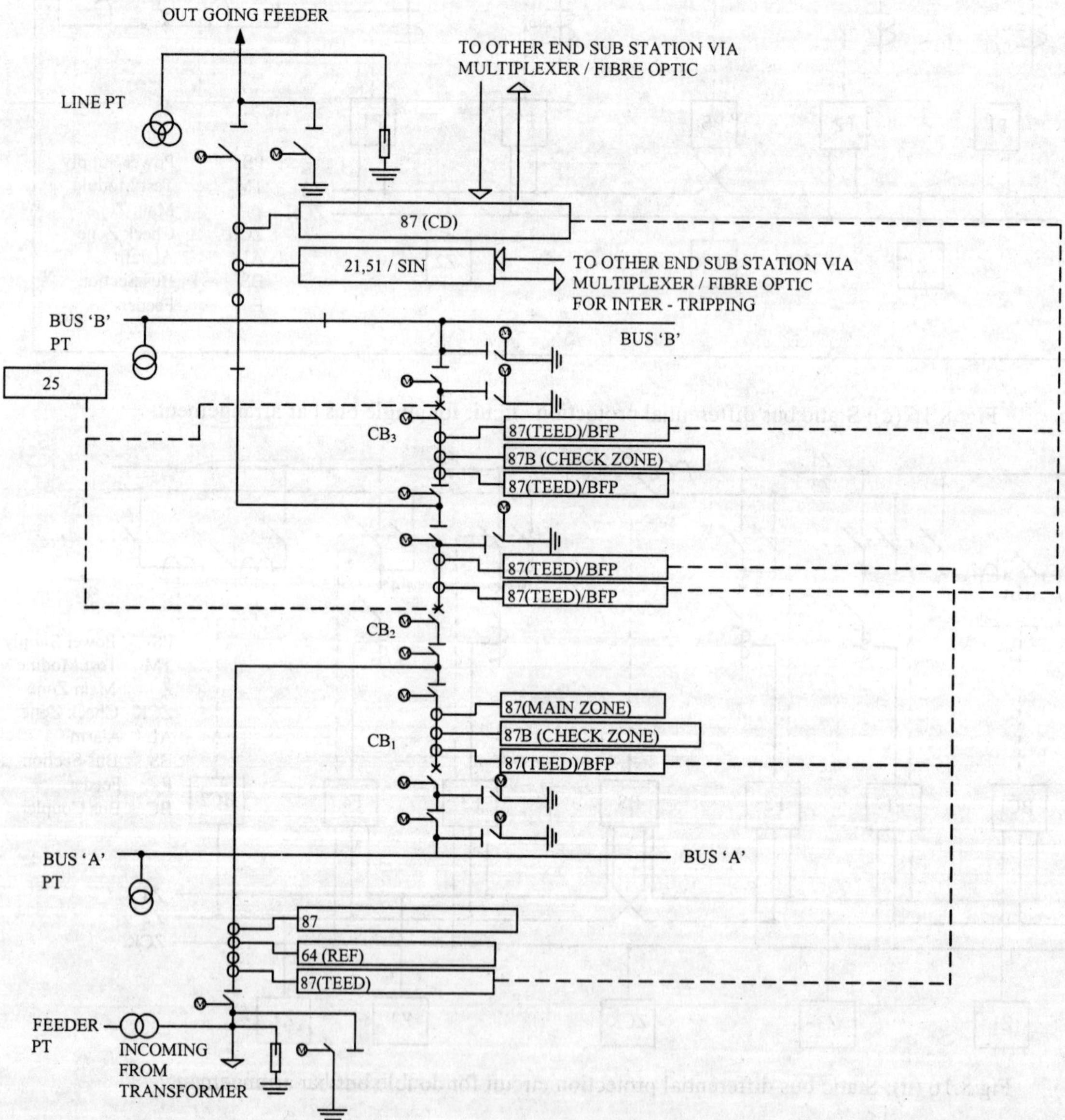

Fig. 8.16 (e): Bus differential protection for one diameter of a double bus one-and-a-half breaker configuration.

High impedance bus differential Relay:

The high impedance differential relay is connected as shown in Figure 8.16 (f) so that under normal operating conditions as well as an external fault the voltage at the relay terminals is approximately zero. In the case of an internal fault, the CT's have, in effect, open-circuited primaries. The source CT's will produce high voltages to drive the fault current through the feeder CT's secondaries. This high voltage will appear at the relay terminals and cause the relay to operate. Following are the tests to be conducted on this relay; Pickup over-voltage; Pickup over-current; Timing over-voltage; Target and seal-in.

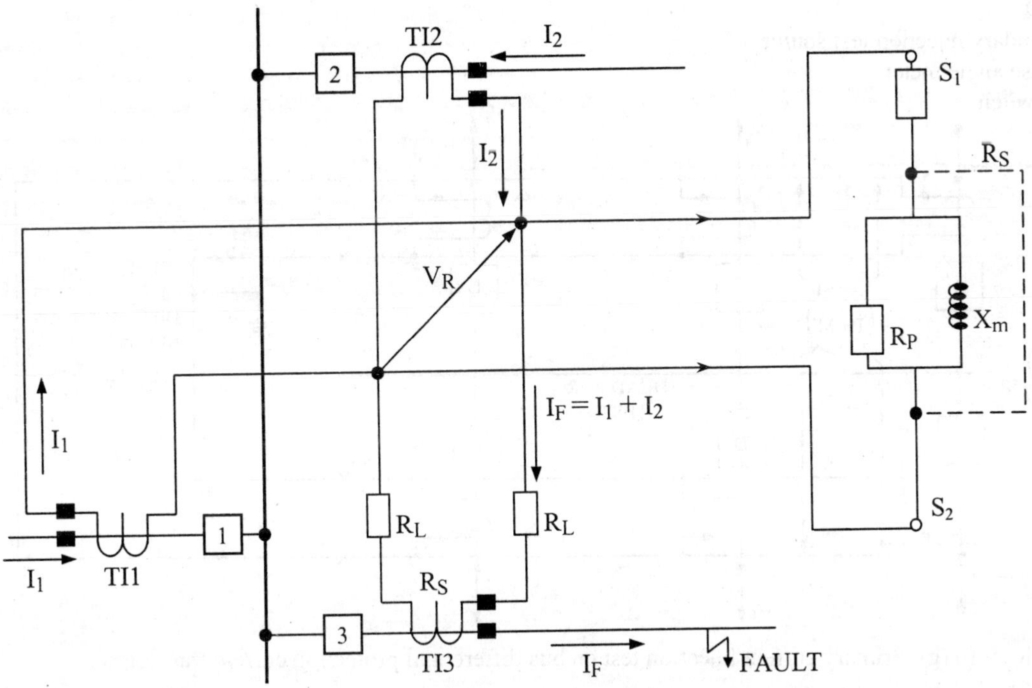

Fig. 8.16 (f): Connection diagram of bus differential voltage relay.

Primary and secondary injection tests on bus differential relay:

Primary and secondary injection testing can be readily applied to most bus differential relaying schemes. The proper application of phase angle meters, standard ammeters and voltmeters, can be extremely useful in measuring secondary quantities to determine proper connections and component integrity. Primary injection testing of this type of relay circuit would consist of applying a suitable current source across each current transformer primary while measuring secondary quantities with suitable meters at the relay location.

As indicated in Figure 8.16 (g) one side of the primary test source could be applied to phase 1 of breaker A, and the other lead applied to phase 1 of breaker B. A current could then be circulated through two current transformers of the phase one circuit, and a comparison made in the secondary of each current transformer with a phase angle meter as shown in figure (g), to determine the phase angle is either in phase or out of phase. This same procedure could then be followed on phase one of other breakers in the scheme while still using breaker A as a reference. Then, of course, the other phases could be checked in a similar manner. In the case of bus differential voltage relay [figure (f)], voltage should be measured instead of currents.

As in other relay circuit testing, the advantage of secondary injection testing of bus differential relays is that it eliminates the need for a high current source. It does not check current transformer polarity. The object of secondary current injection testing in this application is mainly to establish that the phasing of the secondary circuits are correct, and that the relay are properly connected in the secondary circuit. The test is performed on a dead bus, by injecting a current, in the secondary wiring at the current transformer. This is repeated at each current transformer and measurement should be made at each of the three-phase relay locations to insure that the injected quantity appears only in the phase to which it is connected. Continuity of the neutral wire to the switchgear ground should be verified by injecting a current at each of the current transformer neutral terminals.

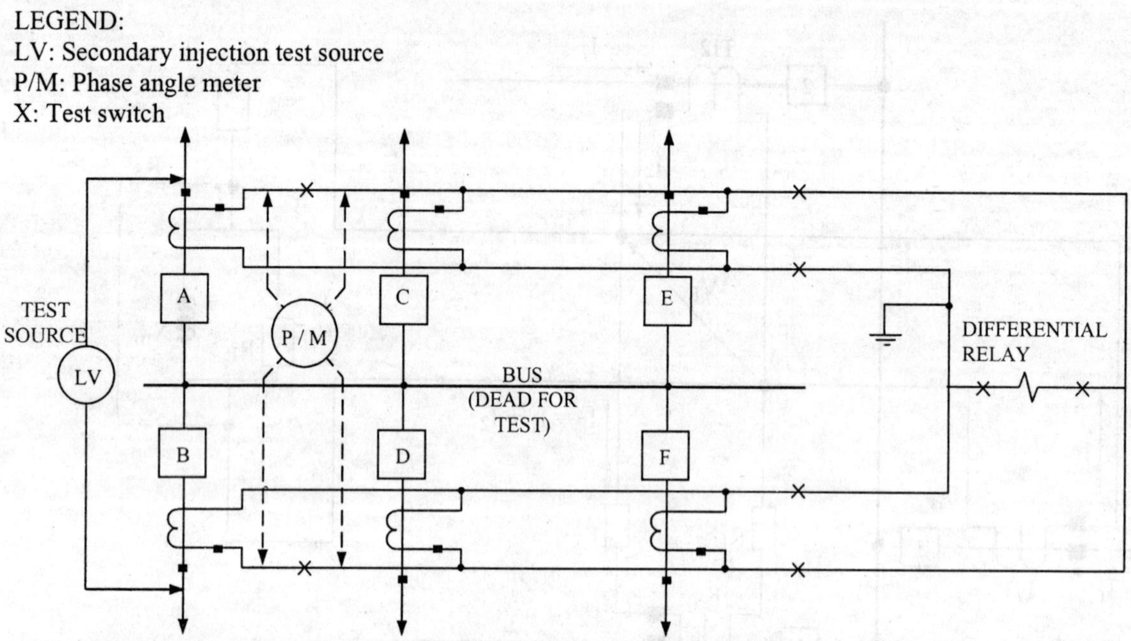

Fig. 8.16 (g): Primary current injection test on bus differential protection current transformer.

8.17 NUMERICAL BUS DIFFERENTIAL PROTECTION FOR HV/EHV SYSTEMS (87B).

The short-circuit protection on buses are characterized by the large number of current measuring inputs. The scope of bus bar protection ranges for each bay in conjunction with one and a half circuit breaker applications to large stations as discussed in figure 8.16 (c). With **Siemens 7UT612 model numerical relay** the current inputs may, also be used to achieve bus-bar protection system for up to 7 feeders. This bus-bar protection functions as a phase-selective protection with 1 or 5 A current transformers, whereby the protected phase is connected as shown in Figure 8.17 (a). All three-phases can therefore be protected by applying three relays. A single phase relaying system can be implemented by connecting the three-phase currents via a summation transformer as shown in Figure 8.17 (b).

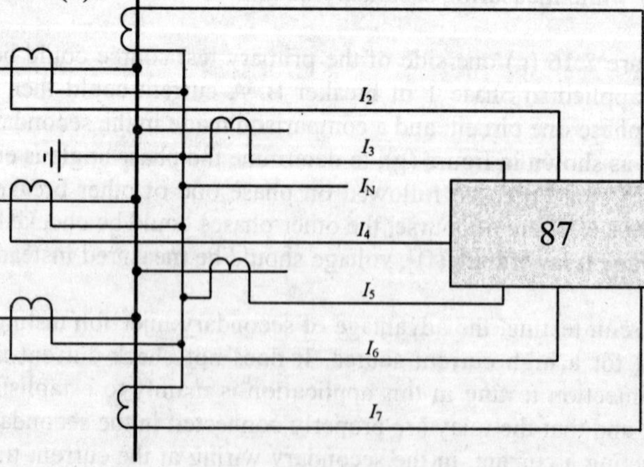

Fig. 8.17 (a): Single line diagram of typical numerical bus differential protection.

The selectivity of the protection can be improved by monitoring the current magnitude in all bays, and only releasing the differential protection trip command when the over-current condition is also met. The security against mal-operation resulting from failures in the current transformer secondary circuits can be improved in this manner. This over-current release may also be used to implement a breaker failure protection. Should the release signal not reset within a settable time, this indicates that a breaker failure condition is present, as the faulty area was not switched off by the bay circuit breaker. After expiry of the time delay the circuit breakers of the in-feeds to the buses may be tripped.

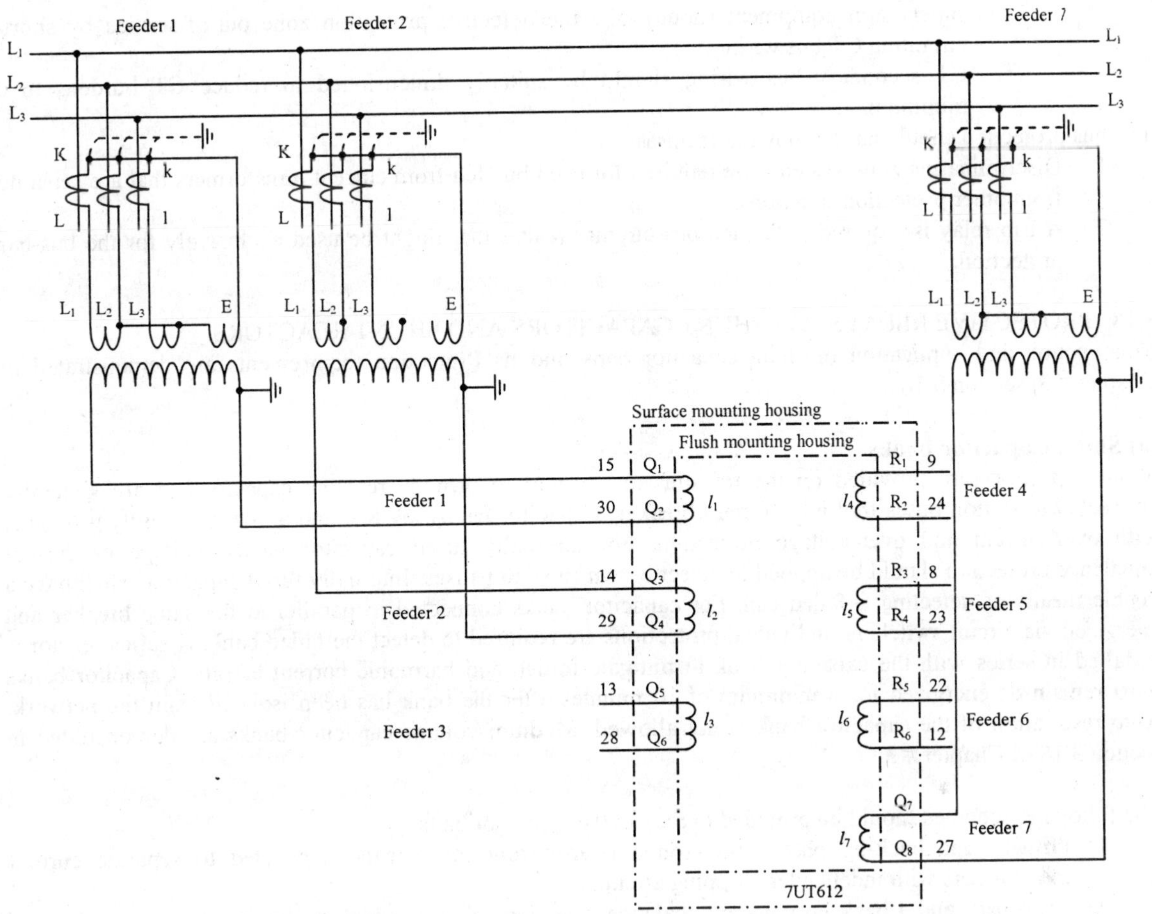

Fig 8.17 (b): Numerical bus differential protection by using summation CT (Courtesy, Siemens Ag).

General features of numerical high-speed bus differential relay:

1. Breaker failure logic, timers and output contacts.
2. Logic to provide a bus-bar protection check zone surrounding the concerned bus section.
3. Tripping circuitry and logic are provided so that only circuit breakers connected to the faulted bus-section are tripped.
4. Programs suitable for use on a personal computer, which can be used to interrogate the relay and communicate settings to the relay. Additional interfacing software and communication protocol's to allow the relay to be controlled and interrogated by a digital substation management system and /or SCADA (Supervisory control and data acquisition) system.
5. To record and retrieve a report of several past fault trips in order of their occurrence. Each report has to contain time, date, measured current etc.

Selection of current transformer for bus protection:

b) Multi-ratio current transformers are preferred. The working ratio can be selected on the basis of maximum load transfer. Un-used CT, secondary winding must be shorted by using suitable shorting links.

c) To cater for the low fault level conditions, the protection sensitivity, allowing for current transformer magnetizing current should not exceed 20% of the rated CT secondary current.

d) The protection stability limit shall not be less than switchgear fault rating.

e) Automatic and continuous supervision of current transformer circuits are provided to give an alarm when the out-of-balance current reaches an undesirable value. Operation of CT supervision equipment should take the defective protection zone out-of-service by short-circuiting CT bus wiring.

f) CT secondary bus wiring should be suitably dimensioned to reduce CT burdens to a minimum.

The bus protection should have following features.

1. Discriminating zone systems are required for each bus fed from current transformers that are separate from other protection functions.
2. A trip relay is required with each bus circuit breaker that might be used exclusively for the bus-bar protection.

8.18 PROTECTIVE RELAYS FOR SHUNT CAPACITORS AND SHUNT REACTORS.

Construction and application of shunt capacitor bank and its Protection requirements are demonstrated in Chapter # 3, section 3.18.

(a) Shunt Capacitor banks

Shunt capacitors are provided on the transmission system to provide reactive capacity and are generally connected to station buses through a circuit breaker. Capacitor banks, 69 KV and above are solidly grounded with over-current and over-voltage protection. For internally fused capacitor banks, voltage or current unbalance protection should be applied to detect blown capacitor fuses. Internally fused capacitors shall have a visible means of detecting a failed can. For capacitor banks connected in parallel to the same breaker and energized via circuit switchers, individual protections are required to detect the failed bank. A series reactor is installed in series with the capacitor bank to mitigate inrush and harmonic current effects. Capacitor banks must remain de-energized for a minimum of 10 minutes after the bank has been isolated from the network. Auto restoration of the capacitor bank is not allowed. Medium voltage capacitor banks are demonstrated in section 3.18 of Chapter # 3.

The following schemes should be provided to protect the capacitor bank:

(1) Primary and back-up phase and ground over-current relays each connected to separate current transformers with independent tripping circuits.

(2) A primary and a back-up voltage unbalance detection scheme, which will prevent the imposition of more than 110% of rated voltage on the individual capacitor cans in the event of multiple fuse blowing. Each scheme should be provided with an independent tripping circuit.

(b) Shunt reactor banks:

Construction and application of shunt reactors are demonstrated in Chapter # 4, section 4.13. Shunt reactors are used to provide inductive reactance to compensate for the effects of high charging current of long open-wire transmission lines and cables. Only oil immersed reactors (Single or three-phase) are used which are generally star-connected and solidly grounded. For reactor banks connected in parallel to the same breaker and energized via circuit switchers, individual protection is required to detect the faulted bank. Reactor banks are to be equipped with auto-isolation equipment to remove the reactor bank from service after a fault condition.

The following schemes should be provided to protect the shunt reactors:

(1) A primary current differential scheme.

(2) A back-up current scheme, preferably Buchholz relay or differential protection utilizing separate current transformers with independent tripping circuit.

(3) Over-temperature tripping device be provided if single phasing, which results in considerable heating, is possible.

<u>Isolation of a faulted shunt reactor tapped to a line</u>

Following schemes are used for isolating a faulted reactor tapped to a line:

(1) Direct transfer trip and a motor-operated disconnect switch to isolate the faulted reactor from the system. Once the motor operated disconnect opens to isolate the faulted reactor, the transmission line is capable of being restored.

(2) Two direct transfer trip schemes to trip the remote terminals and a motor-operated disconnect switch to isolate the faulted reactor. Once the reactor is isolated, the remote terminal is capable of being restored.

8.19 HIGH VOLTAGE DIRECT CURRENT SYSTEM PROTECTION.

HVDC protection shall be capable of protecting the HVDC station from the effects of faults occurring on the interconnected AC system, and protecting the interconnected AC system from faults occurring in the HVDC station zone of protection. HVDC system is demonstrated in section 4.21 to 4.23 of Chapter # 4.

Rectifier / Inverter: The protection applied to the HVDC equipment must mitigate against abnormal voltages and currents in the conversion equipment and the effects these voltages and currents have in the connected AC system. Faults and mis-operation of the DC equipment are isolated within the DC converter and control equipment and must not cause a disturbance on the connected AC system. That is, cascade tripping for DC faults or control malfunctions in the DC system must not occur.

Following relays are used for rectifier protection:

(1) Overload and short circuit protection: Inverse time / Very inverse time over-current relay.
(3) Short circuit protection: Instantaneous high set relay on AC breaker.
(4) Reverse protection on DC breaker to protect against backfire.
(5) Earth fault protection: Instantaneous restricted earth fault relay for rectifier transformers.
(6) Frame leakage protection: High resistance earth fault relay.

AC system and AC transmission lines: The AC system consists of all equipment connected to the AC system and operating with AC voltage. This includes the AC transmission lines emanating to the HVDC station, the converter-transformers. AC filters and interconnecting station bus bar. Protection applied to the AC side of the HVDC station must take in to account the harmonics generated as a result of the conversion process. Protection applied to the AC transmission lines must recognize that the converter station has no inertia, and the distance protection, the HVDC station is to be considered as a load. Therefore, line differential protection is usually applied to protect the connected AC transmission lines. Overreaching distance protection may be applied at the remote terminal set to look in to the converter transformer with a direct transfer trip scheme for the local breaker at the HVDC station.

Converter transformer: The converter transformer [refer figure 4.21 (c) of Chapter # 4] may be a three or four-winding design, depending on the HVDC station requirements. The two secondary windings are usually configured Star and Delta for converter connection as sketched in figure 2.2 (b) of Chapter # 2.. The fourth winding, the tertiary, connects the AC filter banks and any supporting reactor / capacitor banks. The converter transformer protection consists of the same protection as a step-down substation power transformer demonstrated in Chapter # 7. The protection application must take in to consideration the harmonic generated because of the conversion process, either inversion or rectification.

AC Filter banks: Modern HVDC stations employ 12-pulse converter technology as shown in figure 4.2 (b) of Chapter # 4.. Consequently, AC harmonics at frequencies of (12n +/- 1) times the fundamental frequency (50 or 60 Hz.) are generated, where n is an integer. AC filter banks connected to the AC side of the converter station provide a means of sinking the harmonics produced during the conversion process and produce a portion of the reactive power required for the conversion process. Protection of the AC Filter bank is similar to the protection of the shunt capacitor banks described in section 8.18 of this chapter with the additional requirement that the protection must not constrain requirements of the station.

Dynamic over-voltage protection: Dynamic over-voltages occur during switching of the filter banks and shunt capacitor banks. In addition, the shunt connected capacitor banks can increase the remote end open circuit voltages. Over-voltage protection is required at both the HVDC station and the remote ends of the AC transmission lines connected to the HVDC station.

Breaker failure protection: Breaker failure protection could be provided for all HV and EHV breakers in the AC station (Refer Chapter # 7, section 7.11).

8.20 DIFFERENTIAL PROTECTION FOR HVDC TRANSMISSION LINES.

During transient phenomena, a very large charge or discharge current flows on the stray capacitance of the transmission line, especially in a High Voltage Direct Current cable transmission system. Figure 8.20 shows the single line diagram of a typical high-speed differential relay connection employed for HVDC transmission system. The relay eliminates the difficulty of distinguishing between internal and external fault that existed on traditional system,

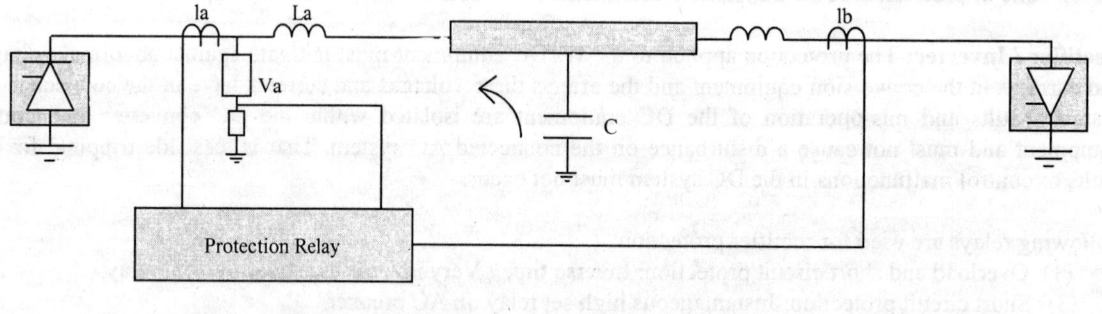

Fig. 8.20: Single line diagram showing differential protection for HVDC cable transmission system.

8.21 FAULT LOCATORS AND DISTURBANCE RECORDERS FOR TRANSMISSION LINES.

Digital fault recorders (DFR) are installed in each transmission line feeder to capture and analyze short transient events, longer-term disturbances, and harmonic records. The high speed, high resolution recording and flexible triggering modes make the DFR ideal for capturing all forms of line transients from conductor clashes, lightning strikes to spikes and sub-cycle distortions.

Function and application of fault locator:

Equipment is connected to the current and voltage circuits employed for the protection and started by the initiation of distance protection or the trip signal to the circuit breaker and measurement (Location of fault with ± 5% accuracy) should be completed before circuit breaker interrupter contacts part. The distance is indicated in digital form and remote transmission in analogue form. However, measurement should not be substantially, affected by the high fault resistance as well as mutual coupling between parallel double circuit lines. Measurement is made in rapid succession in the event of un-successful auto-re-closing of the circuit breaker. Reading will be available in the memory for a reasonable period of time after the occurrence of the fault. Figure 8.21 (a) shows the application diagram of a fault locator.

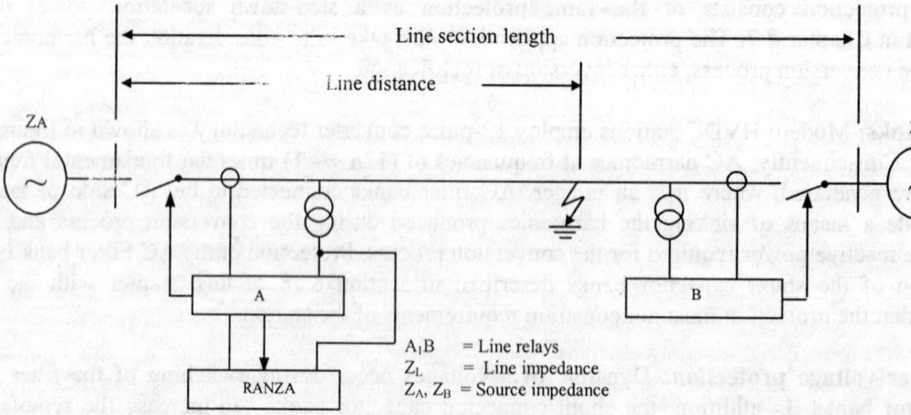

Fig. 8.21 (a): Application diagram of a fault locator.

Function and application of disturbance recorder:

Each feeder of HV/EHV transmission lines are monitored by a disturbance recorder to record graphically the currents and voltages during fault conditions/operation of protective relays. The DFR has provision for:

1. Channels for oscillographic printout and digital data output of recorded data for analysis.
2. Marker channels to record chronologically relay operations.
3. Alarm contacts to indicate, "disturbance recorder operating".
4. Push-button for initiating recording of currents and voltages.

5. Retention of fault information in memory.
6. Recording the events during autoreclosing process.
7. Recording the date and precise time of the occurrence of the fault to the nearest millisecond.

Features of digital fault recorder:

DFR is a fault locator cum disturbance recorder having following functions:

a) Transient fault recorder; post fault analysis to verify protection and circuit breaker operations, fault clearance times
b) Disturbance recorder / logger; extended logging for steady state values, harmonics, and flicker
c) Power quality monitor; voltage and frequency profiles, voltage dips and surges, loss of supply, harmonic content, flicker, voltage and current imbalances.
d) Fault locator; calculates distance to fault based on configurable line model
e) Real time monitor; view analog, digital inputs and computed values in near real time
f) On-line switchgear and circuit breaker monitor; used to identify optimum service time for switchgear operations and predictive maintenance on contact wear.

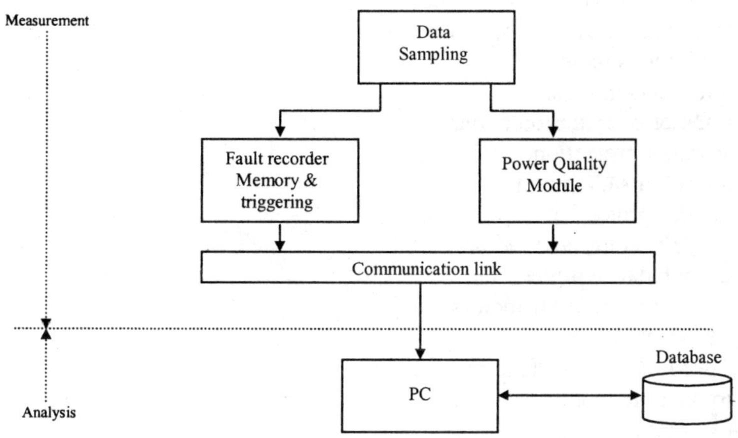

Fig. 8.21: (b): Synoptic diagram for power quality module

Power quality module:

Power quality module shown in Figure 8.21 (b) is implemented as a measurement module embedded in the digital fault recorder (DFR) to measure power quality parameters according to IEC 61000-4. A database stores power quality parameters for the entire network and a software package for post-processing the parameters and verifying the compliance against voltage characteristics or/and compatibility levels. Data comparison is achieved while preserving essential information for the analysis package. Data are stored in the PQ module on a daily basis.

The second task of the PQ module is to log events. When an event occurs, the module generates a concise report with critical data characterizing the event. It is also able to start the DFR recording function providing the end user with the complete waveform acquired at full speed. The module can accumulate data locally. The host polls regularly the module through the DFR communication link, downloads available data and stores it in the database. With the analysis package, the user is able to select nodes in the network according to various criteria. Parameters are represented as histograms, cumulated probability functions, point clouds, raw tables and waveforms for events.

CHAPTER # 9

MEDIUM VOLTAGE MOTORS AND MOTOR PROTECTION RELAYS

CONTENTS:

9.1 MEDIUM VOLTAGE ASYNCHRONOUS MOTORS.

Electric motor is a device used to convert electrical energy in to mechanical energy. There are two different types of motors; (1) synchronous motor; (2) Asynchronous motor. Synchronous motor runs at the same speed of the rotating magnetic field (synchronous speed), whereas asynchronous motor (induction motor) runs at a speed slightly below the synchronous speed because of the slip. Slip in an induction motor is the difference of speed between the rotating magnetic field and the speed of a rotor in an induction motor.

Electric motor components and parts should comply with IEC standard specification 60034, and dimensions in accordance with IEC 72 or NEMA standard. Medium voltage motors are usually manufactured in the voltage range of 3.3 KV to 13.8 KV, 50 or 60 hertz, up to several hundreds of megowatt ranges. These motors are often called as high voltage motor. Degree-of-protection of enclosures are defined in IEC 34 –5, and mounting arrangements are given in IEC 34-7. The terminal boxes shall be suitable for industrial use and include phase insulated, phase segregated and phase separated fault relief type. Method of cooling is described in IEC 34 –6. Asynchronous motors are classified in to (1) Cage motor (2) Wound rotor motor (Slip-ring motor)

Electric motors provide motive power to a wide variety of domestic and industrial machinery. Their versatility, reliability, and economy cannot be equaled by, any other form of drive. Successful motor application depends upon selecting a type of motor, which satisfies the kinetic requirements of the driven machinery. Various types of enclosures (housing) have been standardized by, the National Electrical Manufactures Association (NEMA). The following are the standard enclosure types.

(a) Open Type enclosures: Drip proof, Splash proof, Guarded, Semi-guarded, Drip-proof fully guarded, Externally ventilated, Pipe ventilated, Weather protected type 1 and 2.

(b) Totally enclosed type enclosures: Non ventilated, Fan-cooled, Explosion proof, Dust-ignition proof, Waterproof, Water cooled, Water and air cooled, Air-to-air-cooled, Pipe ventilated, Guarded, and encapsulated.

Figure 9.1 (a) shows classification of AC motors based on its construction and/or applications.

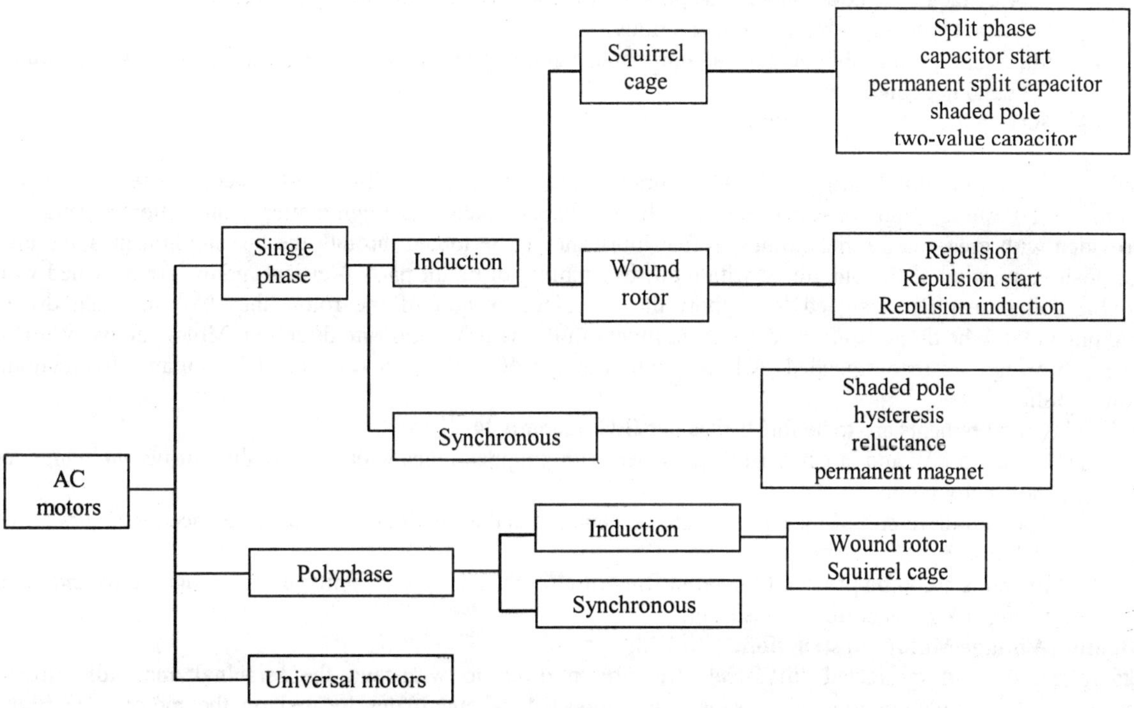

Fig. 9.1 (a): Classification of low voltage and medium voltage AC motors.

Design and operating conditions:

Motor must have sufficient torque for starting and accelerating the maximum load when 80% motor rated voltage is applied to the motor terminals without exceeding the thermal limit of the motor. The permissive locked rotor time shall be greater than the accelerating time, with the motor loaded at 80% rated voltage. Breakdown torque should be adequate to maintain motor operation during a voltage dip of 75% of rated voltage for a minimum period of 60 seconds at rated load and efficiency i.e. a minimum of 180% of full load torque. Locked rotor current, in percent of full load current, should not exceed 650%.

Preferred insulation of winding on motor should be of Class F materials however, the temperature should not exceed Class B limit during normal operation. Winding impregnation by, immersion is preferred. When curing, the motor shall be turned continuously to prevent the formation of voids. The winding shall be treated for fungus and abrasion-resistance. Winding should successfully withstand the conditions existing (meteorological, seismic and environmental) or where, there are atmospheres containing heat, moisture, oil, abrasive dusts, weak acid and sulphur fumes etc. Rated continuous operation (at 80 to 110% voltage) in a 40°C ambient temperature with a motor winding temperature rise by resistance not exceeding 80°C.

Totally enclosed fan cooled motor or totally enclosed non-ventilated motors with degree of protection IP 54 for indoor application and IP55 for outdoor application are suitable for general use. Motors located in hazardous areas are explosion proof manufactured in accordance with IEC 79. Explosion proof motors are provided with drainage to prevent accumulation of water due to condensation and motors 30 KW and above have anti-condensation heaters. Enclosure to the terminal leads for all types of motors are made of cast iron or steel box, having waterproof construction conforming to IP55. Removable gland plates (bolted and gasketed) are provided with cable gland for cable entry. For medium voltage motors leads from motor space heaters, vibration detectors, and stator temperature detectors are brought out in to another marshalling box and provided with grounding terminals for instrument cable shield grounding. Motor leads are permanently marked with terminal arrangements and motor phase identification in alphanumeric designations. Terminal markings of the main cable connections and the arrow showing the direction of rotation of the motor must be marked in accordance with IEC 34-8. Nameplate shall include all motor data required by IEC 34 with following additional information for medium voltage motors.

(1) Service factor includes rated Horse power, voltage, full load current, insulation class etc.
(2) Lubricant type and lubrication instructions.
(3) Maximum permissible number of starts and required cooling period when the motor is started under cold and hot conditions.
(4) Service life: Minimum 30 years.

Ball or roller antifriction bearings (150,000 hours life in accordance with ISO R-281) shall be used (for motors up to 500 HP ratings) and are sealed in dust tight housings to exclude foreign matter. Antifriction bearings are provided with grease and relief fittings so that lubricant can be forced through the bearing housings and also for positive purging of the old grease without disassembling of motor parts. Vertical motors are provided with double roller bearings designed to support the combined weight of the rotor, the shaft mounted driven equipment, and the thrust from the driven equipment in the same or opposite direction. Motors above 500 HP, sleeve bearings are recommended. All AC motors above 500 HP (375 KW) shall be suitable for medium voltage range.

Following requirements are to be fulfilled as per IEC standard 34.

(1) Motors 5 KW and larger must be provided with 2 tapped holes with bolt suitable for two-hole lugs for motor grounding.
(2) The non-drive end of the shaft should be centered and accessible for measuring speed with a portable tachometer.
(3) Eyebolts are to be provided for safe lifting of motors. The screws, bolts, nuts, springs, studs and other fittings are to be corrosion-resistant.

Medium Voltage Motor construction:

Stator frame is of fabricated stiff steel structure in order to withstand the torsional and radial forces encountered in induction motors. Bearings are supported by end plates located on the motor. The fixing positions of the stator shell are optimized to provide maximum support stiffness to accommodate the static and dynamic loads generated during operation of the motor. Bearing selection depends on the shaft speed, bearing loading, required torque transmission etc. All bearings are insulated to eliminate the flow of shaft current. Bearings are of either, grease lubricated, anti-friction rolling element or lubricated journal bearings. The roller bearing would be fitted at the drive end, the ball bearing at the non-drive end. As far as the sleeve bearings are concerned, they can be either self-contained ring lubricated type or forced lubricated type. The lubricating system incorporates a large capacity, finned surface oil reservoir, single ring lubrication and a spherically seated bearing bush.

Stator core is built up from laminations of high permeability, low loss sheet steel, varnished on both sides, rebuilt on a mandrel and then welded to steel members to form a rugged unit, or built in to the fabricated stator frame. High voltage coils are formed in a diamond shape using rectangular copper strips, pre-insulated with enamel, and glass covering. Main insulations provided by mica paper/glass tapes applied as a number of half lapped layers. The coils are fitted in to the stator core (slots), which are then closed with non-magnetic wedges. The end windings are securely lashed and braced with a glass fiber cord to resist short circuit forces arising, and supported with spacers and sometimes with rings made of insulated materials. After the impregnation and baking process, the whole unit forms rigidly supported, fully consolidated, void-free winding. All the high voltage insulation materials shall be Class F conforming to IEC 34 (140°C).

Rotor core is built up from laminations of similar quality as those used for the stator. Core is shrink-fit on a large size shaft, keyed to it and clamped between two end plates to form a rigid assembly. Cage type rotors have electrolytic tough pitch copper bars brazed to the short circuit end rings. The bars are tightly fit in the slots, so that there is no possibility of bar vibration. Rotor windings of wound rotor motors are insulated with class F materials and lap or wave windings (copper bar) are employed. The collector rings of slip-ring motors are of stainless steel, (the surface is centrally grooved to give improved brush performance) and located in a separate compartment outside the drive end bearing. Collector rings (slip rings) are shrink-mounted on a steel hub having fiberglass filled resin. Brush holders are constructed from extruded brass sections, and are mounted on insulated steel spindles carried on a fabricated steel bracket. Springs applying the pressure to the brushes are of the constant tension type eliminating the need to adjust with brush-gear wear. Figure 9.1(b) shows the overview of a complete frameless motor assembly includes rotor, stator, and bearings.

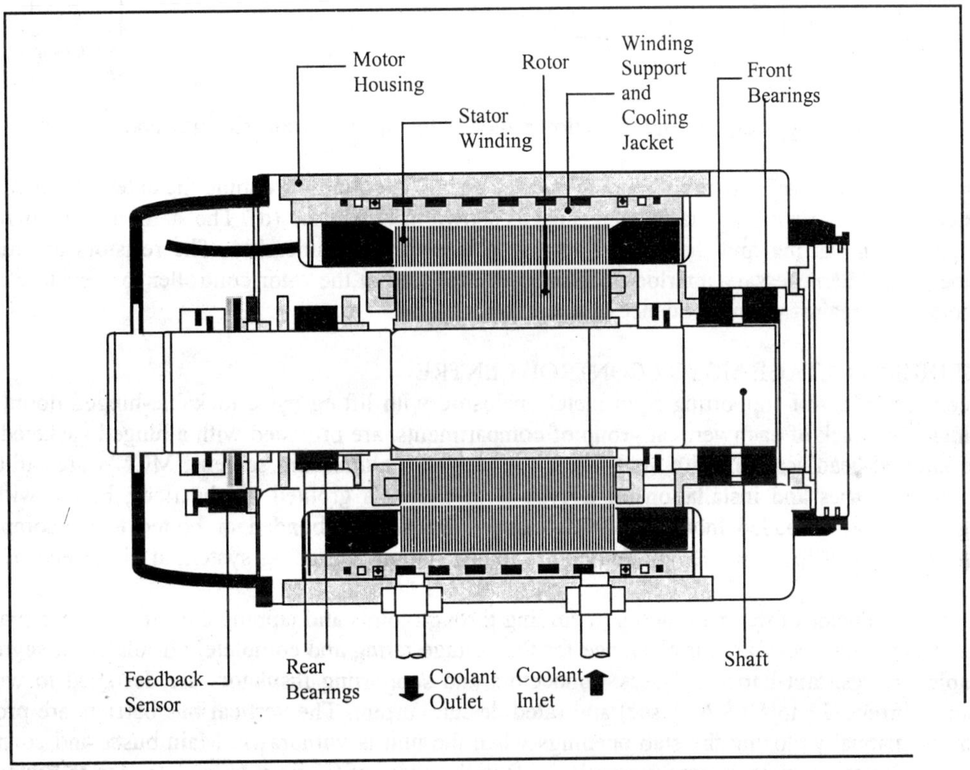

Fig. 9.1 (b): Overview of a frameless motor assembly consists stator, rotor and bearings.

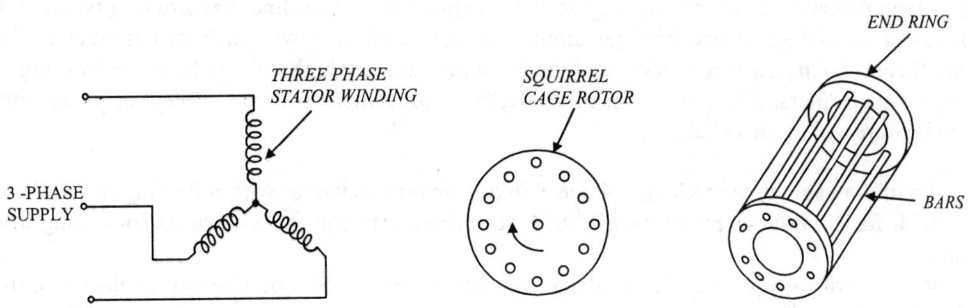

Fig. 9.1 (c): Typical squirrel cage induction motor stator and cage rotor.

Figure 9.1 (c) represents stator and rotor of a typical squirrel cage induction motor. In an induction motor the rotor must have some "slip". The rotor speed must be less than, or lag behind that of the rotating stator flux in order for current to be induced in to the rotor. If an induction motor rotor were to achieve synchronous speed, no lines of force would cut through the rotor, so no current would be induced in the rotor and no torque would be developed.

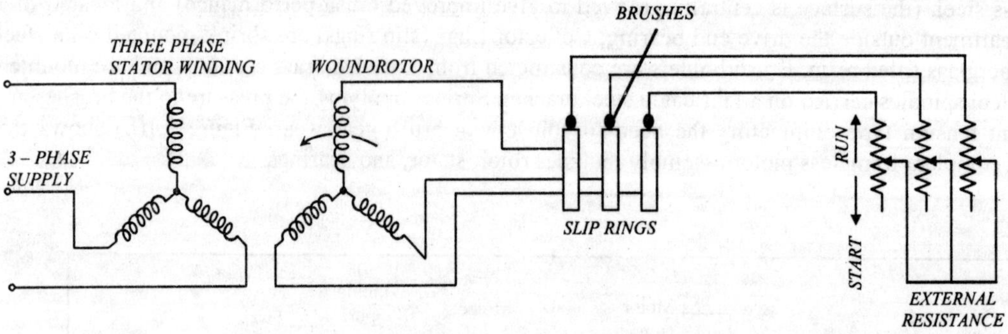

Fig. 9.1 (d): Typical slip ring induction motor stator, wound rotor, slip ring and resistance.

The slip ring motor is well suited for smooth starting drives by suitably stepping the external starting resistance connected to the rotor winding via the slip rings as shown in Figure 9.1 (d). The stator as well as rotor current is limited during starting and the starting torque is increased considerably. The resistors are made of fine nichrome wire. The necessary interlock contacts are provided in the rotor controller to prevent closing of the stator contactor, against wrong sequence of operation.

9.2 MEDIUM VOLTAGE MOTOR CONTROL CENTRE.

MCC consists of a self-supporting rigid metal enclosure with lifting eyes, lockable-hinged doors with piano type hings. The back of each vertical group of compartments, are provided with a hinged gasketed door (with captive knurled-head screws) with ventilation covered with aluminium screens. MCC's are built for top or bottom cable entries and installation on U type steel channels grouted on the floor, bolted with T shaped (sliding type) spring loaded mounting bolts. Copper ground bus bonded or bolted to all compartments is provided throughout the panel length and connected to station grounding system at either end of the ground bus.

Each phase conductor of the main buses (including through joints and tapping connections) are spaced at such intervals to give the necessary air clearance for the voltage rating and completely insulated or segregated with removable fire resistant barriers. Buses, connectors and supporting insulators are designed to withstand the short time current (25 to 50 KA, 1 sec) and rated design current. The vertical bus barriers are provided with shutters for manually closing the stab openings when the unit is withdrawn. Main buses and connections are marked to indicate the phase arrangements R, Y, B in the order of (a) front to back (b) top to bottom (c) left to right as viewed from the switching device. Incoming feeders have a circuit breaker conforming to IEC 947-2 (Standard ratings 400, 630, 800, 1200, 1600, 2000, 2500, 3000 A depending on design rating) with inverse time overload and instantaneous over current trip. Figure 9.2 (a) shows the single line diagram of a typical 6.6 KV Motor control center consisting of one incomer circuit breaker panel and two numbers outgoing feeder panels and one spare feeder. Each outgoing feeder has high breaking capacity high voltage fuses conforming to IEC 60282-1, voltage transformers, SF6 gas insulated contactors and numerical motor protection relay unit, high voltage neon indicators and earth switches.

MCC unit consists of withdrawable type medium voltage SF6 or Vacuum contactor with following interlocks:

(1) Pressure switch for continuous monitoring of SF6 gas pressure to trip the SF6 contactor during low gas pressure.
(2) High voltage, fuse with striker pin and auxiliary contacts to trip the SF6 or Vacuum contactor in the event of fuse blowing.
(3) Mechanical interlocking of the SF6 or Vacuum contactor to prevent racking in or out with contactor energized or closed.

Contactor is a magnetically operated switching device repeatedly establishing and interrupting an electric power circuit. Magnetic contactor is capable of making, carrying and breaking electric current under normal and overload conditions. Medium voltage three-phase contactors comply with IEC 947-4, are suitable for direct on line starting (Utilization category AC3) of electric motors. . Medium voltage contactors are fitted with arc shields and electromagnetic operating mechanism (electrically held-in or mechanically latched types) to hold the contactor closed without requiring a continuous power supply.

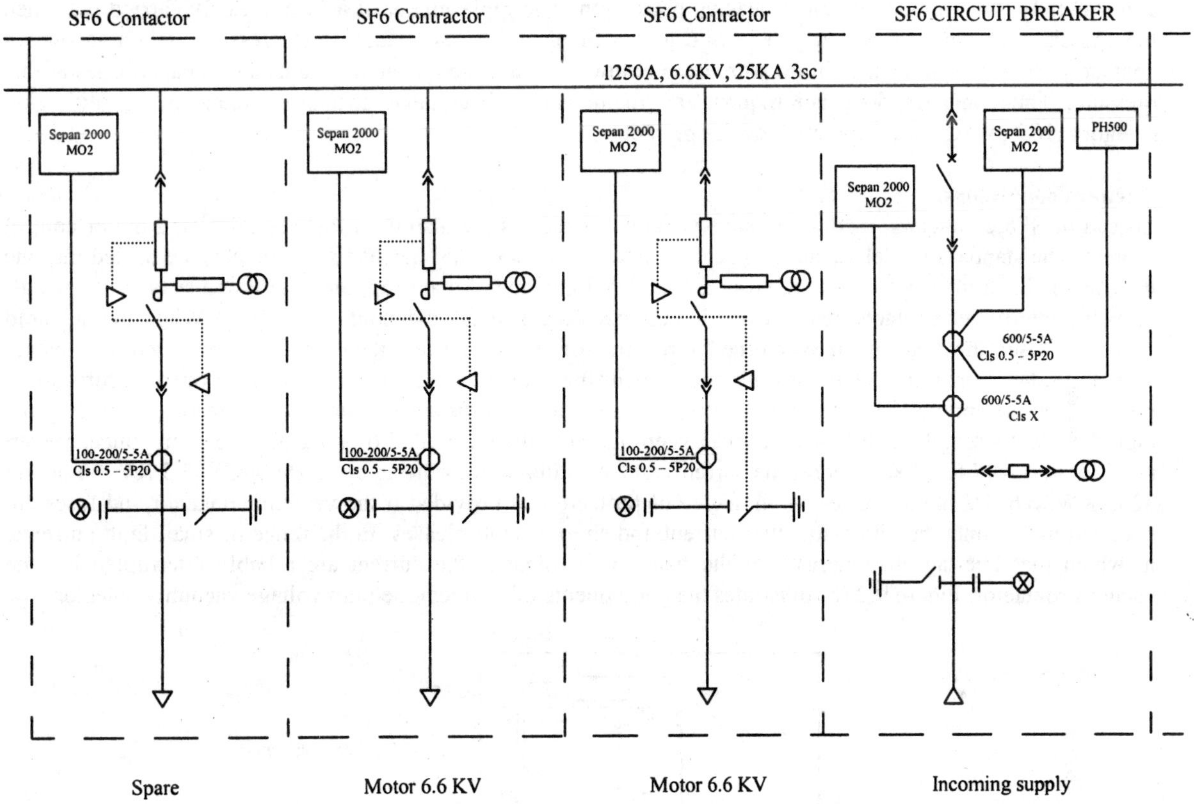

FIG. 9.2 (a): Single line diagram of a typical 6.6 KV motor control center

Maximum switchable power for 400ampere 3.3 KV to 6.6 KV, range withdrawable type SF6 or Vacuum contactor is listed in Table 9.2 (1) below with the assumptions that starting time <10 seconds and starts per hour ⊆ 3 according to IEC 60644.

Table 9.2 (1): Maximum permissible HP loads on 400 A, MV contactor at different voltage levels.

Operating voltage	DOL starting motor HP/KW with 315 A fuse	Transformer load with 315A fuse	Capacitor rating with 315A fuse
3.3 KV	1500HP/1170 KW	1250 KVA	1000 KVAR
4.16 KV	2000HP/1480 KW	1500 KVA	1260 KVAR
5.0 KV	2400HP/1780 KW	1750 KVA	1520 KVAR
5.5 KV	2625HP/1960 KW	2000 KVA	1670 KVAR
6.0 KV	2850HP/2130 KW	2250 KVA	1820 KVAR
6.6 KV	3150HP/2350 KW	2250 KVA	2000 KVAR

When used with 7.2 KV or 12 KV Motor control centers, operating current of 400 ampere contactor is 250 amps and 200 amps respectively, with short time withstand current 50 KA rms / 125 KA peak. For large motors, circuit breakers are used for DOL starting of motors. Contactor differs from a circuit breaker in that it will withstand a very high number of operations (300,000 or more compared to 100,000 for a circuit breaker), has generally lower continuous current ratings and has lower interrupting and making capacities. Contactor is not intended to interrupt fault current on its on and is therefore often used in association with fuses or a circuit breaker.

SF6 insulated contactors:

Medium voltage withdrawable SF6 contactors are equipped with a pressure switch an operation counter and a position indicator and H.V fuses. On the operation of any one fuse, the three poles of the contactor open automatically, thus providing single-phasing protection. The replacement of a fuse is easily carried out when the chassis is in removed position. The SF6 gas is filled at 2.5 bars gauge. The pressure switch actuates a contact in the event of accidental pressure drop below 1.5 bars; the contactor retains all its capabilities at this pressure. The contactor does not require any maintenance. The rated switching frequency to utilization category AC3 or AC4 is 12 operating cycles per hour.

Vacuum contactors:

Instead of SF6 contactors, medium voltage vacuum contactors are also used for manufacturing motor control centers. The standard model vacuum contactors have an AC solenoid mechanism. Contacts are sealed into the interrupter. Each interrupter is installed in an insulated housing. An appropriately designed system of springs, keep the interrupter contacts apart in the de-energized state of the solenoid mechanism. When the solenoid circuit is closed the mechanism overcome the reaction of the springs and the contacts are released for closing. The atmospheric pressure determines not only the closing force of the contacts but also the opening force to be provided by the springs. The low internal pressure and the short distance contract travel made possible by the high dielectric strength of the vacuum break keep the arc voltage small. 3.6 or 7.2 KV Vacuum contactors are rated for 400 A (7 KA 1 sec. short time current) and are suitable for starting up to 1600 KW, 3.3 KV motor and 3200 KW, 6.6 KV motor. A very high degree of protection is provided if the vacuum contactor and fuses are operated in conjunction with static over-current and short circuit releases. In the range of small fault currents, in which the time-lag characteristic of the fuses predominates, the current are reliably interrupted by, the vacuum contactor. Figure 9.2 (b) illustrates the components of a typical medium voltage vacuum contactor.

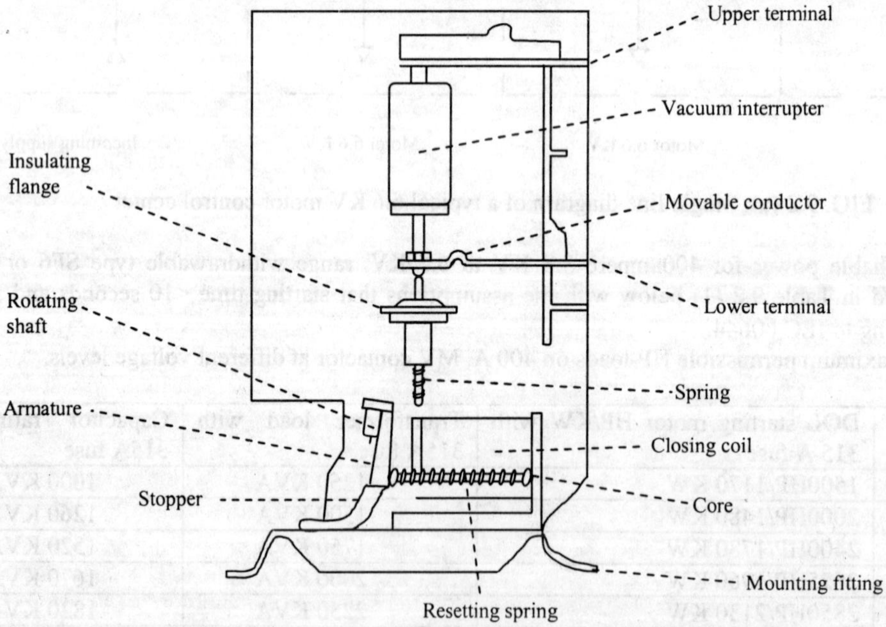

Fig. 9.2 (b): Medium voltage vacuum contactor.

Co-ordination of protection:

The interrupting capacities of the contactors exceed those specified by the relevant IEC standard. For motor starting duty, the contactor forms part of a coordinated protection scheme. Figure 9.2 (c) shows the characteristics (discrimination diagram) of a typical system including High-rupturing current (HRC) fuses (designed for motor protection duty) and an inverse definite minimum time thermal overload relay. [Schematic diagram is shown in Figure 9.2 (d)]. The illustration shows a 900 KW (1200 HP) 3.3 KV motor with a starting time of 12 seconds and a starting current equal to 6 times full load current.

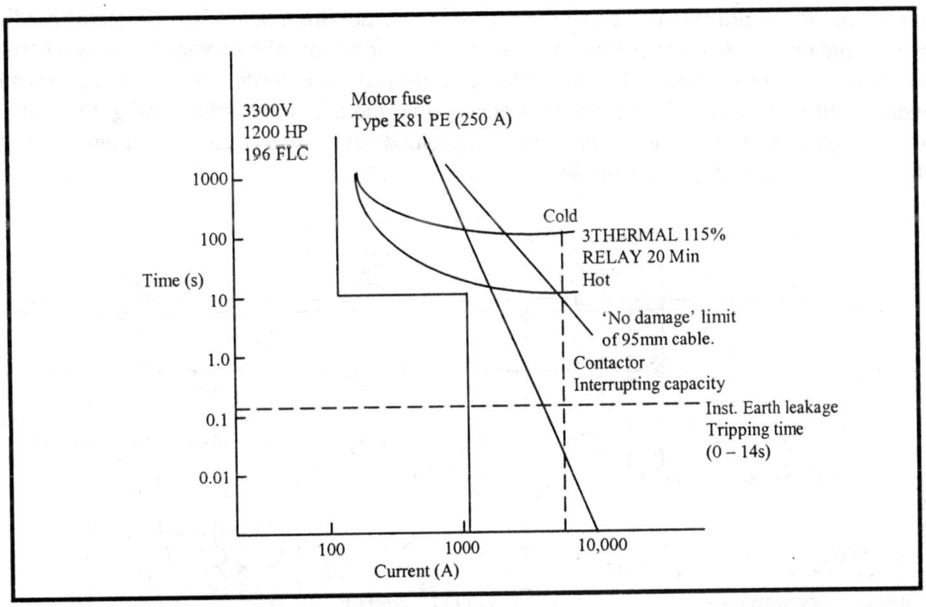

Fig. 9.2 (c): Composite motor protection discrimination diagram.

Motor protection fuses have the ability to withstand repeated starting surges without deterioration and have lower values of current and energy let through under maximum fault conditions when compared with high voltage fuses designed for distribution duty. Fuses incorporates a striker pin should be used. A mechanism associated with the fuses should give a tripping signal to the vacuum contactor in the event of any fuse element blowing. Thermal relay protects the motor against overload and fuses are mean for short circuit protection.

In the mechanical latching contactor, the shunt trip coil and operation counter is connected to DC supply. Whereas the latching coil and closing coil are connected through a rectifier (RD) feeding from AC low voltage supply. Motor protection relay or trip pushbutton can energize the shunt trip coil to de-energize the motor circuit. In the magnetic latching type contactor no shunt trip coil is required.

Medium voltage SF6 contactor uses rotating arc breaking in SF6 gas (Sulphur hexaflouride). A magnetic field causes the arc to rotate between the arcing contacts. The field is created by the passage of the arc through the blow out coil. The rotation movement cools the arc by forced convention. The arc rotation rate depends on the current to be broken. The energy required to extinguish the arc is supplied by the electrical system. At the beginning of the opening operation, the main contacts and arcing contacts are closed. The main circuit is interrupted by the separation of the main contacts. The arcing contacts separate shortly after the main contacts. At the current zero point, the gap between the two arcing rings recovers its original dielectric strength due to the intrinsic properties of SF6 gas.
Figure 9.2 (d) shows the power circuit and control circuit schematic diagram of a medium voltage withdrawable type contactor used in a motor control center. Contactor control circuitry consists of:

(a) Contactor to frame interlock switch: This contact closes when the contactor is in fully engaged position (connected position).
(b) Handle interlock switch: This contact is provided to prevent accidental withdrawal of the contactor when it is energized.
(c) Test run switch: This switch is provided for testing the contactor when the contactor is in the test position. During normal running the switch shall be in the "run" position.

Control relay CR1 is the starting relay, which energize when depressing the start pushbutton. When CR1 is energized, this relay energizes CR2 relay via the NC contacts of thermal overload relay (Device 49) and anti-single-phasing switch contact (operated through the striker pin of the HRC fuses), which in turn energizes

rectifier logic circuit and provide DC supply to the contactor holding-coil. When contactor holding-coil (M) is energized, the contactor closes and seal in coil is energized for sealing the contactor. By de-energizing the seal-in coil the contactor can be opened. The operation counter (ETM) records the number of start/stop operations of the contactor throughout its life. Red lamp indicates that the contactor is ON and green lamp indicates that the contactor is OFF. In large motors the thermal overload relay is replaced by numerical motor protection relays, which provides overall protection for the motor.

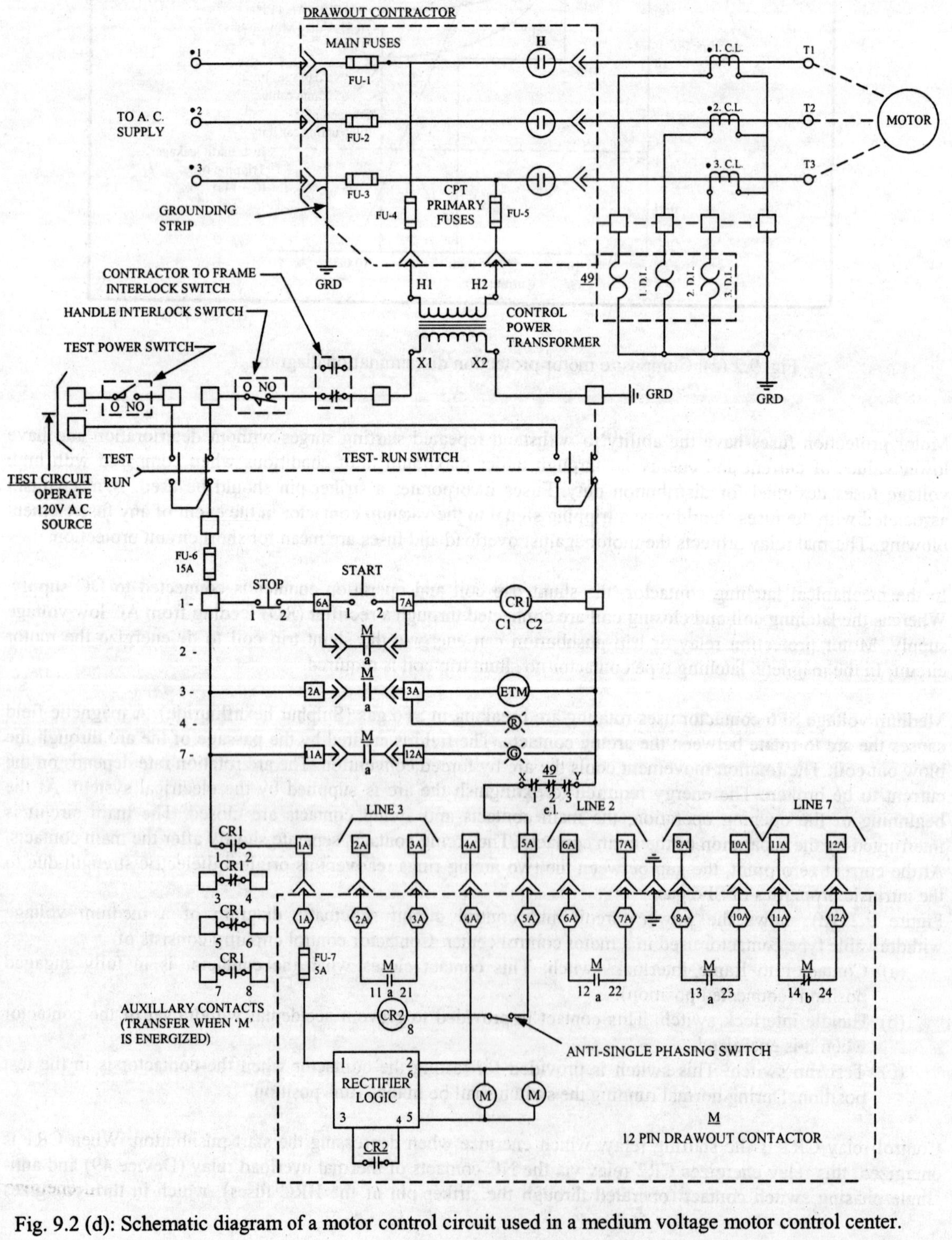

Fig. 9.2 (d): Schematic diagram of a motor control circuit used in a medium voltage motor control center.

Testing and commissioning of MCC:

Factory tests:

1) Continuity and polarity test on all coils and circuits. Check of electrical and mechanical interlocks.
2) Functional tests on all relays. Resistance measurements of all operating coils/tripping coils
3) Check successful operation of trip and close mechanism at specified minimum/maximum control voltage
4) Opening and closing speed of each medium voltage circuit breakers

Site tests: 1) Mechanical operation tests/confirmation of all fuse/breaker/contactor ratings
2) Wiring continuity checks of panel wiring diagram
3) Test charging of all circuits/functional testing of all equipments
4) Operation of all relays, instruments, alarms and trips including relay settings

Maintenance of motor control center:

(1) Enclosures in a marginal atmosphere should be inspected periodically for excessive dust and dirt accumulation as well as corrosive conditions. Periodic cleaning shall be performed for the housings. Paint may be applied in the corroded areas.
(2) Any loose bus bar or cable termination connections will cause overheating, that will lead to equipment failure. Ensure that all joints are properly tightened. Bus bar support insulators should be periodically checked against contamination, cracks and sign of arc tracking. Defective unit must be replaced.
(3) Excessive heat due to loose connections or loose contacts in a disconnector switch can lead to deterioration of the insulation and eventual failure of the device. Overheated conductors and carbonized insulation must be replaced.
(4) Badly worn or pitted contact assembly of the contactors must be replaced. Silver alloy or other metal contacts should be dressed with a fine file or other suitable abrasive, which does not shed abrasive particles.
(5) Protective relays and mechanical / electrical interlocks are to be checked periodically.

9.3 DIRECT-ON-LINE STARTING CONTROL FOR INDUCTION MOTOR.

Figure 9.3 (a) illustrates the power and protection circuit (wiring diagram) of a direct-on-line (DOL) medium voltage induction motor starter with numerical motor protection unit connected through conventional and toroidal current transformers. The circuit consists of high voltage fuses, vacuum or SF6 medium voltage contactor and capacitor for power factor correction, over-current relay, and ammeter with selecter switches.

Motor protection relay introduced in this section is (Schneider Electric, Sepam series 40) a microprocessor controlled numerical protection unit which is a common relay for all levels of voltages and suitable for feeder, motor, generator, transformer and bus protection. When used as a motor protection relay it provides protection against motor internal faults, system faults and load faults. In addition to that monitoring of motor starting conditions and protecting long motor feeders with high capacitance is an added advantage. Relay provides all the necessary electrical measurements and comprehensive power system diagnosis assistance.

Measurements:

- Phase and residual currents
- Phase-to-phase/phase to-neutral and residual voltages
- Frequency, active and reactive power and energy consumption.
- RTD input to measure motor winding temperature

System diagnosis:

- 16 seconds of fault recording configurable for multiple captures and pre-fault memory
- Detailed history of the last 200 alarms and storage of the last five trip reports.
- Current transformer and voltage transformer supervision
- Adoption of control functions by a Boolean logic editor
- Creation of custom alarm messages for each application, and/or in the user's language

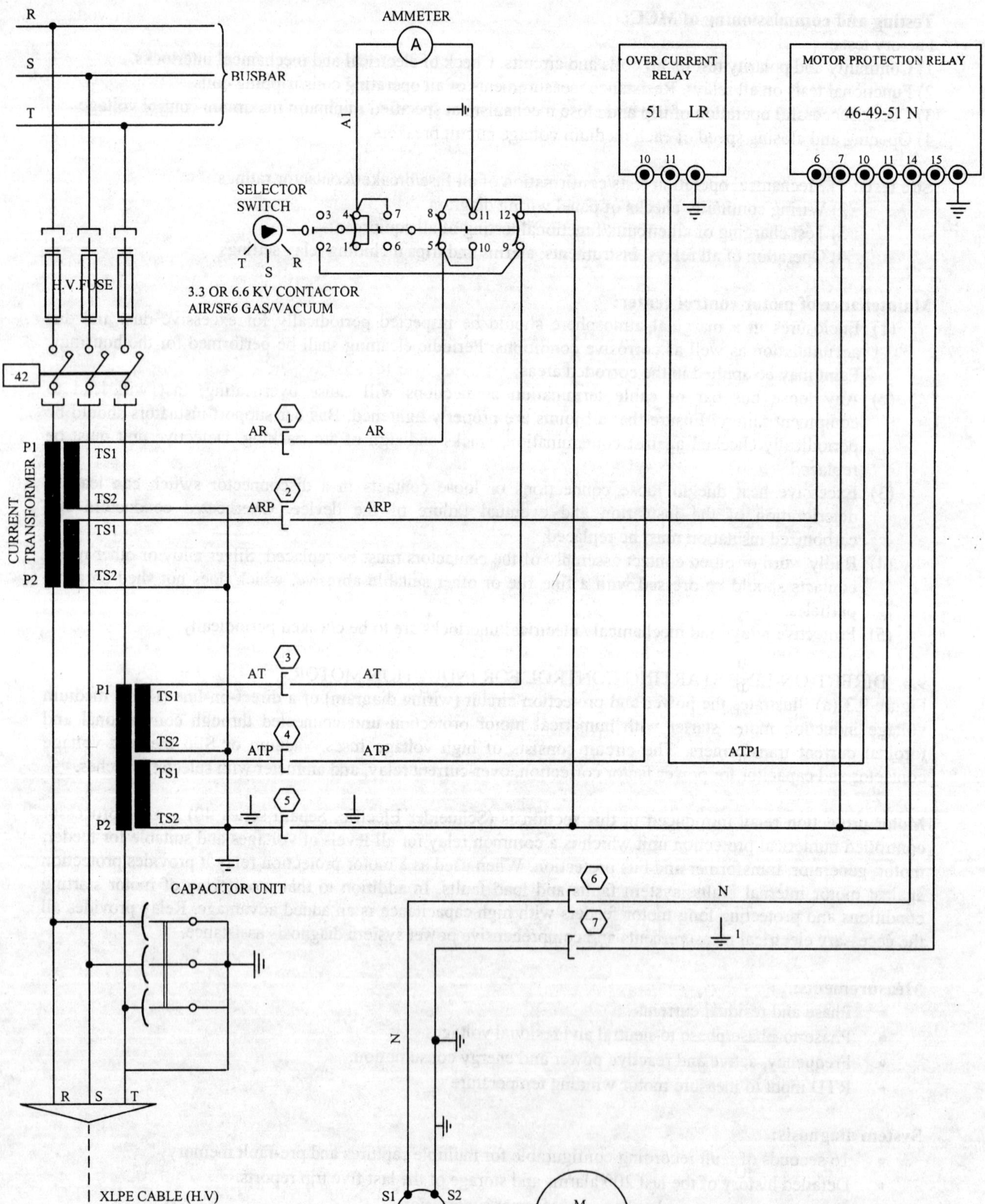

Fig. 9.3 (a): Power circuit wiring diagram of a high voltage contactor starter.

Figure 9.3 (b) illustrates the connection diagram of a numerical motor protection unit for medium voltage induction motor overall protection. The MPU provides following type of protections:

27D: Positive sequence under voltage protection
27/59: Under/over voltage protection
32P: Directional active power protection
37: Phase under current protection
38/49T: Bearing/winding temperature monitoring
40:Directional reactive power protection
46:Negative sequence/unbalance protection
47: Negative sequence/over voltage protection
48/51LR: Locked rotor/Excessive-starting time
50 BF: Breaker failure protection.
50/51: Instantaneous / Time over-current protection
50N/51N: Instantaneous/Time earth fault protection
50G/51G: Instantaneous/Time ground fault sensor
59N: Neutral voltage displacement protection
66: Start per hour monitoring
67N: Directional ground fault protection
81L: Low frequency protection

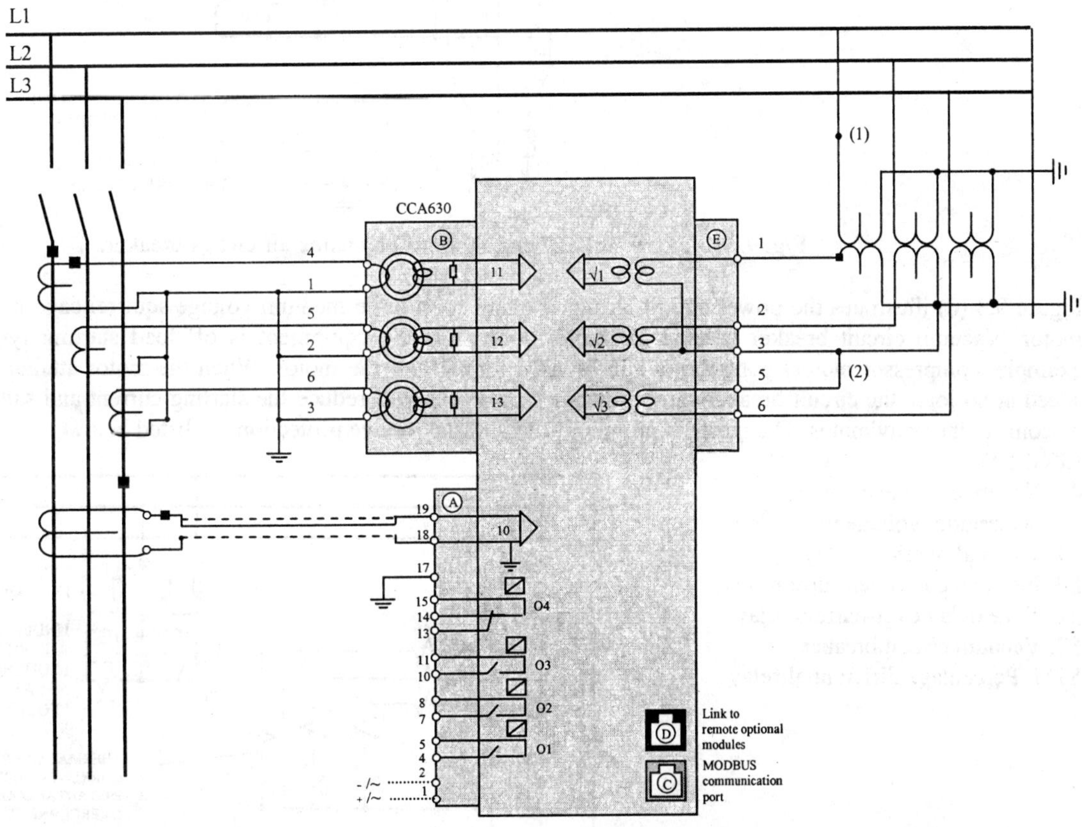

Fig. 9.3 (b): Connection diagram of a numerical motor protection unit (Courtesy Schneider Electric).

Features and benefits:

1. Self-diagnostics for protection assurance
2. Customizable protective settings
3. Graphic LED display
4. Base unit with various User/Machine interface levels (UMI)
5. MODBUS communications for remote management
6. Ethernet/MODBUS Gateways and Web server for automation or supervisory system
7. Power logic system associated with SMS management software

Motor control by using circuit breaker:

Figure 9.3 (c) illustrates the power circuit wiring-diagram for a large low voltage motor. Air circuit breaker is used for motor control.

LEGEND:
27: Under voltage relay
49: Thermal overload relay
50: Instantaneous over-current relay
50G: Earth fault relay
51: Time delay over-current relay
52: Air circuit breaker.

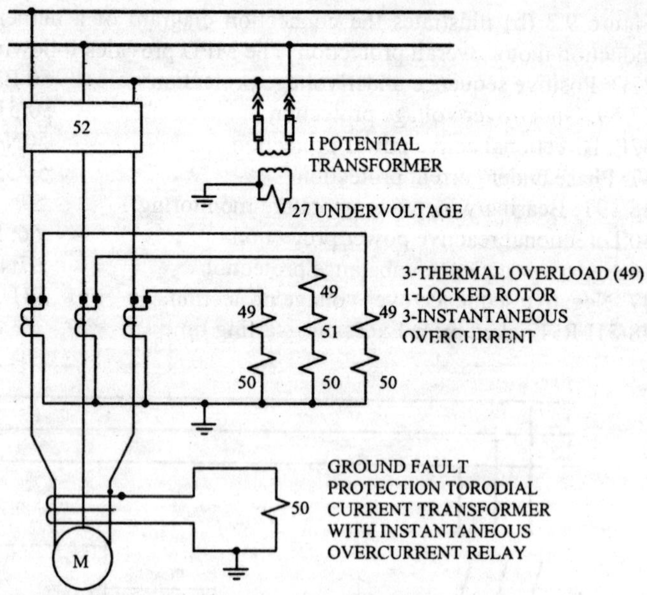

Fig. 9.3 (c): Low Voltage motor control by using air circuit breaker.

Figure 9.3 (d) illustrates the power circuit-wiring diagram for a large medium voltage squirrel cage induction motor. Vacuum circuit breaker is used for motor control. If the equipment is off load starting type, (for example, compressor motor) pony motor can be used for starting the motor. When the motor attains normal speed at no load, the circuit breaker can be switched on which will reduce the starting current and same time disconnect the pony motor. The motor is provided with comprehensive protections as listed below.

LEGEND:
47: Negative sequence relay with under voltage protection
49: Thermal overload relay
50: Instantaneous over-current relay
51: Time delay over-current relay
52: Vacuum circuit breaker
87M: Percentage differential relay

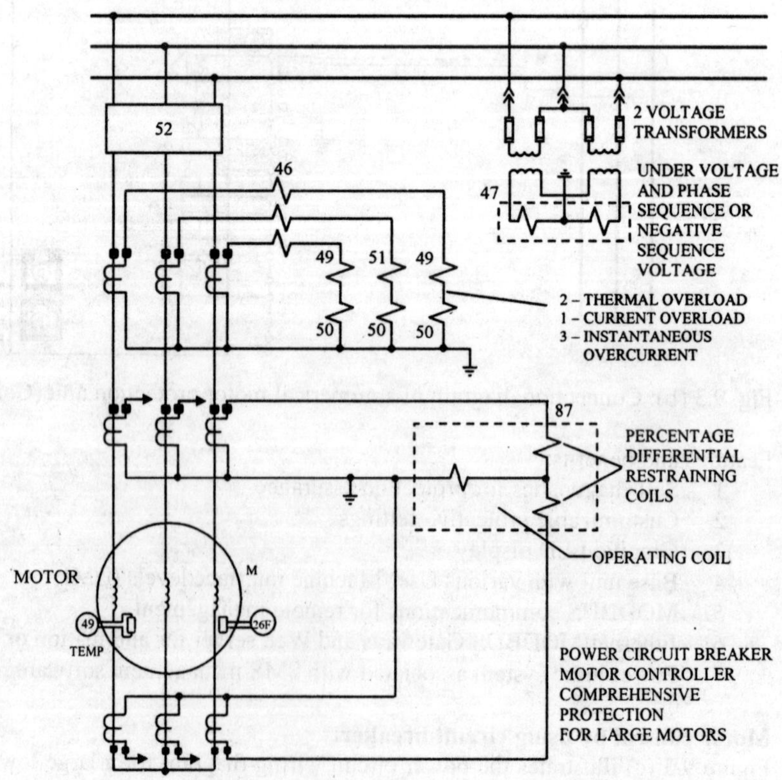

Fig. 9.3 (d): Medium voltage induction motor starting control using vacuum circuit breaker.

For low voltage slip ring induction motor control, the circuit shown in figure 8.3 (c) can be used by, incorporating suitable magnetic contactors in the rotor circuit with necessary interlocking for starting the motor with full resistance connected in the rotor and running with the rotor resistor short-circuited. Similarly, medium voltage slip ring motor can also be controlled by, incorporating suitable medium voltage vacuum contactors in the rotor circuit.

9.4 SELECTION OF RELAYS FOR INDUCTION MOTOR PROTECTION.

Protective relays for medium voltage induction motor protection are shown in the single line diagram depicted in Figure 9.4.

DEVICE NUMBERS:
12: Over-speed
38: Bearing temperature
47: Phase sequence and under-voltage relay
49: Thermal overload relay
50G: Instantaneous earth fault relay
51: IDMT over-current relay
81: Frequency relay
87M: Differential relay

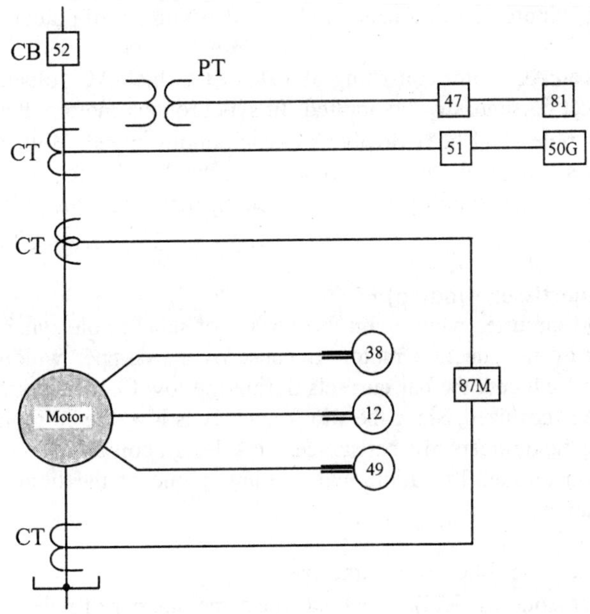

Fig 9.4: Single line diagram for medium voltage induction motor protection.

Protective relays recommended for high voltage induction motor (Cage or wound rotor) protection are listed below.

Table 9.4 (1): Protective relays recommended for protection of squirrel cage or slip ring induction motors.

Device #	Relay title	Relay application	Technical requirements
49	Thermal overload relay	Protection against overheating stator winding	Resistance-temperature detector embedded in the stator winding
47-27	Phase sequence and under voltage protection	Phase sequence and under voltage protection	Three-phase measurement
50BF	Breaker-failure protection	To trip all the relevant breakers	High set over-current relay
50G	Ground fault sensor	Ground fault protection of motor	Using core balance CT
51	IDMT phase over-current relay	Time over-current protection	Protection from overload
81	High/low-frequency relay	Protection against low/high frequency	Single-phase measurement
87M	Differential protection	Detect internal phase-to-phase fault and phase to earth fault	Protect stator winding
12	Over-speed protection	Protection against over-speed	Inductive-proximity probe
38	Bearing-temperature high	Monitor bearing temperature	Resistance-temper detector
39 VB	Vibration monitor	Monitoring bearing vibration	Vibration transducer

9.5 BRUSH TYPE / BRUSHLESS MEDIUM VOLTAGE SYNCHRONOUS MOTORS.

A synchronous motor is an AC rotating machine whose speed is proportional to the frequency. The speed under steady condition is called synchronous speed. The synchronous motor, always run on synchronous speed and has no slip like an induction motor. A synchronous motor has three-phase distributed windings on stator and DC excited field windings on rotor. Synchronous motors have equal number of poles for stator and rotor winding. Synchronous motors does not have any inherent starting torque. The motor is started by using a pony motor to bring the unloaded motor up to synchronous speed or for direct starting the motor is provided with damper windings to develop asynchronous torque. Large (several-hundred MVA) synchronous motors/generators for pumped storage plants are bring up to normal speed by using solid-state converters.
Synchronous speed, Ns = 120f/P rpm.
(rpm = Revolution per minute; f = Frequency in hertz; P = Number of poles)

Synchronous motor is an AC motor consisting of a stator to which AC voltage is applied and a rotor with field winding to which direct current must be applied. In synchronous motors, the stator rotating magnetic field is locked with the rotor poles and both revolve at synchronous speed. With increased load, the load angle δ between the rotor poles and revolving stator field increases, but the speed remains the synchronous speed. If the machine is loaded beyond stability limit, the locking between rotor poles and stator field is lost and the rotor falls out-of step.

Damper winding (Amortissor winding):
It is an additional short-circuited winding on the surface of salient pole synchronous machine similar to a part of squirrel cage rotor of an induction motor. Because of the damper winding, the amplitude of the natural frequency oscillation is reduced, the bar currents during the low frequency sweeping of the air-gap flux across the pole faces must be maximized. Since the slip frequency is low, the currents and the damper effectiveness is maximized by making the dampers low resistance. This design coincides with the requirement for low-starting torque and high pull-in torque. The additional starting torque of the field winding is superimposed on the torque of the damper alone.

Synchronous motors have the following characteristics:

- A wound rotor (rotating field), which has the same number of poles as the stator poles, and is supplied by an external source of direct current. Both brush type and brushless exciters are used to supply the DC field current to the rotor. The rotor current establishes a north/south magnetic pole relationship in the rotor poles enabling the rotor to "lock-in-step" with the rotating stator flux.
- The squirrel-cage Amortisseur winding in the rotor produces *starting torque and accelerating torque* to bring the synchronous motor up to speed.
- When the motor speed reaches approximately 97% of the rated speed, the DC field current is applied to the rotor producing *pull-in torque* and the rotor will pull-in step and " Synchronize" with the rotating flux field in the stator. The motor will run at synchronous speed and produce *synchronous torque.*
- After synchronization, the *pullout torque* cannot be exceeded or the motor will pull out-of-step. Occasionally, if the overload is momentary, the motor will "slip-a-pole" and resynchronize. Pullout protection must be provided otherwise the motor will run as an induction motor drawing high current with the possibility of severe motor damage.

Excitation system:
The rotor of a synchronous motor needs DC field current. The field current is supplied and controlled by the excitation system. Exciters are classified in to slip-ring types and brushless types. The slip-ring type exciter consists of a DC generator, whose output is fed in to the motor field winding through slip rings and stationary brushes as shown in Figure 9.5 (a). Exciter is a DC shunt-generator driven by an AC induction motor. The shunt field of the exciter is separately excited by the solid-state control. Some excitation controls has provision for manual adjustment of the field strength. Other systems automatically regulate the synchronous motor field in a closed loop configuration designed to maintain adequate field strength for varying loads or to maintain a constant power factor. The exciter shunt field is energized when the 52a auxiliary contact of the main breaker closes. In the illustrated-system, the exciter shunt field strength controls the DC output of the exciter, which is picked off by the commutator brushes, bused to the motor slip-ring brushes, and applied via the slip rings to the

main rotating field of the synchronous motor. The synchronous motor starts as an induction motor. When the motor achieves near synchronous speed, the motor field current is applied by the closure of the field application relay (Device # 56).

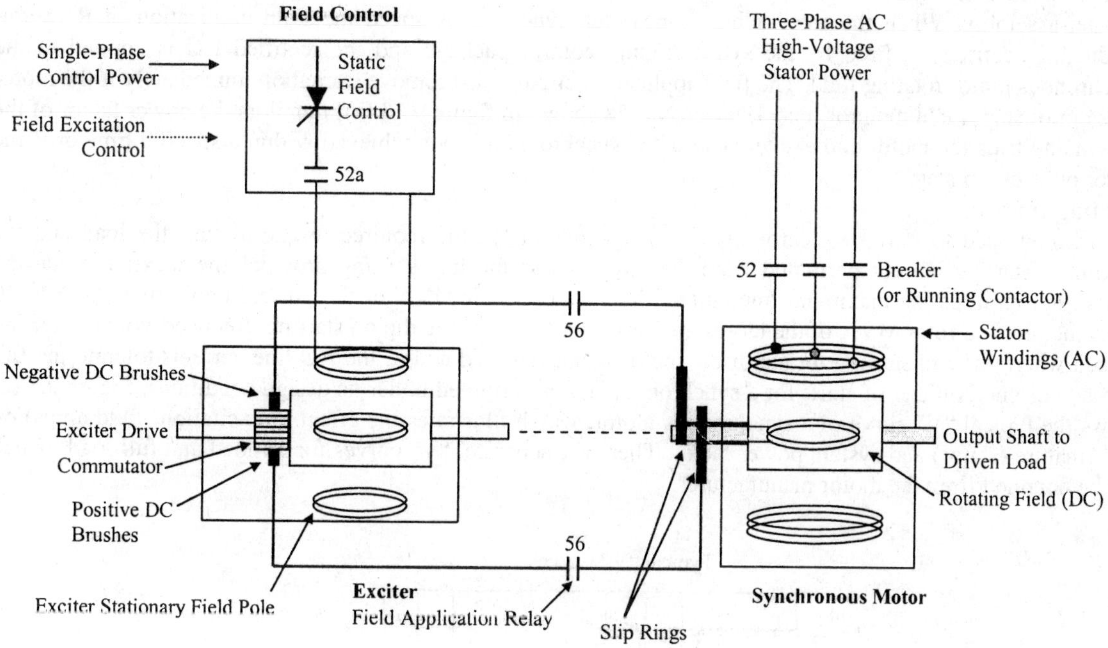

Fig. 9.5 (a): Circuit diagram of a brush type synchronous motor.

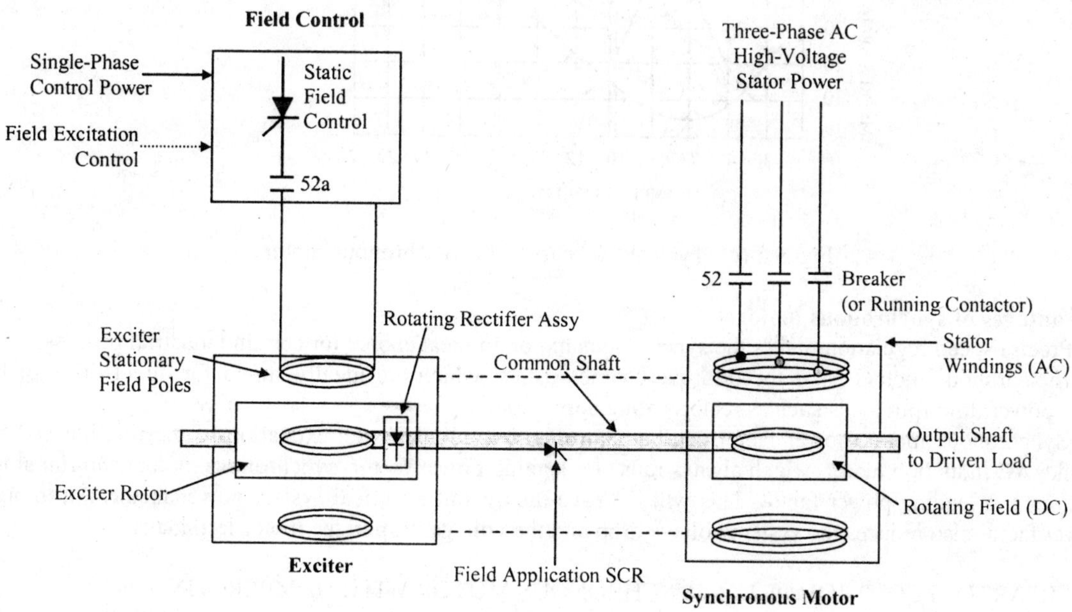

Fig. 9.5 (b): Circuit diagram of a brushless synchronous motor.

Figure 9.5 (b) shows the circuit diagram of a brushless synchronous motor. When the motor is started, by closing the circuit breaker, three-phase supply is applied to the stator windings. The brushless motor starts as an induction motor using an Amortisseur winding in the rotor. The breaker auxiliary NO contact also closes and applies DC output of the solid-state field control to the exciter stationary winding. A three-phase alternating current is induced in the exciter rotor windings and this induced voltage is rectified by the rotating-rectifier-assembly. When the rotor achieves near the synchronous speed the field application SCR (Semi-conducting rectifier) is fired by the synchronizing control package and the rectified DC is applied to the synchronous motor rotating field. The field application circuit must remove excitation immediately if the motor pulls out of step. Field monitor relay [Device No: 78 shown in figure 9.13 (a)] monitors the power factor of the system and trips the motor and exciter field off if synchronism is not achieved within a specific time or if the motor pulls out of step.

Starting control:

The method used to start a synchronous motor depends up on the required torque to start the load and the maximum starting current permitted from the line. Across the line starting provides the maximum starting torque, but requires the maximum line current. The short-circuit MVA of the power supply must be 6 to 10 times the blocked rotor MVA of the largest motor to limit the voltage dip on starting. Reduced-voltage starting is used where the full starting torque of the motor is not required and/or the AC line currents tolerate the full starting current. Number of starts for a synchronous motor is limited under its design conditions. Figure 9.5 (c) shows the typical "V" curve of a synchronous motor, which illustrates the effect of excitation (field amps) on the armature (stator) and system power factor. There are separate "V" curves for no-load and full-load, which can be obtained from the motor manufacturer.

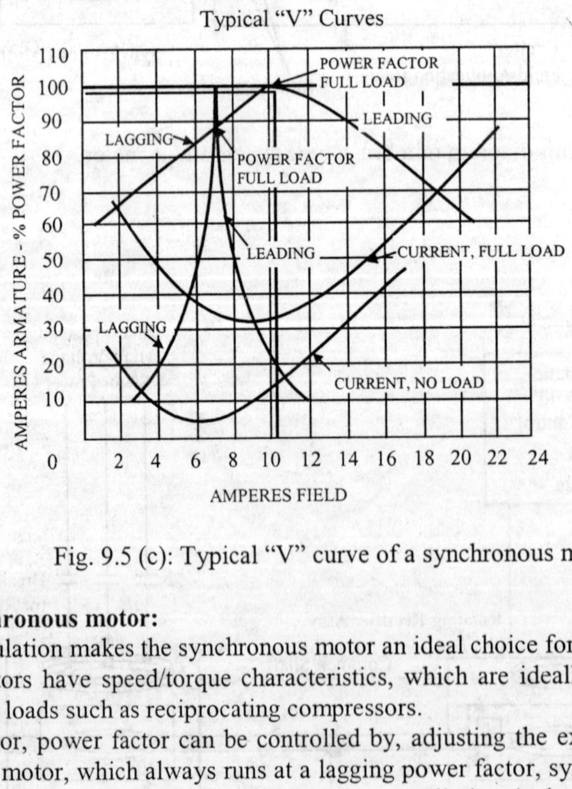

Fig. 9.5 (c): Typical "V" curve of a synchronous motor

Advantages of synchronous motor:

(1) Precise speed regulation makes the synchronous motor an ideal choice for certain industrial process.

(2) Synchronous motors have speed/torque characteristics, which are ideally suited for direct drive of large horsepower, low-rpm loads such as reciprocating compressors.

(3) Synchronous motor, power factor can be controlled by, adjusting the excitation of the rotating DC field. Unlike AC induction motor, which always runs at a lagging power factor, synchronous motors can run at unity or even at a leading power factor. This will improve the overall electrical system power factor. An improved power factor also reduces the system voltage drop and the voltage drop in the motor terminals.

9.6 STARTING CONTROL OF L.V SYNCHRONOUS MOTOR WITH DAMPER WINDING.

In case of induction start-synchronous run motor, the damper winding acts as a squirrel cage rotor and the motor starts on induction-principle. After reaching synchronous speed, the rotor poles locked with stator field and the machine is pulled in to synchronism. Figure 9.6 shows the starting circuit of a low voltage brush type synchronous motor with damper winding. An autotransformer is used for reduced voltage starting, which can be set to supply 50, 65, or 80% of line voltage to the motor on the initial starting stage. The corresponding torque is reduced to 25, 42 or 64 percentages. Reduced-voltage starter connects the motor to a reduced voltage for starting purpose and transfer to full voltage at a speed just below synchronism. This transfer may be controlled by a time delay relay. The field is energized either immediately before or after the full-voltage is applied. Sequence of operation for starting and running of the synchronous motor is listed below.

1. Main field winding is short-circuited.
2. Turn Start-Run switch in to the start position. Reduced voltage through autotransformer is applied to the motor.
3. Motor is started to run up as an induction motor because of the short-circuited damper winding in the rotor.
4. When the motor reaches a steady speed short circuit on the field winding is removed and a DC excitation is applied to the field winding.
5. At rated excitation voltage and rated speed the motor pulled in to synchronism.
6. Apply full supply voltage to the motor by turning the Start-Run switch in to run position.
7. Adjust the power factor to the desired value by varying the DC excitation.
8. By using magnetic contactors, the motor can be switched on automatically.

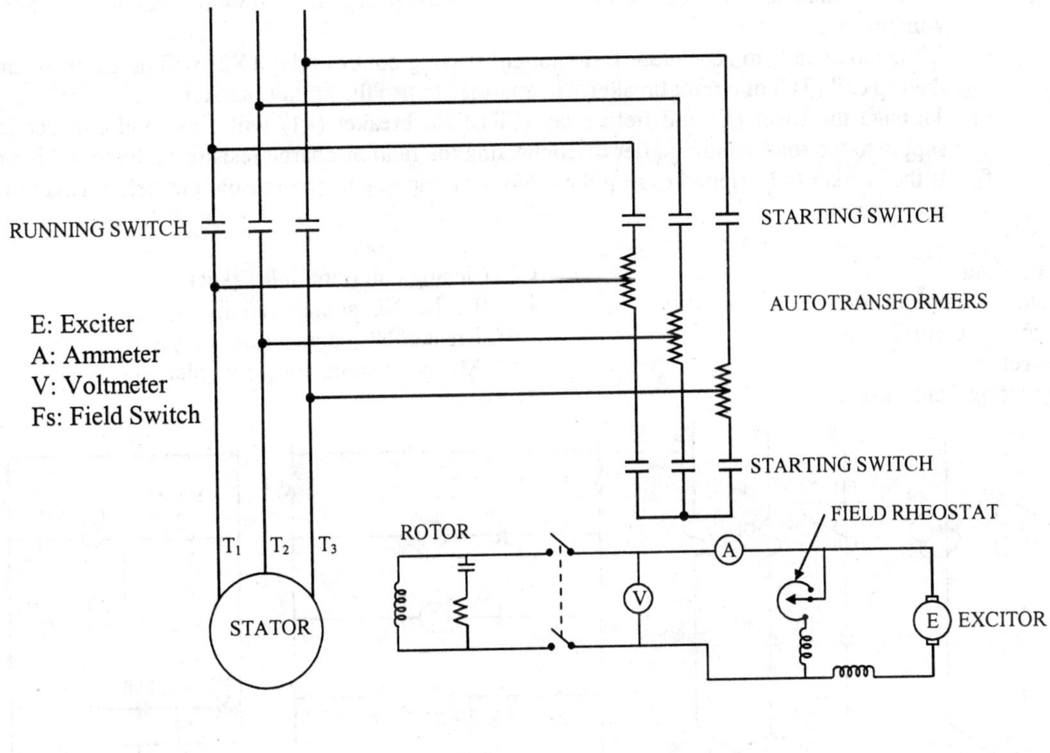

Fig. 9.6: Starting control circuit of low voltage brush type synchronous motor with damper winding.

9.7 STARTING CONTROL OF M.V SYNCHRONOUS MOTOR WITH DAMPER WINDING.

Controllers for synchronous motors have four components: (1) A three-pole starter for the AC stator circuit; (2) A contactor for automatic synchronizing device to control the DC field contactor; (3) A cage winding protective relay to open the AC circuit during failure of synchronizing. Synchronous motor is energized by, closing the main contactor. Rotor is energized by, the field contactor as the motor approaches synchronous speed. Two NO poles of the contactor make the connection to DC excitation, and one normally closed (NC) pole permits dissipation of induced field current during any period of non- synchronous operation. For smooth synchronization, two conditions determine the instant that the DC field is energized: (1) Near by 95% synchronous speed only the DC field is turned on; (2) The rotor poles must be lagging slightly behind stator poles. Synchronizing devices apply DC to the rotor field. Special relay systems can automatically energize the DC contactor when the speed and the rotor and stator poles are in proper relationship. These relays will open if the motor falls out of step because of a momentary overload or voltage dip in the power system. Synchronous operation restored when the voltage dip or overload disappears. Out-of-step protection is provided by a conventional thermal overload device, which is energized whenever rotor remains without rotor field excitation. If, during the start, the motor does not synchronize within a given time period, the relay de-energizes the main contactor. If the motor pulls out-of-step while running and does not resynchronize within the specified time, the relay will disconnect the motor by de-energizing the main contactor.

Figure 9.7 shows the control circuitry of a brush type medium voltage synchronous motor with damper winding and induction motor driven exciter. Synchronous motor starters of the full-voltage type connect the motor directly to the supply lines. The field winding is short-circuited through a discharge resistor during the starting period. The field is connected to the DC lines when the motor is at a speed near synchronous speed. Sequence of operation for starting and running of the synchronous motor is listed below.

a) Start the exciter driven motor by pressing the start pushbutton. Turn the control switch (CS) in to close position. Starting control relay (X2) pickup and opens its contacts in the trip circuit and permits the control circuit for starting the motor.
b) Close the main circuit breaker (52) by pressing the start pushbutton. When the breaker closes, X2 relay drops out.
c) When the breaker is closed the motor starts to run up as induction motor, due to the damper winding.
d) If the motor fails to accelerate fast enough, starting control relay (X2) will de-energize, and the trip coil (TC) of circuit breaker will energize to trip the circuit breaker.
e) Through the timer (T) and field relay (FR) field breaker (41) will close and connect DC supply to the rotor winding after disconnecting the field discharge resistor in the rotor circuit.
f) If the breaker (52) tripped to stop the motor or a trip due to any reason, the field breaker (41) also trips out.

LEGEND:

F: Field winding
FDR: Field discharge resistor
FLR: Field loss-control relay
FR: Field relay
EFR: Excitation field rheostat

CC: Closing coil (circuit breaker)
52a: Breaker NO contact (auxiliary)
52B: Breaker NC contact (auxiliary)
MC: Magnetic contactor (low voltage)
T: Timer

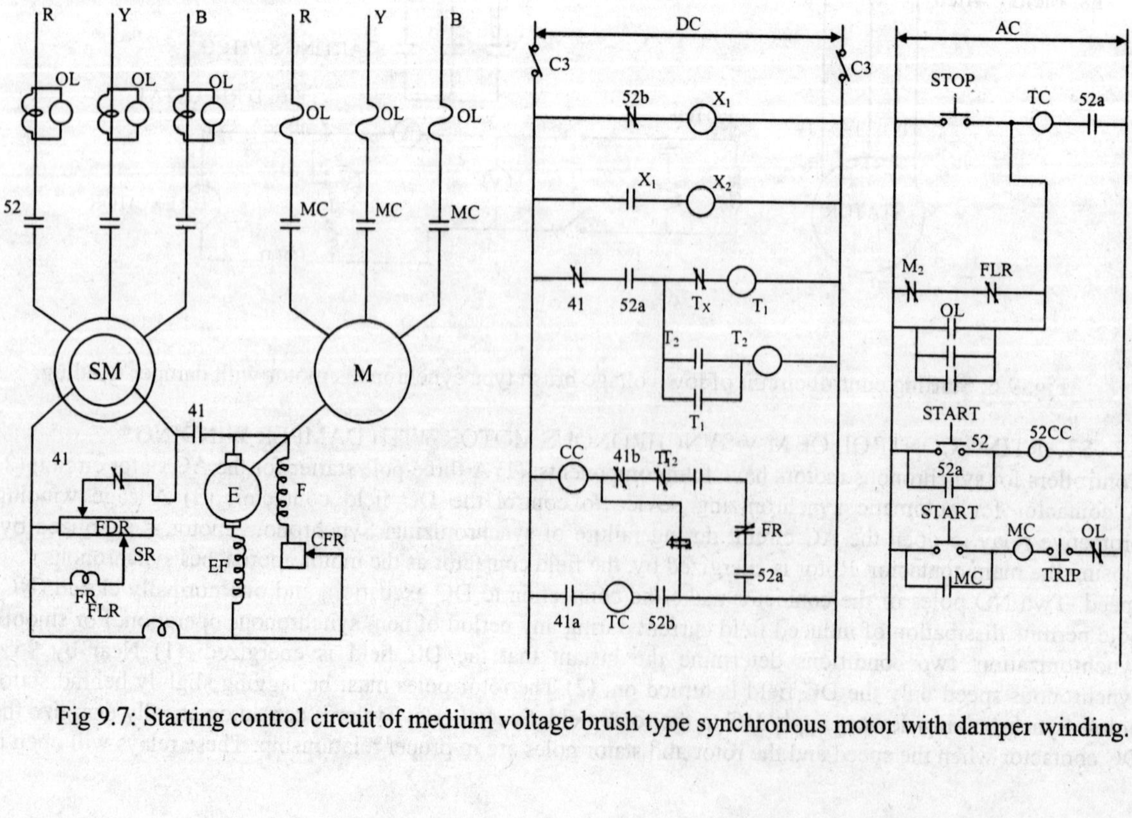

Fig 9.7: Starting control circuit of medium voltage brush type synchronous motor with damper winding.

9.8 STARTING CONTROL OF BRUSH TYPE SYNCHRONOUS MOTORS.

Typical brush type synchronous motor control is shown in Figure 9.8. The general sequence of operation is as follows. Closure of the start pushbutton energizes the line contactor coil M, connecting the motor stator to the AC line and sealing-in around the pushbutton. The motor accelerates as an induction motor with its field connected across its starting (and discharging) resistor. A thermal relay 26F for damper winding protection is in series with the resistor. Should the motor fail to start and accelerate, the relay operates to open the line-contactor coil circuit. It is equally important that the field be applied at the proper speed and at a favorable position of the rotor with respect to the rotating flux in the machine. To accomplish this, coordination is required between the field application or synchronizing relay 56dc and an AC holding coil 56ac. When the line contactor M closes, its auxiliary contact energizes the closing coil 56dc, which energizes the timing relay 2 and opens the field contactor 41coil circuit. The timing relay is used to prevent the application of field until the proper time. When the timer reaches its actuating position, the field application relay closing coil 56dc is de-energized leaving the operation of this relay dependent upon the variable AC voltage signal appearing across the starting resistor as detected by the holding coil 56ac. This relay will drop out when the time interval between half waves of the rectified induced field current exceeds the relay setting. This occurs at 94 - 98% of synchronous speed, at which time its contacts will close, energizing the field contactor 41. Field breaker contacts are make before break types.

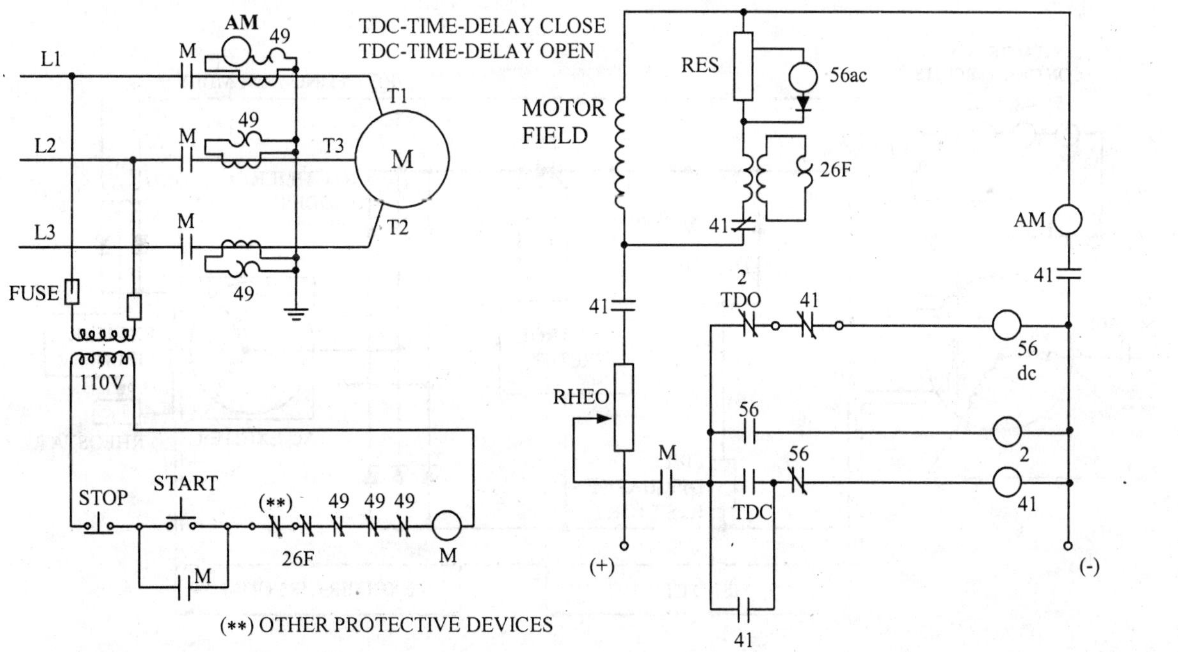

Fig. 9.8: Typical starting-control circuit of brush type synchronous motor without damper winding.

Device 56-Field application relay automatically controls the application of the field excitation to an AC motor at some predetermined point in the slip cycle. This is a frequency relay used to determine that motor speed is 1% - 5% away from synchronous speed, and, in conjunction with a time-delay relay to apply field when conditions are proper to close the field breaker. On some motors, where continuity of service is a factor, this same relay is also used to remove the field during an out-of-step condition and then to automatically reapply the field at the proper time and condition.

Device 53-Exciter or DC generator relay forces the DC machine field excitation to build up during starting or which functions when the machine voltage has built up to a given value. This device checks the presence of DC voltage and is used to protect against loss of excitation for synchronous motors when excitation is obtained from a common bus or separately driven exciter. It may also be used to force voltage build up on a direct connected exciter at the moment of motor synchronization. It is a field voltage check relay set at approximately 90% of rated field voltage.

9.9 STARTING CONTROL OF BRUSHLESS SYNCHRONOUS MOTORS.

The only difference with slip-ring type synchronous motor is that the excitation circuit is assembled on the rotor such that it will rotate when the rotor rotates. Brushes and slip rings are not required as the DC supply, for excitation is obtained from a brushless exciter on the shaft. The semi-controlled bridge with three diodes and three thyristors rectifies the output of the AC exciter generator and supplies the motor field winding. The thyristors act as a switch to open the rectifier during starting and to place in service during running. The AC exciter generator is excited with its own field current. The resistor is permanently connected across the motor field winding during starting and running. It improves the torque characteristics during starting and protects the bridge elements against transient over voltages during running. The capacitor protects the diodes and thyristors against commutation over voltages caused by hole-storage phenomena in conjunction with the inductances of the armature winding of the AC exciter generator.

A typical control circuit, inherent in a brushless type motor and mounted with the rotating equipment, is shown in Figure 9.9. The purpose of the control circuit is to keep the rectifier SCR1 from firing until the induced field-current frequency is very low, representing a close approach to synchronous speed, then to fire the rectifier SCR1 at the proper time, and thus apply excitation to the synchronous motor field. At the same time, the field discharge resistor is removed from the circuit. This is done by the firing characteristic of rectifier SCR2. This frequency sensitive part of the control circuit ensures that the field excitation is applied at the proper pull-in speed for successful synchronizing. Motor field excitation and controls are mounted on the shaft.

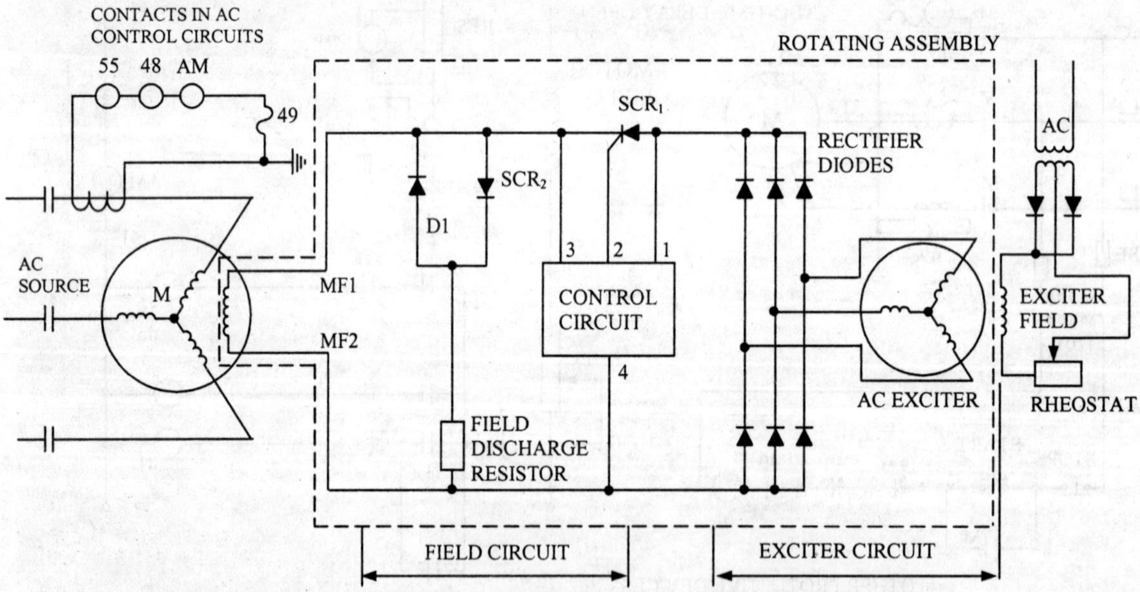

Fig: 9.9: Typical starting-control circuit of brushless synchronous motor.

Device 55: Power factor relay operates when the power factor in an AC circuit rises above or falls below a predetermined value. This relay detects synchronous motor loss of synchronism, which is caused by increased loading or decreased excitation. Loss of synchronism causes the motor to pull out of step with the supply system, producing high line current pulses and possible physical damage to the motor. Some of the relays used have an adjustable power factor angle setting and an adjustable time delay. The relay actuation can be used to remove the synchronous motor from the line or operate an alarm. It is usually set for maximum contact closing-torque when current into the motor lags its unity power factor position by 120° - 150°. It will then operate for conditions occurring when the motor loss synchronism (producing WATT flow out of the motor and VAR flow into the motor), or when the synchronous motor field is lost. The minimum time delay is favored, but the duration of transient effects must be considered when making the time delay setting. Power factor angle relays are put in to service only after the motor has reached synchronizing speed and the field has been applied. This is accomplished by, a timing device in the potential circuit of the relay. The timer allows the potential circuit to be applied to the power factor relay after the time has elapsed for the motor to reach synchronous speed.

Device 48-Incomplete sequence relay is a supervising relay that generally returns the equipment to the normal or off position and locks it out if the normal starting sequence or stopping sequence is not properly completed within a predetermined time.

9.10 NUMERICAL RELAY FOR SYNCHRONOUS MOTOR OVERALL PROTECTION.

Motor protection unit introduced in this section is of General Electric SPM model, which controls starting, synchronizing and protection of collector-ring (brush type) or brushless type synchronous motors. Figure 9.10 shows the functional block diagram of synchronous motor protection unit. The unit provides following protections.

26F: Field over-temperature
27: Under-voltage protection
37: Under current/under power protection
48: Incomplete sequence protection
50: Instantaneous over-current protection
55: Power factor protection and monitoring
56: Field application relay (applies DC to the field)
78: Stalling or out of step protection
86: Lock out relay
94: Tripping relay
96: Auto-loading relay

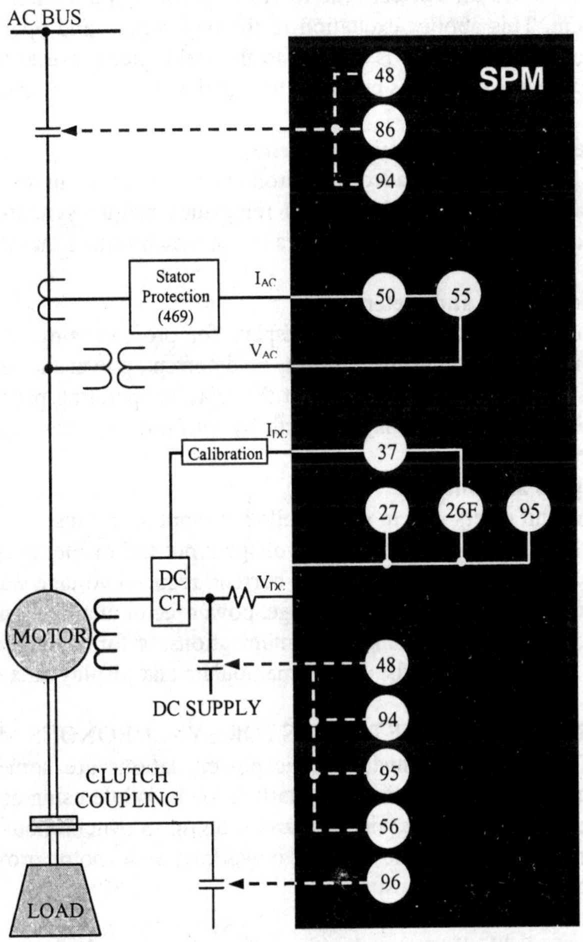

Fig. 9.10: Functional block diagram of synchronous motor protection unit. (Courtesy, General Electric)

Stall/acceleration protection:

Preventing cage-winding overheating during both starting and running out of synchronization conditions. For brushless motors, stall protection is derived from the stator current inputs. Stall protection activates when an operating motor is stopped with power factor protection enabled. For slip-ring motors, speed is determined from the frequency of the induced field current. Stall time can temporarily extend for reduced voltage starting.

Incomplete sequence protection:

If the motor does not synchronize within the programmed time, the incomplete sequence relay (Device No: 48) will operate to trip the breaker.

Power factor pullout protection:

Motor protection and control unit provides power factor settings and also displays the measured leading/lagging power factor. Two modes of pullout protection are available, re-sync mode and ride-thru mode. These modes will be initiated if the lagging power factor drops below the programmed set point, or if a line current surge occurs which is above four times the motor full load current. Re-sync mode operation will cause the field application relay (56) to remove the motor field excitation. The motor will continue to run with the field removed for the set power factor delay time. If re-synchronization does not occur within this time the trip relay (94) will operate and the motor will stop. In ride-thru mode the motor field excitation is not removed immediately, instead, allow the motor to run for the power factor delay time. If the power factor dip or line current surge persists the trip relay will operate and the motor will stop.

Starting and synchronizing:
For slip ring motors the motor protection and control unit detects the proper rotor speed and angle and determines the correct time to close the field application relay (56) based on the percent synchronous slip set point. This applies excitation to the motor field and opens up the field discharge resister loop. For brushless motors, the voltage is applied to the field after a preset time elapses. Power factor pullout protection is then enabled. A contact is provided to signal automatic motor loading.

Reluctance torque synchronizing:
When a lightly loaded synchronous motor pulls in to synchronism before the rotor poles are externally magnetized, this is known as reluctance torque synchronizing. The field application control responds by properly applying excitation if a motor synchronizes on reluctance torque.

Monitoring and metering:
The unit contains an LCD display for programming, displaying trip information, and readout of running parameters such as line current, field current, power factor, field volts and field ohms etc. The unit has built-in test diagnostics to indicate that the relay is operating properly prior to start up of motor. Test mode-allow the user to verify trip relay contacts, system test, squirrel cage protection test, synchronization, power factor test etc.

Inputs and outputs:
The unit offers user to verify following inputs/outputs:
1. Field voltage input, exciter voltage input and exciter current input for slip-ring type motors
2. Motor 'on' input, motor line current, reduced voltage starting input, control power (230V,AC).
3. Power factor reference voltage, power factor analog signal and control signal.
4. RS 485 port for remote communications, or for connection to a DCS, SCADA or PLC.
5. Software allows the user to manipulate and display data on a personnel computer.

9.11 PROTECTIVE RELAYS FOR SYNCHRONOUS MOTOR PROTECTION.

AC generators in hydroelectric power stations are some times using as pumps. Turbine is dewatered by compressed air to reduce the starting loads. While using as a motor, (the generator) starting as induction motor (because of damper winding) and running as synchronous motor. Generator protection relays will protect the synchronous machine when it is working as a motor provided the generator neutral earth connection circuit breaker is in open position.

Figure 9.11 illustrates the single line diagram of synchronous motor protection. The speed of synchronous motor is monitored by, mounting an inductive proximity probe as illustrated in figure 6.20 of Chapter # 6. Bearing over temperature is monitored by, resistance temperature detectors embedded in the stator winding. Machine vibration transducers are employed for monitoring excessive vibration.

DEVICE NUMBER:
12: Over-speed
37: Under current relay
38: high bearing temperature
42: Field circuit breaker for brush type motor.
48: Incomplete sequence
49: Stator winding temperature
50: Instantaneous over-current

50N: Instantaneous earth fault
51: Time delay over-current
51N: Time delay earth fault
52: Main circuit breaker
55: Power factor relay
56: Field application
87M: Differential protection

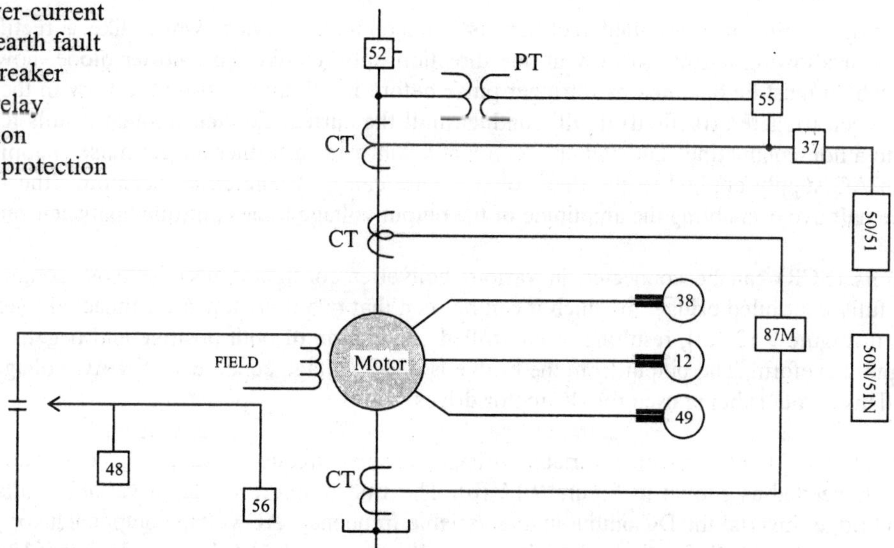

Fig. 9.11: Single line diagram of synchronous motor protection system.

Protective relays recommended for synchronous motor protection, its application and technical requirements are given below.

Table 9.11 (1): Protective relays for synchronous motor protection.

Device #	Relay title	Relay application	Technical requirements
87M	Differential relay	Stator winding internal fault protection	Phase faults and earth faults
50/51	Instantaneous / time over-current relay	Short-circuit/overload protection	High set/IDMT
50N/51N	Instantaneous / time earth fault relay	Earth fault protection	High srt/IDMT
55	Power factor protection relay	Monitoring operating power factor	Motor trips if lagging power factor goes below set value
56	Field application relay	Connect DC excitation to the field	To close (41) DC field breaker of brush type synchronous motor
78	Out-of-step-relay (stalling/swinging)	Protection against out of step (power swinging)	Power-swinging/ voltage dip
49	Stator-winding temperature protection	Stator winding protection	Resistance temperature detector in the winding
37	Undercurrent/under-power relay	Monitoring motor line current	To identify load rejection or single phasing.
48	Incomplete sequence relay	Start sequence protection	If the motor does not synchronize within the set time the relay will initiate to open the circuit breaker.
12	Over-speed	Over-speed protection	Inductive proximity probe
38	Bearing temperature	High bearing temperature	Resistance temperature detectors
39	Vibration	Excessive vibration	Vibration transducers

9.12 FREQUENCY CONVERTER FOR SPEED CONTROL OF M.V MOTORS.

The Thyristor (Silicon controlled rectifier) is semiconductor device, which like a rectifier diode, has the property of allowing current to flow in one direction only. Unlike the rectifier diode, however, it contains a "gate" which must be operated by a trigger pulse before it will allow current to flow in the forward direction. Having been triggered (or fired) it will conduct until the current flowing through it falls to zero, when it will revert to a non-conducting state and only conduct again when a further trigger pulse is applied to the gate. So, with an AC supply applied to the thyristor, the gate can be triggered at any point (the firing angle) in the positive half cycle, enabling the amplitude of the output voltage to be controlled between zero to maximum.

Thyristors (SCR) can be connected in various converter configurations, the most common being the three phase, fully controlled bridge, in which it can be seen that two thyristors are connected to each input phase [as shown in Figure 9.12 (a)], resulting in controlled conduction of both positive and negative half-cycles of the AC input waveform. The output from the bridge is a DC voltage equal to 1.35 x AC voltage x cosine of firing angle. This output is being used for DC motor drives.

To provide the AC motor with a variable voltage, variable frequency supply, a combination of two thyristor bridges is needed as shown in Figure 9.12 (b). The first bridge provides a variable voltage output and the second bridge 'inverts' the DC output in to a variable frequency, AC voltage output. The operation of inversion can be simply described if each thyristor is considered as a switch. As shown in Figure 9.12 (c) the three output terminals are connected alternatively and sequentially via the thyristor 'switches' to the DC positive and negative rails. Variable voltage inverter output wave of each phases are illustrated in Figure 9.12 (d).

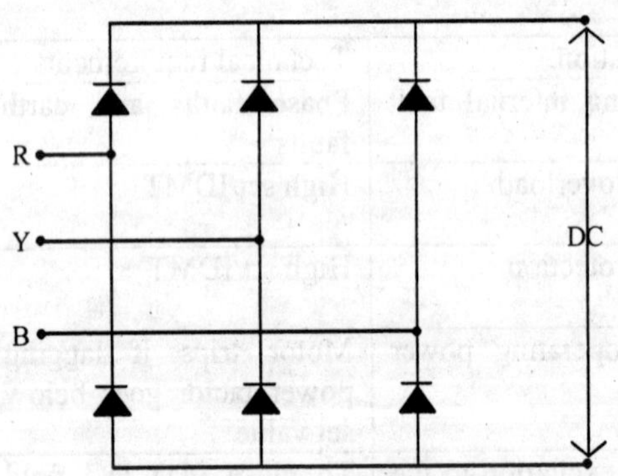

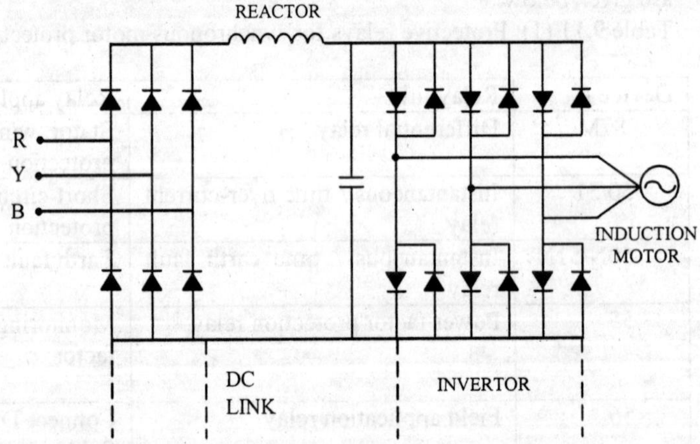

9.12 (a): 3-Phase fully controlled thyristor bridge. Fig. 9.12 (b): Variable-voltage, variable-frequency drive.

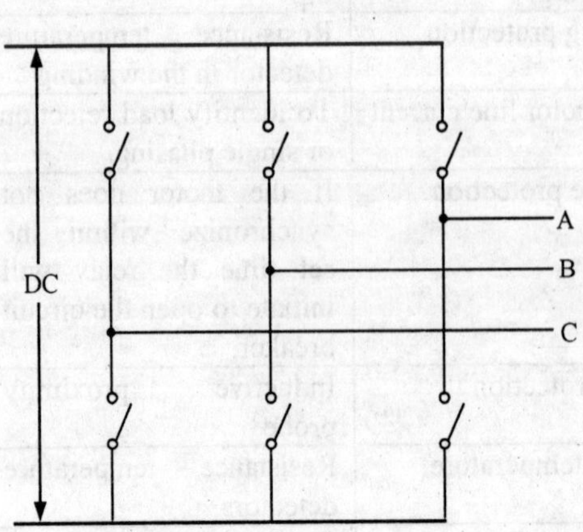

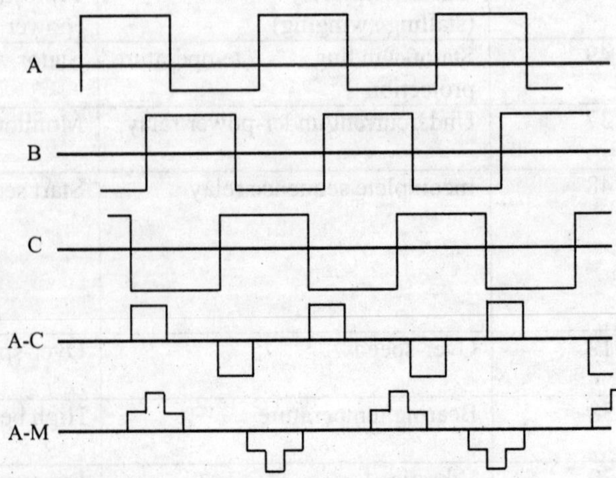

Fig. 9.12 (c): Inverter: Principle of operation. Fig. 9.12 (d): Variable voltage inverter output voltage waves.

When the thyristor (converter bridge) is triggered (or fired) it will conduct only until the current flowing through it falls to zero, when it will revert to the off state. Since the second thyristor-bridge (the inverter) is being supplied from the DC voltage source the current through the thyristor will not naturally fall to zero and switch the thyristor off. A means must be found to force the current to zero and this involves the use of reactors and capacitors referred to as commutation circuits. These effectively reverse bias the conducting thyristor while supplying the load current transiently before the next thyristor is switched on.

The speed control of induction motors using frequency converters gives large benefits for many types of duty, particularly in difficult and hazardous environments. Frequency converter circuit illustrated in Figure 9.12 (e) is designed for speed control of medium voltage squirrel cage induction motor (ASEA drives, model YRRA). The main circuit has on its input side, after the conventional AC supply, a simple diode rectifier followed by a DC filter, consisting of a reactor and a capacitor. The main components of the inverter are the six main thyristors, each with its own bypass or feedback diode, arranged in a six-pulse bridge connection. Conversion from DC to AC takes place in such a way that the three phase terminals are switched in turns with a 120° phase-shift to the plus and minus poles of the DC voltage with the aid of the thyristors.

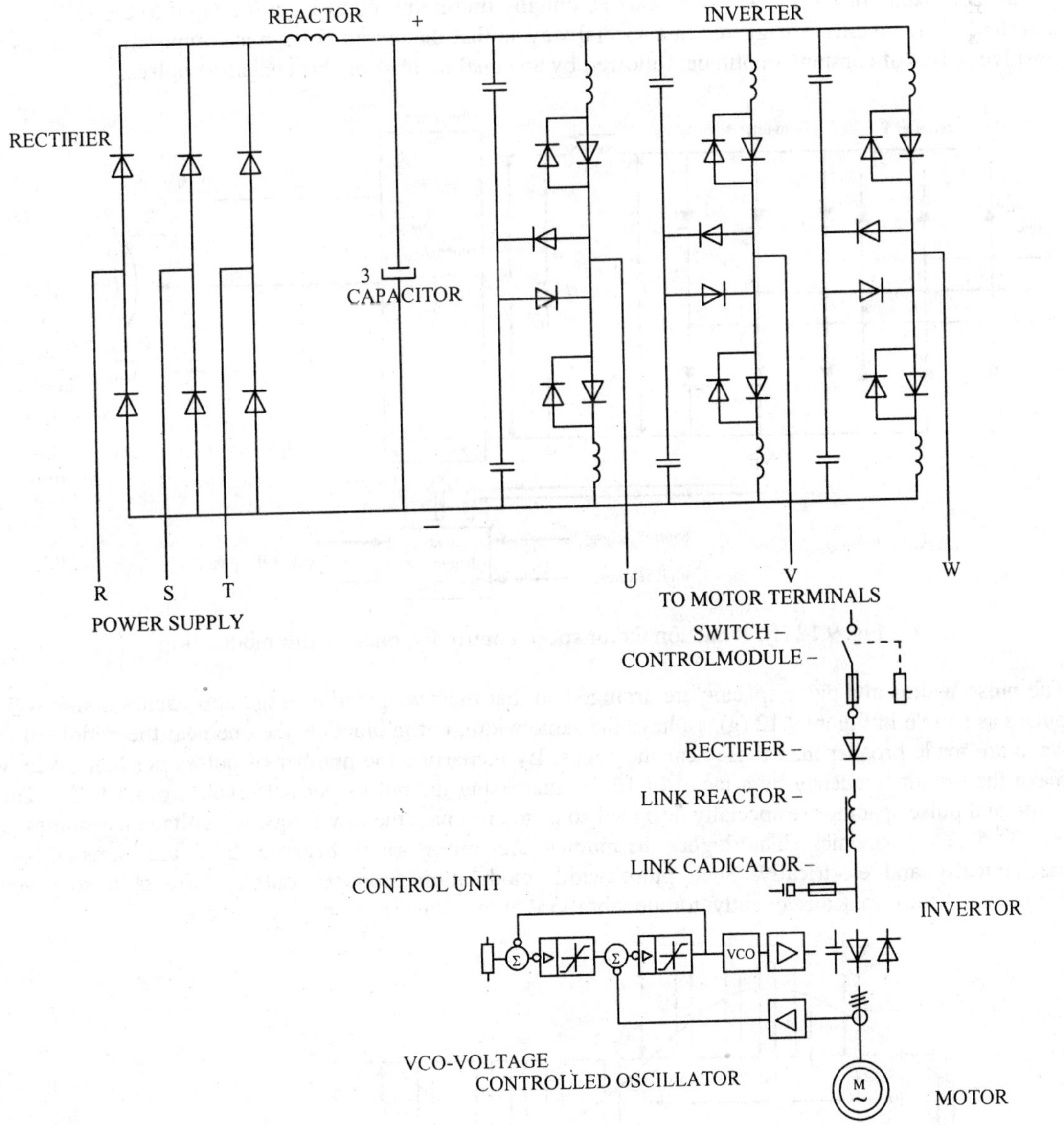

Fig. 9.12 (e): Frequency converter circuit for medium voltage induction motor (Courtesy, ASEA drives).

Since the phases of the motor current are displaced in relation to the voltage, current will flow through the bypass diodes during part of the cycle. To commutate the current from one DC pole to the other, a special commutating circuit is arranged for each phase. This consists of thyristors, capacitors and reactors. When full output voltage is obtained, the main thyristors are conducting for 180° and the line-to-line voltage then consists of voltage pulses 120° long separated by dead intervals of 60°. The fundamental value of the motor voltage (Um) is then related to the line-to-line voltage (Un) of the supply network in the following ways.

Um = 1.05 Un

The frequency converters discussed above create substantial harmonic voltages and currents. When this harmonics flow in the windings they produce torque pulsations that are superimposed on the main driving torque. The pulsations are damped out at moderate and at high speeds owing to mechanical inertia. However, at low speeds, they may produce considerable vibration. Such torque fluctuations are unacceptable, where fine speed control down to zero speed is required. Under these circumstances, the induction motor can be driven by pulse width modulation techniques, which are suitable for induction motors up to several hundreds of horsepower.

Consider the voltage-fed frequency converter system shown in Figure 9.12 (f). A three-phase bridge rectifier 1 produces a fixed voltage E_1, which appears essentially undiminished as E_3 at the input to the self commutated inverter 2. The inverter is triggered in a special way so that the output voltage is composed of a series of short positive pulses of constant amplitude, followed by an equal number of short negative pulses.

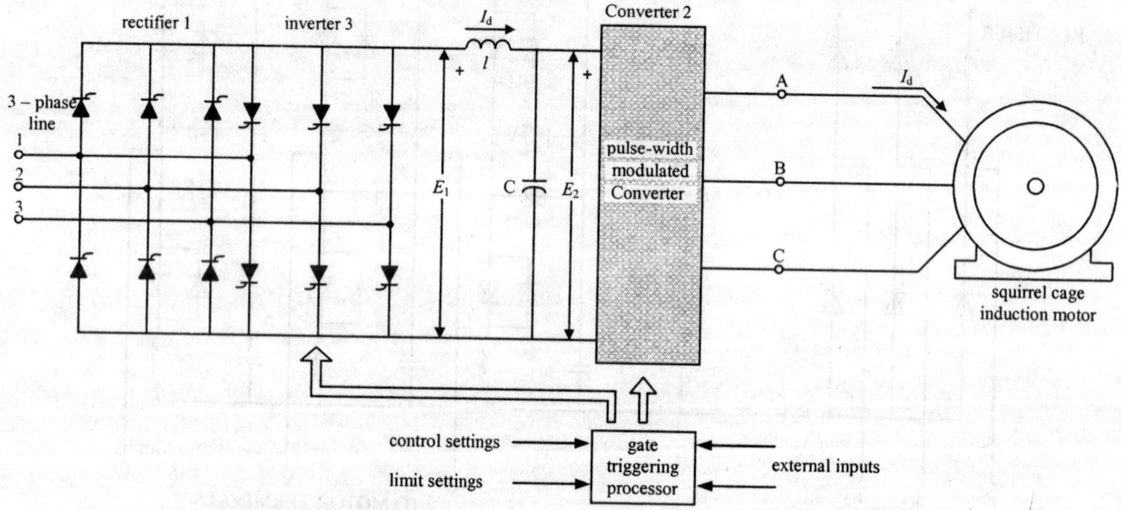

Fig. 9.12 (f): Induction motor speed control by, pulse width modulation.

The pulse widths and pulse spacing are arranged so that their weighted average approaches a sine wave. The pulses as shown in Figure 9.12 (g), all have the same width, but in practice, the one near the middle of the sine wave are made broader than those near the edges. By increasing the number of pulses per half cycle, we can make the output frequency by a factor of 10, by increasing the pulses per half-cycle from 5 to 50. The pulse width and pulse spacing are specially designed so as to eliminate the low frequency voltage harmonics, such as the 3rd,5th,7th harmonics. The higher harmonics are unimportant because they are damped out both mechanically and electrically. Such pulse width modulation produces output currents having very low harmonics distortion. Consequently, torque vibrations at low speeds are greatly reduced.

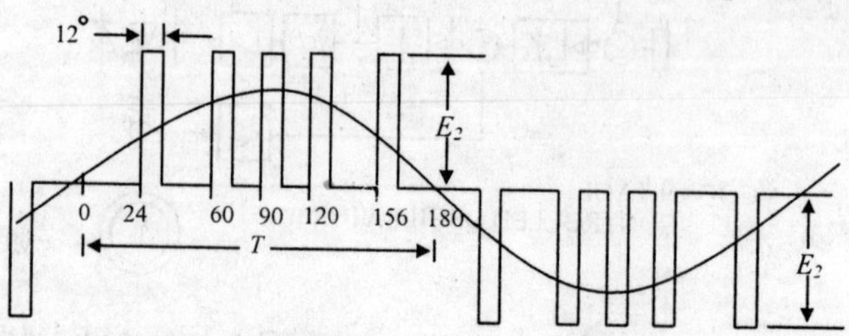

Fig. 9.12 (g): Pulse width modulation: Voltage waveform across one phase.

In some cases, the output voltage has to be reduced while maintaining the same output frequency. This is done by, reducing all the pulse widths in proportion to the desired reduction in output voltage. Thus in Figure 9.12 (h), the pulses are half a wide as in figure (g), yielding an output voltage half a great, but having the same frequency. Therefore vary both output frequency and output voltage using a fixed DC input voltage. As a result, a simple diode bridge rectifier can be used to supply the fixed DC voltage. The power factor of the 3-phase supply line is therefore high.

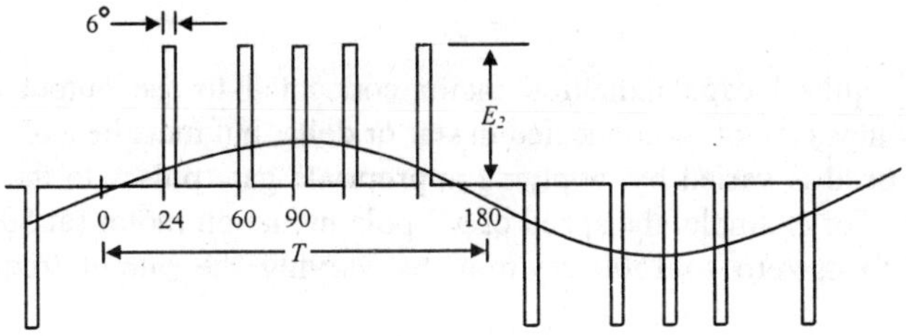

Fig. 9.12 (h): Pulse width modulation: Wave form yielding the frequency but half the voltage.

Regenerative breaking can be achieved, but during such power reversal, current Id [refer figure 9.12 (f)] reverses while the polarity of E_2 remains the same. Hence, an extra inverter 3 has to be placed in reverse parallel with rectifier 1in order to feed power back to the line. Rectifier 1 is automatically blocked while inverter 3 is in operation, and vice versa.

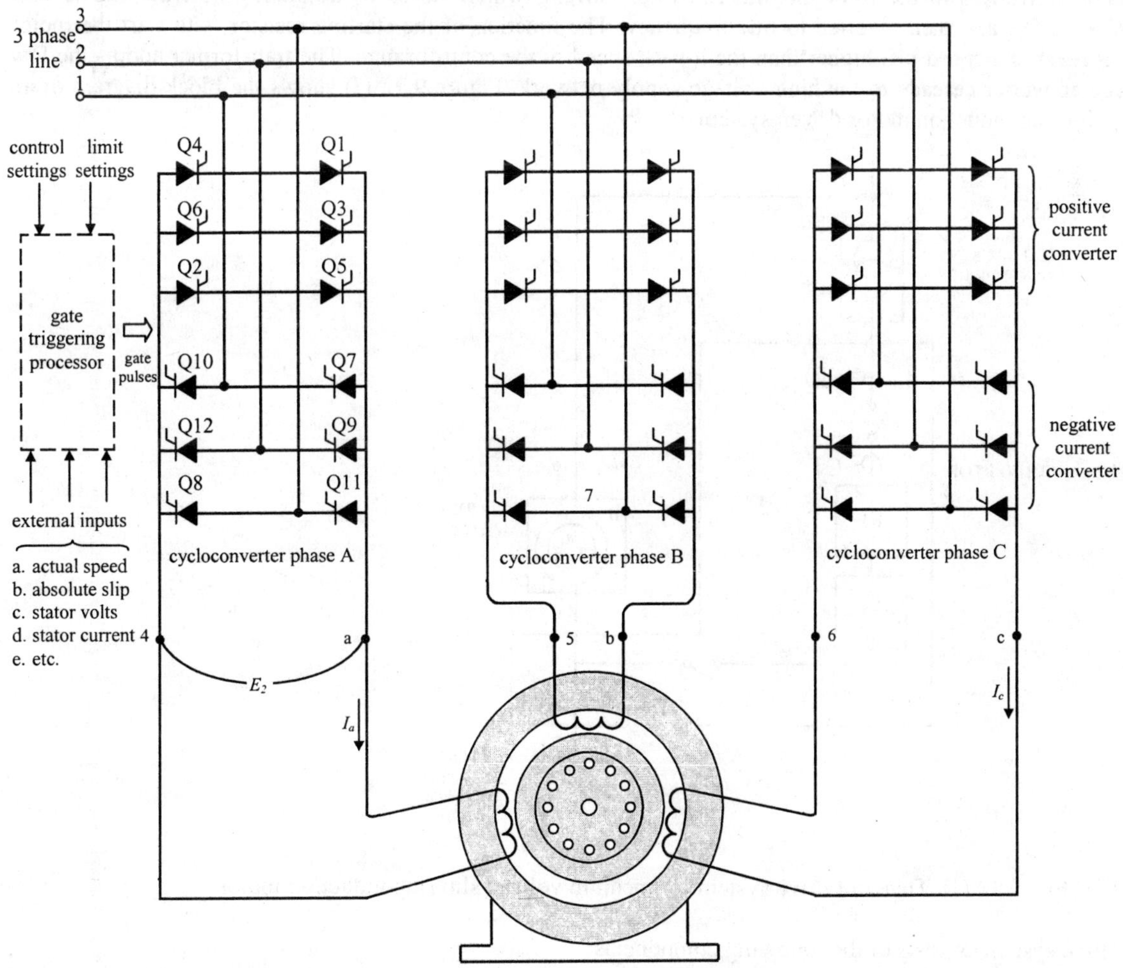

Fig. 9.12 (I): Squirrel cage induction motor fed from a three-phase cycloconverter.

Standard squirrel cage induction motors are almost without exception designed, and have data specified, for duty with constant frequency and voltage. **When such a motor is connected to a variable-frequency non-sinusoidal voltage source, its design data and other characteristics will be changed. The current harmonics, caused by, the voltage waveform, give increased losses. This necessitates de-rating of the output of a conventional motor by 10 to 15% at rated speed.** If the motor is only cooled by, a fan on its own shaft, the load torque at lower speed will further reduced. Vibrations may arise owing to resonance oscillations in some structural part and one must reckon on a higher sound level for a motor fed from a frequency converter.

Figure 9.12 (i) shows a three-phase squirrel cage induction motor connected to the output of a 3-phase cycloconverter, consequently, the windings cannot be connected in star or delta, but must be isolated from each other as shown in the figure. Motor speed is varied by, applying appropriate gate pulses to the thyristors, to vary the output voltage and frequency. For example, the speed of a 2 pole induction motor (at 50 hertz system 120F/P = 3000 rpm) can be varied from zero to 1500 rev/min, by varying the output frequency of the cycloconverter from zero to 25 cycle.

Thyristor controlled drive system for medium voltage slip ring induction motor:
In all processes where it is required to control the flow of gases, liquids, or solid materials, speed control of the drive motors is the only real answer, since it optimizes the drive operation and saves energy. For example, the power required by pumps and fans is reduced in proportion to the cube of the speed, and speed control thus results in major savings of such drives. **It has long been known that the speed of a slip ring induction motor can be controlled by, returning the slip power from the rotor to the mains.** This is done by, thyristor converters in the rotor circuit. The rotor current, which varies in frequency with the slip is first rectified to DC and then inverted to line frequency. The function of the starting resistor is to start the motor until it reaches a speed just higher than the lowest speed in the control range. The transformer adopts the low voltage converter cascade to the high voltage supply network. Figure 9.12 (J) shows the block diagram of an M.V. slip ring induction motor driven system.

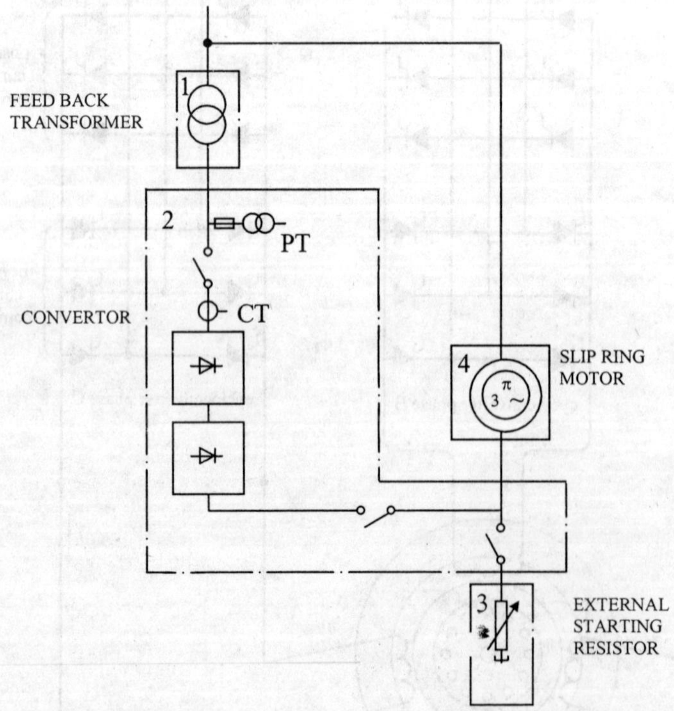

Fig. 9.12 (J): Thyristor drive system for medium voltage slip ring induction motor.

The drive system consists of the following components:

(a) Thyristor unit. The main circuit of the thyristor unit consists of two cascade-connected fully controlled bridges in a 6-pulse 2-way circuit. A fuse is connected in series with each thyristor against short-circuit

protection, and a damping circuit as protection against voltage transients. The firing pulses from the control electronics are fed to the thyristors via firing pulse transformers. The control circuits are thereby galvanically separated from the main circuit. The signals for control and protection are provided via current transformers.
(b) Mains connection unit: For rated current up to 950 A consists of a disconnector switch, fuse and vacuum or SF6 contactor. Above 950 A, circuit breakers are used.
(c) Rotor circuit switching equipment: Contactors are used for rotor current up to 1100 A, and circuit breakers are used for rotor currents above 1100 Amps.
(d) Control equipment: Control equipment for the mains converter consists of a speed controller and a current controller, the output signal of which controls the firing angle to the thyristors. The firing angle for the thyristors in the rotor converter is controlled by means of a filter unit, which receives its input signal from the voltage and current transformers in the rotor circuit.
(e) Protection, operation and monitoring devices: All protection is based on electronics. Faults are indicated by LED's (Light Emitter Displays) and bistable relays, which retain the information in the event of power supply failure. The basic version contains protection against fan failure, over-voltage, under voltage, overload and earth fault. Operational devices, consists of pushbuttons for ON, OFF and de-blocking. A potentiometer is used for manual setting of the speed. For monitoring purposes, indication lamps are provided for indicating RUN status and tripping, and indicating instruments for current, voltage and motor speed.

Speed controlled drive systems for high voltage brushless synchronous motors:
Speed controlled drive system for a brushless synchronous motor is based on that the motor is supplied with variable voltage and frequency from a static frequency converter. The power electronics include a phase-angle-controlled supply converter combined with a machine converter, which has a fixed phase angle. A reactor for smoothing the direct current is located between these two converters. The high voltage thyristors are of puck type assembled between two heat sinks and are located in a cooling duct, through which air is forced by means of a fan. A fuse is connected in series with each thyristor as a protection against external short circuits. A damping circuit is also incorporated to constitute a protection against rapid voltage rises. Figure 9.12 (k) illustrates the schematic diagram of (ASEA type VF2000) drive system for speed control of brushless medium voltage synchronous motor.

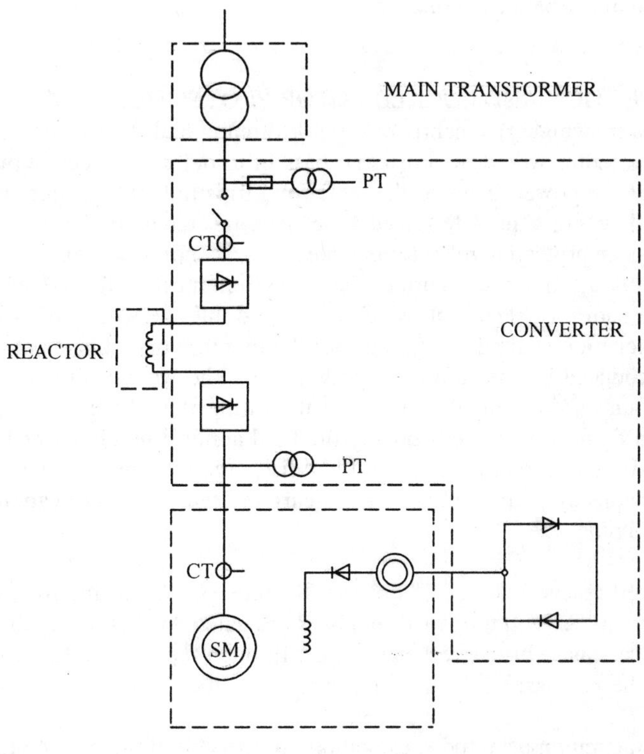

Fig. 9.12 (k): Speed controlled drive system for M.V brushless synchronous motor (Courtesy, ASEA drives).

Thyristor unit is provided with:

a) Current transformers for providing the current response to the control unit.
b) Disconnector with fuses or circuit breaker
c) Fuses for the control circuits.
d) Interfacing transformer for the electronic control units.
e) Process interfacing electronic units.

The firing pulses from the control electronics are led to the thyristors via firing pulse transformers. The control circuits are thus completely galvanically isolated from the power electronics. In addition to generating the firing pulses to the thyristors, the electronic control unit incorporates the following functions. (1) frequency control; (2) current regulation; (3) field regulation; (4) process control.

The drive system consists of the following components:

(a) Protective equipment: The standard protective device consists of (1) instantaneous over-current protection; (2) under voltage protection; (3) earth fault protection; (4) Differential protection; (5) Over speed protection; (6) Blocking protection (if the rotor stalls during a starting attempt); (7) DC over voltage protection (if the voltage in the DC link of the converter become excessive); (8) excitation monitor (dangerous over excitation or under excitation); (9) thyristor monitoring (if any thyristor fails disconnect the system from the power supply).

(b) Monitoring equipment: (1) Status of all protective equipments described above; (2) winding temperature of the synchronous motor; (3) Phase sequence; (4) function of all auxiliary circuits.

Advantages of synchronous motor speed control by using frequency converters;

- Require minimum maintenance because of brushless motors.
- The built-in electronic current limiter enables the motor to start very smoothly, thus minimizing the stresses on the shaft system.
- The motor and frequency converter are always synchronized with each other. This continuous state of synchronism prevents the build-up of disturbing oscillating torque while starting. Lack of oscillating-torques during starting prolongs the service life of the motor.
- Low starting currents results in reduced voltage drops in the supply network. Low starting currents also mean low temperature rise in the windings. An unlimited number of successive starts can therefore be permitted.
- The speed can be controlled with great accuracy within 50% – 100% of the rated speed without necessitating the use of a separate cooling fan.
- High efficiency.

9.13 OUT OF STEP PROTECTION AND LOCKED ROTOR PROTECTION.

With heavy voltage dip (power swinging) synchronous motor running under rated load fall out of step. When synchronism is disturbed, the motor will slow down and pass in to out of step conditions. The field monitor relay (Device # 78) measures the power factor of the motor and trips the motor stator and DC exciter field if synchronism is not achieved within a predetermined time or if the motor pulls out-of-step while running. Schematic diagram of out of step protection relay for brushless synchronous motor is shown in Figure 9.13 (a).

The field application circuit in a synchronous motor excitation system must perform three functions:

(a) Provide a discharge path for the current, which is induced into the wound rotor during start and open this circuit when excitation is applied. During start the motor is operating as an induction motor with the torque being produced by the squirrel cage winding. The wound rotor is also being cut by the rotating stator flux and has a voltage induced in it. During this phase of the start-up SCR2 in the diagram depicted in figure (a) is gated “on” by the field application circuit and provides a discharge path for the induced rotor current through the field discharge resistor (FDR) as shown by the dashed arrow lines. The frequency of this induced rotor current “tells” the application circuit the speed at which the rotor is running.

(b) When the rotor speed reaches above 97% of synchronous speed and the rotor polarity is correct to achieve synchronism, SCR2 will turn “off” and SCR1 is gated “on” allowing the rectified DC current from the rotating three-phase bridge rectifier to flow through the rotating field, as shown by the solid arrows, producing the necessary synchronizing torque for the rotor to pull-in step with the rotating stator flux.

(c) The field application circuit must remove excitation immediately if the motor pulls out of step.

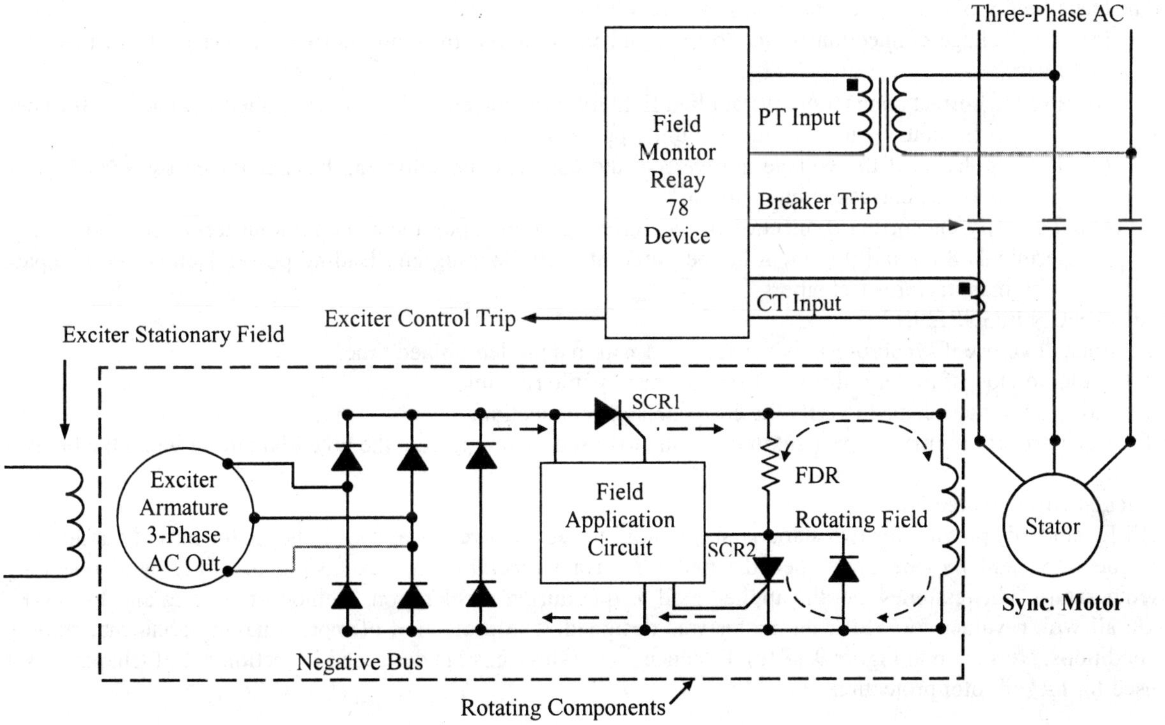

Fig.9.13 (a): Schematic diagram of out of step protection relay for breshless synchronous motor.

Connection diagram of a digital out of step protection relay (field monitoring relay) for a separately synchronous motor protection is shown in Figure 9.13 (b). For the correct connection of the relay, the rotation of the system must be known and a voltage and current of the correct phase relation ship and polarity must be used i.e. potential from phase L_1 and L_2, and current from L_3 as shown in the figure below.

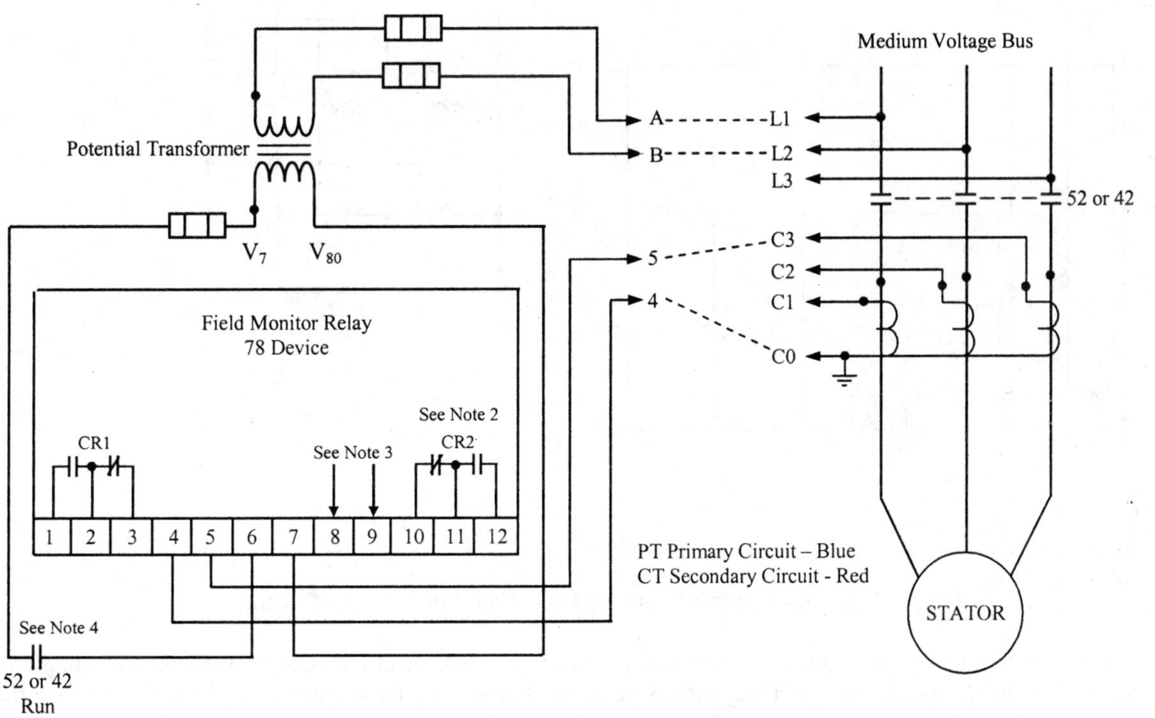

Fig. 9.13 (b): Connection diagram of field monitor relay for separately excited synchronous motor.

The basic field monitor connection criteria are as follows:

(a) The voltage connection is line-to-line, and the required matching current is derived from the otheı phase.

(b) For the correct connection, the applied field monitor current will lead the applied voltage by 90° when the synchronous motor is running at unity power factor.

(c) If the polarity of the voltage is reversed, the correct connection can be maintained by reversing the polarity of the corresponding current.

(d) To verify the correct connection of the current and potential, the analog output terminals of the relay, terminals 8 (-) and 9 (+) can be measured at unity, lagging and leading power factors and compare with manufactures test report.

NOTES ON FIGURE 9.13 (b):

1. Contact to close if synchronism is not achieved within a predetermined time.
2. Contact to close if motor pulls out of synchronism while running.
3. Analog output terminals to verify the correctness of connection.
4. Circuit breaker normally open, auxiliary contact is used to de-energize the potential circuit when the breaker is off.

Locked rotor protection:

IEEE standards provide for two starts in succession, to reset between starts with the motor initially at ambient temperature, and for one start when the motor is at a temperature not exceeding it's rated load operating temperature. This assumes that the applied load torque during acceleration, method of starting and load WK^2 are all within values for which the motor was designed. The protection of motors having abnormal starting conditions, are shown in Figure 9.13 (c). Distance relay (Device # 21) described in section 8.4 of Chapter # 8 is used for locked rotor protection.

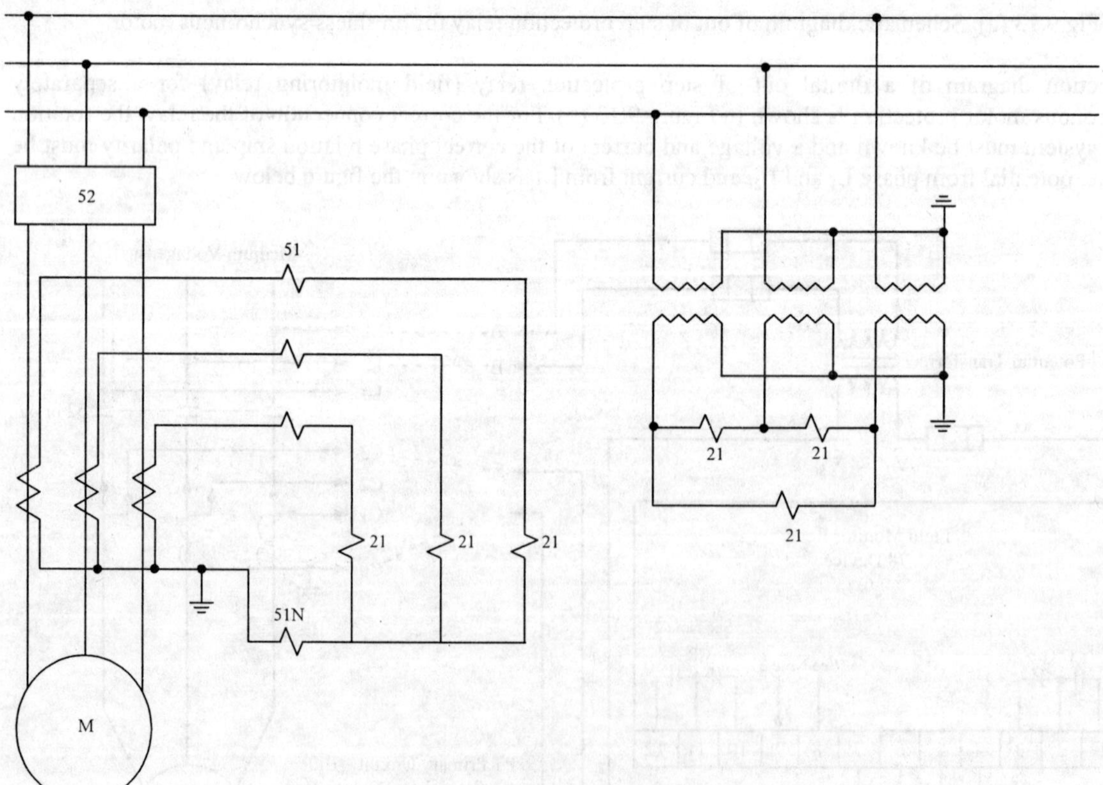

Fig. 9.13 (c): Distance relay used for locked rotor protection of motor.

Repetitive intermittent operation of the motor also can cause mechanical stressing of the stator winding coil ends and of the damper or rotor winding end connections. Minimizing the number of starts will maximize the life of the motor. For automatic operation with a remote control device, it may be necessary to provide a fixed time interval between starts or limit the number of starts within a period of time to ensure safe operation. Locked rotor protection characteristic with time over-current, supervised by a speed switch or a distance relay is illustrated in Figure 9.13 (d).

LEGEND:
12: Over-speed; 21: Distance relay for locked rotor protection; 51: Time over-current relay

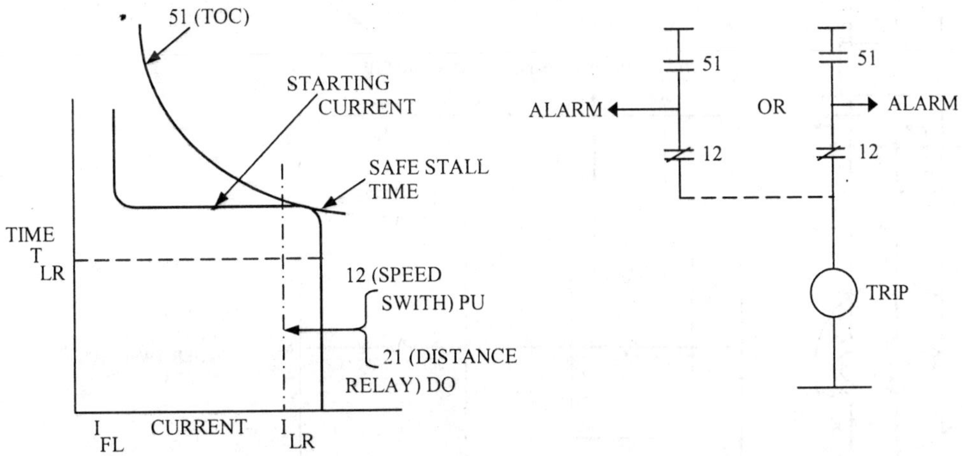

Fig. 9.13 (d): Locked rotor protection with over-current supervised by, speed switch / distance relay.

9.14 DIFFERENTIAL PROTECTION FOR STAR AND DELTA CONNECTED MOTORS.

Differential relay protection is a scheme in which the current entering in a winding is matched against that coming out of the winding. These relays detect low-magnitude fault currents during normal loads and do not trip falsely during high magnitude external faults, or during starting periods. Differential relays cannot detect turn-to-turn faults in the same winding. Connections for differential protection for a star connected motor and delta-connected motor are shown in Figure 9.14 (a) and (b) respectively. The relay responds to the percentage difference between the incoming and outgoing current values. Current transformers (Class 5P20) should have matched characteristics and should not be used for any other purpose. Three current transformers are located within the switchgear panel so as to include the cable within the protected zone. The other three current transformers are located in the motor and connected as shown in the respective figures. Figure (b) need interposing current transformer (for conventional type relays) to match the currents in the star and delta CT's.

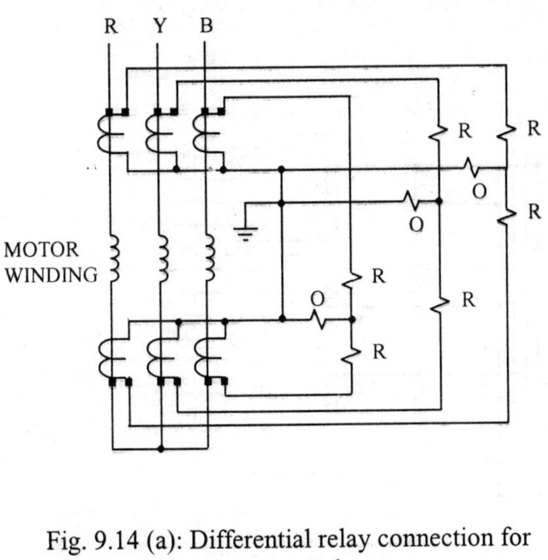

Fig. 9.14 (a): Differential relay connection for star connected motor

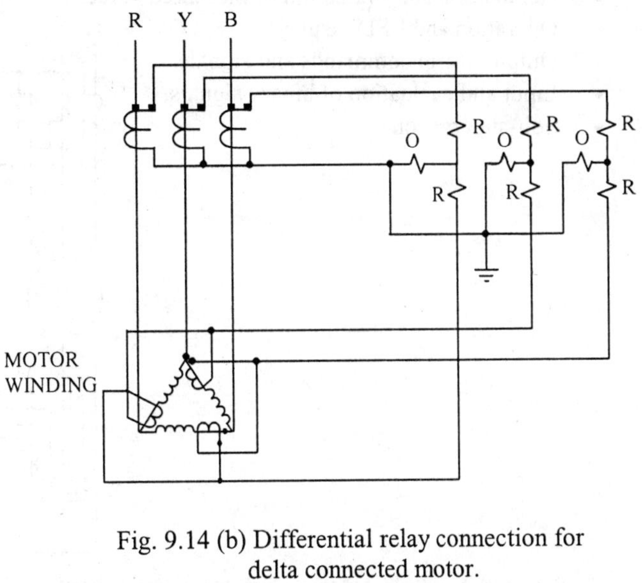

Fig. 9.14 (b) Differential relay connection for delta connected motor.

Figure 9.14 (c) illustrates sensitive differential protection with directional ground relay (Device # 87N) for star connected motors. Relay receives its polarizing signal from a broken delta potential transformer described in figure 5.2 (e) of Chapter # 5.

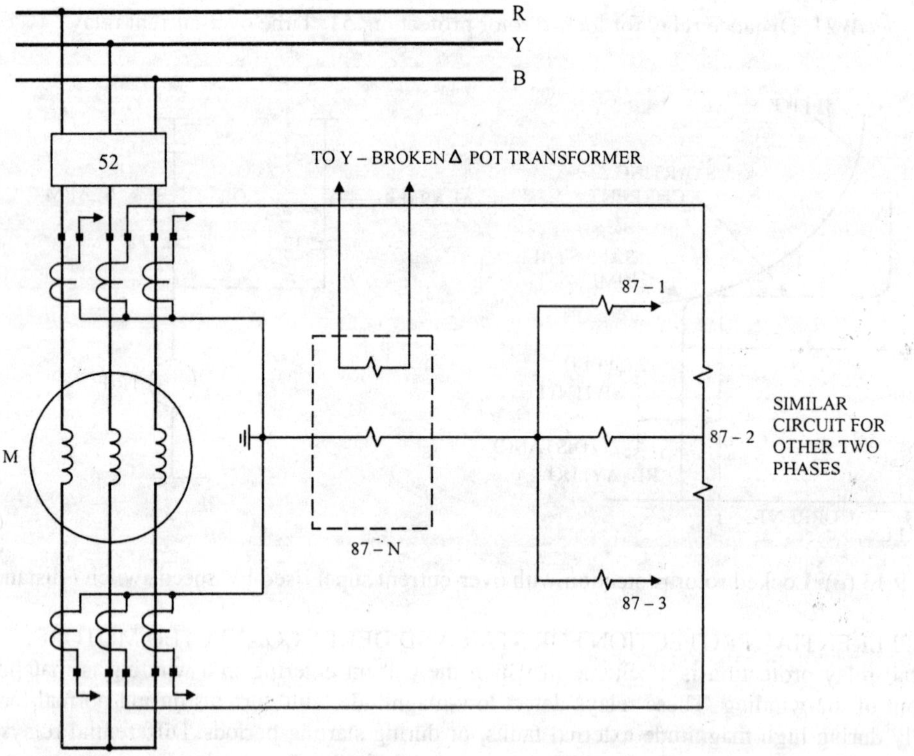

Fig. 9.14 (c): Sensitive differential protection with directional ground relay

Differential protection relay described in Figure 9.14 (d) is **Siemens 7VH60** numerical relay, which is designed for fast and selective differential protection based on the high impedance circulating current principle. It is used for the protection of all type of motors and generators against phase-to-phase and phase-to earth faults in the stator windings. The unit contains all the components needed for:

- Acquisition and evaluation of measured values.
- Operation and LED display.
- Output of trip commands and signals.
- Input and evaluation of binary signals.
- Self-supervision.

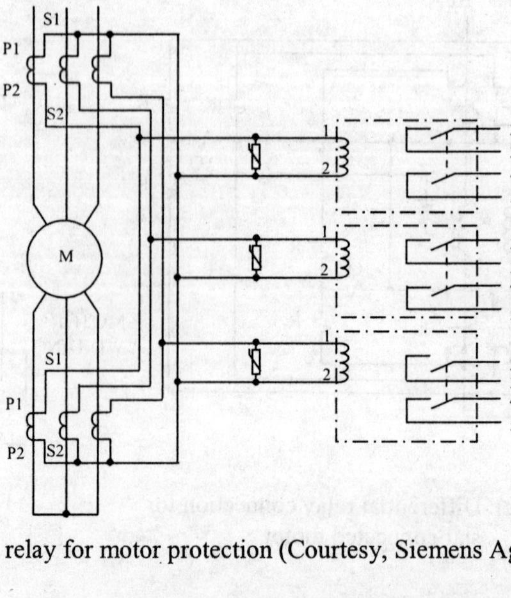

Fig. 9.14 (d): Numerical differential protection relay for motor protection (Courtesy, Siemens Ag).

All protection functions including the DC/DC converter are provided on a printed circuit board. The heavy-duty current plug connector provides automatic shorting of the CT circuits whenever the module is withdrawn. The sensitive relay input (CT connection) transformer galvanically isolates the relay static measuring circuit from the main current transformer. The AC measured current is band-pass-filtered and rectified to a proportional DC voltage. This voltage is monitored by a Schmidt trigger-circuit. If the set DC voltage, equivalent to the relay rated operating current of 20mA is exceeded, then the trigger operates to energize the command output relay as well as the operation indicator. An auxiliary DC supply monitoring circuit consisting of a green LED and an NO/NC relay contact is provided to indicate the status of the DC supply. Figure 9.14 (d) illustrates the connection diagram of high impedance numerical differential relay designed for motor protection. Method of testing differential relay is demonstrated in Chapter # 6, section 6.5, [figure (c) to (k)]. .

9.15 NEGATIVE PHASE SEQUENCE AND CURRENT BALANCE PROTECTION.

Negative sequence current is contributed by the motor or system during an unbalanced voltage condition (for example, open phase, single phase fault or unbalanced load) or when there are shorted turns in the stator winding. These negative sequence currents induce double line-frequency currents that flow in the damper winding or rotor parts. The magnitude of the double line-frequency current depends upon the location of the fault, number of turns shorted, mutual induction, and system and motor impedance. The danger to the rotor parts is a function of the unbalance in the stator current. Figure 9.15 (a) illustrates negative sequence protection for medium voltage motor.

Current balance relay (Device # 60) is an over-current relay that is connected to operate on the differential current from current transformers in the split windings of a motor The relay should be set above the maximum error current caused by winding unbalance. This unbalance can vary with different operating conditions, so it is wise to observe the unbalance under light load, full load, and starting conditions. Ordinary 10% of full load pick-up is secure. A delay of approximately 0.3 sec. for 100% full load current is recommended.

For analysis, during unbalanced conditions the motor can be considered to have two rotors [See Figure 9.15 (b)]. One is the effect resulting from balanced current and the other is the effect of unbalanced current. If perfect current balance existed in each phase of the motor current, then I_1 would be the line current squared with no error in the heating projected from the current. This positive component of current generates the motor output torque or work. The second component of the current is the negative sequence, represented as I_2. It is a three-phase current with reverse phase rotation from that of the AC source. This current generates counter-torque to the motor output torque, or negative work. Because the torque generated by I_2 does not leave the rotor, it is absorbed as heat and therefore has a more significant effect on the rotor heating than the I_1

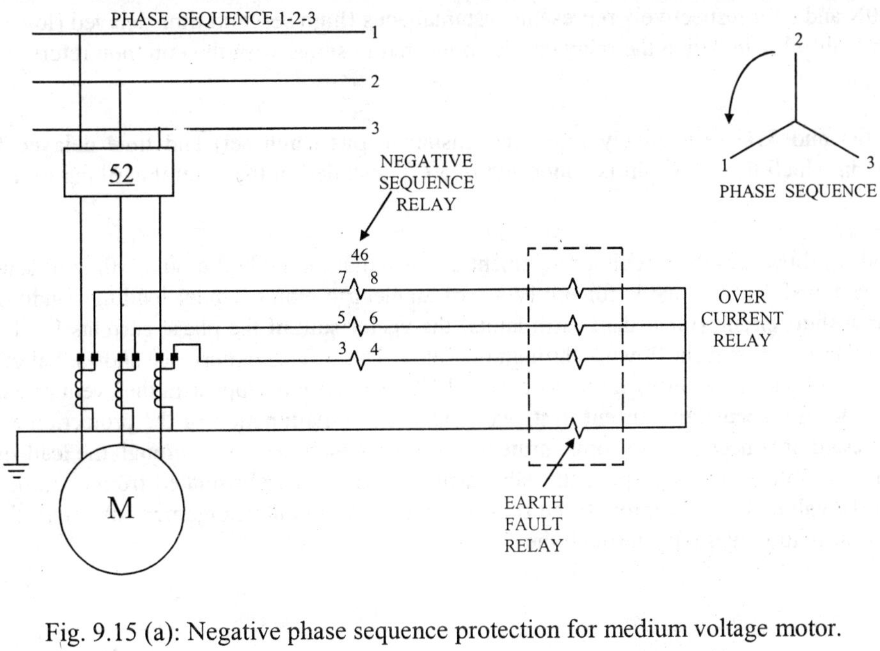

Fig. 9.15 (a): Negative phase sequence protection for medium voltage motor.

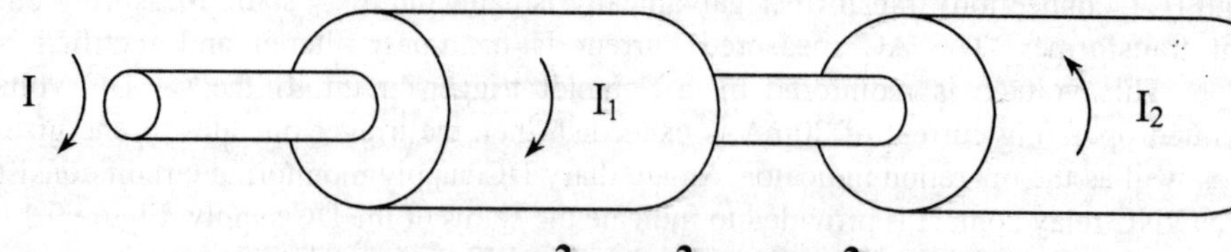

$$I^2 = I_1^2 + KI_2^2$$

Fig. 9.15 (b): Positive and negative sequence current components.

Any 3-phase AC current can be represented by the addition of $I_1 + I_2$. Using vector analysis to determine the positive sequence, one rotates phase B in the positive direction 120 degrees and phase C in the positive direction 240 degrees. [Refer to figure 6.12 (e) & (f) in Chapter # 6]

The formula for $I_1 = \frac{I_A + (I_B + 120) + (I_C + 240)}{3}$

The negative sequence is determined by rotating phase B in the opposite or negative direction for 120 degrees and phase C rotated in the negative direction for 240 degrees. [Refer figure 6.12 (g) of Chapter # 6]

The formula for I becomes $I_2 = \frac{I_A + (I_B - 120) + (I_C - 240)}{3}$

The current squared, as used in the calculation for rotor heat is $I^2 = I^2{}_1 + KI^2{}_2$

Here $I^2{}_2$ is weighted by, K because of the disproportional heating caused by the negative sequence.

9.16 ZERO-SEQUENCE SENSORS FOR EARTH FAULT PROTECTIONOF MOTORS (50G).

There are four different methods of connecting current transformers for earth fault or ground fault protection and are identified as follows:

1. Device number 64: Residual sensing illustrated in figure 5.19 (a) and (b) of Chapter # 5.
2. Device number 50N/51N: Over-current sensing illustrated in figure 9.15 (a), section 9.15 (earth fault protection combined with over-current protection).
3. Device number 50G/51G: Neutral sensing illustrated in figure 7.9 (a) of Chapter # 7 earth fault relay connected to neutral CT.
4. Zero sequence sensing as illustrated in Figure 9.16 (a) and (b).

Device number 50N and 51N respectively represents instantaneous (high set) and time delayed (low set) phase over-current earth fault relay in which the relay coil is connected in series with the common return wire of the CT secondary

Device number 50G and 51G respectively represents instantaneous (high set) and time delayed (low set) ground fault relay, in which the relay coil is connected to a CT installed in the neutral earthing of a generator or transformer.

Figure 9.16 (a) and (b) illustrates the circuit arrangement and installation method of an earth fault sensor (with core balance current transformer) suitable for protection of an electric motor. Under loading conditions, three phase and two phase short circuit (other than earth faults) the vector sum of the phase currents $I_R + I_Y + I_B = 0$, and for that reason there is no current flowing through the relay. The service experience shows that currents I_0, circulating through earth may flow through the cable sheath. These currents, appear in the event of earth faults near the cable and causes a secondary current in its winding and the malfunction of the protection as a result. To prevent the aforesaid, it is necessary to compensate the current, which may pass through the lead sheath and metallic armour of the cable. For this purpose the cable armour and earth are insulated from earth or the earth wire connected to the cable is passed through the sensor window. With an arrangement like that, the current flowing in the cable armour comes back through the earthing wire.

LEGEND (Fig. 9.16b)
1. Cable termination
2. Power cable
3. Gland plate
4. Earth connection
5. Core balance CT

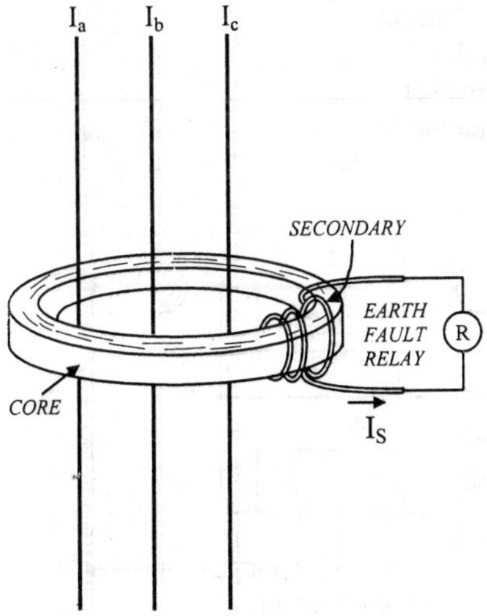

Fig 9.16 (a): Core balance CT

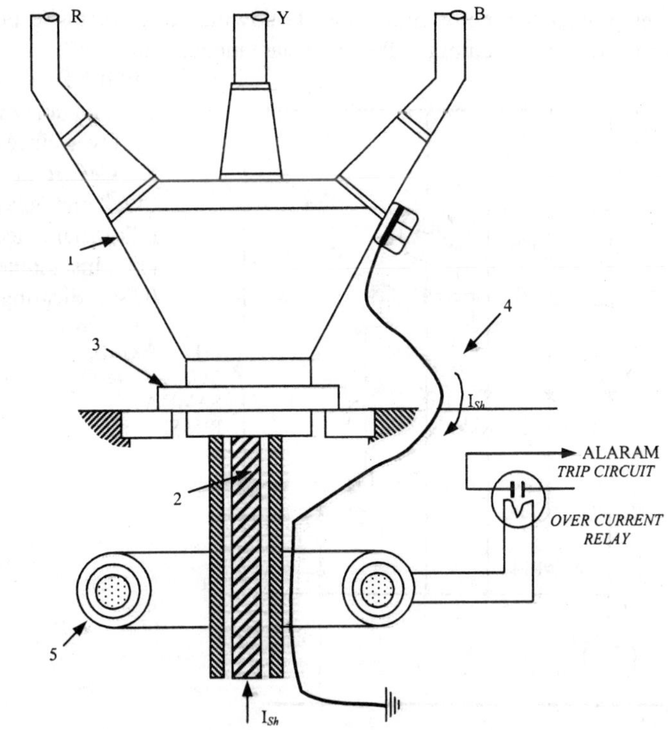

Fig. 9.16 (b): Installation method of zero sequence protection

9.17 INSTANTANEOUS AND TIME DELAY OVERCURRENT RELAY.

Figure 9.17 (a) illustrates the connection diagram of a phase over-current relay designed for motor over-current protection. The relay provides inverse time phase fault protection. IDMT units are supplemented by instantaneous over-current units which when set above the maximum through fault current will provide selective instantaneous clearance for terminal short circuits.

Application: Inverse definite minimum time (IDMT) and instantaneous over-current and / or earth fault protection.

Over-current setting: 50 to 200% range
Earth fault setting: 20 to 80% or 10 to 40% range
Instantaneous setting: 250 to 2000% range
LEGEND:
CO: Time delay element
ITH: Low set instantaneous
ITT: High set instantaneous

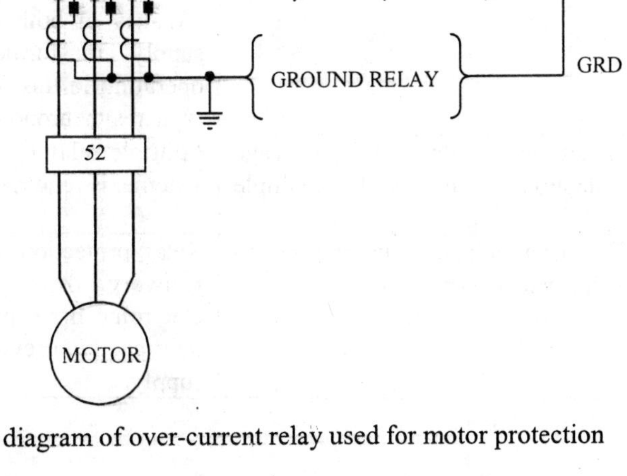

Fig. 9.17 (a): Connection diagram of over-current relay used for motor protection

Figure 9.17 (b) and (c) shows the DC schematic diagram and test connections respectively for over-current relay employed for motor protection. Following tests are to be performed: (1) Zero check (2) Pickup and timing of over-current unit (3) Pickup instantaneous unit.

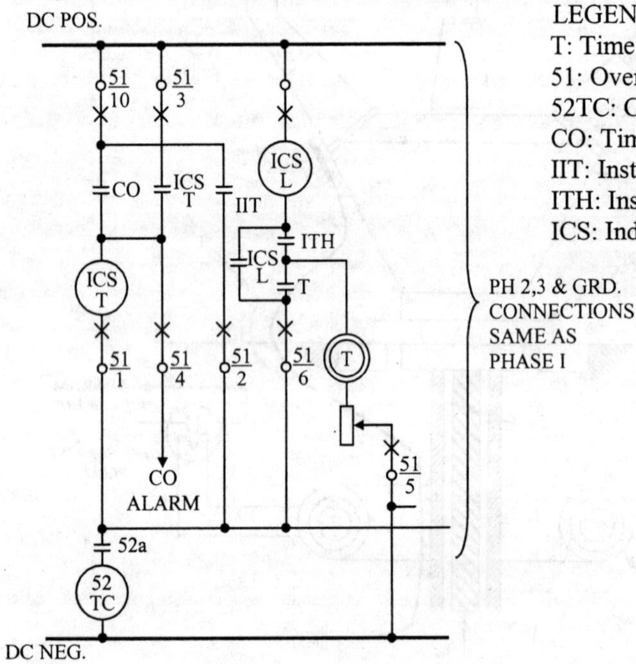

LEGEND:
T: Time delay unit
51: Over-current relay
52TC: Circuit breaker trip coil
CO: Time delay over-current
IIT: Instantaneous high set
ITH: Instantaneous low set
ICS: Indicating contractor

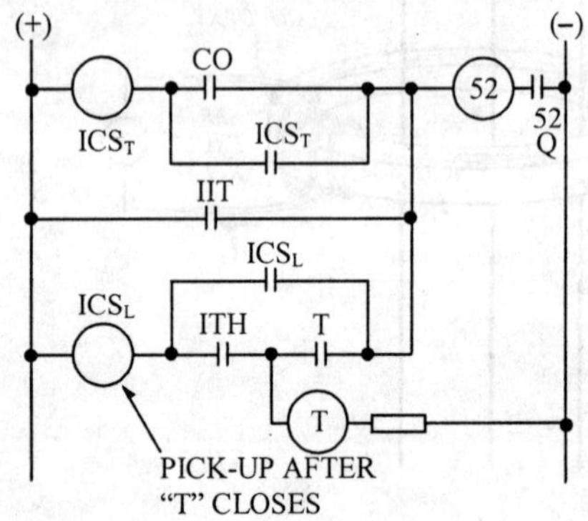

Fig. 9.17 (b): DC schematic diagram of O/C relay

Fig. 9.17 (c): Test connections of DC circuit.

9.18 PROTECTION SCHEMES FOR VARIABLE SPEED MEDIUM VOLTAGE MOTORS.

Table 9.18 (1) below outlines the general protection philosophies as related to various types of motor drives. Most variable frequency drives employ transformer isolated frequency conversion circuitry to drive synchronous and induction motors and therefore, appears as transformer loads on the electrical system to which they are connected. Multiple speed motors contain multiple or tapped windings and relay on contactors to accomplish speed change by way of alteration of the winding configurations.

Table 9.18 (1): Variable speed motor protection philosophy.

Motor type	Protection philosophy
Synchronous or squirrel cage induction motor variable frequency motor drives.	Relay protection similar to transformer protection (phase and ground fault protection). Motor and electronic drive protection should be based on protection interface requirements between the motor / drive and power supply. In many cases, full speed across the line starting or run circuitry or both is employed that bypasses the isolation supply Transformer or converter circuitry or both. While operating in this mode the motor should be protected as a typical synchronous machine or induction machine.
Synchronous or squirrel cage induction motor with multiple speed winding.	Multiple relay CT protection or flux balancing differential scheme, is required.
Slip ring induction motor (Wound rotor induction motor).	Relay protection identical to squirrel cage induction motor recovery drive protection. Supplemental motor and electronic drive protection should be based on protection interface requirements between the motor / drive and power supply.

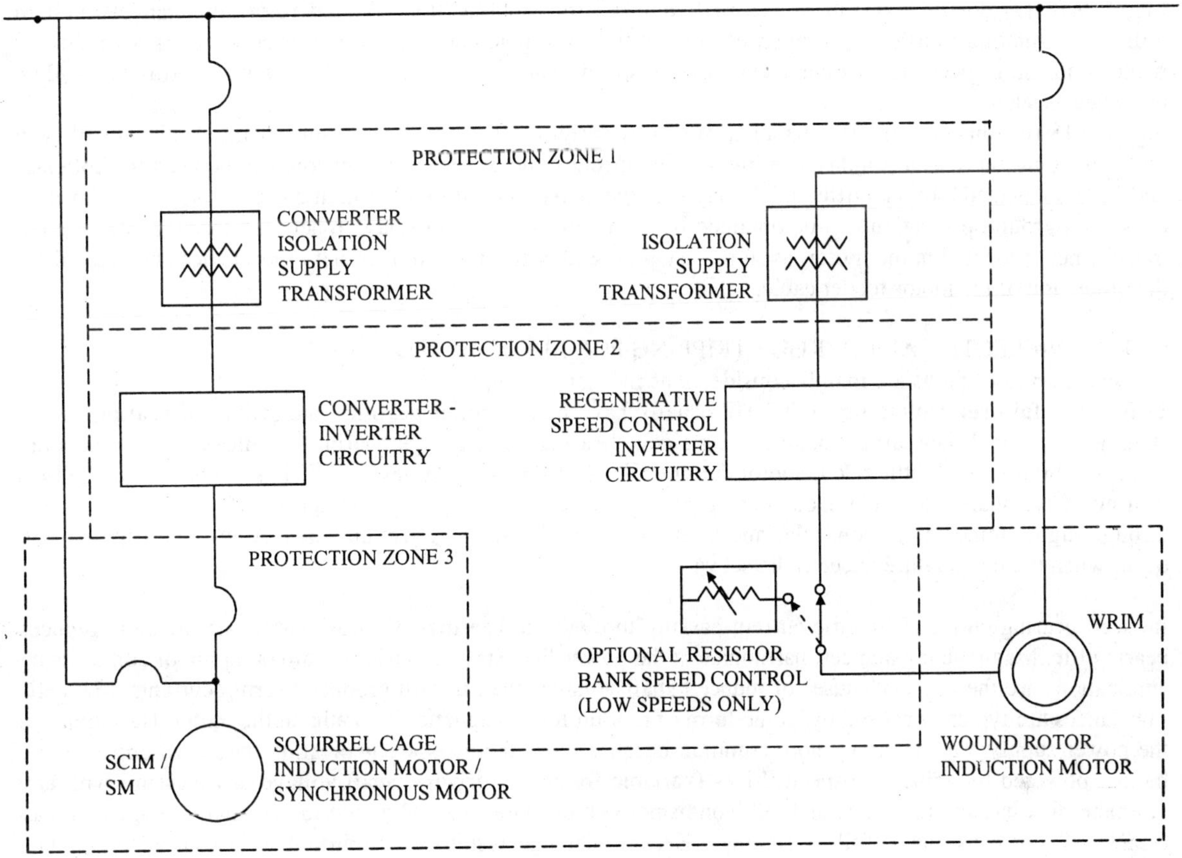

Fig. 9.18 (a): Variable speed motor protection for squirrel cage and slip ring induction motors.

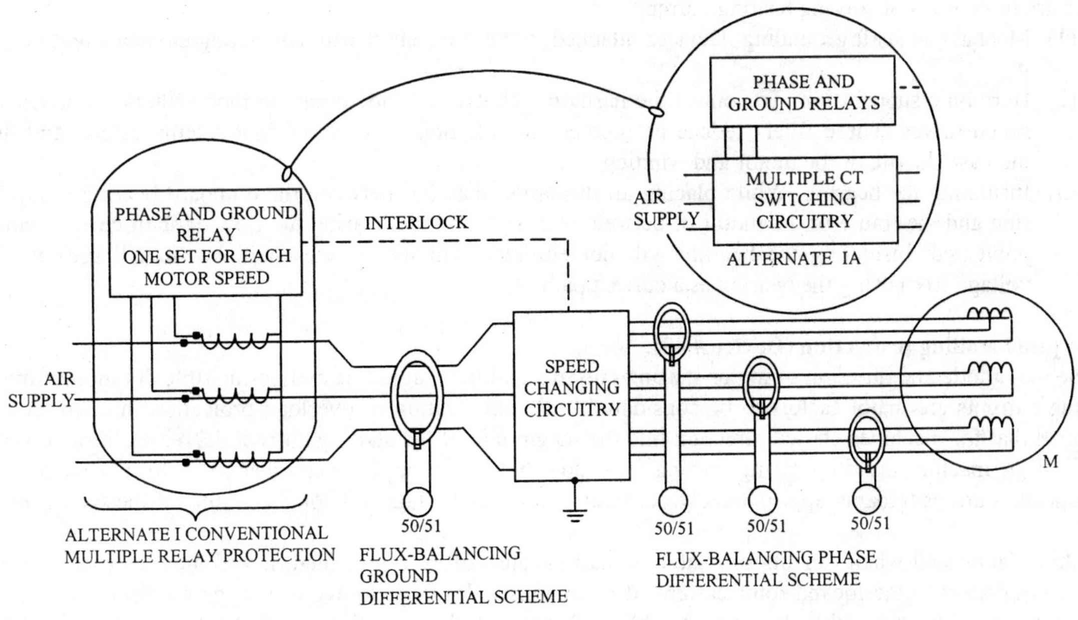

Fig 9.18 (b): Flux balance differential protection for two-speed motors.

Figure 9.18 (a) details two alternatives of two-speed motor protection. Wound rotor slip recovery system utilizes the rotating transformer properties of a wound rotor machine to provide regenerative energy recovery while controlling speed. The wound rotor variable speed motor appears as an induction machine and should be protected as such.

Figure 9.18 (b) illustrates the flux balancing primary current differential protection scheme. Both ends of each motor winding serve as a primary winding of the current transformers. This scheme can be used for both star and delta connected motors. Differential relay sees the differences of internal fault current. Externally sensitive phase and ground protection can be obtained by using an over-current relay. Where the through type current transformer is located in the motor, as in the usual case, this scheme requires that other devices be applied for the protection of the motor feeder cable.

9.19 NON-ELECTRICAL LOCKOUT TRIPPING FOR ELECTRIC MOTORS.

Following types of faults are mainly considered as mechanical faults:

1) Bearing failure: Motors up to 500 HP usually have ball or roller bearings and failure of bearing causes stalling of motor. When large machine using sleeve bearings, a defective bearing is indicated by temperature rise and vibration, with little rise in motor current. Temperature sensing devices (RTD's) embedded in the load bearing (drive shaft side), motor outboard bearing, load case bearing gives adequate warning and protection through digital temperature controller and monitor (refer Chapter # 7, section 7.16). Alarm and tripping will occur when the temperature exceeds the set value.

Induced bearing currents: Electric current passing through the bearings of large motors significantly reduces bearing life. Magnetic imbalances, harmonics in the power line, static electricity from pumping or compressing applications are the primary causes of induced shaft voltages that, in turn produce bearing currents. Magnetic imbalances are typically caused by, some form of non-uniform magnetic flux paths in the motor. Harmonics in the power supply are becoming more common because more facilities are generating their own power, more motors powered by adjustable speed drives (variable frequency drives). Shaft-voltage can measure with any voltmeter that has an impedance of 10,000 ohms per volt or more. Normally, end-to-end shaft voltage less than 0.5 V will not cause harm-full to bearings. Bearing damage results when current is broken at the contact surfaces between rolling elements and raceways. The size of the damage depends on the magnitude of the induced voltage, the impedance of the current path and bearing type.

There are three ways of solving bearing current:

(1) Mechanical shaft grounding: Devices attached to the drive shaft with contacting elements that ground it.

(2) Harmonic suppression: To control the harmonic content provide common mode filters for adjustable speed drives. These filters reduce harmonics, audible noise, vibration, motor temperature, and they increase the life of the motor and winding.

(3) Insulating the bearing. While placing an insulation material between the outboard bearing mounting ring and the frame of the motor or between the shaft and the bearing the flow of shaft current can be prevented. Insulating the bearing will not eliminate voltage on the shaft, but it will prevent that voltage from using the bearing as a current path.

Load jam / stalling protection (Device # 48):

As the magnitude and duration of motor starting currents and the magnitude and permissible duration of motor stalling currents are major factors to be considered in the application of overload protection. It is commonly assumed that for machines started direct on line the magnitude of the starting current decreases linearly as the speed of the machine build up during starting. This does not in fact apply to any machines, for normal designs the starting current remains approximately constant at the initial standstill for 80 – 90% of the total starting time.

Should a motor stall when running or unable to start because of excessive load, it will draw current from the supply equivalent to the locked rotor current. It is obviously desirable to avoid damage by disconnecting the machine as quickly as possible. It is not possible to distinguish the condition from a healthy starting condition purely on a current magnitude basis the only way to overcome the problem is to arrange that the protective device disconnects the motor if the current continues for longer than the normal starting time. Usually a definite-time over-current relay is provided to detect and isolate the motor during load jam condition. This function is instituted only after the motor has started. The load jam pick-up current setting is in multiples of motor's full load current. The definite time delay is adjustable from 0.5 to 10 seconds in steps of 0.1.

Load loss protection (Device # 37):
A definite time undercurrent relay is provided to detect a loss of load condition. The load loss pick up current setting is in multiples of the motor's full load current.

9.20 FAULT LEVEL AT SUPPLY POINTS OF LARGE MOTORS.
The fault level at the point of supply to the installation requires consideration. The minimum fault level, which can occur will affect the operation of the installation, particularly with regard to voltage regulation when starting motors, while the maximum fault level will determine the ratings of equipment installed. All supply systems develop with time the switchgear and other equipment installed must be chosen to be suitable if the external supply system upgrades. The contribution of the installation itself to fault level at the point of common coupling is another important consideration. Rotating plant, either generators or motors will contribute to both make and break fault levels. The contribution of synchronous machines to fault current can be calculated from sub-transient and transient reactance values, and although similar calculations can be carried-out for induction motors. Accurate data are not generally readily available for groups of small motors operating together, as in a typical industrial electrical installation. Generally, induction motor contribution to make fault levels is taken as being equivalent to motor starting current and to break levels as twice the motor full load currents.

When selecting a stand by generator set it is advisable to check that the voltage recovery time after the application of a high transient load is not too long. For normal industrial loads, a voltage dip of 15% is acceptable, with recovery to within 3 percent of the rated voltage in 1 to 1½ second(s), however, for special applications, a voltage recovery to within 3 percent of the rated voltage within ½ second may be called for. A rough guide for voltage dip on a generator assuming a fast acting automatic voltage regulator (AVR) is given by:
Voltage dip per unit value E = Im x (X/100R)
X = Transient reactance of the generator, in percent.
Im = Starting MVA of the motor assuming 1 HP = 1 KVA.
(For DOL starting, 6 times and assisted starting 4 times).
R = MVA rating of the generator
E = Voltage dip expressed in per unit value.
This formula can be used in the initial design stage to determine the maximum size of motor that may be started on a given generator. It is advisable that the motor starting load does not exceed the generator capacity. If several motors are running on the same generator, the total KVA off all motors plus starting KVA of the largest motor, other load connected to the system is to be considered for calculation.

There are many considerations to starting a motor other than effectively connecting it to the line voltage. Nuisance tripping and excessive running currents are signs that a power system is not performing properly. During direct starting, an AC motor will draw typically about 6 times of rated full load current and will last as long, although diminishing in magnitude, as the motor reaches to full speed. If the motor is started with load, inrush current will be drawn for a longer period of time. However, it will not be greater in magnitude than if the motor was started with no load. The power system should be able to supply inrush to any motor connected to the system. If the system does not have sufficient capacity, voltage dip will take place during starting of motors.
A load flow study is especially valuable for a system, which involves multiple load centers. The power flow study is an analysis of the systems capability to adequately supply the load. The study will provide useful information about real and reactive power flow, bus voltages, and power factor etc. Other types of information gained in a load flow study are:

(a) The optimum-tap setting for power transformers.
(b) The need and justification for shunt reactors and/or shunt capacitors.
(c) Optimum size and location of power factor correction equipment.
(d) The possibility and extent of overloads on transformers, generators, and the feeders
(e) The present load on each feeder and location of future load.
(f) System fault level at each bus and feeders.

The load flow study, like all system studies, usually is performed on a digital computer, which produces a printout that lists the required information. The transformer tap positions are selected to insure the correct voltage at critical locations such as motor control centers.

Starting current of electric motor will cause voltage dip. Higher fault level of power supply source indicates that motor can be started with higher starting current with out being heavy voltage dip. Lower fault level of supply means supply is relatively weak.

Fault level MVA = $\sqrt{3}$ x short-circuit current in KA x phase-to-phase voltage in KV
For example, in an 11 KV system, short circuit rating 25 KA.
Fault level = 1.732 x 11 x 25 = 476.3 MVA

The following formula can be used to calculate the short-circuit current available at the secondary terminals of a three phase step down transformer:

$$\text{Short-circuit current in amps Isc} = \frac{\text{KVA} \times 100}{\text{KV} \times \sqrt{3} \times \%Z}$$

KVA = Transformer capacity in Kilovolt ampere given in the transformer nameplate.
KV = Secondary phase-to-phase voltage in Kilovolts.
%Z = Percent impedance of transformer primary lines given in the transformer nameplate.
Isc = Three-phase short circuit current.

For a typical motor load, in addition to the current from the transformer, current will also flow toward the fault, from connected (running) motor which act as generators during a fault. The sub-transient reactance of such motors will determine their contribution to the fault current during the first few cycles after the fault. If exact data of motor is not available an approximate value of 4 times motor full load current is used for motor fault current contribution. Circuit breaker located in the main incoming switchboard and sub-switch board would be required to have an interrupting rating at least equal to the fault current from the transformer secondary plus the fault current contributed by the connected motors.

For example, 1500 KVA 3-phase transformer rated 480 volts 60 Hertz, on low voltage side. Transformer reactance is 5.75% (unlimited primary source). Motor contribution: 100% of transformer capacity.
Full load current = (KVA x 1000) / (Voltage x $\sqrt{3}$) = [1500 x 1000] / [480 x 1.732] = 1804.27 A
Short circuit current = (Full load current x 100) / %Z = [1804.27 x 100] / 5.75 = 31,378.60 A
Motor contribution [considering 100% of transformer full load current] = 1804.27 x 4 = 7217.08
Circuit breaker interrupting current = 31,378.60 + 7217.08 = 38,595.68 Amps = 38.6 KA.

Fault level of supply and circuit breaker ratings are limited to 40 KA (r.m.s) for low and medium voltage motors 1 MW and above. Dry type or mineral oil filled type reactors are connected in series to the feeder or bus bar of medium voltage lines for limiting the current during starting heavy motors or for fault current limiting in systems. Air cored reactors have non-magnetic and magnetic shielding to reduce stray losses. In case of air gapped iron cored reactors adequate clamping of core is provided to reduce noise level. Series connected current limiting reactors are demonstrated in Chapter # 3, section 3.17

9.21 TESTS ON AC MOTORS AND CONVENTIONAL STARTERS.

Tests are to be performed on each motor at the end of production is given below.

(1) No-load test: No-load test reveals the mechanical out-of-balance and correct connections and direction of rotation. Test diagram for squirrel cage induction motor and slip ring induction motor are shown in Figure 9.21 (a) and (b) respectively. Correct nameplate voltage at rated frequency is applied to the motor through a three-phase autotransformer and the measuring circuit consists of voltmeter, ammeter, kilo-wattmeter and power factor meter. For slip ring motor rotor current is measured by inserting an ammeter in the rotor circuit. KW meter reads input power = (iron loss + friction and windage losses). Ammeter shows no-load current (magnetizing current) and PF meter indicates no-load power factor. Copper losses are negligible as the magnetizing current is very low. Slip ring motor start with full design resistance in the circuit and after attaining speed the slip ring is short-circuited.

(2) Full load test: Similar circuits in figure 9.21 (a) and (b) are used for full load test except that the motor is loaded by generator coupled by belt or direct coupling. The output of the generator is measured, and its efficiency at various loads must be known so that the output of the motor can be calculated. KW meter indicates the full load loss.

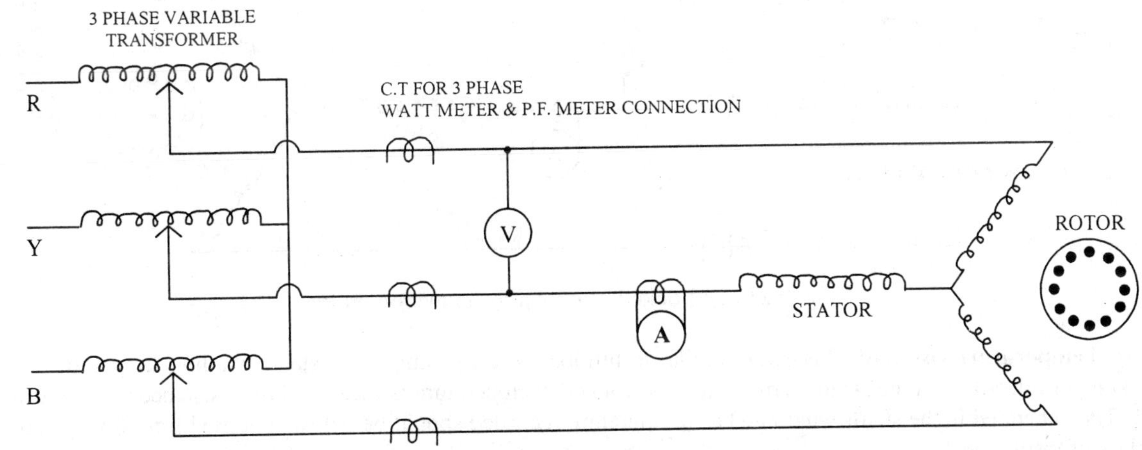

Fig. 9.21 (a): No-load / full load test circuit for squirrel cage induction motor.

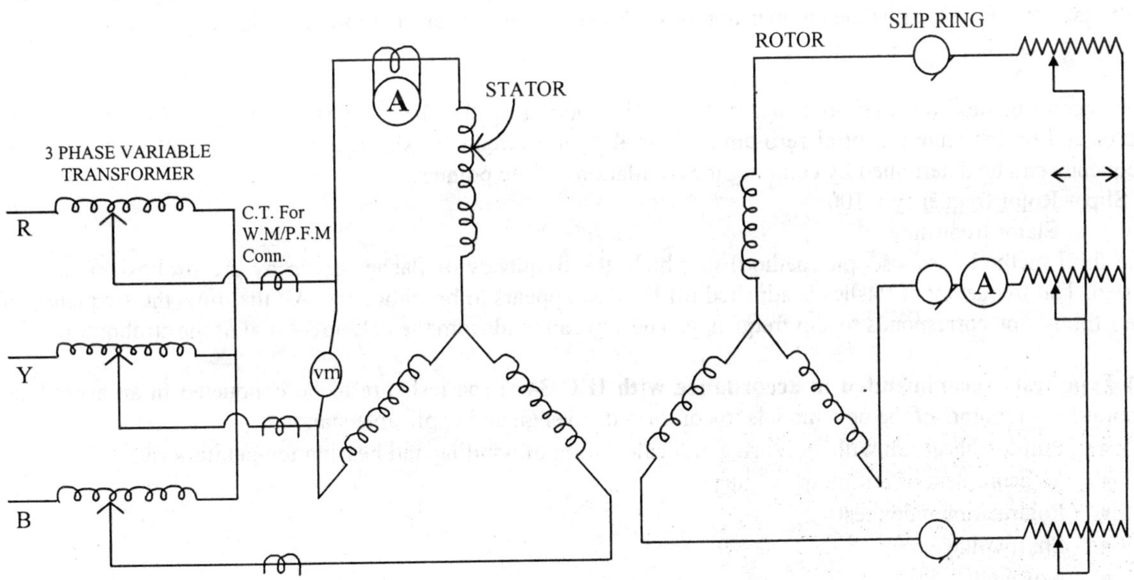

Fig. 9.21 (b): No-load / full load test circuit for slip ring induction motor.

(3) Locked rotor test (Short circuit test): As shown in Figure 9.21 (c), the rotor is locked by a shaft locking device and the stator is supplied through an autotransformer by a reduced voltage at rated frequency. The voltage is gradually increased until stator full load current reads in the ammeter. During locked rotor test, KW meter indicates copper loss (I^2R) at full load stator current.

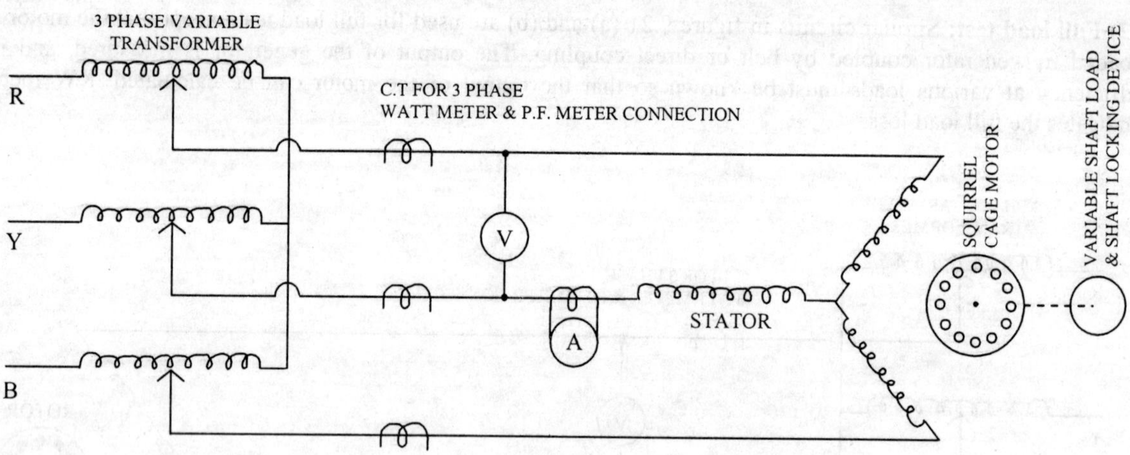

Fig. 9.21 (c): Locked rotor test for induction motor.

(4): Temperature rise test: This test is similar to full load test. Reading of the stator winding temperatures are taken periodically still the steady temperature is reached. Temperature is measured by resistance method using RTDs embedded in the stator winding. The temperature recorded should be below specified limit for particular class of insulation.

Insulation class	Y	A	E	B	F	H	C
Temperature°C	90	105	120	130	155	180	>180

:

(5) Slip measurement: There are three different methods of slip measurements. In the first method actual motor speed (Na) is measured by using a tachometer and the synchronous speed (Ns) is calculated by using the formula 120f / P where P is the number of poles of the motor under test. (f represents the supply frequency).

$$\% \text{ Slip} = \frac{Ns - Na}{Ns} \cdot 100$$

The second method (oscillation measurement) is by measuring the shaft voltage in a squirrel cage induction motor and by inserting a central zero-ammeter in the rotor circuit for slip ring motors. In both case the rotor frequency can be determined by counting the oscillations of the pointer.

$$\% \text{ Slip} = \frac{\text{Rotor frequency}}{\text{Stator frequency}} \times 100$$

The third method (stroboscopic method) in which, the frequency of flashes given by the stroboscope can be varied. The frequency of flashes is adjusted till the disc appears to be stationary. All that time the frequency of the stroboscope corresponds to slip frequency. The slip can read from the calibrated dial of the stroboscope.

(6) Type tests recommended in accordance with IEC 34. Type tests are to be conducted in an accredited laboratory on motors of the new models to conform the design and applicable standard.

- Full load heat run with measuring and calculation of winding and bearing temperature rise.
- Measurement of torque speed curve
- Polarization index test
- Shaft voltage
- Noise level

(7) Routine tests recommended in accordance with IEC 34. Routine tests are conducted at the manufacturer's premises on each motor to conform the performance of the motor.

- Measurement of winding resistance
- No load current, power and speed at rated voltage and frequency
- Locked rotor current and torque
- Mechanical vibration
- Phase sequence and direction of rotation
- Insulation resistance test

- High potential test
- Sleeve bearing inspection
- Physical inspection.

(8) Pre-commissioning/commissioning check:
Following site tests prior to commissioning are recommended for motors to ensure that the machine is free from defects.

1. Measurement of insulation resistance (Use 2.5 KV megger for HV motors)
2. DC resistance measurement (Use wheatstone bridge). For high voltage motors refer Chapter # 1, section 1.13 figure (e) and (f).
3. Check star-delta connection as applicable, cable size and termination, winding continuity etc. Cable tag and equipment identification labels are to be verified.
4. Polarization index is defined as the ratio between the resistance value in 10 minutes and the resistance value in one minute during the process of measurement. Minimum 1.2 is a sign of good insulation. For medium voltage motors 2.5 / 5 KV megger is to be used for conducting the measurement.
   $$\text{Polarization index} = \frac{\text{Insulation resistance obtained after 10 minutes}}{\text{Insulation resistance measured after 1 minute}}$$
5. Earth resistance measurement by using earth tester. The measured value must be below one ohm.
6. High voltage (AC power frequency voltage) test: 1.5 Times motor rated voltage at rated frequency is applied to the motor between phase-to-earth, for a test duration of one minute. Test shall be conducted on each phase as illustrated in Figure 9.21 (d).
7. Check the supply phase sequence based on the direction of rotation marked/required.
8. Vibration test (after commissioning) by using a set of 3-orthogonal accelerometer or vibro-meter.
9. Measurement of audible noise (after commissioning) by using noise level indicator. Measurements are taken at a distance of one metre from the machine surface in direction perpendicular to the shaft.
10. Measurement of no load, full load and starting current etc.

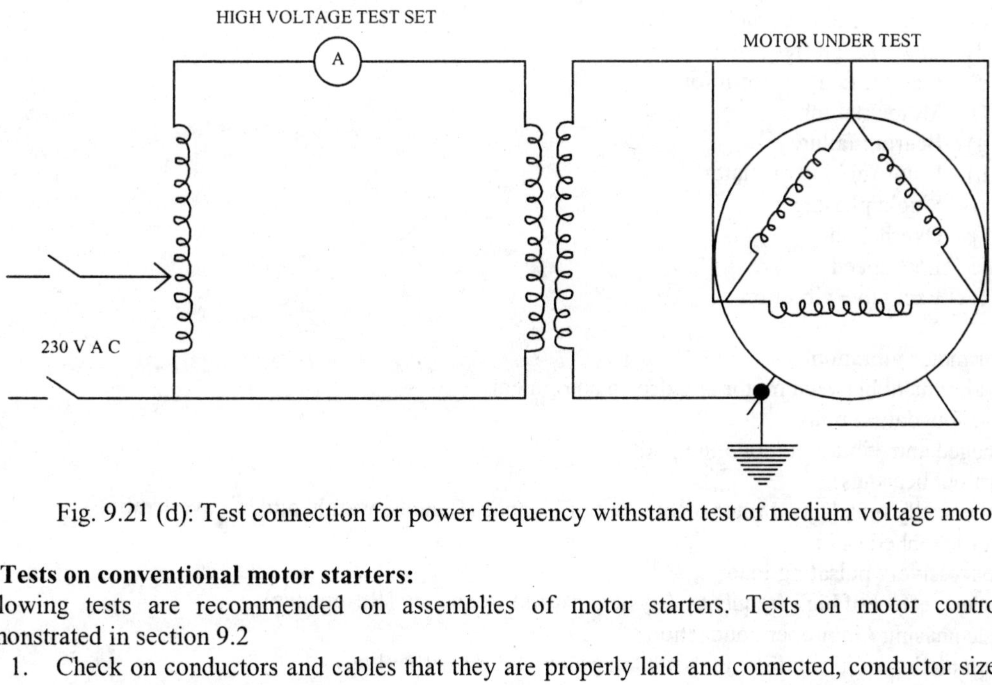

Fig. 9.21 (d): Test connection for power frequency withstand test of medium voltage motor.

(9) Tests on conventional motor starters:
Following tests are recommended on assemblies of motor starters. Tests on motor control center is demonstrated in section 9.2

1. Check on conductors and cables that they are properly laid and connected, conductor sizes are as per specification and drawings.
2. Visual inspection-to-determine degree-of-protection, creepage and clearance distances are maintained.
3. Check on nameplate and marking on components.
4. Test to check the correct function and sequence operation of contactor, timer, starter etc.
5. Electrical functional tests to verify interlocks, protective devices etc.
6. Check the function of protective relays with primary/secondary injection tests.

7. Insulation resistance test (1000 V megger) on power and control wiring excluding electronic devices.
8. Insulation resistance test on power and control cables

9.22 MAINTENANCE, TROUBLE SHOOTING AND REPAIR OF MOTORS.

Part A: Periodical maintenance:

a) General cleaning and blowing of dust by dry compressed air. Tightening all screwed and bolted connections.
b) Checking of air-gap: Excessive variation of air-gap shows that the bearings have worn down. It can be measured by using a feeler-gauge.
c) Alignment of shaft: This can be checked by placing magnetic dial indicators on either side of the coupling while running the motor.
d) Greasing or oiling of bearings: Under normal conditions bearings need lubrication once every six months or as per the equipment manufacturers recommendations. Grease is mainly necessary to protect the bearing against corrosion and to keep away grit and other foreign matter. Oil is used for bush bearings or thrust bearings.
e) Measurements of insulation resistance of windings and polarization index check on AC motor stator.
f) Attention to slip rings, carbon brushes, commutators and starters.
g) Checking whether motor is operating smoothly without vibration and abnormal noise. Noisy running may be caused by the lubricant having run-out, or the ball bearing worn-out. Excessive vibration is due to the disturbance of motor alignment. Abnormal noise may be due to the bend in the shaft.
h) Roller bearing is generally fitted on the driving end of the shaft and ball bearings on the opposite end because roller bearings can take a greater amount of thrust and are therefore better suited than ball bearings for the driving end where the thrust is much greater.

Part B: Trouble-shooting:

1) Abnormal operating conditions:

a) Over voltage
b) Unbalanced voltage
c) Mechanical overloads
d) Low or high frequency
e) Internal fault; stator/rotor
f) Motor stalling
g) Bearing failure
h) Rotor rubbing on stator
i) Single phasing
j) Overheating
k) Low speed
l) Excessive vibration

2) Reasons for motor vibration

a) Mis-alignment between motor and driven equipment
b) Loose foundation bolts
c) Damaged anti-vibration mounting pads
d) Worn-out bearings
e) Mechanically unbalanced rotor / Rotor out of balance (Balance weight added / overhauling)
f) Bent or cranked shaft
g) An excessively pulsating load
h) Magnetic effect of high frequency / system natural frequency (Resonance)
i) Single phasing / improper connection
j) Accumulation of dirt in fan / fan sifted on rotor (After overhauling)
k) Vibration in driven machine
l) Rotor rubbing on stator
m) Accumulation of dirt in fan

3) Reasons for running the motor hot

a) Over load, high or low voltage, unbalanced load

b) Open or short stator coils/rotor coils, turn-to-turn short circuit, grounded stator winding
c) Uneven air-gap, Rotor rubbing on stator, clogged ventilating duct
d) Low frequency / single phasing, unbalanced voltage
e) Failure of cooling system, dirt in motor or ventilating tubes

4) Reasons for running the motor slow
a) Low voltage, low frequency, single phasing
b) Open or shorted stator coils/rotor coils
c) Broken rotor bars, excessive load
d) Too much resistance in the rotor circuit of slip-ring type synchronous motors

5) Reasons for failure to start the motors
a) Excessive load, under voltage, failure of control circuit
b) Blown fuse, single phasing, resetting thermal overload relay after tripping
c) Brush does not touch collector ring or inadequate brush tension (for slip-ring motors).
d) Worn-out contacts or open / burned-out no volt coil of magnetic contactor

6) Reasons for abnormal noise / excessive hum
a) Magnetostruction, aerodynamics
b) Defect in bearings of rotating shaft
c) Speed and power effect / high voltage
d) Ventilation/vibration /unbalanced rotor
e) Broken rotor bar in a squirrel cage motor
f) Excessive wear of sleeve bearings

7) Regular clicking or rapid knocking
a) Foreign matter in air gap (Regular clicking)
b) Bad bearing; dirt in lubricant (Rapid knocking

8) Bearing over-heating
A) Mis-alignment or excessive tension in belt drive
B) Excessive end thrust
C) Too much grease on ball or roller winding
D) Sticking oil ring (sleeve bearing) or oil level too high or low
E) In sufficient lubrication

9) Oil leakage or excessive oil usage
a) Excessive pressure or vacuum in bearing cavity due to blocked heat exchanger tubes
b) Clogged oil return holes in bearings or very high bearing clearance
c) Parts not sealed properly
d) Loose heat exchanger tubes.

Part C: Repair of motors:

1) Static balancing of rotor: In static balancing the rotor is supported on a pair of perfectly horizontal knife-edges. If the rotor is in perfect balance it should rest in any position. If it is not accurately balanced i.e. uneven distribution of weight, the rotor will turn round and come to rest with the heaviest portion in the lowest position, and the hollow portion will occupy the top position. After fixing some counterweight on the top part of the rotor the test can be repeated. This, processes will continue until the rotor can come to rest equally well in the positions. The amount of weight added and its exact location has to be found by the trial and error method, remembering that the greater the distance from the center, the smaller should be the weight. An alternative method is to remove some weight from the heavier portion of the rotor by drilling a hole in the end supports or by chipping as found convenient.

2) Dynamic balancing: Dynamic balancing means carrying out the balancing operation when the rotor is actually rotating to verify the accuracy of balancing at high speed. Special dynamic balancing machines are available by means of which exact amount of weight to be added or removed and its location can be easily

determined. The rotor is mounted on a pair of pedestals carrying spring suspension systems, and driven at any speed required. The machine incorporates a visual indicator, which amplifies the vibration felt on the bearings due to the unbalance of the rotor. A suitable device is also included by means of which a counter-weight of the correct value may be temporarily inserted in the right place on the same shaft to which the rotor is coupled, until the oscillations are neutralized.

3) Impregnation of motor winding: The process of coating electrical windings with insulation varnish is called impregnation. By covering the coils with superior quality insulation varnish, the air spaces are filled-up and sealed. Thus the winding get protected against ingress of moisture. Before applying insulation varnish, the surface to-be applied are perfectly cleaned and free of all dust, oily matter and moisture. Varnish can be applied with a brush (for low voltage motors) and then allowed to dry-up. Few 500 or 1000 watts bulb can be used for heating during the dry-up process.

In the hot dip impregnation method (for high voltage motors) the coil is heated up to a temperature of 80 to 100°C in an electrically heated chamber for 2 to 3 hours. The hot coil winding is then completely immersed in insulating varnish (baking type) and kept immersed for minimum 3 to 4 hours, or until all air bubbles cease. The coil is then removed and after draining out all surplus varnish, the coil is again put back in the heating chamber and kept there at a temperature of 100 to 110°C for at-least 4 hours, by which time the varnish will get completely baked and hard set.

In the vacuum impregnation method all air is first removed out, which ensures that the insulation varnish gets sucked in to the innermost recesses. If the subsequent baking is through, there will be no possibility of entry of humid air from outside in to the winding and, therefore the winding is fully protected and will give a long and trouble free service. The process of vacuum impregnation is demonstrated in Chapter # 1, section 1.14.

9.23 PREVENTIVE MAINTENANCE TESTING OF MOTORS.

For timely detecting a defect and preventing a breakdown during operation each motor should be regularly subjected to preventive maintenance tests throughput its period of service. The aim of these tests and checks is to reveal defects whose presence is impossible to detect by external inspection. If possible preventive maintenance testing and checking should be carried out in the course of a general overhauling during which the rotor is extracted from the stator. The preventive maintenance test comprises the following:

(1) Winding resistance measurement by using a micro-ohmmeter or by voltmeter – ammeter method. The measured values for each phase should not differ by more than 2 percent from those stated in the test report. For wound rotor motor rotor winding resistance also measured and recorded.

(2) Insulation resistance and polarization index value of the winding is to be checked with a 1000 V megger for low voltage motor and 2.5/5KV megger for medium voltage motor. For wound rotor motor rotor insulation resistance is also measured and compare with previous test results. Insulation resistance of rotor rehostat also to be checked and recorded..

(3) Each phase of the stator winding is to be tested by applying power frequency AC voltage between phase and earth (with the other two phases connected to earth) for a period of one minute to check the dielectric strength of the insulation. This test is required only for low voltage motors above 40 KW ratings and all medium voltage motors.

The test voltage to be applied is as follows.

Motor rated voltage: (KV):	0.44	3.3	6.6	11	13.8
Test voltage between phase to earth: (KV):	1.00	5.00	10.00	16.00	21.00

The dielectric strength of the slip ring motor rotor rehostat is tested with 1000 volts for one minute.

(4) The ohmic resistance of the slip ring motor rotor rehostat is measured by using an ohmmeter . It should not differ more than 10% from the value stated in the test certificate. Continuity of its circuit is also checked.

(5) A series of air gap measurements are taken. The size of the air gap at points diametrically opposite to each other should not differ by more than 10% from the average value.

(6) The vibration displacement of the machine is checked and should not exceed the value given below.

Motor rated speed (r.p.m):	3000	1500 and below
Vibration displacement (mm):	0.05	0.10

9.24 DRIVE SYSTEM CONTROL AND SIGNALLING DEVICES.

For control and monitoring of drive systems following devices are employed:
(1) Control stations; (2) Signal lamps with LED's; (3) Selector switches; (4) Push buttons; (5) Limit switches; (6) Proximity switches; (7) Photoelectric detectors; (8) Pneumatic control components; (9) Hydraulic control components.

Control stations: For control of drive system operations following types of control stations are available. Operating heads of control stations are provided with function marking using internationally accepted symbols as illustrated in Figure 9.24 (a). Alternatively standard legend plates with white characters on red background, is fitted.
(a) Metal control stations: A zinc alloy metal enclosure with an assembly of a group of pushbuttons or selector switches etc, dust and damp proof construction with paint finish, suitable for mounting on a wall or frame (Degree of protection IP65).

Following are the advantages of metal control stations:

- Better flexibility and adaptability.
- Excellent shock resistance
- Good electrical safety (earthed base and lid).
- Knockout for cable entry at the bottom (Blanking plates are used for plugging the unused holes).

(b) Double insulated control stations: An insulated built-in coloured Polycarbonate enclosure with an assembly of control and signaling unit (dust and damp protected). Protection of personnel is ensured by double insulation. Following are the advantages:

- Good fire-withstand capability.
- A robust shock resistant unit.
- An easily wired control station with provision for knockouts in the base, sides, top and back.
- Cover and base are interlocked to eliminate risk of inversion.

(c) Light duty pendant control stations: A pendant station for control circuits, with sleeve for control cable 10 to 15 mm diameter, having following features:

- With single action pushbutton operators forming an integral part of the enclosure of compact ergonomic design.
- With double insulated enclosure conforming to IP65, light duty pendant control stations usually used for small hoists, material handling lifts, winches etc.

(d) General-purpose pendant control stations: A range of pendant control stations for control circuits with sleeve for cables 15 to 25 mm diameter, suitable for operation in all conditions with double insulated, increased safety polycarbonate enclosure, compact and light for ease of use. General-purpose pendant control stations are usually used for control of all types of hoist units such as tower cranes, overhead traveling cranes, material handling machinery etc.
(2) Signal lamps with light emitting diodes:
In modern control and monitoring panels, LED's are employed for signaling and indication. The advantages are obvious:

- The radiated light is almost monochromatic, thus the illuminated surface is equal in brightness.
- Power consumption is negligible. Growth and decay of illumination times are measured in nanoseconds, thus new application possibilities exist for flashing or pulsing operation.
- Luminescent diodes possess semi-conductor reliability, i.e, life and reliability are at least compatible with those of associated control gear, often significantly exceeding those values. Thus much higher security of indication of an actual operating condition is ensured than that given by filament lamps.
- Luminescent diodes give 'cold light' with extremely low heat development.
- Luminescent diodes are practically insensitive to shock and vibration effect.

DESCRIPTION	FUNCTION	COLOUR	SYMBOL	SCHEME
1) flush button	START	Green		13 14
	STOP	Red		11 12
1) spring-return mushroom-head button	STOP	Red		11 12
1) stayput mushroom head button (turn to reset)	EMERGENCY STOP	Red	EMERGENCY STOP	11 12
2) spring return buttons	START	green		13 14
	STOP	red		11 12
1) indicator with resistor diode and 127V-2W lamp suitable for 220V a.c. supply	INDICATOR	colourless		X1 X2
	START	green		13 14
2) spring-return buttons	STOP	red		11 12
3) spring-return buttons	FORWARD	green		13 14
	STOP	red		11 12
	BACKWARD	green		13 14
3) spring-return buttons	UP	green		13 14
	STOP	red		11 12
	DOWN	green		13 14

Fig,. 9.24 (a): Universal symbols for motor control stations.

(a) Standard colours for signal lamps:
International standardization of signal lamp colours are brought about by the standard IEC 73.

Table 9.24 (1): Colours for signal lamps and their meanings in accordance with IEC 73.

Colour	Meaning	Explanation	Typical application
Red	Warning or danger	Warning of possible danger or conditions which require careful handling	(1) Failure of a system; (2) Condition exceeds a limit value (3) Important component of a system switched off by a protective device; (4) Danger from live or moving parts.
Yellow	Warning	Change of impending /change of condition	(1) Abnormal condition (e.g, temperature or pressure); (2) Overload, which is permissible only for a short time.
Green	Safety	Indication of correct operational condition or release of further operational sequences	(1) Cooling available; (2) Automatic boiler control operating; (3) Machine ready to start.
Blue	Special information	Blue can have any required meaning except those given for Red, Yellow and Green above	(1) Indication for remote control; (2) Selector in the set-up position.
White	General information	May be used for any purpose not clearly related to one of the other colours or, for example, as confirmation of a condition	

Pilot light means miniature lamp used for indicating and signaling the position of equipments in a control and monitoring panel.

Table 9.24 (2): Colour codes for pilot lights (indication lamps) in accordance with IEC 73.

Colour	Significance	Explanation	Typical applications
Red	Alarm or danger	Warning of potential danger or of a situation requiring quick action.	(1) Lubrication system failure; (2) Essential item of plant stopped by action of protection unit; (3) Danger to persons from exposed live or moving parts.
Yellow	Attention or caution	Change or imminent change of conditions	(1) Abnormal pressure level; (2) Overload acceptable for a short time.
Green	Safety	Indication of a safe condition or permission to proceed.	(1) Cooling liquid circulating; (2) Automatic boiler control in operation (3) Machine ready for start or restart

(3) Selector switches:
Selector switches are available in the following types:

(a) Selector switch designed for selection with indication. Either 2 or 3 position stay-put or spring return. Stay-put switch remain held at the selected position and provide permanent connection. Spring return switch provides momentary connection and returns to off position when the operator releases the hand.

(b) Key operated selector switch designed for use restricted to authorized personnel.

(c) Rotary switches or cam operated switches:

Standard legends for rotary switches are as follows:

English text	Universal inscriptions	Typical application
Forward – Off – Reverse	I - O - I	Forward-reverse control
Manual – Auto	I – II	Standby motor selection
Hand – Off – Auto	I – O – II	Auto – manual selection
Local – Off – Remote	I – O – II	Remote control selection
Off – ON	O – I	Start – stop control
Stop – Start – Run	I – II – III	Star – Delta motor control

(4) Pushbuttons:

Pushbutton is a hand operated spring return button suitable for either front fixing or rear fixing. Pushbuttons are available in the following ranges:

(a) Flush pushbutton designed for general-purpose application.

(b) Booted pushbutton designed for better protection in dusty atmosphere.

(c) Mushroom head pushbutton designed for emergencies or frequent repetitive action (palm operated rather than finger).

(d) Push-pull version.

(e) Illuminated pushbuttons: It is a combination of signaling and control. Recommendations given in Tables 9.24 (2) and (3) apply equally to illuminated pushbuttons. However, the significance of the colour used must comply with both sets of requirements: for pilot lights, when the button is illuminated and for pushbuttons when functioning as a pushbutton. If correct colour selection is difficult a clear lens should be used.

Table 9.24 (3): Colour code for pushbuttons in accordance with IEC 73.

Colour	Significance	Typical application
Red	Action in case of emergency (stop or off)	(1) Emergency stop; (2) General stop; (3) Stop one or several motors; (4) Combined stop / reset
Yellow	Intervention	(1) Manual intervention to prevent abnormal conditions arising; (2) Override function during an automatic cycle.
Green/Black	Start or on	(1) General start; (2) Start one or several motors (3) Start of machine elements; (4) Close an automatic switching device.

Following are the standard texts for pushbuttons and indicating lamps.

Close	Inch	Lower	Open	Reset	Run	Stop
Fast	Jog	Off	Power-on	Reverse	Slow	Up
Forward	Left	On	Raise	Right	Start	Down

Figure 9.24 (b) shows universal symbols for non-illuminated push buttons.

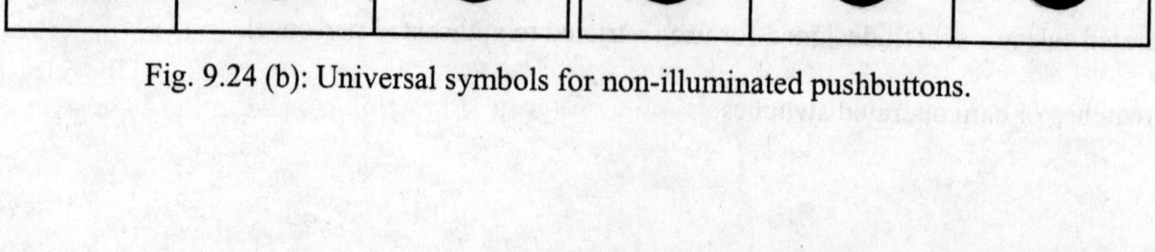

Fig. 9.24 (b): Universal symbols for non-illuminated pushbuttons.

(5) Limit switches:
A switch mechanism that when moved as intended, operates the switch contacts. This mechanism transmits the applied force from the actuating device to the contact block, causing the contact to operate. Contacts are either slow make-slow break type or snap action contacts.

(a) Slow make-slow break contacts: The speed of the contact make / break is dependent on the speed of the operating device. This type of contact is characterized by similar tripping and reset positions in each direction. The recommended minimum plunger speed is 1 mm/second.

(b) Snap action contacts: The speed of the contact make/break is independent on the speed of the operating device. This feature ensures reliable electrical performance even in applications involving low speed actuators. This type of contact is characterized by different tripping and reset points in each direction (differential travel). Differential travel or travel to reset contacts means the distance between the operating point and the release point.

Limit switches with positive opening operation: This contact structure is very similar to snap action contact described above. However, continued operation of the operating mechanism beyond the normal snap action position applies force directly to the normally closed contact (NC) if it has not opened with the snap action mechanism. This helps to ensure opening of even a welded contact. For example, if a contact has a snap action operating point at 40degree rotary movement, the direct opening action point may be at 60degree or more. No direct opening action forces are applied to the normally open (NO) contact.

Switches, which incorporate positive opening operation both in snap action and low break contact assembly, they conform to the recommendations of IEC 2041 or BS 5304 standards. To ensure that the positive opening system, as incorporated within the snap action contact blocks, is operative, the switch must be adjusted to ensure that at least 2 mm of travel beyond the normal operating point is achieved. Where rotary heads are used, this over-travel should be 26degree. For reasons explained above, limit switches with flexible operators cannot be considered as incorporating positive opening operation.

A limit switch must never be used as mechanical stop for machines or drive equipments. Consideration must be given to its maximum travel or operating angle. The actuator should be set or adjusted to provide a certain be given to its maximum travel or operating angle. The actuator should be set or adjusted to provide a certain over-travel after contact operation. This ensures reliable operation. Figure 9.24 (c) and (d) respectively shows front operation and side operation of limit switches. For side operation cams should be designed in such a way so as not to exceed the angular speeds accepted by the limit switch [see figure 9.24 (e)]. Standard cams have a 30degree approach and reset angle as illustrated in Figure 9.24 (e).

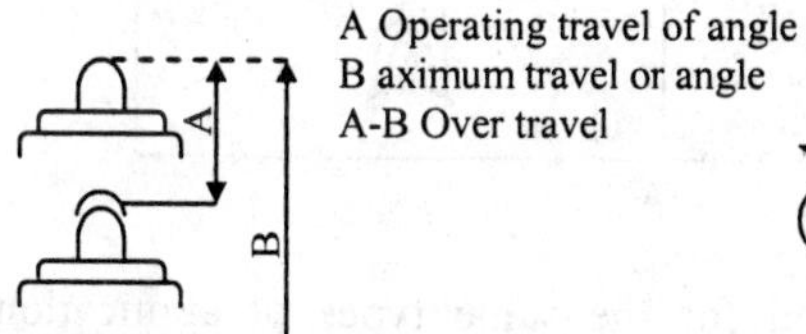

Fig. 9.24 (c): Front operation

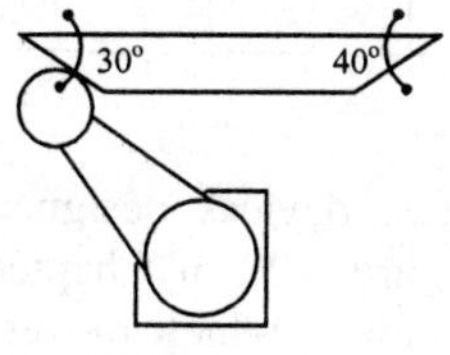

Fig. 9.24 (d): Side operation

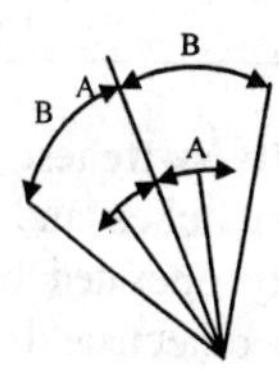

Fig 9.24 (e): Angular movement

Definitions:
(1) Operating position: The position of the actuator when the contacts operate.
(2) Resetting position: The position of the actuator in which the contacts move from the operated position to the "normal" position.
(3) Differential travel: The angle of distance through which the actuator moves from the contact operating position to the actuator resetting position or the distance between the operating point and the release point.
(4) Operating force: The straight-line force in the designated direction applied to the switch actuator to cause the contact to move to the operated position.

Table 9.24 (4): Part 1: Selection guide for operating head of limit switches [Read with Figure 9.24 (f)-(h)]

Type	Utilization	Application	Figure
Steel end plunger head	Actuation from the front only (short travel). Refer Figure 9.24 (f) in this row.	Assembly machines, Machine tools, Lever positioning, Door of trap closing control	
Steel roller plunger head	Front or side actuation (short travel) Refer Figure 9.24 (g) in this row.	Programming, Rotation counting on small-machines, Actuation by linear or rotary cam.	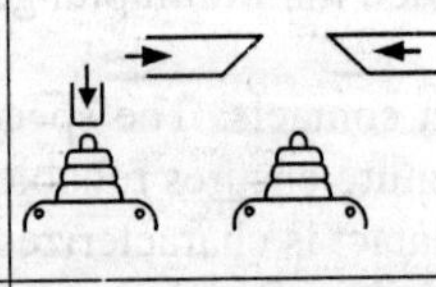
Thermoplastic roller lever head suitable for unidirectional actuation	Side operation in one direction only. Refer Figure 9.24 (h) in this row.	Parcel movement on packing machines, small-material handling machines, Escalators, Public work machinery.	

Table 9.24 (4): Part 2: Selection guide for operating head of limit switches [Read with Figure 9.24 (I)-(k).

Type	Utilization	Application	Figure
Thermoplastic roller lever head actuation from left and right.	Side operation in one or two directions. Refer Figure 9.24 (I) in this row	Forward / reverse movements, Machine tool and production machine carriages, Lifts and services lifts	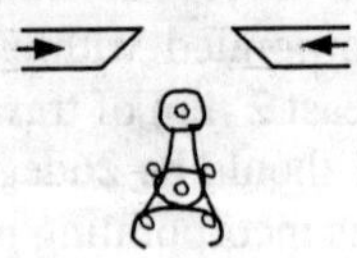
Variable-length thermoplastic roller lever head.	Side operation in one or two directions with adjustment. Refer Figure 9.24 (J) in this row	Hoisting, Material handling, Conveyors.	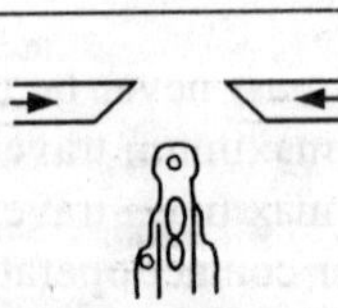
Head with square steel lever	Side operation in one or two directions by irregularly shaped actuators. Refer Figure 9.24 (k) in this row.	Component movement & counting control	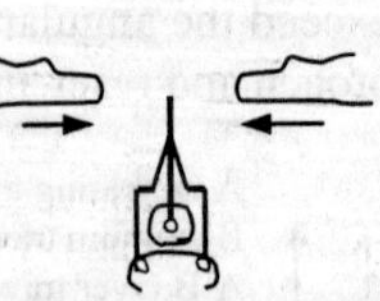

(6) Proximity switches:

Proximity switches and detectors are solid-state devices designed for the same types of applications as mechanically operated limit switches (refer figure 6.20 of Chapter # 6). An inductive proximity switch is designed to detect, and react to any metallic object, which moves in to the immediate area in front of its sensing face. This sensing face comprises a coil, the windings of which are fed by an oscillator, the whole creating an alternating magnetic field in front of the coil. Whenever a metallic object moves in to this field, the resulting induced currents form an additional load and the oscillations cease. This effect is sensed within the switch, and the output changes state. The output devices used give the same effect as the closing and opening of an electrical contact, depending on the model.

Inductive proximity switches are available in the following forms:

(1) Cylindrical small sensing distances with sensing distance 1 mm or 2 mm, used for detecting small objects i.e. to detect tools (drills, taps etc).

(2) Cylindrical medium sensing distance with sensing distance 5 mm or 10 mm, having parts counting capability especially to detect parts in confined spaces where conventional fixing methods would be difficult.
(3) Proximity switches with DIN standard fixing with sensing distance 15mm.
(4) Plug-in compact block type with large sensing range with sensing distance 13 mm to 25 mm.

Proximity switches are, however, particularly suitable for use in the following conditions:
a) Difficult environment: example dusty atmospheres, presences of cutting oil, humidity, steam, shock or vibration.
b) High operating rate: example rapid counting of mass produced parts, monitoring machine rotation speed, etc.
c) Detection without physical contact: example, detection of fragile objects, bottle tops, metallic labels, cigarette packets, etc.
d) Detection of small and / or light objects: example, detection of screws, nuts and bolts, etc.
e) Low voltage and low current switching without bounce: example, input to electronic equipment.

Following are the field of applications of inductive proximity detectors:

- Machine tools: Welding, moulding, and assembling machines; transfer machines; cutting and flanging presses.
- Tyre, paper and cement industries etc.
- Electro-plating.

(7) Photoelectric detectors:
A photoelectric detector comprises a transmitter associated with a photosensitive receiver. The detector of an object is carried out when the transmitted beam is broken or varied in intensity. This signal is then amplified and can be used to drive an external control device. The transmitter source is a light emitting diode (LED), which produces an invisible light beam. The modulated transmission of the LED guarantees a high immunity to external light sources and a practically unlimited operating life. Photoelectric detectors are available in the following forms:
(1) Barrage type AC or DC model: Figure 9.24 (L) illustrates a typical long range sensing (8 M) photoelectric detector, which detect even of reflecting objects with an integral amplifier. Transmitter and receiver are mounted separately.
(2) Reflex type AC or DC model: Figure 9.24 (m) illustrates a typical medium range sensing (2 or 4 metre) photoelectric detector with an integral amplifier. Transmitter and receiver contained within the same compact enclosure.
(3) Direct reflection type AC or DC model: Figure 9.24 (n) illustrates a typical proximity sensing (small distance 0.3 M) photoelectric detector with an integral amplifier. Transmitter and receiver contained in the same compact enclosure. Proximity type detector detects all types of objects.

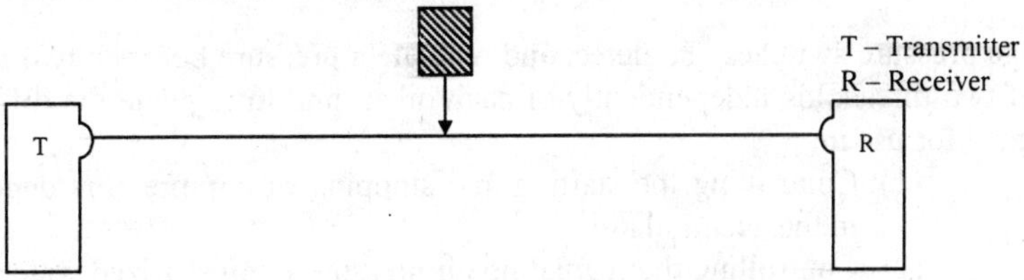

Fig. 9.24 (L): Barrage type photoelectric detector

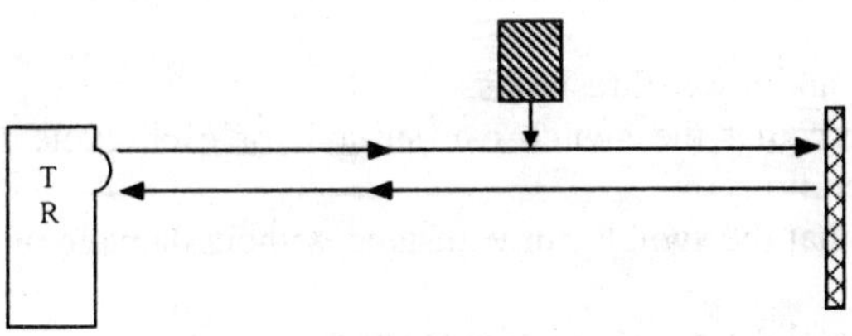

Fig. 9.24 (m): Reflex type photoelectric detector.

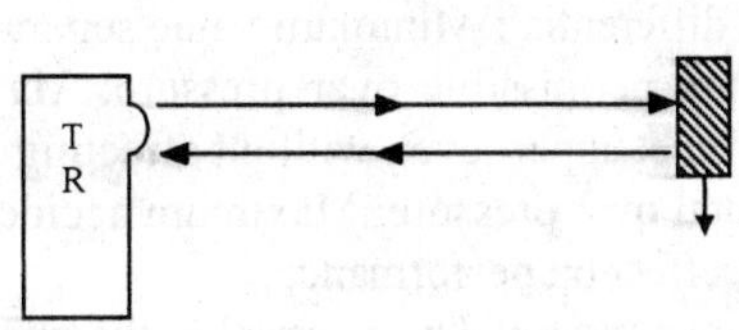

Fig. 9.24 (n): Proximity type detector

Following are the field of applications of photoelectric detectors:

(a) Barrage type (long distance range): Packing machines, labeling, sorting and coding machines etc.

(b) Reflex type (medium distance range): Inspection in the food, chemical, pharmaceutical and textile industries.

(c) Proximity type (small distance range): Postal mail sorting, automatic door control, lifts, escalators etc.

(8) Pneumatic control components:

In parallel with electrical and electronic control, pneumatic control has made a great advance because it forms the most rational means for programming and controlling the operation of air cylinders. Following are the advantages of pneumatic control:

(1) The same industrial air used for both cylinders and controls.

(2) No danger of fire or explosion, no risk of electrocution in a damp environment, no industrial interference.

(3) Elimination of the interface solenoid valves required for electro-pneumatic control.

Following are the control components mainly used in pneumatic technology:

(a) Pneumatic switches and push buttons: Pneumatic switches or pushbuttons are for fixing at the rear of the control desks and control stations. They have the special feature of being modular in composition. Pneumatic valves and electric switches are combined at will in many combinations with a very wide range of control heads.

(b) Miniature limit switches: These rugged pneumatic limit switches are as small as electrical micro-switches, can operate under difficult industrial conditions such as damp, explosive environment, etc., without protections.

(c) Two-stage limit switches: These are intended to provide an air signal under the effect of a mechanical operation and are fitted with ranges of operating heads developed for electrical limit switches. The pneumatic part is a two stage switch body, which makes it possible to obtain a large air flow, using short travels and low forces developed by the operating heads, with snap action at a precise point of travel.

(9) Hydraulic control components:

Pressure and vacuum switches are used to control or regulate a pressure or vacuum level in a hydraulic system. The switch transforms a change of pressure in to an electrical signal "on or off". When the preset pressure is reached, the snap action contact changes state.

Following are the control components mainly used in hydraulic technology.

(a) Fixed range pressure switches: An adjustable pressure setting to provide a high or low-pressure threshold, or to maintain a pressure level. This can be achieved by using the inherent differential of the switch between the trip and reset values at which the contact operates. This is not adjustable. Switches are designed for use in hydraulic circuits for: (1) Lubrication control; (2) Coolant control; (3) Limiting and monitoring the pressure.

(b) Adjustable range pressure switches: To detect and regulate a pressure between two levels (thresholds) or to adjust the levels of two thresholds independently of each other, and to regulate the differential between them. Switches are designed for use in:

(1) Controlling the starting and stopping of compressors depending on the pressure in the accumulator.

(2) Controlling the regulating air pressure in pressurized water distribution systems.

(3) Controlling and regulating the pressure in pipes carrying fluid.

Following definitions are usually applied with hydraulic control:

(a) Differential: Range between upper and lower switching levels obtained after adjustment of the upper level, then setting lower level.

(b) Natural differential: Minimum value separating the upper and lower thresholds.

(c) Maximum permissible over pressure: Maximum pressure that the switch can sustain for each cycle in excess of the set upper level, without affecting its correct operation.

(d) Accidental over pressure: Maximum accidental pressure that the switch can withstand without damage or a detrimental effect on performance.

(e) Maximum pressure: This is equal to the operating pressure plus possible hydraulic surge pressure.

(f) Operating frequency: The maximum permissible operation frequency depends on the size of the pressure switch and the type of actuator used i.e, diaphragm or piston. In general an upper limit of 30 operations per minute should not be exceeded..

(g) Unit of measurements: 1 bar = 10^5 Pa = 0.1 Mpa = 14.5 PSI

Mpa = Mega-passel, and PSI = Pressure per square inch

9.25 DRIVE SYSTEM OPERATION AND SUPERVITION IN POWER STATIONS

The operation of the motor driving various auxiliaries in a power station are supervised by, the shift operators of the section where each unit is installed. According to their application, drive system motors are classified as essential and nonessential. An essential drive system means failure of the drive even for a short period required shutdown of the main unit. Essential drive systems are provided with standby unit to start automatically if the running drive may fail. A nonessential drive means failure of the drive for a certain specified period will not affect the need for shutdown.

Some of the essential drive systems in a thermal power station are the feed water pumps, circulating water pumps, condensate pumps, induced draught fans, forced draught fans, pulverized coal burners etc. Similarly, drive systems in the nonessential category are fuel supply lines, coal pulverizers and fuel system fans, ash disposal equipment, water treatment equipment etc. Even though, the standby units are provided to meet the emergency and place the system in operation during maintenance and repair etc.

In hydroelectric power stations the principal drive system auxiliaries are those supporting the operation of the water turbines and water wheel generators. Among these are the governor oil pressure pumps, lubricating oil pumps, circulating water pumps of the air cooling system, Penstock gate hoisting drive system, Spillway hoisting system, River navigation air compressor etc.

A few examples of essential and nonessential drive systems in a combined cycle gas turbine power plant is listed below.

(a) Gas turbine drives: Gas turbine start motor, boiler feed water pumps, booster pumps, lube oil pumps, oil vapour fans, jacking oil pump, lube oil purifiers, hydraulic oil pumps, offline filter pumps, condenser fans, turning gear, etc.

(b) Steam turbine drives: Auxiliary oil pump, emergency oil pump, oil mist fan, gland steam condenser fan, Noise absorption hood ventilation fans, high-pressure oil pumps, turning gear, and three-phase motor driven valves such as inlet steam temperature control valve, gland steam temperature control valve, drainage closing valve etc.

(c) HRSG (Heat recovery steam generator) drives: Slow down tank transfer pumps, three phase motor driven valves such as steam start-up valve, blow-off valve, feed water stop valve, steam stop valve, steam stop bypass valve, stack damper actuator etc

Station auxiliary drives (Common to all type of power stations): Raw water pumps, water treatment pumps, waste water treatment pumps, Fire water pumps, fire pumps, drinking water pumps, air conditioning system, electrical overhead traveling cranes, workshop machineries, plant air compressors, lifts and hoists etc

Following are the points to be checked while the system is in operation:

(1) When the motor is fitted with sleeve type bearings, the operator must keep watches, the operation of the bearings, seeing that they are not running hot and are receiving sufficient lubrication. No bearing should be allowed to reach a temperature beyond 80°C. In large capacity motors keep a watch over the temperature of the air entering and leaving the motor. The difference between the incoming and outgoing temperature shall be in accordance with the manufacturers test report. Usually 15°C is permissible. High voltage motors are furnished with resistance temperature detectors (RTD) to provide a means for monitoring the temperature of the core steel. The temperature limitation is depending on the insulation class of the winding. For measuring the temperature of the bearings, slip rings etc the thermometer is placed in contact with the surface where the temperature can be expected to its highest value. The thermometer bulb of the capillary tube type thermometer should be wrapped in a strip of tin foil and then lagged on the outside with cotton or other heat insulating material. The temperature can read in the dial when it is constant.

(2) Sleeve type bearings should have their oil replaced at least twice a year. If the oil has become dark and a burnt smell, or small dark particles appear and are felt when it is rubbed between fingers, oil must be replaced by new oil. When the oil is changed the well in the bearing pedestal should be thoroughly rinsed out with kerosene, blown out with air, rinsed with clean oil then only filled with fresh oil. Each bearing should be topped-up to the required level once in a week.

(3) Voltage unbalance: The presence of the supply in all the three phases can be measured from the voltmeter in the panel phase. Unbalancing the voltage will overheat the motor. The effects on motor temperature and amperage draw can be tabulated as follows:

Table 9.25 (1): Effect of voltage unbalance in three-phase AC motors.

Percent voltage unbalance	Percent current rise	Percent temperature rise
0.5	3.8	0.5
1.0	8.0	2.0
1.5	12.5	4.5
2.0	16.75	8.0
2.5	21.0	12.5

The percent of voltage unbalance is defined as 100 times the sum of the deviations of the three voltages from the average without regard to sign, divided by twice the average voltage. In a given 440 volt system phase RY = 434 V, phase YB = 442 V, and phase BR = 456 V.

$$\text{Average} = \frac{434 + 442 + 456}{3} = 444 \text{ V}$$

$$\text{Phase unbalance} = \frac{[(444 - 434) + (444 - 442) + (456 - 444)] \times 100}{2 \times 444} = \frac{(10 + 2 + 12) \times 100}{888} = 2.7\%$$

Another method is:

The percent of voltage unbalance is equal to 100 times the maximum voltage deviation from the average voltage divided by the average voltage. In the above example average voltage is 444 V, and maximum voltage deviation is 456 – 444 = 12 V.

$$\text{Phase unbalance} = \frac{12 \times 100}{444} = 2.7\%$$

Larger motors are provided with phase balancing protection to detect the unbalancing and initiate trip signal to the switching device to isolate the motor. In small motors if nuisance trip outs or repeated trip outs of a motor are experienced and diagnosis of-course motor shows no faults, phase unbalance is a likely cause. For motors of 40 KW and above ratings ammeters are essential. The stator current shall be checked while starting and running.

(4) When a motor fitted with oil ring bearings is started, and while it running its bearing should be watched to see that the oil ring revolve at a normal medium speed. If the revolve slowly or stop, the bearing will receive insufficient oil, and begin to overheat. If they revolve too fast the oil flow will become flashy and some of the oil may leak out from the bearing. The endplay of the shaft in a motor fitted with oil ring bearings should be checked during the no load run. It will be within the range of 0 to 4 mm but compared with the previous reading.

(5) Motors with ball and roller bearings should have grease added to the bearings at least once every six months. When it is done the grease remaining in the bearings should be closely inspected to make sure it has not lost its consistency and shows no signals of contamination by foreign particles.

(6) Motor vibration is checked with the aid of a vibrometer and compare with the previous readings.

(7) A motor general overhaul includes such operation as given bellow.

(a) Isolate power supply and dismantle the motor.
(b) Extracting the rotor after de-coupling the driven load.
(c) Inspecting and checking the condition of stator and rotor.
(d) Cleaning the stator and rotor by dry compressed air.
(e) Rehabbitting sleeve type bearings when the wear is excessive.

(f) Repairing the motor starting and speed control apparatus.
(g) Cleaning and repairing the cooling system.
(h) Performing preventive maintenance tests.
(i) Inspection, repair or replacement of ball and roller bearing
(j) Assembling, re fixing, coupling and alignment.
(k) Test run (no load and on load).

9.26 EMERGENCIES AND TROUBLES IN POWER STATION DRIVE SYSTEM.

To ensure full reliability in operation of the drive systems, it is particularly important to maintain the drive motors in a proper condition. Most of the motor failures occurred in thermal power stations are due to adverse operating conditions, for example, ball and shaft type coal grinding mill motors, the induced draught and forced draught fan motors, the boiler feed and circulating water pump motors, the ash disposal (slurry) pumps and the coal crusher

The main causes of motor failures are:

1) Moisture absorbed by the stator winding: Insulation of the motor due to the presence of steam and water vapours and flooding of the motor due to leakage of water.

2) Incorrect operation: Assume that one of the boiler feed pump driven by an high voltage motor is switched off without closing the delivery valve and the non-return valve or is out of order, the pump impellers becomes to rotate in the reverse direction. When the pump is become necessary again, if the operator switched on the motor, consequently, the rotor winding of this motor will broke down and damage the stator winding also.

(3) Poor maintenance: (a) Failure of protection system / overload relay; (b) Single phasing / voltage unbalance; (c) Lack of lubrication of the bearings; (d) Lack of cooling due to blocking of ventilation system; (e) Breakage of rotor bars due to heavy vibration; (f) Entering oil in the stator windings weakens the insulation resistance

Modern motor practice is such that variance in amperage draw as a result of construction by design will be negligible, but external sources of amperage variance, temperature rise, speed variance and torque decrease should be searched for. It should be kept in mind, however, that voltages higher than normal will increase the inrush current at a rate of about 12% for every 10% voltage increase. The reverse take place if the applied voltage is less than normal rated voltage.

Tracing winding faults on stator and rotor:

(a) Shorted stator coil: After removing rotor energize the three-phase stator winding with single phase 230 or 120 volts AC supply by connecting as shown in Figure 9.26 (a). A portable hummer or hacksaw blade is moved over the stator coils. When the hummer passes above the shorted coil producing humming sound, whereas hacksaw blade vibrates due to flux in the shorted coil.

(b) Earthed stator coil: After removing rotor connect the terminals of stator winding to a low voltage winding as shown in Figure 9.26 (b), through a variable voltage autotransformer of sufficient amperage. Stator should be placed on an insulated platform or dry wood. Apply voltage gradually until the faulty coil is detected by smoke or discoloration. Alternatively a high voltage burn tester can be used to puncture the insulation at the earthed spot. This instrument is connected to low voltage single-phase supply. High voltage is injected between the stator windings and earthed stator body. Gradually increase the voltage and watch the leakage current. At high potential, the insulation at the earthed portion puncture and the set trips automatically.

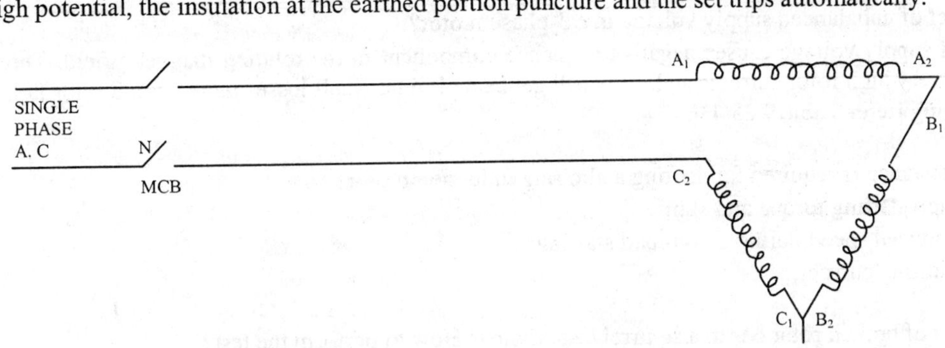

Fig. 9.26 (a): Stator connections for detecting the shorted turns, in an AC motor.

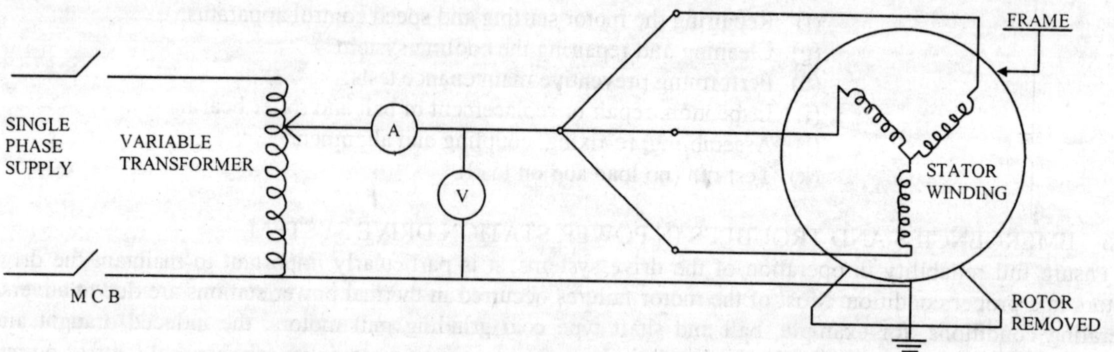

Fig 9.26 (b): Stator connections for detecting the earthed spot, in an AC motor.

(c) Motor checker: Three-phase motor checker is an electronic Oscilloscope, which gives an instant diagnosis. All faults are shown by trace from on the screen. During testing high frequency pulses compare each phases with the other two phases, showing on the oscilloscope screen a sine wave for a good winding and different waveforms for different faults i.e. wrong number of turns, short between coils, earth, open circuit, reversed connections by tracing starting end and finishing ends of the windings.

9.27 QUSTIONS AND ANSWERS ON LV AND HV MOTORS.

Q1. What are the effects of single phasing of a 3-phase induction motor?. How it can be overcome?

- Motor draws more current from the 2 healthy phases (approximately twice);
- Torque developed is reduced, humming sound and vibration;
- Stator winding will get heated because of the unbalanced stator current;
- Rotor gets heated due to the negative phase sequence flux created by the unbalanced stator current;

By using single phasing preventer, single phasing of motor can be avoided in low voltage motors.

Q2. What happened if a 50Hertz 3-phase motor is connected to a 60Hertz 3-phase supply of same voltages?

- Speed increases by 120%. For example at 50 Hz the speed of a 4 pole motor is 120f/p = (120 x 50)/4 = 1500 rpm. Whereas at 60 Hz speed = (120 x 60)/4 = 1800 rpm.
- Starting torque and running torque decreases.
- Bearing life will reduce due to increased speed.

Q3. What is the effect on a motor if the supply voltage is considerably increases?

- Torque increases as torque $T = V^2$
- Slip decreases as slip $S \propto I/V^2$ where I = load current and V = voltage
- Full load current reduces because power $P = \sqrt{3}$ EI cos φ watt. When the voltage increases current will reduce proportionally.
- Starting current increases. At starting no back e.m.f. Starting current $I_{st} = V/Z$. Voltage increases but impedance will not change.
- Insulation failure may occur due to excessive voltage.

Q4. What is the effect of unbalanced supply voltage in a 3-phase motor?

- Unbalanced supply voltage causes negative sequence component in the rotating magnetic field. This will induce very high rotor currents and rotor will get heated. As a result losses increase and rotor fails by overheating [refer Table 9.25(1)].

Q5. Why external resistance is required for starting a slip ring induction motor?

- To obtain high starting torque and slip;
- To start at reduced speed during an on-load starting;
- To reduce starting current;

Q6. What is the effect of broken rotor bar in a squirrel cage motor? How to perform the test?

- Broken rotor bar results abnormal noise, low starting torque, does not reach to rated speed.

- Connect single-phase AC supply to the stator winding (between two phases) through an autotransformer. Adjust current about 30% of full load current. Turn rotor slowly by hand. The current variation occurs if there is a broken rotor bar.

Q7.What are the different methods of starting induction motors? What is the ratio of starting current and full load current in each method of starting?

- Direct-on-line starting (DOL); starting current = 6 to 8 times of full load current.
- Star-delta starting; starting current = 2.5 to 4 times of full load current.
- Reduced voltage starting (Auto-transformer starting); starting current = 2.5 to 3 times of full load current
- Rotor resistance starting for slip-ring induction motors; starting current = 1.5 to 2 times of full load current.
- Part winding motors; starting current = 50% of full winding starting current, but starting torque will also reduce to 50%.
- Direct-on-line reverse/forward starting for reversing of motors; starting current = 6 to 8 times of full load current.
- Solid state AC starting control; starting current = 3 times of full load current

Q8. Explain the method for determining the value of a power factor correction capacitor for a given AC induction motor?

- KVAR (Reactive kilovolt ampere) value of power factor correction capacitor for an induction motor can be derived by using the formula, $KVAR = \frac{\sqrt{3} \times V_L I_0 \times \text{power factor}}{1000}$

V_L = Line to line voltage of the motor
I_0 = No load motor current.

Example: Assume that a motor draws active power 60 KW from a network at 0.6, power factor. For calculating the KVAR value of the capacitor to improve the power factor to 0.8, find the values of Tan ϕ_1 and Tan ϕ_2 by using a engineering calculator or from logarithmic Tables. These values are 1.33 and 0.75 respectively.
Reactive power consumed by the motor at 0.6 PF = 60 x 1.33 = 80 KVAR
Reactive power consumed by the motor at 0.8 PF = 60 x 0.75 = 45 KVAR
Capacitor required = 80 – 45 = 35 KVAR

Q9. What are the different methods of drives commonly used in motors?

- Direct coupling (Rigid or flexible)
- Belt drive
- Chain drive

Q10. Which are the areas where flameproof motors are used? What are the type designations? Why flameproof enclosures are required?

(a) Application:

- Presence of highly inflammable gases, vapours, liquids.
- Presence of combustible dust
- Combustible fiber floating in air
- Highly inflammable liquids like petrol, naptha, benzene, ether etc

(b) Type designations:

(b) Exe: Increased safety;
(c) Exd: Flame proof;
(d) Exn: Non sparking;
(e) Exp: Pressurized

(c) Flameproof enclosures: Flameproof (explosion proof) enclosures are specially designed and built for installations in hazardous locations. The enclosures are gastight and strong enough to withstand the high pressure caused by explosion of gas, which enters the enclosure. The design should be such that the flame or spark within the enclosure should not be carried out of the enclosure.

Q11. What are the different types of thyristorised speed controls for induction motors?

- Variation of stator voltage by controlled AC thyristor control. The supply voltage changed at constant frequency. Wide speed ranges but only intermittent low speeds. Suitable for both squirrel cage and slip ring motors. Speed control range 5:1 (smooth starting).
- Cyclo-converter speed control for 3-phase squirrel cage motors: Two sets of 3-phase controlled rectifiers, firing of thyristors in cyclic order, stator voltage/current controlled fully in magnitude, phase and frequency. High efficiency at about 30 to 50% rated frequency, reversible drives and better control at low speeds.
- Stator frequency control: Speed range 20:1 at constant torque; and 3:1 at constant Horsepower.
- Rotor resistance control by parallel chopper (for slip-ring motors): Rotor circuit resistance varied by means of parallel chopper. Low efficiency at lower speeds.
- Slip power recovery scheme by feedback of power from rotor circuit to supply circuit of slip ring motors. The power from slip ring is rectified smoothed and inverted and fed in to supply circuit. Speed control range 20:1 (good efficiency).

Q12. Define the terms plugging, jogging or inching of motors?

- Plugging of a motor is stopping the motor rapidly by reversing the primary momentarily (any two-phase) connections. Motor produces reverse torque resulting braking.
- Energizing the motor once or repeatedly to obtain slight movements of mechanisms is called jogging or inching. This circuit is essential for the hoist motor control of electrical overhead traveling cranes.

Q13. What are the different methods used for braking a drive motor?

- Friction braking (electromagnetic braking): Brake is applied to the rotor shaft when the electromagnetic brake is de-energized. The shoes/pads are released by spring action. Electromagnetic brake is connected direct to the stator terminals so that whenever the motor is switched on, the brake will simultaneously energize to release the brake shoes. During power failure and while switching off the motor, the electromagnet de-energizes to apply brake to the motor shaft.
- DC injection braking for induction motors: Three phase supply to the stator winding is suddenly replaced with DC supply from the rectifier set. (In case of slip-ring motors, rotor resistance is inserted). DC excitation establishes fixed air-gap flux. This flux gives braking effect.
- Capacitor braking: Three-phase supply to the stator winding is suddenly replaced with supply from three-phase capacitor bank. The induction motor will get self-excited. The load inertia drives the motor with negative slip and the speed drops.

Q14. What are the different methods of speed controls employed for induction motors?

- Pole changing; * By inserting resistance in the rotor circuit (for slip-ring motors only); * Cascade connection;
- By varying frequency; * Thyristor speed control

Q15. What is Ingress Protection (IP) or degree of protection?

- Degree of protection (IP classification) refers to the design and construction of the enclosure. IP code is in two digits.
- The first digit indicates protection against accidental contact with the live or moving parts. The second digit indicates protection against ingress of water, dust and foreign bodies.

Q16. What happens if the rotor of an induction motor achieves synchronous speed?

- Synchronous motors are three-phase AC motors, which run at synchronous speed, without "slip".
- In an induction motor, the rotor must have some "slip" The rotor speed must be less than, or lag behind, that of the rotating stator flux in order for current to be induced into the rotor.
- If an induction motor rotor were to achieve synchronous speed, no lines of force would cut through the rotor, so no current would be induced in the rotor and no torque would be developed.

Q17. Describe the formula for determining the horsepower ratings of a water or oil pump?

- $$\text{Horsepower} = \frac{\text{GPM x Total head in feet}}{\text{3960 x Motor efficiency}}$$

GPM = Gallons per minute

Q18. Describe the formula for finding the external resistance to be connected to the rotor of a slip-ring motor, for starting purposes?

- Ohms per leg for star connected motor = $\frac{\text{Rotor volts} \times \%\ \text{rpm}}{\sqrt{3} \times \text{Rotor amps} \times \%\ \text{HP}}$

* Ohms per leg for delta connected motor = $\frac{\text{Rotor volts} \times \%\ \text{rpm}}{3 \times \text{Rotor amps} \times \%\ \text{HP}}$

% HP is the percentage of rated horsepower required by the minimum load, desired to be carried at the lowest reduced speed.
% RPM is the percent reduction below rated no load speed of the lowest desired reduced speed.
Rotor current (Amps) = (HP x 746) / (√3 x 0.92 x Rotor open circuit voltage)

Q19. Describe the formula for finding the full load current of a squirrel cage or wound rotor induction motor connected either in star or in delta?

- Current (A) = (HP x 746) / (√3 x Line-to-line voltage x Motor efficiency x Power factor).
- Current (A) = (KW x 1000) / (√3 x Line-to-line voltage x Motor efficiency x Power factor).

Q20. Describe the formula for calculating the full load stator current of a synchronous motor?

- $[(\text{KW} \times 1000) / (\sqrt{3} \times \text{Voltage} \times \text{Efficiency} \times \text{Power factor})] \times [\sqrt{1 + \tan^2 \theta}]$

Q21. Describe utilization categories of contactors as per IEC 947?

(a) Alternating current supply:

- AC1: Switching AC loads at unity power factor i.e. heating and lighting loads.
- AC2: Starting, stopping and inching of slip ring motors at ± 2.5 times the motor full load current.
- AC3: Starting and stopping of squirrel cage motors at ± 7 times the motor full load current.
- AC4: Plugging and inching of squirrel cage motors at ± 7 times the motor full load current.
- AC11: Feed-control of magnetic drives, valves, electromagnets (brakes) etc. Rating 10 x rated current.

(b) Direct current supply:

- DC1: Non-inductive or slightly inductive loads: Making and breaking of rated current. L/R = 1 ms.
- DC2: Shunt motor starting, switching off motors during running: Making 2.5 x rated current. Breaking of rated current L/R = 7.5 ms..
- DC3: Shunt motor starting, plugging, reversing, inching: Making and breaking 2.5 times rated current. L/R = 2 ms.
- DC4: Series motor starting, switching of motors during running: Making 2.5 x rated current. Breaking of rated current. L/R = 10 ms.
- DC5: Series motor, starting, plugging, reversing, inching: Making and breaking of 2.5 times the rated current. L/R = 7.5 ms.
- DC11: Feed control of magnetic drives, valves, electromagnets etc. Making and breaking of rated current. L/R (maximum) 300 ms.

Q22. What is an armature shim in a magnetic contactor?

- It is a non magnetic metal insert in the face of a magnetic core intended to prevent the moving armature of a magnetic contactor from coming too close to the core and striking to it, and stick with the core. The armature shim ensures a minimum air gap at all times and prevent chattering the contactor.

Q23. Explain the construction and function of an arc chute in a magnetic contactor? What kind of periodic maintenance is recommended?

- When a contactor opens a circuit carrying current, an arc is drawn from the contact tips. The flame is very hot and should be extinguished quickly. This could be done by, a jet of air with the aid of an arc-chute. It is so constructed that the arc path is split up in to a number of paths so that the heat of the gases is quickly dissipated. It is an insulator, which is suitable for withstanding the severe heat of the arc.

- The internal surfaces of the arc-chute should be examined periodically and thoroughly cleaned and all smoky deposits globules of copper, etc removed at regular intervals. The internal surfaces must be kept smooth and clean by rubbing with coarse canvas or crocus cloth. Avoid the use of sand paper, which may tend to roughen the internal surface.

Q24. What are the different types of single-phase motors available?

- Shaded pole motor
- Split phase motor
- Capacitor start motor, and capacitor start capacitor run motor.
- Synchronous motor: (Reluctance motor, and hysteresis motor)
- Universal motor (work on both AC and DC)

Q25. Explain the function and applications of an AC servomotor?

- These are basically two-phase reversible, induction motors modified for servo operation. They are used in applications requiring rapid and accurate response characteristics. To achieve these characteristics, these induction motors have small diameter, high resistance rotors. The small diameter provides low inertia for fast starts, stops, and reversals. High resistance provides nearly linear speed torque characteristics for accurate control.

Q26. Explain the function and applications of step motors?

- A step motor is a device that converts electrical pulses in to mechanical movements. Conventional motors rotate continuously, but a step motor, when pulsed, rotates (steps) in fixed angular increments. Traditionally, step resolution has ranged from 80 degrees (four steps per revolution) to a fraction of a degree, through 15 degrees (12 steps per revolution) has been most common. Micro step motors are capable of 0.0144 degree steps (25,000 steps/revolution). Step motors are usually used in open loop control systems.
- Permanent magnet step motor: Synchronous inductor motor, which moves in steps when its windings are sequentially energized, or it can operate as a low speed synchronous motor when operated from a two-phase AC power source.
- Variable reluctance step motor: Switched reluctance step motor, which is constructed with a toothed rotor. There are no magnets in the rotor. Depending on the stator design two, three or four phase windings may be used.
- Micro-step motors: These are usually hybrid motors. The rotor consists of an arbor, bearings, and one, two or three sets, or stacks, of toothed cylindrical magnets. The toothed stator is wound so that alternate poles are driven by two separate phase currents. Thus, using digital logic control and bipolar ·ulse width modulation, the motor makes 25000 micro-steps per revolution.

Q27. Explain the function and applications of miniature motors?

- The hollow ironless rotor fits over a stationary magnet system. The copper coils moves, unlike larger motors where the whole coil and magnet system move. The size of the motor varies from 2.5 mm to 38 mm overall diameter. Typical applications include medical systems, semiconductor manufacturing, laser cutting systems, winding machines, robotic handling equipment, motorized potentiometers, aircraft actuators, computer peripherals, bar code scanners, and many others.

Q28. Explain the function and applications of Gear motors?

- Gear motor consists of a motor and speed reducer in an integral assembly. The motor portion of the assembly can be either DC or AC motor. The speed reducer portion can use spur, helical, or worm gears. Gear motor sizes range from fractional horsepower to above 200 hp. The main advantage of a gear motor is that the driving shaft can couple directly to the driven shaft, thus in many situations making belts, chains, or separate speed reducers unnecessary. Field installation is simpler.

Q29: Explain the function and applications of frameless motors?

- Construction of frameless AC motors, electrically, is no different than conventional permanent magnet and induction motors. The frameless designs can be controlled by the same gives as those used to control frame type motors. Frameless motors are delivered as individual components such as rotor, stator and feedback assembly, which are installed as an integral part of a machine. Frameless motors typically have continuous torque ratings from 100 lb-inch to 10,000 lb-inch and speeds from 300 to 20,000 rpm. Frameless motors are widely used in machine tools and high-speed spindles.

Q30. Explain the function and application of direct current motors?

- Direct current motors are used in many industrial applications that require adjustable speed. In uses requiring quick stops, the DC motor can eliminate a mechanical brake (electromagnetic brake). This is done by dynamic braking (motor generated energy fed to a resistor grid), or by generative braking (motor generated energy returned to AC supply). DC motor speed can be controlled smoothly down to zero, followed immediately by acceleration in the opposite direction (without power circuit switching). Also due to high torque-to-inertia ratio, DC motors responds quickly to control signal changes.
- DC motors in all fractional horsepower (Below 1 hp) and low integral horsepower sizes (below 15 hp), have wound fields and are categorized as series-wound, shunt-wound and compound-wound motors. In many motor designs (below 15 hp), permanent magnets are used instead of wound fields. Operating characteristics of permanent magnet motors are similar to those of a shunt wound motors. Field flux, however, is provided by permanent magnets instead current in a winding. Motor torque is directly proportional to armature current over the motor speed range.
- Series-wound motors: As its name implies, this motor has a field that is in series with the armature, (similar to figure 1.17 (d) in Chapter # 1). Series motors are often used to drive high starting torque loads, such as traction vehicles. Torque varies approximately as the square of the current. As the armature gains speed, the counter e.m.f rises, reducing the effective voltage, current, and torque. As the motor shaft load increases, the armature slows to provide sufficient voltage and current to match the load torque. If the load is removed, the motor will race dangerously.
- Shunt-wound motors: Shunt-wound motors are operated from adjustable voltage power supplies. A shunt motor is connected in the same way as a shunt generator (figure 1.17 (d) in Chapter # 1). The shunt field is connected in parallel with the armature windings. The speed remains constant under changing load conditions.
- Compound-wound motors: Compound-wound motor has two field windings one connected in series to the armature and the other connected in parallel as shown in figure 1.17 (d) in Chapter # 1. The shunt field gives the constant speed advantages. The series field gives the advantage of starting with heavy load. By adjusting strength and direction of the series winding relative to the shunt winding, speed-torque characteristics can be made to approximate those of series or shunt motors.

Q31. What are the reasons for chattering an AC magnetic contactor?

- Loose connection in the control circuit.
- Shading rings in the magnetic core is missing.
- Failure of interlocks in the control circuitry.

Q32. What are the reasons for producing humming noise in a magnetic contactor?

- Core surfaces are dirty, not clean.
- Turn-to-turn short-circuit in the holding coil winding.
- Control voltage is less than 90% of the rated voltage.

Q33. While starting an induction motor, it takes five times full load current. When the motor speeds up, the current is reducing to rated current. Why?

- High starting current is drawing because the rotor is at stand still and no back emf is induced in the rotor. To develop starting torque high current is required and motor start with load.
- When the motor speeds up the current reduces to rated current because back emf induced in the rotor opposes the applied voltage. Once the rotor accelerates the starting torque is reduced.

Q34. Why it is essential to employ overload elements in all three-phases of a motor?

- For star-delta or delta-star distribution transformer connections, the current in one of the three secondary lines can become twice that in the other two lines when single phasing occurs.

- When a single-phase motor and three-phase motor are working on the same feeder and one of the two conductors supplying the single phase motor opens, the three-phase motor may supply current to the single-phase motor causing additional current to flow through one of the three-phase windings.
- When two three-phase motors one large and one small are in the same feeder and one conductor opens, both motors could act as phase converters, and either of the two intact phases would carry excessive current to maintain the 3rd phase. The extra current may be large relative to the small motor's full load current, and damage could result.

Q35. Explain the method of determining the direction of rotation or phase sequence of a motor before energizing the motor?

- When more than one 3-phase motors are installed to drive a machine or one shaft is coupled to two motors, it is necessary to predetermine their direction of rotation before connecting to the power supply. Assume that the three phase stator leads are R, Y, and B. Connect one DC voltmeter between phases R-Y and another voltmeter between phases Y-B. Y is the common lead for the two voltmeters. Apply 12 V, battery supply through a resistor between terminals R-B. Polarities of the battery terminals are immaterial. If the motor under test is a slip ring motor, the rotor terminals are to be shorted during the test. When the rotor is at rest, the indications of two voltmeters are constant. When the rotor is caused to rotate by hand or any mechanical means in a given direction the deflection of one voltmeter will increase and the other decrease.
- The stator terminal, which is used as common lead is marked as terminal Y. The stator terminal to which the voltmeter with decreasing indication is connected is marked as terminal R. The 3rd stator terminal to which the voltmeter with increasing indication is marked as terminal B. With this marking the phase rotation is R-Y-B (phase sequence) for the direction in which the rotor was revolved by external means. If the motor is turned in the opposite direction, the deflections of the two voltmeters will be reversed.

Q36. Explain the reasons for using control transformers for motor control?

- Usually, DC control power is used for high voltage motor control as the closing and tripping coils of the circuit breakers are of DC. Where vacuum or SF6 medium voltage contactors are used, AC or DC control power can be selected in the design stage. The reasons for using control transformers are for the safety of plant and personnel.
- 440 volts control wiring has been strictly forbidden in the machine tools, automotive industries, wet areas, locations where foot switches, portable control stations, and pendent controls are being used. 120 or 24 volts control power obtained from an isolation transformer provides greater degree of safety.
- By providing a control transformer [figure 2.2 (J) of Chapter # 2] control circuit can be grounded either on one side or at the midpoint of the secondary. If the control transformer has a midpoint connection, the secondary voltage on either side with respect to ground is 50% of the secondary line-to-line voltage. In both case any ground that would appear on the control circuit would open the fuse or miniature circuit breaker. Moreover, at reduced voltage the fault current will be very low as such damages will be less. Application of control transformer is illustrated in figure 9.2 (d).

Q37. Explain the method of connection to stop pushbutton and start push button? Why the location of the overload contact is preferred in the neutral (grounded side) wire of the control circuit?

- The acceptable practice is the hot wire (phase conductor) of the control circuit goes to stop pushbutton at first. Electrically and operationally, there is no difference if the hot conductor goes to start pushbutton at first. However, the difference is in the saving of one wire run between the pushbutton station and the starter contact, which is used to by pass the start pushbutton when the coil energize. (Refer figure 9.7).
- The location of the overload contact(s) on the groundside of the holding coil of the contactor is specified in NEMA standard. If the overload contact is placed in the hot wire adjacent to the stop pushbutton, this of-course allows the tripping of the contactor when the contactor to open. However, in majority of cases, the remote tripping is wired through cables or wires pulled in conduit, and a ground is more likely to occur. If it does the control fuse will blow but the same time the overload contact or contacts could become welded. Welded or shorted overload contact is difficult and thus

lead to loss of overload protection of the motor. Since the neutral side of the control circuit is grounded, as such no such welding of contact will occur.

Q38. Explain the pros and cons of long distance control circuit?

- Long runs of AC control cables can present two main problems: (1) Motor will not start due to excessive voltage drop; (2) Motor does not stop when the stop pushbutton is depressed. Contactor often fails to dropout because of leakage current through the distributed capacitance between wires of the control circuit. Cable capacitance allows a current to flow, which exceeds the required holding current for the contactor coil, then, the stop button will have no effect. To eliminate this problem, any of the following methods can by tried.
- Use DC control power and DC operated-contactor coil.
- Install a resistance in series with the contactor coil rated at a voltage less than the control circuit voltage. In doing so the coil reactance is reduced and the voltage drop across the coil is reduced when the stop pushbutton is depressed.
- Connect a suitable resistor across the terminals of the holding coil. This would shunt a part of the capacitance current, but it would create heat.
- Connect a capacitance across the coil. Capacitance of the control cable may be measured or obtained from the manufacturers published tables, then a capacitor of slightly higher capacity is to be used. The voltage ratings of the capacitor shall be double the voltage rating of the contactor coil.

Q39. Why it might be desirable to vary the speed of a drive system?

- Increase machine versatility permitting one machine to handle more functions or to work with a wider range of materials.
- Improve product quality and increase productivity by running the machine or process at the optimum speed for a particular material. Thickness, finish etc.
- Maintain a desired speed, sometimes very accurately, with varying loads for more consistent product quality and increased machine utilization.
- Protect machine and products with special starting and stopping capabilities. For example, starting and stopping a conveyor slowly to prevent spilling the items on the conveyor.
- Control, jogging or inching speed for easier, safer machine set-up. Control tension or torque for more constant product quality.

Q40. List five broad categories to be considered when selecting a motor for a particular application?

- Power supply and system frequency.
- The motor's environment at mounting location.
- Type of mounting.
- The nature of the driven load and method of starting and / or speed control.
- The mechanical requirements associated with mounting the motors and connecting / coupling to the driven load.

APPENDICES

1. TECHNICAL DATA FOR XLPE INSULATED IEC STANDARD CABLES UP TO 36 KV.
2. CURRENT RATINGS FOR XLPE INSULATED IEC STANDARD CABLES UP TO 36 KV.
3. TECHNICAL DATA FOR XLPE INSULATED ICEA STANDARD CABLES UP TO 35 KV.
4. CURRENT RATINGS FOR XLPE INSULATED ICEA STANDARD CABLES UP TO 35 KV.
5. INTERNATIONAL STANDARDS ORGANIZATIONS.
6. ABBREVIATIONS USED IN POWER TECHNOLOGY.

APPENDIX # 1

TECHNICAL DATA FOR XLPE INSULATED IEC STANDARD CABLES UP TO 36 KV

CONTENTS:

A1.1. Technical data for XLPE insulated, IEC standard multi-core cables, 600/1000 V
A1.2. Technical data for XLPE insulated, IEC standard three-core cables, 3.6/6 (7.2) KV
A1.3. Technical data for XLPE insulated, IEC standard three-core cables, 6/10 (12) KV
A1.4. Technical data for XLPE insulated, IEC standard three-core cables, 12/20 (24) KV
A1.5. Technical data for XLPE insulated, IEC standard three-core cables, 18/30 (36) KV

A1.1. TECHNICAL DATA FOR XLPE INSULATED, IEC STANDARD MULTI-CORE CABLES, 600/1000 Volts.

Resistance, reactance and impedance for XLPE insulated, (copper conductor) multi-core cable 600/1000 V, conforming to IEC 60502-1 is tabulated in Table A1 (1) below.

Conductor cross section	AC resistance at 90°C, Ω/km	AC resistance at 90°C, Ω/km	Reactance Ω/km	Reactance Ω/km	Impedance Ω/km	Impedance Ω/km
Mm2	50 Hz	60 Hz	50 Hz	60 Hz	50 Hz	60 Hz
2.5	9.45	9.45	0.0976	0.117	9.45	9.45
4	5.88	5.88	0.0921	0.111	5.88	5.88
6	3.93	3.93	0.0850	0.102	3.93	3.93
10	2.33	2.33	0.0807	0.0969	2.33	2.34
16	1.47	1.47	0.0777	0.0932	1.47	1.47
25	0.927	0.927	0.0784	0.0941	0.931	0.932
35	0.668	0.668	0.0757	0.0909	0.673	0.675
50	0.494	0.494	0.0749	0.0899	0.500	0.502
70	0.342	0.343	0.0737	0.0884	0.350	0.354
95	0.247	0.248	0.0719	0.0862	0.257	0.262
120	0.196	0.197	0.0713	0.0856	0.209	0.215
150	0.160	0.160	0.0716	0.0860	0.175	0.182
185	0.128	0.129	0.0717	0.0861	0.147	0.155
240	0.0987	0.0998	0.0709	0.0851	0.122	0.131
300	0.0798	0.0811	0.0713	0.0856	0.107	0.118
400	0.0639	0.0656	0.0707	0.0848	0.0953	0.107

A1.2. TECHNICAL DATA FOR XLPE INSULATED, IEC STANDARD THREE CORE CABLES, 3.6/6 (7.2) KV

Resistance, reactance and impedance for XLPE insulated, (copper conductor) three-core, power cable 3.6/6 (7.2) KV, conforming to IEC 60502-2 is tabulated in Table A1 (2) below.

Conductor cross-section	AC resistance at 90°C, Ω/km	AC resistance at 90°C, Ω/km	Reactance Ω/km	Reactance Ω/km	Impedance Ω/km	Impedance Ω/km
Mm2	50 Hz	60 Hz	50 Hz	60 Hz	50 Hz	60 Hz
16	1.47	1.47	0.111	0.133	1.47	1.47
25	0.927	0.927	0.103	0.124	0.933	0.935
35	0..668	0.668	0.0982	0.118	0.676	0.679
50	0.494	0.494	0.0928	0.111	0.502	0.506
70	0.342	0.342	0.0886	0.106	0.354	0.359
95	0.247	0.247	0.0842	0.1010	0.261	0.267
120	0.196	0.197	0.0819	0.0982	0.213	0.220
150	0.159	0.160	0.0779	0.0959	0.178	0.187
185	0.128	0.129	0.0788	0.0946	0.150	0.160
240	0.0984	0.0993	0.0773	0.0928	0.125	0.136
300	0.0794	0.0805	0.0775	0.0930	0.111	0.123
400	0.0635	0.0649	0.0761	0.0913	0.0991	0.112

A1.3. TECHNICAL DATA FOR XLPE INSULATED, IEC STANDARD THREE CORE CABLES, 6/10 (12) KV

Resistance, reactance and impedance for IEC standard, XLPE insulated, (copper conductor) three-core, power cable, 6/10 (12) KV, conforming to IEC 60502-2 is tabulated in Table A1 (3) below.

Conductor cross-section	AC resistance at 90°C, Ω/km	AC resistance at 90°C, Ω/km	Reactance Ω/km	Reactance Ω/km	Impedance Ω/km	Impedance Ω/km
mm2	50 Hz	60 Hz	50 Hz	60 Hz	50 Hz	60 Hz
25	0.927	0.927	0.120	0.144	0.0935	0.938
35	0.668	0.668	0.114	0.137	0.678	0.682
50	0.494	0.494	0.107	0.129	0.505	0.510
70	0.342	0.342	0.102	0.122	0.357	0.363
95	0.247	0.247	0.0972	0.117	0.265	0.273
120	0.196	0.196	0.0939	0.113	0.217	0.226
150	0.159	0.160	0.0911	0.109	0.183	0.193
185	0.128	0.128	0.0885	0.106	0.155	0.167
240	0.098	0.0988	0.0861	0.103	0.130	0.143
300	0.0791	0.0801	0.0837	0.100	0.115	0.128
400	0.0632	0.0645	0.0809	0.0971	0.103	0.117

A1.4. TECHNICAL DATA FOR XLPE INSULATED, IEC STANDARD THREE CORE CABLES, 12/20 (24) KV

Resistance, reactance and impedance for XLPE insulated, (copper conductor) three-core cable, 12/20 (24) KV, conforming to IEC 60502-2 is tabulated in Table A1 (4) below.

Conductor cross-section	AC resistance at 90°C, Ω/km	AC resistance at 90°C, Ω/km	Reactance Ω/km	Reactance Ω/km	Impedance Ω/km	Impedance Ω/km
mm2	50 Hz	60 Hz	50 Hz	60 Hz	50 Hz	60 Hz
50	0.494	0.494	0.122	0.146	0.508	0.515
70	0.342	0.342	0.115	0.138	0.361	0.369
95	0.247	0.247	0.110	0.132	0.270	0.280
120	0.196	0.196	0.106	0.127	0.222	0.233
150	0.159	0.159	0.102	0.123	0.189	0.201
185	0.128	0.128	0.0989	0.119	0.161	0.175
240	0.0977	0.0984	0.0957	0.115	0.137	0.151
300	0.o787	0.0796	0.0927	0.111	0.122	0.137
400	0.0627	0.0629	0.0890	0.107	0.109	0.124

A1.5. TECHNICAL DATA FOR XLPE INSULATED, IEC STANDARD THREE CORE CABLES, 18/30 (36) KV

Resistance, reactance and impedance for XLPE insulated, (copper conductor) three-core cables, 18/30 (36) KV, conforming to IEC 60502-1 is tabulated in Table A1 (5) below.

Conductor cross-section	AC resistance at 90°C, Ω/km	AC resistance at 90°C, Ω/km	Reactance Ω/km	Reactance Ω/km	Impedance Ω/km	Impedance Ω/km
mm2	50 Hz	60 Hz	50 Hz	60 Hz	50 Hz	60 Hz
50	0.494	0.494	0.136	0.166	0.512	0.520
70	0.342	0.342	0.128	0.154	0.365	0.375
95	0.247	0.247	0.122	0.147	0.275	0.287
120	0.196	0.196	0.118	0.141	0.228	0.242
150	0.159	0.159	0.114	0.137	0.195	0.210
185	0.127	0.128	0.110	0.132	0.168	0.184
240	0.0975	0.0981	0.106	0.127	0.144	0.161
300	0.0784	0.0792	0.102	0.123	0.129	0.146
400	0.0624	0.0634	0.0979	0.118	0.116	0.134

APPENDIX # 2

CURRENT RATINGS FOR XLPE INSULATED IEC STANDARD CABLES UP TO 36 KV

CONTENTS:

A2.1: RATING FACTORS FOR XLPE INSULATED IEC STANDARD CABLES UP TO 36 KV.

Current carrying capacity tabulated in the following tables are applicable for low and medium voltage cables (0.6 KV to 36 KV) manufactured in conformity with International Electro-technical Commission (IEC) standard 60502-1 and 60502-2. Current ratings in each table are calculated under the following basic ambient temperature and cable-laying configuration.

Ambient air temperature: 40°C
Ground temperature: 25°C
Soil thermal resistivity: 1.2°C m/w (metre per watt) or 120°C cm/w
Depth of laying cable: 800mm (trench depth 900mm)

Single core cable 3 in parallel at a spacing of, S=2d. (d= diameter of cable). Multi core cable single installation Maximum permissible conductor temperature for XLPE cable is 90°C at continuous operation and 250°C at short circuit condition. The tabulated value of current ratings and short circuit current ratings in Table A2.2 to A2.5 are for copper conductor cable. **For obtaining the corresponding values for aluminium conductor cable: (1) For current rating, multiply the tabulated value by 0.78**
(2) For short-circuit rating, multiply the tabulated value by 0.65734

Single care cables laid in air means laid on cable tray. Cables laid in ground means laid underground (U/G) direct burial.

Rating factors for other ambient air temperature:

Ambient air temperature: °C	30	35	40	45	50	55	60
Rating factor:	1.10	1.05	1.00	0.94	0.88	0.81	0.73

Rating factors for other ground temperature:

Ground temperature: °C	15	20	25	30	35	40	45
Rating factor:	1.05	1.03	1.00	0.97	0.93	0.89	0.82

A2.2. CURRENT CARRYING CAPACITY FOR XLPE INSULATED, IEC STANDARD CABLES, 600/1000 V

Current carrying capacity and short circuit ratings of XLPE insulated copper conductor power cables 600/1000 volts, conforming to IEC standard 60502-1, is tabulated in Table A2.2

Conductor cross-section	Single core 3 or 4 cables	Two single core/2-core	3 or 4 core cable	Single core 3 or 4 cables	Two single core/2-core	3 or 4 core cable	Short-circuit current: 1sec
mm2	In air: Amps	In air: amps	In air: Amps	U/G: Amps	U/G: Amps	U/G: Amps	Kiloamps
2.5	36	34	29	44	45	37	0.36
4	47	45	38	56	58	49	0.57
6	61	57	48	70	75	61	0.85
10	85	79	66	94	98	81	1.42
16	113	105	88	120	125	100	2.27
25	150	140	115	155	165	135	3.55
35	181	168	141	190	197	162	4.97
50	265	215	178	250	240	200	7.10
70	290	265	220	270	290	240	9.94
95	347	316	263	320	345	285	13.50
120	410	370	300	370	380	325	17.00
150	470	430	350	420	450	370	21.30
185	530	485	409	465	500	410	26.30
240	640	570	480	550	580	480	34.10
300	725	680	574	615	650	535	42.60
400	845	780	670	740	780	640	56.80
500	980			810			71.00
630	1150			945			89.50
800	1380			1100			113.60
1000	1605			1225			142.00

A2.3. CURRENT CARRYING CAPACITY FOR XLPE INSULATED, IEC STANDARD CABLES, >1 TO 12 KV

Current carrying capacity and short circuit current ratings of XLPE insulated copper conductor cable, 3.6/6 (7.2) KV, and 6/10 (12) KV, conforming to IEC standard 60502-2, is given in Table A2.3

Conductor cross-sect:	S/core 3 cables	3 core cable	S/core 3 cables	3-core cable	S/core 3 cables	3-core cable	S/core 3 cables	3-core cable	Short-circuit curr:
KV→→	3.6/6/7.2	3.6/6/7.2	3.6/6/7.2	3.6/6/7.2	6/10/12	6/10/12	6/10/12	6/10/12	1-second
mm2	In air (A)	In air (A)	U/G (A)	U/G (A)	In air (A)	In air (A)	U/G (A)	U/G (A)	Kiloamps
16	120	90	125	105	145	90	122	105	2.27
25	160	120	160	135	185	123	155	135	3.55
35	195	147	188	162	226	153	185	161	4.97
50	245	185	230	200	270	185	223	195	7.10
70	300	225	275	240	340	255	275	235	9.94
95	360	269	326	282	401	282	330	280	13.5
120	410	315	370	320	460	330	371	315	17.00
150	470	360	420	360	540	375	420	360	21.30
185	540	415	472	407	592	430	470	405	26.30
240	630	480	540	470	695	500	548	470	34.10
300	720	550	610	525	820	580	620	530	42.60
400	850	682	710	606	915	695	740	606	56.80
500	970		800		1060		808		71.00
630	1130		940		1230		950		89.50
800	1395		1090		1400		1090		113.60
1000	1640		1230		1650		1230		142.00

A2.4. CURRENT CARRYING CAPACITY FOR XLPE INSULATED IEC STANDARD CABLES >12 TO 24 KV

Current carrying capacity and short circuit ratings for XLPE insulated copper conductor cable, 8.7/15 (17.5) KV, and 12/20 (24) KV, conforming to IEC standard 60502-2 is tabulated in Table A2.(4).

Condu: :area	S/core 3 cables	3-core cable	S/core 3 cables	3-core cable	S/core 3 cables	3-core cable	S/core 3 cables	S/core 3 cables	Short circuit
KV→	8.7/15	8.7/15	8.7/15	8.7/15	12/24	12/24	12/24	12/24	1-sec
Mm2	In air, (A)	In air, (A)	U/G (A)	U/G (A)	In air, (A)	In air, (A)	U/G (A)	U/G (A)	KA
50	279	185	223	195	245	192	240	191	7.10
70	345	255	275	235	303	245	272	230	9.94
95	413	286	320	279	365	289	310	279	13.50
120	465	330	370	315	420	340	365	315	17.00
150	534	375	415	360	479	385	418	355	21.30
185	595	431	470	403	565	435	470	403	26.30
240	713	500	548	470	645	510	545	460	34.10
300	825	580	620	530	735	585	623	520	42.60
400	921	692	740	603	900	692	730	602	56.80
500	1110		810		1010		830		71.00
630	1300		950		1170		946		89.50
800	1450		1090		1400		1100		113.60
1000	1650		1230		1635		1230		142.00

A2.5. CURRENT CARRYING CAPACITY FOR XLPE INSULATED IEC STANDARD CABLES >24 TO 36 KV

Current carrying capacity and short circuit ratings of XLPE insulated copper conductor cable, 18/30 (36) KV, conforming to IEC standard 60502-2, is tabulated in Table A2(5).

Conductor cross sectional area	Single core 3 cables laid in air	3-core cable laid in air/tray	Single core 3 cables laid U/G	3-core cable laid underground	Short circuit current 1 second
mm2	Amps	Amps	Amps	Amps	Kiloamps
50	245	198	225	190	7.10
70	300	245	275	230	9.94
95	365	295	330	275	13.50
120	420	340	370	315	17.00
150	480	385	420	355	21.30
185	565	440	480	400	26.30
240	645	510	550	460	34.10
300	750	585	625	520	42.60
400	900	693	740	600	56.80
500	1010		810		71.00
630	1170		950		89.50
800	1400		1100		113.60
1000	1640		1235		142.00

APPENDIX # 3

ECHNICAL DATA FOR XLPE INSULATED ICEA STANDARD CABLES UP TO 35 KV

CONTENTS:

A3.1. TECHNICAL DATA FOR XLPE INSULATED, ICEA STANDARD MULTI-CORE CABLES, 600 V
Resistance, reactance and impedance for XLPE insulated, (copper conductor) multi-core cables, (600 V) conforming to ICEA standard S-66-524 (NEC), is tabulated in Table A3 (1) below.

Conductor size/gauge	Resistance at 90°C, Ω/km	Resistance at 90°C, Ω/km	Reactance Ω/km	Reactance Ω/km	Impedance Ω/km	Impedance Ω/km	Conductor cross-section
AWG	50 Hz/600V	60 Hz/600V	50 Hz/600V	60 Hz/600V	50 Hz/600V	60 Hz/600V	mm2
14	11.20	11.20	0.0993	0.119	11.20	11.20	2.08
12	7.05	7.05	0.0929	0.112	7.05	7.05	3.31
10	4.42	4.42	0.0872	0.105	4.43	4.43	5.26
8	2.78	2.78	0.0917	0.110	2.78	2.78	8.37
6	1.75	1.75	0.0881	0.106	1.75	1.75	13.30
4	1.10	1.10	0.0832	0.0998	1.11	1.11	21.15
2	0.694	0.694	0.0787	0.0944	0.698	0.701	33.62
1	0.551	0.551	0.0809	0.0970	0.557	0.560	42.41
1/0	0.437	0.437	0.0787	0.0945	0.444	0.447	53.49
2/0	0.348	0.348	0.0769	0.0922	0.356	0.360	67.43
3/0	0.275	0.275	0.0752	0.0902	0.285	0.290	85.01
4/0	0.219	0.220	0.0736	0.0883	0.231	0.231	107.20
MCM							
250	0.186	0.187	0.0744	0.0893	0.200	0.027	127.00
300	0.156	0.157	0.0733	0.0879	0.172	0.180	162.00
350	0.133	0.134	0.0723	0.0868	0.153	0.160	177.00
400	0.117	0.118	0.0716	0.0859	0.137	0.146	203.00
450	0.105	0.106	0.0700	0.0840	0.126	0.135	228.00
500	0.0951	0.0964	0.0646	0.0075	0.115	0.124	253.00
550	0.0864	0.0876	0.0727	0.0873	0.113	0.124	279.00
600	0.0797	0.0810	0.0722	0.0866	0.108	0.119	304.00
650	0.0742	0.0756	0.0718	0.0861	0.103	0.115	329.00
700	0.0694	0.0709	0.0713	0.0856	0.0955	0.111	355.00
800	0.0618	0.0635	0.0706	0.0848	0.0938	0.106	405.00

A3.2. TECHNICAL DATA FOR XLPE INSULATED, ICEA STANDARD MULTI-CORE CABLES, 5 KV

Resistance, reactance and impedance for XLPE insulated, (copper conductor) 3-core cable (5 KV), conforming to ICEA standard S-66- 524 (NEC), is tabulated in Table A3 (2) below.

Conductor size/gauge	Resistance at 90°C, Ω/km	Resistance at 90°C, Ω/km	Reactance Ω/km	Reactance Ω/km	Impedance Ω/km	Impedance Ω/km	Conductor cross-section
AWG	50 Hz/5 kv	60 Hz/5 kv	50 Hz/5 kv	60 Hz/5 kv	50 Hz/5 kv	60 Hz/5 kv	mm2
8	2.78	2.78	0.116	0.139	2.78	2.78	8.37
6	1.75	1.78	0.104	0.124	1.75	1.75	13.30
4	1.10	1.10	0.103	0.113	1.11	1.11	21.15
2	0.694	0.694	0.0951	0.114	0.700	0.703	33.62
1	0.551	0.551	0.0918	0.110	0.558	0.562	42.41
1/0	0.437	0.437	0.0884	0.106	0.445	0.449	53.49
2/0	0.347	0.348	0.0858	0.103	0.358	0.363	67.43
3/0	0.275	0.275	0.0830	0.0996	0.287	0.293	85.01
4/0	0.219	0.219	0.0808	0.0969	0.233	0.240	107.20
MCM							
250	0.186	0.187	0.0793	0.0951	0.202	0.209	127
300	0.156	0.156	0.0782	0.0938	0.174	0.182	152
350	0.133	0.134	0.0769	0.0923	0..154	0.163	177
400	0.117	0.118	0.0757	0.0908	0.153	0.162	203
450	0.105	0.105	0.0748	0.0897	0.129	0.138	228
500	0.0945	0.0956	0.0741	0.0890	0.120	0.131	253
550	0.0863	0.0875	0.0742	0.0891	0.114	0.125	279
600	0.0796	0.0808	0.0739	0.0887	0.109	0.120	304
650	0.0741	0.0755	0.0734	0.0881	0.104	0.116	329
700	0.0693	0.0708	0.0727	0.0872	0.100	0.112	355

A3.3. TECHNICAL DATA FOR XLPE INSULATED, ICEA STANDARD THREE CORE CABLES, 8 KV
Resistance, reactance and impedance for XLPE insulated, (copper conductor) 3-core cables (8 KV).

Conductor size/gaugc	Resistance at 90°C, Ω/km	Resistance at 90°C, Ω/km	Reactance Ω/km	Reactance Ω/km	Impedance Ω/km	Impedance Ω/km	Conductor cross-section
AWG	50 Hz/8 kv	60 Hz/8 kv	50 Hz/8 kv	60 Hz/8 kv	50 Hz/8 kv	60 Hz/8 kv	mm2
6	1.72	1.72	0.112	0.134	1.73	1.73	13.30
4	1.08	1.08	0.111	0.133	1.09	1.09	21.15
2	0.680	0.680	0.102	0.122	0.687	0.691	33.62
1	0.540	0.540	0.0982	0.118	0.549	0.553	42.41
1/0	0.429	0.429	0.0944	0.113	0.439	0.444	53.49
2/0	0.340	0.340	0.0914	0.110	0.352	0.357	67.43
3/0	0.270	0.270	0.0882	0.106	0.284	0.290	85.01
4/0	0.214	0.214	0.0856	0.103	0.230	0.238	107.20
MCM							
250	0.182	0.183	0.0838	0.101	0.201	0.208	127
300	0.152	0.152	0.0824	0.0989	0.173	0.182	152
350	0.130	0.131	0.0810	0.0972	0.153	0.163	177
400	0.115	0.115	0.0795	0.0954	0.140	0.150	203
450	0.102	0.103	0.0784	0.0941	0.129	0.140	228
500	0.0926	0.0936	0.0777	0.0932	0.121	0.132	253
550	0.0847	0.0858	0.0776	0.0931	0.115	0.127	279
600	0.0780	0.0792	0.0771	0.0925	0.110	0.122	304
650	0.0726	0.0738	0.0765	0.0918	0.106	0.118	329
700	0.0691	0.0704	0.0757	0.0909	0.103	0.115	355

A3.4. TECHNICAL DATA FOR XLPE INSULATED, ICEA STANDARD THREE CORE CABLES, 15 KV
Resistance, reactance and impedance for XLPE insulated, (copper conductor) 3-core cables (15 KV).

Conductor size/gauge	Resistance at 90°C, Ω/km	Resistance at 90°C, Ω/km	Reactance Ω/km	Reactance Ω/km	Impedance Ω/km	Impedance Ω/km	Conductor cross-section
AWG	50 Hz/15 kv	60 Hz/15 kv	50 Hz/15 kv	60 Hz/15 kv	50 Hz/15 kv	60 Hz/15 kv	mm2
2	0.694	0.694	0.121	0.146	0.704	0.709	33.62
1	0.551	0.551	0.151	0.182	0.571	0.580	42.41
1/0	0.436	0.437	0.112	0.134	0.450	0.457	53.49
2/0	0.347	0.347	0.107	0.129	0.363	0.371	67.43
3/0	0..275	0.275	0.103	0.124	0.294	0.302	85.01
4/0	0.219	0.219	0.0997	0.120	0.240	0.250	107.2
MCM							
250	0.186	0.186	0.0973	0.117	0.210	0.220	127
300	0.155	0.150	0.0951	0.114	0.182	0.193	152
350	0.133	0.133	0.0931	0.112	0.162	0.174	177
400	0.117	0.117	0.0911	0.109	0.148	0.160	203
450	0.104	0.105	0.0900	0.108	0.138	0.150	226
500	0.0939	0.0947	0.0889	0.107	0.129	0.143	253
550	0.0857	0.0866	0.0877	0.105	0.123	0.136	279
600	0.0789	0.0799	0.0869	0.104	0.117	0.131	304
650	0.0734	0.0745	0.0861	0.103	0.113	0.127	329
700	0.0685	0.0697	0.0850	0.102	0.109	0.124	355

A3.5. TECHNICAL DATA FOR XLPE INSULATED, ICEA STANDARD THREE-CORE CABLES, 25 KV

Resistance, reactance and impedance for XLPE insulated, (copper conductor) 3-core cables (25 KV), conforming to ICEA standard S-66-524 (NEC), is tabulated in Table A3 (5) below.

Conductor size/gauge	Resistance at 90°C, Ω/km	Resistance at 90°C, Ω/km	Reactance Ω/km	Reactance Ω/km	Impedance Ω/km	Impedance Ω/km	Conductor cross-section
AWG	50 Hz/25 kv	60 Hz/25 kv	50 Hz/25 kv	60 Hz/25 kv	50 Hz/25kv	60 Hz/25kv	mm2
1	0.551	0.551	0.130	0.150	0.566	0.573	42.41
1/0	0.436	0.437	0.125	0.150	0.454	0.461	53.49
2/0	0.347	0.347	0.120	0.144	0.367	0.376	67.43
3/0	0.275	0.275	0.115	0.138	0.298	0.308	85.01
4/0	0.219	0.219	0.111	0.133	0.245	0.256	107.20
MCM							
250	0.186	0.186	0.108	0.130	0.215	0.227	127
300	0.155	0.156	0.106	0.127	0.188	0.201	152
350	0.132	0.133	0.103	0.124	0.168	0.182	177
400	0.116	0.117	0.101	0.121	0.154	0.168	203
450	0.104	0.104	0.0993	0.119	0.144	0.158	228
500	0.0937	0.0944	0.0979	0.117	0.136	0.151	253
550	0.0855	0.0862	0.0964	0.116	0.128	0.144	279
600	0.0786	0.0795	0.0954	0.114	0.124	0.139	304
650	0.0731	0.0740	0.0943	0.113	0.119	0.138	329
700	0.0682	0.0692	0.0931	0.107	0.115	0.131	355

A3.6. TECHNICAL DATA FOR XLPE INSULATED, ICEA STANDARD THREE-CORE CABLES, 35 KV

Resistance, reactance and impedance for XLPE insulated, (copper conductor) 3-core cables (35 KV), conforming to ICEA standard S-66-524 (NEC), is tabulated in Table A3 (6) below.

Conductor size/gauge	Resistance at 90°C, Ω/km	Resistance at 90°C, Ω/km	Reactance Ω/km	Reactance Ω/km	Impedance Ω/km	Impedance Ω/km	Conductor cross-section
AWG	50 Hz/35 kv	60 Hz/35 kv	50 Hz/35 kv	60 Hz/35 kv	50 Hz/35 kv	60 Hz/35 kv	Mm2
1/0	0.436	0.436	0.138	0.166	0.458	0.467	42.41
2/0	0.347	0.347	0.136	0.150	0.372	0.382	67.43
3/0	0.275	0.275	0.128	0.154	0.303	0.315	85.01
4/0	0.219	0.219	0.123	0.148	0.250	0.264	107.20
MCM							
250	0.186	0.186	0.120	0.144	0.220	0.235	127
300	0.155	0.155	0.117	0.140	0.194	0.209	152
350	0.132	0.133	0.114	0.137	0.175	0.190	177
400	0.116	0.117	0.111	0.134	0.161	0.177	203
450	0.104	0.104	0.110	0.131	0.151	0.168	228
500	0.0935	0.0941	0.108	0.129	0.143	0.160	253
550	0.0852	0.0859	0.106	0.127	0.136	0.154	279
600	0.0784	0.0791	0.105	0.126	0.131	0.149	304
650	0.0728	0.0736	0.104	0.124	0.127	0.144	327
700	0..0679	0.0688	0.102	0.123	0.123	0.141	355

APPENDIX # 4

CURRENT RATINGS FOR XLPE INSULATED ICEA STANDARD CABLES UP TO 35 KV.

CONTENTS:

A4.1. RATING FACTORS FOR XLPE INSULLATED, ICEA STANDARD CABLES UP TO 35 KV

Current ratings for XLPE insulated copper conductor cables (manufactured in conformity with ICEA specification, National Electrical Code, USA) given in Table A4 (2) & (3) is derived on the basis of following parameters.

Ambient air temperature: 40°C
Ambient earth temperature: 20°C
Load factor: 100%
Thermal resistance: RHO of 90
Conductor operating temperature: 90°C.

Cables laid in air means laid on cable trays or conduits installed under roof or covered cable trench.
Cables buried means buried at a depth of 900mm with sand bedding and backfilling
Cables in underground raceways means through underground ducts or shafts.
For obtaining corresponding current ratings of aluminium conductor cables, multiply the tabulated value by 0.78.
For deriving short circuit current refer formulas given in Appendix # 5 for copper and aluminium conductors.

Rating factors for ambient temperatures:

Ambient air temperature:	30	35	40	45	50	55	60
Factor:	1.10	1.05	1.00	0.94	0.88	0.81	0.73

Rating factors for other earth temperatures:

Ambient earth temperature:	15	20	25	30	35	40	45	50
Factor:	1.03	1.00	0.95	0.91	0.88	0.85	0.79	0.74

A4.2. CURRENT CARRYING CAPACITY FOR XLPE INSULATED ICEA STANDARD CABLES, 0.6 & 5 KV

Current carrying capacity per conductor of 600 and 5000 volts XLPE insulated copper conductor cables manufactured in conformity with ICEA standard S-66-524 specification (NEC) is tabulated in Table A4 (2) below.

Conductor size/gauge	S/core 3 or 4 cables in air 600-5000 V	S/core 3 or 4 cables buried 600-5000 V	S/core 3 or 4 cables in UG Raceway	3-Core cable laid in air 600-5000 V	3-Core cable direct buried 600-5000 V	3-Core cable underground raceway	Conductor cross-section
AWG	Amps	Amps	Amps	Amps	Amps	Amps	mm2
8	83	110	64	59	85	59	8.36
6	110	140	85	79	105	78	13.30
4	145	180	110	105	135	100	21.15
2	190	230	145	140	180	135	33.62
1	225	260	170	160	200	155	42.41
1/0	260	295	195	185	230	175	53.49
2/0	300	335	220	215	260	200	67.43
3/0	345	385	250	250	295	230	85.01
4/0	400	435	290	285	335	265	107.2
MCM							
250	445	470	320	320	365	290	127
350	550	570	385	395	440	355	177
500	695	690	470	485	530	430	253
750	900	895	585	615	650	530	380
1000	1075	980	670	705	730	600	507
1250	1230	1107	775				633
1500	1365	1228	860				760
1750	1495	1345	940				886
2000	1605	1444	1010				1010

NOTE: SQ:MM = 0.0005067 X CIRCULAR MILLS (MCM)

A4.3. CURRENT CARRYING CAPACITY FOR XLPE INSULATED ICEA STANDARD CABLES, 8 TO 35 KV

Current carrying capacity per conductor of 8, 15, 25 and 35 KV, XLPE insulated copper conductor cables manufactured in conformity with ICEA standard S-66-524 specification (NEC), is tabulated in Table A4 (3) below.

Conductor size/gauge	S/core cables (3) laid in air 8 kv to 35 kv	S/core cables (3) buried 8 kv to 35 kv	S/core cables (3) u/ground raceway	3 Core cable laid in air 8 kv to 35 kv	3 Core cable buried 8 kv to 35 kv	3 Core cable u/ground raceway	Conductor cross-section
AWG	Amps	Amps	Amps	Amps	Amps	Amps	mm2
6	110	130	130	93	115	88	13.30
4	150	170	170	120	145	115	21.50
2	195	210	210	165	185	150	33.62
1	225	240	240	185	210	170	42.41
1/0	260	275	275	215	240	195	53.49
2/0	300	310	310	245	270	220	67.43
3/0	345	335	335	285	305	250	85.01
4/0	395	405	406	325	350	285	107.20
MCM							
250	440	440	440	360	380	310	127
350	545	535	535	435	460	375	177
500	680	650	650	535	550	450	253
750	870	805	805	670	665	545	380
1000	1040	930	920	770	750	615	507
1250	1185	1066	960				633
1500	1315	1185	1065				760
1750	1430	1287	1155				886
2000	1535	1380	1250				1010

NOTE: SQ:MM = 0.0005067 X CIRCULAR MILLS (MCM)

APPENDIX 5:

INTERNATIONAL STANDARDS ORGANIZATIONS

ACSE	American Society of Civil Engineers
AIEE	American Institute of Electrical Engineers
ANSI	American National Standards Institution
ASTM	American Society for Testing and Materials
BASEEFA	British Approval Society for Electrical Equipments
BSI	British Standards Institution
CEE	International Commission on rules for the approval of Electrical Equipments
CENELEC	European Committee for Electro-technical Equipment Standards
CSA	Canadian Standards Association
DIN	Deutsche Industrial Norm
EIA	Electronic Industries Association
ENA	European Norm Standards
EPRI	Electric Power Research Institute
ERA	Electrical Research Association
IACS	International Annealed Copper Standards
ICEA	Insulated Cable Engineers Association (USA)
IEC	International Electro-technical Commission
IEE	Institute of Electrical Engineers (UK)
IEEE	Institute of Electrical and Electronic Engineers (USA)
ISI	Indian Standards Institution
ISO	International Organization for Standards
NEC	National Electrical Code
NESC	National Electrical Safety Code
NFPA	National Fire Protection Association
NICR	Nuclear Industry Assessment Committee
NRC	Nuclear Regulatory Commission
NUPIC	Nuclear Procurement Issue Commission
PSB	Productivity Standards Board (Singapore)
SISIR	Singapore Institute of Standards and Industrial Research
UL	Under writers Laboratory
VDE	Verband Deutsher Electrotechniker (German Standard for Product Safety)

NOTE: UL LISTING, CLASSIFICATION AND APPROVAL: Under writers laboratories is an independent organization, which examines, tests, lists, and periodically inspects equipments to appropriates standards.

APPENDIX 6:

ABBREVIATIONS USED IN POWER TECHNOLOGY.

Abbreviation	Stands for:
AAC	All Aluminium Conductor
AAAC	All Aluminium Alloy Conductor
ABCB	Air Blast Circuit Breaker
AC	Alternating Current (Current that reverses its direction of flow periodically)
ACB	Air Circuit Breaker
ACSR	Aluminium Conductor Steel Reinforced
AGC	Automatic Generation Control
AMF	Automatic Mains Failure
AWA	Aluminium Wire Armoured
BCD	Binary Coded Decimal output
BIL	Basic Lightning Impulse insulation level
BOCB	Bulk Oil Circuit Breaker
BSL	Basic Switching Impulse insulation level
BSS	British Standard Specification
CFM	Cubic Feet per Minute (1 CFM = 0.00047 CuM)
CFS	Cubic Feet per Second (1 CFM = 0.0283 CuM) or (449 Gallon/Minute)
CO2	Carbon Dioxide
CP	Code of Practice
CPT	Control Power transformer
CVT	Capacitive Voltage Transformer
DB	Decibel (Unit used to measure the noise level)
DC	Direct current (Current that does not reverse the direction of flow)
DCS	Distributed Control System
DFR	Digital Fault Recorder
DOL	Direct On Line (method for starting of motor)
DSTA	Double Steel Tape Armoured (cable)
DUR	Direct Under-reaching Relays
EHV	Extra High Voltage system
EMI	Electromagnetic interference
EMS	Energy Management System
EMTP	Electromagnetic Transient Program
EPR	Ethylene Propylene Rubber (cable insulation)
ERM	Extensible Ring Main unit
GIS	Gas Insulated Substation/Switchgear
GMCB	Generator Mains Circuit breaker
GPS	Global Positioning System (Clock)
GWH	Gega Watt Hour (1 GWH = 1000 Mega What Hour = 10^6 Kilo Watt Hour)
HDG	Hot Dip Galvanized
HDPE	High Density Polyethylene (cable insulation)
HMI	Human Machine Interface
HOFR	Heat resistant, Oil resistant, Flame Retardant (cable)
HRC	High Rupturing Capacity fuse
HRSG	Heat Recovery Steam Generator
HVAC	High Voltage Alternating Current
HVDC	High Voltage Direct Current
IDMT	Inverse Definite Minimum Time (relay characteristic)
IED	Intelligent Electronic Devices
IGBT	Insulated Gate Bi-polar Transistor

IP	Ingress Protection (Degree of Protection)
IPMC	Integrated Protection Monitoring and Control system
ISDN	Integrated Services Digital Networks
KPa	Kilopascal (Unit of Pressure) [1 KPa = 0.145 PSI and 1 PSI = 51.7 mmHg]
LAN	Local Area Network
LED	Light Emitting Diode
LTT	Light Triggered Thyristor
MCB	Miniature Circuit Breaker
MCCB	Moulded Case Circuit Breaker
MOCB	Minimum Oil Circuit Breaker
NC	Normally Closed Contact (Closed when the breaker is open or off)
NGR	Neutral Grounding Resistor
NO	Normally Open Contact (Closed when the breaker is closed or on)
OFAN	Oil Forced Air Natural
OFWF	Oil Forced Water forced
ONAF	Oil Natural Air Forced
ONAN	Oil Natural Air Natural
OLTC	On-load Tap-changer
OPGW	Optical Power Ground Wire with steel buffer (Fiber optic overhead ground wire)
OTDR	Optical Time Domain Reflectometer
PC	Partial discharge detector
PCB	Polychlorinated Biphenyl
PCD	Pitch Circle diameter
PCS	Protection Circuit Supervising device
PI	Polarization Index (Insulation resistance test)
PLC	Programmable Logic Controller
PLCC	Power Line Carrier Communication
PMCS	Power Management Control System
POR	Permissive Over-reaching Relays
PPM	Particles Per Million
PQ	Power Quality module
PQM	Power Quality Meter
PUR	Permissive Under-reaching Relays
PVC	Polyvinyl Chloride (cable insulation)
RCCB	Residual Current Circuit Breaker
RIV	Radio Influence Voltage
RLDC	Remote Load Dispatch Center
RMU	Ring Main Unit (2R1T, 2R2T, 2R3T) R: Ring feeder; T: Transformer feeder
RPM	Revolution Per Minute
RTD	Resistance Temperature Detector
RTU	Remote Terminal Unit
SCADA	Supervisory Control and Data Acquisition System
SCMS	Substation Control and Monitoring System
SCR	Selicon Controlled Rectifier
SF6	Sulphur Hexaflouride
SMS	Substation Management System
STL	Sequential Tripping Logic
STP	Shielded Twisted Pair (cable)
SWA	Steel Wire Armoured (cable)
SWB	Steel Wire Braided (cable)
TCDS	Transmission Control and Dispatch System
UHV	Ultra High Voltage (above 800 KV)
UPS	Uninterrupted Power Supply

uPVC	Unplasticised Polyvinyl Chloride
UTP	Unshielded Twisted Pair
UV	Ultra Violet or Under Voltage
VCB	Vacuum Circuit Breaker
VDU	Visual Display Unit
WAN	Wide Area Network
XLPE	Cross-linked Polyethylene
y	Admittance measured in Mho
Z	Impedance measured in Ohm

Thermally admissible short circuit current in cables

Particulars of cable	Conductor temperature prior to short circuit (°C)	Maximum short circuit conductor temperature (°C)	Formula
1.1 kV grade copper conductor PVC cable	70	160	$A = 8.7\, I_k \times \sqrt{t}$
11 kV grade copper conductor PVC cable	60	140	$A = 9.0\, I_k \times \sqrt{t}$
33 kV grade copper conductor PVC cable	50	120	$A = 9.3\, I_k \times \sqrt{t}$
1.1 kV grade aluminium conductor PVC cable	70	160	$A = 13.2\, I_k \times \sqrt{t}$
11 kV grade aluminium conductor PVC cable	60	140	$A = 13.5\, I_k \times \sqrt{t}$
33 kV grade aluminium conductor PVC cable	50	120	$A = 14.0\, I_k \times \sqrt{t}$
Bare copper conductor	50	200	$A = 7.0\, I_k \times \sqrt{t}$
Bare aluminium conductor	50	200	$A = 11.2\, I_k \times \sqrt{t}$
11–33 kV grade paper insulated lead covered aluminium (PILCA) conductor cable	65	160	$A = 12.8\, I_k \times \sqrt{t}$
11–33 kV grade XLPE aluminium conductor cable	90	250	$A = 10.64\, I_k \times \sqrt{t}$

where, A = area of conductor (in mm²)
I_k = short circuit current in kA (rms)
t = duration of short circuit

Formulae commonly used in circuit-breakers and relays

$(\text{kVA})_B$ = Base kVA (3-phase); $(\text{kV})_B$ = Base kV (line-to-line); I_B = Base current; Z_B = Base impedance; Z_{PU} = Per unit impedance; Z_{ohm} = Impedance in ohms.

Base current

$$I_B = (\text{kVA})_B \text{ A}$$

Base impedance

$$Z_B = \frac{1000\,(\text{kVA})_B}{\sqrt{3}\, I_B} \text{ ohms} = \frac{1000\,(\text{kV})_B^2}{(\text{kVA})_B} \text{ ohms}$$

Per unit impedance

$$Z_{PU} = \frac{Z_{ohms}}{Z_B} = \frac{Z_{ohms}\,(\text{kVA})_B}{1000\,(\text{kV})_B^2}$$

Impedance

$$Z\% = 100\, Z_{PU}$$

$$Z_{ohms} = \frac{10\,(\text{kV})_B^2}{(\text{kVA})_B} \times Z\%$$

Converting impedance to new voltage base

$$(Z_{\text{ohms}})_2 = \frac{(Z_{\text{ohms}})_1 (\text{kV})_2^2}{(\text{kV})_1^2}$$

When the relay receives star current and star voltage or delta current and delta voltage

$$Z_{\text{sec}} = Z_{\text{relay}} = Z_{\text{pri}} \frac{R_c}{R_v} \text{ ohms}$$

where R_c = current transformer ratio
R_v = potential transformer ratio $V_{\text{pri}} / V_{\text{sec}}$ (both line-to-line or line-to-neutral).

When the relay receives star current and delta voltage

$$Z_{\text{relay}} = \sqrt{3}\, Z_{\text{pri}} \frac{R_c}{R_v} \text{ ohms} = \sqrt{3}\, Z_{\text{sec}}$$

Burden impedance

$$Z = \frac{(V_A)}{(I)^2} = \frac{V^2}{(V_A)} \text{ ohms}$$

where, V_A = volt ampere burden at specified V or I
V = voltage at which burden is specified
I = current at which burden is specified.

Load ohms seen by distant relay

$$Z_{\text{load}} = \frac{1000\,(\text{kV})^2}{\text{kVA}} \times \frac{R_c}{R_v}$$

Voltage across the distance relay for a solid-phase fault at the relay balance point

$$V_{\text{BP}} = \frac{2\, Z_{\text{BP}}\, I_{\text{oo}}}{R_v} = \frac{\sqrt{3}\, Z_{\text{BP}}\, I_{3ø}}{R_v}$$

where,

V_{BP} = secondary line to line voltage across relay
Z_{BP} = primary line to neutral impedance from potential transformer connection to relay balance point
I_{oo} = primary fault current for a phase to phase fault.
$I_{3ø}$ = primary fault current for a 3-phase fault.
R_v = potential transformer ratio.

Maximum prospective short circuit value in a circuit

$$S.C.\,(\text{kA}) = \frac{\text{Transformer (kVA)} \times 100}{\sqrt{3} \times \text{Secondary voltage} \times \%\ \text{Impedance of transformer}}$$

Cable capacities of conduit and trunking

The Institution of Electrical Engineers in their recommendations have worked out the cable capacity of conduits and trunk factors, which will be very helpful in the selection of conduits and trunking for accommodating power cables. Tables 1.0 and 1.1 furnish details for cable capacity of conduits. Table 1.1a and 1.1b furnish details for trunking capacity.

Table 1.0 Cable factors for conduits

Cable Size (mm^2)	Cable factor
1.0	16
1.5	22
2.5	30
4.0	43
6.0	58
10.0	105
16.0	145
25.0	218
35.0	275
50.0	383

Table 1.1 Factors for selection of conduit capacities (IEE)

Conduit length in metres between draw-in boxes	Selection column for straight or number of bends between draw-in boxes																			
	Straight runs Conduit size (mm)					One bend Conduit size (mm)					Two bends Conduit size (mm)					Three bends Conduit size (mm)				
	16	20	25	32	38	16	20	25	32	38	16	20	25	32	38	16	20	25	32	38
1	207	329	571	1000	1234	188	303	543	947	1128	177	286	514	900	–	158	256	463	818	–
2	207	329	571	1000	1234	177	286	514	900	1072	158	256	463	818	–	130	213	388	692	–
3	207	329	571	1000	1234	167	270	487	857	1020	143	233	422	750	–	111	182	333	600	–
4	177	286	514	900	1110	158	256	463	818	973	130	213	388	692	–	97	159	292	529	–
5	171	278	500	878	1082	150	244	442	783	931	120	196	356	643	–	86	141	260	474	–
6	167	270	487	857	1056	143	233	422	750	891	111	182	333	600	–	–	–	–	–	–
7	162	263	475	837	1030	136	222	404	720	855	103	169	311	563	–	–	–	–	–	–
8	158	256	463	818	1005	130	213	388	692	822	97	159	292	529	–	–	–	–	–	–
9	154	250	452	800	980	125	204	373	667	792	91	149	275	500	–	–	–	–	–	–
10	150	244	442	783	956	120	196	358	643	763	86	141	260	474	–	–	–	–	–	–

In order to find out cable capacity of conduit multiply the quantity of each size of cable by cable factor from Table 1.0, add the total factors obtained for each cable size together, then select a factor from the appropriate column Table 1.1 , which factor is equal to, or greater than the total of the cable factors. The conduit size required is given at the top of each column of factors (Table 1.1).

Example 1: Selection of conduit for accommodating following cables, with conduit length equal to 6 m between drawn-in boxes and with bends.

6 Nos. of 1.5 mm^2 cables

4 Nos. of 2.5 mm^2 cables

2 Nos of 4.0 mm² cables
2 Nos of 6.0 mm² cables

From Table 1.9, for 1.5 mm² factor = 22
2.5 mm² factor = 30
4.0 mm² factor = 43
6.0 mm² factor = 58

Total factor = $6 \times 22 + 4 \times 30 + 2 \times 43 + 2 \times 58 = 454$.

From Table 1.1 , cable capacity for the requirements as mentioned in the problems = 32 mm

Table 1.1a Cable factor as per IEE manual for trunking

Cable type	Cable size	Factor
Solid	1.5	7.1
Solid	2.5	10.2
Stranded	1.5	8.1
Stranded	2.5	11.4
Stranded	4	15.2
Stranded	6	22.9
Stranded	10	36.3
Stranded	16	50.3
Stranded	25	75.4
Stranded	35	95
Stranded	50	132.7
Stranded	70	176.7
Stranded	95	227
Stranded	120	284
Stranded	150	346

Table 1.1b Trunking factors as per IEE recommendations

Trunking size (mm)	Factor
75 × 25	738
50 × 37.5	767
100 × 50	993
50 × 50	1037
75 × 37.5	1146
100 × 37.5	1542
75 × 50	1555
100 × 50	2091
75 × 75	2371
150 × 50	3161
100 × 75	3189
100 × 100	4252
150 × 75	4787
150 × 100	6414
150 × 150	9575

INDEX

A

AUTOTRANSFORMER:

B

BUS BAR:

C

D

G

H

I

J

K

L

M

N

O

P

Q

R

S

T